THE PICTORIAL HISTORY OF FORT WAYNE INDIANA

A REVIEW OF
TWO CENTURIES OF OCCUPATION OF THE
REGION ABOUT THE HEAD OF THE
MAUMEE RIVER

By

B. J. GRISWOLD

ILLUSTRATED

WITH HALFTONE ENGRAVINGS
AND THREE HUNDRED PEN DRAWINGS AND MAPS
BY THE AUTHOR

VOLUME II, BIOGRAPHICAL

ALSO THE STORY
OF THE TOWNSHIPS OF ALLEN COUNTY
BY
MRS. SAMUEL R. TAYLOR

CHICAGO
Robert O. Law Company
1917

A Reproduction by UNIGRAPHIC, INC.
4400 Jackson Avenue
Evansville, Indiana 47715

Nineteen Hundred Seventy One

Binding by
Modern Binding Corporation
Portland, Indiana

Publisher's Statement

In issuing these volumes to our subscribers the publishers desire to say a word of appreciation for the editor, Mr. B. J. Griswold. In the course of a long service in like publications, and after laboring with hundreds of writers and editors in many parts of the country, it remains to Mr. Griswold to be esteemed by us the most efficient and in every way the most satisfactory person with whom it has been our province to be associated in a similar line of endeavor. Although relatively a newcomer to Fort Wayne, he has, nevertheless, been able to bring to his work an enthusiasm which usually comes only through long years of intimate association with the locality that is the subject of research. His talents have richly equipped him for preserving not only the verbal story but also the scenic part; and herein is where most histories, both local and general, are remarkably incomplete. The embelishments of these volumes alone make this work unique and valuable, and we entertain no doubt that they will be appreciated and long cherished by those who have been fortunate enough to anticipate their worth.

Mr. Griswold was born October 13, 1873, at Osage, Iowa, the son of James J. and Ruth Velerie (Arnold) Griswold, who still reside there. The father was born in Canada, and the mother in Michigan. After leaving the public school, B. J. Griswold began his newspaper experience in the office of the Osage Weekly News, and was afterward engaged on the staffs of the Waterloo (Iowa) Courier, the Cedar Rapids (Iowa) Gazette, the Terre Haute (Indiana) Tribune, and the Indianapolis (Indiana) Star. He came to Fort Wayne in 1902 and served for nine years as a cartoonist of the Fort Wayne Daily News, and later was engaged in the same capacity with the Fort Wayne Sentinel. Previous to the latter experience he became one of the founders of the Fort Wayne Engraving Company. His present business, the Progressive Advertising Company, was established in 1914. On March 21, 1901, Mr. Griswold was united in marriage with Miss Clara Louise Norton, at Cedar Falls, Iowa. Mr. Griswold is an active member of the Rotary Club, of which he is serving as secretary, and of the Quest Club and the Commercial Club. He is a Scottish Rite Mason and a member of Plymouth Congregational church.

THE PUBLISHERS.

Index to Portraits in This Volume

Barnett, Charles Eldridge	39
Bash, Charles S.	43
Bass, John H.	45
Bass, John H., Residence	48
Bowser, Sylvanus F.	82
Breen, William P.	87
Breuer, William	90
Curdes, Louis F.	120
Deihl, Hugh M.	125
Dreibelbiss, John	144
Duemling, Hermann A.	148
Eckart, Fred	153
Ellison, Thomas E.	160
Eward, Edgar D.	169
Foster, David N.	187
Foster, Samuel M.	190
Fox, Louis	194
Guldlin, Olaf N.	243
Hackett, Edward A. K.	252
Hadley, Robert	256
Haffner, Christian	257
Hanna, Samuel	264
Hayden, Fred J.	279
Hoffman, Edward G.	295
Klaehn, W. Robert	333
Klitzke, William C.	335
Kunkle, Erastus B.	344
Lumbard, Sidney C.	365
Menefee, Charles M.	392
Morris, John	408
Morris, Samuel L., Jr.	409
Perfect, Arthur H.	442
Pidgeon, Charles T.	447
Porter, Miles F.	452
Rockhill, Howell C.	480
Rosenthal, Isaac M.	489
Rosenthal, J. Milton	491
Rosenthal, Maurice I.	492
Rurode, Ernst C.	495
Swinney, Thomas W.	563
Taylor, Robert S.	564
Vesey, William J.	582
Welty, Joel	604
Worden, Charles H.	620
Worden, James L.	622

Biographical Sketches

George F. Aichele is senior member of the firm of Aichele & Son, which conducts in Fort Wayne a substantial and representative business in the manufacturing and handling of cemetery monuments of the best modern type, and the concern has acknowledged leadership in this line of enterprise in Allen county, with a large and well equipped establishment that has the best of facilities for the handling of all classes of monumental and other enduring memorial work on sacred grounds, consecrated to those who have passed forward to "that undiscovered country from whose bourne no traveler returns." Mr. Aichele was born in Wurtenberg, Germany, August 23, 1851, and was a child of three years when he came with his parents to the United States, the voyage across the Atlantic having been made on an old-time sailing vessel of the type then commonly in commission for such transportation service. The family home was established in Kendallville, and there the subject of this review acquired his early education in the public schools. In 1881 he established his home in Fort Wayne and found employment in connection with the line of business of which he is now a prominent representative. He learned the trade of marble and granite cutting in a most thorough way and he has here been established in his indepndent business as a manufacturer of and dealer in cemetery monuments, gravestones, markers, etc., since 1894, the enterprise, built up on the best of service and honorable methods, being now conducted under the firm name of Aichele & Son. Mr. Aichele is a man of broad views and well fortified opinions, takes loyal interest in public affairs of local order and gives his political support to the Socialist party, though he has never had any desire for political activity or public office. In addition to his business he is the owner of valuable real estate in Fort Wayne, including his attractive home property. In the state of New York, in 1874, Mr. Aichele wedded Miss Marie Scheymentki, and they became the parents of three children: Wilhelmina D., Clarence, who is a barber and resident of Fort Wayne, and August C., who is associated with his father in business, as junior member of the firm of Aichele & Son.

John H. Aiken is another of the native sons of Allen county whose ability, ambition and character have brought to him established position as one of the successful and representative members of the bar of the county, and his precedence has been shown also by his able administration on the bench of the superior court of Allen county, a position of which he was the incumbent about two years. Since his retirement from this judicial office he has given his undivided attention to his substantial and important general law business, and he maintains his offices in the Swinney building, Fort Wayne. Judge Aiken was born in Lafayette township, this county, on the 19th of January, 1870, and is a son of John and Martha J. (Trainer) Aiken, the former of whom was born either in Pennsylvania or Eastern Ohio, and the latter was born in one of the eastern counties of the old Buckeye State. John Aiken came to Allen county in 1860 and established his home in Lafayette township, where he owned and improved a good farm. After the lapse of a number of years he sold this property and, after passing an interval in the state of Tennessee, returned to Allen county and engaged in farming in Lake township. He was a Democrat in politics, served as county assessor, and was influential in community affairs. A man of the deepest Christian faith and practice, he served many years as a local preacher in the Methodist Episcopal church, and both he and his wife passed the closing years of their lives in Fort Wayne, the subject of this review being the youngest of their eight children. John H. Aiken passed the period of his childhood and early youth on the home farm and after profiting duly by the advantages of the public schools he took a course in the old Methodist College in Fort Wayne. In consonance with his well defined ambition to prepare himself for the legal profession, he entered the law department of the great University of Michigan, in which he was graduated as a member of the class of 1891 and from which he received his degree of Bachelor of Laws. In May of that year he was admitted to the Indiana bar and established himself in the practice of his profession in Fort Wayne. He was for a time associated with M. V. B. Spencer, and thereafter he conducted an independent practice until 1905, when he formed a partnership with Homer C. Underwood. This alliance continued until 1908, when Judge Aiken removed to Warsaw, the judicial center of Kosciusko county, where for the ensuing three years he was associated in practice with Judge A. G. Wood. He then returned to Fort Wayne, and here his law business has since been of an individual order. As a skilled trial lawyer he has appeared in connection with much important litigation in the various courts of this section of the state, and from 1900 until November, 1902, he gave most effective service on the bench of the Superior court of the county, from which office he retired to give his undivided attention to his large and representative private law business. In 1896 he was appointed county attorney for the poor, and of this position he continued the incumbent four years. In politics Judge Aiken is a stalwart and well fortified advocate of the cause of the Democratic party, and he is actively affiliated with the Masonic fraternity, in which he has received the thirty-second degree of the Scottish Rite, besides being identified with the Ancient Arabic Order, Nobles of the Mystic Shrine. He is also a Knight Templar. On the 1st of September, 1891, was recorded the marriage of Judge Aiken to Miss Lulu Bush, daughter of Dr. Morton W. Bush, of Chelsea, Michigan, and the one child of this union is Arthur L., who is now a resident of the city of Detroit, Michigan.

William Albersmeyer is a native German, born on Nevember 15, 1873, son of Fred and Elizabeth (Heine) Albersmeyer. The father died in Germany and, in 1883, his widow took her family of seven children and came to America, settling in Fort Wayne, where she passed the remainder of her life. The sons and daughters were Fred, Charles, Christ, William, Minnie, Lizette and Hannah. William was sent to live with an uncle in Milan township, after the family located in Fort Wayne, and there had such educational advantages as the public schools offered. He was still in his teens when he took up farming on his own lookout and has since continued to be actively identified with that industry, enjoying a pleasureable degree of success and acquiring possession of ninety acres of the most fertile and productive land in the township. He bought unimproved land and has himself carried on the difficult task of bringing it up to its present high state of cultivation, and his work along the lines of diversified farming is highly creditable to him. Mr. Albersmeyer was married, in 1901, to Miss Sophia Dressler, daughter of August Dressler. Four children have come to them—Esther, Imogard, Elmer and Gertrude. The family have membership in the German Lutheran church and Mr. Albersmeyer is an adherent of the Democratic party in politics.

Samuel Rockwell Alden.—Thirty-eight years have passed since Samuel R. Alden established himself in the practice of law in Fort Wayne. In these years he has been a participant in many of the developing processes that have gone to make that place the prosperous and representative American city it is known to be, and his labors have won for him a position and prominence that might well be envied by his associates. Samuel Rockwell Alden was born in South Wilbraham, Massachusetts, on August 30, 1847, and he is the son of Harlow and Mary Ann (Imson) Alden. Harlow Alden was born in Lyme, New Hampshire. An inventor, dreamer and all-round mechanic, he never made a financial success, though expert in carpentry, cooperage and cabinet work. Disabled during the civil war, in service as sapper and miner, he could not help his son. The mother, spiritual, educated, and energetic, was the formative force in the education and development of her son, and by teaching she was for years the family support. Of mixed descent—English, Scotch, Welsh, German, Dutch and Irish—Samuel R. Alden is a typical American and the twelfth in line from John Alden of Mayflower fame. He came with his parents to Whitewater, Wisconsin, when a small boy and attended the schools in that place. When he had finished his high school course he entered Beloit College, at Beloit, Wisconsin, but his studies were broken off as the result of an injury he sustained in an attempt to stop a runaway. When the Normal School opened at Whitewater, his home town, young Alden began to attend, though he was still suffering from his accident and was able to get about only on crutches. Shortly after that he was appointed to the position of instructor in certain subjects, and for two years taught advanced English and Elocution. His next post was as assistant in Mathematics to Prof. Horace Briggs, at the Buffalo Classical School, a preparatory school for boys. Mr. Alden continued there for two years and in 1874 he went abroad to continue his studies. He attended the University of Leipsic for a year and then entered the University of Heidelberg, after which he spent several months in study in Paris. Returning to his native country he entered Columbia Law School, and he completed a two year course in one year. His admission to the bar of the state of Wisconsin followed shortly afterward and in 1878 he came to Fort Wayne, where he has since been engaged in civil practice, enjoying a marked degree of success and prosperity. Mr. Alden is a prominent Republican and a member of the Baptist church. He has been a Scottish Rite Mason since 1890 and is a member of the Shrine. He has long been a staunch member of the Fort Wayne Commercial Club, and for several years served as president of its predecessor, the Fort Wayne Club. In December, 1884, Mr. Alden was married to Carrie Savin, the daughter of Auguste F. and Sarah J. (Staniford) Savin, of New York City, where Mrs. Alden was born. Three children have been born to Mr. and Mrs. Alden. Whiting, the eldest, is a forester, in the employ of the Canadian Pacific railway and stationed at Calgary, Alberta,

Canada. Dorothy is the wife of Fernand Prussing, a mechanical engineer of Chicago, and, like her new-woman sisters, continues her professional work after marriage. Spencer Thorndyke, a senior at Cornell University, enlisted in the Naval Reserve and is now in the coast patrol guard, stationed at Newport, Rhode Island.

Charles B. Aldrich, recognized as a man of excellent professional attainments, has been engaged in the practice of law in Fort Wayne since 1911 and is one of the prominent and influential younger members of the bar of Allen county. A scion of sterling New England colonial ancestry, he was born at Chattanooga, Massachusetts, on June 12, 1885, and is a son of Charles T. and Susetta (Milan) Aldrich. After due preliminary educational discipline he entered historic old Yale University, and in this institution he was graduated as a member of the class of 1906 and with the degree of Bachelor of Arts. In preparation for his chosen profession he was matriculated in the Chattanooga Law School, in the city of Chattanooga, Tennessee, and from the same he received his degree of Bachelor of Laws in the year 1908. In 1910 he completed an effective post-graduate course in the law school of Yale University, but he had been admitted to the Indiana bar in the year that recorded his graduation in the Chattanooga Law School. In 1911 he engaged in the practice of his profession in Fort Wayne, and since January 1, 1916, has here been a member of the strong and representative law firm of Ryan, Ryan & Aldrich, which controls a substantial and important practice. Mr. Aldrich is a popular member of the Allen County Bar Association and holds membership also in the Indiana State Bar Association. His political allegiance is given to the Democratic party, he and his wife are communicants of the Catholic church, and he is affiliated with the Knights of Pythias, the Benevolent & Protective Order of Elks and the Improved Order of Red Men. On the 9th of July, 1912, was solemnized the marriage of Mr. Aldrich to Miss Juanita Ryan, of Fort Wayne, and the one child of this union is a son, William.

Right Rev. Herman Joseph Alerding, the present bishop of the diocese of Fort Wayne, has been the occupant of that exalted station since his consecration, November 30, 1900, and under his administration the diocese has flourished, the churches have been increased in members, church properties improved, and all kindred interests have progressed most satisfactorily. Bishop Alerding was born in Westphalia, Germany, April 13, 1845, and while he was as yet an infant the family migrated to America, establishing a home at Newport, Kentucky, where the future Bishop attended the parochial schools of Corpus Christi church. Bishop Alerding relates that all the children of the parish, boys and girls, numbering about one hundred and fifty, were taught in one room, by one teacher, which is in striking contrast with the schools of the present day. The education was in every respect strenuous, but the youthful Alerding persisted in his studies, as he had, from his earliest boyhood days, evinced an inclination and a desire to become a priest. He received his first lessons in Latin from Rev. John Voll, pastor of Corpus Christi church at Newport, and from 1858 until 1859 attended the diocesan seminary at Vincennes, Indiana. The second year of his studies was spent in the old St. Thomas Seminary, near Bardstown, Kentucky, and in the fall of 1860 he was sent to St. Meinrad's College and Seminary in Spencer county, Indiana, which institution was conducted by Benedictine Fathers who had come to this country from Einsiedlen, Switzerland. There young Alerding finished his studies and received the Holy Orders from Bishop de St. Palais, the Tonsure and Minor Orders being received on September 18, 1865, Subdeaconship on June 18, 1867, Deaconship on June 21 of the same year and Priesthood on September 22, 1868. After receiving the Holy Orders his first appointment was that of assistant to the Rev. John B. Chasse at St. Joseph's church, in Terre Haute, and there he remained until October 18, 1871. While serving there in that capacity he also had charge of the missions at Rockville and Montezuma, the stations at Rosedale in Parke county and the mission at Sullivan and the station at Farmersburg, in Sullivan county. He was removed to Cambridge City, October 18, 1871, and there he served as the pastor of St. Elizabeth's church until August, 1874. He found a demoralized congregation in this place, but he was able to liquidate the indebtedness on the church property and also to purchase a more favorable site for the erection of a new church building. During his pastorate in Cambridge City he also had charge of the station at Knightstown and Newcastle, in Henry county, and Hagerstown, in Wayne county. The churches at Knightstown and Newcastle were built by him and wholly paid for. In the summer of 1874, Father Alerding was transferred to Indianapolis and appointed to the position of procurator for the newly established St. Joseph's seminary, also serving as pastor for the congregation which had regular services in the seminary chapel. The seminary was abandoned after one year, and later Father Alerding was directed to build a new church. In compliance the present St. Joseph's church was erected and the dedicatory services were held on July 4, 1880. Father Alerding continued as pastor of this charge until 1900, when the See of Fort Wayne became vacant upon the death of Bishop Rademacher, and Father Alerding was appointed to the position, the consecration taking place on November 30 of the same year. In 1901, the first year of his administration, the Bishop's House, at the corner of Lewis and Clinton streets, was erected, and in 1906 a crypt for the burial of church dignitaries was constructed beneath the sanctuary. In 1883 Bishop Alerding published "A History of the Catholic Church in the Diocese of Vincennes," which book " is a monument to his industry and untiring patience," and in 1907 he published "The Diocese of Fort Wayne; a Book of Historical Reference," which increased the debt of gratitude owed him by the thousands of interested members of the Mother Church.

John D. Alleger, proprietor of the Monroeville Breeze and Nestor of the Press in Allen county, was born in Danville, Pennsylvania, August 24, 1854. The year following his birth the parents came to Allen county, and here he has spent his life from that time to the present. The first home of the family was in a small house which stood on the grounds now a part of Concordia College. The father owned and operated a portable sawmill and thus it came about that Mr. Alleger lived in various parts of the county. Acquiring only a rudimentary education, he early began that course of industry which has become a settled characteristic. He went through the bootblack and newsboy period of business, in the former of which he was the first in the city, and in his early 'teens was a coachman for Hon. Hugh McCulloch. In 1869 he took up the printer's calling in the old Fort Wayne Gazette office and with slight variation he has been identified with the newspaper business of the county since that time. He worked for three years in the Monroeville Democrat office and then returned to Fort Wayne, where he remained until 1881, when he resumed his connection in Monroeville. He bought the Democrat, January 1, 1884, and at once changed the name to the Breeze, by which it has been known ever since. He was then without funds, but was enabled to purchase it through the aid of thirty-three citizens who signed a promissory note for $1,000— on which he borrowed the money. The Breeze has been a consistent advocate of Democratic principles though not a slave to partisan rule. In February, 1874, was solemnized his marriage with Malinda Wass, who has borne him three children, named Mrs. Dovie May Noyer (now deceased); William R., and Mrs. Elsie Winifred Battenberg. The son is now associated with the father in conducting the Breeze and thus Mr. Alleger is enabled to give attention to his other interests, among which is a fine farm of seventy-one acres near the town. William R. was married to Susie E. Piller and they have one son—John Carlton— now thirteen years old and a pupil in the high school. Mr. Alleger is, as may be inferred, a Democrat in politics and has held the office of Justice of the Peace for thirty years and through this has come to be known among his acquaintances as Judge Alleger. Fraternally he belongs to the Masons, I. O. O. F., K. of P. and Jr. O. U. A. W.

Albert C. Alter passed his entire life in Fort Wayne and was but forty years of age at the time of his death, which occurred December 7, 1912. The succinct biography of any man may be summed up in the terse expressions that he was born, he lived and he died, but how much is implied aside from this depends upon the man himself and the use he makes of his powers, the attitude which is his toward his fellow men. Mr. Alter achieved independence and success through his own efforts, but over and above this he held himself true and loyal in all of the relations of life, expressed his buoyant nature in kindly thoughts and kindly deeds, and it may well be said that when he passed from the stage of his mortal endeavors the popular estimate of him was shown in the sorrow and regret that came to the hearts of a host of friends who had been drawn to him during the course of his generous and gracious life. To have gained such friends bespeaks the most and best for any man. Albert C. Alter was born at Fort Wayne on October 18, 1872, and was a son of Nicholas and Barbara (Grotenrath) Alter, the former a native of Fort Wayne and the latter of Cleveland, Ohio. The father was one of the pioneer shoe merchants of Fort Wayne, where he continued to reside until his death and where his widow still maintains her home—at 1040 Lake avenue. From an appreciative estimate that was published some time prior to the death of Mr. Alter may consistently be taken the following quotations: "The subject of this sketch is a living proof of the falsity of the assertion that there is nothing in a name. The verb alter, according to wise old Noah Webster and a few other authorities, means the same as 'change,' and this tells in a word just the manner in which Mr. Alter made his money. No, he didn't make it on 'change,' as many another man has done; he simply made it out of change—small change, pennies, nickels and dimes. He started in as a hustling, thrifty newsboy, crying his wares on the very corner of which he is now the boss—a splendid example for the 'newsies' who congregate there daily and make life interesting for those waiting for their cars. We hope they'll all peruse this little story and profit thereby. One day Mr. Alter found himself in charge of the news stand of the Aveline Hotel. Gradually his prosperity increased until he was able to open the present finely equipped cigar and news stand on the busiest corner of the city. All of this and his other evidences of prosperity have been accomplished because he tried to treat everybody right, not forgetting, of course, Mr. Albert C. Alter." Mr. Alter not only thus proved himself a worker when he was a mere boy but he also profited duly by the advantages offered in the public schools of his native city. As a boy he began to assist in the work of his father's shoe store, and later he was for some time employed in the store of A. C. Cott, news dealer. His advancement was shown by his presiding over the news stands in the Aveline Hotel and the Wayne Hotel, and it was in the year 1901 that he opened his cigar and news stand at the corner of Calhoun and Main streets, where he continued to conduct a prosperous business until the time of his death. Mr. Alter was a Democrat in politics, was a communicant of the Catholic church, and was affiliated with the Knights of Columbus and the Benevolent & Protective Order of Elks. On the 20th of November, 1902, was solemnized his marriage to Miss Alice Hunt, who was born and reared in Fort Wayne and who is a daughter of James and Mary (Finan) Hunt, the former of whom has been a resident of Fort Wayne from the time of his birth and the latter, now deceased, was a native of Ohio. Mr. Hunt was for many years one of the successful buyers and shippers of live stock in North Indiana and is now living retired in Fort Wayne. Mr. and Mrs. Alter became the parents of three children, two of whom survive him—Charlotte and Julian. The second child, Albert, died in infancy. On the 15th of November, 1915, Mrs. Alter contracted a second marriage, and her present husband, Harry C. Beekner, a native of Fort Wayne, is a commercial traveling salesman for the C. T. Pidgeon Millinery Company, of this city.

Noah Amstutz is one of the energetic and representative farmers of the younger generation in his native township, is a scion of one of the old nd honored families of Allen county, and in his operations as an agriculturist and stock-grower is bringing to bear the best of modern methods and policies, so that the maximum success attends his farm enterprise, besides which he shows his civic loyalty by taking active and liberal interest in community affairs. He is a son of Jacob and Sophia (Culp) Amstutz, and on other pages of this publication are given adequate data concerning the family history. Born in Springfield township, December 2, 1882, Noah Amstutz passed the period of his childhood and youth under the benignant influences and discipline of the home farm and in the meanwhile did not fail to profit fully by the advantages of the public schools of his native township. A young man of alert mentality and definite ambition, he has never severed his allegiance to the great basic industry of agriculture and through the medium of the same has achieved success that has fully justified this fealty. His independent operations as a farmer were instituted on the old homestead, and he is now the owner of a fine farm of one hundred and fifty-four acres in Section 32, Springfield township, as well as a well-improved additional tract of forty-five acres in Cedar Creek township. The year 1917 finds him serving his second term as one of the progressive and valued members of the Allen county council, and he is aligned as a stalwart advocate and supporter of the cause of the Democratic party. In the time-honored Masonic fraternity his ancient-craft affiliation is with Harlan Lodge No. 296, and he is identified also with other York Rite bodies, has received advancement in the Scottish

Rite and is affiliated also with the Ancient Arabic Order of the Nobles of the Mystic Shrine. In 1902 was solemnized the marriage of Mr. Amstutz to Miss Millie Knight, daughter of Lewis and Christina (Miller) Knight, of Milan township, and the four children of this union are Kenneth, Jeanette, May and Thelma. The attractive rural home of the family is known for its generous hospitality and is about three-fourths of a mile distant from the village of Harlan.

Peter S. Amstutz was born in Springfield township, Allen county, September 27, 1853, on the farm that is now his home, so that he has a record of sixty-four years of continuous residence in the one spot. He is one of the prosperous men of the community, connected prominently with various business enterprises in his district, and is a man highly esteemed of all who know him. He is the son of Peter and Barbara (Schulenger) Amstutz, both natives of Alsace, the French province in Germany. Peter Amstutz, the elder, came to America when he was twenty-two years of age and located in Wayne county, Ohio. His marriage took place in Stark county, Ohio, and after several years of residence there he came to Allen county, Indiana, in 1852, settling on the farm now the home of the subject. Nine children were born to Peter and Barbara Amstutz, of which number only two survive. The children, named in the order of their birth, were John, Joseph, Jacob, Lydia, Barbara, Peter, Jr., Mary, Anna and John, the last named being a prosperous citizen of Wayne county, Ohio. The parents spent their lives in work on their Allen county farm, and prospered according to their labors. When they died the home place went to Peter, Jr., the only other surviving child being established in Wayne county, as has been stated previously. When young Amstutz was eighteen years old he engaged in the implement business, using the home place as a center for his operations. In 1901 the Wabash Railroad, cutting through Springfield township, made Grabill a busy center and Mr. Amstutz moved his business to that point. He has carried on a successful trade in farm implements these many years, besides having found many other important enterprises to identify himself with. He is president of a successful lumber company, director of the People's Store Company and a director of the Woodburn Banking Company, of which concern he was one of the organizers. He is also a stockholder in the Harlan State Bank. In 1879 Mr. Amstutz was married to Anna Roth, who was born in Allen county, daughter of Jacob and Elizabeth (Souder) Roth. Mr. and Mrs. Roth were the parents of five children, of which Mrs. Amstutz was the eldest. The others were Levi, Elizabeth, Lydia and Louisa. Five children were born to Mr. and Mrs. Amstutz. Aaron, the eldest, is located on a farm near Harlan. Delbert G. is also located in that vicinity as a farmer. Harvey is on the old home place. Emma is the wife of Albert Neuenschwander, of Grabill, and Viola, the youngest, is at home with her parents. In 1903 the wife and mother died and in later years Mr. Amstutz married Lydia Grabill, who has since shared his fortunes. Mr. Amstutz is a Republican, prominent in local politics, and a public-spirited citizen first and last. He has served his community ably as a director of the school board and has been supervisor of his township on several occasions, as well as holding other township offices from time to time. In all of them he has displayed an aptitude for public service and has amply earned the regard and esteem in which he has long been held by his fellow citizens and neighbors.

Charles Ashley.—As senior member of the firm of George L. Ashley's Sons, the subject of this review is one of the progressive and successful representatives of the real estate business in his native county, and since the death of their honored father he and his brother, George S., have successfully conducted the substantial business that was founded by the father after he had retired from the office of county recorder, the family having been one of prominence in Allen county for three generations. Charles Ashley was born on a farm in St. Joseph township, this county, a few miles distant from Fort Wayne, and the date of his nativity was March 11, 1876. He is a son of George L. and Josephine (Darling) Ashley, the former of whom was born and reared in this county, where his parents settled in the pioneer days, and the latter was born at Keene, New Hampshire. The parents of George L. Ashley settled in Allen county as pioneers and his father here became a prosperous farmer, with which line of basic industry he continued to be identified until his death. George L. was reared to the sturdy discipline of the farm and in his independent operations as an agriculturist and stockgrower he eventually became the owner of one of the model farms of St. Joseph township. To the management of this homestead he continued to give his attention until he was elected county recorder, in the autumn of 1904, his inviolable hold upon popular confidence and esteem having been significantly shown in this connection, as he successfully overcame at the polls the large and normal Democratic majority and had the distinction of being the only Republican elected to this office in the county during the entire period of its history. He assumed the duties of the office January 1, 1905, and his able administration during the ensuing four years fully demonstrated the consistency of the popular choice of an incumbent. After retiring from office he established himself in the real estate business in Fort Wayne, and his exact and comprehensive knowledge of realty values in this section of the state combined with his executive ability and personal popularity to fortify him splendidly in the development of a substantial business, his two sons having been associated with him in the enterprise which they have effectively continued since his death. George L. Ashley was a man of broad mental ken, of invincible rectitude in all of the relations of life, and held himself true to his high ideals until he passed from the stage of his mortal endeavors, January 5, 1916, the wife of his youth having passed away on the 7th of January, 1879, leaving one son, the immediate subject of this sketch. Mrs. Ashley was a member of the Methodist Episcopal church, as was also her husband. He married, second, Addessa M. Miller and she bore him the following children: Olive E., wife of Arthur J. Smith, of Fort Wayne; Oscar J., died in 1913; George S., junior member of the real estate firm of George L. Ashley's Sons, and Josephine Margaret, wife of Calvin C. Magley, of Fort Wayne. He married, third, Mrs. Zella Culber, who survives him. Mr. Ashley attained to the thirty-second degree in the Ancient Accepted Scottish Rite of Masonry, and it is pleasing to note that he was treasurer of the class of 1912, in which he and his three sons simultaneously received the thirty-second degree and were duly crowned sublime princes of the royal secret. In the public schools of his native county Charles Ashley continued his studies until he had duly availed himself of the advantages of the high school in Fort Wayne, after which he completed a course in a well ordered business college in this city. He continued to be associated in the work and management of the home farm until he was twenty-four years old and when his father was elected county recorder he assumed a position in the recorder's office, in which he served as his father's deputy during the latter's regime of four years, after which he became a member of the firm of George L. Ashley & Sons, in the real estate business in Fort Wayne. After the death of the honored father the present title of George L. Ashley's Sons was adopted, and the firm controls a well ordered and substantial business in the handling of both city and farm property in this section of the state. Mr. Ashley holds himself unwavering in allegiance to the Republican party, and in addition to his affiliation with the Masonic fraternity, as previously intimated, he is identified also with the Tribe of Ben Hur, both he and his wife being members of the Methodist Episcopal church. In 1900 was recorded his marriage to Miss Jessie V. Sweet, who was born and reared in Fort Wayne, and they have two children— Charles L. and Marjorie R.

Mark Ashton, who was born in Maumee township, January 11, 1876, is now numbered among the representative exponents of agricultural and live-stock industry in this township, his excellent farm, comprising seventy-five acres, being well improved and eligibly situated. Mr. Ashton is a son of Ambrose and Mary Annie (Cummins) Ashton, both natives of Ohio, the former having been born in Brown county and the latter in Clermont county, and both having been children at the time of the removal from the old Buckeye state to become pioneer settlers of Allen county, Indiana. After their marriage Ambrose Ashton and his young wife established their home on a farm in Maumee township, and there they passed the remainder of their earnest and industrious lives, the passing years bringing to them a consistent measure of prosperity, the while they had inviolable place in the esteem of all who knew them. They became the parents of seven children, and all are living except Clark, who was a twin of the subject of this sketch and who died at an early age, and Clarence F., the youngest of the number, who is also deceased. The surviving children are George F., Mrs. Nellie A. Doerring, Joseph L., Mrs. Lily D. Keefer, and Mark. The honored father passed from the stage of his mortal endeavors December 24, 1895, the devoted wife and mother having been summoned to eternal rest October 3, 1892. Ambrose Ashton played a large and benignant part in the community life, commanded unqualified confidence and esteem, served as township trustee of Maumee township, and for a number of years held the office of justice of the peace. Mark Ashton is indebted to the public schools of his native county for his early education, and he has been continuously identified with agricultural pursuits from the time of his youth, his independent operations having been instituted on the old home farm, of which his present well improved farm is a part. His political support is given to the Republican party, he is a loyal citizen who gives co-operation in the furtherance of measures and enterprises advanced for the general good of the community, but he has manifested no ambition for public office of any kind. November 1, 1900, stands as the date of the marriage of Mr. Ashton to Miss Lela H. Burrier, who likewise was born and reared in this county and who is a member of a family that was here established in the early pioneer days. She is a daughter of George and Alice (Sanders) Burrier. Mr. and Mrs. Ashton have four children, whose names and respective dates of birth are here designated: Florence M., December 22, 1903; George B., September 20, 1906; Frances L., January 30, 1909; and Forrest C., December 25, 1912.

Austin Augspurger is one of the progressive citizens of Maumee township, with place of residence at Woodburn, where he is engaged in the lumber business and also gives some attention to farming. Mr. Augspurger was born, May 23, 1869, and is a scion of a highly respected family, a number of members of which are residents of the city of Fort Wayne. In the lumber business Mr. Augspurger finds opportunity for the exercise of those qualities of thrift and energy with which he is abundantly endowed, and his activities add to the general spirit of enterprise and endeavor which characterizes the prosperous village of Woodburn.

The Athenaeum—The following interesting treatise on one of Fort Wayne's modern educational institutions outlines the scope and the accomplishments of The Athenaeum—the Teachers' University of Commerce—which is preparing great numbers of young people for success in the business world: "Yesterday's solutions won't solve tomorrow's problems. Yesterday's strategies won't surmount tomorrow's obstacles. Yesterday's means are not adequate to tomorrow's demands. Men, methods, ideas, change with the hour. Humanity moves with the calendar. Efficiency is the watchword of modern enterprise. To perform a task better, and still better than it was ever performed before; to save time; to eliminate waste; to husband material; to conserve human energy; all is the keynote of every successful project, be it corporate or individual. Tasks which appeared infinite twenty-four hours agone are accepted as a common fact a day hence. In the sphere of education, as elsewhere, has the spirit of the age been markedly felt. Theory has culminated in fact; speculation has given place to certainty; concentration has displaced sporadic effort; misdirected energies have been developed into effective forces; methods and systems have been subordinated to results desired. A process of distillation, as it were, has been going on. The great fact of existence has been subjected to the careful scrutiny of the keenest minds, and the result is a scheme of education which more and more nearly approaches the practical; which approximates the instruction of the individual to the needs of real life. Hand and mind are coming to be trained alike to the solution of the struggles which each one must encounter as a sentient being, dependent upon his own powers for subsistence. In this condition began the present worldwide vocational movement of which the modern commercial training institution is a paramountly important part. In the early part of the present century, Mr. W. J. Bowker and Mr. A. B. Sheron, with the prescience which comes only of strenuous experience, perceived the great field open to a school of learning devoted entirely to the higher lines of this great branch of vocational effort, commercial education. Still further did they realize the splendid results which might accrue to such an institution were its student body selected from a class of people whose education and experience were entirely compatible with, and a logical prerequisite to, the assimilation of such knowledge. The Athenaeum, with its splendid body of former teachers in the public schools, was the magnificent results. As 'Mighty Oaks from Tiny Acorns Grow', as great crusades are born in the development of the few, so do gigantic enterprises unfold themselves from small beginnings. The lofty structure is but the duplication of story upon story; the great is but the small built big. The Athenaeum in its incipiency did not differ from a multitude of other great works; its beginning was unpretentious. He who would achieve by new methods must often batter to a breach a granite wall of preconceived opinion and bias prejudice which will try his soul to the uttermost. With men and states, progress sometimes means near-revolution. The world acknowledges but grudgingly a victory in the winning of which she was not invited to actively participate. In this also, the Athenaeum was like to pioneers in other fields who left the broad avenues and blazed new trails; storms often clouded the skies of its earlier days. It promulgated a new plan of education. It held forth a new idea of instruction to the youth, that which eliminated all which did not directly bear upon the pursuit in which he purposed to win his subsistence; all which was not a pertinent and necessary part thereof being discarded. It sought patronage from only an adult class of students, whose age, previous education and experience had peculiarly fitted them to enter upon the study of higher commerce with a full realization of the responsibilities thereof. In this last its student body was finally limited to those individuals who had formerly been teachers in the public schools, and who by reason of such previous employment were most free from undesirable or deterrent temperamental characteristics. Still another departure from the beaten paths was inaugurated in that the institution offered a plan of study to be followed by the student at his home, without the immediate presence of the instructor. Thus were the benefits of the work of the institution placed within the reach of those who, by reason of insufficient financial means were unable to cease their daily employment, and who might otherwise have been prevented from ever securing the education of their choice. With a meagre number of students as a nucleus, class followed upon class; year succeeded year; time sped on as only time can to those whose waking hours are filled with busy toil. With a steadfast faith in the everlasting correctness of its ideals, the institution forged steadily ahead with an ever-widening influence. First from adjacent counties, then from neighboring states, and finally from far-distant places over the entire country came patrons, leaders of their respective communities. In like degree was the staff of the institution increased by the addition of members especially trained to perform the duties assigned to them, until the present organization of nearly three score instructors, secretaries, division superintendents and assistants was perfected. Today, wherever commercial education is known and accepted throughout this broad land, The Athenaeum stands forth to beckon the ambitious on toward greater accomplishment. From the Atlantic to the Pacific, from Canada to the Gulf, come splendid types of men and women to secure the superior benefits to be derived from the magnificent organization of the institution and the unbounded enthusiasm which pervades its every member. With an incomparable student body of former teachers, results are being accomplished which until the most recent years would have been deemed incredible. Here, indeed, has a new standard of business education been unfurled to the world of commerce; here has leadership been won and maintained by the soundest of doctrines—Progress—Efficiency—Attainment."

Alfred T. Bailey is one of the three executive principals of the Banner Laundering Company and has been an energetic and resourceful factor in the development and upbuilding of the prosperous and representative business now controlled by this company, which has one of the most modern and effectively conducted of laundry plants, with facilities of metropolitan order, the Banner laundry being one of the largest and best equipped in northern Indiana and its effective service having gained and retained to it a representative and appreciative patronage. The business had its inception in 1896, when Messrs. Oscar C. Leggett, Adelaide V. Leggett and Alfred T. Bailey opened a modest laundry near the corner of Woodlawn and Calhoun streets. One year later removal was made to 1317 Calhoun street, where the headquarters of the concern were maintained eight years. The business had in the meanwhile greatly expanded and at the expiration of the period noted the company found it virtually necessary to establish larger and better quarters, with the resu t that wise expediency was conserved by the erection of its present substantial two-story building, at 425 East Columbia street. The main building is forty by eighty-three feet in dimensions, the original engine room being thirty-six by thirty feet in dimensions and an addition, thirteen by sixteen feet, having been made to the same. Beginning with a force of only two assistants, the company now gives employment to seventy persons and in the handling of its business nine of the best metropolitan type of wagons are utilized. Oscar C. Leggett, one of the honored founders of this important enterprise, continued his association with the same until his death, which occurred April 26, 1916, and the interested principals of the firm are now Adelaide V. Leggett, Alfred T. Bailey, and Grace E. Bailey. In August, 1915, the company was incorporated under the laws of Indiana and with a capital stock of twenty-five thousand dollars. Alfred T. Bailey was born in Eaton county, Michigan, on August 26, 1869, and acquired his early education in the public schools of Ingham county, that state. His initial business experience was gained as clerk in a general merchandise store at Lansing. Later he held a clerical position in the postoffice at that place, and finally he gained two years of practical and effective experience in the laundry business. In 1896 he came to Fort Wayne and became one of the founders of the Banner Laundering Company, of which he has remained one of the interested principals to the present time, his close application to business having not precluded his taking a loyal interest in civic affairs and in doing his part to further the advancement of his home. He is actively identified with the Fort Wayne Commercial Club and the Rotary lub, and is affiliated with the Masonic fraternity. He and his wife are popular in the social activities of Fort Wayne, Mrs. Bailey, whose maiden name was Grace Davis, having been a resident of this city at the time of their marriage. Their children are Robert L. and Grace Elizabeth.

J. Wade Bailey was born in Newtonville, Essex county, Massachusetts, on August 29, 1879, and is a son of Joseph Tilden and Mabel (Allen) Bailey, both natives of the old Bay state, and both coming from families that date their respective ancestries back to the first settlement of the new world, so that Mr. Bailey may safely claim a purely American genealogy. The elder Bailey was engaged in the banking business in Boston for many years. J. Wade Bailey had his early education in his native city, and when he was graduated from the Newton high school he entered the employ of Fenno Brothers & Childs, then the largest wool dealers in the United States. This firm later sold out to Hartley Brothers, a firm composed of three London and two American merchants, and it may be said in passing that during the panic in the wool market in 1909 this firm failed for about a million and a half dollars. Following that failure Mr. Bailey became connected with the United States Fastener Company, of Boston, and after a year in the Boston offices of the firm he went to Chicago to look after the middle west end of the business, making his headquarters in Chicago for about two and a half years. He left the employ of that firm to engage in the brokerage business, handling manufacturer's lines on a commission basis, and while he was sufficiently successful in the work to warrant his continuation with it, he gave up the business because of the fact that it necessitated constant traveling, a feature that was extremely displeasing to him. Mr. Bailey exchanged his brokerage activities for a connection with the Burroughs Adding Machine Company of Detroit, and going to Peoria, Illinois, was located there for about ten months. He then took a city territory in Chicago for the same company, continuing there for six months, when the company gave him the agency for Northern Indiana, with headquarters at Fort Wayne. Since locating in that territory Mr. Bailey has realized a generous measure of success in his work of popularizing a device which he claims is solely for the purpose of general betterment of business conditions through the installation of twentieth century methods of handling office records, and he believes that the record of such machines already placed by the majority of manufacturing, wholesale and banking houses in that locality stands as an endorsement of that statement. Mr. Bailey was married in Chicago on June 27, 1912, to Miss Florence Tyler, daughter of Edward Tyler, a promoter of Detroit, Michigan. They have one daughter, Bertha Bailey, born October 29, 1913. Mr. Bailey is a Republican, and socially is a member of the Rotary Club of Fort Wayne. He is also a member of the Commercial Club.

Andrew J. Baker is a native son of Fort Wayne, is a representative of one of the old and honored families of this city, and has been for nearly thirty-five years an efficient and valued member of the city fire department, in which he has held the office of captain since 1894. Since 1899 he has held continuously the office of captain at Fire House No. 7, the preceding five years having been marked by his service in a similar capacity at Fire House No. 5. Captain Baker was born in Fort Wayne on March 6, 1859, and is a son of Henry J. and Mary (Doherty) Baker, the former of whom was born in Germany on August 3, 1828, and the latter in the city of Rochester, New York, August 26, 1836. Henry J. Baker was six years of age at the time of his parents' immigration to America and he was reared and educated in Fort Wayne, Indiana. As a young man, associated with two of his brothers, he became prominently concerned with the civic and material interests of Fort Wayne and Allen county, and later in life he became a member of the firm of Murray & Baker, which developed a prosperous enterprise in the manufacturing of mechanical and gas engines. He engaged also in the real estate business and as an exponent of the same did much to further the development and upbuilding of the present metropolis of Allen county. He laid out the plot of land on which is now located the Pennsylvania railroad depot in Fort Wayne, and his name is fittingly honored and perpetuated in the title of Baker street, in that section of the city. He was also in the saw-mill and general lumber business, and furnished the lumber for the Pittsburg Railroad Company shops. For a number of years he was superintendent of the Wabash and Erie Canal with headquarters in Fort Wayne, and he was also one of the Directors and a stockholder in the Fort Wayne, Jackson and Saginaw Railroad. He was essentially a sterling citizen of much energy, progressiveness and versatility. This honored pioneer was but forty-four years of age at the time of his death, in 1872, and he was influential in public affairs of a local order, his allegiance having been given unreservedly to the Democratic party, and though he was not a seeker of public office he served at one time as a director of the northern state penitentiary of Indiana. His widow survived him for more than thirty years and was nearly seventy years of age at the time of her death, in 1904, both having been earnest and consistent communicants of the Catholic church. They became the parents of nine children: Julia, who was born February 12, 1855, is the wife of Charles E. Stapleford, and they maintain their home in the state of Colorado. Mrs. Stapleford is a woman of fine intellectual and literary attainments and is the author of an interesting published volume entitled "Wahseeola," an Indian word that signifies "The Light of the Tribes at the Meeting Waters," and in 1916-17 she is engaged in the preparation for publication of another work entitled "Under the Yoke of Conscience," that is certain to find popular favor and enduring value. Henry J., who was born November 8, 1856, is bookkeeper for the Clifford Brothers Coal Company of Fort Wayne. Catherina likewise resides in Fort Wayne and is the widow of Victor Muller. Captain Andrew J., of this review, was the next in order of birth. Ambrose C., born July 22, 1862, still resides in Fort Wayne. Margaret, born April 27, 1864, is the wife of August Steinbrunner, of this city. Lawrence A. still maintains his home in Fort Wayne, where he was born April 4, 1868. Ellen A., born August 25, 1870, died in 1916. Gertrude F., born February 11, 1872, is the wife of James Orr, of Colorado Springs, Colorado. Captain Andrew J. Baker acquired his early education in the Catholic parochial schools of Fort Wayne, and as a youth he served an apprenticeship to the baker's trade, as if to make even more consistent the name which he bears. He did not long devote his attention to this trade, however, and after quitting the same he was for some time in the employ of the United States Express Company. In 1883, when twenty-four years of age, he became a minuteman in the Fort Wayne fire department, and in 1893 he was made a full-pay member of the department. That his service and executive ability were of high order was made manifest in the following year, when he was promoted to the office of captain and assigned to Fire House No. 5, where he remained until 1899, since which year he has been captain at Fire House No. 7, as previously noted in this context. The Captain is a strict disciplinarian but invariably just and considerate, so that he has the implicit confidence and good will of his co-workers and has made an admirable record of service as one of the resourceful and courageous fire-fighters of his native city. His political affiliation is with the Democratic party and he attends and supports the Catholic church, in the faith of which he was reared and of which his wife is a zealous communicant. On January 28, 1885, wass olemnized the marriage of Captain Baker to Miss Matilda G. Weier, who was born in the city of Cincinnati, Ohio, and who is a daughter of Martin and Amelia (Weaineer) Weier, both natives of Germany. The name of Mrs. Weier's first husband was Richter, and the one child of this union is Benjamin Richter, who is employed as a tinner by the Pennsylvania Railroad Company. Martin Weier, a tanner by trade, established his residence in Fort Wayne in 1861, and here both he and his wife passed the remainder of their lives. Of their six children Louis J. and Eleanor are deceased; Mrs. Baker was the third and was reared and educated in Fort Wayne; Mollie is the wife of Frederick W. Yeager, of Chicago; Hattie is deceased, and Anthony is a resident of North Dakota. Captain and Mrs. Baker have but one child, Louis A., who is now a successful and popular traveling salesman for the Mossman-Yarnelle Company, of Fort Wayne.

BIOGRAPHICAL SKETCHES

Joseph J. Baker has been a resident of Fort Wayne from the time of his birth, is a representative of one of the honored German families that was founded in Allen county in the pioneer days, and from his youth has been closely and worthily associated with business affairs in his native city, where for the long period of thirty-one years he was an efficient and valued employe of the United States Express Company, with which he remained virtually until this corporation closed up its business and retired from the field of enterprise in which it had long been a dominating factor. Mr. Baker is now one of the two interested principals in the Zurbuch-Baker Coal Company, which controls a prosperous wholesale and retail business and in which his coadjutor is Joseph F. Zurbuch, concerning whom individual mention is made on other pages of this volume. Joseph J. Baker was born in Fort Wayne, December 29, 1860, a son of Jacob and Agatha (Mayer) Baker, the former of whom was born in Hesse-Darmstadt, Germany, and the latter in Geisingeny, a town of the German grand duchy of Baden. Jacob Baker came to America as a young man, about the year 1839, and soon afterward became a resident of Fort Wayne, where he engaged in the work of his trade, that of wagonmaker, but soon afterward became the owner of a sawmill, to the operation of which he gave his attention for a term of years, as one of the substantial and valued business men of Fort Wayne. In 1878 he retired from active business and was venerable in years at the time of his death, in August, 1895, his widow having passed to eternal rest on February 4, 1899, and both having been zealous communicants of St. Mary's Catholic church, of which he was a charter member, his political allegiance having been given to the Democratic party. Of the children the eldest is Mary E., who is now Sister Helen of the Catholic sisterhood of Notre Dame and is giving consecrated service at the present time in the city of St. Louis, Missouri; Joseph J., of this sketch, was the second child; Father Joachim is a priest of the Catholic church and holds a pastoral charge at Remington, Jasper county, Indiana; and Johanna is the wife of Henry W. Kohrmann, of Fort Wayne. Joseph J. Baker was afforded the advantages of the excellent parochial schools of St. Mary's church and as a youth entered the employ of the firm of Shaffer & Calbacker, with whom he remained three years. He then entered the local service of the United States Express Company, in the employ of which corporation he continued for thirty-one years, at the expiration of which, in 1914, he became associated with Joseph F. Zurbuch, under the present title of the Zurbuch-Baker Coal Company. He is a loyal and public-spirited citizen and takes deep interest in all things pertaining to the welfare of his native city and county, the while he is found aligned as a staunch supporter of the principles of the Democratic party. Both he and his wife are active communicants of St. Mary's Catholic church, in connection with which he is a member of the Holy Name Society. On November 18, 1890, was solemnized the marriage of Mr. Baker to Miss Elizabeth Miller, daughter of Joseph and Anastasia (Witz) Miller, of Fort Wayne, and they have three children—Helen, who is the wife of Thomas Harkenriter, of Fort Wayne; Leon J., who is attending the United States Naval Academy, at Annapolis, Maryland; and Agneta, who remains at the parental home.

Leonard M. Bane—As one generation has followed another on to the stage of life Allen county has not failed so to recruit its bar as to maintain at all times a high standard for the same, and the city of Fort Wayne has been the home and professional headquarters of many who have been distinguished figures in the history of Indiana jurisprudence. Leonard Morgan Bane is one of the successful and highly esteemed younger members of the Fort Wayne bar, and has been established in the practice of his profession in the Allen county metropolis and seat of government since the autumn of 1908. His close application and recognized ability have resulted in his developing a substantial law business and it is constantly and legitimately increasing in scope and importance from year to year—a condition that denotes the popular estimate placed upon his ability as an advocate and as a well fortified counselor. The ancestors of the Bane family came to Bucks County, Pennsylvania, in the year 1687, from Lancaster, England. The name is Scotch-Irish origin. The great-great uncle of Leonard M. Bane on the Bane side of the family, was a captain of militia and an Indian fighter during the French and Indian war. A great-grandfather, Lot Leonard, of the maternal side of Mr. Bane's ancestral line, was a captain in the Revolutionary war. The grandfather of Mr. Bane on his mother's side was of German descent. Mr. Bane was born in Greene county, Pennsylvania, on November 8, 1880, and is a son of Morgan A. and Mary E. (Bowser) Bane, the former of whom was born in Washington county, Pennsylvania, May 22, 1845, and the latter in Greene county, that state, July 14, 1852. The parents now maintain their home in Washington county, Pennsylvania, where the father is living virtually retired, he having been a successful farmer and also having been for many years engaged in practice as a veterinary surgeon. His political allegiance is given to the Democratic party and while he has always taken a loyal interest in public affairs in his community he has not been a seeker of political office, though he held for twelve years the position of school director. He is affiliated with the Masonic fraternity and he and his wife attend the Christian church. Of the children the eldest is David E., who is a resident of Uniontown, Pennsylvania, where he is successfully engaged in the practice of law; Leonard M., of this review, was the next in order of birth; Seth C. resides in the village of Lock No. 4, Washington county, Pennsylvania, where he holds the position of timekeeper in the American Wire Mills; Orpha R. is principal of the public schools in one of the thriving villages of Fayette county, Pennsylvania; Veronia likewise is a successful teacher in that county; Pearl M. is the wife of Clyde Swaney, of Washington county, Pennsylvania; John R. is engaged in farming near Billings, Montana; and Joseph H. remains at the parental home. Leonard M. Bane acquired his preliminary education in the public schools of Washington county, Pennsylvania, and supplemented this by an effective course in Madison Academy, at Uniontown, that state. Thereafter he was a successful and popular teacher in the public schools of his native state until he initiated his preparation for the legal profession, his service as a teacher having continued for a period of six years. He finally came to Valparaiso, Indiana, where he entered the law department of the Valparaiso University, in which he was graduated as a member of the class of 1907, and from which he received the degree of Bachelor of Laws, his admission to the Indiana bar having been recorded on the 5th of June of that year. On the 13th of November, 1908, he began the independent practice of his profession in Fort Wayne, and by his ability and effective service he has built up an excellent law business that marks him as one of the representative younger members of the Fort Wayne bar. He is affiliated with the Indiana State Bar Association and the Allen County Bar Association, and he has been admitted to practice in the Indiana supreme court as well as in the United States district court for Indiana. Mr. Bane gives unequivocal support to the principles of the Democratic party, and in Fort Wayne he attends and contributes to the support of the Christian church. In the Masonic fraternity his ancient craft affiliation is with Sol D. Bayless Lodge, No. 359, and in the Ancient Accepted Scottish Rite he has received the thirty-second degree, his maximum York Rite affiliation being with Fort Wayne Commandery of Knights Templars, besides which he holds membership in the Ancient Arabic Order of the Nobles of the Mystic Shrine, and is identified with the Knights of Pythias and the Loyal Order of Moose. He is an active member and supporter of the Fort Wayne Commercial Club, and holds membership in the University Club of Fort Wayne and the International Association of Motor clubs.

Mrs. Carrie B. Banning, M. D.—In according recognition to the representative members of the medical profession in Allen county it is in order to pay tribute to Dr. Banning, whose services as a physician and surgeon have been marked by success. Dr. Banning has been engaged in the practice of her profession in Fort Wayne since 1898 and gives virtually her entire attention to the treatment of the diseases of women. A woman of culture, the Doctor takes active interest in civic affairs, and is a woman whose friends are many. Dr. Banning was born at Phelps, Ontario county, New York, on the 11th of February, 1857, and is a daughter of Dr. Calvin Hasselton and Jeanette K. (DeLano) Carpenter, both likewise natives of the old Empire state and both representatives of families that were founded in America in the colonial era, the ancestral record of each family running back in this country to 1638 and both having given valiant soldiers to the patriot forces in the war of the Revolution, so that the Doctor is eligible for and holds membership in the Society of the Daughters of the American Revolution. Dr. Calvin Hasselton Carpenter, a physician and surgeon of much ability, served with distinction as a surgeon with the Union forces in the Civil war, in which he had charge of the Eighteenth Army Corps of the Army of the Potomac, besides having had supervision of hospital boats on the James river, in Virginia. After the close of the war he engaged in the practice of his profession at Geneva, New York, where he became one of the leading exponents of the Allopathy school of medicine and where he died when still a young man, his widow surviving him by many years; his father was one of the prominent clergymen of the Baptist church in the state of New York for many years prior to his death. Dr. Banning, of this sketch, is the elder of the two children, and her only brother, Jay DeLano Carpenter, died at the age of eleven years. Dr. Banning acquired her early education in well ordered private schools and later attended the University of Wisconsin, at Madison. She likewise gave effective service as a teacher in the public schools, and on February 11, 1879, she became the wife of Edmond P. Banning. Within a period of five years' residence in the city of Boston, Massachusettes, she gave special attention to the study of vocal music. Eventually she determined to prepare herself for the profession in which her father had gained distinction. In consonance with this ambition she finally entered the Cleveland University of Medicine and Surgery, at Cleveland, Ohio, and in this institution she was graduated as a member of the class of 1894.

After thus receiving her degree of Doctor of Medicine she was engaged in practice at Willoughby, Ohio, until 1898, in which year she established her home in Fort Wayne. In this city she has impressed the intervening years with faithful service. The Doctor is a medical inspector of the public schools of Fort Wayne and also for the General Electric Company. She is a prominent member in the Indiana Federation of Women's Clubs, besides which she is identified with college sororities. In a professional way she is affiliated with the Indiana Institute of Homeopathy. Of the children of Dr. Banning the first, Lydia, died in infancy; Carina is the wife of William H. Warrington, of Fort Wayne, is a lawyer by profession and the first woman to be admitted to practice in Allen county. Florida is the wife of Charles Hart, of Fort Wayne; and John D. is identified with the Doud real estate agency in this city.

William N. Barden.—The life of William N. Barden, which came to a close on the 21st of April, 1913, was typical of the men who have entered heartily into the life of the community and made valuable contribution to the true social order. Mr. Barden was born in Genesee county, New York, October 22, 1846, a son of Nathaniel and Loretta (Brown) Barden. His father was a native of New Jersey and his mother of the state of New York, and of their four children, Mary, William N., and Loretta are deceised, the only one now living being Charles, who is a resident of Woodland, Illinois. William N. Barden was only sixteen years of age when he contrived to compass his enlistment for service as a defender of the Union in the Civil war. He became a member of the Eighth New York Heavy Artillery, and in this gallant command he continued his faithful and valiant service for a period of three years. The regiment made a glorious record in the eastern campaigns of the great conflict between the North and the South, and took part in every engagement following the battle of Rappahannock with the army corps and division to which it was attached. After the close of his military career Mr. Barden, a gallant young veteran, came to the west and established his residence at Union City, Branch county, Michigan, where he engaged in the work of the carpenter's trade, his desires and ambitions being centered in identifying himself with the higher phases of construction work. Within a few months he was found in Chicago, engaged as a bridge builder. In 1871 he entered the employ of the Pennsylvania Railroad Company, as a constructor of bridges. Later he established himself in business at Valparaiso, Indiana, and while still a resident of that city he re-entered the employ of the Pennsylvania Railroad Company, in the service of which he became eventually locomotive engineer of passenger trains. He was one of the valued and veteran engineers in the employ of the Pennsylvania Railroad Company at the time of his death, and in his forty-three years of faithful and effective service he made a record that inures to his lasting credit and honor. On Christmas day of the year 1872 was solemnized the marriage of Mr. Barden to Miss Nettie Buell, who was born and reared in Branch county, Michigan, and who is a representative of one of the oldest, most numerous and most influential pioneer families of that county. She is a daughter of the late Chauncey and Elmira (Blanchard) Buell, both natives of the state of New York, the father having been born in Chenango county and the mother in Onondaga county. Chauncey Buell settled in the vicinity of Union City, Branch county, Michigan, as one of the pioneer farmers of that section of the state, and he had come to Michigan in 1838, the year following that of its admission as one of the sovereign commonwealths of the Union. He became one of the prominent and influential citizens of Branch county, and there both he and his wife passed the remainder of their lives, both of them having been zealous members of the historic old Congregational church at Union City. Of their five children the eldest was William Henry, who became more familiarly known to his host of friends as "Billie Hank" Buell and who served with honor as a gallant soldier of the Union in the Civil War, in which he was a member of the Fourth Michigan Battery; he is now a resident of the National Soldiers' Home in the city of Milwaukee, Wisconsin; Ira B. became one of the representative farmers and substantial capitalists of Branch county, Michigan, and passed the closing years of his life in Union City, he likewise having been a soldier in the Civil war; Mrs. Barden was the next in order of birth; Frances is deceased; and Elnora is the wife of Phinious I. Simons, of Athens, Calhoun county, Michigan. William N. Barden was a stalwart supporter of the cause of the Republican party, received the thirty-second degree in the Scottish Rite of the Masonic fraternity, was an honored member of the Brotherhood of Locomotive Engineers, and was an active member of the Third Presbyterian church of Fort Wayne, as is also his widow, who takes deep interest in the various departments of church work, her pleasant home being at 206 West Creighton avenue.

Edward A. Barnes, the general superintendent of the Fort Wayne works of the General Electric Company, has been a resident of this city for more than a quarter of a century and has been continuously identified with the electrical business during the entire period of his independent career. He is skilled in both the technical and practical knowledge of applied electricity and in his chosen profession has won distinctive success, as attested by the responsible position of which he is now the incumbent. In his personal career and ancestral history are points of more than passing interest, and in view of the present tragic period of "wars and rumors of war" he can not but feel a measure of satisfaction and pride in reverting to the long and able service given by his father as an officer in the British army. Edward A. Barnes can claim the distinction of Oriental birth, though he is a scion of the staunchest of British ancestry in both the agnatic and distaff lines. He was born at Dhurmsala, India, in June, 1865, and is a son of Major Edward Barnes and Georgiana (Carnegy) Barnes, the former a native of Wales and the latter of Scotland. Major Barnes gave distinguished service as an officer in the English army and was assigned to duty in different colonial dependencies of England from time to time, so that his travels were of wide scope. He was in government service with the army in India at the time of the birth of his son Edward A., of this review, and was in active service in South Africa at the time of his death, his widow having passed the closing years of her life in Fort Wayne, where she remained in the home of her son Edward A. until her death, in 1901. The only other surviving child is Colonel Arthur A. Barnes, who was commander of a Wiltshire regiment in England and who is now with his command in the great European war. Edward A. Barnes was a child of four years when he was taken from India to England, where he received excellent educational advantages and where he gained his preliminary technical training as an electrician. In 1885, when twenty years of age, he came to the United States and established his residence in New York city. There he continued his association with the electrical business until 1889, when he came to

Indiana and established his permanent home in Fort Wayne. Here he took a position with the Fort Wayne General Electric Company, and with this concern he has continued his effective services during the intervening years. The local works of the General Electric Company have owed much to Mr. Barnes for the effective development of the important business of which he is now the general superintendent, and thus he has been a factor in advancing the industrial and commercial prestige of Fort Wayne, where he is known and valued as a loyal citizen, progressive business man and as a captain of industry. In his estimate of the land of his adoption there is naught of equivocation and he is thoroughly in harmony with American sentiment and institutions. His political allegiance is given to the Republican party. He is a communicant of the Protestant Episcopal church, and he holds membership in the Fort Wayne Commercial Club, the Rotary Club, the General Electric Quarter Century Club, and the Country Club, as well as of the American Institute of Electrical Engineers and the American Institute of Metals. On October 16, 1895, was solemnized the marriage of Mr. Barnes to Miss Katherine Steinbrunner, who was born and reared in Fort Wayne and who is a daughter of Robert and Ignatia (Lais) Steinbrunner, both natives of Germany. Mr. and Mrs. Barnes have two children—Georgiana Ignatia Carneay and Katherine Allison Stuart.

Abraham G. Barnett is one of the most venerable of the native sons of Fort Wayne now residing in the city, and he has witnessed the development of the judicial center of Allen county from the status of a mere village to its present proud position as one of the important industrial and commercial centers and attractive cities of the Hoosier state. He is a representative of a family whose name has been identified with the history of Allen county during the long years that have intervened since the war of 1812, and his father was captain of a company that served at the old fort for some time during the progress of the second conflict with Great Britain. Mr. Barnett was born at Fort Wayne November 10, 1832, and is a son of James and Nancy (Welsh) Barnett, whose marriage was here solemnized in the year 1824. James Barnett came to Fort Wayne in 1812, and after having served as captain of a company that was here stationed during a portion of the war of 1812-15 he continued his residence in Fort Wayne after the war had terminated. In the pioneer days he developed a successful business in the hauling of merchandise and other commodities from Dayton, Ohio, to Fort Wayne, and finally he made judicious investments in land in this part of the state. He became one of the successful and influential citizens of Northern Indiana, did much to further civic and industrial development and progress in Allen county, and it was principally through his financial assistance and generosity that the late Samuel Hanna, another of the sterling pioneers of Allen county, was enabled to engage in the mercantile business and thus to lay the foundation of what became one of the large fortunes here accumulated. James Barnett was born in 1785 and died in 1851. His wife was born in 1801 and died in 1857. Of their seven children, four attained to maturity, and of the number only two are now living—Abraham G., of this review, and Mrs. Susan B. Shoaff, who likewise resides in Fort Wayne. Abraham G. Barnett profited by the advantages afforded in the pioneer schools of Fort Wayne and at the age of about seventeen years he here began clerking in the drug store of Watson Wall. In 1852, when twenty years old, he was one of the adventurous spirits who made the long and perilous journey across the plains to California, and four months were demanded in making the trip from St. Joseph, Missouri, the outfitting point, to Placerville, California, a place then known by the significant name of Hangtown. Mr. Barnett was actively associated with gold mining in the pioneer placer camps of California, and his activities included also service as mail carrier and work as a blacksmith. In 1855 he returned to Fort Wayne, where he engaged in the grocery business, besides becoming a successful exponent of agricultural enterprise in his native county. Finally he was appointed United States assessor for the district comprising Allen county, and of this position he continued the incumbent three years. His next occupation was in connection with the operation of a local paper mill, and after severing this alliance he established in Fort Wayne a transfer line. In this field of enterprise he built up a large and prosperous business and to the same he continued to give his general supervision for more than a quarter of a century. Since that time he has lived virtually retired in his attractive home at 2432 South Webster street, and he is one of the well known and highly honored pioneer citizens of Fort Wayne. At the time of the Civil war Mr. Barnett made two attempts to enlist, but on each occasion he was refused the privilege, owing to minor physical ailments. March 3, 1863, he was appointed major in the regular army, but never served. He is the oldest Blue Lodge Mason in Fort Wayne and has taken the York Rite degrees of Masonry and affiliated also with the Scottish Rite. He has always been liberal and public-spirited as a citizen, has maintained lively interest in all things touching the welfare and advancement of his native city and gives his political allegiance to the Republican party. As a young man Mr. Barnett wedded Miss Sarah Elizabeth Angell, who was born at Little Falls, New York, and the maximum loss and bereavement in his life came when his gracious and devoted wife was summoned to eternal rest, in 1906. Of the four children who survive the loved mother, Katherine is the wife of W. Bruce Beamer, of Fort Wayne; Susan M. remains with her venerable father; Byron H. is individually mentioned on other pages; and James W. is the name of the youngest.

Byron H. Barnett was formerly one of the successful exponents of amusement enterprise in his native city of Fort Wayne, where he was for a time associated in the ownership and operation of the Palace theater, a modern home that provides the best grade of entertainments. The business was effectively conducted by the Fort Wayne Lyric Theater Company, of which Mr. Barnett was secretary and treasurer. Byron H. Barnett was born in Fort Wayne, February 14, 1867, and is a son of Abraham G. Barnett, who conducted in this city a successful transfer business and who is a citizen held in unqualified esteem. Byron H. Barnett acquired his youthful education in the Fort Wayne schools and as a young man served an apprenticeship to the machinist's trade, in the Fort Wayne shops of the Pennsylvania Railroad Company. As a railroad man he was for five years employed on the Santa Fe in California, and at the expiration of this period he became associated with his father in the transfer business in Fort Wayne. Finally he here bcame associated with Frank E. Stouder in the ownership of the Lyric theater, and four years later, after having conducted the house most successfully, they disposed of the same and built the handsomely equipped Palace theater, which they conducted under the corporate title previously mentioned and with a substantial and representative supporting patronage. In

politics Mr. Barnett is found arrayed as a loyal supporter of the principles and cause of the Republican party, he and his wife are communicants of the Protestant Episcopal church, he is affiliated with the local organization of the Benevolent & Protective Order of Elks, and in the Masonic fraternity he holds membership in York Rite bodies, including the Fort Wayne Commandery of Knights Templars, besides which he is affiliated also with the adjunct organization, the Ancient Arabic Order, Nobles of the Mystic Shrine. In the Ancient Accepted Scottish Rite of Masonry he has received the thirty-second degree. In 1900 was solemnized the marriage of Mr. Barnett to Miss Catherine Auger, daughter of Louis B. Auger, a pioneer florist and well known citizen of Fort Wayne. Mr. and Mrs. Barnett have one son, Abraham Houston, who was born January 27, 1903, and whose educational advantages include those of the Howe Military Academy, at Howe, Indiana.

Charles Eldridge Barnett, M. D.—One of the functions of this publication is to accord recognition to those who touch closely the communal life of Fort Wayne and Allen county, and under these conditions it is pleasing to give consideration to Dr. Barnett as one of the leading surgeons of the county and state. He is engaged in the practice of surgery in Fort Wayne and his success shows the expediency of concentration of effort in the one department of his profession. Dr. Barnett was born at Wapakoneta, the judicial center of Auglaize county, Ohio, September 30, 1866, and is a son of Rev. William C. and Frances Mead (Sullivan) Barnett, the former a native of Pennsylvania and the latter of Virginia. The father, a man of fine intellectuality and exalted character, gave many years of effective service as a clergyman of the Lutheran church. For many years he was one of the directors of Wittenberg College, and he continued in the active work of the ministry until his death, which occurred in 1898, in the state of Tennessee, his loved wife having died in 1880, at which time the family home was in Kentucky; and of their six children three are living. Dr. Charles Eldridge Barnett was a child of two years when his parents removed from Ohio to Boone county, Kentucky, where he was reared to the age of fifteen yars and where he attended the public schools. Thereafter he was engaged in teaching for a time and finally he entered Edgewood College at Edgewood, Tennesee, in which he was graduated as a member of the class of 1888, with the degree of Bachelor of Science. In preparation for his chosen profession he came to Indiana and entered the Fort Wayne College of Medicine, in which well ordered institution he was graduated in 1890, with the degree of Doctor of Medicine. In 1893 he took an effective post-graduate course in the Chicago Polyclinic, and a few years later he did excellent post-graduate work in the medical department of the University of the South, at Suawanee, Tennessee. The Doctor has made Fort Wayne the scene of his professional activities since 1896 and he has been not only a leader in surgery but has also been influential in the educational work of his profession. He served as a member of the faculty of his alma mater, the Fort Wayne College of Medicine, in which he held the chair of surgical anatomy and genito-urinary surgery until the institution, together with all other medical colleges in the state, was merged into the medical department of the University of Indiana, in which he was made adjunct professor of genito-urinary surgery. The professional novitiate of Dr. Barnett was served at Archer, Nebraska. He is actively identified with the American Medical Association; the Mississippi Valley Medical Association, of which he was vice-president in 1911, as well as chairman of its surgical section; the Indiana State Medical Society; and the Allen County Medical Society, of which he was president during the year 1910-1911. He took a lively interest in the alumni association of Fort Wayne College of Medicine and served at one time as president of the same. The Doctor is a member of the Indiana state committee for the national association of physicians formed for the furtherance of medical preparedness under conditions of war; and of the Council of National Defense under the jurisdiction of the War Department; is a member of the medical officers reserve corps of the United States Army; and is an influential member of the American Society of Urological Surgeons. He is a fellow of the American College of Surgeons. In 1898 he gave definite evidence of his loyalty and patriotism by tendering his service and going forth as assistant surgeon of the One Hundred and Fifty-Seventh Indiana Volunteer Infantry, with the rank of captain. Incidental to the Spanish-American war he continued in active and effective service with this command until the regiment was mustered out, at the close of activities. Dr. Barnett has been a voluminous and an authoritative writer on professional subjects pertaining to the diagnoses and treatment of genito-urinary diseases, especially from the surgical standpoint. After returning from one of his numerous trips to Europe for post-graduate work he gave to the world some new and valuable surgical knowledge by publishing, in 1910, an article entitled, "The Visicule Seminales," which was copied by the leading foreign surgical journals. In 1913 he published an article entitled "Polycistic Kidney," and, as a matter of purely technical judgment on his part, he looks upon these two publications as constituting his most valuable contributions to the literature of his profession. He is one of the Abstract Editors of the Literature of the world under the subject of Genito-Urinary Surgery, also on the advisory board and Colaborator of the Urologic and Cutaneous Review. He is one of the Abstract Editors of Genito-Urinary Surgery in International Abstract of Surgery (Surgery Gynecology and Obstetrics with International Abstract of Surgery). In connection with his study and individual research he continues to make frequent contributions to our leading surgical publications, with his ideals of personal stewardship in thus giving to his confreres the benefits of his fortuitous knowledge. Dr. Barnett has taken post-graduate work in all of the leading surgical centers of Europe, especially Vienna, Austria, and he has traveled in nearly all parts of the civilized world, with a constant view to expanding his knowledge of surgical science and practice. In politics he gives unswerving allegiance to the Democratic party, and in the Masonic fraternity he has completed the circle of both the York and Scottish Rites and belongs to the Mystic Shrine.

James M. Barrett, long connected with the traction systems of northern Indiana in executive positions, has enjoyed for many years an enviable place among the members of the bar of Indiana. For an extended period Mr. Barrett served as the counsel for the several companies that developed into the present Fort Wayne & Northern Indiana Traction Company, and latterly, until 1917, he served as president of this important corporation, which not only owns and operates the Fort Wayne city traction system and a seven-mile extension to Robison Park but also owns and operates two important interurban lines, extending to the south and southwest of Fort Wayne. As an authority on corporation law Mr.

Barrett has gained a high reputation, although his services in other lines have proved to be most efficacious. As the author of the so-called Barrett law, while a member of the Indiana legislature, his name is favorably known throughout the state. James Madison Barrett was born on a farm in LaSalle county, Illinois, February 7, 1852, and is a son of Benjamin and Elizabeth Barrett, both natives of Ireland, where the father was born in the year 1809, a son of William Barrett. James M. Barrett was the eighth in order of birth in a family of eleven children, of whom nine attained to years of maturity. Benjamin Barrett and his wife came from the Emerald Isle to America in 1834. They established their home in Belmont county, Ohio, where the father continued to be engaged in farming until 1848, when removal was made to LaSalle county, Illinois. There the death of Benjamin Barrett occurred in 1876, his widow surviving him by nearly a score of years and having been eighty years of age at the time of her death, in January, 1894. After attending the common schools of his native county, James M. Barrett was given the opportunity of attending the Mendota College, at Mendota, Illinois, and after leaving this institution he entered the University of Michigan, at Ann Arbor, in which he was graduated as a member of the class of 1875. He had pursued a literary course in the university, thus following a natural inclination to acquaint himself with the broad scope of this branch of work undertaken so thoroughly by the Ann Arbor institution. Mr. Barrett's university course was followed by a brief course of study in the law offices of the firm of McCagg, Culver & Butler, prominent Chicago attorneys, and thereafter he spent a period of study at Princeton, Illinois. He was attracted to Fort Wayne in the early weeks of 1876 and reached the city on Washington's birthday anniversary of that year. Shortly after his arrival he was admitted to the bar of Allen county. Mr. Barrett found it advisable to devote his studies largely to the intricacies of corporation law, and his determined action along this line has brought him a designation as a man of keen perception, yet one with a knowledge and appreciation of the rights of men that have won for him the victory in many a hard-fought legal battle. For a considerable period Mr. Barrett was associated in practice with Samuel L. Morris and R. C. Bell, and after the death of the latter the firm of Barrett & Morris continued until the recent addition of Edward G. Hoffman to the personnel of the firm. An extensive suite in the Shoaff building marks the location of this important legal union. For several years before his selection as president of the Fort Wayne & Northern Indiana Traction Company Mr. Barrett served as the counsel for the company. His knowledge of this branch of commercial activity has made his service and advice of incalculable value to other traction systems in which he holds a financial interest. Mr. Barrett is interested in a number of manufacturing industries, including the Packard Company, makers of the famed Packard pianos and player-pianos, and he is a member of the directorate of this concern. In 1896 Mr. Barrett was appointed a member of the board of trustees of Purdue University, at Lafayette, Indiana, by Governor Claude Matthews. He served on the board with former President Benjamin Harrison, who was selected the same year. In 1886 he became the Democratic candidate for state senator, to represent the Fort Wayne district, and his popularity was demonstrated by the splendid majority that was awarded him at the polls. During his first term in the senate he was prominently identified with the creation of many constructive laws. Among the important acts was that which insured for Fort Wayne the choice of his home city as the seat of the Indiana School for Feeble-Minded Youth. During the important session of 1889 Mr. Barrett was the acknowledged leader of his party in the senate, serving as chairman of the judiciary committee and as a member of many other committees whose functions were of marked importance to the success of momentous measures of that session. Senator Barrett was the author of a number of important bills, and proved to be an able and discriminating legislator. Faithful to the interests of the people, he was uniformly recognized as an impartial representative of his district and of the state. Mr. Barrett has achieved a reputation not only as a ready, forceful and eloquent speaker but he has also shown himself to be possessed of great strength of character and thus has ever held an inviolable place in the hearts of the people of his community. Mr. Barrett is a thirty-second degree Mason and a member of the Benevolent & Protective Order of Elks. He finds delight in his affiliation with the Fort Wayne Country Club, and his active interest in civic affairs is suggested by his membership in the Fort Wayne Commercial Club. The recognition of his personal worth is indicated in his membership in the American Academy of Social Science, the American Geographical Society, the American Municipal League, the American Bar Association and the Indiana Bar Association. On the 28th of June, 1877, Mr. Barrett was united in marriage with Miss Marian A. Bond, daughter of Charles D. and Lavinia (Ewing) Bond, of Fort Wayne. Mr. Bond was a former president of the Fort Wayne National Bank, which is now known as the Old National Bank, and his wife was a daughter of Judge Charles W. Ewing, the first attorney to locate in Fort Wayne and one of the earliest judges of the circuit court of Allen county. To James M. Barrett and his wife have been born four children: Florence Ewing, wife of George T. Ladd, of Philadelphia, Pennsylvania; Charles W., master mechanic of the Pennsylvania Railroad shops at Sunbury, Pennsylvania; Walter A., mechanical engineer with the Bass Foundry & Machine Company, Fort Wayne; and James Madison, Jr., now (1917) a student in the University of Michigan, in the literary department of which institution he was graduated in 1916 and in the law department of which he is a member of the class of 1918. James M. Barrett has always been a liberal contributor to every movement for the advancement of Fort Wayne and the state of Indiana, and he is truly counted as one of Indiana's most valuable citizens.

  Louis L. Bart, one of the prominent real estate men of Fort Wayne, Indiana, was born in Mallet Creek, Ohio, a village in Medina county, that state, October 28, 1875. He is of German extraction, his father, Leonard Bart, having been born in Germany, March 31, 1832. He learned the shoemaker trade and conducted a shoe store in Washington, D. C., after his arrival in this country. He espoused the cause of the north in the War of the Rebellion, serving at the battle of Bull Run and others. Later he married Helen Miller, a native of Newark, Licking county, Ohio, and taking his bride to Mallet Creek, established himself in the shoe trade. He conducted a shoe store for thirty-two years, retired, and is still living in the town of his adoption. To him and his wife were born six children, five of whom are living. Louis L. Bart, the subject of this sketch, was educated in the common schools at Mallet Creek, Ohio, and in the high school at York, Ohio, from which institution he was graduated with the class of 1891. Immediately upon

Charles S. Bash

receiving his diploma he interested himself in the profession of telegraphy and followed it for twenty-two years. For fifteen years he was associated with the Nickel Plate Railroad at Fort Wayne, thirteen of which he was train dispatcher. He forsook this calling, however, to take up that of the real estate business, establishing himself in business in 1913. He has met with success in this new pursuit and is now the vice-president of the Wildwood Sales Company But this one office does not require all his time and he is also a director in the Morris Plan Bank, vice-president of the Fort Wayne Real Estate Exchange, and is on the executive committee of the Railroaders' Realty Company. Mr. Bart has always given the Republican party his political support, although he has never entered the lists as a candidate for office. He is a Knight Templar, a thirty-second degree Scottish Rite Mason, and also a member of the Shrine. He is a member of the Commercial Club, serving that organization on the membership committee. On June 29, 1904, was solemnized the marriage of Mr. Bart to Miss Josephine Shuemaker, and this marriage has been blessed with one son, Robert Rosenthal Drayer Bart.

Charles S. Bash.—Measured by its rectitude, its productiveness, its pervading altruism and its material success, the life of the late Charles S. Bash, of Fort Wayne, counted for much, and in this history of the city and county in which he passed the major part of his life and to whose civic and material progress he contributed in large measure, it is most consistent that a review of his career and a tribute to his memory be incorporated. His influence extended in many directions, his broad business activities inured to the commercial prestige of Fort Wayne, and his insistent civic loyalty and progressiveness were not a matter of mere sentiment but of constructive achievement. He marked by distinctive personal accomplishment a place of his own in connection with economic, industrial and social affairs of Allen county, where his name and memory shall be held in lasting honor. Mr. Bash was born at Roanoke, Huntington county, Indiana, July 28, 1853, and at his home in Fort Wayne, he rested from his labors and passed to the life eternal on the 24th of September, 1916, after an illness of several months' duration. Of his attitude in the closing days of his earnest and prolific life the following pertinent statement has been written: "His indomitable courage and his determined refusal to submit to the domination of physical ills were such that until two weeks prior to his death his condition was not thought to be serious." In the year following that of his birth the parents of Mr. Bash removed to Fort Wayne, and here he passed the residue of his life. Here he continued his studies in the public schools until he had duly profited by the advantages of the high school, and soon afterward he became associated with the firm of S. Bash & Company, which was well established in the seed and produce commission business and of which his father, Solomon Bash, was the executive head. This firm was founded in 1868, the interested principals in establishing the business being Solomon Bash, P. D. Smyser, and P. L. McKee. Solomon Bash was long known and honored as one of the representative business men and influential citizens of Fort Wayne and he became president of the commission house of S. Bash & Company after the same was incorporated under the laws of Indiana. Of this office he continued the incumbent until his death, which occurred in 1914. His son, Charles S., subject of this memoir, then assumed control of the extensive and well ordered commission business, of which he became the sole owner, the other members of the company having retired. His intimate and prolonged association with the business thus established in the early days gave to him the strongest of reinforcement in carrying forward the important industrial and commercial enterprise, and in this connection the following estimate is worthy of perpetuation: "Having entered the employ of his father when a young man, he had practically grown up with the business, and his knowledge in this line was so broad and accurate that he was justly considered an authority and that his advice was often solicited and as frequently valued. Few men had a wider or more general acquaintanceship throughout northern Indiana than did Mr. Bash, the nature of his business bringing him into specially close touch with the representative agriculturists in this favored portion of the Hoosier state." A man of splendid force and much reserve energy, Mr. Bash did not limit his activities to the seed and produce business, and his interests became many and varied in connection with commercial, industrial and semi-public enterprises, the while he was known as one of Fort Wayne's most alert, progressive and loyal citizens. Mr. Bash was one of the organizers and incorporators of the Salamoni Mining & Gas Company, and this became one of the most important concerns with which he had constructive alliance. It was essentially due to the zealous and well ordered efforts of Mr. Bash that natural gas was first brought into Fort Wayne, and it was in his home that the first natural gas piped into the city was burned. In that pioneer period of the development of the natural gas industry in northern Indiana, in 1890, the introduction of the gas in Fort Wayne was an event of importance, and many persons assembled to witness the result of the experiment when Mr. Bash lighted the first flame. He had the circumspection and initiative that make for self-confidence, and he was ever ready to support his confidence in concrete action, so that it was characteristic of the man when he became the prime mover in the organization of the natural gas company and the subsequent exploitation and development of the gas resources of this part of the state. In this field was given one evidence of his progressiveness and ready grasping of opportunity, and it is a matter of record that later appreciable financial returns came from the development of the natural gas business throughout the eastern and central parts of Indiana. Mr. Bash was one of the organizers and original stockholders of the Home Telephone & Telegraph Company, and was characteristically resourceful and influential in the upbuilding of its excellent system of service. He was likewise one of the incorporators of the Wayne Knitting Mills and gave to the incipient enterprise the valuable aid that resulted in its development from modest proportions to an important status as one of the leading concerns of its kind in the United States. Mr. Bash established the first fertilizing plant in this section of Indiana, and was for some time a director of the Hamilton National Bank and of the Fort Wayne Electric Works. His judgment was always assured in connection with business affairs and he was always ready to back this judgment by financial co-operation and personal effort in the support of enterprises that tended to advance the general welfare. There were few public enterprises in Fort Wayne in which he did not figure prominently and effectively. Concerning one of the most important undertakings that received his earnest and thoughtful advocacy the following statements have been made: "Just as he caught the vision of what the gas and telephone industries might mean to the commonwealth, so he felt and realized the

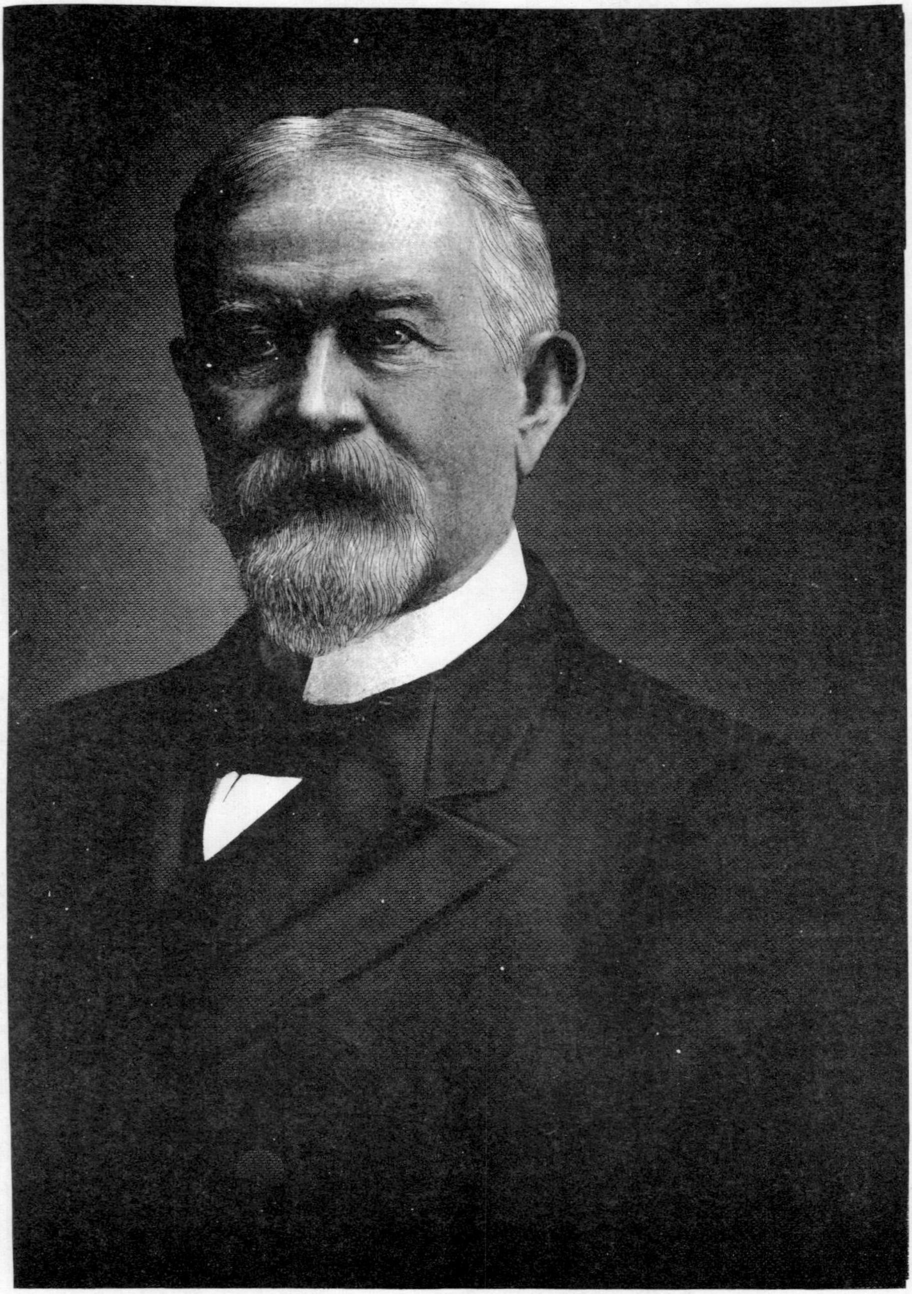

J H Bass

possibilities and value of a barge canal through Fort Wayne. He was one of the pioneer boosters and hardest workers for the so-called Toledo, Fort Wayne & Chicago canal. For years he was a member of the board of directors of the Erie & Michigan Deep Waterways Association, and in December, 1915, he was an influential delegate to the national rivers and harbors congress. In the furtherance of the construction of the canal he made a number of promotive trips with the late Hon. Perry A. Randall and delivered forceful speeches in favor of the project. It was one of his fondest hopes that he might see Lake Erie and Lake Michigan connected with Fort Wayne by a barge canal. He was confident of the ultimate construction of such a waterway. Having been for many years engaged in the shipping business, he could fully gauge the benefits to be derived from such transportation facilities, and he gave unsparingly of his time and money in forwarding the movement." As a broad-minded and public-spirited citizen, Mr. Bash was strongly fortified in his convictions concerning governmental and economic matters and was aligned as a stalwart supporter of the principles of the Republican party. His civic loyalty was clearly shown by the effective service he gave as a member of the municipal board of public works, during the administration of Mayor Oakley, and by his several years' membership on the board of education. His deep interest in the cause of the Republican party became specially noticeable during the national campaigns of 1896 and 1900, when he became associated with Dr. A. E. Bulson, Jr., E. F. Yarnelle, and A. T. Lukens, in forming the "Big Four Quartet," an organization that traveled extensively through this section of the country during each of these campaigns and sang stirring songs in the Republican meetings held to further the cause of President McKinley and that of the party in general. Mr. Bash was a zealous member and supporter of Westminster Presbyterian church, in which his widow retains active membership, and such were his character and services that he signally honored the city in which he spent virtually his entire life and in which the community manifested a sense of personal loss and sorrow when he was summoned from the stage of his mortal endeavors. In April, 1882, was solmenized the marriage of Mr. Bash to Miss Flora E. Orr, who survives him, as do also nine children—Charles S., Jr., Joseph W. and Howard O., all of whom are identified with business affairs in Fort Wayne; Hester, who is the wife of Miles F. Porter, Jr., of this city; Virginia, who is the wife of Hale Bradley, of Huntington, Indiana; Clara, who is the wife of Arthur Schreck, of Fort Wayne; and Misses Lucy, Julia and Marian, who remain with their widowed mother in the beautiful family home in Fort Wayne.

John H. Bass—The name of John H. Bass is inseparably connected, in a most enviable way, with the financial and industrial life of Fort Wayne and the middle west during a period of more than sixty years. The activities of Mr. Bass in his home city date from the year 1852 when, at the age of seventeen, he inaugurated that vigorous, intelligent business career which has raised him to the pinnacle of success and placed his name among the captains of industry. Fort Wayne takes just pride in Mr. Bass as one of her foremost, substantial, progressive citizens. The monster plant of the Bass Foundry & Machine Company, spreading its departments over an area of more than five city squares in length will ever stand as a monument to his genius and ability—for Mr. Bass, unlike many another man similarly situated, has been careful to keep his hands and his mind closely upon the developing business which has grown to such large proportions and has refrained from delegating the care of his larger affairs to others. The Bass Foundry & Machine Company had its inception in 1853, when it was organized as Jones, Bass & Company. John H. Bass came to Fort Wayne in the preceding year from Salem, Livingston county, Kentucky, where he was born, November 9, 1835. Mr. Bass is descended from early families of Virginia and the Carolinas prominently identified with the colonial history of the nation. The grandfather of John H. Bass on the side of the father was Jordan Bass, born in Virginia in 1764, from which state he moved to Christian county, Kentucky, in 1805, in the midst of the troublous conditions which preceded the war of 1812, in which Kentucky and Indiana took such a prominent part. He died in 1853 at the age of eighty-nine years. Sion Bass, father of John H. Bass, was born in Virginia, November 7, 1802. From the age of three, he was a resident of Kentucky and rose to prominence in the conduct of commercial affairs and the owner and cultivator of large areas of farm land. The wife of Sion Bass was Miss Jane Todd, born in Charleston, South Carolina, June 19, 1802, the daughter of John Todd, also a pioneer settler of Kentucky. Sion Bass and wife remained in Kentucky until 1866, when they came to Fort Wayne and spent their closing days with their son, John H. Bass. The mother died August 26, 1874, and the father August 7, 1888. They were the parents of six children, four of whom attained to maturity. John H. Bass is the only surviving member of the family. In this connection it would seem entirely proper to refer briefly to the services and military record of Colonel Sion S. Bass, elder brother of John H. Bass, whose name is held in tender remembrance by the veterans of the Civil war and who have named one of the local posts of the Grand Army of the Republic in his honor. Sion S. Bass, who was born in Kentucky in January, 1827, came to Fort Wayne in 1848, as the first representative of the family to settle in Indiana. To his honor it may be said that he represented the type of pioneer manufacturer who laid the foundation for much of the active development in many lines of endeavor. As a member of the firm of Jones, Bass & Company, which was succeeded by the Fort Wayne Machine Works, he became indirectly one of the founders of the Bass Foundry & Machine Works, which was sold to the Pennsylvania railway for shop purposes and other industries which have resulted from the parent institution. Lincoln's call for volunteers in 1861 appealed to him so strongly that he gave up, with temporary intent, the conduct of his affairs in order to give his services to his country. His first service was in giving assistance to the formation of the famous Thirtieth Indiana volunteers of which he was made colonel. This regiment took an active part in the maneuvers which led up to the battle of Shiloh. Early on the second day of that battle, the regiment, without time to rest from an arduous march to the field, was ordered to advance. Amid a deadly fire, the regiment pushed forward, led by Colonel Bass, who fell with a mortal wound. Many others fell in that fearful advance at Shiloh. The comrades of Colonel Bass, after a brief memorial service, sent the body back to Fort Wayne, where a city already in mourning for many others who sacrificed their lives in that immortal battle, bowed in deeper grief over the fallen leader of the gallant Thirtieth. John H. Bass attended the schools of his native county in Kentucky, and there gave evidence of a strong adaptability for the lines of study which later developed in the modern type of business man. For a time he enjoyed the instruction of a private tutor. He was seventeen years of age when he came to Fort

Wayne, in 1852, to begin his actual commercial career. For a time he was employed in a grocery store, and then served as a bookkeeper for the contracting firm of Samuel and William S. Edsall. Then he joined his brother, Sion S. Bass, as an employe of Jones, Bass & Company, where he served as bookkeeper from 1854 until 1857, when the firm dissolved partnership. During these years, Mr. Bass had, by studying at night, perfected himself as an accountant. In 1857, when investments in Iowa lands proved an attractive venture, he went west and spent $3,700 in the choicest farm lands he could find. He remained two years, watching carefully the real estate conditions, and returned with $15,000 in cash and the deeds to real estate worth $50,000. The close application to the study of business methods fitted him, by the year 1859, to employ his capital, in company with that of Edward L. Force, in the establishment of Bass & Force. The aggregate output of the concern during the first twelve months reached $20,000. This plant stood on the site of the present Pennsylvania railway shops and became the nucleus of this great industrial department of that system. The example of Mr. Bass in venturing the investment of his money in manufacturing enterprises at that time was a great incentive to others to do likewise, with the result that Fort Wayne early became famed as a manufacturing center. Between the years 1860 and 1863 the business was owned and conducted by Mr. Bass and Judge Samuel Hanna. In 1863 Judge Hanna transferred his interests to his son, Horace Hanna, whose death occurred six years later. At that time Mr. Bass purchased the stock held by the Hannas and has since been the sole owner of the business and, under his sole management, it has had a wonderful prosperity. Employment has been given to thousands down through the years, and many of Fort Wayne's substantial citizens have been drawn and held there through their connection with the Bass Foundry & Machine Works. In 1898 the company was incorporated with a capital of $1,500,000, which was later increased to $2,200,000. This corporation owns and operates a branch plant at Rock Run, Alabama, which mines and smelts a large part of the ore used in the products of the Fort Wayne plant. The fine grade of pig iron which is made into car wheels comes largely from the affiliated Alabama concern. From time to time larger and better buildings have been added to the Fort Wayne plant. An average of 2,500 men are employed here, with an annual payroll (1917) of $1,500,000. The tonnage of manufactured material shipped from the two plants aggregates 300,000 tons annually. The chief products of the Fort Wayne plant are car wheels, axles, iron and steel forgings, Corliss engines, boilers, complete power plants and gray iron castings. The product of the Rock Run plant is high grade furnace pig iron. The Fort Wayne plant covers an area of twenty acres. Twenty-five thousand acres of land are included in the Rock Run mining district owned by the company. Raw material from which the Fort Wayne plant produces its finished products is shipped to the city by the train load. The many departments of the business are operated "like clockwork" and the products of the Bass establishments have made a reputation for themselves and Fort Wayne all over America. After Mr. Bass established the Fort Wayne plant on a prosperous basis, he gave a portion of his attention to other lines of industry which indicate his ability in many directions. In 1869 he founded the St. Louis Car Wheel Company, at St. Louis, Missouri, in which he held a controlling interest and served as its president until he disposed of his interest in the company. In 1873 Mr. Bass, despite the conditions which characterized the panic of the period, established an extensive iron works in the city of Chicago, a venture which suggests the qualities in the character of Mr. Bass which enables him to view the future and its possibilities with a keener understanding than that which is vouchsafed to most men of large affairs. Without that degree of daring which characterizes the plunger, but with a marked foresight and sagacity, coupled with good judgment, he recognized the possibilities of the city of Chicago and "got in on the ground floor" just as that city was beginning to recover from the effects of the destructive fire of two years before. The Chicago venture like that in St. Louis proved to be a large paying investment. In addition to the Alabama mining properties, and those already described, Mr. Bass is heavily interested in a large foundry at Lenoir, Tennessee, which is also supplied with raw material from the Alabama mines. During his many years of residence in Fort Wayne Mr. Bass has shown a broad public spirit. He was one of the owners of the original street railway system, when the horse-drawn cars were employed. The Citizens' Street Railway Company was incorporated in 1871, to operate the system. On the 22nd of August, 1887, on the foreclosure of a mortgage for $20,000 executed to Oliver P. Morgan and Edward P. Williams, the property rights and franchises were sold to Mr. Bass and Stephen B. Bond, representing the Fort Wayne Street Railway Company, which was brought into existence to acquire the property. The system then consisted of about two miles of single track on Calhoun street, from Main street to Creighton avenue, on Creighton avenue from Calhoun street to Fairfield avenue, and on Wallace street from Calhoun to Hanna streets. The cars were operated at intervals of twenty minutes. Associated with Mr. Bass and Mr. Bond in this ownership were Jesse L. Williams and Charles D. Bond. These men were the owners of large tracts of land south of the Pennsylvania tracks and east of Calhoun street, and the extension of the line served in the early development of that outlying district. This company owned the street railway lines until August, 1892, when a reorganized company converted the property into an electrically-propelled system. For many years Mr. Bass has been one of the chief stockholders of the First National Bank of Fort Wayne. During thirty years he held the office of president and resigned January 9, 1917. He is also a member of the boards of directors of the Old National Bank and of the Hamilton National Bank. The latter was merged with the First National Bank on April 7, 1917, and the institution is now known as the First and Hamilton National Bank. The beautiful suburban home of Mr. Bass—known as Brookside—is the most widely known estate in this region. In the midst of a large park of three hundred acres with broad areas of artificial lake, the mansion has a most beautiful setting. Here, Mr. Bass maintains a deer and buffalo park, and conducts a large dairy and stock farm. To the breeding of Clydesdale horses and Galloway cattle Mr. Bass has devoted much attention during the past quarter century. Direct importations are made from Europe. Upon this farm are to be found some of the finest specimens of live stock in the world. Exhibits at the Columbian Exposition, Chicago, in 1893, and at the Louisiana Purchase Exposition, St. Louis, in 1904, are noteworthy as receiving many first prizes. In various portions of Allen county, Mr. Bass owns fifteen thousand acres of land, while his land holdings in other parts of Indiana and in other states are extensive. He owns eighteen thousand acres of mineral land in Alabama. In the city of Fort Wayne he possesses a large number of commercial and residential

BROOKSIDE
RESIDENCE OF JOHN H. BASS

properties. So wide are his investment interests that these suggestions must suffice to indicate their aggregate valuation which may be estimated at between five and six millions of dollars. Mr. Bass has ever given his support to the principles of the Democratic party. In 1888 he was chosen as a delegate from Indiana to the national convention of his party and was nominated as presidential elector in that year. Mr. Bass is prominent in Masonic affairs of Indiana; he has been honored with the Thirty-Third degree of the Scottish Rite. He is a member of the First Presbyterian church. Iu 1865 Mr. Bass was united in marriage with Miss Laura H. Lightfoot, daughter of the late Judge George C. and Melinda (Holton) Lightfoot. Mrs. Bass was born in Falmouth, Kentucky, and resided there with her parents at the time of the marriage. Two children have been born to them, Laura Grace, wife of Dr. Gaylord M. Leslie, of Fort Wayne, and John H., whose death occurred August 7, 1891. This brief review of the active life of Mr. Bass suggests nothing of the geniality of the man which has not only surrounded him with the warmest of friends but which has enabled him to establish such a relationship between the executive and the productive departments of his large enterprises as to preserve the highest degree of harmony and consequent efficiency. To him Fort Wayne owes much of the inspiration which has lifted her to a high place among the cities of the middle west.

Conrad Bayer, one of the specially alert and progressive business men of Fort Wayne, has been a resident of this city from his early youth and by his own ability and efforts has risen to a status of prominence and influence in connection with the representative commercial activities of the Summit City. His popularity is unqualified and is indicated in his being more familiarly known as "Coony" Bayer, this pseudonym being utilized in connection with the large and important industrial enterprise which has been developed under his able direction, for he is president and treasurer of the Coony Bayer Cigar Company, which owns and conducts one of the largest cigar manufactories in northern Indiana. This extensive enterprise was founded by him in 1891, and operations were instituted upon a very modest scale, as in this original manufactory he gave employment to but one man, the while he himself vigorously worked also at his trade, after having served a thorough apprenticeship as a cigarmaker. Not only effective service and excellent products were necessary to effect the evolution of the extensive business now controlled by the company of which he is executive head, but also the energy, circumspection and initiative and constructive ability which he was able to bring to bear. He continued business in an individual way until about 1902, when, to meet the constantly increasing demands placed upon his establishment, he effected the organization and incorporation of the present stock company, of which he has been president and treasurer from the beginning, William A. Bayer being superintendent and general manager, and Frederick Bayer the secretary of the company, which was originally incorporated for fifteen thousand dollars. No more pertinent voucher for the splendid expansion of the enterprise can be found than in the fact that in 1914 the capital stock was increased to one hundred thousand dollars, the executive officers remaining the same. In connection with the business and manufacturing departments of this now large industrial and commercial enterprise an average of about seventy-five persons are employed. In 1901 the factory headquarters were established in a building erected for the purpose, at the corner of Wayne and Barr streets, but within a comparatively few years these accommodations proved inadequate, with the result that in 1915 the company erected its present modern building of five stories, at the corner of Calhoun and Lewis streets, the same affording the aggregate floor space of seventeen thousand square feet. The high grade of the products of this manufactory constitutes its best commercial asset, and the annual output of cigars is now in excess of four million, while the trade is constantly being expanded into a broader field. Conrad (Coony) Bayer was born in the Kingdom of Wurtemberg, Germany, on the 27th of November, 1871, and thus he was a lad of about ten years when, in 1881, he accompanied his parents, Michael and Dorothea (Stuber) Bayer, on their immigration to America, the family home having soon afterward been established in Fort Wayne, where he was reared to adult age and where he continued to attend the Lutheran parochial schools until he was eligible for entrance in a local business college, in which he completed an effective course. In the establishment of Dessauer & Company he learned the trade of cigarmaker, and later he was in the employ of W. H. Ortman, engaged in the same line of business. In 1891 he severed this alliance to establish his independent enterprise as a manufacturer of cigars, and from a small beginning he has evolved one of the large and prosperous manufacturing and commercial industries of the metropolis of Allen county, besides having shown his progressiveness and self-reliant energy in connection with other lines of enterprise. He is president of the Bayer Realty Company, and is a member of the directorate of the German-American Bank of Fort Wayne. In politics Mr. Bayer accords staunch allegiance to the Democratic party, he is a valued member of each the Fort Wayne Commercial Club, Rotary Club and Retail Merchants' Association, and is affiliated with the Masonic fraternity, the Independent Order of Odd Fellows, the Benevolent and Protective Order of Elks, the Knights of Pythias, the Order of Buffaloes, and the Turnverein. On September 30, 1901, Mr. Bayer wedded Miss Anna Hofer, daughter of Andreas and Christine Hofer, of Fort Wayne, and the two children of this union are Ralph Conrad, who was born July 12, 1904, and Dorothy Christine, born November 21, 1916.

Mrs. Mary J. Beardsley—It is specially gratifying to present in this history a brief review of the life record of this venerable and revered native daughter of Allen county, who is a representative of one of the best known and most honored pioneer families of the county, her parents having here established their home more than four score years ago. Mrs. Beardsley celebrated in November, 1916, the eighty-third anniversary of her birth, and as she has lived in Allen county all her life it may well be understood that her memory forms an indissoluble link between the pioneer past and the twentieth century of opulent prosperity and progress in this section of the Hoosier state. Mrs. Mary Jane (Wood) Beardsley has the distinction of having been the first white child born in Perry township, this county, and the time of her nativity was November, 1833. She is a daughter of Albert and Nancy (Dunton) Wood, both of whom were born and reared in Jefferson county, New York, where their marriage was solemnized and whence they soon afterward, in 1833, came to Indiana and numbered themselves among the very first settlers in the wilds of what is now Perry township, Allen county, where the father set to himself the herculean task of reclaiming a farm from the forest. Of the twelve children Mrs. Beardsley was the first-born, and in the year that marked the establishing of the new home in Allen county she here gained the prestige of being the first white child born in Perry township, as previously noted. Of the other eleven children, all likewise natives of this county, one died in infancy, and the names of the others are here indicated in their respective order of birth: John Wesley, Richard Freeman, Amos Mason, Oscar B., Julia, Etta, Lucy, Commodore, William and Charles. Besides Mrs. Beardsley only four others of the children are living at the opening of the year 1917—Richard F., who is now a resident of the state of Kansas, where he has been for many years a prosperous farmer; Oscar B., who resides at Monroe, Grant county, Indiana; Lucy, who is the wife of Henry McCarthy, of Columbia City, Whitley county, Indiana; and William, who owns and resides upon his father's old homestead farm in Perry township, one mile west of Huntertown. William Wood is one of the extensive landholders of Allen county and is one of the substantial and representative citizens of his native township. He has five sons, two of whom are successful teachers in the public schools. Albert Wood, father of the gracious pioneer woman to whom this sketch is dedicated, reclaimed much of his land to cultivation and was influential in community affairs during the entire period of his residence in Allen county. He died on his old homestead when he was sixty years of age, and his wife attained to the remarkable age of ninety years. He left to his widow and children the old homestead of one hundred and ten acres, and a part of the tract which he originally obtained from the government is now owned by Henry N. Williams, of Fort Wayne. Mary Jane Wood was reared under the conditions and influences of the pioneer days and acquired her early education in the old-time log schoolhouse, the while she gave active assistance in the domestic activities of the modest but happy pioneer home. In 1849, at Huntertown, was solemnized her marriage to James Oliver Beardsley, and he was fifty-six years of age at the time of his death, in 1878. During all of the long years from the time of her marriage to the present Mrs. Beardsley has lived continuously at Huntertown, save for a period of one year which she passed at Auburn, Dekalb county. Under the administration of President Grant her husband served two terms as postmaster at Huntertown, and for a time he held the position of deputy postmaster, besides having given effective service also as justice of the peace. Mr. Beardsley was a citizen of sterling character and marked ability, and he ever commanded the unqualified confidence and esteem of his fellow men. His political allegiance was given to the Republican party, he was a Master Mason, and was an earnest member of the Universalist church, as is also his widow, who owns and resides in one of the attractive homes of Huntertown and who is surrounded by a host of loyal and appreciative friends who accord to her the most sincere affection. Physical disability prevented Mr. Beardsley from serving as a soldier during the Civil war, but he supported the Union cause to the fullest extent of his ability, besides having paid for a substitute for one of his friends who had been called to the Union service but whose circumstances were such as to make it almost impossible for him to leave home. Mr. and Mrs. Beardsley became the parents of no children, but, lacking filial solicitude on this account, Mrs. Beardsley feels a gracious compensation in the devoted love of her many friends.

Montgomery G. Beaver, one of the essentially progressive and representative business men of his native city of Fort Wayne, is virtually the successor to the substantial lumber business that was here founded by his honored father more than half a century ago, the history of the enterprise having been consecutive and having continued at all times in the control of the Beaver family, so that the extensive and important business now conducted by Montgomery G. Beaver, in the retail lumber trade and the operation of a most modern planing mill, may consistently be noted as one of the pioneer industrial and commercial enterprises of the metropolis and judicial center of Allen county. Mr. Beaver was born in Fort Wayne April 10, 1867, and is a son of Augustus and Mary Emily (Parks) Beaver, both of whom are now deceased, the father having been born in Pennsylvania and the mother in Indiana, in which latter commonwealth their marriage was solemnized. Of their two children the subject of this review is the younger, and his sister, Florence, is the wife of Watson Nicholson, of Ann Arbor, Michigan. Augustus Beaver established himself in the wholesale lumber business at Fort Wayne more than fifty years ago, and as a man of energy, uprightness and sagacity, he developed a most prosperous business, his status as one of the prominent business men and influential citizens of Fort Wayne having been maintained until his death, which occurred when he was about 80 years of age. He contributed materially to the civic and commercial prosperity of the city and county and his name merits an enduring place in the history of Fort Wayne. Montgomery G. Beaver made good use of the advantages afforded in the public schools of Fort Wayne and as a youth became closely associated with his father's lumber business. By personal inclination and ambition, as well as through paternal direction and encouragement, he thoroughly informed himself in all details of the business, and he is a recognized authority in lumber and building material values, as well as in the technical details of manufacturing in this line. At the age of 21 years he was admitted to partnership in his father's business, and after the death of his mother he purchased the entire business, which he has since conducted in an individual and distinctively successful way, the enterprise being now of retail rather than wholesale order and a well equipped planing mill having been operated as an important adjunct of the enterprise. In the spring of 1917 Mr. Beaver completed the erection and equipment of a new planing mill of the best modern standard, the building being of brick and steel construction and thoroughly fire-proof. The plant has its own electrical equipment throughout, the machinery and accessories are of the latest improved order, and the mill has ample capacity for turning out the best work in an expeditious way. The office headquarters of the mill and lumber yards are at 2047 Broadway. In this connection Mr. Beaver gives employment to an average force of from fifteen to twenty men, including a number of skilled operatives in the mill. He is not only an alert, vigorous and progressive business man but also a loyal and public-spirited citizen, with secure place in the confidence and good will of the urban community that has ever represented his home. His political allegiance is given to the Republican party, he is a valued member of the Fort Wayne Commercial Club, in the Masonic fraternity he has received the thirty-second degree of the Ancient Accepted Scottish Rite, besides being affiliated with the Ancient Arabic Order, Nobles of the Mystic Shrine, and both he and his wife are members of Plymouth Congregational church. January 10, 1893, recorded the marriage of Mr. Beaver to Miss Edith R. Cutshall, who likewise was born and reared in Fort Wayne, and whose father, William H. Cutshall, is now a retired farmer of this county, his wife being deceased. Mr. and Mrs. Beaver have one son, Melvin Montgomery, who is associated with his father's lumber business. He was graduated in the University of Michigan, at Ann Arbor, as a member of the class of 1916, and in that institution completed both literary and business courses.

Sylvanus B. Bechtel.—The application of ability and energy to his service with S. F. Bowser & Company has brought to Mr. Bechtel consecutive and noteworthy advancement with this important Fort Wayne concern, and he now holds the exacting and responsible office of general manager, with secure status as one of the representative business men of the younger generation in Allen county's metropolis and judicial center. Mr. Bechtel was born in Barry county, Michigan, June 17, 1878, and the place of his nativity was the fine old homestead farm of his parents, Joseph K. and Mary (Benjamin) Bechtel, the former of whom was born in the province of Ontario, Canada, and the latter in the state of Pennsylvania. The father long held prestige as one of the substantial farmers and honored citizens of southern Michigan, where he continued his identification with the basic industries of agriculture and stock-growing until the time of his death, his widow now being a resident of Toledo, Ohio. Of the children the eldest is William H., who resides at Caro, Tuscola county, Michigan; Barbara is the wife of Guy E. Pierson, of Wayland, Allegan county, that state; Clarence W. died when about 37 years of age; the subject of this review was the next in order of birth; and Roy W. is now a resident of the city of Toledo, Ohio. Sylvanus B. Bechtel continued his studies in the public schools of Michigan until he had completed the prescribed curriculum of the high school at Wayland, in which he was graduated as a member of the class of 1894. Thereafter he proved the solidity and efficacy of his academic discipline by three years of successful service as a teacher in the schools of his native state and after his retirement from the pedagogic profession he went to the city of Grand Rapids, Michigan, where he held a position in the business department of the Daily Democrat until 1899, when he came to Indiana and established his home in Fort Wayne. He arrived in this city in July of that year and entered the employ of S. F. Bowser & Company, his original post in the office of this representative manufacturing concern having been that of correspondent. He was soon given charge of the collection department, and of this position he continued the incumbent until June 1, 1901, when he was promoted to the post of superintendent of salesmen. One year later he was advanced to the management of the mail-order and advertising department; on January 1, 1906, he became assistant general manager; and on the 1st of March, 1914, there came the ultimate in the recognition of his ability and efficient service, when he was appointed to his present important office, that of general manager. The record made by Mr. Bechtel during the period of his association with this company bears its own significance and denotes the fiber and progressiveness of the man himself. In politics Mr. Bechtel is arrayed with the progressive wing of the Republican party; he and his wife hold membership in the South Fort Wayne Baptist church; he is affiliated with York and Scottish Rite bodies of the Masonic fraternity, as well as the adjunct organization, the Ancient Arabic Order, Nobles of the Mystic Shrine, and he is a popular member of the Fort Wayne Commercial Club, the Quest Club, the Fort Wayne Country Club, and the University Club of Fort Wayne. On the 27th of June, 1900, was solemnized the marriage of Mr. Bechtel to Miss Marie M. Russell, who was born in Fort Wayne and who is a daughter of William J. and Mary (Brew) Russell, her parents being now residents of Grand Rapids, Michigan, where her father holds the position of master carpenter for the Grand Rapids & Indiana Railroad. Mr. and Mrs. Bechtel have two children—Kenneth B. and Mary Catherine.

Henry W. Becker has proved a loyal and influential figure in connection with business and civic affairs in his native city of Fort Wayne, where he is now giving characteristically efficient service as a member of the municipal board of public works, an office of which he has been the incumbent continuously since 1905 and in which he has done much to further the efficient and important work of this department of the municipal government. Mr. Becker was born in Fort Wayne February 21, 1859, and is a son of Frederick and Margaret (Jennewein) Becker, both natives of Swaarbrüken, Prussia, Germany, where they were reared and educated and where their marriage was solemnized. The parents of the subject of this review came to America in 1848, a year specially marked by large immigration from Germany to the United States, and the father became one of the successful exponents of the blacksmith trade and business in Fort Wayne, where he commanded unqualified popular esteem and was a substantial citizen at the time of his death, in 1882, at the age of sixty-three years, his widow having survived him by several years and both having been earnest communicants of the Lutheran church, his political convictions having been shown forth in the loyal support which he gave to the cause of the Democratic party. Of the children the eldest is Frederick, Jr., who still resides in Fort Wayne, as do also Minnie, Charles and Mary, Henry W., of this review, being the youngest of the number. Henry W. Becker acquired his early education in the parochial school of the Lutheran church on Barr street, and as a youth he served a thorough apprenticeship to the stonecutter's trade, which, as a skilled artisan, he followed for the long period of twenty years, within which he was concerned in much important contract work in his native city. His induction into public service came when he was chosen deputy assessor of Wayne township, and his effective service in this capacity made him a normal candidate when, in 1900, he was elected township assessor, on the Democratic ticket. Of this office he continued the incumbent four years, and then, in April, 1905, he was appointed a member of the board of public works of Fort Wayne, under the administration of Mayor Henry C. Berghoff. He has received reappointment under each successive mayor and is one of the valued factors in connection with the administration of public affairs in his native city, to which his loyalty is of the most insistent type. As may be inferred from a foregoing statement, he is found arrayed as a staunch advocate of the principles of the Democratic party. On the 3d of September, 1883, was solemnized the marriage of Mr. Becker to Miss Lavina Englert, a daughter of the late Frank Englert, of Fort Wayne, and of the children of this union Magdalin and Margaret still remain at the parental home; Florence is the wife of Paul Lauer, of Fort Wayne; and Henry Roy and Frederick are still members of the parental circle.

William Becker.—The German contingent in Allen county, Indiana, has from the early days been one of prominence and influence in the furtherance of social and industrial advancement and prosperity. He whose name initiates this paragraph was born in the province of Hanover, Germany, October 25, 1860, and was a vigorous and ambitious young man of twenty-three years when he came to America and established his home in Allen county. His parents, Henry and Sophia (Tye) Becker, passed their entire lives in the German fatherland, and of their seven children the subject of this review was the sixth in order of birth; Henry died in Germany; Jacob still resides in his native province; Ferdinand died in Germany; August is a retired grocer residing in Fort Wayne and now gives his attention to the handling of bonds and other high grade securities, he and the subject of this sketch being the only representatives of the immediate family circle in the United States; Minnie and Sophia, the only daughters, both died in their native land. After duly profiting by the advantages offered in the excellent common schools of his home province William Becker there attended the Lutheran parochial schools for four years, after which he completed an effective course in a business college at Petershagen. The promptings of youthful ambitions led him to sever the home ties when he was a young man of twenty-three years, and his success during the intervening period has fully justified his course in immigrating to America and establishing the stage of his activities in Allen county. Here he has become one of the specially energetic and progressive farmers of Adams township, though his original field of activity was in Wayne township, where he lived during the early period of his residence in the county. When Mr. Becker purchased the present model farm of one hundred and thirty acres the place was equipped with eleven primitive log buildings and in general had little suggestion of the thrift and prosperity now in evidence. The old buildings have been replaced by modern structures of the best type, including the attractive and commodious farm residence, which is equipped with modern improvements, including a hot-water heating system, and Mr. Becker has further improved the place by constructing good fences, by clearing away much underbrush and by bringing his land up to the best stage of productiveness. He is essentially one of the vigorous, progressive and successful representatives of the basic industries of agriculture and stock-growing in Allen county, and in all of the relations of life he has so borne himself as to command the confidence and good will of his fellow men. He is a staunch and valiant supporter and advocate of the cause of the Republican party and has been one of its influential representatives in Adams township, where he served one term as township supervisor. He and his wife are active communicants of the German Lutheran church in the village of New Haven, which is about 1½ miles distant from their fine rural home. November 3, 1887, recorded the marriage of Mr. Becker to Miss Sophia Fuelling, who was born and reared in Adams county, Indiana, a daughter of Frederick and Lizetta (Mayland) Fuelling, both of whom were born in Germany, both having been young folk when they became residents of Fort Wayne, Indiana, where their marriage was solemnized and whence they removed to Adams county, where the father passed the remainder of his life as a prosperous farmer, the widowed mother having later returned to Fort Wayne, where she died at a venerable age. Of the children of this honored couple the eldest was Louise, who became the wife of Frederick Kukelhan, both having been killed in a railroad accident at Maples, Allen county, November 9, 1907; Frederick is a resident of Root township, Adams county; William and Charles died in infancy; Mrs. Becker was the next in order of birth; William remains on the old homestead farm in Adams county; Otto died in infancy; Elizabeth is the wife of Gottlieb Berger, who is engaged in the dry goods business in Fort Wayne, with a well appointed establishment on Calhoun street; Ernest maintains his home in Root township, Adams county; and Minnie died in infancy. Mr. and Mrs. Becker have but one child, Arthur, who is associated with his father in the work and management of the home farm; he wedded Miss Edith Behrman, and their two children are Naomi and Wilma.

Fred C. Beckman is a son of Edward Beckman and the grandson of Henry Beckman, who settled in Washington township as early as 1832, spent his life there and there reared his family. Among his children was Edward, who married Eliza Gerding, and they became the parents of ten children—Edward, Louis, Louise, Sophia, Justine, Eliza, Fred C., Herman, Julia and Charlotte. The two named last are deceased, each dying at the age of six years. In 1892 Edward Beckman was elected treasurer of Allen county, was re-elected in 1894 and served in that capacity until January 1, 1897. Fred C. Beckman was born on August 9, 1881, reared in Washington township and educated in its schools. He began farm life on the home place, continuing to make that his home until 1906, when he took up his residence in St. Joseph township. He is living now in that community and is the owner of one hundred and forty acres in Section 6. He has made practically all the improvements himself and the place is in a much better state of productiveness than when it came into his hands. The buildings have been remodeled under his supervision, fences have been erected and tiling has been put in, so that the farm is today one of the fine places of the township. General farming and stock-raising are carried on successfully. Mr. Beckman was married on May 24, 1906, to Miss Amelia Henschen, daughter of Frederick and Amelia (Rehorst) Henschen, farming people of Washington township, where they are still resident. Four children have been born to the Beckman house—Lucile, Herbert, Ruth and Morris. The family are members of St. Paul's Lutheran church at Fort Wayne.

Herman Beckman has been the exponent of progressive methods in his operations as a farmer in Washington township, and his home is one of the finest examples of modern building that is to be found in the township today, if not, indeed, the finest. His farm is up-to-date in every detail and reflects much credit upon its owner. Mr. Beckman is one of the younger farmers of the community. He was born on January 11, 1884, in Washington township, son of Edward and Eliza (Gerding) Beckman, concerning whom extended mention will be found on other pages of this work. Herman Beckman attended the common schools of his native village as a boy and applied himself to farming on the home place, where he is still in charge. He now is the owner of one hundred and seventy acres in Washington township, on which he has carried on progressive and profitable farming that has placed him in the front ranks of the successful men of the village. He has lately completed the erection of a fine modern bungalow, so well planned and carried out that further mention may properly be accorded to it. The place is equipped with every modern convenience, and no city dwelling is better provided with the comforts of urban life than is this farm house of Mr. Beckman's. Electric lights, modern furnace, open plumbing, hot and cold running water, modern laundry equipment in basement with clothes chute from top floors to laundry and service elevators from kitchen to basement, make up some of the labor-saving devices and aids to comfort that are so necessary in these days and so seldom found in the farm home. Mr. Beckman was married, in 1909, to Marie Schow, daughter of Ludwig Schow, concerning whom extended space is given elsewhere in these pages. He and his wife are members of St. Paul's Lutheran church in Fort Wayne and in politics he is a Democrat. He is not active in local politics beyond the demands of good citizenship and has no fraternal affiliations.

John Beckstein is one of the native sons of Allen county who is aiding definitely in the upholding of its prestige along the line of agricultural enterprise and is one of the substantial farmers and representative citizens of St. Joseph township, where he is the owner of a well-improved farm of eighty acres, in Section 29. Mr. Beckstein was born in the township that is now his place of residence and the date of his nativity was August 14, 1861. He is a son of John and Frederica (Bufink) Beckstein, both of whom were born in Germany and were young at the time of coming to America. They settled in St. Joseph township more than half a century ago and the present farm of their son John, of this review, is a part of their old homestead, upon which they continued to reside until their death. Of the children only three are now living—John, George and Henry. The mother passed to the life eternal, in 1877, and the father was one of the venerable and honored pioneer citizens of St. Joseph township at the time of his death, in September, 1914. He whose name introduces this article was reared to the sturdy discipline of the farm, profited duly by the advantages of the schools of his native township, and has never faltered in his allegiance to the basic industry of agriculture, through the medium of which he has achieved definite success. He owns and resides upon a portion of his father's old homestead farm, as previously stated, and upon the same has made numerous improvements that mark the demesne as a model farm. Industry and good management have characterized his activities as an agriculturist and stock-grower, he is independent in politics, has had no inclination toward public office, but takes loyal interest in those things that touch the communal welfare. Both he and his wife hold membership in St. John's Reformed church in the city of Fort Wayne. The home farm is about four miles distant from the city mentioned and receives service on rural mail route No. 15 from the county seat. On November 28, 1894, was solemnized the marriage of Mr. Beckstein to Miss Christina Denges, who likewise was born and reared in this county, a daughter of Christian and Elizabeth (Hansel) Denges, her parents having been children at the time of the imigration of the respective families from Germany to America and both families having established homes in Allen county in the pioneer days. Of the ten children of Mr. and Mrs. Denges five are living—Henry, Christ, Caroline, Sophia and Christina. Mr. and Mrs. Beckstein have five children, namely: Walter, Selma, John, Jr., Edna and Hilda.

George W. Beers has been a resident of Fort Wayne for nearly a quarter of a century and has been specially prominent and influential in the promotion of industrial enterprises—notably along the line of public utilities. It was under his personal direction that the lines of the Postal Telegraph Cable Company were brought into Fort Wayne, he was the chief factor in effecting the organization of the Home Telephone Company, of which he was the first president, and he has not only been a strong, positive and efficient force in the establishing of independent telephone services but has also been prominent in the manufacture and distribution of gas in northern Indiana. He is one of the substantial and valued citizens of Allen county and is entitled to definite representation in this history. Mr. Beers was born in Darke county, Ohio, on the 7th of June, 1859, and is a son of the late William J. and Amanda (Ward) Beers, both of whom passed the closing years of their lives in the old Buckeye state, where the father had been for many years an able and successful member of the bar of Van Wert county. Of the five children only George W. and Kate are now living, and the latter is the wife of Walter S. Allyn, of Cleveland, Ohio. In the public schools of his native state Mr. Beers acquired his early education and as a youth he gained practical experience in surveying and general civil engineering work. In this connection he was associated with the engineering corps that had charge of the construction out of Van Wert of the Cincinnati Northern Railroad. Later he was concerned prominently with timber development enterprises, mainly in the state of West Virginia, and in 1893 he established his permanent home in Fort Wayne. He has done much in furthering enterprises along the line of applied electricity, and, as before stated, he had charge of the extending of the Postal Telegraph lines into Fort Wayne, besides which he was the dominating force in establishing the system of the Home Telephone Company in Allen county and has otherwise been prominently interested in the exploiting and establishing of independent telephone lines. A business man of circumspection, energy and initiative, Mr. Beers has made a most successful record, and as a citizen he has been liberal and progressive. Well fortified in his convictions concerning governmental and economic policies, he is independent in politics and instead of being restricted by mere partisanship he gives his support to men and measures meeting the approval of his judgment. In the Masonic fraternity he is a Knight Templar, a member of the Mystic Shrine and has received also the thirty-second degree of the Ancient Accepted Scottish Rite. Both he and his wife are members of the First Presbyterian church of Fort Wayne. In 1884 was solemnized the marriage of Mr. Beers to Miss Catherine Numbers, who was born at Decatur, Adams county, Indiana, and the two children of this union are Dan N., who is identified with business interests in Fort Wayne, and Ruth, who is the wife of William T. McKay, of this city.

Joseph W. Bell has been a resident of Fort Wayne for nearly forty years and during this long period he has been continuously identified with business interests that have had distinct bearing on the civic and material prosperity of the community. For twenty years he was here engaged in the wholesale saddlery and hardware business, and since his retirement therefrom, in 1911, he has given his attention to the real estate business, in which his operations have been confined to the handling of his own properties, entirely aside from commission transactions. He is the owner of valuable realty in Fort Wayne, both improved and unimproved, and his activities in his present line of enterprise are conducive to further development and progress in the metropolis of Allen county, even as his previous business enterprise contributed to the commercial prestige of Fort Wayne. In the agnatic line Mr. Bell is of sterling Scotch lineage, as a scion of the third generation of the family in America, and in his character and achievement he has manifested the inviolable integrity for which the Scotch people have ever been noted. Joseph William Bell was born at Coshocton, Ohio, and the date of his nativity was December 1, 1853. He is the eldest in a family of three children, and the other two are Mrs. Laura Bell Lewis, of Cleveland, Ohio, and George A. Bell, of Fort Wayne, Indiana. Benjamin Franklin Bell, father of him whose name initiates this article, was born in Glasgow, Scotland, and was but seven years of age at the time of the family immigration to America. He here acquired a liberal education, and his advantages included those of the Ohio Wesleyan University, at Delaware. He prepared himself for and entered the ministry of the Methodist Episcopal church, and he gave many years of earnest, able and consecrated service in the vineyard of the Master. For ten years he was pastor of the Methodist Episcopal church at Delaware, Ohio, and thereafter he held various other pastoral charges, including a number of important order, the closing years of his life having been passed at Wellington, Ohio, where he died at the age of 59 years, his cherished and devoted wife, a woman of singularly gracious personality, having been 48 years of age when she was summoned to the life eternal. At the age of twenty-four years Rev. Benjamin F. Bell wedded Miss Lucinda McMorris, daughter of Joseph McMorris, who was a successful millwright and prominent citizen of Dresden, Muskingum county, Ohio, and concerning the three children of this union due mention has already been made in this context. Joseph W. Bell was signally favored in being reared in a home of culture and refinement and his public school education was supplemented by a course in his father's alma mater, the Ohio Wesleyan University. At the age of twenty-five years he entered the wholesale hardware business at Mansfield, Ohio, where he remained five years. He then, in 1885, came to Fort Wayne, where he has since maintained his home and where for twenty years, as previously noted, he was successfully established in the wholesale hardware and saddlery business. Mr. Bell has always stood exponent of loyal and public-spirited citizenship, has given unfaltering allegiance to the Republican party, has become affiliated with the York, Scottish Rite and Shrine bodies of the Masonic fraternity, is an active member of the Fort Wayne Commercial Club, and both he and his wife were members of the Presbyterian church. On the 26th of December, 1877, was solemnized the marriage of Mr. Bell to Miss Elizabeth Reed, daughter of the late Nicholas S. Reed, of Mansfield, Ohio, and the two children of this union are Guy Reed Bell and Benjamin Rector Bell, both of whom are associated with their father in the real estate business, as representative young men of Fort Wayne.

Henry E. Bell, who has been the popular mail carrier on rural routes Nos. 2 and 5, from the village of New Haven, since 1907, is a scion of one of the well-known families of Allen county, where the marriage of his parents was solemnized, but he claims the Sunflower State as the place of his nativity. He was born in Reno county, Kansas, September 12, 1872, a son of Robert S. and Lucy (Burgess) Bell, the former of whom was born in Pennsylvania and the latter in Allen county, Indiana, where her parents settled in the pioneer days. The mother passed to the life eternal, in 1876, and the subject of this sketch is the eldest of the three children, the other two being Eugene H. and Robert. After their marriage Mr. and Mrs. Robert S. Bell removed to Kansas, where they gained a due quota of pioneer experience, and upon their return to Allen county settled on a farm in Jefferson township. The father became one of the substantial agriculturists of the township, made good improvements on his farm, including the erection of excellent buildings, and he lives in New Haven, the death of his wife having occurred in 1877. Henry E. Bell was about two years old at the time of his parents' return from Kansas to Allen county, where he was reared to manhood on the home farm and where he profited by the advantages offered in the schools of Jefferson township. He continued his active alliance with agricultural enterprise until he assumed his present position as rural mail carrier, in which his service has given unequivocal satisfaction and in which he has made a fine record, as attested by the commendation of the patrons of the two routes which receive his attention. In politics Mr. Bell is a Republican, and he is affiliated at New Haven with the organizations of the Modern Woodmen of America and the Independent Order of Odd Fellows. On October 5, 1898, was solemnized the marriage of Mr. Bell to Matilda J. Cameron. She is a daughter of James and Matilda Cameron, the former of whom was born in Scotland and the latter in Allen county, Indiana, where their marriage was solemnized, Mrs. Bell being the first in a family of seven children and the names of the others being here designated: John A., Martha Maude, Harriett G., one who died in infancy, Lily May, Mary Winona and James Ross. Mr. and Mrs. Bell have no children, but Mrs. Bell has one son by a former marriage—Roy M. Timbrook, who is associated in the conducting of an automobile garage in the city of Fort Wayne.

Gustave Bengs.—The Engineering Company, located at Fort Wayne, of which Gustave Bengs and his brother are the moving spirits, is one of the leading enterprises of its kind in the state. It was organized in 1907, and in 1908 it was incorporated under the laws of the state, at which time the capital stock was increased from $15,000 to $100,000. The company engages in the manufacture of beams, channels, angles, plates, sheets, steel for buildings, iron stairs, ornamental railings and grills, with special attention given to the manufacture of machinery for use in milk condensing, their product in that line being used from coast to coast. The factories are established at the corner of Winter street and the Wabash railroad, and they have most admirable facilities there for the efficient handling of their products. Gustave Bengs is of German origin, born in that country on January 2, 1871, and he is the son of Herman and Anna (Alf) Bengs, both of German birth and ancestry. The father was a stone cutter by trade and came to Fort Wayne with his family in 1883, direct from Germany. The parents, who are no longer living, reared a family of nine children. All survive but two, and the subject was the fourth born in the family. He had his education for the most part in Fort Wayne, attending first the parochial school of the German Lutheran church, and later entering the old Methodist College, where he took a course in mechanical engineering. Following his graduation from that institution Mr. Bengs entered upon an apprenticeship in the Bass Foundry & Machine shop in Fort Wayne, and he served long and faithfully in that shop, adding to his college training valuable experience that has since proved itself of inestimable value to him in his business. Leaving the shop he engaged in business with Frank Gruber in a boiler making enterprise, and after eighteen months sold his interest to his partner, after which he went to Philadelphia and entered the service of the John Baizley Iron Works. He was there for about five years, and from Philadelphia he went to Los Angeles, California, in search of a suitable location for business. He spent six months in that quest and returning to Fort Wayne joined his one-time partner, Frank Gruber, continuing with him for two years. Once more he sold out to his partner, this time to engage in business with his brother, Otto, who is his partner today in the business conducted under the name of The Engineering Company, whose activities have been described in an opening paragraph. The Bengs brothers have every reason to feel pride in their accomplishments in the past ten years as the proprietors of this thriving business, and they have won the confidence and good will of the business interests of the city. Mr. Bengs married Anna Heine in August, 1898. She is a daughter of Fort Wayne, and her family has long been established in the county. Mr. and Mrs. Bengs have three children—Herbert, Raymond and Alfred—fine boys who are growing up in the public schools of the city, and who give promise of splendid futures. The family are members of the German Lutheran church and Mr. Bengs is a Republican in politics, but not a politician.

Edward P. Bennigen, whose well-developed executive ability comes into effective play in his native city, has won by his own ability and efforts a merited advancement in the service of the Pennsylvania Railroad Company, in the freight department of which in the city of Fort Wayne he is now serving as chief bill clerk. Mr. Bennigen was born in Fort Wayne, August 24, 1872, a son of Henry E. and Mary C. (Meyer) Bennigen, the former of whom was born in New Jersey and the latter in Fort Wayne, both having been of sterling German lineage and having passed the closing years of their worthy and unassuming lives in Fort Wayne, the father having been for nineteen years employed as a skilled machinist in the service of the Pennsylvania Railroad Company. He was a sterling citizen who commanded the esteem of all who knew him and both he and his wife were earnest communicants of the Catholic church. Of their nine children the subject of this review is the eldest; Charles F. still resides in Fort Wayne, as does also Bertha, who is the wife of Louis Neef; Agnes is the wife of Edward Wehmeyer, of this city; George W. and Arthur still reside in Fort Wayne; Estella is the wife of Oliver Reed, of this city; Esther died in childhood; and Albert likewise resides in his native city. Edward P. Bennigen acquired his early education in the German parochial schools of the Catholic church in Fort Wayne but began to depend largely upon his own resources when he was a lad of but thirteen years. For a time he was employed in a local clothing store and later found employment along mechanical lines in the Olds Wagon Works, with which he continued his association until 1893. In the following year he entered the service of the Pennsylvania Railroad Company and in 1895 began his work in its freight department, with which he has since been identified and in which he has won advancement to the responsible position of chief bill clerk. He gives his political allegiance to the Republican party, is affiliated with the Knights of Columbus and both he and his wife are communicants of the Cathedral parish of the Catholic church in their home city On June 27, 1906, was solemnized the marriage of Mr. Bennigen to Miss Amelia N. Hitchens, who was born in the city of Cincinnati, Ohio, and they have two children—Elva Mary, who was born July 6, 1907, and Kenneth C., who was born March 19, 1909.

John Benzinger.—Among the many successful and capable farmers of Marion township who claim that prosperous community as their birthplace may be mentioned John Benzinger, who was born in Marion township on June 29, 1859, the son of Fred and Catherine Benzinger. Fred Benzinger was born in New York state of German parents, and he accompanied them to Allen county as a boy. They drove an ox team across the country and experienced many hardships that made the trip a lifelong memory to all who participated and were of sufficient years to remember anything. The family settled on a tract of land in Marion township, and John Benzinger is the owner of that farm today. A single cabin of logs with old time puncheon floor was the first rude home that sheltered the Benzingers, in marked contrast to the commodious dwelling that is the family home of the representative of the name at this time. Fred Benzinger was a farmer all his life, a hard working man and a good citizen, and he was able to accumulate some property during his active years. He was a Democrat and a member of the German Lutheran church, and his children numbered seven. John, the first born, is the immediate subject of this family review. Fred lives in Fort Wayne. May is married. Rosa is the wife of Henry Rievel. Lena is deceased, as is also the seventh child, the latter dying in infancy. John Benzinger had his education in the German Lutheran schools of his community, and early learned to apply himself to the duties that presented themselves in the management of the home place with his father. He continued there until the death of Fred Benzinger, when he inherited the home place, and from then on he gradually accumulated other properties in the township. He carries on diversified farming on a generous scale, enjoying a well merited success in his work. He is a Democrat in politics, prominent in local politics, and a member of the German Lutheran church from infancy. He was married in January, 1888, to Miss Carolina Waterback, who was born in Germany. They have three children—Frederick, William and Mary, the two younger ones still at home with the parents.

Gustav A. Berghoff.—See Rub-No-More.

Hubert Berghoff has been closely associated with his elder brothers, Herman, now of Chicago, Henry, and his younger brother, Gustave, in the development of one of the important industrial enterprises of Fort Wayne, that of the Berghoff Brewing Association, but in 1908 impaired health caused him to retire from active business, though he still is the nominal secretary of the Rub-No-More Soap Company, which has developed in Fort Wayne an extensive and prosperous manufacturing enterprise that adds materially to the city's commercial prestige. Hubert Berghoff was born in the town of Dortmund, Westphalia, Prussia, and the date of his nativity was November 21, 1860, his parents, Anthony and Elizabeth (Boellhauve) Berghoff, having passed their entire lives in that section of the German empire; the father died in 1777 and the mother in 1884. He whose name introduces this article gained his early education in the excellent schools in his native land, and he was nineteen years of age when he severed the home ties and came to America, where, on the 12th of February, 1880, he joined his elder brothers, Herman and Henry, who had established their residence in Fort Wayne and concerning whom further mention is made on other pages of this publication. During the earlier years of his residence in Fort Wayne Hubert Berghoff was associated with the wholesale house of A. C. Trentman, and in 1889 he formed an alliance with his two brothers in establishing the enterprise that has been developed into the extensive business now controlled by the Berghoff Brewing Association. As previously stated, he has been practically retired from active business responsibilities since 1908. Like his brothers, Mr. Berghoff has proved one of the liberal and public-spirited citizens of Fort Wayne and has supported measures and enterprises that have tended to advance the civic and material prosperity of the community. On October 11, 1882, was solemnized his marriage to Miss

Johanna Mayer, daughter of Lawrence Mayer and a representative of one of the old and influential families of Allen county. Of the children of this union the eldest is Hubert, Jr., who is bookkeeper in the offices of the Berghoff Brewing Association; Herman is similarly engaged in the offices of the Rub-No-More Soap Company; Henry E. is secretary and treasurer of the Fort Wayne Carriage Works; and Elizabeth remains at the parental home.

Forrest B. Beyer, of the Beyer Grocery Company, of Fort Wayne, has proved a vital and resourceful factor in the developing of the substantial wholesale business now controlled by this representative commercial concern and is known not only as one of the influential young business men of the metropolis of Allen county but also as one of specially high scholastic and scientific attainments. Mr. Beyer was born at North Manchester, Wabash county, Indiana, May 21, 1886, and is a son of Cyrus C. and Melissa Catherine (Baker) Beyer, who now maintain their home in the city of Kendallville, Noble county, where the father is engaged in the wholesale produce business, besides which he is one of the interested principals in the Beyer Grocery Company, at Fort Wayne. Forrest B. Beyer was a boy at the time of the family removal to Kendallville, where he continued his studies in the public schools until he had completed the curriculum of the high school. In pursuance of his higher educational discipline he entered historic old Yale University, in which he was graduated as a member of the class of 1908 and from which he received the degree of Bachelor of Arts. Later he completed a post-graduate course in Leland Stanford Junior University, at Palo Alto, California, and from this institution he received the degree of Master of Arts. For one year thereafter he served as chemist for the Twenty-Mule Team Borax Company at Alameda, California, and later he held the position of organic chemist for the Bureau of Science at Manila, P. I. In 1913 he came to Fort Wayne and associated himself with the wholesale grocery business then conducted under the title of Beyer Brothers Company, and this alliance he has since continued with marked success, the concern having been reorganized in 1916 under the present title of the Beyer Grocery Company. His associates in the substantial and constantly expanding enterprise are his father, and George H. Crouse and Irvin W. house through its trade territory, and in the establishment itself an Von Gunten. Four traveling salesmen represent this wholesale grocery house through its trade territory; and in the establishment itself an adequate corps of clerical and general assistants is maintained. Mr. Beyer takes lively interest in all things tending to advance the commercial and civic welfare and progress of the Summit City, is an active member of the local Commercial Club and Rotary Club, and is affiliated with the Masonic fraternity. On the 1st of September, 1909, Mr. Beyer wedded Miss Ethel C. Reyher, daughter of Jacob Reyher, of Kendallville, and the one child of this union is Forrest B., Jr., who was born November 5, 1914.

Clarence F. Bicknell.—When Clarence Ford Bicknell came to Fort Wayne, in 1902, to assume the management of the Fort Wayne Daily News, every newspaper in the city entered upon a period of development until, today, no city of its size in America can boast of superior purveyors of the news of the world or more effective wielders of public opinion. Mr. Bicknell was born on a farm near Freelandville, Knox county, Indiana, December 26, 1864. In his native town he attended the public schools and the German Evangelical schools. The death of his father, when Clarence had reached the age of twelve, brought to him early in life the necessity of making his own way in the world, and he commenced by engaging in farm work during his summer vacations while continuing his studies in the winter. At the age of sixteen he began the teaching of a rural school and was engaged for two winters at the same school. The next few years of his experience form an interesting study, but the true philosophy of his activities is shown by the use to which he put his experience. The fact that he was a student in the University of Indiana at Bloomington, from 1883 to 1885, that he left the university at the end of his sophomore year, and, within a short time, was "wiping" engines at night in the roundhouse of the Burlington railroad at Lincoln Nebraska, brings to the mind an inquiry which is readily answered by Mr. Bicknell himself who says that his earnest desire, on leaving school was to "go west and grow up with the country." The Lincoln railroad shops offered the opportunity and Mr. Bicknell grasped it. For seven months, during his work in the roundhouse, he gathered much experience which has been of inestimable value to him in later years. From this work he was advanced to a clerkship in the office of the general superintendent of the road. During his three years in this capacity he perfected himself in stenography and his wider knowledge of the business of the department gave him an advancement to a position in the general passenger department of the Burlington road to Omaha. He remained here for four years, being promoted successively to the positions of head of the advertising department and cashier. In 1893, having for some time wished to enter business for himself, he purchased a weekly newspaper circulated in the towns of Gas City and Jonesboro, Indiana. In 1896, after a successful management of the property, he sold it, and, in connection with his brother, Ernest P. Bicknell, now Director General of Civilian Relief of the American Red Cross Society, purchased a controlling interest in the Terre Haute (Indiana) Tribune, of which publication he served as the business manager. In 1899 he sold the Tribune, but remained under contract as its manager until the spring of 1902, when he came to Fort Wayne and purchased the Fort Wayne Daily News for himself and his brother from William D. Page, its founder. Mr. Bicknell has managed the property with splendid success from the beginning of his connection with it. From a paper of small size and circulation, he has given it a high position of sustained popularity and influence. While a resident of Omaha, Mr. Bicknell, at the age of twenty-three, was united in marriage with Miss Clara A. Sluss, of Bloomington, Indiana. To Mr. and Mrs. Bicknell have been born three daughters, Ruth, Marguerite and Winifred. Mr. Bicknell is a member of the South Wayne Baptist church. He is a Mason, a member of the Scottish Rite body and the Shrine, the Knights of Pythias, the Maccabees, the Commercial Club and the Quest Club. In politics he has always been a staunch exponent of the principles of the Republican party. For two years he occupied the position of chairman of the Republican party of the Twelfth Congressional District. Through the medium of his newspaper, his activity in many organizations, and his wide acquaintanceship, Mr. Bicknell has taken advantage of his exceptional opportunities to support every great public movement which has for its object the good of the many.

Charles L. Biederwolf, the efficient and popular secretary of the Fort Wayne Commercial Club, naturally is unequivocally loyal to

Indiana, as this is his native commonwealth, and he is not only a member of the bar of the state but has also gained broad experience through service as private secretary to two representatives of Indiana in the United States congress, so that, all in all, his activities have been of that broadening type that makes him specially eligible for the furtherance of the high civic ideals and progressive policies of the vigorous organization of which he is now serving as secretary. Mr. Biederwolf was born at Monticello, the judicial center of White county, Indiana, September 27, 1876, and is a son of Michael and Abbie (Snetzer) Biederwolf, both of whom were born in the historic old city of Strassburg, Germany, and were married in Reading, Pennsylvania. Michael Biederwolf was a carpenter by trade but he eventually engaged in the lumber and coal business, in which he developed a prosperous enterprise, both he and his wife having been residents of Monticello at the time of their death and both having been earnest members of the Presbyterian church, the while the father was found arrayed as a staunch supporter of the cause of the Democratic party. Charles L. Biederwolf continued his studies in the public schools of his native place until he had availed himself of the advantages of the high school, and thereafter he attended the Gem City Business College, at Quincy, Illinois, and Wabash College, at Crawfordsville, Indiana, in which latter he was a student for one year. In the prosecution of his law studies he attended the law department of the University of Ohio for two years, as a member of the class of 1898, and he finished his technical course in the law department of the University of Indianapolis in which he was graduated in 1901, and from which he received his degree of Bachelor of Laws, with virtually concomitant admission to the bar of his native state. In 1904 he established his home in Fort Wayne, and thereafter he served in turn as secretary to Hon. Newton W. Gilbert, representative of the Twelfth Indiana district in the United States congress, and the latter's successor, Hon. Clarence C. Gilhams. His secretarial duties involved his residence in the city of Washington during the sessions of congress, and his effective services as secretary gave him a specially close and comprehensive knowledge of public affairs. His incumbency as secretary to Hon. Clarence C. Gilhams terminated in 1909, and on the 26th of March, 1910, he became secretary of the Fort Wayne Commercial Club. In this executive office he has done splendid service in systematizing and vitalizing the work of the club and has aided greatly in making it an influential exponent and promoter of the civic, industrial and commercial interests of Fort Wayne and Allen county. His popularity and the estimate placed on his administrative ability are further shown in his having been chosen secretary also of the Rotary Club of Fort Wayne, which position he held for one year. As implied by his service as secretary to the congressmen previously mentioned, Mr. Biederwolf is staunchly aligned as an advocate and supporter of the cause of the Republican party, and he takes lively interest in the party cause. In addition to his membership in the two representative clubs of which he is secretary, he is a member of the Fort Wayne Country Club, and he is affiliated with the Benevolent & Protective Order of Elks and the Friars. January 28, 1904, gave record of the marriage of Mr. Biederwolf to Miss Katherine Shanahan, daughter of Michael and Mary Shanahan, of Wabash, this state, and both are popular in the social life of their home city. They have no children.

William Bittler has given nearly half a century of effective service in the employ of the Pennsylvania Railroad Company and is one of the veteran men of this corporation in the city of Fort Wayne. Technical and executive ability on his part have not failed of official recognition in the passing years, and, since 1875, he has had full charge of the maintenance and repair work on the water stations of what is known as the western division of the Pennsylvania Lines—between Crestline and Chicago being the line over which he has jurisdiction in his assigned position. He has the status of an expert stone mason, and it was his ability along this line that led to his advancement in the service of the great corporation with which he has been long identified, the while his sterling characteristics and worthy achievement have brought and retained to him the fullest measure of official and popular confidence and good will. Mr. Bittler was born in Berks county, Pennsylvania, December 19, 1850, and in the same historic old commonwealth were born his parents, Reuben and Elizabeth (Smith) Bittler, the father having been a shoemaker by trade and vocation and both he and his wife having been residents of Reading, Pennsylvania, at the time of their death. Of the children Mary, Rebecca and Leah are deceased; Emma still resides at Reading, Pennsylvania; Hannah is the wife of Jacob Wannemaker, of New York city; William, of this review, is the elder of the two sons; and Samuel is a resident of Pennsylvania. As a boy and youth William Bittler gained practical experience and discipline in connection with farm industry in the old Keystone State and in the meanwhile attended the public schools when opportunity offered. At the age of sixteen years he made his way to Tiffin, Ohio, where he worked about eight months as a stone mason, a trade in which his natural predilections and careful application eventually gained to him full qualification as a journeyman. In 1868 he came to Fort Wayne and here was employed at his trade by the late Henry Paul, father of William Paul, who is still a resident of this city. On August 6th of the following year Mr. Bittler took a position as stonemason and pipe man in the employ of the Pennsylvania Railroad Company and then initiated his service in looking after the water stations of the company on the western division. In 1875 his ability and effective service brought to him advancement and from that year to the present he has been in full charge of the work of keeping in proper condition the water stations of the company on the line between Crestline, Ohio, and the city of Chicago. Mr. Bittler is one of the oldest employes of the Pennsylvania Railroad Company attached to the Fort Wayne headquarters, is well known and held in high esteem among the railroad men and the same estimate is placed upon him by all others who know him. He has never swerved in his fealty to and appreciation of Fort Wayne, takes loyal interest in the city's prosperity and progress, has served as a trustee of the municipal water system, is a Democrat in politics, and he and his wife are earnest communicants of the Lutheran church, in the faith of which he was reared. On October 3, 1873, was solemnized the marriage of Mr. Bittler to Miss Mary Jacobs, who was born in Germany and came to America when young. Of the four children of Mr. and Mrs. Bittler the eldest is Edward, who is now assistant cashier of the People's Trust Company of Fort Wayne; George is the recent state treasurer of Indiana; Hannah remains at the parental home; and Herman is identified with business interests in his native city, all of the children having honored the family name and the city of their nativity.

Albert J. Black has been a resident of Allen county from the time of his infancy, has been for many years a successful representative of agricultural industry in Milan township and is a progressive and influential citizen whose secure vantage-place in popular esteem is vouchsafed by his incumbency of the office of county commisioner, to which position he was elected in 1912 and in which he has been the earnest advocate and supporter of measures and enterprises that have conserved the best interests of the county and its people. Mr. Black was born in Erie county, Ohio, on the 18th of June, 1862, and is the only surviving child of Joseph and Matilda (Chester) Black, the former a native of Maryland and the latter of Ohio, their marriage having been solemnized in the Buckeye state and the father having been a sailor on the Great Lakes in his young manhood. The subject of this review was an infant at the time of the family removal from Ohio to Allen county, Indiana, in 1863, and here his father became a substantial farmer and representative citizen of Milan township, where he and his wife passed the residue of their lives. Albert J. Black acquired his early education in the public schools of Allen county, was reared to the invigorating discipline of the farm and during the long intervening years he has not been deflected from the line of close allegiance to the basic industries of agriculture and stock-growing, of which he is now a prominent and enterprising exponent in this county, his well improved farm of one hundred acres being one of the model places of Milan township and being still under his active supervision, though his official duties as county commissioner demanded his presence in Fort Wayne during an appreciable portion of each year during his incumbency of that position. Mr. Black is an active and influential Allen county representative of the Democratic party and prior to his election to the office of county commisioner had served four years as township trustee in Milan township. The marriage of Mr. Black was to Miss Alice M. Swan, who was born and reared in Allen county, and they have two daughters, both of whom have received excellent educational advantages and both of whom have been popular and efficient teachers in the schools of their native county. Senora, the elder daughter, is the wife of Samuel Spindler, of Milan township; and Josephine is the wife of Ray Irving, of the same township.

Louis C. Blase is a popular and successful business man in the metropolis of his native county, where he was local representative of the Cadillac Sales Company for six years, which controlled a substantial business from its headquarters at Fort Wayne. Mr. Blase was born in this county on September 5, 1881, and is a scion of a family whose name has been worthily identified with the history of the county for fully three-quarters of a century. His father, the late Louis Blase, passed virtually his entire life in Allen county, and the widowed mother now resides in the city of Chicago. Louis C. Blase is indebted to the public schools of Fort Wayne for his early educational discipline and is one of the loyal and progressive young business men of this city. He is independent in politics, is an active member of the Fort Wayne Commercial Club, is affiliated with the local lodge of the Benevolent & Protective Order of Elks, holds membership in the Country Club and both he and his wife are communicants of St. Paul's Lutheran church. On January 5, 1916, was solemnized the marriage of Mr. Blase to Miss Ella Beverforden, and they have one child, Barbara. They are popular factors in the social life of their home city.

William Blessing is known as one of the most progressive and successful exponents of agricultural and live-stock industry in his native county, is a scion of a sterling pioneer family, and owns and resides upon the fine old homestead farm, in Section 24, Lake township, which was the place of his birth, the date of his nativity having been December 14, 1861. He is a son of Peter and Catherine (Dush) Blessing, both of whom were born in Germany and were young at the time of the emigration of the respective families to America, the mother's parents having settled near Kendallville, Indiana. Peter Blessing was a sturdy and ambitious youth at the time when he came to the United States and passed the first year in the state of New York. He then came to Allen county, Indiana, and turned his attention to agricultural pursuits. It is a matter of record that this honored pioneer cradled wheat on the ground now comprised in the beautiful suburban residence district known as Bloomingdale—virtually an integral part of the city of Fort Wayne. He eventually became the owner of a farm three miles north of Fort Wayne, but his old homestead is the place now owned and occupied by his son William, the immediate subject of this review. Here he established his residence in 1885, and by the later purchase of additional tracts of land became the owner of one of the large and valuable landed estates of the county, the home farm of William Blessing now comprising one hundred and sixty acres of as finely improved and fertile land as is to be found in this favored section of the Hoosier commonwealth. Peter Blessing contributed, through his energy, ability and civic loyalty, much too the development and progress of Allen county, his was inviolable place in popular confidence and good will, and he continued to reside on his farm until his death, which occurred August 27, 1897, his widow surviving him by a decade and a half and having been venerable in years when she passed to the life eternal, on December 10, 1912. Both were devoted communicants of the Lutheran church and in politics the father was a staunch Democrat. Concerning the children the following brief record is entered: George is a prosperous farmer of Lake township; Henry is deceased; Charles is a representative farmer in Washington township; Mrs. Mary Fick is deceased; William, of this review, was the next in order of birth; John likewise is a successful farmer of Lake township; Elizabeth, Frederick and Otto are deceased. While early accorded his full meed of responsibility in connection with the work of the home farm, William Blessing by no means failed to improve the educational opportunities that were afforded in the school of district No. 5, Lake township. He continued to be actively associated with farm enterprise until he was twenty-five years of age and thereafter devoted eight years to work at the carpenter's trade. He then returned to the old homestead farm and to the same has since continued to give his active and effective supervision, besides which he has added materially to the excellent improvements that had been made by his honored father. He erected the attractive and commodious modern house that is now the family home, has provided a number of minor farm buildings and also erected a silo of large capacity. While utilizing his land for well-ordered agriculture of diversified order Mr. Blessing gives special attention to the raising of the better types of live stock, including short-horn Durham cattle and Chester White swine. He is liberal and loyal in his civic attitude, takes lively interest in local affairs, but has never consented to become a candidate for public office of any kind. His political support is given to the Democratic party and both he and his wife are zealous communicants of St. John's Lutheran church in their home township. April 25, 1907, recorded the marriage of Mr. Blessing to Miss Mary Anderson, who was born in Sweden, a daughter of the late Anders Pearson and Mary (Johnson) Anderson. Of the other children it may be recorded that Christena (Mrs. Johnson) is now a resident of Michigan; Peter resides in the city of Fort Wayne, as does also Mrs. Hannah Rudolphson; and Niels, John, Caroline and Carrie still remain in Sweden. Mr. and Mrs. Blessing have three children—Hilding D., Douglas A. and Astrid M., and the family is one of prominence and popularity in the social activities of the home community.

Maximillian J. Blitz was assigned in 1890 to the position of city ticket agent at Fort Wayne for the New York, Chicago & St. Louis Railroad, which is more commonly known as the Nickel Plate Railroad, and also manager of Kinner's ticket office in Fort Wayne, which office he bought in 1891, though he had in the meanwhile identified himself with other lines of enterprise, through association with which he gradually matured his executive powers, and in 1895 was led to establish and develop his present representative general insurance agency, in connection with which he conducts a substantial real-estate business. Mr. Blitz was born at Cleveland, Ohio, on the 16th of October, 1871, and is a son of Leopold and Sarah (Spear) Blitz, both of whom were born and reared near the city of Berlin, Germany. Leopold Blitz came to America about the year 1842 and both he and his wife passed the closing years of their lives at Cleveland, Ohio, where he had long been a representative merchant and honored and influential citizen. In the public schools of his native town Maximillian J. Blitz acquired his early education, which was supplemented by an effective course in the Spencerian Business College at Cleveland, Ohio. In 1885 he became assistant city ticket agent in Cleveland, Ohio, for the Nickel Plate Railroad, and after serving in this capacity two years he was advanced to the position of assistant ticket agent for the Detroit & Cleveland Steam Navigation Company. This incumbency he retained two years, at the expiration of which, in 1890, he came to Fort Wayne to assume the position of city ticket agent for the same company, with incidental management of Kinner's ticket office. In 1895 he was appointed local agent for the Preferred Accident Insurance Company, of New York, and in the following year he was made district manager for this company for the northern half of Indiana. This experience led to his assuming the agency for other leading insurance companies and eventuated in his developing one of the leading general insurance agencies in the city of Fort Wayne, as previously intimated. He is now general agent for northeastern Indiana for the Hartford Accident & Indemnity Company; general agent for the Lincoln National Life Insurance Company, and local agent for the following named and important companies: The Commercial Union, of New York; the Firemen's Fund, of California; the Niagara Underwriters; the North River Standard Insurance Company, of Hartford, Connecticut; the Sterling Fire Insurance Company, of Indianapolis, and the Standard Live Stock Insurance Company, which likewise has its general offices in the capital city of Indiana. Mr. Blitz maintains spacious and well-appointed offices in the Shoaff Building and in the same gives employment to a corps of six efficient assistants. His business is now of broad scope and has been built up through careful and progressive policies and straightforward dealings, the same forces having been brought to bear also in connection with his substantial real-estate enterprise, which likewise is of a general order. The political proclivities of Mr. Blitz are indicated by the staunch allegiance which he gives to the Republican party, and both he and his wife hold membership in the First Presbyterian Church, of Fort Wayne. In the time-honored Masonic fraternity his ancient craft affiliation is with Wayne Lodge, Ancient Free and Accepted Masons, and he is further actively identified with the local chapter of Royal Arch Masons, the Fort Wayne Commandery of Knights Templars, Fort Wayne Consistory and also the Ancient Arabic Order of the Nobles of the Mystic Shrine, Mizpah Temple. He is likewise an appreciative affiliant of the local lodge of the Benevolent and Protective Order of Elks, and holds membership in the Fort Wayne Commercial Club, the Country Club, and the local Press Club. He takes much interest in military affairs and was an active member of the Fort Wayne Rifles. April 28, 1897, was the date on which was solemnized the marriage of Mr. Blitz to Miss Edith May Barcus, daughter of Hezekiah and Emerilis (Bennett) Barcus, of Fort Wayne. Mr. and Mrs. Blitz have three children, whose names and respective dates of birth are here noted: John Kinner, July 4, 1899; Richard Thompson, January 16, 1902, and Edith Maxine, May 25, 1914.

The Blue Cast Magnetic Springs.—Allen county is to be considered greatly favored in the prestige given by the Blue Cast Magnetic Springs and Sanitarium, which give to the county a reputation for the best of natural and properly amplified facilities for the successful treatment of many of the ills to which human flesh is heir. As the wonderful remedial powers of the waters of the Blue Cast Springs become better and more widely known, in the same ratio is the popularity of the fine sanitarium that has been provided in connection with the same to become more and more one of the leading health meccas of the middle west. No other springs in Indiana can claim waters of greater and more assured medicinal value than those of the Blue Cast Magnetic Springs, and to the splendidly equipped sanitarium are drawn each year greater numbers of health-seekers whose faith in the institution is virtually to be assured through beneficial results. In a publication of this order it is impossible to enter into details concerning the analysis of the Blue Cast waters or the manifold attractions of the sanitarium and its beautiful park, for all these matters are adequately described in the literature sent forth by the institution itself and available to all who make application for the same, but as the developing company has made the institution one of the really great health resorts of Indiana and one that contributes in many ways to the precedence of Allen county, it is but due that a brief review be incorporated in this history of the county. To accomplish this end most consistently the following quotations are taken from an attractive brochure issued by the Blue Cast Magnetic Springs Company: ''Blue Cast Magnetic Springs and Sanitarium are located in beautiful Blue Cast Park, two miles north of Woodburn, Indiana. Woodburn is on the main line of the Wabash Railroad, seventy-five miles from Toledo, Ohio, and fifteen miles from Fort Wayne, Indiana. Direct connections are, therefore, possible with all railroad and interurban lines running into these two traffic centers. Blue Cast Park is on the Maumee river, consists of eighty-five acres, half of which is a fine grove, fronting for over a half mile on the beautiful Maumee river. High banks, splendid scenic views, good boating and fishing, afford most desirable sport and recreation. Blue Cast Magnetic Springs have long been known to residents of the surrounding country, who have enjoyed refreshment and kept in health for many years by partaking of this natural tonic from the crude springs. Now the healthful and invigorating properties of Blue Cast magnetic spring water have become available for the multitudes of sick and ailing and those desirous of continued well being. The name Blue Cast is derived from the very slight bluish tint which distinguishes the water. Another part of the name, Magnetic, is derived from the fact that the water has been endowed by Nature with a peculiar magnetic force rarely found in any mineral water of any kind, the world over. Iron or steel when immersed in this water will become magnetized. This wonderful invigorating force is imparted to those who bathe in Blue Cast water, exerting a powerful tonic and metabolic influence on the cell life of the body. The speedy and popular endorsement of these curative and tonical waters is amply justified by the searching analysis of their properties which has been made by well-known and authoritative chemists. The official analysis establishes beyond a doubt that Blue Cast Magnetic Spring water not only possesses refreshing and exhilarating qualities, but is Nature's own remedy for many common and chronic ailments." The water is further attractive as a high-grade table beverage, and in connection with the sanitarium has provided a bottling department with the best modern facilities, so that the product may readily be shipped to all parts of the country without the slightest deterioration.. From an auhoritative analysis and incidental report made by a leading chemist are taken the following statements: "This is a very fine water for internal medication and is adapted to a wide range of medical uses: the magnesium carbonate is especially good in all stomach disorders and its sulphate acts mildly on the bowels, while the potassium salts aid all the eliminative organs and act as alteratives." Of Blue Cast Sanitarium the following brief description has been given: "The building is a modern, fire-proof, steel and concrete structure, steam heated, electric lighted, with hot and cold Blue Cast Magnetic Spring water in every room. No expense has been spared to carry to the extreme in this sanitarium all the purposes for which it has been constructed,—the comforts of home, rest, recreation and the renewal of the health of patients." The bath facilities are of the best modern type and make provision for the use when expedient of the wonderful magnetic mud that has been impregnated by the springs. An efficient medical staff is maintained in connection with the institution, and there are few health resorts in the United States that can offer greater attractions for recreation and health-building. For full information concerning the institution application should be made to the general manager, George A. Hogue, who is treasurer of the Blue Cast Company and who has been the dominant force in the development of this splendid health resort. George A. Hogue was born at Akron, Summit county, Ohio, on January 17, 1875, and is a son of Albert and Samantha (Rollins) Hogue, both likewise natives of the old Buckeye state, the father having been long employed as an expert machinist in the old Buckeye mower and reaper works at Akron. George A. Hogue is indebted to the educational institutions of his native state for his early scholastic training, and as a youth he became associated with contracting work in railway construction. He initiated his activities along this line in 1892 and eventually became an independent and successful contractor. He obtained and completed the contract for the construction of the line of the Ohio Electric Railway from Lima, Ohio, to Fort Wayne, and had the supervision of all construction work in that connection except the building of the sub-stations. Within his active career as a contractor he built six hundred miles of electric railway— principally in Ohio, Illinois and Indiana. He thus developed to the full his admirable initiative and administrative powers, and when, in 1912, he identified himself with the development and exploiting of the Blue Cast Magnetic Mineral Springs he came to the work splendidly equipped. He effected the organization of the Blue Cast Company, which purchased the land and erected the fine sanitarium now conducted under his direct and effective management, and while the company had the best of medium through which to justify such exploitation it has been in large measure due to the earnest and well-ordered efforts of Mr. Hogue that this fine Allen county institution has been brought before the people of the country and the success of the enterprise made cumulative in character. In politics he is a Republican, and in his civic attitude he is characteristically loyal, progressive and public-spirited. In 1898 he wedded Miss Lua Harrison, daughter of J. B. and Carrie Harrison, of Cleveland, Ohio, and the two children of this union are Earl Harrison Hogue and Bonita Goldie Hogue, the son being now a cadet student in Pillsbury Military Academy, in the state of Minnesota.

William F. Borgmann.—It is signally consistent that in this volume be entered a tribute to the memory of the late William F. Borgmann, who passed his entire life in Allen county, who was a representative of one of the sterling families that was here founded more than half a century ago and whose impregnable hold upon popular confidence and esteem was manifested in all stages of his career, especially during the period of his effective service as chief of the police department of the city of Fort Wayne. He had become associated with his father in the conducting of a prosperous business in Fort Wayne, under the title of the Brown Trucking Company, and his untimely death was the result of a pitiable automobile accident in which he was so severely injured that he died soon afterward. He was born in Fort Wayne on August 7, 1865, and here his death occurred on April 13, 1912. Mr. Borgmann was a son of William and Lesette (Brockmeyer) Borgmann, both of whom were natives of Germany and came to this country when young. The father was a boatman on the old Wabash & Erie Canal when a youth and in later years served for a considerable time as a member of the Fort Wayne police force. Upon his retirement from this service he and his son, William F., became allied in business under the title of the Brown Trucking Company, and with this enterprise he continued to be identified until his death, which occurred in 1908. William F. was the second of a family of five children, all of whom were born and reared in Fort Wayne. He was but fourteen years old when, after having attended school, he began to give his father valuable assistance in the latter's trucking business, and they became very successful along this line, both having been connected with the same until their death. Like his father, William F. Borgmann made a splendid record of faithful and efficient service in the Fort Wayne police department. In 1890 he became a patrolman and not only won promotion in turn to the offices of sergeant and captain but also proved so unmistakably his ability and good judgment that he was finally chosen chief of police. His administration in this important office was most effective and popularly satisfactory, and he continued the incumbent of the post until 1910, when he resigned. In 1898 he had become associated with his father in purchasing an interest in the business under the title of the Brown Trucking Company, and after his retirement from the municipal service gave his attention to this business until his demise. Mr. Borgmann was a most stalwart and loyal advocate and supporter of the cause of the Democratic party and was a consistent communicant of Trinity Lutheran church, earnest in his support of church work and active in the affairs of the parish, of which his widow continues an active communicant. On July 4, 1886, he was united in marriage with Miss Anna Hunche, a native of Lima, Ohio, and a daughter of Henry F. and Anna (Reber) Hunche, both natives of Germany. Henry F. Hunche was born and reared in Germany and came to the United States in 1861. He died. in 1911, his wife having passed away in 1891. Mrs. Borgmann remains a resident of Fort Wayne and maintains the attractive homestead at 420 Fourth street. In the community her circle of friends are legion an entertain for her the warmest regard. In conclusion is entered brief record concerning the children of Mr. and Mrs. Borgmann: Edith is the wife of Paul Charle, of Fort Wayne, and they have three children— John (deceased), William and Virginia. Walter A., who is now his father's successor as president and general manager of the Brown Trucking Company, wedded Miss Pauline Doenges, of Fort Wayne, and they have one son, William W., born May 18, 1913. Irene is the wife of John C. Marshall, of Fort Wayne, and they have two children—Stephen M., born March 24, 1911, and Helen, born January 19, 1913.

Elias H. Bookwalter.—Allen county is favored in having drafted well-qualified officials to direct the various departments of its government, and he whose name introduces this article gave a short but effective service in the office of county recorder, to which position he was elected in the autumn of 1916, his assumption of his official duties having occurred on the 1st of the following January. His incumbency of the position was only for the period of three months, as he died on April 4, 1917, mourned by a large circle of friends. Elias Hubbard Bookwalter was born in Wabash county, Indiana, May 9, 1854, a son of Josiah and Elizabeth (Riley) Bookwalter, the former of whom was born at Eaton, Preble county, Ohio, on April 1, 1827, a date that denotes that his parents were pioneers of that section of the Buckeye State. Josiah Bookwalter was reared and educated in Ohio and, in 1850, came to Indiana and engaged in farming in Wabash county, where he also operated a blacksmith shop. In the autumn of 1866 he came with his family to Allen county and thereafter continued to be engaged in farming in St. Joseph township, until 1870, when he removed to Fort Wayne and became a traveling representative for the Keeler Dental Company. In 1885 he retired from active business life and now resides in the city of Indianapolis, April 1, 1917, marking his attainment of the patriarchal age of ninety years. He is a Republican in politics, having been affiliated with the party during practically the entire period of its existence; he has long been identified with the Independent Order of Odd Fellows; and the passing years have found him a consistent and devoted member of the Methodist Episcopal church. His wife likewise was an earnest member of this religious denomination, her birth having occurred at

Baltimore, Maryland. Josiah Bookwalter is to be given honorable mention as one of the most venerable of the surviving veterans of the Civil War, in which he served as a valiant member of Company E, One Hundred and Thirtieth Indiana Infantry, he having won in the same promotion from private to the office of corporal. He is a member of the Grand Army of the Republic. Of the children the eldest is John A., residing at Indianapolis; Elias H., of this review, was the next in order of birth; Charles A. is one of the influential citizens of Indianapolis and has served as mayor of the capital city; Lucinda is the widow of Newton Cook and resides in Seattle, Washington; and James E. is a resident of Halstead, Harvey county, Kansas. Elias H. Bookwalter gained his rudimentary education in the schools of Wabash county and was about twelve years old at the time of the family removal to Allen county, where he was afforded the advantages of the city schools of Fort Wayne. As a youth he entered the service of the Fort Wayne Journal-Gazette and with this representative newspaper continued to be associated for twenty-eight and one-half years, after which he rounded out his alliance with practical journalism by continuing his connection with the Fort Wayne Sentinel for eighteen and one-half years—or until he assumed the office of county recorder. His broad and varied experience in connection with newspaper business brought to him extensive and accurate knowledge concerning Allen county and its people, and this information proved a fortifying influence in making his administration as county recorder specially efficient and commendable. Mr. Bookwalter was never deflected from the course of loyal allegiance to the Republican party and he gave active service in behalf of its cause. He was affiliated with James B. White Camp No. 152, Sons of Veterans, and Harmony Lodge No. 19, Independent Order of Odd Fellows. In September, 1874, was solemnized the marriage of Mr. Bookwalter to Miss Catherine Perrin, daughter of the late James and Keziah (McWhorter) Perrin, of Bourbon, Marshall county, Indiana, and the only child of this union was Clyde R., who passed his entire life in Fort Wayne and was forty years of age at the time of his death, November 22, 1915. He was married, in 1897, to Stella A. Botzum, of Akron, Ohio, and they have one child, Velma R. Clyde R. Bookwalter was owner of the Fort Wayne Tea & Coffee House and was prominent in fraternal circles.

Rev. John H. Bosch.—The Reformed church in Indiana claims as one of its able, vigorous and zealous clergymen the Rev. John H. Bosch, who has served with utmost fidelity and efficiency as pastor of St. John's Reformed church, of Fort Wayne, since 1895, and whose earnest efforts have done much to forward the spiritual and temporal interests of this old and important parish, the church edifice of which is situated on Washington Boulevard, west. Mr. Bosch was born in the picturesque Rhein Province of Germany, September 8, 1867, and is a son of Henry and Sibilla (Peschken) Bosch, the father having been a prosperous farmer in that favored section of the German empire. He whose name introduces this review found the period of his childhood and early youth compassed by the conditions and influences of the home farm, and his early educational discipline was received in the Lutheran parochial schools of his native province. At the age of twenty years he came to the United States and shortly afterward entered Calvin College, in the city of Cleveland, Ohio, where he prepared himself for matriculation in Heidelberg Theological Seminary, at Tiffin, Ohio. In this latter institution he was graduated as a member of the class of 1894, and prior to this had gone to Chautauqua, New York, where he pursued the special study of the Hebrew language under the private preceptorship of the late and revered Rev. William H. Harper, D. D., who later became president of the great University of Chicago. This effective special course enabled him to complete in two years the prescribed three years' curriculum of the Heidelberg Theological Seminary, and it has been a matter of enduring satisfaction to him that he was thus able to know and receive instruction from Doctor Harper, one of the greatest educators and university executives that America has known. On January 13, 1895, Mr. Bosch was ordained a clergyman of the Reformed church and was duly installed pastor of his present parish, this result having been achieved through the action of "a committee of the Zion's classis of the Synod of the Northwest of the Reformed Church of the United States," and Rev. John Kuelling having been chairman of the ordaining and installing committee. Within the earnest and vigorous pastorate of the present incumbent the parish of St. John's Reformed church, of Fort Wayne, has expended more than thirty thousand dollars in the improving of the church property, and all of this appreciable amount has been paid in full, so that the parish is free from indebtedness. In 1916 was erected a new and modern parsonage, at a cost of eleven thousand dollars. The church has six hundred and seventy-five communicants, implying a congregation of fully one thousand persons. In addition to his zealous pastoral and executive duties Mr. Bosch was for twelve years editor and publisher of a periodical known as Gemeinde Bote, published in the German language. The paper was discontinued, in 1915, but in 1917 it was re-established and is now published in the English language. St. John's Reformed church, of Fort Wayne, was organized, in 1844, by fourteen families as constituent members, and concerning the growth and development of the historic old parish adequate mention is made in the general church history appearing in this publication. The church is identified with the Southwestern Synod, and the assembly of this synod, for 1917, was held in Fort Wayne. St. John's church has the largest congregation of all individual parishes in the synods of either the Southwest or Northwest, and the former synod has been entertained by the historic Fort Wayne church on three different occasions, prior to 1917. Mr. Bosch was for twelve years a member of the board of directors of the Orphans' Home, besides being treasurer of the noble institution, for which he handled in this period funds to the amount of more than one hundred and fifty thousand dollars. At the present time Mr. Bosch is a member of the board of trustees of the Central Publishing House of the Reformed Church of the United States, and he is vice-president of the board, this publishing house being established in the city of Cleveland. Mr. Bosch is a Republican in politics and is known as a broad-gauged, progressive and public-spirited citizen who takes deep interest in civic and governmental affairs, though he has had no desire to take an active part in political maneuvers. He is a devotee of outdoor sports and while in college gained championship honors in tennis. He takes lively interest in base ball, basket-ball, foot ball and all manner of athletics, and he and his wife enjoy to the full the boating, fishing and general pleasures incidental to their annual summer vacations in Northern Michigan, besides which he has indulged in various hunting trips in which he has brought down deer and other large game. In 1899 was solemnized the marriage of Mr. Bosch to Miss Frances R. Schweds, daughter of Rev. F. R. Schweds, D. D., who was pastor of St. John's Reformed church, of Fort Wayne, from 1868 to 1873, and under whose direction the present fine church edifice was erected. Mrs. Bosch was born in the old parsonage of this church and prior to her marriage had been a successful and popular teacher of German in the high school of the city of Terre Haute, Indiana. Mr. and Mrs. Bosch have three children—Aurelia, Paul and Theodore.

John Bostick passed his entire life in Fort Wayne, was a scion of one of the well-known and honored pioneer families of Allen county, and by his character and achievement he reflected dignity upon his native city, where he was long and prominently concerned with business affairs and where he won success through well-directed endeavors. A man of fine attributes of character and genial and kindly disposition, he commanded the high regard of all who knew him and thus set at naught any application of the scriptural aphorism that "a prophet is not without honor save in his own country." Mr. Bostick was born in Fort Wayne June 26, 1847, and here his death occurred two weeks prior to his fifty-fourth birthday anniversary. He was a son of Emanuel and Harriet (Kline) Bostick, who came from Lancaster, Pennsylvania, and established their home in Allen county fully three-fourths of a century ago and who passed the residue of their lives in Fort Wayne, where the father built up a prosperous merchant tailoring business. The third in order of birth in a family of nine children, the subject of this memoir acquired his early education in the public schools of Fort Wayne, and he learned the tailor's trade under the effective direction of his father, by whom he was eventually admitted to partnership and after whose death he continued independently to carry on the successful merchant tailoring business until about 1883, when he engaged in the real estate business. Of this latter and important phase of productive enterprise he continued to be a prominent and successful exponent until the close of his life, and incidentally he did much to further the normal development and upbuilding of his native city, which he had seen grow from a village to a civic and commercial center of metropolitan status. He accumulated an appreciable amount of valuable realty in Fort Wayne and vicinity, and of the same his widow still retains a considerable part, her beautiful home, at 426 East Wayne street, being known for its hospitality as a center of representative social activities. Mr. Bostick was a loyal advocate and supporter of the cause of the Democratic party, was actively affiliated with the time-honored Masonic fraternity and was a zealous communicant of the English Lutheran church, as is also his widow. He passed from the stage of his mortal endeavors on June 12, 1901, in the very prime of his strong and useful manhood and with an unsullied record as a man of sterling character and as a citizen of high ideals. On September 1, 1870, was solemnized the marriage of Mr. Bostick to Miss Louisa Deppeler, who likewise was born and reared in Fort Wayne and whose parents, John and Elizabeth (Weyseit) Deppeler, both natives of the fair little republic of Switzerland, established their home in Fort Wayne many years ago. Mr. Deppeler became one of the representative merchants of this city and was one of the honored and influential citizens of Allen county, both he and his wife having continued their residence in Fort Wayne until their death. Mr. and Mrs. Bostick became the parents of four children, all of whom are living except the first born, Edward, who died at the age of three years and three months. The three surviving sons, Samuel W., John D. and William E., are actively concerned with business affairs in Fort Wayne and the two first mentioned still remain with their widowed mother.

Delbert D. Boston, who is giving effective and loyal service as township trustee of his native township and is engaged in the barber business at Harlan, was born in Springfield township on August 18, 1866, a son of Thomas and Lavina (Snyder) Boston, both natives of the state of Ohio. Thomas Boston was born and reared in Stark county, Ohio, a representative of a sterling pioneer family of that section of the Buckeye State, and was a young man when he came to Allen county, Indiana, and numbered himself among the pioneer exponents of agricultural industry in Springfield township, where his marriage was solemnized and he and his wife passed the remainder of their lives, he having been for many years one of the substantial citizens and representative farmers of the township. He was a Republican in his political proclivities and both he and his wife were consistent members of the Methodist Episcopal church. Mary Ellen, the first of their five children, is deceased, and the survivors are: Myra, Elizabeth, David and Delbert D. He whose name initiates this article was reared to the sturdy discipline of the home farm and in the meanwhile profited by the advantages afforded in the schools of his native township. He continued his association with agricultural enterprise until he was twenty years of age, when he learned the barber's trade, to which he has since devoted his attention. With the exception of two years passed at Findlay, Ohio, he has been engaged in the work of his trade at Harlan during the intervening years, and here he has a well-equipped shop of modern appointments and the best of sanitary provisions, so that his trade is of representative and appreciative order. Mr. Boston is unflagging in his allegiance to the Republican party and in his loyalty to his native township and county. He was elected trustee of Springfield township in November, 1914, and is now the efficient and progressive incumbent of this office. He is affiliated with Harlan Lodge No. 296, Ancient Free & Accepted Masons, he and his wife are active members of the Methodist Episcopal church, and in their home community their circle of friends is limited only by that of their acquaintances. On November 6, 1889, was solemnized the marriage of Mr. Boston to Miss Ella Furney, who was born and reared in this county and is a daughter of Jeremiah and Isabell (Cummings) Furney. Mr. and Mrs. Boston have two children—Beryl, who is the wife of DeGroff N. Swartz, a prosperous farmer of Springfield township; and Donald M., who remains at the parental home.

Daniel Bottenberg, who died March 12, 1917, and who was one of the venerable and revered citizens of Monroe township, is specially entitled to recognition in this history of Allen county, within whose borders he maintained his home from his boyhood and in which he was a representative of a sterling pioneer family. Though he later retired from the arduous labors that long engrossed his time and attention, he continued to reside upon and give a general supervision to his fine farm, which comprises one hundred and sixty acres and which is eligibly situated in Section 22, Monroe township. Mr. Bottenberg was born in Butler county, Ohio, April 19, 1835, and was one of the members of a family of twelve children, only three of whom now survive. He was a son of

Jacob and Nancy (VanHorn) Bottenberg, the former of whom was born in Maryland of German lineage, and the latter in New Jersey, of staunch Holland Dutch ancestry. The parents removed to Ohio in the early '30s and in 1849 they came with their children from Butler county, that state, to Allen county, Indiana, where the father obtained a tract of heavily timbered land, in Marion township, and there he began the reclaiming of a farm under the primitive conditions that marked the pioneer era in the history of the county. His earnest and strenuous efforts brought to him independence and he and his wife lived to see their pioneer log house give place to a more modern and pretentious building. They continued to reside on their farm until he moved to Monmouth and there he died in 1869. Their names merit a place on the roster of the honored pioneers of Allen county. He whose name introduces this review gained his rudimentary education in the common schools of the old Buckeye state and was a lad of about fifteen years at the time of the family removal to Indiana. He assisted his father in the herculean work of reclaiming the old homestead farm and remained at the parental home until he had attained to his legal majority, with a due quota of incidental discipline that tended to broaden his mental horizon. After leaving the home of his parents he farmed rented land for a number of years, and he then purchased his present homestead, which he developed into one of the well-improved and valuable rural estates of Monroe township. As a loyal and liberal citizen he aided in the support of those things that advanced the general welfare of the community and he gave unfaltering allegiance to the Republican party, though he had at no time any desire for public office of any kind. Both he and his wife were zealous members of the Lutheran church in their community and he served the same in the offices of trustee and elder at the time of his death. Through his own well-ordered efforts Mr. Bottenberg made his way to the goal of worthy prosperity and enjoyed the rewards of former years of earnest toil and endeavor, the while both he and his wife rested secure in the high regard of all who knew them. In 1857 was recorded the marriage of Mr. Bottenberg to Miss Elizabeth Lenhart, who was born in Ohio and who is one of the four surviving members of a family of twelve children. Her parents, John and Rebecca (Burroughs) Lenhart, were born, respectively, in the states of Pennsylvania and Maryland, and the father was twelve years of age when he accompanied his parents on their removal to Ohio, where he was reared to adult age. In 1839 John Lenhart removed from Ohio to Adams county, Indiana, where he settled on an embryonic farm in the midst of the almost unbroken forest and there he reclaimed a productive farm. The original family dwelling was a pioneer log house with clapboard roof weighted down with poles, with puncheon floor and wide fireplace as interior provisions, and with door fitted with the old-time latch string that was always left hanging on the outside, as an evidence of the hospitality of the little domicile in which dwelt contentment and happiness. The parents of Mrs. Bottenberg remained on this old homestead until their death. Concerning the five children of Mr. and Mrs. Bottenberg the following brief record is given in conclusion of this sketch: Jason remains with his mother and has the active management of the old home farm; John P. is the second son and is engaged in farming in this county; Nellie is the wife of Henry Bowers; Mary L. is the wife of William C. Foster, and they now reside in the state of Michigan; and Zenus J., the youngest of the children, resides in Monroe township.

Oscar Boulton is one of the native sons of Allen county who has brought to bear a strong and well-poised mentality as well as significant enterprise and progressiveness in the furthering of his successful activities as an agriculturist and stock-grower, and he is now one of the representative exponents of these fundamental industries in his native township of Springfield, where he has made the best of improvements upon his fine farm of one hundred and eighty-five acres, in Sections 27 and 28, the homestead being about one and a half miles distant from the village of Grabill, which is his postoffice address. Mr. Boulton was born in Springfield township, February 2, 1862, a scion of a sterling family that was founded in this county full seventy years ago. He is a son of Henry and Helen (Hatch) Boulton. Henry Boulton was born in England and was fifteen years of age when he came to America with his parents, the home being established in Erie county, Ohio, where he was reared to manhood and whence he came to Allen county, Indiana, in 1847. He purchased a tract of land in Springfield township and from the virgin forest reclaimed a productive farm. There he continued his residence until he had attained to advanced age, when he retired from active labors and established his home in the village of Harlan, where both he and his wife passed the residue of their lives in gracious peace and prosperity and with secure place in the esteem of all who knew them. Louisa, the eldest of their children, is deceased, and all of the others are living, namely: Nettie, Emma, Mary, Flora, Oscar, Ida and Minnie, the subject of this review being the only son. Oscar Boulton was reared to the sturdy and invigorating discipline of the home farm and his alert and vigorous mentality prompted in him such ambition that he was not content with the advancement made by availing himself of the advantages of the public schools, but furthered his academic knowledge by attending for one term the normal department of what is now the great Valparaiso University. That he made good use of the opportunities thus afforded him is evidenced by the effective service which he gave as a representative of the pedagogic profession. For eight years he was in active service as a successful and popular teacher in the public schools of his native county and thereafter turned his attention with equal earnestness and circumspection to farm enterprise, in which he has achieved unequivocal success, his present fine farm of one hundred and eighty-five acres giving definite evidence of thrift and prosperity. In 1917 he purchased a residence in the village of Harlan, where he contemplates making his future home. Mr. Boulton is found aligned as a well-fortified advocate of the principles of the Republican party and takes loyal interest in community affairs, though he has manifested naught of ambition for the honors or emoluments of public office. He attends and supports the Methodist Episcopal church at Grabill, of which his wife is an active member. On April 24, 1890, was recorded the marriage of Mr. Boulton to Miss Isa Burchfield, who likewise was born and reared in this county, a daughter of Joseph and Mary (Safford) Burchfield. Mr. and Mrs. Boulton have no children of their own, but in their home they are carefully rearing an adopted daughter, Julia Hamilton, who accords to them true filial affection.

Jesse W. Bowers, M. D., has fortified himself with that resolute integrity of purpose and that thorough technical preparation which make for unequivocal success in the medical profession, and he is recognized as one of the able and representative physicians and surgeons of the younger generation in the city of Fort Wayne, where he has been established in the general practice of his profession since the summer of 1908 and where his success is on a parity with his unqualified personal popularity. Doctor Bowers was born at Van Wert, Ohio, October 15, 1882, and is a son of George W. and Annie E. (Webb) Bowers, who still reside in that attractive little city of the Buckeye state, the father having been for a number of years identified with railroad operations, later having become an exponent of agricultural industry and being now successfully established as an apiarist at Van Wert, as an enthusiast and authority in bee culture and the producing of the finest grade of honey. Doctor Bowers is indebted to the public schools of his native city for his early educational training, which was supplemented by a course in the Western Ohio Normal School, at Middlepoint, as well as by a thorough course in the Ohio Northern University, at Ada, in which he took a scientific course, as a member of the class of 1901. In preparation for his chosen profession he entered the Eclectic Medical College in the city of Cincinnati, this being one of the foremost schools of the Eclectic system in the Union, and in the same he was graduated as a member of the class of 1908 and with the degree of Doctor of Medicine. He gained valuable experience by serving as an interne in Seton Hospital, Cincinnati, prior to his graduation, and on June 3, 1908, he established his residence in Fort Wayne, where his close application and effective service have resulted in his building up a substantial practice. The Doctor is a member of the State Medical Society and the American Medical Association, has attained the thirty-second degree in the Ancient Accepted Scottish Rite and the York Rite of the Masonic fraternity, besides being affiliated also with the Ancient Arabic Order, Nobles of the Mystic Shrine, the Tribe of Ben Hur and the Modern Woodmen of America. On December 20, 1903, was recorded the marriage of Doctor Bowers to Miss Alby Beck, daughter of Daniel and Margaret (Rank) Beck, of Van Wert, Ohio, and the two children of this union are: Gah, who was born May 20, 1905, and Ferne, who was born January 9, 1908.

William E. Bowers.—One of the progressive and prosperous younger men of New Haven, resident there since 1903, is William E. Bowers, proprietor of the New Haven Tribune and since 1905 manager of the New Haven Telephone Company. Mr. Bowers was born in Jefferson township, Allen county, Indiana, on February 24, 1874, and is the son of David B. and Lucinda (Lesh) Bowers. The father was born in Mansfield, Ohio, and the mother in Lewisville, Ohio. Mr. Bowers was a farmer, coming with his parents to Allen county in 1848, where they bought a farm, locating in Jefferson township. He later purchased the original tract and also added thereto, carrying on active farming operations until 1911, when he retired and moved to Fort Wayne. He died April 9, 1917. Mrs. Bowers died on the home farm in 1906. She and her husband were members of the Methodist Protestant church and were active workers in the church in the years of their residence in Jefferson township. Their children were seven in number. Alfaretta is the wife of J. F. Hathaway, of Fort Wayne. William E., of this review, was the second born. Harry H. lives in Dayton, Ohio. John E. is a resident of Washington, D. C. Glenola is the wife of Earl Schnitz, of Fort Wayne. Arthur died in infancy and Frances died at the age of seventeen years. William E.

Bowers had his education in the schools of Jefferson township, the New Haven and Fort Wayne public schools and the Ohio Normal University at Ada, Ohio, where he took a scientific course. His education finished, he engaged in teaching and for three years was employed in the schools of Jefferson township. He then spent one year in the Marion (Ind.) Law School, after which he taught in the Marion schools for three years and in 1903 came to New Haven and bought the Tribune, which he published successfully until January 1, 1917, when he leased the paper to C. F. Moon. In 1905 he became manager of the Home Telephone Company, of New Haven, and he is now serving as president of the Northeastern Indiana Telephone Association. Mr. Bowers is a Republican in politics, a member of the Methodist Episcopal church, and of the New Haven Commercial Club, one of the live organizations of the town. His fraternal relations are confined to identification with the Modern Woodmen of America. He was married on January 15, 1902, to Miss Pearl Allen, the daughter of Hiram and Amanda (Lancaster) Allen, of Marion, Indiana. Two children have been born to Mr. and Mrs. Bowers—Arthur and Jeannette, now attending school in their home town.

W. J. Bowker.—See Athenaeum.

Allen A. Bowser is first vice-president of the corporation of S. F. Bowser and Company, manufacturers of oil tanks and pumps and one of the most important manufacturing and commercial enterprises of Fort Wayne. He is a nephew of the sterling and representative citizen whose name gives title to this well-known concern. Mr. Bowser was born in DeKalb county, Indiana, on February 19, 1865, and is a son of Alexander and Laurinda (DeVilbiss) Bowser, the former of whom was born in Allen county, the latter in the state of Ohio. The father, a representative of one of the honored pioneer families of this section of Indiana, who is now living retired in Fort Wayne, followed the carpenters' trade for a long period and developed a substantial business as a contractor and builder. Later he and his son Allen, together with Sylvanus F. Bowser, commenced the business in which he continued until his retirement a few years ago. Allen A. Bowser was a child at the time of the family removal to Fort Wayne, where he acquired his early education in the public schools. At sixteen years of age he began working with his father in the carpenter business and at twenty years they started the making of pumps in a barn at the rear of their home. Since this time Mr. Bowser has been an invaluable aid in the extensive industrial enterprise conducted under the incorporated title of S. F. Bowser and Company. His inventive genius has produced many of the ideas of intrinsic value to this company. As first vice-president of this concern he has become an influential figure with secure status as a captain of industry in Fort Wayne. Loyal and progressive in his civic attitude, he is aligned as a stanch supporter of the principles of the Republican party. In 1892 he married Miss Lottie Pierson, who was born and reared in Allen county and who served her community and church nobly until her death in November, 1916. Mr. Bowser himself has served the United Brethren church in many substantial ways, including the superintending of the Sunday school for the past twenty-six years. An only child, Jennie L. Bowser, resides with her father in their beautiful home on East Pontiac Street.

Albert S. Bowser.—Of the younger business men of Fort Wayne, Albert S. Bowser is a most fitting representative. Of unostentatious demeanor, never given to spectacular or pretentious display, Mr. Bowser, in his capacity as secretary of S. F. Bowser & Company and as the manager of the Michigan district in the sales organization of the company, has risen to the best opportunities of his connection with the enterprise founded by his father, S. F. Bowser. He has been actively connected with practically every department of the home office of the concern and is thoroughly acquainted with the details of the immense organization. Mr. Bowser was born in Fort Wayne July 28, 1886, the son of Sylvanus and Sarah F. (Russell) Bowser. A biographical review of S. F. Bowser appears elsewhere in this volume. Albert S. Bowser was educated in the public schools of Fort Wayne, and, following his period in the high school, he entered actively upon his business career with S. F. Bowser & Company, in December, 1906. On the 12th of September, 1907, he was united in marriage with Miss Ida Pearl Kickley, of Fort Wayne. Two children have been born to Mr. and Mrs. Bowser—Bon Silene and Albert S., Jr. Mr. Bowser is a member of the Masonic fraternity, including the Mystic Shrine, and actively connected with the Friars Club and the Country Club. His election to the presidency of the Senate Club in 1917 placed him at the head of one of the live organizations of the younger business and professional men of the city, an honor which bespeaks his popularity among his associates. Mr. and Mrs. Bowser are active members of Plymouth Congregational church.

Sylvanus F. Bowser is a striking example of the stalwart manhood of the middle west—an illustration of the attainment of true success through the application of sterling principles of action. As the head of one of the most widely famed manufacturing institutions of America— one with distribution centers in the capitals of Europe as well as in the chief cities of the United States—his name is known and spoken wherever commercial oils are sold or used. The hundreds of salesmen who tell of the superior merits of the self-measuring oil storage devices manufactured by S. F. Bowser & Company, Inc., not only give a service of untold worth to millions of purchasers but they also spread abroad the good name of Fort Wayne to every quarter of the civilized world. Mr. Bowser is a man of enthusiasm, far-sightedness and of unbounded energy and capacity for thought and work. With high ideals of his duty toward his fellow men, he has built solidly upon the foundation of real success. His fraternal spirit is reflected throughout the organization of the office, the factory and the sales force. Mr. Bowser is a native of Allen county, of which Fort Wayne is the seat of government. He was born in Perry township August 8, 1854, and is a son of John H. and Eliza (Keiger) Bowser, both of whom were born and reared in Pennsylvania, where their marriage was solemnized. They became the parents of thirteen children, of whom six are deceased. John H. Bowser removed from Pennsylvania to Perry township, Allen county, Indiana, in 1833, and here he developed a valuable farm in the midst of the virgin forests. Here he and his wife resided until the close of their days. Sylvanus F. Bowser was reared on the home farm and attended the common schools. In 1882 he became a traveling salesman for the wholesale paper house of W. H. Wells and Brother, of Chicago. It was in 1885, while he was still employed by the Wells concern, that there came to him the idea of the self-measuring oil pump which was an entirely new device, the first of its kind and which was destined to revolutionize the oil handling business of the world. From the time the first pump was made

S. F. Bowser

Mr. Bowser, through the organization of the company after he had thoroughly tested his invention, has constantly overcome all difficulties, until to-day the company's managers are recognized the world over as oil storage and handling experts, producing devices for the small user as well as those demanded by the largest and most complete factory or railroad plant. At the time of his discovery Mr. Bowser—as we find by referring to his own story of the business—had been compelled to refrain from hard manual labor, an account of a physical breakdown, and at this time on account of financial difficulties, he deeded his home to a creditor and engaged for his family small living quarters consistent with his meager means. The story of his struggle against ill health and threatened want, coupled with the courage and energy of the future manufacturer, is one of inspiration and hopefulness to every youth into whose life it may come. Referring to the day when things began to take on a new significance, Mr. Bowser says in his little booklet, entitled "A Dream and a Reality": "It was one morning in the early spring of 1885 that I was going out on a five o'clock train, in pursuit of my business as a salesman. Therefore, I arose at four o'clock, and, among other things, I wanted to leave my wife with a good supply of water for the day. The well from which we got our water was about seventy feet deep, and our means for getting it were somewhat primitive, notwithstanding the same is in use now, here and there through the country, and doubtless forever will be. Over the well was built a little house and up in the roof was a big, grooved swivel-wheel over which the long well rope passed so that a bucket could be made fast to each end of it. By letting one bucket down for water, you at the same time would be drawing up the other bucket full of water. The little house over the well was unusually high. It simply had a roof on it and was not enclosed and the well being deep and the night still and very cold, the steam that came out of the well froze on the ropes thus exposed between the mouth of the well and the roof. Therefore, in order to draw water in this manner, this frozen, frost-covered rope had to pass through my hands, and it being a very cold morning, its sting was added to my hands. I took my grip and made the train. I went to Decatur, twenty-two miles south of Fort Wayne; here I got a team of horses and a sleigh and drove to Pleasant Mills, some six miles southeast. From there I drove to Willshire, Ohio, three and one-half miles farther on. It was on this drive from Pleasant Mills to Willshire that my mind turned to the unpleasantness of drawing water out of this deep well on a cold morning. My thoughts turned to devising some better way, at which time I saw, as it were, a pump cylinder at the bottom of the well sufficiently large to hold a pail of water, the same being provided with a discharge pipe and a pump rod, similar to our present pump, and so arranged that with one full stroke I could discharge a bucketful of water. This looked good to me, and I thought if it was good and practical, maybe I could work up a little business out of it by manufacturing it for the market. Upon returning home I took it up with my brother, who was an engineer on the Pennsylvania Railroad and lived the second door from me, drawing water from the same well. Neither of us being versed in this kind of business, but my brother having an acquaintanceship with a patent-model maker who was quite well versed in mechanics of this sort, we went down and laid the matter before him. He took out of his drawer a little book which treated of subjects of this kind and showed us therein the great pressure that would be necessary to raise the water to the surface from so deep a well, which convinced us that it was absolutely impractical. This settled it, for the moment at least, but when I got out alone and was thinking the matter over, it came to me in almost audible words: 'Why will it not do for oil? It is never far away.' And as this was going through my mind I could see, as it were, an oil tank sitting in the corner of a grocery and I could see another oil tank sitting beneath, in the corner of the basement of the grocery, and as basements are never very deep I felt sure that my pump would work satisfactorily in either of these tanks. So, in a few days, when my brother was in, I took this proposition up with him. He readily agreed with me that in this case the pump would work entirely satisfactorily, but he suggested that everybody was supplied with oil tanks and there would be no market for them. But as my business was selling goods, I did not see it in that way.'' The narrative goes on to tell of the inventor's securing five orders within the following two days, for his pump, which was as yet a dream. None of these orders were filled until three months later, but from that time forward the Bowser pump grew in popular favor until, as in the case of the year 1916, the sales of S. F. Bowser and Company totaled the splendid sum of six and one-half million dollars. The total number of office and factory employes is about 1,200, while the sales force has an aggregate of 550 men scattered over the civilized world. ''A volume could be written of the dark and trying times before the idea came to me,'' says Mr. Bowser, ''and two volumes could be written of the times since; but you will observe that had it not been for these trying times and misfortunes, of which I have had many, together with my broken health, I would not have lost my home, I would still be a traveling man and there would have been no 'Bowser pump' to-day.'' Mr. Bowser has been active for many years in every great movement for the advancement of his fellow men. Daily he is called upon to give his means and his voice to the improvement of the welfare of the people of his own and other communities. Although he is a leader in the conduct of the affairs of the First Baptist Church, his benevolences are widespread. In politics he is a supporter of the principles of the Republican party. On October 11, 1876, Mr. Bowser was united in marriage with Miss Sarah F. Russell, who likewise was born and reared in Allen county and who is a daughter of William and Sarah Russell, residents of Fort Wayne at the time of their death. Mr. and Mrs. Bowser became the parents of six children, as follows: Harry M., Eva C. (now Mrs. Leland F. Johnson), William Hugh (an invalid), Albert S., Ethelyn V. (now Mrs. Daniel G. Milligan) and Mildred L. Bowser. In honor of an invalid son, Mr. and Mrs. Bowser have erected a beautiful place of worship for the Free Methodist denomination, and the same is known as the Hughie Bowser church, the edifice standing near the extensive plant of S. F. Bowser & Company.

Edward B. Boyle has been engaged in business in Hoagland for the past eighteen years and has enjoyed a fair measure of success in that time. Prior to his connection with his present enterprises he was identified with the farming industry, in which he was reared on the home farm of his parents, who were Daniel and Elizabeth (Minick) Boyle, natives of Ireland. They came from their native land in the year 1832, settled in Huntington county, and Mr. Boyle found work on the old canal. After some time spent in that work he had saved enough to make possible the purchase of eighty acres of government land, and from then until his death he was successfully engaged in agriculture in Huntington county. He was a Democrat, a member of the Roman Catholic church, and he died at the age of fifty-six years, leaving four children. Ellen married John Tooley and is deceased. John Patrick was the second born. Edward is the immediate subject of this review, and Mary died in Chicago as the wife of William Thomas. Edward Boyle was educated in the parochial schools at Hesse Cassel, and up to the age of sixteen years spent much of the time with his uncle in that place. He later branched out for himself and up to the age of thirty-two was connected with farming and kindred occupations. In 1899 he engaged in the saloon business in Hoagland, where he has since been successfully established. He is a director in the Hoagland State Bank and is fraternally identified by his membership in the Independent Order of Eagles. A Democrat, he has been influential in local politics, and is a member of the Catholic church at Hoagland. He was married on November 5, 1904, to Mary Schmidt, and they have two children—Robert Patrick and Eugene Charles.

Conrad Branning merits recognition in this history by reason of his status as one of the loyal and popular citizens and substantial farmers of Aboite township, where he is the owner of a well-improved farm of one hundred and sixty acres and where his success has been consonant with the energy and good judgment he has brought to bear in the various departments of his farm enterprise. He was born in Germany, on September 9, 1855, and is a son of Henry and Minnie Branning, who came with their family of nine children to America in the year 1881, their arrival in the port of New York city having been on June 22 of that year. They came forthwith to Indiana and after residing for a time in the vicinity of the city of Vincennes they came to Allen county, where they passed the remainder of their lives, the father having been an industrious and successful farmer. Conrad Branning acquired in his native land his early educational training and there also he learned the mason's trade. He was about twenty-five years of age when he accompanied his parents on their immigration to the United States and for many years he continued to follow the work of his trade, first at Vincennes and later in Fort Wayne. He finally sold his business at Fort Wayne, where he had become a successful contractor, and in 1896 purchased eighty acres of his present homestead farm, the additional eighty acres having been secured at a later date. He has shown his energy and progressiveness in the improving and management of his farm, which is devoted to diversified agriculture and stock-growing and which gives definite evidence of thrift and prosperity. He takes loyal interest in public affairs of a local order and is a staunch Democrat in politics, he and his family being earnest members of the German Lutheran church. On October 10, 1880, was solemnized the marriage of Mr. Branning to Miss Sophia Dammeyer, whose parents passed their entire lives in Germany. Only a few months after their marriage Mr. and Mrs. Branning came to America, and they have been devoted companions and co-workers during the years that have brought to them a generous measure of independence and prosperity. Of their children the first born was Minnie, who died in infancy. The second child likewise was given the name of Minnie, and she is now the wife of Lemuel McKenzie. William, the third child, is deceased. Sophia remains at the parental home. Edmund and

Esther are twins and both are married and well established in life, Edmund having one son, William, and Esther, who is the wife of M. B. Marshall, having two children, Conrad and Catherine. Henry and Louise, the next two of the children, are deceased; and those who remain members of the parental home circle are Ferdinand, Charles, Fritz, Mary, Theodore and Irene.

Charles W. Branstrator was born in Lafayette township on the old William Branstrator place, settled by William Branstrator as long ago as in 1848. He was the father of the subject and he was long and prominently identified with that district, witnessing its development along many lines, and being a contributor to its worthiest advancement. He came from Warren county, Ohio, where the family had long been established in farming activities. William Branstrator married Catherine A. Hill, also of Ohio birth and parentage, and they were the parents of a family of twelve children. Frances E. died on April 13, 1913. Sarah E. is the wife of Henry Cress. Martin Luther died in infancy. Andrew Dallas lives in Fort Wayne. Anna Catherine married George Welbaum. William David is living in Warren county, Ohio, the old family home. Jason D. is a resident of Wayne township. James Calvin died in infancy. George B. Mc. is a resident of Fort Wayne. Charles W. is the subject. Rosa Jane and Della May are deceased. The parents were members of the Unitarian church. Mr. Branstrator was a Mason and was long prominent in his community in a political way, serving as a trustee of the township in the early years after its official formation. He died May 1, 1900, and his wife April 13, 1913. Charles W. Branstrator had better educational advantages than the average farm youth. He followed his high school training with a course in the Fort Wayne College, thereafter spending two years in the University at Valparaiso, where he took a scientific course of study that included engineering. After finishing his university course he taught school from 1890 to 1892, in the latter year being elected to the office of County Surveyor of Allen county and serving as County Surveyor for three consecutive terms. After his term of service he surveyed the Wabash Railroad line from Fort Wayne to Butler, and later spent six months in Oklahoma on an engineering work. Still later he spent some months in Fort Wayne as an engineer and in 1900 came to the home farm. He returned to Fort Wayne, however, but in 1904 once more came back to the old farm, and he may be found there at the present writing, where he has made a name for himself as a feeder of sheep, cattle and hogs. He has been very successful in his stock-farming and feels satisfied that he has found his rightful place in life. Mr. Branstrator is a Mason and a Democrat. He was married on April 14, 1895, to Miss Eda Kimmell, daughter of Jacob and Louisa (Fisher) Kimmell, the father a native of Pleasant township and the mother born in New York city. They were farmers in Pleasant township for many years, and both are now deceased. They had two children—Eda, wife of the subject, and Thomas, who is connected with the electric light plant in Fort Wayne. Nine children were born to Mr. and Mrs. Branstrator, here briefly named in the order of their appearance. Grace K. is a student at Valparaiso University. Helen is at home with the family. Charles is attending the high school in Fort Wayne. The others are Clover Hill, Clara, Mabel, Ann, Sarah Jane and Martha W. All are at home.

William P. Breen

Mrs. Anna Brauneisen is a life-long resident of Indiana and has made her home in Fort Wayne since 1884, when she and her husband opened a grocery store and identified themselves with the community life. When in later years the health of the husband failed Mrs. Brauneisen assumed responsibility for the success of the enterprise and continued to operate it with much success until 1910, when she sold the business and turned her attention exclusively to china painting, which had long been a hobby with her, and which has claimed her attention since then both profitably and pleasureably. She has an ever increasing patronage in Fort Wayne and vicinity, and besides executing orders for the work, she conducts classes in the art of china painting and is generally regarded as an expert along those lines. Her study of ceramics has been a far-reaching one, and it is a subject that claims a large share of her attention, though she has been able to devote some time to real estate operations along very successful lines. She has built and sold two fine residence properties in the city, and is now the owner of a third at No. 2014 Webster Street. She also owns a store building at No. 1602 Wells Street, and some other property in the city. Mr. and Mrs. Brauneisen had one son—a brilliant youth who gave promise of unusual accomplishments in music. He died suddenly at the age of sixteen, just as he was graduated from a local business college. Mrs. Brauneisen is a member of the Roman Catholic church and is devoted to the work of the parish, though the demands her profession make upon her time prevent her from participating to any extent in the social activities of those circles in which she is known and esteemed.

William P. Breen.—Fort Wayne and Allen county are grateful for the influence of the citizenship of a man of the type of William P. Breen, one of the most widely known members of the Indiana bar. Mr. Breen was born in Terre Haute, Vigo county, Indiana, February 13, 1859, the son of James and Margaret (Dunne) Breen, both natives of Ireland, born in 1820 and 1821, respectively. In 1840, the father at the age of twenty, severed the ties which had bound him to the Emerald Isle and came to America. After a brief residence in the east, he came west and settled at Terre Haute, where he remained until 1863, in which year the family removed to Fort Wayne. Mr. Breen not only attained to prominence as one of Fort Wayne's representative business men, engaged in mercantile lines, but he interested himself with marked effect in civic affairs. For a number of years, he served as a member of the city council, and, at the time of his death, was a member of the board of waterworks trustees. This was in 1883. William P. Breen was the only child of James Breen and his wife. He attended the parochial school conducted by the Brothers of the Holy Cross, and followed this with a course in Notre Dame University, from which institution he was graduated in 1877, with the degree of Bachelor of Arts. Upon his return to Fort Wayne, Mr. Breen entered upon a course in the study of law in the offices of Coombs, Morris & Bell, and, in 1879, was admitted to the bar of Indiana. At this time, Mr. Breen was but twenty years of age. From the beginning of his career in the law until November 15, 1882, the time of the death of Judge Warren H. Withers, Mr. Breen was associated with Judge Withers in a most successful practice of his profession, and then, for a period of eleven years, he continued an individual practice of increasing importance, until, in 1893, he formed a co-partnership with John Morris, Jr., son of Judge John Morris. The latter was one of the foremost jurists of his time; his death occurred in 1905. The firm of Breen & Morris, which has continued since its formation, is recognized as one of the most influential in the state of Indiana. The enviable position of Mr. Breen among his fellow-members of the Indiana bar is suggested in his election as president of the Indiana Bar Association for the years 1903 and 1904, as a member of the executive committee of the American Bar Association from 1903 to 1906, and as a delegate to the Universal Congress of Lawyers and Jurists, in 1904, at St. Louis, under the appointment of President Roosevelt, Republican. Although always a vigorous advocate of Democratic principles, Mr. Breen has never sought political honors. His activities have been recognized in his selection as a delegate to the National Democratic Convention at St. Louis, in 1916, and a member of the committee to visit President Woodrow Wilson at Shadow Lawn, New Jersey, in September, 1916, to give him official notification of the action of the convention. Mr. Breen's keen power of thinking, his readiness of speech and his popular method of treating questions of wide importance has given him a place of prominence among the public speakers of Indiana. His opinions and his influence are ever sought by those who feel deeply the need of the co-operation of a man whose word finds weight with the many who seek the truth along many lines of endeavor. On May 28, 1884, Mr. Breen was united in marriage with Miss Odelia Phillips, daughter of Bernard P. and Caroline (Vogel) Phillips, of Fort Wayne. Mr. Breen is the president of one of the city's substantial financial institutions, the People's Trust and Savings Company, of Fort Wayne, which occupies its own modern six-story building, centrally located. He is a member of the Catholic Club, of New York. He is a member of the Fort Wayne Commercial Club and of the Fort Wayne Country Club. Every movement for the substantial betterment of the community finds a stanch advocate in Mr. Breen. No member of the bar has conferred greater honor or distinction upon the profession in Allen county and the state of Indiana. Admittedly a man of resources, he is recognized among the men of his profession as one who is a close student of every element which comes into every case presented for his consideration—quick to recognize and to anticipate difficulties and to overcome them—forceful in the presentation of his arguments—he has gained and held the respect and admiration of all who have in any way been connected with the activities of his professional or private life.

James J. Brennan has been identified with railway affairs since his early youth and his activities have touched both steam and electrical transportation, in the latter department of which he has achieved distinctive success and precedence, as evidenced by the fact that he is at the present time superintendent of transportation for the entire system of the Fort Wayne and Northern Indiana Traction Company, which controls and operates about 230 miles of traction service, in Indiana. He maintains his residence and official headquarters in the city of Fort Wayne and as one of the representative business men of the metropolis of Allen county he is specially entitled to recognition in this history. Mr. Brennan was born in the historic old town of Harper's Ferry, West Virginia, on July 8, 1870, and is a son of Martin and Catherine (McCabe) Brennan, who were residents of West Virginia at the time of their deaths, both having been born in Ireland. Martin Brennan was a youth when he came to the United States, in 1847, and he first established his residence at Charlestown, West Virginia, whence he later removed to Harper's

Ferry. During the major part of his active career he was closely identified with railroad operations and through his industry and well-ordered efforts he won independence and a fair measure of temporal prosperity, both he and his wife having been zealous communicants of the Catholic church. Of their children, Elizabeth still resides at Harper's Ferry; James J., of this review, was the next in order of birth; John resides at Harper's Ferry, and William E. maintains his home at Harrisonburg, Virginia. In his native place James J. Brennan attended school until he was fourteen years of age, when he there entered the employ of the Baltimore & Ohio Railroad Company. He won advancement until he became identified with the train service of this company, and later he was similarly engaged at Pittsburgh, Pennsylvania, in the employ of the Pennsylvania Railroad Company. Later he became identified with the operation of an electric railway at Wheeling, West Virginia, and thereafter his activities in this same direction involved his service in Cleveland, Ohio, and Detroit, Michigan. In 1905 he came to Fort Wayne and assumed the position of superintendent of overhead construction for the Fort Wayne and Northern Indiana Traction Company, and his ability and effective service eventually led to his promotion to his present responsible post, that of superintendent of transportation for the entire local and interurban system of this corporation. He has proved one of the world's workers and his advancement represents the result of his ability, ambition and well-ordered endeavors. In politics Mr. Brennan maintains an independent attitude, he is affiliated with the Knights of Columbus, and both he and his wife are active communicants of the Catholic church. On May 21, 1892, was solemnized the marriage of Mr. Brennan to Miss Bessie Winston, of Wheeling, West Virginia, and of their five children the first two, Cyril and Mary Agnes, are deceased; William Edward is a student in the great University of Michigan, at Ann Arbor, as is also Joseph F.; and Thomas James remains at the parental home.

August Brenneke was a young man of twenty-eight years when he established his home in this county, in 1884, soon after his arrival in America. When he severed the ties that bound him to his native land he came to this country with no definite financial resources and dependent upon his own ability and efforts in making his way to the goal of independence and prosperity. That success has attended him generously within more than thirty years of residence in Allen county is vouched for not only by his influential association with the banking business at Woodburn, but also by his ownership of one of the valuable estates of Maumee township. Mr. Brenneke was born in Germany January 13, 1856, and is a son of Frederick and Caroline (Neward) Brenneke, who passed their entire lives in Germany, the father having been a farmer by vocation. In the excellent schools of his native land August Brenneke received his early educational discipline and there also gained his initial experience in connection with practical farm industry. In 1884 he came to the United States and established his permanent residence in Allen county. Here he bought a tract of cut-over land in Maumee township, and he reclaimed, drained and otherwise improved this property, which is now one of the fine farms of the county. With increasing financial means, Mr. Brenneke continued to make judicious investments in farm land, and he is now the owner of a finely improved estate of two hundred and fifty acres, divided into two farms, each of which is improved with modern buildings and kept up to the highest standard in all respects. Mr. Brenneke has been a man of assertive and self-reliant ambition and enterprise, has ordered his course on a high plane of integrity and honor and has achieved large and well-merited success through his own well-applied energy as a progressive agriculturist and stock-grower. His political support is given to the Republican party, he has served as trustee of Maumee township, and he and his wife are earnest communicants of the Lutheran church. In 1889 Mr. Brenneke wedded Miss Sophia Feusse, daughter of Henry and Margaret Feusse, of Adams county, Indiana, and this gracious union has been blessed with three children: Henry is successfully established in the mercantile business at Woodburn, and Herman and William are, respectively, managers of two of their father's fine farms in Maumee township.

William Breuer.—As the American republic stands to-day pre-eminent among nations in its capacity for the conducting of commercial and industrial affairs of great scope, so does the splendid enterprise of the Berghoff Brewing Company, of Fort Wayne, stand as a conspicuous example of the truth of the above statement, even as it does also of the great value of our German element of citizenship. The history of this representative Fort Wayne concern covers a period of more than thirty years, its business has been at all times conducted with scrupulous integrity both in the matter of maintaining the high standard of production and in the honorable methods employed in all trade transactions. The result has been the upbuilding of a business that far transcends local limitations and that marks the Berghoff Brewing Company as one of the leading institutions of its kind in the Union, the capacity of its extensive and finely equipped plant being tested in supplying the demands of a trade that extends into divers states of the Union and that has made the Berghoff beer famed in such metropolitan centers as the city of Chicago. Of this company William Breuer is vice-president, and prior to giving a brief review of his career it is but consistent that there be entered a resume of the history of the important corporation of which he is thus a valued executive. In the year 1885 the Herman Berghoff Brewing Company was incorporated with a capital stock of one hundred thousand dollars and with Herman Berghoff as president and Hubert Berghoff as secretary and treasurer, the original plant of the company having been established at the corner of Washington Avenue East and Grant Street. The original principals were insistent in bringing the output of the brewery up to the highest German standard, and this policy has been maintained during the long intervening years, so that the Berghoff name now implies the maximum of purity, of proper maturing of all products and of a standard from which there have been all too many lapses in the record of American manufacturing of malt beverages. In 1899 a reorganization of the concern was effected under the title of the Berghoff Brewing Company, and the capitalization was increased to two hundred and fifty thousand dollars of common stock and an equal amount of preferred stock. At this juncture the officers of the company became as here noted: Herman Berghoff, president; Hubert Berghoff, vice-president; Stephen B. Fleming, secretary and treasurer, and William Breuer, superintendent. Three years later each the common and preferred stock was doubled, and at the present time the common stock is represented in the noteworthy sum of seven hundred and fifty thousand dollars, with preferred stock of equal amount. The personnel

Wm Breuer

of the executive corps at the opening of the year 1917 is as here recorded: Gustave A. Berghoff, president; William Breuer, vice-president; Stephen B. Fleming, treasurer, and Martin C. Norton, secretary. All of these officers are likewise directors of the company, and the directorate includes also Charles Weatherhogg and G. R. Johnston. All of the directors are residents of Fort Wayne with the exception of Mr. Fleming, who now maintains his home in New York city, and Mr. Johnston, who resides in the city of Pittsburgh, Pennsylvania. The plant of this great brewery utilizes about one and one-half city blocks, the average annual output is one hundred and eighty thousand barrels of beer and the bottling department turns out an average of one hundred and twenty thousand bottles daily. The company represents not only one of the most important industrial enterprises of Fort Wayne, but is also given the distinction of being the most extensive shipper on the line of the Nickel Plate Railroad. William Breuer was born in Westphalen, Germany, on October 23, 1852, and is a son of Carl Ludwig and Catherine (Helle) Breuer. He was reared and educated in his native province and as a youth served a thorough apprenticeship to the brewer's trade, under the unexcelled German system, his apprenticeship having been initiated May 16, 1866, several months prior to his fourteenth birthday anniversary. In 1881 he came to the United States, and after passing about three months in the city of Rochester, New York, he came to the west and found employment at his trade in the city of Chicago, where he remained about nine months. He then went to Neillsville, the judicial center of Clark county, Wisconsin, where he held a responsible position in a brewery for two years. He then established a brewery at Boscobel, Grant county, that state, where he remained until 1885, when he came to Fort Wayne and assumed the position of superintendent of the plant of the Herman Berghoff Brewing Company, in the development of whose splendid business he has been an influential and valued factor, the while he has gained secure place as one of the representative captains of industry in the metropolis of Allen county, prior data in this review having sufficiently indicated his advancement in the control and management of the affairs of the Berghoff Brewing Company. In politics Mr. Breuer gives unwavering allegiance to the Republican party, he is actively identified with the Fort Wayne Commercial Club, of which he is a trustee, and he is serving as a member of the board of park commissioners of his home city, besides which he is a trustee of Concordia College, one of the important educational institutions of northern Indiana. Both he and his wife are communicants of the German Lutheran church. On November 23, 1884, was solemnized the marriage of Mr. Breuer to Miss Caroline Rodewald, a native of Germany, and they have four children: William, who is actively associated with business affairs in Fort Wayne; Amelia, who is the wife of Kurt Johns, of Newark, New Jersey, and Della and Louise, who remain at the parental home.

Eugene H. Briggs, who exercises important functions in the position of executive assistant in the offices of the great manufacturing establishment of S. F. Bowser & Company, one of the leading industrial concerns of Fort Wayne, is a scion of stanch old colonial stock in New England, on both the paternal and distaff sides. He was born in the city of Boston, Massachusetts, on July 15, 1874, and is a son of Rev. Lewis L. and Mary T. (Howarth) Briggs, the former a native of Providence, Rhode Island, and the latter of Dover, New Hampshire. The father, a man of high intellectual attainments and much oratorical ability, served many years as a clergyman of the Universalist church, his death having occurred in 1893, and his widow survived him by a score of years, she having been summoned to eternal rest in 1913. Of the three children Irene C. is the wife of Thomas G. Rees, of Boston, Massachusetts; Lewis H. died in infancy, and the subject of this review is the youngest of the number. Eugene H. Briggs attended the public schools at Lynn, Massachusetts, and he initiated his business career by assuming a clerical position in a banking institution in the city of Boston, in 1895. He continued his association with banking enterprises until 1910, and in the meanwhile his ability and effective service gained to him consecutive promotion. In the year last mentioned he became factory salesman in New England for the important firm of S. F. Bowser & Company, and in 1913 he came to Fort Wayne, where he now holds the responsible post of executive assistant in the offices of this important concern. Mr. Briggs is found aligned as a loyal advocate of the cause of the Republican party, and at Wakefield, Massachusetts, he still maintains affiliations with Golden Rule Lodge, Ancient Free and Accepted Masons. On October 1, 1900, was solemnized the marriage of Mr. Briggs to Miss May Katherine Wyman, who likewise was born in the city of Boston, and they have two children—Lewis L. and Norma H.

Stillman B. Brokaw has held since the autumn of 1916 a position with the municipal waterworks department of Fort Wayne and takes loyal interest in all things pertaining to the welfare and advancement of his native city. He was born in Fort Wayne and is one of the three surviving children of the late Samuel L. Brokaw, who was born at Galena, Ohio, April 20, 1840, and died in Fort Wayne on April 28, 1907. As a young man Samuel L. Brokaw served as a member of Company K, One Hundred and Eighth Ohio Infantry, with which he served four years, or virtually during the entire period of the great civil conflict through which the integrity of the Union was preserved. He was discharged shortly before the close of the war, as the result of physical disability, and his record was that of a loyal and valiant young soldier of the Union. In 1867 he established his home in Fort Wayne, where he passed the remainder of his life. He was engaged in railroad work during the major portion of the long intervening years and the last ten years of his life were marked by his efficient service as county health officer, in which position he made an admirable record. His widow still resides in Fort Wayne, and with her remain her two daughters, Estella O. and Irene Sinex Brokaw, who, with Stillman B., subject of this review, are the only survivors in a family of nine children. Stillman B. Brokaw was educated in the public schools of Fort Wayne and while yet in his 'teens entered the employ of Albert Tomkinson, who was here engaged in the plumbing business. His work in this connection was so well performed that he won advancement and eventually became an indispensable factor in the business, with which he continued to be associated until he assumed his present municipal position. On May 18, 1910, Mr. Brokaw married Miss Mary E. Tomkinson, a daughter of his employer, Albert Tomkinson, and the one child of this union is Herbert James Brokaw. Mr. Brokaw is a Republican in his political allegiance and is affiliated with the Masonic fraternity. The attractive family home is at 411 Kinnaird Avenue.

Frank I. Brown is a recognized authority in connection with the grades and valuations of lumber and holds the responsible position of lumber agent for all lines of the Pennsylvania Railroad Company of the divisions and branches west of the city of Pittsburgh. He has maintained his home in Fort Wayne for nearly forty years and is one of the well-known and representative citizens of the Allen county metropolis. Mr. Brown was born at South Orange, New Jersey, on June 20, 1856, and is a son of John S. and Adelaide (Freeman) Brown, of whose seven children he is the youngest. The parents were born and reared in New Jersey, with whose history the family names have been identified for many generations, and the father was one of the successful farmers of that state, within whose borders he and his wife continued to reside until their deaths. Frank I. Brown received the advantages of the public schools of New Jersey and also those of the Newark Military Academy, in the metropolis of his native state. As a youth he was concerned with mercantile business in Newark, and in 1880, as a young man of twenty-four years, he came to Fort Wayne and entered the employ of the firm of Hoffman Brothers, for whom he acted as lumber inspector. With this concern he continued his effective services nearly seven years, and he then accepted a position as lumber agent for the Pittsburgh, Chicago & St. Louis Railroad, commonly known as the Nickel Plate. With this company he continued his association in this capacity for twelve years and in January, 1900, he severed this connection to assume his present and similar office in the employ of the Pennsylvania Railroad Company. His official duties cause him to travel extensively, and he is familiar with lumber resources and conditions in the various sections of the Union. Though never a seeker of public office of any kind, Mr. Brown is aligned as a loyal supporter of the cause of the Republican party, and in his home county he is an active and appreciative member of the Fort Wayne Country Club. He is also vice-president of the United States Field Trial Club, of Grand Junction, Tennessee, and is well known as a breeder of English setters. Mr. Brown frequently is called to officiate as judge at the Grand Circuit Field trials. On January 15, 1896, was solemnized his marriage to Miss Anna Bond, of Fort Wayne, no children having been born of their union.

Martin C. Bruick.—The Bruick family, represented in St. Joseph township by Martin C., of this review, had its establishment in America in the year 1834, when his parents—Morris Bruick and Martha Cue—aged nine and seven years, respectively, came with their parents and settled in Adams township. There the young people were reared in the wilderness and, growing up as neighbors and lifelong acquaintances, their marriage followed quite as a matter of course. They settled in the community where they had been reared, became worthy contributors to the industrial life of the township, and were the parents of a family of eight children. They were John, Adam, Anna, Elizabeth, Martin, Henry, William and Jacob, all living at the present writing. The parents are now deceased—his passing being in the year 1887 and hers in 1892. Martin Bruick had a common school training in Adams township and early turned his attention to farming, in which he has since been occupied successfully. He is the owner of one hundred and fifty-four acres in St. Joseph township, on which he may be said to have made all the improvements. He married, in 1892, Sophia Goeglein, daughter of George Goeglein, concerning whom more extended mention will be found on other pages of this work. Seven children have come to Mr. and Mrs. Bruick—Hulda, Luella, Arthur, Amiel, George, Arnold and Carl. The family have membership in the German Lutheran church, and Mr. Bruick is a Democrat in politics.

George H. Buck has been engaged in the fish business in Fort Wayne since 1890 and has built up through effective service a substantial and representative trade, his well-equipped establishment being situated at 720 Harrison street. Mr. Buck was born in the city of Indianapolis, Indiana, July 29, 1861, a son of Charles W. and Louisa (Durfee) Buck, natives of the state of New York and both now deceased, the father having been a railroad man during the greater part of his active life and he and his wife having been residents of Fort Wayne at the time of their death. Of their children the eldest is Lucy, who is the wife of Cyrus Crabbs, of Indianapolis, and the subject of this review was the second in order of birth; Mary is the wife of James Doudrick, of Kansas City, Missouri; Ada is the wife of Frank Cornish, a contractor in Fort Wayne; Edward is a locomotive engineer and now resides in the state of California. He whose name initiates this paragraph acquired his youthful education in the public schools of Indianapolis and Fort Wayne and thereafter was identified with railway service until he established his present business enterprise, in the conducting of which he has shown the care, discrimination and progressiveness that invariably make for success worthy of the name. He and his wife are members of the Methodist Episcopal church, and in the time-honored Masonic fraternity he has received the thirty-second degree of the Ancient Accepted Scottish Rite, besides having completed the circuit of the York Rite, in which his maximum affiliation is with Fort Wayne Commandery of Knights Templars. He is identified also with the Mystic Shrine and the Knights of the Maccabees, and is an active and popular member of the Fort Wayne Commercial Club. The maiden name of the first wife of Mr. Buck was Ella J. Baughman, and she is survived by two daughters—Grace, who is the wife of John Hengstler, of Fort Wayne, and Maude, who is the wife of Walter Kruse, of this city. The second marriage of Mr. Buck was solemnized in 1901, when Miss S. Ellen Uran became his wife. She was born in Michigan and is a daughter of John and Ola (Hayes) Uran. Mr. and Mrs. Buck have one son, George H., Jr.

Ernest F. Bueker, who has been one of the energetic and successful representatives of farm industry in Aboite township, came from Germany to America in 1870, when a youth of about sixteen years, and established his home in Fort Wayne within a short time after his arrival in the United States. In character and ambition he proved himself well equipped for the achieving of success through personal endeavor and for the long period of twenty-two years was engaged in the work of his trade, that of plasterer. Through this medium he gained the financial resources that eventually enabled him to purchase his present farm of eighty acres, where he has erected good buildings and made such other improvements as denote significantly the spirit of thrift and enterprise. As an agriculturist and stock-grower Mr. Bueker won substantial success and still owns his valuable farm property, though he is now living virtually retired in Fort Wayne, where he has a pleasant home at 1923 Hanna street. Loyal to and appreciative of American institutions, Mr. Bueker gives stalwart allegiance to the cause of the Republican party and takes lively interest in public affairs of a local order. He is affiliated with the Masonic fraternity and also with the St. John's Reformed church in Fort Wayne, as was also his wife, who died May 24, 1917. Mr. Bueker was born in Westphalia, Germany, on May 15, 1854, a son of Frederick and Sophia (Buller) Bueker, who came to the United States, in 1871, and settled in Fort Wayne, their son Ernest, of this review, having preceded them to this city by about one year. Here the father engaged in the work of his trade, that of cooper, and here his death occurred in 1886, his devoted wife having been summoned to the life eternal, in 1882, and both having been zealous communicants of the Reformed church. Of their children the eldest is Frederick, who is a retired farmer living in Fort Wayne; Frederica is the wife of Christian Tschannen, a farmer in Aboite township; Caroline and Lottie are deceased; Lizetta is the widow of Henry Hilgeman, deceased; Ernest F., of this sketch, was the next in order of birth; and Henry is deceased. Ernest F. Bueker acquired his early education in the excellent schools of his native land and was an ambitious and self-reliant young man when he severed the ties that bound him to the fatherland and came to the United States, due record having already been given concerning his career since that period. October 3, 1878, recorded his marriage to Miss Lizetta Hildebrand, who was born in Fort Wayne, January 15, 1857, a daughter of William and Marie (Hencheon) Hildebrand, both now deceased. Mr. Hildebrand was for a number of years identified with various lines of business enterprise in the city of Indianapolis and finally removed to Fort Wayne, where he and his wife passed the remainder of their lives. In conclusion is given brief record concerning the children of Mr. and Mrs. Bueker: Minnie is the wife of Charles Stillhorn, of Fort Wayne, and they have two children—Irma and Elmer. Carl, who likewise resides in Fort Wayne, married Miss Minnie Goette, and they have four children—Mildred, Minerva, Nellie and Melba. Edwin resides in Fort Wayne, the maiden name of his wife was Jenette Presler and they have two children—Freda and Kathryn. William, who has charge of the old home farm in Aboite township, wedded Miss Ella Nicholson, and they have one son, William Aaron. Ernest is engaged in farming in Whitley county. Freda is employed as a skilled stenographer in the offices of the S. F. Bowser Company, Fort Wayne, and remains at the parental home. Bertha also makes her home with her father. Matilda is the wife of Edwin Beard, of St. Joseph township.

Frederick J. Bueker is one of the representative farmers of the younger generation in his native township of Washington, and his homestead, comprising one hundred and ten acres, has been by him greatly improved since it came into his possession, so that it is consistently to be designated as one of the model farms of Washington township. He was born in this township March 19, 1879, a son of Frederick W. and Frederica (Oslag) Bueker, both of whom were born in Prussia and were young folk at the time when they came to the United States. The first husband of Mrs. Bueker was William Kolmartin and they became the parents of three children—William, Sophia and Henry J.—of whom only the last mentioned is living, he being one of the successful farmers of Washington township. Mr. Kolmartin died, in 1876, and on February 7, 1877, his widow became the wife of Frederick W. Bueker, the subject of this review being the eldest of the three children of this union; Edward resides on the old homestead farm of his father, and Mrs. Eliza Most is now a resident of the city of Buffalo,

New York. Frederick W. Bueker became one of the substantial exponents of agricultural industry in Washington township and upon his retirement from active labors removed to the city of Fort Wayne, where he and his wife still maintain their home. He whose name initiates this article gained his early education in the public and the Lutheran parochial schools of his native township and as a lad of thirteen years began to render effective aid in the work of the home farm, with the management of which he continued to be associated until he initiated his independent activities as an agriculturist and stock-grower. He purchased his present farm in 1910 and has brought the same under a high state of cultivation, the place being devoted to well ordered agriculture of diversified order. Mr. Bueker erected on his farm the present commodious and attractive residence and also the barn and other farm buildings of minor order. ndustry and progressiveness have brought to him merited prosperity and he is one of the substantial and popular citizens of his native township, his political allegiance being given to th eRepublican party and both he and his wife being active communicants of St. John's Reformed Lutheran church in the city of Fort Wayne, from which their home is about three miles distant, on rural mail route No. 1. On June 27, 1909, Mr. Bueker wedded Miss Sophia Ungerer, who was born and reared in this county, a daughter of George and Magdalena (Hammerbacher) Ungerer, both natives of Bavaria, Germany, their marriage having been solemnized in Allen county about the year 1870. The father is now living retir din Fort Wayne, where he was for a number of years successfully engaged in the contracting business, and his devoted wife passed to the life eternal, March 28, 1912. Mr. and Mrs. Bueker have four children—Carl, Florence, Doris and John.

John Buell has been a resident of Allen county since he was twenty-seven years of age, is now one of the progressive and representative farmers of Aboite township, and his success as one of the world's productive workers has been of unequivocal and meritorious order. He is a citizen who can claim the historic Old Dominion state as the place of his nativity, and he is a scion of one of its old and honored families. Mr. Buell was born on a farm in Rockingham county, Virginia, July 22, 1857, and is a son of William C. and Hannah (Canup) Buell, both of whom passed their entire lives in Virginia, where the father was a representative of agricultural industry during his entire active career. He was long known as one of the most active and influential advocates of the cause of the Republican party in his county and he served two terms as deputy sheriff of Rockingham county. Of his children the eldest was Milton, who served as a soldier in the Civil War, at the age of eighteen years, and who supposedly sacrificed his life in battle, as the other members of the family lost all trace of him within a short time after he had gone to the front; the second child died in infancy and the third was John, subject of this review; Maria became the wife of John Fleming and continued to reside in Virginia until her death; Miss Catherine still maintains her home in Virginia, as does also William, who is a prosperous farmer in Rockingham county; and Sarah Jane likewise remains in the old home state and county. John Buell passed his boyhood days under the turbulent conditions that prevailed in Virginia during the period of and subsequently to the Civil War, and his early education was gained mainly in the old-time subscription schools of his native commonwealth. He continued to assist his father in the operations of the home farm until he had attained to the age of twenty-three years, when he came to the north. He first went to Ohio, where he was employed one year. He was twenty-seven years old when he came to Fort Wayne, Indiana, and here he obtained employment as a locomotive fireman on the Pennsylvania Railroad. He was thus engaged three years, and later was employed by the month at farm work. For one year he worked in a meat market in Fort Wayne, a similar period was given to service as motorman on the street-car lines of the city, and he next worked a year in a blacksmith shop. After his marriage he rented from his father-in-law a farm and continued his operations under these conditions for twelve years. He then purchased forty-six acres in Aboite township, and to the same he has since added until he now has a fine farm of one hundred and sixty-one acres, the same being devoted to well-ordered agriculture and the raising of good livestock. Mr. Buell erected the present modern and attractive house on his homestead, has provided other excellent farm buildings, and is known as one of the vigorous and progressive exponents of farm enterprise in Aboite township. Taking loyal interest in community affairs, he has had no desire for public office, but he is found aligned as a staunch supporter of the cause of the Republican party. On the 4th of March, 1891, Mr. Buell wedded Miss Ida F. Clark, who was born and reared in this county and who is a daughter of Enoch and Anna (Shippey) Clark, both of whom are now deceased. Mr. Clark came from Maryland to Allen county and became one of the successful farmers and stock-growers of this section of the state, besides having given much effective service as a veterinary surgeon. Of the children of Mr. and Mrs. Buell the eldest is Chauncey, who is a skilled mechanic and is employed as such in Fort Wayne; Grace holds a position in a hospital in Fort Wayne; Paul is, in 1917, attending business college in that city; the fourth child, a son, died in infancy; and Oliver is the youngest member of the home circle.

Henry F. Busching.—One of the substantial and prospering farmers of St. Joseph township is Henry F. Busching, who has been devoted to the development of one of the attractive farms of the community in the past years. He is of German birth and parentage, born in Germany on October 4, 1857, son of Karl and Sophia Busching, who lived and died in their native land. They had five children—Mary, Karl, Henry F., Sophia and Minnie. Henry Busching had his education in his native community and came to America in 1881, locating first in Fort Wayne, where he found work on a farm in that vicinity. He later secured employment in the Bass Foundry & Machine Shop was there employed in various capacities until 1882, when he located in St. Joseph township, purchasing fifty acres of farm land and applying himself to its development. This acreage he has since increased by the purchase of another fifty-acre tract, and his farm of one hundred acres is partly improved and on the way to further development. Industry and ambition are salient qualities of his nature and success is bound to be his portion. Indeed, he is already classed with the successful men of the community, and rightly so, in view of his accomplishments from the humble beginnings that were his. Mr. Busching was married, in June, 1882, to Mary Blume, daughter of Henry and Minnie Blume, early settlers in Allen county and highly esteemed among its citizenry. Seven children have been born to the Buschings—Addie, Emma, Mary, Fred, Henry, Herman, and William. Mary died in July, 1914, and the wife and mother passed away on May 5, 1907. The family are Lutherans and members of that church, and take an active part in its activities, as well as in the social affairs of the community. Mr. Busching is independent in politics and an excellent citizen without being active in the politics of his community.

James F. Butt.—One of the foremost men of Maumee township, Allen county, Indiana, is James Butt, born in Erie township, Miami county, on March 25, 1860, on the old Wabash & Erie canal. He is the son of William and Elizabeth (Lesher) Butt and the grandson of William Butt, a pioneer to Allen county from Ohio in 1832. The record of the migrations of the Butt family from 1832 up to 1875 accounts for numerous changes in residence, and a brief recounting of those moves would read something as follows: Came from Pickaway county, Ohio, in 1832; settled in St. Joseph township, Allen county, Indiana, where they farmed until 1846, and then went to Miami county, Indiana, where the son William, father of the subject, remained until 1863, returning in that year to Allen county and settling on a farm in the vicinity of New Haven, where he was engaged in farming until the fall of 1865. He then moved back to Miami county and remained there until 1867. In the spring of that year he came to Allen county once more and there farmed until the death of his wife in February, 1869. In the next year he remarried and took up his residence in Miami county, remained there to 1875, operating a newly acquired farm, and in that year moved to the old home farm in Miami county, where he passed the rest of his days, death claiming him there on March 31, 1907. He was born in Pickaway county, Ohio, on May 10, 1829, and his life was that of a successful and energetic farmer. There were three children of his first marriage: James F., of this review, Ida and Dora. His second wife was the mother of two daughters—Effie and Rose. Mr. Butt was a prominent man in his community always, and wherever he went found his place in the public life of the town and township, and filled numerous public offices during his life time. James F. Butt had the average amount of schooling that is the lot of the country boy, and when he was sixteen he began active farm life on the farm home. He remained on the home place until he was twenty-one, gathering an experience and training that guaranteed him individual success in his own independent career. He came of age in March, 1881, and in June, 1882, bought from his father the home farm of 131 acres in Maumee township, which place has formed the nucleus of his present farm of 491 acres. It is worthy of mention that this 131 acres was deeded by the government to William Butt, grandfather of the subject, in 1832, and has been in the family possession ever since. William Butt, the original owner, did much improvement work on the place, and was himself one of the foremost men of his day in that district. He was one of the charter subscribers to the Fort Wayne Sentinel, a daily newspaper established in 1833, and the first paper that came from the press came into his possession and was cherished by him during his lifetime. The present owner of the old Butt farm is recognized as one of the leading stockmen of Allen county, and he is widely known for the Duroc-Jersey hogs he raises on his place each year, from six to eight hundred head being the yearly product of the place. It is stated on authority that he has sold more hogs yearly than any other man in Indiana, with a similar acreage as a basis of operations. In 1915 he fed 14,000 bushels of corn to that year's hogs. Mr. Butt was married on January 18, 1883, to Miss Lucretia Johnson, the daughter of Edward and Cynthia C. (Pearson) Johnson, who were among the early settlers of Allen county and were prominent in the county all their active lives. Three children have been born to Mr. and Mrs. Butt. Jessie L. is married, and she and her husband live on the home place with the parents. They have two children—Ivan and John. William Edward, the second child of Mr. and Mrs. Butt, is professor of economics in the Kentucky State University. He has two children—Olin and Arthur. James F., Jr., is married and lives in the vicinity of the old home. He is his father's assistant on the home farm. Mr. Butt has taken his place in the public life of the community, and it is a notable fact that he served Maumee township as trustee in 1884 when he was but twenty-four years of age, and held the record then for the youngest trustee in the state. He was re-elected in 1886, and since that time has held other offices of public trust. He is a Democrat in politics, and fraternally has membership in the Independent Order of Odd Fellows, being affiliated with Lodge No. 463 at Antwerp, Ohio.

Frederick C. Buuck is to be consistently designated as one of the representative farmers of Allen county, and his well improved homestead, comprising sixty acres, is eligibly situated in Marion township. That he has proved himself loyally interested in community affairs and has gained secure place in popular esteem is indicated by the fact that he is serving as township trustee, to which office he was elected in 1914. Mr. Buuck was born in Adams county, Indiana, February 18, 1864, a son of Ernest and Sophia (Kleinschmidt) Buuck, both of whom were born in Germany. Ernest Buuck was a lad of seven years when he accompanied his parents on their immigration to the United States and the family home was established in Adams county, Indiana, where he was reared to manhood under the conditions and influences of the pioneer days, assisted in the development of the home farm and profited by the advantages of the schools of the locality and period. He eventually instituted independent operations as a farmer and became one of the prosperous and honored exponents of agricultural industry in Adams county, where he continued to reside until his death, in 1911, his wife having preceded him to the life eternal by about two years, and both having been earnest members of the Lutheran church. Mr. Buuck was a Democrat in politics and was one of the loyal young men of Indiana who went forth in defense of the Union when the Civil war was precipitated on the nation. He enlisted as a private in Company D, Fifty-first Indiana Infantry, and with this gallant command continued in active service at the front until he was so severely wounded as to incapacitate him for further activity, with the result that he was accorded an honorable discharge, after having taken part in a number of severe conflicts. In later years he signalized his abiding interest in his old comrades by retaining affiliation with the Grand Army of the Republic. Frederick C. Buuck, the immediate subject of this review, was the third in orler of birth in a family of eleven children; Louise resides in the city of Richmond, Indiana; Minnie is the widow of Gustav Rumphe and maintains her home in Fort Wayne; Ernst still remains in Adams county; Martin is deceased; William is a prosperous farmer in Adams county; Mary, Sophia and Anna are deceased; Elizabeth is the wife of Christian Mahrnowald, of Jefferson township, Allen county; and Christian resides in Fort Wayne. Frederick C. Buuck grew to adult age under the invigorating discipline of the home farm, continued to assist in its work and management until he was twenty-two years of age and in the meanwhile had not failed to profit by the advantages afforded in the public schools of his native county. Upon leaving the parental home he came to Fort Wayne, where he was employed three years in the shops of the Pennsylvania Railroad. The free and independent life of the farm, though demanding much of arduous toil, made insistent appeal to him and caused him soon to resume his alliance with agricultural industry. He purchased his present homestead of sixty acres, upon which he has made the best of improvements, including the erection of his commodious house and other good farm buildings, and he has so applied his mental and physical powers as to make of his farm industry a distinctive success, his attention having been given to diversified agriculture and to the raising of good live stock. Mr. Buuck is a stalwart in the local camp of the Democratic party, takes lively interest in all that concerns the well-being of his home township and county, and has given most effective service in the office of township trustee. Both he and his wife are earnest communicants of the German Lutheran church. On December 4, 1888, was solemnized the marriage of Mr. Buuck to Miss Mary Doehrmann, daughter of Conrad and Minnie (Zwick) Doehrmann, of Adams county, and the two children of this union, Martin and Freda, still remain at the parental home.

James B. Cahill is junior member of the representative firm of Getz & Cahill, which conducts one of the well appointed undertaking and funeral-directing establishments of Fort Wayne, and on other pages of this work is made individual mention of his associate in the business, Joseph F. Getz. Mr. Cahill was born in Cass county, Indiana, on the 26th of August, 1879, and is a son of James Cahill, who was for a number of years engaged in farming in Cass county and who later removed to the city of Logansport, that county, and entered the service of the Pennsylvania Railroad Company, with which he continued his identification many years. He died October 3, 1899, and his wife is living in Fort Wayne. James B. Cahill acquired his early education in the St. Vincent Catholic parochial schools of Logansport and supplemented the same by a course in Hall's Business College of that city. He then assumed a position in the Logansport offices of the Metropolitan Life Insurance Company, but later prepared himself for the undertaking business, in which connection he acquired a thorough knowledge of the modern system of embalming. For a time he was employed in the undertaking establishment of Potter & Moffitt, in Muncie, this state, and in 1900 came to Fort Wayne, where he entered the employ of the firm of Schone & Veith, being their first licensed embalmer. With this concern he continued his effective services until July, 1908, when he formed a partnership with Joseph Getz and established their present business enterprise, in connection with which they have the most approved facilities for careful and consistent service as embalmers and general funeral directors. Mr. Cahill is affiliated with the Benevolent & Protective Order of Elks, the Knights of Columbus, the Catholic Order of Foresters, the Catholic Benevolent League of Indiana, and of the Holy Name Society of the cathedral parish of the Catholic church in the city of Fort Wayne, both he and his wife being earnest communicants of this parish. He is identified also with the Married Men's Society of the cathedral and is a member of the Retail Merchants' Association of Fort Wayne. On June 22, 1910, was solemnized the marriage of Mr. Cahill to Miss Eleanor Reinhart, who was born at Fort Wayne June 24, 1880, and who was educated in

St. Mary's parochial schools. She is a daughter of Matthias and Anna Marie (Bargus) Reinhart, both deceased.

Stephen A. Callahan is one of the representative younger members of the bar of his native county and since his retirement from the office of assistant prosecuting attorney of Allen county has been engaged in the independent practice of his profession in Fort Wayne, with secure standing and reputation as a resourceful trial lawyer and well fortified counselor. Mr. Callahan was born at Fort Wayne on July 30, 1888, and is a son of James T. and Margaret (Dolan) Callahan, the former a native of Pennsylvania and the latter of Indiana. The father holds the position of chief train dispatcher at Fort Wayne for the New York, Chicago & St. Louis Railroad, and he and his wife have maintained their home in Fort Wayne for thirty years. Of their four children the subject of this review is the third; Winifred remains at the parental home; Frank J. is associated with the Moran Ice Company; and Robert is, in 1917, a student in the Fort Wayne high school. Stephen A. Callahan acquired his early education in the excellent Catholic parochial schools of Fort Wayne and in preparation for his chosen profession entered the law department of the great Valparaiso University, in which he was graduated as a member of the class of 1909 and from which he received his degree of Bachelor of Laws, with virtually coincident admission to the bar of his native state. For two and one-half years after his graduation he was associated with the well known Fort Wayne law firm of Leonard, Rose & Zollars, and he was then appointed deputy prosecuting attorney of the county, a position in which he made an admirable record and from which he finally retired to engage in active general practice in an individual way. Mr. Callahan is a staunch supporter of the cause of the Democratic party, is a communicant of the Catholic church, is affiliated with the Knights of Columbus, the Benevolent & Protective Order of Elks, and the Loyal Order of Moose. May 26, 1914, recorded the marriage of Mr. Callahan to Miss Esther Auger, who likewise was born and reared in Fort Wayne and who is a daughter of Louis and Lydia (Bird) Auger, the former of whom is deceased.

Warren D. Calvin, M. D., is above all else a man of distinct individuality, and that individuality is the positive expression of a strong and loyal nature that in turn exemplifies itself in the true stewardship of good works and kindly deeds. The Doctor is a man of thought and efficient service, and as a true humanitarian he is free from bigotry and intolerance in all of the relations of life. He is one of the essentially representative physicians and surgeons of Allen county and is engaged in the practice of his profession in the city of Fort Wayne. Like many another American who has achieved success and prestige in professional life, Dr. Calvin passed the period of his childhood and youth under the effective and invigorating discipline of the farm, and of the enduring value of this discipline he is deeply appreciative. On the old homestead farm of his father, two and one-half miles distant from Bryan, Williams county, Ohio, Dr. Warren D. Calvin was born, May 27, 1867, his father having been "a farmer good, with corn and beef and plenty," and where he himself early gained a full quota of experience as he "mowed and hoed and held the plow," his active association with the basic industry of agriculture having continued under these benign conditions until he was nineteen years of age, the while he waxed strong of brain and brawn, as he had not failed to make good use of the advantages of the district schools. In this connection it has been recorded that "He attended a country school which at times enrolled more than sixty pupils and which, because of certain local influences involved in the personnel of the patrons of that school, was peculiarly an intellectual rural center. Algebra and Latin were taught at times and from its walls there emerged scores and scores of teachers, many of whom later became able representatives of the legal, medical, pedagogic and ministerial professions, it being worthy of note that one of the students for which this school stood sponsor eventually became United States representative to Mexico." Dr. Calvin expresses his sense of thankfulness for the fortuitous influences that compassed him in the formative period of his youth and he reverts with great satisfaction to the vitalizing privileges that were his in the school above mentioned. He followed the prevailing ambition of the youth of that rural community and put his scholastic attainments to practical test by entering the field of pedagogic service. At the age of seventeen years he assumed charge of his first school, and in the meanwhile he furthered his own education by attending the autumn terms in the high school at Bryan, the judicial center of his native county. When nineteen years of age he devoted a portion of his time as a traveling representative and salesman for A. H. Andrews & Company, manufacturers of school apparatus and furniture, with headquarters in the city of Chicago. His vaulting ambition to gain a liberal education did not overleap the bounds of practical judgment, and it can not be regarded as other than fortunate that the young man was compelled to consult ways and means in the attainment of the desired end and that he was virtually dependent upon his own resources in defraying the expenses of his higher academic and his professional education. In the autumn of 1887 Dr. Calvin entered the preparatory department of Hiram College, of which institution the late General James A. Garfield, former president of the United States, was a graduate and of which he later served at president. In this college the Doctor gave his attention to fortifying himself further for the vocation of teaching, in which field he had at the time a future engagement. However, his desire for a higher education resulted in his continuing his studies in Hiram College until his graduation, as a member of the class of 1892, and with the degree of Bachelor of Science. During his junior and senior years he was associated in the editorial work of the two college publications—the annual and the periodical college paper. In the meanwhile he had formulated definite plans for his future career, and in consonance therewith, in September, 1892, he entered the celebrated Rush Medical College, in the city of Chicago. There he continued his technical studies three years, during which he was joint owner of the college medical journal, besides having been its editor in chief during the last year. He was also the chief promoter and a member of the editorial board of the first medical annual ever published in connection with a medical college. During the summer vacations of his eight collegiate years Dr. Calvin continued his successful service as a traveling salesman for A. H. Andrews & Company, the concern previously mentioned, and from this service he obtained the financial returns necessary for the continuance of his studies. He was graduated in Rush Medical College as a member of the class of 1895, and prior to making a permanent location he determined to gain preliminary experience of a practical and varied order. Thus it was that after receiving his degree of Doctor of Medicine he served his professional novitiate by engaging in active general practice at Canby, Yellow Medicine county, Minnesota, where he remained nine months. This was followed by one year of surgical work of official order along the course of the Chicago drainage canal, which was then in course of construction, his headquarters being at Riverside. Upon completing this service he came to Fort Wayne, where he has been established in the active practice of his profession since April, 1897, and where his unequivocal success offers the best voucher for his ability, discrimination and personal popularity. He gives his attention largely to the phase of practice involved in internal medication and he has long controlled a large and representative practice that denotes him as one of the leading physicians and surgeons of Allen county. Dr. Calvin maintains active and appreciative membership in the American Medical Association, the Mississippi Valley Medical Association, the Tri-State Medical Association, the 12th District Medical Society, the Indiana State Medical Society, and the Allen County Medical Society. He was a member of the faculty of the Ft. Wayne Medical College, and is now (1917) on the Hope Hospital staff. He is medical examiner for eight important life insurance companies and has the distinction of being a member of the United States Medical Reserve Corps, in which he has the rank of first lieutenant. In politics Dr. Calvin believes in supporting men and principles rather than being constrained by strict partisan lines, but if definite political classification were given he would probably be designated as a progressive Republican. In religion the Doctor gives his only denial to the family patronymic, for he goes far afield from the old Calvinistic doctrines and believes that the dogmatic theological creeds are altogether inimical to the interests of mankind, the while he maintains that man's religious nature can incorporate all its wants under the two tenets of the fatherhood of God and the brotherhood of man, untrammeled by creed, ordinances, definite ritualism and mysticism. He believes also that every person should have a vacation from his professional or other vocational work, in order that the mind may dwell upon a different environment and the cells used in the prosecution of his daily employment and thus given a brief and complete rest, with resultant vitalization. In harmony with this conception, Dr. Calvin has taken trips to various parts of the United States and the Canadian provinces, and in each of these digressions he has found it his greatest pleasure to view and contemplate the grand and beautiful spots of nature, especially in the ascending to the mountain heights and fastnesses where nature rules supreme, or at least where the puny handicraft of man is comparatively infinitesimal. In June, 1897, Doctor Calvin wedded Dr. Jessie Carrithers, who is associated with him in practice. Like the average American, Doctor Calvin finds in his ancestral lineage a record that involves the use of the much-discussed hyphen. In short, he is of Scotch, English and Swiss lineage, through being a scion of the Scotch family of McGowan, the English families of Churchill and Kelsey, and the Calvins of Switzerland. Of his forbears who came to America, some established themselves in Puritan New England and some in cavalier Virginia. Later migrations brought other generations of the respective families into contact in the historic old Connecticut Western Reserve of Northern Ohio, and from that section of the old Buckeye state came the first representatives of the Calvin family into Williams county, Ohio, where the subject of this sketch was born.

William H. Carbaugh, well-to-do farmer and veteran of the Civil war, has been a resident of Allen county for more than fifty years. He began his career in this region as a day-laborer, from which phase he advanced to the position of renter, and later to the dignity of owner of his own place, and he has enjoyed a comfortable prosperity as the reward of his honest efforts to gain independence. He was born in Franklin county, Pennsylvania, on January 7, 1840, and is the son of Joseph and Margaret (Miller) Carbaugh, who came to Whitley county in 1856 and passed the remainder of their lives in this region. The father worked for years as a laborer. He and his wife reared a family of five children. They were Mary Elizabeth, deceased; William H., the subject of this sketch; John, who is deceased; Susan Catherine, living in Fort Wayne, and Albert, who died in 1915. William H. Carbaugh had the typical log-school education common to the youth of his time, and he was still quite young when he applied himself to the difficult work of clearing land. He worked at that until he was twenty-two years of age, and then enlisted for service in the Civil war. He was a member of Company E, Eighty-eighth Indiana Infantry, and he served through to the end of the war, participating with his regiment in many of the hard fought engagements of the war, conspicuous among them being Perryville, Stone's River and Chickamaugua. When the war ended he returned home, married soon afterward and with his young wife went to Kansas, where he was engaged in various occupations for two years. They returned to Allen county in 1875 and Mr. Carbaugh applied himself to such work as he could find to do, and for several years was employed as a laborer in the community where he settled. In 1876 he rented a farm and for some years worked on the basis of a renter, when he was able to buy a place of his own. He is living to-day on the forty-acre tract he bought then, and on which he gained a pleasing measure of financial independence. On March 19, 1867, Mr. Carbaugh was married to Miss Elizabeth Johnson, the daughter of James and Rebecca (Baxter) Johnson, who came from Pennsylvania to Ohio and thence to Allen county in 1854. They were farming people and among the best people in their community. A family of fourteen children was reared under their roof. They were Noah, Frances, Isabelle, Harriet, Isaac R., Jacob, Harvey, Abraham, Elizabeth, Lewis, Josiah, Martha, Anna and John. Harvey is living in Lafayette township; Elizabeth is the wife of the subject; Josiah is a resident of Missouri and Anna is living in Wells county, Indiana. The others are deceased. Mr. and Mrs. Carbaugh have three children—Oliver, of Fort Wayne; Frank, of Lafayette township, and Alonzo, of Lagrange county, Indiana, where he is engaged in farming. Frank had three children—William Arthur, Gertrude Marie and Lulah, the last two named surviving. Alonzo has six children—Clarence, Edna, Mildred, Ralph, Glenn and Harold. Edna is the wife of Claude Lovell, of Lagrange, and Glenn died in 1907. Edna Lovell has two children—Alvin Alonzo and Ethel, so that Mr. and Mrs. Carbaugh are distinguished among their friends as great-grandparents.

William L. Carnahan was a man whose character was the positive expression of a strong, loyal and noble nature, and it was given him to leave a last impress upon the civic and business life of the city of Fort Wayne, where he was long and prominently identified with the wholesale boot and shoe business and where his fine character and superior ability made him a resourceful force in furthering the industrial and commercial prestige of the Allen county metropolis. He was one of the most honored and influential business men of the city at the time of his death, which occurred on June 26, 1897, and this history exercises a consistent function when it accords within its pages a tribute to his memory. Mr. Carnahan was a native of Indiana and a representative of a sterling pioneer family of Tippecanoe county, where he was born on March 5, 1837. His father became a representative merchant in what is now the thriving city of Lafayette, that county, and it was in the schools of that place, which was then a mere village, that the subject of this memoir acquired his early education. He later was graduated in the University of Indiana, at Bloomington, and throughout the rest of his long and useful life he was known as a man of fine intellectual attainments as well as of marked business acumen. At the inception of his business career, in 1856, Mr. Carnahan became a pioneer of the state of Nebraska, where he remained three years, during which time he was engaged in the mercantile business in the city of Omaha, besides having served as a clerk in the United States land office at that place. In 1860 he returned to Indiana and established himself in the mercantile business at Delphi, the judicial center of Carroll county. Two years later he returned to Lafayette, where for the ensuing two years he was engaged in the boot and shoe business in a retail way. He then accepted a position as traveling salesman for the firm of Carnahan, Earl & Company, manufacturers of and wholesale dealers in boots and shoes, with factory and general headquarters at Lafayette. Eighteen months later he was given an interest in the business and the title of the firm was then changed to Carnahan Brothers & Company. For five and one-half years thereafter Mr. Carnahan continued his resourceful activities as traveling representative for the firm, and his sterling character, his ability as a salesman and his unqualified popularity proved potent in expanding the business of his firm and popularized its products in a constantly expanding trade territory. In 1872 he came to Fort Wayne and founded the wholesale boot and shoe house of Carnahan, Skinner & Company, and he thereupon assumed the supervision of the clerical and sales departments of the new establishment, his fine administrative ability and thorough technical knowledge giving him special influences in directing the development of the business of the new firm, which was succeeded in 1875 by that of Carnahan, Hanna & Company. He continued as one of the principal and chief executives of this firm and also of its successor, that of Carnahan & Company, which was organized in 1886 and in which his coadjutor was Emmet H. McDonald. He continued as the executive head of the large and prosperous business controlled by this firm until death terminated his activities and brought a close to his long and honorable business career, throughout which his integrity had been inviolable, his progressiveness and energy prodigious and his success unequivocal. The fullest measure of success is ever to be won by loyal and worthy service, and Mr. Carnahan always measured up to the highest standard of business ethics, even as his private life was marked by fine ideals and by kindliness and consideration that won to him the confidence and high regard of all with whom he came in contact. He was essentially a business man, and thus had no desire to enter the turbulence of practical politics or to seek public office, though he gave a staunch allegiance to the cause of the Republican party and was liberal in his civic attitude. He was a consistent member of the Episcopal church, as is also his widow, who still maintains her home in Fort Wayne, a city that is endeared to her by the hallowed memories and associations of the past. In the year 1864 was solemnized the marriage of Mr. Carnahan to Miss Clara L. Hanna, daughter of the late James Bayless Hanna, eldest son of Judge Samuel Hanna, one of the honored pioneer citizens of Allen county, and of this union were born four children, all of whom survive the honored father. Louise is the wife of Dr. Nelson Lloyd Deming, of Litchfield, Connecticut; Robert Hanna Carnahan is one of the representative business men of Fort Wayne, and Clara C. and Virginia C., remain with their widowed mother in the attractive home in Fort Wayne and as popular factors in the representative social life of their native city. The grandchildren of William L. Carnahan are Nelson Lloyd Deming, Jr., and Mary Louise Deming, the children of Dr. and Mrs. Deming, and Robert Hanna Carnahan, William Lumbard Carnahan and Sidney Lumbard Carnahan, children of Robert Hanna Carnahan and Constance Lumbard Carnahan, deceased.

Charles L. Centlivre.—It was given to the subject of this memoir to wield large influence in connection with the upbuilding of one of the now extensive and important industrial enterprises of Fort Wayne, that of the Centlivre Brewing Company. Mr. Centlivre came to Fort Wayne in 1862 and here became associated with his brother, Frank, in the founding of the Centlivre Brewery, the plant and business of which have been developed from a modest nucleus to the point that places the concern among the largest and most successful of its kind in Indiana. Charles L. Centlivre was a man of sterling character, of splendid energy and resourcefulness in business and of that intrinsic and well based civic loyalty that makes for ideal citizenship. Mr. Centlivre was born at Valdien, Canton Dammarie, Arrondissement of Belfort, Haut-Rhin, Alsace, France, on September 27, 1827, and was sixty-seven years of age at the time of his death, in 1895. He was reared and educated in his native province and there learned the cooper's trade under the effective direction of his father. He became a skilled workman through his thorough apprenticeship, and came to America in 1841, the voyage across the Atlantic having been made in one of the primitive sailing vessels of the type common to that period. Mr. Centlivre established his residence in the city of New Orleans, and shortly afterward, when the city became the stage of a frightful epidemic of cholera, returned to his native land. After a comparatively brief visit to the old home he came again to the United States, and on this occasion was accompanied by his father and by two of his brothers. Landing in the port of New York city, the father and sons came to the middle west and made their home at Massillon, Stark county, Ohio. Within a short time Charles L. Centlivre engaged in the work of his trade at Louisville, that county, and in 1850 went to Clayton county, Iowa, where he established a small brewery in the village of McGregor. He was one of the pioneer business men of that section of the Hawkeye state and continued to operate his brewery at McGregor until 1862, when he came to Fort Wayne and formed a partnership with his brother, Frank, in the founding of the Centlivre Brewery. With characteristic energy and thoroughness the brothers applied themselves to the producing of high-grade output and the incidental development of the business. During all the long intervening years the Centlivre Brewing Company has maintained the highest reputation for business policies of the most upright and progressive order and for the turning out of products of the best order. The plant of the company is now one of extensive and thoroughly modern order, and the trade of this pioneer industrial concern is of large volume and most substantial ramifications. Mr. Centlivre gave his splendid energies to the upbuilding of the business and continued his active association with the enterprise until the year prior to his death. He was liberal and public-spirited as a citizen, took lively and constant interest in the welfare of the city in which he long maintained his home, and as a citizen and business man his name and memory are here held in lasting honor. The company of which he was one of the founders now bases its operations on a capital stock of three hundred thousand dollars, his son, Louis C., is president of the corporation, another son, Charles F., is treasurer, and John Ruess is secretary.

John W. Chapman.—One of the foremost men of Hoagland is John W. Chapman, prosperous farmer, now living practically retired from farming activities. For more than half a century he applied himself diligently to agricultural pursuits, and he is to-day enjoying a well earned rest from his labors of those years. Mr. Chapman was born in Pennsylvania on April 19, 1834, and is the son of John and Sarah (Keese) Chapman, both born in that state. They moved to Ohio in 1844; settled on a farm and after four years came to Indiana, settling in Adams county. In 1855 they moved to Allen county, and this section of the state was their home from then until their death. They were the parents of nine children, of which number two are now living. John W. Chapman was reared and schooled in Indiana, and in early manhood turned his attention to farming. From then until the year 1913 he might be said to have labored continuously, and it is gratifying to be able to note that he succeeded admirably in his work. Two fine farms were his at one time, and when he retired from active life, in 1913, he sold one place. The other he still owns, though he takes no part in its management. In 1865 Mr. Chapman married Miss Eunice Harrod. She was born in Allen county, of farming people, and to her and her husband five children were born. They are William, Charles L., Almina, Arminda E. and Delilah. The last named is deceased and Almina is the wife of David McKennan. In 1909 the family suffered the loss of the wife and mother, and the entire community mourned her passing. Mr. Chapman is a Democrat, but has never been an office holder or a seeker after political favors.

Reason Clayton was a small child when his parents brought him from his native state and settled in Allen county, Indiana, and this section of the state has been his home without interruption from that day to this. He was born in Ohio, Wayne county, on September 22, 1847, and is the son of John and Elizabeth Smith Clayton. The father was a Virginian by birth and the mother an Ohioan. As a young man John Clayton left his native state and located in Ohio, where he married, and in 1848 he took his family to Allen county. There the mother died in 1850, leaving four children, two of whom are now living. The father married again, and of six children born of that union all but one are living. He married a third time, and one son was born. In 1897 John Clayton died at his home in Madison township. Reason Clayton left the parental home at the early age of nineteen. He had up to that time attended school with a good deal of regularity, and was qualified, according to the standards of the day, to teach in the district schools in the winter seasons. This he did for a number of years, teaching during the winter months and farming in the summer. In 1888 he bought the farm on which he now lives. It comprises 165 acres in Sections 23 and

24, in Madison township, and is one of the attractive farms of the community. General farming is carried on very successfully, and progressive and productive methods are favored on the Clayton farm. Mr. Clayton is a member of the Knights of Pythias, and is a Democrat in politics. He was married in 1872 to Miss Mary Youse, a native daughter of Allen county, and they are the parents of three children—Otto O., Flora E., and John Fred. Flora lives at home and John is now in Philadelphia in the government service. Mrs. Clayton is a member of the Methodist Episcopal church.

Guy Colerick is herein mentioned as one of the prominent attorneys of the city of Fort Wayne and in the practice of his profession he is well maintaining the prestige of the family name. In the legal circles of Allen county the Colericks have been prominent since the establishment of civil courts there, the first of the family to establish himself in the practice being David H. Colerick, who came from Lancaster, Ohio. He became very prominent as an attorney and as a public spirited citizen, and it seemed that his ability was transmitted to his sons, six of whom were engaged in the practice of law here at one time. One of these sons was Henry Colerick, the father of the subject of this biographical review, and he was widely known as one of the leading trial lawyers in northern Indiana. Guy H. Colerick was born in Fort Wayne, November 20, 1879, and in the public schools of that city obtained his preliminary education. By a process of natural selection he decided upon the law as his profession, and in pursuance of that determination entered the office of his uncle, Walpole G. Colerick, where he remained as a student and a practioner until 1907, having been admitted to the bar soon after attaining his majority. In 1907 he formed a partnership with his father, the late Henry Colerick, and together they were successfully engaged in practice until the death of the latter, in 1909. A partnership was then formed by Guy Colerick and Harry G. Hogan, and this association has continued to the present time, the firm of Colerick & Hogan having a clientele that is representative and of a high order. Mr. Colerick served as city attorney—which position was filled by his honored father for a number of years—from 1906 to 1910, and after a four-year interim he was again appointed to the place, in 1914, and is the present incumbent of that office, serving his second term. Mr. Colerick is a Mason, having attained to the Fourteenth degree of the Scottish Rite, a member of the Loyal Order of Moose and the Benevolent & Protective Order of Elks, in which last organization he is a Past Exalted Ruler. In politics he is a Democrat.

Adam Collis.—For the past thirty-six years Adam Collis has been located in Fort Wayne and during that time was in the employ of the Pennsylvania system in its machine shops for thirty-five years. He has practically watched the city grow up, and almost as many summer suns and winter snows have passed over his head as Fort Wayne herself has experienced. Mr. Collis was born in Cambria county, Pennsylvania, on August 26, 1847, and is the son of Nicholas and Frances (Balwebber) Collis, both born and reared in France. They came to America as young people and Mr. Collis located on a Pennsylvania farm, where he spent the remainder of his life. He was an ambitious and hard working man, and might have passed to a comfortable old age after a life of toil, but was killed in middle life as a result of a runaway accident on his farm. Adam Collis was the only child. When he was about twelve years old the subject moved to Blair county and there went to school a few winter terms. He entered the railroad shops at Altoona, Pennsylvania, and there learned the machinist's trade. He took his first position as a boy of sixteen in the machine shops of the Pennsylvania road at Altoona, and he continued there until 1880, when he came to Fort Wayne, and was here employed by the same company, so that his service with the Pennsylvania road covered a period of more than half a century. He was pensioned in September, 1916. Mr. Collis married Mary Wyrough, of Altoona, Pennsylvania, on January 16, 1872, and they have six children. Frank, the eldest, lives in Edmonton, Canada; John is with the City Water Works in Fort Wayne; James is engaged in mining operations at Prescott, Arizona; Oscar is connected with the Emrich Baking Company, of Fort Wayne; Hugh is a machinist with the Pennsylvania road, located in Fort Wayne, and Mary, the only daughter and the youngest of the family, died at the tender age of four years. Mr. Collis and his sons are Democrats in politics and the family are members of the Catholic church.

Thomas L. Comparet, who holds the office of bookkeeper for the Bass Foundry, an important industrial concern of Fort Wayne, is a representative of sterling pioneer families of this favored section of the Hoosier state and is a scion of a staunch French family that was early settled in Montreal, Canada—fully a century and a quarter ago. He whose name initiates this paragraph was born at Fort Wayne August 1, 1865, and is a son of David F. Comparet, who was born at Fort Wayne on March 6, 1826, when the future metropolis of Allen county was little more than a frontier hamlet. David F. Comparet was a son of Francis and Eleanor (Gnau) Comparet, the former of whom was born at Montreal, Canada, in 1796, it having been given him to become one of the very early settlers of northern Indiana and one of the honored and influential pioneers of Allen county, where he had the distinction of being the first to serve in the office of county commissioner. He was a charter member of the first Masonic lodge organized at Fort Wayne and took deep interest in this fraternity, though he was a communicant of the Catholic church, the rules of which he measurably transgressed when he became a Mason. David F. Comparet became one of the energetic and successful business men of Fort Wayne, where he was engaged in the operation of a flour mill, besides developing a prosperous enterprise in the buying and shipping of grain, hogs and general lines of farm produce. As a young man he wedded Miss Sarah H. Columbia, a daughter of Dana Columbia, who established his residence at Fort Wayne in 1834. David F. Comparet and his wife continued to maintain their home in Fort Wayne until her death, and they became the parents of seven children: Harriet is deceased; Charles is now a resident of the city of Indianapolis; Fannie is deceased; Addie is the wife of Henry W. Matson; William is deceased; Thomas L., of this review, was the next in order of birth, and Thomas is deceased. Thomas L. Comparet acquired his early education in the Fort Wayne schools and when but twelve years of age he began also his experience in connection with the practical affairs of life, by serving as a newsboy for the Fort Wayne Gazette. Later he assumed a clerical position in the employ of the Lake Shore and Michigan Southern Railroad, subsequently being similarly in the service of the Lake Erie and Western Railroad, his labors in these two connection having covered a period of about eight years. For one year thereafter he was in the employ of the Pennsylvania Railroad Company, and he then assumed the position of cashier for the Empire Line. In 1893 he became bookkeeper for the wholesale grocery house of McDonald & Watt, with which concern he thus continued his services until August, 1895, since which time he has held the responsible position of bookkeeper for the Bass Foundry, with high standing as a capable executive and skilled accountant. Mr. Comparet takes loyal interest in all things touching the welfare and progress of his native city and county, is a Republican in his political allegiance, is affiliated with the Masonic fraternity and the Independent Order of Odd Fellows, and both he and his wife are members of the Methodist Episcopal church. On September 25, 1888, was solemnized the marriage of Mr. Comparet to Miss Jennie F. Campbell, who was born and reared in Allen county and who is a daughter of George B. and Lydia (Wass) Campbell, the former a native of the state of New York and the latter of Allen county, Indiana. Mr. Campbell was a popular conductor in the service of the Pennsylvania Railroad Company and was killed in a railway accident, his widow being still a resident of Fort Wayne and Mrs. Comparet being the eldest of their two children: the younger of the children is George E., who resides in Fort Wayne and is cashier in the local offices of the Lake Shore & Michigan Southern Railroad. Of the children of Mr. and Mrs. Comparet the eldest is Irene, who was born October 30, 1890, and who is the wife of Carl Getz, the efficient city forester of Fort Wayne; Myrtle, who was born August, 1893, died in infancy; Irma, who was born August 24, 1896, and Ralph, who was born in 1890, remain at the parental home.

Eli Conrad is a son of Jacob and Elizabeth (Bartch) Conrad, who settled in Allen county, in 1871, and there spent the remaining years of their lives. The son, Eli, was born on February 8, 1879, one of a family of twelve sons and daughters reared on the homestead farm in Cedar Creek township. The others are John, of Wells county, Indiana; Jacob, of Grabill, in Cedar Creek township; Henry, who is deceased; Elizabeth, also deceased; Minnie, the wife of William Shultz, of Fort Wayne; Katherine, the wife of Albert Freis, of Springfield township; Susan, who married Andrew Roth, of Grabill; Lydia, a school teacher in Cedar Creek township; Andrew, of Grabill; Albert, also of that place, and a daughter who died in infancy, and who was the seventh child. Eli and Elizabeth, it should be said, were twins. The father of this family was an Ohioan by birth and a native of Star county, while the mother was of German birth and ancestry. She came to America in girlhood and died in 1886. Eli Conrad remained on the home farm until he reached the age of twenty-two, when he went to St. Joe, Indiana, and there engaged in the implement business. After one year he returned to Cedar Creek township and became identified with the buying and shipping of stock in his county, to which work he has since been devoted with much success. He has also become the owner of a fine farm in Section 18 and his residence is one of the comfortable and spacious ones of his township. Mr. Conrad was married to Lydia Roth on September 4, 1907. She was born in Allen county and is a daughter of Levi and Elizabeth (Witmer) Roth, which family is mentioned elsewhere in the pages of this work as prominent and popular residents of the town of Grabill. To Mr. and Mrs. Conrad two sons have been born—Willard Willmore, born August 20, 1909, and Paul Severn, born on August 15, 1911. Mr. Conrad is a Republican and is prominent in the activities of the local Grange, of which he is a director, and with his wife has membership in the Mission church.

Ernest W. Cook, vice-president and secretary of the Citizens Trust Company, of Fort Wayne, and prominently identified with other local business institutions of representative order, is a scion of staunch Revolutionary stock in America and in all of the relations of life has exemplified true American spirit. His versatility and progressiveness have been shown through his association with varied phases of business enterprise, and he has even endured the strenuous ordeal of close alliance with newspaper enterprise. As one of the loyal citizens and representative business men of Fort Wayne he is properly given definite recognition in this history. Mr. Cook was born at Manchester, Delaware county, Iowa, on February 5, 1861, a date indicating that his parents were numbered among the pioneers of the Hawkeye state. He is a son of Albert H. and Emily J. (Knapp) Cook, the former of whom was born in the vicinity of Saratoga Springs, New York, and the latter in New England, where her ancestors settled in the early colonial days, her paternal grandfather having been a valiant soldier under General Washington in the war of the Revolution. Albert H. Cook and his wife were persons of superior education and both became successful teachers in the public schools, the father having long devoted his attention to service in the pedagogic profession. He died at the age of sixty-eight years and his widow maintains her home in Fort Wayne. He was a stalwart Republican in politics and he was a member of the Methodist Episcopal church, as is also his widow. Of the children the subject of this review is the eldest; Clarence F. is associated with the Overland Automobile Company in Fort Wayne; Rose L., was for twenty-five years employed in the offices of the Tri-State Bank, of Fort Wayne, and Alba is the wife of Jesse F. Patterson, of Logansport, Indiana, her husband being a division superintendent of the Vandalia Railroad. Ernest W. Cook acquired his early education in the public schools of Fort Wayne, Indiana, and his initial business experience was gained when he was a lad of twelve years. At this juncture in his career he vitalized and adorned the independent vocation of newsboy, and later found employment in the office of the Fort Wayne Sentinel, under the direction of William Fleming. He projected his ramifications into all departments of newspaper work, and the experience he thus gained justified the oft-repeated statement that the discipline of a newspaper office is the equivalent of a liberal education. Finally he emancipated himself from the thrall of journalism and became cashier in the Fort Wayne freight house of the Wabash Railroad. Later he was freight and ticket agent for the same road in the city of Defiance, Ohio, and in 1893 he returned to Fort Wayne and became associated with the late Hon. Perry A. Randall and Robert T. McDonald in the purchase of the plant and business of the Ryan Transfer & Storage Company. He was manager of this business about three years, and then sold his interest in the same to assume the office of secretary of the Allen County Loan & Savings Association, in the development of which he wielded much influence and his alliance with which continued until 1899. In 1900 Mr. Cook became identified with the organization and incorporation of the Citizens Trust Company, of Fort Wayne, of which he has served as secretary since that time and of which he has been vice-president also since 1915. He has shown energy and ability in the upbuilding of the business of this substantial and representative financial institution and is a prominent figure in the financial circles of northern Indiana. Mr. Cook has ever been an ardent advocate of the principles of the Republican party, has been an active worker in its ranks and for twenty years served as treasurer of the committee in Allen county. In the Masonic fraternity he has received the thirty-second degree of the Ancient Accepted Scottish Rite, his maximum York Rite affiliation being with Fort Wayne Commandery of Knights Templars, besides which he is a member of the adjunct Masonic body, the Mystic Shrine. He is affiliated also with the local organizations of the Knights of Pythias, the Independent Order of Odd Fellows, and the Benevolent and Protective Order of Elks. Aside from his association with the Citizens Trust Company Mr. Cook is a director of the Lincoln Life Insurance Company and the Trade Mark Title Company, and was for a time treasurer of the Physicians' Defense Company, which latter was merged with the Medical Protective Company. He has been specially zealous and influential in connection with the work of the public schools of Fort Wayne, has been a member of the board of education since 1905 and is now president of the board. Mr. Cook is a man of broad intellectual ken and much literary ability, and he has made many effective contributions to the columns of the Fort Wayne newspaper press—especially in the promotion of high civic ideals and progressive industrial and commercial policies. On September 11, 1880, was solemnized the marriage of Mr. Cook to Miss Charity Carnrike, daughter of John Carnrike, of Fort Wayne, and concerning the children of this union the following brief data are available: Harry L., is assistant superintendent of one of the great steel mills at Gary, Indiana; Frank E., is owner of a restaurant at Seal Beach, California, and Flora E., is the wife of Walter H. Bauer, general manager of the American Chicle Company in the city of New York.

William P. Cooper has the best of reasons for paying the staunchest allegiance to his native city of Fort Wayne and to northern Indiana, for he is a scion of one of the most honored and influential families of this section of the Hoosier commonwealth, his father having settled in Fort Wayne in 1824, when the old fort was still in evidence and when Indians were yet to be found in large numbers in this part of the state. The pioneer house that was erected by his father, in 1835, at the site now designated as 321 East Berry street, Fort Wayne, figures as the birthplace of William Pinkney Cooper, and the date of his nativity was August 27, 1852. His father, Henry Cooper, was born at Havre de Grace, Maryland, in 1793, and was a representative of one of the patrician colonial families of that historic commonwealth. Henry Cooper received in his youth the best of educational advantages, as guaged by the standards of the locality and period, and he became a man of fine intellectual and professional attainments. He was the second lawyer admitted to practice in Allen county, Indiana, and gained precedence as one of the most able and distinguished members of the Indiana bar of the early days, his practice before the supreme court of the state having been for a considerable period larger than that of any other lawyer eligible for practice in that tribunal, at Indianapolis. His name appears frequently in the Blackford reports of the decisions of the supreme court and also in the other early Indiana court reports. By very reason of conditions prevailing in the pioneer days his law business was one of broad itineracy, and extended throughout the various counties of northern Indiana. He made his appearance in the courts at the judicial centers of the various counties by traveling back and forth on horseback, with the old-time saddlebags, in which he carried his requisite legal books. In the same manner he made his journeys to the capital city of the state, and he followed trails through the forests, frequently forded streams and lived up to the full tension of pioneer days in thus making his visitations to such now important centers as Indianapolis, Wabash, Huntington, Goshen, Elkhart and South Bend. He was distinguished for his profound learning, brilliant repartee and dignity of character. He was a man of most gracious personality and for many years his hispitable home, on East Berry street, Fort Wayne, was the stage of much of the representative social life of the little town. Letters which he wrote to his wife from Indianapolis and which are now in the possession of his son, William P., of this review, specially warned her against letting the children play with the Indians, the town at that time having been a mere straggling settlement around the old fort which gave to the present city its name. Henry Cooper's first wife bore the family name of Silvers, and both of their children, Edward and Henry, are deceased. After the death of the wife of his young manhood, Henry Cooper, Sr., wedded Mrs. Eleanor Munson, who was the widow of James P. Munson, and who had two children by her first marriage. The elder of the two, Charles A. Munson, became a prominent citizen of Fort Wayne and served as sheriff of Allen county. At the time of his death, which occurred in Mercy hospital, Chicago, in 1901, Mr. Munson was the western representative in that city of the Fort Wayne Electric Works. He was twice made the Democratic nominee for state auditor of Indiana, but his defeat in each instance was compassed by normal political exigencies. Lucretia M. Munson, the younger of the two children, is the widow of Diedrich Meyers and resides in Fort Wayne. William P. Cooper, of this sketch, is the only child of his father's second marriage, and he was about six months of age at the time of the death of his distinguished sire, in March, 1853. His devoted mother passed away November 19, 1883, at the age of 70 years and 5 months. Mr. Cooper secured his elementary education in the public schools of Fort Wayne, graduating from the high school in 1868. He for a short time served as city editor of the Fort Wayne Gazette and then entered Dartmouth College, where he was graduated in 1873. His taste for literature and his fine critical acumen were recognized at college and, with other honors, he was made class poet. After his graduation he studied law in the Columbia Law School, New York city, and also in the office of Cook & Nassau of that city, and with Hon. Robert Lowry, of Fort Wayne. However, the field of journalism held for him more attraction, and he relinquished his legal studies and began his professional life as city editor of the Fort Wayne News, being also at different times city editor of the Sentinel, the Gazette and the Journal, besides serving efficiently as Fort Wayne correspondent for the metropolitan papers. With a literary style of marked simplicity and directness, his was the rare charm of a "wit that without wounding could hit," but while his humor would lend grace alike to the worst prosaic "locals" or to an important article, his perfect taste was his marked characteristic. In 1888 Mr. Cooper left Fort Wayne to take a position on the editorial staff of the St. Louis Globe-Democrat, where he also did special work covering assignments of importance in and out of St. Louis. Later he returned to Fort Wayne to become managing editor of the Journal for a short time, when he quit journalism and enentered into the insurance business. In this were also exhibited those sterling qualities which insured his former success and in 1895 he was appointed general agent of the New York Life Insurance Company which responsible position he still holds. Socially Mr. Cooper belongs to the Greek letter society, Kappa Kappa Kappa of Dartmouth College, is a member of the Commercial Club, and is a member and ex-president of the Northern Indiana Life Underwriters Association. In June, 1896, he was elected a member of the board of school trustees, serving three years, the last two years as president of the board. In 1901 he was appointed a member of the Board of State Charities, serving under the administrations of both Governor Durbin and Governor Hanley. August 30, 1887, Mr. Cooper was united in marriage with Miss Nellie Brown, of Lafayette, Indiana, a woman of fine intellect and an artist of marked ability, and to them was born, July 10, 1888, a son, Brown, was was graduated in the Fort Wayne high school in 1906, and then entered his father's Alma Mater, Dartmouth College, from which he received, in 1910, the degree of Bachelor of Arts, and has since been associated with his father in the life insurance business. Politically Mr. Cooper is a Democrat, but declined to support the free-silver doctrines of Mr. Bryan and twice voted for McKinley. He represents the best type of citizen and dignified self-respecting manhood.

Thomas B. Coppock, secretary, treasurer and manager of the S. P. Coppock & Sons Lumber Company, is distinctively one of the vigorous and progressive young business men of Fort Wayne and the company of which he is an executive is one of the most important lumber concerns in northern Indiana, with headquarters in the city of Fort Wayne and with branch yards at Memphis, Tennessee, and Tyronza, Arkansas—so that its supply of resources and incidental facilities are of the best. As practical manager of the large yards and general business in Fort Wayne, Thomas B. Coppock has shown exceptional energy and resourcefulness and represents the best type of the aggressive young business men of the twentieth century. The youngest in the family of nine children, Mr. Coppock was born at Beloit, Mahoning county, Ohio, on March 14, 1882, and he is a son of Samuel P. and Anna (Buckman) Coppock, both natives of Pennsylvania. The father became prominently identified with the lumber business in Ohio and in 1898 removed with his family to Fort Wayne, where he established the present business of the S. P. Coppock & Sons Lumber Company, which is incorporated under the laws of Indiana, and in the control of which two of his sons are associated with him. He is one of the representative citizens of Fort Wayne, a broad-guaged business man of wide experience, and one who is liberal and public-spirited in his civic attitude. His wife is now deceased. Thomas B. Coppock is indebted to the public schools of the Buckeye state for his early educational discipline and he was about sixteen years of age at the time of the family removal to Fort Wayne. Here he availed himself of the advantages of the high school and thereafter completed a thorough course in a local business college. Since leaving school he has been actively identified with the business founded by his father, and in the connection he has fully demonstrated his initiative and executive ability. He gives loyal support to the cause of the Republican party, is a member of the Fort Wayne Rotary Club, and in the Masonic fraternity has received the thirty-second degree of the Ancient Accepted Scottish Rite, the York Rite and the Shrine. On May 28, 1908, was solemnized the marriage of Mr. Coppock to Miss Mabel Coverdale, who was born and reared in Fort Wayne, her father, Asahel S. Coverdale, being one of the principals of the grocery firm of Coverdale & Archer, of this city. Mr. and Mrs. Coppock have one child, a daughter, Martha Florence.

John Coutter.—John Coutter's parents were German people who came to America in their youth, married and settled in Dearborn county, Indiana, and there engaged in farming and lived active and wholesome lives for many years. They reared a fine family of eleven children, the subject being the first born, and about five years ago they retired from activities attendant upon farm life and settled down to a quiet and peaceful old age, secure in the esteem and confidence of their many friends and able to enjoy with a good conscience the fruits of their earlier years of toil. They were Andrew and Louise (Meyer) Coutter, and their children are here briefly mentioned as follows: John, the subject of this sketch; Sarah, living in Cincinnati, Ohio; Elizabeth, who is deceased; Carrie, also deceased; Catharine, living in Aurora; Anna; William, also of Aurora, Indiana; Mary, Henry and an infant child are deceased, and Charles, the youngest of the family, lives in Illinois. John Coutter was brought up to farm life, and he and his brothers and sisters had their schooling in the schools of Dearborn county. In 1886, when he was twenty-five years old, he left the home farm, where he had been his father's valued and able assistant, and settled on a rented place, the occasion of his removal being his marriage, which took place in the same year. He rented for ten years and was a successful farmer, despite the fact that he owned no land. In 1896 he returned to the home place, and after a short while bought a farm of ninety-one acres in Pleasant township. He has applied himself with diligence to the work of managing this farm from then to the present time, and has enjoyed a very marked success in the years that have passed. Mr. Coutter was married on February 17, 1886, to Miss Anna Harris, the daughter of John and Margaret (Greave) Harris. They were German people who came to America in young life, and they recall that the trip covered a period of fourteen weeks. As farming people they have been most successful, and they have affiliated themselves with American life in such a manner as to be recognized among the best citizens in their community. They were the parents of a fine family of eleven children, named Henry, Dorothy, Margaret, Mary, Anna, John, William, Sophia, Matilda, William Henry, Benjamin and Fred. Henry and William died, and when the ninth child was born his parents named him William Henry in memory of the others. Anna became the wife of Mr. Coutter, and they have a family of five children—Ernest, Homer, Louise, Clare and Martin. The eldest, Ernest, is located in Fort Wayne, where he is associated as a bookkeeper with the City Lighting Plant; Homer is deceased; Louise married Thaddeus Grossman and the two younger children are still with their parents. Mr. Coutter is a Democrat in politics, and he and his family are members of the Lutheran church, of which faith their families have long been faithful adherents.

David H. Crabill.—The parents of David Crabill are found mentioned at some length in another article in these pages, so that it is sufficient to say at this point that they were David and Sophia (Ridenour) Crabill, and to proceed with data concerning the life and activities of the immediate subject. David H. Crabill was born in Ohio on February 18, 1845, and died on March 25, 1916, at his home in Monroe township, where he had lived for more than a quarter of a century. He was a farmer all his life, as were his parents before him. He had his education in Allen county, where his family had located when he was a small child, and in 1875 he married Mary J. Laughlin, who was born in Lake township,

Allen county, and was the daughter of James and Catherine (Darby) Laughlin, both natives of Pennsylvania who settled in Allen county, Indiana, soon after their marriage. These sturdy people were pioneers in every sense of the word, and they knew Allen county in the early days when its green acres of the present period were covered with dense forest growths. Mr. Laughlin hewed a small open space in the wilderness he chose to locate upon and there built a rude cabin home, with typical puncheon floor and string latch peculiar to the day. There they lived and with the passing years the forest faded away gradually, as a result of the constant labors of Mr. Laughlin and his growing family, so that the time came when they found themselves the possessors of broad acres that yielded rich harvests annually. Of their six children born there, two are now living, and the parents themselves have long since passed on. Following his marriage to Mary Laughlin, the daughter of these pioneers, Mr. Crabill bought a farm of 115 acres in Section eight, Monroe township, and that place has been the family home down to the present day. Mr. Crabill made a point of intelligent farming and as a result enjoyed a pleasureable degree of material success in his work. Six children were born to them—Emma C., Agnes Sophia, John E., Charles L., Frank D., and another who died in infancy. Mr. Crabill died in March, 1916, leaving his widow comfortably established in the family home.

George D. Crane.—There was no element of futility or indirectness in the career of the late George D. Crane, of Fort Wayne, who here maintained his home for half a century and who expressed amidst "all of the changes and chances of this mortal life" the assurance of strong and worthy manhood. He was long known as one of the able and influential exponents of expert accounting and abstracting in Fort Wayne, his sterling character and his unquestioned ability gained to him inviolable confidence and esteem and he was made the administrator or trustee of several large estates in Allen county. He continued his association with his business until his death and was deeply interested in the preparing and maintaining of authentic abstracts of real estate titles in his home county. He was a broad-minded, upright and loyal citizen, was a stalwart advocate of the principles of the Republican party, was a Knight Templar Mason and was an earnest member of the Methodist Episcopal church, as is also his widow. It may consistently be said that he was one of the pioneer business men of Fort Wayne at the time of his demise and it is but consonant that in this history be entered a tribute to his memory. Mr. Crane was born in Montgomery county, New York, on February 6, 1842, and thus he was seventy-four years of age when he was summoned to the life eternal, on June 22, 1916. He was a son of Edward S. and Catherine (Lawson) Crane, both likewise natives of the old Empire state, where the father was a farmer. In 1856 the family removed from New York state to Stephenson county, Illinois, and the parents passed the closing years of their lives at Freeport, that county. Their children were four in number—Adaline, Louisa, Charlotte and George D.—and all are now deceased except Louisa, who remains with Mrs. Crane in the attractive old family home in Fort Wayne and in the most gracious companionship since the death of the revered husband and brother. Mr. Crane gained his early education in the schools of his native state and was a lad of fourteen years at the time of the family removal to Illinois. He continued to attend school at

Freeport and later completed a course in a commercial college. His initial business experience was in the insurance business at Freeport, when he was eventually transferred to Dayton, Ohio, where he remained until he came to Fort Wayne, about the year 1866. Here he became associated with Sanford Lombard in the insurance business, and so continued for a brief period. On February 17, 1869, was solemnized the marriage of Mr. Crane to Mrs. Addie J. (Edsal) Bayless, who has been a resident of Fort Wayne from the time of her birth and who is a daughter of John and Mary (DeKay) Edsal, who were born and reared in New Jersey and who were numbered among the sterling pioneers of Fort Wayne. Mrs. Crane is the only one surviving of a family of three children and she was an infant at the time of her father's death. In her widowhood Mrs. Crane is sustained and comforted by the hallowed memories that touch the long and devoted companionship of her husband and herself, and she is further fortified by the filial solicitude of her two children and by the love of friends who are tried and true. Of the children of Mr. and Mrs. Crane the elder is Harvey E., who holds a position with the Fort Wayne Electric Works; and Alice is the wife of Frank D. Bond, of this city.

George Rockhill Craw is a native son of Fort Wayne who has shown much versatility and resourcefulness as a business man and whose activities have been varied and important in connection with the newspaper and advertising business. He established and developed in the city of Chicago the George R. Craw Advertising Agency, but eventually, in 1913, sold this business to engage in cutlery manufacture, which business he sold in order that he might return to Fort Wayne and assume the supervision of his father's large and important business interests, the impaired health of his sire having brought about the latter's virtual retirement. Upon his return to Fort Wayne George R. Craw assumed, among other responsibilities, the active charge of the Portland furnished apartment building, a fine modern structure owned by his father and aunt. In the spring of 1914 he effected the organization of the Portland Hotel Apartments Company, of which he is now president, secretary and treasurer, as well as manager, his father having been president of the company up to the time of his death, February 14, 1917. George R. Craw was born in Fort Wayne March 10, 1875, and is a son of Edward L. and Maria (Rockhill) Craw, the former a native of Cleveland, Ohio, where his father served as sheriff of Cuyahoga county during the Civil war, and the latter of Fort Wayne, Indiana, where her father, William Rockhill, established his home many years ago, in the early pioneer epoch of the city's history. Edward L. Craw, who at the time of his death was practically retired, was for a long period a prominent exponent of the real estate business in Fort Wayne and did much to advance the physical development and upbuilding of the city. He was one of the honored and influential citizens of the Allen county metropolis and seat of government; served in former years as assistant postmaster of Fort Wayne, a position of which he continued the incumbent sixteen years. He was a staunch supporter of the cause of the Republican party and a communicant of Trinity church, Protestant Episcopal, as was also his wife, who died in 1900. Of the three children the subject of this review is the only survivor, James Edward and Esther Louise having died in infancy. George R. Craw attended the Fort Wayne public schools until he had profited by the advantages of the high school, and at the age of nineteen years became advertising manager of the Fort Wayne Journal-Gazette. In this connection his record was one of successful achievement and after some years of service he went to the city of Cincinnati, Ohio, and became advertising manager for the leading firm of Pettibone Brothers Manufacturing Company, military purveyors and manufacturers of lodge paraphernalia and regalia. After holding this position two years he went to the city of Chicago and assumed the position of editor of the Mail Order Journal. Later he there organized and established the George R. Craw Advertising Agency, and his technical ability and experience enabled him to develop a substantial and prosperous business. After disposing of his interest in this agency he became identified with the cutlery-manufacturing business in Chicago until the ill health of his father led him to return to Fort Wayne, as previously noted. Mr. Craw developed in connection with his newspaper and magazine work in Chicago, special literary ability, and his editorial work was of superior order. He wrote for and conducted special investigations for the Chicago Tribune and wrote for numerous periodicals. He was made a member of the famous Chicago Press Club, and finds satisfaction in maintaining this affiliation since he departed from the western metropolis. His political allegiance is given to the Republican party and he and his wife hold membership in Trinity church, Protestant Episcopal. On July 21, 1913, was solemnized the marriage of Mr. Craw to Miss Blanche Marie Collins, who was born and reared in Chicago, and the one child of this union is a winsome little daughter, Barbara Jane, who was born May 13, 1915.

William H. Crighton, who holds the position of chief draftsman at the Fort Wayne plant of the General Electric Company, is a man of recognized technical and executive ability and is consistently to be designated as one of the unequivocally popular and public-spirited citizens of the Allen county metropolis. Mr. Crighton was born at Fort Wayne on the 19th of October, 1864, and is a son of William and Mary Elizabeth (Kennedy) Crighton, the former of whom was born in Manchester, England, and the latter in Guelf, Canada. William Crighton died January 2, 1917, after many years of active and effective service as a mechanical engineer. He was a staunch Republican in politics and an active member of the Presbyterian church. His wife died March 23, 1909. Of their children, three are deceased—John, Stanley and Grace. The surviving children are: David, Thomas, William H, Jane and Frank. William H. Crighton attended the public schools of Fort Wayne until he had attained the age of sixteen years, when he found employment at the plant of the Kerr-Murray Manufacturing Company, with which he remained about six years, during which he gained practical and varied experience as a draftsman and fortified himself excellently for the profession to which he has continued to give his attention in a successful and influential way. He was thereafter in the employ of the Pennsylvania Railroad Company for several years and, in 1891, he became associated with the drafting department of the General Electric Works at Fort Wayne, with which important concern he is now chief draftsman. He is a Republican in politics and both he and his wife are active members of the First Presbyterian church. On the 4th of June, 1891, was solemnized the marriage of Mr. Crighton to Miss Luretta Esther Hulse, who was born and reared in Fort Wayne, and their three children are Kennethe, Malcolm and Stanley.

Calvin Crow comes of a family of old settlers in Allen county, his paternal grandfather having settled there with his family as early as 1851. Even at that time, it might almost have been said that Wilderness was King, and the section and a half that this sturdy pioneer bought for a homestead was in a state of nature, and afforded ample opportunity for the exercise of the virtues of energy, industry, patience and perseverence, not even omitting the virtue of pluck, which is the inevitable team-mate of the others. The family came from Morrow county, Ohio, where they had been long established, and the grandsire of the subject was long a prominent man in his community, serving as county commissioner of Allen county for many years. He was a Democrat, a staunch Methodist and his family was reared in that faith. James Crow, his son, spent his life in devotion to the farming industry in Lafayette township, and he died there. His widow survives and is now resident in Zanesville. She was Lydia Boelinger in maidenhood. The children of James and Lydia Crow were five in number. Calvin, subject of this sketch, was the first born. Peter, the second child, died in boyhood, and Joseph died in infancy. Michael lives in Wells county, Indiana, where he is engaged in the contracting business, and Martin died at the age of seventeen years. Calvin Crow was born in Lafayette township on December 16, 1861, and was reared on the home farm and educated in the common schools of his native village. He was reared to a thorough knowledge of farm life and the duties attendant upon such life, and when he decided to establish a home of his own, he rented a farm and settled down to make a living from the soil. He prospered and in a few years became the owner of a fine farm of 117 acres, on which he lives at this time. He is reckoned among the capable and progressive farming men of the township today, and is well entitled to the distinction. He is a Democrat, like his father and grandfather, a member of the Odd Fellows and of the Modern Woodmen of America. He was married on June 23, 1887, to Miss Laura Swank, the daughter of Thomas Swank, now deceased. She died on November 12, 1912, and is buried in Zanesville, Indiana. She was the mother of two children—Claude, a prosperous farmer who is married and the father of a little daughter, Helen Marie Crow, and Carrie, the wife of Glenn Kiplinger.

Arnold G. W. Curdes is one of the progressive young business men of his native city of Fort Wayne and though he prepared himself for and did successful work in the legal profession, he has found it more to his taste to give his attention to vigorous business enterprise and is now engaged in the building of high-grade houses in Fort Wayne, as a representative of the Home Builders' Association. Mr. Curdes was born in Fort Wayne on April 2, 1887, and is a son of Louis F. and Clara J. (Harris) Curdes, the former a native of Wittesingen, in Hessen, Germany, where he was born in the year 1863, and the latter was born at Reading, Pennsylvania, in 1865. Further mention of the parents is not demanded in this connection, for on other pages is entered a review of the career of the father, who is a sterling and honored citizen of Fort Wayne. Arnold G. W. Curdes continued his studies in the Fort Wayne public schools until he had completed a course in the high school, and thereafter he attended the Culver Military Academy, the celebrated Indiana school situated on the shores of Lake Maxinkuckee. He next entered the law department of the University of Indiana, in which he was graduated as a member of the class of 1906, and from which he received the degree of

Bachelor of Laws, with virtually coincident admission to the bar of his native state. From 1907 to 1909, inclusive, he was engaged in the general practice of his profession in Fort Wayne, and for the ensuing two years he held the position of general manager of the Fort Wayne Hosiery Company. Since his retirement from this position he has given his attention most successfully to home building enterprise in his native city, and in this field of endeavor he has found ample scope and opportunity for the achieving of success worthy of the name. His political allegiance is given to the Republican party, his religious faith is that of the Lutheran church, and in the time-honored Masonic fraternity his ancient-craft affiliation is with Home Lodge, No. 342, Ancient Free & Accepted Masons. He has received also the thirty-second degree of the Ancient Accepted Scottish Rite of Masonry and is affiliated with Mizpah Temple, Ancient Arabic Order, Nobles of the Mystic Shrine, besides being a member of Concordia Lodge, No. 228, Independent Order of Odd Fellows. On August 18, 1908, was solemnized the marriage of Mr. Curdes to Miss Mabel Edith Wood, daughter of Frank and Margaret (Steinhaur) Wood, of Fort Wayne, and the two children of this union are Virginia Wood Curdes and Louis Arnold Curdes, their respective years of birth having been 1909 and 1910.

Louis F. Curdes has shown in his independent career a vital energy and resourcefulness that have brought to him not only a large measure of success but also a position of prominence and influence in connection with one of the most important lines of enterprise touching the civic and material welfare and progress of the community. As a vigorous representative of the real estate business he has done much to further the advancement and upbuilding of the city of Fort Wayne, and his versatility and his cumulative success are the more gratifying to note by reason of the fact that, coming from Germany to America when a mere youth, he has relied entirely upon his own resources in making his way forward to the goal of independence and prosperity—the record of his advancement offering both lesson and incentive. Louis Frank Curdes was born in the village of Wettesingen, Province of Hessen Cassel, Germany, May 22, 1863, and is a son of Henry and Henrietta (Klingelhofer) Curdes, both of whom passed their entire lives in that section of the German Empire, where the father died in 1873 and the mother in 1887. Louis F. Curdes attended the excellent schools of his native province until he was eleven years of age, and thereafter he continued his higher studies in the well ordered gymnasium at Warburg, Westphalia, and a similar institution at Hademar, in Hessen Nassau. At the age of sixteen years he came to the United States, and after passing a few months in the home of his sister, Mrs. Amelia Brown, at Defiance, Ohio, he came to Fort Wayne to visit another sister, Mrs. Mary Kriger, who died in childbirth only one week after his arrival in the city in which he was destined to gain precedence as a representative business man. After the death of his sister Mr. Curdes was here variously employed for several months, within which period he worked for the White Fruit House, the firm of K. B. Miller & Company, dealers in men's furnishings, and the book store of Sieman Brothers. In 1881 he entered the employ of the Packard Organ Company, with which he continued his association during the ensuing twelve years— or until the financial panic of 1893 brought about so great a curtailment of the company's business that he withdrew from its employ. Ambitious and self-reliant, he carefully consulted ways and means and finally established himself in the real estate business, his early sales having been made

Louis F. Curdes.

on a commission basis. His indomitable energy and honorable methods so expanded his business that in 1895 he was enabled to engage in buying and selling real estate in an independent way. His first venture under these conditions was that of purchasing nineteen lots in the Ewings Grove addition to Fort Wayne, and he was successful in exploiting and selling these properties advantageously. A year or so later he bought one hundred lots in the Industrial Park addition, and, with increasing confidence and characteristic circumspection, he later amplified operations by the purchase of sixty lots in the Swinney addition. To Mr. Curdes is in large measure due the splendid development of these properties and also of seven hundred and forty-four lots of which he assumed control in the beautiful Forest Park addition to the city. His activities have been insistent and cumulative and have included the development of Forest Park boulevard, the Driving Park addition, containing one hundred and five acres, and numerous smaller additions and subdivisions, including Weisser Park, the Driving Park addition likewise continuing its development under his effective supervision. Mr. Curdes has become one of the foremost exponents of real estate interests in Fort Wayne and through his broad operations has shown his faith in the future growth and increasing prosperity of the metropolis and judicial center of Allen county. Concerning his admirable activities in his chosen sphere of enterprise the following pertinent statements have been written: "Mr. Curdes is a man of artistic temperament and talent, and has been able to visualize in his own mind the beautifying of a landscape that to others represented but shrub-covered, barren knolls, and some of Fort Wayne's most beautiful additions and charming drives are but the outgrowth of his planning. He has had and still retains the utmost confidence in the splendid future of Fort Wayne, and the additions which he has so successfully exploited have been planned not only for the present but also for the city that is to be." In politics Mr. Curdes is unwavering in his allegiance to the Republican party, he is an active and influential member of the Fort Wayne Commercial Club, and both he and his wife are communicants of the German Lutheran church. On June 18, 1885, was solemnized the marriage of Mr. Curdes to Miss Clara J. Harris, daughter of John Harris, a prosperous hardware merchant of Fort Wayne. Of the four children of this union Arnold G. W., and Walter L. are associated with their father in the real estate business; Herbert died at the age of ten months; and Helen L., the only daughter, now Mrs. Arthur W. Rose, is a popular factor in the younger social circles of her native city.

Charles E. Dailey followed the blacksmith business in Leo, Cedar Creek township, from 1892 to 1915, when he retired from active labors and settled down to a life of comparative ease. He was born in Cedar Creek township on July 1, 1867, son of Samuel and Mary (McCrory) Dailey, both of Pennsylvania birth. They came to Allen county in about 1846, locating on a wilderness farm in this township and there spent the remainder of their lives. The father died, in 1880, leaving a fine improved farm of one hundred acres, and the mother is now living quietly in Leo, Indiana. They were the parents of seven children. William M. lives in Leo. Dora is the wife of C. L. Hollopeter, of Wooster, Ohio. Franklin met his death by accidental drowning. Charles E. was the fourth child. Sarah became the wife of Samuel Souder, of Michigan. Nevada lives in Fort Wayne, and Abner is located in Grabill. Mr. Dailey stayed on the home farm up to the age of twenty-five years, when he went to St. Joe, Indiana, and there learned the trade of a blacksmith. He worked there for two years, then returned to Allen county and, settling in Leo, built and equipped a modern blacksmith shop, which he operated with all success until he retired, in 1915. Mr. Dailey was married on March 22, 1891, to Miss Nellie Maxfield, who was born in Leo, Indiana, and five children have been born to them. George, the eldest, is located in Detroit, Michigan, and the others—Marjorie, Ronald, Ada and June—are still in the parental home. Mr. Dailey is a Democrat, active in local politics, and was one of the township trustees from 1908 to 1916. He is a Mason and a member of the Eastern Star, his wife also having membership in that branch of Masonry.

John Dalman.—Not all men are permitted to order their lives exactly to their liking but they are the strong and worthy ones who make the best possible use of their powers and wrest from fate the fullest measure of success which conditions impose. He to whom this memoir is dedicated was a man who lived up to the maximum of his ideals and powers of achievement and his sturdy character, his ambition and his industry enabled him to win in his native country a secure vantage-place as a representative farmer and land-holder and as a citizen of more than ordinary influence, this latter assurance having been verified by his effective service as treasurer of Allen county, an office of which he continued the incumbent four years, prior to which he had served nine years as trustee of Pleasant township. Mr. Dalman was born at Fort Wayne on October 13, 1843, and was the eldest of the four children—all sons—of Edwin and Mary (McNeir) Dalman, the former of whom was born in England and the latter in Ontario, Canada. The parents were numbered among the worthy pioneers of Allen county, and here they continued to reside until their death, the father having done his part in connection with the early stages of material and civic development and progress in this now favored section of the Hoosier state. The four sons, John, William, Charles and Thomas, are all deceased. Mr. Dalman early learned the lessons of practical and productive industry, had confidence in his ability to achieve independence through individual effort, and at the age of twenty-one years took unto himself a young wife who was destined to be his loyal and devoted coadjutor and to aid him materially in the accomplishing of their ambitious purposes. At the time of his marriage he settled on a farm of eighty acres, in Pleasant township, and not a little of the true pioneer phase of agricultural development was touched by him in his initial labors as an agriculturist. Self-reliant and indefatigable, he pressed steadily forward toward the goal of success, and at the time of his death was the owner of a valuable and well improved landed estate of two hundred and seven acres—all in Pleasant township. He did much to further the development and advancement of that fine section of Allen county, commanded the unqualified confidence and esteem of all who knew him and made his life count for good in its every relation. The farm property is still owned by his widow, who also owns and occupies one of the attractive residences of Fort Wayne, the same being at 2732 Fairfield avenue, besides which she has other property, both country and city. There was nothing static or vacillating in the nature of Mr. Dalman, and he not only proved himself a worthy member of the world's noble army of productive workers but was also loyal and liberal as a citizen and well fortified in his convictions and opinions. He was a leader in the councils of the Democratic party in Allen county, and, as before stated, was called upon to serve in offices of significant public trust, including that of county treasurer. In the Masonic fraternity he received the thirty-second degree of the Scottish Rite, he was affiliated also with the Independent Order of Odd Fellows, and he was a consistent and devout member of the Christian church, as is also his widow. The gracious marital companionship of Mr. and Mrs. Dalman covered a period of more than forty years, and the relations were severed only when the loved husband and father was summoned to the life eternal, on June 23, 1905. On August 27, 1863, was solemnized the marriage of Mr. Dalman to Miss Louisa Helle, who likewise was born and reared in Allen county and who is a daughter of the late Frederick and Charlotta (Pens) Helle, both natives of Germany, Mrs. Dalman being the youngest of their three children; Frederick and William both are deceased. In conclusion is given brief record concerning the children of Mr. and Mrs. Dalman: Charlotta died in childhood; Jennie L. is the widow of Elgi Rich and resides in Fort Wayne; Merica E. is the wife of Howard Shordon, of Fort Wayne; Edwin F. is actively identified with business interests in Fort Wayne; John W. is associated with the American Steel Foundries, in the city of Chicago; Mary Frances died at the age of two years; and Florence D. is the wife of Jesse Marquardt, of Los Angeles, California.

William E. Dalman was one of eight children born to his parents, William and Rebecca (Osborne) Dalman, early and estimable citizens of Fort Wayne. The elder Dalman came from England as a young man, in 1833, and settled in the original Fort Wayne community, in the days of the old block house. He was a true pioneer, and he spent his remaining years in that locality. He was a shoemaker by trade, and served his apprenticeship in England. He farmed some in Allen county, but for the most part gave his attention to the business of shoe-making, and enjoyed a good deal of well merited success in that work. The children born to William and Rebecca Dalman were James F., a resident of Fort Wayne; Charlotte Jane, deceased; Mary Rebecca, living in Wayne township; Hanna A., the wife of John Corson; Julia, of Fort Wayne; W. E., the subject; Agnes E., of Lagrange, and Matilda Luemma, who is deceased. W. E. Dalman had his schooling in Pleasant township, the family having lived on a farm there for a period of years in his boyhood, and he eventually came into possession of the home place there. In later years he came to own other farms, but the old home was always his headquarters. During his last years he lived retired from active farm life, after enjoying a generous measure of success in his chosen occupation. Mr. Dalman was a Republican in politics, as was his father before him, and he served his township in various official capacities. One office he filled was that of township assessor, and he served from 1896 to 1900. He was married on December 16, 1877, to Miss Mary Bradbury, a native daughter of Pleasant township, and they became the parents of eleven children. Edwin, the eldest, is a farmer and is located in Wayne township; Albert is established in Fort Wayne and is connected with the City Light and Power Company there. Nellie is the wife of William Daffron of Pleasant township. Roy is engaged in farming in Pleasant township. Guy is also connected with the City Light and Power Company in Fort Wayne. Ida married William Ria, a farmer of La Porte county. Arthur is the third of the family to be identified in an industrial way with the Fort Wayne Light and Power Company. The Dalman family is prominent and popular in Pleasant township, and they are likewise well known in Fort Wayne, where various members of the family have identified themselves with the business world, and where numerous representatives of the family of a preceding generation are also to be found.

Rev. Henry Paul Dannecker.—In 1890 the Rev. Henry Paul Dannecker came to Fort Wayne to take charge of St. John's Parish of the Evangelical Lutheran church. He has continued in that position to the present time, and the development of the parish in the past twenty-five years has been a credit alike to the pastor and to the community. The church was established on October 2, 1853. An unpretentious frame building was erected and at the same time they established a parochial school. The little church prospered and in 1861 the old frame structure was razed and a new and more modern building took its place. Again, in 1881, improvements were in order, and a fine brick structure took the place of the preceding frame building. Hand in hand with the growth of the church proper, the parochial school made sturdy development, and the present fine brick school that serves the parish was built in 1897. Three teachers are required to handle an attendance of 150 pupils and the standards of the school are most creditable. The first pastor of the church was Rev. Christian Hochstetter and the first teacher in the school was William Burger. Since those early days five pastors have served the parish. The second was A. Kleingees, who came in 1854 and served until 1857. He was followed by Hugo B. Kuhn, who served until 1861, and was replaced by E. Bauman, whose service continued until 1868. In that year Johannes Kucher came and remained for twenty-one years, and in 1890 the present pastor, Henry Paul Dannecker, assumed charge of the parish, which numbers about 350 families. His services have continued over a period of more than a quarter of a century, and the improvements that have marked his pastorate have been many and varied. St. John's is the second Lutheran church of the city, and with Grace Church is connected with the Ohio Joint Synod. Rev. Henry Paul Dannecker was born in Cincinnati, Ohio, on March 22, 1860, and is a son of Frank and Fredericka (Koch) Dannecker, both of German birth. The mother came from Wuertemburg and the father from Baden, Germany. When Frank Dannecker came to America he located first in Cincinnati, Ohio, and remained there for several years. He married there and there the subject was born. When Henry Dannecker was about seven years old the family moved to Delphos, Ohio, and there the father worked at his trade as a cooper. There were three children—Clara, Henry Paul, and Max, of Van Wert, Ohio. Henry Paul Dannecker had his education in the public schools of Delphos, Ohio, and there learned the printer's trade, at which he worked for three years. He then entered Capital University at Columbus, Ohio, spending four years in study and was graduated in 1881. He engaged in teaching then and spent a year as instructor in a Lutheran parochial school at Youngstown, Ohio, after which he entered the theological seminary at Capital University and was graduated in 1885. He was ordained at New Washington, Ohio, and his first pastorate was at that place, where he spent five years in worthy service. He was then called to Fort Wayne to take charge of St. John's Parish, where he has since continued as has been stated above. Rev. Mr. Dannecker was married on January 14, 1886, to Miss Catherine Schneider, the daughter of William and Catherine (Bachman) Schneider, of Genoa, Ohio. Nine children have been born to them. Theodore, the eldest, has followed in his father's ways and is now

HUGH M. DEIHL

serving as assistant pastor of the church at Marysville, Ohio. Clara is the wife of Otto Sauertig, of Fort Wayne. Anna is deceased. Freda, Luther, Paul, Henry and Catherine are still under the parental roof; and one died in infancy. Mrs. Dannecker's parents were natives of Hessen Castle, Germany, and they came to the United States in 1871, locating in Genoa, Ohio. He was a forester in his homeland, but had retired from service before coming to America, and he was not engaged in active business pursuits after settling in Genoa. Both he and his wife are deceased. Rev. and Mrs. Dannecker have two grandchildren—Marguerite and Marian—the daughters of their eldest son, Theodore.

William Decker is another of the native sons of the fine old Hoosier state who has here found ample scope and opportunity for successful achievement in connection with the basic industries of agriculture and stock-growing, and he is consistently to be designated as one of the representative farmers of Maumee township, where he has maintained his residence since the autumn of 1893 and where he is the owner of a splendidly improved farm of ninety acres. Mr. Decker has shown his progressiveness not only in bringing the farm up to high standard of productiveness but also in the making of the best of permanent improvements, including the erection of one of the best farm residences in the township, the building of good fences and the installing of tile drainage. He takes loyal interest in community affairs, is a Democrat in politics and he and his wife are communicants of the Lutheran church. Mr. Decker was born in Adams county, Indiana, on September 14, 1862, and is a son of Frederick and Mary (Comar) Decker, the former a native of Germany and the latter of Switzerland. The parents came to America in 1852, the voyage having been made on an old-time sailing vessel and thirteen weeks having elapsed ere it reached its destination. Frederick Decker came to Indiana soon after his arrival in the United States and for a time drove mules on the old Wabash and Erie canal. Later he obtained a tract of land in Adams township, where he reclaimed and improved a good farm and he and his wife are now numbered among the venerable pioneer citizens of Adams county, he having celebrated his eighty-fourth birthday anniversary in 1917. Of the five children the subject of this sketch is the eldest and he is the only son, the names of his sisters being here indicated in the respective order of birth: Louisa, Sophia, Anna and Mary. William Decker gained in his boyhood and youth a goodly quota of valuable and invigorating discipline in connection with the work of the home farm, and in the meanwhile he did not fail to profit by the advantages afforded in the public schools of his native county. He continued to be associated with the work and management of his father's farm until his removal to Allen county, and here, as previously stated, he has won for himself a large measure of success in connection with his vigorous operations as a farmer and stock-grower. On January 27, 1888, Mr. Decker wedded Miss Elaine Buuck, who likewise was born and reared in Adams county, and who is a daughter of Louis and Louisa Buuck, early settlers of that county. Mr. and Mrs. Decker became the parents of five children: Paulina is the wife of John Korte, a successful farmer in Milan township; Rudolph and Amy remain at the parental home; Nora died at the age of seventeen days, and the youngest child, a son, died in infancy.

Hugh M. Deihl, whose death occurred in Fort Wayne on August 8, 1913, was a resident of this city for more than half a century, and he walked the path of life with the great simplicity and strength that ever prove an inspiration to honesty and worthy endeavor, the while he was ever loyal to high ideals and was an intuitive optimist and humanitarian. In a quiet and unassuming way he played well his part on the stage of life, and it is but consistent that in this history of the city and county that so long represented his home there shall be entered a tribute to his memory. Not the least of the honors that were his were those gained through loyal service as a soldier of the Union in the Civil war, and his patriotism was reinforced by the knowledge that though he was of staunch German lineage he was a member of a family that was founded in America prior to the war of the Revolution, his parents having passed their entire lives in Pennsylvania and he himself having been born in the city of Philadelphia, on October 23, 1845. He was a son of Charles and Margaret (Martin) Deihl, and concerning the other children the following brief data are available: Mary is the wife of John Smith, of Philadelphia; Charles likewise resides in that city; Peter was the next in order of birth; Mrs. Ella Scott still maintains her home in Philadelphia, as do also Margaret, who is the widow of Joseph Test, and Agnes, who is the youngest of the surviving children; Sarah is deceased. While attending the schools of Philadelphia, Hugh M. Deihl heard his country's call to the defense of the union, and he succeeded, though but sixteen years of age, in being accepted for service in the Union army. He first enlisted for a term of ninety days as a member of a Pennsylvania regiment of infantry, and, after the expiration of his original term, he re-enlisted, his service having continued during practically the entire period of the war, and his valor and fidelity having brought about his promotion to the office of captain. In later years he manifested his abiding interest in his old comrades by means of his appreciative affiliation with the Grand Army of the Republic. Directly after his war service, Mr. Deihl joined the ranks of the world's productive workers by entering upon an apprenticeship to the trade of machinist. Then he came west, and, after remaining in the city of Chicago for a brief period, he came to Fort Wayne and found employment in the shops of the Pennsylvania Railroad Company, his fine mechanical ability making him a skilled and valued employe who commanded substantial compensation for his services. He continued with the railroad company in the Fort Wayne shops for a long period of years and thereafter served thirteen years as chief of the police department of Fort Wayne—an office in which his long incumbency best demonstrates the efficiency of his administration, as well as the high popular estimate placed upon him as a man and a public official. He finally resigned his position as head of the police department and returned to the employ of the Pennsylvania Railroad Company, with which he continued his connection until the time of his death. Mr. Deihl's entire life was guided and governed by the highest principles, his buoyant nature found expression in kindly words and kindly deeds, and he drew to himself the most loyal of friends among all classes. His political allegiance was given to the Democratic party, he was prominently affiliated with the time-honored Masonic fraternity, in which he received the Knights Templars degrees and also the thirty-second degree of the Scottish Rite, as well as those of the Mystic Shrine. He took deep interest in the affairs of the local post of the Grand Army of the Republic and was one of its most popular members. He was affiliated with the Independent Order of Odd Fellows, and for many years prior to his death had been a zealous member of the First Presbyterian church, in which his widow still holds membership.

Shortly after coming to Fort Wayne he was married to Miss Ada Romelia Jones, who was born at Lockport, New York, and who is a representative of an old and honored family of the Empire state. She is a daughter of the late Thomas and Nancy (Guernsey) Jones, and the latter's father, Hon. John Guernsey, served as a member of the state senate of New York, as well as a representative in the United States congress. Mrs. Deihl is the eldest in a family of three children, Fannie J., being the second and John having died at the age of sixteen years. When the silver cord of long and devoted companionship was loosed by the death of Mr. Deihl his widow found the greatest measure of consolation and compensation in the gracious memories of the loving association that had been theirs and of all that he had represented as husband and father. Mrs. Deihl resides at 525 East Berry street, where she delights to extend welcome to her many friends. Mr. and Mrs. Deihl became the parents of two daughters and one son: Lillie is the wife of Hon. James M. Robinson, of Fort Wayne, and Alice M. remains with her widowed mother.

Rev. Joseph F. Delaney, pastor of St. Patrick's Catholic church in Fort Wayne, was born January 15, 1860, at Thompsonville, Conn. He was one of six children born to John and Mary Delaney, the former of whom was a native of Roscrea, County Tipperary, and the latter of the parish of Den, County Cavin, Ireland. His classical and philosophical courses were made at the Niagara University, after which he entered St. Francis' Seminary, Milwaukee. His death breaking after one year, he was sent to St. Vincent's Seminary, Latrobe, Pennsylvania, where he completed his theology. He was ordained priest in the Cathedral at Fort Wayne, by Bishop Dwenger, June 29, 1887. He received his appointment, July 17, as assistant to Very Rev. J. H. Brammer, V. G., at the Cathedral. Two years later he succeeded the Rev. T. M. Leary as pastor of St. Patrick's church. He was named irremovable rector by Bishop Alerding and is a Diocesan Consultor.

David Dennis.—The dignity of labor raises the farmer to a level of importance that corresponds favorably with that occupied by any class of producers. To labor long and faithful years, giving the best of one's ability and talent along any line of endeavor, is to rightly fulfill the destiny of mankind and to make possible a happy and contented age. David Dennis, one of the substantial farmers and highly esteemed citizens of Lafayette township, is a man whose life has been one of constant industry and honorable labor, and though busy about his own affairs at all times, he has never lacked the time to identify himself with the social life of his neighbors or to contribute of his means to the advancement and welfare of his community. He is not a Hoosier by birth, but claims Guernsey, Ohio, as his place of nativity. He was born there on January 1, 1829, and he was seven years of age when the family moved to Monroe county, Ohio, where he continued to be identified with the home life of the family until he was twenty-four years old. His parents were farmers and he had a vigorous and valuable training in the elements of successful farming, so that when he launched out on his own responsibility he was ready to move on to success and independence without passing through the harrowing experiences that beset the early years of many young farmers. It was in 1853 when he left his native state and made the somewhat difficult journey across country to Allen county, Indiana. He drove the entire distance, having a light camping outfit and such equipment as was necessary for such a trip, and arriving in Lafayette township he bought a "forty" of uncleared land, grubbed out a space for a small log cabin and applied himself diligently to the business of making a home for himself and his little family in a new and practically undeveloped district. After some fifteen years of close application to the business in hand, Mr. Dennis had cleared every inch of the land and it was in excellent shape. He sold it to good advantage and bought another farm, this time an eighty-acre place, and it is on that place he is living to-day. It is one of the well developed and highly productive farms of the township and reflects a good deal of credit upon the industry and energy of its owner. Mr. Dennis was married on January 28, 1850, while yet a resident of Ohio, to Miss Elizabeth Bolinger. Nine children were born to them. They were named John, Blanda, Barbara, Marion, Ida Catherine, Ralph D., Margaret, Mary and Edward. The only ones living are Blanda and Edward, the latter of whom lives in New Haven. All were married and reared families, who in turn have families of their own, so that at the present writing Mr. Dennis has sixteen grandchildren and eighteen great-grandchildren. Mrs. Dennis passed away on September 28, 1916, and is buried in Zanesville.

William H. Dennis.—Members of this well known family have been conspicuously identified with the development of Allen county and its agricultural resources during the past seventy-five years, and it is eminently fitting that some mention be made of them in a publication of the nature of this one. Their activities have been praiseworthy to a degree and William H. Dennis has ably carried on the work his father began in 1843, when he first came to Allen county as a pioneer from Pennsylvania. The subject was born on October 22, 1857, and his parents were Jacob and Nancy (Hickman) Dennis, both of Pennsylvania birth and parents. They came from their native state to Indiana in 1843 and settled in Allen county, buying a farm of one hundred acres in Lafayette township, which has since been the center of the family labors and accomplishments. Their early life on this new land was fraught with many difficulties incident only to pioneer life, and residents of the community of the present generation have little realization of what it meant to their parents to establish homes in what is to-day a well-settled and thriving district. Jacob Dennis prospered with the passing years and added land to his holdings from time to time, so that he was excellently equipped to carry on diversified farming on a fairly large scale during the later years of his life. He was a prominent man in his community and served as justice of the peace for many years in Lafayette township. He was generally known as "Squire" Dennis among his associates and his standing in town and county was a creditable one. He was a life-long member of the Methodist Episcopal church, as was also his wife, who was one of the most estimable women of her day in Lafayette township, and who is still remembered for her many excellent qualities of heart and mind. Mr. and Mrs. Dennis reared a family of twelve children, four of whom are deceased, and the others are filling useful places in their various communities. Named in the order of their appearance they are Barbara Ell, who married Amos Busch and is deceased; Martha Anna, the wife of Adam Buscher, of Fort Wayne; John M., who died young; David C., a resident of Roanoke; Mary B., the wife of Nelson Bart, of Fort Wayne; Elizabeth, who is deceased, was the wife of Taylor Bell, and he also is no longer living; William H. is the subject of this review; Albert is deceased; Jacob is a Lafayette township farmer; Alice married Fred Pence, of Huntington; Susan became the wife of Newton Darr; Frank R., lives in Lima, Ohio. William H. Dennis was born in Lafayette township and he had his schooling in the public schools his community afforded. Until 1882, when he was about twenty-five years old, he stayed on the farm home, helping in the management of that place, and then, having married, he branched out for himself. He bought a place of eighty acres in his native community, settled down to independent farming, and from that time his success was assured. He has prospered with the passing years, adding gradually to his land holdings, and to-day has one of the fine farms of the township, where he carries on a progressive and remunerative variety of farming. He has devoted a good deal of special attention to the breeding of Chester White hogs, Durham cattle, Shropshire sheep and Norman and Belgian horses, and the live stock produced on his place is well known for its general quality. Many improvements have been instituted on the farm in the past few years, and a new house and fine barns lately acquired speak definitely of a substantial prosperity that is the aim and ambition of every successful farmer. Mr. Dennis is interested in the Farmers State Bank of Roanoke as a stockholder and at the present time is a member of the township advisory board. He is a Democrat in politics, but does not let his political convictions interfere with his local duty as a citizen. He was married in 1882 to Alice Smalts, daughter of George and Elizabeth Smalts, and they are the parents of four children. Stella and Roy are at home. Celeste is at Fort Wayne and Media is the wife of Jewel Wickliff of Zanesville, Indiana. She has two children, Keith L. and Floyd D.

Robert W. T. DeWald.—From an early stage in its history the city of Fort Wayne has been favored in enlisting men of energy, enterprise, strong initiative and sterling character in the furtherance of civic, industrial and commercial advancement, and in insuring such cumulative precedence there are certain names that are specially prominent and honored in the city's history. Such distinction specially applies to the family of DeWald, and one of the most substantial and important commercial enterprises of the city at the present time is that represented in the extensive business controlled by the wholesale dry-goods corporation of The George DeWald Company, the history of the concern covering a period of nearly three-fourths of a century, so that it is consistently to be designated as one of the pioneer business houses of the Allen county metropolis. Developed along normal and legitimate lines and built up definitely upon honor, the business has stood creditable alike to those who have been in control of the same and also to the city in which its headquarters have been maintained. This representative house has been a leader in commercial and industrial progress in Fort Wayne and in the general annals of the city few names have been more notably and worthily conspicuous as exemplifying civic loyalty and impressive business progressiveness. Robert W. T. DeWald, president of the corporation of The George DeWald Company, was born March 7, 1862, and the place of his nativity was the old family homestead that stood on a now vacant lot adjoining the Fort Wayne postoffice building. His father, George DeWald, was born in Hessen Darmstadt, Germany, on May 14, 1831, and acquired his early education in his native land. At the age of eighteen years he came to America and after remaining for a time in the states of New York and New Jersey he came to Indiana and became one of the representative young business men of Fort Wayne, where he passed the residue of his life and where his death occurred June 27, 1899. In the old Catholic cathedral that stood on the site of the present Library Hall, his marriage to Mrs. Sophia Angeline Netthorst was solemnized February 10, 1861, when he was twenty-nine years of age. His wife was a representative of one of the oldest and most distinguished families of this section of Indiana, her father, Francis D. LaSalle, having been of French lineage and a scion of the historic and partician old family of LaSalle: he came in an early day to old Fort Wayne, where he served as paymaster to the Indians, and it is a matter of historic record that he took a prominent part in conducting the Indians from the settlement when the government made provision for them elsewhere. In 1849 George DeWald engaged in the retail drygoods business in a modest way, and it is specially interesting to note that his original store was on the site of the fine building now owned and occupied by the large wholesale dry-goods house that perpetuates his name. In the early years he was associated in business with Robert Wade Townley and Jonas Townley, who were succeeded by Townley, DeWald and Bend, but eventually he gained sole control of the business and established the firm of George DeWald & Company, this title having since been retained and the concern having been incorporated within a short time after his death. He continued to be actively identified with the business until the close of his life, and the enterprise was continued exclusively along retail lines until the establishment was destroyed by fire, December 27, 1899, about six months subsequently to the death of the honored founder. George DeWald was a man of fine character and much ability. In his business affairs he was the sturdy exponent of progress, and the same held good in his attitude as a loyal and broad-minded citizen. His interest in Fort Wayne was not merely one of sentiment but was manifested in liberality and constructive energy. He did much for the advancement of the city and at all times held to the highest civic ideals. He was essentially a business man and thus had no desire to enter the arena of practical politics, though he was a staunch supporter of the cause of the Democratic party. He and his wife continued their membership in the Cathedral parish of the Catholic church until the founding of St. Patrick's church, when they transferred their membership to this parish, the church edifice being situated on DeWald street, which was named in honor of this sterling pioneer merchant. Mrs. DeWald passed her entire life in Fort Wayne and this revered and gracious gentlewoman was summoned to the "land of the leal" in 1906. Of the children Robert W. T., of this review, is the eldest; Mary E. is the wife of James A. McDonald, and they maintain their home at LaGrange, a suburb of the city of Chicago; Caroline L. is the wife of Henry J. Beuret, of Fort Wayne; Miss Elizabeth M. resides in Fort Wayne, her home being on the site of the old DeWald Square, which was named for her father; George L. is vice-president of The George DeWald Company. Robert W. T. DeWald acquired his youthful education in the parochial and public schools of Fort Wayne and, in 1876, when about fifteen years of age, he initiated his practical training with his father's retail mercantile business. In 1888 he was admitted to partnership, and he has continued his active alliance with the business during the intervening years—a resourceful and valiant force in the development of the large and important enterprise now conducted by the incorporated concern of The George DeWald Company. After the disastrous fire that destroyed the firm's retail store, in the winter of 1899, Mr. DeWald effected a prompt reorganization of the business, and the company was incorporated in January, 1900, under the present title. He became president of the corporation and has continued as its chief executive, his brother being vice-president of the company and William P. Beck being its secretary and treasurer. The wholesale business of The George DeWald Company had its inception in 1900, and the trade of the house, represented by eight traveling salesmen, now extends over a broad territory in Indiana, Ohio and Michigan. Mr. DeWald has not only been one of the prime factors in the upbuilding of this substantial and important commercial enterprise in his native city, but has also given capitalistic and executive co-operation in the upbuilding of other representative business institutions of Fort Wayne. He is vice-president and a member of the executive board of the People's Trust & Savings Company, is a director of the German American National Bank and the German American Trust Company, and is a member of the directorate of the Fort Wayne Morris Plan Bank, the Wayne Oil Tank and Pump Company and the Commercial Investment Company. He is an active and valued member of the Fort Wayne Commercial Club and the Rotary Club, besides being affiliated with the local Country Club. In politics Mr. DeWald gives his allegiance to the Democratic party and both he and his wife are communicants of Catholic Cathedral. On June 25, 1889, was solemnized the marriage of Mr. DeWald to Miss Mollie Henebery, a daughter of Matthew and Mary Henebery, her father being a prominent merchant and banker at Peoria, Illinois. Mr. and Mrs. DeWald have no children.

Daniel W. DeWitt, long a resident of Lafayette township and one of the well established men of the community, was born in Delaware county, Indiana, July 28, 1833. He is a son of Daniel and Rebecca (Thornburg) DeWitt, who came to Indiana from Mercer county, Kentucky, and were farmers all their lives, practically. The elder DeWitt was a soldier in the War of 1812. In 1848 he came to Allen county, bought land and settled down to the unromantic business of founding a home in the wilds of what later came to be Lafayette township. He was an old-time Whig and later a Republican, and through all his life was a substantial factor in the development of those communities with which he found himself identified. To him and his wife were born a family numbering sixteen sons and daughters. Daniel DeWitt was reared in Huntington and Delaware counties and had his education in the schools of the communities wherein he had his residence. The schools were of the primitive type, peculiar to the day, and educations derived within them were meagre indeed. The boy grew up with a thorough working knowledge of farming and was twenty-eight years old when he left the shelter of the family roof tree and turned his attention to independent farming. His first purchase was a tract of fourteen acres, which formed the nucleus of his present comfortable place. There was not an acre of cleared land on it, and he began his private career with as little of material resources as a farmer boy ever set out with, it is safe to say. His first cabin home, built in 1860, had no windows, and they lived in it for some time before a door was hung. But with the passing years Mr. DeWitt achieved real independence and is today one of the most successful men of his township. He was married on February 10, 1860, to Mary Jaxe Hackett, and she bore one son, Don W., who is at present running the home farm, and who is married and the father of three children—Audra Irene, Frances

Justine, and Ruth Elizabeth. Mrs. DeWitt died at a comparatively early age and on December 1, 1886, Mr. DeWitt married Belinda Dennis, daughter of David Dennis, concerning whose family extended mention will be found in other pages. Mr. DeWitt and his son are Republican in politics, and both are leaders in their community. The father has been a member of the Independent Order of Odd Fellows since 1872, and his son is also a member of that fraternal organization.

Harry E. Dial.—"The Farm Man" needs no introduction to Allen county people, for in his capacity as dealer in farm lands, Harry E. Dial has made the acquaintance of practically the entire community. His operations extend through Indiana, Michigan and Ohio, and while he has not confined his real estate activities alone to the sale of farm properties, he specializes in that particular field, and is known as "The Farm Man" to a large and ever-growing clientele. Mr. Dial is a firm believer in the efficiency of printer's ink, and is prepared to vouch for the truth of the well-known saying, "It Pays to Advertise." He was always more or less interested in farms and farming, and his first independent venture was as a farmer. He abandoned his first enterprise for railroad work, but later returned to agricultural life, and continued in it until he came to Fort Wayne in 1912. In that year he established a real estate business in the city, and he has enjoyed a gratifying measure of success in his work. Mr. Dial is a family man, and his marriage to Miss Marion Herr took place in 1894. They have three children—Duayne, Harry, Jr., and Sulvia.

William A. Diffenderfer has been a resident of Allen county since he was a lad of seven years and through his own ability and well directed endeavors has become a prominent figure in connection with the more important business interests of Fort Wayne, where he is now treasurer of the Mossman & Yarnelle Company, a prominent concern here engaged as jobbers in carriages and wagon materials and auto accessories, and where he is also secretary and treasurer of the Wayne Spoke & Bending Company, another of the important industrial corporations of the Allen county metropolis. Mr. Diffenderfer was born at Mount Sterling, Van Buren county, Iowa, on October 25, 1857, and in the schools of the Keystone state he gained his rudimentary education, his parents having been numbered among the pioneers of Van Buren county, Iowa. He is a son of Benjamin O. and Isabella (Alcorn) Diffenderfer, his father, a native of Pennsylvania and a machinist by trade, having gone to Iowa in the pioneer days, returning to Pennsylvania in 1858, and having there remained until 1865, when he came with his family to Allen county, where he and his wife passed the residue of their lives and where he was long employed at his trade in the Fort Wayne shops of the Pennsylvania Railroad. He was a sterling citizen who had inviolable place in popular confidence and good will and both he and his wife were zealous members of the Third Presbyterian church of Fort Wayne, in which he held official position for fully a quarter of a century. Of the two children the subject of this sketch is the elder, and Mary is the wife of James B. Stewart, of Coffeyville, Kansas. As previously intimated, William Diffenderfer was about seven years old at the time of the family removal to Fort Wayne, and here he continued his studies in the public schools until he had completed the curriculum of the high school, in which he was graduated as a member of the class of 1876. Thereafter he proved the basic value of his cholarship by serving a short period as a representative of the pedagogic profession, he having achieved successful work as a teacher in the district schools of Monroe township. Thereafter he devoted three years to the study of law, in the office of the late Judge Colerick, of Fort Wayne, and in 1879 took a position of clerical and executive order in the office of Coombs & Company, engaged in the heavy hardware business in Fort Wayne. This alliance continued a short time when he became associated with the Mossman & Yarnelle Company, with which he has since continued his connection and in which he has become a prominent stockholder. He has aided materially in the furtherance of the company's business and has been treasurer of this well known and representative corporation since 1908. Though he has had no ambition for political preferment Mr. Diffenderfer gives loyal allegiance to the Democratic party and he takes lively interest in public affairs, especially those of his home city and county. In the Masonic fraternity he has received the thirty-second degree of the Ancient Accepted Scottish Rite. Both he and his wife are members of the Third Presbyterian church. In November, 1895, Mr. Diffenderfer wedded Miss Blanche Davis, and she passed to the life eternal September 20, 1897, the one surviving child of this union being Davis A., who is attending the University of Michigan. On November 10, 1909, was solemnized the marriage of Mr. Diffenderfer to Mrs. Harriet M. Riblet, of Fort Wayne. No children have been born to the second marriage.

J. Frank Dinnen, M. D., is established in the successful practice of his profession in his native city of Fort Wayne and is giving special attention to the surgical branch of his profession. Bringing to bear the results of thorough technical training as well as resolute purpose and perhaps inherited predilection, he has gained assured place as one of the able and representative physicians and surgeons of the younger generation in Allen county, his father having long been one of the leading medical practitioners in Fort Wayne. Dr. James Frank Dinnen was born in Fort Wayne on October 25, 1884, a son of Dr. James M. and Catherine (Flemming) Dinnen. Dr. James Dinnen was born in Clermont county, Ohio, and was fourteen months old at the time of his parents' removal to the city of Chicago, where he was reared and educated and his professional education was acquired in the celebrated Rush Medical College, from which he received his degree of Doctor of Medicine. He has been engaged in the practice of his profession in Fort Wayne for many years, is known as one of the most skillful surgeons in northern Indiana and in late years has concentrated his energies largely in the surgical department of professional service. His wife is a representative of one of the honored and influential pioneer families of Allen county, and her father, the late William Flemming, was at one time very prominent in connection with political and general civic affairs in the county, as well as a figure of influence as a capitalist and financier Dr. Dinnen of this review is the youngest in a family of nine children, and the eldest of the number is William, who is now a representative member of the bar of South Bend, this state; Helen remains at the parental home; the next younger daughter is Sister Mary Adele, of the Order of the Sacred Heart; Josephine remains with her parents in Fort Wayne; John Richard is a civil engineer in the service of the Nickel Plate Railroad; and George, Robert and Charles all reside in Fort Wayne. Dr. J. Frank Dinnen acquired his early education in the parochial and public schools and thereafter attended in turn the great Notre Dame University, at South Bend, and the University of Indiana, at Bloomington. In the city of Chicago he completed a course in the medical department of the University of Illinois, in which he was graduated with the degree of Doctor of Medicine. Thereafter he gained valuable clinical experience through two years of service as an interne in St. Elizabeth Hospital, in Chicago, and since September 1, 1909, has been engaged in the practice of his profession at Fort Wayne. The Doctor is serving as a member of the staff of surgeons of the Nickel Plate, the Lake Shore & Michigan Southern, and the Lake Erie & Western Railroads, as well as being retained in similar capacity by all of the traction lines entering or centered in Fort Wayne. He is affiliated with the American Medical Association, the Indiana State Medical Society, the Allen County Medical Society and the American Association of Railway Surgeons. His religious faith is that of the Catholic church.

Frank J. Dix has not been denied the rewards that should attend effective service and distinct technical and executive ability, for he has won advancement to the responsible office of general superintendent of the City Light & Power Company of Fort Wayne, of which position he has been the valued incumbent since July 1, 1908. Mr. Dix claims Fort Wayne as the place of his nativity, his birth having here occurred on October 4, 1866. He is a son of Seth and Esther (Bolger) Dix, who are now venerable and highly honored citizens of this place. Seth Dix was born at Elyria, Ohio, and was a lad of nine years at the time of the family removal to Fort Wayne, where he was reared to adult age and where he gained his education in the public schools of what may be termed the middle pioneer epoch in the history of the metropolis of Allen county. He eventually established a livery and transfer business in the city, and he conducted one of the pioneer hack lines of Fort Wayne, his association with this enterprise having continued for more than a quarter of a century. He has long been a stalwart in the local ranks of the Democratic party and he and his wife are earnest communicants of the Fort Wayne cathedral parish of the Catholic church. Frank J. Dix had the fortuitous influences of the Catholic parochial schools of Fort Wayne in the acquiring of his early educational training, and as a young man he found employment as a locomtive fireman on the New York, Chicago & St. Louis Railroad, commonly known as the Nickel Plate Railroad. After being thus engaged about one year he entered the service of the Jenney Electric Light & Power Company of Fort Wayne, in the employ of which he continued from 1889 to 1908 In the latter year he became chief electrician for the City Light & Power Company, and his ability eventually led to his being appointed general superintendent of this company, as has been previously noted. He has been circumspect and progressive in keeping this public-utility service up to the best modern standard and is one of the well-known and highly esteemed business men of his native city. In neither religion nor politics has he swerved from the faith in which he was reared, and thus he is found aligned as a staunch supporter of the cause of the Democratic party, the while both he and his wife are communicants of the Catholic church. He is a member of the National Association of Municipal Electricians and the Rejuvenated Sons of Jove, is actively identified with the Fort Wayne Commercial Club, and is affiliated with the Benevolent and Protective Order of Elks. On February 8, 1893, was solemnized the marriage of Mr. Dix to Miss Lulu Myer, daughter of Charles F. Myer, of Fort Wayne, and the two children of this union are Martha E. and Dorothy E., both of whom remain at the parental home.

Henry G. Doctor.—The family of which Henry G. Doctor is a representative in Marion township is one of the old established ones of the county, noted for its numbers quite as much as for its stability of character and general good citizenship. Mr. Doctor stands prominently among the retired men of his community, and after many years of strenuous endeavor in the pursuit of agriculture is now to be found living quietly amid the comforts won by his years of earnest effort. He has won the unqualified respect and confidence of his fellows and has not only enjoyed a long life of seventy years, but has made his years count for service to himself, his family and his community. Mr. Doctor was born January 28, 1847, in Marion township, son of Charles and Louisa (Coleman) Doctor. The father came from Germany in young life, in company with his parents, who for a time resided in Pennsylvania. Later they removed to Indiana, making the journey with a one-horse wagon. This wagon carried the camp outfit and the women and children of the little party, and the men walked the entire distance. Roads were bad, and in many places the women dismounted and shared the road with the men folks. The journey was a long and difficult one, fraught with the manifold dangers that beset the path of the overland voyager of the day, but they came through safely and settled in Allen county. The men first found employment in a brick yard, but later Charles Doctor entered land from the government, and at the time of his death, in 1856, was the owner of one hundred and twenty acres of good farm land. To him and his wife were born six children: Margaret, Nathan, Henry G., Mary, William A., and Ellen. Henry G. Doctor was educated in the public schools of Marion township and spent his boyhood and young manhood on the home farm. He was still but a lad, eight years old, when his father died and he early learned to share the burdens that fell upon his mother's shoulders with the death of the head of the family. The old homestead has been his home practically all his life. After the death of his mother, in 1863, he bought the interests of the other heirs to the place and has since retained possession of it. He later purchased the old Nathan Coleman place, and lived on it for a number of years, but subsequently removed to the former home and resided there until he moved to Fort Wayne, in 1900, where he now lives. He has prospered well in his years of devotion to agriculture and is at this time the owner of 570 acres of land in Allen county and 304 acres in Paulding county, Ohio. He also owns a fine home in Fort Wayne, where he lives. Mr. Doctor is a Republican in politics and a member of the German Lutheran church. He was married, December 26, 1865, to Miss Catherine Leydolph, daughter of Fred and Anna Leydolph, and they became the parents of eight children. Charles F. is deceased; Henry J. lives in Marion township. Elizabeth is the wife of William M. Brown, of Adams township. Allen is a farmer in Paulding county, Ohio. Mary married Fred Adam and they live in Adams township, Allen county. Lewis also lives in Adams township. Anna is married to August Bearman, of Marion township. Lucy is the wife of Henry Koehlinger, also of Marion township. Twenty-nine grandchildren have been added to the family in more recent years. Charles F. had a goodly family of eight. They are Rosa, who is the wife of Frank Rice and the mother of a daughter and a son; Henry, Martha (wife of Victor Worm), Walter (deceased), Emma, May, Freda and Paul. Henry Doctor has five children, named Arthur, Della, Elmer, Hulda and Elsie. Elizabeth's three are Melly, married to Ed Berman; Etta and Arthur. Allen has a son, Albert. Lewis has six sons—Arthur, Herbert, Willard, Irwin, Clarence and Walter. Anna is the mother of Elmer, Vera and Mildred, while Lucy has Velma, Paul and Berenice. These are fine young people of much promise, and Mr. and Mrs. Doctor may well be proud of the record of their lives when they contemplate the coming representatives of the name.

Edward W. Dodez, D. D. S., is not only an able exponent of the profession that represents both a science and a mechanic art, but is also one who has made a valuable contribution to the dental profession as a manufacturer of dental remedies and specialties, including his widely-used "Oxpara," which has met with most favorable and well-merited reception and utilization on the part of the members of the profession all over the globe, and it is worthy of special note that it is used in the hospitals in the great war zone of Europe. The doctor has now virtually retired from the active practice of his profession, and is giving his exclusive attention to his well-established and cumulatively successful manufacturing enterprise, with well-equipped establishment at No. 1425 West Main street, in his native city of Fort Wayne. Dr. Edward Wright Dodez was born in Fort Wayne on March 11, 1875, a son of Gustave C. and Helen (Ketterer) Dodez. He attended the public schools of Fort Wayne and also the Westminster Seminary for a time, and in preparation for his chosen profession, entered the college of dentistry of the University of Illinois, this department being located in the city of Chicago. From this school he was graduated as a member of the class of 1899, with the degree of Doctor of Dental Surgery. In the following year he engaged in the practice of his profession in Fort Wayne, and, by his ability, effective service and personal popularity, he built up a large and representative practice, the same continuing to engross his time and attention for about seven years, at the expiration of which time he retired from the active work of his profession to give his supervision to the manufacture of dental remedies and specialties—a line of enterprise in which his success is of a high order. The doctor is an active member of the Commercial Club of Fort Wayne. He is zealous in the support of its high ideals and the progressive policies of the organization, and is serving as a member of its directorate, besides which he is a charter member and one of the organizers of the Fort Wayne Rotary Club. He is a prominent member of the Masonic fraternity. January 24, 1900, recorded the marriage of Dr. Dodez to Miss Lilla May Cramer, daughter of Jeremiah and Josephine (Harlow) Cramer, of Fairbury, Illinois, and of this union have been born four children, all of whom are living except the youngest, Lilla May, who died in infancy. The cheery home circle includes the other children—Edward, Josephine and Helen, the daughters being twins. Westover, the beautiful suburban home of Dr. Dodez, on the Leesburg road, is one of the most attractive places in this vicinity.

Henry J. Doswell, the able and honored superintendent of beautiful Lindenwood Cemetery at Fort Wayne, succeeded his father in this office, in which he has admirably upheld the prestige of the name which he bears, with technical ability and artistic talent that mark him as one of the representative landscape gardeners of his native state. It is a matter of historical interest to record that from the time Lindenwood Cemetery was platted it has been consecutively maintained under the supervision of the Doswells, the father of the present superintendent having assumed charge in 1859 and the beautiful "God's Acre" having been developed and improved under his able management and direction. When he passed to the life eternal, in 1900, he was succeeded by his son, Henry J., and the latter has given equally loyal, earnest and effective service, with the result that Lindenwood is consistently to be designated as one of the most beautiful cemeteries in the state of Indiana. Mr. Doswell was born in Fort Wayne on December 23, 1864, and is a son of John H. and Catherine J. (Humphries) Doswell, both natives of England, where they were reared and educated, the father having been born in the city of London, November 3, 1827, and the mother in Gloucestershire, in April, 1825. In his youth John H. Doswell served a thorough apperticeship under the direction of an able and successful florist in his native land, and he so extended his experience as to gain distinctive ability as a landscape gardener and architect. For a time he was in the employ of W. D. Page, of Southampton, and thereafter he was retained four years as an assistant in the fine gardens of the Earl of Radnor, near Salisbury, in Wiltshire. Upon his retirement from this position he had the distinction and valuable privilege of being employed in the Royal Botanical Gardens at Kew, and later he was head gardener on the estate of Sir William Medlican, at Venhall, Somersetshire. In September, 1852, he immigrated to the United States, and he passed the first winter in Cincinnati, Ohio, where he had charge of the greenhouse of the late William Resor. From the Buckeye state he finally went to Wisconsin, where he purchased a farm and, as a pioneer of that commonwealth, turned his attention to agricultural pursuits. In the autumn of 1859 he returned to Cincinnati, and in the following December came to Fort Wayne to assume charge of the newly established Lindenwood Cemetery, of which he became the first superintendent and landscape architect, the basic design and original beautifying of the cemetery having been perfected under his able direction and his earnest devotion and enthusiastic energy having been the principal medium through which the beautiful cemetery was developed to its present status. He loved his work and his stewardship was in consonance with his sincere and upright character and his appreciation of the sentimental value of his gracious endeavors. In addition to his work at Lindenwood he had charge also, in the summer of 1888, of laying out and initiating the improvement of all of the city park plats of Fort Wayne, and, all in all, the tangible results of his labors during the long years of residence in Fort Wayne constitute a most consistent and enduring monument to the memory of this sterling and honored citizen. The gentle and devoted wife of Mr. Doswell was summoned to eternal rest in July, 1902, both having been devoted communicants of the Protestant Episcopal church. Of their ten children seven are living, in 1917. Henry J. Doswell is indebted to the public schools of Fort Wayne for his early educational discipline, which was here supplemented by a course of study in the old Methodist College. He was signally favored in his youth in being permitted to perfect himself in landscape work under the able and punctilious direction of his father. He was given most careful training, showed a natural predilection for the work and finds satisfaction and pride in the fact that he was chosen the successor of his honored father as superintendent of Lindenwood Cemetery, he having been assistant to his father at the cemetery until the death of the latter, in 1900. Mr. Doswell has not limited his civic loyalty to his service in the line of his profession but takes deep interest in all things pertaining to the welfare and advancement of his native city. He planned the landscape for Lakeside Park. His political allegiance is given to the Republican party. In Masonry he has received the thirty-second degree in the Ancient Accepted Scottish Rite of the Masonic fraternity, his York Rite affiliation being with Fort Wayne Commandery of Knights Templars, and he is identified also with the Independent Order of Odd Fellows and the Modern Woodmen of America. On September 3, 1890, was solemnized the marriage of Mr. Doswell to Miss Mary E. Taylor, who likewise was born and reared in Fort Wayne and who is a daughter of William C. and Mahala (Sudro) Taylor, the father being now a resident of California and the mother being deceased. Mr. and Mrs. Doswell have two children: Harold H. is successfully engaged in the manufacturing of cement burial caskets, in Fort Wayne, and Helen S. is the wife of Arthur E. Kover, of this city.

Wallace E. Doud has in recent years been one of the most prominent and influential figures in connection with the well-ordered physical and civic development and upbuilding of Fort Wayne, and specially important and valuable have been his real estate operations in the platting and exploiting of new additions and subdivisions that have inured greatly to the metropolitan advancement of the chief city of Allen county. Mr. Doud was born on a farm in Defiance county, Ohio, October 25, 1858, and is a son of Linas P. and Clarinda A. (Barden) Doud. His father was born on the shores of beautiful Lake Champlain, in the state of Vermont, and was a scion of a sterling family that was founded in New England in the colonial era. He established his home in Defiance county, Ohio, about the year 1840, and after having been identified with the mercantile business at Defiance about one year he purchased a farm about twelve miles northwest of the county seat, near the present village of Ney. He developed one of the fine farms of the county and was one of the leading citizens of his commnity, his death having occurred on his old homestead, in 1872, and his wife having survived him by nearly thirty years. Of their children, only three are now living: Frank E. and Mildred being still residents of the old Buckeye state and the subject of this review being thus the only representative of the immediate family in Indiana. Wallace E. Doud was reared to the benignant and sturdy discipline of the farm and continued to attend school in his native county until he was sixteen years of age, when he proved himself eligible for pedagogic honors and began teaching in the district schools. Later he fortified himself more fully by a course in a normal college that was then established at Bryan, Ohio, and he continued his effective services as a teacher in the public schools until he had attained to the age of twenty-five years. He then became a representative of the Union Central Life Insurance Company, of Cincinnati, in the service of which he continued until 1894, when he resigned his position and came to Fort Wayne. Here he established an office in the Old National Bank building and engaged, with characteristic vigor and resourcefulness, in the real estate business, of which he has become one of the most influential and successful representatives in Allen county. He retained his original office headquarters until the erection of the modern Shoaff building, when he removed to his present well appointed offices in this fine structure. More than a decade ago Mr. Doud began to specialize in the platting and placing on the market of well defined additions to the city of Fort Wayne, and it is in this field that his greatest achievement has been made. He has sold thousands of lots and his transactions have aggregated millions of dollars, so that it may readily be seen that he has contributed greatly to the development and progress of his home city, while scrupulous integrity has marked his every transaction. Among the more recent additions that have been ably exploited and developed under the direction of Mr. Doud may be noted Pfeiffer Place, comprising nearly six hundred lots; Pontiac Place, with more than five hundred lots, and Calhoun Place, with more than one hundred lots. Mr. Doud was prominently concerned in the organization and incorporation of the City & Suburban Realty Company, the original capital stock of which was ten thousand dollars. The title of the corporation was later changed to the present form, the City & Suburban Building Company, and it now has a capital stock of one hundred and sixty thousand dollars, the while it is undoubtedly doing the leading building business of the city and its environs. Mr. Doud has held the dual office of treasurer and sales manager of this company from the time of its incorporation, and its offices are just across the corridor from the private office in which he conducts his individual real estate business. In the fall of 1916, Mr. Doud became one of the organizers of the Enterprise Building Company. This organization specializes in the erecting of homes which sell at a moderate price. A broad-guaged and progressive citizen, Mr. Doud is aligned as a staunch supporter of the cause of the Republican party, though he has had neither time nor inclination for public office, and he holds membership in the Fort Wayne Commercial Club, of the fine civic and commercial policies of which he is a loyal supporter. He is a director of the Fort Wayne Country Club, is affiliated with the local lodge of the Benevolent and Protective Order of Elks, and has completed the circle of both York and Scottish Rite Masonry up to and including the reception of the thirty-second degree in the latter, besides being affiliated also with the Ancient Arabic Order, Nobles of the Mystic Shrine. He and his wife are zealous members of the Wayne Street Methodist Episcopal church, and he is serving as president of its board of trustees. July 6, 1884, recorded the marriage of Mr. Doud to Miss Fannie J. Van Meter, daughter of Perry H. Van Meter, of Sherwood, Defiance county, Ohio, further reference to the family being made on other pages, in the sketch of the career of her brother, Homer L. Van Meter, of Fort Wayne. Like her husband, Mrs. Doud was formerly a successful and popular teacher, and she was an assistant in the school of which he was superintendent at the time of their marriage. Mr. and Mrs. Doud have two children—Olive A., who is the wife of Raymond W. Ellis, a stock broker at Wilmington, Delaware, and Ethel I., who remains at the parental home.

Frank Doughman—One of the prosperous farming men of Roanoke, who have added their full quota to the agricultural development of that community is Frank Doughman, born in Aboite township, Allen county, on February 17, 1869, and the son of Abraham and Sarah (Henderson) Doughman. The father was a Pennsylvanian by birth and he came to Allen county in his young manhood, in partnership with a twin brother, David D. Doughman, who had accompanied him to the west from their Pennsylvania home. They became the owners of a farm of 147 acres in Aboite township and were prosperous and prominent farming men there for many years. Abraham Doughman was a blacksmith by trade and gave some attention to that work throughout his lifetime. They retired from active life in their later years and were living quietly in the enjoyment of earlier labors at the time when death claimed them. The brothers were Democrats and were lifelong members of the Methodist

Episcopal church. Abraham and Sarah Doughman became the parents of five children. William, the first born, died in childhood. Newton passed away at the age of forty-nine, his death coming very suddenly. Louisa is the wife of William Clark of Aboite township. Clara married John Flaugh and lives in Jefferson township, Whitley county, Indiana. Frank, the youngest, is the subject of this sketch. He was educated in the public schools of his native community and divided his time between his books and the more practical education incident to life on a farm. He had a commendable training in agriculture and when he left home and branched out for himself he rented a farm and applied himself to the task of accumulating sufficient to enable him to become a landowner. Later he bought his present homestead of eighty acres and there he has lived in the successful management of the place. Progressive methods have marked his activities, and he has one of the fine places of the township. Mr. Doughman married on March 5, 1891, Miss Laurina Jane Stoles becoming his wife. She is the daughter of Jacob and Anna (Reindfuse) Stoles, the family having come from Ohio. Mr. Stoles was a native of Bedford county, Pennsylvania, and he settled with his parents in Ohio at the age of eight years, in 1848. He was a shoe-maker by trade, and in his young life taught school for some years. He turned his attention to farming after coming to Indiana and became quite successful in his work in that department of industry. Mr. Stoles was a Civil war veteran, serving three years as a member of Company F, One Hundredth Regiment of Infantry of Ohio, and was a sergeant of his company most of the time. While still a resident of Ohio Mr. Stoles spent some years in the railway service, first as a locomotive fireman and then as engineer. He had one serious collision near Toledo, from which his health suffered to such an extent that he gave up the work and retired to Fort Wayne, where he bought a small farm and passed the remainder of his life on it. Mrs. Stoles still lives on the farm in the vicinity of Fort Wayne. They were the parents of four children. Laurine Jane is the wife of the subject. Clara May lives in Iowa. Frederick W. is principal of the high school at Alexander. Albert Edward is a practicing physician in Fort Wayne. To Mr. and Mrs. Doughman were born four children. Albert, the eldest, lives in Chicago. Anna, Newton and Agnes are still at home with the parents. Mr. Doughman and his family have membership in the Methodist Episcopal church. He is a Democrat in politics and his fraternal relations are confined to membership in the Modern Woodmen of America at Roanoke.

D. Burns Douglass is now numbered among the representative younger members of the Fort Wayne bar and has been established in the general practice of his profession in his native city since the winter of 1905. His ability has been shown in results achieved as a resourceful trial lawyer and well fortified counselor, and his advancement in his profession has been based upon hard work and close application, the while he has shown deep appreciation of and has insistently observed the unwritten code of ethics by which the dignity and distinction of his chosen calling have been upheld. Mr. Douglass was born in Fort Wayne November 24, 1879, and is a son of William B. and Hannah (Clark) Douglass. His father, who was born and reared in New Hampshire, a scion of sterling colonial ancestry, came to Fort Wayne in 1863 and for many years thereafter served as a conductor on the Pennsylvania Railroad lines. He was one of the oldest passenger-train conductors in the service of the company at the time when he retired, and he and his wife are now deceased. Of the three children William V. and Curtis C. are deceased, and thus the subject of this review is the only survivor. D. Burns Douglass continued his studies in the public schools of Fort Wayne until he had completed the curriculum of the high school, and he then went to his father's native state and entered historic old Dartmouth College, in which he was graduated as a member of the class of 1903 and from which he received the degree of Bachelor of Letters. He also pursued a course in the law department of the institution. He took lively interest in the athletic affairs of his alma mater while an undergraduate, and this gave him special facility and judgment when he assumed the position of sporting editor of the Fort Wayne Journal-Gazette, his service in this capacity having covered the season of 1904. In December of 1905 Mr. Douglass was admitted to the bar of his native state, and he has since been actively engaged in the practice of law in Fort Wayne, where he has built up a substantial and representative law business. He is an active member of the Allen County Bar Association and has the confidence and good will of his professional confreres, who are appreciative of the ability which has enabled him to win success in his exacting vocation. In politics Mr. Douglass is a staunch advocate of the principles of the Republican party, and he and his wife are active members of Plymouth Congregational church. In the Masonic fraternity he has received the thirty-second degree of the Ancient Accepted Scottish Rite and now, 1917, is Worshipful Master of Home Lodge Number 342, F. and A. M. He is affiliated also with the Knights of Pythias, besides which he holds membership in the Fort Wayne Commercial Club and the Fortnightly Club. On July 19, 1911, was solemnized the marriage of Mr. Douglass to Miss Marian L. Bridgman, of Northampton, Massachusetts, their acquaintance-ship having been formed while he was a student at Dartmouth College. The two children of this union are William Burns and Robert Bridgman. Mrs. Douglass was born and reared in the old Bay state and is representative of old and distinguished colonial families in New England, that gracious cradle of much of our national history. She is a daughter of Dwight S. and Mary (Lyons) Bridgman, who still restide in their native state of Massachusetts, the mother being a direct descendent of the distinguished Rev. Jonathan Edwards, the historic figure in New England colonial annals, and also of Mary Lyons, who was the founder of Mount Holyoke College, in Massachusetts.

Thomas C. Dowling.—A successful business man prior to his appointment to his present position as postmaster at New Haven, Thomas C. Dowling brought to his duties as a government official an experience that fitted him admirably for the successful administration of the office. He is a native son of New Haven, born there on November 16, 1879, and his parents were Bartholomew and Mary (Moriarty) Dowling. The father was born in county Kerry, Ireland, and the mother was of New Jersey birth. Bartholomew Dowling came to America as a lad of seven years in the year 1849. With his parents he located in Sidney, Ohio, and there had his education in the parochial schools of that community. He was nineteen years old when the Civil war broke out and he promptly enlisted for the three months' period the government asked for the defense of the nation. He began his service on April 27, 1861, as a member of the One Hundred and Twentieth Ohio Infantry, and after a service of one hundred days returned to Sidney and applied himself to work as a tinsmith. After seven years of attention to the work in Sidney he went to Fort Wayne, Indiana, and secured employment with the

Pennsylvania Railroad, and in 1869 came to New Haven, engaging in the hardware and tinning business. He was identified contiuously with the business he then established to the end of his life and the business is still carried on under the same name by his son, James Dowling. Mr. Dowling died on May 13, 1912, when he was seventy years of age. He was a Democrat in politics, a Roman Catholic, a member of the Knights of St. John, and a member of the Ancient Order of Hibernians at Fort Wayne. He was a good citizen, an honorable business man and one of the leaders in thought and action in his community. His passing was a loss to New Haven and he was mourned by all who knew him. His marriage to Miss Mary Moriarty took place on January 8, 1879, in Urbana, Ohio, where she was born and reared. They became the parents of six children. Thomas C., who is the immediate subject of this family review, was the first born. Mae is the wife of Dennis Daly of Fort Wayne. John is a resident of Fort Wayne. Bartholomew is deceased. James is in New Haven, in charge of the business the father left, and William was located in Detroit, but is now with Company E, Twelfth Battery, U. S. A. Thomas C. Dowling had his early schooling in the parochial school of St. John's church in New Haven, after which he attended the Brothers' School of Fort Wayne. His education finished, he secured employment in the offices of the Hibbard-Spencer-Bartlett Company of Chicago, where he spent five years, and gained a comprehensive working knowledge of the hardware business. He then returned to his native place and took charge of the Dowling Hardware Store, relieving his father of much of the responsibility of the place, though the elder gentleman continued the nominal head of the establishment as long as he lived. On March 9, 1915, Mr. Dowling was appointed to the office of postmaster and he quitted the hardware business, leaving his brother, James, in charge. He has since devoted himself exclusively to the duties of his office. Mr. Dowling, like his father, is a staunch Democrat, a member of St. John's Roman Catholic church of New Haven, a member of the Ancient Order of Hibernians, and he is also a member of the Catholic Order of Foresters, and the New Haven Commercial Club. He is one of the up-and-doing young men of the community and has a host of good friends in the town that he has always called home, while his acquaintance throughout the county is wide and varied.

Myron S. Downing.—The full measure of constructive service that justifies success was rendered by the late Myron Sexton Downing, who maintained his home in Allen county during virtually his entire life and who gained distinct prestige as one of the able and representative business men of Fort Wayne. In this city he was engaged in the wholesale baking business at the time of his death, which occurred June 10, 1913, and his character and achievement were such as to make most consistent the brief memorial tribute which it is possible to pay him in this publication. Mr. Downing was born at Sandusky, Ohio, in October, 1859, and was a child at the time when he came to Allen county, Indiana, with his parents, Jeremiah and Cynthia (Sexton) Downing, both of whom were born and reared in the old Buckeye state. Jeremiah Downing became one of the successful farmers of Allen county, and here both he and his wife passed the remainder of their lives, secure in the high esteem of all who knew them. The subject of this memoir was the only child and was accorded good educational advantages in his youth, including those of Heidelberg College, at Tiffin, Ohio. As a young man he proved a successful teacher in the public schools, but he did not long devote his attention to the pedagogic profession. He became identified with the retail clothing business in Fort Wayne, and later he became a traveling salesman for the wholesale cracker and candy house of Louis Fox, in which connection he continued his effective services for many years. He finally was appointed manager of the Fort Wayne plant of the National Biscuit Company, and later purchased the local plant and business, to the control and management of which he continued to give his attention, as a manufacturer and wholesale dealer in standard food products, until the close of his life, his energy, progressiveness and sterling character having made him the ideal business man and his high sense of personal stewardship having dominated his course in all of the relations of life. His political allegiance was given to the Republican party and he was well fortified in his opinions concerning governmental policies and public affairs in general, though he never manifested any desire for official preferment. He was affiliated prominently with the Masonic fraternity and the Benevolent & Protective Order of Elks, and was a valued member of the Fort Wayne Commercial Club. On December 18, 1895, was solemnized the marriage of Mr. Downing to Miss Lewella Donaldson, who was born at Goshen, the judicial center of Elkhart county, Indiana, and who is a daughter of William B. and Annie J. (Ferguson) Donaldson, the latter of whom is deceased and the former has the active management of the business formerly owned by the subject of this memoir. The parents of Mrs. Downing were born in Pennsylvania. No children were born to Mr. and Mrs. Downing and in her pleasant home Mrs. Downing is sustained and comforted by the companionship of her father, who is in charge of the business with which her husband was so actively identified at the time of his death.

Dr. L. Park Drayer.—Possibly the best introduction of a sketch of the life of Dr. L. P. Drayer is a quotation from the columns of the Fort Wayne Journal-Gazette of September 11, 1917, referring to his appointment as secretary of the board of health of the city of Fort Wayne. It says: "Dr. L. P. Drayer, one of the best known practitioners of Fort Wayne, yesterday was named secretary of the city health board by Mayor William J. Hosey, to succeed Dr. John H. Gilpin, now a captain in the Medical Officers' Reserve Corps at Fort Benjamin Harrison. The appointment was accepted by Dr. Drayer only on condition that the entire salary of the office, which is $125 monthly, be paid to Dr. Gilpin. The change is effective at once. Dr. Gilpin's resignation was made necessary because he expects to be absent for the duration of the war. The new secretary was the first health officer ever named in Fort Wayne. It was in 1895 that he was appointed by Mayor Chauncey B. Oakley, the first Republican executive for the city. During the next eight years, he serving two terms, Dr. Drayer organized the health system of the city and put it on the substantial and capable basis of today. He founded the first bacteriological laboratory, which also is the best in Northern Indiana. His work, from 1895 to 1903, put Fort Wayne on the map as a health center, and fruits of his efforts and foresight then have been apparent ever since in the workings of the health department. Although Dr. Drayer is a Republican, Mayor Hosey recognized his merits and the appointment ensued." The foregoing comment suggests not only the capabilities of Dr. Drayer but also the spirit of patriotism and true service which characterizes his activities. No one more than he has contributed to the welfare of the suffering and the needy, though the service has been so quietly performed that it is only when it appears in connection with some great public project like the playground movement or matters connected with the city health department that the people get a glimpse of the truth. Dr. Drayer was born in Hartford City, Indiana, May 4, 1870, son of Dr. Peter and Matilda (Oldfather) Drayer, the former deceased and the latter a resident of Fort Wayne. The childhood of Dr. L. Park Drayer was passed in his native town, where he attended the public schools before entering upon a course in Hanover College. Following this course of preparation, he came to Fort Wayne and became a student in the Fort Wayne Medical College, then one of the foremost institutions of the Middle West. This was in 1892. He remained here one year and then went to Chicago, where he took a course in the College of Physicians and Surgeons. Returning to Fort Wayne, he re-entered the Fort Wayne Medical College and graduated in 1895. By this time his acquaintanceship had grown to such proportions that he decided to locate here permanently. The wisdom of his choice is plainly shown in the marked success which has attended his years of professional duties. Dr. Drayer's position among the members of the profession is indicated by his membership in the county and state medical societies and in the American Medical Association. He is a member of the Central States Pediatric Society, and the American Society of Teachers of Pediatrics, and holds the position of professor of diseases of children in the University of Indiana. As stated in the foregoing quotation, he served as the city chemist and bacteriologist from 1895 to 1902. His activities are by no means confined to his professional field. As a member of the Commercial and of the Rotary Clubs, he has always displayed a keen interest in civic affairs. He is a member of the Fort Wayne Lodge of Elks. Dr. Drayer was married, October 9, 1895, at Madison, Indiana, to Miss Gertrude Greiner, a native of that city. Two children—Gertrude Hillis and L. Park, Jr.—have been born to this union. Dr. and Mrs. Drayer are affiliated with Trinity Episcopal church. The handsome family home is located at the junction of West Berry and Webster streets.

John Dreibelbiss was one who gave to the world distinct assurance of strong and worthy manhood, and his achievement was limited only by the confines that time and opportunity set for every individual person. He was a representative of one of the well known and sterling pioneer families of Allen county, became one of the prominent and successful business men of Fort Wayne and his admirable intellectual powers and business acumen enabled him to win success and to make for himself a place of special influence in connection with the abstract and real estate business in his native county, where he ever commanded unqualified popular confidence and good will, his death having occurred at his home in Fort Wayne on October 7, 1915, and a tribute to his memory being specially consistent as a contribution to this history. Mr. Dreibelbiss was born at Fort Wayne March 24, 1853, and was a son of John P. and Anna (Saurer) Dreibelbiss, the former of whom was born in Bavaria, Germany, November 28, 1829, and the latter in Switzerland, on April 24 of the same year, their marriage having been solemnized in Fort Wayne, and their children having been seven in number, namely: John, Christian G., Christina R., Conrad W., Mary L., Robert B., and Edward D. The honored father died December 31, 1886, and his widow survived him by a number of years. John P. Dreibelbiss was but three years old at the time of his parents' immigration from Bavaria to America, and the family

John Dirbelliss

became early settlers in Fort Wayne, which was then a mere straggling settlement surrounding the old fort which gave title to the fine little city of the present day. The journey from Buffalo, New York, to northern Indiana was made with wagon and ox team, and John P. Dreibelbiss contributed his quota to the development and progress of Allen county along both civic and material lines. He to whom this memoir is dedicated received the best educational advantages afforded in the common schools of Fort Wayne in the period of his childhood and youth, and his alert and receptive mind enabled him eventually to become a man of broad information and mature judgment. Energetic and self-reliant, the youth early turned his attention to work that would enable him to depend largely on his own resources, and for a time he was employed as a clerk in the grocery store of the late Mason Long. Later he was employed by J. B. White, who conducted what was known as the White Fruit Store, and after severing this connection he found employment in a wholesale tea establishment in the city of Chicago, where he remained until this house, together with the greater portion of the business district of the city, was swept away by the historic Chicago fire of 1871. Mr. Dreibelbiss then returned to Fort Wayne, and for some time thereafter gave his attention to farming and floriculture, in the immediate vicinity of the city. Later he resumed the occupation of clerk in a grocery, and in 1883 engaged in the upbuilding of a general abstract business, working out careful and authentic abstracts of title covering all realty in Allen county and making his records the authoritative data in this all important line. He completed the arduous and exacting task of copying from the county's deed, mortgage and court records all requisite data concerning the titles to real estate in every township of the county and then, on January 1, 1887, incorporated his business under the title of the Dreibelbiss Abstract of Title Company. His efforts caused the general public to come to a proper realization of the necessity of obtaining clear titles to property when the same was about to change owners, and the abstract business became an important adjunct of all real estate transactions in the county. Thus it was but natural that Mr. Dreibelbiss should, within a short time, expand the scope of his business to include the handling of real estate, the extending of financial loans upon real estate security and making these departments of his enterprise an important feature of his well ordered activities. He further showed progressive spirit and confidence in the continued growth of Fort Wayne by associating in a financial way with various manufacturing industries in his home city. John Dreibelbiss thus became one of the substantial and valued business men and influential citizens of Fort Wayne, and in his death the city lost an upright, loyal and valued citizen and resourceful and influential man of affairs. In connection with his business he became the author of an excellent little book, to which he gave the title, "Start Right," and in this he concisely and effectively defined the necessity for the authenticating of all titles to real estate, the publication, as placed in popular circulation, having had much influence in furthering the success of the abstract business that was founded by him. He never sought public office but was a staunch supporter of the cause of the Republican party. He attended the Christian Science church. In 1877 Mr. Dreibelbiss wedded Miss Kate M. Darrow, and after her death he contracted a second marriage, Miss Anna Fahlsing then becoming his wife and her home being still maintained in Fort Wayne.

William H. Dreier is one of the veteran and honored business men of Fort Wayne, where he has been identified with the retail drug trade for more than half a century and where, though he is now living virtually retired, he is still president of the well established drug business conducted under the corporate title of The Dreier Drug Company. Mr. Dreier has contributed a generous quota to the civic and material development and progress of the metropolis of Allen county and has long been known as one of the city's representative business men and unassumingly influential citizens, the while his is the further distinction of being a native of the Hoosier state and a scion of one of its honored pioneer families. William H. Dreier was born at Madison, the judicial center of Jefferson county, Indiana, in December, 1842, and is the only surviving member of a family of four children, in which he was the second in order of birth, the others having been Henry, Mary and Joseph. He is a son of Henry and Mary (Mitla) Dreier, both of whom were born in Germany. Upon coming to America Henry Dreier numbered himself among the pioneers of Jefferson county, Indiana, where he reclaimed and improved a farm and where he also conducted for a number of years one of the pioneer hotels in the now thriving little city of Madison, the county seat, both he and his wife having continued their residence in Jefferson county until their death and both having been earnest communicants of the Catholic church. William H. Dreier acquired his preliminary education in the Catholic parochial schools at Madison and supplemented this by higher academic studies in St. Mary's College at Lebanon, Kentucky. After leaving college he returned to his native town of Madison, and after having there been for several years employed as a clerk in a general store he came, about 1863, to Fort Wayne, in company with his brother Henry. They purchased the drug store of Caspar Schoer, and thereafter continued their partnership alliance until the death of Henry Dreier, in 1875. William H. then assumed full control of the prosperous enterprise, and under his effective management it was developed into one of the largest and most important of its kind in Allen county. This pioneer drug business is now conducted under corporate control, and though Mr. Dreier retired from active association with the business in 1911 he still continues president of the company and is a valued counselor in the directing of its policies. He has been one of the liberal and progressive citizens of Fort Wayne, is a stalwart advocate of the cause of the Democratic party but has never been imbued with ambition for political activity or public office. He and his wife are numbered among the most venerable and honored communicants of the Cathedral parish of the Catholic church in their home city, and he has long maintained affiliation with the Knights of Columbus. On November 11, 1875, was solemnized the marriage of Mr. Dreier to Miss Mary Corcoran, who was born and reared in Fort Wayne, where her parents, Patrick and Bridget (Bartley) Corcoran, natives of Ireland, established their residence in the pioneer days, when the present city was a mere village. Mr. Corcoran was here engaged in the grocery business for many years and here he and his wife passed the residue of their worthy and useful lives. Of their five children Mrs. Dreier is the eldest; Frances is the widow of Teles F. Gerow and still resides in Fort Wayne; Owen died in this city, and the next two children died in infancy. To Mr. and Mrs. Dreier were born four children: Loreto is the wife of Edward Gilmartin, Jr., of Fort Wayne; Frances remains at the parental home; Genevieve is deceased; and Mary Alma is the wife of Walter Hamilton, of Fort Wayne.

Charles Frederick Henry Dreyer was born in Germany, November 27, 1843, son of Philip and Engel (Brookmeirer) Dreyer, both of German birth and ancestry, who spent their lives in their native land. They were the parents of five children—Henry, Charles, Sophia, William and Getta. Henry, it should be stated here, served from 1861 to 1864 in the Union army during the Civil war and is now deceased. Getta, the youngest, is also deceased. Charles Dreyer had his education in his native land and came to America in 1870, arriving in Fort Wayne on October 24. He found employment in the blacksmith shop of the Pennsylvania Lines and was fifteen years in that work, coming to Washington township on May 8, 1885. He bought a small farm and devoted his energies to its cultivation. Success followed his efforts and he is today owner of 170 acres in this township. He has developed the land to a high state of productiveness and it is a modern and well kept place in every respect. Mr. Dreyer was married, September 18, 1873, to Miss Christina Salamon, daughter of Charles Salamon, of whom further mention is made on other pages of this publication. Eight children were born to them. William, born on June 18, 1874, died November 8, 1887. Charles was born November 30, 1876. The others are Lizzie, Emma, Anna, Amelia, Frederick and Marie. Mr. Dreyer was highway commissioner of his township for seventeen years and with his family has membership in St. Paul's Lutheran church in Fort Wayne.

Louis Dudenhoefer.—The record of the life of Louis Dudenhoefer is not more eventful to contemplate than is that of the average man of his station and occupation, but it is the achievements of such as he that has made of Allen county the rich and progressive section it is known to be at this time. Mr. Dudenhoefer was born on June 25, 1852, in Marion township, Allen county, and is the son of Philip and Anna (Riel) Dudenhoefer, who came direct from their homes in Germany to Allen county, and two years later settled in Marion township, where they spent the rest of their lives. They bought land, uncleared and unproven, and built a small cabin home in which to begin their independent career as farmers. Mr. Dudenhoefer was industrious and success followed his efforts so that in a short time he was able to add to his original twenty acres by a purchase of one hundred and twenty-three acres near by. In later life he acquired a good deal of town property and the declining years of his life were spent in Fort Wayne, where he died at the age of seventy. His widow survived to the age of eighty-two. They were of the German-Lutheran faith and their children were reared in the same religious belief. They were the parents of Philip, now a resident of Fort Wayne; Louis, the subject of this sketch; Margaret, who married Frank Braber of Fort Wayne, and Francis, who is deceased. Louis Dudenhoefer had his education in the Lutheran schools of his home community and was trained to farm life under the instruction of his father, whose assistant he was for years. When the elder Dudenhoefer retired the son rented the home place and continued as a renter for some years, but in 1904 he bought a farm, where he has since been successfully engaged in stock-farming. Like his father, he is a Democrat, active in local politics, and is a member of the German-Lutheran church. He was married on May 18, 1875, to Miss Lena Geischer, who came of German parents and was herself of German birth, her father having died on shipboard when the family was

148   BIOGRAPHICAL SKETCHES

making the journey from Germany to America. Mrs. Dudenhoefer died in December, 1912, the mother of twelve children. George and Frank are located in Fort Wayne, there engaged together in the grocery business. Henry died in 1913. Frederick and Louis are at home. Mary married Fred Lepper, of Marion township. Nettie is the wife of William Osterhause, also of Marion township. Anna lives in Fort Wayne. Bertha and Gertrude are still at home, while Matilda and Lena, the youngest of the family, are located in Fort Wayne.

Hermann A. Duemling, M. D., has brought to bear in the work of his profession the full powers of a strong and resourceful personality and also the technical ability and skill that have won for him secure vantage-ground as one of the essentially representative physicians and surgeons of Indiana. He is engaged in the active practice of his profession in the city of Fort Wayne, is chief of the staff of surgeons of the Lutheran Hospital, and is an acknowledged leader in the ranks of his profession in northern Indiana, besides being known also as a liberal and public-spirited citizen. Dr. Duemling was born at Addison, Dupage county, Illinois, on the 18th of September, 1871, and is a son of Professor Hermann F. and Jennie (Sulzer) Duemling, the former of whom was born in the historic old town of Magdeburg, Prussia, and the latter at Cedarville, Wisconsin, their marriage having been solemnized in the Badger state. In his native land Hermann F. Duemling received the best of educational advantages and that he was a man of high intellectual attainments is evidenced by the fact that he received the academic degree of Doctor of Philosophy. He came to the United States in 1867 and established his residence in the city of Milwaukee, Wisconsin, where he became an instructor in the city high school. A few years later, after his marriage, he removed to Addison, Illinois, where he was engaged as teacher of mathematics and science in the teachers' seminary. About 1873 he came with his family to Fort Wayne, where he became a valued member of the faculty of Concordia College, as a teacher of mathematics and natural science. Finally he returned to Milwaukee as the chief editor of the "Germania," in which capacity he served for the ensuing period of twelve years—or until the time of his death, which occurred March 13, 1913, his widow still maintaining her home in the Wisconsin metropolis, and being a devout communicant of the Lutheran church, as was also her revered husband. Professor Duemling entered fully into the spirit of American institutions and customs and was a loyal supporter of the principles of the Republican party, his sterling character giving him inviolable place in popular esteem. Of the children the eldest is Dr. Duemling, immediate subject of this review; Enno is the city missionary of Milwaukee; Paula is the widow of Albert C. Koch and she too is a resident of Milwaukee; Jennie is the wife of Dr. Richard Clausen, of that city; Thekla remains at the home of her mother; and Gerhard, a chemist by profession, likewise resides in Milwaukee. Dr. Duemling was a child of about two years at the time of the family removal to Fort Wayne, and here he acquired his rudimentary education in the parochial school of St. Paul's Lutheran church. In 1889 he was graduated in Concordia College, and in consonance with his well defined ambition he then began preparing himself for his chosen profession. He entered the medical department of Washington University, in the city of St. Louis, Missouri, and in the same was graduated in 1892, with the well earned degree of Doctor of Medicine. He has been an enthusiast in his profession and has

H A Duemling

insistently kept in line with the advances made in both medical and surgical science. In 1897 he did most effective post-graduate work in the city of Berlin, Germany, where he studied in and attended the clinics of the Friederich Wilhelm University, his attention having been given principally to an advanced course in surgery. The Doctor served his professional novitiate by establishing himself in practice in Fort Wayne in the year 1892, soon after his graduation, and for the first decade his practice was of general order. Since that time he has confined his service largely to the surgical branch of practice, and in this important field he has gained more than local prestige. High attainments and close and faithful application have constituted the basis of his unequivocal success and have been the source through which he has won high standing in the exacting and humane vocation to which he is devoting himself with all of earnest zeal and self-abnegation. He has been the head of the surgical staff of the Lutheran Hospital in Fort Wayne since 1905, has given most effective service as a member of the city board of health, and is affiliated with the Allen County Medical Society, the Fort Wayne Academy of Medicine, the Indiana State Medical Society, the Tri-State Medical Society, and the American Medical Association. His political allegiance is given to the Republican party and both he and his wife are active communicants of the parish of St. Paul's Lutheran church. On October 5, 1893, was solemnized the marriage of Dr. Duemling to Miss Adeline A. Stuermer, daughter of William and Augusta (Mauth) Stuermer, of Fort Wayne. Mr. Stuermer was born in Brandenburg, Prussia, learned in his native land the trade of cabinet maker, and in the late '60s came to the United States. Many years ago he established his home in Fort Wayne, where he was long employed at his trade in the shops of the Pennsylvania Railroad, his death having occurred May 23, 1892, and his widow being still a resident of Fort Wayne. Dr. and Mrs. Duemling have an interesting family of six children—Editha, Jennie, Werner, Miles, Arnold, and Gerhard. The year 1917 finds Editha, Jennie and Werner as students in the University of Michigan, and Miles in the Fort Wayne high school.

Frank R. Dulin.—The ability, character and achievement of Mr. Dulin have given him established vantage-ground as one of the leading lawyers of the younger generation in the city of Fort Wayne, where he has been engaged in the general practice of his profession since 1903. His standing in the community and as a member of the Allen county bar is assured and enviable, as shown by his having served five years as attorney for the juvenile court of Fort Wayne, under the regime of Judge Edward O'Rourke, and by his having been for four years deputy prosecuting attorney of Allen county, under the administration of Harry H. Hilgemann. Mr. Dulin was born in Boone county, Indiana, on November 6, 1880, and is a son of John A. and Mary A. (Carr) Dulin, the former of whom is now deceased and the latter maintains her home at Lebanon, Ind., the father having devoted the major part of his active career to the fundamental industries of agriculture and stock-growing. He whose name initiates this article was the fifth in order of birth in a family of seven children, all of whom are living. Frank R. Dulin found the period of his childhood and early youth compassed by the sturdy and benign influences of the home farm and he continued his studies in the public schools of his native county until he had availed himself of the advantages of the high school at Lebanon, the county seat. In preparation for his chosen profession he entered the Indiana Law School, at Indianapolis, and in this well ordered institution was graduated as a member of the class of 1902, his reception of the degree of Bachelor of Laws being virtually coincident with his admission to the bar of his native state. For the first year after his graduation he was serving his professional novitiate at Lebanon, judicial center of his native county, where he continued in practice until his removal to Fort Wayne, in 1903. Here he has built up a substantial general law business and gained definite prestige as a versatile and successful trial lawyer. He has appeared in connection with important litigations in the courts of this section of Indiana and the character, scope and cumulative tendency of his law business denotes the popular estimate placed upon him. Mr. Dulin is found arrayed as a loyal and effective advocate of the cause of the Democratic party, he and his wife hold membership in the Baptist church, he is a member of the Fort Wayne Commercial Club and the Country Club, and in the Masonic fraternity his maximum York Rite affiliation is with Fort Wayne Commandery of Knights Templar, besides which he has received the thirty-second degree of the Ancient Accepted Scottish Rite and is affiliated also with the Ancient Arabic Order of the Nobles of the Mystic Shrine. August 28, 1912, recorded the marriage of Mr. Dulin to Miss Della Hughbanks, who likewise was born and reared in Boone county, and who is a daughter of James A. and Luella (Nelson) Hughbanks, well known citizens of that county, where her father is a representative farmer. Mr. and Mrs. Dulin have two children—Frank R., II., and Myrtle.

Thomas Dunkel has been a resident of Allen county since 1904 and is the owner of a well improved farm of one hundred and eight acres, in Sections 14 and 23, Springfield township. Throughout his entire independent career he has been an energetic and successful exemplar of agricultural enterprise, and through the medium of the same has achieved definite prosperity, the while his course has been so ordered in all of the relations of life that he has proved a helpful factor in community affairs and has merited and received the confidence and good will of his fellow men. Mr. Dunkel was born in Pickaway county, Ohio, is the youngest son in a family of eight children, and all of his brothers and sisters still reside in the old home county of Pickaway, namely: Isaac, Malinda, Amos, Jr., Catherine, Laura A. and Amanda J. Mary, the third in order of birth, died in childhood. The parents—Amos and Catherine (Stout) Dunkel—passed their entire lives in Pickaway county, Ohio, the father having been a native of Pickaway township and the mother of Washington township, and they were representatives of sterling pioneer families of that section of the old Buckeye state. Amos Dunkel was a scion of staunch German ancestry and was one of the substantial farmers of his native county during his entire independent career. He whose name initiates this review was born on the old homestead farm of his parents, in Pickaway county, and, as previously intimated, is the only one of the family to have found a theater of successful enterprise outside of his native county, the date of his birth having been August 12, 1861. He is indebted to the common schools of his native county for his early educational discipline and in his youth gained close friendship with honest toil and endeavor, in connection with the work of the home farm. He thus gained at first hand his broad and diversified knowledge of agricultiural and live-stock industry, of which he continued a representative in his native county until January 1, 1904, when, after having disposed of his property in Ohio, he came to Allen county, Indiana, and purchased a farm of eighty acres, in Section 23, Springfield township. He has since bought an additional tract of twenty-eight acres, in Section 14, and is thus the owner of a well improved farm of model type—a demesne that gives every evidence of thrift and prosperity and that constitutes one of the many attractive rural estates of Allen county. His political allegiance is given to the Democratic party and he and his wife hold membership in the Lutheran church. In 1905 was solemnized the marriage of Mr. Dunkel to Miss Barbara Boger, who was born and reared in this county and who is a member of one of its old and honored families. She is a daughter of Samuel and Susanna (Baltz) Boger, who were children at the time when the respective families settled in Springfield township, about the year 1840, at which time the township could claim only six or eight families residing within its borders. The parents of Mrs. Dunkel continued their residence in this township until their death and the names of both merit place on the roster of the honored pioneers of the county. Mr. and Mrs. Dunkel have one child, Ruth.

Charles A. Dunkelberg.—The activities of Charles A. Dunkelberg have brought him into contact with "all sorts and conditions of men." From these he seems to have learned, while his own personality has inspired and taught, with the result that the absorption and cultivation of talents of wide range have not only made him a successful man of business and executive worth but one who counts his warm friends by the hundreds. Fort Wayne knows no home more truly hospitable than that of the Dunkelberg's on South Fairfield avenue. Mr. Dunkelberg was born in Chemung, New York, April 4, 1865, the son of Charles A. and Eliza (Lassen) Dunkelberg, both natives of Germany. At the age of two, Mr. Dunkelberg removed with his parents to the town of Honesdale, Pennsylvania, where the son at the age of twelve was employed for the period of a year in a drug store. After leaving the common schools, he entered Eastman Business College, at Poughkeepsie, New York, and graduated from that institution well equipped with the foundation for a successful business career. He was at this time an expert in stenography, and this accomplishment became a marked factor in his advancement in the business world, and he was one of the first stenographers in northeastern Pennsylvania. He also brought the first typewriter into that section of the state. He had already devoted his attention to a training course in business practice. His first employment, after leaving school, was with the banking and brokerage firm of E. C. Benedict and Company, in New York City, where, as a young man of ready perception and strong character, he was enabled to gain actual experience in the application of the theories gained from the schools. Afterward, he entered the employ of Joseph T. Ryerson and Son, iron merchants, at Chicago. Here he developed the talents which marked him as a man of notable executive ability, and this led to his selection as the steward of the State Hospital for the Insane, at Logansport, Indiana, a position which he filled with entire satisfaction for a period of five years, after which he chose to engage in business in Logansport. He established a wholesale and retail queensware store, and continued in this line for three years. During this period, Mr. Dunkelberg added materially to his knowledge of men and methods, which led to his coming to Fort Wayne to take an important position with S. F. Bowser and Company, world-famed makers of self-measuring oil handling devices. It was in July, 1899, that Mr. Dunkelberg accepted the place of head bookkeeper for the concern. Here his abilities were given full course, and his promotion to the office of superintendent of salesmen was followed by a later advancement to that of secretary and treasurer of the company. His work in these various positions was of untold value to the company at the time when such service figured strongly in the success of the plant and its management. On September 1, 1916, Mr. Dunkelberg resigned his position with S. F. Bowser and Company in order to give his entire time and attention to the management of his large modern dairy farm, located six miles south of Fort Wayne, in Pleasant township, Allen county. Mr. Dunkelberg was united in marriage on May 1, 1895, with Miss Anna C. Crockett, daughter of Franklin and Sarah (Murdock) Crockett, of Lafayette, Ind. To this union have been born four sons—Charles A., Ralph C., Paul C. and David C. Mr. Dunkelberg is a true sportsman. His fondness for hunting "big game" takes him frequently into the Canadian forests, and he has made several trips to Mexico and the southwest on similar quests, the success of which is attested by the collection of mounted specimens of the results of the hunt in the forest and on the plain. The travels of Mr. Dunkelberg have taken him to all portions of the United States and into many sections of Canada and Mexico, and several business trips have required his presence in the capitals of Europe. Mr. Dunkelberg is interested in many Fort Wayne financial and other institutions and his counsel as a member of governing boards has proven to be of the utmost value. His position in business circles of his home city is suggested by his election to the presidency of the Wayne club of Fort Wayne during the year it was united with the Commercial Club. He is active in Masonic circles where he holds the thirty-second degree in the Scottish Rite body, and also is a Knight Templar. He is a member of the Indiana Society of Chicago. Mr. Dunkelberg is a true optimist, and always he displays a delightful fellowship which has won for him countless real friends.

Washington Dunten.—It is now permitted to accord merited tribute to one of the native sons of Allen county who has passed the psalmist's span of three-score years and ten and who has been worthily and prominently identified with civic, industrial and business affairs in the county. He now resides on his attractive homestead farm, in Perry township, about ten miles distant from Huntertown, from which village he receives service on rural mail route No. 2. Mr. Dunten served twelve years as postmaster at Huntertown, from which office he retired in 1913, and for five years was engaged in the dry-goods business in that village. Though now living in virtual retirement, he takes much satisfaction in giving a general supervision to his farm, is favored in the splendid retention of his physical and mental powers and takes a lively interest in all things pertaining to the county which has ever been his home and in the development and progress of which he has played well his part. Mr. Dunten was born at Huntertown, January 26, 1841, at which time the now progressive village was a mere hamlet in the midst of a partially developed agricultural district. He is a son of Ephraim Howard and Pamelia (Hicks) Dunten, the former of whom was born in Jefferson county, New York, and the latter at Hartford, Connecticut, their marriage having been solemnized in the state of Michigan. The parents passed the closing years of their lives in Allen county, where the father died, July 24, 1854, the devoted mother having attained to venerable age and having passed

Fred Ekart

to the life eternal on July 17, 1894, after surviving her husband by fully forty years. The old homestead farm, of forty acres, is that now owned and occupied by the subject of this review, and the father operated in an early day the pioneer hotel in Huntertown, the same having been known as Dunten's Tavern. His first wife was Clarinda Bentley, of Jefferson county, New York, and her death occurred, February 26, 1839. The three children of this union were Louisa, Daniel I. and William H., all of whom are now deceased. Of the four children of the second marriage, Washington Dunten, of this review, is the eldest; Lucy A. is the wife of Jacob Furth, who is president of one of the national banks in the city of Seattle, Washington, as well as president of a railroad company in the west; Lucien, who was born September 10, 1845, died on November 4 of the following year, and his funeral was held from the pioneer Dunten tavern or hotel at Huntertown, the same having been at the time the family home; Ella Medora, who was born February 16, 1849, was about thirty-five years of age at the time of her death. He whose name initiates this review acquired his early education in the pioneer log school house at Huntertown, and his boyhood days were passed in the old-time hotel conducted by his father, though later he began to aid in the work of the home farm, of which he is now the owner. In addition to this old homestead of forty acres he owns an adjoining tract of eighty-eight acres, and the place is one of the well improved and valuable farms of Perry township. Mr. Dunten has been an energetic and successful exponent of agricultural industry and also active in the mercantile business, as previously intimated in this article, besides which he has been known and honored as a man of sterling character and one who has been influential in community affairs. He has designated himself as a Lincoln Republican and has given effective service in the local ranks of his party, besides having held for twelve years the office of postmaster at Huntertown, as previously noted. He was formerly in active affiliation with a Fort Wayne lodge of the Independent Order of Odd Fellows, and he and his wife have been earnest members of the Methodist Episcopal church for fully forty years. November 24, 1866, recorded the marriage of Mr. Dunten to Miss Almena E. Farrand, and she passed to the life eternal on October 29, 1873. Two children were born of this union: Wilna Augusta, who was born October 20, 1869, died December 31, 1891; and Wilbur Howard, who was born August 27, 1872, died June 26, 1909. The second marriage of Mr. Dunten was solemnized October 28, 1874, when Miss Hannah Wilcox, of Coldwater, Branch county, Michigan, became his wife. Mrs. Dunten is a daughter of James R. and Anna (Peckham) Wilcox, who were born in Jefferson county, New York, and became pioneer settlers in Michigan, where ther passed the remainder of their lives. Concerning the three children of Mr. and Mrs. Dunten the following brief record is entered in conclusion of this review: Carrie Louise, who was born April 13, 1880, died August 24, 1899; Ernest W., who was born September 11, 1881, at Coldwater, Michigan, is now a resident of Huntertown; and Lohman Clifford, who was born November 17, 1886, remains at the parental home and has been the popular and efficient carrier on one of the rural mail routes from Huntertown since 1904.

Fred Eckart.—Fred Eckart was brought up in the packing business of which he is now one of the owners, getting his early experience under the guidance of his father, who had established the business, and thus laying a solid foundation for future successes. He is a native son of

Allen county, born here on December 7, 1859, and his parents were Fred and Elizabeth (Linker) Eckart. Mrs. Eckart is a native of Allen county, her parents were Engelhart and Anna (Weisheit) Linker; and she was born in what is known as the Old Fort House in Fort Wayne in 1836, and now lives in the Eckart homestead at 321 East Wayne Street, but the father is of Bavarian birth and parentage. They became the parents of eleven children, ten of whom grew to maturity. Fred is mentioned below; Henry I. died, aged four years; Mrs. Sophia Ober, of Chicago, Ill.; Anna, of Fort Wayne; Reinhart, who died at the age of twenty-six years; Mrs. Matilda Schultheis, of Lima, Ohio; Henry is mentioned elsewhere in this work; Mrs. Caroline Schmidt, of Fort Wayne; Mrs. Henrietta Pfeiffer, of Fort Wayne; and Miss Lucy Eckart and Mrs. Bessie Ranke, of Fort Wayne. Mr. Eckart, whose portrait appears on the preceding page, came to America in early manhood and started up in the butcher business in Fort Wayne, that being the trade he had learned in his native land. He had success and after a few years branched out in the pork packing business. From that small beginning has been developed the present extensive packing industry to which his sons succeeded when he died in 1894. Fred Eckart, the immediate subject of this review, had a somewhat limited schooling, attending the German Lutheran School on Barr Street, Fort Wayne, up to the age of fourteen. He then went into the business with his father to learn the details of the work. He familiarized himself thoroughly with every phase of the business in the plant and then took up the selling end of the enterprise, to which he has given his best energies through the past fifteen years. He has made a study of modern methods in the packing business, and wherever he has found a new idea has put it into play in his own establishment, the result being that the concern has made steady and consistent progress with the passing years. He has evolved some very creditable plans for the pushing of sales into new territory, and all considered, may properly be said to have been an active force in the growth of the industry, which has more than trebled its output in the last twenty years. On June 28, 1888, Mr. Eckart was married to Miss Caroline L. Hostman, the daughter of Christ Hostman, of Fort Wayne. He died, March 1, 1917, aged eighty-two years. They became the parents of one child, Pearl Llva, who died at the age of four days. In Masonry Mr. Eckart has taken both the Scottish and York Rite, and the Shrine. He is also a member of the Knights of Pythias, the Fort Wayne Commercial Club and the Fort Wayne Country Club. He has no party affiliations in politics, but prefers to hold himself free to indulge independent views.

  Henry Eckart, secretary, treasurer and general manager of the Fred Eckart Packing Company, is one of the essentially progressive and representative business men of his native city of Fort Wayne and takes a loyal and helpful interest in all things tending to advance its civic, commercial and industrial prosperity and prestige. Here he was born on the 7th of January, 1867, and he is one of the eleven children of Fred and Elizabeth (Linker) Eckart, the former of whom was born in the Kingdom of Bavaria, Germany, and the latter in the old Fort House that gave title to the present thriving city of Fort Wayne, her parents having been numbered among the very early settlers of Allen county. Frederick Eckart long held precedence as one of the prominent business men of Fort Wayne, where he founded and developed a prosperous packing business. Henry Eckart is indebted to the public schools of Fort Wayne for his early educational training, and in the meanwhile he had become associated with his father's business when he was a lad of but twelve years. He learned the various details of this line of enterprise and continued to be associated with his father's business until he was twenty years of age, when he went to Kansas City, Missouri, where he remained two years, as one of the employes in a leading meat-packing plant. At the expiration of the period noted he returned to Fort Wayne and opened a meat market on Ewing street. He built up a good business in the retail line but finally resumed his alliance with the extensive business of the Fred Eckart Packing Company, to the development and advancement of whose important commercial enterprise he has contributed largely through his progressive policies and marked executive ability, he being now secretary and treasurer, as well as general manager ,of the company. In politics Mr. Eckert maintains an independent attitude, preferring to give his support to men and measures meeting the approval of his judgment rather than to be guided within strict partisan lines. In a general way he advocates the basic principles for which the Democratic party stands sponsor. He and his wife are communicants of the Lutheran church and he is affiliated with the Benevolent and Protective Order of Elks, the Knights of the Maccabees, the Loyal Order of Moose, and the Fraternal Order of Eagles. His wife, whose maiden name was Mamie Voltz, is a native of the city of Rochester, New York, and they have two children—Herbert and Helen.

David S. Eckert, well known in Allen county as a manufacturer of cigars, was born in Fort Wayne on February 4, 1865, and is the son of John C. and Rachel A. (Walters) Eckert. The family was a Pennsylvania one, and the grandparents of the subject, John C. and Sarah (Turner) Eckert, were born and bred in that state. They died in 1844 and 1871, respectively. Their son, John C., the father of the subject, was born in Harrisburg, Pennsylvania, on April 22, 1836, and when he was sixteen years old became identified with the cigar-making industry in Harrisburg. He continued in the work there until 1857, when he moved westward to Ohio, remaining there two years and returning to his home town in 1859. In August, 1862, he enlisted for service in the Union army, joining the One Hundred and Twenty-seventh regiment of Pennsylvania Infantry, that being one of the nineteen regiments called out by the governor of the state for nine months' service. He was mustered out in May, 1863, and in the following September brought his family to Fort Wayne, in which city he passed the remainder of his life. His first work in Fort Wayne was as a cigar-maker, but in 1870 he opened a shop of his own, and his factory at No. 85 Calhoun Street was the scene of much activity in the cigar business. He made a specialty of his Brand 39, which became widely popular wherever his cigars went. On February 8, 1857, Mr. Eckert was married to Miss Rachel A. Walters, who was born in Dauphin county, Pennsylvania, and eight children were born to them, five of whom are yet living. The father died in 1895 and David, the subject of this review, took charge of the business for his mother. At her death, in 1909, it came into his hands, and he has continued as the proprietor of the establishment his father was so long identified with. David Eckert had his education in the Fort Wayne public schools and finished his training with a thorough business course, after which he joined his father in the business, so that he has been identified with the cigar business all the years of his active life. Mr. Eckert was married on April 28, 1903, to Miss Bertha C. Scott, daughter of William L. and Mary Scott. Four children were born to them. Three are living—Mary Katherine, David S., Jr., and Robert William. Mr. Eckert is a Thirty-second degree Mason, with Shriner affiliations, a member of the Elks, the Moose, the Eagles and the Fort Wayne Commercial Club. He is a Democrat in politics and a progressive and enterprising citizen.

Frank W. Edmunds.—The name of Edmunds is one of the oldest and best known in Fort Wayne to-day, its representatives having been identified with the city and its varied activities for the past century. Frank W. Edmunds, the immediate subject of this brief family review, was born in Fort Wayne, and his father, James Edmunds, was also a native son of that city, born there in 1828. James Edmunds in early manhood engaged in the draying business in Fort Wayne, and he was active in that work during the remainder of his life. It is worthy of note that he was the owner of the first spring truck to be operated in his community, a fact that gives indication of a spirit of progress in him that has since been manifested in his son. Mr. Edmunds died in 1874, at the early age of forty-six years. His wife was Mary Smith, also a daughter of Fort Wayne. They were the parents of four children, and their two living sons are Harry Edmunds, a resident of Chicago, and Frank W., mentioned above. Mrs. Edmunds was the grand-daughter of Conrad Smith, who had the distinction of having served from the first call to arms of the Minute Men through to the last day of the American Revolution. His great-grandson, Frank W. Edmunds, is the proud possessor of his official release from the service—a paper that is most interesting in character. Mr. Edmunds was born on November 23, 1869, in Fort Wayne, and had his early education in his home city. He followed his common school training with a course of study in Fort Wayne Methodist College, after which he turned his attention to the study of telegraphy and for two years was engaged in that work. He then became occupied in civil engineering for a period of three years, after which he identified himself with the Fort Wayne Electric Works, where he continued for another three-year period. In 1893 Mr. Edmunds launched out in the business world on his own responsibility, engaging in electrical construction work, and while he started on a small scale, as befitting his circumstances, he is to-day head of the oldest and largest business of its kind in the city of Fort Wayne, employing about sixteen persons. Other interests have claimed his attention, among which might be mentioned the Fresko Chemical Company, of which he is president. Mr. Edmunds is Republican in politics, and is a member of the First Presbyterian Church. He is a thirty-second degree Mason and a member of the Knights of Pythias. He is also a member of the Fort Wayne Country Club, and as a member of the local Commercial Club has been a factor in much of the development work that organization has instigated and carried to completion. In 1911 he married Miss Inez Cecil, of Rome City, Indiana, and they have two sons—Frank, Jr., and William.

John W. Eggeman, judge of the Circuit Court of Allen county, is one of the most influential factors in the development of the highest type of character in the youth of this populous community. His official duties as judge of the Circuit Court carry the responsibilities of judge of the juvenile court, and, in the performance of his work in the latter important field, Judge Eggeman has found the deepest satisfaction, for the reason that it opens an incomprehensibly wide field of true usefulness. Scores of successful young men and women have been able to date the upward turn of their lives from the time the judge has heard their stories in court and given his best thought and attention to eliminating the conditions which have led them into error and wrong. Judge Eggeman was born in Fort Wayne, June 12, 1875, the son of Peter and Catherine (Niezer) Eggeman. Following his years of study in the parochial schools of the city, he attended Taylor University and then entered Notre Dame University. Here he not only became proficient in the several lines of study undertaken to fit him for a life of usefulness, but he attained wide fame as an athlete, notably on the football gridiron. As a youth of six feet and four inches in height, possessed of well-trained muscle guided by a quick-acting mind, his name was known throughout the world of athletics. He graduated from the law department of Notre Dame in 1900 and came immediately to his home city, where he engaged in the general practice of law. For several years he was associated with James B. Harper, a leading member of the bar of Allen county. In 1912 he was elected to serve as the judge of the Circuit Court, succeeding Judge Edward O'Rourke, who had served on the bench for a period of thirty-six successive years. During the active years of Judge Eggeman's service he has displayed highly-developed judicial qualifications which include a keen mind, a knowledge of the spirit of the law, and a true sympathy which fits him to weigh carefully and justly the problems which come before him in his dual capacity. He is an active member of St. Patrick's Catholic parish. As a member of the Allen County Bar Association and one of the founders of the Blackford Club, he has rendered good service. On June 9, 1903, he was united in marriage with Miss Mary Wagner, daughter of John and Elizabeth (Kruse) Wagner, of Lafayette, Indiana. To this union have been born three children —John W., Jr., Robert F. and Mary E. Eggeman. In a recent public address Judge Eggeman presented his views on the question of child delinquency which portrays, perhaps, better than the words of another, the fine mind, the charitable sympathy and the determined purpose of the judge of the juvenile court, before whom are brought the boys and girls of Allen county for examination before other and more severe action can be taken. "Before two months had pased, after I had assumed the bench of the Circuit Court, I became convinced that knowledge of the intricacies of legal procedures was not the only important matter connected with the position," said he. "To my own satisfaction, at least, I soon learned that disputes over material things are not quite so important as endeavoring to make good citizens out of the boys and girls of our community, and if, during my term of office I shall have been instrumental in having the fathers and mothers exercise the proper parental guidance and supervision of the habits of their children, and in instilling in the minds of the members of the different organizations I have addressed a desire to help the children to make good, then I shall be extremely thankful. The proper bringing up of children is not a hobby, but a duty that is owing by every parent, for if we are to have capable and competent men and women we must first have good boys and girls." After entering deeply into the consideration of the influences of heredity and environment, Judge Eggeman gave his reasons for declaring that the surroundings of the child have a greater molding effect upon character than ancestry. "Crime, as such, is not transmitted from our ancestors," declared Judge Eggeman. "A counterfeiter does not hand down a tendency to his offspring to make engraved plates any more than a pickpocket transmits his ability to steal purses from pockets with the skill that defies detection. The only things we acquire through heredity are color, form and structure. We do not inherit mathematical faculties or anything else that we have to acquire. A tendency to steal is no more inherited than a tendency to become a good telegrapher. Drunkenness is not inherited. It is only transitory. While it is true when parents are drunkards we ofttimes find the children drunkards, yet the cause is environment. The parents by example, if not expressly, teach their children to acquire a taste for alcohol." With his views thus expressed, Judge Eggeman appealed to his audience to unite in the great work of placing about the children and the youth the most healthful environments to the end that those whose home surroundings are below the desired standard may be helped to the truest interpretation of manhood and womanhood. "The home," said he, "is where the child must receive its first training. It is remarkable to notice how children absorb and emulate. The conversation and habit of the parent are watched intently, and the manner in which they are reproduced by the children is astonishing. I could picture to you the homes that have come under my observation. Homes that are hells. Homes of debauchery, drunkenness, dishonesty and conflicts. Homes in which the child is taught to lie and steal by direct example. Where the environment is such that, no matter how healthy the brain of the child, it must of necessity become a criminal. Then I could picture to you the home where there is lack of supervision of the intimacies and friendships of the children; evil associations and a failure of the parents to keep in touch with their habits—lack of discipline, encouragement of extravagance and evil example under the parental roof. All these are factors in the spoiling of juvenile character. During the years of 1914 and 1915 we tried an average of two hundred cases each year in the juvenile court of this county and invariably the offenders were reared under the influence of such homes. Some time ago, five boys were brought into court for stealing coal, not for the purpose of keeping warm but to secure money to turn over to their parents. Then we have the parents of the girls who permit them to wander through the streets, and the drift is inevitably downward. Most of the girls come from homes of ignorance coupled with vice. Wrong tendencies, lack of parental control and the lure of all the city's evil agencies combine to bring them to the attention of the law. In most cases, the trouble may be found after a short investigation of the home." Judge Eggeman closed his address by citing a large number of examples which have come under his observation, presenting the great good which has come through the conscientious use of his office and of the establishment of the probationary home in which the boys and girls are cared for amid good surroundings before the sentence to the reform school can be passed. Judge Eggeman in assigning relative importance to the good influences to be thrown about the child, placed the home first. "The next great factor is the Christian religion," said he. "The greatest force for civilization and good in the world to-day is the teaching of the lowly Nazarene."

Albert Egly.—In 1906 Albert Egly brought about the organization of the Grabill State Bank, at which time he became cashier of the new institution. He has continued to hold that position down to the present time, and the success and well being of the bank has been largely attributed to his work. He has been a resident of Grabill for the past fifteen years, coming here in 1901 as bookkeeper for a prominent grain concern, though other labors have claimed his attention between then and the time when he became identified with his present work. Mr. Egly was born in Adams county, Indiana, October 16, 1879, son of Samuel and Fannie (Schindler) Egly, both natives of Adams county and now living in Geneva. They became the parents of five children, of which the subject was the first born. The others are Adam, of Geneva; Katherine, the wife of Ezra Rupel, of Geneva; William, a professor in Bluffton College; and Rachel, living at home. Albert Egly had the usual common school training, followed by a course of study in a well known business college at Valparaiso, Indiana. When he was nineteen years old he engaged in teaching, in which work he was occupied for three years. In 1901 he came to Grabill as bookkeeper for a grain dealer and was in that position for a year. His next work was that of bookkeeper in the Peoples State Bank at Berne, Indiana, which post he held for three years, going thence to the S. F. Bowser Company as assistant manager of the collection department of that firm. After one year in that connection he organized the Grabill State Bank, and since that time (1906) has been cashier of the bank. Mr. Egly is a Democrat, active in local politics, and a leader in the community that has become his home. He is secretary and treasurer of the New Home Telephone Company, and holds a similar office in the Allen County Light and Power Company. He has been a potent force in the work of building up the educational standards of the township and has served as secretary of the local school board for the past three years. On October 17, 1906, Mr. Egly was united in marriage with Miss Anna Stukey, who is of Ohio birth and parentage. They have two children—Robert Paul and Richard Samuel. The family have membership in the Christian church and are leaders in the work of that organization in their community.

Lewis G. Ellingham.—Since he has been a resident of Fort Wayne, beginning with June 1, 1916, when he assumed the active management of the Fort Wayne Journal-Gazette, Lewis G. Ellingham has entered with patriotic earnestness into every substantial effort to further the best interests of the people of this city and the region reached by the enterprising newspaper which he controls. Mr. Ellingham was born on a farm in Wells county, Indiana, February 23, 1868, son of Charles and Hannah (Scotton) Ellingham, both natives of England. The parents removed from the farm into Bluffton, Indiana, when "Lew," as he is popularly known, was a lad of six years. During several years, while he attended the Bluffton schools, Mr. Ellingham was employed in the office of the Bluffton Banner, where his liking for newspaper work was developed into the determination to make it his life work. While he was in his nineteenth year he purchased the Geneva (Indiana) Herald, which he conducted for three years, when he purchased the Winchester (Indiana) Democrat. After three years of service here, he established the Decatur (Indiana) Democratic Press. In 1896, the company purchased the Decatur Democrat and consolidated it with the Democratic Press and the combined publication was issued as the Democrat. Mr. Ellingham became the sole owner of the properties in 1897. He continued the publication of the Democrat, which attained to a prominent and influential place in shaping the political and commercial affairs of the state, until June 1, 1916, when he removed to Fort Wayne to take active charge of the Fort Wayne Journal-Gazette, with Edward G. Hoffman as an associate in the ownership of the publication. Mr. Ellingham's influence in the political affairs of the state is suggested by the fact that, in 1906 and 1908, he served as the Eighth district chairman of the Democratic party with such marked ability as a leader that he became the unanimous choice of the Democrats of Indiana as their candidate for Secretary of State. In the election of 1910 Mr. Ellingham led his ticket and showed a plurality of about 13,000 votes. His service brought him a recognition of confidence, in 1912, and his vote was still larger. Mr. Ellingham's second term ended December 1, 1914. On January 2, 1905, Mr. Ellingham was united in marriage with Miss Nellie Miller, daughter of Colonel and Mrs. M. B. Miller, of Winchester, Indiana. Two children —Winifred and Miller—have been born of this union. Mr. Ellingham is an active member of the Commercial Club of Fort Wayne and of the Fort Wayne Rotary Club. He is a Scottish Rite Mason, a Shriner, and a member of the Knights of Pythias and Elks Lodges. With the family he is a member of the First Presbyterian church of Fort Wayne. At the head of a newspaper of wide influence, Mr. Ellingham is unstinted in his devotion to the promotion of the welfare of his city and state. He has the right idea of the province of a newspaper, and this idea permeates the activities of every person connected with the institution.

Thomas Emmet Ellison, lawyer, was born at LaGrange, Indiana, August 12, 1852, son of Andrew and Susan Miranda (Tuttle) Ellison. Andrew Ellison was born January 11, 1817, at Castlederg, County Tyrone, Ireland, of Scotish-Irish descent. His parents immigrated to America in 1819, and resided in Western New York until 1835, when they came to LaGrange county, where they made their home the remainder of their lives. Andrew was determined to have an education, hence in homespun and homemade clothes, with a linen duster as a dress coat, he pursued his studies at the Ontario Collegiate Institute. The fact that his father was cheated out of a large body of land made him choose the law as a profession. He walked to Wabash, Indiana, where he studied law for nearly a year in the office of Judge J. U. Pettit, and then went on to Indianapolis to be admitted to the bar, in 1843. He resided at LaGrange until his death, November 30, 1896. He was constantly in demand to try difficult and important litigations. He was especially strong before a jury. He travelled the circuit with the Judge, as they did in those days, attending court from forty-two to forty-six weeks in the year, unless it was a political year, when he gave up much of the time to political debate. He never held office, because he wanted to be free from all obligations. His practice in the Supreme Court was not exceeded by any lawyer in the state, from 1853 to 1870. He acquired considerable means and was noted for his generosity and high moral character throughout Northern Indiana. On his mother's side, Thomas E. Ellison was of Winslow descent, which family had much to do with the creation and growth of Massachusetts Colony. While the Winslows are frequently mentioned in English history, they are best known because several came over in the Mayflower, in 1620, or soon thereafter. Edward Winslow, born at Droitwitch, England, in 1560, was the father of nine children. Richard, the eldest, remained in England. Edward, the second, came to America, in 1620, in the Mayflower. He was afterward Governor of Plymouth Colony and a very important personage in the Massachusetts Colony. John came to America and Eleanore remained in England. Kenelm, Mr. Ellison's di-

THOMAS E. ELLISON

rect ancestor, was born April 29, 1599, at Droitwitch, and died September 13, 1672, at Salem, New England.· Gilbert came to America on the Mayflower, but afterwards returned to England. Elizabeth and Magdalen remained in England and Josiah came to Massachusetts, in 1629, and died there in 1636. Kenelm came to this country in the Mayflower, in 1620, and married Eleanore Adams in June, 1632. Of their four children, Kenelm was born about 1635, and died November 11, 1715. By his wife, Demaris, he had eleven children, and of these eleven, John was born about 1701, and died in 1755, having married Bethiah Andrews. Nathaniel, the fourth of the nine children of John and Bethiah Andrews, was born April 22, 1730, and died June 6, 1778, having married Hannah Fitch. Nathaniel fell a victim of a prevailing epidemic while exerting his powerful influence in doing the service of the American armies in the Revolutionary war. (See Blake's Biographical Dictionary). He married Hannah Fitch, of Coventry, Conn., April 9, 1753. They had eleven children. The second, Hannah, was born February 14, 1757, and died May 28, 1802. She married Timothy Tuttle. "Timothy Tuttle was a soldier in the Revolutionary army, in which he served five years and was engaged in many battles, such as Cow Pens, and after the war moved to Willistown, Vermont, then called the Green Mountain Territory, and spent the remainder of his life as a farmer." Of their six children, Richmond, the fourth, was born February 20, 1790, and died at South Bend, Indiana, November 9, 1874. His wife was Lovina Morton, born May 6, 1794, at Winslow, Conn., daughter of Diodate and Jemima Rockwell Morton. She died August 30, 1867, at Mishawaka, Indiana. In 1812, in the war between Great Britain and the United States, Richmond Tuttle was made sergeant in a company called "Dragoons," whose business was scouting and carrying dispatches. Two of his most intimate friends were arrested by the enemy and executed as spies and many in prominent Methodist and just before leaving Brockport, N. Y., he erected the company fell until it was reduced to sixteen. The company was in the battle of Ogdensburg at Sacketts Harbor. Mr. Tuttle was a very a fine Methodist church, for that time, as a reminder of his interest in the town where he had made his home many years. He settled in Mishawaka, Indiana, and was engaged in various business and many church enterprises until the time of his death. His eighth child, Susan Miranda was born September 13, 1829, at Brockport, N. Y. She was married to Andrew Ellison, August 4, 1851, and lived at LaGrange, Indiana, until her death in May, 1913. Thomas E. Ellison was a student at Notre Dame University, in 1868. He attended the University of Michigan in 1872-3-4, being a special of the literary department as well as a regular of the law department, receiving the degree of L. L. B. in 1874. He located in Fort Wayne as a partner of Judge Robert S. Lowry, in 1877. January 10, 1878, he married Emma Sophronia Stockbridge, who died March 23, 1884. They had three children: Robert died in infancy; Phoebe, born September 20, 1880, married Warren Dupre Smith, head of the Department of Geology of the University of Oregon; and Andrew Winslow Stockbridge Ellison, born May 20, 1882, is now connected with the Ford Motor Co., of Detroit, Michigan. For a second wife, the subject of this memo, married Hannah Hall, of Topeka, Kan., Dec. 14, 1887. Mr. Ellison was admitted to the Indiana bar, December 23, 1873, while a resident of LaGrange, Indiana, and he moved to Fort Wayne in February, 1877, and there he has resided ever since. He was admitted to the bar of the United States Circuit Court of Indiana in November, 1880, and to the United States Supreme Court in April, 1890. He was a member of the Board of State Charities of Indiana, 1892-9, and was Vice-President of the National Conference of Charities and Corrections in May, 1898, when it was held in New York City. He has written and delivered many addresses on sociological subjects. He was a member of the Indiana State Senate, 1895-9, and drew the present law as to care of dependent children, since adopted in principle by many of the states. He is also author of the law remodeling the penal system, establishing the parole system and indeterminate sentence. These laws have been especially commended by the International Prison Congress, etc. He was the first president of the Indiana Reformatory, and was a delegate to the International Prison Congress, held at Brussels, Belgium, in 1895, and at Washington, D. C., in 1916. He was also a delegate to the Universal Congress of Lawyers and Judges at the Louisiana Purchase Exposition at St. Louis, Mo., in 1904. He is a member of the American Bar Association and the Indiana Bar Association, is a Democrat in politics and has been prominent in promoting the construction of a waterway between Lake Erie and Michigan by the United States Government.

Miss Julia E. Emanuel.—It is specially gratifying to accord in this publication special recognition to Miss Emanuel, who is the proprietor and active manager of one of the admirably appointed and ably conducted drug stores of Fort Wayne, the same being designated as the Chemist Shop and being eligibly situated in attractive quarters at the corner of Berry and Harrison Streets, the designated number of the establishment being 201 West Berry Street. Miss Emanuel has shown marked technical ability in her chosen profession, for the work of which she carefully educated herself, and she has shown equal ambition and mature judgment as a business woman of exceptional resourcefulness and progressiveness. It may consistently be said that she has an inherent predilection for her present profession and business, for her father was an able physician and surgeon and after his death her mother became successful in the conducting of a drugstore in the former office building of the deceased husband and father. Miss Emanuel was born at Antwerp, Paulding county, Ohio, and is a daughter of Dr. Appeles D. and Emma C. (Kauffman) Emanuel, her father having been a representative physician and surgeon in that county at the time of his death, in 1876, and his widow having thereafter developed in his former office a prosperous drug business, she having been a resident of Antwerp at the time of her death. In the public schools of her native village Miss Emanuel continued her studies until she had availed herself of the advantages of the high school, and she early began to assist in her mother's drugstore, in which she gained her initial knowledge of practical pharmacy. Her self-reliant ambition was shown in her determination to prepare herself fully for the profession in which she has since achieved substantial and merited success, and she finally entered the University of Michigan, at Ann Arbor, in which she was graduated as a member of the class of 1889 and from which she received the degree of Pharmaceutical Chemist. In 1892 Miss Emanuel came to Fort Wayne and for the ensuing ten years was employed in the prescription department in the drugstore of Meyer Brothers, her abiltiy as a chemist and her scrupulous care in the compounding of prescriptions having gained to her the confidence and high esteem of the local representatives of the medical profession as well as of the general public. In 1902 she established her independent business enterprise as a pharmacist, and in 1907 she removed from her original quarters in the Arcade building to her present location, where she has built up a large and representative trade in the handling of drugs, chemicals, toilet articles and general lines of druggist's sundries, and with a most modern and complete prescription department in which the best of service is given. Miss Emanuel is popular in both business and social circles in Fort Wayne and is distinctly a woman of gracious personality, even as she is one of marked business ability.

Stephen C. Emenhiser has been a resident of Allen county from the time of his birth, is a scion of an honored pioneer family, and is to-day one of the representative farmers and stock-growers of Jackson township, where he is the owner of a well-improved farm of one hundred and sixty acres. He purchased this place when he was a young man and shortly prior to his marriage, and his devoted young wife proved his efficient coadjutor when he set to himself the arduous task of reclaiming the land to cultivation, the entire tract having been covered with heavy timber at the time when it came into his possession. Thus through his energy and good management have been made all the improvements that now mark the place as a model farm, the house, barns and other farm buildings having been erected by him and independence and prosperity having crowned his well-ordered endeavors. In connection with diversified agriculture Mr. Emenhiser raises live stock of the better type, including full-blooded Shropshire sheep and Poland-China swine. Mr. Emenhiser has not only been one of the world's productive workers, but has also stood exponent of broad-minded and progressive citizenship. He served one year as township supervisor and for the long period of sixteen years was an influential and valued member of the advisory board of Allen county. His political allegiance is given to the Democratic party, he was formerly in active affiliation with the Improved Order of Red Men, and he and his wife are earnest members of the Evangelical Lutheran church at Monroeville, from which village they have service on rural mail route No. 1. Mr. Emenhiser was born in Madison township, this county, on March 2, 1865, and is a son of Joseph and Adeline (Clark) Emenhiser, the former of whom was born in Pennsylvania, of German ancestry, and the latter in Virginia, of English lineage. The marriage of the parents was solemnized in the state of Ohio, whence they came to Allen county more than half a century ago and established their home on a pioneer farm in Madison township, where they passed the remainder of their lives, in the meanwhile contributing a worthy quota to the social and industrial development and progress of the county. Of their fine family of sixteen children the first born died in infancy; Adam is now deceased; Katherine was the third in order of birth; James is deceased; Mrs. Ameria Smith resides in Hoagland, Indiana; Joseph is deceased; Mrs. Jennie Tood resides in Richmond, Indiana; John is a resident of Jackson township; Adeline is deceased; William is a resident of Texas; Mrs. Abigail Stoneburner resides in Hoagland; Stephen C., of this review, was the next in order of birth; Mrs. Sarah Kantro maintains her home in New York, and Mrs. Minnie Bardey in Buffalo, New York; David is a resident of Hoagland and his twin sister, Delilah, is deceased. Stephen C. Emenhiser acquired his early education in the pioneer schools of Madison township and in the meanwhile assisted in the reclamation and other work of the home farm. He has never severed his allegiance to the great basic industry of husbandry and has for many years been one of the vigorous exemplars of farm enterprise in his native county, as intimated in a preceding division of this article. On October 18, 1890, he married Miss Emma Davidson, daughter of Richard and Mary (Livinston) Davidson, who were born and reared in Licking county, Ohio, and who came to Allen county, Indiana, in 1888. They here resided four years on a farm in Jefferson township and then removed to Kalida, Putnam county, Ohio, where the father passed the remainder of his life and where the widowed mother still resides. Of the children the eldest, Marion, is a resident of Grand Rapids, Michigan; Mrs. Ella Pritchard lives in Ohio; Mrs. Emenhiser was the third child; John and Homer reside in Ohio, the former in the city of Toledo; Mrs. Maude Pratt likewise is a resident of Toledo; James is deceased; Richard is a resident of Bay City, Michigan, and William is deceased. Mr. and Mrs. Emenhiser have seven children: Mrs. Grace Fernet, Mrs. Ada Starehime, Charles, Augustus, Leonard, Stella and Homer. Edward, the fifth child, is deceased, and Augustus, Leonard, Stella and Homer remain at the parental home.

William Emme came direct from his home in Germany to Fort Wayne, where he readily found employment at his trade of cabinetmaker. He was employed constantly by the Pennsylvania Railroad from about 1881. He was born in Germany on March 14, 1848, and his parents were Henry and Christina (Toensing) Emme, both deceased. The father died when William Emme was three years old, and the other children left fatherless at that time were Diederick, now living in Germany; Henry, Sophia and Pauline, all deceased. When he was fourteen years old William Emme was apprenticed to a cabinet-maker in his native community, and he was twenty-four years old when he came to America. After he settled in Fort Wayne he engaged in the carpentering and contracting business and was thus occupied for about nine years, when he found permanent employment in the cabinet work department of the Pennsylvania road. Mr. Emme is employed in the finer work on the coaches, where the skill of a cabinet-maker is in demand. He was pensioned by the company on June 20, 1915. In September, 1876, Mr. Emme was married to Miss Minnie Vollmerding, who, like himself, was born in Germany. Their children are Minnie, Sophia, Fred and Carrie. All four live at home with the parents, and Fred is employed by the Fort Wayne Foundry and Machine Company. The family are members of St. Paul's Lutheran Church, and have a wide circle of friends in the city that has been their home these many years.

Franklin A. Emrick.—In according consideration in this history to those whose ability, character and services have given them assured prestige as representative members of the Allen county bar, there is special reason for offering more than casual recognition to Mr. Emrick, who has served as prosecuting attorney of the county and who has made an enviable record in this office—as a determined, resourceful and well-fortified trial lawyer and as one signally loyal to the public trust reposed in him and to the profession in which he has achieved merited success. Not only technical ability but also hard and persistent work are the mediums through which consistent advancement is made in the legal profession, and Mr. Emrick has lived up to the requirements that insure such prestige. He was born in Pleasant township, this county, on January 30, 1873, and is a son of John P. and Catherine (McFillen) Emrick, who have for many years been substantial farmers and honored citizens of Allen county. In the public schools of his native county Franklin A. Emrick continued his studies until he had completed the curriculum of the Ann Arbor (Michigan) high school, and in the meanwhile he had formulated definite plans for his future career. He began the study of law under effective private preceptorship and was admitted to practice in 1899, but he did not hold as adequate aught else than the most thorough preparation for his chosen vocation, with the result that he entered the literary department of the University of Michigan for one year and then the law department of the same university, at Ann Arbor, leaving there to accept the office of Deputy Prosecuting Attorney in 1899. Of this position he continued the incumbent until January 1, 1904, when he engaged in the general practice of law in Fort Wayne, in partnership with his brother, E. V. Emrick. Within the ensuing decade he was identified with a large amount of important litigation in the courts of this section of Indiana and by his decisive victories added materially to his reputation as a versatile advocate. His ability and his former official experience marked him as a logical candidate for the office of prosecuting attorney of his native county, to which position he was elected in the autumn of 1914 and of which he continued the efficient incumbent until his term expired, December 31, 1917. As public prosecutor he achieved results with the maximum of speed and the minimum of friction, with the result that his record constitutes a worthy part of governmental and legal history of Allen county. Mr. Emrick is a stalwart advocate of the principles and policies for which the Democratic party stands sponsor and he has been active and influential in political affairs in his native county. In the Masonic fraternity he has rounded the circle of each the York and Scottish Rites, besides being affiliated with the Ancient Arabic Order, Nobles of the Mystic Shrine. He is actively identified also with the Knights of Pythias, the Independent Order of Odd Fellows, the Benevolent and Protective Order of Elks, the Loyal Order of Moose, the Fraternal Order of Eagles and the National Union. On June 24, 1904, was recorded the marriage of Mr. Emrick to Miss Mary Ellen Hile, daughter of George Hile, a well-known citizen of Garrett, DeKalb county, and the two children of this union are Franklin A., Jr., and Mary Catherine.

William Emrich, who now lives retired in his attractive home at Huntertown, is one of the venerable and honored citizens of Allen county, within whose borders he has resided since his early youth, a scion of one of the sterling German pioneer families who here settled more than sixty years ago, and he has been one of the vigorous and successful exponents of agricultural enterprise in the country, his old homestead farm, of one hundred and ten acres, having been developed and improved under his energetic management and being one of the fine farms of Perry township. He still owns the property, which is now under the active management of his youngest son, Frank E. Mr. Emrick was born in Baden, Germany, December 17, 1838, a son of Franz and Elizabeth (Hockerberger) Emrich, who came with their children to America in 1852, remained for an interval in Pennsylvania, then removed to Stark county, Ohio, whence, about eighteen months later, they came to Allen county, Indiana. The family home was established on a little farm of thirty acres, in Springfield township, and at the time only two acres of the tract had been cleared. With the passing years Franz Emrich achieved independence and success through his association with agricultural industry, and both he and his wife passed the remainder of their lives in this country, their religious faith having been that of the Lutheran church. Of the three children, the eldest was Elizabeth, whose death occurred in 1905; the subject of this review was the next in order of birth; and George is a resident of Cedar Creek township, this county. William Emrich acquired his early education in the schools of his native land and was a lad of fourteen years at the time of the family immigration to the United States. In Starke county, Ohio, he attended school two months, and hi broader education has been gained under the direction of that greatest of all head-masters, experience. Upon the removal of the family to Allen county he became his father's energetic assistant in the work of the home farm, and later was employed for twelve years on neighboring farms in Springfield township. Frugal and industrious, he carefully conserved his financial resources and eventually was enabled to purchase the fine homestead farm which he still owns, in Perry township. The present substantial improvements on the place were made by him and he long held precedence as one of the enterprising and substantial exponents of agricultural and live-stock industry in Perry township. In October, 1907, he retired from the farm and removed to Huntertown, where he now occupies his attractive and modern home, on Hunter street, the house having been erected by him and being of cement-block construction. His second wife died, in 1909, and Mrs. Amanda Friece now has charge of the domestic affairs of his home. In his young manhood, Mr. Emrich wedded Miss Margaret Holcwarth, who was born in Germany, a daughter of Daniel and Barbara Holcwarth, who settled in Ohio upon coming to America and thence came to Allen county and established their home in Springfield township, where they passed the residue of their lives. Mrs. Emrich died, February 15, 1871, at the birth of her daughter Sarah. She was the mother of five children, all of whom are living, namely: Mrs. Elizabeth Worley; John, of Perry township; Martin, of Fort Wayne; Charles, a resident of Ohio, and Mrs. Sarah Parker, of Perry township. Mr. Emrich married for his second wife Miss Ellen Boger, who was born in Ohio, a daughter of Peter and Catherine (Gruber) Boger, who were natives of Germany and came from Ohio to Allen county, Indiana, in an early day, their home having been in Springfield township at the time of their death. Mrs. Ellen Emrich passed to the life eternal on January 22, 1909, and is survived by two children, Harry A., who is a resident of Fort Wayne, and Frank E., who remains on the old homestead farm, in Perry township. William Emrich has always given his political allegiance to the Democratic party, and while living on his farm he and his wife were active members of the Reformed Lutheran church in Springfield township.

William M. Enslen, M. D., has achieved in his profession the success and precedence that are to be gained only through ability, close and conscientious application and unselfish stewardship that indicates subjective appreciation of the dignity and responsibility of a profession that touches the very destinies of life itself. Doctor Enslen has been established in successful general practice in the city of Fort Wayne for more than a quarter of a century, and the broad scope and representative nature of his professional business indicate alike his ability as a physician and surgeon and his strong hold upon popular confidence and esteem. The Doctor was born in Allen county, Ohio, October 16, 1863, and is a son of John and Mary (Shutts) Enslen, both of whom continued to reside in that county until their death and the remains of both rest in the family graveyard on the old homestead farm. John Enslen was one of the substantial farmers and honored and influential citizens of Allen county, Ohio, was a Democrat in politics and though he had no ambition for public office he served six years as a member of the board of directors of the county farm and infirmary in Allen county, Ohio. He was the first man in that county to own and operate a threshing machine in which steam power was utilized, and he was a progressive and liberal citizen who did much to further the civic and industrial advancement of the county in which he passed the greater part of his life, his parents having established their home in Allen county in 1831 and he having assisted in the reclamation and development of the pioneer farm. Both he and his wife were earnest and consistent members of the Methodist Episcopal Church. Of the eight children Doctor Enslen, of this review, was the fifth in order of birth; Edward, the first born, is deceased; John H. remains in the old home county and is a prosperous merchant in the village of Elida; Columbus E. and Frank M. are twins, the latter a bachelor, and both are locomotive engineers in the service of the Pennsylvania Railroad Company; George S. is engaged in the mercantile business at Lima, the county seat of Allen county, Ohio; Carrie Della is the wife of William Price, a successful farmer of Allen county, Ohio; and Rosa is the widow of John Summers, who was engaged in the mercantile business at Kalida, Putnam county, Ohio, at the time of his death. Dr. William M. Enslen, like many another who has attained to prominence in professional life, found the period of his childhood and early youth compassed by the benignant influences of the farm, and in the meanwhile his alert mentality enabled him to derive the maximum benefits from the advantages afforded him in the public schools. He later attended the institution that is now known as Valparaiso University, at Valparaiso, Indiana, and for several years gave effective service as a teacher in the public schools, principally in rural districts in Ohio. He completed a course in medicine in the Fort Wayne Medical College, and while engaged in teaching school began the study of medicine, under the preceptorship of Doctor Jones, of Gomer, a village in his native county. He came to Fort Wayne and continued his studies under the direction of Doctor Stemen, and finally entered the Fort Wayne Medical College, in which he was graduated as a member of the class of 1890, and from which he received his degree of Doctor of Medicine. During the long intervening years he has continued in the active practice of his profession in Fort Wayne, and his status is such as to mark him as one of the representative physicians and surgeons of this part of the state. The Doctor retains membership in the American Medical Association, the Tri-State Medical Society, the Indiana State Medical Society, the Twelfth District Medical Society, and the Allen County Medical Society. The Doctor is prominently affiliated with both the York and Scottish Rite organizations of the Masonic fraternity, and the Mizpah Temple, A. A. O., N. M. S., he being a member of the first class to take the degrees in this temple. He is a Democrat in his political allegiance and as a public-spirited and loyal citizen gave effective service during the four years he represented the Sixth Ward, of Fort Wayne, as a member of the city council. He and his wife are zealous members of the Methodist Episcopal church and he was specially prominent and influential in the building of the new edifice of the Simpson Methodist Episcopal church in Fort Wayne. On October 15, 1891, was solemnized the marriage of Doctor Enslen to Miss Eva Leist, daughter of George R. Leist, of Elida, Ohio, and the two children of this union are Helen and Myron.

Sankey Everson is vice-president of the Union Grain & Coal Company and has the general management of its modern grain elevator and business in the village of Edgerton, Jackson township. The company operates also a grist mill and elevator at Payne, Ohio, and bases its operations on a capital stock of thirty thousand dollars. Herman H. Roose, of Fort Wayne, is president of the company and J. Y. Stimmel is secretary and treasurer, as well as manager of the mill and elevator at Payne, Ohio. The company was organized about 1903 and was originally incorporated with a capital stock of sixty thousand dollars. The company originally operated not only its present mill and elevators, but also a second elevator and an electric light plant at Payne, Ohio, as well as an elevator at Worstville, Paulding county, Ohio. Of the extra properties the company disposed when it was found expedient to concentrate the business in the present plants, and simultaneously the capital stock was reduced to its present but ample figure. Adjacent to the village of Edgerton, Mr. Everson owns a fine farm of one hundred and twenty-five acres, upon which he has made the best improvements, including the erection of the modern house which constitutes the attractive and hospitable family home, besides which he has otherwise brought the place up to high standard. In connection with his other business activities Mr. Everson has developed a prosperous subsidiary enterprise in the handling of automobile accessories, besides being local agent for the Jackson automobile. His political allegiance is given to the Democratic party, and at Payne, Paulding county, Ohio, he is affiliated with the Knights of Pythias and the lodge of Ancient Free and Accepted Masons. He attends and supports the Methodist Episcopal church, of which his wife is an active member. Mr. Everson was born in Schleswig-Holstein, Germany, November 19, 1871, and there received his early educational discipline under the wonderfully thorough German system. He was thirteen years of age when, in 1884, he accompanied his parents, John and Hannah (Danklefson) Everson, on their immigration to the United States, and the family home was established on a farm in Paulding county, Ohio, much of the land being still covered with a heavy growth of timber, so that he had experience in the arduous work of clearing and reclaiming a number of acres and making the same available for cultivation. The parents resided on his farm about ten years, passed the ensuing eight years at Edgerton, Allen county, Indiana, and then removed to Michigan, in which state they now reside on their excellent farm near Newberry, Luce county. Of their children the subject of this review is the eldest; Momme lives at Port Clinton, Ohio; and Christ, Mrs. Margaret Frederick, August, and Mrs. Sophia McClain reside in Michigan. After coming to the United States Sankey Everson continued his active association with farm industry until he was twenty-one years of age, when he found employment in a stave mill at Edgerton, where he later became manager of the grain elevator of which he still has the supervision, as vice-president of the company controlling the same. In September, 1896, he wedded Miss Marilla Heidebreicht, who was born and reared in Allen county, a daughter of Henry and Henrietta Heidebreicht, who now reside in Edgerton. Mr. Heidebreicht was born in Germany, was young when the family came to America and his marriage was solemnized in Michigan, in which state his wife was born. He served as a valiant soldier of the Union in the Civil war and has ever shown the same spirit of loyalty in the piping times of

E. D. Esmarch

peace as has he also when our nation has recently become involved in the terrific European war. He was formerly identified with the operation of a stave mill in Jackson township, this country, besides which he and his wife conducted for a number of years a popular boarding house at Edgerton, where they are now living in well earned retirement and comfort. Of their four children the eldest is Mrs. Lillie Roose, of Fort Wayne; Henry A. is superintendent of a stave mill at McMillan, Michigan; Mrs. Carrie Phillips resides in Fort Wayne; and Mrs. Everson is the youngest of the number. Mr. and Mrs. Everson have three children —Czerney L., Minta, and Lillian.

Edgar D. Eward has been identified more or less successfully with various business enterprises, but his latest venture seems to be the one that is most satisfactory to him and the one in which he will find activity for the coming years. He came to Fort Wayne in 1913 in the interests of the Consumers' Ice Company, and he has lately arisen to the post of secretary-treasurer and manager of the local concern. The term "self-made" is so hackneyed that one hesitates to apply it in any instance, but the fact remains that Mr. Eward is himself mainly responsible for such success as has been his portion thus far. He was born in Converse, Indiana, on December 18, 1869, and is the son of John W. and Rebecca Jane (York) Eward, natives of Virginia and Indiana, respectively. Mrs. Eward is the daughter of Alfred York, a pioneer of Indiana, who entered land in the vicinity of Monroe in the early days of Indiana settlement, and he rode horseback through a dense swamp from his location in Grant county to Fort Wayne when he went to that point to prove up on his homestead and get his patent. John W. Eward, now living retired at the old home in Converse, practiced law in the early days and was fairly prosperous for his time. He was postmaster at Converse for eight years, and at the present writing is a director in his local bank, and takes an active interest in the affairs of the community, though now in the eightieth year of his life. His life companion still lives and they are enjoying a serene old age in the place that has been their home and the center of their activity for these many years. Five children were born to them. Jessie, the eldest, is the wife of Harry Smith, of SanAntonio, Texas. Edgar of this review is the second born. Fred O. is engaged in the ice and cold-storage business in Marion, Indiana. Homer, the fourth child, died in infancy and Albert died in boyhood. It was a theory of the elder Eward that his sons, being able bodied and possessing health and strength, should make some contribution to their support as soon as they were able to become earners in some degree, and it was expected of the boys that they should earn their own clothes. This rule, while it was doubtless something of a hardship to the boys in a way, may safely be said to have been a corrective influence in their young lives and to have had a tendency to character building that more indulgent methods might not have engendered. When Edgar Eward was twelve years old his father bought a farm in the vicinity of their home and as a boy he spent much of his time at work on the place. The first actual money he ever earned came from his labors on the farm hauling rock, a pastime that many a farmer boy recalls with mingled feelings of pride and resentment, but not all of them can look back to the possession of thirty dollars as a reward for the stone bruises and back aches that accrued from the work. With this sum of money he bought three calves, and from then on he was a stock dealer on a small scale, and realized both pleasure and profit from his activities in that work. When he was eighteen years old he moved back to town from the farm and found employment in a harness shop at the meagre wage of three dollars a week. One year of that work sufficed and he next engaged himself with his uncle in the glass business, where he earned fifteen dollars weekly. He continued with his uncle for three years, learning the glass blower's trade in that time, and for the next ten years was engaged in that work. He left it to engage in the livery business in Matthews, Indiana, but after eight months of that he went back to Converse and there conducted a similar enterprise for the next four years. His next move took him to Marion, where he carried on a successful business in chattel loans for about four years. In 1913 he came to Fort Wayne, here to engage in his present business as manager of the Consumers' Ice Company, as has been previously stated. Mr. Eward was married on March 17, 1898, to Miss Tressie Zirkle, a young woman of many excellent qualities of heart and mind and a native daughter of Indiana. They have two children—Harold and Helen. Mr. Eward is a Republican in politics, and his fraternal affiliations are with the Knights of Pythias, the Elks and the Modern Woodmen and the Maccabees.

Daniel M. Falls.—The firm of Bowser, Prentis & Falls has controlled a successful business in the installing of machinery and in its line has held precedence as one of the most important concerns of the kind in Northern Indiana. The late Daniel M. Falls was employed by the firm for a number of years before he became a member thereof and played an influential part in the development of the business. This firm had the distinction of having installed the machinery used at the Centennial Exposition of 1876, and Mr. Falls was in charge of this important work in the city of Philadelphia. He continued as a member of the firm and as one of the prominent and honorable business men of Fort Wayne until his death, which occurred December 16, 1916. Mr. Falls was born in Pennsylvania, July 3, 1832, and thus was more than eighty years of age at the time of his death. He was a son of Thomas and Barbara (Staufer) Falls, both natives of Germany. The father was a cabinetmaker and came to Fort Wayne in 1843, both he and his wife having passed the remainder of their lives in Allen county and of their nine children the subject of this memoir was the last to survive. As a youth Daniel M. Falls learned the trade of blacksmith, but after having been employed at this trade about two years he became associated with the firm in which eventually he purchased an interest and with which he continued his connection until his death. For some time he was engaged also in the rendering business, but he retired from that field of enterprise in 1905. His old home, in which his death occurred, was erected by him in 1863, and there he continued his residence during the long intervening years. Mr. Falls married Margaret Gormely, a native of Bridgeport, Connecticut, and they became the parents of four children—Charles M., George E., Oliver M. and Etta F. The three first named are deceased and Etta F. is the wife of Calvin K. Rieman, who is factory manager of the S. M. Foster Shirtwaist Company. Mr. and Mrs. Rieman have one child, Carrie K. Mrs. Falls passed to the life eternal, February 22, 1916, and her husband survived her by less than a year, so that in death they were not long divided. Both were earnest communicants of the Protestant Episcopal church, and Mr. Falls was affiliated with the Masonic fraternity, besides having been a charter member of the local lodge of the Independent Order of Odd Fellows.

Earl D. Farr has so applied his technical and executive ability as to win for himself the responsible office of manager of the large and important manufacturing plant of The Boss Manufacturing Company in the city of Fort Wayne, and he is one of the alert, progressive and popular young business men of the Allen county metropolis. Mr. Farr was born in Fulton county, Illinois, on January 5, 1882, and is a son of John and Peninah (Cain) Farr, the former a native of Ohio and the latter of Illinois. The father became a successful exponent of agricultural industry in Fulton county, Illinois, where he is now living retired, his wife having been summoned to the life eternal several years ago. Of their children the first, Arthur, died in infancy; Bertha is the wife of Albert K. Tate and they now reside in the city of Los Angeles, California; Cooper C. resides at Kewanee, Illinois; and the subject of this sketch is the youngest of the number. Earl D. Farr continued his studies in the public schools of his native county until he had duly profited by the advantages afforded in the township high school, and in the meanwhile he gave practical assistance in the work and management of the home farm. At the age of eighteen years he found employment in an Illinois manufactory of farm implements, and later was associated with the printing business conducted by his brother-in-law, Mr. Tate. After severing this alliance he was employed about nine years by the Western Tube Company, at Kewanee, Illinois, and at the same place he then entered the service of the Boss Manufacturing Company, which, in 1912, transferred him to its headquarters in Fort Wayne, where he has since given effective service as manager of the company's well-equipped manufacturing plant. Mr. Farr pays his political allegiance to the Republican party, is affiliated with the Knights of Pythias, and he and his wife hold membership in the Baptist church. June 7, 1905, recorded the marriage of Mr. Farr to Miss Lenna E. Radford, who was born and reared at Kewanee, Henry county, Illinois, and they have three children—Beatrice J., Lillian E., and John R.

Adrian E. Fauve, M. D., has been engaged in the practice of his profession at Fort Wayne since 1906 and his recognized ability and gracious personality mark him as one of the representative physicians and surgeons of this section of the Hoosier state. The Doctor is a scion of fine French stock and takes pride in claiming beautiful France as the place of his nativity, his parents, Louis and Eulalie (Monin) Fauve, being still residents of Bourges, France, where the father is now in the consular service, doing all in his power to uphold his native land in its bitter struggle with opposing forces in the great conflict that is now ravaging and devastating so many European countries. Doctor Fauve was born in Bourges, France, on March 5, 1878, and is the younger in a family of two children, his elder brother, Eugene, being in active service as a gallant soldier of France in the great European war that is raging at the time of this writing, in the spring of 1917. Doctor Fauve was afforded in his native land excellent educational advantages along both academic and professional lines, and he came to America in 1896. He has been indefatigable in fortifying himself for his profession in consonance with its highest modern standards, and he received his degree of Doctor of Medicine from one of the leading institutions of France. Since establishing his home in the United States he has taken effective post-graduate courses in medical institutions both in Indianapolis and Chicago, in which former city he was engaged in the practice of his profession about one year. In 1906 he established himself in general practice at Fort Wayne, and here he has built up a substantial and representative practice, in which he now gives special attention to the diagnosis and treatment of the diseases of the stomach and other digestive organs. His success has been on a parity with his enthusiasm and earnest effort and he has gained high standing in the esteem of his professional confreres. He is actively identified with the American Medical Association, the Indiana State Medical Society, the Twelfth District Medical Society, and the Allen County Medical Society. He is a member of the Medical Reserve Corps of the United States army with the rank of first lieutenant. He is affiliated with both the York and Scottish Rite bodies of the Masonic fraternity. On June 29, 1904, was solemnized the marriage of Doctor Fauve to Miss Mary Etta Juilliard, who was born at Canton, Ohio, and who is of French descent on both the paternal and distaff sides. She is a woman of distinctive culture and talent, having received the advantages of both American and French educational institutions, including those of the convent at Oiseaux, France, and having developed her musical talent through effective study in both America and France. A woman of fine social qualities and gracious presence, she is a popular figure in the representative social life of Fort Wayne. Doctor and Mrs. Fauve have no children.

Franklin J. Federspiel, who conducts a successful and representative general insurance business in Fort Wayne, is a scion of the third generation of the Federspiel family in Allen county, and his father, who likewise was born and reared in Allen county, where he lived retired in the village of New Haven, St. Joseph township until his death, was long and successfully engaged in the conducting of a blacksmith and repair shop, as a skilled artisan and as a man whose fine physical powers found effective balance in his sterling character and strong mentality. The lineage of the Federspiel family traces back to patrician sources in Germany and Switzerland, and it is specially gratifying at this juncture to enter the following data, which are taken from the archives of the official records of the town of Chur, Germany: "The old, noble and aristocratic family of Federspiel comes originally from Switzerland (1257), the Canton Graubundten, where Ulricus von Federspiel first became distinguished. The aforesaid ruled the Bishopric Church in a praiseworthy fashion and by this he became Freiherr (Baron), which the descendants carried on. Yohan Anton Freiherr von Federspiel was then, in the year 1759, made Canon of Chur. Later this family spread out to north Germany. The main colors of the coat-of-arms are silver and blue. Blue in the coat-of-arms means consistency and true devotion towards God. Silver signifies purity, wisdom and innocence. The wings on the helmet mean that the family through praiseworthy deeds raised itself up. The snake is the symbol of wisdom, craft and unity. Taken from Professor Tauhis' Dictionary of Heraldry and the General Heraldry Knowledge of Europe, Vo. V., page 184, Philip Warwitz, heralder and genealogist. Von Federspiel, a Swiss family, from which, as Castle-Colonnel, Lucius Rudolph von Federspiel, in the year 1718, was made a noble." Baltzer Federspiel, grandfather of him whose name introduces this article, was born in Alsace-Lorraine, France, in 1815, and came to America when about fifteen years of age. He settled in New York and when about twenty-one years of age came to Indiana and settled in Allen county. He was a blacksmith by trade and as he found a well-established blacksmith shop in Fort Wayne he went to New Haven, in which village he opened a shop and became a pioneer blacksmith of Adams township, both he and his wife having here remained until their death and his name meriting enduring place on the roll of the honored pioneers of Allen county. Joseph Federspiel, father of the subject of this sketch, was born at New Haven, this county. Here he maintained his home and was virtually his father's successor in the blacksmithing business. He followed his sturdy trade for many years. He was a Democrat in politics and was from his youth an earnest communicant of the Catholic church. As a young man he wedded Miss Catherine Poiry, who was born in Ohio, and her death occurred in 1888. The three children of this union are George C., Frederick B. and Franklin J., all of whom now reside in Fort Wayne. For his second wife Joseph Federspiel married Miss Helen Huth, who is still living, and of this union were born one son and three daughters: Alfred is a resident of New Haven; Catherine is the wife of Alban Schelkner, of New Haven; Clara is the wife of Albert Welling, of New Haven; and Marie is employed as a stenographer in the Dreibelbiss abstract offices, in Fort Wayne. Joseph Federspiel died November 30, 1916. Franklin Joseph Federspiel, the immediate subject of this review, was born at New Haven, this county, March 29, 1877, and he continued his studies in the parochial schools of St. John's Catholic church in that village until he had completed the curriculum thereof. In 1898 he established his residence in Fort Wayne, where he entered the employ of Francis X. Schuhler, who was here engaged in the insurance business and who had developed a substantial enterprise as representative of leading fire, life and accident insurance companies. Upon the death of Mr. Schuhler, in 1906, Mr. Federspiel succeeded to the business, and he has since continued the same with unequivocal success, his clientage being of representative character and the business showing a constantly cumulative tendency under his vigorous and effective direction. He gives his political allegiance to the Democratic party, both he and his wife are zealous communicants of the parish of St. Patrick's Catholic church, and he is affiliated with the following named and representative organizations: The Knights of Columbus, the Catholic Knights of America, the Holy Name Society, the Catholic Benevolent League of Indiana, the French-American Society, the National Union and the Benevolent and Protective Order of Elks. On September 10, 1901, was solemnized the marriage of Mr. Federspiel to Miss Justina Poiry, daughter of Peter Poiry, who was for many years in the employ of the Pennsylvania Railroad Company. Mr. and Mrs. Federspiel have six children, namely: Lucille, Florence, Genevieve, Dorothy, Virginia, and Frank Joseph, Jr.

Charles Feichter has proved himself possessed of that ambition and resourcefulness which make for success in every line of human endeavor and in his native county has found satisfaction and profit in his continued allegiance to the great basic industries of agriculture and stock-growing, of which he is one of the progressive and popular exponents in St. Joseph township, where his homestead farm is a well improved and productive place of forty acres. His parents—Jacob and Rachel Feichter—natives of Germany, may consistently be said to have been pioneers of Allen county, both having been young folks at the time of coming to the county and their marriage having here been solemnized. They established their home on a farm in Lafayette township and there passed the remainder of their earnest and useful lives, secure in the respect and good will of all who knew them. They became the parents of four children—Mary, Lydia, Jacob II., and Charles. He whose name initiates this paragraph learned at first hand the mysteries and intricacies of agricultural industry, for he was reared to the sturdy discipline of the farm and early gained abiding appreciation of the dignity and value of honest toil and endeavor, the while he profited also by the privileges of the local schools of his native township. In his maturer years he continued his farm operations in Lafayette township until 1914, when he removed to his present attractive farm in St. Joseph township, the same being eligibly situated about two and one-half miles distant from Fort Wayne and receiving service on rural mail route No. 14 from that city. In politics Mr. Feichter has always been arrayed in the ranks of the Democratic party, though he has neither desired or held public office; he is affiliated with the Independent Order of Odd Fellows; and he and his wife are active members of the United Brethren church at Nine Mile. In 1897 Mr. Feichter wedded Miss Martha Milledge, daughter of Henry and Minnie (Smith) Milledge, who was born in Ohio and came from that state to Allen county many years ago. Of the ten children born to Mr. and Mrs. Feichter all are living except the youngest, Richard. The names of the other children are here noted in respective order of birth: Effie, Florence, Charles, Jr., Clarence, Clifford, Pearl, Homer, Ruth and Verdonna.

John Ferguson, during his long residence in Fort Wayne, contributed largely and substantially to the welfare of the city, and his death April 9, 1917, was mourned by many who came within the scope of his interests as represented in the financial world and the social circle. Mr. Ferguson was eighty-three years of age at the time of his death, twenty-nine years of that period having been passed as a citizen of Fort Wayne, from the time of his final location here in 1888. Previous to this, however, beginning in 1855, he was a resident of Fort Wayne for a considerable period. John Ferguson was of Scotch-Irish parentage, born June 24, 1834, near Quebec, Canada. The father of Mr. Ferguson, who bore the same name is the son, was a native of Scotland, the place of his birth being Westfield, near Olloa, and the date, 1795. For sixteen years, beginning in 1816, the father followed the life of a sailor. About the year 1830, he came to Canada. Mary Orr, who became his wife, was born in County Armaugh, Ireland, in 1805; she had come to Canada about one year previous to the arrival of Mr. Ferguson. The elder Ferguson and his wife settled upon a farm and there remained until the time of their death. Mrs. Ferguson passed away, March 19, 1879, while her husband remained until February 20, 1883. Mr. Ferguson was a man of great energy and careful habits, and his rugged constitution knew no suffering until just before his death, at four score and eight years. To these parents were born eleven children. The son, John, subject of this memoir, remained on the farm until his twentieth year, when, in 1855, he came to Fort Wayne. Mr. Ferguson laid the foundation for his eminently successful business career during the early years of his residence in Fort Wayne, when he established a large lumber mill in Wells county. During this priod, he secured many large lumber contracts for railroad construction throughout the middle west. After an absence from Fort Wayne of several years, attending to business matters in other portions of the country, Mr. Ferguson returned to this city, in 1888, and resided here continuously until the time of his death. Much of the output of

Mr. Ferguson's lumber mills was shipped to Chicago. His enterprising spirit led him into other investments, many of which have developed into leading Fort Wayne institutions which have contributed materially to the progress of the city. In 1909, Mr. Ferguson established the Ferguson-Palmer Lumber Company, of Paducah, Kentucky. Many of his outside interests, however, were sold during recent years (in order that he might give more intimate attention to important affairs in his home city. During the days of natural gas, Mr. Ferguson was a director of the Natural Gas Company, and for twelve years served as the president of the Bluffton Gravel Road Company. When the Citizens' Trust Company was organized in Fort Wayne, Mr. Ferguson became the first president of that important financial institution. Upon the reorganization of the company, in 1907, he assumed the duties of first vice-president and thus served to the time of his death. Mr. Ferguson's interests in local property were heavy, and he also possessed large tracts of land in Allen, Huntington, Wells and Marshall counties, Indiana, and Lucas county, Ohio. Mr. Ferguson was ever identified with the interests of the Republican party of his county and state, and was a prominent figure in the local fraternal circles. He was actively identified in the Masonic order, being a thirty-second degree Mason, as well as a member of the Mystic Shrine. He was also a member of Harmony lodge, No. 19, Independent Order of Odd Fellows. For many years he was an active member of the First Baptist church. The marriage of Mr. Ferguson to Miss Eliza King was solemnized, November 19, 1861. Mrs. Ferguson was a native of Canada, born in 1837. The following children, born of this union, survive: Mrs. Earl Palmer, of Memphis, Tennessee; Mrs. Lida Vernon, of Fort Wayne; and John King Ferguson and Mrs. Robert S. Robertson, of Paducah Kentucky. Mr. Ferguson was a man of excellent character and his death was a distinct loss to the financial and commercial interests of the city, as well as to the community as a whole, as his charitable nature endeared him to a wide circle of true friends.

Edward L. Feustel has been a resident of Fort Wayne from the time of his birth and through his own ability and energy has here won advancement to a position of prominence and influence in connection with business affairs in general, as is evident when it is stated that he is manager of the Fort Wayne offices of the great national commercial agency of R. G. Dun & Company. As representative of this important concern he has shown marked executive ability and that discrimination which makes him capable of placing accurate estimates upon all lines of business enterprise, and he has assured position as one of the representative young business men of his native city, with a popularity that denotes the estimate placed upon him in his home community. Mr. Feustel was born in Fort Wayne on November 27, 1873, a son of August F. and Sophia D. (Kiefer) Feustel, the former of whom was born in the Kingdom of Saxony, Germany, and the latter in Adams county, Indiana. The father was a gardener by vocation and was long numbered among the sterling and honored citizens of Fort Wayne, where his death occurred November 3, 1893, his wife surviving him and being still a resident of this city. Of their children the eldest is Henry A., of Pittsburgh, Pennsylvania, and the subject of this sketch was the next in order of birth; Adolph J. resides in the city of Detroit, Michigan; George O. is still a resident of Fort Wayne; Katharine C. is the wife of R. B. Garmire, of this city; Frederic F. maintains his home in Detroit, Michigan; Albert

O. is deceased; Robert M. is a resident of Fort Wayne, and is president of the Fort Wayne and Northern Indiana Traction Company; and Oscar is deceased. Edward L. Feustel gained his youthful education in the schools of Fort Wayne and early learned the valuable lessons of personal responsibility and thrift, since, as a mere boy, he delivered daily newspapers, his energy in this line eventually enabling him to render service on four different routes. At the age of fifteen years he became a clerk in a grocery store, and with this line of enterprise continued his active association until he had attained to years of maturity and had developed his powers as a young man of marked business acumen and circumspection. In February, 1896, he entered the service of R. G. Dun & Company, and no further voucher for the efficiency and fidelity of his service is needed than that offered by his advancement to his present responsible position as manager of the local agency and business of this representative concern which figures as the conservator of commercial stability and credits throughout the United States. Mr. Feustel is essentially a business man and subordinates all else to the demands of his present executive position, so that he has had no desire for political activity further than to give loyal support to the Republican party, the while he manifests much interest in all that concerns the well-being of his native city and county. In the Masonic fraternity he has received the thirty-second degree of the Ancient Accepted Scottish Rite, besides being affiliated also with the adjunct organization, the Ancient Arabic Order of the Nobles of the Mystic Shrine. Both he and his wife hold membership in the First Methodist Episcopal church of Fort Wayne. On October 14, 1903, was solemnized the marriage of Mr. Feustel to Miss Edna M. Parham, who was born in the state of Ohio, and their three children are Ruth P., Robert K. and Frederick P.

David C. Fisher.—There are many points of more than cursory interest in the ancestral and personal history of this well-known and highly honored citizen of Fort Wayne, where he has maintained his home for more than half a century, during which he has been consecutively engaged in the real estate business. Of this important line of enterprise Mr. Fisher is now one of the veteran representatives in northern Indiana and through his well-ordered operations, extended over the course of many years, he has contributed much to the development and progress of Fort Wayne and Allen county. It is specially worthy of mention that he is the recognized dean of all who are serving as notary publics in Indiana, his original appointment to this office having been made by Governor Morton, Indiana's chief executive during the Civil War, and by successive reappointments Mr. Fisher has continuously served in this office during the long intervening years since 1865. He is a scion of a family that was founded in America in the colonial days and one or more of his ancestors gave valiant service as patriot soldiers in the great struggle for national independence, so that he is eligible for and loyally affiliated with the Society of the Sons of the American Revolution. In the picturesque village of Little Falls, Herkimer county, New York, David C. Fisher was born on June 25, 1843, and he is a son of James R. and Henrietta (Burnet) Fisher, both likewise natives of the old Empire state of the Union. Mr. Fisher gained his rudimentary education in the common schools of his native state and was a boy of about ten years at the time of the family removal to the city of Chicago, Illinois, in 1853. His father was a skilled cabinetmaker and in Chicago became one of the leading representatives of the undertaking business, the enterprise of which he thus became one of the founders having been continued virtually without interruption to the present time, and the business being now conducted under the title of C. H. Jordan & Company. James R. Fisher and his wife passed the remainder of their lives in Chicago, and his name merits place on the list of the early and representative business men of the great metropolis of the west. Of the five children in the family the subject of this sketch is the oldest; Albert and William B. are deceased; Robert J. resides in Fort Wayne and has been for a long period a traveling representative of the Bass Foundry & Machine Company, of this city; and Henrietta B. is now a resident of Los Angeles, California. David C. Fisher attended school for a time after the family home had been established in Chicago and finally went to Peru, Illinois, where he served as messenger boy for the Western Union Telegraph Company. He made good use of the opportunities afforded him in this connection and finally the company sent him to Dixon, Illinois, where he had charge of its office for several years. He then returned to Chicago, and after having there been engaged in the produce commission business about two years came to Fort Wayne, in 1865. Here he engaged in the real estate business in company with John Hough, and after the latter's death assumed full control of the business, of which he continued as a representative as one of the most venerable and honored exponents of this line of enterprise in this section of the Hoosier commonwealth until January 1, 1917, when he retired. Mr. Fisher has been consistent in all his activities as a reliable and progressive business man and public-spirited citizen and in the county that has long represented his home he has the confidence and good will of all who know him. He is unwavering in his allegiance to the cause of the Republican party and both he and his wife are communicants of the Catholic church. On May 13, 1879, was solemnized the marriage of Mr. Fisher to Miss Dora C. Graham, who was born at Peru, Miami county, Indiana, a member of a sterling and influential pioneer family of that county. Of the three children of Mr. and Mrs. Fisher the first born, Caroline, died in early childhood; John A. died when about three years of age; and David Theodore still resides in Fort Wayne. Mrs. Dora Cecelia (Graham) Fisher is a daughter of John A. and Caroline (Aveline) Graham, the former of whom was born in the city of Baltimore, Maryland, and the latter in historic old Vincennes, Indiana. Mr. Graham came to Indiana in the pioneer days and was one of the early settlers of Peru, Miami county, whence he removed with his family to Logansport, but within a brief period he returned to Peru, where he and his wife passed the remainder of their lives. He was one of the most honored and influential citizens of Miami county, was long a leading member of the bar of that county and was called upon to serve in many important offices of public trust. He prepared and published an interesting and valuable history of Miami county and was one of the venerable citizens of Peru at the time of his death, in 1895, his devoted wife having preceded him to the life eternal. Of their nine children the following brief data are available: Mary J. is the widow of Sylvester Brownell and resides at Peru, this state; Catherine, Richard G., and James Morris are deceased; Alice E. is the widow of Plyny M. Crume, deceased, of Peru; Mrs. Fisher was the next in order of birth; John A. is deceased; Rose Victoria is the wife of Frank M. Dozier, of St. Louis, Missouri; and Caroline A. is the widow of Charles A. Pollock, of Baltimore, Maryland, in which city she still maintains her home.

Hannah Ann (Bowman) Fisher, widow of the late Samuel Fisher, long a prominent resident of Roanoke, and herself one of the foremost women of the community, was born in Columbiana county, Ohio, on November 12, 1835, and is the daughter of Henry and Harriett (Armstrong) Bowman, who were natives of Ohio and Pennsylvania, respectively. Henry Bowman was a prosperous stockman all his active life. He came to Indiana in 1853, at a time when travel was difficult and only hard work was rewarded with any measure of prosperity. He drove his family and household possessions through from Ohio, the familiar ox team and wagon of the day being an important factor in the journey, and in 1852 bought a tract of two hundred acres of wild land. They experienced all the rigors of early life in the wilderness, subjected to the dangers from wild animals and Indians, but they fared well in spite of those difficulties, and became one of the prominent and well-to-do families of the community as the years passed. Mr. Bowman was township trustee for a number of years, and also served some years as postmaster at Aboite. The last ten years of his life were lived in quiet retirement on his home place. Ten children were born to Mr. and Mrs. Bowman. Hannah Ann, the immediate subject of this review, was the first born. Sarah is the wife of Thomas Crawford, of Roanoke. Elizabeth is deceased, also Malinda. Harriet Jane is the fifth child. Mary Elizabeth was the next born. Mathias Walter, Henry, Calvin and Charles are all deceased. Hannah Ann Bowman was married on July 4, 1859, to Samuel Fisher, the son of David and Sarah Jane (Wherry) Fisher, who came from Pennsylvania to Ohio in early life. Samuel was educated in the public schools of his time and worked on his father's farm after the manner of farmers' sons. He came to Allen county in 1852 and found work there, later buying a farm of eighty acres. It was unclaimed land, without a cleared spot large enough to erect a little home upon. The Fisher home was the first plank house in the neighborhood, and was one of the finest places in the community at that time. It was finished throughout in black walnut, that fine old wood of which so much was found in Indiana at that time, and the family lived there for many years. Mr. Fisher was an energetic and progressive man and gained a considerable prominence in his town during his lifetime. He was a Republican and was township supervisor for seven years. He died on January 14, 1911, and his widow is living on the old home place, practically alone. They were the parents of eight children. Ivester lives in Huntington county. Harriett Amanda is deceased. Lucinda Alice became the wife of Hugh McFadden and lives in Aboite township. Ida and Sarah Jane are deceased. Leona Dell married Cyrus Johnson and is a resident of Lafayette township. Mary Luetta is the wife of Talbot G. Foulks, and Henry D. is a resident of Fort Wayne and a conductor on the Pennsylvania road. There are eighteen grandchildren and eighteen great-grandchildren in the family at the present time. Ivester, the eldest child of Mrs. Fisher, has nine children, named Irma, Edna, Elva, Eva, Esther, Marion, Lennie, John and Florence. Lucinda also has nine children, named Edith, Anna, Russell, Otis, Mode, Elizabeth, Fay, Lester and Wilma. The great-grandchildren are as follows: Irma, eldest child of Ivester, now deceased, left Helen, Edna and Eve. Edna, the second daughter of Ivester, has Andra, Francis and Ruth. Elva is the mother of Harley and Maxine. Lennie has one child—Wilhelmina. Edith is the mother of a son, Royal. Anna has three children—Hugh, Helen and Ethel. Etta has four children—Arval, Mabel, Glenn and Wyburn, and the first born of these is the father of one son, Arthur Aaron. Mrs. Fisher has thus, at the age of eighty-two, the distinction of being great-great-grandmother, and she is still enjoying good health and finds much pleasure in the contemplation of the activities of the younger generations that have come up about her.

Robertson J. Fisher.—In the city of Fort Wayne not to know Robertson J. Fisher is virtually to argue oneself unknown, and though he has passed the psalmist's span of three score years and ten he exemplifies most splendidly in both his mental and physical powers the spirit of eternal youth. Buoyant, genial and optimistic, a genuine worker and a lover of his fellow men, he gives patent denial to the years that have passed and he counts as his friends both old and young, with full harmony of interest in the sentiments and ideals of both classes. He has been assertively in and of Fort Wayne for more than a half a century and his memory links the city's primitive past with the twentieth century of opulent prosperity and progress in the capital of Allen county. Since 1864 he has been actively identified with the Bass Foundry & Machine Company, under the varied changes in title and personnel, since 1864, and is now secretary and sales manager of this important industrial concern. At the time of his sixty-sixth birthday anniversary, in 1911, Mr. Fisher consented to give an interview to a representative of the Fort Wayne Sentinel, and it is firmly believed that his host of friends will consider most appropriate the reproduction in this history of his own pertinent and gracious statements concerning his career and his long and close association with Fort Wayne. With minor elimination and paraphrase, therefore, is here given the record which appeared in the Sentinel under date of September 23, 1911, and it is certain that a more interesting personal record could not be offered: "I was born at Little Falls, Herkimer county, New York, September 24, 1845, and am a son of James R. and Henrietta (Burnett) Fisher, the former of whom was born in New York city, in 1818, and the latter was a native of the historic old town of Elizabeth, New Jersey. My father was engaged in business in New York city as an importer of rosewood and mahogany, and he met with large financial loss through the great fire that ravaged the national metropolis in 1835. My parents removed to Chicago in 1853, when I was eight years old. Chicago then had a population of about thirty-five thousand and old Fort Dearborn still occupied a prominent site on the Chicago river. When a small boy I and my companions used to visit the old fortress and pick bullets out of the logs of which it was constructed. The water of Lake Michigan at that time came to the sidewalks on Michigan avenue and the Illinois Central railway tracks were constructed on piling, as was also a part of the depot, which was located at the foot of Lake street. The spring following our removal to Chicago was unusually wet and the waters very high. I paddled a canoe over Madison street, between Clark and State streets, where magnificent buildings are now located. The houses in that part of the city were frame and set upon stilts, and the building in which I attended school was a cheap brick structure located on ground opposite McVicker's theater. My father was engaged in the undertaking business, with a shop and store at Madison and Clark streets, in Chicago. His partner was C. H. Jordan—Fisher & Jordan—and he brought the first iron coffin into Chicago. The firm of C. H. Jordan & Company is still doing business, the proprietors being the sons of my father's partner. My parents died in Chicago—my mother in 1853 and my father in 1857—and in the latter year I went to Elizabeth, New Jersey, to live with a relative. In April, 1861, I came to Fort Wayne to live with my uncle, the late J. D. Nuttman, and later took a position with W. H. Brooks and Charles Hill, who conducted a book and stationery store. I worked there a year and then went into the drug store of Reed & Wall, at Columbia and Calhoun streets. Mr. Reed was colonel of the Forty-fourth Indiana Regiment of Infantry in the Civil War and was at the front during the greater part of my connection with the store, the business being conducted by Watson Wall. That corner was a pretty lively spot while I was there. Fights and riots were frequent and one of them was indelibly impressed upon my memory. In those days drugstore windows were protected by wooden shutters, and it was my duty to put them up in the evening and take them down in the morning. On this particular occasion a riot broke out before I had put up the shutters, and I performed the duty in the midst of flying bricks, stones and pieces of wood. I successfully dodged several bricks and managed to get the windows protected before they were broken, and the valuable stock of 'bear's oil,' used in those days to make the hair grow, was saved; it was made of lard-oil and alcohol. My uncle, J. D. Nuttman, and my brother, William B. Fisher, conducted the Citizens' Bank, where the Old National Bank is now located. In 1867 they organized the First National Bank, which was the first national bank in the state and the eleventh in the United States. I have one of the company's business cards yet, and on it are named the following directors: Samuel Hanna, J. F. W. Meyer, F. Nirdlinger, J. D. Nuttman, John Orff, A. S. Evans, A. D. Brandriff, W. B. Fisher, and John Brown. August 1, 1864, I left Reed & Wall and went to the Bass & Hanna foundry, now the Bass Foundry & Machine Company, and with the exception of a few months spent in Arizona and California I have been with the company since—a period of over forty-seven years (fifty-three years on August 1, 1917). That may appear a long time, but I am not old and feel as active as ever. I mean to live until I reach the one hundred mark. I attribute my activity and good health to my habits. Early to bed and early to rise, eat everything that agrees with me and take a little 'old crow' or its equivalent at dinner and lunch, some physical exercise morning and night, and don't worry. I served in the city council under Mayor H. P. Scherer and Colonel C. B. Oakley, being councilman at large during the latter part of my service. I resigned before the expiration of my term, but was there long enough to find out that I was a jackass, else I would not be there. In 1883 the late C. B. Woodworth and I organized a company for the purpose of prospecting for natural gas and oil, and we put down five wells. As oil and gas developers we were a failure, but we demonstrated the fact that there was plenty of good water underlying the city. Some years ago I took an active interest in the clubs of Fort Wayne and devoted considerable time and money toward establishing the Fort Wayne Club. I was its first president, was honored by a second term, and it was while I was filling this office that the building on Harrison street, now the home of the Commercial Club, was erected. One of the most active men in the club in early days was the Hon. Perry A. Randall, through whose efforts we were able to build. When I came to Fort Wayne there were no sidewalks on Calhoun street south of Berry street. Down Calhoun street was a well-worn plank road, which afforded a veritable shower bath after a storm—the only difference between it and the general kind was that the water was sent upward and was mixed with mud and sand. A part of Berry street also was without sidewalks, and there were none on any of the streets south of that thoroughfare. Charles Taylor, who later became one of the proprietors of the Daily News, and I organized the first baseball club in Fort Wayne and named the same the Kekionga. It became famous in baseball circles in Indiana, Ohio, Michigan, Illinois, Pennsylvania, New York, Massachusetts, New Jersey and Maryland. The history of the famous Kekionga ball team is well known in Fort Wayne. In my capacity as salesman for the Bass Foundry & Machine Company I have traveled more than six hundred and ten thousand miles in the past twenty-five years. I was never injured in all that time, nor was I ever on a train when it was wrecked. I am firmly convinced that I am destined to live a hundred years and that it is a part of the plan of the Ruler of the universe that I shall not be killed or maimed in a wreck." It is not often that a publication of this nature is able to offer so interesting an autobiographical record as the foregoing screed, and it is further significant that the resume has special pertinency in touching the history of Fort Wayne. Mr. Fisher was the fifth in order of birth in a family of six children, and the other two survivors are David C., who resides in Fort Wayne, and Henrietta, who now lives in the city of Los Angeles, California. Mr. Fisher is a Democrat in politics, is affiliated with the Masonic fraternity, holds membership in the Fort Wayne Commercial Club and the Country Club, attends the Presbyterian church, as did also his wife. On October 30, 1866, was solemnized the marriage of Mr. Fisher to Miss Julia Mosby Holton, who was born at Covington, Kentucky, August 11, 1849, and who died at Los Angeles, California, September 18, 1914, her remains being laid to rest in the beautiful Mountain View cemetery at Pasadena, that state. Mrs. Fisher was a woman of most gentle and gracious personality and was loved by all who came within the compass of her influence. She was eligible for membership in both the Society of the Daughters of the American Revolution and the Colonial Dames. She is survived by only one child, Maude F., who is the widow of Lucien E. Walker and who maintains her home at Los Angeles, her only child, Paul E. Walker, being married and having a daughter, so that Mr. Fisher, of this review, has the distinction of being a great-grandfather. He is a scion of families that were founded in America in the colonial era of our national history and is affiliated with the Society of the Sons of the American Revolution, one, his great-grandfather, Colonel David Chambers, of Trenton, New Jersey, having been a gallant officer of the Continental Line in the great struggle that brought independence to the nation.

Philip Fissel was a resident of Fort Wayne for more than two-score years and made his influence felt as a man of sterling character and as a citizen of utmost loyalty and public spirit. He came from Germany to America as a youth and stood as a representative of the best type of the valued German element of citizenship in Allen county, where he gained and retained secure place in popular confidence and good will. He was a man of industrious habits and was for many years actively employed at his trade, that of furniture finisher, as a skilled artisan along which line he was employed by leading Fort Wayne furniture houses that invariably placed high estimate upon his service and his uprightness in all of the relations of life. Mr. Fissel was born in Oldenheim, Rhinhessen, Germany, on June 24, 1847, and his death occurred at his home in Fort Wayne on June 21, 1914, three days prior to the sixty-seventh anniversary of his birth. His parents, George and Katherine (Muehl) Fissel passed their entire lives in the German fatherland, and the father was a weaver by trade, some of the products of his skill being owned and highly prized by the family of the subject of this memoir. Philip Fissel was the fourth in a family of nine children; Mrs. Eva Koch still resides in Germany; Katherine is the wife of John Kemna, of Cincinnati, Ohio; John and George are deceased; Adam resides in Cincinnati; Peter is deceased; Gertrude is the wife of George Fresse, of Cincinnati; and Rosina remains in Germany. Philip Fissel acquired his early education in the excellent schools of his native land, where also he learned the trade of shoemaker. At the age of eighteen years he severed the home ties and came to the United States. He established his residence in the city of Cincinnati, and there learned the trade of furniture finishing, in which he became an expert workman and to which he devoted his attention up to twelve years prior to his death, in later years having lived retired. He established his home in Fort Wayne in 1872, and he identified himself fully and loyally with the community life, both civic and business, so that he was known and honored of men and made for himself a record that shall reflect lasting honor upon his name and memory. He was a staunch and well-fortified supporter of the principles of the Republican party and his religious faith was that of the Reformed church, of which his widow was a devoted adherent. On October 28, 1870, was solemnized the marriage of Mr. Fissel to Miss Anna M. Kuechler, who was born in Germany and who was a daughter of the late Philip Semon Kuechler and Anna Barbara (Kratz) Kuechler. Mrs. Fissel died in Cincinnati, October 17, 1916. In the passing years she had drawn to herself a wide circle of friends, and was sustained and comforted by the filial devotion of her children. Concerning the children of Mr. and Mrs. Fissel brief record is entered in conclusion of this tribute to the honored parents: George John resides in Fort Wayne; Philip died in infancy; Charles Frederick maintains his home in Fort Wayne and is a conductor in the service of the Pennsylvania Railroad Company; Gertrude is a popular teacher in the Franklin school of Fort Wayne; Peter is a painter and decorator by vocation and is engaged in business in Fort Wayne; Rose Ann is the wife of Elmer J. Voirol, of Fort Wayne, her husband being in the employ of the Pennsylvania Railroad Company.

Charles B. Fitch.—To the city of Fort Wayne Charles Byron Fitch is contributing a life of devotion to its constant betterment. No one more clearly than he sees beyond the present and grasps a vision of the Fort Wayne of the future—a Fort Wayne of opportunities for development along every commendable line of human endeavor. On many public occasions, specially since the year 1910, his voice has been raised in pleading for concerted, advanced thought to enable the city of Fort Wayne to come into the full realization and enjoyment of her high place among the cities of the middle west. Of late his special endeavor has been to direct the attention of the public to the need of modern housing conditions for the thousands of new citizens who are drawn to the city through the demands of its enlarging commercial and manufacturing institutions. Mr. Fitch is engaged in the general insurance business in

Fort Wayne and in this line has risen to a place of leadership. He was born in Medina county, Ohio, May 23, 1859, the son of William W. and Aurelia (Brintnall) Fitch. His father was born in Charlemont, Massachusetts, and was twelve years of age when he accompanied his parents on their removal to Ohio, where he was reared to maturity and where he became a successful farmer, his connection with this basic line of industry continuing until his death, in 1867. In Ohio was solemnized his marriage to Miss Aurelia Brintnall, who was born in Seneca county, New York, and of their seven children all are living, in 1917, except one son who died while serving as a soldier of the Union in the Civil war. The first of the Fitch family to reach America from England—the Rev. James Fitch—settled in Rhode Island in 1637, and became one of the founders of that colony. It is related that at one time he sold fifteen thousand acres of land in Massachusetts for one hundred and twenty-five pounds. Nine generations of Fitches since the Rev. James Fitch are easily traceable. There is a clear record of the English ancestry back to the year 1567. Charles B. Fitch, after attending the public schools in Ohio, came in 1873 to Fort Wayne, where he continued his studies. At the age of seventeen years he was engaged in teaching school to gain the means for continuing his studies in the high school. Following his schooling he spent three years in the mercantile and grain business at Avilla, Noble county, Indiana. In 1882, when the Fort Wayne Jenney Electric Light Company—forerunner of the present Fort Wayne plant of the General Electric Company—was organized, he accepted with the institution a position as assistant manager. He remained with the company until 1891, when he entered the life insurance field, as the general agent for northeastern Indiana of the National Life Insurance Company of Montpelier, Vermont. He has continued, with the wide growth of his business, to handle the insurance of this company, while at the same time handling other lines of insurance—including fire, liability and all classes of insurance, all of them having been developed to large proportions. To-day his agency represents some of the strongest and best companies in the world. Mr. Fitch is a recognized authority on insurance matters. For two years he served as actuary of the insurance department of Indiana, under the regime of State Auditor William H. Hart. Mr. Fitch is a member of Plymouth Congregational church. He is a thirty-second degree Scottish Rite Mason, a Knight Templar, of which order he is past commander, a Shriner, and a member of the Lodge of Elks. His membership in the Commercial Club and the Quest Club, of which bodies he has served as president, afford wide opportunity for efforts along commercial and civic lines, and these have no more active and earnest exponents than Mr. Fitch. In politics he is a Republican. The wife of Mr. Fitch was formerly Miss Elizabeth Fryer, a daughter of the late Henry Fryer, of Avilla, Noble county, this state. Mr. and Mrs. Fitch have one daughter, Geraldine, who is ten years of age, in 1917.

Harvey Fitch is another of the native sons of Allen county who has given good account of himself as one of the world's productive workers and is now living virtually retired in the attractive village of Huntertown, Perry township. He is a stockholder in the Farmers' Mutual Telephone Company and is president of the Huntertown Cemetery Association. The lineage of the Fitch family traces back to sterling English origin and the original American representatives of the family came to this country in the colonial period of our national history. Harvey

Fitch was born on a pioneer farm in Perry township, this county, July 15, 1853, a son of Nathaniel and Sarah Elizabeth (Delong) Fitch, the former a native of Pennsylvania and the latter of Ohio, their marriage having been solemnized in Allen county, Indiana. Nathaniel Fitch, Jr., father of the subject of this review, bore the full name of his father, who was a successful agriculturist in Pennsylvania. Reared and educated in the old Keystone State, Nathaniel, Jr., was a young man when he came from Pennsylvania to Allen county, in 1832, and obtained a homestead claim of government land in Perry township, two and one-half miles east of the present village of Huntertown. He was a blacksmith by trade and it is worthy of historic note that he forged the lock irons used on the old canal extending from Fort Wayne to the Wabash river. He reclaimed his farm from the virtual wilderness and became one of the honored and influential citizens of Perry township. His marriage to Miss Sarah Elizabeth Delong was solemnized on June 14, 1840, and they forthwith established their home on the pioneer farm in Perry township, where Mr. Fitch also established a blacksmith shop in which he continuel to do a large amount of work at his trade, being one of the pioneer exponents of this sturdy vocation within the borders of Allen county. His shop is still standing and is one of the pioneer landmarks of this part of the county. Mr. Fitch developed one of the excellent farms of the county, was active in community affairs and served for a number of years as township trustee. He was about seventy years of age at the time of his death and his widow, one of the gracious and revered pioneer women of the county, attained to the venerable age of ninety years. Mr. Fitch left the parental home when he was a lad of but fifteen years, and he bore with him in a bandana handkerchief all of his forldly possessions, except the rifle which he considered an essential part of his equipment. He made the journey from Pennsylvania to Allen county on foot and eventually became one of the largest landholders in this county, his estate at one time having comprised about thirty-two thousand acres, besides which he became the owner of lands in Iowa. He was one of the most vigorous and ambitious of the pioneers of Allen county and in addition to his farm industry and his work as a blacksmith owned and operated a saw mill near the Dekalb county line and developed also a substantial wool-carding business. He was specially well known for his great pedestrian powers, and he almost invariably made trips to and from his farm and Fort Wayne on foot. The ruins of his pioneer saw mill, which was operated by water power, are still to be seen, and in all, he was a sterling and progressive citizen who contributed much to the furtherance of civic and material development and advancement in Allen county. He and his noble wife, who shared with him in the vicissitudes of pioneer life and in the prosperity of later years, her death having occurred, September 6, 1908, became the parents of fourteen children, and thus gave their full quota of hostages to fortune. The eldest son, Perry, wedded Miss Sarah Elizabeth Gloyd, May 12, 1861, and continued his residence in Allen county until his death, April 18, 1900; Matthias, the second son, married Miss Francis Vandalia, December 1, 1867; Charles married Miss Louisa N. Clubb, April 12, 1868; Mary Jane became the wife of Levi Beers, December 24, 1873; Frances wedded Christian Fair, November 26, 1874; Fitilda became the wife of Jerome Gloyd, October 6, 1875; Amos wedded Miss Nancy Elizabeth Hunter, November 27, 1878; **Harvey, of this review,** was the next in order of birth; Sarah Elizabeth became, December 18, 1881, the wife of Irwin Stratton; Emeline became the wife of Allen Monroe Hartsell, December 28, 1881; David Nathaniel wedded Miss Emma Belle Sterling, June 1, 1878; Idealice became the wife of Melvin Arthur Mason, October 8, 1891; Allen married Emeline Green, May 25, 1893; and Nancy died September 1, 1848, as a child. The honored father, Nathaniel Fitch, died June 1, 1877. Harvey Fitch, to whom this review is dedicated, acquired his early education in the district schools and in Perry Center Seminary, an excellent educational institution of the pioneer days in Allen county history. He continued his studies at intervals until he was about eighteen years of age, and in the meanwhile had gained close and effective fellowship with the sturdy work of the farm. He continued as an exponent of agricultural industry in Perry township and after his marriage, at the age of twenty-eight years, he established his residence on a farm of one hundred and sixty acres, hard by the old homestead of his father. Later he purchased a portion of his father's old homestead and there continued his activities as a progressive agriculturist and stockgrower for a period of about fourteen years, within which he had made his farm one of the model rural demesnes of his native township. About 1906 Mr. Fitch removed with his family to his present attractive home at Huntertown, where he has since lived practically retired, though he still gives close supervision to his various real estate and capitalistic interests. His political allegiance is given unreservedly to the Democratic party and he is well fortified in his opinions concerning governmental and economic affairs. He is a charter member of the lodge of Free and Accepted Masons at Huntertown, and both he and his wife are zealous members of the Universalist church. Their home is known for its gracious hospitality and in the same cordial welcome is always assured to their wide circle of friends. On August 30, 1879, was solemnized the marriage of Mr. Fitch to Miss Etta Permelia Parker, who was born and reared in this county, a daughter of the late Dunbar and Permelia Parker, of Huntertown. Mr. and Mrs. Fitch have five children; Audrey, who completed a course in the Angola College and is now with the wife of George Hursh, of Perry township; Nina completed her education in Valparaiso University and is now the wife of Henry A. Emerick, of Fort Wayne; Parker Eugene, who has charge of the old homestead farm of his father and whose final educational discipline was gained in Angola College, wedded Miss Alma Urbine; Cecil completed the curriculum of the Huntertown public schools and is now the wife of Varnie E. McComb, of Huntertown; and Ernest is a member of the class of 1917 in the Fort Wayne Business College.

Monroe W. Fitch & Sons are known among the spirited and successful representatives of the insurance and real estate business in Fort Wayne, Monroe W. Fitch being associated with his two sons—Delmer C. and Eugene M.—under the firm title of Monroe W. Fitch & Sons, with offices at the corner of Berry and Clinton streets. The father was born in Medina county, Ohio, and in his youth rounded out an effective education by attending Oberlin College. For more than twenty years he owned and operated a fine stock farm in Medina county, and from the same made extensive shipments of high-grade horses to the Eastern market. In 1892 he came to Fort Wayne and engaged in the livery business, but after one year abandoned this enterprise to become associated with his brother, Charles B. Fitch, in the fire insurance business. In 1898 the partnership was dissolved and Mr. Fitch then became associated with his two sons, Delmer C. and Eugene M. Fitch, in forming the present representative insurance firm of Monroe W. Fitch & Sons. The office headquarters of the firm were maintained at 86 Calhoun street until June, 1903, when the purchase of the Hartnett Insurance Agency was effected and removal was made to the well appointed office of the latter, at the corner of Berry and Clinton streets, where is now controlled by the firm a large and substantial general insurance and real estate business. Delmer C. Fitch was likewise born at Medina, Ohio, and is a son of Monroe W. and Emma V. Fitch. In the public schools of his native county he continued his studies until he had availed himself fully of the advantages of the Medina high school, after which he came to Fort Wayne and took a clerical position in the shoe store of his uncle. Two years later he advanced from this post to that of clerk in the offices of the Farmers' Loan Association, but within a short interval was prompted to take an assistant superentendency in the local office of the celebrated Prudential Insurance Company. Energy and ability were shown in later association with other leading insurance agencies in Fort Wayne, and finally, in 1898, he became associated with his father and brother, as previously indicated. The Fitch & Sons agency is well managed and well balanced. They do a large fire insurance business, are general agents for Northeastern Indiana for the Maryland Casualty Company, of Baltimore, Md., handling all the business for that company in Northeastern Indiana. They also do a large and profitable life insurance business for the John Hancock Mutual Life Insurance Company, of Boston, as well as quite an extensive loan business, this department being managed by Delmer C. Fitch. The Real Estate Department is headed by Monroe W. and Eugene M. Fitch, they having several able assistants. They do a large city and suburban business. One of the additions being put on at the time this goes to press is the beautiful subdivision and high class, exclusive residence district known as Crestholme Circle, which is already known to be a great success. They have always made a specialty of handling farms over a wide territory in Northeastern Indiana and Northwestern Ohio, having to their credit many of the largest sales ever closed in this section in the land business. Delmer C. Fitch is identified with the Fort Wayne Real Estate Exchange, the Northern Indiana Underwriters Association, and the Indiana Federation of Fire Insurance Agents. In the Masonic fraternity he is affiliated with the Scottish Rite body, as well as with the Mystic Shrine, and he is identified with the Benevolent and Protective Order of Elks, the Knights of Pythias, the Fort Wayne Commercial Club and the Fort Wayne Country Club.

William Fogwell.—One of the fine farms of Allen county is that owned by William Fogwell, now retired from active farming operations. He was long ranked among the most prosperous and progressive farming men of the county and the rest he now enjoys is one that was well earned in a long period of sturdy adherence to his chosen work. Mr. Fogwell son of Samuel and Mathilda (Davis) Fogwell. The parents were born in son of Samuel and Mathilda (David) Fogwell. The parents were born in Maryland, in the vicinity of Hagerstown. In 1839 Samuel Fogwell came to Indiana, settling in Allen county, in 1839, and making Lafayette township his home. He bought a farm and operated it, giving some attention to his trade as a cooper. He prospered and died on the home place, esteemed by all who knew him. His widow survived for a time and died at the old home place. Mr. Fogwell was a Whig in his early days and

David A. Foster

later became a Republican, and he was one of the leaders of his community as long as he lived. He was progressive, energetic and capable and served his township for years as trustee. He was a member of the Universalist church. Eleven children were born to him and his wife. They were named Mary, William, Anna, Eliza, Jacob, Rebecca, Catherine, the widow of Henry Lopshire, Samuel, David, Martha, Alice and Alfred. Mary, Jacob, Rebecca, Samuel, David, Martha and the two youngest are deceased. William Fogwell attended the public schools of Allen county as a boy and divided his time between his studies and his father's farm up to the age of twenty-one years. He then rented a farm and started out on his own responsibility. His success from the beginning was unusual and he was soon able to buy his first piece of land, a tract of seventy-four acres which has continued to be his home from that time to the present. His next purchase was a forty acre tract adjoining, and he has added one tract after another to his holdings until he today is the owner of between four and five hundred acres of the finest land in the county. He specialized largely in stock and dairy farming in the active years of his life, and his fine cattle and hogs were his pride. Mr. Fogwell has retired from active work and the farm is now being conducted by his son. He is a veteran of the Civil war, having spent three years in the service. He enlisted in August, 1862, in Company C, 74th Indiana Infantry, and continued through to the cessation of hostilities. His command participated in many of the severest engagements of the war, among them being Chickamaugua, Missionary Ridge, Lookout Mountain and the Siege of Atlanta. He was wounded in action on July 9, 1864, and on February following re-entered the ranks and continued until the surrender a few months later. He is a Republican, and served his township as supervisor. He was married on September 29, 1856, to Mary, daughter of John Nicodemus of Allen county, and she died leaving eight children. February, 1877, Mr. Fogwell married Miss Julia A. Smith, daughter of Henry Smith, of Huntington county, Indiana, and one son, Richard, has been born to them. He is engaged in carrying on the farm since his father retired. Mr. Fogwell is grandfather to twelve children and a great-grandfather to five. Mrs. Fogwell was born on April 13, 1848.

David N. Foster.—While, for the past forty years, Colonel David N. Foster has been intimately identified with nearly every activity designed for the good of the people of Fort Wayne, he will be best remembered by coming generations as the "father" of the present city park system. It is of such a man that this sketch treats—a type of citizen which has enabled Fort Wayne to take and to maintain a leading position among the municipalities of the middle west. Colonel Foster was born in Coldenham, Orange County, New York, April 24, 1841. At the early age of fourteen, he left his father's farm and commenced his career as a business man in the capacity of "bundle boy" in the store of W. E. Lawrence, an old-time New York City dry goods merchant. In 1859, at the age of eighteen, in company with his brother, Scott Foster, he formed the retail dry goods firm of Foster Brothers, of New York City, which firm, in 1868, turned its attention to the west and opened its first branch establishments. In 1861, Colonel Foster enlisted as a private in the Ninth New York State Militia. With this regiment he saw three years of severe service in the Union army, resigning, at length, because of disability arising from wounds. He was the first volunteer from Orange county, New York, in the Civil war. He came home from the service captain of the company in which he enlisted as a private, having, meanwhile, gone through the lesser grades of corporal, sergeant and lieutenant. In 1871, Colonel Foster came to Indiana and opened the store of Foster Brothers at Terre Haute, which is still in existence. In 1873 he was attracted into the field of newspaperdom and withdrew from the Terre Haute firm. At Grand Rapids, Mich., he established the Saturday Evening Post, a literary and news paper, an enterprise which met with marked success. In 1877, Colonel Foster's attention was directed to the wide-awake city of Fort Wayne, and he sold his newspaper at such a satisfactory figure that he was enabled to re-enter the old firm of Foster Brothers, which had established the Fort Wayne branch in 1868 on a scale that had made the business at once a leader in the city. One of the earliest acts of Colonel Foster which exhibits his public-spiritedness was the effort to secure the passage by the Indiana legislature of 1882 of the Public Library act by which libraries would come under the direct control of the boards of public school trustees, and which should be established through the levying of a special tax by the city council. The present public library and its excellent management are the outgrowth of this pioneer effort. In 1885, Colonel Foster was chosen Department Commander of the Indiana Grand Army of the Republic, in which organization he has been deeply interested and in which his activities have resulted in the accomplishment of splendid benefits to his former brothers in arms. He is a member of the Loyal Legion of the Commandery of Indiana, and in 1895 was its junior vice commander. He was largely instrumental in the establishment of the Indiana State Soldiers' Home at Lafayette, his service as a member of the commission which selected the site and purchased the grounds proving of high value to those of his companions who sought only the highest good of the remaining members of the country's defenders. He helped to prepare the bill which established the home and succeeded in securing its passage by the legislature. Governor Claude Matthews appointed him to serve as a member of the first board of trustees of the institution. He served a second term under the appointment of Governor James A. Mount. In 1891, with a clear vision of Fort Wayne's future growth, Colonel Foster organized the Fort Wayne Land and Improvement Company, which assumed the big task of creating the present beautiful section of the city known as Lakeside. With a firm belief that saloons should not be permitted in residence districts, he advised that the sale of liquors be forever prohibited in that addition, consisting of one hundred and sixty acres, and the company so decided. The same clause was subsequently placed in the provisions of other contiguous and neighboring additions, until an area of five hundred acres in that part of the city never knew the presence of a saloon. In the same year that the Fort Wayne Land and Improvement Company came into existence, Colonel Foster assisted in the organization of the Tri-State Loan and Trust Company as the subscriber for the first twenty-five shares of the company's stock. He was one of the original stockholders which, under the leadership of Theodore F. Thieme, organized the great corporation known as the Wayne Knitting Mills. He was one of the organizers of the German-American National Bank and the German-American Trust Company. He was one of the original stockholders of the Huntington Trust Company, and, in 1907, he organized the People's Trust Company, at Muncie, Indiana, which bought out the People's National bank of that city and succeeded to its business. He assisted in the organization of the Indiana Road Machine Company and the Fort Wayne Furniture Company. The latter concern, like a great many furniture manufactories, met failure in the financial panic of 1893. Colonel Foster was left with something like $50,000 of endorsed paper to pay. It has always been a matter of pride to him that the entire obligation was paid, one hundred cents on the dollar, principal and interest, "and without the loss of a single night's rest." Colonel Foster was an active spirit in the organization of the Fort Wayne Hotel Company which built the Anthony hotel, one of the leading places of entertainment in the middle west. He was one of the organizers of the Commercial Improvement Company, which purchased the Rockhill farm and made possible the large industrial district immediately west of the city, known as Westfield. The object of this company was not to create financial gain but to add greatly to the city's manufacturing interests. At the time of the destruction of the old covered bridge over the Maumee river at East Main street, Colonel Foster led a two years' "fight" which finally resulted in its re-location at Columbia street, thus giving that oldest of business streets a direct approach over the river from the east and north where before it had always had a dead end at Lafayette street. Colonel Foster was one of the leaders in the erection of the splendid home of the Young Women's Christian Association on West Wayne street. He served as a member of the building committee. He is a member of the First Presbyterian church, and was a member of the building committee which erected the present church building. For several years he served as a member of the board of trustees of the church society. For nearly all his life, Colonel Foster has been a Republican, but he uniformly refused political office. In 1912, believing that the management of the Republican party had fallen into the hands of scheming politicians, he joined the movement for the organization of the Progressive party, and was chosen a delegate to the Chicago convention which nominated Theodore Roosevelt for the presidency. For some years he was the president of Hope Hospital association, and has always been active in behalf of this valuable institution. In fact, there has scarcely been any public activity in any direction in Fort Wayne for nearly forty years in which Colonel Foster has not borne an active part. But, as has been suggested before, he believes his most valuable service and that which will longest endure has been performed through his long connection with the Board of Park Commissioners of Fort Wayne. As its president he has given to the duties of the office for many years nearly one-half of his time without other compensation than that which comes from the performance of public service. He will always be remembered as the "father" of the present splendid park system of Fort Wayne. In 1909, in connection with his brother, Samuel M. Foster, he donated to the city Foster Park, the largest, and in some respects the most useful and most beautiful of all the parks of Fort Wayne. He has said that the only praise to which he and his brother are entitled in this connection is the credit of having shown discriminating sense in the selection of a monument which would endure and grow more beautiful and more serviceable as the years go by. Colonel Foster is inclined to think that he was the first of Fort Wayne business men to incorporate a retail business. The D. N. Foster Furniture Company was incorporated in 1884, the business which had heretofore been a partnership having been established in Fort Wayne in 1868. This business he has so efficiently organized that he has often said that he could drop out of its management at any time and it would continue just as successfully without his aid. On January 10, 1878, Colonel Foster was united in marriage with Miss Sara J. Pyne, of Grand Rapids, Mich., daughter of John and Sara Pyne, of Hamilton, N. Y., and to this union were born the following children: Pearl Foster Rahe, wife of Frank J. Rahe, of Los Angeles, California, and Florence Foster Hall, wife of Harvey Hall, of Charleston, West Virginia.

Samuel M. Foster.—The telling of the story of the life and interests of Samuel M. Foster imposes upon the biographer a task of considerable magnitude. Now in his sixty-sixth year (1917), with ample means to "take life easy," Mr. Foster stands today as a leader in those activities which are of the most valuable service to his fellow-men. An estimate of the position of Mr. Foster in the manufacturing, financial and social life of Fort Wayne and Indiana can best be gained through a consideration of the means of the development of his fortunes down through the years. Such a review will make clear the steps which have led to the enviable place he has so long occupied in this community—steps which have often presented such a rugged and forbidding aspect as would daunt a man of less stable character. Mr. Foster was born in Coldenham, Orange county, New York, December 12, 1851, the son of John L. and Harriet (Scott) Foster. He was the youngest of seven children, six of whom were boys. At the age of fourteen he went to New York and entered upon employment in a dry goods store conducted by his brothers, but, three years afterward, he located at Troy, New York, where, at the age of twenty-one, he formed a partnership with his brother, the late A. Z. Foster, in the retail dry goods business. The brother was, in his latter years, a successful merchant at Terre Haute, Indiana. The Troy venture proved to be profitable, and, two years later, Samuel M. Foster found himself financially able to carry out a plan to secure a collegiate education. He sold his interests in the Troy establishment and entered Yale, at New Haven, Connecticut. The fact that during the conduct of his regular work, Mr. Foster was able to find the time to serve as one of the editors of the Yale Courant suggests the energetic application of the student during that period. Incidentally, he won an appointment on the junior exhibition, earned the high honor of a selection as one of the Townsend men from a competitive class of one hundred and thirty-two, and was named by the faculty as one of ten to represent the class on the platform on the occasion of commencement day. On June 26, 1879, Mr. Foster received the degree of Bachelor of Arts, and graduated fourteenth in a class composed originally of two hundred members. Mr. Foster came to Fort Wayne in the fall of 1879, and entered the law office of Judge Robert S. Taylor. He had not determined the nature of his life work, but was aware of the value of an education along the line which the reading of the law would provide. At this same time, he was concerned with regard to the condition of his health, which had become impaired during the closing strenuous days of his work at Yale, and he determined to abandon for the time, at least, the more or less confining work of the law office and to enter upon a career in journalism. The way was opened at Dayton, Ohio, where the Saturday Evening Record was established, with Mr. Foster as its editor and proprietor. The experience was brief, and it appears to have convinced Mr. Foster that a continuance in this line

David M. Foster

at that time would have been ruinous to both health and purse. In 1880, the Record—now the Dayton Daily Herald—was sold, and Mr. Foster returned to Fort Wayne and resumed his connection with Foster Brothers, who had launched upon the commercial sea in the middle west. In 1882, the firm was dissolved by the withdrawal of Scott Foster, who went to New York to assume the duties as president of a bank, and the business of the firm was then divided, Samuel M. Foster succeeding to the charge of the firm's dry goods department. It was while encountering reverses in the business world that Mr. Foster, with rare good fortune, became "the father of the shirt waist" which laid the foundation of his fortune and provided the women of the world with the most useful and the most universally-worn garment ever devised. Referring to this most interesting period, Mr. Foster, in an interview published in 1904, said: "It's the same old story. Necessity was the mother of invention. I was in the retail dry goods business over on Calhoun street, between Main and Berry. I had precious little capital, and most of it was borrowed. Rent was high and trade was dull. It was a perfect case of 'expenses like New York and business like New Haven.' 'A general flavor of mild decay' pervaded the establishment, and there was great danger that the business would dry up and blow away. For months I was on the ragged edge, and couldn't see anything in the future but failure in business and the humiliation of not being able to pay my debts. Clerks stood around and waited for customers who wouldn't come. My own time was taken up largely in trying to devise some plan to stem the current that was slowly, but I could see was surely, carrying me into water beyond my depth. One day in the winter of 1884-5, when the thermometer was too low to read, and a customer was as scarce as natural gas, I just happened to recall that during the preceding summer I had bought some boys' unlaundered shirt waists that were good sellers and hard to get. I fell to wondering whether we could not make some for the next season, using the materials from the store and having the clerks cut them out. There wasn't one left in stock, but inquiry among the clerks revealed the fact that one of them had one at home in the wardrobe of his little boy. When he brought it to the store the next day it was a sorry-looking object, worn out and faded by many washings. But I wish I had it today. I would be tempted to have it handsomely framed and installed among those who have been my best friends. How little it takes to change the current of men's lives! How small a thing will sometimes turn failure aside and bring success in its stead, or vice versa! It fairly makes one shudder to think how much often depends upon the way we decide the merest trifle. Perhaps the same small measure of success would have followed along some other chain of events, but we can 'never measure the might have been.' Be that as it may, the little rag of a shirt waist was the start of what little material success I may have met with. What did I do with it? Well, I took it and with my own hands ripped it apart, and from the different parts made something resembling patterns. Then I cut one out and one of the clerks sewed it together. When it was done it was like the boy who was to wear it, 'fearfully and wonderfully made.' Then we guessed how much bigger the larger sizes should be and how much smaller the smaller ones. Then we skirmished about to find 'kids' of the average sizes for the various ages from four to fourteen years. After pegging along in this way for a while we eventually secured patterns for a line of sizes. I think I did all the work myself. Then we started to make up a little stock. We didn't even know how to go about cutting them out. We used pocket knives and scissors, and cut about three thicknesses of cloth at a time. Now often we cut sixty at one time and do it easier than when we used to cut three. Everything was petty and crude, but we didn't know any better. About this time I remember one day my brother, D. N. Foster, and George W. Pixley came in, and, finding me haggling away with a jack-knife, remarked with mingled pity and disgust, 'Well, that's great work for a Yale graduate to be at.' However, necessity, like the lawyers, 'knows no law,' and I had to keep at it. After getting a lot cut, we gave them out to women to make. Our idea up to this time was merely to make enough for our own use, but one day it occurred to me that I might sell some to other merchants. So I mailed a sample to about half a dozen dry goods firms that I knew of, together with a personal letter. I remember very well the result. We received three orders for twenty-five dozen each. The receipt of these three orders quite elated me. I figured they cost me $1.50 per dozen, not counting the time of the clerks, and we sold them for $2 a dozen. Other small orders came in, and I quickly set about increasing our facilities. I found out how to cut them and hired a cutter. He is with us yet. We made just one thing, a boys' calico shirt waist at $2 a dozen. The first season we sold three thousand dozen, clearing $1,500, but what was made in the shirt waist business was being promptly lost in the dry goods business, and then some. The second year we sold six thousand dozen, the profits from which promptly again went down the same rathole. About this time I made up my mind to get out of the dry goods business in any way possible short of setting fire to the store. It took a year to accomplish this, but at last it was achieved, and I came out with a whole skin and good credit, but not much except faith and hope. This was in December, 1886. Since then it has been smooth sailing, but I have often thought that I worked harder and more intelligently when I was going down hill than I have ever since. So you see, as I said before, it was the old story of necessity being the mother of invention. Had I been making a living in the dry goods business I would have been there yet, but because I wasn't I had to devise something else. So, a fellow doesn't ever know what is best for him, or, as the believer in special providence puts it: 'Behind a frowning countenance God often hides a smiling face!' Well, who invented the ladies' shirt waist? Nobody. Like Topsy, it 'just grew.' I have told you we started making boys' shirt waists in December, 1886. By the summer of 1889 we had so developed the business that we were making quite a line of styles in the various sizes, the largest being fourteen years. Along in the spring of that year we found ourselves receiving many reorders for the largest sizes only. As the price was based on the average size, and as a fourteen cost about double what a four did, orders for nothing but big sizes left us holding the bag at a great rate. Some requests came for sixteens. We knew boys of that size and age didn't wear shirt waists, so we set on foot an inquiry to ascertain what had created the demand. We discovered that the boys' sisters were buying these large sizes and wearing them to play croquet and lawn tennis, or to go picnicking in. Soon they began asking for longer sleeves and smaller necks. We took the hint and made something especially adapted for the girls. The next year we made quite a line that met with ready sale, but it was a year or two before we broke loose, and every woman took to wearing them. As we know it, the shirt waist is an American garment. It originated here and has always been much more generally worn in this country than in Europe. Later, the separate silk waist came into vogue, and, since its advent, it has had a considerable influence on the wash waists. I do not claim that we made the first shirt waists that were ever made in this country, but I know of no one who made them before we did. Probably some other manufacturers had an experience similar to ours at about the same time, and responded to the demand about as we did. Certainly, we were the first parties west of New York to take up the manufacture of this garment which has been of such value to feminine humanity. Something like five or six successful factories have been started either directly or indirectly as the result of ours." The shirt waist factory of the S. M. Foster Company is now one of Fort Wayne's leading manufacturing institutions. The foundation of the German-American National bank, in 1904, with Mr. Foster as its president, has left the conduct of the manufacturing business largely to his associates, while his personal attention is centered more closely upon the business of the bank. For a long time Mr. Foster was the president of one of the city's most important manufacturing enterprises, the Wayne Knitting Mills, and he now holds the place of chairman of the board of directors of the institution. Besides his large stock interests in various Fort Wayne institutions, he is one of the owners of the plant of the Western Gas Construction Company, makers of gas holders and gas-making apparatus; he holds a valuable interest in the Fort Wayne Box Company, makers of paper boxes and cartons. Besides the presidency of the German-American National bank, Mr. Foster holds a like position with the German-American Trust Company, a state institution with a south side branch. Ever since the creation of the Lincoln National Life Insurance Company, now recognized as one of the best-managed and most rapidly growing institutions of its kind in America, he has held the responsible position of president. Mr. Foster, when asked to state the most important item of his activities as it bears upon the public good, refers to an incident of about twenty years ago when he precipitated a fight for the principle that interest on public funds should not pass into the hands of the official in charge of the public's business, but should belong to the people and be used for their benefit. On this issue Mr. Foster was elected a member of the Fort Wayne board of school trustees. After a prolonged contest, funds that had long passed into private pockets were diverted to public uses. His fight resulted in the present depository law which requires that interest on all public funds is to be turned back to the public. Mr. Foster served one term as school trustee, and with the interest received during that time, together with his salary as trustee, the site of the present public library was purchased. This was done in 1895. That the opposition to Mr. Foster's stand was decidedly strong is shown by the fact that 204 ballots were required to elect him and the session of the city council extended to the hour of 2 o'clock in the morning. In 1913, Mr. Foster was offered by President Woodrow Wilson the position of ambassador to the Argentine Republic, but he declined the honor. In company with his wife, Mr. Foster, in 1907, visited southern Europe, and, during 1909, they visited "the land of the midnight sun." In 1912 they made a voyage around the world. Mr. Foster was married in June, 1881, to Margaret Harrison, of Fort

Wayne. They have one daughter, Alice Harrison, the wife of Fred H. McCulloch, grandson of Hugh McCulloch, the first controller of the currency of the United States and the secretary of the treasury under three presidents. Mr. Foster is prominent in Masonic circles as a holder of the Thirty-second degree in the Scottish rite. He is an Elk, a Moose, a member of the Fortnightly club, president of Hope Hospital Association and president of the Associated Charities, and is affiliated with many other important movements. In 1911 Governor Marshall appointed him a trustee of Purdue University, in which capacity he is still serving. Governor Samuel M. Ralston, in 1916, appointed Mr. Foster as a member of the Indiana Centennial Commission having in charge the state-wide celebration of the one hundredth anniversary of the admission of Indiana to the sisterhood of states. The fondness of Mr. Foster for fine horses is shown in his favorite pastime of horseback riding. During recent years Mr. Foster has devoted much time to the subject of taxation, and it is through his efforts that the attention of the people of Indiana is called to many unjust features of the present statutes. In 1915, Mr. Foster sold his fine home on West Wayne street to the Loyal Order of Moose and erected two attractive homes on South Fairfield avenue, one for himself and wife and the other for his daughter. In 1909, in connection with his brother, David N. Foster, he gave to the city of Fort Wayne, Foster Park, the largest and in some regards the finest of the public parks. Foster Park will preserve forever the name of the brothers who in this way, as in many others, have given of their best selves to the upbuilding of their home city.

Louis Fox.—The many interests and activities of Louis Fox are the most suggestive evidences of his efforts to bring to a high standard of success those enterprises which have required the combination of intellect and means to insure their growth and stability. During the period of his entire life in Fort Wayne, Mr. Fox has exerted a splendid influence upon the development of many enterprises in which have been required those sterling elements which he has known so well how to provide. He was born in Fort Wayne, March 8, 1852, a son of George and Mary Fox. The father was a native of Germany, and the mother came from Switzerland. They engaged in the confectionery and baking business, beginning in 1863, and continued in it with growing success. The father died on October 13, 1892. The mother died, August 10, 1891. Three children were born to George and Mary Fox, namely, August L. and Joseph V., both deceased, and Louis, the subject of this sketch. Louis Fox received his education in the Catholic and public schools of Fort Wayne. He fitted himself for a commercial career by attending business college. His first endeavors in the business world were with the wholesale grocery and confectionery house of Huestis & Hamilton, where he gave special attention to the details of the candy trade, which better fitted him to engage with his father in the manufacture of confectionery and baked goods. This connection was continued until June 1, 1877, when Mr. Fox formed a partnership with H. J. Trentman in a wholesale cracker and confectionery establishment. In 1882, he purchased Mr. Trentman's interests and conducted the business alone until June 11, 1890, when the United States Baking Company bought the business and engaged Mr. Fox as manager; he was also a director in the purchasing concern. In 1898, the United States Baking Company sold its interests to the National Biscuit Company, and Mr. Fox

Louis Fox

continued as manager of this concern until June 1, 1902, when he resigned and retired from active business. "I have passed by fiftieth birthday," said Mr. Fox, "and I desired to retire from active business, this being my twenty-fifth year in the cracker and candy business in Fort Wayne." His retirement did not remove him from the active business world, for Mr. Fox is that type of energetic, aggressive personality that cannot be satisfied with retirement. His many business interests which are closely connected with the development of his home city and those of other cities to which his influence has spread, have kept him active in the business world. He is at the present time the president of the Hartford City (Indiana) Paper Company, one of the truly prosperous manufacturing institutions of the State; vice-president of the Tri-State Loan & Trust Company, one of Fort Wayne's strongest financial institutions; president of the Medical Protective Company, the largest insurance company engaged exclusively in that class of insurance; president of the Fort Wayne Postal Telegraph Company; president of the Fort Wayne District Telegraph Company; president of the Brazil (Indiana) Gas Company; a director of the First and Hamilton National Bank; a director of the Wayne Knitting Mills; a director of the Commercial Land & Improvement Company; a director of the Fort Wayne Corrugated Paper Company, director of Wayne Paper Goods Company, director Deister's Miner Supply Company, president Tatahuicapa Plantation Company, president of the Lake Erie & Fort Wayne Railroad Company, a trustee of the Catholic Cemetery Association, and a trustee of St. Paul's Catholic Church. A consideration of these and the many incidental connections of Mr. Fox with the activities of his home city is convincing evidence of the appreciation of his clear mind, his agreeable personality and his substantial citizenship. Among the most recent enterprises of our city for which Mr. Fox is wholly responsible is the erection of a mammoth department store building on the northeast corner of Calhoun and Washington streets. This building will be the largest and best equipped store building in Northern Indiana. The property, when completed, will represent an investment of more than one million dollars and is a distinct advance in the upbuilding of this city and an undertaking for which Mr. Fox has received the high commendation of all who are interested in the growth of Fort Wayne. Mr. Fox was married on September 2, 1875, to Sophia Lau, daughter of Thomas and Mary Lau. Mr. Lau was an architect and builder of Fort Wayne. To Louis Fox and wife were born three children: Rose M., wife of Charles M. Niezer, to whom have been born one son, Louis Fox, and two daughters, Rosemary Lau and Margaret Sarah. Robert L. and Oscar A. Fox, sons of Mr. and Mrs. Fox, are engaged in business in Fort Wayne under the firm name of Fox Brothers & Company, retail dealers in furniture and house furnishings. Robert L. married Edna Reuss, daughter of John B. and Amelia Reuss, of this city, and they have one daughter, Virginia Mary. Oscar A. was united in marriage with Alma Zangerle, daughter of a prominent furniture manufacturer of Chicago, and they thave two daughters—Aneta Lucille and Nancy Alma—and one son, Louis Arthur. Louis Fox is a staunch adherent to principles of the Democratic party. He is a member of the Fort Wayne Lodge of Elks, of the Fort Wayne Country Club, of the Commercial Club, The Knights of Columbus, and of St. Paul's Catholic Church. The confidence of the citizens of Fort Wayne in Louis Fox as a desirable leader of the people is shown in their frequent appeals to him to serve in large official capacities. His inclinations have caused him to decline the nomination for the mayoralty on several occasions. He has, however, served as a member of the city council from the sixth ward, and there gave the benefit of his voice and influence to the making of a greater Fort Wayne. As a member of the city Board of Park Commissioners, he has done much to bring about a development of the present splendid park and boulevard system. His business experience has not been without its discouraging circumstances. In 1889, for example, a fire destroyed in its entirety his factory building, located at Calhoun and Jefferson streets. Mr. Fox merely used this as an occasion for expansion and larger endeavor. His home life has been of the happiest. Mrs. Fox was called from earth, September 21, 1914. In the enjoyment of her companionship Mr. Fox had made a number of European voyages, visits to Mexico, Central and South America and other portions of the old and new world. There now remains the memory of this companionship and the presence of the children and grandchildren to add to the pleasure of his later days.

Henry Franke established, in 1893, his present thriving business industry in Fort Wayne, where he has a well-equipped and essentially modern plant devoted to the manufacturing of special lines of lumber products, particular attention being given to the output of high-grade interior finish, the same being used almost entirely by local contractors and builders in Allen county. Ability and well-ordered energy have made the enterprise a most prosperous one and the establishment is situated at 1215 Hugh street. In initiating the business Mr. Franke began operations with a modest equipment driven by horse power. Later he utilized steam power and, keeping in touch with modern progress, he now operates his machinery by electricity. He gives employment to an average force of sixteen persons and is one of the reliable and highly esteemed business men of the city that has been his home for nearly forty years. Henry Franke was born at Petershagen, Westphalia, Germany, on September 8, 1857, and is a son of Christian and Sophia (Uphoff) Franke, both of whom passed their entire lives in that section of the great empire of Germany, the father having been a carpenter by trade and vocation. He whose name introduces this review gained his early education in the schools of his native town, principally in the Lutheran parochial schools, and thereafter learned the carpenter's trade under the effective direction of his father. In 1881, when twenty-three years of age, he severed the home ties and set forth to make his way in America, where he felt assured of better opportunities for gaining independence through individual effort. In that year he established his home in Fort Wayne, and here he worked at the carpenter's trade with Charles Krudorf for some time. Later he engaged independently in business as a contractor and builder, and in 1893 he founded his present excellent business enterprise, as previously noted. About 1902 he also established at Wayne Trace, this county, the Farmers' Lumber & Shingle Company, and in the control of this business likewise he has been definitely successful. Mr. Franke is always ready to aid in the support of those things that tend to advance the welfare of the community, but he has had no desire for public office or the affairs of politics. Both he and his wife are zealous members of Emanuel Lutheran church. February 22, 1882, recorded the marriage of Mr. Franke to Miss Wilhelmina Graeper, daughter of William Graeper, of Westphalia, Germany, where Mrs. Franke was born and reared, as was also her husband. Of the three children of this ideal union the eldest is William, who is actively identified with Fort Wayne business interests. He wedded Miss Marie Hartwig and they have four children— Henry, Esther, Florence and Richard. Bertha, the second of the children, is the wife of George Buehler, of Toledo, Ohio, and Emma, the youngest child, remains at the parental home.

Eldridge Franklin has proved himself an efficient and versatile factor in connection with practical electrical enterprise and now holds the position of superintendent of overhead construction in the light and power department of the Fort Wayne & Northern Indiana Traction Company, with residence and official headquarters in the city of Fort Wayne. His technical knowledge of applied electricity is equaled by his practical and executive ability and he is one of the representative young men in the employ of the important corporation mentioned. Mr. Franklin was born in Chariton county, Missouri, on April 13, 1889, and is a son of Marcellus and Anna (Davis) Franklin, both of whom were born and reared in Missouri, where they passed their entire lives, the father having been a contractor during the major part of his active business career. They became the parents of seven children, of whom the first born, Maggie, is deceased; Arthur Frederick resides in the city of Omaha, Nebraska; Eldridge, of this sketch, was the next in order of birth; Edward Earl maintains his home at Moberly, Missouri; Florence is the wife of William Meyers, of Delphi, Carroll county, Indiana; and Thomas died in childhood. Eldridge Franklin gained his early education in the public schools of his native state and was a lad of thirteen years at the time of his mother's death. He was then taken into the home of his maternal grandparents, on whose farm, in Chariton county, Missouri, he remained two years, in the meanwhile continuing to attend school. In his native county he finally entered Salisbury University, in which excellent institution he continued his studies three years, with special attention given to electrical engineering. Upon leaving the university Mr. Franklin came to Indiana and assumed a position in the employ of Delphi Electrical Company, at the judicial center of Carroll county. He continued in the service of this company until January 1, 1909, when he came to Fort Wayne and entered the employ of the Fort Wayne & Northern Indiana Traction Company, with which he has since been connected and with which his ability and effective service have led to his advancement to the position noted in the opening lines of this article. Mr. Franklin is found aligned as a loyal supporter of the cause of the Republican party, he and his wife are communicants of St. Patrick's Catholic church, and he is affiliated with the Knights of Pythias, the Improved Order of Red Men, the Independent Order of Odd Fellows, and the Tribe of Ben Hur. In 1904 was solemnized the marriage of Mr. Franklin to Miss Mary Sales, who was born and reared at Delphi, this state, and they became the parents of three children—Esther Mary, Thomas Marcellus, and Eldridge, Jr., the last mentioned having died in infancy.

Henry Frech.—More than sixty years ago, when he was a lad of about ten years, this venerable citizen of Fort Wayne accompanied his parents on their immigration from Germany to America, in 1853, and the family home was establisher on a pioneed farm in Aboite township, this county. Here the subject of this review lived up to the full tension involved in reclaiming from the forest a productive farm and eventually it devolved upon him to develop a farm for himself. In the most significant way did he honor and show his loyalty to the land of his adoption when the Civil war was precipitated, for he was one of the sturdy young men who went forth from Allen county to do valiant service in defense of the Union. As a soldier of the republic he made a record that shall ever reflect distinction and honor upon his name. Mr. Frech was born in the Kingdom of Wurtemberg, Germany, October 8, 1843, and thus he has now passed the psalmist's span of three score years and ten, so that, having borne the heat and burden of the day, he has justified himself to the world and well merits the gracious peace and prosperity that attend him now that he has retired from the active responsibilities that long developed upon him. He is a son of Henry and Christina (Exter) Frech, of whose six children four attained to maturity, the subject of this review being now the only survivor of this sterling pioneer family of Allen county. The other three who grew to maturity in this county and who have passed from the stage of life's mortal endeavors were Frederick, John and Christina. Upon coming to Allen county, in 1854, Henry Frech, Sr., purchased eighty acres of timbered land in Aboite township, and his initial work was to make a clearing for the little log house which he built as the family home. He eventually improved a productive farm and on this old homestead he and his wife passed the remainder of their lives, their names meriting enduring place on the roll of the sterling pioneers of Allen county. Both were zealous communicants of the Lutheran church and in politics he became a staunch supporter of the cause of the Democratic party. Henry Frech, Jr., the immediate subject of this sketch, acquired his rudimentary education in his native land and as a boy attended for a time the pioneer district school in Aboite township, though he early found that the arduous work of the home farm demanded the greater part of his attention. He did well his part in reclaiming the land and continued to assist his father until there came the call of higher duty, with the outbreak of the Civil war. In 1862, at the age of eighteen years, he enlisted as a private in Company B, Twelfth Indiana Infantry, and with this gallant command continued in service until the close of the war, when he received his honorable discharge. He took part in many of the important engagements marking the progress of the great conflict and was always found at the post of duty. He took part in battles at Richmond, Kentucky, Vicksburg, Mississippi and Jackson, Mississippi, and in connection with the memorable Atlanta campaign he participated in the battles of Missionary Ridge, New Hope Church and Kenesaw Mountain, as well as the siege and capture of Atlanta July 22-28, 1864. Thereafter he was with his command in the engagements at Jonesboro, Savannah, Columbia, Bentonville and Raleigh, in connection with Sherman's historic march to the sea, and within his military career he was in every southern state except Texas and Florida. He marched more than six thousand miles, and Frank Aveline, the original captain of his company, met death in the battle of Missionary Ridge. Mr. Frech witnessed and assisted in the burning of the city of Columbia, South Carolina, and after the final surrender took part in the Grand Review, in the city of Washington. After his return to Fort Wayne Mr. Frech was here engaged in the ice business for a time and then bought eighty acres of unimproved land in Aboite township. His first domicile was a primitive log house which he erected on his land, and he cleared an dimproved the farm, to which he later added forty acres. He made this one of the fine farms of the township and the excellent buildings that now mark the place were erected by him. He remained on the old homestead until 1912, since which time he has lived retired in Fort Wayne, where his home is at 754 West Superior street. Mr. Frech has never faltered in his allegiance to the Republican party and his first vote for president was cast for President Lincoln, he having been at the time in service as a soldier of the Union. He has vitalized the more gracious memories and associations of his military career through forty years of appreciative affiliation with the Grand Army of the Republic, in Sion S. Bass Post, No. 40, at Fort Wayne. He was reared in the faith of the Lutheran church and has ever held to the same, as did also his loved and devoted wife, the supreme loss and bereavement in his life having come when she was summoned to eternal rest June 13, 1914. On October 4, 1870, was solemnized the marriage of Mr. Frech to Miss Jennie Birely, a daughter of David and Anna (Bowser) Birely, who came from Pennsylvania to Allen county many years ago and here passed the residue of their lives. Concerning the children of Mr. and Mrs. Frech brief record is entered in conclusion of this review: Frank is the owner of a valuable ranch in the state of Colorado, where he maintains his home; Anna is the wife of John Clark, of Perry township; Ida is the wife of Grant Simmons, of Huntington county; Charles resides upon and operates the old homestead farm, in Aboite township; Jessie is the wife of Henry William McMaken, of Aboite township; and Florence is the wife of Carl Garting, a farmer of Lake township. Mr. Frech receives from his children the deepest filial devotion and takes just pride in the fact that he has twenty-one grand-children.

Charles Freese has been for many years actively identified with the drug business in his native city of Fort Wayne and is now one of the leading exponents of this important line of retail enterprise in Allen county. In 1910 he organized the Dreier Drug Company, which took over the old established Dreier drug store, at 526 Calhoun street, and he has since continued as the active executive and manager of the well-ordered establishment, which is kept up to the best metropolitan standard and which receives a representative supporting patronage, besides which they also own a drug store at 1402 Calhoun street. Mr. Freese was born in Fort Wayne August 2, 1860, and is a son of William A. and Sophia (Rehling) Freese, both of whom were born in Germany and were young folk at the time when they came to America, about the year 1847, and numbered themselves among the pioneers of Allen county, Indiana. Here their acquaintanceship was formed and here their marriage was solemnized, at Fort Wayne, in 1853. Of their three children the subject of this review is the youngest; Amelia is the wife of George Nill, of Fort Wayne; and William A., Jr., likewise resides in this city. The father gave his attention principally to lumber manufacturing during the period of his residence in Indiana, was a sterling representative of that fine element of German citizenship and progress of Allen county, and he was comparatively a young man at the time of his death, in 1861. His wife survived him by more than half a century and was one of the venerable pioneer women of Allen county at the time of her death, in May, 1914. Both of the parents were lifelong and earnest communicants of the Lutheran church. Charles Freese made good use of the advantages offered by the public schools of Fort Wayne and, in 1877, when about seventeen years of age, entered upon a practical apprenticeship in the Dreier drug store. Within his four years' service in this establishment he gained a thorough technical knowledge of pharmacy and upon severing his connection with the Dreier firm went to the city of Chicago, where he held a position in a similar establishment for the ensuing two years. He then returned to Fort Wayne and for virtually a quarter of a century thereafter continued in the employ of the Meyer Brothers' Drug Company. He is thus to be considered as one of the veteran representatives of the drug business in his native city, and upon leaving the Meyer company's employ he purchased the old established Dreier drug store, in which he had served his apprenticeship, and in 1910 effected the organization of the Dreier Drug Company, of which he is vice-president. His wide acquaintanceship and unqualified personal popularity have proved potent in expanding the business of the company and as practical manager of the establishment he has brought to it a large contingent of new and appreciative patrons. Mr. Freese is a staunch Republican, but has never had any ambition for public office or for the activities of so-called practical politics. He is a member of the Fort Wayne Rotary Club and is affiliated with the local lodge of the Benevolent and Protective Order of Elks. Both he and his wife hold membership in the English Lutheran church. In 1906 Mr. Freese wedded Miss Louise Bulmahn, who likewise was born and reared in Fort Wayne, and who is a daughter of Henry E. Bulmahn.

Henry F. Freese, one of the representative young business men of Allen county, is secretary and treasurer of the New Haven Floral Company, which has a large and modern plant at New Haven and is one of the leading concerns engaged in high-grade floriculture in Northern Indiana. Adequate description of the green houses and business of the company is given on other pages, in the sketch of the career of the vice-president and general manager of the company, Herman J. C. Leitz. Henry F. Freese was born in the city of Fort Wayne, April 18, 1891, son of August and Christina (Kiel) Freese, both natives of Munden, Kingdom of Hanover, Germany, whence they came to America and established their home in Fort Wayne, about the year 1881. August Freese was engaged in the retail grocery business in this city for a number of years and is now at the head of a substantial wholesale liquor business in Fort Wayne, his loyalty and progressiveness being denoted by his active membership in the Fort Wayne Commercial Club. Both he and his wife are communicants of the parish of Emmaus German Lutheran church. Concerning their children brief record is here given: Fred is deceased; August remains at the parental home; Herman is deceased; Henry F., of this sketch, was the fourth; Wilma and Esther are with their parents; Elsie is deceased; and Lydia is the youngest member of the parental home circle. Henry F. Freese gained his early education in the Lutheran parochial schools in Fort Wayne and thereafter completed an effective course in the International Business College, one of the well conducted educational institutions of Fort Wayne, where also he availed himself of the advantages of Concordia College. After leaving school he was employed two and one-half years in the Fort Wayne plant of the General Electric Company, as an office assistant, and for two years thereafter held a position in the office of the firm of Freese & Gale, of which his father is senior member. He next was employed two years in the offices of the Cushion Heel Shoe Company, at Fort Wayne, and in February, 1914, became secretary and treasurer of the New Haven Floral Company, to the affairs of which he has since given his close attention. In politics he is an independent voter, he is one of the vital and progressive members of the New Haven Commercial Club and he still retains membership in Emmaus Lutheran church in Fort Wayne, as does he also in various clubs and subsidiary organizations of this flourishing parish. On November 16, 1915, was solemnized the marriage of Mr. Freese to Miss Louise M. Yergens, daughter of Gustav and Minnie (Klett) Yergens, of Fort Wayne, and they make of their pleasant home in New Haven a veritable center of generous hospitality.

John Freiburger.—After years of conscientious application to the industry of farming, John Freiburger found himself in a position where he might retire and enjoy the fruits of his labors. He has lived quietly on his home farm in Sheldon since 1877. Mr. Freiburger was born in Alsace, France, on April 1, 1849, and in 1855 came with his parents to American shores, settling soon thereafter in Allen county, Indiana. He was reared to farm life and as a young man spent some little time in Fort Wayne. He was devoted to the country, however, and in 1897 bought a small farm of seventy-five acres in Pleasant township, to which, in later years, he was able to add a forty-acre tract, and on this acreage he carried on successful farming activities for many years. He is a progressive man in agriculture and his farm is one of the well-kept and highly productive places in the township. On September 30, 1873, Mr. Freiburger married Miss Mary Miller, the daughter of Christian and Lena (Rupp) Miller. The father, it may be said, was of French birth and parentage, but the mother was of Russian ancestry. They were among the early pioneer settlers in Allen county, and dated their coming from some time in the thirties. They knew all the privations and dangers common to the people of their day who braved the wilds in their desire to establish independent homes in a new land, and their names go down in the history of Allen county among those of her pioneer sons and daughters. Seven children came to them, all deceased but two—Catherine of Fort Wayne, and Mary, the wife of the subject. The others were Lou, Frank, Andrew, John and Albert. John Freiburger was himself one of a large family of thirteen children. Barney, the eldest, lives in Fort Wayne. Theresa is deceased. John came next. Ignatius is no longer living. Joseph is living in Fort Wayne. George died in March, 1914. Mary M. and Caroline have their homes in Fort Wayne. Peter is located in Wisconsin, Antony is established in Grand Rapids, Michigan. The three youngest children died in childhood. To Mr. and Mrs. Freiburger have come thirteen children. Catherine lives in Lafayette, Indiana. Albert and Clara are identified with Fort Wayne. Edward is located in Lafayette. He is a priest in the Roman Catholic church, and serves in his priestly capacity at St. Joseph's Orphan Asylum. Ignatius lives in Ossian. Laurette is in Alliance, Ohio. Mary has honored the family by her entrance into a sisterhood, Providence. Ambrose lives in Sheldon. Ida died June 11, 1914. Rose, Eugene, Estella and Priscilla are still members of the family home. All are members of the Roman Catholic church, and Mr. Freiburger is a Democrat in his political faith.

Anselm Fuelber is one of the specially honored and influential representatives of the sterling German element of citizenship that has contributed much to the civic and material advancement and prosperity of Fort Wayne. He is a man of fine intellectual and professional attainments, has been prominently concerned with newspaper enterprise in Fort Wayne, but he is now giving his attention principally to the practice of law and to the insurance business. He is known and valued as one of the loyal and public-spirited citizens of Fort Wayne and is definitely entitled to specific recognition in this history of Allen county. A member of a family of five children, Mr. Fuelber is the only representative of the family to have established a home in the United States, he being the youngest of the children and his mother having died at the time of his birth. His father, Edward Fuelber, was a prosperous farmer in Germany, and there passed his entire life. He whose name initiates this article was born in Germany on April 19, 1851, and in his native land received excellent educational advantages, including a course in the law department of the great University of Berlin, in which he was graduated as a member of the class of 1875, with the degree of Bachelor of Laws. In 1878, as a young man of twenty-seven years, Mr. Fuelber came to America and for the first four years maintained his residence in the city of New Haven, Connecticut. He then passed a year at Cincinnati, Ohio, from which city he came to Fort Wayne in 1883. The greater part of his active business career has been marked by close and effective alliance with newspaper enterprise, and as a writer he has proved specially strong in a literary sense as well as influential in the directing of popular sentiment and action. For twenty-five years he was connected with the Fort Wayne Staats Zeitung, and for four years thereafter was manager and editor-in-chief of the Fort Wayne Abend Post. Since his retirement from active journalistic work he has given his attention primarily to the insurance business, besides which he is making effective application of his ability as a lawyer, though he has held his professional ability in this line as incidental and supplemental to his activities in connection with other fields of business. Well fortified in his political convictions, Mr. Fuelber has been an effective advocate of the principles and policies of the Democratic party, but he is not constrained by strict partisanship and is a stalwart supporter of the policy of a high protective tariff for the country of his adoption, as he has made a close study of governmental and economic questions. He holds membership in representative German societies in his home city and also is affiliated with the local lodge of the Benevolent and Protective Order of Elks. His interest in local affairs has been loyal and insistent and he served three years as a trustee of the Fort Wayne board of education, the Bloomingdale, Washington and Smart school buildings having been erected while he was the incumbent of this office. In 1885 was solemnized the marriage of Mr. Fuelber to Miss Anna Rath, who was born in Germany and who accompanied her parents, Dr. August Rath and Caroline (Adam) Rath on their immigration to America, the family home having been established at Fort Wayne in 1877 and the parents having here passed the residue of their lives, Doctor Rath having become one of the representative physicians and surgeons of this city. Mr. and Mrs. Fuelber have one son, Otto E., who is engaged in the law business in Fort Wayne, as a member of the firm of Harper & Fuelber, with offices in the Shoaff building; he wedded Miss Edna McClaren, of Ann Arbor, Michigan, and they have two children—McClaren A., and Harriet.

Otto E. Fuelber is making his native city of Fort Wayne the stage of his successful endeavors as one of the well-fortified and ambitious younger members of the Allen county bar, and in the practice of his profession is associated with James B. Harper, this alliance having obtained since 1912, the year of his graduation in the law school. Mr.

Fuelber was born in Fort Wayne on February 24, 1890, and is a son of Anselm and Anna (Rath) Fuelber, who still reside in this city. He profited duly by the advantages afforded in the public schools and the International Business College of Fort Wayne, and in the meanwhile had formulated definite plans for his future career. Following the course of his ambition, he entered the law department of the great University of Michigan, at Ann Arbor, in which he was graduated as a member of the class of 1912 and from which he received his degree of Bachelor of Laws. He was forthwith admitted to the bar of his native state and has since been engaged in active practice in his native city, where he is proving himself resourceful and successful both as a trial lawyer and as a counselor well grounded in the involved science of jurisprudence. Mr. Fuelber is aligned as a staunch advocate of the cause of the Democratic party and takes an active interest in local affairs of a public order. On June 6, 1913, was recorded his marriage to Miss Edna MacLaren, daughter of Henry and Harriet B. MacLaren, of Ann Arbor, Michigan, and they have two children—MacLaren A., who was born January 18, 1915, and Harriet, who was born April 28, 1916.

John F. Fuelling is one of the progressive farmers and loyal citizens claimed by Milan township, his being one of the large and well improved landed estates of Allen county, and his achievements having marked him as a man of special energy, enterprise and mature judgment. He is a scion of a sterling pioneer family of Northern Indiana and was born on a farm in Adams county, this state, May 17, 1851, a son of John H. and Catherine (Rheinhart) Fuelling, both natives of the state of Georgia and both young when they came to Indiana, the respective familiies having established residence in Allen county in the early pioneer days. John H. Fuelling was a lad of sixteen years at the time of the family removal to Allen county and both he and his father assisted in the work on the old Wabash & Erie canal, which gave to Fort Wayne its first definite medium of transportation. As a young man John H. Fuelling entered claim to a tract of government land in Adams county, where he reclaimed a productive farm from the forest and both he and his wife passed the remainder of their lives, secure in the respect of all who know them and prospered in the passing years by their earnest and effective industry. Of their ten children the second Angel died October 16, 1916. The first-born, Elizabeth, died in childhood; Clamor is the third born; Amelia is deceased; the subject of this sketch was the fifth in order of birth; and the others are Sophia, Jacob, Henry, Lusetta, Charles and Martin. John F. Fuelling was reared to the sturdy discipline of the pioneer farm and is indebted to the district schools of his native county for his early educational discipline. In early manhood he removed to Michigan, and in that state continued his activities as a farmer until 1888, when he came to Allen county and purchased two hundred and sixty acres of land in Section 18, Milan township, and Section 6, Maumee township. Later he purchased an additional fifty acres in Section 13, Milan township, and on this extensive and valuable rural estate has made the best of improvements, so that it constitutes one of the valuable farm properties of Northern Indiana. As an agriculturist and stock-grower Mr. Fuelling brings to bear progressive policies and scientific methods, and thus receives the maximum returns from his farm enterprise. His political allegiance is given to the Democratic party. The marriage of Mr. Fuelling was to Miss Louisa Catherine Wolf, who was born and reared in

Michigan, the date of her nativity having been August 10, 1858. Her parents, Frederick and Henrietta (Hackstadt) Wolf, were born in Germany, but were young at the time of the immigration of the respective families to America, their marriage having been solemnized in Michigan, where Mr. Wolf long continued as a representative farmer and where he passed the remainder of his life, his widow being still a resident of the Wolverine State. Mr. and Mrs. Wolf became the parents of four children: Rose and Alfred are deceased; Mrs. Fuelling was the next in order of birth; and Amanda was the last born. Mr. and Mrs. Fuelling became the parents of ten children, all of whom are living except the sixth, Theodore, who died at the age of one year. The names of the other children are here indicated in respective order of birth: Caroline, Amelia, John, Lewis, Henry, Martin, Charles, Fritz and Bertha.

Henry Gallmeyer.—In writing of the prosperous young farming men of this section, mention should properly be made of Henry Gallmeyer, one of the more successful and well known men of his generation in Milan township. He was born in Allen county, Indiana, August 16, 1880, a son of Fred and Christina (Brockmiller) Gallmeyer, the father a native-born German and the mother a daughter of Adams township in Allen county. Fred Gallmeyer came to America in young manhood and settled in Fort Wayne, where he met and married Christina Brockmiller, and they settled on a farm in Milan township soon after their marriage, there spending the rest of their lives. They were parents of twelve children—Fred, William, Henry, Hanna, Minnie, Elizabeth, Amelia, Sophia, Tena, Emma and two others who died in infancy. All of the ten named are living, with the exception of Emma. The children were educated in the schools of Milan township, and Henry Gallmeyer was introduced to farm life on the home place, of which he later became the owner, and he is today carrying on successful farming operations on the old homestead farm. He was married, in 1912, to Dora Myers, a daughter of John and Anna (Merriman) Myers, both of German birth and ancestry, who came to America in 1874 and settled on a farm in Henry county, Ohio, later coming to Allen county, Indiana, and settling in Milan township, where they are spending the closing years of their lives in the home of their daughter, Mrs. Gallmeyer. Mr. Gallmeyer and his wife are members of the German Lutheran church, and are prominent in the good works of that body. They have a wide circle of friends in and about their home community, where their industry and general good citizenship have won for them admirable positions.

Robert B. Garmire, the present efficient court reporter for the Allen county court, has fortified his accuracy and marked facility in stenographic work by an experience of broad and important order, involving his employment in his profession in many different sections of the United States. He was born at LaGrange, Indiana, October 10, 1876, and is a son of Jacob and Sarah (Young) Garmire. The father and mother were born and reared in England and were among the pioneers of LaGrange county, Indiana, where the father established his home in 1840 and where he reclaimed from the veritable wilderness a valuable farm, the while he lived up to the full tension of pioneer life in the early days, the original home having been a primitive log house and deer and other wild game being much in evidence. Jacob Garmire was of German ancestry, though he was born in England, as noted, and both he and his wife continued to reside in LaGrange county until their death, their religious faith having been that of the Evangelical Lutheran church and his political allegiance having been given to the Republican party. Of the children the eldest is Preston, who is now a prosperous ranch owner and substantial agriculturist in the state of California; Ida is the wife of John J. Arnold, who is in the rural mail service, and they maintain their home in Fort Wayne; Luther is a resident of California; Estella is the wife of Frank Taylor and they reside in the state of Michigan; Horace B. is in Texas; Mary is the wife of George Jenkins, of Michigan; Emma is the wife of George Myers, of LaGrange, Indiana; Sylvia is deceased; and Robert B., of this review, is the youngest of the number. In the public schools of his native county Robert B. Garmire continued his studies until his graduation in the high school, and as a member of the class of 1897 he was graduated in the old Fort Wayne Business College, which has lapsed in organization. For four years thereafter he was employed in the offices of the Pennsylvania Railroad at Fort Wayne; for the period of eighteen months thereafter he was on a ranch in the state of California; he then returned to the employ of the Pennsylvania Railroad Company, but resigned his position about a year later, and for the ensuing twelve years was engaged in the mail-order business, at Fort Wayne. In 1913 he opened in this city a public stenographic office, and in this connection he handled a large amount of important work, including that of legal documents. In September, 1916, there came consistent recognition of his ability and character in his appointment to his present position, that of official reporter of the Allen county court. He had previously served twelve years as deputy coroner of Allen county. Mr. Garmire is a staunch advocate and supporter of the cause of the Democratic party, has received the thirty-second degree of Scottish Rite Masonry, besides being affiliated with the Mystic Shrine, in which he is first lieutenant of the Shrine Patrol of Mizpah Temple, at Fort Wayne, besides which he is a past chancellor of the Knights of Pythias. On June 21, 1900, Mr. Garmire wedded Miss Kathryn Feustel, daughter of August and Sophia (Kiefer) Feustel, of Fort Wayne, and the three children of this union are Mildred, Dorothy and Robert B., Jr.

William Clayton Geake, a prominent attorney of Allen county and a resident of Fort Wayne, was born in Toledo, Ohio. He is a son of William and Alice (Clayton) Geake. He received his preliminary education in the public schools and in the old Methodist College in Fort Wayne, and then entered the University of Michigan, as a law student, and graduated with the class of 1900, being admitted to the Indiana bar the same year. He then returned to Fort Wayne and opened an office for the practice of his profession, soon obtaining a fine clientage and becoming one of the legal lights of the county. In his political relations he is allied with the Republican party and from 1903 to 1907 served as Deputy Attorney-General of Indiana under Charles W. Miller. He has also served as a member of the Republican State Executive Committee, and he is frequently called to sit as special judge in the Superior Court of Allen county. Mr. Geake was married April 9, 1903, at Middletown, Pa., to Miss Anna O. Keener, and of this union two children have been born —Mary Catherine and William Keener. Mr. and Mrs. Geake are active members of Trinity Episcopal Church, in which he formerly served as vestryman, and in fraternal affairs he is especially prominent in Masonic circles. He has served as master of the Blue Lodge, filled other offices in both the local and Grand Lodge, and has been a member of the Supreme Council of the Scottish Rite. In 1916, at Pittsburgh, Pa., he had conferred upon him the Thirty-third degree.

Julius Gehrig.—One of the pioneer citizens of the town of Grabill, in Allen county, is Julius Gehrig, who was one of the organizers of the Grabill Lumber Company and is now the head and front of that progressive and prospering concern. Practically every industry in the community has felt the touch of this man of affairs, and he has done much to further the best interests of the town in its various departments of civic and industrial life. Mr. Gehrig was born in Upper Sandusky, Ohio, April 11, 1866, son of William and Louisa (Kipfer) Gehrig. The father was a native of Switzerland and the mother of Ohio. Some time after their marriage they located in Wisconsin and there lived on a farm. The father there met his death in a runaway accident, and the mother, practically among strangers, gave up the place and returned to Ohio, where she might be among her own people. The children who grew to manhood are John, a resident of Woodburn, Indiana; Julius, of this review; Theodore, of Cedar Creek township, and Ferdinand, also of that place. After the family had returned to Ohio Julius was sent to live with an uncle, who was a farmer, and he had much practical experience there up to the age of fifteen years, when he went to live on a neighboring farm for a year. In 1883 the mother moved to Indiana and bought a farm in Cedar Creek township and this place, with the help of her four sturdy sons, she was able to operate very successfully for a number of years. It was an eighty-acre place, which they made to pay for itself in a comparatively short time, after which they established a brick yard on it and conducted a brick business for some years. They built a brick house on the homestead, Julius Gehrig doing practically all the carpenter work on it. His aptitude for the work was so marked that after finishing the house he turned his attention to carpentry and for ten years was engaged in that work. When the town of Grabill was established, Mr. Gehrig was one of the foremost men in the organization work that went on and he was instrumental in establishing the Grabill Lumber Company, of which he is now secretary-treasurer and manager. Other industries with which he is prominently connected are the Home Telephone Company, the Power & Light Company and the Grabill Realty Company, in all of which he is a shareholder and a member of the board of directors. He is also a director in the Grabill State Bank, one of the sturdy financial concerns of the county. Mr. Gehrig is a Democrat and a member of the Reformed church. He married Lydia Ringenberg, an Allen county girl, April 10, 1915, and one son has been born to them—Robert Lee, born May 8, 1916. Mr. and Mrs. Gehrig have a wide circle of friends and acquaintances in Grabill and Allen county and their home is one of the social centers of their community.

William F. Geller.—The purposeful and worthy ambition that makes for definite action has been significantly manifested in the career of Mr. Geller, who is one of the representative business men and valued and progressive citizens of Fort Wayne and who is a native son of this city as well as a scion of an honored pioneer family of Allen county. He has by his technical and executive ability and well-ordered efforts built up a large and prosperous business enterprise that is the leading one of the kind in Fort Wayne, his well-equipped and essentially modern bakery, at the corner of Broadway and Washington streets, having the best of facilities for the manufacturing of staple food products as well as a wide variety of fancy cakes and other fine table delicacies. In connection with the general functions of the enterprise has been developed a metropolitan catering department, and the establishment is one that is creditable alike to its owner and to the city in which it is situated. Mr. Geller was president of the Indiana Master Bakers' Association for 1916-17, and is now (1917) president of the Tri-State Master Bakers' Association. William F. Geller was born in Fort Wayne on March 17, 1859, and is a son of Theodore and Catherine M. Geller, both of whom continued their residence in this city until their death. The father was born in Germany, was a piano-finisher by trade and established his home in Fort Wayne more than half a century ago. He had previously lived in the state of New York, and it was from the old Empire state that he went forth to render gallant service as a soldier of the Union in the Civil War, in which he was a member of Company H, Seventh New York Infantry, his service having continued during practically the entire period of the great conflict between the states of the north and the south. He whose name introduces this article gained his early education in the public schools and he was eighteen years of age when he entered upon a practical apprenticeship to the baker's trade, in the old-time Fort Wayne bakery owned and conducted by the late Christian Hoftner. He fortified himself thoroughly in all details of his trade and continued in service at the Hoftner bakery until he attained to his legal majority, when he put his technical knowledge to practical use and also showed his self-reliance and enterprise by engaging in business in an independent way. In 1881 he opened a small bakery a few doors to the south of his present establishment, and since 1887 has conducted his substantial business from the present headquarters, in which he gives employment to a corps of thirty-five persons. Mr. Geller has shown much progressiveness and initiative ability in the developing of his large and prosperous business and has not only achieved substantial success but has also made the same a medium for expressing in a practical way his civic loyalty and public spirit, though he has manifested no desire for public office. His political allegiance is given to the Republican party, he is affiliated with the Knights of Pythias, the Modern Woodmen of America, and the National Union, and he and his wife are communicants of Christ church parish of the Lutheran church. In 1882 was solemnized the marriage of Mr. Geller to Miss Cecelia M. Neal, who was born and reared in Darke county, Ohio, her father having been a representative farmer in Jefferson township, Allen county. Mr. and Mrs. Geller have four children—Mabel, Willard H., Walter N., and Arthur E. Mabel is the wife of Leo E. Danuser, of Detroit, Michigan, and the three sons still remain in their native city of Fort Wayne.

Anna C. Genth is the representative of a family that came to Allen county many years ago and has been identified with the growth and progress of the county from then down to the present date. She is the daughter of Lewis and Catherine Witzgall, who were of German birth and ancestry, and who settled first in Stark county, Ohio, and later in Allen county, Indiana. The father was a weaver by trade and worked some at that industry, but for the most part devoted himself to farming, in which he found a pleasing success. Coming to Allen county, they bought forty acres of land, later adding an eighty-acre tract to their holdings, and they lived on their farm home until death claimed them, when they were well advanced in years, though the latter years of their lives were spent in quiet retirement from farm duties. They were the parents of six children. William lives in Pleasant township, Anna C. is the subject of this sketch, Martin is deceased, Caroline lives in North Dakota, Lewis is settled in Marion township, and Katie is the wife of Jake Kimmell. Anna C. Witzgall married William August Genth on January 9, 1874. He was a son of Adam Genth, who came from Germany in young manhood and settled on land in Allen county, there spending the remainder of his life. William A. Genth was born in Allen county on March 18, 1848, educated in the schools of his native community, and reared to a thorough knowledge of farm life under the instructions of his father. After he left the parental roof he was employed for a number of years, and then bought a farm of his own to which he took his young wife. His first purchase was a sixty-acre tract, and he was able a little later on to add one hundred and twenty acres to his holdings. Prior to his marriage, he devoted some years to his trade as a carpenter, having learned that trade after he left home, and he built the house that was the family residence for years. He was a Democrat and a member of the Evangelical church. In 1913 he retired from active life, his health being not as good as usual, and he died on March 20, 1916, at the family home. Six children were born to Mr. and Mrs. Genth. Frank lives in Lafayette township. William is on the home place. Walter lives in Lafayette township. Albert is also on the home place, as is Adolphus, the youngest of the six. Katie, the fifth child, died in infancy. Frank, the eldest son, is married and has five children—Edna, Richard, Russell, Marie and Noll. William has two children—Valda and Ruth, while Walter has a family of six—Mabel, Howard, Roy, Clyde, Virgil and Anna. Mrs. Genth has lived a life of quiet industry and is counted among the more dependable women of her community, where she has a host of staunch friends who have shared in the beneficient influence shed by her lif and works.

Rev. Samuel Gerig, who gave earnest and effective service as a clergyman of the Missionary church and was a scion of one of the well known and honored families of Allen county, was engaged in the work of the ministry in the west at the time of his death, which occurred Aug. 23, 1909, but he ever payed a tribute of loyalty and affection to his native county and looked upon the same as his home until the time when he passed from the stage of life's mortal endeavors, his window now maintaining her residence at Woodburn, one of the attractive and prosperous villages of Allen county. Mr. Gerig was a man of strong mentality, broad and practical in his views, and his consecrated labors in the vineyard of the Divine Master were fruitful in good. Concerning the Gerig family of Allen county adequate data are given in other articles in this volume, and thus it is not necessary to enter into geneological details in this memoir. Samuel Gerig was born on a farm near Grabill, in Springfield township, this county, and the date of his nativity was October 15, 1876, so that he was but thirty-two years of age when he was summoned to eternal rest. His father, Joseph Gerig, gained precedence as one of the representative farmers and substantial citizens of Springfield township and the family name has been long and worthily identified with the history of Allen county. He whose name introduces this review was reared to the sturdy discipline of the farm and received his youthful education in the public schools of Springfield township. His initial activities of an independent order were in connection with agricultural industry, and his deep Christian faith and his high sense of personal stewardship early led him to enter the ministry of the Missionary church, as a representative of which he served as pastor of the church at Woodburn. Upon leaving his native state he engaged in active ministerial service in Missouri and Kansas, and his faithful labors in these states covered a period of seven years. He was residing in Kansas at the time of his death, after which his widow returned to Allen county, where she has since maintained her home. Mr. Gerig was a loyal supporter of the cause of the Republican party and was a young man who commanded unqualified popular confidence and esteem, both as a clergyman and as a citizen. On June 1, 1899, was solemnized his marriage to Miss Lavina Klopfenstein, who likewise was born and reared in Allen county, a daughter of Joseph and Anna (Stukey) Klopfenstein, adequate mention of the family being given on other pages of this work, in the sketch of Joseph Klopfenstein, a half-brother of Mrs. Gerig. Mr. and Mrs. Gerig became the parents of five children, all of whom remain with their widowed mother in the pleasant home at Woodburn, their names being here given in respective order of their birth: Frieda, Jesse, Harry, Walter and Irene. Mrs. Gerig earnestly aided her husband in his service as a clergyman and is a zealous adherent of the Missionary church.

Frederick W. Gerke has been a resident of Allen county since his boyhood, is a representative of one of the old and honored German families of the county and is the fortunate owner of one of the specially fine farms of St. Joseph township. Known as one of the most enterprising and progressive farmers of that township and, without ambition for public office of any kind, he has been influential in community affairs, with secure place in popular esteem. Frederick William Gerke was born in the Kingdom of Hanover, Germany, January 27, 1850, a son of Henry and Dora (Mandel) Gerke, who immigrated to America in 1855, and first settled in Jackson county, Indiana, where they remained four years. The family home was then established in Dubois county, Indiana, where the father continued his association with agricultural pursuits for six years. Removal was then made to Allen county, in 1864, and Henry Gerke purchased a tract of land in St. Joseph township, where he developed one of the excellent farms of the county and became one of the substantial agriculturists and valued citizens of his township. He achieved through his industry and good management a large measure of material prosperity and when well advanced in years retired from active labors and removed to the city of Fort Wayne, where he and his wife passed the remainder of their lives in the generous peace and comfort that justly rewarded former years of earnest endeavor, both having been devoted communicants of the German Lutheran church. They became the parents of three children—John, Anna E. and Frederick W. He whose name introduces this review was about four years old at the time of the family immigration to the United States, and he attended school in both Dubois and Allen counties, while he gained his full quota of youthful experience in connection with the work of the home farm. In 1882 he rented from his father sixty acres of his present farm, in Section 29, St. Joseph township, and eventually purchased the property, to which he had added forty acres, so that his splendidly improved farm now comprises one hundred acres. He erected on the place his modern and commodious brick residence and other farm buildings of superior order, and everything about the place indicates thrift and good management, the farm being given over to diversified agriculture and stock-raising. Taking deep interest in community affairs, but imbued with no desire for public office, Mr. Gerke is independent in politics and gives his support to men and measures meeting the approval of his judgment. He and his wife are active members of the German Lutheran church at Goeglein. In 1882 was solemnized the marriage of Mr. Gerke to Miss Mary Rebber, daughter of Christopher and Clara (Rohe) Rebber, both of whom were born in Germany, Mr. Rebber having been for many years one of the substantial farmers of Allen county. Mr. and Mrs. Gerke have one son, Henry C., who is engaged in farming at home in St. Joe township, his wife, whose maiden name was Addie Busching, being a daughter of Henry F. Busching, concerning whom individual mention is made on other pages of this publication.

Joseph F. Getz, senior member of the firm of Getz & Cahill, which conducts one of the leading undertaking establishments of Fort Wayne, at 1031 Calhoun street, has as his associate in the business James B. Cahill, and the enterprise was established by them on September 1, 1907. Mr. Getz was born at Mahoning, Mahoning county, Ohio, September 1, 1860, a son of Charles and Anastasia (Weaver) Getz, who were born and reared in Baden Baden, Germany, where their marriage was solemnized, and they immigrated to America in 1848. They first established their home at New Albany, Franklin county, Ohio, and later removed to Mahoning county, where the father engaged in farming, besides having operated coal mines of which he was the owner. He was a Democrat in his political proclivities and both he and his wife were communicants of the Catholic church, their home having been maintained in the old Buckeye State until the time of their death. Of their children, Angeline is the wife of Joseph Schriver, of Salem, Columbiana county, Ohio; Henry, Charles and Joseph F. are all residents of Fort Wayne; August resides at Salem, Ohio, as does also Frances, who is the wife of Herman Vonimon, and Frank likewise maintains his home at Salem; Florence, the youngest of the children is the wife of Carl Baker, of Akron, Ohio. Joseph F. Getz acquired his early education in the schools of Salem, Ohio, and continued his residence in his native state until 1879, when he established his home in Fort Wayne. He was about nineteen years of age at the time and for three years gave his attention primarily to the buying and shipping of live stock, in connection with which line of enterprise he traveled somewhat widely through the rural districts of Indiana. Thereafter he was employed on a stock farm in Allen county about three years, and for a comparatively equal period was in other employment. He then entered the local service of the Adams Express Company in Fort Wayne, in which connection he continued two years. For a year thereafter he was identified with the retail grocery business and then conducted a retail liquor business five years. For fourteen years after his retirement from this field of enterprise he conducted a prosperous retail cigar business, upon disposing of which he became associated with Mr. Cahill in the establishing of their present business as undertakers, embalmers and funeral directors, with facilities of the best standard in all particulars. Mr. Getz gives allegiance to the Democratc party, he and his wife are communicants of the Cathedral parish of the Catholic church, and he is affiliated with the Knights of Columbus, the Fraternal Order of Eagles, the Benevolent & Protective Order of Elks, the Tribe of Ben Hur, and the U. T. C. On May 25, 1886, was solemnized the marriage of Mr. Getz to Miss Louise Perriguey, daughter of Felix and Caroline (Vosier) Perriguey, of Fort Wayne, and they have five children: Bernadette is the wife of William Baughman, of Fort Wayne; Edna is the wife of Harry Miller, of this city; and Arthur, Hilda and Clarence remain at the parental home.

Benjamin F. Geyer, sales manager of the Wayne Oil Tank Company, is one of the younger men who are making distinctive impress on the business life of Fort Wayne. He was born at Plymouth, Indiana, May 7, 1882, his parents being Ferdinand F. and Augusta M. (Wollenhaupt) Geyer, the former having been born in 1847 in Wurtemberg, Germany, and the latter in 1856 at Dayton, Ohio. Benjamin F. was educated in the public schools of his native town and of Monroeville, Indiana, the family having moved to the latter place. From the local schools he went to Indiana University for three years. He taught in the high school of Monroeville in 1903-4, and then took a special course in advertising at Chicago for two years, concurrent with which he was employed in the office of the Western Electric Company. Returning to Monroeville he taught another year and in 1907 took a position with Bowser & Company. Here he made an excellent record and had become assistant advertising manager when, in 1912, he relinquished that place to become advertising manager of the Wayne Oil Tank Company. Since then his progress has continued and from 1914 he has been sales manager of this concern. Under his guidance the business has already increased upwards of 300 per cent. Mr. Geyer was married August 24, 1909, to Blanche M., daughter of Josiah B. and Mary (Bauserman) Miller. They are members of Simpson M. E. church and he is a member of the Masonic order, having been Worshipful Master of Monroeville Lodge, No. 293.

Henry W. Gibson.—One of the Marion township farmers who were brought up on the soil and have a life-long acquaintance with it is Henry W. Gibson, the son of David and Mary (Reichard) Gibson, pioneers to Marion township from Pennsylvania as early as the year 1864. They were sturdy and industrious people and acquired a good deal of land in and about Marion township during the years of their residence there, and prospered in accordance with their efforts. Mr. Gibson was an early Whig and a Democrat from the demise of the first-named party. He was Roman Catholic in his church relations, as was also his wife, and they reared a family of ten children, of whom only the subject is living at this writing. The others were named John, Lydia, Mary, David, Daniel, Theresa, Sarah, Susanna and Frank. Henry W. Gibson was born in Pennsylvania on March 28, 1847, and accompanied his parents to Indiana in 1864. He was educated for the most part in the parochial schools, and spent his young life at home on the family farm, working with his father and doing his full share toward making the farm a success. On the death of the father he inherited a tract of one hundred and forty acres, and he has spent his life thus far in the development of the agricultural industry in Marion township. Excellent buildings are a feature of his property, and he carries on a successful business in stock-farming. Mr. Gibson was married on January 14, 1873, to Miss Mary Hipler, the daughter of John and Catherine (Daneberger) Hipler, who came to America from Germany in their young lives and settled in Indiana. Mr. and Mrs. Gibson became the parents of ten children. Theresa is the wife of William Smith, and they make their home in Fort Wayne. John is also located in Fort Wayne. Henry, Jr., is at home with his parents. Frank lives in Marion township on a farm. Rosa is in Fort Wayne.

Clemens is in Fort Wayne also, and the four younger children—Leo, Ambrose, Mary Marie and Emmett—are to be found in the family home. The eldest daughter, Theresa Smith, has four children—Irvin, Eve, Ralph and Willard. John also has four children—Mildred, Elmer, Arnold and Normand. Frank has three children—Oscar, Monroe and Ruth.

Mrs. Lucy Gibson, widow of the late David W. Gibson and daughter of Edward F. and Margaret (Denney) Farrell, was born in Muskingum county, Ohio, on May 20, 1833, and came with her parents to Allen county, Indiana, in 1849. They were farmers and lived prosperously and contentedly on their Allen county farm for the remainder of their lives. Mr. Farrell was a Democrat, active in the party ranks, and a member of the Roman Catholic church, as was also his wife. They were the parents of a family of ten children, of whom only two are living. Briefly named, in the order of their appearance, they were Mary M., Margaret, Catherine, Lucy, Elizabeth, Dennis, Edward, Charles, John and Frank. Lucy is the immediate subject of this review. Edward is living in the state of Illinois, and Frank, the youngest of the family, is in Hammond, Indiana. Lucy Farrell was married on February 14, 1865, to David W. Gibson, who was born on March 5, 1838, in Pennsylvania, and was the son of David Gibson, who came to Allen county in the early part of the nineteenth century, bought land and established himself in the farming industry of the county. He was a successful man and his son shared in that prosperity as well. He lived retired for some years prior to his death, which took place on February 2, 1912. He was a Democrat and a member of the board of trustees of Marion township for some years, also serving as township assessor for two terms. He was a man of considerable prominence in his community, and his passing was a decided loss in the township. He was a lifelong member of the Roman Catholic church and at the time of his passing had membership in the church at Hessen Cassel. To Mr. and Mrs. Gibson were born four children. Agnes is the wife of Frank Wyss. Edward is a resident of Marion township. Henry and Helen are twins, and both are to be found with the mother on the home place, which Henry has managed for some years. Mrs. Gibson has fourteen grandchildren to her credit. The eldest daughter, Agnes, has eight children, named Charlotte, Celestine, Stella, Frank, Aloysius, Clarence, Viola and Verby. Edward has three sons—Walter, Andrew and Marchant. Henry's children are Irene, Russel and Rodger. Mrs. Gibson is well known in and about Marion township and has a host of staunch friends wherever her endearing and estimable qualities are known.

Howard M. Gieseking is a young man who has shown marked initiative and executive ability and has brought the same to bear most effectively in connection with farm industry in his native county. He is one of the most extensive and successful agriculturists and stock-growers in Lake township and insistently utilizes the same careful and well ordered business principles that make for success in commercial enterprise but that are far too often neglected in connection with the fundamental enterprises of which he is an essentially representative exponent. In the livestock department of his farm operations Mr. Gieseking makes a thorough inventory each year and knows to a dollar what gain his stock is making each month. The same methods are followed so far as consistent in other departments of farm activity, and thus it is not strange that Mr. Gieseking is known as a thoroughly progressive business man, even as he is a loyal and public-spirited citizen. He is associated with certain of his neighbors in the ownership of a modern threshing outfit, and the fine traction engine that is a part of the equipment is utilized for power. The enterprising farmers who are the owners of this excellent outfit have proved in its operations the value of the investment, for they not only thresh their own grain at minimum cost but also gain an appreciable return for work done for other farmers. The cattle shipped from the farm of Mr. Gieseking, in 1916, were pronounced by an authority from Purdue University to be the best in the state. This is but one assurance of the high standard which he maintains in all phases of his farm business, and it is specially gratifying to accord to him merited consideration in this history. On the old homestead that is an integral part of his present valuable landed estate of three hundred and seventy acres, in Lake township, Howard M. Gieseking was born on June 1, 1882, a son of William F. and Lydia E. (Larimore) Gieseking, both likewise natives of Allen county and representatives of sterling pioneer families of the same. William F. Gieseking, long one of the representative and honored citizens of the county, still resides on the old homestead with his son, Howard M., his devoted wife having passed away in 1907. He has lived on this farm the major part of his life, reclaimed much of the land from a semi-improved condition and marked the passing years with large and worthy achievement, so that he accumulated a large estate and incidentally did much to further civic and industrial progress in his native county. All of the land of this extensive property, with the exception of fifty acres, lies along the Goshen road, and it is one of the best farm properties in Lake township. Howard M. Gieseking acquired his preliminary education in the district schools of Lake township and supplemented this by direct and special courses in the high school at Churubusco. Since he was eighteen years of age he has exercised his energy and administrative ability in connection with the operations of the fine homestead farm of which he is now the owner, the property having been purchasd by him in 1914. He was the fourth in order of birth in a family of five children—Mary, Charles, Alice, Howard M., and John—and the only other of the number now living is Alice, whose home is at Pueblo, Colorado, and her husband is a traveling representative for the Burroughs Adding Machine Company, of Detroit, Michigan. After he had purchased the farm from his father, as above noted, the subject of this review began the raising and feeding of pureblood white-faced Hereford cattle and pure-bred Duroc-Jersey swine. He adopted the scientific methods of feeding advocated in connection with the agricultural department of Purdue Univerity, and the balanced and selected system of rations has proved its value in no uncertain way in his operations. For the May market, in 1917, Mr. Gieseking had thirty-nine steers, twenty-two grade heifers, and for the July market one hundred and five hogs. On his farm he has two of the best type of silos, with an aggregate capacity of four hundred and forty tons. The horse barn on the model farm is forty-four by sixty feet in dimensions; the cattle barn is one hundred and forty by thirty feet; and the sheep barn is sixty by thirty-two feet in dimensions. A cement floored feeding yard is eighty-two by one hundred and thirty-five feet in dimensions; the granary and feed mill is thirty-two by twenty-two feet; and a private dynamo and full incidental equipment affords modern lighting facilities for both house and the barns, besides supplying power for the feed mill and other purposes. Thorough system obtains in every department of the farm operations, and the owner gives a most active and efficient supervision to all details. He employs from three to five men, according to season demands, and it has been consistently said that he individually does the work of two men, so indefatigable his energy and so great his enthusiasm as a representative of the noble art of husbandry. Mr. Gieseking is an exemplar, and that in a most practical and productive way, of the best systems of scientific agriculture and stockgrowing, is a leader in the advocating and use of modern methods and appliances, and is setting an example well worthy of emulation on the part of all who would achieve the maximum of success through farm enterprise. His farm has a traction engine of modern type and all other mechanical equipments are the best that can be obtained, so that the Gieseking farm is a veritable model and one that is a source of general pride to Allen county. Mr. Gieseking is a Republican in politics, as is also his honored father, and he is affiliated with the Masonic fraternity and the Benevolent and Protective Order of Elks. On December 24, 1912, was solemnized the marriage of Mr. Gieseking to Miss Georgia M. Teagarden, who was born and reared in this county, as were also her parents, Marion and Alice (Jackson) Teagarden, the former of whom is deceased and the latter resides in the city of Fort Wayne. Mrs. Gieseking is the youngest in a family of six children, and Harvey is the eldest. Thomas is deceased; Edward resides in Fort Wayne, as does also May and Edna remains with her widowed mother. Mr. and Mrs. Gieseking have no children. Their beautiful home is known for its gracious hospitality and is a center of much of the representative social life of the community.

Charles E. Gilbert has established a unique and notably successful business in Fort Wayne, in which his only son, Harold H., is his associate in conducting what has been significantly designated as The Letter Shop. The offices of the firm are located in the Lincoln Life Insurance Building and the best facilities are here afforded for the handling of all kinds of typewritten work, with special attention given to multigraphing letters and other documents. Employment is given to a corps of seven assistants, and the business has met a distinct demand by its service, with the result that it has become a substantial enterprise of important order, touching, as it does, all lines of human interest—religious, fraternal, educational, professional and commercial. Charles E. Gilbert was born in Rockcreek township, Wells county, Indiana, on January 25, 1873, and is a son of Emanuel and Lydia Anne (Schoch) Gilbert, the father, now deceased, having been a carpenter by trade and also one of the successful farmers and influential citizens of Wells county. Charles E. Gilbert passed the period of his childhood and early youth on the home farm and is indebted to the public schools of his native county for his early education, besides which he attended the Indiana State Normal School at Marion for one year. January 4, 1894, was solemnized the marriage of Mr. Gilbert to Miss Mary Catherine Harker, daughter of David and Sarah (Teeple) Harker, of Portland, Jay county, Indiana, and the one child of this union is Harold Harker Gilbert. For a number of years Mr. Gilbert was a representative of the International Correspondence Schools, of Scranton, Pennsylvania. In 1905 he established his residence and business headquarters in Fort Wayne. On April 1, 1908, he showed his initiative, ability and progressiveness by founding The Letter Shop, and he has made of the enterprise a signal success, as previously intimated in this article. In 1915 he admitted his only son to partnership in the business, and the latter has proved a valuable young coadjutor. Mr. Gilbert, also his son, is affiliated with Wayne Lodge No. 25, Ancient Free and Accepted Masons, and in addition both have had conferred the degrees of the Ancient Accepted Scottish Rite and are also affiliated with the Ancient Arabic Order, Nobles of the Mystic Shrine.

Guy J. Gilbert has proved a resourceful and successful exponent of the life-insurance business and in the city of Fort Wayne he maintains his official headquarters as general agent for the Lincoln Life Insurance Company, of which he had previously served as special representative. Mr. Gilbert was born at Worthington, Franklin county, Ohio, on August 17, 1871, and is a son of Theodore R. and Ellen L. (Johnson) Gilbert, the father having been likewise a native of the Buckeye state and having devoted the major part of his active business career to mercantile enterprise, he having been a resident of Angola, Indiana, at the time of his death. He whose name introduces this article gained his early education in the public schools of Angola, Indiana, to which place his parents removed when he was a child. As a youth he served for a time as a clerk in the mail-order department of the Angola postoffice, and in 1899 he established his residence in Fort Wayne, where for twelve years he was employed in the money order division of the postoffice. He then put in one year with the Wildwood building concern. Later he passed eight months in the city of Mobile, Alabama, in the service of the Alabama Farm Land Company, and since that time has been actively and successfully associated with the Lincoln Life Insurance Company, with which he rose from the position of special representative to that of general agent, with headquarters in Fort Wayne. Mr. Gilbert is an active member of the Fort Wayne Commercial Club, holds membership in the local lodge of the Benevolent and Protective Order of Elks, and is affiliated with the Scottish Rite bodies of the Masonic fraternity, as is he also with the adjunct organization, the Ancient Arabic Order of the Nobles of the Mystic Shrine. Mr. Gilbert was married in September, 1897, to Miss Ida E. Kurrle, of Kendallville, Indiana. She is a daughter of Jacob and Katherine Kurrle. They have three children as follows: Donald C., Paul H. and Robert B.

John Gilbert was a man who held himself true and loyal in all of the relations of life and who marked the passing years with earnest and successful achievement that denoted him as a citizen of worth in the community. He was long numbered among the well-known and substantial business men of Fort Wayne and here maintained his home for nearly thirty-seven years, his age at the time of his death having been seventy years and his passing having been counted a distinct loss in the community life. Mr. Gilbert was born in Tachau, Bohemia, Austria, of German parentage, and the date of his nativity was March 9, 1833. He was about nine years of age at the time of his father's death, but the devoted mother lived for many years thereafter. He and his brother Edward entered upon their school work in Ratisbon, Bavaria, where they attended an important educational institution for three years. Within a comparatively short time thereafter an uncle who had established himself in business in New York city, as an importer, sent for the two boys, and thus the subject of this memoir was enabled to continue his educational pursuits in Brooklyn, New York, and eventually to be graduated in pharmacy. Young, ambitious and purposeful, he found employment in a drug store, and his experience was eventually extended to touch both the retail and wholesale phases of the drug business. From New York city he responded to a call from London, Ontario, Canada, and after having there been employed one year as prescription clerk in a drug store, he turned his face westward and located in Rockford, Illinois, where he was similarly engaged for two years and where he then became the proprietor of a drug store, which he conducted until 1866. While a resident of Rockford, Mr. Gilbert met and married Harriet P. Mandeville, his devoted companion and helpmeet until the close of his life. The ceremony took place May 27, 1861. Mrs. Gilbert was the daughter of Michael and Elsie Marie (Corey) Mandeville, who passed the closing years of their life in Rockford, where the daughter attended the private and public schools of the city, and where her educational advantages included those of Rockford College. The Mandeville family was founded in America in colonial days and the lineage traces back to French-Huguenot origin. The father of Mrs. Gilbert was long a successful exponent of agricultural industry in Winnebago county. He and his wife were born and reared in the state of New York. In 1866 Mr. Gilbert established his home in Fort Wayne. He became general manager of the wholesale and retail drug business of the firm of Meyer Brothers & Company. With this representative Fort Wayne concern he continued his alliance fourteen years, and for the ensuing eleven years he held the position of district manager for the Standard Oil Company, in which connection he made a characteristically admirable record. His death occurred September 21, 1903. Mr. Gilbert gave loyal allegiance to the Republican party and always manifested a broad-minded interest in public affairs, both national and local. He was a man whose abiding Christian faith was shown in good works and unfailing toleration and kindliness. He was an earnest and influential member of Plymouth Congregational church, in which his widow still retains active membership, both having been charter members of this now representative religious organization of Fort Wayne. He was a deacon of this church from the time of its organization until his death. For many years Mr. Gilbert maintained active and appreciative affiliation with the Masonic fraternity and he was well known and highly honored in both the business and social circles of the community that so long represented his home. Besides the widow, Mr. Gilbert is survived by an adopted daughter, Gertrude, who is the wife of Pierre Plantinga, of Cleveland, Ohio. Mrs. Gilbert finds in the devotion of her many friends in Fort Wayne a measure of solace and consolation now that the husband of her youth has passed forward to the "land of the leal," and she delights in extending to her friends the hospitality of her pleasant home, at 916 West Washington street. Among the beneficent acts of Mrs. Gilbert, and one which suggests the kindly spirit which has ever pervaded her life, comes down from the year 1910, when she presented to the city of Rockford the Mandeville home and the beautiful surroundings, consisting of three acres of wooded land. The spot is known as Mandeville park.

George W. Gillie, who assumed the office of sheriff of Allen county on January 1, 1917, is giving an administration that fully justified the popular choice of the incumbent, and he has become specially well known also as a skilled veterinary surgeon, in which connection he was a deputy state veterinarian from 1909 to 1913, besides which he is serving at the present time as a government inspector for the national bureau of animal industry. Doctor Gillie has been a resident of Allen county since his childhood, is a scion of fine Scottish lineage and in his character and achievement is a young man who is distinctly exemplifying the sterling traits of the race of which he is a representative. He was born in Berwickshire, Scotland, August 15, 1880, and in that same section of the land of hills and heather were born and reared his parents, James and Janet (Taylor) Gillie. James Gillie became a successful agriculturist and stock-grower in his native land and there continued his residence until June, 1882, when he came with his family to the United States, and established his residence at Kankakee, Illinois, where he soon afterward was made superintendent of construction in the building of the Illinois asylum for the insane. In 1884 he came to Allen county, Indiana, and for sixteen years thereafter was a substantial exponent of agricultural and live-stock industry in Washington townshp. For the ensuing ten years he farmed in St. Joseph township, where he then purchased a well-improved farm of one hundred and sixty acres. To this place he continued to give his effective supervision until his death, which occurred October 29, 1911, and his widow still remains on the homestad farm. He was a man of lofty integrity and marked energy, was a Republican in politics and was a member of the Plymouth Congregational church in Fort Wayne, as is also his widow. Mr. Gillie was known for his broad mental ken and for his loyal interest in community affairs. In the Masonic fraternity his ancient-craft affiliation was with Summit City Lodge, in Fort Wayne, and he was a member of the Fort Wayne Commandery of Knights Templars, besides being affiliated with the Scottish Rite branch of Masonry. He was one of the early members of the Caledonian Society of Allen county and in 1889 he effected the organization of the Allen County Plowing Association. Of the children the present sheriff of the county is the eldest; Peter is likewise a veterinary surgeon and is engaged in the practice of his profession at Mansfield, Ohio; Janet died at the age of seven and Jean at the age of six years; John A. is one of the successful farmers of St. Joseph township; Margaret is the wife of Joseph Pearson, of Ogden, Boone county, Iowa; Agnes is the wife of Arthur Boerger, of Fort Wayne; Harold likewise resides in this city; and James S. remains with his widowed mother on the farm in St. Joseph township. Dr. George W. Gillie was afforded the advantages of the public schools of Fort Wayne and also attended the International Business College in this city. In 1901 he completed a short course in dairy science and industry at Purdue University, Lafayette, this state, and in-preparation for his chosen profession entered the University of Ohio, at Columbus, in which he was graduated in 1907, with the degree of Doctor of Veterinary Surgery. In the following year he was appointed milk inspector for Allen county, of which position he continued the incumbent until 1913. He engaged also in the general practice of his profession and from 1909 to 1913 was retained in the position of deputy state veterinarian. He continued in the practice of his profession until the autumn of 1916, and his retirement therefrom came when he was, at that time, elected sheriff of the county, the duties of which office he assumed January 1, 1917. The Doctor is aligned as a staunch advocate of the principles of the Republican party, is identified with the Indiana State Veterinary Association, is affiliated with both York and Scottish Rite bodies of the Masonic fraternity, as well as the adjunct organization, the Mystic Shrine, and both he and his wife are popular factors in the social life of their home city. On June 25, 1908, was solemnized the marriage of Doctor Gillie to Miss Grace Nannette Merion, who was born and reared in the city of Columbus, Ohio, where she was graduated in the state university on the day that her marriage occurred, she being a daughter of Charles and Emma (Kienzle) Merion. Doctor and Mrs. Gillie have two daughters, Jean M. and Charlotte M.

Claude F. Gladieux, of New Haven, is a representative of one of the honored and influential pioneer families of Allen county and was born on the old homestead farm of his father, in Jefferson township, February 6, 1866. He is a son of Francis and Mary (Lamont) Gladieux, both natives of the now stricken province of Alsace, France, which became a part of German territory after the close of the Franco-Prussian war and has become the stage of tragic military operations incidental to the present great European war. Francis Gladieux was but seven years old when he accompanied his parents to America and the family home was first established in Stark county, Ohio, whence, two years later, removal was made to Allen county, Indiana. Peter Gladieux, father of Francis, obtained a tract of land in Jefferson township and there instituted the development of a farm, both he and his wife having there passed the remainder of their lives, as sterling pioneers of the county. Francis Gladieux was reared to manhood on the home farm, received the advantages of the common schools of the locality and period and finally became one of the most successful farmers of the county, his death having occurred on the old homestead, in December, 1916, and his widow still remaining on the place, which is endeared to her by the gracious memories of the past. Francis Gladieux wielded much influence in public affairs in Allen county, served nine years as county commissioner and was for one term a member of the Indiana legislature. On other pages of this publication is entered a specific tribute to his memory, and thus further review of his career is not required in the present article. Claude Francis Gladieux gained physical and mental vigor through his youthful association with the work of the home farm and through his studies in the public schools of his native township. He continued to assist in the affairs of his father's farm until he had attained to the age of twenty-nine years, and thereafter continued independent operations as a farmer until 1914. In August, 1915, he established his present business enterprise at New Haven. He gives his allegiance to the Democratic party, is a member of the French-American Society of Allen county, and he and his wife are communicants of the Catholic church, in the faith of which they were carefully reared. On January 8, 1894, was solemnized the marriage of Mr. Gladieux to Miss Jennie Giriodot, who likewise was born and reared in Jefferson township, a daughter of Jules and Mary (Borsnet) Giriodot, both natives of France. The father is now one of the honored retired farmers of Jefferson township and the devoted wife and mother has passed to the life eternal. Mr. and Mrs. Gladieux have six children: Ruth is the wife of Eugene Martin, of Indianapolis, and they have two children—Thelma and Ronald; Lottie is the wife of Nicholas Martin, of Fort Wayne; and Pearl, Aldine, Gladys and Lillian remain at the parental home.

Francis Gladieux.—The character and achievement of the late Francis Gladieux marked him as one of the honored and influential citizens of Allen county and he was one of the county's oldest and most successful farmers at the time of his death, which occurred October 17, 1916, at his fine rural home in Jefferson township. That he held inviolable place in popular esteem needs no further voucher than the statement that he served three terms as county commissioner, 1874 to 1882, and that he represented Allen county in the lower house of the Indiana legislature. Mr. Gladieux was born in Alsace, France, on October 8, 1837, and thus was seventy-nine years of age when he was summoned to the life eternal. He was a lad of seven years when he accompanied his parents to America and the family home was established in Stark county, Ohio, whence removal was made to Allen county, Indiana, in 1853. The subject of this memoir thus gained experience in connection with the pioneer period in the history of this county and he passed the remainder of his long and useful life in Jefferson township, where he became one of the leading exponents of agricultural industry and where he achieved a high degree of material prosperity. In 1860 he wedded Miss Mary Lamont, who proved his devoted companion and helpmeet, and they celebrated their golden wedding anniversary in 1910, the event having been one of notable order in the annals of Jefferson township. Mrs. Gladieux still survives the husband of her youth, as do also six of their nine children—Louis, Frank, Amiel C., Edward and Mesdames Emmett Ternet and Louis Roussel. He is survived also by thirty grandchildren and three great-grandchildren. He was a devoted communicant of St. Louis' Catholic church at Besancon, as is also his venerable widow. A man of superabundant energy and fine mentality, Mr. Gladieux was well qualified for leadership in popular sentiment and action, and he was long one of the influential representatives of the Democratic party in Allen county. In addition to his effective service in the legislature and as a member of the board of county commissioners he was for twelve years trustee of Jefferson township and for four years township assessor. He had resided on his old homestead farm for the long period of fifty-six years and was the owner of some of the largest and best improved farms along the Lincoln highway, in which connection it should be observed that he was one of the first men to advocate and further the construction of good roads in the eastern part of the county. He lived a godly and righteous life and now that he rests from his labors his name is held in endearing veneration in the county that so long represented his home and was the stage of his successful endeavors as one of the world's constructive workers.

Frank P. Glazier, attorney-at-law and abstractor in Fort Wayne, was born at Mexico, Miami county, Indiana, January 2, 1867. His parents were Harlow and Eliza (Chapman) Glazier. After receiving his education in the public schools of his native place and at Wabash, Indiana, he began his active course in business as an employe in the factories of Mexico and Wabash, to the latter of which the family moved in 1882. Having qualified himself for the duties of deputy recorder of the county, he was appointed to that place in 1900 and filled it satisfactorily for four years. In 1905 he came to Fort Wayne and became associated with the Dreibelbiss Abstract Company, where he has remained until the present time. Mr. Glazier has made a study of law as it relates to real estate and has been admitted to the bar of Allen county, his practice being confined to the branch of law in which he has specialized. He was married June 30, 1908, to Elizabeth T., daughter of Francis and Marion (Stirling) Burgess. They are members of the Presbyterian church. Mr. Glazier is a member of the Masonic and I. O. O. F. fraternities, in the former of which he has attained the thirty-second degree of the Ancient Accepted Scottish Rite.

C. M. Glock, M. D.—The village of Arcola is favored in claiming as one of its most progressive and public-spirited citizens the able and representative physician whose name introduces this paragraph and who is signally dignifying the profession in which his honored father gained precedence and distinction in Allen county. Dr. Glock not only controls a substantial practice as a physician and surgeon but is also prominent in connection with business affairs in his home village, where he is president of the Arcola State Bank, in the organization of which he assisted, in 1912, and in the development of the business of which he has wielded much influence, especially through his inviolable place in popular confidence and esteem. Dr. Glock was born at Cedarville, Cedar Creek township, this county, in the year 1876, the youngest in a family of four children, his mother having died within a few months after his birth. The other three children are Laurinda, Josephine and Otto. The Doctor is a son of Dr. Frederick Glock and Margaret (Watkins) Glock, the former of whom was born in Wells county, Indiana, and the latter in the ancient fortified city of Hyderbad, India, her parents having been Christian missionaries in the Orient. Dr. Frederick Glock completed a thorough course in the Miami Medical College, at Cincinnati, Ohio, in which he was graduated as a member of the class of 1868. Thereafter he continued in the active and successful practice of his profession, as one of the leading and honored physicians of Allen county, until the close of his life. In the earlier period of his professional service he resided at Cedarville, but later engaged in practice in the city of Fort Wayne, where his death occurred, October 25, 1886, his wife having passed away in 1877. Dr. C. M. Glock was an infant at the time of his mother's death and was only ten years of age when his father likewise passed from the stage of life's mortal endeavors. He was afforded the advantages of the excellent public schools of Allen county and thereafter completed a course in pharmacy at Purdue University, in the city of Lafayette. His experience as a pharmacist quickened his ambition for the discipline that would open to him a wider and more beneficent field of endeavor, and he finally entered the Fort Wayne Medical College, in which he was graduated as a member of the class of 1903 and received the degree of Doctor of Medicine. Thereafter he gained valuable experience by serving eighteen months as an interne in the Indiana state school for feeble-minded children, at Fort Wayne, and then established his residence at Arcola, where his ability, earnest ministrations and personal popularity have conspired to develop for him a large and representative general practice. He is a liberal and progressive citizen and in politics gives unswerving allegiance to the Democratic party. In 1903 the Doctor wedded Miss Goldie Tilbury, who was born and reared in this county, as were also her parents, Scott and Dora (Parker) Tilbury, members of old and honored families of the county. Dr. and Mrs. Glock have one child—Margaret.

George Goeglein.—Fifty years of continuous and honored identification with the affairs of his community place George Goeglein indisputably among the foremost men of St. Joseph township. Representative of the finest type of Allen county pioneers, he has spent his life thus far in the conduct and operation of a general merchandise business, with some attention to farming in later years. He has been a leader in his home town through half a century of development, and much credit is due to him for his worthy efforts and accomplishments in his community. He has served in local offices on numerous occasions and was one of the organizers of the German Lutheran church of which he is a member, while other enterprises pertinent to the well-being of his community have never lacked his patronage and encouragement. He has, in short, been a leader in his township, and has enjoyed the confidence and honest esteem of his fellow citizens through all the years of his activities among them. Mr. Goeglein is a native Ohioan, born in Meigs county, June 21, 1840, a son of Daniel and Magdalene (Ryder) Goeglein, both natives of Oppenheim-on-the-Rhine, in Germany. They came to Ohio in the springtime of 1838 and there, in Henry county, settled down to farm life, where they spent the remainder of their active careers. In later life they moved to St. Joseph township, in Allen county, Indiana, and took up their residence in the home of their son, George, the subject of this review, where they spent their declining years. George was the youngest of their seven children, the others being Elizabeth, Margaret, Katherine, Jacob, John and Philip, all deceased. George Goeglein had his schooling in the common schools of Meigs county, Ohio, and was twenty-five years of age when he came to Allen county and began an independent career. He thought he was destined for farm life and accordingly rented a farm and started a crop, but fortune had other plans for him, it seemed, for a long illness prevented him from giving his farm any attention after the crop was put in the ground, in consequence of which he was not especially busy at harvest time. He then turned his attention to the general merchandise business and started a general store in what has in later years come to be known as Goeglein. He began in a small way, carrying a general stock, and for the past fifty years has continued in that business in his community, realizing no small measure of prosperity, and in his position as merchant in the village coming to have an intimacy and understanding with his fellows denied to many another in the community. Mr. Goeglein never quite relinquished his ambition to become a farmer and in later years acquired a farm, which he has developed to a splendid degree, so that it is one of the finest farms in the community, though its acreage is not large. Mr. Goeglein, however, has emphasized a truth that many another successful farmer has demonstrated—that sixty-five acres, properly managed, is a more creditable possession than sixty-five acres farmed in a slip-shod manner. Modern buildings mark the place as the property of a successful farmer, and the fences are most creditable. The place is tiled and in every way brought up to the highest agricultural standards of a successful farming country. Mr. Goeglein married Katie Savage, a daughter of Conrad and Mary Savage, both native-born Germans and early settlers in the state of Ohio. The father died in Ohio and Mrs. Savage passed her declining years in the home of her daughter, Mrs. Goeglein. Nine children were born to Mr. and Mrs. Goeglein, and they reared two adopted daughters as well. The children, named in order of their birth, are: John, George A., Valentine C., William G., Gottlieb, Frederick, Theodore, Katie, and Sophia. The adopted daughters are Kate and Carrie. Add to this goodly family his own parents and those of his wife, and it will be seen that Mr. Goeglein was a man who enjoyed family life and welcomed such responsibilities of a domestic nature as came his way. Mr. Goeglein is a Democrat in politics, active in a local way, but not a participant in the more far-reaching activities of his party.

John J. Goldsmith, the efficient and popular young proprietor of the Hoosier Garage, at Harlan, Springfield township, was born in Cedar Creek township, this county, March 30, 1890, a son of Christopher C. and Lydia (Zimmerman) Goldsmith. Christopher C. Goldsmith was born in Hartford township, Adams county, Indiana, June 10, 1856, a son of Jacob and Susanna (Egly) Goldsmith, both of whom were born in Germany and came to America when young. They became the parents of ten children, namely: Joseph, Henry, Susanna, Jacob, Katherine, Lena, Christopher C., Amos, Rachel and one who died in infancy. Jacob, Katherine and Amos are now deceased. Jacob Goldsmith learned in his youth the carpenter's trade, to which he devoted his attention for several years. He then engaged in farming in Butler county, Ohio, whence he finally came to Indiana and established himself as a farmer in Adams county. He later came with his family to Allen county, where he continued his association with agricultural industry and where both he and his wife passed the remainder of their lives, both having been earnest members of the Mennonite church. Christopher C. Goldsmith gained his early education in the common schools of Adams and Allen counties and eventually became one of the substantial and representative farmers of Cedar Creek township, where he continued his active allegiance to the basic industry of agriculture until 1904, when he sold his farm and became essentially the first settler in the village of Grabill, Springfield township, where he engaged in the hardware business, his store having been the first building erected in the village. Three years later he removed to Harlan, where he engaged in the same line of business, a stock of general merchandise having been added four years later, and he was associated with John H. Zimmerman in the conducting of a substantial and prosperous hardware and general merchandise business under the firm name of J. H. Zimmerman & Co. He is a stalwart supporter of the cause of the Republican party and both he and his wife are active members of the Methodist Episcopal church. They became the parents of five children—John J., David L., Frank, Benjamin and Rose—and of the number David and Benjamin are deceased. In February, 1889, was solemnized the marriage of Mr. Goldsmith to Miss Lydia Zimmerman, who was born in Tippecanoe county, this state, a daughter of John and Lena (Slagel) Zimmerman, who were born and reared in Germany, where their marriage was solemnized. Upon coming to America they first settled in Missouri, whence they later came to Indiana and located in Tippecanoe county, where they passed the remainder of their lives, Mr. Zimmerman having there become a substantial farmer. They had the following children—Josephine, Nicholas, Lena, Mary, Joseph, Kate, John, Lydia, Rose, Elizabeth, Leah, Benjamin and Sarah. John J. Goldsmith continued his studies in the public schools until he had profited by the advantages of the Harlan High School, and thereafter completed a three months' course in the commercial department of Valparaiso University. In 1909 he assumed the position of bookkeeper in the bank at Grabill, and after serving in this capacity one year and eight months he removed to Harlan and assumed the responsible office of cashier of the Harlan State Bank, in which position he served from 1911 until January 1, 1917, and in which he did much to further the upbuilding of this substantial financial institution. The Hoosier Garage, at Harlan, to which he now devotes his attention, is a modern garage building of cement-block construction, the same having been erected by him in the autumn of 1916. Mr. Goldsmith is one of the loyal and progressive young men of Harlan, is influential in community affairs, is a Democrat in his political adherency, and holds membership in the Methodist Episcopal church. On November 27, 1913, was solemnized the marriage of Mr. Goldsmith to Miss Joy M. Shutt, who was born and reared in DeKalb county, Indiana, a daughter of William and Francis (Houck) Shutt, who were born in DeKalb county, this state, and both of whom are now deceased.

Joseph Grabill may be said to be the father of the little town that bears his name, for it was he who laid it out, in 1901, a part of his home place being in the original townsite. Mr. Grabill organized the bank and in other ways played a prominent part in making a prosperous village of the new community. He was born in Springfield township on January 16, 1886, son of Joseph and Magdalene (Gerig) Grabill, both of them natives of Germany who came to America after their marriage and settled in Allen county, almost immediately thereafter. They had seven sons and daughters. David is a resident of Grabill. Joseph was the second child. Anna married Jacob Conrad. Lydia is the wife of Peter Amstutz. Jacob lives in Springfield, Indiana. Noah is a Grabill resident and Samuel is located in Berne, Indiana. Joseph Grabill has been devoted to farm life to a considerable extent and has been very successful in that enterprise, as well as along other lines to which he has given his attention. He has a fine home in the community and is identified with some of the leading industrial and financial enterprises in the village, being a stockholder and director in the Grabill Bank and the Grabill Grain Company. His connection with the organization of the town in the earlier days has already been touched upon. Mr. Grabill was married first to Miss Emma Sanders, daughter of Christ Sanders, and one daughter, Lily, was born of this union, and she is the wife of Noah Roth, of Grabill. Mr. Grabill was married, second, on March 28, 1897, to Miss Katherine Nafcigger, born in Henry county, Ohio. She died on September 8, 1911, the mother of three children—Priscilla, Wilma May and Clifford Louis— all of whom are at home. Mrs. Grabill was a devoted wife and mother and her passing was a great loss to the entire community as well as to the family she left. Mr. Grabill and his children have membership in the Grabill Mission church and he is a member of its board of directors.

Jeremiah B. Grabner conducts a prosperous general merchandise business in the village of Edgerton, Jackson township, and is serving also as trustee of the township, a fact that denotes unequivocally the high regard in which he is held in the community that has ever represented his home. He was born in this township on July 10, 1872, son of Peter N. and Louisa (Hurtle) Grabner, both of whom were born in Germany, whence they came with their parents to the United States when they were young. Settlement was first made in the state of Ohio, and Peter N. Grabner was a youth when he came to Allen county and established his home in Fort Wayne. For more than a quarter of a century he served as a locomotive engineer in the employ of the Pennsylvania Railroad Company, and after retiring from this position established his home on a farm in Jackson township, where both he and his wife passed the remainder of their lives—sterling citizens who commanded the high regard of all who knew them. Of their eleven children the first born, Emma, is deceased; Henry is engaged in the successful practice of law in Fort Wayne, as one of the representative members of the Allen county bar; Jacob and John are deceased; Mrs. Louise Rood is the next in order of birth; Mrs. Susan Shiffman is a resident of the state of Oklahoma; Samuel is the next; Jeremiah B. is the immediate subject of this sketch; Albert and Adeline are deceased; and Mrs. Minnie Smith is the youngest. Jeremiah B. Grabner acquired his early education in the schools of Jackson township and continued to be associated in the work and management of the home farm until he was twenty-four years of age, when he established his present mercantile business at Edgerton, the same having been made a prosperous enterprise under his effective management. He is a stalwart in the local camp of the Democratic party, has been influential in public affairs of a local order, and in November, 1914, was elected trustee of Jackson township, for a term of four years. He had previously served nine years as township assessor and two years as constable. He is affiliated with the Modern Woodmen of America and with the Improved Order of Red Men. February 6, 1902, recorded the marriage of Mr. Grabner to Miss Jennie Stolder, daughter of Peter and Mary (Voroil) Stolder, both of whom were residents of Jackson township at the time of their death and were children when the respective families established homes in Allen county. Mr. Stolder was born in Switzerland and his wife was a native of France. They are survived by five children—Julian, Louis, Mrs. Louisa Spieth, Mrs. Jennie Grabner, and Justine. Mr. and Mrs. Grabner have six children, all of whom remain at the parental home—Edith, Carl, Ethel, Ruth, Daniel and Oliver.

Fred Graeber came from his German fatherland to America when he was a young man of about twenty-seven years, and after landing in New York city, in 1898, he came forthwith to Allen county, where he joined his brother William, who had established a home in Fort Wayne in the year 1882. He whose name introduces this sketch had the energy, ambition and resourcefulness that make for worthy achievement and definite success, and he has become known and honored as one of the progressive farmers and stock-growers of Maumee township, where he owns a well improved farm of one hundred and fifty-three acres, besides an additional tract of eighty acres in Milan township. On this extensive landed estate he is bringing forth the best results in both agricultural and live-stock enterprise, and he is giving special atention to the raising of fine Belgian horses, in connection with which department of enterprise he owns a Belgian stallion of the best type. He has identified himself most fully and loyally with community affairs and is deeply appreciative of the institutions and advantages of the land of his adoption. His political support is given to the cause of the Republican party and he and his wife are zealous communicants of the Lutheran church. Fred Graeber is the younger in a family of five children, and the eldest of the number is William, who came to Allen county in 1882, as noted above; Louisa and Henrietta remain in Germany; and Henry is deceased. Mr. Graeber was born in Dilingen, Germany, on February 25, 1871, and is a son of William and Romina (Hocker) Graeber, who passed their entire lives in that section of the great German empire, the father having been a farmer by vocation. Mr. Graeber has made the best of improvements on his farm property and in his varied operations represents the most progressive methods and policies involved in twentieth-century agriculturism and stock-raising. On April 12, 1899, was solemnized his marriage to Miss Romina Bohnke, who is a daughter of Fred and Wilhelmina (Logaeman) Bohnke, who were born in Germany and whose marriage was solemnized in the city of Cincinnati, Ohio. In 1891 they came to Allen county, but they later removed to Adams county, where Mr. Bohnke passed the remainder of his life and where his widow still maintains her home. Mr. and Mrs. Graeber have four children—Herman, Alvina, Luetta, and Minnie—and the pleasant family home is known for its generous hospitality and good cheer.

Philip Graf.—The late Philip Graf was for many years engaged in the grocery business in Fort Wayne, and was still occupied in that enterprise when death claimed him on September 11, 1910. He was a prosperous and prominent man in the city and was a dependable citizen and a credit to the community as long as he lived. He reared a fine family of sons and daughters who are filling places of usefulness wherever they are found, and viewed from the standpoint of worth, his career in Fort Wayne was a highly successful one. Mr. Graf was born in Ohio on September 8, 1854, and he died when in the prime of life. He was the son of John and Barbara (Ranning) Graf, both of them born and reared in Germany, and John Graf came to Fort Wayne to settle when Philip was a lad of three years. The father was in the employ of the Pennsylvania road from that time until the end of his life. Six children were born to him and his wife, but not one of the number is living today. The first independent work Philip Graf carried on was in a trunk factory on Columbia street in Fort Wayne, and he was there seven years. His next venture was in the grocery business. He had saved something from his seven years of labor in the factory and invested it in a small grocery store at 1813 Lafayette street. Some time later he erected a more roomy store on the site, and he carried on a thriving grocery business there up to the time of his death. The place is still carried on under the name of the Graf Grocery. After his marriage Mr. Graf built a fine home at 1930 Lafayette street, and his widow is living there today. Mr. Graf was married on May 13, 1879, to Miss Sophia Wessel, who was born in Michigan and came to Fort Wayne with her parents when she was about two years old. The Wessels are still living in Fort Wayne, and have lately celebrated their sixty-first wedding anniversary. Mr. Wessel was a stationary engineer for many years, and has been retired from the service for some time. He and his wife, who was before her marriage Elizabeth Keintz, have traveled extensively in this country and Europe, having crossed the Atlantic ocean fifteen times. He is now eighty-four and his wife seventy-eight years of age. To Mr. and Mrs. Graf were born eleven children. They were named Philip, Elizabeth, Anna, Florence, Joseph, Philip, Marie, Laurette, Gertrude, Gerald and Charles. The first five named are dead, as are also the two youngest—Gertrude and Gerald. Philip Junior was named in honor of his father and is now employed by the Armour Packing Company at Chicago as a mechanical engineer. Marie, the seventh child, is the wife of Amiel Bail of Fort Wayne, and Laurette is married to Joseph Lill, of St. Louis, Missouri. Mr. Graf was a Democrat all his life and a Catholic, with membership in St. Peter's church, in Fort Wayne, which he helped to build and which he always supported most generously. He was a member of its board of trustees at the time of his death. Fraternally, he had membership in the Benevolent and Protective Order of Elks, and was one of the most popular members of that organization. He died while he might be said to be in the very prime of his life, and his passing was mourned by many who knew him for an honest gentleman, a good citizen and a staunch friend.

Frank C. Graffe is one of the progressive and dependable men of the younger set in Fort Wayne, his native city. He has been in the employ of the General Electric Works, since 1903, as a movement maker on watches and later was advanced to the post of supervisor of stock and materials entering into the make-up of the product of his department. Mr. Graffe was born on February 15, 1880, son of George and Mary Elizabeth (Boone) Graffe, the father a native New Yorker and the mother born in Wayne township, Allen county, Indiana. George Graffe, however, came to Fort Wayne as an infant in arms and spent his mature years in the hardware business. He was a tinner by trade, and his knowledge of that work fitted admirably into his later activities as a dealer in hardware in Fort Wayne. He died in his home city and his widow still survives. Seven children were born to them; Rose is the wife of Frank A. Willis, of Jersey City, New Jersey; Clara is the widow of John V. Kessell of Fort Wayne; Julian B. is located in Oklahoma City, Oklahoma. Two daughters, Daisy and Amelia, have shed lustre on the family name by their vocations in the church, both being Sisters of Providence in Chicago. The sixth child was Frank C .and the youngest is Henry J., of Fort Wayne. Frank Graffe had his education in Cathedral Parochial school and engaged in the jewelry business with his uncle when he left his studies. Later, he went to Princeton, Indiana, and was there employed in the Princeton Clock Works for two years, finishing his training in the business, after which he accepted a position as manager of a jewelry establishment in Brooklyn, New York, where he demained for a year and a half. Returning to Fort Wayne for a brief period, he was offered a position in Logansport with J. E. Taylor, where he was engaged until 1903, when he returned once more to his home city and there became identified with the General Electric Works as has already been stated. In 1903 Mr. Graffe was married in Logansport to Miss Laura M. Tucker, who was born and reared in that place. Their marriage took place on February 24. Mr. and Mrs. Graffe adopted two boys—Stephen and Raymond—and the latter met his death in an automobile accident on October 2, 1915. Mr. Graffe is a Democrat in politics, a member of the Roman Catholic church and the Knights of Columbus.

Samuel Wilson Greenland, general manager of the Fort Wayne and Northern Indiana Traction Company since 1911, is conceded to be one of the rising young men in his particular field. He has already filled a number of positions of some importance and he came to the present company as purchasing agent, bearing recommendations of the most pleasing character. Mr. Greenland is a native of Pennsylvania, born in Clarion, that state, on April 27, 1879, and he is the son of Walter W. and Sadie E. (Wilson) Greenland. Both were of Pennsylvania families, the father being born in Huntington county and the mother in Clarion county. Walter W. Greenland was engaged in the lumber and oil business all his life. He died in 1894, and his widow survives him, living at present in Clarion, Pennsylvania. Five children came to them as follows: Bird W., now deceased; Walter Jr., of Moberly, Missouri, there connected with the Wabash railroad; Elizabeth, the wife of W. S. Stephenson, of Roanoke, Virginia; Samuel Wilson of this review, and J. Allen, who is general freight and passenger agent for the Fort Wayne and Northern Indiana Traction Company, of which the subject is general manager. As a growing boy at home, Mr. Greenland attended the public schools of Clarion. He later attended Pennsylvania Military College at Chester, Pennsylvania, and he had his technical training in Pennsylvania State College. He completed a course in electrical engineering there, after which he engaged for a short time in the lumber business in Pittsburgh. He was next associated with the Bell Telephone Company, being located first at Pittsburgh, then at Wheeling and still later in eastern Ohio. In 1905 he was associated with Robert W. Watson at Harrisburg, Pennsylvania, in electric railway engineering, and in 1907 he went to Columbus, Mississippi, as general manager of the Columbus Railway Light and Power Company, and in 1911 was called to Fort Wayne to accept the position of purchasing agent for the Fort Wayne and Northern Indiana Traction Company. His appointment to the office of general manager followed soon after, and he is occupying that position at this time. Mr. Greenland was married September 14, 1909, to Miss Mary Elizabeth Fox, of Bridgeport, Ohio, where she was born and reared. They have three children—Samuel Wilson, Jr., Sarah Elizabeth and Mary Fox. Mr. Greenland is a thirty-second degree Mason, with Knight Templar and Shriner affiliations, and is also a member of the Benevolent and Protective Order of Elks. He and his wife have membership in the Methodist Episcopal church and have an active part in the good works of that body.

Frank Greenwell, M. D., is to be be designated not only as one of the leading physicians and surgeons of his native county, where he has been established in the practice of his profession for the past forty years, but he has also been a signally prominent and influential figure in public affairs in the county, his maximum political preferment having come when he was elected a member of the senate of the Indiana legislature. His broad mental grasp and indomitable energy have found effective play in his support of measures and enterprises tending to advance the civic and industrial progress and prosperity of his native county, and his capacity for the giving of active service in varied lines has demonstrated his versatility and his civic loyalty, and that without impairing in the least his allegiance to the profession in which he has achieved prestige and unequivocal success. Dr. Greenwell was born in Perry township, this county, April 8, 1851, a son of George and Elizabeth (Blickenstaff) Greenwell, both natives of the state of Maryland. The father was left an orphan when about ten years of age, and prior to coming to Indiana had lived for a number of years in Ohio, where his elder children were born. About the year 1848 he became one of the pioneers of Allen county, where he obtained a tract of land and instituted the development of a farm from a virtual wilderness. He continued as one of the substantial exponents of agricultural industry in this county until his death, at the age of seventy-two years, and his name merits high place on the roll of those sterling pioneers who contributed generously to civic and industrial development and progress in this now favored section of the Hoosier State. His political support was given to the Democratic party. His wife was fifty-eight years of age at the time of her death. Of their five children two died in early childhood, and the other three still survive, the two brothers of Dr. Greenwell being Christian L. and George W., both of whom are representative farmers in Allen county. Dr. Greenwell passed the period of his childhood and early youth on the old home farm and after profiting duly by the advantages afforded in the public schools of the locality and period pursued a higher academic course in the Methodist College at Fort Wayne. In consonance with his ambition and well formulated plans, he then entered the medical department of historic old Western Reserve University, in the city of Cleveland, Ohio, and in this institution was graduated as a member of the class of 1876 and with the degree of Doctor of Medicine. In that same Centennial year he established his residence at Huntertown, Allen county, where he has since continued in the active general practice of his profession and has served long, faithfully and effectively in the alleviation of human suffering and distress, his practice having extended over a wide section of country normally tributary to Huntertown. He has kept in close touch with the advances made in medical and surigal science and still gives much time to the study of the best standard and periodical literature of his profession, besides maintaining affiliation with the Allen County Medical Society, the Indiana State Medical Society and the American Medical Association. In the midst of the many exactions of his professional service the Doctor has found time and opportunity to exert potent influence in community affairs of a public order and has been a leader in the local camp of the Democratic party. He served two years as county councilman at large, and in 1910 was elected representative of his district in the state senate, in which he served the regular term of four years and was an influential figure in the legislative sessions of 1911 and 1913. In the senate he was the staunch advocate of much constructive and progressive legislation. He was the author of the present Indiana law governing cold-storage institutions and business and championed this bill with characteristic energy and effectiveness, besides which he framed the Indiana park law, the enactment of which has met with representative popular endorsement. The Indiana cold-storage law has been the pattern on which many other states have formed similar legislative enactments. Dr. Greenwell was one of the organizers and incorporators of the Huntertown State Bank, in 1913; was its first president and served in this executive office two years. He was re-elected for a third term but felt constrained to retire from the position, owing to the exigent demands placed upon him in the work of his profession, the claims of which he has never subordinated to any other interests. In 1910 he was concerned in the organization of the Huntertown Grain Company, and has served consecutively as president of this corporation except during one year when he was able to prevail upon his associates to release him from the responsibilities involved. The Doctor is at the present time president also of the Huntertown Live Stock Association, which was organized August 2, 1916, and there have been few matters of importance in his home community that have not enlisted his attention and felt his benignant and loyal influence. On May 26, 1876, the year that marked his reception of the degree of Doctor of Medicine, was solemnized the marriage of Dr. Greenwell to Miss Mary Jane Hunter, who was born and reared in this county and is a daughter of the late William T. Hunter, of Huntertown, a village that was named in honor of this representative pioneer family. Dr. and Mrs. Greenwell became the parents of two children, of whom one is living, Eloise, who is the wife of Henry Nelson, their home being at Huntertown and Mr. Nelson having come to Indiana from Windsor, Massachusetts, a suburb of the city of Boston. Mr. and Mrs. Nelson have one child, Mary Elizabeth. In years of continuous practice Dr. Greenwell may consistently be termed the dean of his profession in his native county, even as he is known and honored as a representative citizen.

Charles E. Greer is one of the progressive young business men of Fort Wayne, where he has through his own ability and well ordered efforts achieved definite success and a position of influence in local business enterprise, this fact being assured when it is stated that he is now vice-president of the Seavey Hardware Company, one of the leading wholesale and retail concerns in this line of retail trade in the metropolis of his native county. Mr. Greer was born in Fort Wayne on September 24, 1874 and attended the public schools of Fort Wayne until he was fourteen years of age, when he found employment in the local factory in which at that time wagon and carriage spokes were manufactured; and a few years later he entered the employ of the Seavey Hardware Company, in the year 1892. He began his service in the position of order clerk, later was a salesman in the retail department, next assumed the position of receiving clerk, later served as stock clerk and as representative of the house as a traveling salesman. His course has been marked by well earned advancement and he has been indefatigable in his work, careful in informing himself thoroughly in all details of the business and full of energy and progressiveness. He finally became buyer for the concern and, since 1914, has been vice-president of the Seavey Hardware Company, with established vantage place as one of the representative business men and loyal and valued citizens of Fort Wayne. Mr. Greer has had no desire to enter the arena of practical politics but is thoroughly public-spirited and takes deep interest in all things pertaining to the welfare of his native city and county.

Chester Greer.—Fifty-four years of continuous residence in Lafayette township and vicinity have established Chester Greer firmly in his community, where he has been conspicuously identified with the agriculture and business interests of the district since he first identified himself with life as an independent factor. He has been prosperous, and is today connected with various moneyed interests, aside from his farming activities, and he has been associated with the civic life of his township in useful and important capacities. He was born in Pleasant township on February 16, 1863, the son of Thomas and Sarah (Shives) Greer, who were born in Carroll county, Indiana, in the vicinity of Delphi. The paternal grandfather of the subject was a native son of Ireland, who came to America in boyhood, settling in 1841 and identifying the family name with the fortunes of Pleasant township in 1842. He was Thomas Greer, and he was truly a pioneer in the community wherein he ended his days. He helped to lay out Pleasant township, and the first township election was held at his home. He was a Democrat, always active in politics, and was a leader in his community as long as he lived. When he first located in Pleasant township he bought eighty acres of canal land and there built a home for his family. He died July 4, 1910, and his wife passed away October 29, 1902. Thomas Greer following in the useful career his father had begun and took his place as a prominent and dependable man in the community. He was also active in local politics and served first as township assessor for four years and later as county assessor for a similar period. He devoted his agricultural activities mainly to stock-farming, and was very successful in that work. He was a member of the Presbyterian church and was high in Masonry, both he and his father having attained to the thirty-second degree of that order. In later life Thomas Greer lived retired from active farm life, and he died July 7, 1910. To him and his wife twelve sons and daughters were born. John, the first born, is a member of the Fort Wayne police force. Sarah J. is the wife of William Gray, of Ohio. Chester is the subject of this family review. Mary died in infancy. William is a resident of Salt Lake City. Thomas lives in

Fort Wayne. Ellen, George, Joseph and Charles are deceased. Clara is a graduate nurse in Fort Wayne. Cora married Ray Keyser of Lafayette township. Chester Greer was brought up on his father's farm and had the usual farm training. His education was limited to the schools of his community, and when he reached manhood he rented a farm and turned his attention to the business of gaining material independence along the lines for which his training best fitted him. He rented a farm for six years and, in 1898, bought a place of eighty acres in Lafayette township, where he has since made his home. He has made much progress in the years of his residence there and his success in stock-farming is an accepted fact wherever he is known. He is a Democrat and was township assessor of Lafayette township for ten years. He has long had membership in the Christian church and his fraternal connections are with the Independent Order of Odd Fellows and the Modern Woodmen, being a charter member of the latter order at Zanesville. Mr. Greer is a stockholder in the Uniondale Rural Telephone Company and for four years was treasurer of the company, while he has been a member of its board of directors for nine years. He was married on October 5, 1889, to Miss Sarah J. Earl, a daughter of Charles and Margaret (Cartwright) Earl, and to them have come six children. Margaret is the wife of Samuel G. Zirkle, of Marion township. Edith married William T. McAllister, of Marion township. Nora is in training in Hope Hospital in Fort Wayne. Sarah Fern and Ruth are now attending the high school in Roanoke, and Naomi, the youngest, is at home with the parents.

Julian C. Gremaux.—One of the capable and progressive young farmers of Jefferson township and a native son of his community is Julian C. Gremaux, trustee of his township and a citizen of much merit. He was born in Jefferson township on August 31, 1885, son of Arsene and Melinda (Reuille) Gremaux, both of French birth and ancestry. They came to America as children, the mother being only four years old when she was transplanted with her family from their native France to American soil. The parents after marriage settled in Jefferson township and are living there at the present time. They were ambitious people and succeeded in establishing a home in their new country, their successes enabling them to educate their children in some degree and to help them to become established in life. They reared a fine family of eight children, all living at this writing, and named as follows: Francis E., Mary, Adeline, Annie, Alice, Julian C., Lois and Clem. Annie and Alice, it should be stated, are twins. Julian C. Gremaux was educated in the schools of Jefferson township and at a business college in Fort Wayne. After completing his studies he turned his attention to the business of farming, settling on a farm in Section 24, where he is still living and enjoying a very satisfactory and well merited success. General farming and stock raising occupy him, and he has taken his place among the foremost farming men of his community in the brief period in which he has been identified with the work as an independent operator. October 6, 1914, Mr. Gremaux was married to Miss Eleanor Voirol, daughter of Louis and Mary (Bardy) Voirol, Jackson township people, still resident there, and two children have been born to them—Veronica and Eleanor. The family are communicants of the Catholic church and Mr. Gremaux is a Democrat in politics. He is now serving in the office of trustee of Jefferson township, having been elected, in 1914, for a four year term. He has given a creditable service to his community in that office and takes his place among the representative and progressive men of the township.

Euclid Eugene Griest.—The Griest family, of which Euclid Eugene Griest is a representative, dates its settlement in America back to a date prior to the coming of William Penn. John Griest was the first of the name to leave England. He was a Quaker, or Friend, and was driven out of his native land because of his religious belief. Like many another, he came to the new world as a seeker after religious freedom and found it in Lancaster county, Pennsylvania, where he established a home and reared a family, worshipping God according to the dictates of his own conscience, without interference from any. All of the name in America today are said to be direct descendants of that brave pioneer. It is not clear just when the family made its first migration from Pennsylvania into the middle west, but in about 1820 we find the grandfather of the subject established in the state of Ohio. Later he moved to Iowa, and there he died when his son, A. P. Griest, father of the subject, was about fourteen years of age. Following the death of the father, the little family returned to Quaker City, Ohio, and the boy worked at odd jobs about the town for a few years. He was still in his teens when he made up his mind to better his condition somehow, and he did it by following a course of study in Duff's Business College in Pittsburgh. He completed a course of training in bookkeeping in three months, after which he held a position as instructor in the college for a few months. He then went to Baltimore, Maryland, there to accept a position with a commission house, and he was with that concern for two years, coming back at the end of that time to take a position as agent for the Baltimore and Ohio Railroad at their station in Quaker City, Ohio, his former home. From that time on Mr. Griest continued in the railroad service in one capacity or another. From his Quaker City office he was promoted to the post of agent at Shawnee, was later moved to Plymouth and still later to Zanesville, the latter station being then one of the largest stations on the B. & O. By that time Mr. Griest had come to feel that he had reached the end of his advancement with the B. & O., and he resigned from its service in 1887 to accept a position as clerk in the auditor's office of the Cleveland & Marietta Railway Company, at Cambridge, Ohio. About a year afterward he was appointed acting auditor, and a year later became auditor for the road, continuing in that office until January 1, 1900, when that road was absorbed by the Pennsylvania system. At that time he was made auditor's traveling agent, in which capacity he served until January 1, 1903, when he was appointed to the position of auditor of the ore and coal freight receipts for the Pennsylvania Lines at Pittsburg. On January 1, 1917, he was appointed auditor of miscellaneous accounts. He died January 15, 1917. On August 27, 1878, Mr. Griest was married to Miss Arabella Moore, like himself a native of Quaker City, Ohio, the marriage taking place in that community. Five children were born to them. Ethel and Kate are deceased. Milton Moore is sales manager for the Carnegie Coal Company at Pittsburg. Helen is the wife of H. T. Cook, manager of the order department of the American Sheet & Tin Plate Company, of Chicago. Euclid Eugene, the third born, is the immediate subject of this family review. He was born in Zanesville, Ohio, on November 28, 1882, and had his early education in the schools of Cambridge, Ohio, though his advantages in that early period were limited, for he dropped out of the high school during his first year and went to work in a department store. A suspicion that he was not exactly suited to department store life led him to withdraw from that field, and he was seventeen years old when in June, 1899, he entered the employ of the Cleveland & Marietta Railroad Company as a clerk and messenger in the auditor's office. On January 1st following this office was transferred to Pittsburgh, and he entered the office of the division freight agent at Cambridge as clerk. A little later he served as a machinist's apprentice in the shops of the Pittsburgh, Cincinnati, Chicago & St. Louis, remaining there as apprentice and full fledged machinist until October 1, 1904. It should be remarked that during the last four months of his service as an apprentice Mr. Griest was assigned to special work under the master mechanic, in charge of the machinery, taking out the steam engines and installing motors in connection with the work of changing the shop from steam to electric drive. This work completed, he was assigned to re-arrange the piece work prices, and work in connection with the introduction of high speed steel and generally improving shop methods. Not content with his accomplishments thus far, young Griest resigned from the service and on October 1, 1904, entered the school of mechanical engineering at Purdue University. He was graduated from that institution in June, 1907. On July following he entered upon the duties of designer for the Crucible Steel Company of America, with offices at Pittsburg, in which position he remained until November 1, 1907, when he left the Crucible Steel people and entered the employ of the Erie Railroad as foreman of their machine shops at Hornell, New York. On February 1, 1908, Mr. Griest came to Fort Wayne as assistant machine shop foreman for the Pennsylvania Lines. A year later he was promoted to the office of assistant master mechanic, which position he held up to the time of his appointment to his present post as master mechanic, on January 1, 1915. It should be remarked here that the shops at Fort Wayne are the largest of the northwest system of the Pennsylvania Lines, employing about 2,300 men, and are among the principal shops of the entire system. Mr. Griest succeeded B. Fitzpatrick, under whom he had served as assistant master mechanic, and he was the logical successor to the post made vacant by the death of the veteran master. On September 8, 1909, Mr. Griest was married to Miss Marianna Lindley, the daughter of Charles W. Lindley, a retired farmer of Bloomingdale, Indiana. She was a graduate of Purdue University, also of the class of 1907. They have one daughter—Miriam, born April 4, 1914. Mr. and Mrs. Griest are both representatives of old Quaker families and are themselves adherents of the faith, but as that denomination is not sufficiently numerous in Fort Wayne to warrant the maintenance of a church, they have united with the First Presbyterian church of Fort Wayne and are loyal and active members of that body. Mr. Griest is a Republican, but has manifested no political ambitions at any time. He is a Mason, well advanced, and in Fort Wayne has membership in the Commercial Club, the Country Club and the Rotary Club. He has shown himself genuinely interested in the affairs of the Young Men's Christian Association and served as a member of the central board of that organization, as well as having served as a trustee and as a member of the building committee. In the fall of 1916 he was elected president of the Association. In line with his work he is chairman of the executive committee of the International Railway General Foreman's Association. He is a director in the Citizens Trust Company and a director in the Fort Wayne

Morris Plan Company. It may be said that Mr. Griest has been identified with railroad work to the exclusion of all other lines of endeavor since he was seventeen years old, though an exception of one brief period might be named. During his university career he spent one vacation season, from June 1 to October 1, 1906, in a trip to Alaska, where he was engaged in the investigation of mines and investment propositions, in the interests of the New York Development Company. In that period he made a brief but agreeable acquaintance with the Alaska and British Columbia districts.

John E. Griffin is the owner of the fine old homestead farm on which he was born and reared and which is eligibly situated in Section 2, Perry township, and is not only a scion of one of the honored pioneer families of Allen county but has also proved conclusively that to him is not applicable the scriptural aphorism that "a prophet is not without honor save in his own country," for, while claiming no prophetic powers, he has secure place in popular confidence and esteem, as indicated by the fact that the year 1917 finds him the loyal and valued incumbent of the office of township trustee of his native township. On his present homestead farm Mr. Griffin was born, November 14, 1870, a son of Alanson C. and Henrietta (Surfus) Griffin. His father, who is now one of the venerable and honored pioneer citizens of Allen county, was born in Union county, New York, June 29, 1836, and still resides in Perry township, to the development and progress of which section of the country he has contributed his full quota. His wife was born and reared in Perry township and here passed her entire life, her parents having been numbered among the early pioneers of the county. She was born in 1844 and was called to the life eternal in 1876, her lineage having traced back to German origin. The original American representatives of the Griffin family came from England and the paternal grandfather of the subject of this review was a successful carpenter and contractor in Union county, New York. His son, Alanson C., likewise learned the carpenter's trade, but the major part of his active career was marked by close and successful association with agricultural industry, of which he became a leading exponent in Allen county. John E. Griffin was the fourth in a family of six children, all of whom are living. John E. Griffin was reared to the sturdy discipline of the farm and acquired his early education in the schools of Perry township. He continued thereafter to assist his father in the management and work of the farm until 1895, when he assumed control of its operation. Later he purchased the place, which is well improved, and has proved himself one of the most vigorous, progressive and successful farmers of his native township, the fine farm being devoted to diversified agriculture and stock-growing. Mr. Griffin gives special attention to the raising of short-horn cattle and is actively identified with the Indiana Short-horn Breeders' Association. He has been one of the influential workers in the local ranks of the Democratic party, served several years as a member of the advisory board of Perry township, and since 1914 has held the office of township trustee. He is affiliated with the Masonic fraternity and he and his wife are zealous members of the Church of God. In 1895 was solemnized the marriage of Mr. Griffin to Miss Alda Lige, daughter of Samuel J. and Nancy Jane (Bailey) Lige, her father being a prominent farmer of Jackson township, DeKalb county. Mr. and Mrs. Griffin have two children—Velma M. and Erma W. Mr. Griffin is a loyal supporter of all measures and enterprises tending to advance the best interests of his home county, is a vigorous worker and sagacious man, and finds his chief recreation in occasional hunting and fishing trips and in enjoying with his family the facilities and pleasures afforded by his fine automobile.

William M. Griffin.—The position of William M. Griffin in the commercial and financial activities of Fort Wayne affords him an exceptional opportunity to exert a decided influence in the forward movement of the city toward a higher place among the municipalities of the middle west. Always an active leader along business and industrial lines, the worth of Mr. Griffin was recognized in a marked degree, when, in March, 1913, the Commercial Club of Fort Wayne, which had chosen him to serve as its president in 1914, voted to revise its constitution in order to permit his re-election to the highest executive position in the organization. During the years of his presidency the club enjoyed exceptional growth in numbers and influence in the upbuilding of the welfare of the city. The growth from a membership of three hundred to more than one thousand took place during Mr. Griffin's administration. Mr. Griffin is a native of Brimfield, Noble county, Indiana. After attending the schools there he served for several years as an instructor in the schools of the county and then removed to Kalamazoo, Michigan, in which city he resided at the time of the outbreak of the Spanish-American war. As a member of Company E, of the Thirty-second Michigan volunteers, he served during the campaign in the south. Shortly after his honorable discharge he came to Fort Wayne and entered upon a commercial career. He is the president of the Wayne Oil Tank and Pump Company, manufacturers of self-measuring oil-handling equipment and devices, which have a nation-wide sale. The business, under the general management of Mr. Griffin, who is surrounded by men of experience and skill, has grown to great proportions. The growth of the popularity of the automobile, the increasingly stringent laws governing the handling and storage of oil, and the widespread demand for modern systems of handling oil, have combined to bring prosperity to this growing concern. Mr. Griffin is a director in several of the leading financial and commercial institutions of Fort Wayne, and his counsel is an important factor in the progress of the interests with which he is connected. He is a charter member of the Fort Wayne Rotary Club, a member of the Fort Wayne Country Club, of the Chicago Athletic Association, the Chicago Automobile Club, and the Columbia Club of Indianapolis. In June, 1902, Mr. Griffin was united in marriage with Maud C. Merillat, and they have one child, Jack M. The Griffin home on South Fairfield avenue is one of the handsomest residence properties in Fort Wayne.

Aristide Grosjean.—Within the pages of this history will be found individual reference to a number of the members of the Grosjean family, whose name has been identified with the annals of Allen county during a period of virtually three-fourths of a century, and he whose name initiates this paragraph is well upholding the prestige of the patronymic. He was born on the old homestead farm of his father, a short distance from Fort Wayne, in Washington township, and the date of his nativity was September 15, 1864. His parents, John B. and Mary (Poirson) Grosjean, were both born in the French province of Alsace-Lorraine, which became a part of German territory after the close of the Franco-Prussian war and which is again the stage of sanguinary conflict in the deplorable European war that is now raging. John B. Grosjean was about fourteen years old at the time of the family immigration to the United States and it was fully seventy years ago that he numbered himself among the energetic farmers of Allen county, Indiana, where he achieved success through his well directed endeavors and where both he and his wife died when venerable in years. Concerning their children brief data are given on other pages, in the sketch of the career of their son, John B. Aristide Grosjean found his childhood and youth compassed by the benignant and invigorating influences of the home farm and his early educational advantages were those afforded in the public schools of Allen county. When about twenty years of age he became associated with his brothers, Julian and Edward, in the lumber business at Wallen, this county, and after the lapse of eight years he purchased his brothers' interests in the business. He continued to operate the saw mill and conduct a general lumber business in an individual way for the ensuing eight years, at the expiration of which he sold the plant and business and removed to Fort Wayne, where he devoted about eighteen months to the retail grocery trade. For the next year he was engaged in the sale of farm implements and machinery, and his next occupation was that of foreman of city trucking operations, a position which he held for eighteen months. Since that time he has been actively engaged in cement construction work, as one of the representative and successful exponents of this important line of enterprise in the metropolis of his native county. He takes a lively interest in all things touching the welfare of his home city and native county, is a Republican in politics and both he and his wife hold membership in the Congregational church. On October 22, 1889, was solemnized the marriage of Mr. Grosjean to Miss Sarah Little, who was born and reared at Fort Wayne and who likewise is of distinguished French ancestry on the distaff side, her maternal grandfather, Colonel Louis Humbert, having served as a gallant officer in the French army under the great Napoleon and having taken prominent part in the Napoleonic wars. Mrs. Grosjean is a daughter of Alfred and Mary E. (Humbert) Little, the former of whom was born in Maryland and the latter in Ohio, the father having devoted the major part of his active career to the painter's trade and business and having resided for several years past in the home of his daughter Sarah, wife of the subject of this sketch, his wife being deceased and Mrs. Grosjean being the elder of their two children; Grace, the younger daughter, is the wife of George A. Stephans, of Cleveland, Ohio. Mr. and Mrs. Grosjean have two children, Wadge and Amber, both of whom remain at the parental home, and the former is associated with his father in the cement contracting business.

John B. Grosjean is another of the native sons of Allen county who has proved definitely alert and resourceful in connection with business activities and who is now one of the substantial citizens of Fort Wayne, where he conducts a large and prosperous business as a general contractor in cement-construction work. He was born on the old homestead farm of his father, in Washington township, a few miles distant from Fort Wayne, and the date of his nativity was September 14, 1850, so that he may consistently be termed a scion of one of the pioneer families of Allen county. He is a son of John B. and Mary (Poirson) Grosjean, both of whom were born in Alsace-Lorraine, France, now a German province and the stage of much of the stupendous and horrible military activities of the present great European war. John B. Grosjean, a representative of sterling old French stock, was a lad of about fourteen years when he accompanied his parents to America, and he was reared to manhood in the United States. As a young man he became one of the industrious exponents of agricultural enterprise in Allen county, where he improved a good farm near Fort Wayne, and he passed the later years of his long and useful life in retirement and in the enjoyment of the rewards of his former earnest toil and endeavor. Both he and his wife were venerable in age at the time of their death and the names of both are held in lasting honor in the county that so long represented their home. Of their children the eldest is Felix, who is a representative farmer in Washington township, this county; John B., of this review, was the next in order of birth; Celia and Joseph are deceased; Edward is a resident of Fort Wayne; Felicia is the wife of John Irving, of Los Angeles, California; Mary is the wife of Benjamin Christian, of Fort Wayne; Julian, who likewise maintains his home in Fort Wayne, is individually mentioned in other pages; Aristide is likewise mentioned; Ella is deceased; Clara is the wife of William Morrison, of Fort Wayne; and Frank died in childhood. John B. Grosjean acquired his early education in the public schools and continued to be associated with his father in the operations of the home farm until he had attained to his legal majority. For a period of about eight years thereafter he was actively and successfully identified with the lumber business and the operation of saw mills. He finally erected a saw mill at Wallen, this county, and after operating the same about four years established a tile manufactory at Arcola, Lake township, where later he erected also a grain elevator, which latter he operated only one year. He continued to give his attention to the tile business about ten years, and then disposed of his interest in the well established enterprise, besides selling also three farms which he had purchased in the county. He then, in 1900, established his residence in the city of Fort Wayne, where for the first year he gave his attention to the retail grocery business. After his retirement from this line of enterprise he was for four years engaged in the real estate business, and he then established his present cement business, which has been developed to substantial proportions and involves various kinds of cement construction work, including the building of cement walks and also architectural concrete work. Mr. Grosjean is one of the progressive and highly esteemed business men of the Allen county metropolis, is liberal and public-spirited as a citizen, and though he is a staunch supporter of the cause of the Republican party he has had no ambition for political office of any kind. Both he and his wife hold membership in the Methodist Episcopal church. For his first wife Mr. Grosjean wedded Miss Mary Hudson, who was born and reared in Fort Wayne, and she passed to the life eternal in 1880, having become the mother of two children—Edgar, who resides in Fort Wayne, and Abbie, who died in childhood. On March 30, 1882, was solemnized the marriage of Mr. Grosjean to Miss Mary Cook, who was born at Fort Wayne and who is a daughter of Jacob and Elizabeth (Pegg) Cook, both natives of the state of New York. Jacob Cook was a boy of eight years when his parents became pioneer settlers of Fort Wayne, where he was reared to maturity, and he eventually became one of the prosperous farmers of Allen county, where both he and his wife passed the residue of their lives. Of their eight children the first three—Carrie, Clarence and Arthur—are deceased, Mrs. Grosjean having been the fourth child; James is deceased; Jennie resides in Fort Wayne; George is a resident of the state of Michigan; and Etta is the wife of Frederick Lemon, of Allen county. Mr. and Mrs. Grosjean became the parents of three children, of whom the first two—Ernest and Ralph—are deceased; and the third, Velma, is, in 1916-17, attending the James Millekin college at Decatur, Illinois.

Julian Grosjean, who is a successful and representative contractor in concrete construction work, with headquarters in the city of Fort Wayne, has been a resident of Allen county from the time of his birth, which occurred on his father's old homestead farm, in Washington township, a few miles distant from Fort Wayne, August 5, 1862. He is a son of John B. and Mary (Poisson) Grosjean, both of whom, as the names definitely indicate, having been of French ancestry, and they were born in the province of Alsace-Lorraine, France, a district that is now a German province. John B. Grosjean was a lad of about fourteen years when he came to America and settled in Allen county, Indiana, about seventy years ago, his energy and ability having enabled him to gain place as one of the representative farmers of Washington township. Both he and his wife attained to venerable age and were honored pioneer citizens of the county at the time of their death. Of their children the eldest is Felix, a prosperous farmer of Washington township; John B. is specifically mentioned on other pages; Cleia and Joseph are deceased; Edward is identified with business activities in Fort Wayne; Felicia is the wife of John Irving, of Los Angeles, California; Mary is the wife of Benjamin McQuiston, of Fort Wayne; Julian, of this review, was the next in order of birth; Aristide is individually mentioned elsewhere in this publication; Ella is deceased; Clara is the wife of William Morrison, of Fort Wayne; and Frank died in childhood. Julian Grosjean was reared to the sturdy discipline of the home farm and in the meanwhile made good use of the advantages afforded in the public schools of his native county. At the age of twenty-one years he became concerned in the operation of a saw mill and continued thus to be identified with the manufacturing of lumber for a period of about ten years. For three years thereafter he was engaged in the grocery business in Fort Wayne, and after his retirement from this line of enterprise devoted five years to buying lumber for the Studebakers. He then engaged in his present line of businss, and as a contractor in modern concrete work has erected several high-grade buildings, besides giving attention also to all other general lines of cement construction, his successful operations giving him place as one of the substantial business men of his native county, where he has secure vantage-ground in popular esteem. Mr. Grosjean is a Republican in politics, is affiliated with the Tribe of Ben Hur, and both he and his wife hold membership in the Methodist Episcopal church. August 21, 1888, recorded the marriage of Mr. Grosjean to Miss Grace M. Sechler, who was born at Ossian, Wells county, Indiana, and was a child at the time of the family removal to Allen county. She is a daughter of the late Jacob and Catherine C. (Horn) Sechler, her father having been for many years a prosperous merchant in Fort Wayne and Huntertown, and her maternal grandfather, Hon. Patrick Horn, having served as a representative in the lower house of the Indiana legislature. Mrs. Grosjean was the fourth in order of birth in a family of five children, the first born having been Cyrilus, who is deceased; Milo H. is a resident of Fort Wayne and Charles of Sugar Loaf, Colorado; and Nellie is the wife of Charles W. Warcup, of Marshalltown, Iowa. Mr. and Mrs. Grosjean have four children—Ethel, Arthur, Harold and Bernice.

Asa G. Grosvenor.—Technical ability, executive and initiative energy and a high sense of civic loyalty make Asa Walters Grosvenor specially eligible for the office of which he is now the valued incumbent, that of county surveyor of Allen county, a position to which he was elected in November, 1916, and the duties of which he assumed on the first of the following January. Mr. Grosvenor's reputation as a civil and construction engineer far transcends local limitations and he has been identified with a large amount of important engineering work since establishing his home in Fort Wayne, even as he had been previously in the state of New York and elsewhere. Mr. Grosvenor has the unique distinction of reverting to Constantinople, Turkey, as the place of his nativity, his birth having there occurred, November 7, 1875. In 1867 his father became a member of the faculty of Robert College in that oriental city, where he continued his effective educational service for a period of twenty years, at the expiration of which he returned to the United States and assumed the chair of international law in historic old Amherst College, Massachusetts, where he still remains as a revered professor emeritus. This distinguished educator, Professor Edwin A. Grosvenor, was born at Newburyport, Massachusetts, and his wife is a native of Millbury, that state, both being representatives of fine old colonial stock in New England, that gracious cradle of much of our national history. Professor Grosvenor was graduated in Andover Theological Seminary and was ordained a clergyman of the Congregational church, as a representative of which he went forth as a missionary and educator in Constantinople. He is a Democrat in his political allegiance and is affiliated with the Psi Upsilon college fraternity. He has given exalted service as a clergyman and educator, and, now venerable in years, he is revered alike for his noble character and his fine intellectual attainments. Of the three children, Asa W., of this review, is the eldest; Gilbert H. and Edwin P. are twins, the former being now in the newspaper business in Washington and the latter is associated with Harry W. Taft in New York City. Asa W. Grosvenor was reared in a home of distinctive culture and this in itself could not but prove a fortuitous condition and a spur to intellectual achievement. In early life he left his native city in the far Orient and carried forward his educational work in the United States until he received, in 1897, the degree of Bachelor of Science from Amherst College. He forthwith entered the celebrated Massachusetts Institute of Technology, and in the same was graduated with the class of 1899. Thereafter, under civil service, he held for two years a position as supervising architect in connection with the government at Washington, and for six years thereafter held the post of civil engineer on the lines of the Pennsylvania Railroad, west of Pittsburgh. He was thereafter assistant engineer in Ohio, and at New Castle, Pennsylvania, and finally was assigned to headquarters in the service of the Pennsylvania Company at Fort Wayne. He finally resigned his position to accept the post of superintendent of construction of tunnels under the East river, New York city, in the employ of S. Pearson & Son, of London, England, the celebrated firm of contractors. After giving effective service in this important capacity and one year of professional work as assistant engineer in the employ of the New York Central Railroad, Mr. Grosvenor came again to Fort Wayne, where, in March, 1909, he opened an office and engaged in the work of his profession as a civil and consulting engineer and supervisor of construction. He has designed and directed the construction of many fine concrete bridges, has made special surveys for floor protection work and designed the buildings of the Fort Wayne Oil & Supply Company. In this city he was the designer also of the Harrison street bridge, and at Wabash, Indiana, designed and supervised the construction of a modern concrete bridge seven hundred feet in length, over the Wabash river. Though he gives close attention to his official duties as county surveyor of Allen county he is able to continue effectively his general professional work, in connection with which he has worthily won his success and prestige. Mr. Grosvenor is a Republican in his political proclivities, he and his wife are members of the First Presbyterian church of Fort Wayne, he is affiliated with Sol D. Bayless Lodge, No. 359, Ancient Free & Accepted Masons, and also with the Psi Upsilon college fraternity. October 27, 1904, recorded the marriage of Mr. Grosvenor to Miss Gertrude King Hanna, daughter of Oliver S. and Mary Ellen (Nuttman) Hanna, of Fort Wayne, and of the three children of this union two are living, Juliet Hanna and Florence Walters. The only son, Jonathan Holman, died at the age of two years.

Charles Grotrian.—One of the older residents of Madison township is Charles Grotrian, retired farmer and veteran of the Civil war, and a resident of Allen county since he came to America, in 1854, as a lad of fifteen years. He is the son of Fred and Wilhelmina (Hassel) Grotrian, both of German birth, who settled on a farm in Allen county when they reached America with their little family. They lived quietly and prospered agreeably, and saw their closing days on the farm they acquired on coming into the county. They were the parents of six children, four of them now living. Charles Grotrian attended school in Allen county, and the most of his educational advantages were found after he came to his adopted country. When the Civil war was fairly well advanced he enlisted for service in the Ninety-first Indiana Volunteers, serving till the close of hostilities, when he returned to his home and engaged in farming. He gradually acquired land and when he retired from active life, in 1906, he was the owner of two hundred and twenty acres of the finest land in the county. He moved to Maples, in Jefferson township, and is living there at this time. Mr. Grotrian is a Democrat, but not active in politics. He was married in 1863 to Miss Henrietta Gable, a native German, and they are the parents of nine children—Charles A., Fred H., Frank and Daniel, twins; Wilhelmina, Henrietta and Clara. The eighth and ninth born are deceased. Mr. and Mrs. Grotrian are members of the German Lutheran church.

James O. Grove, D. C., is a thoroughly skilled and successful exponent of the benignant system of chiropractic, which has proven a splendid aid in the alleviation of human suffering and in the eradicating of many of the ills to which human flesh is heir. He is an enthusiast in his profession and in the practice of the same is well established in the city of Fort Wayne, as one of the leading representatives of the chiropractic school in Indiana. Dr. Grove was born in Perry county, Ohio, March 29, 1874, and is a son of Hiram and Leah (Boyer) Grove, the latter of whom is deceased. Hiram Grove, of German lineage, was born and reared in Perry county, Ohio, a scion of a sterling pioneer family of that section of the Buckeye state, and during his entire active career he has given close allegiance to the basic industry of agriculture, of which he continued a prominent and honored exponent in his native county. He is the owner of a farm in Adams county, Indiana, served sixteen years as county trustee in Darke county, Ohio, is a Democrat in his political proclivities and is affiliated with the Masonic fraternity. Of the children the eldest, Harry, is now a resident of Oklahoma; Noah resides at Sturgis, Michigan; Mary is the wife of William Klipstein, residing in Ohio; James O., of this review, was the next in order of birth; Charles is in Texas; Orrin in Oklahoma; John died in infancy; George and Grover reside in the state of Oklahoma; and William and Ralph died in infancy. Dr. Grove is indebted to the public schools of Ohio for his early education, and in the earlier period of his business career he was a traveling salesman for a firm engaged in the flour trade. Later he was identified actively with the buying and shipping of grain for a period of ten years, with headquarters at Lagrange, Indiana, and finally he became deeply impressed with the consistency and value of the comparatively new system of chiropractics, with the result that he went to the city of Grand Rapids, Michigan, where he entered the Michigan College of Chiropractics, in which he was graduated in 1912 and from which he received his degree of Doctor of Chiropractics. In March of that year he opened an office in Fort Wayne, and here he has built up a substantial practice of representative order, his success having fully justified his choice of profession. He is a director of the Indiana State Association of Chiropractic and has been influential in the furtherance of the system of practice with which he has identified himself with characteristic earnestness and enthusiasm. He is a Scottish Rite Mason and a Shriner. On March 3, 1903, was solemnized the marriage of Dr. Grove to Miss Beryl Glazier, and they have four children: Doris, James O., Jr., Clark and Leah Marguerite.

Herman H. Grubb is one of the substantial business men and influential citizens of his native county and now resides in the fine little city of New Haven, in Adams township. He is vice-president of the New Haven State Bank and, since 1911, has given effective service in the office of superintendent of the Wabash Valley Utilities Co. Mr. Grubb was born at Harlan, this county, October 26, 1869, a son of Ira I. and Mary Elizabeth (Oberholtzer) Grubb. Ira I. Grubb was born in Pennsylvania, June 3, 1838, and in the employ of the Pennsylvania Railroad Company came to Indiana when a young man. At the time of the Civil war he owned and operated a wagon shop at Harlan, and thereafter he purchased the old Oberholtzer homestead farm of one hundred and sixty acres, in Springfield township, where he continued to give his attention successfully to agricultural enterprise during the residue of his active life. He died November 24, 1911, at the age of seventy-three years, the loved wife of his youth having passed away at the age of fifty-three years and both having been earnest members of the Evangelical Lutheran church. He was a Democrat in politics and was affiliated with the Masonic fraternity—a man of sterling character and a loyal citizen who was respected by all who knew him. Of the children the eldest is Charles C., who remains on the old homestead farm; Lockie L. is the wife of J. C. Hursh, of Auburn, Indiana; Herman H., of this sketch, was the next in order of birth; Berne B. resides in the city of Lafayette, this state; and Mary J. is the wife of Rev. S. E. Slater, of Auburn, Indiana. After having availed himself of the advantages of the public schools, Herman H. Grubb attended the university at Valparaiso, Indiana, and thereafter was employed for some time in his brother's grocery store at Harlan. For one year he operated a creamery in that village and for three years thereafter was engaged in the hardware and lumber business at St. Joseph, this state. For six years he operated a saw mill and handle factory at St. Joe, and then sold the plant and business and, in 1904, removed to New Haven, where he was associated with C. W. Sperry in the same line of industrial enterprise until 1911. He then sold his interest in the business and has since held the office of superintendent of the Wabash Valley Utilities Co., as previously stated in this article. A staunch advocate of the cause of the Democratic party, Mr. Grubb has not been ambitious for political office, though he gave six years of effective service as a member of the village council of New Haven. In the Masonic fraternity he has received the thirty-second degree of the Scottish Rite, besides being affiliated with the Mystic Shrine, the Knights of Pythias, and the Modern Woodmen of America. He is one of the active and valued members of the New Haven Commercial Club. In addition to his banking interests he purchased the old Herrick homestead of one hundred acres, in Springfield township, and gives to the same a general supervision. June 4, 1892, recorded the marriage of Mr. Grubb to Miss Harriet Herrick, who likewise was born and reared in Allen county, and the one child of this union is a son, C. Glenn, who remains at the parental home. Mrs. Grubb is a daughter of Arona and Mary (Boger) Herrick, the former of whom was born in the state of New York and the latter in Ohio. Mr. Herrick came to Allen county, Indiana, about 1848, purchased a tract of land near Harlan and became one of the pioneer farmers of the county. In 1864 he went forth in defense of the Union, as a member of Company D, One Hundred and Fifty-fifth Indiana Infantry, and in his army service contracted illness from which he never recuperated fully, his death having occurred in 1876: His wife long survived him and was venerable in years at the time of her death, July 4, 1912. Mr. Herrick was a stalwart Republican and was affiliated with the Masonic fraternity. Mrs. Grubb was the fifth in a family of six children and was born on the old homestead farm near Harlan, a property now owned by her husband, the date of her nativity having been January 6, 1870. The eldest of the children, Andrew, is deceased, as is also Delia A.; Ida S. is the wife of O. D. Applegate, of this county; and Catherine and William are deceased.

Frank J. Gruber has become one of the representative figures in connection with the industrial and general business activities of his native city and his civic liberality and progressiveness are on a parity with his ability and successful achievement as a captain of industry, he being the proprietor of the Frank Gruber Boiler Works, which represents one of the important industrial enterprises of Fort Wayne. Mr. Gruber was born in this city on the 13th of July, 1865, and is a son of Michael and Veronica (Huhn) Gruber, both of whom were born in Germany, though both were young at the time of the immigration of the respective families to America. Michael Gruber was afforded the advantages of the excellent schools of his native land and was sixteen years of age at the time of his disembarkation in the port of New York city. He remained in the national metropolis six years and there thoroughly skilled himself as a workman at the tailor's trade. At the expiration of the period noted he came to Indiana and established his residence in Fort Wayne. Here he was employed at his trade in the Nurdlinger tailoring establishment, and later in that of Townley Brothers. About the year 1871 he established a retail grocery at the corner of Wilt and Van Buren streets, and here he built up a substantial business, his active connection with the same having continued until about fifteen years prior to his death, and the business being still conducted at that location by one of his sons. A severe attack of smallpox prevented his enlistment for service in the Civil war, though it was his loyal ambition to go forth in defense of the Union. The original home of Michael Gruber after he had established his residence in Fort Wayne was one block west of the Bluffton plank road, now known as Broadway, in the city of Fort Wayne. After he established his grocery business he removed to the house which he had built some time before engaging in the grocery business next to his store, and this old homestead, at 722 Wilt street, is now owned and occupied by his son, Edward J., who also owns and conducts the grocery business established by the father. It was in this house that Frank Gruber, the immediate subject of this review, was born. Michael Gruber was one of the well known citizens of Fort Wayne and the community was deeply shocked when he met a tragic death, at the age of seventy-two years. He was struck by an engine while walking on the tracks of the Pennsylvania Railroad near Fort Wayne, and died shortly afterward as the result of his injuries, his loved and devoted wife having survived him by only eight months and having been sixty-nine years of age when she too was summoned to the life eternal, both having been lifelong and zealous communicants of the Catholic church. Of their nine children the first two died in infancy; Elizabeth, who by her devoted consecration is known as Sister M. Veronica, is a member of the Catholic sisterhood of the Poor Handmaids of Christ, and is a teacher in one of the Catholic parochial schools of the city of Chicago; Frank J., of this sketch, was the next in order of birth; Jacob J. is employed as a skilled patternmaker at the Fort Wayne Electric Works; Veronica is the wife of John Winbaugh, of Fort Wayne; Edward J. resides at the old family homestead and conducts the grocery business established by his father, as has been previously stated in this context; Michael J. died one week prior to the demise of his mother and was twenty-seven years of age at the time; Carrie is the wife of George Welch, of Fort Wayne. Frank J. Gruber gained his early educational discipline in the excellent parochial school of St. Paul's Catholic church, on Washington street, and he began his practical experience as a worker when but thirteen years old. At this juncture in his career he found employment in the Shurrick stave factory, but shortly afterward entered service in the Olds spoke manufactory, on Lafayette street, where he was employed one year. For the purpose of learning thoroughly the boilermaker's trade he then entered upon an apprenticeship in the establishment of the firm of Kerr-Murray, where he gained practical experience. About one year later he entered the boiler shop of the Bass Foundry & Machine Works, where he completed his apprenticeship and where he continued to be employed about eighteen years, though for a short interval he had been employed in the Matthews Boiler Works, in the city of South Bend. Later he was employed at his trade for a time at Terre Haute, in the shops of the Vandalia Railroad Company. In 1895 Mr. Gruber and Gustave Bengs established in Fort Wayne the National Boiler & Sheet Iron Works, and his original plant, one of modest order, having occupied the land on which now stands the city gas tank. After the lapse of one year he purchased his partner's interest in the business and changed the title

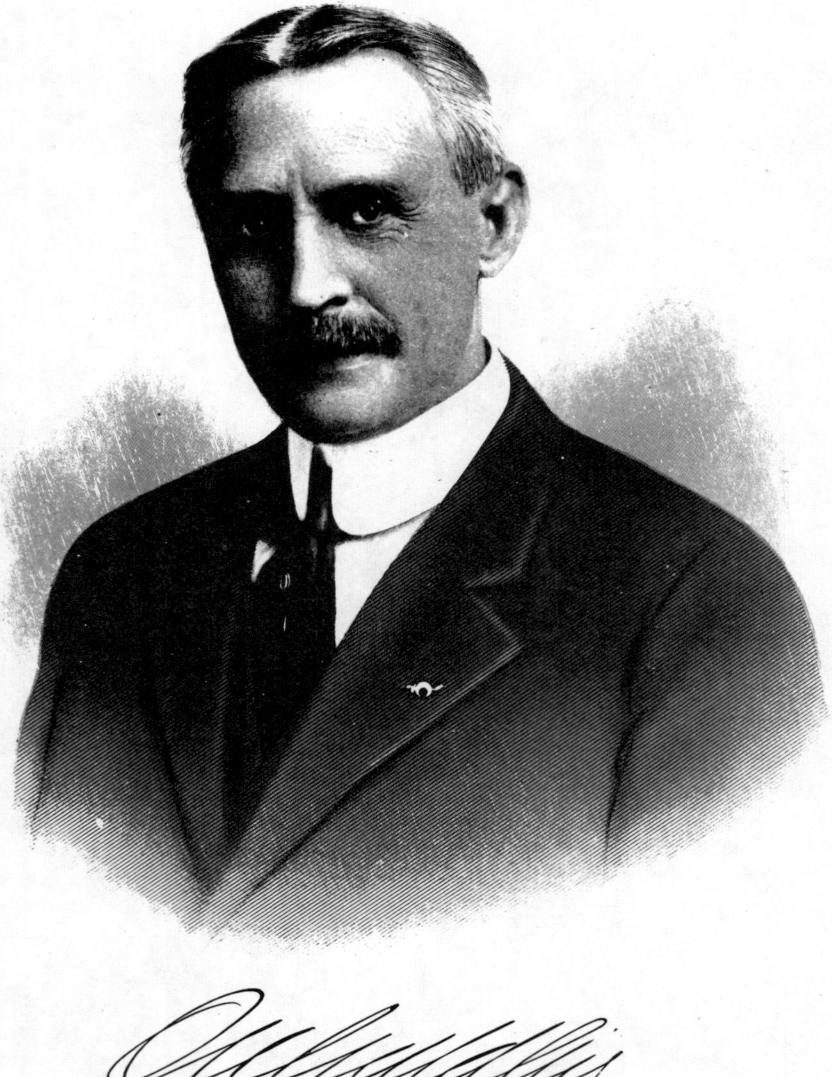

of the concern to Gruber Boiler Works. Under this name the enterprise was continued nine years, and it had in the meanwhile grown to be one of substantial order. At the expiration of that period Mr. Gruber admitted Gustave Bengs to partnership, whereupon the title was changed to the Gruber & Bengs Iron Works. About one year later Mr. Bengs organized an engineering company, with which he is still identified. The thriving business of Mr. Gruber has since been conducted by him in an independent way and under the title of the Frank Gruber Boiler Works, the establishment being situated on North Barr street at the corner of Duck street, and the main shop being sixty-two by one hundred and fifty feet in dimensions. The plant has the most modern equipment and facilities for the turning out of boilers, tanks and sheet-iron work of every description, and its provisions include the best devices for welding and cutting by the oxygen-acetylene gas method. Mr. Gruber has proved a most energetic and resourceful business man and is one of the world's great army of productive workers. His political allegiance is given to the Democratic party, and he and his wife are zealous communicants of the parish of St. Patrick's Catholic church. On September 18, 1886, was solemnized the marriage of Mr. Gruber to Miss Louisa Zimmerman, who likewise was born and reared in Fort Wayne, and they have five children—Stella, Irma, Helen, Lenore, and Frank J., Jr. Stella is now the wife of Albert Derheimer, of Fort Wayne, and all of the other children are still members of the gracious home circle.

Olaf N. Guldlin, M. E.—The success which the true American holds in highest estimation is that which has been achieved through individual ability and well directed effort, and he whose name introduces this review has measured fully up to the high standard thus set in the land of his adoption, the while he is a scion of the fine Scandinavian stock from which America has had much to gain and nothing to lose. Through his exceptional technical ability and his executive and administrative talent he has become one of the leading captains of industry in the city of Fort Wayne, and his reputation in his chosen sphere of endeavor far transcends local confines, to mark him an influential figure in the field of industrial enterprise in which he has earnestly and worthily directed his activities. In 1885 Mr. Guldlin established his residence in Fort Wayne, and in 1888 he became the founder of the now extensive and important industrial enterprise conducted under the title of the Western Gas Construction Company, of which noteworthy corporation he has been president from its inception. A man of sterling character, his ambition has caused him to direct his course along a normal and important line of enterprise for which his technical ability specially qualifies him, and he has been significantly the architect of his own fortunes—the builder of the ladder on which he has risen to the plane of large achievement and well merited success. Mr. Guldlin was born in the fine old city of Christiana, Norway, on December 6, 1858, and there he was reared to adult age, the while he was given excellent opportunities for the proper development of his alert mental faculties and natural mechanical talent. He applied himself with characteristic diligence as a student in the Technical College in the city of Bergen, in his native land, and later in the celebrated Polytechnikum in the city of Munchen, Bavaria, Germany, after about a year's practical experience in the iron works of A. L. Thune at Christiana. He then, at the age of twenty-one years, severed the ties that bound him to home and fatherland and set forth, with high aspirations and indomitable courage, to make for himself a place in the United States, which he wisely looked upon as a country of broader opportunities. Soon after his arrival in America Mr. Guldlin found employment in the engineering department of the celebrated Baldwin Locomotive Works, in the city of Philadelphia, and with this concern he remained two and a half years. His ambitious purpose and recognized ability conserved his advancement at that time, even as they have in the successive stages of his vigorous and productive career, and upon leaving Philadelphia he accepted the position of engineer for James R. Smedberg, of Lancaster, Pennsylvania, then a celebrated gas engineer. In 1885 he assumed the post of engineer for the Kerr-Murray Manufacturing Company, at Fort Wayne, Indiana, and, as previously noted, he here initiated, in 1888, an independent business. It was in this year that he and his associates, W. A. Croxton and Frank D. Moses, here opened an office as mechanical and consulting engineers. It was through this medium that he was finally enabled to establish the modest enterprise that has been developed into the present extensive industry controlled by the Western Gas Construction Company. Within the first year after he had opened his office in Fort Wayne Mr. Guldlin entered into a contract for the erection of a large fuel-gas plant in the city of Akron, Ohio, members of the Lloyd family of Detroit, Michigan, having been interested principals in the enterprise. When, in 1890, Mr. Guldlin determined to expand his field of operations by effecting an incorporation of the business which he had established in Fort Wayne, he was fortunate in obtaining the ready co-operation of Messrs. Gordon W. and Ernest F. Lloyd, who were associated with him in the incorporation of the Western Gas Construction Company, of which he became president, Gordon W. Lloyd treasurer, and Ernest F. Lloyd secretary. In January, 1902, he purchased the interests of the Lloyds, and the company then became distinctively local in the personnel of its stockholders and with the following corps of officers, which is still maintained: Olaf N. Guldlin, president; Samuel M. Foster, vice-president; Charles McCulloch, secretary; and J. Ross McCulloch, treasurer. The following brief record concerning this representative industrial concern is well worthy of perpetuation in this connection: "The history of this business has been one of continuous growth, and operations were initiated in a small machine shop, sixty-five by one hundred feet in dimensions, that was erected in 1893. In the same year was erected also a small building for the accommodation of the general offices and the draughting department. In 1895 the machine shop was enlarged to a length of two hundred and fifty feet, and five years later it was found necessary to add a foundry and wrought-iron shop, in order properly to care for the increasing business. Two years later equally exigent demands resulted in the reconstruction and enlargement of all departments of the plant, and from time to time additions have continued to be made until the finely equipped institution now covers about thirteen acres of ground. The object of the business, or rather its chief function, is the construction of gas works machinery and apparatus, for city as well as coke oven works, and the business of the company now extends into the most diverse sections of the Union, with facilities that make it possible for the concern to handle contracts of practically the maximum magnitude. The shops in Fort Wayne now give employment to more than four hundred persons, most of whom are skilled and highly paid artisans, while the field force, engaged in the erection of gas plants on contract, is of about equal numerical strength. Of all institutions devoted exclusively to the manufacturing of gas apparatus, the plant of the Western Gas Construction Company is now the largest in the world, and in addition to its extensive domestic business the company now sends its products into the European countries, South America, Australia and the Philippine Islands. Mr. Guldlin's fame as an expert in his particular line of business is now international. In 1900 he was a delegate from the Western Gas Association to the international gas congress held in the city of Paris, France. The exhibition made by his company at the Louisiana Purchase Exposition, at St. Louis, in 1904, won for the company three grand prizes, five gold medals and four silver medals, after a proper demonstration of the methods of operation in appling the various devices to practical use in gas plants. In addition were received two gold and one bronze medals for exhibits of auxiliary apparatus used by the company in its construction work. To Mr. Guldlin personally was awarded a grand prize, with diploma, in recognition of his inventions and developments in the gas industry. The exhibit was visited by gas engineers from all parts of the world. He was also appointed a member of the international jury of awards, and at the conclusion of the exposition he received from its president, Hon. David R. Francis, a personal letter attested by Walter B. Stevens, secrtary of th xposition, advising him that by direction of the Louisiana Purchase Exposition Company a commemorative diploma and medal had been conferred upon him in appreciation of his services. Mr. Guldlin was likewise instrumental in having his company represented by an effective exhibit at the Panama-Pacific Exposition, San Francisco, in 1915, and on this exhibit was awarded the medal of honor, two gold medals and two silver medals, besides which Mr. Guldlin was personally awarded a gold medal. In politics this vigorous and loyal citizen has been unswerving and well fortified in his allegiance to the Republican party, though he is essentially a business man and has no ambition for political preferment. In the time-honored Masonic fraternity he has received the royal-arch degrees, and in the Ancient Accepted Scottish Rite has attained the thirty-second degree, besides being affiliated with the Ancient Arabic Order, Nobles of the Mystic Shrine, and being a life member of the Benevolent & Protective Order of Elks. Among the more notable scientific and social organizations with which he is further identified may be mentioned the following named: The American Society of Mechanical Engineers; the American Gas Institute; The Pacific Coast Gas Association and the specific organizations of the same order in the states of Indiana, Illinois, Michigan and Wisconsin; the American Academy of Political and Social Science; the American Political Science Association; American Economic Association; the Rejuvenated Sons of Jove, in which his membership number is 61; the Lotus Club of New York city; the Missouri Athletic Club of St. Louis; and the Cosmos Club of San Francisco. On August 28, 1889, was solemnized the marriage of Mr. Guldlin to Miss Addie L. Bleekman, who was born at Stratford, Fulton county, New York, in November, 1863, who is a representative of one of the old families of the Empire state, and who was a child at the time of her parents' removal to Indiana, the family home being established in Fort Wayne. She is a daughter of Jerome and Henrietta (Sixbey) Bleekman, the former of whom is now deceased, and the mother resides in Fort Wayne. Mrs. Guldlin continued her studies in the Fort Wayne public schools until she was graduated from the high school, and in 1888 she was graduated Ph. B. in Buchtel College, at Akron, Ohio, an institution now known as Municipal University of Akron. She is a woman of most gracious personality, of distinctive culture and of high civic ideals. While in college she became affiliated with the Eta Chapter of the Delta Gamma sorority, and from a brief sketch of her life which appeared in a publication devoted to that organization are taken the following extracts: "Mrs. Guldlin is very active in club work, particularly in modernizing, simplifying and dignifying home work and home industries. Mrs. Guldlin has been on many boards and committees and has held in connection with club work many offices, both state and national. As chairman of the home-economics department of the General Federation of Women's Clubs, she was instrumental in making this department a vital and established division of the activities of the federation. In this work she traveled extensively, during which time she lectured in many states, especially on the relation of home economics to the public schools and to all other institutions of a community." From still another source is drawn the following estimate of this noble and gracious gentlewoman: "After her marriage Mrs. Guldlin applied the same energy and study to mastering the intricacies of housekeeping and home-building, and the practical knowledge which she thus gained has led her to take an active interest in the domestic-science department of the women's clubs of Fort Wayne. It was her active interest in the home economics subject, which foresaw the great need of a scientific knowledge of home-making for the masses, which prepared her for her work. With this realization she studied the history of the movement in the United States, what it had done, what it hoped to achieve, and she became acquainted with the recognized leaders of home economics. With their active co-operation she was able to carry forward the work of her department and make it a vital thing in the home club and community life. She became an authority on this subject and was made chairman of the home-economic department of the Women's League of Fort Wayne. Later she was made chairman of the same department of the Indiana Union of Literary Clubs, and afterward chairman of the home-economic department of the Indiana State Federation of Women's Clubs. In 1906 came to her further and merited distinction, in being chosen the executive head of the same department for the General Federation of Women's Clubs. Both Mr. and Mrs. Guldlin have been specially active in their efforts to further civic improvements, and it was largely through their unselfish and well directed efforts that, in 1911, the children's playground on Van Buren street, Fort Wayne, was constructed and equipped. The idea originated with Mrs. Guldlin, and through her club associations she disseminated her views on the subject until the public became convinced of the merit of the proposition and funds were donated for the desired object. For weeks Mr. Guldlin personally supervised and directed the work of grading and equipping the land that had been obtained for the purpose, along the St. Mary's river, and in addition to this he and his wife contributed liberally to the fund needed for the achievement of the desired ends. The members of the committee of the playgrounds association, in token of the efforts put forth by both Mr. and Mrs. Guldlin in the furtherance of this admirable work, insisted on giving to the new resort for the children the title of the Mr. and Mrs. Guldlin Playgrounds."

It is believed that by quotations from various sources may best be conveyed an idea of the personality and splendid services of Mrs. Guldin, and thus in conclusion of this article the publisher finds pleasure and consistency in making excerpts, with minor elimination and paraphrase, from an appreciative article that was written by W. M. Herschell and that appeared in the Indianapolis News of October 14, 1911: "When the Indiana State Federation of Women's Clubs meets in annual convention at Indianapolis, October 24-6, there will be among those present an energetic little woman who proudly points to the fact that she is a citizen of Fort Wayne; and, in turn, Fort Wayne can proudly point to Mrs. Olaf N. Guldlin, for she has placed that city on the map of womanly achievement. Mrs. Guldlin is the chairman of the home-economics committee of the General Federation of Women's Clubs, and has spread the gospel of good housekeeping in every section of the United States. The rise of Mrs. Guldlin into prominence as an American club woman is the result of her belief in her own household philosophy. She first attracted national attention among women when she read a paper on household economics before the general federation when it met in Boston, five years ago. This live-wire Fort Wayne woman read her paper and instantly found herself in the club limelight. She was praised for her views on household economics and, following the introduction of a resolution to abolish the household-economics department because of lack of interest in it, made a stand for its retention that reflected credit on her. She declared the women's clubs of the United States could not afford to abolish any department of interest in the upbuilding of home life. So emphatic was she in her stand for the principle of home economics that she was elected chairman of the department, and, to-day, there is no branch of womanly effort that is receiving more attention. This energetic Fort Wayne woman who tackled the job of making the work effective has made the work effective! When the general federation met in Cincinnati, in May, 1910, no woman was as pleasantly discussed as Mrs. Guldlin. Her name was heard in committee meetings, in the lobbies and in every place where clubwomen gathered to talk. When the hour set aside in the convention for the discussion of household economics arrived, Mrs. Decker, a leading clubwoman of Denver, took the platform and the writer heard her pay a tribute to Mrs. Guldlin that must have made the heart of every Hoosier woman throb with pride. This talk fairly brought the convention to its feet in approving Mrs. Guldlin's work. Mrs. Guldlin is a little woman, but she is a dynamo of energy. Her rise as an American clubwoman has not been self-sought. She has gone on doing her work and her friends have done the boosting. As an advocate of right living she has worked so earnestly that to-day her mail is almost as heavy as that of any business firm in Fort Wayne. From every quarter—town and country—she gets letters asking for information concerning home economics. She collects ideas from clubs all over the country and then passes them on. She keeps no good ideas to herself in order to trade on them when the next general federation meets. Day in and day out she and her fellow-laborers in the cause are seeking to have domestic science taught in every American public school and to amplify the work in every other consistent and practical avenue. Mr. and Mrs. Guldlin spread the spirit of their home happiness over Fort Wayne. For instance, there is a large playground that bears their name, a testimonial to their worthiness as citizens. Mr. and Mrs.

Guldlin are childless, but they have several children in their keeping for rearing and education. They love children, and every boy and girl in Fort Wayne knows it. Their beautiful home extends its gracious hospitality and good cheer to old and young alike, and the most intimate friends of the popular chatelaine of this home know her heart is bent on bettering conditions in American homes and making life brighter for all humankind." It may further be added that Mrs. Guldlin is state director and district chairman of the Woman's Franchise League, was a member of the centennial committee of the Indiana State Federation of Women's Clubs at the time of the centennial anniversary of the admission of Indiana to statehood, is president of the Fortnightly Club, a member of the executive committee of the Women's League, and in her home city is an active and valued member of the College Club, the City Franchise League, the Art Association, the Associated Charity and Rescue Mission, and of the advisory committee of the vocational school board.

George C. Gump.—One of the fine farms of Perry township is that owned and occupied by George Calvert Gump, and his prominent status as one of the substantial and progressive exponents of agricultural and live-stock industry in his native county is the more interesting by reason of the fact that his present homestead is the one on which he was born and reared, the date of his nativity having been July 31, 1868. His parents were young when they came to Allen county, where their marriage was solemnized, and it was about the year 1856 when they established their residence on the well improved farm now owned by the subject of this review. At that time the land was little more than a forest and the father set to himself the herculean task of reclaiming the farm from a virtual wilderness. Indomitable energy and determination brought steady progress in their train and eventually the farm yielded forth its generous increase from season to season, and peace and prosperity found here an abiding place. The parents, George and Harriet (Agenbroad) Gump, were honored pioneer citizens of Allen county, Indiana, at the time of their death. George Gump was a man of strong individuality and mature judgment, was influential in community affairs and commanded the unqualified esteem of all who knew him. He served two terms as trustee of Perry township and was always ready to lend his co-operation in the furtherance of measures and enterprises projected for the general good of the community. Of the fine family of thirteen children, two died in infancy; Frank, eldest of the number, is engaged in farming in Nebraska; Mrs. Priscilla Jackson is a resident of Churubusco; Mrs. Margaret Pulver is deceased; Mrs. Alice Flannigan resides in Perry township; Mrs. Jane Hursh maintains her home in Perry township; Madison and Marion reside respectively in Auburn, Indiana, and in Perry township; George C., of this sketch, was the next in order of birth; Mrs. Effie Belot is deceased; Mrs. Cora Shambaugh is a resident of Fort Wayne; and Celestia is deceased. George C. Gump was reared to manhood on the old home farm, early began to contribute his quota to its work, and his youthful educational advantages were those of the common schools of the locality and period. The old homestead has continued as the stage of his vigorous and effective activities of independent order, and the property, comprising one hundred and eighty-four acres, in Section 15, Perry township, came into his possession after the death of his father, he having purchased the interests of the other heirs. He has made numerous and valuable improvements on the place, including the erection of his commodious and modern residence, which is of cement construction, and which is one of the model farm homes of Perry township. Mr. Gump is progressive and liberal in his civic attitude, is a Democrat in politics, but has never desired or held public office of any description. September 3, 1896, recorded the marriage of Mr. Gump to Miss Ivy B. Moudy, who was born and reared in Cedar Creek township, this county, a daughter of the late Martin and Martha (Updyke) Moudy, who passed their entire lives in this county, where the respective families were founded in the early pioneer period. Mrs. Gump is one of a family of seven children, and the only other surviving members of the same are Mrs. Sylvia Van Zile and Mrs. Nora Treese. Mr. and Mrs. Gump have seven children, all of whom remain at the parental home, namely: Russell J., Forrest R., Clara B., Martha E., George E., Walter C., and Eva F.

Charles H. Gumpper is a native son of Fort Wayne, a scion of one of the sterling old families of Allen county, and through his energy, ability and well-directed endeavors has gained a position of prominence as one of the representative business men of the city that has been his home from the time of his birth and to which his loyalty is of the most intense order. He is president of the Grace Construction Company, which has developed a substantial and important business in the installing of asphalt and other types of street paving and which has successfully completed many large contracts, both in Fort Wayne and elsewhere. The company has done the street paving in virtually all of the new additions to the city of Fort Wayne, including the Harrison Hill, the Driving Park and the Weisser Park additions, besides the asphalt paving on State street and other thoroughfares of the city. The company gives employment to an average force of two hundred and fifty persons and is essentially one of the strong and important industrial concerns of the Summit City. The company was incorporated in 1910, with a capital stock of fifty thousand dollars, and its official corps from the beginning has been as here noted: Charles H. Gumpper, president; Mrs. Martin J. Grace, vice-president; and Martin J. Grace, secretary, treasurer and general manager. Charles H. Gumpper was born in Fort Wayne on December 6, 1867, and is a son of Christian C. and Sarah C. (Arnold) Gumpper, the former a native of Pennsylvania and the latter of Ohio. Christian C. Gumpper established his residence in Fort Wayne about the year 1865, and for about a decade thereafter continued in the employ of the Pennsylvania Railroad Company. He then engaged in the confectionery business, with which he continued his connection about thirty-five years, within which period he built up a large and prosperous enterprise that marked him as one of the representative business men of the city. He passed the closing years of his long and useful life in well-earned retirement, his death having occurred in 1896, and his venerable widow still maintaining her residence in Fort Wayne. Mr. Gumpper was a stalwart supporter of the cause of the Republi party and was a zealous member of the Grace Reformed church, in which he was an elder at the time of his death and of which his widow continued an earnest communicant. Of the three children, Ada is the wife of Harry A. Keplinger, of Fort Wayne; Charles H., of this review, was the next in order of birth; and Frederick C. is now a resident of Detroit, Michigan. After having duly profited by the advantages of the public schools Charles H. Gumpper completed an effective course in the Fort Wayne

Business College, and for one year thereafter was in the employ of the Keystone Grocery Company. For the ensuing seven years he held a clerical and executive position in the offices of the Nickel Plate Railroad, and for a quarter of a century thereafter was associated with Conrad Neireiter in the insurance business in Fort Wayne. In 1910 he became one of the organizers and incorporators of the Grace Construction Company, of which he has since been the president and to the affairs of which he gives the major part of his time and attention. In politics Mr. Gumpper holds himself aside from strict partisan lines and as an independent gives his support to the men and measures meeting his approval as a liberal and progressive citizen. He is affiliated with the Masonic fraternity, including the Mystic Shrine, and he and his wife are active members of Grace Reformed church. On December 9, 1891, was solemnized the marriage of Mr. Gumpper to Miss Emma Neireiter, daughter of Conrad and Harriet (Lepper) Neireiter, of Fort Wayne, and the four children of this union are Ruth J., Howard, Ada and Dorothy.

Jacob D. Gumpper has made a splendid record in connection with business affairs of broad scope and his activities have touched many and varied lines of enterprise during the course of his long and productive business career. He has maintained his residence in Fort Wayne for nearly forty years, was for nearly a score of years one of the most successful traveling salesmen for the Bowser Pump & Tank Company, which is one of the most important industrial and commercial concerns of Fort Wayne, and he is now retained as instructor of salesmen for this representative corporation. He is one of the well-known and highly esteemed citizens who specially merits recognition in this history. Mr. Gumpper was born at Chicora, Butler county, Pennsylvania, on April 26, 1848, and is a son of Christian C. and Dorothea (Aldinger) Gumpper, both of whom continued their residence in the old Keystone state until their death and both of whom were earnest communicants of the German Lutheran church. Christian C. Gumpper was born and reared in Germany and came to the United States about the year 1816. He was for many years one of the sterling citizens and prominent business men of Chicora, Pennsylvania, where his death occurred, and for years he was there engaged in the hotel business. Of the children, Christian C., Jr., Gottlieb and Henry C. are deceased; Frederica is the widow of Theodore Craig and resides at East Butler, Pennsylvania; and the subject of this sketch is the youngest of the children. Jacob D. Gumpper gained his youthful education in the schools of his native town and as a lad of thirteen years initiated his association with the practical affairs of business by taking a position in a general store at East Brady's Bend, Pennsylvania, where he remained thus engaged four years. For six years thereafter he was a traveling salesman for a Pittsburgh wholesale grocery house, which he thus represented through northeastern Pennsylvania. After retiring from this position he was for five years independently engaged in the general merchandise business at Carbon Center, Pennsylvania, and for five or six years thereafter was identified with the oil-producing industry in the Pennsylvania fields. He was connected with the Bradford District Oil Exchange in the old Keystone state during the period immediately prior to his removal to Fort Wayne, Indiana, where he established his residence in 1879 and where he was successfully established in the retail grocery business until 1897. It is specially worthy of record in this connection that he purchased for use in his store the first oil tank that was manufactured by S. F. Bowser, founder of the great manufacturing business that has since been developed from a modest nucleus. This purchase was made by Mr. Gumpper on September 5, 1885, and indicated his early appreciation of the value of the invention upon which has been built up the extensive business of the Bowser Company of the present day. In September, 1897, Mr. Gumpper sold his grocery business and became a traveling representative for the Bowser Company, the oil tanks and pumps of which he introduced into many different states of the Union. In this connection he made a splendid record as a salesman, and in his travels he visited nearly all states of the Union. His services as a traveling representative continued until September, 1914, and it may well be understood that his broad and varied experience makes him a valuable factor in his present executive position with the Bowser Company, that of instructor of salesmen. Mr. Gumpper is aligned as a loyal supporter of the cause of the Republican party, is affiliated with Home Lodge, Ancient Free and Accepted Masons, and with the Knights of Pythias, and both he and his wife hold membership in the Third Presbyterian church of Fort Wayne. June 26, 1888, recorded the marriage of Mr. Gumpper to Miss Laura M. Dickinson, daughter of Philomen C. and Emma (Thompson) Dickinson, of Fort Wayne, and the one child of this union is Harold D., who is in the employ of the Buda Electric Company in the city of Chicago.

James Hager Haberly.—Among the many rising young men of affairs in Fort Wayne today James Hager Haberly stands well in the foreground. He identified himself early with the Fort Wayne Electric Works and there received a general training that fitted him for his present position as general manager of the Fort Wayne Engineering and Manufacturing Company, with which he has been identified since 1908. Mr. Haberly is the son of George W. and Frances M. (Stimpson) Haberly, and he was born in Terre Haute, Indiana, on December 16, 1879. George W. Haberly was a native Ohioan and the mother was of New York state birth and ancestry. They were the parents of five children—Frances M., Louise Elizabeth, George W., Samuel S. and James H. Haberly of this review. When he was a small lad the father died and, in 1898, the mother married Col. Robert S. Robertson, who died in 1906. Mrs. Robertson is now a resident of Fort Wayne. James Hager Haberly had his early schooling in the schools of Terre Haute, at about the age of fourteen entering Howe Military Academy at Howe, Indiana, from which institution he was graduated with the class of 1898. He was then nineteen years old, and instead of carrying his education through a university course he chose to identify himself at once with life's work as a student in the Fort Wayne Electric Works. He continued with that concern for ten years, filling various positions in the factory and as a member of the sales force. It was his aim to neglect no phase of the business, and the ten years he spent with that concern were filled to the full with the task of gathering experience. This diligence and ambition brought a timely reward, for when the Fort Wayne Engineering and Manufacturing Company was incorporated he was elected treasurer and general manager of the company. This was in 1908. The products of the Fort Wayne Engineering and Manufacturing Company consist of water systems, farm lighting plants and garage air systems. The business began in a small way, it may be said, and now has a plant covering about three acres of ground, with eight large and modern factory buildings. It supplies electric lighting systems for farmers, also current for the operation of their small power motors, and it is safe to say that this firm has contributed largely to the comfort and well being of the farming element of Allen county. Mr. Haberly was married October 23, 1906, to Miss Alma Elizabeth Paul, the daughter of Henry C. Paul, of whom extended mention will be found elsewhere in these pages. Mr. and Mrs. Haberly have one son, Henry Paul. The family have membership in Trinity Episcopal church and Mr. Haberly has served the church as vestryman. He is a member of the Sons of the American Revolution and is now president of Anthony Wayne chapter of the local body. He is a member of the Country Club, the Quest Club, and is president of the Fort Wayne & Decatur Traction Company. He is a Republican in politics.

Edward A. K. Hackett.—A man of noble character and splendid ability, the late Edward Alexander Kelly Hackett lifted himself to the plane of high and worthy achievement and became one of the prominent and influential figures in Indiana journalism and in the directing of popular sentiment and action. By his forceful individuality and fine intellectuality he became a leader in the newspaper business in the Hoosier state, and from 1880 until his death, which occurred **August 28, 1916,** he was owner and publisher of the Fort Wayne Sentinel, which under his able supervision was maintained at a high standard and became one of the most influential daily papers of the state. For a number of years he was also the owner of the Indianapolis Sentinel, which reached its greatest success and influence under his control, and above all this he was dominated by the exalted integrity of purpose and the high ideals that make for enlightened and useful citizenship. He was one of Fort Wayne's most distinguished and honored citizens, and this history would stultify its consistency were there failure to pay within its pages a tribute to his memory and to offer at least a brief review of his career. His final illness was of very brief duration and renal calculus was the immediate cause of his death. Mr. Hackett was born at Bloomfield, Pennsylvania, June 29, 1851, and was a scion of one of the old and honored families of the historic Keystone state. He made the best possible use of the advantages afforded in the public schools of his native state and in his youth was enabled to supplement this discipline by a course of higher study in Bloomfield Academy, in his home county of Perry. It has consistently been said that the discipline of a newspaper office is tantamount to a liberal education, and this further reinforcement came to Mr. Hackett, for as a young man he learned the printer's trade in the office of the Perry County Democrat, a weekly paper published at New Bloomfield. After thus gaining working facility in the "art preservative of all arts" he was employed at his trade in leading newspaper offices in Philadelphia, Pittsburgh and other eastern cities, and at the age of twenty-three years came to Indiana and established his residence at Bluffton, judicial center of Wells county. There he purchased a half interest in the Bluffton Banner, and within a short time came into sole control as editor and publisher of this paper. Energy and progressiveness characterized his entire career, and thus it may readily be understood that he made of this enterprise a definite success, thus opening the way to broader and more influential activity in connection with the newspaper business in northern Indiana. In 1880 Mr. Hackett came to Fort Wayne and purchased from William Fleming the plant

E. A. K. Hackett

and business of the Fort Wayne Sentinel, his successful genius finding in this connection adequate scope for productive action, as shown in the fact that he developed the Sentinel into one of the most prosperous and influential daily papers in this section of the state and made the same potent in the fostering and advancing of community interests along both civic and material lines. He continued as owner of the plant and business of the Sentinel until the time of his death and the property is one of the most valuable of its kind in northern Indiana at the present time. As a writer Mr. Hackett was forceful, sure and circumspect, so that his editorial utterances carried weight not only in local affairs but also in exemplifying the best political thought and polity, his allegiance having been given to the Democratic party. From an editorial published at the time of his demise are taken the following extracts, which give supplemental information concerning his specially successful and broad-gauged business career: "Mr. Hackett started the American Farmer, which for several years was published in the Sentinel office and later sold to a big publishing company. He was also at one time interested in the Indianapolis Sentinel, disposing of his interests several years before it suspended publication. Several years ago he established the Hackett Medical College at Canton, China, placing his eldest daughter, Dr. Martha Hackett, in charge. Mr. Hackett owned the Indianapolis Sentinel at the same time he owned the Fort Wayne Sentinel. The former paper was sold to Belford, Clark & Company, and then Mr. Hackett returned to Fort Wayne and devoted his entire attention to the local publication." The deep Christian faith of Mr. Hackett guided and governed his course in all of the relations of life and was essentially a faith not only of sentiment but also of service. He was earnest in the support of all moral agencies, including the cause of temperance, and was actively identified with the Winona Assembly and Summer Schools Association, at Winona Lake, Indiana. He was one of the most earnest and honored members of the First Presbyterian church of Fort Wayne, was an elder in the same at the time of his death and had also given characteristically effective service as superintendent of its Sunday school. Concerning him the following appreciative and merited statement has been made: "He took an active part in every movement which tended to the betterment of Fort Wayne, and his death comes as a loss to the entire city." As a young man Mr. Hackett wedded Miss Mary A. Melsheimer, whose father was a representative physician and surgeon engaged in practice at Bluffton, Wells county, and she passed to eternal rest in April, 1898. Of the children of this union the first born, Susan, died in infancy; the second child, Martha, is a talented physician and has charge of the hospital that was founded by her father in the city of Canton, China, as previously noted; Helen, the youngest of the children, is the wife of John C. Johnson, of Los Angeles, California, and they have two children—May Alice and John Edward. On October 16, 1900, was solemnized the marriage of Mr. Hackett to Miss Susie Emma Reid, who was born at Greenville, Bond county, Illinois, where she was reared and educated and where she completed a course in Almira College of that city. A woman of culture and gracious personality, she continues to occupy a secure place in connection with the representative social and religious activities of Fort Wayne, where she is a devoted member of the First Presbyterian church. With her in the beautiful home remain her three children—Catherine Reid, Edward A. K., Jr., and Wayne. Mrs. Hackett is a daughter of Colonel John B and Emma T. (Holden) Reid, long numbered among the most honored residents of Greenville, Illinois, her father having gained his military title through gallant service as a soldier and officer on the Union side during the Civil War.

Alva O. Hadley.—A model farm is, in the opinion of those who have seen the Hadley farm in Section 30, Marion township, one that conforms to the standards of that place. Mr. Hadley has one of the finest and best-kept stock farms in Allen county, and he is known widely among the breeders of blooded Belgian horses, Holstein cattle and Duroc-Jersey hogs as one of the most progressive and successful men in the business. The buildings on the farm are the last word in point of convenience and sanitation, and reflect the progressiveness and capability of the owner of the place. Alva O. Hadley was born June 30, 1862, in Clermont county, Ohio, and is the son of Parley P. and Martha H. (Snell) Hadley. The father was of English parentage and the mother came of Pennsylvania Dutch blood. In 1869, Parley Hadley went to Crawford county, Kansas, and settled on a tract of land of one hundred and sixty acres. He applied himself to farming operations, adding another quarter-section in time, and conducted a very successful cattle business for a good many years. He was a carpenter by trade, but spent more time in agricultural pursuits than in devotion to his trade, and was considered a very successful man, well-to-do for his day. He was a veteran of the Civil War and his service covered the entire period of hostilities. He enlisted when the first call for troops came and was discharged after the surrender, in the spring of 1865. He was with Sherman on the March to the Sea and participated in many of the bloodiest battles of the war. He arose during his service from the rank of private to that of Captain. Mrs. Hadley died in March, 1882, and in 1890 Mr. Hadley returned to Ohio, where he spent the remaining years of his life in quiet retirement. He died in September, 1908. After the death of the subject's mother, Mr. Hadley married again, Martha Engle becoming his wife, and two children were born to them. Mabel married Joseph Carr and Harrison died in April, 1909. The children of the first marriage were six in number and mention of them is made briefly as follows: Elizah Ann is the wife of George Cunningham, of Kansas. Alva O., the subject of this review, was the second child. Amanda Bell died when she was eighteen years of age. George died in childhood. Ida passed away in 1909. John is living in Fort Wayne, and is connected prominently with the Fort Wayne Dairy Company. Alva Hadley was a small boy when the family moved to Kansas and he had his early education in the schools of the Sunflower State. He lived on his father's farm to the age of twenty-one, when he branched out for himself on a rented farm. In 1894 he bought his first land. It was a small farm of seventy-two acres, which he sold some time later and bought his present farm of eighty acres in Section 30, Marion township, Allen county. All his life he has given his attention to the production of blooded stock, and his Belgian mares and stallions are among the finest to be found in the state. Mr. Hadley is Republican in politics and a member of the Methodist Episcopal church. His fraternal affiliations are with the Masons and he and his wife are affiliated with the Eastern Star. He is also a member of the Modern Woodmen of America. He was married on July 1, 1883, to Miss Euphemia Davidson, daughter of Anderson Davidson, of Scotland, and Anna B. (Miller) Davidson. The father was of Scotch parentage. He died young in years and his widow moved from Ohio to Wells county, Indiana, bringing her five children with her. They were: Rosa, wife of J. W. Snider, living in Fort Wayne at this writing; Elizabeth, the wife of L. Springer, of Fort Wayne; Simon, who died in Fort Wayne February 12, 1916; Ella, who died in Kansas; and Euphemia, the wife of Mr. Hadley. Mr. and Mrs. Hadley are the parents of four children—Guy, Gladys, May, Ray and Adoniram W. Guy is located in Marion township, and the two younger children are at home with the parents. Ray P. married Ermal, daughter of William Comer, of Pleasant township.

Arthur L. Hadley.—Among the men who have given long service with the Fort Wayne plant of the General Electric Company and who have contributed of their intelligent efforts toward the advancement of electrical knowledge and the practical application of their studies, is Arthur L. Hadley, chief engineer of the great institution in Fort Wayne. Mr. Hadley has been connected with the works in this city since 1889 and has contributed much to the development of the big plant and its output—which have made the name of Fort Wayne known in all quarters of the civilized world. Mr. Hadley was born in Templeton, Massachusetts, October 19, 1867, and is a son of Lucien N. and Jeanette (Bourn) Hadley, the former a native of Canaan, New Hampshire, and the latter of Templeton, Massachusetts. Lucien N. Hadley was a successful furniture manufacturer and lumber dealer. Arthur L. Hadley continued to attend the public schools of Templeton until his graduation in the high school, as a member of the class of 1885, and then, following a natural inclination, he entered upon a period of study in the Worcester Polytechnical Institute at Worcester, Massachusetts. There he took a course in mechanical engineering that opened a way for special attention to matters electrical—a field of study and experimentation that particularly appealed to him. He was graduated in the institute as a member of the class of 1889 and with the degree of Bachelor of Science. After leaving school there was afforded to him the opportunity of spending a few months in the electric-lighting plant at Gardner, Massachusetts, and there his privileges for the further study of electrical matters developed in him the determination to devote his future studies to this line. In Fort Wayne at that time was established the Fort Wayne Electric Light Company, the forerunner of the present immense plant of the General Electric Company. Men of the type of Mr. Hadley were required for the development of the business, and he came to Fort Wayne November 11, 1889, to take charge of the transformer-testing department. He gave his attention to development work, ever seeking new and improved ways of applying principles which the electrical field constantly provides for men of peculiar ability. These efforts were begun on electric storage batteries, under the general supervision of M. M. M. Slattery. Then, in the departments headed by C. S. Bradley and F. S. Hunting, he engaged in experimental work on three-phase motors, with marked success. He served for a period as the assistant to James J. Wood, in designing transformers and alternating-current and direct-current machines. In many lines of experimental and development work Mr. Hadley has added much to the success of the products of the General Electric plant in Fort Wayne. He now has charge of the apparatus-engineering department, which includes the designing of all alternating-current and direct-current generators and also all direct-current motors except those of the small-motor department of the works. Mr. Hadley is an active member of the American Institute of Electrical Engineers. He is a member of the Fort Wayne Electro-Technic Club, the Mutual Benefit Relief Association of the great electric works, the Fort Wayne Commercial Club and the University Club. He is a thirty-second degree Mason and a member of the Mystic Shrine. He is a loyal member of Plymouth Congregational church. In 1895 Mr. Hadley wedded Miss Nellie M. Richey, daughter of Amos Richey, of Fort Wayne, and the three children of this union are Gladys, Norman and Elizabeth, all of whom are members of the family circle at the parental home, on South Hoagland avenue.

Robert Hadley.—Though he died within about three years after establishing his residence in the city of Fort Wayne the late Robert Hadley made a definite impression on this community both through his sterling personality and distinctive business ability. He was the founder of the prosperous retail furniture business that is still conducted under the title of Hadley & Company and in which his interests are now held by his widow. Mr. Hadley was born in the fine old city of Lexington, Kentucky, on July 4, 1870, and was a scion of fine old southern ancestry. He acquired his youthful education in the schools of his native city and after completing the curriculum of the high school he there became actively identified with the retail furniture business. Later he was connected with similar enterprise in St. Louis, Missouri, and Indianapolis, Indiana, from which latter city he removed to Minneapolis, Minnesota. His next change of residence was made in his removal to Toledo, Ohio, and from that city he came to Fort Wayne in 1912, in which year he became the organizer of the firm of Hadley & Company and opened one of the really metropolitan furniture stores of this part of the Hoosier state. To the management of this business he continued to give his close attention until his untimely death, May 1, 1915, about two months prior to the forty-fifth anniversary of his birth. Mr. Hadley was an alert and progressive business man and his genial personality gained to him the staunch friendship of those with whom he came in contact in the various relations of life. His political allegiance was given to the Republican party and he was affiliated with the Benevolent and Protective Order of Elks and the Loyal Order of Moose. On February 6, 1902, was solemnized the marriage of Mr. Hadley to Miss Kate Opergfell, who was born and reared in the city of St. Louis, Missouri, the younger in a family of two children, her brother, George, being still a resident of St. Louis. Mr. and Mrs. Hadley became the parents of four children, all of whom survive the honored father and remain with their widowed mother in Fort Wayne, their names being here entered in the respective order of their birth: Edwin Charles, Adele Helen, Robert Harold, and Virginia Jane.

George M. Haffner is now the executive head and general manager of one of the important pioneer business enterprises in the city of Fort Wayne, and as president of the Haffner Star Bakery he is the virtual successor of his honored father, who founded the business more than half a century ago. In all the years that have passed since the enterprise was initiated in a comparatively modest way, the Haffner establishment has been maintained at the highest standard consonant with conditions and demands, and the Haffner Star Bakery of the present day is thoroughly metropolitan in all of its facilities, in the grade of its products and in careful and progressive management. Christian Haffner, whose portrait appears herewith, was the founder of the extensive

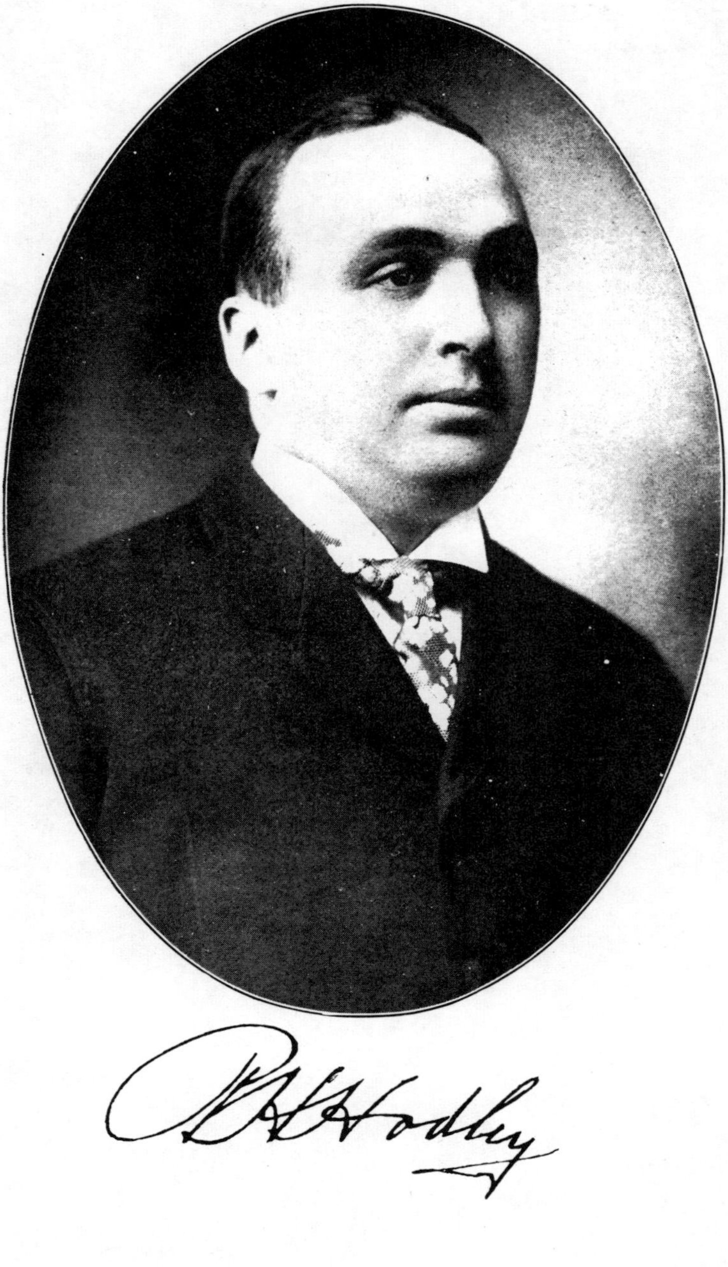

business now controlled by the Haffner Star Bakery and the father of the present president of the company conducting the enterprise. He was born at Marbach, Kingdom of Wurtemberg, Germany, on August 19, 1835, and his death occurred at his home in Fort Wayne, April 29, 1893, so that he was fifty-seven years of age when he was summoned from the stage of life's mortal endeavors. He was afforded the advantages of the schools of his native land and was twenty years of age when he came to the United States, in 1855. After tarrying a few weeks in the city of Philadelphia he made his way to Cincinnati, Ohio, where he found employment at his trade, that of baker. When the Civil War was precipitated he promptly showed his loyalty to the land of his adoption, as he was among the first to enlist in response to President Lincoln's call for volunteers. He enrolled himself as a private in the Ninth Ohio Infantry, with which he proceeded to the front and with which he continued in active service three months. Severe illness then incapacitated him for further active service in the field, but it was a matter of deep satisfaction to him that he was able to bring his trade into play and to continue his service to the nation by acting as baker for his Government. In 1865, about the time of the close of the war, Christian Haffner came to Fort Wayne and purchased a half interest in the Wolroff bakery, which was situated on East Main street, opposite the present No. 1 fire-department station. Finally he purchased Mr. Wolroff's interest in the business and later admitted C. W. Jacobs to partnership in the same. This alliance continued until 1869, when the partnership was dissolved and Mr. Haffner built a new bakery plant at the corner of Harrison and Berry streets. There he continued successful operations about twenty years, and, in 1890, about three years prior to his death, he found the establishment inadequate to meet the demands placed upon it by the constantly expanding trade, and accordingly showed his enterprise and good judgment by removing to the building now occupied by the Haffner Star Bakery, at 333-5 East Lewis street, where he was able to install a larger and more improved equipment and where he continued at the head of the more prosperous business until his death. Thereafter his widow continued the business, which was placed under the direct and effective management of their son, George M., and under these conditions the enterprise was conducted until June 1, 1900, when George M. assumed a definite partnership relation. On September 1, 1914, as a matter of commercial expediency, the business was incorporated under the title of the Haffner Star Bakery, and with a capital stock of fifty thousand dollars, all of which is retained by members of the Haffner family, the widow of the honored founder being vice-president of the company. George M., the eldest son, is president, treasurer and manager, Clarence M. and Frederick C., younger sons, are stockholders and directors of the company, and the former holds the office of secretary of the same. The finely equipped plant has the best of facilities in both the bread and cake departments, and the fullest assortment of modern bakery goods is at all times available in supplying the large wholesale and retail trade of the concern, they being the pioneer leaders of the famous ten-cent "Hol-Tayto-Loaf" bread. The progressive policies of the company are indicated in preparations to double the capacity of the plant within the near future. In the establishment employment is given to about thirty persons, an appreciable trade is controlled in the wholesale line in the territory normally tributary to Fort Wayne, and the business of the company, in 1916, aggregated over one hundred and twenty thousand dollars. The establishment maintains and supplies six distinct city routes in Fort Wayne, with automobile delivery facilities, including an electric truck. Christian Haffner was known and honored as a man of sterling character, of marked business energy and capacity and of utmost civic loyalty. His political allegiance was given to the Republican party, he was a member of the Lutheran church, and he was affiliated with Concordia Lodge No. 228, Independent Order of Odd Fellows. In December, 1867, Mr. Haffner wedded Miss Mary Feist, of Columbia City, Indiana, and concerning the children of this union the following brief record is entered: Herman died in childhood; Emma died at the age of forty-six years on November 10, 1914; George M. is the immediate subject of this review; Frederick C. is a director of the Haffner Star Bakery; Edward J. is deceased; Rose M. is the wife of John F. Wagner, of Fort Wayne; Arthur C. L. is a resident of the city of Chicago; and Clarence M. is secretary of the corporation. George M. Haffner was born in Fort Wayne on March 7, 1870, and he acquired his early education in the public, Reformed Lutheran and Catholic parochial schools of his native city. As a boy he began to assist in his father's bakery, and his experience continued until he had served a most thorough apprenticeship under the discriminating and careful direction of his father. That he has been dominated by ambition to learn the baking business in every detail and to fortify himself in scientific knowledge pertinent thereto is shown by his having taken a course in a well-conducted technical baking institute in the city of Milwaukee, Wisconsin, and also a course of pertinent lectures delivered by members of the faculty of Purdue College, at Lafayette, Indiana, where also he attended the conference called for th purpose of founding a technical baking school in connection with the institution. In the administration of the affairs of the company of which he is president Mr. Haffner has shown not only a thorough technical knowledge of the business but also much initiative and executive ability, as well as the progressiveness that makes for the achievement of large and better results. He takes loyal interest in all things touching the welfare and advancement of his native city, is a Democrat in his political proclivities, is a member of the board of directors of the Fort Wayne Commercial Club, has served as president of the Fort Wayne Retail Merchants' Association, is a prominent member of the Indiana Master Bakers' Association, of which he has been president two terms, and is identified also with the national association of master bakers, of which he also served one year as president. He holds membership in the Rotary Club, has given service as president of St. Aloysius Young Men's Society and was for three years president of St. Charles-Baromeo Relief Society. He is an active member of St. Mary's Athletic Club and is captain of the bowling team of the same. Both he and his wife are earnest communicants of St. Mary's parish of the Catholic church. On October 12, 1898, was solemnized the marriage of Mr. Haffner to Miss Helen Catherine Noll, daughter of Benedict R. Noll, of Fort Wayne, and of the seven children of this union all are living except the fourth, Helen, who died in infancy. The surviving children of the ideal home circle are Rozella, Bernadette, Herman G., Eugene, Alma and Florence.

Arthur Fletcher Hall.—Few men who have come to Fort Wayne within the period of recent years have entered so enthusiastically and effectively into the varied activities of the city as has Arthur Fletcher

CHRISTIAN HAFFNER

Hall, vice-president and general manager of the Lincoln National Life Insurance Company. Without a suggestion of selfish interest and with the enthusiasm of one who finds his highest enjoyment in true service, Mr. Hall has given much to Fort Wayne that is of permanent good, for he is interested actively in every project which suggests true municipal and social progress. He was born in Baxter Springs, Kansas, on May 11, 1872, the son of Truman and Harriet (Beeler) Hall. The father died there and the family returned to the mother's home, Indianapolis, Indiana. Here, Arthur F. Hall received his educational training in the common and high schools. At the age of seventeen, upon the completion of his high school course, he entered the employment of the Indianapolis Journal, then one of the leading newspapers of the middle west, and continued with the institution for a period of fifteen years, during which time, through his keenness of perception of the possibilities of the work entrusted to him, he occupied every position in the business department of the publication. The training he received here, and which continued at the time he was serving as assistant business manager in 1904, when the property was purchased by new interests, laid the foundation upon which was built his later success. Leaving the business department of the Journal, Mr. Hall entered the agency ranks of the Equitable Life Assurance Society of New York. In 1905 Mr. Hall determined to make a greater place for himself in the insurance world. He came to Fort Wayne and, through his ability to convince men of his thorough equipment to organize a great life insurance company, he at once entered upon the plans which resulted in making Fort Wayne the home of the widely-known Lincoln National Life Insurance Company, now grown to a proud place in the insurance world. Early in its history the "Insurance Press" said, "The future of the Lincoln Life is in the hands of men who know how." The years have proven the wisdom of the statement—and Arthur F. Hall has been the guiding spirit of the great institution's upward progress. From the beginning, Mr. Hall has served as the general manager, as well as the vice-president of the institution. His important work with the Lincoln Life, however, has not absorbed all his energies. His well-ordered mind fits him to give attention not only to the important activities of the city but to its pleasures as well. He is busy in Masonic circles. As a member of the Blue Lodge, the Scottish Rite and the York Rite, he has helped to make the order a greater power for good. While serving as potentate of Mizpah Temple, A. A. O. N. Mystic Shrine, he added greatly to the popularity of the order in Fort Wayne. His interests are suggested also in his membership in the Rotary Club, the Commercial Club and the Quest Club, of Fort Wayne, and the Columbia Club, of Indianapolis. He is an active member of the Fort Wayne Country Club, of which organization he has served as president. He is a member of the Trinity Episcopal church, of which body he has served as vestryman. His interest in financial affairs is suggested by his connection with the German-American National bank and the Morris Plan bank as a director. In politics he is a Republican. During the memorable campaign to raise a fund of $300,000 for the erection of a building for the Young Men's Christian Association, Mr. Hall served as the captain of one of two sections which succeeded in raising forty thousand dollars in excess of the designated goal. In June, 1898, Mr. Hall was united in marriage with Miss Una Fletcher, daughter of Dr. William B. and Agnes (O'Brien) Fletcher, of Indianapolis. To them have been born three children: Arthur F. Hall, Jr., 1902; William Fletcher Hall, 1905, and Aileen Hall, 1913. This family occupies "Beechwood," one of the most attractive of the south side homes in Fort Wayne.

Chester I. Hall.—The profession of electrical engineering has an able and popular young representative in Fort Wayne in the person of Chester Irving Hall, who here holds a responsible position with the General Electric Company. Mr. Hall claims the Sunflower State as the place of his nativity, he having been born in the city of Topeka, Kansas. He is a son of Irving and Ella Carrie (Martin) Hall, both of whom were born at Grand Rapids, Mich., where the respective families settled in the pioneer days. The Hall family was founded in New England in the colonial era of American history, and Elias Hall, grandfather of the subject of this review, was born in the state of Massachusetts, and he settled in Michigan many years ago, the remainder of his life having been passed in that state. Irving Hall devoted the major part of his active business career to retail merchandizing and was a resident of Chicago, Illinois, at the time of his death, in 1905, his wife and daughter now being residents of Chicago. Chester I. Hall acquired his preliminary education in the public schools and his technical training in the University of Illinois, in which he prepared himself for his present profession, that of electrical engineer. He did his initiative professional work in the city of Chicago and has been a resident of Fort Wayne since 1913. At Benton Harbor, Michigan, in 1912, was solemnized his marriage to Miss Lillian Mess, who was born in the city of Chicago, and the two children of this union are John Irving, born at High Lake, Illinois, in 1913, and Warren Chester, born at Fort Wayne, Indiana, in 1916.

Allen Hamilton, who is now serving with loyal efficiency as township trustee of Wayne township and who thus has an important part in directing the governmental affairs of the city of Fort Wayne also, has been a resident of Allen county from the time of his birth and is a representative of a family whose name has been worthily linked with the history of this county for an approximate period of seventy years, so that upon him rests a modicum of ancestral pioneer honors, this likewise being true in the maternal line. Mr. Hamilton was born in the village of Leo, Cedar Creek township, this county, on July 14, 1848, and is a son of James Montgomery Hamilton and Johanna (Breckenridge) Hamilton, the former of whom was born in Ireland and the latter at Brookville, Franklin county, Indiana, where her parents were pioneer settlers. James M. Hamilton was born in the year 1822 and acquired his elementary education in his native land. He was a lad of twelve years when he accompanied his parents to the United States, in 1834, and he became one of the pioneer exponents of agricultural industry in Allen county, Indiana, where he established his home when still a young man. He was engaged in farming in Washington township at the time of his death, in 1864, and was one of the highly esteemed men of that section of Allen county, his political support having been given to the Republican party and both he and his wife having been earnest members of the Methodist Episcopal church. Mrs. Hamilton survived the husband of her youth by nearly half a century and was eighty-six years of age at the time of her death, in 1913, she having been one of the venerable and revered pioneer women of Allen county. Allen Hamilton acquired his early education in the common schools of Washington township and later attended the Jefferson school in Fort Wayne, as did he also the Methodist College for a short interval. He was a youth of sixteen years at the time of his father's death and he remained with his mother on the old homestead farm, in Washington township, until 1870, when he entered upon an apprenticeship to the trade of machinist, in the Fort Wayne shops of the Pennsylvania Railroad. He became a specially skilled artisan and continued in the employ of the Pennsylvania Railroad Company for nearly half a century, virtually all of his service having been in the Fort Wayne shops, and his final retirement, after an association of forty-six years, having occurred August 19, 1916. Mr. Hamilton has been influential in public affairs in his home city and county for many years and has been a zealous and loyal advocate of the principles of the Democratic party. He is now serving as trustee of Wayne township, to which office he was appointed, August 18, 1916, and he has served also as a member of the county council, as a member of the municipal council of Fort Wayne, in which latter body he represented the Second ward, and for six years he was a member of the Fort Wayne board of education. In each of these positions of public trust his course has been directed with a high sense of stewardship and with a constant desire to conserve and advance the best interests of the community. He is now nearing the scriptural span of three score years and ten, but his mental and physical powers have not appreciably signalized the passing of the years, his sane and industrious life having been such as to leave him hale and strong as the shadows begin to lengthen from the crimson west. Mr. Hamilton has been in active affiliation with the Independent Order of Odd Fellows since 1873 and he is one of the well-known and unequivocally popular native sons of Allen county. On September 2, 1875, wa ssolemnized the marriage of Mr. Hamilton to Miss Cecilia Fink, daughter of the late Charles and Elizabeth Fink, of Fort Wayne. Mr. and Mrs. Hamilton have four children: James M. is now a resident of the city of Cleveland, Ohio; Walter G. and Frank G. still reside in Fort Wayne; and Edmund C. is a resident of the city of Chicago.

Oliver S. Hanna.—A representative of one of the oldest and most prominent of the permanent families of Fort Wayne, Oliver S. Hanna has remained an active factor in the commercial and financial circles of the city through a period marked by a wonderful physical development in his native place. Mr. Hanna was born in Fort Wayne, August 12, 1847, the son of James B. and Mary King (Fairfield) Hanna. James B. Hanna was the oldest son of Judge Samuel Hanna—admittedly Fort Wayne's foremost citizen of all times—and Eliza Taylor Hanna. He was born in Fort Wayne, June 11, 1823. For several years in the pioneer days of the village Judge Samuel Hanna and James B. Hanna, under the firm name of S. Hanna and Son, were engaged in mercantile trade here. James B. Hanna died in 1851, at the age of twenty-eight years. The wife of James B. Hanna was born September 8, 1823, at Kennebunkport, Maine, a descendant from two prominent families of the "Pine Tree" state, the Fairfields and the Kings. To James B. Hanna and wife were born three children: Clara L. (Mrs. W. L. Carnahan, of Fort Wayne), Oliver S. and James T., the latter deceased. Oliver S. Hanna was educated in the public schools of Fort Wayne and later at Stamford, Connecticut, and Poughkeepsie, New York. On December 4, 1878, he was united in marriage with Mary Ella Nuttman. To this union two children have been born: Gertrude King, now Mrs. Asa W. Grosvenor, of Fort Wayne, and Julia N., now Mrs. Creighton H. Williams, of Fort Wayne. The commercial career of Mr. Hanna was begun in the First National Bank of Fort Wayne, of which institution he became a director. Later, he entered the wholesale boot and shoe house of Carnahan, Hanna & Company. Afterward, he organized the wholesale dry goods and notion house of Hanna, Wiler & Company. In 1882 Mr. Hanna entered into co-partnership with James D. Nuttman in the establishment of the banking institution of Nuttman & Company, the presidency of which he has held during a period of years. Mr. Hanna is a Republican in politics, though he has not entered actively into political affairs. He is a member of the congregation of the First Presbyterian church. He is a member of Mizpah Temple, A. A. O. N., Mystic Shrine, having taken both York and Scottish Rite degrees. He is a loyal member of the Commercial Club of Fort Wayne.

Hon. Robert Blair Hanna is of the third generation of the Hanna family of Fort Wayne, and it would indeed be difficult to write a history of Fort Wayne without writing a large portion of the history of that branch of the Hanna family. He was born on his father's farm, located on the east bank of the St. Mary's river in Washington township, Allen county, Indiana. His father was Henry Clay Hanna, a son of Samuel Hanna, whose history is recorded elsewhere in this work. His mother was a daughter of William W. Carson, born in Castel Bar, Ireland, then moved to Crossinalina, where he served as a military officer of high rank, then immigrated to Cobourg, Canada, with his family, where he followed farming and where Elizabeth Catharine Carson was born. After the death of her father, she and her mother came to Fort Wayne to live with her brother, William W., who as town attorney drafted Fort Wayne's first city charter, served as a Democratic member of the Indiana legislature and as judge of the common pleas court of Allen county. Her's was a family poor in purse but rich in culture, and she was indeed a woman of unusually fine social qualities and a most devoted daughter, wife and mother. Robert's parents were married October 25, 1854, in the little brick house still situated near the northeast corner of Barr and Berry streets. To their union were born eight children: Samuel Carson Hanna, born December 18, 1855, died December 31, 1855; Joseph Thomas Hanna, born February 18, 1857; Henry Clay Hanna, Jr., born June 11, 1858; Minnie Eliza Hanna, born April 18, 1862, died December 13, 1871; Charlotte Hanna, born August 16, 1864, died February 20, 1884; Annie Louise Hanna, born January 19, 1866, died September 15, 1893; Robert Blair Hanna, born March 25, 1868; and Elizabeth Catharine Hanna, born December 31, 1870, died December 15, 1872. The father died July 25, 1881, at the age of fifty-two years, five months and seven days, and the mother died September 8, 1916, at the age of eighty-seven years, five months and twenty days. For the first seven years of his school life, R. B. Hanna attended the German-Lutheran school on Barr street; then the public grade and high schools and the Fort Wayne Business College. After reading law for three years in the office of his brother, Henry C. Hanna, and being admitted to the bar in 1890, he formed a partnership with his brother and was with him for several years, and then alone he continued successfully in the practice of law until being appointed postmaster in 1906. Public affairs attracted "Bob" Hanna early and in 1892 he was elected to the city council as a Republican candidate by a majority of 62 from the then first ward, which was strongly Democratic. He was largely instrumental in establishing many municipal improvements and civic policies, including garbage collection and crematory system; establishment of a fund for a suitable covered market to be erected on the space donated to the city for that purpose by his Grandfather Hanna; leasing the life estate reserved to his heirs by Col. Swinney when he willed to Fort Wayne what is today Swinney park; building the lake and beautifying the grounds around the reservoir, now known as Reservoir park; starting the Anthony Wayne monument fund, and on July 25, 1893, he introduced the resolution which looked to securing for the people interest on the school funds, which was finally accomplished upon the election of Samuel M. Foster to the school board. While only twenty-four years old, and politically a minority member, he was made a member of the councilmanic commission which controlled the police and fire departments. Shortly before the close of his term, the council was called upon to fill the vacancy caused by the death of Mayor Charles A. Zollinger; politically the council stood 12 Democrats, 8 Republicans, and the final ballot stood 12 for Henry P. Scherer and 8 for R. B. Hanna. In 1898, he was nominated, in his absence and against his wishes, a candidate for state senator on the Republican ticket in the Democratic county of Allen. He ran 1,500 ahead of others on his ticket, carrying the Democratic city of Fort Wayne but losing the county by 900. During the campaign he advocated placing justices of the peace on a salary instead of allowing them fees, and at the session of the legislature, two years later, he secured the passage of the bill he had framed reducing the number of justices of the peace for Fort Wayne and placing them on a salary. He was one of the organizers of the Fort Wayne club in 1892 (afterwards the Anthony Wayne club), and of The Fort Wayne Commercial club in 1899, and a director in each for several years before and after their consolidation into the present Commercial Club of Fort Wayne. He was secretary of the Fort Wayne Commercial club for five years. The bringing of factories and interurban electric roads to Fort Wayne; the arbitration and satisfactory adjustment of the long disputed gas question; the elevation of the railroad tracks; and the building of the Anthony hotel were among the many questions with which the club successfully dealt during Mr. Hanna's term as secretary, and the famous "Made-in-Fort-Wayne Exposition" given during that time was his idea. Mr. Hanna was appointed postmaster of Fort Wayne January 18, 1906, and he was re-appointed May 1, 1911. He devoted all of his time to his official duties and at the time he re-appointed him, President Taft said that his record was one of the very best in the whole United States. Upon retiring as postmaster he was given a surprise banquet and presented with a diamond ring by the postoffice employees—the ring being of Masonic design as Mr. Hanna is a member of Sol D. Bayless Lodge No. 359 F. and A. M. and a Scottish Rite Mason of the thirty-second degree. Truthfully, indeed, has it been said that "Wherever the spirit of civic patriotism breathes in Fort Wayne 'Bob' Hanna is sure to be found," for no sooner had he resigned as secretary of the Commercial club than he found himself in the non-salaried position of secretary of the Fort Wayne Civic Improvement Association, an organization then recently promoted by the Commercial club. The activities of this association resulted in a community-wide civic awakening, a civic revival, in which practically every organization of men and women in the city took part, and the civic pride of the people was stirred as never before. Mr. Hanna is a student of community problems, and the vast amount of civic, community and public welfare work which he has done in Fort Wayne during the past twenty years can only be suggested here. He is now giving of his time and talents as a member of the Allen county Liberty Loan executive committee; the Fort Wayne Red Cross subscription committee; chairman of the Rotary club intensive farming and city lot gardening committee, and in many other ways and along still other patriotic lines. As a public speaker, Mr. Hanna is much in demand at Republican political meetings, community gatherings and business and professional men's meetings and banquets, both in Fort Wayne and in nearby cities and towns. He is engaged in business, with an office at 919 Shoaff building, under the title of realty engineering, the nature of which brings into play his legal training, his ability to plan and organize and promote, his knowledge of modern city planning, particularly as it relates to laying out new additions to the city. One of the adjuncts to his business is his connection with the Bedford Stone & Construction Co., which is one of the largest building companies in the country. Robert Blair Hanna and Eva Theodosia Nelson were married in Trinity church, Fort Wayne, February 2, 1906. Her father was Amos DeGroff Nelson, former sheriff of Allen county, a son of Isaac DeGroff Nelson, commissioner of statehouse construction at Indianapolis and president of Lindenwood cemetery association, in which stands a handsome monument erected to his memory by that association. DeGroff was a brother of the late William R. Nelson, owner and editor of the Kansas City Star; DeGroff Nelson's mother was Elizabeth Rockhill, a daughter of William Rockhill, who was a representative in the United States congress. Mrs. Hanna's mother was Helen Catharine, daughter of Samuel Edsall, at one time elected to the Indiana legislature from Allen county on the Democratic ticket and also a member of the state militia; her mother was Cynthia Harrison, who was a cousin of William Henry Harrison. To Mr. and Mrs. Hanna's union has been born two children, Robert Blair, Jr., born January 19, 1907, and Agnes Taylor, born September 15, 1912. The family attends the Trinity Protestant Episcopal church.

Samuel Hanna.—"Judge Hanna belonged to the higher type of the pioneer class of men. He was a planter and builder, more than a legislator. He had the hope, the courage, the forethought, the fertility of resource, the unfaltering purpose and will that characterize the planters of colonies and the founders of cities." So spoke the Hon. Joseph K. Edgerton on the 12th day of June, 1866, the day after the death of the man whose name stands above every other in the history of the city which bears the name of Fort Wayne. To one who knows not the story, it is held out as an example of all that makes for real, true usefulness in every phase of society and in every condition of men. Samuel Hanna was born October 18, 1797, in Scott county, Kentucky, just three years after General Wayne completed the building of the fort 'round which grew the village which developed into the modern city. His father, James Hanna, removed to Dayton, Ohio, in 1804, and purchased a farm lying just outside the town. Here Samuel assisted in clearing the land and laying the foundation for the family's future years of work and enjoyment of the home. The educational advantages were limited, but the boy was given every opportunity to attend the schools of the neighborhood. His earliest employment away from home was that of post-rider, delivering newspapers from the place of publication to the more

Engraved by J.C. Buttre

Yours Affectionately
Saml. Hanna

distant subscribers. His journey carried him to many points in western Ohio. This was before the postal delivery system was in contemplation in these sections. In his nineteenth year, Samuel Hanna occupied the position of clerk in a store in Piqua, Ohio. He and another young man, also a minor, bought out the proprietor, giving their notes for $3,000. Soon after these notes were transferred to an innocent purchaser. About the same time, the goods were taken from them by writ of attachment, leaving the young men without means and heavily in debt. Hanna's partner soon relieved himself of liability by the plea of infancy. Not so, Samuel Hanna. Although his friends advised him in the same course, representing that he had been swindled, he nobly declined, declaring he would pay the last dollar of the debt. It was paid in full with interest. The incident is quoted to show the character of the man as manifested all through his eventful life. After teaching a country school for a time, he attended an Indian treaty council at St. Mary's Ohio, in the capacity of sutler—a person licensed to provide the representatives of the United States with supplies of various kinds—and, with his brother, Thomas, hauled the goods from Troy, Ohio. The small profits from this venture formed the foundation of his future fortune. His success in this direction also determined him upon the plan to locate at Fort Wayne, then a little village huddled about the old stockaded fort. He arrived in 1819, while in his twenty-second year, and just one year before the troops evacuated the fort. The place at that time was but an Indian trading post, with few white inhabitants. Immediately, he entered upon mercantile pursuits in a small way in partnership with his brother-in-law, James Barnett, in a log building located on a spot which is now described as the northwest corner of Barr and Columbia streets. The town had not yet been laid out, and the streets were merely the trails which had served the Indians and the soldiers for many years. By a course of fair dealing, first with his Indian customers and then with the whites, he acquired a high degree of regard and consideration on the part of the people among whom he lived so many years. From the moment he came to Fort Wayne, Samuel Hanna, at all times and on all occasions, evinced a strong desire to build up the town, to advance its material interests in every way, and to improve and develop the resources of the surrounding country, and though not inattentive to his own interests, the cardinal purpose was kept steadily in view during his whole life. In all meetings of the people for the promotion of the public welfare, he was always a conspicuous and leading actor. He early conceived the indispensable necessity of opening and improving roads and other facilities for travel and inter-communication; but to fully appreciate his designs in this respect, it is necessary to revert to the condition of things at that time. The chief supply of provisions and almost every necessity of life had to be brought from a distance, mostly from Miami county, Ohio, by way of St. Mary's, being transported by wagon to the latter place and thence to Fort Wayne by flat-boats down the St. Mary's river. The difficulties attending the transportation of goods by these means is inconceivable in the present day. The facilities for obtaining goods for sale in the Hanna store were little or no better. They were, mostly, purchased in New York and Boston and brought up the Maumee in pirogues, a most laborious task, or packed through the wilderness from Detroit, on horses. Soon after locating in Fort Wayne, Samuel Hanna was appointed agent of the American Fur Company, a responsible position which he filled with credit. When Allen county was formed he was one of the two first associate judges of the Circuit Court. During these years he extended his trading operations to Lafayette and Wabash, Indiana, where he was connected with his brothers, Joseph and Hugh. He purchased large tracts of land in the Wabash valley. Students of the development of the plan to construct the Wabash and Erie canal unite in the declaration that while the idea of the waterway may have originated in the mind of the great Washington, it remained for Samuel Hanna to point out the practicability of the enterprise and to devote his energies to the completion of the work. It was while in familiar conversation with David Burr in a little summer house attached to the Hanna home that the canal subject appears to have assumed a definite shape. Hanna and Burr opened correspondence with the Indiana senators and representatives in congress and secured their favor and influence for the great undertaking. These efforts resulted, in 1827, in a grant by congress to the state of Indiana of each alternate section of land for six miles on each side of the proposed line, through its whole length, to aid in the construction of the canal. Against powerful opposition Judge Hanna, now elected to serve in the state legislature, fought the plan through to success. The state first appropriated one thousand dollars to purchase the necessary surveying instruments and procured the survey and location of the summit level of the waterway. Judge Hanna was selected as a member of the canal commission. He went to New York, purchased the engineering instruments and returned by way of Detroit, from which place he rode on horseback. Judge Hanna and Mr. Burr surveyed the feeder canal to connect the waterway with the St. Joseph river. The legislature acted favorably on their report and the work was ordered continued to the end. Judge Hanna was fund commissioner for the canal for several years and negotiated for most of the money with which the work was carried on. Perhaps the wisdom and ability of Judge Hanna were never more strikingly displayed in any single act of his life than in the establishment and organization of the State Bank of Indiana. When the derangement of the currency and financial embarrassment, consequent upon the veto of the United States Bank and other kindred measures occurred, he was a member of the state legislature. The president had recommended the creation of more state banks to supply the circulation, retired by the closing of that institution. Accordingly, a charter was introduced into the state legislature of such a character that Judge Hanna and other judicious members thought it ought not to pass. He opposed its passage with great power and ability, and was principally instrumental in defeating it; but it was clearly seen that a charter of some kind would pass the next session. A committee was appointed to prepare a proper charter during the vacation, to be presented when the legislature again convened. Judge Hanna was made chairman of the committee and to him was confided the duty of drafting the proposed new charter. It passed both houses with but little opposition. Thus was created the State Bank of Indiana. A branch was at once established at Fort Wayne, of which Judge Hanna was president, much of the time, and Hon. Hugh McCulloch, cashier, during the whole time of its continuance. In 1836 Judge Hanna purchased the large remaining land interest of Barr and McCorkle, adjoining and surrounding the plat of Fort Wayne and comprising much of the most valuable downtown real estate of today. For several years he devoted himself to the

Fort Wayne Branch bank, to the management and improvement of his estate, and to the enjoyment of his domestic and social relations; accepting, occasionally, a seat in the legislature. At this time the roads leading to Fort Wayne were in a wretched condition most of the time and their improvement became a matter of vital necessity. The plan of "planking," which had come into vogue in the east, was seized by Judge Hanna with avidity and acted upon with his accustomed promptness and energy. Through his efforts the Fort Wayne and Lima Plank Road Company was formed and money borrowed chiefly from the Branch bank was used to construct the highway. The first attempt to let contracts proved a failure. In order to give the work a start Judge Hanna took the first ten miles north of Fort Wayne and went personally into the work, superintending, directing and with his own hands assisting in the most laborious operations. Others followed his example and the road was built within the two succeeding years, to Ontario, a distance of fifty miles from Fort Wayne. This was the first work of the kind ever undertaken in northern Indiana. Judge Hanna then took active part in the construction of the Piqua plank road and others. When the builders of the Pennsylvania & Ohio railroad reached the town of Crestline, in Ohio, and it was proposed to extend it to Fort Wayne under the name of the Ohio & Indiana railroad, Judge Hanna was ready with his powerful co-operation. He was largely instrumental in inducing the people of Allen county to vote a subscription of $100,000 to its capital stock. This was the turning point of the great enterprise. In 1852, in connection with Pliny Hoagland and William Mitchell, he took the whole construction contract from Crestline to Fort Wayne, one hundred and thirty-two miles, and entered immediately upon the prosecution of the work. The funds of the company became exhausted. Doctor Merriman, president of the road, resigned, disheartened. Judge Hanna was elected to succeed him. In three days he was in the eastern cities, pledging his individual credit and that of his coadjutors, Hoagland and Mitchell, for funds. This effected, he hastened without delay to Montreal and Quebec to redeem railroad iron that had been forfeited for non-payment of transportation charges. Work was resumed. In November, 1854, the cars from Pittsburgh and Philadelphia came rolling into Fort Wayne. In the autumn of 1852, while encumbered with the building and financial embarrassments of the Ohio & Indiana railroad, the Fort Wayne & Chicago Railroad Company was organized and Judge Hanna was elected president. The financial difficulties of this road were also most burdensome, but the greater the pressure the greater Judge Hanna's resources appeared to develop and come to his rescue. Judge Hanna effected the consolidation of the three properties which formed the beginning of the great Pennsylvania Railroad system of today. The accomplishment of Judge Hanna is best understood from a review of the year's efforts. In the beginning it became apparent to many of the stockholders, as well as managers of the separate corporations extending from Pittsburgh to Chicago, and which, in fact, for all practical and business purposes, formed but one line, that the interests and convenience of each, as well as of the public, would be promoted by merging their separate existence into one great consolidated company. Judge Hanna early and earnestly espoused the cause of consolidation, and a meeting was called at Fort Wayne to consider and act upon the subject. Contrary to expectation, considerable opposition to the projected consolidation manifested itself at this meeting, headed and managed by the shrewd and talented Charles L. Boalt, encouraged and assisted by others hardly less astute. The debate was animated and exciting. The best talent on both sides was warmly enlisted. The contest extended to considerable length and its issue appeared doubtful. Before the debate closed Judge Hanna rose for a final appeal. No one who heard that brief effort will forget it. It was a condensed array of facts and arguments—a splendid outburst of burning, earnest eloquence. The opposition was literally crushed out. The vote resulted in a large majority for consolidation—many who had opposed it in the beginning voting in its favor. Thus, on the first day of August, 1856, the three minor corporations were obliterated on terms satisfactory to themselves and the great Pittsburgh, Fort Wayne & Chicago Railway Company succeeded to their franchises and liabilities. While Judge Hanna, who was elected to serve as vice-president of the Pittsburgh, Fort Wayne & Chicago (Pennsylvania) railroad, would never yield an iota of the interests of the company to any outside consideration, he was not unmindful of the interests of Fort Wayne. Hence his untiring efforts in establishing the immense railroad shops and manufactories of his city. Upon the organization of the Grand Rapids & Indiana Railroad Company, Judge Hanna was elected to serve as its president. He accepted with reluctance. He seemed to have a foreboding that his life's work was drawing to a close. When he was leaving his home to attend a meeting of the board of directors at Grand Rapids, less than two months before his demise, the remark was made that he would return president of the company. He replied, "No, that cannot be. The responsibility is too great; I cannot accept it." He was elected, however. Judge Hanna's efforts for the improvement of both town and country were not confined to those of a public nature, but his means were always freely advanced for the promotion of private and individual enterprise. In partnership with James Barnett he established the first grist mill on the St. Mary's river. The woolen factory of French, Hanna & Company, the extensive foundry and machine shops of Bass and Hanna (now the Bass Foundry and Machine Company's plant), the hub, spoke and bending factory of Olds, Hanna & Company, as well as many others, may be cited as instances of his wider interests. Many persons were essentially aided in their early efforts by the use of Judge Hanna's capital. With the utmost charity and good-will towards all Christian denominations, Judge Hanna's religious training was in the faith and spirit of the Presbyterian church of which his father was an elder for half a century. The organization of the First Presbyterian church, in 1831, had his hearty co-operation and support, though he did not become a member until 1843. He was then selected as a ruling elder, a position he held during the remainder of his lifetime. The last illness of Judge Hanna was of short duration, covering only five days. His demise came on June 11, 1866. The city council passed resolutions of sorrow which found an echo in the heart of every citizen. The bells of all churches were tolled and, amid sombre draperies on every side, a procession two miles in length followed his mortal remains to their last resting place in Lindenwood cemetery. Thus ended the pure and noble life of one whose name will ever be cherished by the citizens of Fort Wayne. March 7, 1822, at Fort Wayne, Judge Hanna was united in marriage with Miss Eliza Taylor, who was born in Buffalo, New York, in 1803, the daughter of Israel and Mary Taylor, natives of Massachusetts. She came to Fort Wayne in 1820, from Dayton, Ohio, on a visit with her sister, Mrs. Laura Suttenfield. Mrs. Hanna possessed nobility of character, great personal courage and the ability to handle the affairs of home and society with ease. Although delicate in appearance, she possessed a strong constitution and was very active all her life. She died, February 12, 1888, at Fort Wayne in the Hanna homestead, still occupied by her daughter, Mrs. Fred J. Hayden. Following are the children of Judge and Mrs. Hanna: Jesse Bayless, member of the firm of S. Hanna & Sons, general merchandise; Amos Thomas, also a member of this firm; Henry Clay, at one time engaged in the grocery business and also a partner in the firm of N. G. and H. G. Olds and Company; Charles, a partner in the firm of French, Hanna & Company, manufacturers of woollen goods; Samuel Teford, associated with his father in the railroad business as private secretary while he was president of the Grand Rapids and Indiana road; Samuel T., a public-spirited citizen who served at one time as a member of the city council; Horace Hovey, a partner of John H. Bass in the firm known as Bass & Hanna; William Willis, a partner in the firm of French, Hanna and Company; Hugh Taylor, whose death occurred in 1915; and Eliza, the only daughter, the widow of Hon. Fred J. Hayden, the only surviving child of Judge and Mrs. Hanna. Mrs. Hayden retains the old homestead in the same manner as when her distinguished father and her respected mother welcomed and entertained their hosts of frinds in the years of the past. The air of hospitality and good fellowship is apparent today as in the yesterdays, and the fond memories of earlier years give to the splendid old mansion a value above that of the more common things which we call real treasures.

Edward Happel is a scion of the second generation of the Happel family in Allen county, with whose industrial and civic affairs the family name has been identified for approximately seventy years. The parents of Mr. Happel established their home on a pioneer farm in Lake township, this county, about the year 1848; the father reclaimed from a semi-wilderness a productive farm, and here he and his wife passed the remainder of their lives, sterling and industrious citizens who wrested from the hands of fate a due measure of prosperity and independence and at all times merited and commanded the confidence and respect of all who knew them. He whose name initiates this paragraph has not only upheld but expanded the prestige of the family name in connection with the basic industries of agriculture and stock-growing in his native county. He was born on the old homestead farm of his parents, in Lake township, and the date of his nativity was April 4, 1855. He is a son of Frederick and Henrietta (Bitting) Happel, both of whom were born and reared in Berks county, Pennsylvania—representatives of sterling old German families that were early founded in the Keystone State. The parents of Mr. Happel were married in their native county and, as before stated, came to Allen county, Indiana, about the year 1848. Frederick Happel contributed his quota to the industrial and social development and progress of the county, and both he and his wife attained to venerable age. Of their five children the eldest is Mrs. Catherine A. Anderson; and the second in order of birth is Mrs. Amanda Onick, both being still residents of Indiana; Minerva and Edward were twins and the former is now deceased, she having been the wife of George Blessing; and Mrs. Sylvia Draker is the youngest of the number. The parents were life-long and zealous communicants of the Lutheran church. The early educational advantages of Edward Happel were limited to a somewhat irregular attendance in the rural schools of Lake township and he continued to be associated with the work and management of his father's farm until he finally purchased the property. He remained on the old homestead for three years after his marriage, which occurred in 1880, and then sold the property and purchased a farm of one hundred and eleven acres, eligibly situated on the Goshen road. Later he added forty-six acres to the area of his estate, which is situated in Sections 2 and 3, Lake township, and his energy and good judgment have been shown in the installing of many improvements on the place and in keeping the same up to a high modern standard. Eighty-eight acres are under a high state of cultivation and devoted to diversified agriculture, and Mr. Happel also gives attention to the raising of live stock, which he has made a profitable department of his farm enterprise. He is loyal and progressive as a citizen and has been influential in community affairs of a public order. The secure place which he holds in popular esteem is indicated by the fact that he served four years as township trustee of his native township. His political allegiance is given to the Republican party and both he and his wife are communicants and active and valued members of St. John's Lutheran church in Lake township. On November 11, 1880, was solemnized the marriage of Mr. Happel to Miss Louisa Lamley, who likewise was born and reared in this county, a daughter of the late Gottlieb and Margaret Lamley, of Lake township. Of Mr. and Mrs. Happel's interesting family of children it is gratifying to note that all are living except the youngest, William, who died in infancy, and Katherine, the eldest, who was the wife of J. W. Rapp; Rosa is the wife of George Felger, and they reside in Lake township; John is engaged in farming in Lake township; Lavina is the wife of Ed Hagan, of Lake township; Anna is the wife of Ed Blessing, of the same township; Arthur remains at the parental home and assists in the management of the farm; Ruth is the wife of William Schmidt, of Lake township; Dave is at home, and Lena and Jacob are also members of the gracious family circle of the parental home.

Frank J. Harber was born in Pleasant township, Allen county, Indiana, on April 24, 1860, and his life thus far has been passed practically within the borders of his native community. He is the son of Nicholas and Margaret (Tracy) Harber, both of whom came from Germany as young people, and who settled in Allen county soon after their marriage. They were industrious young people and, desirous of owning land and a home of their own, entered land under the homestead laws, thus coming into ownership of one hundred and sixty acres of wild land in Pleasant township. Nicholas Harber had courage and young energy, and his wife was his equal in those sturdy qualities. They knew many hardships in those early years while they were making a farm out of that tract of wild land, and frugal living was the order of the day. For years the elder Harber was wont to tell, he saw little or no money, year in and out. They literally got their living from the soil. Salt, at one time during those years reached a record price of sixteen dollars a barrel, and he relates that they distilled salt from the black ash trees that grew abundantly on the land, and so supplied that ever present need without the outlay of actual money. Wild game abounded in the woods, and venison in those days was every man's legitimate food. Mr. Harber tells that he has sold venison in the villages for one cent a pound, and would sometimes get as much as fifty or seventy-five cents for the hide. The wild turkey, plentiful then, but now practically extinct, would bring twenty-five cents in the village market. It was by such means as these that the early settlers found a means to secure those necessities that could not be coaxed from the soil during the early years when they had not cleared enough land to enable them to farm in real earnest. Nicholas Harber had three brothers and two sisters, and with him they shared in the pioneer life of their day and contributed their full share to the development and upbuilding of the communities in which they settled. Mr. Harber's success is a fair sample of what they were able to accomplish in their lifetimes. He added a good deal of land to his original holdings. First was a tract of a hundred and sixty acres, for which he paid the sum of $1.25 per acre. Later he secured a half section, so that his holdings aggregated one section, or 640 acres. To Mr. and Mrs. Harber were born five children: Martin, John H., Gerhard, George and Frank J., the last named being the immediate subject of this review. All were educated in the common schools of their community and in the parochial school, and they received better educational advantages than many of the youth of their native community. Up to the age of twenty-six Frank Harber stayed on the home farm as his father's assistant. On the death of his father he inherited one hundred and eighty acres, and he has there carried on successful farming down to the present time. Modern and commodious dwelling and barns manifest the progressive character of Mr. Harber's farming, and in addition to being one of the successful young farmers in the township he is identified somewhat prominently with business enterprises of the community. He has served as president of the local telephone company for five years, a concern in which he holds considerable stock, and is interested in a mining venture in Nevada that promises well for future gains. Mr. Harber and his family are members of the Roman Catholic church, and he is Republican in his politics. He was married on May 25, 1886, to Miss Maggie Buff, daughter of Anthony and Susan (Reiniger) Buff who were early comers to Allen county from Pennsylvania. The day of wolves and Indians was in their time, and they shared in the privations and the pleasures that marked the lives of every pioneer of their period. Mr. Buff was a farmer, but he kept a tavern, as it was called then, for years. They were prominent and estimable people in their day, and their children have followed them in the worthy ambitions they manifested. Mr. and Mrs. Harber have four children and one grandchild. Callistus, the eldest, is married and has a daughter, Thelma. The others are Dorothy, Ethel and John G., all living at home.

Martin Harber.—The Harber family is of German ancestry and the parents of Martin Harber came from Germany in their young life. They were Nicholas and Theresa (Gerhard) Harber, and they settled in Marion township in the early days of its development. They were ambitious and industrious people and came to be among the well-to-do farmers of their community. Mr. Harber bought and sold land and at the time of his death was owner of about seven hundred acres in the county, being counted among the wealthy men of his community. He was a Democrat, active to some extent in party politics, and the family were adherents of the Roman Catholic faith, with membership in the local church. More extended mention of them and of their children will be found in a sketch of Frank J. Harber. Martin Harber was born in Allen county,

Indiana, November 4, 1852. He acquired his education in the public and parochial schools of this county and has engaged in agricultural pursuits practically all his life. For some years, however, he has been living retired in Fort Wayne, having won a competency during his active career to enjoy a well deserved rest. On June 10, 1880, he married Miss Catherine Mischo, a daughter of Michael and Catherine Mischo, who came from Germany to New York, and thence to Allen county, settling in Fort Wayne, where the father was engaged as a stone mason for many years. To Mr. and Mrs. Harber were born eight children: Anna M. Clara M., Edward N. M., Albert J., Frances M., William G., George C., and Bertha M. The mother of this family died September 7, 1900. Mr. Harber, although retired from active business, is one of the progressive and enterprising men of Allen county, and is numbered with the substantial citizens of Fort Wayne. He owns two hundred and three acres of well improved land in Pleasant township as well as a comfortable home in Fort Wayne, where he resides.

Robert F. Harding, a representative of the younger active citizens of Fort Wayne, has given freely of his talents and energy to the betterment of his home city. His responsible place in the development of the world-famed Fort Wayne plant of the General Electric Company has been filled with a degree of completeness which tells plainly of his value to this important center of industrial activity. Mr. Harding is a native of Logansport, Indiana, where he was born, September 9, 1870. He is a son of Daniel F. and Mary A. (Fleming) Harding, who came to America from the north of Ireland in 1869. The value of the elder Mr. Harding's contribution to the upbuilding of Fort Wayne is shown by the honors bestowed upon him by the people of Fort Wayne in his election to the office of mayor. At the beginning of his career, however, Mr. Harding, who reached Fort Wayne in the early '70s, found his services in demand as a civil engineer, and latterly he was connected in this capacity with what is now known as the Lake Erie & Western Railroad at the time of its construction. Following his connection with the Lake Erie & Western road, he became connected with the Pennsylvania railroad, then known as the Pittsburg, Fort Wayne and Chicago Railroad, and served with this important concern for a period. When he gave up railroad work, Mr. Harding entered upon a prosperous career in the insurance business in Fort Wayne and became an important factor in this field. Mr. Harding's death occurred in 1912. The widow, who has devoted her best life to the betterment of those about her, has been a leader in many religious efforts for the good of the many. Robert F. Harding attended the public schools of Fort Wayne and then was employed in a dry goods store as salesman until his true field of effort was opened in one of the departments of the present General Electric Company's plant, formerly known as the Fort Wayne Jenney Electric Light Works, the Fort Wayne Electric Corporation and the Fort Wayne Electric Works. After serving in various clerkships, Mr. Harding became the superintendent of an important department and has, for several years, served as purchasing agent of the company's immense Fort Wayne plant.

Edward Harper, an honored citizen and representative business man of New Haven, Adams township, has been established in the undertaking and funeral-directing business in this village for nearly thirty years and the enterprise is now conducted under the firm name of Edward Harper & Son, his only son being his able coadjutor. The incidental equipment of the Harper undertaking establishment is of the best modern type, with scientific embalming facilities and with automobile hearse and ambulance service. Edward Harper is a native of Allen county and a representative of a family that here settled in the pioneer days—more than sixty years ago. He was born on the pioneer farm of his father, in Jefferson township, and the date of his nativity was March 26, 1855. In this county his parents, William and Mary (Hunter) Harper, continued to reside until their death, and their names merit enduring place on the roll of the sterling pioneers of the county. The father was born in Ireland and the mother in Erie County, Pennsylvania. Of their twelve children the eldest, Rebecca, died in 1865; John was a resident of Allen county at the time of his death, in 1913; John, Hamilton, James and Samuel were gallant soldiers of the Union in the Civil war and all are now deceased, as are also William, Hugh, Mary and Matilda; William and Mary and Matilda having all died in the year 1854; Edward, the immediate subject of this review, was the eleventh in order of birth; and Robert Emmett, the youngest of the number, owns and resides on the old homestead farm in Jefferson township. The childhood and youth of Edward Harper were compassed by the environs and influences of the home farm, in the work of which he early began to assist, and in the meanwhile he made effective use of the advantages of the public schools of the locality and period. After leaving the farm he learned the carpenter's trade, to which he continued to devote his attention for a period of twelve years. He finally met with a fall that resulted in permanent injury to his right hip and prevented his further activities as a carpenter and builder. Under these conditions he established his home at New Haven and engaged in the undertaking business, which has continued to receive his attention during the long intervening years, the enterprise having been founded by him in March, 1889, and the highest standard of service having been maintained at all times. The close and sympathetic relations that have been promoted between Mr. Harper and the other citizens of the community have given him specially secure place in the confidence and esteem of all who know him, and it may consistently be said that his circle of friends is limited only by that of his acquaintances. His political views are indicated in the loyal support which he gives to the cause of the Republican party. On January 1, 1883, was solemnized the marriage of Mr. Harper to Miss Martha A. Shull, daughter of Jacob and Melinda (McCulloch) Shull, who were well known residents of Grant county until Mrs. Shull's death, when the father moved to Jefferson township, and whose three surviving children are Mrs. Florence E. Burkhold, Mrs. Harper and Mrs. Mary Ross, of Fort Wayne. Mr. and Mrs. Harper have two children, Emmett E., who is associated with his father in business and concerning whom more specific mention will be made; and Etta May, who remains at the parental home, being employed as bookkeeper in the office of the Rice Cereal Company in Fort Wayne. Emmett E. Harper was born in Jefferson township, this county, September 18, 1884, and his early educational discipline was acquired in the public schools of New Haven. Later he completed a course in the International Business College in the city of Fort Wayne. From the time of initiating his active career he has been closely associated with his father in the undertaking business and he is the junior member of the firm of Edward Harper & Son, which holds license No. 732 issued by the Indiana State Board of Embalmers. October

18, 1908, recorded the marriage of Emmett E. Harper to Miss Fannie G. Greenawalt, who likewise was born and reared in Allen county and who is the eldest of the four children of Oliver J. and Ella (Jackson) Greenawalt; Hazel, the second child, is the wife of Mr. Hickner, who holds in 1917 the position of principal of the public schools in the city of Valparaiso, Indiana; George R. is principal of the schools of Norway, Michigan; and Mary, who remains in Allen county, has likewise made an excellent record as a school teacher. Mr. and Mrs. Harper have three children—George Edward, Bruce Morris and Mary Elaine.

Morse Harrod, M. D., has been established in the general practice of his profession in the city of Fort Wayne for a quarter of a century and is known and honored as one of the able and representative physicians and surgeons of his native county, the broad scope of his practice indicating the high estimate placed upon him as a man and as an exponent of his exacting profession. The Doctor was born on a farm in Allen county, April 4, 1866, a son of Morgan and Belinda (Beam) Harrod, the former of whom was born in Knox county, Ohio, August 3, 1826, and the latter in Allen county, Indiana, September 16, 1832, she having here continued to maintain her home during the long intervening years and being now one of the venerable and revered representatives of a sterling pioneer family of the county. Morgan Harrod passed the major part of his life in Allen county and was long numbered among the progressive farmers and influential citizens, his death having occurred one day prior to the eighty-second anniversary of his birth. He passed to the life eternal on August 2, 1908, after a life of signal integrity and usefulness. The Harrod family was founded in America in the colonial days and John Harrod, an uncle of the late Morgan Harrod, was a patriot soldier in the war of the Revolution. Dr. Harrod is of a family of eight sons and three daughters, and all of the number are living, except two of the sons. The Doctor was reared to the sturdy discipline of the home farm and after he had made good use of the advantages of the public schools his ambition led him to prepare himself for the profession in which he has achieved distinctive success and precedence. He entered the celebrated Eclectic Medical College in the city of Cincinnati, Ohio, and in this institution was graduated as a member of the class of 1891, since which time he has been continuously engaged in the general practice of his profession in Fort Wayne, where he has also become an interested principal in a number of business enterprises of important order. He served as county coroner from 1892 to 1896, is a Democrat in his political allegiance, has received in the Masonic fraternity the thirty-second degree of the Ancient Accepted Scottish Rite, and both he and his wife hold membership in the Baptist church. On May 31, 1888, was recorded the marriage of Dr. Harrod to Miss Jennie L. Lipes, who likewise was born and reared in this county, a daughter of D. D. and Mary J. (Somers) Lipes, the former of whom is deceased and the latter resides in the city of Fort Wayne. Dr. and Mrs. Harrod have three children, concerning whom brief record is entered in conclusion of this review: Camilla is the wife of Sidney H. Karn and they have one daughter, Jean Elizabeth. Wayne Allen Harrod was graduated in the Fort Wayne High School and in the Guggenheim Institute of Mining Engineers, at Golden, Colorado, and is now holding a responsible position as a mining engineer at Keddie, California. Velma June, the youngest of the children, remains at the parental home.

Jonathan Hart.—When it is stated that on the 17th of April, 1917, this sterling and honored citizen of Monroe township celebrated the eightieth anniversary of his birth and that he has been a resident of Allen county since he was a lad of twelve years, it becomes evident that he is a representative of one of the county's pioneer families and that his memory constitutes a gracious link between the primitive past and the twentieth century of opulent prosperity in this now favored section of the Hoosier state. Mr. Hart has been one of the world's prolific workers and it was entirely through his own ability and efforts that he made his way to the place of material prosperity and well merited independence. For more than half a century he has maintained his home on his present well improved farm, which comprises eighty acres and which is eligibly situated in Section 16, Monroe township. This land was largely covered with timber when he purchased the property, and his original dwelling was a little log house of the primitive type. With the passing years his energetic and timely labors brought about the reclamation of his land and its development into one of the specific centers of prosperous agricultural and live-stock industry in the county, the while increasing prosperity was made manifest in the substantial buildings with which he improved the place. Now veneral in years, he has given over to others the heavy labors and responsibilities that were long his portion, but vigorous of mind and physical powers to a degree that gives denial to his age, he still takes vital interest in the affairs of his farm and in all that concerns the welfare of the township and county to whose development and progress he has contributed his quota. In his farm enterprise he achieved special success as a grower and feeder of live stock of all kinds and was a leader in the industrial progress of his township, even as he has been one of its influential citizens. He is a Democrat in politics and served at one time as supervisor of Monroe township. Mr. Hart was born in Ashland county, Ohio, April 17, 1837, and is a son of George and Sarah (Friedline) Hart, who were natives of Pennsylvania and who became early settlers in Ashland county, Ohio, whence they came to Indiana and established their home on one of the pioneer and embryonic farms of Allen county in the year 1849. Here they passed the remainder of their lives, and of their ten children only four are now living. Jonathan Hart has profited much from the discipline given in the broad school of experience but his specific education was limited to a somewhat irregular attendance in the common schools of Ohio. After the family removal to Allen county he attended the pioneer schools for brief intervals, and in connection with the reclaiming and other work of his father's farm he gained full fellowship with arduous toil. He remained at the parental home until he had attained to his legal majority and then purchased his present farm, which he has made one of the valuable places of Monroe township. In 1861 Mr. Hart wedded Miss Sarah W. Hines, and this devoted wife and helpmeet of his young manhood was his faithful companion for nearly forty years, the gracious ties being severed when she passed to the life eternal, in 1898. They became the parents of four children: O. P., Wayne M., William and Jeanette, all of whom are living except the last named. In 1901 Mr. Hart married Mrs. Virginia E. (Hines) Gerian, a sister of his first wife and the widow of Jonas L. Gerian, and she died in 1904. By her first marriage Mrs. Hart had seven children, all of whom are living, namely: Lucy M., Elmer S.,

Israel M., Daniel H., Wilson F., William, and Clyde E. Of these children five now reside in California and two in Michigan.

Arthur Harter.—In Section 12, Springfield township, is situated the finely improved and well ordered farm of Mr. Harter, the same comprising one hundred and fifty acres of most fertile and productive land and constituting one of the valuable rural properties of the county. Mr. Harter is a representative of one of the old and honored families of Allen county and his maternal grandparents were numbered among the very early pioneer settlers of this favored section of the state, where they established their home, in Springfield township, in the year 1837. Arthur Harter was born on the old homestead farm of his father, in Springfield township, and the date of his nativity was November 22, 1862. He is a son of William and Lucinda (Hall) Harter, both of whom were born in Stark county, Ohio, and the latter was but two years old at the time of her parents' removal to Allen county, Indiana, where she was reared under the conditions and influences of the pioneer era. William Harter, a scion of one of the influential pioneer families of Stark county, Ohio, was there reared to adult age and was a young man when he came to Indiana and found employment as a moulder in the original Bass foundry, besides which he did skillful work as a millwright and expert mechanic along other lines. After his marriage he settled on a farm in Springfield township, where he developed one of the excellent places of this part of the county and continued to reside, a sterling and highly honored citizen, until his death, which occurred in February, 1916, his cherished and devoted wife having passed to the life eternal May 19, 1895. Of their five children the four who survive are Olive Esther, Arthur, Mildred Lucinda, and Isaac. Emma, the youngest of the number, died in childhood. The father was a Republican in politics, was influential in connection with community affairs of a public order, and both he and his wife were consistent members of the Methodist Episcopal church. Through youthful association with the work of the home farm and through his attendance in the public schools of his native township, Arthur Harter waxed strong in physical and mental power and well fortified himself for the active duties and responsibilities of life. He had continued during the intervening years his close and effective alliance with the fundamental and all-important industries of agriculture and stock-growing, and is known as one of the substantial and aggressive exponents of the same in his native county. While he has shown loyal interest in all things touching the welfare of his home township and county and is a stalwart advocate of the principles of the Republican party, he has never desired or held public office. Both he and his wife are active members of the Methodist Episcopal church at Hicksville, and he is affiliated with the lodge of Knights of Pythias at Spencerville, Dekalb county. On December 24, 1885, was solemnized the marriage of Mr. Harter to Miss Ella Shutt, who was born and reared in this county, a daughter of George and Mary Ann (Houk) Shutt, both of whom were born in Ohio and were children when the respective parents numbered themselves among the pioneer settlers of Allen county. George Shutt was the youngest in a family of eight children, and the names of the other children are here noted: John, Daniel, Levi, Samuel, Joseph, Jacob and William—a remarkable family of sturdy sons. The names of the children of George and Mary Ann Shutt are here designated: Gertrude, Hattie, Mortimer, Lillie, Ella. Mr. and Mrs. Harter became the parents of two children, of whom the elder, Stella, is deceased, and the younger is George

William, he remaining at the parental home and being an ambitious and popular young man who is associated with his father in the work and management of the farm.

Jacob Hartman has been a resident of Allen county from the time of his birth, which occurred on the old homestead farm in Marion township, September 11, 1862, and after having been for nearly a quarter of a century engaged in the retail grocery business in Fort Wayne he here, in 1908, established himself in his present business, that of real estate and insurance, the insurance department of his enterprise being confined largely to fire and casualty indemnity. He has been one of the successful business men and public-spirited citizens of Fort Wayne, where he is well known and highly esteemed, and since January 1, 1914, has served consecutively as councilman at large on the municipal board of aldermen. His political allegiance has been exemplified in staunch support of the cause of the Democratic party, he and his wife are communicants of St. Mary's Catholic church, and he is an active member of the Catholic Benevolent League of Indiana. Joseph Hartman, father of the subject of this review, was born in Germany, about the year 1838, and was reared and educated in his native land. At the age of eighteen years he severed the home ties and set forth to seek his fortunes in America. Soon after landing in the United States he made his way to Toledo, Ohio, and in that vicinity he found employment at farm work. He carefully husbanded his earnings and finally came to Allen county, Indiana, and purchased a farm in Marion township. He developed one of the valuable farms of that section of the county and was one of its specially successful exponents of the basic industries of agriculture and stock-growing during the remainder of his long, worthy and useful life, his death having occurred October 17, 1899, and his name meriting high place on the roll of the sterling pioneers of the county. In 1860 he wedded Miss Caroline Hoffman, who was born in the city of Cincinnati, Ohio, and who died in Fort Wayne March 10, 1915, both holding earnestly to the faith of the Catholic church. Of their ten children all are living except one. Jacob Hartman, the immediate subject of this sketch, continued to be associated in the work and management of the home farm until he had attained to his legal majority and in the meanwhile he made good use of the advantages afforded in the public schools of the locality. At the age of twenty-two years he became identified with mercantile enterprise in Fort Wayne, and here he conducted a grocery store continuously for about twenty-four years. He retired from this business in 1908, since which time he has given his attention to the real estate and insurance business, as previously noted in this context. In 1883 was solemnized the marriage of Mr. Hartman to Miss Anna Ankenbruck, a daughter of Bernard and Catherine Ankenbruck, of Fort Wayne, and of this union have been born four sons and four daughters; Augusta is the wife of Joseph J. Hake, of Fort Wayne; And. J. wedded Miss Edith Auer and they reside in this city; and Jacob, Jr., Marie, Elsie, William, Leo and Irma G. remain at the parental home.

Allen Monroe Hartzell, president of the New Haven State Bank, was born in New Haven, Allen county, Indiana, on August 25, 1856, and is the son of Levi and Mary (Souders) Hartzell, both of them born in Miami county, Ohio. The father came to Allen county in 1840, locating in what is now New Haven, where he bought land and devoted himself to farming, as well as conducting a grist and saw mill. He died in 1871 at the age of fifty-eight years and his widow survived him until January 5, 1905, when she was aged eighty-five years and five days. Their children were seven in number. Joshua is a resident of Marion, Indiana. Elias lives in Hoagland, Indiana. Susan is the wife of Dr. L. L. Null, of New Haven. Jennie married T. C. Shilling, of Troy, Ohio. John R. lives in New Haven. Allen M. was the next, and Warren S., the seventh and youngest child, died at the age of forty years. Allen M. Hartzell had his education in the public schools of New Haven and in the old Methodist College in Fort Wayne. He taught in the public schools for about two years after finishing his studies and then entered the law offices of Robert Shatton in Fort Wayne, where he spent seven years. From that experience he turned to farming and dairying in his native community and that enterprise held his attention successfully until he turned his activities to the banking business, with which he has since been successfully identified. On December 28, 1881, Mr. Hartzell was married to Miss Emmaline Fitch, daughter of Nathaniel Fitch, of Huntertown, Indiana. Mr. Hartzell is a Republican in politics, a thirty-second degree Mason, and a Shriner. The New Haven State Bank was organized on October 29, 1909, and opened for business December 6, 1909. It opened with a capital stock of $25,000, which was increased, in 1916, to $35,000. The first president was Allen M. Hartzell and he still holds that office. The present board of directors includes H. H. Grubb, Ira B. Sleet, A. M. Hartzell, A. R. Schmitker, Josiah Adams, D. B. Nail, and Paul Vonderau, and is made up of practically the same body of men who served when the bank was first organized. Paul Vonderau succeeded his father on the death of the latter, and D. B. Nail serves now in the place of Christ Heine, who was a member of the original board. This gives evidence of a harmonious organization, and indeed, that element has entered largely into the success and growth of the institution. When the bank was organized, T. Thimlar was made vice-president, and on January 2, 1915, he was succeeded in that office by Herman H. Grubb, who now serves in that capacity. The bank building is a commodious structure of brick, with two floors and basement, and a floor space of 22 x 58 feet. It is thoroughly modern, well equipped, and has every facility for the handling of the volume of business that passes through it daily. An idea of the growth of the bank may be gleaned from the following figures: Deposits for 1910 were $128,000; in 1911, $178,000; in 1912, $210,000; in 1913, $256,000; in 1914, $279,000; in 1915, $298,000; in 1916, $349,000; and in 1917, $400,000. Its exchange banks are the Fifth Third National Bank of Cincinnati, Ohio, and the First and Hamilton National Bank of Fort Wayne, Indiana.

Carl M. Hassold, cashier of the Hoagland State Bank since October, 1915, is a young man well known in that community. He was born in Huntington, Indiana, on September 25, 1880, and is a son of Rev. Stephen and Margaret (Weber) Hassold. The father is of German birth, having come to America when a child of four years, and the mother was born in Indiana. They lived in Huntington county sixteen years, in DeKalb county eighteen years, and for four years have made their home in Allen county; and at this writing Reverend Mr. Hassold is pastor of a Lutheran church in Madison township. Their son, Carl M., had his education in the German Lutheran schools of Huntington, Indiana, and in the Fort Wayne college, from which he was graduated in 1902. He then entered Concordia Seminary to study for the ministry and, in 1905, having

Fred J. Hayden

qualified for the ministry, assumed the pastorate of a Lutheran church in Ohio. He spent four years in that state and a similar period in ministerial work in Portland, Oregon. His health failed and he withdrew from the ministry. Some months later he returned to Allen county and, in October, 1915, was offered the position of cashier of the Hoagland State Bank. He accepted the post and has continued to discharge the duties of cashier in a capable and altogether satisfactory manner. His success may properly be said to be of his own making, for he had little or no help in getting his education, and he has worked diligently for such benefits as have come his way. Mr. Hassold is Republican in politics and is unmarried.

Fred Hauke has proved himself possessed of that healthy ambition that is certain to be fruitful in worthy achievement, and he is now numbered among the successful farmers of Maumee township, where he owns and resides upon a fine farm of eighty-four acres, in Section 5, besides which he is the owner of another good farm, of eighty acres, in Milan township. He was about twenty-five years of age when he came from his German fatherland to America, in 1885, and he established his home in Fort Wayne. Here he was employed twelve years as a skilled mechanic in a boiler shop, and at the expiration of that period he purchased his present homestead farm in Maumee township. Much of the land was cleared by him and upon the place he has made the best of permanent improvements, including farm buildings, fences, tile drainage, etc., the while his success in his farm enterprise has been in consonance with his indomitable energy and progressive policies. Mr. Hauke was born and reared in Birda, Germany, and is the eldest in a family of four children, William having died in 1915 and Henry in 1913, and Minnie being a resident of Mindan, Germany. The parents, Christ and Minnie (Koene) Hauke, passed their entire lives in Germany. In the excellent schools of his native land Fred Hauke received his youthful education, and his ambition and self-reliance manifested themselves when he set forth to seek his fortune in America, as previously noted. He has improved both of his farms and gives his attention to diversified agriculture and to the raising of good types of live stock. He is a Republican in his political allegiance, and both he and his wife are active members of the Lutheran church. In 1889 Mr. Hauke returned to Germany, and shortly afterward was there solemnized his mariage to Miss Anna Ripper, who accompanied him on his return to America and who has proved a devoted helpmeet to him as he has advanced toward the goal of prosperity and independence. They have six children—Edward, Arthur, Elmer, Anna, Adelia and Freda.

Fred J. Hayden.—The name of Fred J. Hayden is worthy of a prominent place in the list of men whose true worth has made Fort Wayne and Indiana most clearly entitled to superior recognition. As a man devoted to the public interests he contributed generously of his talents and ability to further the interests of all the people. As a business man his influence tended to raise to a high plane the interests with which he was connected. Fred J. Hayden was born at Coburg, in the province of Ontario, Canada, the son of Rev. William and Jane (Kirsop) Hayden, both natives of England. His parents, ever interested in his advancement, provided the means for excellent educational advantages in his home town, after which he entered Victoria College, where he was graduated as a member of the class of 1864. Two years afterward he was honored by his alma mater with the degree of Master of Arts. Following the period of his graduation, Mr. Hayden's abilities while still a youth were recognized in his connection with the Cobourg and Marmora Railway and Mining Company, as its secretary, which position he held for a number of years. He resigned his connection with this concern in 1874 and came directly to Fort Wayne, which was his residence until the time of his death, thirty-two years later. He early identified himself with the best element of the city in its civic and social life and lost no time in taking the steps to qualify as a citizen of the United States. In 1884 Mr. Hayden was elected as the representative of the people of Allen county in the Indiana house of representatives, and here, for two terms, he served with signal efficiency. In 1888 still higher appreciation and honor was accorded him in his election as state senator to represent the counties of Allen and Whitley. At the latter election he was given an unusually large and flattering majority, and his capabilities for the high office were manifested during the two sessions of his service in the senate. As a member of this body he was active in securing the passage of the Australian election law, in 1889, and of the new tax law, in 1891. These two enactments were considered a splendid advance step in modern legislation. Soon after locating in Fort Wayne Mr. Hayden became connected prominently with the management of the First National bank as a member of its directorate, and he identified himself with the management of a number of large estates in Fort Wayne, a business which he conducted with much credit to himself and profit to his clients. When the matter of holding the World's Columbian Exposition, in 1893, was agitated and when the most dependable and intelligent men of the various states were called upon to take an active part in furthering the great enterprise, Mr. Hayden was among the first to receive recognition. In May, 1891, he was appointed by Governor Hovey as one of the World's Fair Commissioners, and in June of the same year, at the initial session of the commission, he was unanimously elected treasurer of the Board of World's Fair Managers of Indiana, which responsible and exacting office he filled to the entire satisfaction of the commission and the people of his state. It has been very truthfully claimed that it was owing to the careful and conservative management of the funds appropriated for this magnificent enterprise by the state that Indiana was enabled to make such a typical and representative showing and to keep its building open until the close of the exposition period. It is worthy of record in this connection that when all accounts were finally adjusted and all expenses met, Mr. Hayden was enabled to turn back into the state treasury nearly two thousand dollars. The selection of Mr. Hayden, a Democrat, by Governor Hovey, a Republican, to serve in this connection discloses the governor's ability to recognize dependability and public spirit regardless of party affiliations. As a university graduate, together with practical application of the principles learned in the home and in the school, Mr. Hayden was particularly well fitted, by reason of his many sterling qualities of heart and mind, to fittingly fill the varying positions to which he was called. In 1873 was solemnized the marriage of Mr. Hayden to Miss Eliza Hanna, the only daughter of the late Judge Samuel Hanna, for many years recognized as Fort Wayne's foremost citizen, and their home on East Lewis street was the scene of much social activity during the lifetime of Mr. Hayden. His death occurred December 30, 1906, and his passing was widely mourned throughout the state. He was a Mason of high degree, and in the matter of church affiliation it should be stated that he was reared in the Congregational faith, became a member of the Church of England, and when he became a resident of Fort Wayne he became a member of the Presbyterian church, in the advancement of whose interests he gave much of his time and those more material benefits without which any institution prospers but indifferently.

Owen N. Heaton.—Judge Heaton has played a large and benignant role in connection with the civic and material advancement of his native county and is a scion of one of the best known and most honored pioneer families of Allen county, his paternal grandfather, Jesse Heaton, having come from the state of New York to Indiana early in the second decade following the admission of the Hoosier commonwealth to the Union. He became one of the earliest settlers in Dearborn county, where he obtained a tract of government land and continued his residence until 1833, when he came to Allen county and purchased a tract of three hundred and twenty acres of wild land, in what is now Marion township. The major part of this tract was covered with heavy timber, the nearest neighbors were a band of Indians, under Chief Godfrey, and thus the sturdy pioneer was called upon to face the vicissitudes and herculean labors that were involved in initiating the development of a farm from the primitive wilderness. Jesse Heaton did well his part in furthering the social and material development of the county; here he and his wife passed the residue of their lives, and the names of both merit enduring place on the roll of the sterling pioneers of the county. Judge Heaton of this review has long been numbered among the representative members of the Allen county bar. His activities have not been confined to service as a lawyer and jurist but have also touched definitely the civic, political and business phases of the county's history, involving special prominence in connection with the affairs of the Republican party in this section of the state. He effected the organization of the Citizens Trust Company of Fort Wayne, of which he is now the president, and his has been a dominating influence in developing the same into one of the most important financial and fiduciary institutions of northern Indiana. Judge Heaton was born on the old homestead farm of his father, in Marion township, this county, and the date of his nativity was September 2, 1860. He is a son of Jesse and Samantha C. (Larkin) Heaton, and his father was long known and honored as one of the most substantial and progressive exponents of agricultural and live-stock industry in the county, as well as a liberal and public-spirited citizen who was specially influential in the furtherance of the cause of the Republican party, in the establishing of good schools and in supporting all measures and enterprises legitimately advanced for the general good of the community. He was the owner of one of the well improved and valuable landed estates of Allen county and during the later years of his active life gave his attention principally to the raising of live stock of superior type. He was a man of indefatigable industry, of broad mental ken and of that sterling character that ever comr s objective confidence and approbation. He was affiliated with the Masonic fraternity for many years and served as master of the lodge of Ancient Free & Accepted Masons in the village of Poe. He was a member of the Methodist Episcopal church and his memory is revered by all who came within the sphere of his kindly influence. Mr. Heaton passed from the stage of life's mortal endeavors in 1889, and his widow resides in Fort Wayne, being now in her eighty-fifth year. Concerning their children the following brief data are available: Freeman died in childhood; Charles E. was engaged in the successful practice of his profession at Fort Wayne and was a skilled physician and surgeon of prominence at the time of his death; Margaret D. is a resident of Fort Wayne; Judge Heaton of this review was the next in order of birth; Elmer and Etta are deceased; Mary is the wife of Homer B. Smitley, of Fort Wayne; Ellis J. is a successful contractor and builder in Fort Wayne; Luella May resides in Fort Wayne; Benjamin F. is one of the prominent members of the Allen county bar and is associated in practice with his brother, Owen N., immediate subject of this sketch; and Pearl is the wife of George Allen, of Fort Wayne. Judge Heaton found the period of his childhood and youth compassed by the invigorating influences and discipline of the home farm and while attending the public schools continued to assist in the work of the farm during the summer vacations. In 1884 he completed a course in Fort Wayne College, and then began, with characteristic energy and ambition, the study of law, under effective private preceptorship. He made rapid and assured advancement in the assimilation of the science of jurisprudence and, in 1886, was admitted to the bar as one eligible for practice in the various courts of Indiana, including the federal tribunals in the state. He forthwith engaged in active general practice in Fort Wayne, and his powers as a resourceful and versatile trial lawyer have been put to many an important test through his association with many leading causes brought into litigation in the various courts, including the supreme court of the state. He continued to give his close attention to his large and representative law practice until he was elected to the bench of the superior court of Allen county, on which he served from 1902 to 1910—the longest tenure of office that the history of the county records in connection with an incumbent elected on the Republican ticket. The admirable record of Judge Heaton on the bench has become an integral part of the judicial history of the county. Upon retiring from the superior bench Judge Heaton was made the Republican candidate for representative of this district in the United States congress, and though he was unable to overcome the large and normal Democratic majority he was defeated by a small margin of votes. In 1899 Judge Heaton effected the organization of the Citizens' Trust Company of Fort Wayne, which was incorporated with a capital of two hundred thousand dollars, and he served as vice-president and a director until 1910, when he was elected to his present office, that of president. Under his regime as chief executive of this important institution its assets have been increased from five hundred thousand to more than two million dollars, this substantial and consecutive growth designating it as one of the strong and important financial institutions of the state. Giving close attention to his executive duties in this connection, Judge Heaton still continues in the active practice of his profession, with well merited status as one of the strong and influential members of the Indiana bar. He is affiliated with both the York and Scottish Rite bodies of the Masonic fraternity and also with the Knights of Pythias and the Benevolent & Protective Order of Elks. On August 23, 1889, was solemnized the marriage of Judge Heaton to Miss Katherine Russell, daughter of Benton C. and Sarah (Amidon) Russell, of Branch county, Michigan, and the one child of this union is Miss Dorothy Russell Heaton, who was graduated in the Fort Wayne high school and who is, in 1917, a student in Washington College, in the city of Washington, D. C.

Gottlieb H. Heine.—Even the brief data possible of incorporation in this sketch will show conclusively that Mr. Heine has proved himself a young man of assertive initiative and executive ability, and he is consistently to be designated as one of the progressive and valued young business men of his native city. He is now president of the Meyer Brothers Company, which conducts a chain of six well equipped retail drug stores, four of which are in the city of Fort Wayne, one at Anderson, and one at Kokomo, so that the company is one of the prominent and representative concerns in this line of business enterprise in the state. Mr. Heine has become influential also in other fields of business, being treasurer of the Meridian Amusement Company at Anderson and vice-president and treasurer of the company of the same title at Danville, Illinois, both operating moving-picture establishments of the best grade. Mr. Heine was born in Fort Wayne, January 10, 1878, and is a son of Fred W. and Augusta (Stoppenhagen) Heine, the former of whom was born in Germany and the latter in Adams county, Indiana. The father was for many years a resident of Fort Wayne, where he was long employed as a skilled car-builder in the shops of the Pennsylvania Railroad, and here his death occurred, his widow being still a resident of Fort Wayne. Gottlieb H. Heine was afforded the advantages of the parochial schools of the Lutheran church in Fort Wayne and here supplemented this discipline by a higher course of study in Concordia College. His initial business experience was of clerical order and, in 1897, he became stenographer and assistant bookkeeper in the retail drug establishment of Meyer Brothers & Company, of which position he continued the incumbent three years. He then became a principal in effecting the reorganization and expansion of the business, under the present title of the Meyer Brothers Company, of which he became treasurer and general manager. His resourcefulness and energy resulted in bringing to bear most progressive policies in the conducting of the business and, about 1910, he became president of the company, of which office he has since continued in tenure, this company now having a chain of six retail stores, as has previously been noted in this article. Mr. Heine is essentially and emphatically a business man and, though he takes loyal interest in public affairs, especially those pertaining to his native city, he has never had any predilection for public office and is independent in his political proclivities. He was reared in the faith of the Lutheran church, of which he is a communicant, and is a member of the Fort Wayne Commercial Club and the Quest Club. In 1901 was solemnized the marriage of Mr. Heine to Miss Etta Littleton, daughter of Charles J. and Maria (Babbitt) Littleton, of Sandusky, Ohio, both of whom are now deceased. Mr. and Mrs. Heine have two sons—Harold and Elwood.

Anthony W. Heit has been identified closely with the industrial and commercial interests of Fort Wayne during practically his entire active career and is now one of the interested principals in the Heit-Miller-Lau Company, which here controls a large and important industrial enterprise in the manufacturing of high grade confectionery and specialties. Through his own initiative and constructive ability Mr. Heit has gained secure vantage-ground as one of the representative business men of his native city and for many years has also been quietly influential in civic affairs. Mr. Heit was born in Fort Wayne May 23, 1860, and is a son of Anthony and Josephine (Most) Heit, both of whom were born in Germany. Anthony W. Heit acquired his rudimentary education in the public schools of Fort Wayne but he early became largely dependent upon his own resources, as he was but eleven years old at the time of his father's death. Thus his broader education has been that gained under the preceptorship of that wisest of all head-masters, experience, and well has he profited by this discipline. When a lad of fifteen years he became identified with the candy-manufacturing business in the city of Toledo, Ohio, and with the exception of an interval of three years has been concerned with this line of business enterprise during the long intervening period. The interval mentioned, from 1878 to 1881, found him employed in the Fort Wayne office of the Empire Fast Freight Line, and upon severing this association, May 1, 1881, he took a position as traveling salesman for the firm of Trentman & Fox, manufacturing confectioners and cracker bakers. With this firm and its successors he continued his alliance until September 1, 1902, when he became associated in the purchase of the confectionery department and incidental good will of the Fort Wayne branch of the National Biscuit Company, and the enterprise has since been successfully conducted under the title of the Heit-Miller-Lau Company. Mr. Heit continued "on the road" as traveling salesman for the new company until 1907, when he came to the house headquarters, where he has since held the position of manager. In the well equipped factory the company gives employment to a force varying from sixty-five to one hundred and twenty-five persons, and efficient salesmen are retained in representing the house throughout its trade territory—in Indiana, Ohio and Michigan. In addition to his connection with this important commercial enterprise Mr. Heit is a stockholder and director of the First and Hamilton National Bank of Fort Wayne. Taking a lively interest in all that concerns the welfare and advancement of his native city and also in public affairs in general, Mr. Heit has designated himself an independent Republican in politics, but he has had no ambition for political activity or public office. He is a valued member of the Fort Wayne Commercial Club, holds membership also in the Country Club and the Quest Club, and in the Masonic fraternity has received the thirty-second degree of the Ancient Accepted Scottish Rite. On October 8, 1886, was recorded the marriage of Mr. Heit to Miss Nellie Roelle, who likewise was born and reared in Fort Wayne and who is a daughter of Frank and Caroline (Stake) Roelle, both now deceased. Mr. and Mrs. Heit became the parents of two children—Edna, who is the wife of Herbert W. Fee, of Fort Wayne, and Howard J., who died at the age of twenty-two months.

James Heliotes is one of the substantial and progressive business men of Fort Wayne, where he has developed a large and prosperous business as a manufacturer of and dealer in high-grade confectionery. His well equipped factory is situated at 1314 Calhoun street and is designated as the Columbia Candy Factory, and at 1002 Calhoun street is located his attractive retail establishment, known as the Columbia Candy Kitchen. Mr. Heliotes was born in Greece, November 20, 1881, a son of John and Lena (George) Heliotes. He was a lad of about twelve years when he immigrated to the United States, in 1894, and joined an uncle who was successfully established as a candy manufacturer in the city of Chicago. In the western metropolis Mr. Heliotes remained seventeen years, and in this interval gained a thorough knowledge of all details of candy manufacturing, in the establishment of his uncle. In 1912 he came to Fort Wayne and purchased his present retail confectionery store, shortly afterward establishing his modern factory, through which he supplies an extensive wholesale trade as well as his own retail store, his annual business having now attained to an average aggregate of about thirty thousand dollars and its scope and importance being such as to mark him as one of the progressive young business men of the Allen county metropolis, where he has gained secure place in popular confidence and esteem. Further evidence of his success is that given in his being financially interested in other prosperous mercantile enterprises, not only in Fort Wayne but also in the states of Ohio and Illinois. Mr. Heliotes is a Republican in his political adherency, he and his wife are active communicants of the Orthodox Greek Catholic church and he is affiliated with the Benevolent & Protective Order of Elks, the Knights of Pythias, and the Loyal Order of Moose. His further business alliances in Fort Wayne include a half interest in each the Summit City Restaurant and the Metropolitan Lunch Room. The maiden name of the wife of Mr. Heliotes was Amanda Lambrakes, and she likewise is a native of Greece, in which historic land both received their early education. They have three children—George, John and Angelus.

John C. Heller is an able and influential exponent of a line of business enterprise that has most important bearing upon the general prosperity and progress of Allen county, as he is president of the Allen County Abstract Company, the excellent records of which conserve most perfectly the surety and legitimacy of all real estate transactions in this favored section of the Hoosier state. John Conrad Heller was born at Port Mitchell, Indiana, on January 23, 1861, and is a son of Thomas S. and Carrie M. (Nill) Heller, the former of whom was born in Pennsylvania, of German ancestry, and the latter in Allen county, Indiana, where her parents settled in the pioneer days and where she is now one of the venerable native daughters of the county, her home being in the city of Fort Wayne. Thomas S. Heller came to Indiana from Bushkill, Pike county, Pennsylvania, and he was long known and honored as one of the representative and influential citizens of Allen county, where he continued his residence until his death, when sixty-one years of age. Here was solemnized his marriage to Miss Carrie M. Nill, and of their six children the subject of this review is the first born; George M. is deceased; Flora remains with her widowed and venerable mother at the pleasant home in Fort Wayne; William likewise resides in this city; Ada is the widow of Charles J. Bulger and now resides with her mother and older sister; and Louise is the wife of Edwin J. Lindman, of Fort Wayne. John C. Heller acquired his early education in the public schools of Monroeville, this county, and there also served his novitiate in connection with practical business affairs as an assistant in the general merchandise store conducted by his father. He finally assumed entire charge of the store, and when his father was elected county recorder and the family removed to Fort Wayne, the judicial center of the county, he assumed the position of deputy recorder. In this connection he gained ample and valuable experience in regard to real estate in Allen county, and when about twenty-three years of age he became associated with the abstract business, with which he has since continued to be identified and as a representative of which he is now president of the Allen County Abstract Company, as previously noted. The records of the company are recognized as authoritative in regard to all realty in the county, and they greatly facilitate all real estate transactions besides making the incidental titles clear and unassailable. Mr. Heller, both as a business man and as a loyal and public-spirited citizen, is well upholding a family name that has long been honored in Allen county. His political allegiance is given to the Democratic party, he and his wife are communicants of the English Lutheran church, and in the time-honored Masonic fraternity he has received the thirty-second degree of the Ancient Accepted Scottish Rite, besides being affiliated with the Ancient Arabic Order of the Nobles of the Mystic Shrine, Mizpah Temple, and the Knights of Pythias. On May 20, 1885, was solemnized the marriage of Mr. Heller to Miss Hattie V. Shell, a daughter of the late Franklin V. V. Shell, who was a representative member of the bar of Allen county, he having been originally engaged in the practice of law at Monroeville and having later established himself in practice at Fort Wayne, where his death occurred. Mr. and Mrs. Heller have one son, Eugene L., who was born June 22, 1900, and who is now a member of the class of 1918 in the Fort Wayne high school.

Edward A. Helmcke, who is treasurer of the Wayne Knitting Mills and who has contributed much to the permanent development of the great industrial enterprise of which adequate description has been given on other pages, was born in the principality of Lübeck, Germany, on March 9, 1862, and is a son of Wilhelm Helmcke. In his native land he received excellent educational advantages, including those of the Katharineum Gymnasium, and as a youth entered upon an apprenticeship in a mercantile establishment in his home city. After one year of service in the German army he went, in 1884, to Venezuela, South America, under a three years' contract for service as clerk for Mestern & Company, at Puerto Cabello. At the expiration of this period he came to the United States and established his residence in the city of St. Paul, Minnesota, where for the ensuing ten years he held the position of cashier in the large fur establishment of Gordon & Ferguson. He then went to New York city, where for eighteen months he held a responsible position with a prominent commission firm doing business with Mexico, and in June, 1898, he came to Fort Wayne and entered the employ of the Wayne Knitting Mills, in a clerical capacity. His ability as an executive and aggressive business man led to his becoming one of the stockholders of the corporation, and of the same he has served as treasurer since 1902. He is identified with the Fort Wayne Commercial Club, the Fort Wayne Country Club, and also with the Lincoln Yacht Club in the city of Chicago. Mr. Helmcke is significantly loyal to his home city and takes lively interest in all things pertaining to its welfare and advancement. He is one of the popular business men of Fort Wayne and is one of the strong and vigorous executives who have aided in the upbuilding of one of the city's greatest industrial and commercial enterprises. Mr. Helmcke's name is enrolled on the list of eligible bachelors in Fort Wayne.

Henry Dietrich Helmke came to America as a lad of sixteen years. He was born in Germany on November 12, 1860, son of Henry and Margarette (Hohnemann) Helmke, both native Germans, where they were all their lives identified with farm life. They had a family of ten children, named Mary, Minnie, Henry, Fred, Henry D., Herman, Anna, William, George and an infant who died unnamed. Henry D. Helmke had some education in his home land, and when he was sixteen he embarked for New York alone, intent upon seeking what prosperity he might find in a new world. Arriving in New York he soon after set out for Henry county, Ohio, where he remained until 1903, a period of twenty-seven years, when he came to Allen county and located on a farm in Maumee township. He bought 130 acres in Section 34, and with characteristic diligence applied himself to the task of reclaiming that wilderness tract and making a productive and habitable place of it. The success of his undertaking is everywhere apparent today, and the improvements he has effected are well in keeping with the best standards set by modern agriculturists of this section of the state. Mr. Helmke was married November 27, 1884, to Miss Katie Schroder. She died October 15, 1885, leaving a daughter, Katie. On September 3, 1886, Mr. Helmke was married to Miss Minnie Rohrs, daughter of Henry and Mary Rohrs, both native Germans who came to America in 1859, following their marriage. They settled in Defiance county, Ohio, and there spent the rest of their lives. The father was born on October 30, 1824, and died on February 10, 1901, and the mother, who was born February 19, 1834, died on August 20, 1903. They had ten children, named Fred, Henry, Minnie, Herman, William, Anna, Mary, Sophia, George and Katy. To Mr. and Mrs. Helmke were born nine children. They are Nora, Mary, Anna, Dorothea, Ernest, Henry, Frank, Otto, Martin and Hellen. Dorothea died when she was three and a half years old, but the others are living at this time. Mr. Helmke and his wife and children are members of the German Lutheran church and he is a Democrat in politics. He has been active in local government and has served his township ably for four years as a member of the Maumee township advisory board. His influence in the community has always been for the best good of the greatest number and he has done his full share in the development and advancement of Maumee township since he came to be a resident in it.

James A. Henderson, who resides on his well improved farm of eighty acres, in Springfield township, is now one of the venerable citizens of the county that has been his home since he was a lad of about ten years and which he represented as a gallant soldier of the Union in the Civil war. A sterling citizen who has made his life count for good in all its relations, he is well known and commands unqualified esteem in Allen county, and is specially entitled to definite recognition in this history of the county. Mr. Henderson was born in Mahoning county, Ohio, July 8, 1841, a son of John and Elizabeth (Zimmerman) Henderson, both natives of Pennsylvania. In 1851 John Henderson came with his family from Ohio to Allen county and here made settlement in Milan township, where he reclaimed and improved a good farm and he and his wife passed the remainder of their lives, both having been well advanced in years at the time of their death and having been honored pioneer citizens of this favored section of the Hoosier state. Of their family of children, the first died in infancy, as did also the second child. Of those now living the subject of this review is the eldest, he having been seventh in order of birth, and the other surviving members of the once numerous family are Hattie, John and David. The names of those deceased are as here noted: Josiah, Mary, George, Sarah, and Joseph. James A. Henderson gained his rudimentary scholastic discipline in his native county and, as before stated, was ten years old at the time of the family removal to Allen county, where he further prosecuted his studies in the pioneer rural schools of Milan township. He assisted in the work of the home farm until he initiated his independent career in the same line of industrial enterprise. He had not yet celebrated his twentieth birthday anniversary when the Civil war was precipitated on the nation, and such was his youthful patriotism and loyalty that he responded to President Lincoln's call for volunteers. In October, 1861, he enlisted as a private in Company E, Thirtieth Indiana Infantry, with which he proceeded to the front and with which he lived up to the full tension of the great internecine conflict. He participated in many engagements, including a number of the important battles marking the progress of the war, his command having been assigned to the Army of the Cumberland. He was with his regiment in the great Atlanta campaign and with General Sherman in his subsequent and ever memorable march from Atlanta to the sea. He was mustered out at Indianapolis, in October, 1864, and received his honorable discharge, after having been in active service for three years and eleven days. In later years he has vitalized the more gracious memories and associations of his military career by his affiliation with that noble organization, the Grand Army of the Republic, and his record as a soldier of the Union shall ever reflect honor upon his name. After the close of the war Mr. Henderson returned to Allen county, and for ten years thereafter was engaged in the saw mill and lumbering business. Prior to identifying himself with this enterprise he had continued his association with agricultural industry. In 1880 Mr. Henderson traded his saw mill for eighty acres of land in Springfield township, and this tract constitutes his present homestead farm. He reclaimed to cultivation the greater part of the land that had not previously been thus improved, and also made many other substantial improvements, especially in the erection of substantial farm buildings and in providing those accessories that mark the energetic and progressive agriculturist and stock-grower. He still takes a lively interest in the varied activities of the home farm, but the general control and management of the same is now given over to his younger son. He has been a loyal citizen in the "piping times of peace," even as he was when he went forth to aid in the preservation of the nation's integrity, and both he and his wife are zealous members of the Lutheran church, his political support being given to the Democratic party. On June 8, 1871, was solemnized the marriage of Mr. Henderson to Miss Mary J. Richards, who was born in Pennsylvania, as were also her parents, Solomon and Matilda (McIntyre) Richards, who came from the old Keystone state to Allen county, in 1862, and settled on a farm in Milan township, where they passed the residue of their lives. They became the parents of eight children, namely: Lucinda, John, Mary J., Smith, Alfred, Allen (deceased), Matilda (deceased), and Ella. Mr. and Mrs. Henderson have two children: Earl M. is engaged in the drug business in the city of Indianapolis, and Burt W. has the active management of the home farm.

William D. Henderson is a native son of Fort Wayne who is especially entitled to recognition in this history, for he is not only a scion of old and honored pioneer families of Allen county but has also achieved distinctive priority as one of the leading business men and influential citizens of Fort Wayne. Here his capitalistic interests are of varied and important order, here his civic loyalty has been manifested in his effective service in municipal offices, and here he has long and successfully conducted a substantial hay, grain and seed business. His paternal grandfather, Zenas Henderson, was one of the sterling pioneers of Allen county, and the same is true concerning his distinguished maternal grandfather, the late Colonel Louis Humbert, who was born and reared in France and who served as an officer in the army of the great Napoleon, with whose forces he participated in the historic battle of Waterloo. He established his home in Fort Wayne when the present city was a mere village, and here he passed the residue of his life, a citizen of fine character and much ability. At one time he owned and conducted a hotel known as the Spencer House, on Calhoun street opposite the court house. One of Colonel Humbert's sons served as a gallant soldier of the Union in the Civil war, as did also one of the paternal uncles of him whose name introduces this review. Within a block distant from his present business establishment William D. Henderson was born, March 26, 1859, and he is a son of William D. and Angeline (Humbert) Henderson, of whose six children only one other is living—Mrs. Kittie (Henderson) Long, who is the widow of Mason Long and who remains in Fort Wayne. Mrs. Angeline (Humbert) Henderson, who was born July 19, 1833, has been a resident of Fort Wayne from her early youth and such is her gentle and gracious personality that she is held in affectionate regard by all who have come within the compass of her benign influence. William D. Henderson, Sr., was born at Fort Wayne and was a young man of about thirty-six years at the time of his death, in 1866. He received his education in the pioneer schools of Allen county, where his parents remained until their death, and he had become one of the representative merchants of Fort Wayne, where he was engaged in the grocery business, on Columbia street, at the time of his demise. To the public schools of Fort Wayne William D. Henderson of this review is indebted for his early educational discipline, and he was a lad of about seven years at the time of his father's death. After leaving school he entered the local shops of the Pennsylvania Railroad, where he learned the tinner's and coppersmith's trades, to which he continued to give his attention until he was twenty-three years of age. He then, on February 7, 1882, established in a modest way his present hay, grain and seed business, which under his able and progressive management has been expanded to large proportions and constitutes one of the important mercantile enterprises of his native city. It is worthy of mention that he founded the business with a capital of only one hundred and seventeen dollars, and that on the original site he still conducts the enterprise in a substantial and modern building which is owned by him and which is a three-story structure, forty by one hundred and ten feet in dimensions, in the very center of the business district of the city. In addition to controlling this extensive and prosperous business Mr. Henderson is a director of the Citizens' Trust Company, is a member of the executive board of the Fort Wayne Oil & Supply Company, and is a stockholder of the First National Bank of Fort Wayne. Zealous and loyal in promoting and supporting measures and enterprises tending to advance the civic and material prosperity of his home city and county and taking a lively interest in municipal affairs, Mr. Henderson is aligned as a well fortified advocate of the cause of the Democratic party and has been influential in its local councils. He has represented the first ward as a member of the city council and has also served effectively as a member of the municipal board of public safety. He is an active and valued member of the Fort Wayne Commercial Club and is affiliated with the Knights of Pythias. On October 9, 1888, was solemnized the marriage of Mr. Henderson to Miss Emma Neuenschwander, who was born at what was then Newville, but now Vera Cruz, Wells county, this state, and who is a daughter of the late Isaac and Caroline (Liebmann) Neuenschwander. Mr. and Mrs. Henderson have two children—Irma Ruth and Josephine.

Gustav F. Hilgeman, who is one of the representative contractors and builders of his native city of Fort Wayne, where he was born September 6, 1869, learned the carpenter's trade under the effective direction of his father, who is now one of the venerable and honored citizens of the Allen county metropolis, and prior to engaging in the contracting business in an independent way the subject of this review had served about eight years as an efficient and popular member of the Fort Wayne fire department. Mr. Hilgeman is a son of Jacob William and Bernardine (Peters) Hilgeman, both of whom were born in Germany and the latter of whom was summoned to the life eternal when seventy-three years of age. Jacob W. Hilgeman was reared and educated in his native land and came to America about the year 1855. He has been for many years a well known and substantial citizen of Fort Wayne, where he is now living retired, after a specially successful career as one of the leading contractors and builders in this city. This venerable citizen celebrated his eighty-second birthday anniversary in 1916. He is steadfast in his allegiance to the Republican party and is a zealous member of the German Reformed church, as was also his devoted wife. Of the children, the first born, Caroline, is deceased; Henry still resides in Fort Wayne; Gustav F., of this review, was the next in order of birth; Louisa is the wife of John Stocks, of this city. Gustav F. Hilgeman gained his early education in the public schools of his native city and in the meanwhile, as a lad of thirteen years, he initiated his practical apprenticeship to the trade of carpenter, under the punctilious and careful direction of his father. He continued his association with the work of his trade until 1894, when he became a member of the city fire department, his efficient services with which continued until 1902, when he resigned his position and became associated with his brother Henry in contracting and building. They erected many high-class private residences, a number of school buildings and business structures and were contractors in the erection of the fine Anthony Hotel at Fort Wayne, this being one of the most modern hotel buildings in this section of the state. The brothers finally dissolved partnership and Gustav F. has since continued in control of a substantial and representative contracting and building business in an independent way. He is a staunch advocate of the cause of the Republican party, is loyal and progressive as a citizen, and is a member of the German Reformed church, his wife being a communicant of St. Paul's Lutheran church. On February 28, 1906, was solemnized the marriage of Mr. Hilgeman to Miss Mary Kolb, who was born and reared in Fort Wayne, a daughter of John A. and Mary B. (Knees) Kolb, the former of whom was born in the Kingdom of Bavaria, Germany, and the latter in Fort Wayne, where her parents settled many years ago. Mr. and Mrs. Kolb still reside in Fort Wayne, where he is living retired, and here he was in the employ of the Pennsylvania Railroad Company until 1912, when he severed his alliance on account of advanced age, he having been a resident of Fort Wayne since 1853. His wife died in 1881. Of the three children Mrs. Hilgeman is the eldest and prior to her marriage she had been for ten years an efficient and popular saleswoman in the well known Frank dry goods establishment of Fort Wayne; Edward H. still resides in this city and is traveling salesman for the Eckart Packing House; and Della is the wife of Harry Starke. Mr. and Mrs. Hilgeman have no children.

Harry H. Hilgemann is one of the successful lawyers of Fort Wayne and Allen county. He took his place in his chosen profession in 1903 and for two years conducted an independent practice. In 1905 he associated himself in a co-partnership with Clyde M. Gandy, well known in and about Fort Wayne, and this partnership continued until December 1, 1908. Mr. Hilgemann is the son of Henry F. and Lisette (Bueker) Hilgemann, and was born on August 19, 1881, in Fort Wayne. His mother was of German birth, born in Teklenberg, Germany, on April 2, 1852. Henry F. Hilgemann, his father, was born in Fort Wayne, Indiana, on January 30, 1851. For years he conducted a grocery and meat market on West Jefferson street in his home city, and he was a public-spirited citizen all his life. He served in the city council from 1888 to 1890, and built up a creditable record as a public servant in that brief period. He died January 7, 1904, and his wife is still living and makes her home with her son, the subject of this review. Harry H. Hilgemann had his elementary schooling in the public schools of his native city and was graduated from the high school in 1900. In the same year he entered the law department of the University of Michigan and was graduated in 1903 with the degree of L. L. B. Returning to his home he read law for a few months in the office of Zollars & Zollars, well known attorneys of Fort Wayne, and then became associated with the late Judge Robert Lowry. In him Mr. Hilgemann found a most admirable preceptor. He was the associate of the Judge at the time of his admission to the bar of Indiana, in 1903, and continued so until the death of that gentleman, in 1904. He is now engaged in the practice of his profession, with offices at Rooms 604-5-6-7-8, Peoples Trust Building. Mr. Hilgemann has had a very creditable public record thus far. He served as deputy prosecuting attorney from 1908 to 1912, and so well did he manage the duties of his office that he was elected to the post of prosecuting attorney, serving from 1912 to 1916. As prosecutor and deputy he has prosecuted and assisted in the prosecution of fifteen homicide cases, in every one of which a conviction was secured. Special mention might fittingly be made of his activities in the investigation and successful prosecution of a so-called arson trust, which had a nation-wide activity. He was also instrumental in breaking up the traffic in habit-forming drugs and was a leader in bringing about stricter laws governing the use and sale of such drugs. Under his administration of the office a rigid enforcement of laws relating to wife-desertion and child-neglect was brought about, and he gave his attention successfully to the making of better laws governing those phases of existence. All considered his eight years as deputy and prosecutor were big with worthy activity in the discharge of his duty and his administration was conceded by all to have been a most successful one. In the spring of 1916 Mr. Hilgemann was a candidate for the Democratic nomination for Congress against the then incumbent, but was defeated at the primaries by the narrow margin of 219 votes in the six counties of his district. Mr. Hilgemann is a prominent Mason, with affiliations in the A. F. & A. M., Fort Wayne Consistory, Mizpah Temple, Ancient Arabic Order, Nobles of the Mystic Shrine. He is also a member of the Elks, the Loyal Order of Moose, and of the St. Joe Athletic Club. On July 24, 1909, Mr. Hilgemann was married to Miss Minnie E. Horn, daughter of John L. and Nettie M. (Bain) Horn, of Spencerville, Indiana. They have their home at 1124 Ewing street, in Fort Wayne.

Chester J. Hinton is one of the popular and representative business men of the younger generation in his native city of Fort Wayne, where he conducts a modern coffee store at 1818 Calhoun street, the establishment having the most approved appliances for the roasting, grinding and sale of coffee products, and its exceptionally excellent service has gained for it a substantial and representative patronage, though Mr. Hinton founded the business only a comparatively short time ago—in January, 1916. Chester John Hinton was born in Fort Wayne on August 24, 1893, and is a son of John C. and Anna (Welten) Hinton, both of whom were natives of this city, the respective families having been founded in Allen county many years ago. The mother of Mr. Hinton still resides in Fort Wayne. The father's death occurred December 17, 1916, following an illness of one day. The elder Mr. Hinton was for thirty years successfully established in the restaurant business, though he had previously served as passenger-train conductor for the Pennsylvania Railroad Company. All of their five children still remain in Fort Wayne, with the exception of Lucille A., who resides at Lansing, Michigan, and their names are here indicated in the respective order of their birth: Verna C., Walter H., Chester J., Lucille A., and Eveline I. Chester J. Hinton attended the public schools of Fort Wayne until he had completed a three years' course in the high school, and, in 1911, when eighteen years of age, he assumed the position of bookkeeper in the First National Bank of Fort Wayne. He was assistant teller in this representative financial institution when he resigned his position, in 1913, and went to the city of Chicago, where he applied himself with characteristic energy to learning the various grades of coffee, the roasting of the same and its proper preparation for the retail trade. He is an expert in this line of business and has been specially successful in the conducting of his attractive Fort Wayne store, which he established in January, 1916, as previously noted. He is one of the vigorous young supporters of the cause of the Republican party, takes a vital interest in all things pertaining to the civic and material welfare of his native city and is one of Fort Wayne's popular young bachelors and business men. He holds membership in the Third Presbyterian church.

James C. Hipple began his active business career in association with his father, who was long a prominent builder and contractor in Long Island, New York, where the family resided. When he was twenty-five years old Mr. Hipple left that field and became connected with the Edison laboratory at Menlo Park, New Jersey. Thereafter his rise was rapid, and he was later connected with some of the largest manufacturers of incandescent lamps in America. Mr. Hipple was born in Long Island, New York, on December 14, 1854, son of John and Elizabeth (Thomas) Hipple. John Hipple was of German origin and his wife was born in Wales. Neither is living at this time, and only four of their nine children survive. It was in 1879 that James Hipple left his father's employ and found work in the Edison laboratory at Menlo Park, New Jersey, and he spent his time while there to such good advantage that two years later they sent him to Paris in charge of an exhibition of their product, and he remained there two and a half years, disposing of French rights in the Edison patents. While there he established a plant for the manufacture of Edison lamps. On his return to America he spent a brief vacation period of two months at home and then went to Dresden, Germany, to establish a plant for the company. He was five years in Germany on business for his house, and when he returned he went into the world-famed Edison laboratory at Orange, New Jersey, spending about a year and a half there in research work. Mr. Hipple was next associated with the Hamson Lamp Works for about three years, after which he joined forces with E. G. Acheson in the manufacture of carborundum, a material of which Mr. Hipple was the inventor and which is a substance known to be harder than emery and used as a substitute for that product. They were engaged in this business for about a year at Niagara, and Mr. Hipple left the work to go to Germany for the purpose of protecting valuable patents they owned. He was there about three years, and when he returned to America entered the employ of the General Electric Company at Harrison, New Jersey. The company sent him from there to Toledo, Ohio, to take charge of their factory at that point, and in 1911 he was transferred to Fort Wayne in charge of their interests in this city, which position he was filling at the time of his death, which occurred April 28, 1917. Mr. Hipple was married on July 4, 1881, to Miss Cathrine Caples, of Long Island, New York. One child was born to them —William C. Hipple, whose birth occurred in Paris, France. This son possesses the same tastes and inclinations as his father and is employed by the Westinghouse Lamp Company in New Jersey. He is a capable and ambitious young man, and his accomplishments thus far in his chosen work indicate that he will one day rival his father in the success of his career. Mr. Hipple was a Democrat and a man of sound business principles. During their residence in Fort Wayne Mr. Hipple and his wife made a host of frineds.

David F. Hiser.—Success has attended the well-directed efforts of David F. Hiser, who has passed his life thus far within the confines of Allen county. He was born in Pleasant township November 12, 1860, and is the son of George W. and Barbara (Hare) Hiser, who were of German birth and parentage, and who came to America with their respective families in young life and were thereafter identified with the industrial life of Pleasant township, where they settled on farm land. George Hiser early acquired land and continually added to it during the years of his active life as a farmer. He also interested himself in town property in Poe, where he lives retired today at the age of eighty-four years. He has been a Democrat since becoming a voter and is a life-long member of the German Lutheran church, in which he reared his children. They were seven in number, and David F. is the eldest. The others are Mary Ann, the wife of Frank Hickour, living on the old home place; William, of Fort Wayne; Margaret, married to Gustave Felps, of Martin's Ferry, Ohio; Ezra, of Poe, Indiana; John, living near Columbia City, and Allie, who lives with her aged father in Poe. David F. Hiser attended the public schools of his native community as a boy and shared his time between his studies and the duties that fell to his lot on the home farm, where, as the eldest of the children, he had a greater responsibility than the average youth of his day. When he was twenty-seven years old he left the home farm and launched out for himself as a renter. After seven years he bought a farm of eight acres and achieved independence with that purchase. He has since added two purchases of forty and one hundred and twenty acres, so that he has a comfortably large place for the exercise of his industry. Mr. Hiser is one of the successful men of his community and is interested in a financial way in the Hoagland State Bank. He was married on November 8, 1887, to Miss Julia C. Reehling, daughter of Jacob and Margaret (Sherer) Reehling, German people, both now deceased. They lived for years in Pleasant township and were among the most highly esteemed people of their community. Mr. Reehling, commonly known as Squire Reehling, was prominent in local politics as a member of the Democratic party and was a person of some importance in his township. The children of Mr. and Mrs. Hiser are Maud, married to Clement Smith, and Lauretta, who is the wife of Frank Harkless. Mrs. Smith has a son, named Brice, and Lauretta is the mother of two little daughters—Viola and Julia Frances. Mr. Hiser is at the present writing (1917) engaged in the building of a fine new dwelling house on his farm, which promises to be one of the most attractive homes in the community. New barns also will be fitting accompaniments to the residence and the standard of the Hiser place, always well to the front, will be considerably augmented by these improvements.

William H Hiser.—In fifty-five years of continuous residence in Allen county the Hiser family has come to be identified permanently with its agricultural record and has found a place for itself well worthy of the labors the various members of the family have expended in the development of those communities with which they have been connected. William H. Hiser was born in Montgomery county, Ohio, on October 1, 1852, and is a son of Christopher and Susan (Troxel)) Hiser. The father, as a boy in his native county, had practically no advantages, and whatever he accomplished was through his own exertions and energies. He was a distiller by trade, but when he came to Allen county, in 1861, he turned his attention to farming and was thereafter identified with that field of enterprise. He established his family on an eighty-acre farm and there they lived and enjoyed the fruits of their labors, rearing a fine family and bearing their full share of the burdens of community life in that early period. Mr. Hiser was a leader in his township and served for a number of years as supervisor. Ten children were reared in the Hiser home. Lewis is deceased; William H. was the second born; Savilla Ann is deceased; Samuel is a resident of Fort Wayne; Idylla married Robert Ewert, of Lafayette; Joseph W. is located in Indianapolis; John is deceased. The others are Martha Ella, Louisa and Margaret. William H. Hiser was twenty-eight years old when he withdrew from the family circle and turned his attention to the task of carving out a career for himself. He naturally chose farming, for it was in that industry that all his training had been gained. He rented for some years, then bought 116 acres, where he is living at this time. Between the years 1892 and 1894 he was a resident of Fort Wayne, but returned in the latter year to his farm and there has since carried on diversified farming with all of success. His farm is one of the best developed in the community and its comfortable dwelling and spacious barns reflect the progressive spirit of the owner. Mr. Hiser is a Democrat in politics and is at present a member of the township advisory board. He has always evinced a wholesome interest in the civic affairs of his community and shirks no public duty that comes his way. He was married on November 18, 1880, to Miss Elizabeth Scherer, daughter of Jacob and Mary Scherer, who were of German ancestry and who are now deceased. Mrs. Hiser is one of the most estimable and dependable women in the

E V Hoffman

village and with her husband shares the confidence and esteem of a wide circle of friends and acquaintances. They have no children.

Edward G. Hoffman.—Whether the activities of Edward G. Hoffman are studied with special reference to his service as a member of the Democratic national central committee, as an attorney, as a business man or as a loyal citizen, there comes such revelation of the salient points of his character as to indicate that he is always found amply fortified to discharge his assigned duties with thoroughness and competency. No man in Fort Wayne has more fully measured up to the true standard of modern citizenship. Fourteen years ago Mr. Hoffman was graduated in the law department of the University of Michigan. He engaged at once in practice at Fort Wayne, as a member of the firm of Ballou & Hoffman, and this professional alliance continued until February, 1914, when he withdrew and became a member of the representative law firm of Barrett, Morris & Hoffman. Mr. Hoffman was born in Springfield township, Allen county, Indiana, October 1, 1878, and is a son of George W. and Anna (Stabler) Hoffman. George W. Hoffman was of German birth and ancestry. He came to America as a young man and, in 1851, settled in Allen county, where he became well known in farming and lumbering circles. Here he passed the remainder of his life and was in his sixty-third year at the time of his death, in 1906. By his first marriage he was the father of one son, and his second wife, mother of Edward G. Hoffman of this review, had one son by her first marriage. Dr. Gideon Hoffman, eldest son of the late George W. Hoffman, is successfully engaged in the practice of his profession, and Henry Weicker is the son of Mrs. Hoffman's first marriage, he being a prosperous farmer in Milan township, this county. Of the two children of George W. and Anna (Stabler) Hoffman, Edward G., immediate subject of this sketch, is the elder, and John C. likewise is a representative member of the Allen county bar, engaged in practice in Fort Wayne. The venerable mother now maintains her home at Maysville, this county, her birth having occurred in Canada. Edward G. Hoffman acquired his early education in the schools of Springfield township and the Maysville high school. Thereafter he entered Valparaiso University, in which he was graduated as a member of the class of 1900 and from which he received the degrees of both Bachelor of Science and Bachelor of Arts. In consonance with his ambition and well matured plans he then entered the law department of the University of Michigan, and in this celebrated institution was graduated in 1903, with the degree of Bachelor of Laws. His initial service in the practice of his profession was given in Fort Wayne, where he became a member of the firm of Ballou, Hoffman & Romberg, which became one of best known law firms in the city during the period of his alliance therewith. In February, 1914, as previously noted, Mr. Hoffman withdrew from this firm and entered into partnership with two other able and well known attorneys of Fort Wayne, under the firm name of Barrett, Morris & Hoffman. This firm has its offices in the Shoaff building and controls a general law business, though to a certain extent special attention is given to corporation law, in which branch of practice Mr. Hoffman has won not a little distinction. Mr. Hoffman is secretary and treasurer of the Deister Machine Company, is secretary and treasurer of the Fort Wayne Journal-Gazette Company, and is a director of the Tri-State Loan & Trust Company. He has shown himself to be an efficient business man as well as a skilled lawyer, and his record amply disproves the common belief that a man can not achieve success in both business and professional life. Mr. Hoffman is a thirty-third degree Mason and is affiliated also with the Elks, the Moose and the Knights of Pythias. He is a member of the Fort Wayne Commercial Club, the Quest Club, the Fort Wayne Country Club, the University Club of Fort Wayne, and the Indiana Society of Chicago. He also retains affiliation with the Sigma Nu college fraternity. A prominent and influential representative of the Democratic party, Mr. Hoffman is now a member of the Democratic national committee, in which position he succeeded Hon. Thomas Taggart, ex-United States senator from Indiana. On May 7, 1912, Mr. Hoffman wedded Miss Emily R. Hoffman, a daughter of William Henry and Maizie (Evans) Hoffman, both of whom are now deceased. Mrs. Hoffman has the distinction of being a niece of Admiral Reynolds, of the United States Navy, and of the General Reynolds who lost his life while in command of his regiment in the battle of Gettysburg, he having been one of the gallant officers of the Union in the Civil war. Mr. and Mrs. Hoffman have one daughter, Anne Katharine, who was born December 26, 1914, and one son, Edward G. Hoffman, Jr., born August 30, 1916. Mr. and Mrs. Hoffman are members of the Presbyterian church and he is a member of the board of trustees of the church with which they maintain affiliation. Mrs. Hoffman was born and reared in Fort Wayne and has a wide circle of friends in and about the city, while her husband has won to himself the confidence and esteem of an ever increasing number in the years of his establishment here.

G. Max Hofmann is one of the representative business men of Fort Wayne and in the land of his adoption has found opportunity so to use his technical and executive powers as to gain prestige as one of the men of industry in the Hoosier state. He is an expert in connection with scientific and practical details of the gas industry and business, has given efficient service as general superintendent of the Fort Wayne Gas Company, is president of the Western Engineering & Construction Company, of this city, and also of the National Steel Casting Company, of Montpelier, Blackford county, Indiana. A man of superabundant energy and progressiveness, he has shown great capacity for the developing and upbuilding of enterprises of broad scope and importance, but the manifold exactions placed upon him in these connections have not in the least curbed his genial and buoyant nature, so that he has been appreciative of the fine amenities of social life and has gained a host of friends. Mr. Hofmann was born in Dresden, Germany, on November 4, 1857, and is a son of C. A. and Juliane Henrietta Hofmann. In his fatherland he was afforded the best educational advantages, including those of one of the leading colleges in the city of Dresden, and he developed fully his scientific and mechanical talents by acquiring a thorough education as mining engineer. In 1883 Mr. Hofmann came to the United States and soon after his arrival established his residence in Fort Wayne. Later he entered the service of the extensive Bass foundry, at Fort Wayne, which institution he represented for a time in its iron-ore fields in Alabama, in his professional capacity of mining engineer. With the inception and initial development of the natural gas resources in the field about Pittsburgh, he went into that Pennsylvania field as an expert. Later he returned to Indiana and became associated as chief engineer with the Consumers' Gas Company, of Indianapolis. After remaining thus engaged in the Indiana capital city for a period of three years he returned to Fort Wayne, in 1889, and assumed the position of superintendent and technical expert for the Fort Wayne Gas Company, with which corporation he continued his active alliance for a period of twenty years: He has been a prominent figure in the development of the natural gas resources of Indiana and other states and has been concerned also in other important public utility enterprises, including the telephone business. In the latter connection it should be noted that he is a director of the companies that control the independent telephone lines in Fort Wayne and its vicinity and a director of the Old National Bank, a director of the Marion and Bluffton Traction Company, is president of the Fort Wayne Testing Laboratory Company, and president of the Fort Wayne Freie Presse Co., besides being president of the Western Engineering & Construction Company and the National Steel Casting Company, as previously noted in this context. Entering fully into the spirit of American institutions and systems, Mr. Hofmann has aligned himself as a stalwart advocate of the principles of the Republican party. In the time-honored Masonic fraternity he has received the thirty-second degree of the Ancient Accepted Scottish Rite and those of the Ancient Arabic Order, Nobles of the Mystic Shrine, besides which he is actively affiliated wth the Benevolent and Protective Order of Elks and Royal Arcanum. On August 28, 1880, was solemnized the marriage of Mr. Hofmann with Miss Bertha Schulze, of Dresden, Germany, and to this union seven children were born, of whom two survive, as follows: Lothar Hofmann, who was born in Germany, December 22, 1881, and graduated from the University of Wisconsin in the chemical engineering course. He also studied six years in various parts of Europe and is now a resident of Florida; Roland Paul Hofmann was born April 12, 1890, in Fort Wayne. He is a graduate from the DePauw university and attended the Universities of Michigan and Wisconsin. He now owns and operates a large fruit and dairy farm in Orange county, Indiana. The wife of Roland Paul Hofmann was formerly Miss Frances Zabel, of Omaha, Nebraska. G. Max Hofmann, of late years, spends his winter in Florida, where he owns a beautiful home in Palm Beach, besides which he has various financial interests in that state.

William Hoffman was born December 24, 1886, on the farm he now owns and occupies. He is a son of Henry and Henrietta (Herdengan) Hoffman, of German birth, who came to America in 1868, locating in Allen county. A little later on, when they had prospered to some extent, they bought a farm of 159 acres in Madison township, which represents the family home at this writing. The mother died in 1903, but the father still lives and makes his home with his son. They reared there a family of nine children, all living. William alone elected to remain on the home place, and when he had finished his schooling in the common schools of Allen county he turned his attention to farming in real earnest. Not long after he had reached his majority he bought the old homestead and has since continued successfully in his work. Mr. Hoffman specializes somewhat in cattle and makes a practice of buying and feeding cattle for the market. Progressive methods have characterized his work and he is counted among the most progressive and up-to-date farmers in the county today. Mr. Hoffman is a Democrat. At the present writing he is unmarried.

Francis M. Hogan in this history is consistently accorded recognition as one of the representative younger members of the bar of his native city of Fort Wayne. In the general practice of law he has built up a substantial practice, the constantly cumulative tendency of which vouches for his technical ability and personal popularity. He whose name initiates this paragraph was born in Fort Wayne on August 3, 1888, and is a son of Hugh T. and Mary Elizabeth (Fitzgibbon) Hogan, the former a native of Ireland and the latter of the state of Ohio. Hugh T. Hogan was a boy at the time of the family immigration from the fair Emerald Isle to America and the home was established in the city of Rochester, New York, in which state he was reared to adult age. Mr. Hogan served in his youth a thorough apprenticeship and became a skilled mechanic. He came to Fort Wayne about the year 1870 and has long been a valued and popular employe in the local shops of the Pennsylvania railroad, where he is now a general foreman and master mechanic. He has retained the fullest measure of popular esteem in the city that has long been his home and the stage of his earnest endeavors, he is a Republican in his political adherency and he served at one time as a member of the board of trustees of the municipal waterworks system of Fort Wayne. He is one of the zealous communicants of the Cathedral parish of the Catholic church, as was also his devoted wife, whose death occurred several years ago. Of the children, John and Robert died in infancy; Hugh P. is general foreman in the Baltimore & Ohio Railroad shops in the city of Cincinnati; Margaret is the wife of Gustave Stieglitz, of Bedford, Indiana; Harry G. is a member of the law firm of Colerick & Hogan; Genevieve is deceased; and Francis M., of this review, is the youngest of the number. Francis M. Hogan gained his early education in the schools of the Fort Wayne Cathedral parish of the Catholic church, his discipline including also a high school course, and as a youth he served an apprenticeship as a machinist in the Pennsylvania Railroad shops. He followed his trade a comparatively brief interval and later was identified for a short time with the insurance business. His experience has also included effective service as a newspaper reporter, both in Fort Wayne and in the city of Valparaiso, where he simultaneously was a student in Valparaiso University. After he had formulated definite plans for his future career he entered the law department of the great Notre Dame University at South Bend, Indiana, and in this institution he was graduated as a member of the class of 1914, his admission to the bar of his native state having been virtually concomitant with his reception of the degree of Bachelor of Laws. He forthwith returned to Fort Wayne, where he has since been individually engaged actively in the legal profession and also has been associated in successful practice with his brother Harry G. Hogan and Guy Colerick, and they have gained enviable place as able trial lawyers and well equipped counselors, as indicated in the extent and representative character of their clientele. Mr. Hogan is a stalwart and enthusiastic advocate of the principles of the Republican party, holds membership in the Fort Wayne Commercial Club, the Friars' Club, the University Club and the One Hundred Per Cent. Club, and is affiliated with the Knights of Columbus and the Royal League and Ancient Order of Hibernians. He is an active communicant and loyal supporter of the Cathedral parish of the Catholic church in his native city and is one of Allen county's popular young bachelors.

Harry G. Hogan, member of the vigorous and successful law firm of Colerick & Hogan, has proved in his achievement that he made a wise choice of vocation and has definite vantage ground as one of the prominent younger members of the Fort Wayne bar. Mr. Hogan is duly proud to claim Fort Wayne as the place of his nativity, his birth having here occurred May 4, 1881. He is a son of Hugh T. and Mary Elizabeth (Fitzgibbon) Hogan, the former of whom has long been a valued employe and executive in the local shops of the Pennsylvania Railroad, where he was general foreman, his wife having passed to eternal rest when about fifty-eight years of age, and both having become earnest communicants of Fort Wayne Cathedral parish of the Catholic church many years ago, Mrs. Hogan having been born in Ohio, and Hugh T. Hogan being a native of the Emerald Isle, whence his parents came to America when he was a boy. He was reared and educated in the city of Rochester, New York, where also he learned the trade of machinist, and about the year 1870 established his residence in Fort Wayne, where he has since continued in the employ of the Pennsylvania Railroad Company, being now one of the veterans in the service of this great corporation. He is a loyal citizen who has taken lively interest in community affairs, is a Republican in politics and served at one time as a trustee of the city waterworks. Of the children in this well known family John and Robert died in infancy; Hugh P. is general foreman in the Baltimore & Ohio Railroad shops in the city of Cincinnati; Margaret is the wife of Gustave Stieglitz, of Bedford, Indiana; Harry G., of this sketch was the next in order of birth; Genevieve is deceased; and Francis M. is individually mentioned on other pages of this work. To the Catholic parochial schools of his native city Harry G. Hogan is indebted for his early educational discipline, and thereafter he was employed for a time in the drafting rooms of the Fort Wayne plant of the Western Electric Works. His ambition, however, lay along different lines and was essentially one of action, so that he finally entered the law department of Notre Dame University, at South Bend, in which he was graduated as a member of the class of 1904, his reception of the degree of Bachelor of Laws having been practically concomitant with his admission to the bar. His initial experience in the practical work of his profession was gained through his assocation with the Fort Wayne law firm of Harper & Eggemann. After practicing a few years, in 1910 he formed a partnership with Guy Colerick, under the firm name of Colerick & Hogan. From 1910 to 1913 he served as city attorney. The firm controls a very successful practice of general order. Mr. Hogan has been an active worker in behalf of the principles of the Republican party, and in addition to having served as secretary of the county committee of the party in 1906 he was chairman of the speaking bureau of the Republican contingent in the city campaign of 1905. In 1908 he was made chairman of the Republican county committee, and in this connection he showed much finesse in maneuvering the political forces at his command. In 1909 he was vice-chairman of the city committee of the party and in 1916 was again able to render efficient service through his incumbency of the position of chairman of the Republican executive committee of the Twelfth congressional district. Mr. Hogan is a loyal and active member of the Fort Wayne Commercial Club, holds membership in the Fort Wayne Country Club, as does he also in the influential Columbia Club in the city of Indianapolis; he is a communicant of Cathedral parish of the Catholic church and is affiliated with the Ancient Order of Hibernians, the Benevolent and Protective Order of Elks, the Knights of Columbus, the Loyal Order of Moose, and the Royal League. On November 28, 1916, was solemnized the marriage of Mr. Hogan to Miss Virginia S. Olds, daughter of William and Margaret E. (Simonson) Olds, well known citizens of Fort Wayne.

David H. Hogg is a man of excellent intellectual and professional attainments and the same energy and determined purpose that led him to provide largely the means that enabled him to acquire his higher literary and technical education have been potent in securing to him strong vantage ground as one of the representative members of the Fort Wayne bar. He has been established in the practice of his profession in Fort Wayne since June, 1913, and is now the junior member of the law firm of Macbeth & Hogg, which controls a substantial and well ordered law business. Mr. Hogg was born in Jackson county, Indiana, and is a son of Nelson and Nancy Hogg, his father having been a farmer by vocation and having served as a valiant soldier of the Union in the Civil war. That Mr. Hogg was early imbued with ambition and capacity for assimilative study is shown in the fact that he was graduated from high school when but fifteen years of age. As previously intimated, he depended largely upon his own resources in acquiring his higher education, and in 1909 was graduated in the University of Indiana with the degree of Bachelor of Arts. In 1912 he received from the law department of the same institution the degree of Bachelor of Laws, and in the meanwhile he had taught history and Latin in high school to aid in defraying his collegiate expenses. In June, 1913, Mr. Hogg opened a law office in Fort Wayne, and his diligence and ability combined with his sterling character to gain to him a supporting patronage that made his professional novitiate one of comparatively brief duration. On January 1, 1916, Mr. Hogg and Jesse Macbeth formed a partnership for the practice of law under the firm name of Macbeth & Hogg. He has subbordinated all else to the work of his profession and thus has not sought political preferment, though he accords staunch allegiance to the Republican party. He is a valued and appreciative member of the Allen County Bar Association, is affiliated with the Masonic fraternity, the Knights of Pythias and the Independent Order of Odd Fellows, and is a member of the First Baptist church, of Fort Wayne. In the Sunday School of that church he is teacher of the Men's Bible class, which has been developed under his leadership until it is the largest of the kind in Fort Wayne, and which has totaled one hundred and sixty members at the time of this writing, in the spring of 1917. Mr. Hogg and his mother reside on West Jefferson street and he delivers numerous addresses in this section of Indiana.

Hogue, G. A., (See Blue Cast).

J. F. Hollopeter has been established in the hardware and implement business since 1911, and has enjoyed a very gratifying success in that enterprise in the past five years. He has been a resident of Allen county practically all his life and has been identified with various other lines of activity, but in his present venture he seems to have become permanently established. Mr. Hollopeter was born in Cedarville, Allen county, Indiana, June 17, 1880, son of Mathias and Mary E. (Stevick) Hollopeter, both of Pennsylvania birth. The father came to Allen county as a young man and was engaged in lumbering and farming for years. He died in 1898, but the mother still lives and has her home at Leo, Indiana. Six children were born to these worthy people, here briefly named as follows: Milton is a resident of Jennings county, Indiana; Bert is located in Fort Wayne; J. F., of this review, was the third child; Lester is located in business in Fort Wayne; Mabel is the wife of Clyde McEwen, of Leo; and Lois is married to William Snyder, of Huntertown, Indiana. Both parents had children by a former marriage. The two children of the father's early marriage, Charles and Allie, are deceased. There were four children of the mother's first marriage—Morton, George, Ole and Homer. The two eldest are residents of Leo and the two younger ones are deceased. When he was seventeen years old young Hollopeter identified himself with farm life and was active in that work until 1900, when he moved to Muncie, Indiana, and there was connected with a planing mill in a mechanical capacity for three years. In 1904 he went to Fort Wayne and was in the employ of the electric street railway company there for about four years, going from that place to Dewitt, Arkansas, where he was for five years manager of the local telephone company. In 1911 he returned to his native state and county, locating in Grabill, where he opened an establishment devoted to the sale of hardware and farm implements. His very gratifying success at this work has already been noted in a previous paragraph. In addition to his activities as a merchant Mr. Hollopeter runs a hotel at Grabill with much success. In 1900 Mr. Hollopeter married Miss Daisy May Hill, and they have two children —Helen and Stanley. A Democrat in politics, Mr. Hollopeter finds time to devote to the party interests in his community, and his influence in his home town has been a helpful and progressive power. He has served as justice of the peace in Cedar Creek township for the past six years. He is a member of the Modern Woodmen, but has no other fraternal affiliations.

Rev. George H. Horstman, pastor of St. Andrew's Catholic church, was born at Fort Wayne, November 15, 1872. From the seventh to the fourteenth year of his age he attended St. Mary's parochial school. In 1888 he began his classical studies in St. Lawrence's College, Mount Calvary, Wisconsin. In 1892 he was sent to Mount St. Mary's Seminary, Cincinnati, for the study of philosophy and theology, and was ordained priest by Bishop Rademacher at Fort Wayne, June 24, 1897. His appointments were: Assistant at St. Mary's church, Michigan city, till August, 1900; pastor of Reynolds and its missions from August, 1900, to July, 1905; pastor at Remington from July 4, 1905, until July 6, 1910, when he came to Fort Wayne as pastor of the newly organized St. Andrew's Catholic church, in which charge he has continued up to the present time.

Victor A. Huguenard.—The late Victor A. Huguenard was born at Crourchaton Departement de-la-Haute-Saone, France, as the name very strongly suggests, and he died March 5, 1915, when he was in the seventy-sixth year of his life. He was a son of Peter Claude and Frances (Boley) Huguenard, and was about twelve years of age when he accompanied his parents from France to the United States. The family came to Allen county, Indiana, and settled on a farm near Fort Wayne, where the subject of this memoir gained in his youth practical experience in farm work, under the direction of his father. When he reached years of responsibility he launched out into farming on his own account and succeeded admirably in his independent operations as an exponent of agricultural industry. In 1886 he removed to the city of Fort Wayne and here opened a feed barn, the same having been conducted by him for several years and up to the time of his retirement from active business. April 9, 1894, Mr. Huguenard wedded Miss Eugenia Masson, and her death occurred July 1, 1898, the only child of this union being Joseph Victor, who was born February 26, 1897. On October 17, 1900, was solemnized the marriage of Mr. Huguenard to Miss Mary Jane Leonard, of Fort Wayne, and she still maintains her home in this city. Mrs. Huguenard is a daughter of William and Hanora (Carroll) Leonard. William Leonard, who was a gunsmith by trade, came to Fort Wayne in

1853 and as a skilled artisan became a pioneer exponent of his trade in Allen county, both he and his wife having passed the remainder of their lives in Fort Wayne. No children were born of the second marriage of Mr. Huguenard. He was a splendid type of the loyal American citizen and his influence as a man and as a citizen was helpful and uplifting in the community. He had a host of staunch friends in and about Allen county and his passing was mourned by all who knew him.

Elwin M. Hulse, one of the younger members of the Fort Wayne legal fraternity, was twenty-five years old when he was admitted to the bar, in 1900, and he has been engaged in active practice here down to the present time (1917). He was fortunate in becoming the associate of his uncle, Judge R. S. Taylor, when he was ready to identify himself with his profession as a practitioner, and this firm has gained a considerable prominence in the patent field, their activities being devoted largely to that phase of legal practice. Born January 1, 1875, in Fort Wayne, Elwin M. Hulse is the son of William L. and Sophia (Taylor) Hulse. The father was born in New Jersey on November 4, 1835, and the mother in Cincinnati, Ohio, July 25, 1845. Mr. Hulse came to Fort Wayne as early as 1857 and was engaged in that city for the remainder of his life as a mechanic, barring only a period of four years which he spent in service during the Civil war. He enlisted in the Fifth Indiana Battery during the first months of the war and was active in the service until peace was declared. He participated in many of the most hotly contested battles of the war and was with Sherman on his March to the Sea. Mr. Hulse died in Fort Wayne in 1905 and his widow survives him. They were the parents of three children. Luretta, the first born, is the wife of William H. Crighton. William S. was the second child and Elwin M. of this review is the third and youngest. Young Hulse attended the public schools of Fort Wayne and when he had finished his high school training entered Purdue University, following that period of study with a law course in the University of Michigan at Ann Arbor. His subsequent activities down to date have been touched upon in a preceding paragraph. It is sufficient to say here that his professional career thus far has been attended by a pleasing measure of success, and it is generally conceded by his associates that he has not yet reached the summit of his achievements. Mr. Hulse is prominent as a member of the Masonic order, in which he is well advanced, and he is a member of the Rotary and Commercial Clubs. He was married November 26, 1902, to Miss Grace Harding, daughter of Daniel L. and Mary (Fleming) Harding. Both were born in Ireland. Mr. Harding died in 1912, but Mrs. Harding still lives and has her home in Fort Wayne, where their daughter, Mrs. Hulse, was born and reared. Two sons have been born to Mr. and Mrs. Hulse—Stewart H. and Edward L.—both students in the local schools. Mr. and Mrs. Hulse are members of the First Presbyterian church of Fort Wayne and have an active part in the work of that body. They are Republicans in their political faith.

Rev. Chrysostom Hummer, pastor of the Church of the Most Precious Blood, in Fort Wayne, was born March 9, 1866, at Luxemburg, Stearns county, Minnesota. He pursued his studies at St. Charles Seminary, Carthagena, Ohio, and was ordained priest by the Most Rev. W. H. Elder, D. D., June 21, 1893. He taught one year at St. Joseph's Indian and Normal School. From June, 1894, to Sepetmber, 1896, he was pastor of St. Michael's church, at Kalida, Ohio, and from 1896 to January, 1903, was professor at St. Joseph's College, Collegeville, Indiana, from which position he was transferred to his present charge, the pastorate of the Church of the Most Precious Blood, at Fort Wayne.

Fred S. Hunting.—A more likeable man than Fred Stanley Hunting or one more worthy of real friends is not enrolled among the citizenship of Fort Wayne. A type of man whose success is due entirely to his own strength of character and tireless energy, he has won an enviable place in the commercial life of Fort Wayne and a recognized position of honor in the higher circles of manufacturing and electrical engineering in America. A brief review of his life should prove an inspiration to him who feels handicapped by the lack of financial means to "land" in a desirable place in the modern scheme of things. Mr. Hunting was born in East Templeton, Worcester county, Massachusetts, September 30, 1867, the son of William and Martha D. Hunting, both natives of the old Bay state and descendants of English stock. It is worthy of note that conditions rendered it necessary that the son spend his vacation period and the Saturdays, which are usually passed in play, in working beside his father in one of the chair factories which have given that section of Massachusetts a name as a chair-manufacturing center of importance. Today Mr. Hunting looks back upon those preparatory years as a character-forming and habit-building period in which he learned the value of a dollar and the true worth of time. He adheres firmly to the belief that the years from twelve to twenty are virtually important in the laying of the foundation of a life of active worth. From factory conditions he learned much that in later years has aided him to understand clearly the problems of the thousands of men employed in the Fort Wayne works of the General Electric Company, of which he is the general manager, and to deal with these problems in a just and intelligent manner. In the course of time, after his graduation in the Templeton high school, Mr. Hunting entered the Worcester Polytechnic Institute at Worcester, Massachusetts, an institution founded by John Boynton, a resident of Templeton, and there he developed his latent talent along the lines of engineering and applied electricity. So well did he apply himself at the institute that upon graduating, in 1888, with the degree of Bachelor of Science, he was awarded, on account of scholarship, one of the six seventy-five dollar prizes from the graduate-aid fund. Small as the amount may seem to the man of today, it was a godsend to the youth of 1888, and it is probable that the granting of the award gave to Fort Wayne one of its most aggressive men, for it provided the necessary means whereby he was able to accept a position in a city far distant from his native locality, when the opportunity came. Fortunately, he found a waiting position in the drafting department of the Fort Wayne "Jenney" Electric Light Company, which has since developed into one of the plants of the General Electric Company. Mr. Hunting came to Fort Wayne in October, 1888. In 1890 he was given the place of assistant to M. M. M. Slattery, then chief electrician of the works. Two years later he was advanced by appointment to the position of assistant to C. S. Bradley, who was then experimenting with multiphase apparatus. In the following year Mr. Hunting was elevated to the position of chief engineer of the engineering department of the Fort Wayne Electric Company, and he continued the incumbent of the same when the institution became the Fort Wayne Electrical Corporation. In January, 1899, he was made vice-president and sales manager of the corporation. In May of the same year, when the business was reorganized, he assumed the important duties of treasurer and sales manager of the Fort Wayne Electric Works. During these years, through Mr. Hunting's keen knowledge of men and of the times, as well as his thorough acquaintanceship with the productive phase of the electrical business, the high-class products of the Fort Wayne works were distributed to all parts of the United States and the name of Fort Wayne became synonymous with the finest grade of electrical machinery and apparatus. When the plant was made a part of the great General Electric Company's properties Mr. Hunting became the general manager of the Fort Wayne works, which are now by far the largest manufacturing industry in Fort Wayne. Mr. Hunting is a thirty-second degree Mason, a member of the Fort Wayne Country Club, of the Fort Wayne Commercial Club, and of the Fortnightly Club. In politics he is a Republican. He is an active member of the Plymouth Congregational church. In banking circles his abilities are recognized in his membership on the board of directors of the First National Bank and of the Tri-State Loan & Trust Company. Mr. Hunting's position among the leading manufacturing and electrical men of the country is suggested by his membership in the Electrical Manufacturers' Club of New York, his connection as a Fellow of the American Institute of Electrical Engineers, which maintains its headquarters in New York city and of which he served as a vice-president in 1914 and 1915, and by his being a member of the board of governors of the Electric Power Club, a national association of electrical manufacturers. He is also a member of the Mohawk Club of Schenectady, New York, in which city is maintained the main office of the General Electric Company. Mr. Hunting has been twice married. A few months after coming to Fort Wayne he returned to the east and wedded Miss Harriet Alzina Sawyer, of East Templeton, Massachusetts. Three children were born of this union—Ralph W., of Los Angeles, California; Lawrence S., of the same city, and Harold Stanley, of Fort Wayne. Mrs. Hunting passed away on June 26, 1904. On June 10, 1907, was solemnized the marriage of Mr. Hunting to Miss Elma Pearl Balthis, of Chicago, and the one child of this union is a son, William Fred. The family home is on Washington boulevard west, corner of Nelson street.

George W. Husted was one of the native sons of Allen county who gave to the world assurance of strong and worthy manhood and who marked the passing years with productive energy. As a citizen he held to the things that are good and true and though he never sought the great white light of publicity and was content to pursue the even tenor of his way with a high sense of personal stewardship, he represented the best in the communal life, instinctively exemplified the Golden Rule and gained and retained the confidence and esteem of his fellow men. He was one of the representative farmers of Maumee township for many years prior to his death, which occurred January 26, 1907, and his character and accomplishment were such as to make specially consistent the memorial tribute here paid to him. He was a representative of one of the old and honored families of Allen county and was born on a farm in Maumee township, January 4, 1862, the eldest in a family of ten children, namely: George W., James M., Solomon L., William, Charles L., Frank L., Grosvenor, Frederick A., Alvin R. (deceased) and Dora Margaret. The parents, Louis B. and Margaret Jane (Swisher) Husted, were both natives of the state of New York and became early settlers in Allen county, Indiana, where the father reclaimed and improved one of the productive farms of Maumee township, and there both passed the residue of their lives, their religious faith having been that of the Lutheran church. The subject of this memoir found the period of his childhood and youth compassed by the invigorating and benignant influences of the home farm, so that he early learned the lessons of practical industry and gained an enduring appreciation of the dignity of honest toil and endeavor, the while he did not fail to make good use of the advantages of the public schools of the locality and period. He gave his entire active life to agricultural pursuits and was one of the substantial farmers and influential citizens of his native township at the time of his death, his energy and ability having enabled him to accumulate a fine farm of 150 acres and his progressiveness having been manifested in both the agricultural and live-stock departments of the farm enterprise. Though he had no ambition for public office he was at all times ready to lend his co-operation in support of measures and enterprises projected for the general good of the community, was a Republican in politics and served four years as assessor of Maumee township. The old homestead farm is still in the possession of his widow and children and is under the active management of his younger son. Mr. Husted was a communicant and earnest supporter of the Lutheran church, as is also his widow, and his life was thoroughly in harmony with the Christian faith which he thus held. On October 10, 1883, was solemnized the marriage of Mr. Husted to Miss Pamelia Horner, who likewise was born and reared in Maumee township, the date of her nativity having been February 14, 1864. Mrs. Husted is a daughter of James and Sarah Ellen (Mackey) Horner, and the other two children are Sabina E. and William E. The father was a native of Pennsylvania, whence he went to Kentucky, in which state his marriage was solemnized. Upon coming to Allen county, more than half a century ago, he settled in Maumee township, where he became a prosperous exponent of agricultural industry, both he and his wife having passed the remainder of their lives on their old homestead firm. Mr. Horner's first wife died prior to his removal to Kentucky, and of this union were born seven children, of whom only three are living—Missouri Ann, Dorcas J., and Viola Bella. The sixth child died in infancy and the others who are now deceased were Darias E., Frances and Artemas. Of the four children of Mr. and Mrs. Husted the eldest is Alva G., who is now a resident of Cleveland, Ohio; Donald has charge of the old home farm; and Vada Pearl and Bessie Opal remain with their widowed mother, who now has an attractive home in the village of Woodburn and whose circle of friends in her native county is limited only by that of her acquaintances.

Clifford J. Hutchinson.—Efficiency and progressiveness have marked the regime of Mr. Hutchinson in the important office of manager of the advertising department of the Perfection Biscuit Company, of Fort Wayne, and he has shown much versatility and initiative in his chosen field of activity. He was born in Fort Wayne on March 8, 1890, and is a son of Frank and Blanche (Hood) Hutchinson, his paternal ancestors having come to America from London, England, about 1810, and having settled in Pennsylvania, and the maternal ancestors having likewise come from England in an early day. George Hood, maternal grandfather of Mr. Hutchinson, established his home on a pioneer farm in Allen county, Indiana, about the year 1850, and it was his to represent this county as a valiant soldier in the Civil war. The paternal grandfather likewise came to Allen county in the early '50s, and he became a prosperous farmer as well as a successful buyer and shipper of grain and live stock. Frank Hutchinson was reared and educated in Allen county, and for the past forty years has conducted in Fort Wayne a successful business as a contractor in interior decoration of houses. He whose name introduces this article was afforded the advantages of the admirable public schools of Fort Wayne, including the high school, and he perfected through his own application and varied experience his ability as an expert accountant, it having been his to give close study to the business or profession during his association with several important business institutions. For seven years he effectively handled the affairs of the cost-accounting department of the Perfection Biscuit Company, and he was then, in 1916, promoted to his present responsible position, that of manager of the company's advertising department. He is one of the alert and popular young business men of his native city, is a Republican in his political allegiance, is affiliated with both the York and Scottish Rite divisions of the Masonic fraternity, and holds membership in the first Baptist church of Fort Wayne. He is president of the Associated Christian Workers, composed of all of the young people's societies of the Protestant churches of Fort Wayne, and he is also an active worker in the local Young Men's Christian Association, is a member of the executive committee of the Men's Christian League, is treasurer of the Fort Wayne Sunday School Association, is scout master for Troop 7 of the Indiana Boy Scouts, and is one of the two delegates from Indiana to the Northern Baptist Convention. These statements show conclusively the enthusiasm and earnest zeal of Mr. Hutchinson in connection with religious service and his high civic and social ideals are shown in his general attitude as one of the loyal and progressive young men of Allen county, his circle of friends being coincident with that of his acquaintances.

Max Irmscher.—More than thirty years ago a German youth of seventeen years left his native land, came to the United States and established his home in Fort Wayne. In Germany he had served an apprenticeship to the trade of blacksmith and thus, equipped with energy, ambition and resolute purpose, as well as with sterling character and a thorough knowledge of his trade, he found little difficulty in obtaining employment in the city of his adoption. That young man was Max Irmscher, whose ability and progressiveness have enabled him to make for himself secure vantage ground as one of the representative contractors and builders of the metropolis of Allen county, and in this important domain of constructive enterprise he has shown as great facility as he manifested in the earlier work of his original trade. Mr. Irmscher was born in Saxony, Germany, and is a son of Gottfried and Augusta Irmscher, his father having been a farmer by vocation and having passed his entire life in Germany, where the venerable wife and mother still lives. Of the children the eldest is Emma, who remains in the German fatherland and is the wife of Carl Kretchmer; Anton came to the United States and was a resident of Fort Wayne at the time of his death; Ida is the wife of Professor Fred Graffe, of Leipsic, Germany; Alma is the wife of Robert Wolf and they reside in Germany; Max, of this review, was the next in order of birth; Gustav is deceased; and Hulda and Arthur remain at the old home in Germany. Max Irmscher acquired his early education in the excellent schools of his native land and was but fourteen years old when he left the parental home and entered upon an apprenticeship to the blacksmith's trade. Within the ensuing period of about two and one-half years he had become a skillful workman, and soon afterward, in 1883, he severed the home ties and set forth to seek his fortunes in America, where he felt assured of better opportunities for winning independence and prosperity through his own efforts. Soon after his arrival in the port of New York city he came to Fort Wayne, and after here following his trade about six months began acquiring the trade of brickmason. In this line of work he soon became skilled and finally engaged in contracting in an independent way, in the construction of brick buildings and in other general mason contracting. He became also one of the organizers of the Fort Wayne Brick & Tile Company, but this incidental enterprise did not reach successful issue until he became associated with others in buying the stock and establishing the business on a firm foundation. The original corporate name is retained and Mr. Irmscher is vice-president of the company, which now controls a substantial business in the manufacturing of brick and tile. He gives the major part of his time and attention to general contracting and building, and in this section of the state are to be found many fine structures that have been erected by him, among them being the Jefferson school, the Harmar school and the Concordia and Third Presbyterian churches, all in Fort Wayne. He assisted in the erection also of the Rudisill school, erected the Regal building and, in 1916, completed the contract for the erection of the Freiburger builing, a modern four-story brick and cement structure, sixty by one hundred and fifty feet in lateral dimensions and with deep basement. Fidelity to the terms of all contracts has marked his course at all times and has combined with skilled workmanship and business acumen to gain to him an unassailable reputation and the confidence and good will of all with whom he has had dealings. It is much that he has so worthily achieved within the years of his residence at Fort Wayne, and he has identified himself fully and loyally with the interests of this fine little Indiana city. He owns and occupies a fine two-story brick residence at 2103 Forest Park boulevard, and this attractive home is known for its cordial and unassuming hospitality and good cheer. Mr. Irmscher is independent in political affairs and both he and his wife are earnest communicants of St. Paul's Lutheran church. On December 19, 1889, Mr. Irmscher wedded Miss Sophia Heger, who was born and reared in Fort Wayne; and they have seven children—George, Arthur, Max, Jr., Hilda, Malinda, Martha and Sophia. Arthur is a graduate of Purdue University and the other children also have received excellent educational advantages.

George Jacobs was a lad of about sixteen years when he came with his parents from Germany to the United States and the family home was established in the city of Fort Wayne, where he has since continued his residence and where he has been prominent in musical circles, both as a talented musician and also as the owner and conductor of a well equipped music store, to the management of which he now gives his attention as one of the leaders in this line of enterprise in the Allen county metropolis. Mr. Jacobs was born in Hohnhousen, Germany, on May 6, 1857, and is a son of George and Hannah (Sauer) Jacobs, who were born and reared in that same section of the great German empire, where the father continued to be identified with the brewing business until 1872, when he came with his family to the United States and established his residence in Fort Wayne. He entered the employ of the Pennsylvania Railroad Company, with the service of which he continued to be identified until his death, which occurred March 10, 1887, his widow passing to the life eternal in 1889, and both having been earnest communicants of the Lutheran church. Of their nine children the eldest is

Andrew, who still resides in Fort Wayne; Mary is the wife of William Bittler, of this city.; Dorothy is deceased; George, Jr., of this review, was the next in order of birth; Barbara is the wife of John Sauertig, of Fort Wayne; Mary resides with her sister Barbara; Carrie is the wife of George Hill, of Fort Wayne; and the next two children were twin sons who died in infancy. He to whom this sketch is dedicated gained his early education in the excellent schools of his native land and was about sixteen years old at the time of the family immigration to America, as previously noted. He furthered his education by attending for a time the public schools of Fort Wayne and in early youth manifested marked musical talent, his love for music having been reinforced by the ambitious purpose that caused him to apply himself and become skilled in orchestral and band interpretations. In earlier years he was a member of leading organizations of this order in Fort Wayne and, since 1890, he has conducted his representative music store on Calhoun street, where he displays the best standard types of pianos and other musical instruments, talking machines, musical merchandise, etc. The excellent and reliable service which this popular music house has given at all times has gained to it a large and appreciative patronage of representative order, and the proprietor has thus gained place as one of the substantial business men of the city that has long been his home and in which his circle of friends is coincident with that of his acquaintances. Though essentially loyal and progressive as a citizen and independent in his political views, Mr. Jacobs has manifested naught of desire for public office of any kind. He and his wife are zealous communicants of St. John's Lutheran church, of whose board of trustees he has been treasurer since 1910. May 6, 1883, recorded the marriage of Mr. Jacobs to Miss Mary Rapp, who was born and reared in Fort Wayne and who is a daughter of the late George Rapp. Of the five children of Mr. and Mrs. Jacobs the eldest is George W., who is associated with his father's music store; Mamie and Edith remain at the parental home, as do also Esther and Helen, the former of whom is a popular teacher in the public schools and the latter is one of the talented young musicians of the city.

William E. James, editor and publisher of the Harlan Herald, has gained prestige as one of the able representatives of the newspaper fraternity in the county that has been his home from the time of his birth, he having been born at Harlan, Springfield township, May 14, 1875, the place having then been known as Maysville. He is a son of George T. and Arretta (Dorsey) James, the former of whom was born in Harford county, Maryland, December 11, 1851, and the latter was born and reared in Scipio township, Allen county, Indiana, a daughter of William and Martha (Tanner) Dorsey, early settlers of that township, Mr. Dorsey having been a native of England and his wife of the state of Ohio. George T. James is a son of William and Mary H. (Lilly) James, both of whom were born and reared in Maryland, where their marriage was solemnized and they continued to reside until 1863, when they came to Indiana and settled in Springfield township, Allen county, their home having been established in the little hamlet of Maysville, from which was evolved the now thriving and attractive village of Harlan. William James was a skilled carpenter and became a successful contractor and builder in Allen county, his entire active life having been marked by his close association with the work of his trade, besides which he was a licensed exhorter or local clergyman of the Methodist Episcopal church and served long and faithfully as an earnest church worker until his death, in 1899. His five children were: George T., Spencer V., Leroy, Lily and Dora. George T. James gained his rudimentary education in his native state and was a lad of about twelve years at the time of the family removal to Allen county, Indiana, where he continued his studies in the village schools of Maysville, or Harlan of the present day. As a youth he here was identified with farm industry for a period of seven years and then established himself in the general merchandise business at Harlan. He built up a prosperous enterprise and conducted a general store for fifteen years, at the expiration of which he eliminated the dry-goods department. He has since continued to conduct a prosperous business in the handling of groceries and provisions and is one of the leading merchants and representative citizens of Harlan. He is a Republican in politics, has served as a member of the advisory board of Springfield township, is affiliated with the local lodge of the Independent Order of Odd Fellows at Harlan and he and his wife are earnest members of the Methodist Episcopal church. In 1871 was solemnized his marriage to Miss Arretta A. Dorsey, and they have seven children—Ellis E., William E., Bertha, Arta, Edith, Lela and Byron. William E. James is indebted to the public schools of his native village for his early educational discipline and as a lad became a clerk in his father's store, his service in this capacity having continued several years. He then gained a practical knowledge of the "art preservative of all arts" in a local newspaper office, and has since continued his allegiance to journalism, in connection with which he has achieved success and prestige, as he has been editor and publisher of the Harlan Herald since 1912 and has made the paper an effective exponent of local interests as well as a forceful supporter of the principles of the Republican party. Though he is distinctively progressive and public-spirited as a citizen and wields much influence in community affairs he has manifested no ambition for political office of any kind. He is affiliated with the local lodges of the Masonic fraternity and the Independent Order of Odd Fellows, and both he and his wife are communicants of the Lutheran church. On February 22, 1911, was recorded the marriage of Mr. James to Miss Mary L. Ankrim, who was born and reared in Indiana, a daughter of Richard Ankrim, her father having been born in Ohio and now residing near Harlan. Mr. and Mrs. James have a fine little son, Wilton E., who was born September 15, 1912.

Leland F. Johnson is a mechanical engineer and an able executive, as is clearly demonstrated by his present incumbency of the position of manager of the engineering department in the extensive plant of S. F. Bowser & Company, which represents one of the most important industrial concerns in the city of Fort Wayne. Mr. Johnson has been long and successfully identified with practical engineering work and is one of the progressive men and loyal and public-spirited citizens of the metropolis of Allen county, with secure place in popular confidence and good will. Mr. Johnson was born at Ossian, Wells county, this state, on November 20, 1876, and is a son of Benjamin F. and Mary Catherine (Fox) Johnson, who now maintain their home at Crawfordsville, Indiana, where the father is serving in the office of township trustee at the time of this writing, in the early part of the year 1917. Professor Benjamin F. Johnson is a man of high intellectual attainments and virtually his entire career has been marked by his close and effective identification with the pedagogic profession. He has made an admirable reputation as a teacher in the public schools of Indiana and also as a member of the faculties of higher institutions of learning, with secure vantage-place as one of the representative figures in Indiana educational circles. Of the three children the subject of this sketch was the second in order of birth, and the other two, Louise Martha and Edward M., still remain at the parental home. As may readily be inferred, Leland F. Johnson was reared under the benignant influences of a home of distinctive culture and refinement, and he continued his studies in the public schools until his graduation in the high school. He then entered Purdue University, at Lafayette, and in this institution was graduated as a member of the class of 1898, with the degree of Bachelor of Science in Mechanical Engineering. After leaving college Mr. Johnson held the position of assistant foreman in the machine shops of the Pennsylvania Railroad Company for two years, and thereafter continued his services with this great corporation in the capacity of round-house foreman in turn at Cleveland, Wellsville and Alliance, Ohio. Thereafter he held the post of assistant master mechanic of the company's shops at Allegheny, Pennsylvania, and later as master mechanic at Toledo, Ohio. In 1907 he entered the employ of the S. F. Bowser Company, of Fort Wayne, with which important concern he has since remained and in the extensive plant of which he is now manager of the engineering department. He is a Republican in his political proclivities and both he and his wife hold membership in the Baptist church. On October 17, 1907, was solemnized the marriage of Mr. Johnson to Miss Eva Cherrell Bowser, daughter of Sylvanus F. Bowser, the influential Fort Wayne captain of industry and one of whom individual mention is made on other pages of this work. Mr. and Mrs. Johnson have two children—Leland Fox, Jr., and Robert Bowser.

Benjamin F. Jones is actively associated with the painting and decorating business established and conducted in the city of Fort Wayne by his brother, Oliver S., of whom individual mention is made on other pages of this work, and he himself is likewise entitled to recognition in this history of his native city and county. Mr. Jones was born in Fort Wayne on September 21, 1871, a son of John and Ada (Taylor) Jones, both of whom are now deceased, the father having been somewhat more than forty years of age at the time of his death and the mother having passed to eternal rest more than thirty years ago. John Jones was born in Wales and was a child at the time of the family immigration to America, the home having been established in Fort Wayne when he was about seven years of age. Here he was reared to manhood and became known as a skilled machinist. He was employed in the shops of the Wabash Railroad at Fort Wayne for many years prior to his death and was a man whose sterling integrity gave him secure place in popular esteem. Of the children, Oliver S., with whom the subject of this sketch is now associated in business, is the eldest, and the second, Miss Eva, has presided over the domestic affairs of the family home since the death of her loved mother, Benjamin F., the next in order of birth, being still a bachelor and a member of the home circle at the residence formerly occupied by the parents; Mary is married and resides in the city of Chicago; John L. still resides in Fort Wayne; Charles now lives at Los Angeles, California; and Ada is the wife of Andrew Leeuw, of Fort Wayne. Benjamin F. Jones continued to attend the public schools of Fort Wayne until he was about sixteen years of age, and then, in 1887, found employment in the Fort Wayne Folding Bed Works, on Columbia street, in the finishing department of which manufactory he continued to be employed until 1896. He then assumed a position in the finishing department at the Packard Organ Works, another of the important industrial concerns of Fort Wayne, and this association continued until 1903, when he identified himself with the bridge-building department of the Wabash Railroad. Later he formed his present association with the substantial painting and decorating business that has been developed by his eldest brother, in which connection he finds a desirable field for the exercising of his mechanical and executive ability. His political support is given to the Republican party, he is affiliated with the Junior Order of United American Mechanics, and, like others of the family, he holds membership in the Plymouth Congregational church in his native city.

Fremont L. Jones.—In the personal and family history of Mr. Jones there are to be found many points of special interest as pertaining to the great state of Indiana and also to the city of Fort Wayne. In an individual way he has played a large and benignant part in connection with important business enterprises in Fort Wayne and his entire career has been marked by earnest and worthy endeavor and by the finest type of civic loyalty. He was born at Jonesboro, Grant county, Indiana, on August 10, 1855, and that now thriving little city was platted and founded by his grandfather, Obediah Jones, in whose honor the place was named. David W. Jones, father of the subject of this review, was born at Raleigh, North Carolina, and was a youth at the time of the family immigration to Indiana, where his father became one of the influential pioneers of Grant county. David W. Jones learned the printer's trade and became a prominent figure in the newspaper business in Indiana. In this connection it is specially interesting to record that in his office was printed the first specific history of Fort Wayne. He came to Fort Wayne in 1863 and was the founder of the Fort Wayne Daily Gazette, which he conducted with characteristic ability. He and his wife passed the closing years of their lives in Fort Wayne. Of their eight children five are living and two sons and one daughter maintain their home in Fort Wayne. The maiden name of the gracious and loved wife and mother was Jane Atkinson. Fremont L. Jones was a lad of about eight years at the time of the family removal to Fort Wayne, where he attended the public schools of the period, as well as the old Methodist Episcopal College, which in its day was one of the leading educational institutions in northern Indiana. During vacations he worked in his father's newspaper office and gained a good knowledge of the mysteries of the "art preservative of all arts." He figures in a most significant way as a pioneer in the laundry business in Fort Wayne, where his identification with this important line of enterprise has continued for fully forty years. He served one year as an apprentice in the laundry of Rice & Pierce, at Grand Rapids, Michigan, and upon his return to Fort Wayne formed a partnership with another ambitious young man and established a modest laundry, with limited capitalistic resources. This was the first steam laundry to be placed in operation in Fort Wayne, and during the long intervening years Mr. Jones has kept pace with the general march of growth and progress, with the result that his laundry today is of the best metropolitan order, with improved facilities and with a corps of more than seventy employes. Mr. Jones was one of the organizers of the Lincoln National Life Insurance Company, the home office of which is in Fort Wayne, and he is a member of its directorate at the present time. He has been for more than thirty years a member of the National Laundrymen's Association and has in his possession a photograph of the group of laundrymen who founded the organization, in 1883, he having been one of these organizers. He assisted also in the organization of the Allen County Loan & Savings Association, which became a thriving organization of its day, and the interested principals in which later founded the Citizens' Trust Company, of which Mr. Jones is a director, this company having assumed control of the business of the Allen County Loan & Savings Association. Mr. Jones was likewise one of the organizers of the Tri-State Loan & Trust Company and the Van Arnam Manufacturing Company, of which latter he is still a director. He is a stockholder in the First and Hamilton National Bank, leading financial institution of Fort Wayne, and in manifold other ways he has shown his liberality and public spirit in the development and support of local institutions of important order. He is the executive head of the Troy Dry Cleaning Company, of which he was the founder. In politics Mr. Jones has ever given stalwart allegiance to the Republican party and both he and his wife have long been members of the Wayne Street Methodist Episcopal church in Fort Wayne. In the Masonic fraternity he has received the thirty-second degree of the Ancient Accepted Scottish Rite and has been specially appreciative of the teachings and history of the various York Rite as well as the Scottish Rite bodies, besides maintaining affiliation also with the Mystic Shrine. He is a valued member of the Fort Wayne Commercial Club and the Quest Club. In the year 1879 was solemnized the marriage of Mr. Jones to Miss Gertrude M. Hatch, who was born at Huntertown, this county, and who is a daughter of the late Newman B. and Abigail (Parker) Hatch. In conclusion are given brief data concerning the children of Mr. and Mrs. Jones: Bessie is the wife of Charles F. Thayer, of Charlotte, North Carolina; David V. has charge of the Troy Dry Cleaning Company's business, this concern having been founded by his father, as previously noted; Ralph L. is proprietor of the Fort Wayne Office Towel Supply Company; Walter B. is the superintendent of his father's laundry; Leon B. is in the United States marine corps, and Donald H. is an officer in the United States army.

John G. B. Jones.—The career of Mr. Jones has been a varied and interesting one. An alien by birth, he has proved himself a true American in both spirit and letter, and Fort Wayne today has not a man who exceeds him in the quality of his citizenship. He has in turn identified himself with the various careers of teacher, soldier, business man and lawyer. In the latter field he found himself to be in his proper element and, since 1911, has been engaged in legal practice in Fort Wayne. John G. B. Jones was born in Seacombe, Cheshire, England, on March 5, 1874, a son of John Milner and Mary Sophia (Denison) Jones, both now deceased. The father was born in the year 1832, in Pudsey, Yorkshire, England, and he died at Seacombe, Cheshire, England, November 8, 1888. He never came to America, but soon after his death his widow followed her sons to American shores and died here in 1902. The three living children of these parents are John G. B., of this review; Arthur K., living at Kendallville, Indiana, and Richard B., of Egremont, Cheshire, England. John G. B. Jones as a boy at home in England attended the Wallasey Board School of Seacombe. He finished there in 1890, soon after which he came to America, being then sixteen years of age. He was located in Rome City, Indiana, and began to attend school there soon after his arrival. For six months he attended the common school and the next year entered high school, continuing for two years as a student. He did not graduate, but turned his attention to teaching and for two years was employed in that work. He went to England on a visit when he was about twenty years old, going over in May, 1894, and returning the following September. He then took up teaching again and spent two years more in that profession. He cast his first presidential vote as an American citizen in LaPorte, Indiana, for William Jennings Bryan. By that time he had made up his mind that he wanted to study law and he entered the offices of Lieutenant Governor Mortimer Nye, carrying on his studies diligently for two years. When the Spanish-American war broke out he promptly enlisted for service with the One Hundred and Sixty-first Indiana Volunteers and was in the service until October, 1899, when he was honorably discharged. School-teaching again took the young man's attention and he was engaged in the LaPorte schools one year. In 1900 he returned to Rome City, Indiana, and there engaged in the milk and ice business, in which he continued for four years, enjoying a fair degree of prosperity. He was not satisfied to confine himself to a business career, however, and in 1904 entered the University of Indiana. He was four years in that institution, graduating in 1908, following which he entered the law school of Harvard University and was graduated in 1911. He first practiced law in Gary, Indiana, with R. O. Johnson, now mayor of that thriving and progressive little city, and after one year came to Fort Wayne. From then until now he has carried on a general practice in this city and is rapidly making a name and place for himself in the ranks of his profession. In 1912 he became the local representative for Bradstreet's Commercial Agency and still carries on that work in connection with his general practice. Mr. Jones has specialized in real estate law and is considered an authority in that department. Mr. Jones is the owner of a farm in the vicinity of Rome City and finds both pleasure and profit in the indulgence of his inclinations in that direction. He is a Democrat, a member of the Methodist Episcopal church, and his fraternal relations are with the Masons and the Sons of St. George, an English order of prominence; also Past Commander of the Spanish American War Veterans, and a member of the University Club. While attending the University of Indiana he was treasurer of his class in both his sophomore and senior years and was otherwise prominent in the student body. He was married on Christmas day, 1898, to Mary Lilian Clock, daughter of George W. and Mary J. (Shourds) Clock, both now deceased. They were a Rome City family of prominence, and Mrs. Jones was born and reared there. Martha M. Shourds, an aunt of Mrs. Jones, was a well known and much loved school teacher of Noble county in the seventies, and she was a woman of true Christian character, possessing many noble traits of heart and mind, and her name is well known to many prominent families of this city. Mr. and Mrs. Jones are popular and prominent in the circles they move in and have a host of friends in the city they have come to know as home.

Oliver S. Jones has gained definite place as one of the substantial business men of his native city of Fort Wayne, where he was born December 29, 1867, and where he controls a representative general contracting business as a painter and frescoer. He is a son of John and Ada (Taylor)

Jones, the former of whom was born in Wales and the latter in Ohio, she having been a lineal descendant of Zachary Taylor, who was elected president of the United States in 1848 and whose death occurred in 1850, about one year after his inauguration. John Jones was a lad of seven years when he came with his parents to Fort Wayne, where he served a thorough apprenticeship to the machinist's trade and was for a long period employed in the shops of the Wabash Railroad. He was but little more than forty years of age at the time of his death and his widow survived him by a number of years. Of their children, Oliver S., of this review, was the first born; Eva and Benjamin F. still reside in Fort Wayne; Mary is the wife of Robert Fuelgraff, of Chicago; John L. resides in Fort Wayne and Charles in Los Angeles, California; and Ada is the wife of Andrew Leeuw, of Fort Wayne. Oliver S. Jones duly profited by the advantages afforded in the public schools of his native city and as a youth entered upon an apprenticeship to the painter's trade, in which he acquired high proficiency, and he has continued in the work of his trade, besides amplifying his scope of operations by the execution of contracts for the most approved modern type of fresco work. Of these important lines of business enterprise he is now one of the prominent and successful exponents in Fort Wayne, where he is firmly entrenched in popular confidence and good will. His political allegiance is given to the Republican party, he has received in the Masonic fraternity the thirty-second degree of the Ancient Accepted Scottish Rite, after having completed the circle of the York Rite, in which his maximum affiliation is with Fort Wayne Commandery of Knights Templars, and he is a member also of the Ancient Arabic Order of the Nobles of the Mystic Shrine, besides being affiliated with the Benevolent and Protective Order of Elks and the Independent Order of Odd Fellows. Both he and his wife are active members of Plymouth Congregational church in their home city. Mr. Jones was actively identified with the Indiana National Guard for twenty-seven years, at the expiration of which he resigned his membership. With his command he enlisted for service in the Spanish-American war, in which he was second lieutenant of the Twenty-eighth Indiana Battery. On March 8, 1909, Mr. Jones wedded Birdie Gouty, who was born and reared in Fort Wayne and whose death here occurred on January 4, 1914, she being survived by no children. On April 25, 1916, was solemnized the marriage of Mr. Jones to Miss May Siems, who was born in New York city and who is the popular chatelaine of their attractive home.

Noah A. Joray.—By very reason of its eligible situation in the midst of as fine a farming district as is to be found in the Hoosier state, the thriving village of Sheldon, in Pleasant township, is the logical and de facto center of a substantial and noteworthy activity along the normal mercantile lines essential in such a community. He whose name introduces this article is recognized as one of the progressive and representative merchants of the village, where he conducts a well-equipped hardware establishment of which he has been the proprietor since the spring of 1915. He has a well-selected stock of heavy and shelf hardware, stoves, ranges, etc., with departments devoted also to the handling of paints and oils, farm implements and machinery, and other accessories demanded in modern farm enterprise. Mr. Joray was born at Vera Cruz, Wells county, Indiana, on December 13, 1876, and is a son of Samuel and Esther (Baughman) Joray, the former of whom was born in the picturesque canton of Berne, Switzerland, and the latter in the state of Ohio. Samuel Joray came to the United States in 1844 and for forty years was successfully established in business as a wagonmaker at Vera Cruz, Wells county, where he passed the closing period of his life in well-earned retirement, his death having there occurred on January 8, 1914, and his widow being still a resident of.Wells county. Mr. Joray was independent in politics and was a zealous member of the Christian church, as is also his venerable widow. Of their children the eldest is Sarah, who is the wife of Peter Shoemaker, of Wells county; Victor is deceased; Robert is still a resident of Wells county; Seralda is deceased; Noah A., of this review, was the next in order of birth; and Harvey and George are twins, the former being a resident of Wells county and the latter of Huntington county. Noah A. Joray is indebted to the public schools of his native county for his early educational training and as a youth there worked in a barber shop at Bluffton, the county seat, for a period of one year. During the following two years he was employed in the machine shops of the Bass Company, at Fort Wayne, and he next remained for a time on the old homestead farm of his father. His next medium of activity was a clerkship in a mercantile establishment at Goshen, and later he continued his association with the work of the home farm until 1915, when he removed to Sheldon and purchased of the firm of Reift and Rupright his present hardware business. He has made numerous improvements in the store, keeps his stock up to the best standard and controls a substantial and prosperous business. His political allegiance is given to the Republican party, and he and his wife are specially zealous members of the local Methodist Episcopal church, of which he is a trustee as well as superintendent of its Sunday school. On August 31, 1897, was solemnized the marriage of Mr. Joray to Miss Sarah E. Myers, daughter of Seth and Anna (Rogers) Myers, of Wells county. The two chlidren of this union are Hattie M. and Margaret, and both remain at the parental home.

Anton Kalbacher.—Coming from Germany to the United States in company with his parents when he was a lad of eleven years, the late Anton Kalbacher first became a resident of Delphos, Ohio, and in the following year began to depend largely upon his own resources. He was in the most significant and worthy sense the architect of his own fortune, and it was given him to achieve large and noteworthy success as one of the influential and honored business men of the city of Fort Wayne, to the upbuilding and advancement of which he contributed in generous measure. Here he established his residence in 1855 and here he continued to maintain his home until his death, which occurred April 7, 1904. Mr. Kalbacher was born in Germany on August 24, 1841, and received his rudimentary education in his native land, his alert mentality having enabled him to gain a broader education through the experiences and associations of a long, active and useful life as one of the world's productive workers. Upon coming to Fort Wayne, in 1855, he fo d employment in the establishment of Bever and Dunham, pioneer flour merchants. He continued his identification with this line of enterprise for many years and his energy and ability made his success of cumulative order from year to year. In 1878 he erected in Fort Wayne a substantial two-story brick building, in which he established himself in the dry-goods and grocery business. In 1882 he purchased the Sedgwick flour mills, later known as the St. Joseph mills, and these he successfully operated until 1887, when he sold the plant and business. It was in the year 1882 that he also became associated with William Pollhoff in the general grain and flour business, and with this enterprise he continued to be identified four years. During the later years of his life he gave his attention principally to the supervision of his varied properties and capitalistic interests, and he was one of the unassuming but honored and influential citizens of Allen county when death set its seal upon his mortal lips. He was well fortified in his opinions concerning governmental policies and public affairs of a local order, and his political allegiance was given to the Democratic party. Both he and his wife were zealous and devoted communicants of St. Mary's Catholic church, of which he served as a trustee, and both were active in all departments of the parish work. Their fine old homestead in Fort Wayne was that in which Mrs. Kalbacher was born, as were also all of her children, and she survived him by more than a decade, her summons to the life eternal having come on August 31, 1916, and her gentle and gracious personality gained to her the affectionate regard of all who came within the sphere of her influence. On October 19, 1865, was solemnized the marriage of Mr. Kalbacher to Miss Jane Schobe, who was born in Fort Wayne on June 17, 1845, a daughter of Eberhardt and Maria Angel (Daman) Schobe, who were of German ancestry and who were sterling pioneers of Fort Wayne, where they continued to reside until their death, which occurred in the old homestead which became the residence of Mr. and Mrs. Kalbacher, who likewise died there, the ancient dwelling, in an excellent state of preservation, having been held by the two families for the long period of seventy-six years. Of the children of Mr. and Mrs. Kalbacher the eldest is Aquineta, who is now mother superior of the Academy of Our Lady, in the city of Chicago, this being one of the largest Catholic schools of its kind in the entire west; Katherine M. is the wife of Thomas McKiernan, of Fort Wayne; Theresa and Leonore remain in the ancestral homestead in this city; Edward is deceased; and two children died in infancy. All of the children were most carefully reared in the faith of the Catholic church and all of those surviving continue as zealous communicants of this great mother church of Christendom.

William Kammeyer was a sturdy and ambitious man of thirty-five years when he came from Germany to America, and though his financial resources were reduced to the lowest figure at the time of his arrival in the land of his adoption, he was fortified with energy and determination and has won independence and definite success through his own efforts. This is indicated when it is stated that he is now the owner of one of the valuable farms of Allen county, his homestead place, in Maumee township, besides being the owner also of another excellent farm in the same township, this place being now under the active management of his son. To have achieved such worthy success through individual effort denotes the sterling character and determined purpose of Mr. Kammeyer, and he well merits consideration in this history of Allen county, where he has won to himself a wide circle of loyal friends. He was born in Germany on October 18, 1860, and is a son of Frederick and Sophia (Ehlerding) Kammeyer, the former of whom passed his entire life in that section of the German empire. The widowed mother came to the United States in 1901, when venerable in years, and here passed the remainder of her life in the homes of her children who had preceded her to this country. The subject of this review was the third in a family of five children. In the schools of his native land William Kammeyer gained his early education and as a youth did not lack full fellowship with arduous toil and endeavor. He was employed as a day laborer and also in general farm work and continued his activities in his native land until 1895, when, at the age of thirty-five years, he came to America, where he felt assured of better opportunities for the achieving of independence through personal effort. Soon after his arrival he came to Indiana and established his residence in Fort Wayne. Here he found employment in the Bass foundry, at a wage of ninety-six cents a day, and later was employed for a time by the city. Finally he rented a farm in the adjoining county of Wells, where he remained one year under these conditions. He then purchased forty acres of land in that county, and after finally selling this property, a few years later, returned to Allen county and purchased a farm of eighty acres in Milan township. Six years later his status was such that he was justified in the purchasing of an additional sixty acres, in the same township, and four years later he sold the latter tract, the while he traded the eighty acres for one hundred and ninety-five acres of virtually unimproved land. Of this tract he later disposed, and his next purchase was of a farm of one hundred acres in Maumee township. To the improvement and operation of this place he continued to give his vigorous attention for six years, and it is now under the direct supervision of his son, as previously stated. At the expiration of the period noted Mr. Kammeyer bought his present attractive homestead farm of sixty acres, the same being eligibly situated on the north side of the river and having formerly been known as the Ashton farm. Here he has to a certain degree abated the arduous labors that were so long his portion, but he still gives active service in the general management of the homestead, with loyal and effective assistance on the part of three of his sons. Mr. Kammeyer is always ready to do his part in the support of measures and enterprises advanced for the general good of the community, but he has never sought public office of any kind and is independent in his political attitude. He and his family hold earnestly to the faith of the Lutheran church. In 1886 Mr. Kammeyer wedded, at the old home in Germany, Miss Sophia Roemke, daughter of the late Frederick and Minnie (Dommeyer) Roemke, who passed their entire lives in Germany. Mr. and Mrs. Kammeyer have six children—Ernest, Louisa, Sophia, William, Frederick and Walter.

Richard M. Kaough has had the initiative and executive ability to develop a specially prosperous enterprise in connection with a line of enterprise that is now one of important order in all sections of the United States, and it is pleasing to note that in this achievement he has not found it expedient to wander outside the limits of his native county. He is at the head of the firm of R. M. Kaough and Company, which controls a substantial wholesale and retail business in the handling of automobile tires and accessories and the well-equipped establishment of which has a department especially devoted to the vulcanizing of tires, employment being given to a force of ten assistants and the building occupied, at 224 West Main street, having been erected for the purpose to which it is now applied, the structure, of modern design and facilities, having been completed in 1911. Mr. Kaough established the enterprise in September, 1908, and the title of the Fort Wayne Vulcanizing Works was retained until August 1, 1916, when the scope of the business was expanded and the present firm name adopted. Mr. Kaough at first confined his operations exclusively to the vulcanizing of tires and gave employment to only two persons. His enterprise grew apace and he gained such vantage ground in the confidence of his appreciative patronage that he finally found it expedient to make his business include the handling of standard brands of automobile tires and general lines of automobile accessories both at wholesale and retail, the while he provided even better facilities for the vulcanizing department. The success of the expanded business has fully justified the course which he took in making the business one of more comprehensive order. Richard M. Kaough was born in Aboite township, Allen county, Indiana, on June 17, 1882, and has become well known as one of the alert and progressive young business men of the metropolis of his native county. He is a son of James and Mary (Biemer) Kaough, who now reside in Fort Wayne, the father having long been a representative farmer of Allen county and having now retired from active association with this fundamental industry. Richard M. Kaough was reared to the sturdy discipline of the home farm, profited duly by the advantages of the public schools and remained closely associated with agricultural enterprise until he had attained to his legal majority. He then learned the trade of blacksmith and finally purchased the shop in which he had served his apprenticeship. He conducted the business successfully for six years and then sold the shop, which was located at 247 Pearl street, and initiated his present prosperous business in Fort Wayne. Mr. Kaough is independent in his political attitude, but takes loyal interest in public affairs, especially those of a local order, and in his home city holds membership in the Commercial Club and the Rotary Club. On January 25, 1910, Mr. Kaough wedded Miss Vida E. Bowers, daughter of John S. and Mary (Laman) Bowers, of Decatur, Adams county, and they have one child, Edwin.

Dr. Daniel E. Kauffman, one of the prominent medical practitioners of Monroeville, was born in the State of Ohio, March 4, 1862. His father followed the vocation of a prosperous farmer, was a Buckeye by birth and served with distinction as captain of a company in the Civil War. His death occurred October 23, 1863. Ten children were born to the parents of Doctor Kauffman. After completing his preliminary educational training Doctor Kauffman entered Taylor Medical University in which he graduated in the class of 1891. He began his professional practice in Rome City, Indiana, but later went to Payne, Ohio. There he remained until 1905, building up meantime a lucrative practice, and then located in Monroeville, where he has since continued. He is recognized by the medical fraternity as one of the eminent surgeons and physicians in this section of Indiana. Doctor Kauffman espouses the cause of the Democratic party and has done much to bring about the success of the party at the polls. Fraternally he is identified with the Knights of Columbus, the Red Men, and he also is a member of the County, State, and American medical associations. He and his family are members of the Catholic church. Doctor Kauffman was united in marriage to Miss Taresia G. Brady, the accomplished daughter of Peter Brady, a member of a prominent pioneer family in the State of Ohio. Four children have blessed this union: Clara, who is the wife of C. W. Harris, of Toledo, Ohio; Taresia, who is the wife of Fred Schaab, of

Fort Wayne, Indiana; Rose, who is the wife of Louis Pile, also a resident of Fort Wayne; and Daniel, who is a corporal in the First Indiana Battery of Field Artillery. The Doctor owns a fine home in Monroeville in one of the beautiful residence districts of the village.

Robert E. Kaufman maintains his residence at New Haven and has developed a prosperous business as one of the leading buyers and shippers of live stock in Allen county. He was born in Whitley county, Indiana, March 21, 1866, and is a son of Henry and Samantha (Bell) Kaufman, the former a native of Wayne county, Ohio, and the latter of Williams county, that state. Henry Kaufman established his residence in Whitley county, Indiana, in 1845, and became one of the pioneer farmers of the county, besides which he was long known as a successful buyer and shipper of live stock. Both he and his wife continued their residence in Whitley county until their death, and both were active members of the United Brethren church, he having been a Democrat in politics and having been affiliated with the Masonic fraternity. Of the children the eldest is Albert, who is a resident of Storm Lake, Iowa; Francis M. resides in Fort Wayne and Webster at Sheldon, Indiana; William, Lorinda and Jennie died in early childhood; Robert E., of this review, was the next in order of birth; Harrison S. is a resident of Warsaw, this state; and John is deceased. Robert E. Kaufman passed his childhood and youth on the old home farm and profited duly by the advantages of the public schools of his native county, after which he attended what is now known as Valparaiso University, besides having been for a time a student in the old Chicago University. Thereafter he was some time a resident of Eugene City, Oregon, and upon coming to Allen county, Indiana, passed two years in Fort Wayne as a stock buyer. In 1904 he removed to the village of New Haven, and here he has since continued his successful activities as a buyer and shipper of livestock, in which enterprise he is associated with his brother, Francis M., who resides in Fort Wayne. Mr. Kaufman is a staunch advocate of the principles of the Democratic party and he formerly served as a member of the municipal council of New Haven. He is affiliated with the Modern Woodmen of America and both he and his wife hold membership in the Congregational church. April 24, 1893, marked the marriage of Mr. Kaufman to Miss Chloetta Clark, daughter of Rev. Horace and Susan (Lenhart) Clark, of Eugene City, Oregon, and the only child of this union was Beatrice Leonore, who died at the age of twelve years.

George V. Kell.—With all of appreciative consistency may it be said that Hon. George V. Kell is one of the prominent, influential and representative citizens of his native county, and his loyalty and progressiveness have been shown along lines that have tended greatly to conserve civic and material advancement and prosperity in his home county and state. The owner of a splendidly improved landed estate in Eel River township, Mr. Kell here stands exemplar of the best in modern and scientific agricultural and live-stock industry; he is president of the Farmer Mutual Fire Insurance Association; is a member of the directorate of the Citizens' Trust Company of Fort Wayne, and has not only represented Allen county in the lower branch of the state legislature but has also given equally loyal and public-spirited service as a member of the state senate. Thus it will be seen that there are many salient points that make consonant the according of special recognition to this sterling and popular citizen within the pages of this history. He is a scion of one of the sterling pioneer families of Allen county and on the old homestead of his parents, in Perry township, this county, his birth occurred, February 3, 1846. While the ancestry of Mr. Kell is in large measure of German order he takes pride in reverting to the fact that his great-great-grandmother on the paternal side was a near kinswoman of the Empress Josephine, wife of Napoleon Bonaparte. Mr. Kell is a son of Jacob and Mary Katherine (Weimer) Kell, the former of whom was born in Germany and the latter was a native of Ohio, but of German ancestry. The father of Mr. Kell settled in Allen county when much of this section of the state was little more than a forest wilderness, and developed a productive farm in Perry township, where both he and his wife passed the residue of their earnest and useful lives. George V. Kell was reared to the invigorating discipline of the pioneer farm and in his youth was favored in receiving good educational advantages, as he was able to attend the Perry Center Seminary, which occupied a site on one corner of his father's farm and which was in its day one of the best educational institutions in Indiana. Mr. Kell's father and two other specially liberal and influential citizens of the county established this admirable school and for a considerable period provided for its maintenance. The principal of the seminary was Professor Timothy Titus Tilden, who had been graduated in Dartmouth College and was an educator of exceptional ability and enthusiasm, his name meriting high place in the records of educational history in Indiana. At the age of sixteen years George V. Kell completed the curriculum of this excellent school, and in the meanwhile the Civil war had been precipitated. He was unable to prevail upon his parents to permit him to enlist and go forth as a soldier of the Union, as he was but fifteen years old when the war began, and this parental refusal did not dampen his youthful patriotism and loyalty, though it made impossible their desired fruition in action. Until he had attained to his legal majority Mr. Kell continued to assist in the work and management of the home farm during the summer seasons and during the intervening winters did effective service as a teacher in the district schools. At the age of twenty-one years, in 1867, was solemnized his marriage to Miss Alice Hatch, and their bridal tour or honeymoon trip was made through the medium of a team and covered wagon, a veritable "prairie schooner," which afforded them transportation from Indiana to Taylor county, Iowa, where they became pioneer settlers and Mr. Kell purchased a tract of two hundred and forty acres of land. To the reclaiming, improving and operation of this farm he continued to give his attention for the ensuing six years, and the ill health of Mrs. Kell then led them to return from the west to the old home in Allen county. Here they established themselves on the present rural demesne which still constitutes the home place, and the fine estate comprises two hundred acres of the most fertile land in Eel River township, the while the improvements of permanent order are of the best type, including a large and attractive farm residence that has become widely known as a center of generous and unostentatious hospitality, with Mrs. Kell as its gracious and popular chatelaine. Apropos of Mr. Kell's sojourn in Iowa in the pioneer days, it may be noted that while there he again gave his attention to teaching school for a time, and an indication of the sparsely settled condition of the country in that period is conveyed in the statement that his school district embraced four townships in four different counties and that in this pioneer district, comprehensive in area, there were only twelve children to be mustered as pupils in the little school house. Mr. Kell became influential in public affairs in his community and, though he was the only Democrat in his township, his popularity was such that he was elected township trustee, an office of which he continued the incumbent four years. He was still a resident of Iowa at the time of the national election of 1872, notable as that in which Horace Greeley appeared as presidential condidate on a fusion ticket, against General Grant, the Republican candidate, Charles O'Conor, of New York, as the "straight-out" Democratic candidate, besides which a Temperance candidate was in the field also. In this election Mr. Kell gave his support to O'Conor, and from that time to the present has invariably voted the regular Democratic ticket in all national elections as well as in state elections. He has been one of the strenuous and well fortified workers in the ranks of his party, has been a delegate to many of its state and congressional conventions in Indiana, has been a member of the executive committee of the party for this state and has served with characteristic loyalty and ability in both houses of the Indiana legislature, in which his record has become a very part of the legislative history of this commonwealth. While a member of the house of representatives he became widely known as the author of the Kell bill for the promotion and regulation of farmers' mutual fire insurance companies, and he also introduced and ably championed several other bills that came to enactment and have proved of enduring value to the state. While in the senate he earnestly supported the Nicholson bill, for the regulation of the liquor traffic in the state, though his championship of this measure brought protest from some of the leaders of his party. Without fear or favor, in his legislative career, as in all other relations of a signally active and useful life, Mr. Kell invariably took his stand in consonance with his judgment and conscientious convictions, and to do the right as he has seen the right has been an intrinsic functioning of his very nature. He and his wife have long been zealous members of the Methodist Episcopal church and for nearly forty years he has been a member of the board of trustees of the church of this denomination at Huntertown, which thriving little city is his postoffice address. He is affiliated with the Masonic fraternity, including Scottish Rite bodies, and was formerly an active member of the Patrons of Husbandry. In connection with his well ordered operations as a progressive agriculturist and stock-grower Mr. Kell has achieved more than local prominence and reputation in the breeding of standard-bred horses, and from his farm have gone forth many fine roadsters as well as trotting horses that have made excellent turf records. The marriage of Mr. Kell to Miss Alice Hatch was solemnized in 1867, as before noted, and Mrs. Kell likewise was born and reared in Allen county, her parents, Newman and Abigail Hatch, having come to this county in the pioneer days from the state of New York. Mr. and Mrs. Kell became the parents of eight children, all of whom are living, namely: Gertrude, Louise, Jessie E., Beatrice, George Robert, Frank B., Dorothy, and Walter. Dorothy was for four years a successful teacher in the schools of the Philippine Islands and is now the wife of J. C. Rundles, of Eel River township.

Henry E. Kellermeier, who resides upon his fine homestead farm of one hundred and sixty-nine acres, will celebrate, in 1918, the seventieth anniversary of his birth, has been a resident of Allen county all his life and is a representative of two of the very early pioneer families of the county, within whose borders both his paternal and maternal grandparents established their home when this section of the Hoosier state was little more than an untrammeled forest wilderness. Of the farm of Mr. Kellermeier the portion on which is established the residence of the family is in Maumee township, and the remaining eighty-two acres lie across the line in Milan township. The place has been equipped by its present owner with good buildings and other permanent improvements, and here he has achieved success and independence through his well-directed activities as an agriculturist and stock-grower, the younger of his two sons now having the active management of the farm. Mr. Kellermeier was born in Fort Wayne in the year 1849, and is a son of Louis and Gecina (Brookmeier) Kellermeier, both of whom were born in Germany and were young when the respective families immigrated to America and became pioneer settlers in Allen county. Louis Kellermeier became one of the substantial farmers of the county and here he and his wife passed the remainder of their lives, both having attained to venerable age and having been earnest communicants of the Lutheran church. This honored pioneer couple became the parents of nine children, of whom the subject of this review was the first born. The youngest two are deceased, and the names of the other children are here designated: Amelia, William, Minnie, Christ, Mary and John. He whose name introduces this sketch acquired his early education in the schools of Fort Wayne and in his youth there learned the carpenter's trade, to which he continued to devote his attention for a few years. He then engaged in farming in Milan township for a period of ten years and for the ensuing four years was similarly engaged in Adams township. He then returned to Fort Wayne, but two years later he removed to his present farm, where he has since maintained his home and where the results of his energetic and able management of the various departments of farm enterprise are in distinct evidence. He has always been a stalwart supporter of the cause of the Democratic party and he and his family hold zealously to the faith of the Lutheran church. Mr. Kellermeier has been active and influential in the support of measures that have conserved civic and material progress in his home township and county and he served three terms as supervisor of Maumee township. In 1879 was solemnized his marriage to Miss Katie Weber, a daughter of Louis Weber, who was a sterling pioneer of this county. Mr. and Mrs. Kellermeier have two children: Edward, who is a prosperous farmer in Milan township, wedded Miss Carrie Thiele, of Seymour, Jackson county. Theodore, who has the active supervision of the old homestead farm, married Miss Orna Gerber, and they have one child, Miss Carrie, at home.

Robert E. Kelly is one of the well-known and distinctively popular citizens of Fort Wayne, where he is now serving as chairman of the municipal board of public works. Further evidence of his secure place in popular esteem was given when he was elected county recorder of Allen county, an office in which he served four years and in which he gave a most efficient and uniformly satisfactory administration. In the old family homestead that stood on the same city lot as does his present attractive residence, Robert E. Kelly was born on October 27, 1864, and he is a son of Thomas F. and Margaret (Clark) Kelly, the former of whom was born in Ireland and the latter in the state of Ohio. Thomas F. Kelly was reared and educated in his native land and was a young man when he emigrated to America. In 1858 he came to Fort Wayne and for a time was employed on the old-time canal which was a medium of transportation in that pioneer period and was captain on the state boat. Later he was identified with other lines of enterprise, a sterling, industrious and unassuming man whose upright character gave to him strong vantage-place in the confidence and good will of his fellow men. He served in an Indiana regiment during the war between the states, and was honorably discharged at the close of the war. He was a member of Sion S. Bass Post, G. A. R. He continued his residence in Fort Wayne until his death, whic occurred in 1893, and his venerable widow passed to the life eternal in 1911, both having been devoted communicants of the Catholic church. Of their two children the subject of this review is the elder, and the second was Edward, who died in infancy. Robert E. Kelly gained his early education in the Catholic parochial schools of Fort Wayne and was not yet fifteen years old when he found employment as a messenger boy for the Fort Wayne, Cincinnati and Louisville Railroad. He worked his way forward to the position of locomotive fireman and when twenty-one years of age attained to the dignity of locomotive engineer. He served for a term of years as engineer of passenger trains and was thus engaged until 1908, when he was elected county recorder of his native county, an office of which he continued the incumbent four years, as previously noted in this context. For about one year after his retirement from this office he was not actively engaged, but in 1914 was appointed a member of the Fort Wayne board of public works, of which he is serving as chairman at the time of this writing and in which he is giving specially loyal and circumspect service. Mr. Kelly gives his political allegiance to the Democratic party and both he and his wife are earnest communicants of the Catholic church, he being now a trustee of the parish of the Church of the Precious Blood. Mr. Kelly is affiliated with the Catholic Knights of America and the Knights of Columbus and is also a popular and influential member of the Ancient Order of Hibernians, for which he served as treasurer of the Indiana state organization for two terms. He still maintains affiliation with the Brotherhood of Locomotive Engineers and has served as secretary of the local organization of the same. On May 15, 1888, was solemnized the marriage of Mr. Kelly to Miss Ellen Ryan, who was born at Rushville, Indiana, and concerning the children of this union the following brief data are given: Thomas J. was graduated in Purdue University as a mechanical engineer and in the work of his profession is now employed by the Northern Indiana Gas and Electric Company, with headquarters in Fort Wayne; Marie is the wife of Edward Disser, of Fort Wayne; Genevieve died in early childhood; and Josephine, Robert J., Laurence W., Anna and Katherine remain members of the parental home circle.

William Aden Kelsey, who for the last twenty years has ably served as secretary of the Farmers' Mutual Fire Insurance Association, was born in Rush county, Indiana, May 4, 1842, and is a son of Aden and Rebecca (Broadway) Kelsey. They were born in Montgomery county, Ohio, in the years 1803 and 1804, and there they were married February 9, 1826. They removed to Rush county, Indiana, in 1837, and there the father died in 1846. The mother died in Allen county, Indiana, June 2, 1888. They were the parents of seven children: Mary, Samuel B., James T., Sarah E., Caroline, William A. and Isaac H., all of whom are now deceased with the exception of the subject, William Aden Kelsey, whose education was secured in the common schools and at the old Methodist College in Fort Wayne. He left his books to enlist in the Union army in the Civil War, in 1861, and served as a private soldier in Company E, Forty-fourth Indiana, and as Captain of Company G, One Hundred and Fifty-second Indiana infantry. He was discharged from the service in August, 1865. Mr. Kelsey married Emma Richard, daughter of Mrs. Elizabeth Richard, October 15, 1868. Three children were born to them: Frank R., the eldest, died in November, 1913. Louis M. is engaged in the United States railway mail service, and Arthur is at home. Mrs. Kelsey died on the 14th day of February, 1915. Mr. Kelsey, who has lived in Allen county for the past sixty-three years, owns farming property in Aboite township, of which he served for several years as trustee. He has always been a warm advocate of public improvements, and many years ago was active in putting through the first gravel road in the county, which was the forerunner of the present splendid system of roads of which Allen county is justly proud. He had much to do with the establishment of free mail delivery in the rural districts. Many years before the United States government became interested in this matter, he formed a co-operative organization among his neighbors, who, at their own expense, delivered their mail at their own homes from Fort Wayne, a distance of twelve miles. This experiment proved so satisfactory that its results were presented to the government of the United States with the request that it select some suitable place to test the possibilities of a system of free rural mail delivery. This request was granted, the success of which was so gratifying that it resulted in the adoption of the present rural mail delivery service that extends throughout the land. Mr. Kelsey is a member of the West Jefferson Street Church of Christ. In politics he is a Republican and he is one of the oldest members of Harmony Lodge No. 19, I. O. O. F. He is a charter member and past commander of Lawton-Wayne Post No. 271, Department of Indiana, G. A. R., a member of the State encampment of the G. A. R. and, at its meeting held in Evansville in May, 1916, was elected Junior Vice Department Commander for the State of Indiana.

Alonzo G. Kendall is the owner of one of the extensive and specially valuable landed estates of Allen county and has been a man of large affairs during the major part of his active career. Prior to coming to Allen county he had become the owner of three hundred and twenty acres of excellent land in McClain county, Illinois, and he has also an appreciable tract of land in Missouri. In 1910, with characteristic progressiveness and mature judgment, he came to Allen county, where he purchased from the Ellison estate three hundred and seventy-six acres of land in Aboite township, his homestead place, a veritable model, being situated nine miles distant from Fort Wayne on rural mail route No. 8. For a time he here conducted the largest dairy farm in the county, but he now gives his attention principally to the raising of superior live stock and the propagation of sugar beets, in which latter department of his farm enterprise he had in the season of 1916 one hundred and one acres of sugar beets, which gave a substantial and profitable yield. He raises the best types of cattle and swine, and of the latter he makes a specialty of the spotted Poland-China type, with registration of all that he breeds. In addition to his other large interests Mr. Kendall is a stockholder of the Sterling Sales Company, at Auburn, DeKalb county, Indiana. While a resident of Illinois he was a stockholder and executive officer of a number of important stock and grain companies. Mr. Kendall has shown his liberality and progressiveness, not only in connection with his private affairs but also as a loyal and public-spirited citizen, and he has proved a valuable acquisition to Allen county. His political allegiance is given to the Republican party and he and his wife hold membership in the Methodist Episcopal church. Mr. Kendall was born in McLean county, Illinois, on July 20, 1860, and is a son of Thomas Jefferson Kendall and Margaret (Michael) Kendall. The father was born in the vicinity of Zanesville, Ohio, and was a boy at the time of the family removal to McLean county, Illinois, where he was reared and educated and where he eventually became a specially successful farmer and an honored and influential citizen of his community, his landed estate in that county at the time of his death having comprised two hundred acres. He was a stalwart Republican and was a lifelong member of the Methodist Episcopal church, as was also his wife, she having survived him by several years. Of their children the subject of this review is the eldest; Mollie is the wife of George Welsh, a prosperous farmer in Missouri; Sadie is the wife of Guy Lawrence, of Danville, Illinois; and William remains on the old homestead farm in McLean county, Illinois. Alonzo G. Kendall found requisition for his services in connection with the work of the home farm while he was a boy and youth and in the meantime profited by the advantages afforded in the public schools of his native county. In initiating his independent career as a farmer and stock-grower he rented land and under these conditions continued his energetic activities several years. He then purchased a farm of his own, in McClain county, Illinois, and in that state, as previously noted, eventually became the owner of three hundred and twenty acres of valuable land. In 1887 was solemnized the marriage of Mr. Kendall to Miss Hattie M. Hall, who likewise was born and reared in Illinois, a daughter of the late Henry J. M. and Minerva (Gapin) Hall, both of whom were of Scotch lineage and continued their residence in Illinois until their death. Of the children of Mr. and Mrs. Kendall it is to be recorded that Minnie Minerva is the wife of C. R. Benjamin, of Logansport, Indiana, and Thomas Henry, Roy A. and Arthur William remain at the parental home.

Harry F. Kennerk, of the representative Fort Wayne law firm of Kennerk and Somers, has by his character and achievement gained a secure vantage-place that gives him precedence as one of the able and successful members of the bar of his native county, and further interest attaches to his career by reason of his being a scion of one of the sterling pioneer families of Allen county, his father, Timothy Kennerk, having been the first white child born in Pleasant township, this county, and being now one of the venerable and honored citizens of Marion township, where he still resides on the old homestead farm that was the birthplace of all of his children, of whom seven are living. The devoted wife and mother, whose maiden name was Mary Harrigan, was born in County Limerick, Ireland, and she was summoned to the life eternal on February 20, 1914, her memory being revered by all who came within the compass of her gracious influence. She was a devout communicant of the Catholic church, as is also her husband. Timothy Kennerk was reared under the conditions of the pioneer epoch in the history of Allen county, where he continued his association with farm enterprise until February 19, 1863, when he became a member of a company that on that date set forth from Fort Wayne with ox teams and wagons and initiated the long and perilous journey across the plains to Montana, which was then the center of a genuine stampede of gold-seekers. The Fort Wayne company made the trip by a new route, covered a distance of seven hundred miles and arrived in Montana on August 14, 1863. Mr. Kennerk was successful in his quest for gold, as a pioneer in the historic placer mines of Montana, and on his return to Indiana, in 1865, he brought with him gold dust to the value of six thousand five hundred dollars, which he took to Philadelphia and sold to the great capitalist, Jay Gould. He then returned to Allen county and purchased the fine old homestead farm on which he still resides, as one of the venerable and influential pioneer citizens of the county. Harry F. Kennerk was born on the homestead above mentioned, in Marion township, and the date of his nativity was June 12, 1873. After having profited by the advantages of the public schools he attended for two terms the Tri-State Normal School at Angola, Steuben county, later was for two terms a student in what is now Valparaiso University, and for one year he attended DePauw University, in which he completed his academic or literary education. In preparation for his chosen profession he was matriculated in the Indiana Law School, at Indianapolis, in which he was a member of the class of 1900. He was admitted to the bar in that year and in September formed a law partnership with Herbert L. Somers, with whom he has since been successfully associated in practice in Fort Wayne, where they control a substantial and important law business and where he gives special attention to commercial law. Mr. Kennerk is an active member of the Allen County Bar Association, is a Democrat in his political allegiance, and both he and his wife are communicants of the Catholic church. On September 11, 1904, was solemnized the marriage of Mr. Kennerk to Miss Nora Wickens, who was born at North Vernon, Indiana, a daughter of Patrick and Hannah Wickens, the former of whom is now deceased. Mr. and Mrs. Kennerk have six sons and one daughter, namely: Gregory T., H. Hugh, Owen J., Mary Helen, Terrence Daniel, and David Wickens and Perry Anthony, who are twins.

Edgar H. Kilbourne.—Even a cursory review of the career of this representative young business man of Fort Wayne reveals conclusively the fact that from his boyhood he has shown remarkable self-reliance and resourcefulness. He has been virtually dependent upon his own resources since he was a lad of nine years, and long before he had attained to his legal majority he had held in connection with business enterprises a number of responsible positions usually assigned to persons of greater age and experience. This signifies that his alert mind and definite ambition had enabled him to rise above the average plane and to profit more fully from experience than the average person. There is lesson and incentive in the story of his progress, and even this brief sketch offers data of adequate order to reveal this. Edgar Hamilton Kilbourne, now a prominent and successful exponent of the real estate business in Fort Wayne, was born in the city of Baltimore, Maryland, on April 12, 1885, and is a son of Lawrence W. and Amelia Ellsworth (Burton) Kilbourne, both of whom are now deceased, the father likewise having been a native of Baltimore. Of the seven children three are living. Edgar H. Kilbourne attended the public schools of his native city until he had entered upon the first year of study in the grammar school. At the age of nine years he left the parental home and made provision for his own support by serving as a newsboy in his native city. He followed this vocation until he had attained to the age of eleven years, and for the ensuing two months he was employed in a grocery store, his compensation being one and one-half dollars a week. He was supposed also to have been provided with his board, but his employer failed to make good this important item of expense. The ensuing two months found the vigorous and ambitious boy employed in a dairy-lunch room, and for the next three weeks he applied himself to the operation of a foot-power press used in dieing yeast-powder boxes in a Baltimore tin factory. He next found employment in a cigar store, where he worked two weeks, and for two months thereafter was employed in a toy store. By way of change and determination to advance, he thereafter worked two months in a pretzel factory. His next occupation was with Wells Brothers' Butter and Egg Store as bundle boy and doing other work in connection with a butter and egg store, and this service continued about two months. All this time he was striving to find a position that would yield him sufficient income so that he might make progress toward the goal of independence, and finally he was attracted by a sign indicating that boys were wanted to learn the trade of harnessmaking in the establishment of O'Connor and Startzman. He promptly made application at the factory, was accepted, and within the following two and one-half years he had learned the trade thoroughly—an apprenticeship of less duration than that usually required to attain to this result. At this juncture the firm dissolved partnership and the heads of the various departments in the factory went with Mr. Startzman, Jr., a member of the original firm. Mr. Kilbourne was selected to take charge of the packing and shipping department under the new regime and also was made assistant buyer. Six months later the factory was virtually destroyed by fire and business was not resumed. Under these conditions Mr. Kilbourne obtained a similar position with the firm of O. F. Day, Son and Company, engaged in the same line of business in Baltimore. Shortly afterward, when but fifteen years of age, he decided to come to the west, and, with him decision and action have ever gone hand in hand. He wrote and dispatched eighteen letters, addressed to different business concerns at various points—from Pittsburgh to San Francisco. That he presented his case effectively is shown by the fact that he received replies from all except one of the letters and was definitely tendered in the connection five different jobs. Of these five he accepted that which offered the lowest salary but apparently the best prospects for the future. Thus it was that he made his way to the city of Detroit, Michigan, and entered the employ of the firm of Pierson and Hough, engaged in the manufacture of harness, horse collars and saddlery. The ambitious youth proved his value and within a few months was earning and receiving a salary of one hundred and twenty-five dollars a month as assistant buyer for the concern, under H. L. Pierson, the senior member thereof. He had the supervision of the work of the city and suburban salesmen, and when commercial expedience brought about the incorporation of the business five of the department heads were admitted as members of the new company, including Mr. Kilbourne. With the Pierson-Hough Company Mr. Kilbourne continued his alliance until he was twenty years of age and he then became associated with three other men who were at the head of departments in the business and they engaged in the same line of business in an independent way, Ed O'Neill, of Birmingham, Michigan, likewise becoming a principal and the enterprise being incorporated under the title of the Oakland Harness Company. Before the new business had been definitely established Mr. Kilbourne received from Fort Wayne a proposition to come to this city and effect a reorganization of the Johns-Thompson Saddlery Company, which was accomplished. At this juncture Mr. Pierson, of the Pierson-Hough Company, of Detroit, also made to Mr. Kilbourne and F. B. Thompson an offer to represent his concern in Fort Wayne. This offer was accepted and an office duly opened in Fort Wayne, where Mr. Pierson consented to the local representatives likewise establishing for themselves a merchandise brokerage business. Under these conditions Mr. Kilbourne applied himself with characteristic energy and progressiveness from October 1, 1907, until 1913, when Mr. Thompson returned to Detroit to enter the real estate business. For the ensuing year Mr. Kilbourne conducted an independent real estate business in Fort Wayne, and he then formed a partnership with C. E. Perry, under the firm name of Kilbourne and Perry. The office of the new firm was originally established in the Old National Bank building, from which removal was later made to the present eligible quarters in the modern Shoaff building, from which well-appointed offices the firm now conducts a substantial, well-ordered and very successful general real estate and financial business. Mr. Kilbourne is one of the vigorous and representative young business men and popular citizens of Fort Wayne and his loyalty to the city of his adoption is one of appreciation and of unwavering confidence in the still greater future of the Allen county metropolis. His political allegiance is given to the Republican party, and he has held various official chairs in the different bodies of both the York and Scottish Rites of the Masonic fraternity, in the latter of which he has received the thirty-second degree. He is also serving, in 1917, as captain of Mizpah Arab Patrol connected with Mizpah Temple of the Ancient Arabic Order of the Nobles of the Mystic Shrine, of which he is Chief Rabban. He is affiliated also with the local lodge of the Benevolent and Protective Order of Elks, is one of the vital and influential members of the Fort Wayne Commercial Club, in which he has been elected on the Board of Directors, and he holds membership in the Fort Wayne Country Club, the Rotary Club and the local organization of the Anti-Tuberculosis League. He is also Chairman of the Board of Examiners of the Officers' Reserve Corps Military Training Camps Association. In 1909 was solemnized the marriage of Mr. Kilbourne to Miss Bertha A. Deininger, of Decatur, Indiana, she being a daughter of Ulrich Deininger, a well-known citizen of that place. Mr. and Mrs. Kilbourne have no children, but the attractive home circle is amplified by the presence of Mrs. Lavinia Garnet, a sister of Mr. Kilbourne.

Milton G. Kimmel comes of a family that has been established in Indiana since 1837, and from then down to the present time has been creditably identified with its agricultural industry. His maternal grandfather, John Ogden, of whom more extended mention is made in the personal sketch devoted to Robert Kimmel, brother of the subject, was one of the substantial farming men of Wells county to the end of his days, after his advent there in 1837, and he passed away in 1891, one of the best known and most highly esteemed men of his county. Milton G. Kimmel is the son of David T. and Sarah A. (Ogden) Kimmel. He was born on the old family homestead, July 17, 1851, and was reared to farm life, devoting himself to that vocation until about twenty-three years of age. He then removed to Fort Wayne, where he became identified with the

Packard Piano Company, with which he has since been associated in the capacity of engineer. Mr. Kimmel was married, November 5, 1874, to Maria Hoke, a daughter of John A. and Elizabeth (Weaver) Hoke, natives of Pennsylvania and pioneers of Allen county, having removed here in 1860. To Mr. and Mrs. Kimmel were born eleven children, five of whom died in infancy. Those who grew to maturity are Anna J., who became the wife of Frederick Trevey, and is now deceased; Charles A. is also deceased; Harriet E. is the widow of the late Albert Hartsein, of Fort Wayne; Cora M. is the wife of Henry Mills, of Fort Wayne; Harman G. is a butcher in the United States navy, and Frederick I. is also in the United States navy, in the capacity of baker. Mr. and Mrs. Kimmel also have four grand-children: William G., George R. and Sarah C. Trevy, and Velma H. Mills. Mr. Kimmel is numbered with the progressive and enterprising citizens of Fort Wayne and is identified in many ways with matters which have to do with the progress and betterment of the city. He maintains a pleasant home at 3232 Indiana avenue, where he and his wife are surrounded by a host of warm friends, and have sufficient means to keep the wolf from their door.

Robert Kimmel was reared on a farm and since he was twenty-one years old has operated his own land. He has been successful and prosperous and takes his proper place among the leading agricultural men of Pleasant township. He was born on December 22, 1865, and is a son of David T. and Sarah A. (Ogden) Kimmel, who came from Stark county, Ohio, to Allen county, Indiana, in 1840. They located first in Wayne township, spending about a year there, and then moved to Pleasant township, where the family has since been represented creditably. David Kimmel knew many hardships and privations in the early years of his residence in Allen county, and his prosperity was the result of his own well-directed efforts and his unfailing energy and continued toil. The gentleman farmer was unknown in those pioneer days, and the methods that won success then are obsolete in the farming world today for the most part. Robert I. Kimmel was the seventh child in a family of eight born to his parents. Milton G., the first born, is found mentioned elsewhere in the pages of this work. He is located in Fort Wayne and is connected prominently with the Packard Piano Company. John M. is located in Des Moines, Iowa. Martha married Amos Lawrence of Fort Wayne and is deceased. Mary Jane is the wife of Jacob Fieghman and lives in Huntington county, Indiana. Lucy R. is deceased. Jacob C. lives in Fort Wayne, and Harriet E. lives in Bensen, Nebraska, and is the wife of LeRoy Herndeen. Robert Kimmel as a boy attended the schools of Pleasant township, and under his father's able instruction on the farm learned much on the home place that fitted him for his career as a farmer in later years. He comes of sturdy stock, and it should be said here that his maternal grandfather, John Ogden, came to Indiana as early as the year 1837. He was a native Pennsylvanian, born on October 9, 1807, and was of English ancestry. His education was meagre, so far as books were concerned, but he was a man of splendid mentality and was self taught along many lines, and all his life held a prominent place in his community. He married young, the date of that event being May 27, 1828, and Martha Swavanger became his wife. They were courageous and ambitious and, in 1837, set out for Indiana, in the hope of finding greater advantages than their own state afforded. The trip across the country in that early day was a matter of considerable moment, and it speaks well of their native hardihood that they were willing to undertake it in the face of the difficulties they knew they must encounter. Arriving in Wells county, they entered government land and in course of time were the possessors of one of the fine homes of their district. Ten children were born to them, one of them being the mother of the subject. Mr. Ogden was always a prominent man in his community, a leader in its political activities, and an ardent Democrat. He died in 1891, on the 19th day of January, when he was eighty-four years of age. Robert Kimmel was married on January 7, 1891, to Miss Susan Fieghman, daughter of Solomon and Mary (Silvius) Fieghman, who were of German ancestry. They lived for many years in Lafayette township and there carried on farming operations. Mr. Fieghman died July 18, 1903, and is survived by his widow and children. To Mr. and Mrs. Kimmel have come six children. Elvin Ray married Miss Florence Rutter and they have one child—Mildred May. Clifford, Forest, Verdona May, Charles R. and Kenneth F. are all at home, and are young people of much promise.

Elmer King is to be consistently designated as one of the representative and progressive young business men of Allen county and is here successfully established in the produce business, with residence and headquarters at Woodburn, Maumee township. In the handling of general lines of farm produce and dairy products he is a representative of the well-known firm of Miller Brothers, of Cleveland, Ohio, and to the headquarters of this concern in the Ohio metropolis he consigns the major part of the produce which he buys in his assigned territory. Mr. King was born in Livingston county, Illinois, October 20, 1890, and is a son of Samuel and Lena (Rediger) King, who were likewise natives of that county, where the respective families were founded many years ago. Samuel King has made farming his vocation throughout his entire active career and continued his residence in his native county until 1906, when he removed with his family to Allen county, Indiana, and settled on a farm in Maumee township. Two years later he removed to Fulton county, Ohio, where he has since been a successful exponent of agricultural enterprise, his home being in the vicinity of the village of Fayette, and his loved and devoted wife having there died on July 29, 1916. They became the parents of twelve children, namely: Mattie, Elmer, Clara, Aaron, Joseph, Samuel, Jr., Ella, Anna, Phoebe, Irving, Harvey, and Martha. All of the children, except the last named, survive the mother. Elmer King gained his early education in the public schools of his native county and was about sixteen years of age at the time of the family removal to Allen county, Indiana. Here he gave his attention to farm activities for a period of three years, and since that time has been successfully established in the produce business at Woodburn, where his energy, progressiveness and sterling characteristics have gained to him unqualified popular confidence and esteem. His political support is given to the Republican party, but he has had no ambition for political activity or public office. In 1912 was recorded the marriage of Mr. King to Miss Lucy Stucky, who was born and reared in Allen county, a daughter of Moses and Mary (Gerig) Stucky, well-known citizens of Maumee township. Mr. and Mrs. King have no children.

Josiah King, who for many years was identified with the milling business at Roanoke, Indiana, and since his retirement, in 1888, has been numbered with the prominent citizens of Fort Wayne, takes pleasure in looking back upon a busy and eventful career that has stood for progress all along the line and marks him as a man of ambition and industry. He was born in Quebec, Canada, October 29, 1834, a son of Diamond and Frances (Allen) King, who were born respectively in Buxton, Maine, April 25, 1813, and near Kinsale, Ireland, May 20, 1815. The latter immigrated to America, in 1833, and soon afterward became the wife of Diamond King, whose parents had settled in Canada when he was eight years of age. He grew to manhood in Quebec, there met and married his wife, and in 1836 came to Allen county and purchased land in the wilderness of Pleasant township. He was accompanied to Fort Wayne by Thomas Ferguson, an uncle of the late John Ferguson, the well known lumber man, and the journey was made on foot from Toledo, Ohio, to this city. In 1841, after Mr. King had erected a cabin on his land and made little improvements, he returned to Canada, and in 1843 sold his interests in that country and returned to Allen county with his family and settled upon his land in Pleasant township. Here he continued to make his home until 1851, when he went to Oregon and Washington, and remained in that western country for about fourteen years, his eldest daughter accompanying him on his journey. In 1864 he returned, via the Isthmus of Panama, to Allen county and once more settled on his home place in Pleasant township, and there passed the remainder of his life, dying January 6, 1908, having removed to the city of Fort Wayne some years previous. He was an old-time Whig and later a Republican, and at all times was loyal to his party. He was a life-long member of the Baptist church, and was a man of the highest type of character who was ever ready to do his part in the world's work for civilization and progress. Josiah King was reared a farmer and had but little educational advantages, there being no schools of any consequence in Pleasant township until he had nearly reached his majority. He worked on the home place until he was twenty years of age, when he decided to seek his fortune in Chicago. He first found employment at a salary of ten dollars per month, but after a short time engaged in sailing on the lakes, his salary then being twenty dollars a month. On September 16, 1854, he was shipwrecked, five vessels and their crews going down near the Calumet in an equinoxial gale. He with some others made their way to shore and walked to Chicago. He gave his shoes to his captain, who was an old man, and himself walked to the city barefooted. Mr. King recalls that his only earthly possessions were vested in a dollar he had in his pocket. He found employment in Chicago again and for some years was engaged in carpenter work. Returning to Allen county he was employed as a millwright in his home community. Imbued with the patriotism characteristic of the true American, he offered his services in defense of the Union soon after the breaking out of the Civil war. On August 5, 1862, he enlisted in Company F, Eighty-eighth Indiana Infantry (Captain, I. H. LeFevre, who was killed at the battle of Chicamauga). He was mustered in as corporal and later promoted to sergeant, and on May 15, 1864, was advanced to the rank of first lieutenant, being honorably discharged for disability, January 11, 1865. He saw much activity during the two and a half years of his service, participating in many hard fought battles, among which were Perryville, Kentucky, Stone River, Tennessee, Chicamauga, Georgia, Lookout Mountain, Tennessee, Resaca, Georgia, Kenesaw Mountain, Georgia, and many other minor engagements. He suffered an attack of erysipelas during the last few months of his service, which terminated in rheumatism and heart trouble, that disabled him from further service. After the close of his military career he engaged in the mercantile business at Chillecotha, Missouri, for about a year and a half, then returned to Allen county and became identified with the industrial life of the country; and from then until his retirement, in 1888, was one of the active business men of the country. He was employed in various capacities for some years, including the operation of a sawmill. In 1873 he sold his mill and, in 1875, went to Roanoke, where in partnership with James O. Ward he erected a flour mill and continued its successful operation until 1888. In 1887 Mr. Ward sold his interest to William Stults, of Huntington, Indiana, and he was Mr. King's partner for a short time. In 1892 Mr. King disposed of his interest in the mill to L. M. Dague, and retired from the business. During the years of his connection with this enterprise he witnessed the mill's evolution from an old-fashioned burr mill to the modern rolling mill, and the success of the establishment was due largely to his progressive industry and untiring efforts. Though now in the declining years of his life, he still enjoys complete mental activity, and is identified in many ways with matters which have to do with the progress and betterment of the country. Since 1888 he has been a resident of the city of Fort Wayne, living at 818 Wilt street, where he owns a pleasant little home, surrounded by a host of warm friends and sufficient means to keep the wolf from his door.

Thomas A. King.—Among the prominent agriculurists of Allen county, Indiana, none are more worthy of mention in a work of this character than the late Thomas A. King, of Fort Wayne. He was born in Pleasant township, this county, February 17, 1848. His parents, Diamond and Frances (Allen) King, were natives of Maine and Ireland, respectively, though they were pioneers of Allen county and were numbered among the enterprising and substantial citizens of the county. He acquired his education in the public schools of Pleasant township and was still a school boy when the Civil war broke out. He enlisted in Company E, One Hundred and Forty-second Indiana Infantry, and served as a brave and fearless soldier until honorably discharged, acquitting himself in a manner highly creditable to himself and his country. On returning to civil life he again turned his attention to farming in Pleasant township, and for many years was one of the progressive and enterprising men of that section of the county. In 1915 he retired from active business and removed to Fort Wayne, where he afterward resided until his death, February 11, 1917. Besides his various property interests in this city he also had an interest in the grain elevators at Sheldon, and was one of the active grain men of the county. Mr. King was married, in 1872, to Miss Merica E. Dalman, and they became the parents of six children, as follows: Frederick D., of Fort Wayne; Frances, wife of Simon P. Genth, of Lafayette township; Thomas E., of Fort Wayne; Jessie, wife of Gideon Ringenberg; Fern E., wife of Sherman Crowell, and Alma G., wife of Charles Lopshire. The mother of this family died in 1912.

Mrs. Elizabeth Kirkhoff.—One of the honored and estimable residents of Sheldon is Mrs. Elizabeth Kirkhoff, widow of Louis Kirkhoff and the daughter of Jacob and Elizabeth (Houser) Minck. The father was a native German, born in Hessen, Darmstadt, and the mother was of American birth and parentage. They came to Allen county as young people and played an important part in the development of the agri-

W. Robert Klaehn

cultural resources of their community. Louis Kirkhoff, who became the husband of Elizabeth Minck, was a native son of Pleasant township, born there on July 18, 1871, and was a son of Christian Kirkhoff. He was reared and schooled in Pleasant township, and when he married settled on the home place of his father and continued to develop the farm that had occupied his father's attention for the greater part of his life. To Mr. and Mrs. Kirkhoff were born eight children. They are Raymond, Linus, Frances, Henry, Laura, Victor, Clara and Mary. Linus is located at Grayling, Michigan, in the United States army; Frances is in Fort Wayne; Henry is in Virginia, and the others are still on the home place with the widowed mother. The husband died November 11, 1915. The family have membership in the Roman Catholic church and have an excellent standing in their community and the county.

Chester S. Kitch is one of the progressive young business men who has gained place among the prominent and successful representatives of real estate enterprise in Allen county and he is achieving a splendid work in the development of residence properties in Fort Wayne, where he gives special attention to the building of attractive and well-constructed houses which he sells to home-seekers upon most advantageous terms, including a minimum cash payment and regular monthly installments thereafter until the property passes into the full ownership of the appreciative home-maker who, in many instances, would have otherwise been unable to compass this altogether desirable and legitimate end. The C. S. Kitch Company also handles with discrimination approved second-mortgage loans on real estate security, as well as bonds, stocks, equities and life-insurance policies, and in connection with the real estate enterprise is conducted a well-ordered fire-insurance business, the agency acting specially as underwriters for the Providence Insurance Company of Washington, D. C. Mr. Kitch initiated his present business activities in 1909, when he purchased the established real estate business of Stultz and Company and adopted the present title of the C. S. Kitch Company. He is one of the aggressive, liberal and essentially representative young business men of Fort Wayne and is contributing much to the physical development and upbuilding of the city and its environs. Mr. Kitch was born at Huntington, Indiana, February 27, 1883, and is a son of John Kitch, a well-known citizen and business man of Huntington county. After having properly availed himself of the public school advantages in his native city he took a higher course of study in Northwestern University, at Evanston, Illinois, and he thereafter went to the city of Indianapolis, where he entered the service of the company operating the interurban electric railway line between the capital city and Terre Haute. For five years he held the office of district freight and passenger agent for the Indianapolis and Eastern interurban system, and of this responsible position he continued the incumbent until he came to Fort Wayne and engaged in his present line of business enterprise, in 1908. Mr. Kitch is a Republican in politics, is one of the alert and progressive members of the Fort Wayne Commercial Club, and is a popular member of the local lodge of the Benevolent and Protective Order of Elks. On April 15, 1909, he married Miss Agnes Naughton, of Lafayette, Indiana, and they have one child, Jack D.

W. Robert Klaehn is a representative of one of the old and honored German-French families of Allen county, has been a resident of Fort Wayne from the time of his birth and has for a long period of years been engaged in the undertaking business. Close application during exceptionally long business hours eventually brought such impairment to the health of Mr. Klaehn that he was admonished by his family physician to abate his business activities to a certain extent, and under these conditions he admitted to partnership, in March, 1911, his present valued coadjutor, Albert E. Melching, who has relieved him of the more arduous and exacting duties involved in the conducting of the business. In a house that stood at the northeast corner of Washington and VanBuren streets, Fort Wayne, W. Robert Klaehn was born on February 28, 1858. His earlier education was acquired in the Lutheran parochial schools of St. Paul's and the Emanuel churches, and was supplemented by high academic study in Concordia College, as well as a course in the Fort Wayne Business College. In 1876 he became associated with the undertaking business of Hall and Klaehn, his father, Julius J. Klaehn, having been the junior member of this firm. Upon the death of the honored father, in 1880, the widowed mother believed that the subject of this sketch was yet too young to assume full control of the business, and the same was sold to the firm of Scheumann and Schoppman. In 1888 Mr. Klaehn purchased the interest of Schoppman, but the original firm title was continued until 1898, when Mr. Klaehn purchased the interest of Mr. Scheumann and assumed full control of the business. He thereafter conducted the enterprise in an individual way until his health made it expedient to admit his present partner to an alliance which has proved most harmonious and successful to both, the firm name being now Klaehn and Melching. Julius J. Klaehn, father of him to whom this review is dedicated, was born in the Kingdom of Saxony, Germany, and came to America in 1852, in which year he established his residence in Fort Wayne. Here he was associated for a time with the business of John A. Miller, and, in 1862, engaged in the furniture business in an independent way, on Harrison street. He later became a member of the firm of Hall and Klaehn, and the business gradually was concentrated and confined to undertaking and funeral directing. Mr. Klaehn died, January 1, 1880, and his devoted wife did not long survive him, as she was summoned to the life eternal on the 24th of October, 1882, both having been devout communicants of the Lutheran church. The maiden name of Mrs. Klaehn was Wilhelmina Schmidt and she was born in the province of Alsace-Lorraine, which was then a part of French territory. Of the six children in the family three are now living, the subject of this sketch being the only surviving son; Frances is the wife of William Griebel, of Fort Wayne; and Flora is the wife of Rev. John Griebel, who is a clergyman of the Lutheran church, their home being at Perryville, Missouri. W. Robert Klaehn gives his political support to the Republican party and both he and his wife are earnest communicants of Emanuel Lutheran church, of which he is a trustee. On May 15, 1885, Mr. Klaehn wedded Miss Julia Breimeyer, who was born and reared in Fort Wayne, a daughter of Henry and Sophia (Busse) Breimeyer, well-known citizens who settled in Fort Wayne many years ago and who here passed the residue of their lives. Mr. and Mrs. Klaehn became the parents of eleven children, all of whom are living except two, who died in infancy. Julius is associated with his father in business; Arthur is in the employ of the Fort Wayne Plumbing and Heating Company, is married and has three children; Robert holds a position in the offices of the German-American National Bank of Fort Wayne, of which bank

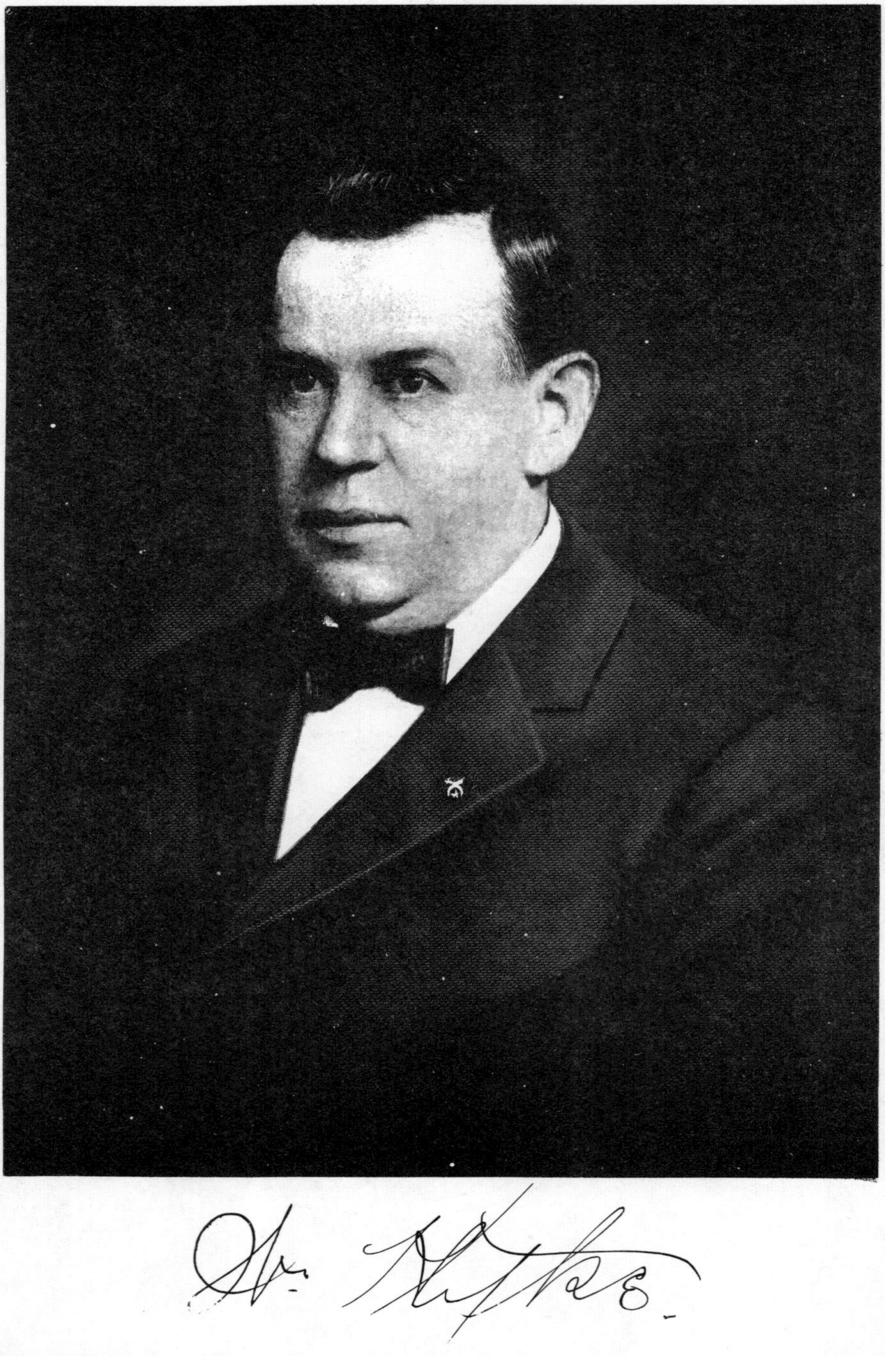

his father is a director; Edna is the wife of Henry J. Herbst, assistant superintendent at Thieme Brothers' silk mill, Fort Wayne, and they have one daughter; Walter is in the employ of the Fort Wayne Oil and Supply Company; Loretta, Beatrice, Mildred and Ruth remain at the parental home.

Jacob Klett was a sterling citizen who, in 1877, founded the large and important lumber business now conducted under the title of Jacob Klett and Sons, and this is now the oldest concern doing business on Pearl street in the city of Fort Wayne, the sons having control of the enterprise and having shown their filial loyalty and appreciation by retaining, since the death of their honored father, the original firm name. The late Jacob Klett, who made a definite impress as one of the staunch business men and loyal citizens of Fort Wayne, was born in Germany on September 13, 1831, and he was reared and educated in his Fatherland, whence, in 1852, about the time of attaining to his legal majority, he came to the United States, a strong and ambitious young man who was animated by a determination to make for himself a place of independence and prosperity in the land of his adoption. About one year after his arrival in America he came to Indiana and established his residence in Fort Wayne. For the first few years he was employed in driving an old-time stage on a line operated by a man named Angel, and thereafter he gained valuable experience while in the employ of the firm of Clark & Rhinesmith, engaged in the lumber business. He did not follow a mere routine, but was alert in absorbing and assimilating knowledge of the various details of the business, so that he was properly fortified when he decided to engage in the same line of business enterprise in an independent way. In 1877, as previously noted, he became the founder of the business that still perpetuates his name and that is conducted by his three sons under the title of Jacob Klett and Sons, the enterprise having its headquarters in the same location that Mr. Klett established the business virtually forty years ago. He applied himself with characteristic energy and progressiveness until he had developed a prosperous lumber business of a general order, and, in 1883, he admitted to partnership his eldest son, John A. William B., another son, was made a member of the firm in 1889, and, in 1898, after the death of the father, a third son, John G., likewise was admitted to partnership, these three constituting the interested principals in the present firm. In addition to maintaining at the yard a large stock of lumber of all kinds and also general lines of building material, the firm also operates a planing mill which was established by the concern about the year 1889 and which is situated at the corner of Wells and Superior streets. In the handling of its business the firm gives employment to an average of twenty persons, and the sons are fully upholding the honors of the family name. The maiden name of Mrs. Klett was Louise P. Sautter, and she survived her husband by about twelve years, he having passed away on July 3, 1896, and her death having occurred January 23, 1908. Of their children three sons and two daughters are now living.

William C. Klitzke was in the very prime of his strong and useful manhood when he was summoned from the stage of his mortal endeavors, but he had already accomplished a man's work in the world and had left a definite impress on the business activities of the city of Fort Wayne, though he had here maintained his home for less than a decade.

His ability and his sterling attributes of character gave him inviolable place in the confidence and good will of those with whom he came in contact in the various relations of life, and many were the staunch friends who felt a sense of personal loss and bereavement when he passed to the life eternal. Mr. Klitzke was born in the city of Chicago, Illinois, on February 3, 1874, and thus was but little more than forty-three years of age when he passed away, his death having occurred at his home in Fort Wayne on February 17, 1916. He was a son of Ferdinand and Augusta Klitzke, both of whom were born in Germany and both of whom survive him, their home being now in the city of Hammond, Indiana, and the father being a representative lumber buyer of that place. Of the other children it may be recorded that John is a resident of Fort Wayne; Herman lives in the city of Chicago; Emil is identified with business affairs in Fort Wayne; and Louis and Paul reside at Hammond, Indiana. The subject of this brief memoir gained his early education in the public schools and in his youth identified himself with practical business affairs. He remained at the parental home until April 14, 1900, when was solemnized his marriage to Miss Ida Mundt, who was born in Germany but was a child at the time of the family emigration to America. She is a daughter of Herman and Freda Mundt, both of whom are now deceased, the father having been a carpenter by trade and having been a resident of Hammond at the time of his death. His devoted wife survived him and was called to the life eternal in October, 1914. They became the parents of five children: Minnie is the wife of Earl Maske, of Fort Wayne; Alice is the wife of Frederick Smith, of this city; Millie is the wife of Patrick Butler, of St. Louis, Missouri; Herman resides at Hammond, Indiana; and Mrs. Klitzke is the eldest of the number. After his marriage Mr. Klitzke was identified with business interests in Hammond until 1907, when he came to Fort Wayne and assumed the active management of the affairs of the Fort Wayne Dairy Company, of which he was vice-president and treasurer at the time of his death, a substantial and prosperous enterprise having been developed under his progressive and well-ordered management and the company still represents one of the important industrial enterprises of the Allen county metropolis. Mr. Klitzke was a Democrat in politics, but never manifested aught of ambition for public office. He was reared in the faith of the Lutheran church, and was affiliated with the Masonic fraternity, including the Shrine, and the Benevolent and Protective Order of Elks. He is survived by no children, but his widow still maintains her home in Fort Wayne and continues actively in the management of the business of her late husband, besides which she is a stockholder in the Fort Wayne Transfer Company.

David N. Klopfenstein.—The townsite of Grabill is located on what was the birthplace of David N. Klopfenstein—the homestead of his parents, Joseph and Fannie (Schlatler) Klopfenstein, who spent their maturer years upon it and there ended their days. After the farm came into the possession of the son David, he began to dispose of it, bit by bit, for building sites and retains only the spot on which the family residence stood. Mr. Klopfenstein was born on July 25, 1866, one of seven children born to his parents. Jacob, the eldest, lives in Archbold, Ohio. The second child, a daughter, died in infancy. David N., of this review, was the third born. Joseph is a resident of Grabill. Katherine married Frank Hauser, a minister, now located in Cleveland, Ohio. The two youngest were twins, John Henry and Berg, the former being a minister of the Gospel and located in Kansas in his work. David Klopfenstein had the usual farm training and country schooling that goes with rural life, and when he was old enough to begin to make his own way in the world, went to work at the carpenter's trade, in which he continued to the age of twenty-five years. He then spent a year in Kansas and two years in Oklahoma and, in 1896, returned to the family home in Grabill, making that his headquarters and finding work as a carpenter in the county. He is still engaged in that work, but specializes in fence building, and has built a large part of the modern fences to be found on Allen county farms. For a few years after he settled on the old homestead place he farmed with much success, but the eventual sale of the greater part of the highly improved land brought an end to that enterprise. In 1884 Mr. Klopfenstein built a cider mill on the homestead farm, since which time he has operated it in season every year with the exception of three seasons. On November 2, 1899, Mr. Klopfenstein married Caroline Roth Goldsmith, the widow of Amos Goldsmith. Three children have blessed their home—Elizabeth May, born August 5, 1901; Joseph John, born June 19, 1903; and Bernice Blye, born February 28, 1906. The family have membership in the Mission church and have an active part in the labors of that organization in their community. Mr. Klopfenstein is independent in his political views and takes no part in politics beyond that dictated by the demands of good citizenship.

Joseph A. Klopfenstein.—The Klopfenstein family has already been mentioned at some length in a sketch of David N., a brother of the subject, so that it will suffice to say in regard to the parentage of the subject that he is a son of Joseph and Fannie (Schlatler) Klopfenstein, people of Adams county birth, and farming people all their lives. The homestead farm, on their death, became the property of David Klopfenstein, and has since been sold in small parcels for building spots in the growing village of Grabill. Joseph Klopfenstein was born there on July 25, 1867, and lived on the home place until he reached the age of twenty-one, when he married and established a home of his own. Katherine Yaggy became his wife on November 6, 1890. She was born in Allen county and is a daughter of Andrew and Elizabeth (Sanders) Yaggy, native Ohioans who came to Allen county in their young days and there spent the remainder of their lives. They were the parents of a fine family of children, briefly named as follows: Hannah, the wife of John Roth, of Berne, Indiana; Henry, of Woodburn, Indiana; Andrew, of the same place; Katherine, the wife of the subject; Menno, located in Arizona; John, of Woodburn; and Sarah, the wife of Rev. Henry Klopfenstein, of Mineola, Kansas, a brother of the subject. The mother of this family, by a previous marriage to Jacob Roth, had five children. Anna, the eldest, is deceased. Levi is a resident of Springfield township. Elizabeth lives in Grabill. Louisa is the wife of Jacob Klopfenstein, of Grabill, and Lydia married David Grabill, of Grabill. Joseph and Katherine (Yaggy) Klopfenstein have seven children. Menno, the first born, named for his maternal uncle, lives in Grabill. Jesse is in Fort Wayne, with the General Electric Works at that point. Two pairs of twins followed—Howard and Homer, and Rufus and Reuben. Rufus is in Fort Wayne in the employ of the General Electric Works, but the other three boys are at home in Grabill. Mary-Anna, the youngest child, is also at home with her parents. Mr. Klopfenstein has long been engaged in the manufacturing of tile in Grabill and has a very successful and growing plant there. He is associated in the business with his brother, David N., and his sons also are of much help to him in the operation of the plant. He and his family are members of the Mission church and he has served for years as a member of the Grabill school board. He has no political affiliations, sharing with his brother David a belief that community welfare can best be served without allegiance to party lines.

Charles S. Knight did a man's work in a manly way and his entire life was one marked by rectitude and honor, so that he measured up to the highest standard demanded for the commanding of popular respect and approbation. He became closely identified with the civic and business affairs of Fort Wayne, where his widow still maintains her home, but in the closing period of his life he was giving his attention principally to the zinc-mining industry, in the vicinity of Marion, Crittenden county, Kentucky. He was well known and highly honored in Fort Wayne and it is but consistent that in this history of Allen county be entered tribute to him as a man of fine character and as a citizen of the utmost loyalty. Charles S. Knight was born in Columbus, Ohio, on November 24, 1846, a son of Willard and Elizabeth (Matier) Knight, both natives of Pennsylvania. The father was long identified with railway affairs and was connected with the Hocking Valley Railroad for many years prior to his death, both he and his wife having been residents of Ohio at the time of their death. He to whom this memoir is dedicated acquired his early education in the common schools of Pennsylvania and Ohio and in the latter state gained his preliminary business experience. In 1882 he established his residence in Fort Wayne, and here he was in the employ of the Fort Wayne Gas Company until he accepted the position as a salesman for the Fort Wayne Electric Company with which he continued to be identified many years, his alliance with this important industrial enterprise having continued for some time after the local plant and business had been absorbed and made a part of the organization of the General Electric Company. It was after a reorganization of the business in Fort Wayne that he became interested in zinc mining in Kentucky, but he continued to maintain his home in Fort Wayne until his death, which occurred August 14, 1899. Mr. Knight was a well fortified advocate of the principles for which the Democratic party stands sponsor in a basic way, he received the thirty-second degree in the Ancient Accepted Scottish Rite of Masonry, was affiliated also with the Benevolent & Protective Order of Elks, and he attended and gave liberal support to the Presbyterian church, of which his widow has been an active member for many years. On August 2, 1870, was solemnized the marriage of Mr. Knight to Miss Alice Cheney, who was born at Defiance, Ohio, and who is a daughter of James and Nancy (Evans) Cheney, natives, respectively, of Vermont and Ohio. Mr. Cheney was a young man when he made his way from New England to Toledo, Ohio, and he soon located at Defiance, that state, where he presently became one of the leading contractors in connection with the construction of the old Wabash and Erie canal. He maintained his residence at Defiance about ten years and in 1854 removed to Fort Wayne, where he engaged in the banking business. In 1856 he removed with his family to Logansport, Indiana, where he engaged in the banking business. He was one of twenty men who supervised the starting of national banks in Indiana. Later he became interested financially in the Fort Wayne gas works, and in 1882 he came to Fort Wayne to assume the supervision of the business of the gas company, of which he was the president. He continued as one of the substantial capitalists and honored and influential citizens of Fort Wayne until his death, December 13, 1903, at the venerable age of eighty-six years, his wife having passed to the life eternal on June 27, 1895, at the age of seventy-one years, and the memories of both are revered by all who came within the sphere of their benign influence. Of their four children the eldest is Helen, who is the wife of John A. Kimberley, their home being in Neenah, Wisconsin; Willard is now a resident of Redlands, California; Mary C. is the wife of John C. Nelson, of Logansport, Indiana; and Mrs. Knight is the youngest of the number. Mr. and Mrs. Knight became the parents of six children, of whom the first born, Willard C., died at the age of forty-four years; James C. is prominently identified with business interests at Jackson, Tennessee; Elizabeth is the wife of Frederick C. Peters, of Fort Wayne; Helen C. is the wife of Dr. Allan Hamilton, a representative physician of Fort Wayne; Mary is the wife of Frederick E. Hoffman, of this city; and Alice Stuart remains with her widowed mother in their pleasant home in Fort Wayne.

Otto Knoblauch has been a resident of Allen county since 1881 and here his ability and business sagacity have enabled him to achieve large and merited success. He is one of the venerable and honored citizens of the village of Woodburn, Maumee township, where he formerly operated a saw mill and conducted a general store, and where he now gives his attention to the real estate business. He is one of the large landholders of the county, owning eight hundred acres of valuable farm property, and through his varied activities he has contributed his quota to the civic and material progress and prosperity of the county. Though he has passed the psalmist's span of three score years and ten he retains splendid mental and physical vigor—the reward for right living and right thinking. As one of the substantial and valued citizens of Allen county he is eminently entitled to representation in this history. Mr. Knoblauch was born in Osterburg, Kingdom of Saxony, Germany, in the year 1846, a son of William and Charlotte (Schroeder) Knoblauch, who came with their children to America in 1868 and settled in Lenawee county, Michigan, where they passed the remainder of their lives, the father having been a farmer by vocation during his entire active career. William Knoblauch was twice married and his first wife was comparatively a young woman at the time of her death. They became the parents of four children—William, Frederick, Charlotte and Elizabeth, all of whom are deceased. Of the second marriage were born four children—Herman, Otto, Ludwig, and August. Of these children Herman is deceased. Otto Knoblauch gained his youthful education in the excellent schools of his native land and was twenty-two years of age when he accompanied his parents on their immigration to the United States. He continued to be associated with agricultural industry in Lenawee county, Michigan, until 1881, when he came to Allen county, Indiana, and established his residence at Woodburn. There he became the owner and operator of a saw mill and also conducted a general merchandise store, his active connection with these enterprises having continued until 1898, when he retired. He has since devoted his attention principally to the buying, selling and improving of farm and village property in this section of the county, and he has been one of the honored and influential citizens of Woodburn, where he held for six years the office of postmaster. He is independent in politics and he and his wife are zealous communicants of the Lutheran church. On June 2, 1879, was solemnized the marriage of Mr. Knoblauch to Miss Margaret Flack, daughter of Charles and Margaret (Messerer) Flack, at that time residents of Detroit, Michigan. The parents of Mrs. Knoblauch were born in Germany and were young folk when they came to America, in 1852. Mr. Flack was a cabinetmaker by trade and for many years was actively engaged in the work of his trade in the city of Detroit, Michigan. Mrs. Knoblauch was the first born in a family of five children, the others being Elise, Ernest, Mary and Charles, all of whom are living except the last mentioned. The loved mother is deceased and the venerable father now resides in the home of Mr. and Mrs. Knoblauch, who accord to him true filial solicitude. Mr. and Mrs. Knoblauch became the parents of ten children, whose names are here entered in the respective order of birth: Ernest, Carl, Anna, Elise, Albert, Carl (second of the name), Emma, one who died in infancy, Clara and Walter. Carl, first of that name, died in infancy, and Albert is also deceased, so that the surviving children are seven in number.

George Koehlinger was four years old when he accompanied his parents on their journey from the German Fatherland to America, in 1849. He was born in Germany, July 26, 1845, son of Henry and Christine (Weber) Koehlinger, both reared in Germany and there married. They came to Allen county very soon after their arrival on American shores and made their home there the rest of their lives, settling in Adams township after a long and tedious as well as perilous journey by ox team overland. They bought a farm of eighty acres, for which they paid the small sum of two dollars per acre, and there settled down to the quiet of farm life. They prospered and came to be leaders in their community. The father, who was a Republican and a member of the German Lutheran church, died at the age of sixty-five, leaving a family of nine children, of whom only four are living. Named in the order of their birth they are Jacob, Philip, Mary, Peter, Henry, Catherine, Elizabeth, George and Frederick. The five first named are deceased, and it is worthy of mention that Henry, the fifth son, was a soldier in the Civil war. Catherine is the wife of Frederick Collinger. Elizabeth lives in New Haven. George is the subject of this sketch, and Frederick is living retired. Mr. Koehlinger attended the German Lutheran schools of his community as a boy, but his education was meagre, and his young life was for the most part spent on the home farm where he ably assisted his father in the management of the place. In time he bought the farm home, and since that time has bought and sold a good many parcels of farm land in Adams township. He is profitably engaged in stock farming and has made an unqualified success of his farming career. He is a Democrat in politics and was for seven years a member of the advisory board of his township. Mr. Koehlinger has all the ear-marks of a good citizen and his identification with his home community has been a commendable and satisfactory one, viewed from all standpoints. He was married on June 6, 1867, to Miss Mary Lepper, daughter of George and Julia Lepper. Mrs. Koehlinger died on October 26, 1907, the mother of three children— Elizabeth, May and Henry. The first named is the wife of Christ Dennges, of Fort Wayne, and the mother of four children, named Arthur, Otto, Christ and Walter. May married Henry Gerhard of Fort Wayne and has Henry, Hulda, Elmer and Clarence. Henry is also married and his three children are Velma, Paul and Berenice. Henry, it should be said, is engaged in the operation of the old home farm, owned and operated by his father, the subject, for many years. He is a successful farmer and reflects much of the careful training received while he was his father's assistant.

Robert Koerber.—Switzerland has through so many generations been famed for her watches that the mention of the one name invariably suggests the other. And so it is quite in keeping that the father of Robert Koerber should have been a watch-maker, for he was born in Switzerland, was there reared and there served his apprenticeship under an expert watch-maker. Frederick Koerber came, with his wife, Elizabeth (Koerber) Koerber, in the year 1887, to America, settling first in Lima, Ohio, where they remained a year and then moved to Fort Wayne. There they spent the remainder of their lives, the father passing out in 1902 and the mother in 1914. They were the parents of five children—Frederick, Robert, Jacob, Bertha and Walter—all residents of Fort Wayne, with the single exception of Frederick, who makes his home in Colorado. Robert was born in Switzerland on March 7, 1880, and was seven years old when he accompanied his parents to America. He attended the public schools of Lima, Ohio, and Fort Wayne, up to the age of fourteen, when he undertook to learn the trade of a cigar-maker. He was not sufficiently enthusiastic about the work to wish to continue in it indefinitely, and when he was seventeen he entered upon a jewelry apprenticeship under his father, who was at that time in the employ of H. C. Graffe & Company, then a prominent firm in the city but no longer in business. When Mr. Koerber was twenty-one years old he engaged in business with Eugene George Trenkley, now deceased, and the concern has grown with the passing years so that today the Trenkley & Koerber, Inc., jewelry store is one of the prominent places in the heart of the retail district of Fort Wayne. Mr. Koerber was married on August 20, 1902, to Miss Mary M. Volmer, daughter of Mrs. Mary Volmer, of Fort Wayne. Their children are Robert Frederick, Harold and Marcella Elizabeth, aged thirteen, ten and seven years, respectively. The family have membership in Plymouth Congregational church and Mr. Koerber is a Scottish Rite Mason and a Shriner. He is also prominent as a member of the Quest Club, the Rotary Club, the Country Club, the Commercial Club and the Merchants' Association. Mr. and Mrs. Koerber claim a wide circle of friends in their home city and are warmly received in whatever circle they appear.

Christian Koester claims Fort Wayne as his birthplace, and has passed his life thus far within the confines of Allen county. He was born in the city named above on December 30, 1857, son of Christian and Minnie (Stillhorn) Koester, both born and reared in Germany. They came to Allen county in young life, settled in Fort Wayne and there had their home until 1880, when they came to St. Joseph township and are there resident at this writing. Mr. Koester was successfully engaged for many years in the lime and stone business in Fort Wayne, but in St. Joseph township turned his attention to agriculture, in which he enjoyed a very commendable success. The only child of these people is Christian Koester, the subject. He had his early education in the schools of Fort Wayne, and in 1875 came to St. Joseph township and settled on the farm, which is his home today. He has been successful in farm life, owns one hundred and fifty-one acres of highly cultivated land in one piece and eighty acres in another, both places being well developed and highly productive. The home place is one of the finest in the township, with a modern brick dwelling house and all other buildings accordingly. The house is most pleasantly situated in the midst of a pine grove, and its appointments are wholly modern and indicative of the good judgment of its owner. Mr. Koester is engaged in general farming and stockraising and his place is second to none in the township in point of productiveness and appearance. Mr. Koester was married, in 1880, to Miss Mary Gerke, daughter of John and Mary (Meyer) Gerke, both of German birth and early settlers in St. Joseph township, Allen county. To Mr. and Mrs. Koester nine children were born, all living at this writing. They are Minnie, Emma, Fred, Harry, Carl, George, Elmer, Marie and Paul. Mr. Koester has not identified himself with public life in his community to any extent, having been satisfied with the duties of good citizenship without permitting himself to participate in the political life of his township. He has allied himself with no lodges, but has been a lifelong member of the German Lutheran church, as is also his wife, and their children were reared in the same faith. The family is among the most dependable element in the town and they have played a conspicuous part in the upbuilding and development of their community in its most creditable aspects.

Rev. Herman B. Kohlmeier, pastor of the Lutheran Evangelical church at New Haven, was born in Houston county, Minnesota, December 19, 1871. His parents were Henry F. and Katherine (Burmester) Kohlmeier. He received his primary education in schools near his home and then attended Concordia College at Milwaukee four years, then two years in the school of the same name at Fort Wayne. Succeeding this he continued his studies at Concordia Seminary at St. Louis, Missouri, where he graduated in 1894. Having thus prepared himself he accepted the pastorate of a church at Pipestone, Minnesota. After six years he came to Indiana and took charge of the churches at Garrett and Auburn. In December, 1907, he came to New Haven, where he has met with marked success. Since coming here he has improved the property very much, having built a new brick parsonage and a fine new school house where, with an assistant, he conducts a school with upwards of sixty pupils, taking them through the seventh grade. Besides this he has a church at Monroeville. Rev. Kohlmeier was married November 18, 1896, to Alvina Lange, at Weyauwega, Wisconsin. They had no children, but adopted a girl now named Irene. Mrs. Kohlmeier died March 1, 1904. His second marriage occurred August 24, 1905, when Lydia Boettcher, of Jericho Springs, Mo., became his wife. She has borne him nine children, named Theodore, Paul Gerhard, Natalie, Ruth, Esther, Johanna, Lydia, and twin girls Beata and Tabea.

Elias Kohr is a representative of a family that was long established in Maryland and which first settled in Allen county in 1850. He is a son of Samuel Kohr, born May 20, 1808, and for many years prominent in the development process that converted this section of the county from a wilderness state into a blooming garden. The elder Kohr was a staunch Republican in later life and was a member of the United Brethren church to the end of his days. His children numbered eight, and of that family only three are living. Named in order of their birth they were George, Catherine, Sarah, William, Nancy, Jacob, Elias and Jole. Sarah lives in Wells county, as does also Nancy, and Elias, the immediate subject of this sketch, is the other surviving child. He was born in Ohio, February 28, 1847, and was reared to farm life, gaining such meager education as was available to the country boy of his day. He volunteered for service in the Civil war in the spring of 1864, and served to the end of hostilities as a member of Company D, One Hundred and Thirty-seventh Infantry of Indiana. The war over, he settled on land in Lafayette township, buying eighty acres of virgin land, on which he gradually made the necessary improvements to bring it into a state of productiveness. He has today one of the attractive places in the township and is counted among the prosperous farming men of the district. He was married on February 16, 1871, to Miss Nancy Hamilton, daughter of Benjamin Hamilton, and eight children have been born to them. Harry S. is dead. Alwildia is the wife of J. E. Plummer. Francis H. was the third child and Wire M. the fourth. Jonathan is deceased and the remaining children are John C., Monteville D. and Julia E., she being the wife of B. H. Pierson of Janesville. Alwildia is the mother of three children—Arnold F., Doyle and Wilma, while Francis has Cecil Dayton and Herman Oliver. Julia (Kohr) Pierson has one child—Vilas M.

Edward H. Kruse, M. D.—The old-time popular prejudice against the young physician and surgeon has been largely obliterated in recent years, and this result has been accomplished by the effective service and earnest enthusiasm of the younger representatives of the most exacting and responsible of all professions. Long experience brings its rewards in efficiency, but modern medical and surgical science demands of even the tyro a most thorough and comprehensive preliminary preparation and clinical experience. Dr. Kruse is one of the able physicians of Fort Wayne, in which city he was born on June 15, 1883. He is a son of William and Dorothea (Busching) Kruse, both of whom were born in Germany, and at the time of his death the father was one of the successful business men and honored and influential citizens of Fort Wayne, where he had long been engaged in the contracting business and where his widow still maintains her home. Of their six children three are living—Frederick, Dr. Edward H. and Waller, all of whom reside in their native city of Fort Wayne. Dr. Kruse gained his preliminary education in the Lutheran parochial schools of Fort Wayne, and in preparation for his chosen profession entered the Indiana Medical College, in the city of Indianapolis. In this institution he was graduated as a member of the class of 1906, and after having thus gained his degree of Doctor of Medicine he further fortified himself by effective post-graduate work for two years in leading medical and surgical institutions in the cities of Berlin and Vienna, Germany. This was the final preparation. He established himself in practice upon his return from Germany, in 1909. During the four years, from 1912 to 1915, the Doctor held the office of coroner of Allen county, and since his retirement his co-operation has been retained, as he is now serving as deputy coroner. He is actively identified with the Allen County Medical Society, the Indiana State Medical Society, and the American Medical Association. In politics he pays his allegiance to the Democratic party, his religious faith is that of the Lutheran church, and he is a loyal member of the Fort Wayne Commercial Club. The Doctor maintains his offices in a building at the corner of Berry and Clinton streets. In December, 1912, was solemnized the marriage of Dr. Kruse to Miss Geneva Maxfield, who was born at Angola, Steuben county, Indiana, a daughter of Samuel Maxfield, and the two children of this union are Dorothy Lou, and Geneva.

Erastus B. Kunkle was one of those strong and loyal men who always faced the right way with the right spirit, and by very nature and integrity of purpose he helped to carry the victorious attitude in all of the relations of a signally earnest and useful career. He was a man of marked inventive genius and revealed this talent in a legitimate and productive way that made him a useful citizen and that brought to him a large and merited success and prosperity. He was one of the veritable captains of industry in Fort Wayne, where he developed a substantial industrial enterprise in the manufacturing of valuable mechanical devices and appliances of his own invention, and his character and services marked him as the model citizen, so that his name and memory are held in lasting honor in the city that was long the stage of his productive activities and to the interests of which he was loyal at all times. Erastus Boise Kunkle was born in Westmoreland county, Pennsylvania, on the 14th of December, 1836, and thus was nearly seventy-seven years of age when, on August 2, 1913, he was summoned to the life eternal, after a life replete with kindliness, sympathy and good deeds, as well as one filled with large and worthy achievement of a practical order. His parents, Leonard and Harriet (Boise) Kunkle, passed their entire lives in the old Keystone state, within whose borders he himself was reared and educated, besides there learning in his youth the trade of machinist. In 1862, as a skilled artisan, he went to Alliance, Stark county, Ohio, where he worked at his trade for two years. He then, in 1864, came to Fort Wayne, where for eleven years he was employed in the locomotive department of the shops of the Pennsylvania Railroad. In the meanwhile he had given much thought and much of his leisure time to study and experimentation and finally effected the invention of the celebrated Kunkle lock-up pop safety valve, to the manufacturing of which he began to devote his attention in January, 1876, after having duly patented the invention, to which he subsequently added numerous other inventions of valuable order and expanded his manufacturing to include the turning out of his various devices. The improved inventions that he thus placed on the market met with unqualified favor, for their superiority and practical value could not fail to gain recognition, and in association with his brother-in-law, W. D. Bostick, he built up one of the substantial and important industrial enterprises of Fort Wayne. He continued his active association with his manufacturing business until his death, and since that time the enterprise has been continued successfully by his former partner and by Mrs. Kunkle, who is a sister of the latter and the widow of the honored founder of the business. Mr. Kunkle was a man of broad and well fortified views, loyal and progressive in his civic attitude, and a staunch advocate of the principles of the Democratic party. He had no desire for political office, but his civic loyalty was such that he was gratified to serve as a member of the board of waterworks commissioners of Fort Wayne and otherwise to do all in his power to further the well being of his home city. He was a deacon and trustee of the English Lutheran church of Fort Wayne, of which his widow continues a devoted communicant. On October 22, 1868, was solemnized the marriage of Mr. Kunkle to Miss Louisa E. Bostick, who was born in Lancaster county, Pennsylvania, daughter of the late Emmanuel and Harriet (Kline) Bostick, who were residents of Fort Wayne at the time of their death. Of the children of Mr. and Mrs. Kunkle, Ella A. remains with her widowed mother in the attractive home provided by the devoted husband and

E. B. Kunkle

father whose memory they revere; Eva H. is the wife of Chancey Griffith, of Fort Wayne; Blanche M. is now a resident of the city of Chicago; Lulu C. is the wife of Otis E. Goodman, of Los Angeles, California; Edith P. is the wife of Charles Merrill, of Princeton, West Virginia; Laura is the wife of Adolph Schumaker, of Fort Wayne; and Frances A. died in infancy.

John F. Kurtz.—That man who justifies himself to the world and to himself through years of earnest and productive industry well merits the gracious environment of peace and prosperity when the shadows of his life begin to lengthen gradually from that golden west where the sunset gates are open wide. Such a sterling representative of the world's great army of workers is John F. Kurtz, who long held prestige as one of the energetic, resourceful and successful exponents of agricultural industry in Allen county and who, now venerable in years, is living in merited retirement in an attractive village home at Harlan, Springfield township. Mr. Kurtz was born in the Kingdom of Wurtemburg, Germany, August 10, 1840, a son of John and Barbara (Stokes) Kurtz, who immigrated to America, in 1841, and settled in Lancaster county, Pennsylvania, where they continued to reside seven years. They then removed to Richland county, Ohio, and sixteen years later, in 1871, came to Allen county, Indiana, and settled on a farm in Milan township, where they passed the remainder of their lives, both having attained to advanced age and both having been devoted members of the German Lutheran church, the entire active career of the father after coming to America having been marked by his close and effective association with farm industry. Of the seven children the subject of this sketch is the eldest; Eliza is deceased, and the others are still living—Martha, Mary, Kate, Henry and Arthur. John F. Kurtz was about six months of age at the time of the family immigration to the United States and in Ohio was reared to adult age, the while he made good use of the advantages afforded in the common schools of the period. He accompanied his parents on their removal to Allen county, and after having been for fifteen years identified with the work and management of the old homestead farm of his father, in Milan township, purchased his present well improved farm of sixty-two acres, which lies adjacent to the village of Harlan, in Springfield township. He still resides on this well improved farm, but for several years past has lived virtually retired, in the enjoyment of the rewards of former years of earnest and honorable endeavor. He has had no ambition for public office or political activity but is aligned as a loyal supporter of the cause of the Democratic party and has always done his part in the furtherance of those things that conserve the communal welfare. He is affiliated with Harlan Lodge, No. 331, Independent Order of Odd Fellows, and both he and his wife hold membership in the Methodist Episcopal church. In 1876 was solemnized the marriage of Mr. Kurtz to Miss Mary Swift, who was born and reared in this county, a daughter of the late Philetus and Caroline (Kutts) Swift, natives of New England and early pioneer settlers in Allen county, Indiana. Mr. and Mrs. Kurtz have five children—Eva, Agnes, Carrie, Annie, and Gaylord.

Christ Lamle.—Another of the sterling native sons of Allen county who has here achieved definite success as a progressive and energetic exponent of agricultural and live-stock enterprise is he whose name introduces this paragraph and whose well improved farm is eligibly situated in Section 12, Lake township, on rural mail route No. 4 from the city of

Fort Wayne. He is a popular representative of one of the honored pioneer families of the county and his venerable father is now living retired in the city of Fort Wayne. Mr. Lamle was born in this county, March 20, 1866, a son of Gottlieb and Magdalina (Erman) Lamle, both of whom were born in the Kingdom of Wurtemburg, Germany, and were young folk when they came to America, their marriage having been solemnized in Allen county, Indiana. They settled first on a farm in Wayne township and later the father continued his activities as a farmer in Aboite and Lake townships. He and his wife lived up to the full tension of pioneer life, endured many hardships and privations but were sustained by unwavering courage and ambition, as well as by mutual love and devotion, so that they gradually won for themselves and their children definite independence and prosperity. Gottlieb Lamle used oxen in clearing his land in the early days and in later years often recalls incidents of the pioneer period in Allen county history, especially one in which he was able to rescue his wife from death when she was pursued and beleaguered by a pack of wolves. Mrs. Lamle had set forth, barefooted, to bring in the cattle on the pioneer farm, and a large pack of wolves trailed her by her bloody footprints. Becoming aware of her imminent danger, she took refuge in a tree, and by good fortune her husband found her when he set out for the search at night, his lantern and the axe which he carried having proved adequate in driving off the ferocious beasts, which were thus cheated of their prey. Mr. Lamle was long numbered among the energetic and successful farmers of the county and is now one of the venerable and revered pioneer citizens of Fort Wayne, his cherished and devoted wife having passed to the life eternal on March 17, 1914. Of their eleven children the eldest, William, is now a resident of California; John M. is a farmer in Washington township; Mrs. Louise Happle and Mrs. Katie Fritz reside in Lake township; Gottlieb, Jr., is deceased; George, Christ, David and Andrew are all prosperous farmers in Lake township; Gottlieb (second of the name) resides in Fort Wayne; and Magdalena is deceased. Christ Lamle gained his early education in the rural schools of Lake township and was associated with his father in the work and management of the home farm until his marriage, in the autumn of 1891. For a short time thereafter he and his wife lived at Churubusco, Whitley county, and upon their return to Allen county established their home on the Randall farm, in Lake township. Two years later they removed thence to the Henry M. Williams farm, and later were on a farm in Cedar Creek township. Two years thereafter found them on a farm in Washington township and they then removed to their present farm, which comprises ninety-seven acres and is commonly known as the Litchfield farm. Mr. Lamle has made various improvements on this homestead, including the installing of a considerable amount of tile drain-pipe, and he is recognized as one of the energetic and circumspect representatives of farm enterprise in Lake township. Diversified agriculture receives his careful attention and he is making a specialty also of the raising of Duroc-Jersey swine. He is aligned as a supporter of the cause of the Democratic party and is affiliated with the lodge of Ancient Free & Accepted Masons at Huntertown. On November 18, 1891, Mr. Lamle wedded Miss Malena Huguenard, who was born and reared in Washington township, this county, a daughter of August and Mary (Humbert) Huguenard, both natives of France and residents of Washington township for many years, the devoted wife and mother having there died on the old homestead farm, June 2, 1900, and the father having thereafter lived retired in the city of Fort Wayne until his death, which occurred June 17, 1916. Mrs. Lamle was the fourth in a family of six children; Louisa, the eldest, is deceased; Felix and Mary still reside in Allen county; Alexander was killed in an accident in the electric power house in Fort Wayne; and Frank died young. Mr. and Mrs. Lamle have no children.

Rev. August H. L. Lange, the able and honored pastor of Concordia Evangelical Lutheran church of Fort Wayne, was born in the city of St. Louis, Missouri, on January 5, 1864, son of Louis and Margaret (Schmidt) Lange, both of whom were born in Hessen, Germany. In his youth Louis Lange learned the printer's trade and for many years was editor and publisher of Die Abend Schule, a semi-monthly, illustrated family magazine that is still published in St. Louis and that under his management gained a wide circulation among the German-speaking people of the United States and Canada. With this splendid publication Mr. Lange continued his active association until his death, which occurred in St. Louis in 1894, his wife surviving him by a number of years and both having been most devout communicants of the Evangelical Lutheran church. Of their twelve children only three are now living, and of the number the subject of this review is the eldest; Theodore succeeded his father as publisher of Die Abend Schule and is still conducting this excellent periodical; and Pauline is the wife of Otto Doederlein, of Chicago. Another of the sons was the late Hon. Louis Lange, of Chicago, who was for a number of years publisher and editor of a weekly political review known as Die Rundschau, and who served four years, 1893-7, as American consul in the city of Bremen, Germany, his death having occurred in 1898. Rev. August H. L. Lange acquired his preliminary education in the German Lutheran parochial schools of his native city, thereafter pursued a higher academic course in Concordia College, Fort Wayne, Indiana, and his ecclesiastical and philosophical studies in preparation for the ministry were completed in Concordia Theological Seminary, St. Louis, Missouri. He was ordained a clergyman of the Evangelical Lutheran church in 1886, in the Missouri synod, and his first pastoral charge was at Fremont, Nebraska, where he continued his services five years. For the ensuing three years he was assistant pastor of Zion Lutheran church in the city of Chicago, and simultaneously he assisted his brother, the late Hon. Louis Lange, as co-editor of Die Rundschau, a publication previously mentioned in this context. In 1894 Mr. Lange accepted a call to the position of assistant pastor of Bethlehem Lutheran church, in the city of St. Louis, and incidentally he assisted in the editorial work and management of Die Abend Schule, the periodical that was so long published by his honored father, who was a man of fine intellectual attainments. He continued his pastoral service in his native city until 1896, when he accepted a call to assume the pastoral charge of the eastern district of St. Paul's Lutheran church in Fort Wayne, where he has maintained his residence since that time and where his consecrated zeal and devotion have been prolific in the development and vitalizing of the work of his present parish, which was formally organized on January 1, 1900, as Concordia church, and which now has about twelve hundred communicants, making it one of the large and important Lutheran parishes of Indiana. Mr. Lange also has ex-officio direction of the parochial school, which retains in service five efficient teachers and has an enrollment of three hundred and twelve pupils in 1917. He is president also of the board of trustees of his alma mater, Concordia College; is second vice-president of the central district of the Lutheran synod of Missouri; is secretary of the Lutheran Hospital board of trustees, Fort Wayne; and secretary of the Luther Institute of this city. It will thus be seen that the exacting ministerial and executive duties devolving upon Mr. Lange make full demands upon his energy, thought and time, but his enthusiasm and zeal have proved equal to all such demands and he is indefatigable in his labors in the vineyard of the Divine Master and in the service of his fellow men. As was said of one of the distinguished public men of England, he "can toil terribly" and in addition to all his other service he has found time and opportunity to do a large amount of literary work of enduring value. Thus it may be noted that he is author of the following named works: "The Life of Luther," "The Holy Land," "The Declaration of Principles of the Ministers of the Lutheran Synod on the Separation of Church and State." He has given numerous editorial and other contributions to leading German publications in America and has been called upon to deliver secular lectures in various cities of the Union. Mr. Lange is a man of fine literary appreciation and ability, a close student of science, history and general literature of the best order, and his private library is one of the largest and most select in Fort Wayne. A man of broad and well ordered views concerning civic, governmental and economic affairs, he has insistently and ably advocated the policy of absolute segregation of the affairs of church and state. In 1887 was solemnized the marriage of Mr. Lange to Miss Magdalena Wagner, daughter of Rev. Anton Wagner, of Chicago, and she was summoned to the life eternal in 1895, the only child of this union being Paula, who is now the wife of Rev. Frederick Lindemann, of New York city. In 1896 Mr. Lange wedded Miss Betty Lange, daughter of Professor Rudolph Lange, a member of the faculty of Concordia Theological Seminary, St. Louis, Missouri, and the four children of this union are Clara, Anna, Hedwig, and Magdalena.

August J. Lanternier has been a resident of Fort Wayne since his boyhood and here he early became associated with the gardening enterprise that was established by his father in the pioneer days. During the long intervening years he has continued his close and appreciative association with the gracious products of the soil, his knowledge of plant propagation is authoritative, he long controlled a large and representative business as a horticulturist and general market gardner, and since 1901 has been one of the leading florists of the metropolis of Allen county. He discontinued his general gardening enterprise when he turned his attention to the propagation of flowers and decorative plants, and in the latter field of enterprise he has been specially successful, as he is an expert in the growing of the gracious products that now have his fostering care and is an enthusiast in floriculture. His modern greenhouses have an area of about thirty-five thousand square feet and his hotbeds are about twenty-five hundred square feet in their gross area, besides which he keeps up large propagating beds and keeps his establishment up to the most approved modern standard in all departments, his retail store, in which are handled the finest of cut flowers and decorative plants, being situated at 1203 Calhoun street. Mr. Lanternier was born in Vouhnan, France, on June 12, 1844, son of Joseph and Mary (Juillard) Lanternier, the former of whom was a skilled gardener in his native land,

and who became one of the pioneer exponents of this kind of enterprise in Allen county, Indiana, where he established the family home in 1854, when his son, August J., of this review, was a lad of about ten years. He developed a most prosperous business as a skilled horticulturist and market gardener and his field of operations was the grounds now owned and occupied by the greenhouses and other departments of the florist business conducted by his son, August J. He was a man of gracious personality and sterling character and won to himself the loyal friendship of the community in which he maintained his home for nearly forty years, his death having occurred about the year 1891, and his son, August J., having succeeded to the business. He was an earnest communicant of the Catholic church, as was also his wife, who preceded him to the life eternal. August J. Lanternier acquired his rudimentary education in his native land and after the family home was established in Fort Wayne he attended the Catholic parochial schools for a time. In 1858, as a lad of fourteen years, he became actively associated with his father's gardening enterprise, and during the long years that have since passed he has continued operations on the old homestead place which his father purchased more than sixty years ago and upon which he has made such improvements as to give him prestige as one of the leading exponents of floriculture in northern Indiana. He has had no desire for political activity or preferment, though he is most loyal in his civic attitude and takes deep interest in all that concerns the welfare of his home city. Both he and his family are communicants of the Catholic church. On the 29th of June, 1865, was solemnized his marriage to Miss Amelia Gerardot, daughter of the late Joseph Gerardot, who was of sterling French lineage and who was one of the representative farmers of Jefferson township, this county, in the early days. In conclusion is given brief record concerning the children of Mr. and Mrs. Lanternier: Mary is the wife of George Mohl, of Fort Wayne; Cecelia is the wife of Virgil Racine, of this city; Helena died after attaining to adult age; Louise died in infancy; Louis and Mond are identified with their father's business interests in Fort Wayne; Clara is the wife of Frank Myers, of this city; John, Joseph and Clement still remain in and pay loyal allegiance to their native city; and the two last named are associated with their father, while John is a bookkeeper and stenographer; and Irene is the wife of Edward O'Connor, of Fort Wayne.

Abner Lantz, who is serving most efficiently as trustee of his native township and is one of the representative citizens and successful farmers of Milan township, has passed his entire life in Allen county, where his parents established their home more than sixty years ago and the family name has always stood exponent of loyal and progressive citizenship. Mr. Lantz was born in Milan township on March 15, 1864, a son of Christian and Mary (Hatt) Lantz, both of whom were born in Canton Berne, Switzerland, and were young at the time of the immigration of the respective families to America, their marriage having been solemnized in Ohio. From the old Buckeye state Christian Lantz and his wife came to Allen county many years ago and established their home in Milan township, where he reclaimed and improved a good farm and continued to reside until his death, which occurred in December, 1899, his widow having been summoned to eternal rest in November, 1905, when venerable in years and both having ever commanded the high regard of all who knew them, their religious faith having been that of the Methodist Episcopal church. Of their children the eldest is Mrs. Sophia Froelich, who resides in West Virginia; Mrs. Elizabeth Saunders maintains her home in the state of Oregon; Mrs. Bertha Schwartz still resides in Allen county; Christian is deceased; Joel is a resident of Iowa; and Abner, of this review, is the youngest of the number. Abner Lantz early began to contribute his quota to the work of the home farm and in the meanwhile profited fully by the advantages afforded in the public schools of Milan township. He continued to be associated in the management of his father's farm until his marriage, shortly before his twenty-eighth birthday anniversary, and thereafter farmed on rented land until 1910, when he purchased and removed to his present farm, which comprises twenty acres and is eligibly situated in Milan township. He has made many improvements on the place, including the erection of a modern house and barn, good fences and the installing of tile drainage. Here are manifest definite thrift and prosperity and Mr. Lantz is consistently to be noted as one of the substantial exponents of progressive and scientific farm enterprise in his native county. He is equally vigorous and loyal in his civic stewardship and the appreciation of this fact was significantly shown on January 1, 1915, when he assumed the office of township trustee, for a term of four years, his administration having fully justified the popular choice of an incumbent. His political faith is that of the Democratic party and both he and his wife are zealous and valued members of the Methodist Episcopal church at Milan Center. On February 9, 1892, was solemnized the marriage of Mr. Lantz to Miss Nona Freeman, daughter of the late Samuel and Mary (Lytle) Freeman, who were honored residents of Allen county at the time of their death, the father having been a native of this county and the mother of the city of Logansport, Indiana. Of their four children, Mrs. Lantz was the second in order of birth; Mrs. Josephine DeHaven is a resident of Tulsa, Oklahoma; Samuel departed from Allen county a number of years ago and the other members of the family have unfortunately lost all trace of him; and Elizabeth is a popular teacher in the public schools of Fort Wayne. Mr. and Mrs. Lantz have an interesting family of seven children—Albert F., Ruth E., Frank A., Perry D., Naomi J., Nan, and Gertrude H. Albert F., the eldest son, wedded Miss Mae Hutker and they reside in Milan township, their twin daughters—Margaret and Marjorie—having been born September 29, 1915, and thus giving to the subject of this sketch his first claim to the title of grandfather. Another daughter, Dora, has been born to Albert F. and wife. Ruth E. married George W. Moss, of Cedarville; and Frank A. married Stella Smith, daughter of Mathias Smith, and they live in Milan township.

Thomas Lau is a progressive business man who has shown himself fortified in the elements of personality that conserve worthy and genuine success in connection with the practical affairs of life, and he has today a secure status as one of the influential men of affairs in his native city of Fort Wayne, where he is an interested principal in the Heit-Miller-Lau Company, which is engaged in the manufacturing of confectionery and table delicacies on an extensive scale and of which adequate description is given on other pages, in the sketch of the career of Anthony W. Heit. Mr. Lau is also the executive head of the Lau Building Company, which is doing an important service in furthering the physical development and advancement, as well as the incidental civic prosperity of Fort Wayne, his associates in this company being Oscar and Robert Fox and Mrs.

Charles Niezer. Mr. Lau was born in Fort Wayne on November 29, 1860, son of Thomas and Mary (Schilling) Lau, both natives of Germany, the father having been born in Bavaria and the mother in Baden and both having been residents of Fort Wayne for many years prior to their death. Thomas Lau, Sr., was an architect of fine talent and in connection with the work of his profession became one of the representative contractors and builders of Fort Wayne, his political support having been given to the Democratic party and both he and his wife having been devout communicants of the Catholic church. Of their ten children six are now living. He whose name initiates this review is indebted to well ordered Catholic schools in Fort Wayne for his early educational discipline and his initial business experience was gained through his association with the Greenbaum insurance agency, with which he was connected six months. He then entered the employ of Louis Fox, who was engaged in the manufacturing of crackers and candies, and with this concern he continued until the plant and business were sold to the United States Baking Company, which later consolidated with the National Biscuit Company. In 1902 the present Heit-Miller-Lau Company purchased the local establishment of the National Biscuit Company, and the business has since been successfully continued on an extensive scale, a description of the plant and its activities being given in the previously mentioned sketch of Anthony W. Heit, the administrative head of the company. The genius of productive service has marked the career of Mr. Lau, and he has at all times held high place in the confidence and good will of the community in which he has lived from the time of his birth and in which he has won advancement through his own well directed endeavors. In a generic way he gives his support to the principles of the Democratic party, but in local affairs he supports men and measures meeting the approval of his judgment and without reference to strict partisan lines. He is affiliated with the Fort Wayne Lodge of the Benevolent & Protective Order of Elks. October 10, 1893, recorded the marriage of Mr. Lau to Miss Caroline Nessel, who was born at Kendallville, Indiana, daughter of the late Christian Nessel. Mr. and Mrs. Lau have one daughter, Miss Helen, who remains at the parental home and who is a popular factor in the social activities of her native city.

George E. Lawrence.—Three generations of the Lawrence family have called Allen county "home" since Jacob Lawrence, the pioneer ancestor, migrated from his native community in Wayne county, Ohio, and settled in Lafayette township. The family is one of pure German extraction, three brothers Lawrence having emigrated from Germany in 1735 and settled in eastern Pennsylvania. From that region they came west to Ohio and were established there for many years. In fact, many of the name and family will be found today in Wayne county, Ohio, and elsewhere in the Buckeye state. The last three generations have been farming men, but prior to that the men of this fine old American family were identified with ship-building and merchandising, being successful and prosperous in those fields. George E. Lawrence was born in Lafayette township on August 13, 1865, son of John J. and Mary (Shank) Lawrence. The mother was born in Huntington county, Indiana, June 12, 1844, and the father in Wayne county, Ohio, January 25, 1837. He came to Allen county with his father at a time when it was almost a virgin wilderness. The Indian was the only human inhabitant and the wilderness trails were the sole means of travel. When John Lawrence married and took his bride to their new home, they lived in a rude but comfortable log cabin, built with his own hands, and located on a spot from which he had cleared the timber of the growth of countless years. He was one of five children born to his parents. The others were George B., David, Milo and Amos. The last named is living at 1418 East Lewis street, Fort Wayne, Indiana. The family is a long lived one, and the mother of these men was an Ohian by birth, of Scotch ancestry, and lived to be sixty-nine years old. She was a most estimable character and her sons came to man's estate possessed of many sterling qualities that were the inheritance of a noble mother. She, Mary (Shank) Lawrence, was one of seven children, the others being Wilfred, Anna, Valira, George J., John and Ella. John J. and Mary (Shank) Lawrence reared a family of nine children. Elma M., the eldest, is the wife of Frank Jones. George E., the subject of this family review, was the second born. John and Rose, next in order of birth, are both deceased. William is deceased. Ella is the wife of M. M. Knight, of Bibbis, Indiana. Cora married John Shellin and is deceased. Effie is the wife of Elmer Settesmyer, of Roanoke, Indiana. Mildred E. married Alrick Wickeffer and died in March, 1914. George E. Lawrence is one of the foremost men of his community and is identified with the leading financial and industrial activities of the township. He is a director and stockholder in the Farmers' State Bank at Roanoke, owner of some city property in Huntington and Marion, and a farm in Michigan, and is now living retired from active business. He has traveled quite extensively in the west. He is a Democrat, though not especially active in politics, and his fraternal activities are confined to the K. O. T. M., of which he has long been a member. On May 10, 1910, John J. Lawrence died and is buried at Zanesville. He was seventy-three years of age at the time of his death and his widow still survives him. Both were life-long members of the Church of God, and Mrs. Lawrence still retains an active interest in the work of the church.

John Lawrence.—The family of which John Lawrence is the immediate representative has been established in Allen county since 1863, when George and Elizabeth (Geitgey) Lawrence settled here, coming from Wayne county, Ohio. They were early land-holders in the county, though Mr. Lawrence did not give much time to farm life. He was prominent in the county and state and served as a member of the state legislature two terms, and for fifteen years was employed as an adjuster in the service of the Mutual Life Insurance Company. John Lawrence was one of their five children. The others were Oliver, Alice, Ida and Grover, of which the last named is the only living one. John Lawrence may be said to be self-educated. He spent more time in boyhood on his father's farm than in the pursuit of book-knowledge, and he is today in charge of the home place and carries on an extensive stock-farming enterprise. He was married on November 25, 1880, to Miss Alice Feighner, daughter of Jacob Feighner. Mr. and Mrs. Lawrence have four children. Dora is the wife of Albert S. Ewert, of Lafayette township. Elizabeth Rebecca married Samuel Albery Krumma, of Lafayette township. Carrie Pearl married Frank Jackson and Ethel May is living at home. Five grandchildren add distinction to the lives of Mr. and Mrs. Lawrence. Dora is the mother of Ruth Marie, Lawrence Lewis and Noel Edward. Elizabeth has a son, born August 18, 1917. Carrie claims a pair of twin daughters, named Mary Fay and Fairy May. Oliver Lawrence, the deceased brother of the subject, left one son, who has three children—Frank, Charles and Helene. Grover, who lives in Fort Wayne, has a daughter, Elizabeth Sylvia. Alice left a daughter, Cora May, who also has a daughter named Alice. Ida (Lawrence) Pontius left a son—Laurence W. Pontius. The Lawrence family is well established in the county and Mr. Lawrence, subject of this brief family sketch, is identified with various business enterprises in and about his township.

John T. Leach, Jr., foreman of engine repairs in the shops of the Pennsylvania Lines in Fort Wayne, is one of the city's own sons, born there on February 23d, 1882. His parents were John L. and Mary E. (Loftus) Leach, the former of English birth and the latter of Ohio, and they died in 1903 and 1888, respectively. Mr. Leach was employed for about twenty-five years in the boiler works of the Pennsylvania system and was one of the valued employees of the road at that point. Seven children were born to Mr. and Mrs. Leach. Jane E. lives at home and keeps up the establishment for her brothers and sister. Mary E. is deceased. James is employed in the motive power department of the Pennsylvania Lines; John T. is the fourth child; Edward D. is a veterinary surgeon in Fort Wayne. Bertha V. is teacher of English in the Fort Wayne high school. She graduated from the high school and the DePauw University. Sadie is a stenographer and bookkeeper for the Southern Express Company at Tampa, Florida. John T. Leach had a common school education and three years in high school. In 1900 he took a position in the office of the master mechanic of the Pennsylvania Railroad, but after a year entered the machine shops as an apprentice. He served the prescribed time, coming out a licensed machinist, and after some service along general lines was made foreman of the locomotive repair department. He makes his home with his sister and brothers at the family residence on Creighton avenue. Mr. Leach is a Republican and his fraternal affiliations are with the Masonic order and the Independent Order of Odd Fellows. He is one of the capable and reliable young men who have made good in their home city and he has a wide circle of friends in his native community.

Herman J. C. Leitz, vice-president and general manager of the New Haven Floral Company, has been actively identified with this concern from the time of its organization, on the 1st of April, 1912, and has been a dominating factor in the development of the prosperous enterprise. In founding the business there were associated with him Henry F. Herman, Rev. H. B. Kohlmeyer, Henry F. Heine and Miss Sophia L. Herman, and operations were initiated with a capital stock of ten thousand dollars. After the lapse of two years Henry F. and Sophia L. Herman sold their interest in the corporation, as did also Mr. Heine, and at this juncture August F. and Henry F. Freese and Theodore Thimlar became interested principals. Together with Mr. Leitz and Rev. H. B. Kohlmeyer these gentlemen now control the substantial business, which is one of the thriving and important industrial enterprises of the village of New Haven. The capital stock has been increased to thirty thousand dollars and the officers of the company are as here designated: August F. Freese, president; Herman J. C. Leitz, vice-president and general manager; and Henry F. Freese, secretary and treasurer. The company have fifty thousand square feet of glass in their greenhouses and propagating conservatories, and the splendid growth of the business is shown in this ample provision, for at the beginning there were but ten thousand square feet of glass in the greenhouses, each year having been marked by an amplification of the facilities. Special attention is given to the propagating of the best types of roses, carnations and chrysanthemums and also the providing of bedding stock for spring planting. The out-put of these fine conservatories is sold mainly at wholesale to the retail dealers in the city of Fort Wayne and the enterprise is one of the largest and most successful of the kind in Allen county. Herman J. C. Leitz was born at Farnham, Erie county, New York, on April 12, 1880, and is a son of Herman and Adeline (Herr) Leitz, the former of whom was born at Collinsville, Illinois, and the latter at Kingsville, Maryland. The father is now engaged in the general merchandise business at Fort Morgan, Colorado, and he has the honorable distinction of having served as a valiant soldier of the Union during the entire period of the Civil war. After the war he went to Buffalo, New York, and later he was engaged in the general merchandising business at Farnham, that state. In 1886 he came with his family to Fort Wayne, and later he removed to Fort Morgan, Colorado, where he and his wife have since maintained their home. Herman J. C. Leitz gained the major part of his early education in the parochial schools of Emanuel Lutheran church in Fort Wayne and as a youth began working for the Flick Floral Company. Later he was employed eighteen years in the Vesey greenhouses and at the expiration of this period removed from Fort Wayne to New Haven and became associated in the organization of the company of which he is now vice-president and general manager. He is not only an expert but also an enthusiast in floriculture, and his success in his chosen field of enterprise has been the due reward of earnest effort. He is a Republican in politics, is serving, in 1917, as a member of the municipal board of trustees of New Haven, is the leader of the New Haven Cornet Band and is one of the staunch supporters of the progressive civic policies of the New Haven Commercial Club, of which he is an influential member. August 4, 1904, recorded the marriage of Mr. Leitz to Miss Lena Beyer, daughter of George M. and Lena (Cramer) Beyer, of Altenburg, Missouri, and the three children of this union are Walter E., Helen Mae, and Herman E.

John W. Liggett is consistently to be designated as one of the representative young business men of his native city of Fort Wayne, where he is president of the Singmaster Printing Company, which conducts a finely equipped general job-printing establishment. The enterprise was founded more than a quarter of a century ago, and about 1896 Joseph M. Singmaster purchased the business of the concern, in which he had previously been an interested principal, as a member of the Lipes, Nelson & Singmaster Printing Company. Mr. Singmaster, who was long numbered among the sterling citizens and successful business men of Fort Wayne, died on March 26, 1914, and the business was inherited by his daughter, Mary S., wife of him whose name initiates this article. Mr. Liggett was elected president of the company, which had been incorporated in December, 1904, with a capital stock of five thousand dollars. Mr. Singmaster was elected president of the company and served in this capacity until his death, the while Lewis W. Munson was secretary and treasurer. After the death of Mr. Singmaster a virtual reorganization took place, and the present executive corps of the company is as here noted: John W. Liggett, president; James A. Liggett, vice-president; and Mrs. Mary S. Liggett, secretary and treasurer. The company has a modern plant of the most approved equipment and its effective service has retained to it a substantial and representative supporting patronage. John W. Liggett was born in Fort Wayne on October 4, 1884, and is a son of James and Frances E. (Davis) Liggett, both natives of the state of Ohio. James Liggett became identified with the manufacturing of carriages after he had established his residence in Fort Wayne, and later he here conducted a successful livery business. Later he removed to Hammond, this state, where he holds a position as a government revenue officer, his wife being deceased. He is a Republican in politics and formerly served as superintendent of the police department of Fort Wayne. He is affiliated with the Independent Order of Odd Fellows and is a member of the Baptist church, as was also his wife. Of their children the eldest is Phortes C., who is a resident of Fort Wayne; Grace resides in the city of Chicago; James A. is vice-president of the Singmaster Printing Company; Blanche B. resides at Gary, Indiana; the subject of this review was the next in order of birth; and Frances Nellie is the wife of Charles McKee, of Lincoln, Nebraska. John W. Liggett made good use of the advantages of the public schools of Fort Wayne, including the high school, and as a youth he here entered the service of the Western Gas & Construction Company, as a machinist. After a service of eighteen months he went to Logansport, this state, where for two months he was in the employ of the Reutenberg Motor Company. He then returned to Fort Wayne and for the ensuing eighteen months was here employed at the Fort Wayne Electric Works. For two years thereafter he was employed as a skilled machinist in the local shops of the Pennsylvania Railroad, in which service he continued two years. For the ensuing two years he was again employed at the Fort Wayne Electric Works, and he then engaged in the laundry business as one of the interested principals of the Union Laundry Company. In 1907 Mr. Liggett again entered the employ of the Pennsylvania Railroad Company, with which he continued two years, the following four and one-half years having found him identified with industrial activities in the state of California, whence he then came back to assume his present position as president of the Singmaster Printing Company. He is secretary of the Master Printers' Association of Fort Wayne, is an active member of the Fort Wayne Commercial Club, is affiliated with the Independent Order of Odd Fellows and the National Union, the Masonic order as a Shriner and Knight Templar, and both he and his wife are members of the English Lutheran church. On January 1, 1906, was solemnized the marriage of Mr. Liggett to Miss Mary S. Singmaster, and they have two children—James J. and Mary E.

C. Ross Lindemuth has gained precedence as one of the able young civil engineers of his native county and state and after giving five years of effective service in the position of deputy surveyor of Allen county he became, in the autumn of 1916, the Democratic candidate for the position of county surveyor, for which his technical ability and prior experience eminently qualified him. Mr. Lindemuth was born on the old homestead farm of his parents, in Maumee township, Allen county, on January 1, 1886, a son of Albert C. and Josephine (Snyder) Lindemuth, both of whom were born in Onondaga county, New York. Albert C. Lindemuth established his residence in Allen county about the year 1870, and he has not only been one of the successful farmers of the county but has also been prominently concerned with a substantial tile-manufacturing business, both he and his wife being still residents of this county and both being active members of the Evangelical Lutheran church. Elmer, their first child, is deceased; Ernest G. is still identified with agricultural pursuits in Maumee township; C. Ross, of this review, was the next in order of birth; Albert M. is principal of the high school at Defiance, Ohio; Amy D. remains at the parental home and is principal of the high school in the village of Monroeville; and Addie L. remains at the parental home. C. Ross Lindemuth continued his studies in the public schools of Allen county until his graduation in the high school at Antwerp, as a member of the class of 1904. Thereafter he put his scholastic acquirements to practical test and use by devoting three years to successful service as a teacher in the district schools of his native county, after which he entered the Northern Ohio Normal School, at Ada, in which he completed an effective three years' course and in which he was graduated in 1910 as a civil engineer. For one year thereafter he continued his pedagogic service, as superintendent of the high school at Antwerp, in which he himself had been graduated, and in the spring of 1911 he was appointed deputy surveyor of Allen county, a position of which he continued the efficient and resourceful incumbent until he became a candidate for advancement to the office of county surveyor, as previously noted. Mr. Lindemuth is a young man of excellent intellectual and professional attainment, is loyal and progressive in his civic attitude, and is a staunch advocate of the principles and policies for which the Democratic party stands sponsor. He is affiliated with the Masonic fraternity, the Benevolent & Protective Order of Elks, and the Loyal Order of Moose, and he is distinctively popular in both business and social circles in his native county. He and his wife are communicants of the Evangelical Lutheran church. On June 1, 1910, was solemnized the marriage of Mr. Lindemuth to Miss Alta H. Harris, who was born and reared at Antwerp, this county, and they have two children—Hollis Charlotte, born August 12, 1911, and Martha Jane, born May 9, 1916.

George W. Lindemuth, who is now successfully engaged in the real estate and insurance business in the city of Fort Wayne, as one of the prominent and influential exponents of these lines of enterprise, has been a resident of Allen county from the time of his birth and is a scion of a sterling family whose name has been identified with the civic and industrial annals of the county for more than half a century. He was born in Scipio township, this county, August 17, 1866, a son of Michael and Sarah (Nevinger) Lindemuth, both natives of Pennsylvania and of staunch German lineage. From the old Keystone state Michael Lindemuth went to Ohio when a young man and there continued his association with agricultural pursuits, near Germantown, Montgomery county, until 1862, when he came to Allen county, Indiana, and purchased a tract of virtually unimproved land, in Scipio township. There he developed one of the productive farms of the county and stood at all times exemplar of the most loyal citizenship, as well as of those sterling characteristics that invariably beget popular confidence and good will. He was a Democrat in politics, and, as a man of ability and mature judgment, was called upon to serve in the office of justice of the peace, of which he continued the incumbent for twenty-four years. Both he and his wife were devout communicants of the German Lutheran church, his death having occurred August 22, 1887, and the loved wife and mother is also deceased. Of their children, the eldest is William, a resident of Germantown, Ohio; Samuel maintains his home at Bunker Hill, Miami county, Indiana; James B.

resides at Lagrange, this state; Albert C. lives at Antwerp, Ohio; Clayton A. is a resident of Woodburn, Allen county, Indiana; Laird V. resides in the city of Seattle, Washington; Edward is one of the successful farmers of Allen county, in Maumee township; Vance E. is a resident of Defiance county, Ohio; Frank B. lives at Wolcottville, Lagrange county, Indiana; George W., of this review, is the youngest of the sons; Mary is the wife of John Boyer, of Germantown, Ohio; and DeEtte is the wife of Charles Overmeyer, of Fort Wayne. It is pleasing to note that all of the twelve children are now living, and it may be stated also that the youngest is now more than two score years of age. George W. Lindemuth was reared to the sturdy discipline of the home farm and that in his youth he made good use of the advantages afforded in the public schools of Allen county is indicated by the fact that as a young man he devoted several years to successful work as a teacher in the district schools—principally during the winter terms. For ten years thereafter he continued his active association with the basic industry of agriculture, and thereafter served as deputy sheriff of his native county. In 1906, as candidate on the Democratic ticket, he was elected county auditor, and in this office served with characteristic loyalty and efficiency. After the close of his administration as county auditor he traveled for a time, for the purpose of recuperating his impaired health, and in 1914 engaged in the real estate and insurance business in Fort Wayne, a field of enterprise in which he has achieved definite success, with attendant operations of important order in the handling of both city and farm property. Since May 17, 1915, he has held the important office of chief fish and game commissioner of Northern Indiana, and in the same, a state office, he is giving a most effective administration. As previously intimated, Mr. Lindemuth is aligned as a staunch supporter of the cause of the Democratic party, and in a fraternal way has received the ancient-craft, capitular and chivalric degrees of Masonry, in which his maximum affiliation is with Fort Wayne Commandery of Knights Templars, besides which he is a member also of the Mystic Shrine and is similarly identified with the local organizations of the Knights of Pythias, the Benevolent & Protective Order of Elks and the Loyal Order of Moose. His interest in virile sports is indicated by his membership in the St. Joe Athletic Club. On March 24, 1892, Mr. Lindemuth wedded Miss Mina Boulton, daughter of Henry and Helen (Hatch) Boulton, of Harlan, this county, both parents being now deceased. Mr. Boulton came from England to the United States, in 1847, and he long held prestige as one of the specially successful farmers and property-owners of Allen county, where he died, in 1915, at the patriarchal age of ninety-four years. Concerning the children of Mr. and Mrs. Lindemuth the following brief data are available: Mildred died at the age of eight years; George Ray is an electrical engineer; Carl B. is a student in a dental college in the city of Indianapolis; Maurice H. remains at the parental home and is attending the public schools.

Charles G. Linden.—He whose name introduces this review is the younger of the two surviving sons of the late George W. Linden, to whom a memoir is dedicated in the preceding paragraph. Mr. Linden was born on the homestead farm in Jefferson township, this county, and the date of his nativity was November 19, 1887. After having profited fully by the advantages of the public schools of New Haven he completed an effective course in the International Business College in the city of Fort Wayne. For three years thereafter he was absent from his native county, the period having been passed in California and other western states and in the Canadian northwest. After his return to Allen county Mr. Linden gave his attention for eight years to the management of the old homestead farm, and in January, 1913, he accepted the position of assistant cashier of the New Haven State Bank, of which office he has since continued the efficient and popular incumbent. He is affiliated with Home Lodge No. 312, at Fort Wayne, of the Ancient Free and Accepted Masons, and he also maintains affiliation with the various bodies of the Ancient Accepted Scottish Rite of Masonry. He is a member of the New Haven lodge of the Independent Order of Odd Fellows, is a Republican in politics, is serving, in 1917, as city clerk of New Haven, and is one of the representative young business men of his native county, his name being still enrolled on the list of eligible young bachelors of the county.

George W. Linden was one of the venerable and revered pioneer citizens of Allen county at the time of his death, which occurred June 26, 1914, in the village of New Haven, and he was eighty-six years of age when he was thus summoned from the stage of life's mortal endeavors. A man of sterling character and strong mentality, he showed throughout his earnest and industrious life a high sense of personal stewardship, and he contributed his full quota to the civic and industrial development and upbuilding of Allen county. There are many features of more than passing interest in connection with his personal and family history, and it is gratifying to present in this publication a brief tribute to his memory. George Washington Linden was born in the city of Rochester, New York, on June 7, 1828, a son of James and Sarah Linden, the former a native of Ireland and the latter of the state of New York, where their marriage was solemnized. James Linden was reared and educated in his native land and was a sturdy young man when he came to America, as a British soldier, at the time of the war of 1812. That his loyalty was deflected to the American cause at the time of this second conflict with Great Britain is indicated that he gave to one of his sons, the subject of this memoir, the name of George Washington, though he had continued his military service in the English ranks until the close of the war. After the war he continued his residence in the state of New York until 1832, when he removed with his family to the Territory of Michigan, which was not admitted as one of the sovereign states of the Union until five years thereafter. In the Wolverine state he was thus an early pioneer settler, and there he and his wife passed the remainder of their lives. They became the parents of twelve children, and of the number only two are now living—Judson and Emmett. George W. Linden was four years of age at the time of the family removal to Michigan, and there he acquired a limited education in the pioneer schools. At the age of fifteen years, prompted by adventurous spirit and self-reliance, he ran away from home, and it was at this stage in his career, in 1843, that he made his way up the old Wabash and Erie canal to Allen County, Indiana. Here he found employment, principally at farm work, until he was able to purchase land of his own and initiate independent operations as an agriculturist. He applied himself vigorously and effectively to the reclaiming of land from the virgin forest that then covered much of the county, and finally, in 1870, he established his residence on the now fine old Linden homestead farm in Jefferson township. Here he developed and improved one of the best farms of the county and on the same continued to reside until 1912, when he retired from active responsibilities in connection therewith and removed to the village of New Haven, where his death occurred about two years later, on June 26, 1914. Mr. Linden was always known for his loyalty and public spirit and was influential in community affairs, besides which it was given him to render valiant service as a soldier of the Union during the later period of the Civil war. He served one term as trustee of Milan township and held for a number of years the office of justice of the peace. He was a Republican in politics and was affiliated with the Masonic and Odd Fellows' lodges at New Haven. In 1864 Mr. Linden enlisted in the Seventh Indiana Battery of Light Artillery and latter was transferred to the Eleventh Battery, as nearly all of his comrades in the gallant Seventh had been killed in action. He was in the thick of the fray in a number of fiercely contested engagements marking the progress of the great conflict and continued in the service until the close of the war, when he received his honorable discharge. In later years he vitalized his interest in and association with his former comrades in arms by maintaining appreciative affiliation with the Grand Army of the Republic. Mr. Linden became one of the stockholders of the J. F. Shell Loan & Investment Company, of Fort Wayne, and, with the other stockholders, he encountered heavy financial loss in this connection through the mismanagement of the company's business, the stockholders having been called upon to make good the company's securities that were held by banking institutions in the city of Cleveland and elsewhere. To meet these assessments Mr. Linden was compelled to dispose of nine hundred acres of valuable land in Allen county, his aggregate holdings having been ten hundred and fifty-six acres. These unfortunate reverses resulted in his estate being comprised at the time of his death in one hundred and forty-five acres of land in Jefferson township and his home property in the village of New Haven. The maiden name of the first wife of Mr. Linden was Pauline Johnson, and she died while a young woman, leaving no children. By his second marriage, to Sarah McIntosh, he became the father of one child, George W., Jr., who is now a resident of the city of Fort Wayne. After the death of his second wife Mr. Linden eventually contracted a third marriage. On January 1, 1884, he wedded Miss Natalie C. Goehling, who survives him and who still maintains her home in New Haven, this county. Of the six children of this union four survive the honored father, namely: Josephine, Charles G., Mary and Etta. Nettie, the third in order of birth and Antonia the fourth died in childhood. Mr. Linden exemplified in his daily life and service the faith which he earnestly professed as a member of the Methodist Episcopal church, of which his widow continues a zealous member. Mrs. Linden is a daughter of Rev. Charles and Abbeta (Kleinbeck) Goehling and was born at Brooklyn, N. Y. Rev. Charles Goehling was a man of fine intellectuality and served for many years as a clergyman of the German Lutheran church, with all of consecrated devotion. He was born and reared in Germany, where he was graduated in the great Heidelberg University and where also he prepared himself for the ministry. After receiving holy orders as a clergyman of the German Lutheran church he came to America and thereafter held various important pastoral charges—in Brooklyn, New York; on Staten Island, that state, where he remained twenty-five years; and later at Erie and Girard, Pennsylvania. He passed the closing years of his life in well earned and serene retirement at New Haven, Allen county, Indiana, where he died, November 16, 1905, at a venerable age. His wife preceded him to the life eternal and of their five children three are living—Henrietta, Josephine and Mrs. Natalie C. Linden, widow of the subject of this memoir. The two sons, Charles and Frederick, are deceased.

Edward L. Litot.—In the year 1895 Edward L. Litot returned to Fort Wayne, the city of his birth and early training, to associate himself with the Pennsylvania Railroad in the important position of boiler inspector in its boiler shops. In addition to his duties in that department he is inspector of piece work in the shops, so that he finds himself amply occupied in his particular field. Mr. Litot was born in Fort Wayne on January 12, 1868, son of George A. and Lucine (Beuret) Litot, the former a native of Alsace-Loraine (France) and the latter of Berne, Switzerland. They met and married in Fort Wayne, the father having come to America in 1848, direct to Fort Wayne, where he went to work at his trade, that of a miller. For twenty-seven years he operated the well known Rudisill Grist Mill. He and his wife died in Fort Wayne. Eleven children came to them, of which number nine survive. They are Joseph V., of Fort Wayne; Mary M., the wife of Joseph Rondot, of Stockton, California; Eugene, a resident of Wilkesburg, Pennsylvania; Louis A., living in Cleveland, Ohio; Edward L., the immediate subject of this review; John B., of Des Moines, Iowa; Peter J., of Fort Wayne; George J., of Atlantic City, New Jersey, and Josephine, the wife of Joseph Girardot, of Fort Wayne. Two sons died in boyhood. Edward L. Litot had fairly good schooling advantages in his youth and when he had quitted school entered a boiler shop in Fort Wayne as an apprentice to the trade. He spent seven years in the Fort Wayne shops and some time later he went to Alliance, Ohio, where he remained for a year in similar work, returning to Fort Wayne to accept his present position as inspector of boilers and piece work in the Pennsylvania shops. His record of twenty-one years in that position is one that speaks volumes for his efficiency and general ability in his work and he enjoys the confidence and good will of employers and employees alike. On June 6, 1894, Mr. Litot was united in marriage with Anna M. Maguire, of Whitley county, Indiana. Five children have been born to them—Frances, John, Helen, Rosella and William, of which number the three first named survive. Mr. Litot is a Democrat, a member of the Royal League, and he and his family are communicants of the Catholic church.

Edward J. Longfield has achieved distinctive success in his chosen sphere of business and in addition to being proprietor of the popular and well managed Terminal Restaurant in the city of Fort Wayne is also retained as steward of the Standard Club, one of the representative social and business organizations of the city. Mr. Longfield was born at Plymouth, Indiana, August 24, 1873, son of John and Emma L. Longfield. His father, who was a wheel-finisher by trade, served as a loyal and valiant soldier of the Union in the Civil war as a member of the Eighteenth infantry regiment of the regular army, and his service continued during the entire period of the war. He lived up to the full tension of the great conflict and in the battle of Stone's River was wounded. After the war John Longfield continued his residence in the town of Plymouth until 1874, when he removed with his family to Fort Wayne. Of his two children who attained to maturity the subject of this review is the elder, and the other was William J., whose death occurred August 2, 1916. Edward J. Longfield was not yet one year old at the time of the family removal to Fort Wayne, and here he received his early education in the Catholic parochial schools, including that conducted by the Christian Brothers. After leaving school he found employment in the factory of the Olds Wheel Company, with which he continued his association several years. He then took a position with the D. C. Fisher Insurance agency, with which he was connected nine years, in general clerical and executive capacity. He next accepted a position as clerk for the Wayne Club, of which he was soon afterward appointed manager. His next position was in the meter department of the Fort Wayne Electric Company, and four years later he resigned his position to assume that of manager of the Standard Club. Six years later he resigned this post in favor of his only brother, the late William J. Longfield, and he then, in 1905, established the Terminal Restaurant, which he has made one of the popular and successful institutions of the kind in Fort Wayne. Upon the death of his brother, on August 2, 1916, he was prevailed upon to resume the position of steward and manager of the Standard Club, and of this position he continues the incumbent, besides giving close and effective attention to the conducting of his restaurant business. Mr. Longfield is a Republican in politics, and is a communicant of the Fort Wayne Cathedral parish of the Catholic church. At the time of the Spanish-American war, in 1898, Mr. Longfield entered service in the capacity of hospital steward, and later private in the One Hundred and Fifty-seventh Indiana Infantry, with which he continued his service until the command was mustered out and he was accorded his honorable discharge. He is a popular and appreciative affiliate of the United Spanish American War Veterans Association. In 1902 was solemnized the marriage of Mr. Longfield to Miss Edith E. Aiken, daughter of Charles Aiken, of Fort Wayne. They have no children. Mr. Longfield is a baseball enthusiast and finds his chief recreation during the season in attending ball games and in fishing excursions, with a distinct predilection for out-doors sports.

Oliver J. Lopshire.—The Lopshires came from Ohio to Indiana and have been successfully identified with the agricultural activities of Allen county. Oliver J. Lopshire, the subject, is a son of George and Margaret (Miller) Lopshire and was born in Lafayette township, Allen county, on November 8, 1850. His parents lived through the pioneer stage of development and during their active years cleared and developed an eighty-acre farm, bringing it up to a high state of productiveness during their lifetimes and adding their full quota to the best interests of the community wherein they lived and moved. They had six children. Frances, the first born, is deceased. Oliver J. is the immediate subject. David is deceased. Sarah became the wife of Frederick Bishop. George is a prosperous Allen county farmer. Lewis lives retired in Fort Wayne. Oliver Lopshire had little educational training, attending the old log cabin schools of the village perhaps three months in every year while he was a lad and spending the rest of the time at work on the home farm. After he had launched out for himself he rented a place, some time later buying forty acres, to which, in later and more successful years he added eighty acres and still later another tract of eighteen acres. He has carried on diversified farming with much success and the labors of his active years are everywhere apparent in the excellent condition of his farm. It was on October 23, 1873, that Mr. Lopshire married Elizabeth Bishop, the daughter of John and Charlotte (Keller) Bishop, who were natives of Pennsylvania and later pioneers to Indiana, where they both passed the last years of their lives. Seven children came to Mr. and Mrs. Lopshire. Frank lives on the home farm. Rosa is the wife of Edward Dalman of Wayne township; Minnie died in 1905; Ada married Frank Kohr of Wayne township; George is located in Allen county; Laura is deceased and Charles is at home. Frank is married and has two little daughters—Florence and Hazel. Rosa also has two children—Verdona and Virgil. Minnie, who died as the wife of Frank Neunemacher, left a son, Russell. Ada has two children—Cecil and Herman. George has two sons named Paul and Alvin. Laura, the wife of Frank Bishop, left three children—Donald, Lucile and Pauline. Mr. Lopshire is a man who has always enjoyed the esteem and confidence of his fellow men and has taken a praiseworthy part in the civic activities of his township for many years. He is a Republican, true to the party in the matter of national issues, but in local politics he makes no party distinction, satisfied with what seems to him to stand for the best interests of the community, regardless of who is sponsor for it. He has lived well and to excellent purpose and his influence in his neighborhood has always been a creditable one.

Cyrus J. Lose.—Contributing definitely to the success of Mr. Lose as a progressive representative of the printing and engraving business in his native city are his technical knowledge, his close application and his personal popularity. He has built up a prosperous general job-printing and engraving business in Fort Wayne, where he has a well-equipped plant in a suite of four rooms of the building at 818-20 Calhoun street. He gives employment to seven persons, with an excellent corps of skilled job compositors and expert pressmen, and in his general printing and engraving enterprise he gives his close and discriminating personal supervision to all details, so that the high-grade output of his establishment constitutes one of its best commercial assets. Mr. Lose was born and reared in Fort Wayne, to whose public schools he is indebted for his early educational discipline. On July 15, 1876, he properly observed the anniversary of our national independence by assuming the dignified position of errand boy in the office of the Fort Wayne Gazette, and on January 1 of the following year he entered upon a practical apprenticeship to the printer's trade, in which he became a skilled workman within the eight years that he continued in the service of the Gazette office. After severing this association he was for several years employed in the job-printing department of the Fort Wayne Journal, and he next passed ten months in the employ of the Fort Wayne office of the Western Newspaper Union. Thereafter he was continuously with the Journal job department until July 15, 1903, when he retired from this position. The next day he established in one room a modest job-printing office, and from this beginning has developed his present modern job office, which he keeps up to the best standard in equipment of type fonts, paper stock and accessories and press facilities, with a department specially devoted to engraving. Mr. Lose has been an ambitious worker during his entire active business career and has fully merited the unequivocal success which he has achieved in his independent enterprise. He is a loyal and valued member of the Fort Wayne Commercial Club, has received the maximum degrees of York Rite Masonry, as a member of the Fort Wayne Commandery of Knights Templars, besides having attained to the thirty-second degree of the Ancient Accepted Scottish Rite of the time-honored fraternity and being also identified with the Ancient Arabic Order, Nobles of the Mystic Shrine, the Knights of Pythias, and the Independent Order of Odd Fellows. Both he and his wife are active communicants of Trinity Lutheran church. The 13th of September, 1893, gave record of the marriage of Mr. Lose to Miss Edith Cothrell, of Fort Wayne, and they have two children—Ralph and Kathryn. The son is now a member of the class of 1919 in the agricultural department of Purdue University, at Lafayette, this state, and the daughter is attending the high school at Fort Wayne.

Martin Luecke.—Concordia College, Fort Wayne, Indiana, is one of the largest and most influential Lutheran educational institutions in America. Dr. Martin Luecke is its president. The thousands of students from all portions of America who have come under the instruction of this splendid school have felt the marked advantage of the influence of Doctor Luecke throughout their college course. He is a man equipped by temperament, education and experience to inspire in the student the cultivation of those qualities which make for the highest and best citizenship. Concordia college was founded in the year 1839, in Perry county, Missouri, by Lutheran refugees from Saxony. The rapid growth of the school from its beginning in a log cabin determined its founders upon its removal to a more suitable location, and the city of St. Louis was selected as the most desirable site for the institution. However, as time went on, the town of Fort Wayne, in 1861, especially on account of the Civil War, was deemed to be a still better location for the school and here it was located, taking the place of a Lutheran seminary which had been established on a portion of the present campus. The growth of Concordia college to its present splendid position of supremacy among the Lutheran schools of America has been due to careful, conservative management and true service in fitting its students for their life work. Most of the students of Concordia enter the theological department, but the college prepares young men for many other useful and learned professions. There are now eighteen handsome, substantial buildings on the Concordia campus, six residences, lecture hall, dormitory, dining hall with stewards' quarters and kitchen, gymnasium, heating plant, swimming pool, shower baths, hospital, and armory, with social rooms. Much of the physical growth of the college has been accomplished during the administration of Doctor Luecke. In these years of service the student body advanced notably along many lines, and, latterly, the organization of the young men as a battalion under the instruction and command of a United States army officer has proved to be a notable forward step. Doctor Luecke was born in Sheboygan county, Wisconsin, June 22, 1859, the son of Christian and Emily (Von Henning) Luecke. He was graduated from the preparatory department of Concordia college in 1878, and, three years later, from Concordia Theological Seminary at St. Louis. In the latter year (1881) he was ordained as an Evangelical Lutheran minister and entered upon his clerical duties as the pastor of the church of his denomination in Bethalto, Illinois. At the close of four years of effective work in this field he accepted the pastorate of the church at Troy, Illinois, and here he remained to perform valuable service for a period of eight years, when, in 1892, he was summoned to the charge of an important congregation in the Illinois capital, Springfield. During this period he also held several important positions in the synods of Missouri, Ohio and other states. While a resident of Springfield he founded the Springfield Hospital and Training school, in 1897. In 1903. Doctor Luecke was called to the presidency of Concordia college, Fort Wayne, where he has served as executive head of the institution at the same time that he has given his personal attention to the classes in the study of the New Testament, Greek, Sacred History and Religion. During his busiest years Doctor Luecke has given to the world a number of valuable historical and literary works, including the following: "A History of the Civil War of the United States" (1892), "History of Concordia Seminary at Springfield" (1896), "A Synopsis of the Holy History of the Old and New Testaments" (1906), and "A Short Life of Christ" (1911).

Martin H. Luecke.—No member of the bar of Allen county occupies a more enviable position than Martin H. Luecke. As a representative of the younger group of Fort Wayne lawyers, none more clearly than he personifies the truest type of leadership in his profession, a condition due largely, no doubt, to the early determination to attain a high degree of proficiency as a specialist in limited lines of a many-sided profession. Mr. Luecke devotes his attention to civil and probate practice, in which branches of activity he has attained recognized superiority. His well-ordered mind enables him not only to cope at all times with the problems of the many cases to which his skill is summoned, but he finds it his keenest pleasure and satisfaction to contribute much of his time and energy to the public good, a trait which finds one expression in his devotion to the cause of good roads throughout the state of Indiana. Mr. Luecke's endeavors in this direction were begun in 1913. By midsummer of 1917, he had organized the work in two-thirds of the townships in Allen county, acting under the authority of the board of county commissioners. These splendid efforts drew him into the larger field of the state, and, as chairman of the Indiana commission on laying out the main trails and market highways of the state, he has been supported by the State Highway Commission to such an extent that the greater portion of the state has been thoroughly mapped. This success reflects Mr. Luecke's ability as an organizer and leader in the larger affairs of public life. Mr. Luecke was born in Bethalto, Illinois, May 23, 1883, son of Dr. Martin Luecke, president of Concordia College, of Fort Wayne, the leading Lutheran educational institution in America. The father is the subject of biographical mention in another portion of this work. Dr. Luecke served as the pastor of the Lutheran church at Bethalto during the childhood years of the son. Martin H. Luecke was graduated from the high school of Springfield, Illinois, which had become the home of the family upon the removal from Bethalto. An eagerness for learning prompted him to pursue his studies through Illinois Western University, at Bloomington, and from that institution he graduated with honors. During the period of his residence in Springfield, Mr. Luecke served as Deputy County Treasurer of Sangamon county, and as Assistant State Librarian under appointment of Governor Richard Yates. In 1903, Mr. Luecke came to Fort Wayne and was admitted to the practice of law. Under appointment of John W. Eggeman, judge of the Circuit Court of Allen county, he has served as probate commissioner of the county. In the years of his professional career Mr. Luecke has been associated with Zollars & Zollars, James M. Robinson, and William C. Geake, and, for a considerable time, has been associated with Edward O'Rourke, who, for a period of thirty-six years, occupied the bench of the circuit court of Allen county. The firm of O'Rourke & Luecke occupies a modern suite of offices in the Tri-State Building on Court street, opposite the court house. Mr. Luecke has ever taken a lively interest in the political

Sidney C. Lumbard

affairs of the city, county, district and state. As the chairman of the Democratic central committee of the Twelfth Congressional District, he is one of the most valued members of the state central committee of his party. Mr. Luecke is a member of the Commercial Club of Fort Wayne, and an active worker on important committees in that organization. As the first president and one of the organizers of the Fort Wayne Rotary Club, he has assisted in giving to the city one of its most valued and aggressive organizations of service. Through the medium of the Hoosier State Automobile Association, which he is serving as first vice-president, he has been enabled to carry forward much of his good roads program. In his capacity as the Allen county counsel of the Lincoln Highway Association, he has contributed much to the success of that great enterprise. On June 2, 1908, Mr. Luecke was united in marriage with Miss Emma M. Foellinger, daughter of Adolph Foellinger, of Fort Wayne. To Mr. and Mrs. Luecke a daughter, Marguerite F., was born July 9, 1910. The family home is at No. 322 West Woodland avenue. Mr. and Mrs. Luecke are members of the Lutheran church.

Sidney C. Lumbard.—A man is rich or poor according to what he is, not according to what he has, and gauged by this significant metewand the life of the late Sidney C. Lumbard was one of opulence, for he measured up to the highest standard of true, loyal and noble manhood and left to the world the heritage of worthy thoughts and worthy deeds. He left a strong impress upon the business and social fabric of Fort Wayne, in which city the major portion of his life was spent, and such were his character and influence that it is specially consistent that in this history be entered a tribute to his memory. At the time of his death, which occurred March 11, 1899, he was one of the foremost exponents of the real estate and insurance business in this section of Indiana, and since he passed from the stage of life's mortal endeavors his widow has successfully continued the insurance business to which he long gave his close attention. Mr. Lumbard was born in the city of Brooklyn, New York, on May 27, 1849, and thus was nearly fifty years of age at the time of his demise. He acquired his early education in the old Empire state and was a lad of about fourteen years at the time when his parents established their home in Fort Wayne, in 1863. His parents, Sanford and Mary Ann (Babcock) Lumbard, here passed the residue of their lives, and the father was one of the influential insurance men of Fort Wayne at the time of his death. Sidney C. continued his studies in the Fort Wayne schools until he completed three years of the curriculum of the high school, and at the age of eighteen years he entered his father's insurance office, in which he gained the thorough knowledge which later was to enable him to become one of the leading representatives of this line of enterprise in northern Indiana. His father was local agent for several insurance companies, but finally became special agent for the Phœnix Fire Insurance Company of Brooklyn, New York, his son, Sidney C., assuming the local agency for the various companies and, in the year 1871, forming a partnership with John S. Irwin in the general insurance and real estate business. He gained precedence as one of the strongest and best-known local insurance underwriters in northern Indiana, his real estate operations expanded to broad scope and importance and he had large investments and interests in Allen county realty at the time of his death. He was a man of fine mentality and well fortified opinions, and his sterling character and mature judgment caused his advice and counsel to be often sought in connection with business and civic affairs. His course in all of the relations of life was guided and governed by lofty ideals, and his genial and kindly personality gained to him the high regard of all who came within the sphere of his influence. He had no desire for the honors or emoluments of political office, but was a staunch supporter of the cause of the Democratic party, his religious views being in accord with the tenets of the Baptist church, in the faith of which he was reared. He was affiliated with both the York and Scottish Rite bodies of the Masonic fraternity, and was at all times persona grata in both business and social circles of the community which was long the stage of his earnest and prolific endeavors. In June, 1870, was solemnized the marriage of Mr. Lumbard to Miss Adelia Lynn, who was born at Bluffton, the judicial center of Wells county, Indiana, daughter of the late Lewis and Martha (Hutchinson) Lynn. Mr. and Mrs. Lumbard became the parents of three children: Mrs. Eugene H. Olds, Mrs. Robert H. Carnahan, who died in 1906, and Francis S. Lumbard. Since the death of her husband Mrs. Lumbard has continued the insurance business which he built up and has shown marked ability and circumspection in her practical association with this important line of enterprise, the while she is a popular figure in the social life of the community.

Dr. John Edward McArdle, since 1909 established in the general practice of medicine and surgery in Fort Wayne, was born in Monroeville, Allen county, on November 22, 1884, and is the son of Peter and Mary (English) McArdle, concerning which family more extended mention is to be found in other pages of this work. Doctor McArdle as a boy attended the Monroeville high school and was graduated therefrom in 1903, following which he entered the Indiana Medical College at Indianapolis and was graduated from that institution in 1907 with the degree M. D. He served an internship of two years in St. Joseph Hospital, in Fort Wayne, following his graduation, after which he became associated with Doctor Drayer in the general practice of medicine and surgery in Fort Wayne, where he is now located. Doctor McArdle was married on September 6, 1910, to Miss Henrietta Grimme, daughter of G. B. Grimme, a well-known merchant tailor of Fort Wayne. Three boys have been born to Doctor and Mrs. McArdle—Edward, John and Richard. The family have membership in St. Patrick's Roman Catholic church, and Doctor McArdle is a member of the Knights of Columbus, the Elks, the Moose and the Friars Club. He is a Democrat and served from 1915 to 1917 as coroner of Allen county.

Peter McArdle.—The year 1875 marked the advent of Peter McArdle in Allen county, Indiana. Prior to that time he had been gathering experience in American ways in the states of New York and Kentucky. Allen county seemed better suited to him than any of the other places he had tested out, and he was content to settle on a farm in Monroe township, where he has since lived and devoted his energies to the development of a fine farm of two hundred acres of fertile Indiana land. Mr. McArdle is of Irish birth and parentage, born in Arbagh, Ireland, on June 22, 1847, son of Owen J. and Annie (McKinley) McArdle. The parents spent their lives in their native community, rearing a family of thirteen children, of which number only the subject is alive today. Peter McArdle was reared and educated in the community of his birth and was twenty-two years old when he struck out for himself in quest of such favors as America had to offer to a young and ambitious Irishman. He spent two years in New York city and, in 1871, moved on to Kentucky. Returning to New York he gave another year to life in the great metropolis and then turned his face to the west, locating, in 1875, in Allen county, on a rented farm. A few years of moderate prosperity as a renter made it possible for him to purchase the property on which he is now living. This fine place of two hundred acres is located in Section 18, Monroe township, and it is one of the finest improved pieces of land in the community. Success has followed Mr. McArdle's efforts and he is today one of the solid citizens of the township which has represented his home for the past thirty-five years. Energy, good management and thrift have played an important part in his rise in the scale of material prosperity, and he stands high in the regard of his fellow citizens in the township. Mr. McArdle was married in February, 1881, to Miss Maggie English, who was born and reared in Ohio, and of the nine children that came to them eight are now living. The family are members of the Roman Catholic church, and Mr. McArdle is a Democrat.

David O. McComb.—In connection with the high standard of efficiency maintained in the public schools of Allen county there is no need for indirection or conjecture in determining the strength and benignancy of the influence wielded by Mr. McComb, who is now the efficient and valued incumbent of the office of county superintendent of schools, of which position he has been in tenure since his election, in 1913, and in which he has achieved a splendid work in systematizing and advancing all departments of school service in his jurisdiction—notably in advancing the centralization plan, which carries with it the high-school work, his service and progressive policies along this line having resulted in the centralizing of the one-room district schools of the county and in bringing the work of the same up to the most efficient status. Under his regime all departments of school work in the county have been unified and strengthened, and he has proved not only a resourceful exponent of pedagogy but also versatile and enthusiastic as an executive. Mr. McComb was born on a farm in Perry township, this county, June 11, 1872, son of James and Margaret (Simonton) McComb. James McComb was born in Ireland, of Scottish ancestry, and was about three years old when his parents emigrated to the United States, his mother having died about two years later. As a boy he was bound out, or indentured, to a family in Clermont county, Ohio, and he was reared to manhood in the old Buckeye state, where he made good use of such limited educational advantages as were afforded him. After his marriage he came to Allen county, Indiana, about the year 1850, and purchased two hundred acres of wild land, in Perry township. Here his diligence, energy and progressiveness eventually enabled him to reclaim and improve one of the fine farms of the county, and he so ordered his course in all of the relations of life as to merit and receive the unqualified confidence and good will of the community. He was a Democrat in his political proclivities, was influential in local affairs of a public order and served two terms as trustee of Perry township, an office to which he was first elected in 1888. Both he and his wife were active and consistent members of the United Brethren church. Of the children the eldest is Robert S., a farmer in the state of Washington; Mary is the widow of John J. Rundles and resides in Perry township; James I. is a prosperous farmer in Perry township; Thomas C. is a farmer in Kent county, Michigan; Morton T. is engaged in the general merchandise business at Huntertown, Perry township; William S. was a successful physician and surgeon engaged in practice at Sheldon, this county, at the time of his death; Emma is the widow of Samuel H. Davis and maintains her home in St. Joseph township; Hiram E. is a successful farmer in Kalamazoo county, Michigan; John S. resides in Perry township; and David O., of this review, is the youngest of the number. The boyhood and youth of David O. McComb were compassed by the invigorating influences of the home farm and after he had availed himself of the advantages of the public schools of his native township his ambition for a higher education was such that he determined to acquire the same, though he realized that in attaining this end he must needs depend largely on his own resources. He attended Taylor University, at Upland, Indiana, one year, and later was a student in the normal university at Angola. Self-application has been largely the medium through which he has gained his liberal education and he has become one of the representative and influential figures in pedagogic circles in his native commonwealth, where he devoted twenty years to effective service as a teacher in the public schools, his activities in this line having been initiated in 1894 and much of his service in the early years having been in the district schools of Allen county. In 1911 Mr. McComb was appointed deputy county auditor, under the administration of Calvin H. Brown, and of this position he continued the incumbent two years. He was soon afterward, in March, 1913, elected to the office of county superintendent of schools, and to the duties of this position he has since devoted himself with characteristic energy and enthusiasm, the tangible results of his efforts constituting the best voucher for the efficiency of his administration, which has met with unequivocal popular approval. He has served at various times in the office of justice of the peace, but he has made educational work his vocation and finds in the same his maximum satisfaction and award. In politics Mr. McComb gives his allegiance to the Democratic party, and though he was reared in the faith of the United Brethren church he is now an active member of the Evangelical Association. He is affiliated with the lodge of Ancient Free and Accepted Masons at Huntertown and, since 1914, has served as president of Fort Wayne Council of the National Union, a fraternal insurance order. On Christmas day of the year 1900 was solemnized the marriage of Mr. McComb to Miss Anna C. Matsch, who was born and reared in Allen county and who is of German lineage. Mr. and Mrs. McComb have three children—James C., Walter A., and Dorothy Mae. The family home in Fort Wayne is known for its culture and is a center of hospitality.

George W. McComb.—General farming and stock-raising have claimed the attention of George W. McComb since he settled on his present farm in Cedar Creek township, in 1906, and he has been enjoying a very gratifying success in the work. A Kentuckian by birth, he is a son of Joseph and Elizabeth (Berry) McComb, both of Kentucky birth and ancestry, and all their lives engaged in farming. George McComb was one of the six children of his parents, and his natal day was December 18, 1877. The others are Belle, the wife of James Paugh, of Lagrange, Kentucky; Ella, the wife of Nicholas Brown, of Westport, Kentucky; James, Joseph Milton and Cleveland. The mother of this family died in 1889, when the subject was a lad of twelve years, and the father lived until January 13, 1916. The death of the mother brought inevitable changes in the management of the family, and George McComb at the age of twelve went to work for his living, receiving his keep and a wage of five dollars a month for his labors. When he was seventeen years old he went to Edgar county, Illinois, and worked on a farm for some years, in 1906 coming to Cedar Creek township, where he bought a farm of seventy-nine acres in section 29. He settled down in earnest to the work of improving the place, and the ten years spent there have seen many changes in the general appearance of the place. October 18, 1899, Mr. McComb married Iva Ann Rebecca Boyers, born in Edgar county, Illinois, daughter of George W. and Josephine (Willhoit) Boyers. She was one of eleven children. The children are as follows: Leroy and Emerson Lee, residents of Boise, Idaho; Florence, deceased; Emma Isador, wife of William Parkison, of Edgar county; Edward Otis; Retta Hammett, wife of Hilton Kirkham, all of Illinois; Iva, wife of the subject; Clarabelle, George, Sylvan, and Josie, all of Edgar county. To Mr. and Mrs. McComb have been born seven children. They are Theodore Clifton, born August 2, 1900; Josephine Lucille, born January 7, 1902; Donovan, born November 8, 1904; Joseph Owen, born April 25, 1906; George Walter, born November 8, 1908; Ernest Harold, born November 27, 1911; and Susan Mary, born April 24, 1914. Mr. McComb is a Democrat, more or less active in county politics, and is now serving as chairman of the Cedar Creek Agricultural society, one of the live organizations of the county in that particular field. He is a member of the Modern Woodmen of America and of the Baptist church, while his wife has membership in the Christian church.

Merton T. McComb has been a resident of Allen county from the time of his birth, is a representative of one of the old and honored families of this section of the state and has marked the passing years with worthy achievement, including service as a successful and popular teacher in the public schools and progressive activities along normal lines of business enterprise. He is now one of the prominent merchants of Huntertown, in Perry township, and is influential in community affairs, as a broad-minded and progressive citizen of the utmost civic loyalty. His birth occurred in Perry township, September 13, 1861, and he is a son of James and Margaret (Simonton) McComb, the former born near Belfast, Ireland, of remote Scottish ancestry, and the latter was born in Clermont county, Ohio, in which state their marriage was solemnized. Mrs. McComb was a daughter of Theophilus Simonton, who was a prosperous farmer in that county, whence he removed to the vicinity of Cincinnati, though he later returned to his fine old homestead farm, where he passed the remainder of his life and where he died at the patriarchal age of ninety-one years. James McComb was three years of age at the time of his parents' immigration from the Emerald Isle to America, and the family home was established in Cincinnati, Ohio, where the devoted mother died shortly afterward. James was thus a child when he was adopted by James Newbro, in whose home he was reared to manhood, in the meanwhile receiving the advantages of the common schools of the Buckeye state. James Newbro finally came to Allen county, Indiana, and became a pioneer farmer of Perry township. He died in Effingham, Illinois. James McComb accompanied his foster-father on the removal to Allen county, at the age of twenty-two years, and his young wife came with him to the new home in the Hoosier state. He purchased a tract of land in Perry township and there developed one of the valuable farms of the county, the property being still in the possession of the McComb family. He was a man of strong individuality and sterling integrity, was influential in his community and served four years as trustee of Perry township. He remained on his old homestead until his death, at the age of seventy-eight years, and his widow was eighty-one years of age when she too was called to the life eternal. They became the parents of ten children, and the family name has continued to be prominently and worthily identified with the history of Allen county. Robert, the eldest son, is now a resident of Seattle; Thomas C. resides in Grand Rapids, Mich.; John S. is a farmer in Perry township; Mary is the wife of John Rundels, of Huntertown; James I. is a farmer in Perry township; Merton T., of this review, was the next in order of birth; Emma is the wife of Samuel Davis, of St. Joseph township; Dr. William S. was graduated in the Fort Wayne Medical College and was engaged in the practice of his profession in his native county at the time of his death, which occurred when he was but thirty-three years of age; Hiram, now of Huntertown; David O., who resides in Fort Wayne, is serving as superintendent of education for Allen county. Merton T. McComb acquired his early education in the schools of Perry township, and in the meanwhile gained close fellowship with the invigorating work of the home farm. In pursuance of higher academic discipline he attended for one year the Methodist College at Fort Wayne, and for ten years thereafter he was an able and popular representative of the pedagogic profession, having taught for three years in the district schools of Perry township and for seven years in the schools of White county. About 1889 Mr. McComb resumed his active association with farm industry, and was one of the progressive agriculturists and stock-growers of his native township until 1904, when he purchased the well established general merchandise business of Dr. Frank Greenwell, at Huntertown, where he continued with unequivocal success until 1916, when he sold it to his brother, Hiram E. He is one of the representative men and loyal and public-spirited citizens of the village. He assisted in the organization of the Huntertown State Bank, was one of the members of its original directorate. In the autumn of 1916 he became prominently identified with the organization of the Huntertown Agricultural society, and he is always to be found aligned as a staunch supporter of measures and enterprises advanced for the general good of the community. On March 17, 1890, was solemnized the marriage of Mr. McComb to Miss Rosetta, daughter of Philander Bush, of White county, and concerning the five children of this union the following brief data are consistently entered: Elsie, who was graduated in the Fort Wayne Business College after having fully profited by the advantages of the public schools, is now the wife of Ralph Jones, of Fort Wayne; Verine E., whose educational acquirement included a course in the Fort Wayne high school; James Lynn likewise had the advantages of the Fort Wayne high school and he is now engaged in the automobile business at Huntertown; Lydia B. was graduated in the Fort Wayne high school and is now a member of the class of 1917 in the Lakeside School, at Fort Wayne; and Glenn is attending the public schools of Huntertown.

Charles McCulloch.—During the period of three-quarters of a century, Charles McCulloch, banker, born and reared in his home city, has witnessed the growth of the place from a frontier village to a municipality of metropolitan proportions. In this same period Mr. McCulloch, passing from the years of childhood to maturity, has ever stood as a loyal, active element in the making of the greater Fort Wayne of today—Indiana's second city. Born during the period of the building of the Wabash and Erie canal, he was a child of three years when traffic on this great artificial waterway, with Fort Wayne as the center of activity, was opened between Lake Erie and the Ohio river. During his youth the first railroads were built, connecting Fort Wayne with Chicago and the East. The memory of these early days of development remains clear in the mind of Mr. McCulloch and much written history of the period has received the light of his reminiscent reviews of conditions of former times. The father of Charles McCulloch—Judge Hugh McCulloch—was ever an inspiration to the son in the accomplishment of high ideals. Rising from the plane of a frontier village lawyer and banker to the loftiest place of trust in the nation's world of finance, Hugh McCulloch became the man to whom was entrusted the responsible task of steering the Ship of State through troublous financial waters during the period of the Civil War and the succeeding days of reconstruction. Hugh McCulloch came to Fort Wayne on horseback in the spring of 1833. He has just completed a course in law and had chosen Fort Wayne as a likely place for the practice of his profession. His services as judge of the probate court of Allen county were cut short by his appointment, in 1835, as the cashier of the Fort Wayne branch of the State Bank of Indiana. With the reorganization of the Bank of the State of Indiana he was elected to serve as the president of the central institution. In 1863, Salmon P. Chase, secretary of the treasury of the United States, summoned Judge McCulloch to the national capital and offered him the office of the first comptroller of the currency of the United States. The acceptance and the appointment by President Lincoln followed. Mr. McCulloch's successful method of organizing the newly created department and the national banking system, by which the state banks throughout the Union were superseded by national banks, has given him the appellation of "the father of the national banking system." In the formation of his second cabinet President Lincoln selected Judge McCulloch as secretary of the treasury, in which position, during the succeeding administration of President Johnson, he coped successfully with the nation's financial problems during the period of reconstruction, and he served in the same position in the cabinet of President Arthur. In 1870, Judge McCulloch went to London, England, as the resident and managing partner of Jay Cook, McCulloch and Company. Judge McCulloch was born in Kennebunk, Maine, in 1808. His marriage with Sarah Man was solemnized in Fort Wayne. Charles McCulloch was born in Fort Wayne, September 3, 1840. For a period he was under the instruction of a private tutor and later graduated from the Fort Wayne public schools. During his youth and early manhood he became closely connected with the banking business, since the family residence was connected with the original building in which the branch bank was located at the southwest corner of East Main and Clinton streets. Under the instruction of his father he early acquired a taste for the line of effort which had marked the success of Judge McCulloch. Mr. McCulloch served as the president of the Hamilton bank and its successor, the Hamilton National bank, his connection dating from 1874. The original private banking house of Allen Hamilton and Company was founded in 1853 by Allen Hamilton, Hugh McCulloch and Jesse L. Williams. Upon the reorganization of the institution, in 1874, Charles McCulloch was elected president. The merging of the institution into the Hamilton National bank took place in November, 1879, and the final reorganization occurred in 1899. The institution was blessed with a history of prosperity and soundness which gave it a high place among the banking institutions of the middle west. On the 7th of April, 1917, the Hamilton National bank was merged with the First National bank, the combined institution assuming the name, First and Hamilton National bank. Mr. McCulloch has always been interested in public affairs. Independent in politics, he has given the weight of his support in all instances in which his judgment pointed to a man or a principle which would best serve the people. He served as a member of the board of trustees which established and constructed the original municipal waterworks plant which has developed into the present valuable property. The city council took initial action in the matter of the waterworks plant in the spring of 1876, when a lively controversy raged over the proposition to secure the water supply from the abandoned Wabash and Erie canal feeder, connecting with the St. Joseph river. The plans prepared by J. D. Cook, of Toledo, Ohio, in 1879, were adopted by a popular election of 3,094 to 561, and the application of these plans formed the foundation of the present system in which Mr. McCulloch took a prominent part. The initial cost of the system was $236,865. The first deep wells were sunk in 1888. At later periods Mr. McCulloch served two terms as a member of the city council. Mr. McCulloch is a member of Fort Wayne lodge of Masons and a Thirty-second degree member of the Scottish Rite body. He is a member of the Commercial Club and of the Fort Wayne Country Club. On the 20th of June, 1865, Mr. McCulloch was united in marriage with Miss Sada F. Ross, daughter of John and Clara Ross, of Vincennes, Indiana. To this union was born one son, John Ross McCulloch, now vice-president of the First and Hamilton National bank. Some time following the death of Mrs. McCulloch Charles McCulloch was united in marriage with Miss Ada Willison, of Beloit, Wisconsin. One son Fred H. McCulloch, treasurer of the Electrical Supply and Fixture Company, was born of this union. The present Mrs. McCulloch was formerly Mrs. Lucy L. Phillips. The family home, located at the corner of West Wayne and Ewing streets, was secured a few years ago by the congregation of the First Church of Christ, Scientist, after which Mr. McCulloch established a new modern home immediately adjoining the property on the north.

Fred H. McCulloch, treasurer and manager of the Electric Supply and Fixture Company, Fort Wayne, is a popular representative of one of the old and honored families of this city, where his paternal grandfather settled about three-fourths of a century ago, when the future metropolis of Allen county was but a village in the midst of a section of Indiana that was in the pioneer stage of civic and material development. He whose name initiates this paragraph was born at what is now 336 East Berry street, Fort Wayne, and the date of his nativity was July 22, 1884. He is a son of Charles and Ada (Willison) McCulloch, the former of whom was born at Fort Wayne on September 3, 1840, and the latter at Massillon, Stark county, Ohio, in 1850. On other pages of this work is entered a review of the career and genealogy of Charles McCulloch, and thus it is unnecessary to repeat the data in the present article. Fred H. McCulloch is indebted to the public schools of Fort Wayne for his early educational discipline, and he took a five-year course in the

Hill School, Pottstown, Pennsylvania. At the age of nineteen years he entered the Sheffield Scientific School of historic old Yale University and in this institution completed a thorough course in mechanical engineering. He was graduated as a member of the class of 1907 and received the degree of Bachelor of Philosophy. His initial experience of a practical order was gained in the Fort Wayne machine shops of the Western Gas Construction Company and later served as a messenger in the Hamilton National bank of this city. Upon leaving this position he became treasurer of the Wayne Steel Refrigerator Company, with which he continued his connection until 1909, when he assumed his present position of treasurer and manager of the Electric Supply and Fixture Company, of Fort Wayne, which has developed under his able and progressive supervision into a substantial business that makes it a valuable addition to the industrial and commercial activities of Fort Wayne. Mr. McCulloch naturally takes lively and loyal interest in all things pertaining to the welfare and advancement of his native city, is a Democrat in his political allegiance and is an active member of the local Commercial Club and the Rotary Club. In a professional way he holds membership in the American Illuminating Engineering Society and in his fraternal relations is affiliated with the Benevolent and Protective Order of Elks, the Rejuvenated Sons of Jove, and the Loyal Order of Moose. He is a member of the Fort Wayne Country Club, and his wife holds membership in the First Presbyterian church, in which he is a member of the Men's Club. On October 16, 1907, was solemnized the marriage of Mr. McCulloch to Miss Alice Foster, daughter of Samuel M. and Margaret (Harrison) Foster, of Fort Wayne, and the one child of this union is Betty Foster McCulloch, born September 5, 1908.

Hugh McFadden has won for himself definite vantage-place as one of the successful exponents of agricultural and live-stock industry in Allen county, where he is the owner of one of the well-improved farms of Aboite township. He was born in Sandusky county, Ohio, on September 24, 1860, a son of John and Elizabeth (Reinic) McFadden, the former of Irish birth and the latter of German lineage. John McFadden was born and reared in Ireland and was a young man when he came to the United States. He landed in the port of New York city and within a short time thereafter made his way westward and established his residence in Sandusky county, Ohio, where for several years he was engaged in farming. About the year 1882 he came with his family to Allen county, Indiana, where he identified himself with lumbering operations and became the owner of a sawmill. He operated the mill several years and during the closing period of his life lived retired, in the city of Fort Wayne, where both he and his wife died, his political support having been given to the Democratic party and his religious faith having been that of the Catholic church. Of the children the eldest is James Henry, who is now living virtually retired at Roanoke, Huntington county, this state; Alvina is the wife of Henry Smith, a farmer in Lafayette township, Allen county; Hugh, of this review, was the next in order of birth; and Elsie is the wife of John K. Smith, of Huntington county. Hugh McFadden was reared to adult age in the old Buckeye state and received his early education in the Ohio public schools. He gained familiarity with the work of the home farm and initiated his independent career as a farmer on rented land. In 1884 he came to Allen county and became a teamster in connection with his father's sawmill. Later he passed eighteen months on the Bass farm, and after that followed various occupations until about the time of his marriage. He then resumed farming operations and, in 1904, purchased his present excellent farm, which comprises one hundred and sixty acres and upon which he has made substantial improvements, including the erection of modern farm buildings. He gives his attention to diversified agriculture and to the raising of good live stock, in which latter department of his vigorous farm enterprise he gives special attention to the raising of Duroc-Jersey swine. His political allegiance is given to the Democratic party and he is affiliated with lodge No. 275 of the Independent Order of Odd Fellows at Roanoke, Huntington county. April 8, 1887, recorded the marriage of Mr. McFadden to Miss Alice Fisher, daughter of Samuel and Hannah A. Fisher, concerning whom specific mention is made on other pages of this work. Mr. and Mrs. McFadden have nine children: Edith is the wife of Alvin J. Stauffer, of Aboite township; Anna is the wife of Carl Jennings, of Ontario, Canada; Russell is associated in the work and management of the home farm; Otis is now a resident of Essex, province of Ontario, Canada; and the other children are still at the parental home—Mode, Elizabeth, Fay, Lester and Wilma.

Reuben S. McFarren has been identified with farm life in the states of Ohio, Illinois and Indiana, and has found more of success and advancement in his Indiana years than in any of the others. He is a native of Ohio, born in Stark county on August 26, 1837, son of William and Polly (Ritter) McFarren. The family moved from Stark county to Noble county, Indiana, and after a brief residence there went to Illinois, where they spent five years and then returned to Indiana and settled in Wabash county. The later years of the parents were spent in the home of the son Reuben, after he had acquired independent means. They were members of the United Brethren church, and Mr. McFarren was a Republican in politics. Reuben S. was one of nine children born to his parents. Jeremiah, William and Jacob are deceased. Matilda lives in Lagrange county. Jane is deceased. Reuben S. was the next born. Franklin died in infancy. Sanford is located in Oregon, and Julia Anna, the youngest of the nine, died in infancy. Reuben S. McFarren had his schooling in the old log schools that served in his boyhood days, and he farmed with his father in the family moves from Ohio to Indiana and thence to Illinois and back to Indiana. He married, June 20, 1862, and then branched out for himself, settling on a farm in Sparta township, Noble county, which was his home until he came to Allen county, Lafayette township, his present home. His place, which is limited to one hundred and twenty-three acres, is one of the well-kept and highly improved ones of the township and has yielded a satisfactory return to its owner for the labors expended on it. At the present time Mr. McFarren is living retired, but he is nevertheless closely identified with the civic life of his town and township. He has taken a prominent part in local politics and is counted among the best-informed men of his community on topics of the day. His marriage to Miss Serena Sholty took place on June 20, 1862. She is a native Ohioan like himself, and it was while a resident of Stark county that he made her acquaintance. They are the parents of five children, four of whom are living, and all filling places of usefulness in their respective communities today. They are Oliver P. Morton, a resident of Roanoke; Lily May, living at home; Delphy, the wife of Harry Brock, of Huntington county; and William H., living in Lafayette. Rosa E., born August 10, 1875, died in June, 1876.

James Marshall McKay.—Among the distinguished men of Indiana who have left the impress of their individuality upon the mercantile and industrial life of the country, none are more worthy of mention in the history of Fort Wayne and Allen county than the late James M. McKay, president of the wholesale grocery firm of G. E. Bursley and Company, of this city. His labors not only constituted a potent factor in the commercial and industrial interests of Fort Wayne, but were an inspiring influence, and, even though he has passed from the scene of earthly activities, his work remains as a force for good in the community. He not only achieved notable success in business, but in his home, in social and public life, he was kind and courteous, and no citizen of this city was more respected or enjoyed to a greater degree the confidence of the people, or more richly deserved the regard in which he was held. Mr. McKay was born in Ingersoll, Canada, January 21, 1856, a son of Neil and Nancy (Young) McKay, and he fully exemplified the sturdy, enterprising character for which the people of that country have always been noted. He came to Fort Wayne at the age of thirteen years, and thenceforward his life and enterprises were blended with the growth of this city. While a young man he was engaged with his father in the railroad contracting business and later in the retail grocery trade. In 1887 he associated himself with the late Gilbert E. Bursley in establishing the wholesale grocery firm of G. E. Bursley and Company, of which he remained an active factor until the time of his demise. For thirty years his time and energy were devoted to the building up of the enterprise with which he was associated, and his name in connection with any transaction was always a guaranty of straightforward and honorable dealing. This great concern is one of the largest enterprises of its kind in northern Indiana and is not only a leader in the wholesale grocery trade both at home and abroad, but is the wonderful outgrowth of a small business established three decades ago. The success of the firm in a large measure has been due to Mr. McKay's superior merchandising ability and executive judgment, and a just portion of the present prosperity of the house may be attributed to his quiet faithfulness and untiring efforts. Fort Wayne is indebted to her many keen business men for her prosperity and the place she occupies among the leading cities of the state, and to none more than James M. McKay. A man of unusual public spirit, interested in local affairs and proud of the city in which much of his activities and mature manhood were passed, he was a strong factor in the furtherance of any measure which had for its aim the advancement of the people or the betterment of existing conditions. He was a man of strong convictions of what is right and wrong and was unfaltering in his opposition to a course which he deemed inimical to the best interests of the country, and he was entirely fearless of criticism and public opinion when he believed he was right. He was actively identified with nearly every movement that had for its object the welfare and advancement of civic interests, and no worthy projects were attempted during his residence in Fort Wayne to which he did not contribute largely of his time and financial support. He was active in church and Sunday School work and for many years was a ruling elder in the First Presbyterian church of this city. He was also especially interested in the Y. M. C. A. and gave freely to its support. On October 1, 1885, Mr. McKay was united in marriage with Miss Elizabeth J. McFee, of Fort Wayne, a daughter of William and Margaret (Christy) McFee, pioneers of this city, and they became the parents of three sons: Neil Aldrich, William Thompson and James Marshall, Jr. The first two named are associated with the firm of G. E. Bursley and Company and the last is in the officers' reserve training camp at Indianapolis. Although unostentatious in manner, Mr. McKay had many warm friends and was everywhere recognized as a man of the highest type of character. Though prominent in social circles, he was devoted to the pleasures of home life and his happiest moments were always spent at his own fireside. He found a pleasure in promp' the welfare of his family and was a kind and indulgent husband and father. His career was one that redounds to his credit and places his name high in the estimation of his fellowmen. It was also one of which his family has a just reason to be proud, for never was a man's success due more to his own native ability and less to outward circumstances. Nothing came to him by chance. He reaped only where he sowed, and the harvest, with its valued aftermath, came to him alone through energy, industry and perseverance.' In business life he was alert, sagacious and reliable. As a citizen he was honorable, prompt and true to every engagement, and his death, which occurred June 25, 1917, removed from Fort Wayne one of its most valued citizens. The originality and profound grasp of his intellect command respect, and yet these were not all of the man. In every relation of life were shown the light that comes from justness, generosity, truth, high sense of honor, proper respect for self, and a sensitive thoughtfulness for others. What a magnificent legacy such a man leaves to the generations who shall come after him! To sketch in detail Mr. McKay's active business career would be a task of no small moment, however agreeable and interesting. It must suffice to say in conclusion that his labors were of the most earnest character, that they were exceedingly comprehensive, and that they contributed in an important degree to the development of the commercial and industrial prosperity and wealth of the city in which they were performed and in no slight measure to the material advantage of the entire country. Although making no claim to greater credit than that which belongs to one who, by wise and persistent effort, advanced his own fortune and at the same time that of many others, who shares in one way or another in his enterprises, a discriminating public sentiment will not fail to accord him a front rank among the commercial benefactors of the nation.

Robert B. McKeeman, M. D., has found in his native county ample field for successful achievement in his exacting profession and has won secure place as a representative physician and surgeon in the city of Fort Wayne. He was born near Hoagland, Allen county, on February 27, 1874, a son of David C. and Margaret (McConahey) McKeeman, natives of County Antrim, Ireland. David C. McKeeman was reared and educated in Ireland and came to America when a young man. He remained for a time in the vicinity of Albany, New York, and then came to Indiana and purchased a farm near Hoagland, Allen county. He became one of the prosperous exponents of agricultural and live-stock industry in this county and here he and his wife passed the residue of their lives—possessed of those sterling attributes of character that invariably beget popular confidence and respect. Mr. McKeeman was a Republican in politics and both he and his wife were lifelong members of the Presbyterian church. Of their children the first three—John,

Catherine and Margaret—are deceased; Jennie is the wife of Henry Dauer, of Decatur, this state; Nancy is the wife of Robert Mercer, of Poe, Allen county; Belle and James are deceased; William Alexander, Ella and David C., Jr., reside in Fort Wayne; and Dr. Robert B., of this review, is the youngest of the number. Passing his childhood and early youth on the home farm, Doctor McKeeman made good use of the advantages of the public schools in the village of Hoagland and thereafter attended Taylor University, at Upland, this state, and the normal school at Marion. After two years of successful service as a teacher in the schools of Allen county he was able to follow the course of his ambition and to enter the Fort Wayne Medical College, which is now an integral part of the medical department of the University of Indiana. In this institution he was graduated in 1897, and, after thus receiving his degree of Doctor of Medicine, engaged in practice at Monroe, Adams county, where he remained until 1900, since which time he has been engaged in practice in Fort Wayne, where he has developed a substantial and representative professional business. The Doctor is identified with the Allen County Medical Society, the Indiana State Medical Society and the Tri-State Medical Society. His political allegiance is given to the Republican party, he and his wife are members of the Third Presbyterian church of Fort Wayne, and in the time-honored Masonic fraternity he has received the thirty-second degree of the Scottish Rite. October 5, 1897, was made an eventful day in the life of Doctor McKeeman, since then was solemnized his marriage to Miss Susan M. Hocker, a daughter of Joseph and Jesteen Hocker, of Monroe, Adams county, and the four children of this union are L. Stanford, Lillian Theodosia,, Donald H. C. and Ruth Beatrice.

William M. McKinnie.—The vital urge and inspiration of genuine ambition and talent marked the career of William Mark McKinnie, who was long numbered among the representative business men and best-known and most popular citizens of Fort Wayne, and who became a national figure in connection with the hotel business, in which line of enterprise his father also had achieved success and high reputation. Playing a strong and loyal part in connection with the civic and business life of Fort Wayne, generous, considerate and possessed of an affability that won to him the staunchest of friends, Mr. McKinnie was a man whose loss was felt with a sense of personal bereavement in the city that had long been his home, his death having occurred, July 1, 1913, and it is specially consonant that in this history be entered a tribute to his memory. Mr. McKinnie was born at Rochester, Beaver county, Pennsylvania, September 5, 1858, and was a boy at the time of the family removal to Fort Wayne, where he was reared and educated and where he passed the remainder of his life, save for a few years' residence in the city of Pittsburgh, Pennsylvania. He was one of the five children born to Captain Henry McKinnie and Malinda (Bean) McKinnie, whose marriage was solemnized at Rochester, Pennsylvania, on January 1, 1851. Concerning the other children it may be recorded that Emma died in infancy; Frank H. was a resident of Sewickley, Pennsylvania, and is now deceased; Esther was the wife of Dr. Charles F. Bingham, a representative physician in the city of Pittsburgh, where her death occurred; and George B. was assistant manager of the Hotel Anderson, at Pittsburgh, at the time of his death. Captain McKinnie died at his beautiful home in Sewickley, Pennsylvania, October 1, 1899, and his widow survived him by several years. He was born at Poland, Mahoning county, Ohio, December 26,

1822, and his father was a pioneer tavernkeeper at Youngstown, the judicial center of that county, where also he served a number of years as postmaster. Captain McKinnie was reared and educated at Youngstown, and it is worthy of note that in his youth he received instruction in penmanship from John Spencer, whose name is perpetuated in the Spencerian system of penmanship and also in the long famous Spencerian pens. The following quotations from an article published at the time of the death of Captain McKinnie are worthy of reproduction in this connection: "While still a youth Captain McKinnie became engaged as a clerk for Reed and Parks, a famous commission house that operated a chain of warehouses on the old Pennsylvania and Ohio canal, and he was given charge of the Youngstown warehouse and business of the firm, in the employ of which he continued a number of years. During one of his trips from Cleveland he brought Jennie Lind, the famous singer, to Pittsburgh, and in late years he often spoke of his horseback trips from Youngstown to Pittsburgh to deposit the firm's money in the banks of the latter city. In 1845 Captain McKinnie entered the steamboat business, running for many years between Pittsburgh and New Orleans as clerk on some of the largest and most famous packet-boats of the day. He was clerk of the Great Republic, the largest packet of the day on her first trip, and for a long time he was clerk and captain of the Sunny Side. During the early days of the Civil War he operated the Sunny Side as a government transport and as a hospital and supply boat. He was at Vicksburg, Pittsburg Landing and Fort Donelson during the famous engagements at these points, and his boat was burned by the Confederate guerrillas at Island No. 10, Captain McKinnie having a thrilling escape from the burning wreck. After the destruction of his boat he returned to Pittsburgh, and, in 1863, purchased the railroad eating house on the Pittsburgh, Fort Wayne and Chicago Railroad at Fort Wayne, Indiana. He retained his interest in this business and the old-time McKinnie House at the railroad station until his death. In 1876 Captain McKinnie opened the Monmouth House at Spring Lake Beach, New Jersey; in 1877 he started the Manhattan Beach Hotel, on Long Island, and in 1879 the Oriental Hotel at the same beach. He operated both houses until 1892 and became personally acquainted with most of the prominent business men of the country and was a personal friend of Gen. W. T. Sherman. In 1879 Captain McKinnie became associated with Colonel Samuel Kiefer in assuming charge of the Grand Central Hotel in New York city, but they retired from the control of the same about eighteen months later. In 1880 Captain McKinnie and his son Frank H. opened the Neal House, Columbus, Ohio, and operated the same about ten years. In 1884 the Captain, in partnership with his brother-in-law, E. L. Bean, secured the lease on the Hotel Anderson, in Pittsburgh, and he retained the active management of the same until three years prior to his death; he relinquished the management to his oldest son, Frank H. He devoted his energies exclusively to his hotel interests, his only outside connection being as a stockholder of the National Bank of Western Pennsylvania. As a young man he became affiliated with the Masonic fraternity, and in Pittsburgh he attended and supported St. Andrew's Episcopal church. William M. McKinnie, the subject of this memoir, well upheld the prestige of the family name both as a citizen and as a prominent exponent of the hotel business. He early became associated with his father in the operation of the old McKinnie Hotel at the Pennsylvania Railroad station in Fort Wayne, and after his father removed to Pittsburgh William M. took charge of the railroad eating house, of which he continued the owner until about 1903, when the Pennsylvania Company assumed control of all such places along its system. A quarter of a century before his death Mr. McKinnie opened the Wayne Hotel, which he conducted ten years, with brilliant success, and which he made one of the leading hotels of Indiana. For several years after his retirement he gave his attention prrincipally to the management of his important real estate interests in Fort Wayne and Allen county, and, in 1904, went to Pittsburgh, Pennsylvania, where he succeeded his father and brother as proprietor of the Hotel Anderson. In 1910 he sold his interests in this business and returned to Fort Wayne, where he was successfully engaged in the real estate business until his death. His health had been much impaired for a number of months prior to his demise, and the immediate cause of his death was pernicious anaemia. A man of broad mental ken and well-fortified convictions, Mr. McKinnie was distinctively a business man and had no ambition for political preferment. He was a communicant of the Catholic church, as is also his widow. On June 1, 1887, was solemnized the marriage of Mr. McKinnie to Miss Georgie Fleming, a daughter of William and Helen F. (Mayer) Fleming, of Fort Wayne, Mr. Fleming having been one of the honored and influential citizens of Allen county for many years prior to his death. Mrs. McKinnie still maintains her home in Fort Wayne. Of the children of Mr. and Mrs. McKinnie four survive the honored father—Linda M., Gerald, Carlotta and Fleming. In conclusion the following quotations are taken from an editorial that appeared in a Fort Wayne paper at the time of the death of Mr. McKinnie: "The feeling of sadness that pervades the community is not confined alone to manifestations of sympathy for the bereaved family, but is an evidence of genuine regret at the passing of a beloved friend and companion, a progressive citizen, a man whose heart o'erflowed with the milk of human kindness and whose sympathies were decidedly cosmopolitan. Mr. McKinnie was active in the business and social life of Fort Wayne, gave willing aid to any movement for the betterment of his home city, and his passing will leave a void that only time will fill."

Martha McMahon.—One of the recent comers to Allen county is Mrs. Martha McMahon, widow of the late William C. McMahon, who died at his home in Pleasant township on September 1, 1907. They came to Allen county in 1906, after more than fifty years of residence in Illinois. Mrs. McMahon was born on January 15, 1847, near Montreal, Quebec, daughter of Richard and J. (McMahon) Perry. The family came to Illinois in 1850 and there made their home for many years. Martha Perry married William C. McMahon on January 18, 1865. He was born in Philadelphia on June 30, 1838, son of Samuel and Eliza (Caldwell) McMahon, both born in Ireland, whence they came to America in youth. Their son, William C., was a veteran of the Civil war, having served three years in the 106th Illinois Infantry as a member of Company D, participating in many of the memorable engagements of the long and bloody war. He was a farmer practically all his life, successful and prosperous, and was a man of no little influence in his home community. He was a Republican and a member of the Methodist Episcopal church. To him and his wife were born nine children. Eliza Jane is the wife of J. C. Newlin; Charles C. lives in Illinois, his native state; Edward Lloyd died in young life; Harvey L. is a farmer in Pleasant township; William is engaged in the grain and lumber business in Georgetown,

Illinois; Flora B. is the wife of Doctor Merrell, of Marshalltown, Iowa; Hattie E. married C. H. Loos, of Fort Wayne; John R. lives on the home farm with his widowed mother, who finds a good deal of pleasure in the grandchildren that are springing up about her. Eliza is the mother of Samuel C. Charles has one daughter, Hattie Bell. Harvey has a son named Harold H. William has three children,—Edward, Mary and Katherine. Flora is the mother of Mary E. and Robert Perry. Hattie has a daughter named Martha Annette. John has one son, William C., named in honor of the grandsire, William C. McMahon, who died soon after coming to make his home in Pleasant township among his children. He is buried in the cemetery at Ossian, Indiana.

Henry William McMaken was born and reared in Adams township, Allen county, Indiana, the date of his nativity being December 14, 1874. He is a son of Henry Clay and Frances (Link) McMaken and his grandfather was born in the old Fort. Henry C. followed farming and became the owner of a fine farm, from the active duties of which he is now retired. His children are Lucy, Luella, Dora (son), Helene, Elizabeth, and Henry W. The last named was educated in the public schools and pursued the duties of the farm with his father. In 1901 he bought eighty acres of land and has continued in the general farming until the present time. April 4, 1900, he was married to Jessie, daughter of Henry and Martha J. (Birely) Frech, and they have six children: Henry, Ruth, Herbert, Margaret, Wilma, Edith. Mr. McMaken is one of the energetic and prosperous farmers who takes a deep interest in all affairs of his community and usually votes for the principles of the Republican party.

Edward J. McOscar, M. D.—Through character and stewardship Dr. McOscar has proved himself well fortified for the achieving of worthy success in his profession and is now to be consistently designated as one of the successful physicians and surgeons of Fort Wayne, where he has been established in practice for thirty years and is now giving his attention almost exclusively to the surgical branch of his profession. The Doctor was born in Dekalb county, Indiana, November 14, 1860, being the third in order of birth of seven sons, born to John and Mary (Skilling) McOscar, who were born in the state of Pennsylvania—the former near Harrisburg, in 1822, and the latter in the city of Philadelphia, in 1834. John McOscar accompanied his parents on their removal from Stark county, Ohio, to Dekalb county, Indiana, in 1845, and his father, Hugh McOscar, there obtained a tract of government land, in which connection he became one of the pioneer agriculturists of that section of the state. John McOscar was long numbered among the representative farmers and substantial citizens of DeKalb county, where he continued to reside until his death. He was a man of strong intellectual powers and much business ability and so ordered his life as to command popular esteem. It may be noted that he was one of the pioneer teachers in the common schools of DeKalb county, with the history of which county the family name has been long and prominently identified. Prior to their marriage his wife likewise had been a popular teacher in the schools of DeKalb county, to which county she came with her parents, in 1846, from Ashland county, Ohio, and after the death of her husband, in 1887, she removed to Fort Wayne, where she continued to reside with her son, Dr. Edward J., subject of this review, until her death, which occurred, October 27, 1910. Mrs. McOscar was a woman of fine mental ken and personality, she had traveled somewhat extensively, and to the close of her life continued to take lively interest in matters pertaining to the improving of civic conditions. The public schools of his native county afforded Dr. McOscar his early educational advantages and eventually he showed his spirit of reciprocity by teaching in the schools of the county for two years. In preparing himself for his chosen profession he was fortunate in being able to enter the historic old Jefferson Medical College, in the city of Philadelphia, and in this admirable institution was graduated as a member of the class of 1884. After thus receiving his degree of Doctor of Medicine he gained most valuable clinical experience through two years of service in the hospital connected with his alma mater and in the Philadelphia Polyclinic Hospital. In 1886 he came to Fort Wayne and his novitiate was of briefer duration than is usual in his profession, as he soon built up a successful practice. He has continued his professional activities in an independent or individual way during the long intervening years. The Doctor has taken effective post-graduate work in leading institutions in New York city, Philadelphia and Chicago, as well as in the great medical and surgical institutions of Berlin and Vienna, his trip abroad for this purpose having been made in 1908 and his primary object having been to advance his skill in surgery, to which department of practice he has since given his special attention. The Doctor has indulged himself in extensive travels, largely for pleasure, and thus has visited the Canadian provinces, Mexico, the West Indies, Panama, the northern portion of South America, and the Bahama and the Hawaiian islands. In 1912 he visited Japan, China and the Philippine Islands, and on the homeward trip crossed Siberia and visited Moscow, Petrograd and other points of interest in Continental Europe. He has found his travels both a pleasure and an inspiration, as well as a medium for the accumulation of knowledge and fortifying experience along cosmopolitan lines. Dr. McOscar is a member of the American Medical Association, the Congress of Clinical Surgeons of America, the Indiana State Medical Society and the Fort Wayne Medical Society. He is a member of the surgical staff retained by the Grand Rapids & Indiana Railroad, is a consulting surgeon for the Wabash Railroad, and he served three years as surgeon for the Pennsylvania Railroad Company. He is local medical examiner for several leading life insurance companies. The Doctor pays loyal allegiance to the cause of the Democratic party, is a communicant of the Fort Wayne Cathedral parish of the Catholic church, holds membership in the Commercial Club and the Country Club, and is affiliated with the Knights of Columbus, the Benevolent and Protective Order of Elks and the Knights of the Maccabees.

Jesse Macbeth, successful young lawyer of Fort Wayne and a resident of that city since 1900, is the eldest of six children born to David F. and Samantha (Macbeth) Smith. The separation of the parents resulted in a division of the family name, the mother and children holding to the maternal family name of Macbeth. She was a daughter of Samuel Patterson Macbeth and the granddaughter of Samuel Hamilton Macbeth, of Brown county, Ohio. Jesse Macbeth was born on a farm near Felicity, Ohio, October 10, 1877. He had his early schooling in the common schools in Clermont and Warren counties, Ohio, later attending the National Normal University, Central Normal College, Valparaiso and Indiana Universities, and the John Marshall Law School. He won diplomas from Central Normal College and the law school above named. After teaching school two terms in his native state, Mr. Macbeth located in Fort Wayne, in 1900, there engaging in teaching for six years. He then took up the practice of law and has enjoyed a very creditable success in that field. He has been active in fraternal and educational organizations and was for six years a member of the Fort Wayne Board of Education, serving the city well in that capacity. His fraternal activities are with the Masonic order, and he is a past grand master of the Independent Order of Odd Fellows for the state of Indiana. A Democrat, he has done his full share in advancing party interests, but has never been a seeker after political honors. In 1903 Mr. Macbeth married Miss Agnes Kurtz, of Harlan, Allen county, Indiana, and they are the parents of five children—Cecil, Alice, James, Esther and George. Since January 1, 1916, Mr. Macbeth has been associated with David H. Hogg, under the firm name of Macbeth and Hogg.

Charles A. Mailand.—The Mailand family came to Allen county in the year 1837 and was identified with this region in its earliest stages of agricultural development. Men and women of the name have from then down to the present time contributed liberally and loyally of their best to the upbuilding of their respective communities and have found their reward in material benefits as well as in the consciousness of duty well performed. Charles A. Mailand, who is the immediate subject of this sketch devoted to the family, was born on August 13, 1864, in Marion township, son of Carl and Berhardina (Berning) Mailand, who came to Allen county as children in company of their respective families. Carl Mailand came of German parents and was a member of the German Lutheran church, as were his parents before him. He acquired land in Allen county and settled down to the business of stock raising, in which he enjoyed a worthy success, and he acquired a good deal of property during his lifetime. He was a participating witness in some of the greatest changes the county passed through in the days of her development from a wilderness to a productive farming region and was wont to tell how, when a boy on his father's farm, they always went to their work armed with knife and gun, partly for the sake of protection and partly because desirable game abounded and it was considered a good plan to be prepared, even in those days. Deer were plentiful, and were frequently shot from the windows of the cabin home, and the Indian in those early times was a constant menace to the happiness and well being of the pioneer settlers. Charles A. Mailand was one of nine children born to his parents. Lazetta and Henry W., the two eldest, are deceased. Louisa married Henry Swartz and lives in Fort Wayne; Ferdinand, Amelia, Sophia and Minnie are no longer living, and Berhardina married Fred H. Meyer, of Pleasant township. Charles A. was the youngest of the family. He was educated in the common schools of Marion township and was employed on the home farm until his marriage. At that time he was the recipient of a gift of one hundred and twenty acres of land from his father, it being the custom of the elder Mailand to present each of his children with some land on their marriage. Young Mailand later added one hundred and eight acres and has for years carried on a successful business in stock farming. He has kept up the standard of his place to a pleasing degree and his farm is a modern one in every respect. Mr. Mailand has extended his interests into other channels and was a director in the Hoagland State Bank. He was married on October 23, 1890, to Miss Johanna Meyer, the daughter of J. C. Meyer, who is mentioned at some length in other pages of this work. The Mailands have five children—Alvina, Herman C., Luella, William and Herbert, all at home.

James Mallo was born in Pleasant township and has passed his life thus far within its borders. His natal day is August 24, 1869, and he is a son of George J. and Jane (Dalman) Mallo. The father was born in Buffalo, New York, in the year 1848, and came to Allen county, Indiana, in 1859. He gave his attention mainly to farming enterprises and when the Civil War broke out enlisted and gave one year to service in the Union army. Returning to the pursuits of peace, he came, in time, to own some land in Pleasant township and there spent a good many quiet but busy years in devotion to the business of agriculture. He is now living retired in Fort Wayne, enjoying the comforts won by years of earnest effort. He is Republican in politics and an adherent of the Christian Science faith. To him and his wife seven children were born. Ellen is the wife of Marion Ake; May is the second born; Agnes married Henry Wheeling; Judia is deceased, as are also Mary and Charles. James, the youngest, is the immediate subject of this sketch. He had his education in the schools of Pleasant township and gave his young years to agricultural activities on the farm of his father. He bought forty acres in Lafayette township and there has his home today, where he is engaged in diversified farming and enjoying a very comfortable success in his chosen work. He was married in August, 1893, to Miss Catherine Suter, daughter of Jacob Suter, an old and honored resident of Allen county, who died in 1910, after a life devoted to the pursuits of agriculture, in which he was very successful. The children of James and Catherine Mallo are Clara, Ethel, Ralph and Clarence. Clara is the wife of Elmer Krouse and is the mother of one child. The three others— Ethel, Ralph and Clarence—are still members of the home family and are young people of much promise.

August E. Martin has been a resident of Allen county from the time of his birth, has contributed materially to the advancement of agricultural industry in the county, and is now a successful exponent of the real estate business, with residence and business headquarters in the city of Fort Wayne. On the homestead farm of his father, in Perry township, this county, August E. Martin was born August 17, 1868, and the family name has been worthily linked with civic and industrial advancement in the county for more than half a century. Mr. Martin is a son of August J. and Josephine (Rassat) Martin, both of whom were born in France, both having passed the final decade of their lives in Fort Wayne. The original settlement of the Martin family was made in Stark county, Ohio, from which they finally came to Allen county. The first American representatives of the Rassat family settled in the state of New York, and came thence to Allen county. Mr. Martin was thirteen and his wife nine years of age at the time of the removal of the respective families to America. August J. Martin finally purchased land in Perry township, and on this homestead he and his wife continued to reside until they had attained to advanced age. They became the parents of nine children: Frank, Julian, Alexander, Charles (who died at the age of nine years), Henry, Nestor, August E., Louise, and Josephine. Louise is the wife of Frank Laurent, of Fort Wayne, and Josephine is the wife of Thomas Kehoe, who is with the Overland Automobile Company in Cleveland, Ohio. August E. Martin acquired his preliminary education in the public schools of his native township and supplemented this training by an effective course of study in the Academy of the Sacred Heart. He continued to be associated with the work and management of the home farm and after his marriage he was engaged independently for a period of twelve years. He then established his residence upon a farm of two hundred acres in Washington township, and upon this he made many improvements, including good buildings, an effective drainage system and substantial fences. On March 1, 1908, he removed with his family to Fort Wayne. He still owns one of the fine farms of the county and gives much attention to the buying and selling of farm property, and has general supervision of operations on his farm. Upon his removal to Fort Wayne Mr. Martin identified himself with the substantial and prosperous real estate business of the Monroe Fitch Company, and he still continues active in this important line of enterprise. As a loyal and progressive citizen he gives staunch allegiance to the Democratic party but he has never sought or held public office. He is affiliated with Fort Wayne Lodge, No. 155, Benevolent & Protective Order of Elks; is identified with the Franco-American Society of Allen county; and both he and his wife are communicants of the Fort Wayne Cathedral parish of the Catholic church. On January 11, 1888, was solemnized the marriage of Mr. Martin to Miss Maude E., a daughter of Solomon and Emma (Kryder) Kell, the former a native of Stark county, Ohio, and the latter of Cedar Creek township, this county. Mrs. Kell passed to the life eternal July 30, 1910, and Mr. Kell's death occurred January 31, 1915. The children of Mr. and Mrs. Martin are Floyd, the wife of John Gillie, of Fort Wayne; Francis remains at the parental home; Scott, the maiden name of whose wife was Bessie Payne, is in the employ of the Tepper Dry Goods Company, of Fort Wayne; Maurice is now a resident of Troy, Ohio; and August E., Jr., is at the parental home.

David Martin has passed the ninety-first milestone on the journey of life and is one of the most venerable and honored citizens of Allen county. For more than sixty years he has maintained his residence on the old homestead farm which he reclaimed from the forest wilds of Monroe township, and as a man of exalted integrity of character and superior intellectual ability has been a leader in thought and action and has done much to further the social and material development and progress of his home township and county. A veritable patriarch, he is revered in the community in which he has long lived and labored to goodly ends and of which he is a pioneer, his reminiscences in regard to the early days in Allen county being graphic and interesting and well worthy of perpetuation in the history of this section of the Hoosier state. Mr. Martin is a scion of families that were founded in America in the colonial era, and his parents were sterling pioneers of Ohio. He was born on a pioneer farm in Licking county, Ohio, the date of his nativity having been July 29, 1826, and he is the only survivor of the eight children born to John and Margaret (Mesecup) Martin, the former a native of Pennsylvania and the latter of Hagerstown, Maryland. From the old Keystone state the parents removed to Ohio in an early day and became pioneer settlers in Licking county, where the father obtained a tract of wild land and instituted the arduous work of reclaiming a farm. On this old homestead he and his noble wife passed the residue of their lives, worthy in stewardship and achievement and honored by all who knew them. David Martin was reared under the conditions and influence of the pioneer period in the history of the old Buckeye state, and through ambitious predilection and close application he acquired an education far superior to that of the average youth of the locality and period. He continued his residence in Ohio until 1851 and then, as a young man of twenty-five years, came to Allen county, Indiana, and valiantly girded himself to meet the duties and responsibilities that devolved upon him as a virtual pioneer. He was able to give most effective and valued service as a representative of the pedagogic profession and for a number of years continued as a successful and popular teacher in the schools of the county during the winter months, the while he devoted his attention to farm work during the intervening summer seasons. In the autumn of the year 1853 was solemnized his marriage, the lady of his choice being likewise born in Ohio. After his marriage Mr. Martin settled on his present homestead farm, in Sections 16 and 19, Monroe township, the tract at the time having been heavily timbered and his original domicile having been a primitive log house, an unpretentious dwelling, but one in which peace, comfort and happiness found abiding place and from which emanated kindliness, good cheer and gracious Christian faith and influence. With the passing years the earnest and arduous labors of Mr. Martin resulted in the reclamation and improving of what is now one of the fine farms of Monroe township, the tract of one hundred and sixty acres having good buildings and its general appearance fully indicating the thrift and good management that have marked its development and the directing of the various departments of farm enterprise. Though his venerable years cause Mr. Martin to be an observer rather than an active force in connection with the affairs of his farm, his mental faculties have remained alert and incisive and right living has given him remarkably well-preserved physical powers, so that he still takes a lively interest in the operations of his old homestead and also in community affairs in general. He has given allegiance to the Republican party during virtually the entire period of its existence and no man has been more influential or held in greater veneration in Monroe township than this patriarchal pioneer, whose life has been one of consecrated stewardship as a citizen and as the friend and counselor of his fellow men. He has held many fiduciary positions at various stages in his career, served three terms as public administrator for Monroe township, and at one time he served four months on the grand jury. As young folk both he and his wife became earnest and devout members of the Methodist Episcopal church, constant in faith and instant in good works. For more than twenty years he has been licensed as a local preacher of this religious denomination, and it has thus been his to give counsel, comfort and solace to those in affliction, to guide his fellow men to Christian righteousness and to exalt the service of the Divine Master in whose vineyard he has accounted himself a humble worker. The devoted companionship of Mr. Martin and his gracious wife continued for more than sixty years and was dissolved only when the loved wife and mother was summoned to eternal rest, her death, in October, 1915, having been the supreme loss and bereavement in the life of the venerable citizen to whom this review is dedicated and who holds himself firm in faith and Christian fortitude in the gracious evening of a signally long and useful life. Mr. and Mrs. Martin became the parents of thirteen children, the names of whoi follow: Al, Susan (deceased), Margaret Jane (deceased), Florella, Samuel, William, David, Jr., Oliver, Joseph, John B., Nancy and Mary Ellen.

Frank C. Martin.—One of the most gratifying and consistent phases in the compilation of this history has been that it has been possible to incorporate within its pages specific mention of so appreciable a number of the representative exponents of farm industry in the county, and especially those who stand as scions of sterling pioneer families of this favored section of the old Hoosier commonwealth. Such an one as Mr. Martin, who is one of the most substantial and progressive farmers and stock-growers of Perry township, where his well improved farm, comprising one hundred and sixty acres, is eligibly situated in Section 35. His memory links the pioneer past with the present period of opulent prosperity and progress in Allen county, and in his youth he had his full share of the arduous work pertinent to the reclaiming of a farm from a virtual forest wilderness. He has been in the most significant sense one of the world's productive workers and has achieved success and substantial prosperity through his own ability and efforts. On both the paternal and distaff sides Mr. Martin is a scion of pioneer families that were founded in Allen county in a very early day, and there is much of interest attaching to his genealogical history. Mr. Martin was born in Perry township, this county, January 29, 1855, a son of August J. and Josephine (Rassatt) Martin, both of whom were born in France, the stage of much of the stupendous military operations in the great European war that is fiercely raging at the time of this writing. August J. Martin was a lad of twelve years at the time of the family immigration to America and his future wife was eleven years old when she accompanied her parents to this country. The Martins came to Stark county, Ohio, and the Rassatts settled in New York state, and it was from those localities that these two families came, by medium of stage and ferry boat, to Allen county, Indiana—about the year 1844. Settlement was first made at Fort Wayne, which was then little more than a forest hamlet that clustered about the site of the old fort that gave to the present city its name. On the south line of Perry township August J. Martin purchased a tract of heavily timbered land, at the rate of one dollar and twenty-five cents an acre, and there instituted the reclaiming of a farm from the wilderness. He bore the full tension of pioneer life and aided in laying the foundation for the great superstructure of prosperity that later generations in the county were to enjoy, both he and his wife having passed the remainder of their lives on the old homestead farm. Of the children the subject of this sketch is the first born, and the other surviving members are Jules J., Alexander, Henry, Nestor, August E., Mrs. Louise Laurent, and Mrs. Josephine Cahoe. Charles is deceased. The boyhood and youth of Frank C. Martin were passed under the conditions and influences of the pioneer epoch in Allen county history, and it was his to gain the fullest fellowship with arduous toil and endeavor, to endure hardships with fortitude and to gain experience at first hand. He assisted his father in clearing and otherwise improving the home farm, his educational advantages were very limited, but his ambition and vital mentality were such as to overcome this handicap in large measure, for he has made the best use of self-discipline and has become a man of broad mental ken and mature judgment. He has studied and read with discrimination and speaks and reads French as well as English, thus showing a loyalty to the land of his ancestors. With the passing years Mr. Martin made his labors count for advancement toward the goal of definite independence and prosperity, and he is now the fortunate owner of one of the finely improved and valuable farms of his native township and county. As a youth he assisted in the erection of the log house that was the family abode for a long term of years, and it is interesting to note that he and his brother Jules felled the trees and hewed the timber that were utilized in the construction of the present barn on his farm. He has since remodeled the structure, and has also modernized the house on his farm. When he reverts to the conditions that were in evidence in the pioneer days and then recalls that at the present time he utilizes in his farm enterprise the best of modern implements and machinery, even including a traction engine, Mr. Martin must realize that he has himself been an exponent of progress and has played well his part in furthering civic and industrial prosperity in his native county. In connection with well ordered agriculture of diversified character Mr. Martin has been specially successful as a breeder and grower of fine live stock, including short-horn cattle, Poland-China swine, and registered Cotswold sheep. The buildings on his farm are of a type that further indicates his progressiveness, and everything about the place betokens thrift and prosperity. In a general way Mr. Martin supports the Democratic party, but in local affairs is independent of partisan lines and votes for men and measures meeting the approval of his judgment. He and his wife are zealous communicants of St. Vincent's Catholic church in Washington township. It is pleasing to note that Mr. Martin has given to his fine homestead the attractive and consistent name of Oak Lane Farm. On May 8, 1877, was solemnized the marriage of Mr. Martin to Miss Louise A. Urbine, daughter of John B. and Adele (Litot) Urbine, natives of Alsace-Lorraine, France, which is now a German province. The parents of Mrs. Martin were young when they came with their parents to America and established their home in Allen county, and both the paternal and maternal grandfathers of Mrs. Martin assisted in the construction of the pioneer canal that afforded to Fort Wayne its first definite medium for transportation, besides which the paternal grandmother likewise assisted in the arduous work, with payment equal to that paid to her husband, and she sturdily used a wheelbarrow and other primitive implements with remarkable vigor. The parents of Mrs. Martin were honored members of the farming community in Perry township until their death and their names merit enduring place on the roll of the honored pioneers of the county. Their surviving children are James, Mrs. Mary Morrell, Mrs. Louise A. Martin, and Mrs. Clara Bobay. Frank is deceased. In conclusion is given record concerning the large and interesting family of Mr. and Mrs. Martin: Leonore L. was born September 30, 1877, and on February 13, 1900, became the wife of Victor Sordelet. They reside in Perry township and have three children—Alfred, Hubert and Crystal. Florence I., who remains at the parental home, was born August 3, 1879. Stella M., who was born November 26, 1880, is the wife of Edward Schrader, of New Haven, their marriage having been solemnized May 1, 1900. They became the parents of six children, all of whom are living except the fourth, Robert. The names of the surviving children are Walter, Frank, Edna, Maurice and John. Alice M., the fourth child of Mr. and Mrs. Martin, was born October 15, 1882, and remains a member of the home circle. Grace A., born November 14, 1884, is the wife of George Hardest, of New Haven, their marriage having occurred July 26, 1911. Clarence A., who was born September 10, 1888, resides in Bluffton. His marriage to Miss Adeline Sordelet was made a matter of record on November 25, 1916. Frances H., who was born May 17, 1891, was united in marriage to John B. Surface, March 5, 1912, and her death occurred on the 23d of the following month. Eunice F., born May 17, 1891, a twin of Frances H., became the wife of Adlore Carl, July 2, 1912, and they have three children—Hazel, Martin and Wanda. Edith C., born February 27, 1895; Viola J., born February 15, 1898; and Margaret J., born April 4, 1900, are the younger members of the gracious home circle. Louise B. died at the age of four months and Moses E., who was born September 1, 1892, died September 10, 1901.

Henry J. Martin.—Another of the native sons of Allen county who has built up a secure position for himself through well-directed efforts and the application of commendable zeal is Henry J. Martin, born in Perry township, Allen county, on July 27, 1863. He is a son of August J. and Josephine (Rasett) Martin, both natives of France, who came to America in youth, settled with their families in Allen county and there met and married. They came as young people to Fort Wayne, in 1845, and later located in Perry township, there identifying themselves with the agricultural activities of the community and continuing to be thus employed through the remainder of their useful and honorable careers. They retired, in 1898, but lived only a brief period thereafter. They were the parents of eight children—Frank, Julius, Alexander, Henry J., Nestor, August E., Loren and Josephine. Henry J. Martin had his education in the Perry township schools, in common with his brothers and sisters, and early identified himself with the farm life of Perry township, later on settling in Washington township. He finally came to St. Joseph township and has since had his home here. He is today owner of a fine farm of two hundred and ten acres in what is known as the Richardville Reservation, and his is one of the fine improved farms in the township. In 1887 Mr. Martin married Matilda Pepe, daughter of Lewis and Mary (Petregney) Pepe, both of French birth and parentage. They came with their respective families to Allen county in 1833 and were thereafter identified with the development of this region. Mr. and Mrs. Pepe were the parents of ten children—Louisa, Emily, Ellen, Angeline, Joseph, Alfred, Alexander S., Flora and Harriet. The third, fourth, fifth, sixth and tenth named are deceased. To Mr. and Mrs. Martin have been born four children. Georgia married William Blume, of St. Joseph township. Hubert married Esther Sordelet. Charles and Gerald are unmarried and share the family home. The parents, with their children, are members of the Roman Catholic church, and Mr. Martin is a Democrat in politics.

Edward Coy Martz, postmaster of Grabill since 1914, and one of the well-known citizens of Cedar Creek township, is a native son of Adams county, born on July 23, 1881, and the eldest child of his parents, George W. and Magdalene (Kessler) Martz. The father was born in Adams county, Indiana, and the mother in Celina, Ohio. She is deceased, but the father still lives at Berne, Indiana, where he is engaged in farming, in which industry he has been engaged all his active life. The children of George and Magdalene Martz are five in number and are named as follows: Edward Coy, the subject of this review; Thurman, a resident of Joplin, Missouri; Bessie, the wife of Menno Wittner, of Berne, Indiana; Ira, of Portland, Indiana, and Ferdinand, also of that place. Edward C. Martz had the usual experience of the farmer boy and up to the age of sixteen had opportunity to become fairly well acquainted with the joys and discomforts of farm life. He left home when he had passed his sixteenth birthday and applied himself to carpenter work for about three years, after which he turned his attention to the barber's trade and was engaged in that work for something like nine years. He was still occupied in that field when he was appointed to fill the office of postmaster at Grabill, July 22, 1914, receiving his appointment at the hands of President Wilson. He is still discharging the duties of that office and has acquitted himself most commendably in the service of the government. Mr. Martz was married on August 29, 1905, to Miss Grace Vergil Hill, a young woman of Adams county, and they have three children—Hester, Bessie and Edward, Jr. Mr. Martz is a Democrat and is active in local politics. His only fraternal affiliations are with the Modern Woodman of America, in which he has long been a member of Leo Camp 10121.

George E. Mason and his father, Joseph S., were native sons of Allen county, and the family was established in this district in the early days of the nineteenth century by Frank Mason, the paternal grandfather of the subject. He left his native state of Pennsylvania as a young man and made the long wilderness journey overland with an ox team. This intrepid pioneer acquired title to a tract of government land and established a home where he reared a family that has done its full share in the later development of Allen county. Joseph, the father of the subject, was reared to farm life, had little schooling, and in youth settled down in Wayne township, where he was born and occupied himself with the cultivation of a wilderness farm, much as his father had done. He acquired more and better land in later years, and branched out into stock-farming, in which he was prosperous and successful. He gave some time to stock-buying also, and was known to be a capable veterinary surgeon in his time. Though not schooled in the work, he had a natural talent for it and was depended upon in his community and thereabouts by his fellow citizens. Mr. Mason was a Republican in politics, though he never aspired to political favors. He married Catherine Sites and they were the parents of two children—George E. and Bell, who is the wife of Dr. Daniel Sled, of Fort Wayne. George E. Mason was born in Wayne township, this county, December 18, 1856. He acquired a substantial education in the district schools of his community and a practical training in the business of farming at the hands of his father, who died in 1904. After his marriage, in 1884, he rented a farm of two hundred and forty-two acres in Lafayette township, where he settled and carried on extensive farming and stock raising. He purchased this farm in 1886, and resided on it until he retired and moved to Fort Wayne in 1913; though he still owns the farm, and also owns a fine home at 1206 Dayton avenue, this city, where he lives. Mr. Mason was married on January 11, 1884, to Miss Catherine Baker, daughter of one George Baker, an Englishman and a resident of Fort Wayne. Six children were born to the Masons. Joseph is a prosperous farmer in Wayne township, now living on and conducting the old family homestead. Roy is an employe of the Fort Wayne street car company. Harley is in the employ of the city electric light company in Fort Wayne. Ida married Norman Prince, of Wayne township. Montgomery is in the employ of the Wayne Oil Tank and Pump Company. William McKinley, the youngest of the six, is living with the parents in Fort Wayne, and is also in the employ of the city electric light company. Ten grandchildren add to the joys of the elder Masons. Joseph has five children, named

James, Wayne, Velma, John and George. Roy has a son named Harold. Harley is also the father of a son, George. Montgomery has a little daughter, called Virginia, and Ida has two sons—George and Roy.

John W. Meeks, who is now engaged in the insurance business at Monroeville, has been a resident of Allen county from the time of his birth and is a representative of a well known pioneer family of Monroe township, where the place of his nativity was a primitive log cabin of the type common to the pioneer days. He has now passed the scriptural span of three score years and ten and thus it may well be understood that his memory forms a definite link between the pioneer past and the present period of august and stable prosperity in Allen county. He further honored his native state by going forth as a soldier of the Union in the Civil war, and as one of the prominent and honored citizens of the county he is well entitled to recognition in this history. Mr. Meeks was born in Monroe township, January 13, 1843, a son of Thomas and Nancy (Bartlett) Meeks, who were born and reared in West Virginia, where their marriage was solemnized, and who came to Allen county, Indiana, in the year 1840. The father purchased a tract of heavily timbered land in Monroe township, and for the property he paid at the rate of one dollar and twenty-five cents an acre. For a domicile he erected a log cabin of the true pioneer order, the little dwelling having had a roof of clapboards or shakes, the floor having been of puncheon, the chimney of the old-time fireplace having been of stick and mud construction, and the entrance door, with its latchstring, having always been gladly opened to extend hospitality to neighbors or the worthy wayfarer. Thomas Meeks and his noble wife lived up to the full tension of pioneer life, and with unremitting toil he effected the reclamation of his farm from the wilderness. He developed his homestead into a productive tract and on this place he and his wife passed the remainder of their lives, their names meriting enduring place on the roster of the sterling pioneers of Allen county. They became the parents of six sons and four daughters, and of the number two sons and three daughters are living at the time of this writing, in 1917. John W. Meeks reverts with no small degree of reminiscent satisfaction to the experience which was his in the pioneer period of Allen county history, and it is still more pleasing to him that he has been able to witness and aid in the development and progress of his native county, along both civic and industrial lines. From the little log-cabin home he went forth in his boyhood to gain his rudimentary education in the pioneer schools of Monroe township, and he so applied himself as to lay a substantial foundation for the broader education which he has since gained in the school of practical experience. Mr. Meeks was eighteen years of age when the Civil war was precipitated and forthwith gave evidence of his youthful loyalty and patriotism by responding to President Lincoln's call for volunteers. At the second call in 1861, he enlisted as a private in Company D, Thirtieth Indiana Infantry, and continued in active service for a period of three years. He took part in numerous engagements, including a number of the important battles marking the progress of the conflict, and for a time was assigned to detail duty in the quartermaster's department. He was mustered out and received his honorable discharge in the city of Indianapolis, and then returned to Allen county and resolutely turned his attention once more to winning the gracious victories which peace ever has in store, "no less renowned than war." For a number of years Mr. Meeks continued his successful activities as one of the representative farmers of

Monroe township, and later engaged in the buying and shipping of live stock, to which line of industrial enterprise he applied himself about three years. For twelve years thereafter he controlled a successful meat-market business at Monroeville, and in this village he continues to reside as one of its best known and distinctly influential citizens. Here he is now engaged in the insurance business, besides which he is a notary public. He formerly owned a well improved landed estate in his native township, and at the present time is the owner of seven valuable residences properties in Monroeville, each of these properties being improved with good houses and other buildings. Mr. Meeks is a staunch Republican in politics; he and his wife are active and valued members of the Methodist Episcopal church at Monroeville, of which he has served as trustee and steward for fully thirty-seven years, and he has long been affiliated with the local lodge, No. 283, of the Independent Order of Odd Fellows, in which he has passed all of the official chairs. His continued interest in his old comrades of the Civil war is shown by his appreciative affiliation with the Grand Army of the Republic. In the year 1864, was solemnized the marriage of Mr. Meeks to Miss Mary C. Dobbs, who was born in Allen county, Kentucky, whence she came with her parents to Indiana when she was a girl. Mr. and Mrs. Meeks had but one child, Mary Idella, and the supreme loss and bereavement of their wedded life was that which came when their cherished daughter passed to eternal rest at the early age of ten years.

Charles A. Meigs has developed through service of the most effective order a substantial and important business as one of the leading optometrists and manufacturing opticians of Fort Wayne, where he engaged in the practice of his profession in December, 1905, with headquarters on Calhoun street. He came to Fort Wayne from his native city of Chicago and was thoroughly fortified in his equipment as a scientific optometrist, so that he soon built up a prosperous business. His retail establishment is now situated at 1012 Calhoun street and he has amplified in a significant way his operations in his chosen line of enterprise and has become the executive head of the Fort Wayne Optical Company, which occupies the entire second floor of the Lyric building, at the same location —1012 Calhoun street—and which has control of a substantial manufacturing and wholesale trade in the manufacturing of lenses for the correction of all irregularities of vision. For the grinding of prescription and other lenses the establishment is equipped with the most modern facilities, the company imports basic lenses and other accessories in a direct way, and its dealings are entirely with physicians, oculists, opticians and professional optometrists, two traveling representatives being employed and the house force numbering eleven persons. This important manufacturing concern was established in 1909, the business is incorporated with a capital of ten thousand dollars and Morris Blau is the general manager. The factory at the beginning employed but two men, but the enterprise has shown a substantial and consecutive expansion in scope and importance and is now one of the prominent industrial corporations of Fort Wayne, its trade territory embracing Indiana, Ohio, Michigan and Illinois. Mr. Meigs is consistently to be designated as an eyesight specialist and has gained the highest reputation in the diagnosis and correction of errors of refraction in the vision. He not only has his prescription lenses manufactured in a direct way in the establishment, but also has the best facilities for supplying the mountings and properly adjusting all lenses, so that the absolutely perfect correction is assured in every instance. He has individually patented an improved nose piece for what are commonly designated as nose glasses, the device being easy of manipulation, secure in its grip and designed in such forms as to make the adjustment always accurate in focal distance and maintaining the unwavering alignment of cylindrical and other special lens for the correction of astigmatism and other irregularities aside from myopia and presbyopia. The Doctor gives special attention also to the prescribing, manufacturing and adjusting of kryptok and other bifocal lenses and also those of colored type, for the elimination of eye strain. In his retail establishment he employs nine assistants and his representative supporting patronage attests the higher popular estimate placed upon him and his work. Dr. Meigs was born in the city of Chicago, on July 25, 1880, and his father, John Stanley Meigs, a native of the state of New York, was long engaged in the optical business in Chicago, where his death occurred. Dr. Charles A. Meigs was afforded the advantages of the public schools of his native city and his original technical experience in connection with the optical business was gained under the effective direction of his father. He attended school also at St. Johns, Vermont, took a special course of professional study under the preceptorship of Dr. Earl J. Brown, a prominent oculist and optician of Chicago, and in 1898 was graduated in the Northern Illinois Optical College. Thereafter he was employed in the old and celebrated optical establishment of L. Manasse, of Chicago, until 1905, when he came to Fort Wayne and initiated the business which he has since developed to large and substantial proportions and to which he gives his close attention and the careful personal inspection and supervision that insures to patrons effective service in every instance. The Doctor is a loyal and appreciative member of the Fort Wayne Commercial Club, a member of the Rotary and Quest Clubs and an officer in several of the Masonic bodies.

Charles M. Menefee, who has been engaged in the foundry business for a full quarter of a century and who is one of the prominent representatives of this line of industrial enterprise in the city of Fort Wayne, was born in Greene county, Ohio, on September 4, 1857, a son of William Henry Menefee and Laurena (Deneal) Menefee, natives of the Old Dominion state, where the former was born in 1833 and the latter in 1837, dates that indicate that the respective families were founded in Virginia in an early day. Charles Milton Menefee, the immediate subject of this sketch, received limited educational advantages in his youth, but has made good this handicap to a large extent through his active association with business affairs during the course of a significantly busy and useful career. In his youth he learned the various details of the foundry industry and through his alliance with this domain of enterprise has long been one of the successful business men of Fort Wayne, where he has applied himself earnestly and where he has at all times commanded unqualified esteem. He is a Republican in politics and both he and his wife hold membership in the United Brethren church. The maiden name of Mrs. Menefee was Mary Elizabeth Allen, and the children of Mr. Menefee and his wife are ten in number, namely: Harry B., Oscar F., James W., Earl H., Edith, Rebecca, Mary, Amy, Leah, and Allen. Edith is the wife of Edwin M. Pfeiffer; Mary is the wife of Kenneth Harbaugh; Leah is the wife of Clarence Coover; and Rebecca is the wife of F. E. Wilmore.

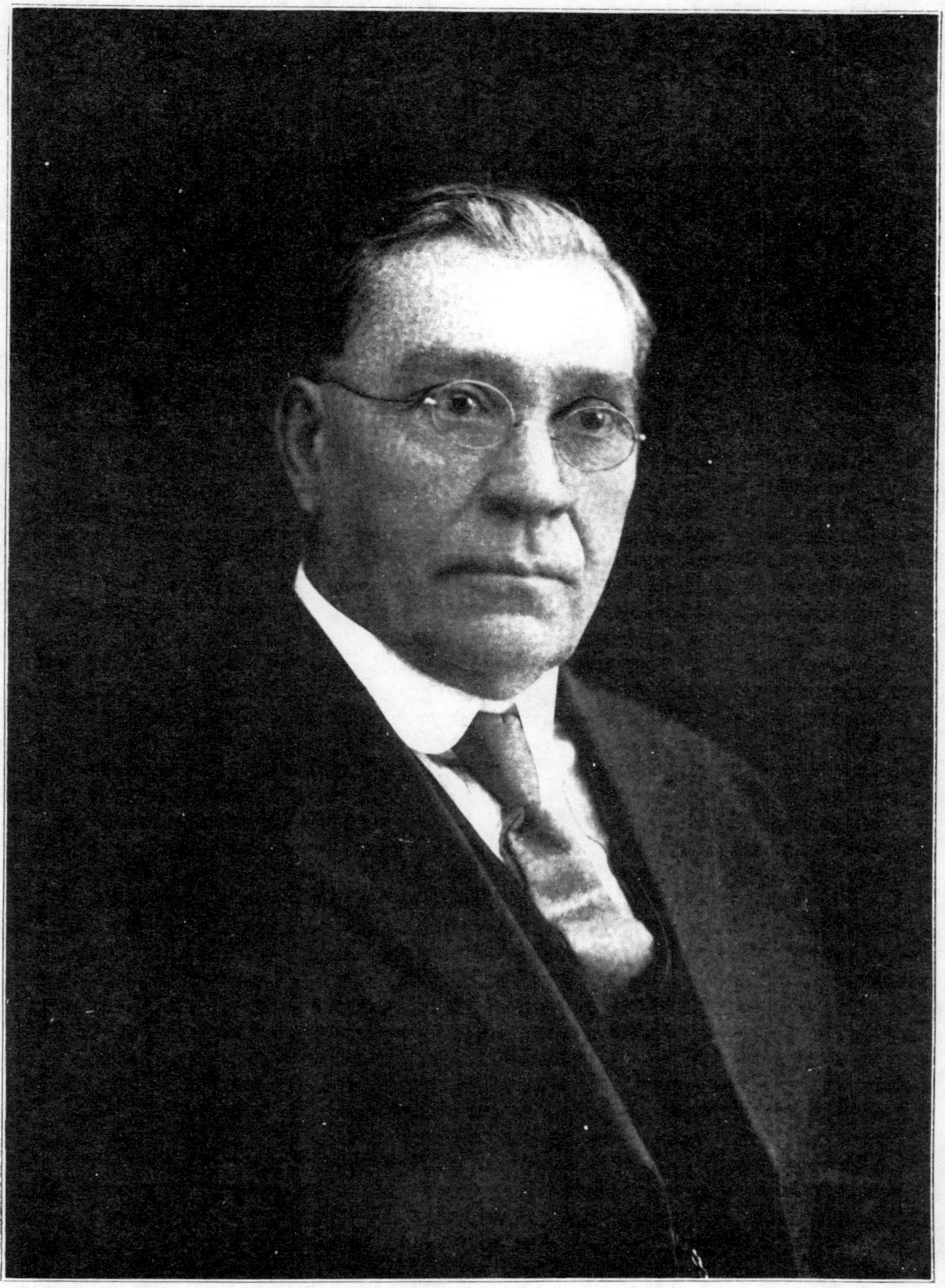

C. M. Menefee

Dr. D. J. Mercer came to Poe in 1902 and here established himself in the practice of his profession. He has built up an extensive following in the community and stands well among his fellows throughout the county. He is an Allen county product, born in Madison township on December 13, 1878, son of Robert and Nancy (McKeeman) Mercer, themselves natives of Allen county and among the representative people of their community. Doctor Mercer was one of five children—three sons and two daughters, one of the daughters being deceased. He was educated in the schools of Madison township, and following his high school training entered Fort Wayne Medical School, from which he was graduated with the class of 1901. The young M. D. practiced his profession at Helmer one year and then came to Poe, where he has since been established. He is progressive in his work and has made a practice of attending Chicago clinics whenever possible, so that he has kept well abreast of the times in a professional way. Doctor Mercer was married on November 14, 1901, to Miss Nettie B. Fry, daughter of Jacob Fry, of Fort Wayne, Allen county, and they have three children—Charles Robert, David John and Harriet Elizabeth. The doctor is a Scottish Rite Mason and is affiliated with various Fort Wayne bodies of the order.

Robert Mercer, though a painter and decorator by trade, has devoted his energies mainly to the farming industry, in which he has achieved a very creditable success and is counted among the foremost men of his community today in point of his accomplishments in agriculture. He was born in Hancock county, Ohio, on May 31, 1854, son of Jacob and Harriett (Whitcomb) Mercer. The father came from Amsterdam, Holland, as a small boy, in company with his parents, and with them settled in Hancock county, Ohio. He devoted himself to farm life and as a young man bought an eighty-acre farm, which he later sold and came to Allen county, Indiana, settling in Marion township in 1858. He bought a farm of eighty acres, to which he later was able to add a purchase of three forties, and for years was counted among the foremost farming men of his community. He was a Democrat in politics and a member of the Methodist Episcopal church. He had three children—Robert, Eliza Jane and Rebecca. The first named is the subject of this brief family sketch. The second married William Van Horn and is now deceased, while Rebecca is the wife of Michael Flaugh, a Madison township farmer. Robert Mercer attended the public schools of Marion township and was also privileged to attend what was known as a "select" school at Middletown. He was the leader of a singing school for some years in young manhood and continued on the home farm until he was twenty-three years old. He then bought eighty acres of farm land in his home community and settled down to farm life, which industry has claimed the greater part of his energies up to the present time. He is one of the well-thought-of men of his township and his standing is excellent wherever he is known. A Democrat, he served his party as delegate at two National Conventions and has always taken an intelligent interest in local politics. He and his family are members of the Methodist Episcopal church and he is a Scottish Rite Mason, affiliated with Masonic bodies in his home village of Poe and also in Fort Wayne. He was married on February 28, 1876, to Miss Nancy McKeeman, daughter of David C. and Marguerite (McConahey) McKeeman, who came from Ireland and who were well-to-do farmers of Hoagland, now both deceased. They were the parents of twelve children, named John, Catherine, Margaret, Jennie, Nancy, Belle, James, William, Alexander, David C., Ella, and Robert B. Nancy is the wife of the subject and Robert B. is a practicing physician in Fort Wayne. To Mr. and Mrs. Mercer five children were born. David J. is engaged in medical practice in Poe, and brief mention is accorded him in other pages of this work. Robert F. is located in Fort Wayne. Marguerite May is deceased. Verba E. is the wife of Charles Sherer and Leslie Bud is at home with his parents. Doctor Mercer has three children—Charles Robert, David John and Harriett Elizabeth. Robert also has three children. Margaret, deceased daughter of Mr. and Mrs. Mercer, was married and left a son, Delbert. Verba is the mother of four, named Pearl, May, Alberta and Ruth. The Mercer family, it will be seen, is one that has contributed full measure to the development of the county, and the individual members are living well up to the standards set for them in their early homes.

James R. Meriwether.—How little could the many friends of the late James Read Meriwether have realized that tragedy stalked at his heels when, on January 20, 1908, he set forth to make an inspection of his summer cottage at Rome City, and how pitiable was his fate was not revealed for some little time. It is supposed that in lighting the gasolene stove in the cottage his clothing became ignited, and when his body was discovered it was found that he had been burned to death in the fire that destroyed his cottage. Mr. Meriwether had long been one of the well-known and highly honored citizens of Fort Wayne, his genial, kindly and buoyant nature having drawn to him the staunchest of friends, the circle of which was limited only by that of his acquaintances. He had been long and prominently associated with the executive control of the Grand Rapids & Indiana Railroad, and at the time of his death was chief clerk to the division superintendent, Mr. Hudson, with headquarters in Fort Wayne, where the general offices of the company have long been established. Mr. Meriwether was a scion of a family whose name has been identified with American history since the colonial era and was born at Jeffersonville, the judicial center of Clark county, Indiana, in the year 1859—a son of James B. and Martha Agnes (Read) Meriwether. He was afforded in his youth excellent educational advantages, including those of the Eastman Business College at Poughkeepsie, New York; Purdue College, Indiana; and one of the prominent educational institutions in Wisconsin. Upon coming to Fort Wayne Mr. Meriwether found clerical employment in the offices of the Grand Rapids & Indiana Railroad, and his ability and faithful service brought to him consecutive advancement until he was finally appointed chief clerk to the division superintendent, of which position he continued the incumbent until his death, the road having in the meanwhile come into control of the Pennsylvania Railroad Company. In politics Mr. Meriwether gave his allegiance to the Democratic party, though he had no ambition for political office. He was actively affiliated with the Fort Wayne Commercial Club and other representative civic organizations in his home city, and he was an earnest communicant of the Protestant Episcopal church. On November 12, 1889, was solemnized the marriage of Mr. Meriwether to Miss Georgia Maier, who was born and reared in Fort Wayne and who is a daughter of John George and Elizabeth Jane (Taylor) Maier, her father having been one of the early and influential pioneers of Allen county and having ever commanded high place in popular confidence and good will. Mr. Meriwether is survived by two children—James Maier and Martha Jane—who remain with their widowed mother in the attractive home at 1238 West Wayne street, Mrs. Meriwether having been a resident of Fort Wayne from the time of her birth.

William Edmund Metcalf.—William Edmund Metcalf began the general merchandise business in Poe April 1, 1914, when he withdrew from the teaching profession in which he had been active for about ten years. His success in his new enterprise has been a pleasing one thus far, commensurate with the investments he has made in it in every way, and his future in the field of merchandise is a pleasant outlook. Mr. Metcalf was born in Perry township on October 29, 1881, and is the son of Martin V. and Mary Elizabeth Metcalf, who came from Ashland county, Ohio, in 1849. Mr. Metcalf was a prosperous farmer. He began in a small way with a government tract of one hundred and sixty acres, later inheriting a seventy-acre farm and still later adding another eighty through purchase. He was a leader in his community always. A Democrat in politics he was a member of the county board for four years and served well in that office. He was a member of the United Brethren church, with his family, and he died on December 28, 1911. His widow survives him. They were the parents of three sons. Samuel was educated for the medical profession was engaged in practice in Fort Wayne when he died. William Edmund was the second son and Martin V. the third and youngest. William Edmund Metcalf, with his brothers, had his early schooling in the common schools of his community. Finishing with the high school, he entered the Tri-State College, where he pursued a scientific course, and later he went to Valparaiso University. His studies there equipped him admirably for educational work and for nine years thereafter he was employed as principal in various schools in Allen and other counties in this part of the state. He spent one year as principal of the schools at Harlan, Indiana; two years in a similar capacity at Huntington; three years at Leo; one year in Wayne township and two years at Hoagland. In 1914 the opportunity to engage in mercantile pursuits presented itself, and Mr. Metcalf did not hesitate about making the venture. He carried a general merchandise stock, succeeding Homer Brown in the business he had conducted in Poe, and later increased the stock to a great extent, bringing up the general standard of the establishment and increasing the volume of business. Mr. Metcalf is a Democrat and takes a genuine interest in the political affairs of his community. He is a member of the Methodist Episcopal church, as is also his wife, and is a member of the Masonic fraternity and the Knighths of Pythias. He was married on August 11, 1907, to Allie, daughter of George and Susan (Galloway) Hollopeter, who came to Indiana from Ohio, their native state, and spent the best years of their lives in Cedar Creek township.

Fred H. Meyer, who takes a prominent place among the agricultural men of Pleasant township, has been a resident of his community since boyhood. He was born in Adams township, Allen county, on August 6, 1867, son of John C. Meyer, a successful Adams township farming man, who came with his family to Pleasant township in 1876 and there passed the remainder of his life. The boy Fred had his education in the local schools and lived on the home farm to the age of twenty-four years. At that time his father presented him with a highly improved farm of 150 acres and the young man stepped out to farm on his own responsibility. He has prospered with the passing years and has devoted himself to the pursuits of general farming, with special attention to stock-raising. When he undertook independent farming Mr. Meyer also undertook the duties of a family man and married on November 5, 1891, Miss Bernhardena Mailand, daughter of Carl and Bernhardena (Berning) Mailand, natives of Germany who settled on a farm in Adams county and later settled in Allen county. They were the owners of a very fine farm of about 240 acres and were among the prosperous people of their community. In later life they retired from active farm life and lived quietly, enjoying the fruits of earlier labors. Mr. and Mrs. Meyer have six children and three grand-children. Lawrence, their eldest, is a railroad man. Agnes married Theodore Greiner, and the others share the parental home as yet. They are Irene, Edna, Carl and Edward. The son Lawrence has three little daughters—Dorothea, Eileen and Donald. The family have membership in the German Lutheran church and Mr. Meyer is a staunch Democrat. He is a man of influence in his community and with his family enjoys the esteem and confidence of all who share in his acquaintance.

George Meyers.—Lafayette township, in Allen county, has in George Meyers one of the well established and successful farming men of the community. He is an Ohioan by birth, born in Franklin county, Ohio, September 4, 1857, son of Jacob and Laura (Ebbert) Meyers. The father died in Marshall county, Indiana, July 15, 1870, and his widow survived until the spring of 1916. The family came to Indiana in 1861, locating first in Marshall county and engaging in a farming venture that was more or less successful. Of eight children born to Mr. and Mrs. Meyers, three survive. Named in the order of their appearance the children were: Harriet, George, Anna, Mary, Catherine, Amanda, Ella, Caroline and Lucinda. The first, fourth, fifth, sixth and seventh are deceased. George is the subject of this review; Anna is the wife of Peter Kayser, of Lafayette township, and Lucinda is married to Harley Myers. George Meyers was a lad of thirteen years when his father died and from that time to young manhood continued on the home place as manager of the farm his father left them. He had some schooling, but his advantages were limited, owing to the conditions existing in his community along educational lines at the time when he should have been having his early training. Mr. Meyers first owned land in Wells county, Indiana, and he bought first one piece and then another until he was the owner of several pieces of valuable Indiana farm land. In 1900 he bought his present farm of eighty acres and since that time has been actively engaged in its improvement and development along modern lines. It is one of the finest places in the township today and reflects the energy and progressiveness of its owner in many respects. Mr. Meyers carries on diversified farming and has enjoyed a very pleasing measure of success in his vocation. He is one of the foremost men of his community and is now serving as a trustee of Lafayette township. He is a Democrat and a member of the Church of God. He was married on April 18, 1878, to Miss L. Michael, daughter of Gottlieb and Salina (Broeckbeck) Michael, both of German parents and both now deceased. Mrs. Meyers was one of their seven children—the others being Elizabeth, Catherine, John, Carl, Mary and Christina. To Mr. and Mrs. Meyers nine children have come. Elnora, the first born, is the wife of E. O. Nicholson. Loreta is married to Clark Bradbury, of Fort Wayne. Jacob Frederick is the third in order of birth. Desse May is married to Webert Blumer, of Lafayette township. Gertrude is the wife of Homer Corll, of Zanesville, Ohio.

Josephine Chloe, Lela Viola, Cecil and Gerald are at home with the parents. The family has long enjoyed the esteem and confidence of a wide circle of friends and acquaintances in the county, and especially in Roanoke is its standing a highly satisfactory and commendable one.

Henry J. Meyer, born on March 21, 1871, in Adams township, Allen county, Indiana, is a son of John C. and Mary (Schroeder) Meyer, native born Germans who came to America as children in company with their parents. They settled in Adams township after marriage and there spent their active years. Henry Meyer had his education in the Adams township schools, including a high school course, and spent a year and a half as a student in Concordia College. He early turned his energies to farm life and settled on a farm of 222 acres, which he has since made his home and the center of his activities. He has improved the place vastly since it came into his possession, remodeling the dwelling and barns, improving the soil and bringing the standard of the place up to the highest point. He manifests a good deal of pride in the Durham cattle bred on his farm, a feature to which he has given a good deal of attention. Mr. Meyer is a Democrat in politics and a member of the German Lutheran church. He was married on June 6, 1898, to Miss Louisa Frier, daughter of Paul and Anna (Gelke) Frier, who are of German parentage and are now living retired in Fort Wayne. Mr. and Mrs. Meyer have four children—Esther, Lydia, Christoph and Henry, Jr.

Robert Millard has been a resident of Fort Wayne for more than a quarter of a century and as a man of initiative and executive ability and wide and varied commercial experience has become one of the prominent figures among those who are upholding the city's prestige as an industrial and distributing center. He is one of the interested principals in the firm of Moellering Brothers & Millard, which is here engaged in the wholesale grocery business and which constitutes one of the solid and important commercial concerns of northern Indiana, its trade extending into Michigan and Ohio. Mr. Millard was born at Adrian, the judicial center of Lenawee county, Michigan, August 15, 1856, a son of Alfred L. and Harriet (Truax) Millard, both of whom were born in the state of New York but the marriage of whom was solemnized in Michigan, the Truax family having been one of special prominence in the pioneer period of the history of the Wolverine commonwealth. Alfred L. long held prestige as one of the able and representative members of the Michigan bar, to which he was admitted by the supreme court at its first session after Michigan was admitted to statehood, and was influential in public affairs in the state, within whose borders he continued to reside until his death, in 1900, at the venerable age of eighty-six years, the wife of his young manhood having passed away at the age of fifty years. He married, second, Miss Grace Grieve, of Perry, New York, who bore him one child, a daughter, Miss Grace Millard, a prominent educator of Detroit, Michigan. Robert Millard profited fully by the advantages afforded in the public schools of his native city and at the age of eighteen years found employment in a wholesale dry goods house in the city of Toledo, Ohio, where he remained thus engaged two years. For five years thereafter he held a position with a leading wholesale grocery house in the same city, and for the next several years was successfully established in independent business as a broker in grocery supplies and specialties—first in Toledo and later in the city of New York. In 1891 he engaged in the same line of jobbing trade in Fort Wayne and two years later became a member of the firm of Moellering Brothers & Millard, with whom he has since continued his connection and to the upbuilding of the business of which he has been able to contribute much, as his thorough knowledge of the details of the business is equal to his recognized progressiveness and administrative ability. He is vice-president of the German-American Trust Company, a member of the local board of directors of the Fort Wayne Rollinm Mill Corporation and of the Lincoln National Life Insurance Company. He is one of the active and appreciative members of the Fort Wayne Commercial Club and at one time its president; holds membership in the Fort Wayne Country Club, is a staunch Republican in his political proclivities and attends and supports the Presbyterian church, as does also his wife. In October, 1893, was solemnized the marriage of Mr. Millard to Miss Ellen Easley, who was born in Lafayette, Indiana.

Edward C. Miller.—Fort Wayne has for her postmaster one of her native sons and a man who has been largely identified with the manufacturing interests of the city in the past thirteen years. From 1903 to 1915 Mr. Miller was manager of the Fort Wayne Brick Company and withdrew from that position to enter upon the duties of his new office of postmaster following his appointment, in May, 1915. Edward C. Miller was born in Allen county, Indiana, November 30, 1872, son of Samuel and Matilda Miller. The father was born on January 14, 1850, in Wells county, Indiana, and was eighteen years old when he came to Allen county, Indiana, where he established himself in business and in Fort Wayne was for years the proprietor of the Fort Wayne Journal, one of the representative news sheets of the city. He died in 1887, young in years, but with a splendid record for progressiveness and general good-citizenship that is reflected in the career of his son. His wife, the mother of Edward Miller, was of Ohio birth and parentage, her family coming from Columbus and settling in Fort Wayne in 1863. She was born in September, 1856, and is still living in Fort Wayne. Three children were born to Mr. and Mrs. Miller. Edward C., of this review; D. O., now living in Washington, D. C., and Glo D., the wife of E. J. Ricke, of Fort Wayne. Edward C. Miller had his education in the public schools of Fort Wayne. He was fifteen years old when his father died, and he left school then to take his place in the ranks of labor as carrier of a paper route on the Journal, of which his father had been the publisher. He did not remain long in that position, but soon found inside work, and his first position of responsibility was that of bookkeeper for the Western Fruit Company. From that firm he went to the Randall Wheel Company and, in 1893, accepted a post as traveling salesman with the McIntosh-Huntington Company of Cleveland. He was similarly employed by the Bassett-Presley Steel and Iron Company of Cleveland for a number of years, and, in 1903, became manager of the Fort Wayne Brick Company, a well established concern of his native city. Under his management the industry made creditable advancement and came to be one of the leading industrial plants of the city. Mr. Miller was honored, in May, 1915, by his appointment to the office of postmaster of the city and he is today serving capably and creditably in that position. His business experience had given him a training that is most essential in the equipment of the candidate for such an office, and, considered from every viewpoint, his appointment was a happy one. Various other interests have a share in Mr. Miller's attentions. Among them is the Fort Wayne Concrete Tile

Company, of which he is secretary and treasurer, and he is a director in the Morris Plan Banking Company. The Fort Wayne Commercial Club has had an enthusiastic and spirited member in him and he is now serving the organization as a director. Public-spiritedness has been a dominant trait in his make-up and he has been a leader in his community from earliest manhood. He was only twenty-six years of age when he was elected to membership in the city council and he held that office continuously until 1903. When the Centennial was celebrated in Fort Wayne, in June, 1916, Mr. Miller was general chairman of the executive body, and it is not too much to say that it was largely through his labors that the occasion proved to be the tremendous success it was generally conceded to have been. Mr. Miller is a Democrat and a leader in county politics. His fraternal relations are with the Masonic order, in which he has lately taken the thirty-third degree, the Benevolent and Protective Order of Elks and the Loyal Order of Moose. He is also a member of the Rotary Club and the Quest Club, representative social organizations of the city. On March 12, 1893, Mr. Miller was married to Nellie H. Fahlsing, daughter of Charles W. and Henrietta E. (Zollars) Fahlsing. She was born in Fort Wayne and there educated. Mr. and Mrs. Miller have one daughter, named Ednell, the name being an unusual and specially pleasing combination of the Christian names of the parents.

Rev. Jacob W. Miller has been the able, devoted and honored pastor of the parish of St. Paul's Evangelical Lutheran church in Fort Wayne since 1896, and his zealous labors have inured to the spiritual and temporal prosperity of this important parish, even as they have proved equally benignant in other pastoral charges that have been his. He is one of the influential figures in the council and synod of the Evangelical Lutheran church and the parish over which he is in charge is the largest of the Lutheran church organizations in Fort Wayne. He is president of the Evangelical Lutheran School Association of Fort Wayne, Indiana, which organization has established and is efficiently conducting the Fort Wayne Luther Institute, a high-class business college that provides an admirable two-year curriculum. Rev. Jacob William Miller was born at Cove, Garrett county, Maryland, on the 16th of September, 1860, a son of Melchior J. and Barbara (Everlein) Miller, the former born in Hessen-Darmstadt, Germany, and the latter in Maryland, of Bavarian ancestry. The subject of this review is the second child and eldest son in a family of twelve children, of whom eight are still living. He received his early education in the parochial and public schools of Accident, Maryland, and at the age of fifteen years came to Fort Wayne and entered Concordia College, in which staunch institution he completed the full six-year course. In 1881 he entered Concordia Theological Seminary, St. Louis, Missouri, and in the same was graduated as a member of the class of 1884, his ordination as a clergyman of the Evangelical Lutheran church having taken place the same year. In the autumn of 1884 he received a call to the church at Stuttgart, Arkansas, and there continued his service until 1889, his pastoral work having been amplified by his serving simultaneously as missionary of his denomination in eastern Arkansas. In 1889 he was called to the pastorate of the Evangelical Lutheran church in the city of Little Rock, Arkansas, and there continued his earnest labors until impaired health made it expedient for him to seek a change of climate. Accordingly, in 1893, he accepted a call to Zion's Lutheran church in the city of St. Paul, Minnesota, where he retained this incumbency until 1896, the year that marked his call to his present pastorate in Fort Wayne, upon the death of Rev. Henry G. Sauer, whom he succeeded. The largest Lutheran church in Fort Wayne, St. Paul's, has twenty-two hundred communicants, with an incidental membership of fully six hundred more persons in the parish organization. Since 1910 Mr. Miller has had as his able and valued coadjutor his son, Rev. Paul F. Miller, who is assistant pastor, and who is doing splendid work in the furtherance of the varied interests and activities of the important parish. The parochial school of St. Paul's church is one in which the pastor and parishioners take just pride, the same having an enrollment of three hundred pupils and retaining a corps of eight men teachers. Mr. Miller holds, in 1917, the office of first vice-president of the German Evangelical Lutheran Synod of Missouri, Ohio, Indiana and other states. He is liberal and public-spirited as a citizen and maintains an independent political attitude. He takes deep interest in civic affairs in his home city and is zealous in his efforts to aid and uplift humanity, with enduring charity and tolerance and with abiding sympathy for "all sorts and conditions of men." In 1886 Mr. Miller wedded Miss Katherine Goehringer, of Accident, Maryland, and she was summoned to the life eternal in 1889, being survived by two sons, Rev. Paul F., who is his father's assistant, as above noted, and Theodore, who is pricer in the Fort Wayne Drug Company. The second marriage of Mr. Miller was solemnized in 1891, when Miss Clara Schachameyer, of Chicago, became his wife. Her death occurred in 1900, and of the four children of this union three are living—Martine, Ada and Walther. In 1903 Mr. Miller married Miss Mary Burkhart, of Accident, Maryland, and the five children of this marriage are Henry, Frederick, Margaret, Ruth and Gertrude.

Rev. William Caspar Miller, of Fort Wayne, is a son of William M. and Mary J. (Ackermann) Miller, and was born at Lafayette, Indiana, January 16, 1869. He attended St. Boniface's parochial school until thirteen years old. He then entered St. Francis' Gymnasium at Cincinnati, and later St. Gregory Seminary at Cedar Point, Ohio, where he completed his classical course. His philosophical and theological courses were made at Mount St. Mary's of the West Seminary at Cincinnati. He was ordained priest by Bishop Alerding in the Cathedral at Fort Wayne, May 24, 1902. After this he traveled in Europe and at Rome had audiences with Pope Leo XIII., August 2 and 7. During the illness of Rev. Dominic Duehmig, he had charge of the parish at Avilla from October 1, 1902, to February 1, 1903. He was then made assistant to the pastor of St. Mary's church at Michigan City. On August 28, 1906, he was transferred to the Bishop's House in Fort Wayne, where he has since remained doing the work of an assistant at the Cathedral and secretarial work under the Bishop's direction.

Samuel Mills is one of the substantial retired farmers and venerable pioneer citizens of Allen county, and for the past twenty years he has maintained his home in the pleasant village of Harlan, Springfield township, where he is a stockholder and director of the Harlan State Bank. Mr. Mills was born in Jefferson county, New York, October 21, 1837, and is a son of Jedediah A. and Jane (Forsyth) Mills, the former of whom was born in the state of New York and the latter in Ireland, she having been a child at the time of her parents' immigration to the United States and the family home having been established in New York state, where was solemnized her marriage to Jedediah A. Mills. In the spring of 1853 they came to Allen county, Indiana, and settled in Springfield township, where Mr. Mills engaged in farming, but he was killed four years later in a runaway accident, he having been thrown from the wagon when he lost control of his frightened team and his injuries having been such that he died shortly afterward, his wife having survived him by many years and having remained in Allen county until her death. They became the parents of four children, Mary, Nancy, William and Samuel, and all now deceased except the last named and youngest, who is the immediate subject of this review. Samuel Mills gained his early education in the schools of the old Empire state and was about sixteen years of age at the time of the family removal to Allen county. After his father's death, four years later, he assumed much of the responsibility involved in the improving and operations of the home farm, and with the passing years he became one of the most successful exponents of agricultural industry in Springfield township, where he accumulated a fine landed estate, and where he continued his vigorous operations as a progressive agriculturist and stock-grower until 1896, since which time he and his wife have resided in the attractive home which he then purchased in the village of Harlan. He is still the owner of valuable farm property in the county and gives a general supervision to his varied property and capitalistic interests, including his service as a member of the directorate of the Harlan State Bank, of which he is one of the leading stockholders. Mr. Mills is an implacable adversary of the liquor traffic and shows his consistency by giving staunch and loyal support to the cause of the Prohibition party. August 21, 1861, was solemnized the marriage of Mr. Mills to Miss Brown, who was born in Allen county on August 13, 1838, a daughter of William and Elizabeth (Miller) Brown, who were honored pioneer settlers of the county. Mr. and Mrs. Mills became the parents of seven children, all of whom are living except the first born, Charles. The names of the surviving children are here given in the respective order of their birth: Samuel, Jr., Abbie, Jeremiah, Alice, William and Jesse.

John Mohr.—From his youth until his death, which occurred July 27, 1906, Mr. Mohr was actively identified with the Hamilton National Bank of Fort Wayne and for many years prior to his demise had served as the able and honored cashier of this representative financial institution of his native city. His course in all of the relations of life was guided and governed by inviolable integrity and high ideals, he commanded unqualified popular respect and was one of the unostentatiously influential business men and loyal citizens of Fort Wayne during the period of a long and significantly useful career. He passed his entire life in the metropolis of Allen county and was a scion of one of the city's sterling pioneer families, his parents having been John and Helen (Witz) Mohr and his father having been for a protracted period successfully established in the boot and shoe business in Fort Wayne, where both he and his wife remained until their death. Of their six children the first was Louis, who is deceased; Adeline is the widow of Clay Taylor and still maintains her home in Fort Wayne; John, subject of this memoir, was the next in order of birth; and Joseph and Conrad, twins, likewise are deceased. The parents were earnest communicants of the Catholic church and their son John thus received his early education in the parochial schools and in a school conducted by one of the brotherhoods of the Catholic church. When but fourteen years of age he became a messenger and general clerical assistant in the Hamilton National Bank, and by faithful and efficient service won advancement through the various grades of promotion until he became cashier of the institution, of which important and exacting executive office he continued the valued and honored incumbent until his death. He was one of the solid and influential figures in the financial circles of this section of the state, was a man of broad information and mature judgment, and his consideration and gracious personality gained to him the confidence and good will of all with whom he came in contact. He was liberal and public-spirited in his civic attitude, was a Democrat in politics and though he had no ambition for public office his civic loyalty was such that he consented to serve as a member of the city council, in which he first represented the Seventh and later the Second ward. He was affiliated with the local organizations of the Benevolent & Protective Order of Elks and the Fraternal Order of Eagles, and was a devout communicant of the Catholic church, in which he held membership in the Cathedral parish, his widow being still an active communicant of this parish. On October 6, 1874, was solemnized the marriage of Mr. Mohr to Miss Hannah Helena Nettlehorst, who was born and reared in Fort Wayne, a daughter of the late Charles and Sophia A. (LaSelle) Nettlehorst, the latter having been a daughter of Francis D. LaSelle. Charles Nettlehorst was engaged in the hardware business at Fort Wayne at the time of his death, which occurred when he was a young man of thirty-two years, and his young widow later became the wife of George DeWald, who was born in Germany, and both passed the closing years of their lives in Fort Wayne, further data concerning the family being given on other pages, in the sketch of the career of Robert DeWald. Mrs. Mohr is the elder of the two children of her mother's first marriage, and the younger child, Francis, died in infancy. Mr. and Mrs. Mohr became the parents of two children, both of whom survive the honored father: Frank X. holds an executive position with the First and Hamilton National Bank, and Helen Sophia is the wife of Detlef Ferdinand Urbahns, who is employed in the same banking institution. Mrs. Mohr has been a resident of Fort Wayne from the time of her birth and in her widowhood is sustained and comforted by the filial devotion of her children, by the affectionate regard of her many friends and by the gracious memories and associations of the past.

Rev. William E. Moll, the able and revered pastor of Emanuel Lutheran church in Fort Wayne, has not only shown the utmost zeal and devotion in the work of his high calling but also stands exponent of broadminded and progressive citizenship, so that he has made his benignant influence extend in various directions. The prosperous parish over which he is placed in charge has found its spiritual and temporal affairs effectively administered by him, and it is interesting to record that this church was founded in the year that recorded also the birth of its present pastor. The organization of Emanuel church was effected in July, 1867, and its first pastor was Rev. William S. Stubnatzi. In the following year the devotion and liberality of the little church organization were shown in the erection of the substantial brick edifice which is still utilized by the congregation, but upon which many improvements have been made in the passing years. The original parish school was opened before the church building had been completed, and soon afterward the present school building was erected. Emmanuel church has played an important part in the spiritual and civic life of Fort Wayne, and the history of the parish school has been marked by splendid growth as well as by efficiency of work during the long period of its history. In 1880 Rev. C. Gross assumed the pastorate, and his devoted ministrations continued for nearly a quarter of a century. In the harvest of the Divine Master he bore the heat and burden of the day and left enduring results of consecrated zeal, his retirement from the pastorate having occurred in 1903, in which year he was succeeded by the present incumbent, so that in the half century of its noble history Emmanuel church has had but three shepherds. Three hundred families are represented in the parish organization, the present enrollment in the parish school is eighty-five pupils, and three efficient and zealous teachers are employed. The attractive parish house was erected in 1882 and is of substantial brick construction. Rev. William Ernest Moll was born in the city of Detroit, Michigan, September 3, 1867, a son of Conrad and Renata (Fuerbringer) Moll, the former born in Bavaria, Germany, and the latter in the state of Illinois. Conrad Moll came to the United States in 1846, as a lad of seven years, and the family home was established in the state of Michigan. He provided ways and means through which to acquire a liberal education, and in Concordia College, at Fort Wayne, completed the thorough philosophical and theological course that qualified him for ordination as a clergyman of the Lutheran church, in the faith of which he had been carefully reared. He gave many years of faithful and consecrated service in the ministry and in the same rested from his labors only when death put its seal upon his mortal lips and he passed forward to the life eternal, in 1899, his widow being still a resident of Detroit, Michigan. Of the children the first born was Otto A., who is deceased, and the subject of this review was the second child; Theodore M. resides at Norway, Michigan; Clara remains with her widowed mother; Gustave W. is a resident of Foster City, Michigan; Richard P. remains with his mother in Detroit; Walter L. resides in Fort Wayne; Agnes is at the maternal home; Kurt is deceased; and Nettie is the youngest member of the family circle at the home in Detroit. After having fully profited by the advantages of the Lutheran parochial schools and the public schools of his native city, Rev. William E. Moll came to Fort Wayne and entered Concordia College, his father's alma mater, in which, as a member of the class of 1886, he continued his studies six years. He then went to St. Louis, Missouri, where he entered the theological department of Concordia College, in which he was graduated in 1889 and incidental to which was soon afterward ordained a clergyman of the Lutheran church. In the same year he became pastor of a church at Kirkwood, Missouri, where he remained until 1895; thereafter he held a charge at Dunkirk, New York, until 1897; and his next pastoral incumbency was at Ottawa, Province of Ontario, Canada, where he continued his effective services until he accepted his present pastorate, in 1903. Taking loyal interest in community affairs and also those of governmental order, Mr. Moll is non-partisan in politics and gives support to men and measures meeting the approval of his judgment. On July 6, 1892, was solemnized his marriage to Miss Clara L. Keyl, who was born and reared on Staten Island, New York, a daughter of Stephen and Magdalene (Walther) Keyl. The two children of this union are Conrad S. and Esther M., who are still members of the gracious home circle.

Clyde F. Moon.—It is perhaps true that the average citizen in any given community fails to realize to how appreciable a degree the local newspaper, if properly conducted, exercises most important functions as an exponent of the diversified interests of that community and how great and benignant its influence in the furtherance and safe-guarding of local civic and material well-being. Specially potent is the influence thus exerted by the newspapers of the smaller cities and different villages, and perhaps equally pronounced is the lack of popular appreciation, so that oftimes the ambitious editor and publisher is constrained in a professional way to look upon "virtue as its own reward." He whose name introduces this paragraph has effectively mustered his forces as one of the representative newspaper men of Allen county and is not only the editor and publisher of the Woodburn News, at Woodburn, the principal town of Maumee township, but also has editorial management and general control of the New Haven Tribune, at New Haven, Adams township, and the Grabill Review, at Grabill, Cedar Creek township. He is a practical exponent of the "art preservative of all arts" and has proved himself a strong editorial writer and able business man, with the result that he has not only achieved success in his chosen field of endeavor but has also brought his papers to such high standard as to gain to them unqualified popular approval and support. Mr. Moon was born at Hesperia, Oceana county, Michigan, on January 25, 1885, and is a son of Thomas and Harriet (Madison) Moon, the former of whom was born in the state of New York and the latter in Michigan, where her parents settled in the pioneer period of the history of that state. Thomas Moon was reared and educated in the old Empire state and upon his removal to Michigan established his residence in Montcalm county, where his marriage was solemnized and where he continued to reside fifteen years, within which he worked at the carpenter's trade and for a time conducted a bakery. He finally removed with his family to Hesperia, that state, where he became an active and representative business man and highly honored citizen and where he continued to maintain his home until his death, which occurred in 1898. His widow now resides in the home of her son, Clyde F., subject of this review, at Woodburn, and is accorded the deepest filial love and solicitude by all of her children. Of the children the first three—Myrta, Ruth and Lena—are deceased, and besides Clyde F., three others survive the honored father, namely: Clarence, Flora and Altha. Clyde F. Moon is indebted to the public schools of his native state for his early educational discipline, and at the age of eighteen years he entered upon an apprenticeship to the printer's trade in the office of the Hesperia Union at Hesperia, Michigan. The intricacies and mysteries of the printer's art did not baffle him and he familiarized himself thoroughly with all details of the country newspaper business. He finally purchased and became editor and publisher of the paper in whose office he had learned his trade, and there remained until 1910, when he sold the plant and business and established his residence at Woodburn, Allen county, Indiana, where he purchased the Woodburn News, a weekly paper which he has made a model and through which he has effectively exploited and conserved community interests. His office is a thoroughly modern plant, with excellent equipment in both newspaper and job departments, and this is assured when it is stated that he utilizes in his establishment the Linotype machine. In 1916 Mr. Moon likewise assumed the editorial management of the New Haven Tribune, of which he now has full control, the paper being printed in his Woodburn office. Mr. Moon is not only one of the able and alert newspaper men of Allen county but is also distinctively progressive, loyal and public-spirited in his civic attitude. He has not sought political preferment, but both in a personal way and through the columns of his papers has been a resourceful advocate of the cause of the Democratic party. He is affiliated with the National Union and both he and his wife hold membership in the Missionary church. On June 12, 1912, was solemnized the marriage of Mr. Moon to Miss Clara Yaggy, who was born and reared in Allen county, a daughter of David and Mary (Schlatter) Yaggy, representatives of old and honored families of this county. Mr. and Mrs. Moon have two children—Doris and Arametha.

Luie H. Moore has shown his distinct initiative and executive ability in building up his present substantial and representative real estate business in the city of Fort Wayne, and upon his records are at all times to be found most desirable investments in both city and country realty, the while his agency negotiates equitable exchanges of property and gives attention to rentals, collections, etc. Mr. Moore was born at Hicksville, Defiance county, Ohio, April 26, 1874, a son of James and Elizabeth (Lindsey) Moore, natives of Noble county, Ohio, and representatives of old and honored families of the Buckeye state. James Moore was long numbered among the prosperous farmers of Ohio and eventually removed to the state of Washington, where he is now living virtually retired. He has always given staunch allegiance to the Republican party, has held minor public offices, is affiliated with the Masonic fraternity and is a member of the United Brethren church, as was also his wife, whose death occurred in Defiance county, Ohio, December 30, 1905. Of the children Samuel L. is a resident of Haviland, Ohio, and Findley maintains his home in Hicksville, Ohio. Luie H., of this review, was the next in order of birth; and Mary is the wife of Henry Carey, a successful farmer near Hicksville, Ohio. Luie H. Moore passed his childhood and early youth on the home farm and acquired his preliminary education in the public schools of his native county. He supplemented this training by a course in Otterbein University, at Westerville, Ohio, and in 1893 identified himself with a retail hardware establishment at Haviland, Ohio. In 1895 he assumed the position of traveling salesman for the Evansville Stove Works, of Evansville, Indiana, and later gave equally vigorous and effective service as claim agent for the Bankers' Life Insurance Company, with residence and headquarters in Fort Wayne. In 1911 he established himself in the general real estate business in Fort Wayne, and his energy and progressiveness have resulted in the development of a substantial and prosperous enterprise, in connection with which he has effected many important real estate transfers in Fort Wayne and other parts of Allen county. His political allegiance is given unequivocally to the Republican party. During the gubernatorial campaign of Governor James B. Goodrich, in 1916, he was manager of the Twelfth district. In Masonry he has taken the Scottish and York Rites and the Shrine, besides which he is affiliated also with the Knights of Pythias, both he and his wife being members of the Christian church. July 6, 1904, recorded the marriage of Mr. Moore to Miss Mildred M. Fish, daughter of Orlando and Eliza (Confeur) Fish, of Groverhill, Paulding county, Ohio. Mr. and Mrs. Moore have one child, Evelyn, born in 1914.

Rev. G. J. Mooreman.—It was in September, 1916, that Rev. Fr. Gorge J. Mooreman came to his present position as priest in charge of Besancon St. Louis parish in Jefferson township, and he has ably conducted the affairs of church and school since that time. About one hundred and forty families make up his charge, and the school numbers about one hundred and twenty pupils, with four Sisters of Notre Dame looking after their instruction. Father Mooreman is a native of Indiana, born in Greensburg, Decatur county, October 8, 1883, and he is the son of Joseph and Christine (Hill) Mooreman, natives of the state of Ohio. Father Mooreman had his early schooling in the common schools of Greensburg, after which he went to St. Joseph's College, Illinois, for his academic work, and then to St. Meinrad's in Spencer county, Indiana, where he had his philosophy and theology training. He was ordained to the priesthood and his first service was in the position of assistant at the Cathedral in Fort Wayne, serving there from 1908 to 1911, when he was sent to Kendallville, continuing in service there until January 14, 1914. His next post was at Huntington, Indiana, as assistant to Father Noll, and he served there until September, 1916, when as above stated, he came to his present duties in charge of St. Louis parish. His earlier work was designed to give him an experience that has served him well in his labors in his present post, and he finds much to occupy him in the management of church and school. His influence, not only among the members of his parish, but in the entire community, has been of a high order, and he stands in the forefront of the citizenry of New Haven and of Jefferson township, with a pleasing record for service in civic affairs that marks him as a leader in the ranks of his fellows.

Peter A. Moran was one of the substantial and representative business men of his native city at the time of his death, which occurred December 3, 1907, and he passed his entire life in Fort Wayne, a scion of a sterling pioneer family and a citizen who ordered his course upon the highest plane of integrity and honor, so that his was secure place in popular confidence and esteem. Mr. Moran was born in Fort Wayne on April 13, 1855, and was a son of Peter and Rachel (Nusbaum) Moran, the former of whom was born in County Meath, Ireland, in 1818, and the latter of whom was born in Frederick county, Maryland. Peter Moran, the father, was reared and educated in his native land and was a youth of seventeen years when he immigrated to the United States and established his residence in the state of Maryland, where his marriage was solemnized and where he continued to maintain his home until about 1847, when he came to Indiana and located in Fort Wayne, where he found employment in the pioneer tannery conducted by Mr. Fry. He was an expert tanner and continued to be identified with the work of his trade until 1860, when he engaged in the ice business, as one of the early exponents of this line of enterprise in Fort Wayne. He developed a prosperous business and to the same he continued to give his attention until his death, which occurred on the 17th of November, 1880, his wife having survived him by a number of years and both having been earnest communicants of the Cathedral parish of the Catholic church in their home city. Of their children the first was Mary Ann, who died in childhood; Margaret is the wife of Albert Dittoe, of Fort Wayne; William and Mary Ellen are deceased; Peter A., subject of this memoir, was the next in order of birth; and James Eli likewise is deceased. Peter A. Moran acquired his early education in the parochial school conducted by the Catholic brothers in connection with the Cathedral, and as a youth he learned the tinner's trade. Later he became associated with his father's ice business and upon the death of his honored sire he succeded to the ownership of the well established and prosperous business, with which he continued his active identification until his death—a man of energy, progressiveness, integrity and genial personality, and one whose circle of friends was virtually coincident with that of his acquaintances. Mr. Moran was a staunch supporter and advocate of the cause of the Democratic party, was a zealous communicant of the Catholic church, as a member of the Cathedral parish, and was affiliated with the Catholic Knights of America. On May 24, 1881, was solemnized the marriage of Mr. Moran to Miss Mary E. Baker, who was born September 10, 1859, and was reared in Fort Wayne, where she still maintains her home and where she is an active communicant of the Cathedral parish. Mrs. Moran was educated at St. Augustine's Academy, conducted by the Sisters of Providence, in Fort Wayne. Of the children of this union, Peter J. and Bernard A. are active young business men of Fort Wayne; Mary M. is the wife of Frank Callahan, of this city; Gertrude died in infancy, as did also Alphonsus; Celeste died at the age of ten years and Thomas at the age of six years; and Amelia remains with her widowed mother. Mrs. Moran is a daughter of the late John and Mary (Faust) Baker, the former of whom was born in the historic old city of Worms, in the beautiful Rhine district of Germany, the date of his nativity having been October 17, 1817. He was reared and educated in his fatherland and as a youth of seventeen years he came to America and established his residence in the city of Pittsburgh, Pnnsylvania. In 1848 he became a resident of Fort Wayne, where he was a pioneer wagonmaker and where he continued to be actively identified with enterprise in this line until a short time prior to his death, which occurred on February 19, 1895, at which time he was known and honored as one of the sterling pioneer citizens of the Allen county metropolis. He was a staunch Democrat in politics and both he and his wife were communicants of St. Mary's Catholic church. Mrs. Baker was born in the city of Baltimore, Maryland, on July 25, 1824, and her death occurred February 24, 1909.

Peter C. Morganthaler has achieved in his native city of Fort Wayne a position of marked prominence and influence as an exponent of electrical engineering enterprise and is now managing engineer of the meter department of the General Electric Works of Fort Wayne. He was born in this city on August 28, 1879, a son of Peter and Ella (Clifford) Morganthaler, the former of whom was born at Massillon, Stark county, Ohio, and the latter at Concord, New Hampshire, she being now a resident of the city of Chicago. Peter Morganthaler, Sr., was reared and educated in his native state and established his residence at Fort Wayne, Indiana, in 1865. He engaged in the mercantile business here and was one of the pioneer merchants and honored and influential citizens of Fort Wayne at the time of his death, on October 1, 1892, his widow being now a resident of Chicago, as previously noted. Of their five children the first born was Zillah, who died in childhood; Clifford and Calot now reside in the city of San Francisco, California; the subject of this sketch was the next in order of birth; and Russell is deceased. Peter C. Morganthaler is indebted to the public schools of Fort Wayne for his early educational discipline, which was supplemented by an effective course in the Chicago Manual Training School. In 1897, when eighteen years of age, he entered the employ of the General Electric Company at Fort Wayne, and two years later became a traveling representative for this corporation. In this capacity he continued his service until 1902, when, to further his technical knowledge, he identified himself with the meter-manufacturing department of the business. He was punctilious and characteristically ambitious in this connection and gradually won his way forward until he was given his present responsible office of managing engineer of the meter department. As a practical and scientific electrician he is affiliated with the American Institute of Electrical Engineers. His political allegiance is given to the Republican party and he and his wife are active members of the First Presbyterian church of Fort Wayne. On February 1, 1900, was solemnized the marriage of Mr. Morganthaler to Miss Evelyn Rossell, who was born in Wabash county, Indiana, but who was seven years old at the time of the family removal to Fort Wayne, where she was reared and educated. She is a daughter of Joseph Amos and Lulu (Miles) Rossell, the former of whom was born in Wabash county and the latter in the city of Logansport, this state. Mr. and Mrs. Rossell still maintain their home in Fort Wayne and he is a traveling commercial salesman for a wholesale shoe house. Of the children, Mrs. Morganthaler is the elder, and the younger is Della, who is the wife of Ernst C. Rurode, Jr., concerning whom individual mention is made on other pages of this work. Of the two children of Mr. and Mrs. Morganthaler the first, a daughter, died in infancy, and the one surviving is a fine little son, Joseph Cornell.

Dr. Elmer E. Morris was born in Mahoning county, Ohio, on March 23, 1868, son of Jonathan L. and Hannah (Mitchener) Morris. He is directly descended from Robert Morris, an early American financier and famed as a signer of the Declaration of Independence. Jonathan Morris was born in Beaver, Pennsylvania, and the mother came from Westchester, Pennsylvania. Both parents were of the William Penn type of Quaker. They were farming people and devoted their lives to that industry. The father died at Alliance, Ohio, in 1902, and the mother still lives, sharing a home with her son, Dr. Morris, of this review. The two sons of these people entered the medical profession and Dr. Isaac E. Morris, the second son, is established in practice in Fort Wayne. Dr. Elmer E. Morris had his early education in the public schools of Alliance, Ohio, and later attended Mount Union College, the Tri-State Normal at Angola, Indiana, and the University of Cincinnati. He was graduated from the Ohio College of Dental Surgery in dentistry in 1898 and, in 1902, took his medical degree in the Eclectic Medical Institute at Cincinnati. He practiced dentistry in Cincinnati for a brief time, then took up the practice of medicine in 1902, locating at Hoagland, where he spent nine years in his work. In 1911 he came to New Haven and engaged in general practice. He has enjoyed a pleasing measure of popular confidence and esteem and has a secure place in the community he so recently settled in. Doctor Morris is a member of the directorate of the Peoples' State Bank of New Haven and is now vice-president of the institution. He is a Republican in politics, a member of Plymouth Congregational church in Fort Wayne, member of the New Haven Commercial Club, member of the County Medical Association, a member of the Masonic fraternity with all degrees up to and including the thirty-second Knight Templar and a Shriner. He was married on June 20, 1901, to Miss Addie E. Smith, daughter of Doctor Smith, of Hoagland, who was one time auditor of Allen county. Doctor and Mrs. Morris have three children—Joseph E. Bernice and Jean W.

John Morris is widely recognized as one of the most prominent members of the bar of northeastern Indiana. As a man, a loyal citizen

John Morris

Samuel L. Morris, Jr.

and able lawyer he is held in the highest regard. His father, the late Judge John Morris, was one of the leading lawyers and jurists of Indiana for many years, and attention to a review of his life has been given in connection with the sketch of the career of Stephen Morris, on other pages of this publication. John Morris was born in Fort Wayne, on March 24, 1860, and the maiden name of his mother was Theresa J. Farr, she having been a resident of New Lisbon, Ohio, at the time of her marriage. In 1844 the parents of Mr. Morris came from Ohio and established their home at New Auburn, Dekalb county, Indiana, and in 1857 they came to Fort Wayne, where occurred, three years later, the birth of their son, John, the immediate subject of this review. Following his course in the public schools Mr. Morris entered upon a course in the law department of the great University of Michigan, at Ann Arbor, in which institution he was a member of the class of 1883. He studied law also in the office of his father and Judge William H. Coombs and this effective preceptorship continued three years. It was under these fortuitous conditions that he laid the foundation for the successful career that has been his in the later years of his vigorous professional activities. In June, 1886, Mr. Morris formed a law partnership with Charles H. Worden, and this alliance continued until May 22, 1893, when Mr. Morris retired from the firm and entered into a professional partnership with William P. Breen, the firm of Breen & Morris, having since held an important place among the strong legal firms of Indiana. They occupy an extensive suite of offices on the second floor of the People's Trust building. Mr. Morris is a director of the People's Trust & Savings Association. In politics he has always been a staunch supporter of the principles of the Republican party. In 1889 he was appointed to the office of deputy clerk of the United States court for this district, and of this position he continued the incumbent until the selection of Thomas J. Logan as his successor. He is affiliated with the Scottish Rite bodies of the Masonic fraternity, as well as with the local lodge of the Benevolent and Protective Order of Elks. He is actively identified with the Allen County Bar Association, the Indiana Bar Association and the American Law Association. He has at all times evinced a deep and loyal interest in civic and political affairs, holds membership in the Fort Wayne Commercial Club and is also a member of the Columbia Club, a representative social and political organization in the city of Indianapolis. He finds satisfaction also in maintaining membership in the Fort Wayne Country Club and is one of the well-known and popular citizens of his native city and county.

Samuel L. Morris, Jr.—Descended from a long line of distinguished jurists, Samuel L. Morris, Jr., of Fort Wayne, already has attained to an enviable place among the leading men of the bar of Indiana. Mr. Morris was born in Fort Wayne, September 22, 1884, son of Samuel L. and Carrie E. (Ambos) Morris. His grandfather, the late Judge John Morris, who was long a leading practitioner of the bar of Allen county and of Indiana and whose place among his fellows was recognized in his selection as the representative man to lay the corner stone of the Allen county courthouse, was one of the ablest of the pioneer lawyers of Indiana. At a critical time in the history of the state he was summoned to the capital to serve as a commissioner of the supreme court of Indiana, and in this capacity gave to the state splendid service. Samuel L. Morris, son of Judge John Morris and father of Samuel L. Morris, Jr., was born at Auburn, Dekalb county, Indiana, in 1851. He has long held a prominent place among the attorneys of Indiana, his practice being confined largely to corporation cases. He is a member of the firm of Barrett, Morris & Hoffman, of Fort Wayne. His wife was born at Columbus, Ohio, and of their four children the following data are entered: Gertrude E. is the wife of Percy G. Olds; John is deceased; Samuel L., Jr., was the next in order of birth; and Jeanette is the wife of Joseph Lyle Tucker, treasurer of the International Business College in Fort Wayne. Following his graduation in the Fort Wayne high school, in 1904, Samuel L. Morris, Jr., entered the offices of Barrett & Morris, where he studied law for five years. In 1907 he was admitted to practice before the bar of Allen county. In 1909 he opened an office in the Shoaff building, where he practiced law until the latter part of 1915, when he formed a partnership with Albert E. Thomas and Howard L. Townsend, under the firm name of Thomas, Townsend & Morris, with offices at 721-726 Shoaff building. This firm has a large miscellaneous practice and is considered one of the strongest in the city. Mr. Morris has been admitted to practice in the supreme and appellate courts of Indiana, the United States district court for the district of Indiana, the United States circuit court of appeals for the Seventh circuit and the supreme court of the United States. He is general attorney for the Midland Engineering Company of Fort Wayne, Indiana, and the attorney at Fort Wayne for the Sinclair Refining Company of Illinois, which is a subsidiary company of the Sinclair Oil and Refining Company of New York. He is a member of the Indiana State Bar Association, the American Bar Association, the American Society of International Law, the Masonic order and the Phi Alpha Psi fraternity. He is a staunch supporter of the principles of the Democratic party. His church affiliation is with the congregation of Trinity parish, Protestant Episcopal. Mr. Morris has ever been a close student of the law and is recognized as one of the ablest of the younger members of the bar of northern Indiana. His law library, comprising more than twelve hundred volumes, is one of the most valuable collections in the state. On December 10, 1913, Mr. Morris was united in marriage with Miss Helen Margaret Good, daughter of Dr. and Mrs. Charles H. Good, of Huntington, Indiana. Mrs. Morris, a young woman of many admirable qualities and most gracious personality, is an accomplished pianist. Mr. and Mrs. Morris have one son, Samuel L. Morris, III. The family home is at No. 1002 Wildwood avenue.

Stephen Morris.—As a member of the Morris family which has left the impress of the higher character of its representatives upon the life and development of Fort Wayne, down through the years, Stephen Morris, cashier of the Old National Bank of Fort Wayne has contributed his full share. Mr. Morris was born in Auburn, DeKalb county, Indiana, November 17, 1856, and was brought to Fort Wayne when he was but six months old. He has resided here continuously ever since. His grandfather, Jonathan Morris, was a native of Loudoun county, Virginia, where he was born, June 9, 1788. While yet a young man, Jonathan Morris removed to Columbiana county, Ohio, and settled on a farm near New Lisbon. He there married Miss Sarah Snyder, who was born in 1790. The death of Jonathan Morris occurred in 1865; his wife died in 1875. John Morris, son of Jonathan Morris, and father of Stephen Morris, was born on the farm near New Lisbon, December 6, 1816. Following his schooling, he studied law in the office of William D. Ewing, in New Lisbon, and was admitted, in 1844, to practice at the bar of Columbiana county. In 1844 he removed to Auburn, DeKalb county,

Indiana, where he opened an office for the practice of his profession. His success here laid the foundation for a long life of usefulness and service to the people of northeastern Indiana as well as the state at large. His first political honors came in his election as judge of the Court of Common Pleas, the district at that time comprising a number of counties in the northeastern portion of the state. In 1857 Judge Morris removed to Fort Wayne, where the remainder of his life was passed. In April, 1881, he was appointed by Judge James L. Worden, with whom he was at one time associated in the practice of the law, as one of the five supreme court commissioners who were called to assist the state Supreme Court at Indianapolis to undertake the important work of disposing of a large budget of cases. The appointment was noteworthy, in that Judge Morris was a staunch republican, while Judge Worden, who made the appointment, was a democrat. The explanation comes with an understanding of Judge Worden's appreciation of the ability of his former associate. The written opinions of Judge Morris in the Indiana Reports frequently are cited as authority in the settlement of legal questions. Judge Morris died in 1906. To him and his wife were born seven children; namely, Mrs. Woodworth, of Fort Collins, Colorado; Edward, whose death occurred when six years of age; Samuel L. of Fort Wayne, a leading attorney of the Allen county bar; Mary, residing at home; Stephen, the subject of this sketch; John, of Fort Wayne, a prominent figure in the legal fraternity of Allen county; Mrs. Julia M. Barnes, of Detroit, and one child who died in infancy. Stephen Morris received his education in the public schools of Fort Wayne and in the Methodist college, a prominent Fort Wayne institution of the earlier days. At the age of nineteen years he entered the employ of the Old National Bank, in which institution he served through successive positions of greater importance until he reached the responsible office of cashier. On August 23, 1882, Mr. Morris married Miss Anna B. Miller, of Fort Wayne, daughter of John and Sarah Miller. The children born of this union are J. R. and Stephen, Jr. In politics Mr. Morris has always been a staunch Republican. As a member of the Commercial Club of Fort Wayne, and in other ways, Mr. Morris has ever displayed a loyalty to Fort Wayne interests.

William S. Morris maintained his home in Fort Wayne nearly a quarter of a century, was long a prominent and influential figure in connection with practical railway operations, and in all of the relations of life gave assurance of strong and noble manhood, so that he commanded the confidence and good will of his fellow men, the while he played well his part as a loyal and public-spirited citizen. After years of earnest and effective endeavor he felt justified in retiring from active business and executive alliances, about 1909, and thereafter continued to reside in his pleasant home in Fort Wayne until his death, which occurred June 15, 1915. William Samuel Morris was born in the city of Chicago, Illinois, on March 4, 1857, and was a son of Samuel and Frances (Webster) Morris, his father having been one of the pioneer passenger train engineers on the line of the Chicago, Rock Island & Pacific Railroad. He was in the prime of life at the time of his death and his widow subsequently contracted a second marriage, the name of her second husband having been Swasey and two children having been born of this union—Grace, who became the wife of Richard D. Morgan, of Richmond, Virginia, and Arthur, who died at the age of twelve years. William S. Morris profited by the advantages of the public schools of

Chicago and also the Cook County Normal School, and his original mechanical training and practical experience in connection with the railroad business were gained in the shops of the Housatonic Railroad at Fall River, Massachusetts, under the direction of his uncle, Chauncey R. Morris, who attained to high reputation as a mechanical engineer and who held for many years the position of master mechanic of the Fort Wayne shops of the Wabash Railroad. About the year 1885 William S. Morris established his home in Fort Wayne and here held for several years the position of master mechanic in the Wabash Railroad shops. Within the course of his long and varied experience as a railroad man of marked ability he was associated with various railway companies, including the Pere Marquette, the Erie and the Chesapeake & Ohio. In the employ of the last mentioned company he held the position of superintendent of motive power and subsequently consulting engineer, and while he was thus engaged he was a delegate to the meeting of the International Railway Association held at Berne, Switzerland, in 1910. His wife and two children accompanied him abroad and after the adjournment of the convention mentioned the family made an extended and interesting trip through various European countries. Mr. Morris achieved unqualified success as a practical railway man and executive and was an active and popular member of the American Railway Guild, of which he served one term as president, as well as of the Mechanical Engineers' Association of New York. He held the position of superintendent of motive power in the service of both the Chesapeake & Ohio and the Erie Railroads. His political allegiance was given to the Republican party and through many sources he manifested his deep and helpful interest in the welfare and advancement of Fort Wayne, where he was a valued member of the Commercial Club. Mr. Morris was an earnest and zealous churchman of the Protestant Episcopal church and served many years as a member of the vestry of Trinity church in Fort Wayne, of which he was for some time the junior warden. In the time honored Masonic fraternity he was affiliated with both the York and Scottish Rite bodies. His first wife, whose maiden name was Lillie Ward, was a daughter of Horatio N. Ward, of Fort Wayne, and she is survived by one child, Helen, who is the wife of Bernard M. Jones, of Richmond, Virginia. The second marriage of Mr. Morris was solemnized November 9, 1898, when Miss Grace M. White became his wife. Mrs. Morris was born and reared in Fort Wayne and is a daughter of Captain James B. White, one of the well known and highly esteemed citizens of Allen county. The one child of the second marriage of the honored subject of this memoir is William, who was born March 21, 1900, at Richmond, Va. The family home is maintained at 813 West Berry street.

Edward Moser, M. D.—Though Dr. Moser has been a resident of Indiana since his childhood he can claim the fair little republic of Switzerland as the place of his nativity, his birth having there occurred, in the canton of Berne, on January 12, 1874. He has been engaged in the active general practice of his profession at Woodburn, Allen county, since June 13, 1906, and is recognized as one of the able and representative physicians and surgeons of the county, his substantial practice extending throughout the territory normally tributary to his home village. The Doctor is the second in order of birth in a family of twelve children, all of whom are living, and he is a son of Jacob S. and Mary Ann (Studer) Moser, who continued their residence in Switzerland until April, 1881, when they came with their children to America and settled on a farm near Berne, Adams county, Indiana—a locality known for its fine element of Swiss citizens, as the name of the village of Berne well denotes. The father became one of the substantial farmers and honored citizens of Adams county and is now living retired in the village of Berne, his devoted wife having passed away in 1898. Of the twelve children the eldest is Rev. Louis A., who is a clergyman of the German Reformed church, and, as before stated, Dr. Moser, of this review was the second child. The names of the other children are here entered: Jacob J., Herman F., Rudolph, Martha, Leah, Arnold, Lydia, Lena, Leo and Louise. Dr. Moser was about seven years old at the time of the family immigration to the United States and was reared under the invigorating descipline of the home farm, in Adams county, Indiana, where also he profited fully by the advantages afforded in the public schools. His ambition has ever been one of action, and thus he was not satisfied with less than a liberal education, in the attaining of which he was finally moved to prepare himself also for the exacting profession in which he is now giving most effective service. He attended the normal school at Portland, Jay county, for one term and thereafter was for three terms engaged in successful pedagogic work, as teacher in the district schools of Adams county. In 1902 he entered the Indiana Medical College, at Indianapolis, where he continued his studies one year. During the following three years he was a zealous student in the Hahnemann Homeopathic Medical College and Hospital, in the city of Chicago, and in this fine institution he was graduated as a member of the class of 1906. Within a few days after having thus received his degree of Doctor of Medicine he established his residence at Woodburn, where he has since been engaged in general practice and where his ability and gracious personality have enabled him to build up a large and representative practice. He is one of the able exponents of the beneficient Homeopathic school of medicine in northern Indiana and continues a close student of the best in standard and periodical literature pertaining to medical and surgical science, with the advances in which he thus keeps in effective touch. He maintains affiliation with the American Institute of Homeopathy and is a member also of the Allen County Medical Society and the Indiana State Medical Society. His political allegiance is given to the Republican party and he and his wife are active members of the Missionary church. October 8, 1898, recorded the marriage of Dr. Moser to Miss Mary Neuenschwander, daughter of Christian Neuenschwander, a well known citizen of Adams county, and she passed to the life eternal on February 5, 1902. Of the two children, Viola died in infancy and Frances Effie remains at the paternal home. On September 18, 1904, was solemnized the marriage of Dr. Moser to Miss Mary Egly, who was born and reared in Allen county and who is a daughter of Jacob and Lydia (Musser) Egly, the family being representative by more explicit mention on other pages of this publication. Dr. and Mrs. Moser have three children—Madeline, Marion Edward and Richard Donald.

Edwin R. Moser.—The village of Woodburn, Maumee township, is situated in the midst of one of the finest agricultural districts of northern Indiana and as a trading and industrial center it is one of the vigorous and thriving towns of Allen county. It is but natural that here the principal industrial and commercial enterprise should be that represented by the Woodburn Elevator and Milling Company, which has developed a large and substantial business, with grain elevator and mills of the best modern facilities. As secretary and treasurer of this company Mr. Moser is one of the representative business men of this part of the county, even as he is one of the prominent exponents of the grain business in northern Indiana. Edwin R. Moser was born in Moniteau county, Missouri, on June 2, 1872, a son of Abraham J. and Caroline (Welty) Moser, both of whom were born in Wayne county, Ohio, and both of whom were young at the time of the removal of the respective families to Missouri. In the latter state Abraham J. Moser passed the remainder of his life, and he was long numbered among the representative farmers and honored citizens of Moniteau county. His widow now resides at Fort Morgan, Colorado. Of the ten children the subject of this review was the second in order of birth, and all of the others still survive the honored father, namely: Martha, Esther, Oscar, Elizabeth, Dennis, Lawrence, Edna, Elvin and Orrin. Edwin R. Moser early gained practical experience in connection with the varied activities of the home farm, and his youthful education was acquired in the public schools of his native state. As an independent young farmer in Missouri he continued operations four years, and he then, in 1898, came to Allen county, Indiana, and established his home at Woodburn, where he engaged in the buying and shipping of grain and eventually became one of the leading stockholders and executives of the Woodburn Elevator and Milling Company, to the affairs of which he now gives his close and effective attention. He is a Democrat in his political allegiance and he and his wife hold membership in the Missionary Baptist church. On September 14, 1902, Mr. Moser wedded Miss Elizabeth Rothgeb, a daughter of Jesse and Mary (Rushart) Rothgeb, natives of Ohio. Mr. Rothgeb has been a successful farmer in Allen county, Indiana, and he now resides in the village of Gar Creek, this county, where he is engaged in the general merchandise business, is station agent for the Wabash Railroad, and is serving as postmaster. Mrs. Rothgeb is deceased. Mr. and Mrs. Moser have no children.

William E. Mossman.—The name of William E. Mossman comes instinctively to the mind of the people of Fort Wayne when the subject of broad service to the greatest number presents itself for consideration. With a keen appreciation of the true monument which a man, during his lifetime, is enabled to rear to endure beyond the years of a lifetime, Mr. Mossman has chosen to manifest his munificence in a way to attract the least attention and yet continue its good influence through the succeeding years. As an example of this it is necessary only to refer to his gift of $50,000 to the fund for the establishment of the new building of the Young Men's Christian Association and the gift of the fund to add a modern swimming pool to the equipment of the Young Women's Christian Association. Mr. Mossman, ever active in the forward movements of the city, has entered earnestly into every worthy cause in which he could lend assistance either through the contribution of his personal efforts or his means. His connection with the industrial and financial life of Fort Wayne has enabled him to exert a particularly valuable influence through these channels. About eighty years ago the Mossman family located in Whitley county, Indiana, and it has been identified with that section in varied lines of activity from then down to the present day. Others of the name found their ways into Allen and adjoining counties, but none of them, perhaps, have been more successful in their business ventures than has William E. Mossman, who is an influential factor in many prominent enterprises in Allen county and numerous other localities. Mr. Mossman is of Hoosier birth, born on a Whitley county farm on September 17, 1843, son of Francis and Rheua (Conner) Mossman. The mother was of Virginian birth and parentage, but Francis Mossman was born in Pennsylvania and came with his parents into Ohio in the old Western Reserve days. He was reared there and came to Indiana in 1838, pre-empting homestead land in Whitley county in about 1840 and settling down to farm life with his young wife. They prospered comfortably and were happy enough to be content to spend the rest of their lives on their farm. The mother died there in 1887 and the father survived her until 1904. Of the nine children born to them five are living at this writing (1917). William E. Mossman was reared to farm life and had such educational advantages as the county offered in those times. He was a young man of ambition and when about twenty-six years old determined to get into business on his own responsibility, being no longer content with the farm and its opportunities. He chose to identify himself with the mercantile business as a dealer in groceries and provisions and for three years continued to enjoy moderate success. He then turned his attention to other lines, engaging in the manufacture of hardwood lumber. Here he found himself, it seems, for Mr. Mossman has continued to be active in that industry from then until now. In recent years, however, he has given less attention to the mill business than heretofore, and his mills at Memphis, Tennessee, represent practically his only remaining interest in that enterprise. These mills operating under the name of Mossman Lumber Company, are one of the large industries of Memphis. Other industrial fields have claimed his attention, and the Wayne Knitting Mills, one of the leading concerns of its kind in Fort Wayne, has known him as vice-president and director for the past fifteen years. Another prominent enterprise to which he gives a considerable time and attention is the Mossman-Yarnelle Company, a wholesale heavy hardware house of Fort Wayne, in which he has been the senior partner since 1885, when he bought out the interests of Frank Alderman. The firm was then known by the name, Alderman and Yarnelle, but with the advent of Mr. Mossman into the business it took on its present style of title. He is also president of the Dudlo Manufacturing Company, a firm that specializes in enameling copper wires and making insulation coils, and it may be said in passing that this concern is growing into one of the largest of the manufacturing industries of Fort Wayne. Financial institutions, too, have come in for a share in Mr. Mossman's attention. He is a director in the Old National Bank of Fort Wayne, and twenty-five years ago he lent material aid in the organization of the Tri-State Loan and Trust Company, of which he has been vice-president and a director ever since. In all of these enterprises no little credit is due to Mr. Mossman for the very creditable advancement that has been theirs in the years that he has been connected with them. The quality of what is usually termed "foresight," coupled with his splendid business integrity and good judgment, have resulted in a combination that seldom fails of singular success, and Mr. Mossman's associates have had reason to view their connection with him with a deal of satisfaction. Mr. Mossman, in 1868, married Miss Lois Douglas, of Whitley county, daughter of Smith Douglas, a pioneer farmer of that district. Three children are theirs—Paul, Stella and Ethel. Stella is the wife of George A. Philbrick, of Fort Wayne, and Ethel married George Jacobs, who is manager of the Dudlo Manufacturing Company. Mr. Mossman and his family are members of the Congregational church and he is a Republican, a thirty-second degree Mason, with Shrine affiliations, and a member of the Fort Wayne Commercial Club.

Raymond J. Mourey is one of the native sons of Allen county whose progressiveness has been demonstrated not only in the management of his individual business affairs but also in his liberality and public spirit as a citizen. His present fine farm of one hundred and sixty acres, in Sections 18 and 19, Jackson township, includes the old homestead on which he was born and reared, and he is a member of a sterling French pioneer family of this county, where his father established his residence in 1850. It is specially interesting to record that the father, Paul Mourey, now resides with the subject of this review and is one of the patriarchal pioneer citizens of the county: he celebrated the ninetieth anniversary of his birth on March 30, 1917. He whose name initiates this paragraph is one of the most energetic and enterprising exponents of agricultural and live-stock industry in Jackson township and has been influential in public affairs of a local order, especially in the furthering of the construction of good roads in the county, besides which he has been called upon to serve in various offices of public trust, indicating the popular appreciation of his ability and his sterling character. Mr. Mourey was born in Jackson township on August 17, 1868, a son of Paul and Frances (Vuilleman) Mourey, both of whom were born in Abbenaus, Department of Doubs, in northeastern France, where they were reared to maturity and their marriage was solemnized. As previous reference to his venerable age denotes, Paul Mourey was born in the year 1827 and was a young man of about twenty-three years when he severed the ties that bound him to his native land and set forth to seek his fortunes in America. It was in 1850 that he established his home in Allen county, and he found employment in Fort Wayne. At that time wages were diminutive, and it was not until 1862 that he had accumulated sufficient money and made such other provisions as to justify his sending for his young wife, who had remained in France until he should be able to pay the expense of her journey to America. Mrs. Mourey arrived in Fort Wayne by way of the old canal, and she and her husband then located on an embryonic farm of forty acres, in Jackson township. The land had virtually no improvements and most of the same was covered with a heavy growth of timber. Mr. Mourey worked early and late in improving the property and was eventually able to purchase an adjoining tract of forty acres. The old homestead of eighty acres, as previously stated, is now an integral part of the fine landed estate that constitutes Fairview Stock Farm, the present place of residence of the subject of this sketch. On the original homestead Paul Mourey remained until 1885, when he removed to a farm of forty acres in Jefferson township. There the wife of his youth was summoned to the life eternal on August 26, 1889, and July 29, 1891, recorded the marriage of Mr. Mourey to Rose Mougier. The second wife died, January 7, 1916, and the venerable father has since resided in the home of his son Raymond, who accords to him the deepest filial solicitude. Of the six children of the first marriage the first three died in France, as infants. Frank was the first born after the mother had come to America, and he died at the age of two years; Raymond J., of this sketch, was the next in order of birth; and Octavia died at the age of two years. No children were born of the second marriage, and thus Raymond J. is the only surviving child. To the district schools of Jackson township Mr. Mourey is indebted for his early education, which was supplemented by his attending a business college in Fort Wayne for one term. After leaving the home farm he established a general store at Payne, Paulding county, Ohio, and there continued his mercantile activities six years—or until his store was destroyed by fire, on July 4, 1898. He soon afterward returned to the old home farm in Jackson township and has increased its area until he now has a well-improved place of one hundred and sixty acres, the same being devoted to diversified agriculture and to the raising of the finer type of live stock. As a stock-grower Mr. Mourey has been specially progressive and successful and thus has consistently given to his farm the title of Fairview Stock Farm. When he returned to the farm the buildings on the same were represented by a primitive log house and a pig-pen, the while a considerable part of the land was still covered with timber and underbrush. The vigor and enterprise of the owner are now evidenced in a commodious modern house of cement-block construction, a fine barn and other substantial farm buildings, all of which have been erected by Mr. Mourey, who has installed also an effective system of tile drainage, built good fences and otherwise shown his spirit of thrift and his good judgment. He has been one of the active and influential figures in the Allen county ranks of the Democratic party and for ten years was a member of the Jackson township Democratic committee. From 1901 to 1905 he was a member of the advisory committee of the township and thereafter served four years as township trustee, with marked loyalty and efficiency. Since 1914 he has held the office of county ditch commissioner. He was one of the foremost advocates and supporters of the good-roads movement in Jackson township and, with the loyal co-operation of four or five other progressive men of the township, succeeded in getting from the county an appropriation for the construction of twenty-one miles of stone road in Jackson township. The land of the township is largely prairie soil, and while specially fertile was in large part originally of low level, so that proper drainage has been necessary, while the construction of stone roads was almost imperative if the township was to come fully into its own. Mr. Mourey is an appreciative and valued member of the French-American Society in Fort Wayne—in fact, is a charter member of the same. He and his family are communicants of the Besancon St. Louis Catholic church, on the Ridge road. On April 26, 1892, was solemnized the marriage of Mr. Mourey to Miss Ellen Lamont, who likewise was born and reared in Allen county and who, like himself, is of sterling French lineage. Mrs. Mourey is a daughter of Alphonse and Victoria (Gladieaux) Lamont, the former of whom was born in Alsace-Lorraine, France, and the latter in Stark county, Ohio. Alphonse Lamont was four years of age when the family came to America and has been a resident of Allen county since his youth, his marriage having here been solemnized. His home is near the Besancon Catholic church, in Jefferson township, and he has for many years been one of the representative farmers of that township, where he is known and honored as a venerable pioneer citizen at the present day, his devoted wife having passed away, May 21, 1901. Of their children the first, Louis, died at the age of two years; Charles is a farmer in Jefferson township; Mrs. Mourey, wife of the subject of this review, was the third child; Mrs. Ida Maire resides in Trumbull county, Ohio; Justin resides on the old homestead farm, of which he has the management; Mrs. Rosalie Burns resides in Jackson township; John and Clement are engaged in the automobile trade in Fort Wayne; and Ernest and Clarence still reside in Jefferson township. All of the children are married except John. In conclusion is entered brief record concerning the children of Mr. and Mrs. Mourey: Leonard R., born October 10, 1893, is a resident of Jackson township. He married Miss Eva Dodane, and their one child is a daughter, Helen. Amelia E., born January 7, 1895, is the wife of Arthur Oberley, of Jefferson township, and they have a daughter, Esther. Cecelia R., born June 17, 1898, remains at the parental home and is a successful and popular teacher in the district schools of Jackson township. Paul A., born May 17, 1901, and Edna E., born July 21, 1903, remain at the parental home; Clarence was born June 7, 1911, and died on the 14th of the same month; Francis L., born January 24, 1909, is the youngest member of the gracious family circle of the parental home.

John J. Muir.—A signally varied and interesting career has been that of this Fort Wayne scion of fine old Scottish ancestry, and his special technical ability has brought to him positions of distinctive executive responsibility. Since the early part of 1897, with the exception of an interim of six years, he has held the office of mechanical superintendent of the Bass Foundry and Machine Company, one of the most important industrial and commercial concerns lending prestige to the city of Fort Wayne. Mr. Muir was born in Waterford, Ireland, of Scottish parentage, and was a child at the time of his parents' removal to the fine old city of Glasgow, Scotland, where as a boy and youth he was afforded the advantages of Blythswood Academy. He furthered his technical education by effective courses of study in Andersonian University and the College of Science and Arts, besides taking a course in naval architecture in Glasgow University. Thoroughness and mature judgment have dominated his course from his youth to the present time, and thus he consistently served a definite and effective apprenticeship in the line of marine engineering, his privileges in this field having been given him in the representative establishment of the firm of Muir and Houston, of Glasgow, of which his father was the senior member. After completing his apprenticeship he gained somewhat more than two years' practical experience in sea-going engineering on trans-Atlantic passenger steamers. He then assumed a position in the engine-drafting department of the famous Fairfield Shipbuilding and Engineering Company's works, in the city of Glasgow, and later received appointment to the position of deputy superintending engineer under a three-year contract or agreement with the India General Steam Navigation Company, of Calcutta, East India. On completing his term of service in this responsible position Mr. Muir became the incumbent of the office of assistant manager with the firm of John King and Company, Limited, shipbuilders and general contractors and engineers, at Howrah, Bengal, India. The conditions in the Orient caused his health finally to become so much impaired that he was virtually compelled to relinquish the position last mentioned, and, in 1893, he came to the United States and established his residence in Fort Wayne. For two and one-half years he was employed in the engineering department and drafting room of the Fort Wayne Electric Works, and then, in June, 1895, assumed the position of draftsman in the great Fort Wayne plant of the Bass Foundry and Machine Company. Early in 1897 he was appointed mechanical superintendent for this company, of which important office he is the incumbent at the present time, though from 1901 to 1907 he was in the employ of other concerns. During this interval he served successively as mechanical engineer for the Sun Oil Company, at Marcus Hook, Pennsylvania, and steam expert engineer with the American Sheet and Tin Plate Company, a subsidiary concern of the United States Steel Corporation. On January 6, 1898, he was married to Mrs. Lee Ella Dodez-Nutting, daughter of Mr. and Mrs. G. C. Dodez, of this city, who died May 9, 1899. There were no children by this marriage. December 25, 1907, at Trinity Episcopal church, Pittsburgh, he was married to Miss Elizabeth S. White, whose father was a prominent journalist of Glasgow, Scotland. There are three daughters by this marriage—Elizabeth R., Janet J. and Alice M. Mr. Muir has been for a long period an active member of the American Society of Mechanical Engineers, the American Association for the Advancement of Science and the Engineers' Society of Western Pennsylvania. He is a thorough cosmopolitan, as the foregoing brief record fully indicates; is a man of fine intellectual attainments and technical knowledge, and his genial personality has gained to him the staunchest of friends in the business and social circles of Fort Wayne.

Henry W. Muldoon.—When the father of Henry W. Muldoon came from his native land in his young manhood, he settled promptly in Marion township and there acquired three hundred acres of farm land in that community and applied himself with all diligence to the task of making a productive farm of it. He succeeded in his efforts most admirably and was known among the most successful farmers of the township for many years. He was Henry Muldoon and his wife was Jane Drew, and they came from Ireland as young people. They were ardent Catholics and Mr. Muldoon was a Democrat in politics from the time of his coming to America to the end of his days. They reared a family of nine children. Alice, the first born, became the wife of Louis Miller, of Wells county. Mary married Marcellus Rauner and both are deceased. Henry W., the subject of this brief review, was the third born. Charles came next and is a farmer in Marion township. Jane is the wife of Isadore Rauner, of Fort Wayne. Elliott lives in Pleasant township. Elizabeth is the widow of William Drew, of Fort Wayne. William is located in Chicago and Albert is a resident of Fort Wayne. Henry W. Muldoon had his early schooling in Marion township and followed that with attendance at the Brothers' School in Fort Wayne. He early identified himself with farm work in an independent capacity and his first purchase was a place of one hundred and twenty acres in Marion township, to which he has added fifty-seven acres, all of which is in an excellent state of improvement and is highly productive, yielding its owner a nice profit annually. Mr. Muldoon has made many attractive improvements in the various buildings on his place, and the tenor of the farm is of a decidedly upward tendency. Mr. Muldoon is a Democrat in politics and a member of the Roman Catholic church. He was married on January 16, 1883, to Miss Gertrude Herber, daughter of Garrett and Gertrude (Wolf) Herber, farmers of Marion township for many years, and both now deceased. Five children were born to Mr. and Mrs. Muldoon. Elva is the wife of Hubert Clever, of Pleasant township; Frank is his father's able assistant on the home farm; Oliver and Marie are also at home, and Grover, the youngest, died at the age of twenty years. Elva is the mother of three children—Farma, Ena and Violet, while Frank, who married Dora Fox, has two children—Beulah, born March 11, 1916, and Delbert, born June 10, 1917. Oliver married Marguerite Barva, daughter of Joseph Farmer, of Cedar Creek township.

Samuel E. Mulholland.—Fort Wayne has enrolled among its "live-wire" younger business men Samuel E. Mulholland. Identified with every public movement which has marked the progress of the city since he came to Fort Wayne, in 1908, he has assisted in the lasting and substantial movements enabling the city to hold its place among the live communities of the country. Mr. Mulholland is a native son of Indiana and has made his way forward to a status of prominence and influence in connection with important business affairs in Fort Wayne, where he is vice-president of the Northern Indiana Gas and Electric Company, besides being general manager of its southern division. Mr. Mulholland was born in Cass county, Indiana, on September 13, 1866, a son of Henry and Mary A. (Panabaker) Mulholland, the former of whom was born in Belfast, Ireland, and the latter at Lancaster, Ohio. The father was long engaged in the sawmill and general lumbering business and was a resident of Logansport, Cass county, at the time of his death, his widow still maintaining her home in that city. Samuel E. Mulholland is their only child. After having made good use of the advantages afforded in the public schools of Logansport, Mr. Mulholland became actively associated with the newspaper business in that city, where he was employed with the old Logansport Journal. After his retirement from this alliance with journalistic enterprise he held for several years an executive position in the First National Bank of Logansport. The ensuing five or six years found him engaged as chief bookkeeper for the firm of Wiler and Wise, of Logansport, and, in 1895, he allied himself with the Murdock gas interests in the same city. Later he was transferred to Lima, Ohio, where he continued his association with the same concern for seven years. For two years thereafter he had charge of the street railway system of South Bend, Indiana. In 1908 he came to Fort Wayne, where he succeeded Henry C. Paul as the general manager of the system of gas supply which had previously been controlled by the Fort Wayne Gas Company and its successor, the Indiana Lighting Company. His alliance was continued at the time the property was purchased by the Northern Indiana Gas and Electric Company, of which he became vice-president, as well as general manager of the southern division, in March, 1916. The corporation owns and operates ten or more gas, electric-light and water-power plants in the state. Within the period of his residence in Fort Wayne Mr. Mulholland has become interested also in local real estate, in which he has made judicious investments. He is also a member of the directorate of the German-American National Bank of Fort Wayne. His political allegiance is given to the Democratic party. He has received the thirty-second degree of the Ancient Accepted Rite of the Masonic fraternity, as well as being affiliated with the Mystic Shrine, the Benevolent and Protective Order of Elks, and the Commercial, Rotary and Quest Clubs of Fort Wayne. On October 20, 1892, was solemnized the marriage of Mr. Mulholland to Miss Flora Murdock, daughter of Andrew J. and Margaret (Chadwick) Murdock, of Logansport. Andrew J. Murdock was for many years one of the influential capitalists and business men of Logansport, where he had been engaged in the mercantile business and where he was president of the First National Bank for a long time prior to his death. Mr. and Mrs. Mulholland have two sons—Andrew Murdock and Henry Eric.

J. Frank Mungovan has been influential in governmental affairs in his native city and county and has also become prominently identified with local business interests. In 1905 he was elected city clerk of Fort Wayne, and after serving four years in this important municipal office there came to him further manifestation of popular confidence and esteem, in that he was elected municipal judge, an office of which he continued the incumbent four years and in which he gave a most effective administration. Further interest attaches to his career by reason of the fact that he is a representative of a family that was founded in Fort Wayne more than sixty years ago, as indicated by the fact that here his birth occurred on August 11, 1857. He is now associated with James Ryan in the ownership of one of the leading undertaking establishments in Fort Wayne, and the well-appointed headquarters of the firm of Mungovan and Ryan is at 1908-10 Calhoun street. Mr. Mungovan is a son of Thomas and Mary (Fox) Mungovan, both of whom are now deceased. The father was born in Ireland and the mother in Lancaster, Pennsylvania. Thomas Mungovan was a skilled artisan and was employed as a tool dresser in the shops of the Wabash Railroad about fifty-five years. He was one of the venerable and honored citizens of Fort Wayne at the time of his death, in 1914, and of his fine family of ten children all are living, except one. To the parochial and public schools of Fort Wayne J. Frank Mungovan is indebted for his early educational training, and as a youth he found employment in a local grocery establishment. In service for others and in independent business he continued his association with the retail grocery trade in Fort Wayne for a quarter of a century. He then entered the employ of the McCormick Harvester Company and was with this great Chicago corporation for four years after its business had been consolidated with others to constitute the International Harvester Company. Soon after this, in 1905, he was elected city clerk of Fort Wayne, and in this capacity and that of judge of the city court he continued in the municipal service for a consecutive period of eight years. In 1914 he purchased an interest in the undertaking business of James Ryan, with whom he has since been associated under the firm name of Mungovan and Ryan. He is a stalwart in the local camp of the Republican party, he and his family are communicants of St. Patrick's Catholic church, and he is affiliated with the Knights of Columbus, the Ancient Order of Hibernians and the Holy Name Society of St. Patrick's parish. On May 20, 1886, was solemnized the marriage of Mr. Mungovan to Miss Caroline Fry, who likewise was born and reared in Fort Wayne and is a daughter of Jacob and Mary (Phillips) Fry, both now deceased. Mr. and Mrs. Mungovan have eight children. Genevieve is the widow of Frank J. Kindler and resides in Fort Wayne; Harry, Raymond and Donald are all married and well established in life; and at the parental home remain Magdalene, Franklin and Caroline, who are twins, and Thomas, who is the youngest of the number.

Adolph C. Muntzinger.—Adolph C. Muntzinger, proprietor of the furniture establishment in Fort Wayne that bears his name, was born in Van Wert county, Ohio, December 15, 1880, a son of Ernest and Elizabeth (Stamm) Muntzinger. The father was born in Germany and came to America in 1865, locating in Van Wert county and engaging in farming. He married there and reared a family of five children, all living but one. The parents still live on their farm in Ohio, and are active and hale for people of their years. Adolph Muntzinger had his early education in the public schools of his native county, finished the high school course of his home town, and then entered college. When he was twenty-one years old he came to Fort Wayne and found employment with the Indiana Furniture Company for the ensuing five years, after which he went to Bryan, Ohio, and there engaged in the furniture business on his own responsibility. After three years he disposed of the business, returned to Fort Wayne and established the Muntzinger Furniture Company, which he has since conducted very successfully, his place being recognized throughout the county as one of the thoroughly up-to-the-minute furniture stores of the city. Mr. Muntzinger is a member of the Lutheran church and in politics is a Democrat. He was married May 17, 1917, to Clara, daughter of Joseph Brudi, of New Haven.

Abel L. Murchland.—The late Abel L. Murchland was a native Virginian, born there on December 29, 1856, and he was a son of James and Martha M. (James) Murchland, also born in that state. The parents moved into Adams county, Indiana, when their son, Abel, was a small child, and settled on a farm, but later came to Allen county, where they ended their days after quiet and uneventful lives of farmer folk. They reared a family of thirteen children, of which number four are living at this time. Abel Murchland was reared in Allen county and there had such education as he was privileged to gather. He was married, in 1885, to Miss Jennie C. Erwin, a daughter of R. K. and Margaret (Armstrong) Erwin, both of Ohio birth and parentage. Their daughter, Jennie, was born in Allen county, whence they came soon after their marriage, and where they passed the rest of their lives. Mr. and Mrs. Murchland, after their marriage, followed the custom of impecunious couples of country origin, and, having no farm of their own, rented one. They were able to save enough in a few years to purchase a farm in Monroe township and that place still represents the family home. It is a prosperous place of eighty acres, with comfortable dwelling and other buildings, and has been highly improved in every respect. Seven children were born to Mr. and Mrs. Murchland there. They are Richard Lee, now deceased; Frank E.; Dottie B., the wife of Walter Barkley; Ross K.; Guy F., who is farming the homestead; Mildred A. and Mary M. The husband and father died on January 6, 1913, at the comparatively early age of fifty-seven years. He was a lifelong member of the United Brethren church, and his family likewise are adherents of that faith.

Darwin S. Myers has been a resident of Fort Wayne from the time of his birth and for more than thirty years he has been in the employ of what is now designated as the Fort Wayne Department of the General Electric Company, in the gigantic plant of which he is the executive head of the alternator section. Through the various changes that have marked the up-building of the most important industrial enterprise in Fort Wayne Mr. Myers has continued his services with marked efficiency and his technical and executive ability have not lacked consistent recognition, as indicated by the important position of which he is now the incumbent. Mr. Myers is the youngest in a family of three children, the eldest, Meigs, being deceased, and Herschel. The parents, Dr. William H. and Mary Ann (Van Swenger) Myers, were natives of Ohio and established their home in Fort Wayne in the year 1851, the remainder of their lives being passed in this city, where Dr. Myers, a man of fine scientific and professional attainments, gained precedence as one of the most distinguished physicians and surgeons of Indiana. It is a matter of record in medical history that he performed the first Caesarian operation in Indiana, the same being the third delicate operation of this type to be recorded as performed in the entire world. Darwin S. Myers acquired his youthful education in the Fort Wayne schools and was further fortified by having been reared in a home of distinctive culture and refinement. He initiated his active business career as an employe in the Meyer Brothers drug establishment, with which he remained two years, and in 1884 he found employment in the plant of the Fort Wayne Electric Company, his connection with the concern having been consecutive during the intervening years and his being now secure status as one of the able and valued executives in the local establishment of the General Electric Company. Though he takes loyal interest in public affairs and all that touches the welfare of his native city, Mr. Myers is independent in politics and has had no desire to become a candidate for public office. Both he and his wife hold membership in the Methodist Episcopal church. On December 3, 1891, was solemnized the marriage of Mr. Myers to Miss May Mahin, who was born and reared in Indiana, and who is a daughter of Rev. A. E. and Catherine Mahin, the former of whom is deceased and the latter of whom now resides in Huntington, this state. For six years Rev. Mahin was presiding elder of the conference district that includes Allen county, and he was the revered pastor of the Wayne Street Methodist Episcopal church for several years. Mrs. Myers is the youngest in a family of five children; John W. is now a resident of Denver, Colorado; Sadie is the wife of C. E. Smith, of Moores Hill, Dearborn county, Indiana; Elizabeth is the wife of M. W. Kimball, of North Dakota; and Schuyler is deceased. Mr. and Mrs. Myers became the parents of four children—Mary, Catherine, Ruth E., Darwin S., Jr., and Elizabeth Jane. All are living except Ruth E., who died in early childhood.

Charles J. Naughton is one of the three interested principals in the partnership concern that conducts a loan and credit business under the title of the Fort Wayne Credit Company, and special attention is given to real estate loans and the handling of securities of diversified order. He was born in the city of Lafayette, Tippecanoe county, Indiana, March 10, 1890, and is a son of Daniel and Mary (West) Naughton, who were born and reared in the city of Albany, New York, where their marriage was solemnized. Upon coming to the west the father was for a time engaged in the retail grocery business in the city of Chicago, and later he became one of the prominent business men of Lafayette, Indiana, where he and his wife still reside and where he is now living virtually retired. Of the children the subject of this review is the youngest; Agnes is the wife of Chester Kitch, of Fort Wayne; John resides in the city of Indianapolis; and William remains at the parental home, the religious faith of the family being that of the Catholic church. After completing the curriculum of the Catholic parochial schools of his native city, Charles J. Naughton there continued his studies in the high school and later took a course in the Union Business College, one of the excellent institutions of Lafayette. He came to Fort Wayne in 1909 and entered the employ of the Fort Wayne Credit Company, in which he was later admitted to partnership; the other two principals at the present time being his father-in-law, Sherman Stults, and O. W. Lake. Mr. Naughton is a Democrat in politics, is affiliated with the Ancient Order of Hibernians and the Benevolent & Protective Order of Elks, and both he and his wife are communicants of the Cathedral parish of the Catholic church. On April 26, 1911, was solemnized the marriage of Mr. Naughton to Miss Virginia Stults, a daughter of Sherman and Ione (Windle) Stults, who maintain their home at Huntington, Indiana. Mr. and Mrs. Naughton have one child, William S., who was born August 7, 1912.

Herman C. Neilsberg, who holds the office of manager for the firm of Walsh and Company, engaged in general insurance business in Fort Wayne, has proved himself a young man of versatility and has been identified with various business concerns of important order, the while he has developed marked resourcefulness as an executive and capable man of business. Herman Charles Neilsberg was born in the city of Chicago, Illinois, on February 5, 1880, a scion of fine Swedish ancestry on both the paternal and distaff sides. His parents, Samuel and Matilda (Anderson) Neilsberg, were both born in Sweden and came to America about half a century ago, when they were young. The parents still reside in Chicago, where the father is living retired, after a successful career as a contractor in that city. He was educated in Germany, his father having been a lawyer by profession and connected with the diplomatic service between Sweden and Germany. The maternal ancestors of the subject of this review were prominently identified with the military service of Sweden, and one of his uncles was a captain in the Swedish army. Mr. Neilsberg was the second in order of birth in a family of four children; Jennie S. is the wife of Theodore Hass, of Chicago; Hattie M. remains at the parental home; and Minnie is the wife of Earl L. Garns, of Chicago. Herman C. Neilsberg profited by the advantages of the public schools of his native city, including the Hyde Park high school, and thereafter took a one year's course in Armour Institute and a law course in the LaSalle University, in 1910. Prior to having fortified himself by his study in the latter Chicago institution he had held various positions in his native city—principally of clerical order. In 1900 he was employed in the Chicago general offices of the Illinois Central Railroad and in 1902 was similarly employed at Elkhart, Indiana, in the service of the New York Central Lines. From 1903 to 1907 he was a clerical executive in the offices of the Hawley-Downdraft Furnace Company, of Chicago, of which he became assistant secretary. On account of impaired health he resigned this office, in 1907, and returned to Elkhart, Indiana, where he engaged in the real estate and insurance business. There he remained thus engaged until the spring of 1913, when he came to Fort Wayne and entered the employ of the firm of Walsh and Company, of which he is now manager. By reason of the service of his maternal ancestors and relatives Mr. Neilsberg apparently inherited a predilection for military affairs. At least it is to be recorded that, in 1898, he enlisted as a member of the celebrated First Infantry Regiment of the Illinois National Guard, at the inception of the Spanish-American war, and after the mobilization at Camp Lincoln, at Springfield, was transferred to the First Illinois Cavalry, with which he was mustered into the United States service and with which he served until the close of the war. Thereafter he continued an active member of the First Cavalry Regiment of the Illinois National Guard until 1903, when he was honorably discharged, by reason of leaving the state. Mr. Neilsberg is loyal and progressive as a citizen but is not constrained by strict partisan lines in politics. He has the staunchest of friends in both business and social circles.

Samuel W. Newell, president and manager of the Indiana Paint and Varnish Company, was born in Ontario, Canada, August 1, 1870, son of James and Nancy (Johnson) Newell, natives of Canada, where they passed their entire lives. They were the parents of five children, four of whom are living at this time. Samuel Newell had a common school education, passing through high school, and he had his first introduction to the hardware business in 1893, when he came to Detroit from Ontario and continued there until 1904. During six years of that time he was engaged as a traveling salesman in the paint and varnish line and in that time gained a thorough knowledge of the business, so that he was particularly well qualified to launch a business venture of his own when he came to Fort Wayne, in 1905 ,and engaged in the sale of paint and varnish under the firm name of the Indiana Paint and Varnish Company. He became president of the concern and has since continued in that office, as well as having charge of the business of the firm in a managerial capacity. This is one of the thriving concerns of its kind in Fort Wayne and its success may properly be said to be due to the efforts of Mr. Newell. On December 27, 1905, Mr. Newell was married to Miss Anna M. Swayze, daughter of John P. and Sophronia Swayze, Michigan people still resident there. Four children have been born to the Newells—James S., Samuel Foster, John D. and Rae C. Mr. and Mrs. Newell have membership in the Third Presbyterian church of Fort Wayne and he is clerk of the church at the present time. He is a thirty-second degree Mason and a member of the Quest Club of Fort Wayne, as well as being a member of the Commercial Club.

Herman C. Nieter, who now holds precedence as one of the vigorous and successful exponents of the agricultural and live-stock industry in St. Joseph township, was born in Germany, on January 1, 1850, and in the following year his parents came to America and established their home in Allen county, where he has continued to reside during the long intervening years and where he has contributed his quota to civic and industrial development and progress. Mr. Nieter is a son of Christian and Dorothy (Horstmeyer) Nieter, the latter of whom died within a comparatively few years after the home had been established in Allen county, Indiana, the subject of this review being the younger of the two children, and his brother Henry being now a resident of Fort Wayne. The father ultimately contracted a second marriage and of the same were born three children—Christ, Frederick and Minnie, Frederick being deceased. He whose name introduces this sketch acquired his early education in the public schools of Fort Wayne and after attaining to years of maturity engaged in the trucking business in that city. With this line of enterprise he continued to be identified until 1912, when he purchased his present farm of eighty acres, eligibly situated in St. Joseph township and five and a half miles distant from Fort Wayne, on rural mail route No. 15 from that city. He has made many substantial improvements on the place, including the erection of a good barn, the building of proper fences and the installing of a system of tile drainage. In connection with general agricultural enterprises Mr. Nieter is proving successful also in the raising of Shorthorn cattle, Poland-China swine and Bronze turkeys. In politics Mr. Nieter is found arrayed as a supporter of the principles of the Democratic party, he is a Protestant in his religious views, and in the city of Fort Wayne maintains affiliation with the lodges of the Benevolent and Protective

Order of Elks and the Independent Order of Odd Fellows. On June 2, 1882, was solemnized the marriage of Mr. Nieter to Miss Lizette Stillhorn, who was born and reared in this county, and of the three children of this union—Grace, William and Edward—only the one daughter is living.

Charles M. Niezer has the intellectual and technical equipment that has enabled him to achieve success and prestige as one of the representative members of the bar of his native county. He is engaged in the practice of his profession in Fort Wayne. He is a scion of the third generation of the Niezer family in Allen county, where his paternal grandfather, a native of Germany, settled in the pioneer days and became one of the county's staunch exponents of civic and industrial development and progress. The family has been one of prominence and influence in the county during a period of fully three-fourths of a century. Charles M. Niezer was born at Monroeville, Monroe township, this county, on March 31, 1877, a son of John Bernard Niezer and Sarah T. (Eyanson) Niezer. Both parents died in Fort Wayne, the father, September 15, 1912, and the mother, December 16, 1915. The names of the six children of the family are here designated in the respective order of birth. John T., Maurice C., Charles M., Louise H. Kroeff, George B., and Marguerite C. Andrews. John Bernard Niezer was born in Milan township, this county, July 21, 1846. He became one of the influential citizens of his native county, where he achieved worthy success through his active association with mercantile enterprise and the banking business. As a supporter of the principles of the Democratic party he was a prominent figure in local politics and served many years as township trustee. Popular confidence and esteem were further shown in his selection to the office of county auditor, of which important position he was the efficient incumbent for a term of four years—1886-90. He was the organizer of the Citizens' State Bank of Monroeville, the first banking institution founded in Allen county outside of the city of Fort Wayne. He served as president of that bank from the time of its incorporation until his death. During the closing years of his life he lived virtually retired in Fort Wayne. He was one of the organizers of the German-American National Bank and the German-American Trust Company, and was a director of each at the time of his death. Sarah T. Niezer, the mother, was born in Philadelphia, Pennsylvania, March 22, 1845, of a pioneer family. Her ancestors were among the first settlers in the colony of Maryland and served as soldiers in the Revolutionary war. Both father and mother were sincere communicants of the Catholic church. Charles M. Niezer acquired his preliminary education in the public and parochial schools of his native county and his higher academic advantages were of the best order, as he pursued his studies not only in the great Notre Dame University at South Bend but also in the University of Indiana, at Bloomington. In preparation for his chosen profession he entered Columbia University, in New York city, and was graduated as a member of the class of 1901, with the degree of Master of Arts. He had previously received the degrees of Bachelor of Arts and Laws. Admitted to the bar of his native state, in 1901, Mr. Niezer forthwith engaged in the general practice of his profession in Fort Wayne, and his energy, ambition and ability have gained for him success. Mr. Niezer is aligned as a loyal and effective advocate of the cause of the Democratic party, he is affiliated with the Knights of Columbus and the Benevolent and Protective Order of Elks, and both he and his wife are communicants of the Fort Wayne Cathedral parish of the Catholic church. On October 18, 1906, was solemnized the marriage of Mr. Niezer to Miss Rose Fox, daughter of Louis and Sophie (Lau) Fox, of Fort Wayne, and they have three children, whose names and respective dates of birth are here indicated: Louis Fox, September 10, 1907; Rosemary Lau, May 6, 1909; and Margaret Sarah, September 3, 1910.

Maurice C. Niezer.—It was in the year 1843 that the German ancestors of Maurice C. Niezer emigrated from Germany and settled in Allen county, Indiana, there engaging in farming activities. They were Bernard H. and Christinea Niezer, born in 1809 and 1816, respectively. Of their seven children, John B. was the fourth, born on July 21, 1846, and he was the father of the subject. He was seven years of age when he accompanied his parents to Fort Wayne, and such schooling as John Niezer had was gained between then and his fourteenth year, for when he was fourteen years old he was apprenticed to a tinner in Fort Wayne. When he had completed his apprenticeship he worked at the trade of a tinsmith for seven years, quitting the work, in 1866, to settle in Monroeville, where he established a small hardware business. He was successful, but withdrew in later years from that field to establish himself in the hay, grain and coal business, in 1886. That enterprise, too, was high prosperous, and his sons—Maurice C., first named in this brief family review, and George B.—are today in control of the business established by their father. John Niezer was a man prominent in his community as long as he lived. He served his township as a trustee for a term of three years, succeeding himself in the office in 1882, and for seven years he was treasurer of the Monroeville school board. In September, 1886, he was nominated by the Democratic party from six candidates for nomination for the office of County Auditor and was elected by a very comfortable majority. He served the county most capably in that office, and when he retired there was none who had aught but praise for his official record. Mr. Niezer was married, in 1869, to Miss Sarah T. Eyanson, who was born in Philadelphia in 1846, and six children were born to them: John T., Maurice C., Charles M., Louisa H., George B. and Marguerite C. Maurice C. Niezer was born in Monroeville, Allen county, August 23, 1874, and was reared in that community. He attended the schools of his home community and when he had finished his high school training took a course of study in the McDermott-Whiteleather Business College at Fort Wayne, graduating in 1893. His first position was in the employ of his father, who was then engaged in the wool, hay and grain business, and he continued there, studying the work from all sides. In 1909 he moved to Fort Wayne and incorporated the business, his father having in that year turned the reins of management over to him and his brother, George B. They have since that time branched out considerably and today conduct a thriving business in hay, grain, seed and coal. The father died, September 15, 1912. Mr. Niezer, in common with others of the family, is an adherent of the Roman Catholic faith and attends the Fort Wayne Catholic Cathedral. He is also a member of the Knights of Columbus and of the Elks. He is a Democrat in politics and is unmarried at this time.

Daniel B. Ninde is one of the genial and successful attorneys of Fort Wayne, where he was born July 28, 1870. His parents were Lindley M. and Beulah (Puckett) Ninde, the former of whom was long a distinguished and able lawyer of the Allen county bar. Daniel B. was educated in the schools of his native city and there entered the United States naval academy at Anapolis, where he graduated in 1891. Being one of the honor men of his class he was permitted to resign in accordance with the regulations then prevailing. Succeeding this he attended at Harvard one year and after another year at the University of Michigan he graduated in the College of Law. Thus admirably equipped he took up the practice of law in the office of his father and brother, at Fort Wayne. This partnership continued until 1907, so far as his brother was concerned, but the father passed to the life eternal in 1901. He was elected prosecuting attorney for Allen county in 1904 and filled that office for two years. Mr. Ninde has preferred the quiet and orderly life of a private citizen and has not sought for higher political preferment. At the present time he is attorney for the Lincoln Life Insurance Company, one of the foremost institutions of its kind in the middle west. He has been three times married. The first time was with Rose, daughter of Prof. I. N. Demmon, of Ann Arbor, Michigan. His second wife was Mary C. Coe, of Durham, New Hampshire, a prominent family that came to New England in early colonial days. His marriage with his present wife occurred January 18, 1913. She was Margaret Coe, a sister of Mary C. They have two children, named Murray C. and Richard. Mr. Ninde is a member of the Masonic fraternity, in which he has attained the thirty-second degree in the Scottish Rite.

Lee J. Ninde, who is now giving his attention principally to the real estate business, achieved secure status as one of the representative younger members of the bar of his native city and county prior to entering upon his present business activities and as a lawyer he well upheld the prestige of the family name, his father having been for many years one of the distinguished members of the bar of Allen county and having served for a number of terms on the bench of the superior court of the county. Lee J. Ninde was born in Fort Wayne on January 8, 1874, a son of Judge Lindley M. and Beulah C. (Puckett) Ninde, the former a native of Warren county, Ohio, and the latter of Winchester, Randolph county, Indiana. Judge Ninde was reared and educated in the old Buckeye state and his law course was taken in Farmer's College, in the city of Cincinnati. In 1851 he established his home in Fort Wayne and here his energy, ability and sterling character gained to him definite success in his chosen profession, of which he became one of the leading representatives in northern Indiana. He was long and actively engaged in the practice of law, besides having served as judge of the superior court of the county, and he was a citizen who was influential in the civic and political affairs of this section of the state, the while he maintained inviolable hold upon popular confidence and esteem in the community that represented his home for half a century. He was a stalwart in the camp of the Republican party, a lawyer of high attainments, a loyal and public-spirited citizen and a man who ordered his course upon a lofty plane of integrity and honor. He was a birthright member of the Society of Friends, but both he and his wife were zealous members of the Presbyterian church for many years prior to their death. Mrs. Ninde died in the spring of 1892 and the Judge died in the summer of 1901—one of the venerable and revered pioneer lawyers and jurists of Allen county. Of the children the following brief record is consistently entered. Harry W. is now a resident of Laramie, Wyoming; Daniel B. is engaged in the practice of law in Fort Wayne; Lee J., of this review, was the next in order of birth; Helen died in 1882 and Jane in 1894.

Lee J. Ninde acquired his early education in the public schools of Fort Wayne and after leaving the high school became a student in historic old Phillips-Exeter Academy, at Exeter, New Hampshire. In preparing himself for his chosen profession he entered Harvard University, in which he was enrolled as a member of the class of 1895. For the ensuing twelve years he was engaged in the active general practice of his profession in Fort Wayne and within this period appeared in connection with much important litigation in the various courts. Upon his retirement from the work of his profession he brought his powers effectively to bear in the real estate business, of which he has continued a prominent, successful and progressive representative. In 1910 Mr. Ninde organized the Wildwood Builders' Company, of which he became president, and this company has carried forward the development and upbuilding of one of the finest suburban residential districts of Fort Wayne. He is a member of the Fort Wayne Real Estate Board, the Indiana Real Estate Association, and the National Real Estate Association. He has served as president of the local board and also as president of the Indiana Real Estate Association. His political allegiance is given to the Republican party, he is affiliated with the Masonic fraternity and the Knights of Pythias, and is a loyal and valued member of the Fort Wayne Commercial Club and the Fort Wayne Country Club. On October 8, 1900, was solemnized the marriage of Mr. Ninde to Miss Joel A. Roberts, daughter of Willis and Moffett (Peacock) Roberts, of Mobile, Alabama. Mrs. Ninde, a woman of most gracious personality, became a popular factor in the leading social life of Fort Wayne, and here her death occurred, March 7, 1916, no children having been born of the union.

Emil Nitzsche, who has been a resident of Washington township and identified conspicuously with its agricultural activities since 1899, is of foreign birth and ancestry, claiming Jahna, in Germany, as his birthplace, His natal day was April 17, 1864, and he is the son of, William and Herenia (Auerche) Nitzsche, both of them born in Germany, and the father died there in 1874. The mother is still a resident of their native community and has married a second time. Emil Nitzsche was the second child of his mother's first marriage. The others were Ernestine, Amelia and Franz, all deceased. There are three children of the second marriage—Ida, Emma and Anna, all living at this time. Emil Nitzsche had his education in Germany. He was eighteen years old when he came to America, settling in Allen county, Indiana, in 1882. He was first employed in a brass foundry in Fort Wayne and spent fourteen years in that work. He came to Washington township, in 1899, settling on a small farm in Section 28. He has farmed prosperously and today has a farm of eighty acres, finely improved, and representative of the most modern methods in agriculture. Dairy farming constitutes his principal interest and his Holstein and Jersey cattle are among the finest to be found in the county. Mr. Nitzsche married on May 19, 1887. He chose Louisa Beineke, daughter of Henry and Fredericka (Powers) Beineke for his wife. Seven children have been born to them. Frank married Clara Korstman and they have two children—Robert and Herbert. Anna became the wife of Charles Weise and they have a daughter named Ruth. William and George were twins and are both deceased. William grew to young manhood and was in his twenty-second year when death called him, but George was an infant of three months when he died. Marguerite is the wife of Monroe Clapstattle. Esther and Elsie married brothers, Robert and George Fritz. Neither has children. Mr.

Nitzsche is a member of the Bruederlicher Verein at Fort Wayne and, with his wife and children, is a member of the German Lutheran church. He takes no active part in politics beyond the dictates of good citizenship.

Harry C. Offutt is an ambitious and progressive young man who has gained prominence and success as a civil engineer of special ability and aggressiveness, and it has been within his province to achieve status as one of the thoroughly representative business men maintaining headquarters in the city of Fort Wayne. Here, in February, 1914, he became associated in the organizing of the Indiana Engineering and Construction Company, and there is no medium of inconsistency in stating that this has become one of the important and specially successful corporations of its kind in the Hoosier state. Retaining in its employ a force of two hundred persons, including five skilled civil and mechanical engineers, the company has from the beginning stood exponent of energy, circumspection and progressive policies, with the result that it has completed many important contracts in the line of civil, mechanical and electrical engineering work and also in the construction of high-grade buildings of the most modern type, among which there may be mentioned the following Fort Wayne structures: The Gates and the Gauntt buildings, two of the most modern business blocks in the city; the Boys' Cathedral School, the large barn of the Fort Wayne Transfer Company, three buildings of the plant of the General Electric Company at Fort Wayne, Indiana, and the large barn of the Brown Transfer Company. Besides this the company has constructed seven fine bridges on the line of the Fort Wayne and Northern Indiana Railway. The company has the best of facilities for the completion of the largest contracts in its domain of enterprise and is contributing materially to the business prestige of Fort Wayne. Operations are based on a capital stock of ten thousand dollars, the company is incorporated under the Indiana laws, and Mr. Offutt is its president and treasurer. Harry C. Offutt was born in Mercer county, Pennsylvania, January 18, 1882, and was but two years old at the time of the death of his father, Thomas P. Offutt, who had been a prominent merchant in the county mentioned. Harry C. Offutt obtained his early education in the public schools of his native county and thereafter completed a thorough course in civil engineering at the Pennsylvania State College, in which institution he was graduated as a member of the class of 1905. Thereafter he was engaged for a time in professional work in the city of Pittsburgh, after which he was for four months the incumbent of a position in the office of the chief engineer of the Grand Rapids and Indiana Railroad, in the city of Grand Rapids, Michigan. He then established his residence in Fort Wayne and for the ensuing four years was assistant engineer of the maintenance of way department of the Southern division of the railroad just mentioned. The next four years found him as vice-president of the Beers-Offutt Construction Company, of Fort Wayne, and at the expiration of this period he became one of the organizers of the Indiana Engineering and Construction Company, of which he has since been president and treasurer and in the development of the substantial business of which he has effectively used his technical and executive ability. Mr. Offutt is a loyal and popular member of the Fort Wayne Commercial Club, and in the Masonic fraternity has received the thirty-second degree of the Scottish Rite, besides being affiliated also with the Ancient Arabic

Order, Nobles of the Mystic Shrine. He was married, in June, 1907, to Jane McKinney Magee, of Harrisville, Butler county, Pennsylvania. One boy, Harry C. Offutt, Jr., was born January 14, 1914.

Edward O'Rourke, of Fort Wayne, was born in Newark, New Jersey, October 13, 1840, and is one of eight children born to Christopher and Ellen (Flannagan) O'Rourke. He received his education in the public schools of Ohio and was also a student in the Methodist College of Fort Wayne, where he spent three years studying Latin and mathematics. He began reading law in the office of Worden & Morris, of Fort Wayne, in 1865, and the next year was admitted to the bar, since which time he has been a member at Fort Wayne. In 1867 he was elected prosecutor and served five years. After his retirement from the office of prosecutor he practiced until 1876, when he was elected judge of the Thirty-eighth district. He held this position by six successive elections for thirty-six years, and when his term expired, in 1912, he formed a partnership with Martin H. Luecke, which still continues. It is interesting to note in this connection that Judge O'Rourke served longer on the Circuit bench than any other judge in the state of Indiana. He is a member of the Allen County, Indiana State and American Bar Associations, a thirty-second degree Mason, and a Democrat in politics. The degree of Doctor of Law was conferred on the subject of this sketch by Taylor University. Judge O'Rourke married Ada L. Abrams, and they are the parents of five children: Thomas, Helen, Clara, Mary and Edward, Jr. The family home is at 420 East Washington street, Fort Wayne, Indiana..

Charles W. Orr has, in an active career of thirty years, demonstrated his ability both as a merchant and a farmer. Farming has proved more attractive to him than other lines of enterprise and he has given his undivided attention to stock farming on his fine farm of more than two hundred acres of the best land in Lafayette township. Mr. Orr was born in Carroll county, Indiana, December 9, 1861, and his parents were William and Priscilla (Die) Orr, Ohioans of Scotch-Irish parentage. The father was a farmer all his life—first in Tippecanoe county and later in Carroll county. He migrated to the latter county, in 1862, and was a pioneer settler in his community, where he bought one hundred acres of uncleared land and devoted himself tirelessly to its care and cultivation for the rest of his life. He died there in 1877, one of the most estimable men of his community and a leader among his fellows. He was a Democrat in politics and a life-long member of the Methodist Episcopal church. To him and his wife were born six children. Etta, the eldest, died in 1870. Lyda died unmarried in 1907. Charles is the immediate subject of this family review. Franklin is a resident of Lafayette township. Edward is deceased, as is also Cora, the youngest of the family, who became the wife of Noah David, of Parks Hill, Clinton county, Indiana. Charles W. Orr had his education in the public schools of Carroll county, and it is understood that his advantages in an educational way were not greater than were those of the average farm boy of his period. He was his father's assistant, as the eldest son is apt to be, and after the death of the elder Orr, in 1877, he remained on the home place and directed the work of the farm in his mother's interests. He was occupied thus until his marriage, after which he worked by the day for about two years and then rented a farm and undertook the achievement of independence. His first place was a forty-acre **farm,**

and after four years of renting he was able to buy a "forty," which he later sold for an "eighty." He continued for years to buy and sell, each time adding something to his holdings, so that since 1885 he has increased his holdings from forty to 300 acres. Trading land was more or less of a hobby with him, but he always bettered himself in a deal, it is said, and when, in 1916, he engaged in business in Bluffton, he continued long enough to prove his ability and then sold the business for a farm of one hundred and sixty acres in Wells county. His two hundred acre farm in Lafayette township is one of the show places of the village and reflects much credit upon him. Its house and barns are modern and spacious, well kept and attractive, and mark the place for one of the progressive ones of the township. Mr. Orr was married in September, 1882, to Miss Ada Blinn, daughter of Adam Blinn, an Ohio farmer, and to them have been born eleven children. Arthur is a resident of Indianapolis. Luther lives in Huntington, Indiana. Walter is on the home farm. Oliver is located in Indianapolis, where he is in the employ of the International Airship Company. Grace became the wife of Samuel Payr, of Fort Wayne. William and L. D. are at home. Anna is at present (1917) attending a business college in Fort Wayne. Frederick, Agnes and Edward are still at home. Four grandchildren have been added to the family name, as follows: Luther has a son named Mark. Walter has one child—Catherine Marie. Samuel has a son called Vernon and Oliver has one child named Irel. Mr. Orr is a Republican, and he is a member of the Methodist Episcopal church, in which his wife also has membership, and in which his family was reared. The sons and daughters of Mr. and Mrs. Orr have thus far brought only credit on the family name, and wherever they have gone have found places for themselves that speak well for their ideals and ambitions.

John F. Oswald, successful farmer and now assessor of Washington township, is the owner of the old Oswald homestead, on which he was reared and which claimed his early labors during the period in which it was being developed from a tract of wild land to a productive and profit-yielding farm. Mr. Oswald was born in Washington township on November 4, 1863, son of John M. and Sophia (Henry) Oswald, natives of Georgia and Pennsylvania, respectively. They met and married in Allen county when young people of the age of twenty years, settled on the farm where they reared their children, attained comparative material wealth and finally died. Their children were Mary E., who died in 1910, and John F., of this review. John F. Oswald had a common school training and early identified himself actively with the business of farming. With the death of his parents he came into ownership of the home place of one hundred and twenty acres, and his later labors have carried on the development work he assisted his father with in earlier years. He has enjoyed a pleasing success in his farming activities and stands well to the forefront among the prosperous farmers of his township. He was married on April 20, 1892, to Martha A. Newman, daughter of Barney and Elizabeth (Klaena) Newman. The father was a German by birth who came to Ohio and there met and married his wife. They were the parents of seven children, Mrs. Oswald being the youngest of the family. The others, named in the order of their appearance, are William, Edward (died October 3, 1911), Matilda, Louis, George and Elizabeth. The living ones are filling positions to which life has called them, in one field or another. Four children were born to Mr. and Mrs.

Oswald. They are Grace E., William McKinley, Edwin O. and James M., all living at the present writing. Mr. Oswald has been a prominent man in his township for many years and has filled the office of township assessor since 1914, when he was elected for a four-year term. Prior to his election he had served six years as deputy assessor. He is Republican in politics, a member of the Independent Order of Odd Fellows, with affiliations at Harmony, and of the Modern Woodmen of America, lodge No. 3127, at Fort Wayne. He and his family are members of the Bethany Presbyterian church in their community.

Harry E. Overmeyer, secretary and general manager of the Woodburn Tile and Brick Company, is known as one of the vigorous and progressive business men of the younger generation in his native county and has been primarily influential in the development and upbuilding of one of the most important industrial enterprises of the fine little city of Woodburn. Mr. Overmeyer was born in Maumee township, this county, on November 17, 1887, a son of George and Abbie E. (Applegate) Overmeyer, who now reside at Woodburn. George Overmeyer was born and reared in Henry county, Ohio, and his wife is a native of Allen county, Indiana, the Applegate family having been here founded in the early pioneer period of the county's history. He whose name initiates this paragraph was the third in a family of four children, and the others are Ada, Bertha and Ethel. Harry E. Overmeyer profited duly by the advantages afforded in the public schools and in connection with the enterprise with which he is now identified has shown the energy and resourcefulness that mark the truly progressive and successful business men. The Woodburn Tile and Brick Company has a fine modern plant and owns the land from which it derives the materials with which to carry on its manufacturing operations, the output capacity being one hundred and fifty thousand tile and twenty-five thousand brick per day. This company was incorporated, in 1904, with a capital stock of eighteen thousand five hundred dollars and its officers are as here noted: Henry Schleppermann, president and treasurer; Henry Cook, vice-president; and Harry E. Overmeyer, secretary and general manager. Mr. Overmeyer is loyal and progressive, not only as a business man but also as a citizen, and the popular appreciation of his attitude in the latter respect was manifested when, in the spring of 1908, he was elected a member of the village council of Woodburn, a position in which he is giving characteristically effective service. His political allegiance is given to the Republican party and he is affiliated with the lodge of Ancient Free and Accepted Masons at Harlan, as well as with the organizations of the Improved Order of Red Men and the Modern Woodmen of America at Woodburn. May 25, 1908, recorded the marriage of Mr. Overmeyer to Miss Minnie Schleppermann, who was born and reared in this county and who is a daughter of Henry and Augusta Schleppermann, who were born in Germany and now reside in their attractive home in Woodburn, this county. Mr. and Mrs. Overmeyer have two children—Mildred and Doris.

Fred B. Owen, who has demonstrated his scientific and technical ability as a well fortified electrical engineer, has been in the employ of the General Electric Company of Fort Wayne since 1903, and since the early part of the year 1916 has held a position in the standardizing department of the company's well equipped plant. He has the distinction not only of being a native of the historic old city of Providence, Rhode

Island, where he was born February 11, 1874, but he is also a scion of fine old colonial ancestry along more than one genealogical line, he being of the eighth generation in descent from Roger Williams, the first white settler within the present limits of Rhode Island. Mr. Owen is a son of John A. and Julia Estelle (Mowry) Owen, both of whom were born and reared in Rhode Island. In the public schools of his native city Mr. Owen acquired his preliminary education and in 1896 he was graduated in the celebrated Massachusetts Institute of Technology, in the city of Boston. In the same year he entered the employ of the Narragansett Electrical Company, of Providence, Rhode Island, and he continued his service in the meter department of the plant of this corporation for a period of six and one-half years, at the expiration of which, in 1903, he came to Fort Wayne and associated himself with the Fort Wayne Electric Works. In that year he took a position in the meter department, in which he continued his activities until 1916, when he was transferred to a position in the standardizing department, with the operations of which he continues to be identified. He has become a popular factor in the business and social circles of Fort Wayne, is loyal and progressive as a citizen and is independent in politics. He is serving as secretary of Home Lodge, No. 342, Ancient Free & Accepted Masons, and is affiliated also with Fort Wayne Chapter of Royal Arch Masons. On September 23, 1899, was solemnized the marriage of Mr. Owen to Miss Ida M. Tift, who was born and reared in the state of Connecticut and whose original colonial ancestors came to America on the ship Ann, a virtual companion or consort of the historic Mayflower. Mrs. Owen is a daughter of William Henry and C. Emily Jane (Mitchell) Tift, who still maintain their home in Connecticut. Mr. and Mrs. Owen have one daughter, Estelle Brown.

The Packard Piano Company.—This is one of the leading manufactories of Fort Wayne. It started, in 1871, when the Fort Wayne Organ Company was organized with a capital of $24,000 and with L. M. Ninde as president, I. T. Packard as secretary and S. B. Bond as treasurer. Those holding office on the board of directors at that time were L. M. Ninde, J. H. Bass, S. B. Bond, C. D. Bond, H. F. Talbot, R. F. Keith and number of practical organ men, came here immediately after the Chicago I. T. Packard. Messrs. Packard, Keith and Talbot, together with a fire and interested a number of Fort Wayne capitalists, including the above named, also Charles McCulloch, J. A. Fay and O. A. Simons. I. T. Packard held some valuable organ construction patents and it was for that reason that his name was given to the product. The factory was located in South Wayne, on the corner of Fairfield and Organ avenues, a place considered at that time to be at the end of nowhere. Only twenty-five to thirty men were employed and the production of organs began on a very small scale. S. B. Bond took charge of the financial management from the very start. Mr. Packard was the first superintendent. On his death, in 1875, R. F. Keith became superintendent, G. E. Bursley became business manager and secretary, in 1872, and remained in that capacity until 1882, when he resigned on account of ill health. S. B. Bond was elected general manager in addition to his being the president since 1873 and remained at the head of the company until his death in 1907. J. H. Bass was one of the originators of the company, has been one of its largest stockholders and a director from the very start and has always been a loyal supporter and adviser. He is the only living member of the original board of directors, on which board he has served continuously since 1871. Albert S. Bond, the oldest son of S. B. Bond, began his work for the company in 1879. He worked his way up from the bench through the various departments of the factory, also in the office and on the road as traveling salesman, and was made superintendent, in 1886, and secretary and treasurer in 1893, and had an important part in the general management years before that. He has been the capable head of the business for years and its success is very largely due to his broad knowledge and fair mindedness. He was president of the National Piano Manufacturers' Association of America in the years 1911 and 1912. C. J. Scheimann started with the company as office boy, in 1877, after spending a year in the office, and worked for over a year at the manufacturing end of the business, then returned to the office and has seen it grow from a small to an extensive office. He has been treasurer and sales manager, also a director in the company, for a number of years. He made two trips to Europe in the interest of the business, in 1900 and 1907, and to him a goodly share of credit is due for what success has been achieved. W. H. Wiebke started with the company, in 1885, in the office and has developed into an exceptionally able and competent office and financial man, also a director in the company. H. W. Bond started to work in the factory in 1887, is a thoroughly trained factory man, became superintendent in 1906 and is also a director in the company. S. C. Bond began his work in the Packard factory, in 1897, and worked through the factory and has been assistant superintendent since 1906, and is a director in the company. J. M. Kuhns joined the Packard forces in 1901. He became secretary in 1905 and is a director in the company. J. M. Barrett, J. D. Bond, C. E. Bond, M. W. Simons, G. M. Leslie and Jessie M. Bond served on the board of directors and C. E. Bond was secretary for a number of years. J. M. Barrett, through his important office as attorney and legal adviser, has furthered the interest of the company greatly. A large and profitable organ business was built up and the fame of the Packard organs soon spread all over the world. In 1893, owing to the fact that the demand for reed organs was diminishing and there being a greater demand for pianos, the company embarked into the manufacture of pianos, changing the firm name to The Packard Company, in 1899. The demand for organs kept diminishing, and from the fact that several other large manufacturing concerns had sprung up under the name of Packard in various lines and who practically adopted this company's style of lettering and trademark, the name of the company was changed to The Packard Piano Company, in 1915, and has been prospering and building up a very extensive business in grands, uprights and player pianos, which it ships not only throughout this country but also to a number of foreign countries. The Packard quality has been attested to by many of the most prominent musicians and is evidenced by its use in over three hundred of the leading schools of music, conservatories and colleges. From the small capital of $24,000 it increased to its present capital of $720,000, besides a handsome surplus. It has factories containing a floor space of 117,000 square feet and its plant and lumber yards cover five acres of ground which, through the growth of the city, are now located in one of the most desirable residence districts. The Packard for years has taken pride in having its factory and grounds properly parked and is exceptionally attractive in appearance. The Packard workmen form the Packard Family. They are working under advanced conditions, where they have a say in matters, and under the

Packard policy not only the hands but the brains and heart of every workman are thoroughly enlisted; and this is probably the reason why the Packard quality is so exceptionally good and why this company throughout the trade is acknowledged one of the very highest from an artistic as well as a commercial and financial standpoint. When the company started manufacturing pianos it also opened a retail store under the name of The Packard Music House, which is the leading business of its kind in northern Indiana, located on the northeast corner of Washington and Calhoun streets, Fort Wayne, Indiana, and for many years has been under the able management of H. A. Achenbach. The present officers of the company are: A. S. Bond, president and director; J. H. Bass, vice-president and director; J. M. Kuhns, secretary and director; C. J. Scheimann, treasurer and director; W. H. Wiebke, assistant treasurer and director; H. W. Bond, superintendent and director; S. C. Bond, assistant superintendent and director; J. M. Barrett, attorney and director, and G. M. Leslie, director.

George Pancake, who died January 14, 1908, is well remembered in and about Monroeville, where he lived for almost forty years on an eighty-acre farm, the present home of his widow. He was a thrifty man and prospered accordingly, and while he was retiring and unpretentious, he was a lifelong influence for good in his home community. He was born in Ohio on February 3, 1847, and died on January 14, 1908. His parents were Aaron and Julia (Throckmorton) Pancake, both native Ohioans who removed to Van Wert county, Ohio, in 1851, and there they passed the closing years of their lives. Of their twelve children five are living at this writing. George Pancake was educated in Ohio and there married Susan Crabill, in 1869, when he was twenty-two years of age. She was born in Champaign county, Ohio, and was the daughter of David and Sophia (Ridenour) Crabill, native Virginians who came to Ohio in their early married life, later locating in Allen county, Indiana, where they died when well advanced in years. After his marriage George Pancake came to Allen county, Indiana, bought a farm of eighty acres and settled down to make the best of such opportunities as were his. He prospered and spent many happy years on his home in Monroe township. There his three children were born and reared and there he died, at the age of sixty-five years, on January 14, 1908. He is buried in the Odd Fellows' Cemetery in Monroe township. His widow and two daughters, Alice and May, are still living in the home he made for them, and his son, William, is making his way in the world on his own responsibility. The family are members of the Lutheran church in Monroe township and Mr. Pancake was a Democrat.

William Pape.—The firm established by William Pape, in 1896, under the name of Pape-Bremer & Company, has in recent years been turned over to the sons, William and Theodore, the father living in retirement. The business is a general painting and paper hanging firm and is one of the most reliable of its kind in Fort Wayne. William Pape was born in Germany on February 4, 1841, and came to America with his father, in 1850, settling in Fort Wayne, where the father engaged in the contracting business. He was prosperous enough to buy a home on Madison street, but when he died, about 1860, he left his wife and son otherwise unprovided for, so that William Pape, at the age of fifteen, found himself facing the necessity of matching his young wits and strength against the world in an effort to provide support for himself and his mother in a strange land. He began it with wood-sawing. It was hard work and the pay was small, but he was strong of heart as well of limb and was able to eke out a living and sometimes even save a little for the future. In the early months of the Civil War he enlisted in Company B,, Thirty-fifth Indiana Infantry, and served through to the end of the four-year conflict. Returning to his home in Fort Wayne at the close of the war, he found work in a hotel, continuing in it for about three years. He later engaged in the painting and paper-hanging business, continuing in it successfully for many years. He was married in the latter sixties to Miss Louisa Gaulmeyer and three children were born to them. The eldest, a daughter, died in infancy, and the others are William C. and Theodore, who, in 1904, took over the business and are now carrying on the firm of Pape & Sons, established in 1896 under the name of Pape-Bremer Company, with Mr. Pape at the helm. The business establishment of the firm is at 223 East Wayne street, but the firm is owner of considerable other real estate in the city. Following the death of Mrs. Pape, Mr. Pape married Carrie Wilson, in June, 1908. She is a daughter of Charles and Mary (Wagner) Wilson and is the only surviving member of their large family of nine children. Mr. Pape is a Democrat and a member of the Lutheran church, in which he has long been active and prominent as a worker. He is now living retired from business activities, interesting himself in the affairs of the firm in a purely advisory capacity. He came up, step-by-step, from a youthful poverty into the comforts of an honorable prosperity, and none is better prepared than he to appreciate the blessings of an old age that is lacking in the hardships that marked his earlier years.

The Paragon Cooperage Company is a comparatively new concern that represents one of the important industrial and commercial enterprises of Fort Wayne, its functions being the manufacturing and wholesale dealing in cooperage products of all kinds. The company, which is not incorporated and which is a partnership concern, has not only its well established headquarters in Fort Wayne, but also has well equipped manufacturing and distributing plants in the states of Arkansas, Missouri and New York. The enterprise was established in March 7, 1910, and the interested principals from the inception have been Charles A Spanley and John E. O'Connor, of both of whom more specific mention will be made in this article. The company gives employment to a force of about one hundred persons and progressive and reliable policies have been the forces that have enabled the company to develop a substantial and prosperous business that shows a constantly cumulative tendency as marking objective appreciation of its facilities and effective services. Charles A. Spanley, senior member of the firm, was born in Fort Wayne on April 26, 1881, and both he and his coadjutor are numbered among the aggressive and enterprising young business men of their native city and state. Mr. Spanley is a son of Martin and Sophia (Gephart) Spanley, both of whom were born and reared in Wayne township, this county, and are representatives of sterling pioneer families. Martin Spanley devoted the major part of his active life to farming and he and his wife still reside in Wayne township, where he is now living virtually retired after many years of successful association with the basic industry of agriculture. He is a Republican in politics and both he and his wife are earnest communicants of the Catholic church. Charles A. Spanley gained his early education in the parochial school of St. Mary's Catholic church in Fort Wayne and later took an effective course in the International Business College of Fort Wayne, Indiana. For a short time he was in the employ of the G. E. Bursley Company and later in that of the Fort Wayne & Northern Indiana Traction Company, and then completed his course in the business college, after which he was for eighteen months in the employ of the Horton Manufacturing Company. About four years were then given by him to service in the employ of the Pennsylvania Railroad Company, and he then became associated with the Noble Cooperage Company, in the employ of which he continued eight years, or until he became associated with Mr. O'Conner in establishing their present business, under the title of the Paragon Cooperage Company. Mr. Spanley is a Republican in politics, holds membership in the Fort Wayne Commercial Club and the celebrated Columbia Club of Indianapolis, and is affiliated with the Fort Wayne Lodge of the Benevolent and Protective Order of Elks. John E. O'Connor was born in Fort Wayne on December 11, 1887, a son of Stephen and Louise (Bercot) O'Connor, the former of whom was born in Ireland and the latter in Allen county, Indiana, where her parents established their home many years ago. Stephen O'Connor came to Fort Wayne within a short time after the close of the Civil war and had been long and actively concerned with business affairs in this city, where he was secretary of the old S. C. Lumbard Company. John E. O'Connor is indebted to the parochial school of the Catholic Cathedral parish of Fort Wayne for his early educational advantages, and his initial activity in connection with business affairs was as an employe in the local offices of the Western Union Telegraph Company. He then found employment in the establishment of the Noble Cooperage Company and in this connection gained the practical experience that has effectively qualified him for independent enterprise along the same industrial line. He continued with the Noble Cooperage Company until 1910, when, as already noted, he became associated with Mr. Spanley in the development and upbuilding of their now thriving business conducted under the title of the Paragon Cooperage Company. His political convictions are in harmony with the tenets of the Republican party and he and his wife are communicants of the Cathedral parish of the Immaculate Conception. Mr. O'Connor is affiliated with the Knights of Columbus, and the Benevolent and Protective Order of Elks, the Friars, and holds membership in the Fort Wayne Country Club. On November 30, 1912, was solemnized the marriage of Mr. O'Connor to Miss Clara Lassus, daughter of the late John B. Lassus, of Fort Wayne, and they have two children—Mary Louise and John E., Jr.

James S. Peddicord is one of the energetic and progressive young representatives of the real estate business in the city of Fort Wayne, and his well ordered operations include the handling of reality on commission and also the development and exploitation of new and desirable residential and industrial tracts. At the time of this writing he is giving special attention to the development of Shady Brook Addition to Fort Wayne and Penn Park Addition at Hamilton Lake, a favored summer resort of this section of Indiana. He has also conceived and planned Kensington Park, work on which is now under way and which will be one of the most highly improved and attractive residence sections in the city. His success is the direct result of his own ability and well directed enterprise and he is one of the effective and popular exponents of real estate enterprise in Allen county. James Sheldon Peddicord was born in Indiana county, Pennsylvania, on October 17, 1883, and both of his parents—John and Sarah Peddicord—died during his infancy. The orphan child was taken into the home of an aunt, but when he was four years of age he was sent to the orphan's home maintained under the auspices of the Evangelical Association or church at Flat Rock, Ohio, where he remained seven years and gained his early educational discipline, which was supplemented by his attending the public schools of Seneca county, in which the previously mentioned home is situated. Finally he entered the Tri-State College, at Angola, Indiana, where he took a classical and commercial course, the latter of which he completed when twenty-one years of age. He soon afterward established his residence at Fort Wayne, where for four years he was in the employ of the Bass Foundry and Machine Company. He then, early in the year 1909, engaged in the real estate business with offices in the Shoaff building, where he continued to maintain his headquarters and centered his constantly expanding business. He has made an excellent reputation for resourcefulness and reliability in this important field of business enterprise and has achieved success that is worthy of the name. Mr. Peddicord is a republican in his political proclivities, was reared in the faith of the Evangelical Association, and in his business and social relations is an appreciative and popular member of the Fort Wayne Real Estate Exchange, of which organization he was secretary during the first two years of its existance, and also a member of the Fort Wayne Commercial Club. His name is still enrolled on the list of eligible young bachelors in the metropolis of Allen county.

Charles J. Pequignot, who is numbered among the progressive and representative exponents of farm enterprise in his native county, has owned and operated his present well improved farm of eighty-four acres, in Aboite township, since 1902. He is of French lineage, as the name indicates, and is a scion of a family that was founded in Allen county in the pioneer days, his paternal grandfather having come to America from France and having established a home in Allen county, where he reclaimed a farm from the virtual wilderness and where he and his wife continued to reside until their death. Charles J. Pequignot was born in St. Joseph township, this county, on December 6, 1877, a son of Frank and Anna (Lauers) Pequignot, both of whom were born in that township, where they were reared to maturity and their marriage was solemnized. Frank Pequignot was long numbered among the representative farmers of his native township, and since leaving the farm he and his wife have maintained their home in the neighboring town of Roanoke, in Huntington county, where he is living retired. Mr. Pequignot has always been aligned with the Democratic party and he and his wife are earnest communicants of the Catholic church. Of their children the subject of this review is the eldest; Sarah is the wife of George Lumway, a farmer in Lake township; Christina resides in the city of Fort Wayne; John is a farmer; Elizabeth is the wife of Samuel Deal, of Fort Wayne; Agnes is the wife of Samuel Kelter, of that city; Nora is the wife of Louis Hines, of Jefferson township, Whitley county; William D. is a farmer in Aboite township and is individually mentioned on other pages of this volume; and Harry is with his parents in the village of Roanoke. Charles J. Pequignot acquired his youthful education in the parochial and public schools and thereafter continued to assist his father in the work of the home farm until he initiated his independent career by renting land and engaging in the same line of enterprise on his own account. He operated a rented farm twelve years and then, in 1902, purchased his present farm, upon which he has made good improvements, the general air of thrift and prosperity which prevades the place giving evidence of his energy and good management. He gives his political allegiance to the Democratic party and he and his wife are communicants of the Catholic church. On October 11, 1890, Mr. Pequignot wedded Miss Julia Lovine, who likewise was born and reared in this county. She is a daughter of Frederick and Addie Lovine, the former of whom came to Fort Wayne from Buffalo, New York; he was a molder by trade but after having been employed at his trade in Fort Wayne for a number of years located on a farm, impaired health having prompted this action on his part. He has now retired from active labors, but he and his wife still reside on their pleasant homestead farm, north of Fort Wayne. When Mr. Lovine removed to the farm he took with him two of his brothers who were blind and for them provided a good home during the remainder of their lives. His first wife, whose maiden name was Minnie Mulching, bore him one child, Charles, who died young. Of the children of the second marriage the eldest is Alice, who is the wife of Charles Weaver, their home being in the state of Colorado; Frederick resides in Fort Wayne; Julia, wife of the subject of this sketch, was the next in order of birth; John remains at the parental home and has charge of the farm; George lives at Huntertown, this county; Cora is the wife of Marion Griswold, of Washington township; William is associated in the work and management of his father's farm; Delia is the wife of Guy Kniss, of Huntertown; and Mary is the wife of John Irwin, of Eel River township. Mr. and Mrs. Pequignot became the parents of four children: Zenetia is the wife of Claude Kinder, of Arcola, this county, and they have four children—Charles, Bernice, Charles and Earl; Earl, the second child of Mr. Pequignot, remains at the parental home; Arthur, who resides in Fort Wayne, is married and has one son; Ansel; and Oscar is deceased.

Henry C. Pequignot is one of the representative business men of the younger generation in Fort Wayne and through his energetic and progressive activities is contributing much to the civic and material advancement of his native city and county, where he conducts a substantial real estate and insurance business and has done effective service in the improving of city realty, as a builder of high grade houses, the same being placed on the market on such terms as to enable the home-seeker to make provision for his family and add to his value as a citizen. Mr. Pequignot is a scion of sterling French ancestry and a representative of an honored pioneer family of Allen county, his grandfather, Joseph C. Pequignot, having come to America from Paris, France, and, as a man of much technical ability, having been one of the engineers retained in the construction of the old-time canal from Fort Wayne to the mouth of the Maumee river. He whose name initiates this article was born in Fort Wayne on November 3, 1882, a son of Charles C. and Josephine F. (Greve) Pequignot, both of whom were born in the city of Paris, France. Charles C. was a lad of about nine years when he accompanied his parents on their immigration to America, about the year 1857, and soon afterward the family home was established in Allen county, his father assuming his executive duties as an engineer in the construction of the canal. Charles C. was afforded the advantages of the Catholic parochial schools and St. Vincent's Academy, of Fort Wayne and was one of the prominent and successful representatives of agricultural industry in Allen county, where he continued his activities as a successful farmer until the close of his long, worthy and useful life, his death having occurred October 16, 1915, and his widow being now a resident of Fort Wayne. He served in Company C, One Hundred Forty-second Indiana Infantry, having enlisted June 1, 1862, and was discharged at Nashville, Tenn., July 14, 1865. He was a staunch supporter of the cause of the Republican party, was a public-spirited citizen of broad mental grasp and his name merits enduring place on the roll of the sterling pioneers of Allen county, where he lived and labored to goodly ends. He was a devout communicant of St. Peter's Catholic church in Fort Wayne, as is also his widow. At this juncture are entered brief data concerning their children: Mary is the wife of Frank Runyon, of Perry township, this county; Eleanora is the wife of John Myers, of Fort Wayne; Ellen is the wife of Edward Littlefield, of this city; Julian C. is a prosperous farmer in St. Joseph township; Della is the wife of Oliver York, of Fort Wayne; Henry C., of this sketch, was the next in order of birth; Louise is the wife of Frank Sordlett and they maintain their home in the city of Chicago; Cedonia is the wife of Theodore Bohen, of Fort Wayne; Albert F. and Robert likewise reside in this city; and Edna is the wife of Robert Fleckenstein, of Fort Wayne. Henry C. Pequignot acquired his early education in the Catholic parochial schools of his native city and later attended the Kentucky State Normal School in the fine old city of Lexington. As a youth he learned the art of telegraphy and as a skilled operator was in railway service four years, principally in the employ of the Wabash Railroad Company. Thereafter he was employed in the Fort Wayne real estate office of Isaac D'Isay and later studied law and was admitted to the bar, his knowledge of jurisprudence having proved of much value to him in connection with the substantial real estate business which he has developed in an independent way, his activities in this field of enterprise having been initiated in 1906. He handles both city and farm property and his books show at all times most desirable investments, with many opportunities for the exchange of properties. In connection with his real estate operations he has proved successful as a builder and has improved a number of properties in Fort Wayne. In connection with his real estate enterprise he maintains a department devoted to fire insurance, and in the latter line is agent for a number of substantial and well known companies. Progressive both as a citizen and as a business man, Mr. Pequignot is found aligned as a stalwart in the local camp of the Republican party, and both he and his wife are communicants of the Catholic Cathedral parish of Fort Wayne. In a fraternal way he is affiliated with the Knights of Columbus and the Benevolent and Protective Order of Elks. On June 28, 1904, was solemnized the marriage of Mr. Pequignot to Miss Anna Isenbarger, daughter of Henry C. and Sarah (Bruss) Isenbarger, of Huntington, Indiana, and the five children of this union are: Geraldine, Eugene, Robert, Mildred and Marjorie.

William D. Pequignot, who is one of the progressive and popular farmers of the younger generation in Aboite township, where he resides upon one hundred acres of land that is a part of his father's estate, is a scion of the third generation of one of the sterling pioneer families of Allen county, where his paternal grandfather settled in an early day, shortly after immigrating to America from France. Mr. Pequignot was born in Lake township, this county, on October 1, 1886, a son of Frank and Anna (Lauers) Pequignot, who now reside in the village of Roanoke, Huntington county, where the father is living retired. Frank Pequignot was born and reared in St. Joseph township, this county, as was also his wife, and was for many years one of the prominent and successful farmers of the county, where he still owns a valuable landed estate, both he and his wife being communicants of the Catholic church, and his political support being given to the Democratic party. Charles J., the eldest of their children, is the subject of an individual review on other pages of this work; Sarah is the wife of George Lumway, of Lake township; Christina resides in Fort Wayne; John is another of the successful farmers of the county; Elizabeth is the wife of Samuel Deal, of Fort Wayne; Agnes is the wife of Samuel Kelter, of that city; Nora is the wife of Louis Hines, of Jefferson township; William D., of this review, was the next in order of birth; and Harry remains at the parental home. William D. Pequignot acquired his early education in the public schools of his home township and from his youth to the present his activities have been in connection with the affairs of the fine farm properties owned by his father, from whom he now rents to well improved farm of one hundred acres, the same being by him utilized effectively for diversified agriculture and stock-growing. He is one of the loyal and public-spirited young men of his native county, pays his allegiance to the Democratic party, and he and his wife are communicants of the Catholic church. September 26, 1909, recorded the marriage of Mr. Pequignot to Miss Celia Hines, daughter of Michael and Catherine Hines, the former of whom is deceased and the latter resides in the village of Roanoke. Mr. and Mrs. Pequignot have four children, Marietta, Harold, Paul and James.

Arthur H. Perfect.—In following out a unique policy of living, Arthur H. Perfect has developed a means of becoming naturally a citizen of exceptional value to his home city. That policy may be described as a devotion to his business affairs to such a degree that the material gains therefrom have provided him with the means to do the largest amount of good to the greatest number. His plan is in marked variance with that of the man whose material success tends to the development of habits of selfishness and narrowness of view of true service to others. No one denies that Mr. Perfect has proven to be a marked success in the business world. Everyone admits, in the same thought, that his service to the people of his home city has been widely and wisely manifested. Mr. Perfect is the president of A. H. Perfect & Company, one of the foremost wholesale grocery establishments of this portion of the middle west. He was born January 16, 1865, in Olive Green, Delaware county, Ohio, son of Emory and Lucy (Moyer) Perfect. Later, the family removed to Wilmington, Ohio, where Arthur H. Perfect was educated in the common schools. At the age of sixteen, however, he entered upon his commercial experiences, beginning with employment in a Wilmington dry goods store where he was employed for three years. Going then to Springfield, Ohio, he entered upon the study of stenography and typewriting, combined with business instruction, devoting his evenings to the work which proved of such essential value to him in later years. For seven years he was employed in the offices of The Thomas Manufacturing Company at Springfield. Opportunity then came to him to engage in the wholesale grocery business at Findlay, Ohio, with a partner, the firm name being Evans, Perfect & Company. When the occasion for advancement arose, Mr. Perfect sold his interests to his partner and established a wholesale grocery house at Madison, Wisconsin. While passing through Fort Wayne, at this time, Mr. Perfect learned of the closing of the wholesale grocery establishment of McDonald & Watt, and he called at the place to ascertain whether or no

Arthur H. Perfect

a portion of the stock would be usable in connection with his Madison venture. This visit of investigation revised all his plans. He became convinced that Fort Wayne was a more suitable center for a wholesale grocery than Madison and so the Summit City claimed him as one of her wide-awake and aggressive business men. The co-partnership of Arthur H. Perfect, Harry A. Perfect, T. Guy Perfect and H. H. Eavey, under the name of A. H. Perfect & Company, was formed in April, 1896, and this organization was continued until March, 1907, when the firm was incorporated under the same name, with Arthur H. Perfect, president; H. H. Eavey, first vice-president; T. Guy Perfect, second vice-president; Harry A. Perfect, secretary-treasurer. The original capitalization was for $200,000. For a considerable period the company occupied large quarters at the northeast corner of West Columbia and Harrison streets. Later, the present building at the corner of Clay and East Columbia streets was erected for the special use of the Perfect concern, and recently the company purchased a large tract of ground on Old Fort Place, east of Lafayette street, where a modern building of immense proportions is soon to be erected. The company employs seventeen road salesmen and thirty-five men in the house. It is the center of distribution of vast quantities of well-known brands of foodstuffs, prominent among which are the "Perfect" brands along many choice lines. This brief outline suggests the fact that Mr. Perfect has prospered, but an analysis of his methods brings the added knowledge that his success is firmly founded upon strictly honorable business methods, backed by a thorough knowledge of his field and the way in which its needs may best be met. Ever since he came to Fort Wayne Mr. Perfect has been identified strongly with all the forward movements which have marked the recent years. During the campaign of June, 1916, when the city of Fort Wayne drew to itself attention from all parts of America because of the success of the campaign to raise $300,000 to establish a Young Men's Christian Association, Mr. Perfect served as the general chairman of the organization, and it is needless to observe that the breaking of the world's record in a ten-day's canvass for funds was in no small degree dependent upon the policies and the activities of the executive head of the organization. In his capacity as president of the Associated Charities—the central "clearing house" of the city's benevolent organizations—Mr. Perfect has given splendid service. His connection as an elder in the First Presbyterian church affords wide opportunities for the kind of work which suits best his inclinations and his talents. In Masonic circles he is also active. In the Scottish Rite he holds the Thirty-second degree and he is deeply interested in the Shrine. He is a member of the Commercial club of Fort Wayne and the Columbia club of Indianapolis. No movement in the general interest of his city or state fails to receive the active support of Mr. Perfect. With no desire for leadership, he is ofttimes called to places of responsibility when difficult problems for the public welfare are to be solved. On January 31, 1889, Mr. Perfect was united in marriage with Miss Maude Eavey, daughter of H. H. Eavey, of Xenia, Ohio. Henry Eavey Perfect, a son, possessing traits which promised much for a future of usefulness, lived only to the age of twelve. A second son, Frederick Eugene Perfect, a student at Howe Military Academy, is of the type of young man to profit well by the training of home and school and to rise to a desirable place in society. The Perfect family home on West Wayne street is one of the newer substantial residence properties on that pretty thoroughfare. The family cottage on the shore of Sylvan Lake, Rome City, Indiana, which claims attention during the warmer months, is one of the delightful spots at this popular resort. Mr. Perfect spends much of his time at his summer home, where, in the place of passing the hours in restful ease, he finds a more pleasing diversion in the care of his flowers and a model vegetable garden.

Ely E. Perry is recognized as a lawyer of excellent attainments and has been engaged in the practice of his profession in the city of Fort Wayne since 1902. He gives special attention to real estate law and is one of the prominent exponents of this branch of practice in the metropolis and judicial center of Allen county. In connection with his law business he has concerned himself vigorously with the improving of local realty, as a builder of high grade houses in the south side of the city. Ely Emerson Perry was born on a farm near Belle Plaine, Marshall county, Illinois, and the date of his nativity was August 12, 1876. He is a son of William John and Jennie (Moore) Perry, the former a native of Marshall county and the latter of Woodford county, Illinois. The father was one of the representative farmers of his native county at the time of his death, was a scion of one of the old and influential families of that section of Illinois, and his widow now resides in the city of Los Angeles, California, the subject of this review bieng the younger of their two children, and the daughter, Lillian, being the wife of Charles Ong, of Varna, Marshall county, Illinois. Ely E. Perry continued his studies in the public schools of his native state until he had completed a course in the high school at Washburn, Woodford county, after which he pursued higher academic studies in the Illinois State Normal School at Normal. For two years after leaving this institution he was a successful teacher in the public schools at Varna, Woodford county, and then entered the law department of Rock River University, at Dixon, Illinois, in which he was graduated as a member of the class of 1902, and from which he received the degree of Bachelor of Laws. During two years of his law course he held the position of secretary to Judge Watts, the dean of the law school. In 1902 Mr. Perry established his residence in Fort Wayne and for six months was associated with the well known law firm of Ninde Brothers. Thereafter he was for two years associated in practice with Herman Brown, under the firm name of Brown & Perry, and since that time has conducted an individual practice, the same having grown to be one of successful and important order, especially in the domain of real estate law, to which he gives almost exclusive attention, though he has made for himself a reputation as a skilled trial lawyer and circumspect and well informed general counselor. Mr. Perry has been prominently identified with the material development of the south side of Fort Wayne, where he has erected and sold a number of high grade houses, his association with this line of enterprise being still continued in an effective way. His political allegiance is given to the Democratic party, he and his wife hold membership in the Methodist Episcopal church, he is a loyal member of the Fort Wayne Commercial Club and the University Club, and in the Masonic fraternity has received the thirty-second degree of the Ancient Accepted Scottish Rite, besides being affiliated with the Ancient Arabic Order, Nobles of the Mystic Shrine. On November 7, 1903, was solemnized the marriage of Mr. Perry to Miss Robina A. Pierce, who was born in the state of Kansas, and whose parents, Alfred R. and Emma (Eason) Pierce, now reside on Kinnaird avenue, Fort Wayne, the father being a retired druggist. Mr. and Mrs. Perry have one daughter, Hester Lillian, who is attending the public schools.

Frank C. Pfeiffer, of Aboite township, is one of the prosperous and well known farmers of that section of Allen county. He was born July 2, 1866, in Washington township and is a son of Charles G. and Abigail (Williams) Pfeiffer. The father came from Wurtemburg, Germany, with his parents when eight years old. After a residence in Buffalo for five years the family came to Allen county, where land was bought, a homestead of 160 acres. This was cleared and improved by the toil of all grown members of the family and subsequently another twenty-four acre tract was added. Charles and Abigail Pfeiffer were members of the Lutheran church, and reared a family of nine children, as named in the sketch of George L., following this. Of these, George L. and Ivory K. are elsewhere mentioned in nearby pages of this volume. Frank C. attended the schools of his neighborhood and assisted in the strenuous duties of farm life until he grew to manhood, and after renting for a time he bought eighty acres of his present farm. By application and industry he has greatly improved this with modern buildings, and it is one of the stock-raising places of Aboite township. June 17, 1891, he was married to Edith, daughter of Valentine and Emaline (Pettit) Mann, natives of Pennsylvania and Indiana respectively. Mr. and Mrs. Pfeiffer are parents of the following children: Evelyn and Lucile, in Fort Wayne; Walter, Laurine and Ralph at home.

George L. Pfeiffer.—Among the substantial citizens and farmers of Washington township, none are more worthy of mention in a publication of the nature of this one than is George L. Pfeiffer, who has stood solidly for development and progress in his community through all his maturer years. He is a native son of Allen county, born on September 18, 1853, son of Charles and Abigail F. (Sutton) Pfeiffer, natives of Germany and Pennsylvania, respectively. Coming first to Ohio after his arrival on American shores, Charles Pfeiffer later came to Allen county, Indiana, where he met and married his wife, and there they made their home as long as they lived. They were parents of nine children. John, the eldest, is deceased; the second child was George L., of this review, after whom came Emma, Charles A., William H. and Clara, who were twins, Frank C., Ivory K. and Arthur W. George L., in common with his brothers and sisters, had his education in the district schools of his native community in Washington township, finishing in the schools of Fort Wayne. He turned his attention to farming when he had finished his studies, and from then to the present time has devoted his energies to farm life, with the exceptoin of a two-year period when he was engaged in the teaming business in Fort Wayne. Today Mr. Pfeiffer is the owner of ninety-one acres in Washington township, highly improved from every viewpoint, and is counted among the foremost farms of the community. He was married on March 24, 1887, to Miss Althea L. Cartwright, daughter of James M. and Elizabeth M. (Ferris) Cartwright, the father a native of Ohio and the mother of New York state. She came to Allen county when she was thirteen years of age and he was a young man when he settled here, first locating in Aboite township and, in 1865, moving to Wayne township, where he spent five years, still later settling in Lake township. They were the parents of thirteen children, named as follows:

Walton, Lavina, Jennie, Felicia, Adeline, Warren, Anna, Ida, Elizabeth, Althea, Jessie, Charles and Dora. Walton, Adeline and Elizabeth are deceased. Mr. and Mrs. Pfeiffer are parents of nine children. They are Elmer, Howard, Charles, Earl, Raymond, Ross, Althea, Warren and Jessie. Mr. Pfeiffer has served his township in the office of assessor and is a Republican in politics. He is a member of the English Lutheran church at Fort Wayne, as are also the members of his family.

Ivory K. Pfeiffer is another of the prosperous and well-to-do sons of Charles G. and Abigail Pfeiffer, who are more extensively noticed in the memoir of Frank C. Pfeiffer on an earlier page of this volume. Ivory K. received his education in the schools of Washington township, Allen county, where he was born April 19, 1871. He grew to manhood in the active labors of the farm, than which there is none better for the physical and mental development. For several years he followed agricultural pursuits as an independent operator on land rented from his father and father-in-law. In 1906 he purchased his present home farm in Aboite township, where he has erected modern house, barn, silo and other requisite improvements, which go to make a first-class farming and stock-raising establishment. He advocates the principles of the Republican party and belongs to the Lutheran church and to the Redmen. September 3, 1896, he espoused Sophia, daughter of Edward and Marie Beckman, and they have these children: Edna, Frederick, Ervin, Florence, Melvin, Mildred and Verda, all at home.

Artemas W. Pickard has gained in his native city a position of distinct prominence and influence in connection with industrial and commercial activities of important order, as shown in his tenure of the office of assistant treasurer and manager of the Fort Wayne Foundry and Machine Company, with which he identified himself in 1891, at which time the business was conducted under the title of the Fort Wayne Iron Works. The company maintains a well-equipped plant with the most approved modern facilities and controls a substantial and prosperous business, so that it stands representative in the industrial life of the city. In addition to this alliance Mr. Pickard also holds the office of secretary of the Pickard House Furnishing Company, which has developed a very successful retail business and is one of the leading concerns of its kind in northern Indiana. Mr. Pickard is emphatically progressive and liberal, both as a business man and as a citizen, and he is always ready to give his support to measures and enterprises tending to advance the well-being of his native city and county. On January 4, 1893, Mr. Pickard was united in marriage with Miss Adah Gray, of Fort Wayne, a daughter of Mr. and Mrs. James P. Gray, and they have one son, Artemas Gray, now (1917) a student in the University of Michigan. Mr. Pickard is an active member of the Fort Wayne Commercial Club and the local Rotary Club, as well as the Country Club, and is affiliated with the Benevolent and Protective Order of Elks. Mr. Pickard was born in Fort Wayne on September 7, 1869, a son of Thomas R. Pickard, who was identified with the Bass Foundry and Machine Company for over fifty years. He continued his studies in the public schools until he had duly profited by the advantages of the high school, and as a youth entered the employ of the Bass Foundry and Machine Company, with which concern he remained until he became identified, in 1891, with the Fort Wayne Foundry and Machine Company, a J. H. Bass corporation.

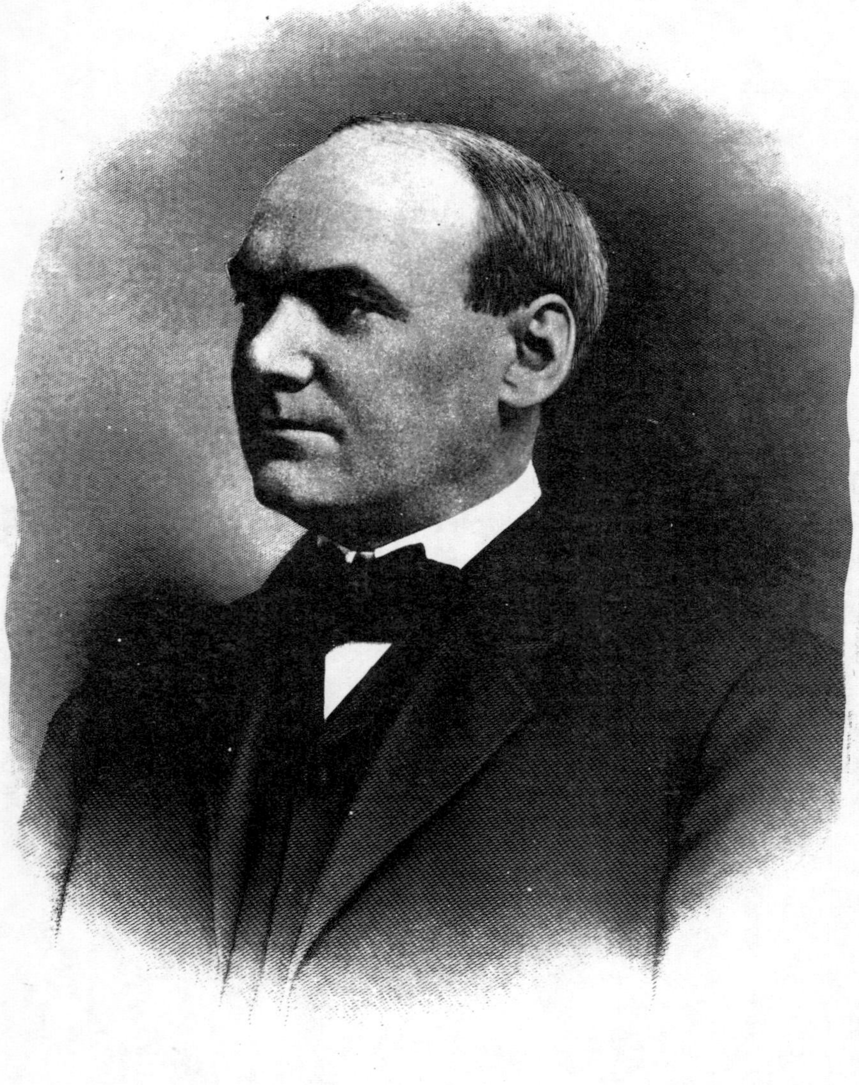

A. T. Pidgeon

Charles T. Pidgeon, who is president of the C. T. Pidgeon Millinery Company and treasurer of the C. T. Pidgeon Realty Company, is consistently to be designated as one of the influential and progressive business men of Fort Wayne and his ability and sterling character have been shown in his admirable achievement in connection with business interests of importance. Mr. Pidgeon was born in Clinton county, Ohio, February 12, 1863, a son of Rev. John M. and Caroline P. (Thompson) Pidgeon, natives of Guilford county, North Caroline, where the former was born, February 2, 1833, and the latter in the year 1842, their home being now at Jamestown, Greene county, Ohio, where the father is living retired, after a quarter of a century of devoted service as a minister in that noble religious organization, the Society of Friends, of which both he and his wife are birthright members. He whose name introduces this article acquired his early education in the public schools of Ohio and supplemented the same by an effective course in Earlham college, an admirable institution maintained under the auspices of the Society of Friends, at Richmond, Indiana. He gave two years of effective service as a teacher in the public schools and thereafter was in the railway mail service for a period of four years. In January, 1888, he became associated with the wholesale millinery house of Adams and Armstrong, whose establishment was then situated on Calhoun street, Fort Wayne. Three years later he established his residence in the city of Cleveland, Ohio, and from that point continued as a traveling salesman for the same firm for one year. On July 1, 1893, he was admitted to partnership in the business, the corporate title of the concern having been changed to James A. Armstrong & Company. He continued as vice-president of the company until January 1, 1901, when he purchased the interests of his associates, Messrs. Armstrong and Turner, changed the title to the C. T. Pidgeon Millinery Company and assumed the office of president of the corporation. Under his effective management as chief executive the trade of the house has been greatly expanded, making it a leader in lines of commercial business centered in Fort Wayne. The progressiveness of Mr. Pidgeon has further been exemplified through his association with the C. T. Pidgeon Realty Company, of which he is treasurer and which has valuable holdings in the Allen county metropolis. He is a loyal and valued member of the Fort Wayne Commercial Club; is a Republican in politics, and both he and his wife are active members of the Congregational church. On November 21, 1900, was solemnized the marriage of Mr. Pidgeon to Miss Maude B. Keplinger, who was born and reared in Fort Wayne, a daughter of Jacob and Elizabeth Keplinger, both of whom are now deceased. Mr. and Mrs. Pidgeon have one daughter, Mervyn G.

Ogden Pierce.—The late Ogden Pierce was a resident of Fort Wayne for a quarter of a century prior to his death and was identified with the city in a business way during practically all that time. He came of a family that was established in Allen county as early as 1844, and his early years were passed in this section of the state, so that he was in no sense a stranger to Fort Wayne prior to the time when he settled there in business. Mr. Pierce was born on May 19, 1830, in Athens-on-the Hudson, New York state, and died on May 16, 1905, so that he lacked but three days of seeing his seventy-fifth birthday anniversary. He was the son of Dr. Eli and Sarah (Burgess) Pierce. The father was a native of the old Bay state and the mother was of English birth and parentage.

They came to Allen county, in 1844, and Doctor Pierce was at one time the owner of about four thousand acres of land in the county. He farmed some, but devoted himself mainly to the practice of his profession, and was a man highly esteemed of all who knew him in the district in which he practiced. Doctor and Mrs. Pierce were the parents of seven children, all of whom are deceased. When the subject was about sixteen years of age he began to teach school in the winter seasons. He was educated by private tutors and in the John Greer School. When a young man he went to Milwaukee, Wisconsin, and became a member of the Board of Trade in that city and there remained for some years. He then returned to Allen county and, locating in the vicinity of Fort Wayne, turned his attention to farming. After two or three years he gave up the simple life and went into the postal service, continuing in that work from 1871 to 1885. In that year he joined F. L. Jones in a business venture and they became the proprietors and owners of the Troy Laundry. They continued in that business successfully and Mr. Pierce was thus occupied at the time of his death. On July 3, 1871, Mr. Pierce was married to Miss Martha A. Jones, daughter of David W. Jones, and to Mr. and Mrs. Pierce five children were born. Ogden, the eldest, is train master for the Nickel Plate Railroad with headquarters at Fort Wayne. Ethel is the wife of Alexander S. Reid, of Richmond, Indiana. Robert Burgess lives in Cleveland, Ohio, where he is city manager for the Kelly-Springfield Rubber Company. Howard H. is assistant ticket agent in the office of the Pennsylvania Lines in Fort Wayne. Martha Burgess lives at home. Mr. Pierce was a Mason and a lifelong member of the Episcopal church. He enjoyed the friendship of a wide circle of the representative people of Fort Wayne and his passing was mourned by all who had shared in his acquaintance.

George W. Pixley.—The contribution of George W. Pixley to the industrial, fraternal, mercantile and financial development of Fort Wayne includes a vast number of interests which can only be suggested in a brief sketch of his busy career. His keen perception of the value of opportunities, his consistent faith in Fort Wayne and his exemplification of the highest type of citizenship is best gained through a careful consideration of his accomplishments in many fields. George Whiting Pixley was born in Kirkland, Oneida county, New York, March 1, 1834. His parents were David and Charlotte (Mygatt) Pixley, natives of New York state, where they continued to reside throughout their lifetime. Mr. Pixley received the foundation of his education in the Clinton Liberal Institute at Clinton, New York, and from this institution entered upon his business career extending through many years. For a period of four years he served as a clerk in Utica, New York, in the State Canal Department, where his varied duties opened his vision to larger possibilities. For fifteen years thereafter, however, he devoted his attention to farm work. One year was then spent in Troy, New York, and from this city he came direct to Fort Wayne, Indiana, in 1876, at a time when the town was blossoming into evidences of larger city opportunities. Here he engaged in the clothing business and continued for nine years under the firm name of Owen, Pixley and Company. Then he and his brother succeeded to the business of Owen, Pixley and Company, which was thereafter known as Pixley and Company. The firm occupied a building on Court street, until 1889, when the erection by Mr. Pixley of the Pixley-Long block on East Berry street, at the head of Court street, provided new and larger quarters for the conduct of the business. Here Mr. Pixley continued to guide the affairs of the enterprise to greater success, until about 1906, when he gave the business to a nephew who was named for him, a resident of Utica, New York. The new owner continued the business until 1914, when it was sold to the firm of Stellhorn and Neireiter. During his years of effort in the retail trade Mr. Pixley was regarded as a strict adherent to honest business principles, which gave to his enterprise a firm standing and a reputation for reliability and progress. In 1889, at the time of relinquishing the management of the clothing store, he cast about for some method whereby he could gratify the wishes of men who desired to become property owners. While Fort Wayne has many citizens financially well-to-do, its population, for the most part, is made up of men whose salaries preclude the possibility of their paying cash for a home. These were the men Mr. Pixley desired to aid, so, interesting other citizens in his project, he organized the Tri-State Building and Loan Association and was its president during all its life. Its mission met with instantaneous favor and the association developed until it became the largest of its kind in the state of Indiana. From this association which had forged to the financial fore in Indiana sprang the Tri-State Loan and Trust Company, for the old association was merged with the Fort Wayne Trust Company, another financial institution in which Mr. Pixley was active. On December 28, 1870, Mr. Pixley was united in marriage with Miss Sarah A. Lewis, of Kirkland, New York, daughter of Chauncey E. and Electra Lewis. They have one daughter, Louise, who shares with her parents the happiness of their beautiful home on West Wayne street. Mr. Pixley is one of the charter members of all of the different bodies of Scottish Rite Masonry and has served as treasurer of the same continuously. For years he has held the honorary thirty-third degree of the Scottish Rite. He is an attendant of Plymouth Congregational church, holds a lively interest in political affairs and serves in the ranks of the Republican party. However, his energies are displayed in a quiet every-day effort to be of real service in the circles in which he moves, and where those who know him best appreciate the kindliness and helpful motives which govern his daily life.

The Pollak Waist Company, successor of the Paragon Manufacturing Company, represents one of the prominent manufacturing industries of the city of Fort Wayne, and the products of its factory, presented to the retail trade through the medium of a corps of eleven traveling salesmen, have proved their own best advertising, the "Wayne Maid Waist" being of recognized superiority in design and workmanship and the factory's annual output of ladies' waists being now of extensive order, the while the trade of the concern shows a constantly cumulative tendency. In the factory employment is given to three hundred and fifty persons and the trade of the company extends into the most diverse sections of the United States. The Pollak Waist Company was incorporated in 1910, with a capital stock of thirty thousand dollars, and the business has been carried forward with marked energy and progressiveness, as its success fully denotes. Those concerned in the organization of the company, as successors of the Paragon Manufacturing Company, whose business and plant were purchased by the new corporation, are the same principals who constitute the present executive corps, Herman H. Pollak being president of the company; Robert M. Pollak, vice-president; and M. Charles McDougal, secretary and treasurer. All of these officers had been residents of Cleveland, Ohio, prior to establishing the present thriving industrial and commercial enterprise in Fort Wayne, and the latter city has had much to gain and nothing to lose by their interposition in its business activities. Robert M. Pollak, vice-president of the company, was born in the city of Cleveland, Ohio, on the 13th of January, 1884, and his early educational advantages were those afforded in the public schools of the fair Forest City of the Buckeye state. After leaving school he gained broad and practical experience as an employe in a waist manufactory in his native city, where he finally became associated in the establishing of an independent enterprise of the same order, their operations having been continued in Cleveland until 1910, when they came to Fort Wayne and consolidated their business with that of the Paragon Manufacturing Company, under the present corporate title of the Pollak Waist Company. The technical knowledge and executive ability of Robert M. Pollak have made him a vigorous and progressive figure in connection with the development of the substantial business now controlled by the company and he is one of the popular and representative young business men of Fort Wayne, where he is an active member of the Commercial Club and also of the Country Club.

Herman A. Popp is making an excellent record as an executive of one of the important and successful educational institutions of Fort Wayne, where he has held the office of vice-president of the International Business College since 1899. Mr. Popp was born on a farm in Cedar Creek township, Allen county, Indiana, September 11, 1872, a son of Frederick and Barbara (Zehndner) Popp, both of whom were born in Germany and are now deceased, their surviving children being eight in number. Frederick Popp came to America when a young man and became one of the substantial farmers and highly honored citizens of Allen county, where for many years he lived and labored upon his own and well-improved farm. He was born March 6, 1827, and died, February 13, 1901, while visiting the land of his birth, his remains being laid to rest in his native country and his wife having passed the closing years of her life in Allen county. After having profited fully by the advantages of the public schools of his home county Herman A. Popp pursued a higher course of study in Taylor University, which was at that time located in Fort Wayne. Upon completing his education at the above named university, he taught in the public schools for a period of three and one-half years. He then retired from public school work to complete a thorough course in the business college of which he is now vice-president and to the upbuilding of which he has contributed in a large measure. He is a director of the Protective Electrical Supply Company of Fort Wayne and he and Mr. Staples, president of the International Business College, are associated also in the conducting of similar institutions in the cities of Elkhart and South Bend. They are pioneers in this line of educational enterprise in northern Indiana and the colleges conducted under their direction are of the best standard maintained in the middle west. Mr. Popp is independent in politics, is an active member of the Fort Wayne Commercial Club and he and his wife hold membership in the Wayne Street Methodist Episcopal church. On September 11, 1895, was solemnized the marriage of Mr. Popp to Miss Eunice Matilda Chapman, who was born in Perry township, this county, a daughter of Solomon and Hannah Chapman, her father being one of the substantial farmers of the township mentioned. Mr. and Mrs. Popp have three children—Homer G., Herbert Leslie and Ralph Emerson.

Jacob Popp has passed the past forty-seven years of his life on the farm on which he was born on February 11, 1870. It is located in Section 30, Cedar Creek township, and was the property of his parents—Frederick and Anna Barbara (Zehender) Popp. They were born in Bavaria and came to America in about 1845, locating soon thereafter in Allen county and settling on the farm in Cedar Creek township which became the property of their son Jacob in more recent years. The mother died in July, 1899, and the father soon after returned to Germany, where he passed away on February 13, 1901. They were the parents of eleven children, of which number eight survive. Jacob always stayed on the home farm and after the death of the parents the place was divided up and eighty acres fell to his share. He later added thirty-three acres more, so that he has a very comfortable tract of land at his command. He carries on general farming and dairying, giving special attention to the Jersey as an aid to profitable dairying, and he is one of the successful men in the township in his work. Mr. Popp was married on November 9, 1899, to Miss Leila Otto, who was born in Allen county and is well and favorably known throughout the county. She is the daughter of Franklin Pierce and Delila (Foltz) Otto, both of them native Indianians, and is one of their three daughters. The others are Artie Meece, the wife of Kelsey D. Fitch, of Fort Wayne, and Josie Velda, wife of August Schlatler, of Perry township. Mr. and Mrs. Popp have three children. Otto Emmett was born April 17, 1901; Arthur Jenning on August 22, 1902, and Mabel Marie on September 25, 1906. Robinson Chapel has their staunch religious support as members, and they have many friends in their home community and throughout the county where both have been known from childhood. Mr. Popp is a Democrat in politics, but not active in those matters beyond the demands of good citizenship.

Hiram Porter, one of the valued citizens of Allen county whose memory of pioneer days reaches back over a more extended period of years than those of all but a few others in northern Indiana, was born in Scioto county, Ohio, November 17, 1826, son of John and Sarah (Null) Porter. At the time of this writing, in 1917, Hiram Porter is thus nearly ninety-one years of age. To this first marriage of John Porter were born four children—Elizabeth, Hiram, Samuel and William Harrison. The children of a second marriage of John Porter—with Bethena Goings—were Christian, Hannah, Eliza, Anna, Allen, George, Joseph, Matilda, John, James, Ellen, David and two pairs of twins who died in infancy. John Porter came to Allen county, in 1833, and settled on the Breckenridge farm in St. Joseph township, on the site of the present Indiana School for Feeble Minded Youth. After clearing a few acres for cultivation he removed to the Archer farm, in Washington township, in 1836. Three years later Mr. Porter located on the Coldwater road, on the farm now owned by Mr. Rodenbeck, and in 1842 settled on the John Archer farm, where he cleared forty acres of land. Then Mr. Porter purchased eighty acres near the Lima road, in Washington township, where he resided until his death. Here he cleared a large area of land and erected a substantial log house. Hiram Porter received his earlier education in the country schools and later came to Fort Wayne, where he attended the old Methodist College. He remembers with pleasure Professors Samuel Brenton and R. D. Robinson. For sixteen years Mr. Porter taught school during the winter months and engaged in farming during the intervening summer seasons. In 1859-1861 he taught the Fletter school in St. Joseph township, No. 1. At the time of the homecoming celebration of old teachers of the county, in 1915, he was the only teacher present whose services extended back to the year 1861. Five of his pupils of that year enlisted in the Union army and all returned from the service. At the time of the roll call, in 1915, no one responded when the names of fifty-five of Mr. Porter's pupils of 1859 and fifty-eight of 1861 were called, nor were any of the patrons of the school present. Mr. Porter tells of the spot where Little Turtle, the Indian chief, is buried, as he remembers it being pointed out by Jack Hackley. He is an authority also on Johnnie Appleseed (John Chapman), who frequently visited the Porter home. He remembers the day of the burial of Johnnie Appleseed in the Archer cemetery. On February 26, 1857, Mr. Porter married Miss Hester Arnold, daughter of Elijah and Julia Ann (Mickey) Arnold, and their devoted companionship of more than half a century was broken by the death of Mrs. Porter, on June 23, 1910. After his marriage Mr. Porter continued to teach school and to cultivate the Schwartz farm in St. Joseph township. He was prevented through a physical defect from enlisting for service in the Civil War. He improved the farm on the Ann Hackley reservation and lived here until his retirement from active life, in 1890, at which time he took up his residence in the Fort Wayne residential district of Bloomingdale, on Putnam street. In 1900 he removed to his present home in Washington township. To Hiram Porter and his wife were born eleven children: John Elijah, Melissa Jane, Henry Allen, James Sylvester, William Louis, Sarah Elizabeth, Oliver Franklin, Bethena May, Hiram, Jr., Charles Walter, and Mary Viola. Mr. Porter has been a member of the Masonic fraternity since 1882. He is a Protestant in his religious views and has always been a staunch Republican in politics. In his advanced years Mr. Porter is in vigorous physical and mental health and is very active for a man of such patriarchal age.

Miles F. Porter, M. D., has been engaged in the practice of his profession in the city of Fort Wayne for nearly forty years and is with all consistency to be designated as one of the representative physicians and surgeons of Indiana. He has achieved special prestige as a surgeon and, since 1896, has given his attention almost exclusively to the surgical branch of his profession, in which connection he is professor of surgery in the Indiana University School of Medicine, in the city of Indianapolis. In his character and services he has signally honored a profession that was likewise dignified by the able interposition of his father and his paternal grandfather, and the names of few, if any, families have been longer or more prominently identified with the history of the medical profession in Indiana. Dr. Miles Fuller Porter was born at Decatur, judicial center of Adams county, Indiana, on September 27, 1856, a son of Dr. John Pomeroy Porter and Elizabeth (Darwin) Porter, whose marriage was solemnized in that place. Dr. John P. Porter received excellent educational advantages along both academic and professional lines, and in 1856 was graduated in the celebrated Rush Medical College, in the city of Chicago. Thereafter he was associated in practice with his father, Dr. Alexander Porter, a pioneer physician at Decatur, until the outbreak of the Civil War gave to him a higher call for service. He became assistant surgeon of the Eighty-ninth Indiana Infantry, and he virtually sacrificed his life in defense of the Union, as he continued his efficient

Miles F. Porter

and faithful services with his regiment until he was shot and killed by guerrillas in Missouri, in the autumn of 1864. He whose name initiates this review was a lad of about eight years at the time of his father's death and his ambition was early directed along the line of service that had been that of his father and grandfather. He acquired his early education in the schools of his native town and in eastern Ohio, and under private tutors gained an excellent knowledge of both Latin and German. He finally entered the Medical College of Ohio, at Cincinnati, and in this institution was graduated as a member of the class of 1878. After thus receiving his degree of Doctor of Medicine he served a professional novitiate of one year at Geneva, Adams county, Indiana, and he then came to Fort Wayne, where he has continued his able professional activities during the long intervening years and where his personal popularity has ever been on a parity with his recognized fidelity and ability in his exacting profession. The Doctor has held as satisfactory to himself nothing save the maximum fortification for the work of his chosen calling, and this implies that he has been a close and appreciative student and that he has kept in full touch with the advances made in medical and surgical science, the while he has gained high reputation as a surgeon. In addition to effective work in the educational branch of his profession, as a member of the faculty of the Indiana University School of Medicine, he has been actively identified with and influential in numerous professional organizations of representative order. He holds membership in the Allen County Medical Society and the Indiana State Medical Society, of which latter he has served as president; he was formerly president of the American Association of Obstetricians and Gynecologists; he is a trustee of the American Medical Association and is an active and appreciative member of the American Surgical Association. Doctor Porter is essentially loyal and public-spirited as a citizen, but has had neither time nor inclination for public office and is independent in politics. He is affiliated with the Masonic fraternity and he and his wife hold membership in the Wayne Street Methodist Episcopal church. On June 19, 1878, was solemnized the marriage of Doctor Porter to Miss Lillian Anne Wilding, daughter of James and Anne Wilding, of Fort Wayne, and of the children of this union the first born, Grace, is deceased; Lucile is the wife of Dr. Ben Perley Weaver, of this city; Charles D. is now a resident of Pittsburgh, Pennsylvania; Clara is the wife of Page Yarnelle, of Fort Wayne; Dr. Miles F., Jr., is individually mentioned immediately following this; and James P. and Elizabeth remain at the parental home.

Miles F. Porter, Jr., M. D., is, in line of direct descent, a scion of the fourth generation of the Porter family to be a representative of the medical profession in the state of Indiana, his father, Dr. Miles F. Porter, being at the present time one of the representative physicians and surgeons of the Hoosier commonwealth and being engaged in the practice of his profession as one of the foremost surgeons in the city of Fort Wayne. Concerning him individual mention is made on other pages of this volume, with further reference to other generations of the family that have given able physicians to this state. He whose name initiates this paragraph is one of the well-fortified, successful and popular physicians and surgeons of the younger generation in his native city of Fort Wayne, where he was born, January 30, 1887. He continued his studies in the public schools until he had completed a course in the Fort Wayne high school, and then entered Williams College, in which historic old Massachusetts institution he was graduated, in 1907, and from which he received the degree of Bachelor of Arts. In preparation for the profession that had been honored by the services of his father, his paternal grandfather and great-grandfather, he was then matriculated in the medical department of Harvard University, in which he was graduated as a member of the class of 1911 and from which he acquired his well-earned degree of Doctor of Medicine. On his return to Fort Wayne he became associated in practice with his father, Doctor McCaskey and Doctor Weaver, and this effective alliance has since continued, the while his cumulative success has fully justified his choice of vocation and also enabled him well to uphold the professional prestige of the family name. He maintains affiliation with the Allen County Medical Society, the Indiana State Medical Society and the American Medical Association. Both he and his wife maintain membership in the Wayne Street Methodist Episcopal church. The Doctor naturally takes loyal interest in all things touching the welfare of his native city and county and is independent in his political status. On April 11, 1912, was recorded the marriage of Doctor Porter to Miss Hester Bash, daughter of Charles S. and Flora (Orr) Bash, of Fort Wayne, and the two children of this union are Nancy Ellen, who was born, March 11, 1913, and Lucy Jane, who was born May 23, 1914.

Milton J. Porter, the executive head of the substantial enterprise carried on in the city of Fort Wayne under the title of the Porter Construction Company, is a progressive business man who is well entitled to recognition in this history. He was born at Marion, the judicial center of Grant county, Indiana, on August 27, 1861, a son of Reuben W. and Rachel Jane (Willard) Porter, natives of Indiana and representatives of sterling pioneer families of this state. Reuben W. Porter developed a prosperous business as a mover of houses and other buildings and both he and his wife passed the closing years of their lives at Marion, Grant county. Of their children the subject of this review was the second in order of birth; Adelia is the wife of Louis Powell, of Dayton, Ohio; Ezra is deceased; and William still resides at Marion, Grant county. Milton J. Porter acquired his education in the public schools of his native county and as a youth became associated with his father's house-moving business and with the handling of heavy machinery, which was made an adjunct of the enterprise. He continued his connection with his father's business until he had attained to his legal majority and has since devoted the major part of his time and attention to the line of enterprise to which he was thoroughly trained in this alliance. In 1910 he established himself in the same line of business in the city of Fort Wayne, and here has developed a prosperous business under the title of the Porter Construction Company, his contracting being now of wide scope in its direct and incidental lines and his local investments including his attractive residence property. Mr. Porter in a political way has a reason for the faith that is in him and signalizes this by staunch support of the cause of the Republican party. Both he and his wife hold membership in the Congregational church and he is affiliated with the Masonic fraternity, the Tribe of Ben Hur, the Woodmen of the World and the Independent Order of Odd Fellows, including its uniformed rank of Patriarchs Militant. July 1, 1882, recorded the marriage of Mr. Porter to Miss Nora D. Patterson, who was born in the city of Indianapolis, a daughter of Robert and Nancy C. Patterson, and the six children of this union are: James W., Robert, Laurence (deceased), Marguerite, Paul C., connected with the Porter Construction Company; Charles Milton and Ocalena B. All of the surviving children reside in Fort Wayne with the exception of James W., who maintains his home at Marion, Grant county. Marguerite is the wife of Percy Shockley, who is a traveling salesman for the Heit-Miller-Lau Company, manufacturing confectioners, and the other children remain at the parental home.

Christ Prange is a popular representative of that fine German element of citizenship that has played a very important and benignant part in the development and upbuilding of Allen county along both civic and industrial lines, and his fine dairy farm, in Washington township, is the old homestead on which he was born, the date of his nativity having been June 14, 1869. He is a son of Charles and Sophia (Brinkman) Prange, both of whom were born in Germany and came with their parents to America when they were yet children. The marriage of the parents was solemnized, January 4, 1855, and they settled in Washington township, this county, where they passed the residue of their lives—earnest, upright and industrious folk who commanded the high esteem of all who knew them and who achieved definite success and prosperity through their long and active association with farm enterprise. Mrs. Prange passed to the life eternal on July 27, 1904, and the honored husband and father preceded her, as his death occurred March 20, 1897, both having been lifelong and consistent members of the German Lutheran church. They became the parents of six children, namely: Henry, William, Charles, Sophia, Frederick and Christ. All of the children are living, in 1917, except William and Charles. Christ Prange was an alert and vigorous boy who did well his part in assisting in the work of the home farm and who made good use of the advantages afforded in the public schools of his native township. He has continued to pay honor and tribute to the basic industries of agriculture and stock-growing, remains on the old homestead, which comprises one hundred and two acres, and is giving special attention to the dairy department of his farm enterprise. He has a fine dairy herd of eighteen head of excellent cows at the time of this writing, in the spring of 1917, and finds a ready demand for his dairy products in the city of Fort Wayne. He has made the best of improvements on the home farm, including a large house of modern design and facilities, and has provided the most scientific equipment for the conducting of his dairy business under the best sanitary conditions. He is a man of energy and progressiveness, as the appearance of his beautiful farm well attests, and though he takes loyal interest in all that touches the social and material welfare of the community and is a staunch supporter of the cause of the Democratic party he has never manifested any desire for public office of any kind. Both he and his wife are active communicants and liberal supporters of the German Lutheran church at West Jefferson. On June 19, 1899, was recorded the marriage of Mr. Prange to Miss Louisa Prange, a daughter of Henry and Minnie (Millbrook) Prange, of Washington township, this county, and she is the popular chatelaine of one of the beautiful rural homes of her native county. Mr. and Mrs. Prange have no children, but in their pleasant home they delight in extending welcome to the young folk of the community as well as to their many friends of mature years.

Rev. John R. Quinlan, rector of the Cathedral at Fort Wayne, was born April 19, 1858, at Valparaiso, Indiana, son of Michael and Hannah (Shanahan) Quinlan, both natives of Ireland. They came to America with their respective families and were married at Valparaiso, Indiana. Michael Shanahan worked as a foreman in the construction of the Pittsburgh, Fort Wayne & Chicago railroad, a relative, P. T. Clifford, having a contract in the construction work. The mother of Rev. Quinlan died when he was about two years old, and in 1861 his father enlisted in the United States regular army. He served throughout the period of the Civil war, participating in the battles of Shiloh, Gettysburg, Lookout Mountain and many other noted engagements. After the close of the war he received an honorable discharge from the army and returned to Valparaiso, where he married and later removed to the state of Kansas, engaging in farming there until his death, in 1905. Rev. Quinlan was educated in the parochial schools of Valparaiso and took his classical course at the St. Francis Seminary, near Milwaukee, Wisconsin, in which institution he graduated with the class of 1890, being ordained to the priesthood on June 22 of that year. He came to Fort Wayne, on July 4 following, to receive his commission, and was appointed by Bishop Dwenger as assistant pastor of the Fort Wayne Cathedral. He remained in this position eight years and was then sent to Huntington, where he established St. Mary's parish, building a church, school, residence and Sisters' house. He remained in Huntington three and one-half years and then was recalled, on March 10, 1901, to Fort Wayne, where he was made rector of the Cathedral. Six months later he suffered a nervous breakdown and in consequence was given a temporary release from his duties and returned to Huntington, where he remained until July 6, 1910. Having fully recovered he again came to Fort Wayne, took up the duties of rector of the Cathedral and has remained in that position to the present time.

Christian Rahdert is one of the younger farming men of Washington township, who, in a community of prosperous men, has found a place among them well meriting his labors since he turned his attention to the serious business of life. He has progressed with each succeeding year and his holdings today are well worthy of mention. Mr. Rahdert is a native son of his home community, born in Washington township on June 27, 1876, and his parents were Fred C. and Martha N. (Arney) Rahdert. The father was German born, it should be said, and the mother was an Allen county girl, coming of one of the old established families in this part of the state. Fred Rahdert came to Allen county as a young man and there met and married his wife. They established a home in Washington township, reared a family of ten children, and made themselves a part of the community life in every way. Their children were Mary, Louise, Sophia, Anna, Martha, Christian, Amelia, Fred, Eunice and Emma. Sophia and Fred are deceased. Christian Rahdert was schooled in the Washington township schools and his advantages were of necessity limited. He early identified himself with farm life and has since continued in that industry, enjoying more than average success and acquiring title to one hundred and twenty acres of fine land in his native township. He has made many improvements on the place and has a fine home. He married in 1902, Eliza Kramer being the girl of his choice. Concerning her family mention is to be found in a sketch referring to her father, Charles Kramer, elsewhere in this work. Mr. and

Mrs. Rahdert became the parents of two children, Wilmer and Verna, and the wife and mother died on February 22, 1913. Mr. Rahdert married a second time, Sophia Rosebrock becoming his wife on March 24, 1914. She is a daughter of Christopher and Marie (Stroubil) Rosebrock, the parents natives of Germany. There are three children of the second marriage—Frederick, born January 23, 1915, Paul, born March 28, 1916, and Martha, born March 18, 1917. Mr. and Mrs. Rahdert are members of St. Paul's Lutheran church at Fort Wayne.

Frank C. Rahe passed his entire life in Fort Wayne, gained secure status as one of the city's representative business men, and was a citizen whose sterling character and worthy achievement gained to him the inviolable confidence and esteem of all who knew him. His father, Carl Rahe, was born and reared in Germany and upon coming to America became one of the pioneers of Fort Wayne, where he and his wife passed the remainder of their lives. He to whom this memoir is dedicated was born in Fort Wayne on January 23, 1853, and here his death occurred on July 10, 1900, his mortal remains being laid to rest in the beautiful Lindenwood cemetery. He was a lifelong and earnest communicant of the Lutheran church, and his widow, who still resides in Fort Wayne, continues an active and devoted member of the same religious organization. Mr. Rahe acquired his youthful education in the Lutheran parochial schools and the public schools of Fort Wayne, and in finding a field for successful activity in the commercial world finally engaged in the manufacturing of cigars, of which line of enterprise he continued as a prominent and successful representative in Fort Wayne until the time of his death. By energy and good management he built up a large and prosperous business and as a citizen was always ready to lend his influence and co-operation in the support of measures and enterprises projected for the general good of his native city and county. Though he had no desire for political activity or public office he gave a staunch support to the cause of the Democratic party, and, as previously noted, his religious faith was that of the Lutheran church. In the year 1881 was solemnized the marriage of Mr. Rahe to Miss Katherine Pierman, who was born in Germany and was a child of four years at the time of her parents' immigration to the United States. She is a daughter of Zachariah and Emma (Feldman) Pierman, who were residents of Allen county, near Maysville, at the time of their death. Mrs. Rahe is the owner of three valuable residence properties in Fort Wayne, including her own attractive home, and the city is endeared to her by the memories and associations of the past. Two children were born to Mr. and Mrs. Rahe—William Frank and Frederick C. (twins). The former died at the age of one week and the latter is bookkeeper for Wolf and Dessauer. He married Miss Elizabeth Popp and they have one son, James Franklin.

Frank J. Rahe.—One of the prosperous and rising young business men of Fort Wayne today is Frank J. Rahe. He began his business career at the age of thirteen, starting out in the employ of the D. N. Foster Furniture Company. One promotion followed another until today Mr. Rahe is treasurer and manager of that well-known concern. Mr. Rahe was born on March 3, 1881, in Cincinnati, Ohio, son of Henry and Amelia (Ellerman) Rahe. The father was born in Germany, coming to America in 1852, and for years was engaged in the contracting business in Cincinnati and Fort Wayne. The mother was born in Brookville, Indiana, and with her husband is now deceased. They were the parents of six children. Elizabeth is the wife of Henry Wiegmann, of Fort Wayne. Edward is established in business. Ella lives in Fort Wayne. Emma is the wife of H. L. Dunkle, of St. Joe, Indiana. Frank J. was the next in order of birth, and Will is living in Fort Wayne. Frank J. Rahe attended the German Lutheran school and also the public schools of Fort Wayne up to the age of thirteen, when he left his books for the serious business of life. As stated above, he went to work for the D. N. Foster Furniture Company and from that time on his rise was rapid. He was a hard worker, determined to succeed from the beginning, and his present important position has come to him as his just due in return for faithful service, cheerfully rendered. Mr. Rahe is Republican in politics and a member of the Presbyterian church. He has served as president of the Merchants' Association, in 1910-11, and was president of the Indiana Retail Furniture Association in 1912-13. He is a member of the Rotary Club, the Commercial Club and the Modern Woodmen of America. He was married, in 1905, to Miss Claire Pearl Foster, daughter of D. N. Foster, who is mentioned elsewhere in these pages. Two children have come to Mr. and Mrs. Rahe—Maxine Foster and David Foster Rahe.

John H. Rahe was for a long period of years one of the prominent business men and representative citizens of Fort Wayne, where he conducted a furniture store that received a substantial and appreciative patronage. He was a youth of eighteen years when he came from his native Germany and established his home in Fort Wayne, where he learned the trade of cabinetmaking, becoming a skilled workman and from the work of his trade being gradually advanced into the general furniture business of retail order. He was a man of the highest integrity, resolute, ambitious and endowed with excellent judgment, so that success came to him as a natural prerogative. He had no desire to come into the white light of publicity, but was most loyal and liberal as a citizen and took abiding interest in all things pertaining to the welfare of the city in which he maintained his home for nearly sixty years and in which his death occurred on February 27, 1911, his remains being laid to rest in the beautiful Concordia cemetery. He had been a lifelong and earnest communicant of the Lutheran church and was active in the support of the same, his widow likewise being a devoted member of this fine religious organization. Mr. Rahe was born in Germany on November 26, 1835, and thus had celebrated his seventy-sixth birthday anniversary about two months prior to his death. He was reared and educated in his native land and was eighteen years of age when he severed the home ties and set forth to seek his fortunes in America. Soon after his arrival in the United States he came to Fort Wayne, where he applied himself vigorously to the work of the cabinetmaker's trade until the time when he established himself in the furniture business. Of this line of retail enterprise he continued a successful and popular exponent for fully thirty years and through his association with the same gained substantial prosperity, the while he figured as one of the prominent merchants of the city. He was generous and kindly in all of the relations of life and his circle of friends was limited only by that of his acquaintances. Though he had no desire to take part in active politics or to become a candidate for public office of any description, he was always ready to lend his influence and co-operation in the furtherance of the social and material prosperity of Fort Wayne, and his political allegiance was given to the Democratic party. His strong and noble character manifested itself most luminously in the precincts of his home, and none could have been more devoted as husband and father, the fine residence which he provided being still occupied by his widow, to whom Fort Wayne is endeared by the gracious memories and association of the past. In 1859 was solemnized the marriage of Mr. Rahe to Miss Sophia Blase, who was born in Germany and was a young woman of twenty-two years when she came to the United States. Mr. and Mrs. Rahe became the parents of one son, Henry, who is now a resident of the city of Detroit, Michigan, and whose only child, May Stella, now lives in the home of her paternal grandmother, Mrs. Rahe, to whom she accords solicitude and companionship.

Alfred L. Randall is a citizen who has shown in deeds as well as words his loyal interest in his native city and county and is one of the prominent representatives of the automobile trade in Fort Wayne, his having been the first commercial garage established in the city. He was born in Fort Wayne on November 18, 1867, a son of Franklin P. and Mary J. (Read) Randall, honored pioneer citizens of Fort Wayne at the time of their death. Franklin P. Randall was born in the state of New York and became a resident of Allen county, Indiana, in 1835. He was one of the prominent and influential citizens of Fort Wayne and the high place that he held in popular confidence and esteem is indicated in the fact that he served fourteen years as mayor of the city, a record that has been equaled by no other man who has been the executive head of the municipal government. He was engaged in the insurance business for a long period and was about eighty years of age at the time of his death. Of his ten children six are living, in 1917. Alfred L. Randall attended the public schools until he had profited by the advantages of the Fort Wayne high school and thereafter attended the old Methodist College and Taylor University, in which latter he was a student for two years. After his school days he was employed in a local plumbing establishment two years and for the ensuing two years was employed in the office of the Kerr Murray Manufacturing Company. The next three years found him the incumbent of the position of cashier for the Seavey Hardware Company, and then, in 1893, he here established himself in the bicycle business. He continued one of the prominent representatives of this line of business in northern Indiana until the bicycle had begun to wane in popularity, and, in 1902, he established the first automobile garage and salesroom in his native city; he developed a prosperous business as agent for various makes of automobiles until the fall of 1916, when he disposed of his business, but still continued to represent automobile trucks, etc., in this field. He erected and owns the modern theater building of the Jefferson Theater Company, of which he is president. Mr. Randall is president of the Fort Wayne board of education, is president of the Fort Wayne Auto Trade Association, is secretary of the Fort Wayne Motor Club, and in his handling of automobiles is president of the Randall Sales Corporation. Mr. Randall is affiliated with the Benevolent and Protective Order of Elks, is one of the loyal and progressive members of the Fort Wayne Commercial Club, in which he is a member of the Lincoln Highway Committee, and is also actively identified with the local Rotary Club. His political allegiance is given to the Democratic party and both he and his wife are communicants of the Protestant Episcopal church. On November 5, 1890, was solemnized the marriage of Mr. Randall to Miss Grace Greenwood Hayden, daughter of John W. Hayden, who is engaged in the real estate business in Fort Wayne. Mr. and Mrs. Randall have five children: Mary is the wife of Capt. Charles T. Williams, of the U. S. Army Engineers' Corps, of Washington, D. C., and Phyllis, Virginia, Sarah Grace and Alfred H. remain at the parental home.

Frank M. Randall, who, in the office of city engineer, is one of the able and popular executives in connection with municipal affairs in his native city of Fort Wayne, has also the further distinction of being a scion of one of the honored pioneer families of this section of the Hoosier state. His father, the late Franklin P. Randall, came to Allen county nearly eighty years ago and was one of the able and influential pioneers of Fort Wayne, even as he was one of the leading members of the bar of this section of the state in the formative period of the history of Allen county and its present fine metropolis. Franklin P. Randall was born in Madison county, New York, on June 2, 1812, and was a scion of the seventh generation of the Randall family in America, the original progenitors having come from England and here established residence in the early colonial period of our national history. His grandfather on the paternal side was a gallant soldier of the Continental Line in the war of the Revolution and was an officer of a regiment that took part in the battle of Saratoga, besides which he was a personal witness of the surrender of General Burgoyne. The father of Franklin P. Randall was an officer of the patriot forces that participated in the war of 1812, after the close of which he resumed his active association with agricultural pursuits, in Madison county, New York, where he and his wife passed the residue of their lives. In his youth Franklin P. Randall received good educational advantages, and in this connection it may be noted that he attended both Cortland and Hamilton Academies, excellent New York educational institutions of the day. For a time he was engaged successfully in the teaching of school in his native state and then began the study of law under the effective preceptorship of Judge Ellis Lewis, who served fourteen years as chief justice of the supreme court of the state of New York. In February, 1838, Mr. Randall was admitted to the New York bar and a few months later came to Indiana and established his home at Fort Wayne, which was then a small village. He became closely, worthily and prominently identified with the development and progress of this section of Indiana, with loyal interest in all things touching the civic and material advancement of the community, and his character and ability made him a dominant force in connection with public affairs in the pioneer village and county. Very soon after he had established his residence at Fort Wayne he was called upon to serve in public office, and thereafter, during the long period of his residence in Allen county, he gave much of his time and effective attention to service in public offices of varied orders. He was one of the best known and most honored pioneer citizens of Fort Wayne at the time of his death, in 1892, and his name must ever be given significant distinction in the recorded history of the city and county in which he so long lived and labored unselfishly, loyally and effectively, with a supreme sense of personal stewardship in connection with those things that make for the general good of the community. Mr. Randall was a young man at the time of his marriage to Miss Mary J. Read, who was born in Kentucky, and who was one of the venerable and revered pioneer women of Fort Wayne at the time of her death, in 1913. Frank M. Randall, the immediate subject of this review, was born in Fort Wayne and in the public schools of his native city continued his studies until he had completed the curriculum of the high school. He then entered Purdue University, at Lafayette, in which he completed a thorough course in mathematics and civil engineering. Thereafter his first specific application of his technical knowledge was achieved when he became associated with a surveying corps that was engaged in railway construction work in Ohio. Later he was identified also with the engineering corps of the Nickel Plate Railroad. In 1891 the city council of Fort Wayne tendered him the office of city engineer, and of this important position he has since continued the efficient and valued incumbent. Within his long period of service he has accomplished a large amount of important municipal engineer work of various kinds, and his administration has been signally discriminating, practical and progressive. Within his regime have been made vast improvements and extensions in the paving of the streets of Fort Wayne, the establishing and amplifying of the modern sewerage system, and other important work whose superiority clearly demonstrates his technical ability and executive resourcefulness. He has permitted no work to pass muster without being held to the highest possible standard, and his native city owes to him much for the effective service he has given during the period of its most remarkable development and progress along both civic and material lines, the progressive trend of the city being still vigorous and normal and his loyalty to his home city being of the most insistent order. He has been unswerving in his allegiance to his chosen profession and thus has had no inclination to enter the arena of so-called practical politics, though he gives a staunch support to the cause of the Democratic party. In 1884 was solemnized the marriage of Mr. Randall to Miss Calla Embury, and they have three children: Ruth is a successful and popular teacher in the high school of the city of Detroit, Michigan; May is the wife of Austin Melchers, of Detroit; and Franklin P. is a member of the class of 1917 in the law department of the great University of Michigan, at Ann Arbor.

William F. Ranke.—The fiscal affairs of Allen county are being carefully and effectively conserved under the administration of Captain Ranke as treasurer of the county, and he is now serving his second term in this office, a fact that vouches for the inviolable place which is his in popular confidence and good will in his native county, and this objective attitude being the more significant when it is understood that in the election of 1916 he was the only Democrat elected to office on the county ticket. Captain Ranke, whose military title was gained through effective service with the Indiana National Guard and as an officer in the Spanish-American war, was born in Fort Wayne on January 20, 1865, and is a scion of one of the old and honored German families of northern Indiana. He is a son of William and Sophia W. (Jacob) Ranke, both natives of Germany, where the former was born, September 16, 1838, and the latter, February 18, 1845. Captain Ranke gained his preliminary education in the Lutheran parochial schools of Fort Wayne and thereafter attended the old Methodist Episcopal College in this city and also Concordia College. In 1885 he was graduated in the department of pharmacy of the University of Michigan and thereafter continued his active identification with the drug business in Fort Wayne until January 1, 1908, when he became an employe in the office of the treasurer of Allen county. His ability enabled him to profit fully by the technical experience thus gained, and thus he was a normal and specially eligible candidate when he was elected to the office of county treasurer in 1914. In his first term he fully justified the popular choice of an incumbent, and the estimate placed upon his administration was significantly shown when he was re-elected, in 1916, as the only successful candidate on the Democratic ticket in the county, his friends and admirers having rallied to his standard without reference to partisan lines. Captain Ranke has been one of the influential figures in Democratic politics in this section of the state and has been closely identified with the maneuvering of political forces in his native county. In 1906 he was elected senator from Allen county and served during the legislative sessions of 1907, 1908 and 1909, his record having been marked by characteristic loyalty to his constituency and by effective influence in the furtherance of wise legislation. Captain Ranke's identification with the Indiana National Guard had its inception in 1887, when he became a private in Battery E. In this fine organization he won promotion to the office of captain, and when the Spanish-American war broke out he enlisted with his command, which became the Twenty-eighth Battery of Indiana Volunteers. He served as captain of this battery from the time of its enrollment in the United States volunteer service, on April 26, 1898, until the organization was mustered out, on the 31st of the following October. The battery was mobilized in one of the southern reserve camps and was not called to the stage of active warfare in Cuba, much to the regret of its members. In 1899 President McKinley appointed Captain Ranke a captain in the Thirty-ninth United States Infantry, but he resigned this commission and did not join the regiment, owing to the exigencies of his private business affairs. The Captain is past department commander of the Indiana Department of the United Spanish War Veterans, is an active member of the Military Order of Foreign Wars, and also of the Naval and Military Order of the Spanish-American War. He is affiliated with the Benevolent and Protective Order of Elks and other fraternal organizations, and his religious faith is that of the Lutheran church. When the serried ranks of the eligible bachelors of Allen county pass in review it will be noted that Captain Ranke marches therein with true military nerve and precision.

Lyman H. Ransom is one of the most venerable and honored of the active business men of Fort Wayne, where he has maintained his home for more than forty years and now holds the dual office of secretary and treasurer of the Fort Wayne Mercantile Accident Association, a corporation that controls a large and important business in the extending of indemnity along clearly defined lines of insurance, the published literature of the association giving adequate data concerning the province and service of the association. Mr. Ransom is a scion of one of the honored pioneer families of the state of Michigan, his parents having there established their residence in the territorial period of the history of that commonwealth. He was born on a pioneer farm near Sturgis, St. Joseph county, Michigan, on July 17, 1837—the year that marked the admission of that state to the Union—and he is a son of Henry M. and Betsey P. (Banning) Ransom, who were born and reared in Connecticut, where their marriage was solemnized, both having been representatives of families that were founded in New England in the colonial era of our national history. Upon his removal to the wilds of southern

Michigan Henry M. Ransom became one of the pioneer farmers of St. Joseph county, where he reclaimed his farm from the forest and became a substantial and influential citizen, both he and his wife having continued their residence in the Wolverine state until their death. Lyman H. Ransom was reared to the sturdy discipline of the pioneer farm and in addition to availing himself of the advantages of the common schools of the locality and period also pursued a higher course in a well-ordered academy at LaGrange, Indiana—a place not far distant from that of his birth. That he made good use of his scholastic opportunities was demonstrated in the success which attended his pedagogic efforts during the period of about five years that he was a teacher in the common schools of southern Michigan and northern Indiana. He finally engaged in the hardware business at Burr Oak, an attractive village of his native county, and after a period of seven years sold his stock and business and became a traveling salesman for a wholesale hardware house of New York. In 1874 he established his residence in Fort Wayne. For the ensuing seven years he was a traveling representative of the firm of Prescott Brothers and Company, here engaged in the hardware business, and after severing this association he passed ten years in similar service for the firm of Morgan and Beach, also of Fort Wayne. In 1899 he assumed his present position, that of secretary and treasurer of the Fort Wayne Mercantile Accident Association, and has been primarily instrumental in the development and upbuilding of the substantial business now controlled by the representative corporation. Mr. Ransom has from his youth given staunch allegiance to the Republican party and has shown himself at all times a broad-gauged and progressive citizen, the while he has been accorded the full measure of popular confidence and good will. On May 14, 1862, Mr. Ransom wedded Miss Jennie L. Duncan, daughter of Alonzo Duncan, of Coldwater, the judicial center of Branch county, Michigan. Mrs. Ransom was summoned to the life eternal on September 6, 1913, and of the four children of this union only the eldest, Newell H., of Fort Wayne, is living. The names of the deceased children are here designated: Nellie P., Edward P., and Maude N. On January 26, 1915, was solemnized the marriage of Mr. Ransom to Mrs. Hannah Gross, of Fort Wayne, and she is the popular chatelaine of their pleasant home.

Carl L. Rastetter.—When the late Carl L. Rastetter left the Fatherland and made his way to America, he settled in Fort Wayne, there establishing himself in the drug business. He knew no other American city as home, for he spent the remainder of his life in the community in which he settled upon his arrival on our shores. He was a prosperous merchant and a good citizen, and Fort Wayne lost a desirable and estimable member of society when Death claimed him. Mr. Rastetter was born in Germany on March 18, 1866, and died at his home on December 3, 1911. He was a son of William J. and Mathilde Rastetter, both now deceased. The father was for many years director of a prominent German institution of learning. Carl L., of this review, was one of three children of his parents. He was the eldest, and the others are Anna, the wife of Prof. O. Reans, of Constance, Germany, and Gustav, of Breslau, Germany. Mr. Rastetter was just twenty-four years of age when he came to America. He had been well educated in his native land—was a graduate of the Polytechnic and an accomplished linguist. When he located in Fort Wayne he decided that a practical business enterprise might be more remunerative than the educational field, and he accordingly established himself in the drug business at East Washington and Harmar streets. He continued to conduct a successful drug business at that place up to the time of his death. Mr. Rastetter was married on February 1, 1893, to Miss Rose Miller, of Fort Wayne. She was a daughter of John J. and Barbara (Weber) Miller, both natives of Germany. The father was a jeweler by trade and was engaged in the jewelry business in Fort Wayne, where he was one of the earliest settlers. Mrs. Rastetter was one of the five children of her parents and the youngest of the family. The others were John, of Chicago; Erwin, of Fort Wayne; Anna, who died in Fort Wayne, and Angela, the wife of John Lennart, of Fort Wayne. To Mr. and Mrs. Rastetter five children came. The eldest, Erwin, is living in Detroit. Hilda, Anna, Carl and John are still at home with their mother. Mr. Rastetter was a Democrat in politics and adhered to the faith of his fathers, the Roman Catholic church. During his life in Fort Wayne he accumulated a considerable property and the family home is located at 915 East Washington street.

Charles A. Rastetter.—Real estate is the basis of all security and in every community of populous order there is imperative demand for the interposition of dealers and agents of vigorous enterprise in controlling or directing real estate transactions, as such operations touch the most vital civic and material interests of the communal life. In his native city of Fort Wayne Mr. Rastetter is an able and progressive representative of the real estate business and as a young man of marked energy, initiative and good judgment has not only succeeded in developing a substantial business but has gained the confidence and good will of all with whom he has had dealings. He was born in Fort Wayne on October 21, 1883, a son of Louis and Elizabeth (Howenstein) Rastetter. Louis Rastetter was born and reared in Germany and was a young man when he came to the United States and established his residence in Fort Wayne, where he found employment at his trade, that of machinist. He was an exceptionally skilled artisan and it is worthy of historic note in this connection that he manufactured the clocks that long and effectively marked the passing hours in the tower of the old courthouse of Allen county. He later engaged in the manufacturing of carriages and long held secure vantage-ground as one of the substantial business men and highly esteemed citizens of Fort Wayne, where he died in February, 1898, at the age of sixty-four years, his widow still maintaining her residence in their old homestead, on Broadway. He was a stalwart Republican in his political proclivities and was affiliated with the Ancient Order of United Workmen. His venerable widow has been a devoted communicant for many years of the Salem Reformed church. Of the four children the subject of this review was the third in order of birth and all still reside in Fort Wayne: William C. is here engaged in the manufacturing business; Helen is the wife of John Wilkins; and Mary Ann remains with her widowed mother in the old homestead. Charles A. Rastetter continued his studies in the public schools of Fort Wayne until he had profited by the advantages of the high school and thereafter completed a course in the Fort Wayne Business College. For many years he was associated with the work and management of his father's carriage factory, and, since 1913, has been engaged in the real estate business. He handles both city and farm property, has gained a substantial clientage and upon his books are represented at all times most desirable investments and properties for exchange. He gives attention also to collections and rentals of an order consonant with his general real estate operations. Mr. Rastetter is found aligned as a staunch supporter of the cause of the Republican party, is affiliated with the Benevolent and Protective Order of Elks, also Masonic Order, is a member of the United Commercial Travelers' Association and C. T. M. A., and both he and his wife are communicants of Salem Reformed church, also a member of the consistory; of the Sunday school of which he is serving as treasurer for a second time in 1916-17. In 1911 was solemnized the marriage of Mr. Rastetter to Miss Sarah Meschberger, daughter of Fred Meschberger, of Fort Wayne, and their pleasant home is known for its hospitality. Mr. Rastetter is secretary of the appraisement committee of the Fort Wayne Real Estate Board, having been appointed as a member of the same for a period of three years.

Henry A. Rathge was born in Germany on September 25, 1864, a son of Cort and Mary (Feldman(Rathge, who came from Germany to America, and in 1878 settled in Henry county, Ohio. They lived in that region until the death of the mother, in 1889, when the father moved to Allen county and at the present writing makes his home with his son William, a resident of Maumee township. He was the father of five children, named Fred, Henry A., Herman, William and Diedrick. Henry Rathge had his early schooling in Germany, being ten years old when the family came to America, and he added something to his education in the schools of Henry county. He early learned the carpenter trade, in which he became proficient, and followed the trade for thirteen years in Ohio. In 1903 he came to Allen county, Indiana, gave up his trade and bought a farm of one hundred and seventy-three acres in Sections 34-5 of Maumee township. He has lived there from then to the present time and has cleared, tiled, fenced and otherwise improved the land so that it is today one of the fine places in the township. Modern buildings maintain the general high standard of the place and general farming and stock-raising are the enterprises to which the owner and manager devotes his energies. Mr. Rathge was married on November 22, 1906, to Alvina Theek, daughter of Christ and Caroline (Ettleben) Theek, German born people who came to America in 1883, settled in Defiance county, Ohio, and the father became a successful brick-mason there. To Mr. and Mrs. Rathge three children have come. They are named Evelyn, Esther and Harold. Mr. and Mrs. Rathge and the children are members of the German Lutheran church and Mr. Rathge has served as a member of the Advisory Board of Maumee township for the past four years. He is a Democrat and takes a proper interest in local politics, though in no sense a politician. He has no fraternal affiliations.

George F. Rauh.—Among the successful and well-known farmers of St. Joseph township George F. Rauh has, in nineteen years of continuous residence and activity, found a secure place and many friends. He is one of the quiet, steady-going men of the community, always to be relied upon and certain to be found supporting those measures and movements designed to wield a beneficent influence and to better civic life. He was born in Germany on April 2, 1861, a son of Nicholas and Elizabeth (Miller) Rauh, both of whom passed their lives in their native country. George Rauh had his early schooling there and was twenty-two years old when he came to America in 1883, settling at once in Fort Wayne, where he continued to reside until 1889. In that year he married Sabine Schrumm, daughter of Jacob Schrumm. Her parents were from Ireland. After his marriage Mr. Rauh moved to St. Joseph township, where he bought eighty acres of land and settled down to farm life. He has enjoyed a pleasing measure of success, developing his farm to a high degree and carrying on general farming and stock raising. He has never been openly active in politics, though he votes the Democratic ticket as a rule, and has held no offices in the community. He and his wife are members of the German Lutheran church and are among its staunch supporters. They have no children.

Edwin H. Redding, auditor and assistant secretary of the Lincoln Life Insurance Company in the city of Fort Wayne, has won advancement and prestige in connection with this line of business enterprise and is one of its able exponents in his native state. Mr. Redding was born at Bluffton, the judicial center of Wells county, Indiana, on November 12, 1880, a son of William A. and Caroline (Elick) Redding, who still reside in that county, the father being a representative farmer and also having given most effective service as county commissioner, his incumbency of this important office indicating definitely that he is one of the honored and influential citizens of Wells county. After having availed himself of the advantages of the public schools of Bluffton Edwin H. Redding prosecuted a higher course of study in Valparaiso University and later completed an effective course in Voorhees Business College, in the city of Indianapolis. After leaving the latter institution he served for a short time as stenographer for the Big Four Railroad, in its office at Mattoon, Illinois, and then returned to the capital city of Indiana, where he held for eighteen months a position as clerk and stenographer in the offices of the George T. Evans Mining Company. He next initiated his association with the insurance business by assuming the position of assistant cashier in the Indianapolis offices of the Equitable Life Assurance Society of New York city, an office of which he continued the incumbent four years. At the expiration of this period, in 1906, he came to Fort Wayne to accept a similar position in the offices of the Lincoln Life Insurance Company, and his efficient service led to his being advanced, in 1911, to his present responsible office of auditor and assistant secretary of this important company. He has entered fully into the progressive spirit and business vitality of the Allen county metropolis and judicial center and is an active member of the Fort Wayne Commercial Club. On May 17, 1909, was solemnized the marriage of Mr. Redding to Miss Bernice Pommert, daughter of Joseph and Etta Pommert, of Auburn, DeKalb county, and the one child of this union is a fine little son, Robert.

Adam A. Reinhart.—In connection with the history of Fort Wayne and Allen county far more than cursory interest attaches to the representative citizen and influential business man whose name introduces this article, for on both the paternal and distaff sides he is a scion of sterling pioneer stock in this city and county, his father having been a young man when he became a resident of Fort Wayne, soon after arriving in America, his emigration to the United States having occurred in 1849, in which year he established his home in Fort Wayne. The maternal grandfather of Adam A. Reinhart was one of the earliest settlers of what is now the judicial center and metropolis of Allen county, and this section of the state was a primitive wilderness at the time, with but few white settlers to dispute dominion with the Indians. Mr. Reinhart has been a resident of Fort Wayne from the time of his birth, which here occurred, June 2, 1868, and is now one of the leading merchants and progressive and valued citizens of his native city, where he is associated with James L. Shields in the conducting of a most prosperous clothing and men's furnishing business, under the title of the Shields Clothing Company, he being the junior member of the firm. Matthias Reinhart, father of the subject of this review, was born in Germany, in the year 1831, and thus was about eighteen years of age when, in 1849, he immigrated to America and became a resident of Fort Wayne. He was a shoemaker by trade and with the passing years became one of the successful business men of the city in which he passed the remainder of his life and in which he commanded unqualified popular esteem, his death having occurred in 1891. His wife, whose maiden name was Anna Bargus, was born in a log house that stood on the site of the present Palace theater in Fort Wayne and was the first child born of German parentage in Allen county. Her father, Martin Bargus, came to Fort Wayne, in 1824, and made the long and arduous journey from New York to Fort Wayne with an ox team and a wagon. His marriage was solemnized when he was a youth of twenty years and the nuptial ceremony was performed in the old Anthony Wayne fort, by an itinerant missionary. Mr. Bargus assisted in the construction of the old canal that had much to do with furthering the development of Fort Wayne and which was an important medium of transportation in the pioneer days. He was a skilled workman at the carpenter's trade and utilized his mechanical ability by the construction of many of the old-time wheelbarrows used in the pioneer community. At the time of his arrival in Fort Wayne Mr. Bargus wore a seemly German coat and waistcoat gaily ornamented with brass buttons, and the Indians manifested great admiration for the buttons, which they proceeded to cut from his garments. Because he made no objection to their taking of the buttons they gave to him, in their own language, the title of the "Blessed Dutchman." During the great cholera epidemic that many years ago ravaged Allen county, Mr. Bargus personally escaped attack and was able to do noble service in the stricken community, not only in caring for the afflicted but also in making the coffins for the victims of the scourge and assisting in the burial of the dead, it having been his melancholy duty to render this service for his loved and devoted wife, who was among those who succumbed to the dread malady. He was a charter member and earnest communicant of St. Mary's Catholic church in Fort Wayne, as were also the parents of Mr. Reinhart, subject of this review. The mother of Mr. Reinhart survived her husband and was venerable in years at the time of her death. Of the ten children Adam A. is the eldest of the four now living; Mary and John likewise continue their residence in Fort Wayne, the latter being a traveling salesman by occupation; and Laura is the wife of James B. Cahill, who is engaged in the undertaking business in Fort Wayne. Adam A. Reinhart is indebted to the parochial schools of St. Mary's church for his early educational training, and after leaving school became identified with mercantile enterprise in his native city, where he has won advancement to secure position as one of the representative business men of Allen county. For a number of years he was independently engaged in the conducting of a general haberdashing business and finally formed a partnership with James L. Shields, with whom he has since continued to be associated in the conducting of one of the leading clothing stores of the city, the establishment of the Shields Clothing Company being essentially metropolitan in its equipment and service and its trade being of substantial and representative order. Mr. Reinhart naturally takes loyal interest in all that touches the welfare and progress of his native city and county, his political allegiance being given to the Democratic party and both he and his wife being zealous communicants of the Catholic church. In a fraternal way he is affiliated with the Knights of Columbus and the Loyal Order of Moose. On August 8, 1893, was solemnized the marriage of Mr. Reinhart to Miss Elizabeth Heiny, who likewise was born and reared in Fort Wayne and is a daughter of the late Nicholas and Mary M. (Schele) Heiny, her father having been for a long period engaged in the grocery business in this city, where both he and his wife died. Mr. and Mrs. Reinhart have four children: Margaret remains at the parental home; Edward is in the employ of S. F. Bowser and Company; Marie is in the employ of the Lincoln Life Insurance Company as stenographer, and Jeanette Laura Josephine is the youngest.

Charles J. Reuss, the efficient and popular assistant secretary of the Centlivre Brewing Company, is one of the representative young business men of his native city of Fort Wayne, where he was born July 2, 1880, a son of John B. and Amelia (Centlivre) Reuss, the former of German and the latter of French lineage. John B. Reuss was born at Bad Kissengen, Germany, and was fifteen years of age when he came to the United States and established his residence in Cincinnati, whence he later came to Fort Wayne. He learned the jeweler's trade in his youth but eventually became identified with the business of the Centlivre Brewing Company, of which important Fort Wayne corporation he is now secretary. He is one of the city's progressive and influential business men, is a Democrat in politics and both he and his wife are communicants of the Fort Wayne Cathedral parish of the Catholic church, as are also their five children. Charles J. Reuss gained his early education in the parochial school of St. Mary's church and in that conducted by the Christian Brothers. At the age of fourteen years he entered the great Notre Dame University at South Bend, where he continued his studies for the ensuing six years. In 1900 he left the university, while in his junior year, and became a clerk in the offices of the Centlivre Brewing Company, his advancement to his present office, that of assistant secretary, have been recorded in 1913. Mr. Reuss is one of the popular young bachelors of Allen county, is an active member of the Fort Wayne Commercial Club, the Country Club and the Rotary Club, and is affiliated with the Benevolent & Protective Order of Elks, besides holding membership in the local Rifle and Revolver Club. His political allegiance is given unreservedly to the Democratic party and he is a communicant of the Cathedral parish of the Catholic church. He finds his chief recreation and diversion in periodical hunting and fishing trips and as a progressive young citizen takes loyal interest in all that concerns the welfare of his home city and county.

John B. Reuss.—A vivid and buoyant personality is that of this well known citizen and influential business man of Fort Wayne, and through his own ability and efforts he has made his way forward to the goal of prosperity and to a commanding place in connection with business affairs of broad scope and importance. Mr. Reuss has been a resident of Fort Wayne for more than forty years, is secretary of the C. L. Centlivre Brewing Company, and his prominence as an influential figure in the civic and commercial life of Fort Wayne is further indicated by his being a stockholder and director in the Home Telephone Company, The Tri-State Loan & Trust Company and a number of other important corporations. In his close association with the social and industrial progress of Fort Wayne he has brought to bear the full force of a tense, vital and resourceful individuality, and his civic loyalty has been shown in divers avenues of enterprise and promotive energy. Mr. Reuss was born on April 1, 1851, in Kissingen, a prominent European watering place in Bavaria, Germany, made famous chiefly through its medicinal springs which bubble up in sparkling profusion from nature's laboratory, for the purpose of curing various human ills. In the excellent schools of his native land Mr. Reuss acquired his youthful education, and, in 1865, just at the termination of the great Civil war in the United States, through the influence of an uncle, a piano manufacturer in Cincinnati, Ohio, he came to America and established his residence in the Ohio city, where he soon accepted a position with H. Duhme & Company, a large jewelry manufacturing firm. In 1874 he came to Fort Wayne and entered the employ of George J. E. Meyer, who was then one of the city's leading jewelers. In November of 1876 Mr. Reuss was married to Miss Amelia M. Centlivre, of Fort Wayne, and to this union were born five children. During the long intervening years Mr. Reuss has continued his vigorous identification with business activities in Fort Wayne, and in 1891 he became one of the interested principals in the C. L. Centlivre Brewing Company, of which he has served as secretary since its incorporation, in 1895. It has been consistently said that "much of the success of the enterprise is due to the efforts of Mr. Reuss, whose wide acquaintance and unqualified popularity have been potent in furthering the upbuilding of the large and prosperous industrial enterprise." He has had much to do with the development of Fort Wayne along both industrial and commercial lines, is cosmopolitan in his tastes, and his experience, as he has traveled extensively, "there being few points of interest in the civilized portions of the globe that have not been visited by him." He is one of the vital and valued members of the Fort Wayne Lodge of the Benevolent and Protective Order of Elks, with which he has been affiliated during practically the entire period of its existence. He is an adept and enthusiest in floriculture and in this gracious domain of nature's finest art he finds both satisfaction and recreation.

William Richard is a representative of one of the old and honored families of Allen county, has personally contributed his quota to the upholding of the agricultural and live-stock prestige of the county and is now living virtually retired in the village of New Haven, though he still owns his well improved farm in Jefferson township. A man of vigor and poise, he is not content to be inactive and gives his attention to service in connection with the New Haven postoffice, besides which he is the owner of a half interest in the Happy Hour theater, an attractive amusement resort of the village. Mr. Richard was born in Jefferson township, this county, on February 4, 1859, a son of Christian and Elizabeth (Ditzeller) Richard, both of whom were born in Germany and were children at the time of the immigration of the respective families to America, the original settlement having been made in Pennsylvania and removal from the old Keystone state to Ohio having occurred a number of years later. The parents of Mr. Richard married in Ohio and thence came to Allen county, Indiana, and numbered themselves among the pioneers of Jefferson township. The father obtained a tract of heavily timbered land and reclaimed the same into one of the productive farms of the county. The passing years brought to him independence and prosperity and on his old homestead he erected an attractive farm house, in which he and his wife passed the closing years of their lives. He signalized his loyalty and patriotism by serving as a soldier of the Union in the Civil war. He enlisted as a member of an Indiana regiment and his arduous service as a soldier left him broken in health, with the result that after the war he continued a virtual invalid until his death, which occurred in 1870, at the age of forty-eight years, his wife having been about sixty-eight years old at the time of her death. Of their ten children Hannah and Henry are deceased; Eli is a resident of Monroeville, and Caroline of New Haven; William, of this review, was the next in order of birth; Mandy, Susan, Mary and Lydia are still living; and Adeline died in infancy. William Richard was afforded the advantages of the public schools of Maples, Jefferson township, and continued to assist in the work and management of the home farm until he initiated his independent operations as a farmer. He became the owner of a farm northeast of Maples, and reclaimed much of the land that had not been improved, besides which he erected substantial buildings and finally developed the place into one of the model farms of Jefferson township, the same being still in his possession and comprising eighty acres. He continued his active operations as a farmer for thirty years and then removed with his wife to New Haven, where he has since lived practically retired, a sterling citizen who has gained prosperity through his own efforts and commands unqualified popular esteem. His political support is given to the Republican party, but he has never desired or held public office. On March 1, 1883, was recorded the marriage of Mr. Richard to Miss Caroline Hannah Dünger, daughter of Robert and Sophia (Alspaugh) Dünger, who were born in Germany and who were young at the time of the immigration of their parents to America, their marriage having been solemnized in Pennsylvania. From the old Keystone state Mr. and Mrs. Dünger came to Allen county, Indiana, and established their home on a farm in Madison township, where they passed the remainder of their lives. Mr. and Mrs. Dünger became the parents of eight children, of whom the first, fifth and sixth, John, Robert and Edward, are deceased. The surviving children are Frederick, Conrad, Caroline, Henry Phillip and Sophia. To Mr. and Mrs. Richard were born seven children: Aday May, deceased; Elmer, married Alice Turnet; William and Lottie Sophia died in infancy; Viola Belle married Alton Yarian, of Fort Wayne; Lodemma married Clark David, of Fort Wayne; and Maud Esther married Paul Augspurger, of Woodburn, Ind.

Henry Riebersal, who is now one of the substantial and progressive farmers of Maumee township, was born in the Kingdom of Hanover, Germany, on February 5, 1865, but has been a resident of the United States since he was a lad of five years, his mother having died when he was virtually an infant. He is a son of Frederick Riebersal, who was born and reared in Hanover and there continued his alliance with agricultural industry until 1872, when he came with his motherless children to America and established his home on a farm in Defiance county, Ohio, where he remained until his death, about five years later, in 1877. Of his three children the first born, Heinrich, is deceased; Herman is the second born; and the subject of this review is the youngest of the number. Henry Riebersal acquired his early education in the public schools of Defiance county, Ohio, and was but twelve years old when he was doubly orphaned by the death of his honored father. Thus he early became largely dependent on his own resources and has proved himself well equipped for the responsibilities that thus devolved upon him, for he was won definite success and prosperity through his continued association with the great fundamental industries of agriculture and stock-growing. His first independent operations as a farmer were prosecuted in Henry county, Ohio, where he remained thus engaged for seven years. He then, in 1903, came to Allen county, Indiana, and purchased his present farm of eighty acres, in Section 27, Maumee township. Virtually the entire tract was covered with timber and underbrush when it came into his possession, and through his energy and good management he has reclaimed the greater portions to cultivation, has properly fenced the property, has installed an excellent system of tile drainage, and has erected modern farm buildings—all of which stand in evidence of his indomitable perseverence, his vigorous and well defined purpose and his progressive policies. Mr. Riebersal is a Republican in politics, is loyal and liberal as a citizen, and he and his wife are communicants of the Lutheran church. In the year 1898 was solemnized the marriage of Mr. Riebersal to Miss Sophia Marden, daughter of Henry and Sophia Marden, both natives of Germany and well known and honored old-time citizens of Allen county. Mr. and Mrs. Riebersal have a fine family of eight children, namely: Frederick, Henry, Jr., Emma, Sophia, Amelia, Carl, Martin, Hattie.

John M. E. Riedel has developed most effectively a native talent and has become an able and successful representative of a profession that touches most closely the physical attractiveness and civic progress and prosperity of the community. As a skilled architect he is one of the leading exponents of this profession in northern Indiana, with residence and office headquarters in the city of Fort Wayne, and besides being licensed as an architect in Indiana has gained the same recognition also in the states of Michigan, Illinois and New York. Mr. Riedel was born in the city of St. Louis, Missouri, on December 2, 1865, a son of John and Margaret (Beyer) Riedel, both natives of Germany. In the year following that of the birth of the subject of this review his parents came to Fort Wayne and his father, a man of fine intellectual attainments and noble character, became a teacher in the parochial schools of St. Paul's Lutheran church. He continued his earnest and effective services in the pedagogic profession, and in connection with the parochial schools mentioned, for the long period of forty-seven years, and there is no need for uncertainty or conjecture in defining the enduring value of his faithful services, his name being held in lasting honor and reverent affection in the city that was so long his home and in which his death occurred in March, 1916, after he had attained to the venerable age of eighty-two years. His aged widow resides in Detroit and is loved by all who have come within the compass of her gracious influence. She is a devout communicant of the Lutheran church, as was also her husband, and he gave his political allegiance to the Democratic party. Of the children, John M. E., of this review, is the eldest; Catherine is the wife of Rev. B. Henry Succop, who is, in 1917, the pastor of the Lutheran church at Ionia, Michigan; Rev. J. Paul is a resident of Brooklyn, New York; and Rev. Christian G. and William P. maintain their home in the city of Detroit, Michigan. John M. E. Riedel was an infant at the time of the family removal to Fort Wayne and here gained his preliminary education in the parochial schools of St. Paul's Lutheran church and largely under the direct and careful preceptorship of his father. Later he pursued a high course of study in Concordia College, and then entered the offices of the firm of T. J. Tolan & Sons, of Fort Wayne, for the purpose of studying architecture. Under these conditions he applied himself with diligence and appreciation for a period of about three years and made good use of the opportunities afforded him for the study of and practical work in the profession that represents both an art and a science. He continued his experience and study for three and one-half years in the offices of H. W. Matson, another representative architect in Fort Wayne, and by this time had admirably fortified himself for his chosen profession. On January 2, 1889, Mr. Riedel established himself independently in business as an architect, and his unequivocal success affords the best evidence of his ability and of his unqualified loyalty to the vocation of his choice. He has designed and supervised the construction of many fine buildings of both public and private order, and among the number may be designated the buildings of Concordia College, the Centlivre Hotel, the Lyric theatre, the Trinity Lutheran church edifice, the parochial school of St. Paul's Lutheran church, and the fine residence of H. A. Duemling—all of these being in Fort Wayne. His professional service has been enlisted outside the borders of his home county and state and the buildings which he has designed mark him as an architect of much technical skill and artistic talent. He has continued a close student of architectural art and has developed a number of original conceptions in his work as a designer. Mr. Riedel has thus contributed much to the physical attractiveness of his home city, and as a citizen is most loyal and public-spirited. In politics he holds himself aside from strict partisan lines, he and his wife are active communicants of St. Paul's Lutheran church, and he is an appreciative and valued member of the Fort Wayne Commercial Club. In 1902 was solemnized the marriage of Mr. Riedel to Miss Helen M. Achard, of New York City, and they have one son, Carl R., who remains at the parental home.

Sylvenus J. Roberts, who is conducting a prosperous retail lumber business at Woodburn, Maumee township, is a scion of one of the well known pioneer families whose name has been prominently and worthily linked with the development and progress of Allen county, he himself being of the fourth generation of the family in this county and his birth having occurred at Harlan, Springfield township, October 1, 1879. He is a son of William H. and Elmira (Taylor) Roberts, the former a native of Allen county and the latter of Huntington county, this state, their home at the present time being at Columbia City, the judicial center of Whitley county, where the father is engaged in the real estate business. William H. Roberts was reared to manhood in Allen county and is a son of Frank Roberts, who passed his entire life in this county, his parents having been pioneer settlers in Springfield township, and the family having been one of prominence in connection with agricultural enterprise and loyal and worthy citizenship, as one generation has followed another on to the stage of life's activities. William H. Roberts continued his successful activities as farmer near Harlan, this county, until 1904, when he removed to Columbia City, where he has since been substantially established in the real estate business, his political support being given to the Republican party and both he and his wife being earnest members of the M. E. church. The subject of this sketch is the eldest in a family of ten children, all of whom are living, and the names of the other children are here entered in the respective order of their birth: Frank H., Elmira, Orville, Willis, Leona, Ralph, Elbridge, Frances and Ignota. He whose name introduces this article acquired his early education in the public schools of Springfield township and as a boy and youth gained a full quota of practical experience in connection with the work of the home farm. At the age of twenty-one years he began an apprenticeship to the carpenter's trade and became a skilled artisan and a successful contractor and builder. He continued to follow his trade until 1910, when he engaged in the lumber business at Woodburn, his prior experience specially qualifying him for this line of enterprise, in which his success has been unequivocal. In his well equipped yards are to be found the various grades of lumber and general building material, and his correct business methods and policies have gained to him a substantial trade. He is always ready to give support to those measures and enterprises that tend to advance the civic and material welfare of the community, is a Republican in politics and he and his wife hold membership in the Missionary church. On October 20, 1898, Mr. Roberts wedded Miss Salome Sprunger, who was born and reared in this county, adequate mention of the family being given on other pages, in the sketch of Alvin A. Sprunger, who is a brother of Mrs. Roberts and who is serving as postmaster at Woodburn. Mr. and Mrs. Roberts have four children—Wilmer S., Glenn B., Ronald and Evans Lee, born April 10, 1917.

Col. Robert S. Robertson.—Fort Wayne and Allen county have been especially fortunate in the exceptionally high quality of their citizenship, and for this splendid prevailing condition much credit goes naturally to the leaders of thought and action among the people. One of the foremost of these was the late Colonel Robert S. Robertson, whose substantial activities touched many phases of development throughout the state of Indiana. Robert Stoddart Robertson was born April 16, 1839, in North Argyle, New York, the son of Nicholas and Martha Hume (Stoddart) Robertson. The paternal grandfather, Robert Robertson, was born in October, 1755, in Kinross-shire, Scotland, on the estate of "Touchie Miln," which had been inherited by several generations of the family, from their ancestor, Robert Robertson, of 1470. In 1793, the year previous to the erection and establishment of old Fort Wayne, the grandfather of Colonel Robertson came to the United States and settled in Washington county, New York, where he resided until his death in November, 1840. Nicholas Robertson, father of Colonel Robertson, was born in North Argyle, May 12, 1803, and his death occurred there in 1896. He served as postmaster of the town and as a justice of the peace for many years. He was for a number of years engaged in business as a cabinet-maker; later he was a mill owner and operator. On May 27, 1831, Nicholas Robertson was united in marriage with Miss Martha Hume Stoddart, a native of New York city, born in March, 1812, the daughter of Robert and Ann

(Hume) Stoddart. Her lineage traces on both paternal and maternal lines to two prominent Scottish families, the Stoddarts and the Humes. Robert S. Robertson, after attending the common schools of Argyle, entered upon a course of study in Argyle Academy. He early developed a fondness for the choicest literature, and decided upon the law as a profession, although, during his boyhood days, his time was passed between his school work and employment in his father's mill. In 1859, the way was opened for a course of study in the law office of Hon. James Gibson, in Salem, New York. In the following year, he went to New York City and entered the law office of Hon. Charles Crary, and in this same year he was admitted to the bar of New York. The active practice of his profession was opened at Whitehall, New York, in 1861, where he succeeded to the professional place of Hon. John H. Boyd, member of congress, who was retiring from the practice. But before his affairs assumed definite shape, Lincoln's call for volunteers summoned him to the defense of the nation's colors and he devoted his efforts to the raising of a company, which was summoned to Albany and remained there until its members were called to unite with other bodies to fill out their ranks. Colonel Robertson gladly entered the service as a private of Company I, Ninety-third regiment, New York Volunteer Infantry. Before leaving the state, he was appointed orderly sergeant. He participated in all of the campaigns, battles and skirmishes in which his regiment participated and won high honors because of "gallant and meritorious service in the field." He was promoted to a lieutenancy in April, 1862, to first lieutenant in May, 1863, and later he received two brevet commissions, one from President Lincoln conferring the rank of captain of United States volunteers, and another from the governor of New York, breveting him colonel of New York volunteers. He served as personal aide to General Nelson A. Miles while the latter was in command of the famous fighting First brigade, First division, Second Army corps, and while so serving was twice wounded, the first time at Spottsylvania Courthouse, May 12, 1864, where he was struck on the knee by a musket ball, and again on the 31st of the same month at Totopotomoy Creek, where he was shot from his horse in a charge, a minie ball passing through his abdomen from the front of the right hip to the back of the left. He continued his service, though for a period his death seemed a certainty, but because of the wounds, which gave fresh trouble during the siege of Petersburg, September 3, 1864, he was discharged "for disability from wounds received in action." Subsequently, Colonel Robertson received the "Congressional Medal of Honor" for services rendered at Corbin's Bridge, Virginia, May 8, 1864. Following his war service, Colonel Robertson located in Washington, D. C., where he became a member of the firm of Crocker, Robertson & Bramhall. During this time he made the close acquaintanceship of Vice-President Schuyler Colfax, of Indiana, and became interested in that stateman's estimate of the advantage of citizenship in the Hoosier state. He came to Fort Wayne in 1866, where he resided continually until his death. Colonel Robertson's capabilities enabled him to win immediate popularity because of his true worth as a public-spirited citizen. He was elected to serve as city attorney in 1867, 1868 and 1869. In 1868 he received the nomination to the office of state senator, but the normal Democratic majority could not be overcome. From 1871 to 1876 he served as United States commissioner and register in bankruptcy, and in the latter year he was nominated for lieutenant-governor of Indiana, with Godlove S. Orth as candidate for governor. Orth was compelled to resign from the ticket and Benjamin Harrison took the place. The ticket was defeated. In 1886, General M. D. Manson resigned the lieutenant-governorship, and, in the ensuing election, Colonel Robertson was chosen as his successor. He took the oath of office, but the Democrats, who had decided to regard the election as unauthorized by law, forbade him to assume the duties of presiding officer, a duty prescribed as a function of the office. The Democrats were in the majority. Two injunction suits to prevent the action of the Democrats ensued, and when Colonel Robertson sought a second time to take his office he was forcibly excluded from the senate chamber. But for the council of Colonel Robertson that his friends remain calm during the ensuing excitement, some regrettable act might have been done. Colonel Robertson continued to exercise all the functions of his office except that of presiding officer of the senate. While holding this office, Colonel Robertson was for two successive years elected president of the state board of equalization, a place which had hitherto invariably been filled by the governor of the state. In 1889 President Harrison appointed Colonel Robertson a member of the Utah commission, and he served in this connection until 1894. Early in the period of his residence in Fort Wayne, Colonel Robertson formed a professional connection with Judge Lindley M. Ninde and Judge Robert S. Taylor, under the name of Ninde, Taylor & Robertson. In 1868 this firm was dissolved, and Colonel Robertson formed a partnership with David P. Whedon, under the name of Whedon & Robertson; this relationship ceased in 1871, when Mr. Whedon removed to Utah. Soon afterward, the firm of Lowry, Robertson & O'Rourke (Robert Lowry, Colonel Robertson and Edward O'Rourke) was formed, and this continued until 1876, when Judge Lowry was elevated to the bench. Judge O'Rourke received similar preferment the following year. For a period of years thereafter, Colonel Robertson was associated in practice with James B. Harper, but, in 1894, he became associated with William S. O'Rourke. Always, Colonel Robertson was recognized as a lawyer of the highest, truest type. In July, 1865, at Whitehall, New York, Colonel Robertson was united in marriage with Miss Elizabeth H. Miller, whose grandfather came to New York in 1804. To this union were born Nicholas Alexander, of Eureka, Utah; Louise, wife of William H. Shambaugh; Robert Strowan, of Paducah, Kentucky; Mabel, wife of Ernest F. Loyd, of Detroit, Michigan; Annie M., wife of William N. Whitely, of Springfield, Missouri. Mrs. Elizabeth Robertson died in May, 1896. In August, 1898, Colonel Robertson was united in marriage with Mrs. Frances M. Haberly (nee Stinson). Mrs. Robertson has attained to a wide reputation as an authority on art. Her published works have found a place among the finest works in their line. As a student of the exhibits of the foreign galleries, Mrs. Robertson has taken many companies of travelers to all portions of Europe. As a lecturer on art, her grasp of the subject has given her popularity in many parts of America. Colonel Robertson was ever an earnest supporter of the principles of the Republican party. He became a member of the Masonic order in 1862, and attained to the Thirty-second degree of the Scottish Rite. In 1866 he joined the Grand Army of the Republic, and was ever an active leader in the affairs of the order in the state. In 1882 he joined the Ohio Commandery of the Military Order of the Loyal Legion, and, subsequently, in 1888, he became a charter member of the Indiana Commandery, and a member of the Medal of Honor Legion. He was ever an active member of the Fortnightly club of Fort Wayne. Colonel Robertson was long a member of the American Association for the Advancement of Science, the Indiana State Historical Society and the Congress Internationale des Americanistes, of Europe. Always an appreciative student of history, Colonel Robertson gave especial attention to the fascinating story of the development of the region of the Maumee and Wabash valleys, and much of the record of those who have gone before has been preserved through his efforts to place those records in permanent form. His contributions to the reports of the Smithsonian Institution, the North American Review, the Magazine of History and other publications, are notable. The death of Colonel Robertson removed from Fort Wayne and Allen county a citizen through whose efforts much of the advancement of affairs along many lines of endeavor were brought to a high state of accomplishment.

Amasa S. Robinson.—In 1836 Jonathan Robinson, a native Ohioan, moved into Indiana and settled on land in Madison township. It was virgin territory, heavily timbered, and it was the work of many long and trying years to reclaim those acres. Jonathan Robinson, however, was the possessor of all the sturdy pioneer instincts that were so essential in the development of the country, and he was able, with the passing years, to transform the wilderness into a productive farm and made his home on those acres until the day of his death. His wife was Sarah J. Shafer, also of Ohio birth, and of their ten children, two are living at this writing. Amasa S. Robinson was born on the Madison township farm in Allen county on January 7, 1849, and was reared and educated in the county. He completed a course in the high school nearest to his home and when sixteen years old went to work as a teacher in the local schools. He spent some years in that profession, and, in 1900, engaged in the ice cream business in Monroeville, where he has since conducted a successful and constantly growing enterprise. He is well established and prosperous and has won and held the confidence of the public in a most gratifying manner. Mr. Robinson is a Scottish Rite Mason and has held many important offices in the various bodies with which he is affiliated as a Mason. A Democrat, he has been active in local politics and served his township eleven years as assessor and five years as trustee. To his duties in both these offices he brought a character of service that made for a commendable degree of efficiency, and, in 1915, was appointed to the office of postmaster in Monroeville, of which office he is still the occupant. Mr. Robinson has been twice married. In 1875 he married Miss Sarah Master, who died in 1880, leaving one son. In 1881 he married Miss Lillie Peckham. Seven children were born to them and of that number five are still living. Of the sons, Clyde L. is assistant cashier of the First National Bank at Ashland, Ohio; Ralph A. is employed as a railway clerk and has been so engaged for the past nine years, and Harry A. is assistant postmaster under his father.

Frank S. Robinson, who is one of the representative farmers of Wayne township, is well upholding the prestige of a family name that has been most prominently and worthily linked with Allen county history since the time when this section of the state was little more than an untrammeled wilderness and when the present city of Fort Wayne was represented only by a frontier fort and Indian trading post. It is thus a matter of consistency, even as it is of definite gratification, to be able to record in this publication definite recognition to this honored pioneer family of which Frank S. is a scion of the third generation in the county. Horney Robinson, grandfather of him whose name introduces this article, was born in Fayette county, Ohio, on June 22, 1806, a son of Thomas Robinson, who likewise was a native of Ohio, his father having been one of the very early settlers in the Buckeye state and having been a valiant soldier in the war of 1812. Horney Robinson was a vigorous youth of about twenty years when, in 1826, he came to Allen county, Indiana, and numbered himself among its early pioneer settlers. He was well fortified for the labors and responsibilities of pioneer life in a virtual wilderness, and in 1832 obtained one hundred and twenty-six acres of heavily timbered land in what is now Aboite township. Here he applied himself vigorously to the reclaiming of a farm, here he did well his part in the furtherance of civic and material development and progress, and with the passing years prosperity attended his well ordered activities. He was one of the successful farmers and best known and most honored citizens of Aboite township, and on the old homestead place, now one of historic interest, he and his wife passed the remainder of their lives. In 1829 was solemnized his marriage to Miss Catherine Freshour, who was born in Pennsylvania, and she preceded him to eternal rest by more than twenty years, her death having occurred February 27, 1864, and he having been one of the most venerable pioneer citizens of the county at the time of his death, July 22, 1887. They were most devout and zealous members of the Methodist Episcopal church and were prominently concerned in establishing its pioneer organization in Allen county, their home having been always open to extend welcome and generous hospitality to the itinerant clergymen who visited the county in the early days. Of the children of this sterling pioneer couple it is possible to give brief record at this juncture: Sarah J. is the wife of Milton N. Ward, of Topeka, Kansas; Warren, father of Frank S., immediate subject of this review, will be more specifically mentioned farther on in this context; William is deceased; Frank became a clergyman of the Methodist Episcopal church and is a resident of Muncie; and Samantha is the wife of Dr. Moffett, a well known physician long engaged in practice in the city of Lafayette, Indiana. Warren Robinson was born in Pleasant township, this county, on November 30, 1834, and his early education was gained in the pioneer schools and in the old Methodist College, which was in its day a leading educational institution of northern Indiana, established at Fort Wayne. He became a man of strong intellectual force and in early years was a successful and popular teacher in the schools of this section of the state, his activities in the pedagogic profession having continued six years. In 1861 he turned his attention to farming and to the buying and shipping of live stock and was very successful in both lines of enterprise. He was known and honored as one of the upright, steadfast and loyal citizens of his native county, was influential in community affairs and commanded the unqualified esteem of all who knew him. At the time of his death he was the owner of a valuable landed estate of two hundred acres, principally in Aboite township. He was a well fortified and earnest advocate of the principles of the Republican party and was a lifelong and earnest member of the Methodist Episcopal church. His death occurred May 11, 1908, and his wife, whose maiden name was Sarah Fields, is now deceased. He is survived by one son and one daughter, children of his first marriage. Frank S. Robinson, to whom this review is dedicated, was born in Wayne township, this county, on November 29, 1869, and is indebted to the public schools for his early educational discipline. He continued to assist his father in the work and management of the latter's extensive farm property until he was about twenty-one years of age, and thereafter was engaged in farming in the state of Iowa for fourteen years and for two years in Colorado. He turned to Allen county in 1914 and from his father's estate inherited a portion of his present fine farm, which comprises one hundred and thirty-seven acres. Mr. Robinson has naught of inertia or apathy in his make-up and has always been a vigorous worker, his success having been in large measure achieved through his own ability and efforts. On his farm he has erected a commodious house of modern design and facilities, besides which he has remodeled the barn and made other substantial improvements. He is one of the progressive farmers of Wayne township, gives special attention to the raising and feeding of good live stock, and in his native county his circle of friends is limited only by that of his acquaintances. He is affiliated with the Masonic and Odd Fellows fraternities, is a Republican in his political proclivities, and both he and his wife are active members of the Methodist Episcopal church. On February 20, 1895, was solemnized the marriage of Mr. Robinson to Miss Olive B. Schannon, who was born in Muscatine county, Iowa, February 20, 1876, daughter of Daniel and Sarah (Raupe) Schannon, who were born in New Jersey and became pioneers of Iowa. Mr. Schannon, who is now living retired in the Hawkeye state, was for many years engaged in farming and stock-raising on an extensive scale and is a veteran of the Union service in the Civil war, his wife being deceased. Mr. and Mrs. Robinson have one daughter, Zetta S., who is the wife of G. Herbert Lopshire, associated with her father in the management of the home farm, and they have one son, Warren R., named in honor of his maternal grandfather.

Mrs. Mary E. Robinsen was born in Union township, Wells county, Indiana, on August 6, 1862, daughter of Charles and Margaret (Cartwright) Carl. Her father was a successful stock buyer in his community and shipped to both home and foreign markets. She was the youngest child in a family of twelve, the others being James, John, Henry, Earl, Freeman, George, Robert, Charles, Stephen, Frank and Sarah Jane. All are living but the second, fourth, seventh and tenth in order of naming. Mary, the youngest child and the subject of this family review, was reared on her father's farm and in young womanhood married William M. Robinson, who was born in Pleasant township on March 2, 1860. He was a son of William L. and Nancy Viola (Kemel) Robinson, and was reared on the farm of his parents and educated in the district schools of his day and age. He was for years associated with his father in farm life and when he launched out independently he bought a seventy-acre farm and applied himself to its management. Later he acquired the old homestead farm and that became his home for the remainder of his life, during which time he made many substantial and commendable improvements about the place. Mr. Robinson was a Democrat in politics and a member of the Methodist Episcopal church. To him and his wife were born five children. Samuel is living in Pleasant township. He is married and has three children—Julia Marie, Will Edmund and Viola. Charles Cleveland farms the old home place and his children are Virginia May, and Mary Emula. Edith May married Guy Brindes and they have two children—Vadoma Almeda and Jule Woodrow. Lula Jane is the wife of Jay Wickliff and they have six children—Ralph Irwin, Blanche May, Clarence William, Zola Marie, Earl Clifford, and Clara Almeda.

Henry A. Rockhill.—Success finds fertile ground along every avenue of endeavor. A healthy ambition will take root anywhere, and he who is possessed of such ambition will overcome the obstacles of time and place and make for himself a place of independence. He whose name introduces this review has been significantly one of the world's workers and has depended entirely on his own resources in making his way to the goal of success and definite prosperity. He is a native son of Allen county, is now numbered among its successful exponents of agricultural industry, and is a scion of a pioneer family of the county. His early advantages were most limited, he had early fellowship with arduous toil and endeavor, and he permitted nothing to curb his indomitable energy and ambition, so that advancement came to him as a natural prerogative. He has overcome the handicaps of earlier years, is a man of mature judgment and sterling character, is influential in community affairs of a public nature and has been called upon to serve in township offices of trust. His well improved farm is situated in Section 35, Lake township, on rural mail route No. 5 from the city of Fort Wayne. Mr. Rockhill was born January 21, 1859, a son of Joseph and Sarah J. (Russell) Rockhill. His father came to Allen county in 1830 and became one of the pioneer farmers on the Goshen road, where he cleared what is known as the Hoboken farm, to the improvement and cultivation of which he gave his attention for ten years. He took and completed the contract for the construction of the original Leesburg plank road and in payment for this service received one hundred and sixty acres of land in Green township, Noble county. He removed to this place, reclaimed and improved the same, and there he and his wife passed the remainder of their lives, his death having occurred in March, 1892, when he was of venerable age, and his old homestead farm being now owned by James Russell. Of the eight children those now living are Edward W., James W., Henry A., Mary Rebecca, and Louise, who is the wife of R. K. Erwin, of Fort Wayne. The names of the deceased children are as follows: Charles, John and Thomas. The boyhood and early youth of Henry A. Rockhill were marked by close application to work, much of which was of arduous order, and his early educational advantages were limited to a desultory attendance in the Hadley school. In the austere school of experience and hard knocks he matured the judgment that now indicates him as a man of strong mentality and well poised individuality, and he has made the best of every opportunity that has been presented. For thirty-five years he gave his attention to teaming, logging and the operation of a threshing outfit finally, his having been the first steam thresher in the local fields. Through well ordered incidental transactions he was ultimately able to assume the ownership of his present fine farm, which comprises one hundred and fourteen acres of the fertile land of Lake township. He has made excellent improvements on the homestead, including the erection of good farm buildings, and is one of the progressive and successful representatives of agricultural and live-stock enterprise in his native county. He has been active and influential in the local councils of the Democratic party, has secure place in popular esteem and has served one term as township assessor, besides having been for one term township trustee. Both he and his wife are active communicants of the Catholic church at Arcola. On February 21, 1882, was solemnized the marriage of Mr. Rockhill to Miss Mary Cavalier, who was born and reared in this county and is a daughter of Victor and Marie (Manier) Cavalier, the former of whom is deceased and the latter now resides in Fort Wayne. Of the seven children of Mr. and Mrs. Rockhill four died in infancy and one, Mary Maria, at the age of seven years. Of the two surviving children the elder is Joseph V., who is a resident of Aboite township, and the younger, Frank H., is telegraph operator for the Pennsylvania Railroad station at Arcola, this county.

Howell C. Rockhill is not only a native of Fort Wayne and prominently identified with the industrial and commercial interests of the city but his is the distinction also of being a scion of a family whose name has been influentially identified with the history of Allen county for more than ninety years. He himself has been a leading figure in the furtherance of the industrial prestige of Fort Wayne, where his capitalistic and executive interests have been of broad scope and importance and where he has effectively upheld the honors of the name which he bears, both as a successful man of affairs and as a liberal and progressive citizen. Howell Cobb Rockhill was born within the present corporate limits of Fort Wayne, and the date of his nativity was January 10, 1856. He is a son of William and Elizabeth (Hill) Rockhill, the former of whom was born at Burlington, New Jersey, February 10, 1793, and the latter at Baltimore, Maryland, on June 28, 1820. The paternal grandparents were Joseph and Mary (Davis) Rockhill, the former of whom was born in New Jersey, in 1765, a descendant of the Rockhill family that settled in the new world about the middle of the seventeenth century. Mary Davis was born in 1768. Joseph and Mary Rockhill died in Fort Wayne. William Rockhill became one of the pioneer settlers of Allen county, Indiana, where he established his home in 1822, when he was a young man of twenty-nine years. Here he entered claim to a large tract of government land, the eastern limit of which is now Broadway in the city of Fort Wayne. Here he instituted the reclamation of his land from the virtual wilderness and became eventually one of the leading exponents of agricultural industry in the county. Of him the following estimate has been written: "He was a man of great strength of character and integrity of purpose, and he took a leading part in the early organization of the county government as well as in the city government of Fort Wayne, a few years later." This sterling pioneer was well equipped for leadership in popular sentiment and action and he became one of the most honored and influential citizens of the county. In 1844 he was elected to the state senate, and in the following year was elected representative of his district in the United States Congress, his service in each of these offices having been rendered with characteristic ability and fidelity. Mr. Rockhill was a staunch advocate of the principles of the Democratic party and in addition to having served in the state senate and as a representative in congress he held also the position of representative of Allen county in the lower house of the legislature and served as county commissioner, as trustee of Wayne township and as member of the school board of the city of Fort Wayne, in which he was deeply interested. He died on January 15, 1865, about one month prior to the seventy-second anniversary of his birth, and his

H C Rockhill

wife was called to the life eternal May 9, 1859, in her thirty-ninth year. Of their seven children the subject of this review is the youngest of the five who attained to years of maturity. William Wright was born August 2, 1849; Ann Maria was born December 7, 1851, and was the wife of Edward L. Craw; and Hugh McCulloch and Jesse David Bright, twins, were born July 31, 1853. All the brothers are residents of Fort Wayne. Howell C. Rockhill acquired his early education in the public schools of Fort Wayne and it has been his privilege to witness and aid in the development of the mere village into a fine city of metropolitan significance. He was graduated in the Fort Wayne high school as a member of the class of 1873, and thereafter attended the Shattuck Military Academy at Faribault, Minnesota. After leaving school, together with his brothers, he began farming and stock-raising on a tract of unbroken land just outside the city limits of Fort Wayne and was extensively engaged in raising trotting horses and Holstein cattle under the firm name of Rockhill Bros. & Fleming. Later he assumed the position of manager of the Journal Company, publishers of the Fort Wayne Journal-Gazette. He long continued his alliance with this representative newspaper enterprise in his native county and in the meanwhile had extended his interests into other important fields. He had become a director of the Fort Wayne Iron & Steel Company and, in September, 1905, resigned his position as manager of the Journal Company to assume that of receiver for the industrial corporation just mentioned. He gave vigorous assistance in the reorganization of the concern under the present title of the Fort Wayne Rolling Mills Company and became vice-president, treasurer and active manager of the new corporation, in which position he has since continued to serve, the while he has brought to bear much executive resourcefulness in the upbuilding of one of the important industrial and commercial enterprises of his native city. He is likewise an interested principal in several other representative financial and manufacturing institutions of Fort Wáyne, being a director of the Fort Wayne Box Company, the Citizens' Trust Company, the Fort Wayne Transfer Company, vice-president and general manager of the Lake Erie and Fort Wayne Railroad Company, an industrial road serving with switching facilities a large factory district at the junction west of Fort Wayne, besides which he is treasurer of the Lincoln National Life Insurance Company, of which he was one of the organizers. Mr. Rockhill is an appreciative and valued member of the Fort Wayne Commercial Club and the Rotary Club, holds membership also in the Country Club, and is emphatically progressive and public-spirited in his civic attitude, though he has manifested no ambition for public office. In politics he supports the Democratic party in a generic way but does not permit himself to be hedged in by strict partisan lines. On November 21, 1906, was solemnized the marriage of Mr. Rockhill to Miss Ophelia Valette Rurode, who likewise was born and reared at Fort Wayne, and their two children are: Elizabeth Oglesby, born February 20, 1908, and William Rurode, born November 28, 1911. The residence of Mr. Rockhill is at 1337 West Wayne Street.

Wesley S. Roebuck.—Much credit attaches to Wesley S. Roebuck because of his achievements in the field of agricultural activities in St. Joseph township, where he has one of the finest farms to be found in the state. His place is unique in that it is one among a very few irrigated farms to be found east of the Mississippi river, and that he has labored progressively and effectively is evidenced by the fact that Purdue University recognizes his farm as one of the finest examples of modern agriculture in the state in point of soil productiveness and general up-to-dateness. Wesley S. Roebuck was born in Mercer county, Ohio, November 4, 1861, son of Ransom and Rebecca (Scoles) Roebuck. The father was born in Fayette county, Ohio, and the mother in Knox county, Ohio. Both were of Scotch descent and came of sturdy and honorable families who had been identified with the pioneer development of the state of Ohio in most creditable manner. Ransom Roebuck accompanied his family from Fayette county into Mercer county, Ohio, when he was a small boy and saw phases of pioneer life that were matters of fact with him and his generation but which would be thrilling adventures to the youth of the present day, who find much enjoyment in the perusal of those tales relating to the life and experiences of the men of two generations ago. As a boy young Roebuck, father of the subject, was wont to accompany his father on many adventurous trips. The father operated a reel or push boat on the Maumee river in those days, and young Ransom was frequently his companion on his trips to old Fort Wayne, in 1819 and 1820, when the present thriving city was merely the site of the fort and boasted a few bark shanties here and there in the vicinity of the main buildings. The elder Roebuck was a government agent and his duties comprised those of looking after the locating of immigrants, as well as looking out for the Indians. He personally handled the money with which the government paid the Indians, and his son Ransom often assisted him in bringing it to Fort Wayne. The money was always gold, tied up in packages of about what an average man could lift with ease, and it was sent through without guards of any sort. Never, in the years that Mr. Roebuck had charge of that work, was there any miscarriage of his plans, the delivery of the gold always being made promptly and safely. Ransom Roebuck was active in farm life in Mercer county for many years and was fairly prosperous all his days. He had a family of twelve children. Wesley Roebuck had his education in the common schools of Mercer county, Ohio, and taught in the schools of his community for a time, as did many of the wide-awake young men of his period, after which he went to Colorado and there settled on a government claim on which he lived long enough to get a government patent to it. Returning to his home, he settled a little later in Mercer county and, in 1894, located at New Haven, where he engaged in commercial gardening. For eight years he operated on rented land, after which he bought eighty-two acres in St. Joseph township, and there has continued engaged in active farming on a highly developed scale of action. As has been said, his farm is one of the few irrigated places to be found east of the Mississippi river, and it is an example of what may be accomplished along those lines with a little well-placed effort. Mr. Roebuck has a number of modern hot houses and his cement reservoir has a capacity of 350,000 gallons. The reservoir is filled from the river one-half a mile distant, a six-inch pipe carrying the water in and a 20-horsepower gas engine being employed to do the work. The entire farm is piped with miles of smaller pipe, and the mellow waters of the Maumee river are distributed at will over the land. Mr. Roebuck married Elizabeth Yokum, daughter of Milton and Mary H. Yokum, who were born and reared in Ohio. Two children have come to them. Ada is the wife of Kelly Blume, of St. Joseph township, and Bransom lives at home with his parents. Mr. Roebuck is a Mason of the Scottish Rite branch and is a member of the Shrine at Fort Wayne. Politically he is a Socialist of the best type. All his life he has combined thinking with doing, and the results are highly creditable to him.

Carl J. Roemke is a native son of Allen county, born in Milan township on September 14, 1892, and his parents were Conrad and Wilhelmina Roemke, concerning whom definite and more extended mention will be found elsewhere in this publication. The subject was educated in Allen county schools and had a thorough training in the business of agriculture under his father, and is at this writing operating a farm he rents from the elder Roemke. It is a place of one hundred and twenty acres, and under Mr. Roemke's management is helping to maintain the general high standards set in agricultural circles in the county. Mr. Roemke was married on September 20, 1914, to Miss Dora Reckeweg, daughter of Diederich and Louise (Cartie) Reckeweg, both native-born Germans who came to America as young people. They married in Fort Wayne and have spent practically all their lives as farmers in Milan township. They were the parents of ten children, named William, Louisa, Wilhelmina, Carrie, Fred and Carl, who are twins, Emma, Anna, Dora and Arthur. All are living at this writing. Mr. Roemke and his wife have one child —Willard, born August 8, 1916. They are members of the German Lutheran church and active workers in the parish. Mr. Roemke has no political affiliations, and holds no offices or no lodge memberships.

Conrad Frederick Roemke.—Another of the prosperous and energetic sons of Conrad and Wilhelmina Roemke is Conrad F., born in Milan township, Allen county on May 26, 1883, and much of his life a resident of his native community. He had his education in the district schools of the county and early initiated his career as a farmer in Maumee township, where he operated for three years. He then went to Kansas where he spent ten years in farming activities, afterward returning to Maumee township and is there engaged in the management of a rented farm of eighty acres. He has prospered and has a creditable standing among his fellow citizens as a farmer of no little enterprise. He was married on April 5, 1909, to Belva, daughter of Charles and Rachel (Fritts) Lloyd. Charles Lloyd is an Ohioan by birth and his wife is a native of Indiana. They were married in Kansas, where they had gone with their parents, and there they spent the greater part of their lives. They had six children—Arthur D., Maude Ethel, Roy Wesley, Frank Wesley and Belva, wife of the subject. To Mr. and Mrs. Roemke have come four children. Marjorie Lavon was born January 20, 1910; Georgia Pearl, February 22, 1912; Charles Conrad, September 26, 1914, and Evelyn on August 12, 1916. Mr. Roemke is a member of the Modern Woodmen of America at Woodburn and of the Kriesstolznau Verein, also at Woodburn. He and his family have membership in the German Lutheran church, and Mr. Roemke is a Republican in his political affiliations.

Conrad Roemke is another of the sterling and energetic citizens who have aided in developing and upholding the prestige of agricultural industry in Allen county and here has worked his way forward from a position of modest financial resources to secure status as one of the representative farmers and substantial and valued citizens of Maumee township, his well improved landed estate now comprising three hundred and seventy acres and his attention being given to diversified agriculture and stock-raising, in both of which departments of farm enterprise his success has been excellent, as he has employed scientific methods and the most approved of modern facilities. His homestead farm is improved with modern buildings and thrift and prosperity are shown forth in all phases of his farm industry. As a loyal and progressive citizen he gives his support to the Democratic party, he and his wife are communicants of the Lutheran church, and at Woodburn, a village about two and three-quarter miles distant from his home farm, he is affiliated with the Verein Kreisstolzenau. Rev. Roemke was born at Lande, Germany, October 9, 1857, a son of Conrad and Wilhelmina (Myer) Roemke, both of whom passed their entire lives in Germany, where the father followed the vocation of shepherd throughout his active career. Of the five children the subject of this sketch was the second in order of birth, and the names of the others are as here noted: Frederick, William, Eliza and Wilhelmina. The father was twice married and the two children of the second union are Carl and Louisa. In the schools of his native land Conrad Roemke of this review acquired his early education and there became his father's assistant in the latter's pastoral activities when he was a mere boy. He continued to give service as a shepherd until 1882, when, at the age of twenty-five years, he came to America and established his residence in Fort Wayne. Here he was employed in a brick yard four and one-half months and then leased the farm of John Peoples in Milan township. There he applied himself with characteristic diligence and good judgment for the ensuing four years and in the meanwhile carefully husbanded his financial resources. His next change was made when he removed to the Black farm, in the same township, and there he remained five and one-half years. In the meanwhile he had purchased ninety-two acres in Maumee township, from William Meyer, and in 1892 he removed to this place, where he remained until 1902 and then sold and bought the Hamm place of 120 acres and in 1906 he bought a tract of land of eighty acres in section 17, but in 1915 moved to his present home of 170 acres. Mr. Roemke has been one of the worlds productive workers, and by his energy and ability has added to his landed property until he now owns three hundred and seventy acres, as previously noted. On November 11, 1881, was solemnized the marriage of Mr. Roemke to Miss Wilhelmina Kammeier, daughter of Henry and Sophia (Koenig) Kammeier, well known residents of Neuinknick. Of the eight children of Mr. and Mrs. Roemke all are living except the second, William, who died in childhood. The names of the surviving children are here noted: Conrad F., Carl J., William H., (second of the name), Henry, Wilhelmina, Louisa and Meta.

William Roemke.—As the second decade of the twentieth century draws toward its close the world is rocked and upheaved by the most devastating war in the annals of time, and in the midst of unrest and clamor, uncertainties and the disruption of normal conditions, he is to be considered the most fortunate of men who owns and operates a good farm, who is able to do his part earnestly and quietly in behalf of humanity and to offer through the medium of his successful enterprise the goodly products that must ever represent succor and sustaining power to all sorts and conditions of men. Never in the world's history has so much depended upon the work and service of the farmer as at the present, and among the substantial exponents of agricultural industry in Allen county Mr. Roemke is one of those who expresses in his earnest and well directed endeavors his sense of personal stewardship and responsibility. He is the owner of one of the excellent farms of Maumee township and is a loyal and enterprising citizen who is true to American institutions and all they imply, with a civic loyalty that is direct and unqualified. Mr. Roemke was born in Lahde, Germany, on January 8, 1863, a son of Conrad and Wilhelmina Roemke, further record concerning the family being given on other pages of this publication, in the sketch dedicated to Conrad Roemke. William Roemke acquired his early education in the schools of his native land and was a youth of nineteen years when he came to America. He arrived in Allen county, May 1, 1882, and established his residence in the city of Fort Wayne, where for the first year he was employed in a brick yard. The following year found him engaged in teaming, and for the ensuing six years he farmed on rented land—in St. Joseph and Milan township. In the meanwhile he has carefully conserved the financial returns from his industrious labors and after his marriage continued to operate a rented farm in Milan township for a period of three years. He then purchased eighty-four and one-half acres in Section 8, Maumee township and has made this place one of the model farms of the county. He has made the best of permanent improvements, including the erection of a modern and commodious brick house of two stories, the supplying of other excellent farm buildings and the construction of good fences, as well as adequate tile-drainage facilities. His landed estate now comprises three hundred and fifty acres and is one of the valuable farm properties of this section of the state. Mr. Roemke gives his attention to diversified agriculture and the raising of good live stock, and has been specially successful in the raising of fine horses. His political allegiance is given to the Democratic party and he served eighty years as a member of the advisory board of Maumee township. He and his family hold membership in the Lutheran church and he is affiliated with the Verein Kreisstolzenau at Woodburn, which village is his postoffice address. In the year 1889 was solemnized the marriage of Mr. Roemke to Miss Mata Rahmann, daughter of Henry and Greta Rahmann, who were born and reared in Germany and there wedded, after which they came to America and settled in Allen county, Indiana, many years ago. Mr. and Mrs. Roemke have twelve children, and all are certain to uphold fully the honors of the family name. Their names are here entered in the respective order of birth: John, Charles, Minnie, Louisa, Emma, William, Jr., Matie, Frederick, Ida, Christian, Ernest and Henry.

Hubert H. Rogers.—The city of Fort Wayne is signally fortunate in having added to its representative business enterprises so well equipped and thoroughly modern an optical establishment as that here conducted by Mr. Rogers, who is a thoroughly scientific and experienced optometrist and who has in the Fort Wayne headquarters the best of facilities for the examination and proper diagnosis of all visual irregularities and for correcting the same with accurate lenses that are ground in the establishment itself. In his chosen profession he has had wide experience and has achieved unqualified success, and he not only has direct charge of the Fort Wayne business which he established, in September, 1915, but also the supervision of branch establishments at Springfield, Illinois and Lima, Ohio, with a corps of employes in the three branches that totals fifteen persons, each skilled in his respective functions. Mr. Rogers was born in the city of Indianapolis, Indiana, on January 17, 1879, a son of Edwin St. George Rogers and Catherine M. Rogers, his father having long been a representative member of the bar of Indiana's capital city. Hubert H. Rogers acquired his early education in the publci schools of his native city and in preparing himself for his chosen profession went to New York city, where he completed a most effective course of study and practical work under the preceptorship of Andrew J. Cross, one of the prominent optometrists of the national metropolis. Thereafter he held for three years a position as manager in the extension optical establishment of M. J. Harris, of New York city, and at the expiration of this period, in 1915, came to Fort Wayne and founded the excellently appointed establishment from which he now controls a large and representative supporting patronage, based upon effective service and fair and honorable dealings. Mr. Rogers has identified himself thoroughly with the civic and business life of Fort Wayne, is an active and popular member of the Commercial Club, holds membership also in the Country Club, and in the Masonic fraternity he has completed the circle of both the York and Scottish Rites, in the latter of which he has received the thirty-second degree, besides maintaining affiliation with the Ancient Arabic Order of the Nobles of the Mystic Shrine.

William H. Rohan.—No citizen of Fort Wayne enjoys a wider or more desirable acquaintanceship than William H. Rohan, general manager of the important department store of Wolf & Dessauer. Promiently connected for many years with leading financial and banking institutions, Mr. Rohan, by the cultivation of native qualifications of true friendliness, has made for himself a sure place in the commercial world with its unlimited opportunities for an ever-widening influence. Mr. Rohan was born in Fort Wayne, September 21, 1872, son of Captain John H. and Theresa (O'Brien) Rohan. The father was born in County Clare, Ireland, June 24, 1839, son of John and Bridget Rohan, with whom he came to America in 1845. The family first located in Burlington, Vermont, but, three years later, removed to Milwaukee, Wisconsin. In early life John H. Rohan learned the trade of a wood finisher and followed it in Milwaukee until 1859 and afterward in Buffalo, New York. Lincoln's appeal for volunteers for the war was the occasion for his enlistment, in 1862, with Company D of the One Hundred and Sixteenth New York regiment. He served until the close of the rebellion, during which time he was twice severely wounded. Captain Rohan was mustred out of the service at Washington, D. C., in June, 1865. Returning to Milwaukee, he was engaged in the retail grocery business for three years, when the opportunity was opened for a return to his trade of finisher of wood in the factory of the Burdett Organ Company, in Chicago. He remained with this concern until the disastrious fire of 1871, after which he came to Fort Wayne, which was already recognized as a wideawake city, and took employment with the Fort Wayne Organ Company, which has developed into the great plant of the Packard Company, makers of pianos and player pianos. Here he served as the foreman of a department for many years. His election as treasurer of Allen county showed the wide popularity he attained during the succeeding years. Captain Rohan was united in marriage, in May, 1868, with Mary Ann Theresa O'Brien, daughter of Lawrence and Mary O'Brien. Nine children were born to Captain and Mrs. Rohan, five of whom are living: Mrs. James Hughes, of Chicago; William H., the subject of this sketch; Agnes, of Chicago; J. Frank, of Fort Wayne, and Edward, who is an engineer in the United States navy. Captain Rohan died in 1906 and Mrs. Rohan in 1908. William H. Rohan was educated in the parochial schools of Fort Wayne, from which he was graduated at the age of sixteen years. Shortly after this he turned his attention to commercial pursuits and secured a position with the wholesale establishment of the George DeWald Company, dealers in dry goods and general merchandise, as city accountant. Then a favorable opening in the official force of the White National Bank, of Fort Wayne, enabled him to enter that institution as a bookkeeper. He remained with the White bank for a period of thirteen years, during which time his acquaintanceship among all classes of citizens was greatly broadened, and then he relinquished the place to enter the office of his father, who had been elected to the treasurership of Allen county. While William H. Rohan was employed in the county treasurer's office the absence of Assistant Cashier Detzer, of the White National Bank, left a vacancy in the bank, and no greater tribute to the worth of Mr. Rohan can be cited than the action of the bank management in holding open this place for Mr. Rohan until his work with his father should have been completed. Returning then to the bank, he continued his services until 1906, when that institution was absorbed by the First National Bank, when he was offered the position of assistant cashier of the Old National Bank of Fort Wayne. He accepted the place, and at the end of the first year was made the cashier of the institution. In 1914, the board of directors further recognized his worth in placing him in the office of vice president; at the same time he was made a member of the directorate. Mr. Rohan remained with the Old National Bank until April, 1916, when he resigned to accept the responsible position of general manager of the Wolf & Dessauer's establishment, the foremost retail dry goods and department store in Northern Indiana. He remains, however, as a director of the Old National Bank. Messrs. Sam Wolf and Myron E. Dessauer, in acquiring the business association of Mr. Rohan, have shown marked judgment, for with the rapid growth of the city and the material expansion of the business, the added responsibilities of the management of the business calls for just such co-operation as Mr. Rohan is best fitted to provide. The erection of a half-million-dollar six-story building to house the enlarging business of the Wolf & Dessauer store in 1917, is such as to suggest the bigness of the men who are to guide its destiny. Mr. Rohan's position is one to call forth and develop inherent faculties for expansion and salesmanship as well as judgment in the purchase of goods to meet the ever-changing conditions of the times, and none who know him doubt his ability to meet these exacting requirements. In October, 1896, Mr. Rohan was united in marriage with Miss Josephine Manuel, daughter of Jules Manuel, of Fort Wayne. Two children have been born of this union, Margery and Maurice. Mr. Rohan is a member of St. Patrick's Catholic church, and is a member of the Knights of Columbus order. He is a member of the Commercial Club, the Quest Club and other organizations designed for the general good. In politics, Mr. Rohan is independent, always throwing the weight of his influence for the man of true worth, without regard to partisan connections.

William Roller was born in Pleasant township, Allen county, Indiana, on February 9, 1866, son of John and Anna (Ernst) Roller. The father was a native German, born in 1823, and came to America in 1850, locating first in Ohio and later migrating to Allen county, where he bought a farm of eighty acres and settled down to the peaceful but arduous duties of farming in a new country. He was prosperous, being both diligent and progressive, and to his original purchase later added an equal amount, so that he came to own one of the better farms in his township, of which he was one of the earliest settlers. He recalls the time when the court house site of today was a wheat field and has been a witness to many important changes in the topographical aspect of the county. He and his wife were the parents of eleven children, who were named Mary, Catherine, Caroline, John, Jacob, Sarah, Regina, William, Eliabeth, Emma, and a child who died in infancy. Of this goodly family seven survive. William Roller had such education as the schools of his day provided and was his father's helper at home until he was twenty-seven years old, when he married and settled on a rented farm in Lafayette township. After several years of renting he bought a place of his own and has since been actively engaged in diversified farming, in which he has been comfortably successful. Mr. Roller is a Republican in his politics, a member of the German Lutheran Church, with his family, and is in addition to his farming interests a stockholder in the Equity Elevator Company at Sheldon. He was married on June 6, 1893, to Miss Clara Riehle, daughter of Christ and Mary (Fox) Riehle, who were natives of Germany. The father was a blacksmith by trade and came to America, leaving his family in Germany. He bought a farm and prepared a home for them here, where they later joined him, and they have since been residents of Pleasant township. Mrs. Roller was one of their children, the others being Christina, the wife of George Harber, of Pleasant township; Elizabeth, now deceased; Minnie, who married R. Minick, a Pleasant township farmer; and Caroline, the wife of Henry Cleever, of Allen county. Five children have been born to Mr. and Mrs. Roller—Elmer, Cline, Calvin, Reuben and Mary Ann, all living at home with the exception of Cline, who died in 1899.

Anthony F. Rose was born in Washington township and has passed his life thus far within its borders. He has lived quietly on the farm his parents settled when they came to this region, and since the death of the mother and father has shared the old homestead with a sister, neither of them having married. They are among the substantial and dependable people of the community and have contributed in a commendable measure to the development of the township. Mr. Rose was born on January 17, 1850, son of Charles W. and Christine (Muesing) Rose, natives of Germany who came to America as children and were married in Washington township, settled on new land and spent the remainder of their lives in developing and upbuilding a home. They reared a family of twelve children, four of whom are living today. Named in the order of their birth they are Louisa, Anthony F., Lena and Amelia. The others, who died on the home farm, were Sophia, Eliza, Christina, Charles, Christian and three others who died in infancy. Anthony F. Rose was educated in the Washington township schools and early learned to apply himself to farm work on the home place. He inherited the family home on the death of his parents and is today the owner of 185 acres of fertile land in Washington township, where he carries on general farming and stock raising. He and his sister, who has shared the old home with him, are members of St. Paul's Lutheran church and take their place among the best people of the community.

Theodore W. C. Rose.—One of the younger native sons of Washington township is Theodore W. C. Rose, born here on October 13, 1870. His parents were Christian F. and Christina (Brinkman) Rose, natives of Germany who came to America in their youth and met and married after attaining young manhood and womanhood. They first settled on a Washington township farm, continuing as residents there until 1871, when they took up their residence in St. Joseph township, in Allen county, there residing until death claimed them. They were active in

Yours truly
J. N. Rosenthal, M.D.
1902

farming work all their lives and played a creditable part in the development of those communities with which they identified themselvs as workers. They were the parents of ten children—Charles, Mary, Christian, Frederick, William, Louisa, Henry, Minnie, Gottlieb and Theodore, the subject. William and Gottlieb are deceased, but all the others are living in and about Allen county. Theodore Rose had his early education in the common schools of Allen county and early identified himself with farm life in St. Joseph township, where he is still living. He is now owner of 172 acres of excellent land in the community, on which all modern improvements have been made by him, and the place boasts a fine dwelling, commodious barns, fences, tiling and such other improvements as go to make up a well-kept and profitable piece of farm property. Mr. Rose was married on October 11, 1894, to Miss Emma Kramer, daughter of Charles and Sophia (Rose) Kramer. Mr. Ksamer is a native of Lucas county, Ohio, and his wife of Allen county. He came with his parents as a boy from Ohio, settling in Allen county and here married, reared his family and lived his life to its end as a St. Joseph township farmer. He was for ten years in the employ of the Wabash Railroad, but left that work for the more attractive and independent vocation of farming, in which he was very successful. To him and his wife were born nine children—Charles, Emma, the wife of Mr. Rose; Eliza, who is deceased; Albert, Ida, deceased; Adolph, deceased; Henry, Amanda, and Arthur. The mother died in 1907 and the father in December, 1910. Mr. and Mrs. Rose have three children—Neva, Herbert and Alma. All are at home. Mr. Rose is a Democrat in politics and for twelve consecutive years has served as a member of the St. Joseph township advisory board, and it is presumable that the quality of his service in that position may be measured by the fact of his recurring election to the office. He and his family have membership in St. Paul's Lutheran church of Fort Wayne.

Isaac M. Rosenthal, M. D.—Often we are called upon to judge the character of a man through the study of his spoken words to which utterance was given at a time when he feared that the close of his earthly days was near at hand and when the mind turned to thoughts which may have been foreign to him in times of health and strength. But the truer estimate is gained from the words of a man at a time when, in the full vigor of mind and body, he reveals his normal self. The late Dr. Isaac M. Rosenthal has left a record of his innermost thoughts, inscribed in a most novel and unique manner. On August 30, 1895, during a sojourn at Mackinac Island, there was offered to him the opportunity to leave, for the edification of his children, a record of his voice. "Without advance preparation," says Dr. Maurice I. Rosenthal, his son, "my father spoke the words which are treasured by the children above all that we could possibly possess." The record follows: "My Dear Ones All: My last will and testament you will find to be an expression of my impartial love and my desire to be just to you all. If I have failed therein, it is but through the limited, very limited, wisdom given to all that are earthborn. My soul soars higher. This is to be to you as a voice from the Unknown Beyond. I will request that you do not mourn for me but rejoice with me. After our bereavement, I still love and live with you and for you; but to be again united with that true, loving, pure, heavenly soul is happiness beyond human comprehension. Think of me, as we did of dear Mother; imagine that we, in spirit, are with you, to love, guide and protect you. Remember all that was good and noble in my earthly career.

Do not forget, but forgive, all the errors, evils and shortcomings of my ways upon earth. Follow the good and avoid the evil. Love and protect one another, thereby giving eternal joy and bliss to your parents in the Unknown Beyond, as you did whilst we dwelled in body with you. Peace on earth and good will to all. 'Osch Sholom Bim'ro'mov Hoo Ya'ases Sholom Olenu v' al Kol Odom V'imroo Amen! (May He who bringeth peace to pass in the highest give peace to us and all men and say Amen.)''

Dr. Isaac M. Rosenthal, for many years before his death, October 29, 1906, at the age of seventy-seven years, had enjoyed a place among the best surgeons of Indiana. The story of his life is one of interest and inspiration. On October 31, 1831, Dr. Rosenthal was born in the little village of Lauphin, Wurtemberg, Germany. Here he passed his childhood years and was afforded exceptional advantages along both academic and professional lines. From the time of his boyhood years Dr. Rosenthal's inclination was toward the medical profession, a propensity which manifested itself with unmistakable clearness in his earliest years. His mother died while he was but a boy, and the father came to America to make a home for his children and to give to them the advantages which the new world promised to many another son of Germany. Having accomplished the task of preparing to receive the children, it was his pleasure, in 1847, to send for them. They landed in Philadelphia, and here, for a time, they resided. Isaac M. Rosenthal then removed to Oberlin, Ohio, where he was enabled to continue his medical studies under a preceptor, Dr. Maxwell. It was in Oberlin that the young man experienced his first practice, for he devoted himself closely to his studies and was frequently permitted to take active charge of cases, under the watchful care of Dr. Maxwell. Upon the earliest opportunity he entered the medical department of the Western Reserve University, and his aptness and previous application to the study of medicine enabled him to complete his course in 1852, when he located at Bedford, Ohio, where he began the practice of his profession and there remained for four years. In 1856 he removed to Indianapolis, Indiana, and continued with the same high degree of success which had characterized his earlier efforts. In 1860, conditions at Fort Wayne offered a special inducement to him to locate here, and this city proved to be the goal of his permanent success. At that time Fort Wayne was a city of about seven thousand population. The contemporaries of Dr. Rosenthal at the time he began his services in Fort Wayne were Dr. Woodworth, Dr. Myers, Dr. Bowen, Dr. McCulloch, Dr. Brooks, Dr. Smith, Dr. Josse, Dr. Schmitz, and others who have been a credit to the profession in Indiana in the years agone. For many years after his selection of Fort Wayne as a permanent place of residence Dr. Rosenthal was one of the foremost surgeons in northern Indiana. His personal and professional standing was always of the highest order. He served numerous terms as president of the Allen County Medical Society, and one term as vice president of the Indiana State Medical Society. For eight years he was a member of the Fort Wayne board of health, and for a considerable period served as county physician. In truth, during the nearly half a century of his residence in Fort Wayne he continued as one of the leading physicians and surgeons of this section of the state, and his noble character, combined with his professional ability, gave him an inviolable place in the confidence and esteem of the community in which he lived long and in which he labored with utmost zeal and devotion. He had much to do with the systematizing and development of the service of St. Joseph Hospital and was the head of its staff

J. Milton Rosenthal

of physicians and surgeons for many years prior to his death. It was in this incident of his professional career that Dr. Rosenthal took greatest pride. He was a supporter of the principles of the Democratic party and took an active interest in the affairs of the nation, state and city. He was a member of the Independent Order of Odd Fellows. Both Dr. and Mrs. Rosenthal were prominent in the affairs of Achduth Veshalom Synagogue congregation. Dr. Rosenthal's place in the medical world is suggested by his connection with the American Medical Association, the Indiana State Medical Society and the Allen County Medical Society. The wife of Dr. Rosenthal was formerly Miss Adele Rauh, with whom he was united in marriage, November 30, 1857, at Cincinnati, Ohio. Mrs. Rosenthal died, in 1895, at the age of sixty years. Dr. and Mrs. Rosenthal were the parents of seven children. These were Dr. Charles H., who was a successful doctor of dental surgery at Cincinnati, Ohio, at the time of his death; Rebecca, the wife of Joseph Lohman, of Fort Wayne; Edward A., who was successfully established in the practice of law at Chicago at the time of his death; Minnie, the wife of Cyrus Arnold, of Detroit, Michigan; Dr. Maurice I., the widely known surgeon of Fort Wayne; Hattie, the wife of Louis Frankel, of Chicago; and John Milton, a representative dental practitioner of Fort Wayne.

J. Milton Rosenthal, D. D. S.—A leading practioner of dental surgery is Dr. J. Milton Rosenthal, who maintains a modern suite in the Utility Building. Dr. Rosenthal was born January 25, 1875, and has always resided in this city. He is the son of Dr. Isaac M. and Adelle (Rauh) Rosenthal. Dr. Isaac M. Rosenthal, whose name is held in the fondest memory by thousands of Fort Wayne people, as well as members of the medical profession throughout Indiana, was one of the foremost physicians and surgeons of his day. His life forms the subject of an extended biography in this volume. Following his course of study in the public and high schools of his home city, Dr. J. Milton Rosenthal entered the University of Michigan at Ann Arbor in 1894 and was graduated with the degree of Doctor of Dental Surgery in the class of 1897. He returned to Fort Wayne and in August of 1897 opened an office on Harrison street opposite the Commercial Club building between Berry and Wayne streets. Here he remained for five years, after which he took possession of a suite in the Flick building on West Berry street and remained for a period of about ten years. In 1911 he located in the People's Trust building on Calhoun street and there remained until the summer of 1917, when he took quarters, modern in every respect, in the new Utility building on East Wayne street, between Calhoun and Clinton streets. The complete equipment of Dr. Rosenthal's new office is a silent proclamation of his thorough acquaintanceship with the most advanced points of practice and service in dental surgery. Dr. Rosenthal gives special attention to orthodontia (straightening teeth) and oral surgery. He is dental surgeon to St. Joseph and Fort Wayne Lutheran hospitals. Dr. Rosenthal is an active member of the Isaac Knapp Coterie of Fort Wayne; the Twelfth District Dental Association; the Northern Indiana Dental Association, and the Indiana State and the National Associations. He is a member of the Fort Wayne Lodge of Elks and the I. O. O. F. lodge. He is actively connected with the Fort Wayne Country club and the University Club of Fort Wayne. He is a member of the Achduoth Vesholom congregation. Although never taking an active part in politics he has always been a Democrat. On January 21, 1908, he was united in marriage with Miss Ruth Loewenstein, also a resident of Fort Wayne, the daughter of Jacob and Dora Loewenstein. To Dr. and Mrs. Rosenthal have been born two sons, J. Milton Rosenthal, Jr., born October 7, 1909, and Edward Charles Rosenthal, born December 28, 1916. The family home is located at 338 West Berry street.

Maurice I. Rosenthal, M. D., F. A. C. S.—In the city of Fort Wayne where he was born Doctor Maurice I. Rosenthal is giving added distinction to the profession in which his father, Doctor Isaac M. Rosenthal, attained to the highest honors. Doctor Rosenthal has succeeded his father as the surgeon to the Saint Joseph Hospital in Fort Wayne, one of the noble institutions of this city whose hospital ranks among the best in the middle west. Doctor Rosenthal was born in Fort Wayne on April 9, 1869, son of Doctor Isaac M. and Adele (Rauh) Rosenthal, the names of both of whom are held in lasting honor in Allen county. Doctor Isaac M. Rosenthal is the subject of a biographical essay in another portion of this work. Doctor Maurice I. Rosenthal attended the public schools in Fort Wayne until he completed the curriculum of the high school and then entered the Ohio Medical College, medical department of the Cincinnati university, from which institution he graduated in 1889. Immediately after his graduation at Cincinnati he went to Europe, where he further pursued his studies at the University of Berlin and the University of Strasburg, in Germany, and at the University of Prague, in Bohemia. In 1892 the doctor returned to the United States and for the ensuing decade was engaged in active general practice in Fort Wayne. Since the expiration of that period he has specialized in surgery and his success has amply justified his concentration of effort in this department of professional service. In 1902 he again visited the European schools of medicine, taking special studies in Berne, Switzerland, and in Vienna, Austria. Doctor Rosenthal has furnished a number of contributions to medical literature. He is a member of the American Medical Association, the Mississippi Valley Medical Association, the Tri-State Medical Society, the Indiana State Medical Society, and the Allen County Medical Society, besides which he is a Fellow of the American College of Surgeons and the American Association of Gynecologysts and Obstetricians. He is affiliated with the Masonic fraternity, the Knights of Pythias and the Benevolent and Protective Order of Elks, and an active member of the Commercial Club, the Country Club and the University club. Subordinating all else to the demands of his profession, Doctor Rosenthal has had no desire to enter the arena of practical politics, although he gives allegiance to the Democratic party and takes loyal interest in all things pertaining to the civic and material welfare of the community. His name is still enrolled on the list of eligible bachelors of his native city.

Louis G. Rosselot.—One of the long established and reliable families of St. Joseph township is represented by Louis G. Rosselot, who was born there November 16, 1858, son of Louis and Sophia (Racine) Rosselot, natives of France and Switzerland, respectively. As young people they immigrated to America and met and married in St. Joseph township, which community represented their home and the scene of their activities through the remainder of their lives. They were sturdy people, possessing many admirable attributes of heart and mind, and they added their full share to the community welfare during their years as residents of St. Joseph township. Seven children were born to them. Louis, the subject, was the first born. Then followed Charles, Henry, Mary, Sophia, Amelia and Lucy. All reached years of maturity and added much to the comfort and well-being of their parents, both of whom are now deceased.

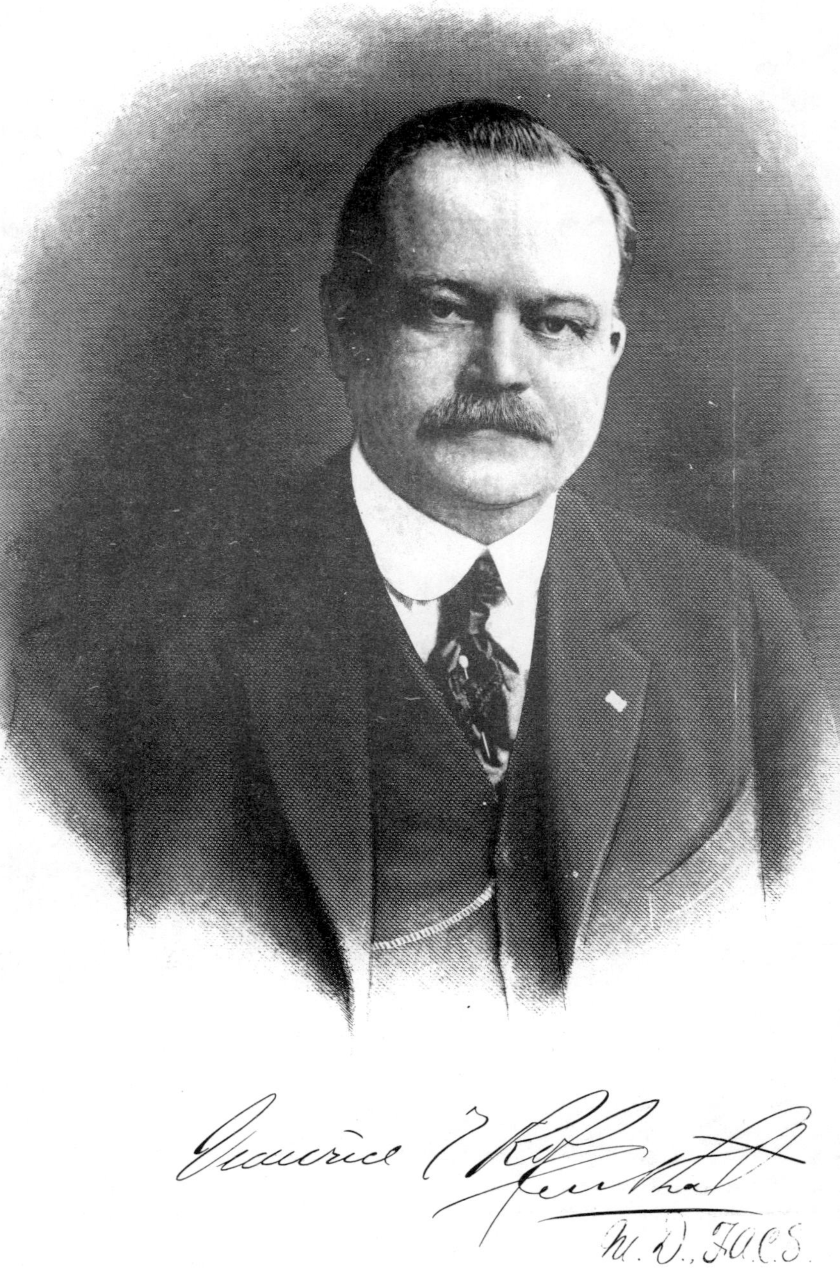
M.D., F.A.C.S.

The subject had his education in the common schools of his home community and when in his 'teens turned his attention to work in the paper mills. He spent twelve years in that industry and then abandoned it for the more congenial occupation of farming. He returned to the old homestead, where he has since devoted himself exclusively to farming, and the appearance of the eighty-acre tract he works is ample evidence and proof of the wisdom of his later choice of an occupation. Mr. Rosselot was united in marriage with Miss Anna Ream, in 1884. She is a daughter of John and Anna (Kramer) Ream, German people who came from the Fatherland in their young married life and settled in Mercer county, Ohio, later locating in Allen county, Indiana, where they passed the last ten years of their lives. To Mr. and Mrs. Rosselot four children have been born. They are Louis, Clarence, Georgia and Alma. The family have membership in the English Lutheran church and the husband and father is an adherent of the Republican party in the matter of politics.

Dr. Charles Joseph Rothschild.—Dr. Charles Joseph Rothschild, one of the younger men of his profession in Fort Wayne, and coroner of Allen county, may with all propriety be spoken of as a leader in his profession in Allen county today, and his successes thus far in his career give promise of a brilliant future in his chosen field of usefulness. Dr. Rothschild was born in Fort Wayne, May 28, 1881, son of Henry and Sophia (Rauh) Rothschild, both of German birth and parentage. The father was born in Wurtemburg on December 4, 1835, and resides in Fort Wayne, and the mother in Landau, April 26, 1841, and she died March 3, 1917. Dr. Rothschild was their only child and they viewed his promising career with a good deal of well merited satisfaction. Charles Joseph Rothschild was given a public school training, and when he had finished with the high school and its prescribed courses entered the University of Michigan and was graduated from the medical school of the University in 1905. Returning to Fort Wayne he associated himself with Doctor Maurice I. Rosenthal, continuing for three years, after which he went to Europe and spent two years in post graduate work. During that time Doctor Rothschild was clinical assistant in the Royal and Imperial Woman's clinic of the University Hospital at the University of Vienna and an interne in Rudolfiner Haus in Vienna, and had the opportunity to study under the most noted master pathologists of Berlin, Vienna and London. He improved his time and in the two years spent abroad gathered a fund of information that a less ambitious student would not have gleaned in a much longer period. Returning, in 1910, to Fort Wayne, he established offices in the Peoples' Trust Building, where he conducted a general practice in medicine and surgery until July, 1917, when he moved into the Utility building, where he maintains a modern office. Doctor Rothschild is a member of the American Medical Association, the Indiana State Medical Association, the Northern Tri-State Medical Association, the Fort Wayne Medical Society, and the Fort Wayne Academy of Medicine. In 1909 he was chairman of the executive committee of the American Medical Association of Vienna, Austria, and he is a member of the local Country Club, the Fort Wayne Commercial Club, is a charter member of Kiwanis and of the University club, is a member of the Independent Order of B'Nai B'Rith, the Benevolent and protective Order of Elks and the Knights of Pythias. He is Republican in politics, and in March, 1916, was nominated by his party for the office of county coroner, and was elected by a handsome majority.

Charles P. Roy is a popular representative of one of the numerous families given to Allen county many years ago by France, the great nation with which the United States has become allied in the terrific European war that is making the second decade of the twentieth century a climacteric period in this world's history. Mr. Roy was born in Washington township, this county, on February 22, 1862, and is a son of Felix and Elizabeth (Martin) Roy, both natives of France and both children at the time of the immigration of the respective families to America. Felix Roy was seven years old when he came with his parents to the United States, and after remaining for a time in Ohio removal was made to Allen county, Indiana, at a period that gives to the Roy family a measure of pioneer prestige. The Martin family likewise was early founded in the county, and the marriage of the parents of the subject of this review was solemnized in Perry township. Thereafter they resided on a farm in Washington township until 1868, when removal was made to Perry township, where the father developed a good farm and became one of the valued and substantial citizens of the county in which he was reared to manhood. He continued his active association with agricultural pursuits until his death, which occurred March 9, 1891, and his widow passed to eternal rest on June 20, 1909, both having been devout and consistent communicants of the Catholic church. Of the children the eldest is Joseph C., who is a resident of Indianapolis; Julian J. and Frank D. are deceased; Charles P.; John B. and Henry L. are deceased; Mrs. Amelia Fox is a resident of Fort Wayne; Alexander C. maintains his home in the city of Chicago; Edward resides in Fort Wayne; Mary died in infancy; Alice resides in Fort Wayne; and Albert is deceased. To the public schools of Perry township Charles P. Roy is indebted for his early educational training, and he continued thereafter his association with the work and management of the home farm until the death of his honored father. About one month earlier had been solemnized the marriage of the subject of this review, in 1891, and it was in the spring of that year that he purchased his present farm of eighty acres, eligibly situated in Section 28, Perry township. Under the energetic and well ordered management of Mr. Roy this homestead has been made one of the model farms of Perry township, as he has erected excellent buildings, including a modern house and barn, and has brought all departments and facilities of the farm up to the most approved standard of twentieth-century husbandry, with due relative attention given to diversified agriculture and to the raising of excellent types of live stock. Mr. Roy is a Democrat in politics, is liberal and progressive as a citizen, takes lively interest in community affairs and served six years as trustee of Perry township—a preferment that indicates alike his ability, his civic loyalty and his personal popularity. He is a member of the French-American Society in the city of Fort Wayne and both he and his wife are active communicants of St. Vincent Catholic church, in Washington township. On February 10, 1891, was solemnized the marriage of Mr. Roy to Miss Olive G. Schuler, who likewise was born and reared in this county, and was a daughter of John and Sarah (Coolman) Schuler, the former of whom is living retired in the city of Fort Wayne, where the death of the loved wife and mother occurred on January 21, 1916. Mr. Schuler was born on shipboard while his parents were en route across the Atlantic from Germany to America, and the family home was first established in Pennsylvania, whence removal later was made to Ohio. In the pioneer

E. C. Rurode

days John Schuler settled in St. Joseph township, Allen county, and later he became one of the substantial farmers of Cedar Creek township, where he continued his productive activities until his removal to Fort Wayne, about the year 1903. Of his five children the eldest, William G., is a prosperous farmer in Perry township; Olive G., wife of the subject of this review, was the next in order of birth; Mrs. Gertrude Roeger and Royal are residents of Fort Wayne; and Leah is the wife of Dr. William O. Smith, of Hoagland, this county. Mr. and Mrs. Roy have three children, all of whom remain at the parental home—Mabel Gertrude, Velma Leona, and Hilda Alma.

The Rub-No-More Company.—To note those enterprises which stand representative in their respective lines of industry as bearing upon the precedence and commercial activity of the city of Fort Wayne is one of the prime functions of this publication, and thus particular recognition is consistently given to the company whose title is given above and which represents one of the more important industrial and commercial enterprises of the metropolis of Allen county. Continued and cumulative success is the ultimate criterion of merit and reliability in the industrial world, and the priority maintained by the Rub-No-More Company stands in evidence of its well authorized claims as being one of the leading concerns of its kind in the United States. The business of this important company had its inception about the year 1880 and was formerly conducted under the title of the Summit City Soap Works. The interested principals in the establishing and developing of the enterprise were John O'Rourke, Brutus Burrie and Caspar Miller, who continued the controlling forces until 1883, when the expansion of the business led to the formation of a stock company, of which the late Hon. Perry Randall became president; Henry Graffe, vice-president; and Brutus Burrie, secretary and treasurer. Thereafter the enterprise was continued under the title of the Summit City Soap Works and under the above mentioned executive management until 1892, when the plant and business were purchased by Gustave A. Berghoff, who has been one of the most progressive and resourceful figures in the development of the industrial interests of Fort Wayne and who retained for the concern the title of the Summit City Soap Works, until 1905, when he expanded the scope of operations and effected the organization of the present Rub-No-More Company, of which he has continued the president. Henry C. Berghoff is vice president of the company; Hubert Berghoff is secretary, and Albert Jauch is treasurer. Since Mr. Berghoff assumed control of the business and gave to it the spur of his incisive energy and progressiveness, new and well equipped buildings have been provided, the plant now covering about three acres of ground, with a frontage of one thousand feet along the Nickel Plate railroad. The special output of the plant is now the superior product known as Rub-No-More Washing Powder and the establishment proper gives employment to a force of about one hundred and thirty persons; the while the company's corps of forty traveling salesmen represent its interests in thirty-five states of the Union. The recognized superiority of the washing powder manufactured by this concern has given to it a cumulative demand wherever it has been introduced, and the Rub-No-More Company has done much to carry the commercial prestige of Fort Wayne into the most diverse sections of the United States.

Ernst C. Rurode.—Few men of Fort Wayne of today have been as closely connected with the development of the city since Civil war times as Ernst C. Rurode, who holds a most enviable place in the forefront of the men who have been engaged in mercantile pursuits of Northern Indiana. For half a century he has been an active participant in the commercial interests of the city, and during that time has had a part in the wonderful transformation of the place from a town into a modern city. Mr. Rurode is a native of Germany, born May 4, 1838, at Hanover. His parents were Henry and Katherine (Hoyer) Rurode, both born in Germany. The father was engaged in agricultural pursuits. The same longing for the opportunities which brought hundreds of others from the Fatherland to America caused Mr. Rurode, in 1854, to break the old home ties and sail for the United States. For a period he remained in New York city, in the belief that here his fortune would be made. But the west seemed to offer superior advantages, so he came to Indiana and went directly to Terre Haute. From there, in 1860, just before the breaking out of the Civil war, he transferred his interests to Fort Wayne where, in company with John MacDougal and L. B. Root, he opened the New York Store which has continued ever since as one of the leading commercial houses of the region. Following the death of Mr. Root, in 1897, Mr. Rurode became the sole owner of the business, which has since been conducted under the name of the Rurode Dry Goods Company. Mr. Rurode is the president of the reorganized company; Ernest C. Rurode, Jr., vice president, and Charles A. T. Krimmel, secretary and treasurer. Mr. Rurode's business career, extending down through the half century since the Civil war, has been characterized by various problems of the times, and these form an interesting study for him who would weigh them and compare them with the ever-changing conditions in other fields of endeavor. Through it all Mr. Rurode, ever applying the truest principles of trade, has maintained the place of his business among the best of its kind. Never stooping to questionable business methods, he has always held firmly the confidence of the people of Fort Wayne and the entire northern part of the Hoosier state. In one marked line of effort has Mr. Rurode witnessed a wonderful development—namely, in the methods of advertising. Always conducting his business on a fair and square basis, Mr. Rurode, always a believer in publicity for the upbuilding of his trade, has clung steadfastly to the principle of truth in advertising, even in the old days when many advertisers believed that in order to prosper it was necessary to tear down the prosperity of a competitor. The wife of Mr. Rurode was formerly Miss Emeline Wilson Peddicord, daughter of the oldest banker in the state; she was a niece of Governor Oglesby, of Illinois. Mrs. Rurode died, May 2, 1916. By this union four children were born: One daughter who died in infancy; Valette, wife of Howell C. Rockhill, treasurer of the Fort Wayne Rolling Mills Co., and treasurer of the Lincoln National Life Insurance Co.; Emeline Prather, at home, and Ernst C., Jr., of whom this volume contains a biographical sketch. Mr. Rurode is interested in a number of Fort Wayne enterprises, though he has given a great share of his time to his dry goods business. He is president of the Fort Wayne Hotel Company, which owns the Anthony hotel. He is a Scottish Rite Mason and a member of the Mystic Shrine. He is a member of the English Lutheran church.

Ernst C. Rurode, Jr.—Among the progressive younger business men of Fort Wayne is Ernst C. Rurode, Jr., vice president of the Rurode Dry Goods Company, one of the leading retail establishments of northern Indiana. Mr. Rurode was born in Fort Wayne, July 18, 1885, son of

Ernst C. and Emeline (Peddicord) Rurode. A sketch of the father, who, through a long period of years, has maintained a prominent place among the merchants of northern Indiana, is to be found elsewhere in this volume. After the completion of his course of study in the public schools, Ernst C. Rurode, Jr., attended Culver Military Academy, at Culver, Indiana, and then entered upon a course in the Lawrenceville Preparatory School, in Lawrenceville, New Jersey. At a time when the advantages of travel were designed to make the most lasting impressions upon the mind of the young man, the way was opened to him for an extended European sojourn, which included visits to Germany, France, Switzerland and England. Upon his return he immediately entered upon an active commercial life by assuming a position of trust with the Rurode Dry Goods Company, of which his father was the active head. Through successive steps he attained to the position of treasurer of the company. On June 10, 1910, Mr. Rurode was united in marriage with Miss Della Rossell, of Fort Wayne, daughter of Joseph and Lulu (Miles) Rossell, natives of Wabash county and Logansport, Indiana, respectively, but now residents of Fort Wayne. Mr. Rossell is a well-known traveling salesman for a leading shoe house. Two children have been born to Mr. and Mrs. Rurode—Ernst C., the third, and Joseph Rossell Rurode. In politics, Mr. Rurode is a republican. He is an active member of the Masonic order, being a Scottish Rite Mason and a member of the Mystic Shrine. He is also a member of the Elks lodge. Mr. and Mrs. Rurode are members of the Presbyterian church.

Mrs. Fronica Sack.—Mrs. Fronica Sack comes of a family that was established in Pleasant township in the early forties and has contributed generously to the development of the agricultural resources of the community and to those other communities within the county with which its members have been identified. Mrs. Sack was born in Sheldon, Pleasant township, December 19, 1849, and is a daughter of Joseph and Barbara (Schonbill) Miller. They were of German birth and came to America in young life. They met and married in Fort Wayne, and soon afterward came to Pleasant township, where they bought land and settled down to the quiet of farm life. They owned eighty-five acres of land that later came to be of exceptional value and began life in a two-story log cabin that was more pretentious than the cabin homes of most of their neighbors. Mr. Miller died at the early age of forty-five years, leaving his widow and a family of eight children. They were Fronica, Joseph, Mary, Catherine, Rosa, Anna, Lena and Jacob. Joseph and Catherine are deceased. Mary is the wife of Barney Frieberger of Fort Wayne. Rosa married George Minick, of Monroeville, Indiana. Anna is the wife of Harry Shife, of Fort Wayne. Lena married Charles Minick, who died in October, 1915. Jacob lives in Adams county, Indiana; Fronica Miller was married January 10, 1870, to Henry Sack, son of Henry Sack, who was a farmer of German parentage and a resident of Hessen Castle. In the parochial schools of that community Henry, Jr., had his early schooling, and when he had finished his education joined his father in the operation of the home farm of one hundred and sixty acres, which he inherited on the death of his parents. He later sold half of the place, but the remaining half was kept for a home, and he spent the best years of his life in the development of that property. He was a prominent man in his community, a Democrat in politics, member of the Catholic church, and an estimable and worthy citizen. He died on November 20, 1899. He and his wife were the parents of a family numbering thirteen children. Henry, Jr., the first born, died April 8, 1900. Mary married George Sorg and is living in Pleasant township. Joseph is in Toledo, Ohio. Lena is the wife of John Scherschal, of Milan township; Rosa died in 1897; Catherine married Walter McEwen and they lived in Fort Wayne. John and Anthony are residents of Fort Wayne, also. Elizabeth is the wife of Corey Kaymeyer. Clara died as the wife of Joe Middleton. Matilda married John Wayandt and they live on the home place with Mrs. Sack. Charley is also at home with the widowed mother and Jacob is living in Fort Wayne. Mrs. Sack is enriched by the possession of fourteen grandchildren. Mary has five children—named Andrew, Alice, Walter, Herman and Arthur. Joseph's children are Chester and Esther. Lena has Elmer, Florence, Francis and Walter. Catherine's three are Elsie, Robert and Esther, while Clara has a son and a daughter—Thomas and Agnes.

Henry Brooke Sale, vice-president and treasurer of the Hoffman Brothers Company, has a place among the prominent business men of Fort Wayne, where he has been established since 1909. Mr. Sale is a son of John W. and Ann Eliza (Hoffman) Sale, the former born in Warren county, Indiana, August 30, 1844, and the mother in Maryland on September 7, 1848. They were married in Fort Wayne, in 1871, and the father was for many years engaged in the lumber business, in which he enjoyed a very gratifying success. He was living retired, however, at the time of his death, in 1914—seven years after the passing of the mother. They were the parents of three children. Francis B. is a resident of Fort Wayne, Indiana. Jessamine is the wife of John H. Nixon. Henry Brooke, the oldest child, was born on August 1, 1873, and had his early schooling in Howe School, at Lima, Indiana. Later, when he was fitted for the pursuit of higher studies, he entered Purdue University. At the age of twenty years young Sale entered the business world in the employ of Hoffman Brothers. In 1897 he identified himself with the United Telephone Company at Bluffton and for a year and a half held the position of secretary of that company. At the end of that time he went to Indianapolis as superintendent of the then new long distance telephone company, remaining there until 1905. When he left he was vice president and general manager of the New Long Distance Telephone Company and Indianapolis Telephone Company, his advance with that concern having been marked by its rapidity. Mr. Sale was next identified in business as a member of the Sale-Blackledge-Nellis Company, which he was instrumental in organizing, in 1906, for the manufacture of catsup and other canned goods. This concern is still in business with factories at Effingham, Illinois, and Brazil, Indiana, and sales department in Indianapolis. In 1909 Mr. Sale returned to Fort Wayne to become secretary and treasurer of the Hoffman Brothers Company and on the death of A. E. Hoffman, in 1913, became vice president and treasurer of the concern, which position he now fills. Mr. Sale married on March 24, 1898, Miss Charlotte Lowry, a native of Fort Wayne and daughter of Judge Robert Lowry. They are membes of the First Presbyterian Church of Fort Wayne and Mr. Sale is a thirty-second degree Mason, a member of the University Club of Indianapolis, the Indianapolis Country Club, the Fort Wayne Country Club and the Fort Wayne Commercial Club. He is a man who manifests a wholesome interest in the civic advancement of his home community and may be depended upon to lend material aid in those movements calculated to enhance the civic welfare of the city.

Charles Salomon.—Three generations of the Salomon family have been active in the industrial life of Washington township since the first of the name came from Germany and settled here, and a fourth generation is growing up in the community today. Charles Salomon represents the third generation and has taken a prominent place in the civic life of his community for some time. He was supervisor of his township for four years and is now serving as assistant superintendent of highways, and has been prominently identified with the work on the Lincoln Highway and the Lima Road. He is also identified with farm life in the township and is the owner of a farm of 127 acres, where he carries on general farming with much success. He is a son of Karl and Louise (Winkelmeier) Salomon and was born in Fort Wayne on July 4, 1875. His parents were native Germans and Karl Salomon was the son of Anthony and Christina (Giesking) Salomon. Anthony Salomon came to America in 1865, settling soon thereafter in Washington township, where he passed the remainder of his life. He was father of six children —Karl, Christine, Christ, Minnie, Lizzie and Marie, all living at this writing and heads of families in Allen county. Karl Salomon settled in Fort Wayne when he came to America and was for fifteen years engaged as a workman in the boiler shops of the Pennsylvania railroad before he came to Washington township, in 1883, and settled on a farm. He is still operating his place of 127 acres, in Section 15, and has one of the fine places in the township. He married on November 15, 1874, Miss Lizzie Winkelmeier, and they were parents of four children—Charles, of this review, and three others who are deceased. Charles Salomon had his early education in Fort Wayne and moved to the farm home of his parents as a boy. He has since been identified with the life of the community in a manner creditable alike to himself and the township, and has demonstrated the high order of his citizenship in definite terms. He is a successful farmer and is accounted as one of the foremost men of the township today. On May 25, 1899, Mr. Salomon was married to Martha Rahdert, daughter of Fred Rahdert. Mr. and Mrs. Salomon have four children—Karl, Hilda, Emma and Velma. All are living at home and enjoying the advantages afforded by the schools of the township. Mr. Salomon is a Republican in politics and he and his family have membership in St. Paul's Lutheran church in Fort Wayne.

Christian Salomon.—It is both gratifying and significant to note that there is a goodly quota of the youth of Allen county who have here found in their mature years ample scope for successful endeavor and have no desire to abate their allegiance to and appreciation of the county. Such a one is Mr. Salomon, who owns and resides upon the fine old homestead farm, in Washington township, which was the place on which he was reared and which is property of whose possession any man might well be proud. Mr. Salomon was born, May 10, 1856, in Westphalen, Germany, a son of Anthony and Christena (Eseking) Salomon, the family having immigrated to America, in 1871, and the home having been established on the farm now owned and occupied by the subject of this review. The original tract comprised one hundred acres, and to the same has been added thirty-three adjoining acres, and much of the land was reclaimed and improved by the honored father, who was effectively aided by the only son, Christian, of this sketch. As increasing prosperity justified such action, the best of improvements were gradually made on the homestead, and here the parents passed the remainder of their lives, earnest, kindly and industrious folk who commanded the high regard of all who knew them and both devout communicants of the German Lutheran church. The father's death occurred, September 25, 1884, and the loved wife and mother did not long survive him, as she too passed to the life eternal on February 23, 1886. Of the five children the eldest is he whose name introduces this article; Mrs. Christena Drier and Mrs. Minnie Gerding are still residents of Allen county, as is also Mrs. Louise Drier, whose home is in Fort Wayne; and Mary is the wife of Rev. Ed. E. Arendt, who is a Lutheran missionary residing in the city of Hong Kong, China. Christian Salomon acquired his early education in his native land and was a lad of about fifteen years when the family came to America and established a home in Allen county. He was reared to manhood on his present farm and the same has received his effective labors and management during the entire course of his youth and mature years, his marriage having been solemnized about one year prior to the death of his honored father and the entire control of the farm having been his since that time. In later years he has been severely afflicted with rheumatism and has passed the active management of the farm over to his sons, who are well upholding the honors of the family name as sterling young men and progressive farmers. The present commodious and attractive house on the farm was erected by the subject of this sketch, and he has made many other excellent improvements of permanent order, including the construction of fences and the installation of tile drainage. He has taken deep interest in community affairs, is a Democrat in politics and served four years as road superintendent, with characteristic efficiency. Both he and his wife are active members of the German Lutheran church in the city of Fort Wayne. October 25, 1883, recorded the marriage of Mr. Salomon to Miss Dorothea Bashelier, daughter of Louis and Dorothea (Mollet) Bashelier, who were born in Germany and were for many years residents of Allen county, where the father was a prosperous farmer of Washington township, his death having occurred, April 5, 1913, and his wife having passed away, May 5, 1890, the three surviving children being Mrs. Salomon, Frederick and Henry. Mr. and Mrs. Salomon have four children: Anna, the only daughter, is the wife of Henry S. Kramer, of St. Joseph township, this county; and Edward, Henry and Walter are associated in the management of the home farm.

Felix Schanz is a well known and popular business man of Fort Wayne, where he has maintained his home for nearly forty years and his ability and progressiveness have won to him a place as one of the leading exponents of modern photographic art in the United States. His photographic studio, at 309-311 West Washington Boulevard, is one of the best appointed in the United States, with the most approved equipment in all departments and with numerous features that make it absolutely unique. The attractive and modern studio building was erected by Mr. Schanz in 1914 and was designed by him with special reference to meeting fully the demands of the best type of modern photography in all of its branches. The studio has gained national reputation among photographers, and each year many prominent representatives of the profession visit the establishment to survey its facilities and the splendid appointments. Provision is made for the best of accommodations for the making of photographs, with a department for sittings on each the first and the second floors, together with the most complete and attractive arrangements for the desired toilet changes demanded in securing the most effective results from different poses and with varying accessories.

On the first floor it is possible to drive directly in with an automobile and to obtain pictures of the machine and its occupants. The equipment of the studio includes also the most modern facilities for the production of the moving-picture photography, and no similar establishment in the Union can claim a superior equipment for the producing of the highest grade of photographs, as well as the most attractive specimens of the lower-priced type when demanded. It is much to have given to Fort Wayne such a splendid center of art production as the Schanz studio, and the popular proprietor caters successfully to the most cultured tastes and aesthetic ideals of his extensive and representative clientele, the while he has the satisfaction of knowing that he has provided his home city with a studio that is not excelled in even the leading metropolitan centers of the country. In connection with his business he has devoted time and thought to the study of an experimentation in photographic art in all of its phases, has not been content to follow the leadership of others and has discovered and devised many methods and accessories to advance the general effectiveness of photographic reproduction. He is both an expert and a connoisseur, both a practical business man and an appreciative patron of art. Few citizens of Fort Wayne are better known in the community and none can claim a circle of more loyal friends. Mr. Schanz was born in France on April 15, 1861, a son of C. and Catherine (Hauter) Schanz, both of whom are now deceased. The father was born in Alsace-Lorraine and his death occurred when the subject of this review was a child. Felix Schanz was reared in France until about five years of age, was educated in Germany, and was eighteen years of age when, in the autumn of 1879, he came to the United States. He landed in the port of the national metropolis and remained in New York city nearly three years, his attention being there given to electrical and photographic work. In the autumn of 1881 he came to Fort Wayne and here installed at the Centlivre brewery plant the first electric calling bell system thus placed in commission in this city. He continued his connection with this line of enterprise a short time and then became associated with the photographic business of F. R. Barrows, with whom he remained three years. For the ensuing three years he was connected with the Star photograph gallery and then opened a studio of his own, in rooms above the old Eckart meat market, on Calhoun street, the site now occupied by the Frank dry-goods store. Two and one half years later he removed to better quarters, at 922 Calhoun street, and there remained twenty-six years, or until his removal to his present fine studio building, where, as he personally has stated, he feels specially gratified to note that the patronage which he enjoyed at the old stand has followed him to the new. Mr. Schanz is cosmopolitan in his tastes, genial and gracious in his personality, independent in his political proclivities, and a loyal and appreciative American citizen as a resdent of the city of his adoption. On the 15th of May, 1890, was solemnized the marriage of Mr. Schanz to Miss Mary Schmoll, who was born and reared in Fort Wayne and whose father, Gottlieb Schmoll, was here in the employ of the Pennsylvania Railroad Company for many years, his death having occurred in the year 1900. Mr. and Mrs. Schanz have three children: Dr. Robert Schanz is a member of the medical and surgical staff of the Lutheran hospital in Fort Wayne; Paul is a traveling representative for an important optical house in Fort Wayne; and Elfreda has most graciously and successfully had charge of the reception room of her father's studio since 1913, with the result that she has become well known to the many patrons and has gained unqualified popularity in her native city.

Gottlieb E. C. Schaper, a representative of one of the old and honored German families of Allen county, was born in Adams township, this county, on December 19, 1864, and not only has the satisfaction of being at the present time the owner and operator of the fine old homestead farm which was the place of his nativity, but also has the distinction of being, in 1917, trustee of Adams township, an office in which he has given characteristically loyal and efficient service in the furtherance and maintenance of the civic and industrial interests of his home township and native county. Mr. Schaper is a son of Ernest and Mary (Broadtmeler) Schaper, both of whom were born in Germany. Ernest Schaper came to America about the year 1829 and he became one of the pioneer settlers of Allen county, Indiana, where he first located in Wayne township. Later he purchased a tract of wild land in Adams township, and there he reclaimed a productive farm, to the management of which he continued to devote his attention until his death. He was a sturdy and upright citizen who did well his part in the civic and industrial life of the community and he achieved success worthy of the name. He was sixty years of age at the time of his death and his name merits high place on the roll of the sterling pioneers of the county, his widow, now venerable in years, remaining with her son Gottlieb, in whose home she is accorded the deepest filial love and solicitude. She has been a life-long communicant of the German Lutheran church, as was also her husband, and he was a Democrat in his political allegiance. Of the three children the subject of this sketch is the youngest; Frederick is one of the substantial farmers and valued citizens of Adams township; and Mary is the wife of Conrad Frosh, likewise one of the representative agriculturists of that township. Reared to manhood under the benignant and invigorating influences of the home farm, Gottlieb E. C. Schaper likewise profited fully from the discipline which he received in the public schools of his native township. He has never wavered in his allegiance to the basic industries of agriculture and stock-growing and as owner of the old homestead farm he is one of the successful and progressive exponents of these important lines of enterprise in Allen county—a steadfast and loyal citizen who commands the respect and confidence of the community. As a stalwart supporter of the cause of the Democratic party he has been influential in public affairs in his township, and in 1914 he was elected trustee of Adams township, of which position he is now the incumbent, his present term expiring in 1918. His finely improved farm is situated about three and one-half miles distant from Fort Wayne, and there he receives service on rural mail route No. 12. Both he and his wife are active members of the Lutheran church and their attractive home is known for its hospitality and good cheer. On April 23, 1893, was solemnized the marriage of Mr. Schaper to Miss Dora Mueller, who likewise was born in Chicago township, a daughter of Rudolph and Berdina Mueller. At the parental home still remain the six children, namely: Irwin, Martin, Gottlieb, Hilda, Edna and Elsie.

William H. Scheiman has been prominently concerned with governmental and general civic affairs in his native county and city, has held various positions of public trust, including that of county treasurer, and as an influential exponent of the real estate business has done much to further the civic and material advancement of Fort Wayne, where he is vice-president and general manager of the City & Suburban Company, one of the leading real estate organizations of Allen county. Mr. Scheiman was born in Fort Wayne on the 10th of February, 1873, a son of Frederick and Sophia (Koester) Scheiman. Frederick Scheiman was born in Germany and came to America in 1840. He became one of the pioneers of Fort Wayne, where he established himself in the work of his trade, that of tailor, and long continued as one of the successful business men and highly honored citizens of this community, in which both he and his wife passed the closing years of their lives, both having been communicants of St. Paul's Lutheran church and his political allegiance having been given to the Democratic party. His wife's brother, Christian Koester, was prominently associated with the late William Paul in the development of lime quarries at Huntington and Wabash, the original representative of the Koester family in Allen county having come from Hanover, Germany, on a sailing vessel that required three months to make the voyage across the Atlantic. Of the children of Frederick Scheiman and wife, the eldest is Henry, who is now a resident of Grand Rapids, Michigan, and who is assistant treasurer of the Grand Rapids & Indiana Railroad Company; Frederick E. W. and Charles J. remain in Fort Wayne, and the latter is treasurer of the Packard Piano Company; Dora likewise resides in Fort Wayne; and William H., of this sketch, is the youngest of the number. William H. Scheiman acquired his early education in the local parochial schools of the German Lutheran church and his advancement in the business world has been won entirely through his own ability and efforts. After leaving school he obtained a position as office boy in the real estate offices of E. L. Craw and in each successive stage of progress has made the best possible use of the opportunities that have been presented. He expanded his practical knowledge of business affairs and in his youth made good record for himself as bookkeeper for the wholesale grocery house of G. E. Bursley & Company and as credit man in the hardware establishment of Pfeiffer & Schlatter. Thereafter he was for some time connected with a Fort Wayne lithographing enterprise and finally became assistant county treasurer, under the administration of Treasurer Rohan. Later he was assistant to the superintendent of the Indiana State School for the Feeble Minded, in Fort Wayne, and in 1906, as candidate on the Democratic ticket, was elected county treasurer. His efficient administration led to his re-election at the expiration of his first term and he retired from this office at the close of his second term, in 1911. Mr. Scheiman is now giving the major part of his time and attention to the extensive and important real estate business controlled by the City & Suburban Company, of which he is vice-president and general manager, as previously noted. He is president of the Fort Wayne Real Estate Board at the time of this writing, in 1917, is a director of the Fort Wayne Commercial Club, and is president of the Quest Club. In November, 1899, Mr. Scheiman wedded Miss Margaret Lang, whose death occurred in 1903 and who is survived by no children. On November 28, 1908, was solemnized the marriage of Mr. Scheiman to Miss Ada Thomas, daughter of Enoch and Mary Thomas, of Fort Wayne. Mrs. Thomas, who is now deceased, was a member of one of the old and honored families of Fort Wayne. Mr. and Mrs. Scheiman have two children—William Thomas and Elsie Margaret.

Charles J. Scheimann is emphatically to be designated as one of the representative figures in the industrial and commercial life of his native city of Fort Wayne, where through his own ability and well directed endeavors he has risen from the stage of small beginnings to a plane of commanding influence in connection with a number of the largest and most important industries of the city. After leaving school Mr. Scheimann became office boy in the employ of the Fort Wayne Organ Company, which was then an important local institution controlled by Messrs. Gilbert E. Bursley and Stephen B. Bond. Later he was employed for some time in the company's factory, but after gaining practical knowledge of the details of manufacturing he returned to the office department, in which his experience and his executive ability came more effectively into play. He thus became closely associated with the development and upbuilding of the business and since 1897 has held the office of treasurer of the Packard Piano Company, which important manufacturing concern of Fort Wayne is a direct outgrowth of the Fort Wayne Organ Company. Mr. Scheimann is a director not only of the Packard Piano Company but also of the Meyer Brothers Company, engaged in the wholesale and retail drug business; a director of the National Steel Castings Company, at Montpelier, Indiana; a director and one of the largest stockholders of the Vapor Stove Company, of Detroit, Michigan; secretary and a director of the Fort Wayne Freie Presse; and a director of the Ideal Automobile & Sales Company, of Fort Wayne. For the past nineteen years (1917) Mr. Scheimann has been a trustee of Concordia College, one of the noble educational institutions maintained in Fort Wayne under the auspices of the Lutheran church, and he has the general supervision of the fiscal affairs of the college. The political allegiance of Mr. Scheimann is given to the Democratic party and he is known and honored as one of the liberal and progressive citizens of Allen county, as well as one of the most influential business men of Fort Wayne. Hs is an earnest communicant of St. Paul's Lutheran church; he was the first president of the Walther League, in the club house and schools of which he has shown the deepest and most liberal interest, and he is a valued member also of the Fort Wayne Commercial Club, the Country Club and the Quest Club, besides which he was formerly president of the interesting Fort Wayne musical organization known as the Apollo Club. He has played a large part in the upbuilding of the extensive manufacturing and commercial business controlled by the Packard Piano Company, and in the interest of this splendid Fort Wayne institution has made two trips to Europe. Charles J. Scheimann was born in Fort Wayne on October 24, 1862, a son of Frederick and Sophia (Koester) Scheimann, the former of whom was born in Prussia and the latter in the Kingdom of Hanover, Germany. The father was a tailor by trade and after coming to the United States worked at this trade for some time in the cities of New York and Brooklyn. The family home was established in Fort Wayne very early in the '60s. He was a merchant tailor and here lived practically retired during the closing years of his honorable and useful life, having died in 1889, and his wife survived until 1906; both were devoted communicants of St. Paul's Lutheran church, the while his political views were shown in his staunch support of the cause of the Democratic party. Of the children, Henry F. resides in the city of Grand Rapids, Michigan, where he holds the office of assistant treasurer of the Grand Rapids & Indiana Railroad; and Fred

E. W. is prominently identified with business interests in Fort Wayne; he was treasurer of the old Street Car Company and later was treasurer of the Salamonie Mining and Gas Company, and is now connected with the Northern Indiana Gas & Electric Company. Charles J., of this review, was the next in order of birth; Dora remains with her brother Charles, whose wife is deceased; and William H. is ex-county treasurer of Allen county and now vice-president and general manager of the City and Suburban Building Company. Charles J. Scheimann acquired his preliminary education in the parochial schools of St. Paul's Lutheran church of Fort Wayne and thereafter attended Concordia College, of which he is now a trustee. On November 3, 1890, at Los Angeles, California, he married Miss Elise Koester, who passed away four months after her marriage, since which time Mr. Scheimann maintained a home with his mother and sister, Dora, in charge, until the death of the former, since which time the latter has been the hostess. He served one season as conductor on the first open, or summer, street car placed in commission in Fort Wayne and then completed a course in the Powers Business College. Soon afterward he became associated with the Fort Wayne Organ Company, and his career from that time forward has been outlined in the earlier portion of this record.

Benjamin B. Schlatler.—One of the prominent farmers of Spencerville in Cedar Creek township is Benjamin B. Schlatler, born in Allen county on March 16 and the son of Christian and Barbara (Gerig) Schlatler, both of German birth and parentage. In about 1848 the father located in Cedar Creek township, immediately following his arrival in America, and there met and married Barbara Gerig. They spent their lives in devotion to rural life and the upbringing of their family of six children, and both have now passed to their reward. Their children are here briefly mentioned as follows: Christ lives in Washington. Benjamin B. was the second born. Joseph died in youth, as did Andrew. David is a resident of Fort Wayne and Mary is the wife of David Dever, of Colorado. Benjamin Schlatler remained at home after the others had gone out into the world and in later years, when the old homestead came into his ownership, he added to it other land in the township, so that he has a considerable acreage under cultivation. He is a successful farmer, intent upon realizing the best results from the labor and money expended in the operation of his acres, and has brought up the standard of Cedar Creek agriculture appreciably in recent years. His fine brick dwelling house and modern and commodious barns indicate the measure of his success in his chosen work. On May 2, 1880, Mr. Schlatler married Christine McCartney, a native of Allen county and daughter of James and Parthena (Lee) McCartney, both of Ohio, who came to Allen county as early as 1847. They located on Cedar Creek and later moved into Leo, in Cedar Creek township, and were long and successfully engaged in farming there. They were pioneers in the truest sense and knew this district when it was a veritable wilderness. Eight children were reared in their home. Hannah, the first born, is dead. Eliza is the wife of Jacob Zechner, of DeKalb county. William is living in Illinois. The fourth child was Christine, wife of the subject. Louis lives in Cedar Creek township. Mary is deceased. Alice is the wife of Paul Metz, of Chicago. Charles died in infancy. Mr. and Mr. Schlatler have one son, James Leroy, born July 9, 1888, and he is now engaged in carrying on the work of the home farm, the father having lately withdrawn to some extent from its management. Both father and son are staunch Democrats and members of the Methodist church. They are men of excellent qualities and are citizens of a high order in their community. The family is highly esteemed in the community with which it has so long been identified and enjoy the friendship of a wide circle in town and county.

Christ S. Schlatter is the owner of one of the well improved landed estates of Springfield township and has long been known as one of the representative agriculturists and loyal and progressive citizens of the county that has been his place of residence since he was a child of about three years. He was born in Mulhausen, Germany, October 18, 1851, and in 1854 his parents, Benedict and Elizabeth (Garrick) Schlatter, immigrated to America and became pioneer settlers of Allen county, Indiana. They established their home in Cedar Creek township, where the father girded himself valiantly for the arduous work of reclaiming a farm from the forest, both he and his wife having passed the remainder of their lives on the old homestead, which he brought to profitable productiveness. The names of the ten children in this sterling pioneer family are here noted: Benedict, Jr., Josph, Christ S., Anna, Fanny, Kate, Elizabeth, Mary, Lydia, and Jonas. He whose name introduces this paragraph was reared to adult age in Cedar Creek township, where he early began to assist in the work of the pioneer farm, and where he received his youthful educational discipline in the common schools of the day. He continued as an exemplar of agricultural enterprise in Cedar Creek township until 1886, when he removed to Springfield township and purchased a tract of ninety-two acres, in Section 33. Later he bought an adjoining twenty-five acres in the same township, and finally he added to his landed estate one hundred acres in Section 34 of the same township, so that he now owns a valuable farm property of two hundred and seventeen acres. With characteristic energy and discrimination Mr. Schlatter has marked the passing years not only by successful farm enterprise but also by the providing of the best of permanent improvements on his farm property. He erected the commodious and attractive brick residence that constitutes the family home, and the barns and other buildings are of a type that is consonant with the fine house, all buildings being lighted by the modern electric plant which Mr. Schlatter has provided for the purpose. That a man whose management of his private business affairs has been so effective should be called upon to give co-operation in the directing of governmental matters in the community was virtually a foregone conclusion, and thus it is to be recorded that Mr. Schlatter served one term as township supervisor, with characteristic loyalty and efficiency. In politics he is not constrained by partisan dictates but gives his support to men and measures meeting the approval of his judgment. He and his family hold membership in the Mennonite church. In 1877 Mr. Schlatter wedded Miss Anna Yoder, whose death occurred in the year 1897. Of the five children of this union all are living except the second, Solomon, whose death occurred in 1914. The names of the other children are as follows: David J., Leah, Sylvia, and Joseph. In the year 1899 was solemnized the marriage of Mr. Schlatter to Miss Katie Gerig, who was born in Springfield township, this county, June 26, 1870, and who is a daughter of Joseph and Katie (Nofciger) Gerig, the former a native of Germany and the latter of the state of Ohio, where their marriage was solemnized and whence they came to Allen county and established their home in Springfield township, where they passed the remainder of their lives. Their children were ten in number, namely: John, Joseph, Anna (deceased), Katie (Mrs. Schlatter), Joel and Aaron (both deceased), Daniel, Samuel (deceased), Mary, and Elizabeth. Of the three children of Mr. and Mrs. Schlatter the two surviving are George and Jesse, Elmer, the first born, having died in childhood.

Cleveland S. Schlatter is conducting a prosperous mortgage loan business in the city of Fort Wayne and has proved himself a straightforward and versatile young business man, besides which he is a lawyer, having been admitted to the bar in October, 1916. Mr. Schlatter was born in the village of Leo, this county, on May 23, 1884, a son of Christian J. and Elizabeth (Carnahan) Schlatter, who now reside in the state of Washington, where the father is successfully engaged in farming. Cleveland S. Schlatter is indebted to the public schools of his native village for his early educational discipline, which included that of the high school, and later pursued higher academic studies in the Valparaiso University, the great Indiana institution in the city of Valparaiso. In his early youth Mr. Schlatter entered upon an apprenticeship to the tinner's trade, in a hardware establishment at Leo, and to this trade gave his attention four years. In 1907 he established his residence in Fort Wayne, where he became identified with the Peoples Loan Company, his experience being such as to equip him fully for independent operations in the same line when, on November 10, 1914, he established the Independent Loan Company. He is also engaged in the active practice of law and has been energetic and ambitious in his technical reading, with the result that he has gained excellent knowledge of the science of jurisprudence. He has essayed definite activity in the domain of politics and gives his allegiance to the Democratic party, and is now (spring of 1917) a candidate for city judge. On April 9, 1910, Mr. Schlatter wedded Miss Lola C. Landis, a daughter of William and Hattie (Campbell) Landis, of Fort Wayne. The two children of this union are Woodrow H., who was named in honor of President Wilson, even as his father was given similar recognition of Democratic paternal predilections, his birth having occurred in the year that recorded the first election of Grover Cleveland to the presidency of the United States; and Florence L.

David J. Schlatter has proved his resourcefulness and progressive spirit by developing in his native township of Springfield a specially substantial business as a commercial gardener. He has made a close study of horticulture and brings to bear in his operations scientific and practical methods that insure the best results in the propagation of the various vegetables, for which he finds a ready demand in the city of Fort Wayne, where his supporting trade is principally centralized. His fine little farm of forty acres, in Section 33, Springfield township, is almost entirely devoted to horticultural enterprise and is one of the veritable garden spots of the county in both a literal and visual sense. Mr. Schlatter has made the best of modern improvements on the place, including the erection of an attractive and commodious house which he has equipped with the best of modern facilities, including furnace heat and electric lighting system, the home being about five miles distant from the village of Grabill, which is his postoffice address. Mr. Schlatter is a representative of one of the well known and honored families of Springfield township, where he was born, April 24, 1880, a son of Christ S. and Anna (Yoder) Schlatter, his father having long been one of the representative farmers of this township. After having profited fully by the advantages of the public schools of his native township Mr. Schlatter gave his attention to general agricultural pursuits until he found that he was not physically fortified to withstand the intense heat and heavy labors entailed in general farm work. Under these conditions he consulted expediency by turning his attention to commercial gardening, and the success that has attended his enterprise has fully justified his choice of industrial vocation. Exercising his franchise in harmony with his earnest conviction, he gives his allegiance unreservedly to the Prohibition party, and both he and his wife are zealous members of the Church of Christ, Mrs. Schlatter, whose maiden name was Malinda Myers, having been born on the farm which they now own and occupy and their marriage having been solemnized February 5, 1902, and she is a daughter of John and Rose Myers, sterling residents of Springfield township.

August C. Schmidt.—The late August C. Schmidt had his introduction to America at the early age of seven years, when he came with his parents from their home in Germany and settled on a farm in Allen county. This section of the state has represented the family home since their arrival on American shores, in 1849, and their connection with the community has at all times been a creditable one. The parents of August Schmidt were John G. and Sophia H. (Hommer) Schmidt, born and reared in Germany. A wagonmaker by trade, John Schmidt continued in his chosen work after settling here and enjoyed a fair measure of prosperity during his lifetime. The son, August C., was born in Germany on July 7, 1842, and was educated in Allen county. Coming of age he naturalized duly, and in the second year of the Civil War enlisted in Company I, Eighty-ninth Indiana Infantry, and continued in the service through to the end of the war. He was a participant in many hard-fought engagements, and his wartime experience differed from that of his fellows only in that he escaped without injury of any sort during the period of his service. He was mustered out at Mobile, Alabama, in July, 1865, returning at once to his Allen county home, where he settled down to the quiet pursuits of farm life, in Marion township. In 1871 the young man married Miss Sophia Meyers. She was an Allen county girl, the daughter of J. D. and Sarah Jane (Dehaven) Meyers. The father was of German birth. He came to America in early manhood, married, settled on a farm and there he and his wife spent their remaining days, enjoying to the end the respect and confidence of their friends and associates in the community. After the marriage of Mr. Schmidt to Sophia Meyers he rented a farm in Marion township and settled down to make what he could of such resources as were at his command. What he lacked in money he made up in courage and energy and after twelve years became the owner of an eighty-acre farm in section ten, Monroe township, where he spent his remaining years busily engaged in the work of developing the place. When he passed on, August 14, 1901, he left to his widow a comfortable home and she has since resided there, carrying on the place capably and successfully. Mrs. Schmidt has made some improvements on her own responsibility since the farm came under her control, chief among which is a fine modern dwelling that reflects much credit upon her Eleven children were born to Mr. and Mrs. Schmidt, all but two of whom are living at this writing. They are here named in the order of their borth: John E. deceased; William A.; Minnie, the wife of Charles H. Van Horn; Emma C., the wife of T. J. Sheehan; Amelia, deceased; David H.; Harvey C., of Fort Wayne; Tilla M., married to J. B. Sheehan; Lucy H., the wife of Frank Neadstine; Frances M., living at home, and Goldie E., who is also at home with the mother.

Rev. Carl H. Schnepel.—The general historical division of this publication offers in a specific way adequate data concerning the various religious organizations in Allen county, and thus it is not requisite that in the article at hand be given detailed record concerning St. Mark's Lutheran church at Sheldon, of which the honored pastor is he whose name initiates this paragraph. Supplemental information, however, may be briefly given. In 1914 there was installed in the fine church edifice a new and model pipe organ, at a cost of fifteen hundred dollars, and within the past four years improvements upon the house utilized as a home for the teachers in the parochial school have involved an expenditure of about one thousand dollars. Under the regime of Mr. Schnepel the parish has been signally prosperous in both its spiritual and temporal affairs, and since 1912 the annual offerings for benevolent purposes have been increased from $450 to $950. The earnest zeal and loyalty of the members of the parish are at all times in evidence, and each year the voting members customarily appear on one or more occasions to make necessary repairs and improvements upon the church property. F. G. Doepping, who had been for more than a decade an able and valued teacher in the parish school, departed on August 2, 1916, to engage in similar professional service in the city of Oshkosh, Wisconsin, and his successor, who arrived on the 22d of the same month, is C. F. Stadelmann, who came to this field from Holland, Dubois county, Indiana. The close of the year 1916 found fifty-two pupils enrolled in the parish school, in which the work is carried forward to the eighth grade as defined in the curriculum of the public schools of the city. In the parish schools special attention is given to religious instruction and counsel and also to the teaching of the German language. In the church services are conducted in both German and English, and in lieu of a Sunday school each Sabbath the pastor gives to the congregation, including the children, a half hour of instruction in the scripture and the lessons drawn therefrom. St. Mark's church has at the time of this writing 225 communicants, with a congregation appreciably in excess of this number. Rev. Carl H. Schnepel was born at Aschwarden, province of Hanover, Germany, on August 26, 1873, a son of C. H. and Meta (Bahr) Schnepel, who were born in that same province of Prussia, where they passed their entire lives, the father having been a gardener by profession and vocation and having passed to the life eternal in 1914, the mother of the subject of this review having died when the latter was an infant. Rev. Carl H. Schnepel was reared and educated in his native land, and, in 1889, he came to the United States and prepared to fit himself for the work of the ministry of the Lutheran church, in the faith of which he had been carefully reared. After passing one year in New York city he removed to the city of Chicago, and within a short time thereafter entered the Lutheran Seminary or divinity school in the city of St. Paul, Minnesota, in which institution he was graduated as a member of the class of 1896, a year which recorded also his ordination as a clergyman of the Lutheran church. His first pastoral charge was at Fort Jennings, Ohio, where he remained in faithful service until December, 1901, when he assumed a pastorate at Belmont, Wisconsin, where he remained until he assumed his present important charge at Sheldon, Allen county, in September, 1912. He has brought to bear in his ministerial work fine intellectual powers, earnest consecration and a high sense of stewardship, and his executive ability has been such as effectively to supplement his gracious and devoted service in the spiritual field of his labors. He has vitalized all departments of the parish work of St. Mark's church and has the earnest co-operations of his flock. On June 14, 1899, was solemnized the marriage of Mr. Schnepel to Miss Lena Rausch, who was born in Bavaria, Germany, June 27, 1875, and was ten years of age at the time of the family imigration to America. Her parents, Iudwig and Magdalina (Guth) Rausch, firse settled in Pennsylvania and later in Kansas, from which latter state they finally removed to Celina, Ohio. The death of Mr. Rausch occurred before the family moved to their new home, he having been a railway official in his native land and having been a man of superior ability. His widow now resides in the home of the honored subject of this review, Mr. and Mrs. Schnepel have five children, whose names and respective dates of borth are here noted: Rosa, October 9, 1899; Carl, December 9, 1903; Emil, August 4, 1909; Olga, March 23, 1913; and Frieda, September 6, 1916.

Ludwig Schowe.—Ludwig Schowe is a native of Washington township, born within its borders on October 26, 1846, and has been a continuous resident of the place throughout his lifetime. His parents, Ernest and Sophia (Hilgeman) Schowe, were of Prussian birth, and came to Allen county from their native land as young people. They married, in 1843, settled in Washington township, and carried on farming with some success until the death of the husband and father, in 1854. Later the widow remarried. Of the first marriage there were four children— Henry, Sophia, Katherine and Ludwig of this review. Ludwig Schowe had a common school education in his native community and his active career began in the work of conducting the home place, which his father left at his death. Today Mr. Schowe owns two hundred and fourteen acres of land in Washington township, on which he has made all the improvements, and his farm home is one of the well-kept and profitable places in the township today. On April 4, 1872, Mr. Schowe married Sophia Nieman. Mrs. Schowe passed away on March 4, 1874, and some time later Mr. Schowe was united in marriage with Miss Frederika Wegman, daughter of William and Sophia (Gerdothage) Wegman, long natives of Germany. Eleven children blessed the home of Ludwig Schowe. Of his first marriage there was one and of the second ten. Named in order of their birth the children are Sophia, Amelia, Emma, John, William, Marie, Benjamin, Clara, Edwin, Raymond and Lester. Emma, John, Benjamin and Raymond are deceased. Mr. Schowe has served his township as assessor in years past, and has taken his place among the dependable citizens of the township through all his mature years. He is Republican in politics, and is a member of St. John's Reformed church in Fort Wayne.

W. Frank Schrader, M. D., for more than twenty years one of the well known physicians of Fort Wayne, was born April 8, 1868, in Kenton, Ohio. His parents were Henry and Hariet (Gary) Schrader. In the schools of his native town Dr. Schrader received his early education and this was followed by courses in the normal schools at Ada and Middlepoint, Ohio. Thus equipped he began teaching in Kenton and thence he went in a like capacity to the Northwestern Normal College at Middlepoint. In 1891 he came to Fort Wayne and became instructor in the old Methodist College, now Taylor University, at Upland. In this last named institution he took up the study of medicine, which he pursued diligently until 1894, when he was graduated. He took special courses in Boston and New York. On returning to Fort Wayne he began the practice of his profession and was the first interne in Hope Hospital. In his school and pedagogic days Dr. Schrader had devoted much time to public speaking and kindred subjects and in this connection he was frequently called on for elocutionary entertainment. By money thus earned he was enabled to finish his education in his profession. His practice was of a general character until about five years ago, since which time his activities have been limited to the treatment of rectal diseases. He has contributed numerous articles to various magazines and to medical journals, all of his writings being characterized by a lucid and entertaining style and by clear thinking. He was married October 10, 1904, to Elizabeth Abbee, of Chicago. Mrs. Schrader is widely known as a pen artist and is a woman of superior talent and marked intellectuality. Dr. Schrader is a member of the Masonic fraternity and of the Presbyterian church.

Charles Schroeder passed his entire life in Fort Wayne, where he long held secure vantage-place as one of the city's representative business men and liberal and progressive citizens. During virtually the entire period of his active career he was here engaged in the retail drug business and his technical ability and personal popularity greatly conserved the success of the enterprise, he having been one of the leading druggists of his native city at the time of his death, which occurred, April 20, 1906. His sterling character and personality won to him the staunchest of friends, and his death was recognized as causing a distinct loss to the business and social circles of the Allen county metropolis. Mr. Schroeder was born in Fort Wayne, February 4, 1860, and thus was in the very prime of his strong and useful manhood when death set its seal upon his mortal lips. His parents, Louis and Elise (Rippe) Schroeder, were both born in Germany and established their home in Fort Wayne more than half a century ago, the remainder of their lives having been passed in this city, where they lived and wrought to goodly ends. Of their two children the subject of this memoir was the younger, and the older is Louis S. C. Charles Schroeder made good use of the advantages afforded in the public schools of Fort Wayne and thereafter further fortified himself by completing a course in a business college in his native city. In 1877 he became associated with his brother, Louis S. C., in the drug business, and soon developed his knowledge of the manifold details of this line of enterprise and became a skilled pharmacist. He was a vigorous and resourceful business man and through effective service not only brought substantial success to his mercantile enterprise, but also firmly entrenched himself in the confidence and good will of all who knew him. He had no ambition for practical politics or official preferment, but was loyal and liberal as a citizen and gave his political support to the cause of the Democratic party. He was affiliated with the Knights of Pythias. On October 4, 1883, was solemnized the marriage of Mr. Schroeder to Miss Louise D. Lahmeyer, who likewise was born and reared in Fort Wayne and whose parents, Daniel and Caroline (Mayer) Lahmeyer, came to the United States from their German fatherland in 1847 and 1852, respectively, and established their home in Fort Wayne. The father was a carpenter by trade until his death occurred, in 1888, his venerable widow being still a resident of Fort Wayne. Of their three children Mrs. Schroeder was the first born; John died when about thirteen years of age; and Carl is actively identified with Fort Wayne business interests. Mr. Schroeder is survived by one son, Carl Louis, who was born, January 14, 1889, and is now a member of the reportorial staff of the Fort Wayne Daily News; he continued his studies in the public schools until his graduation in the Fort Wayne high school and thereafter was for three years a student in the great University of Michigan, at Ann Arbor, Michigan. He married, June 21, 1916, Miss Dorothy Kilgore, of Fort Wayne, and they have one child, Charles William, born April 16, 1917. Since the death of her honored husband Mrs. Schroeder has found a measure of reconciliation and compensation in the gracious memories of their years of devoted companionship, and in her native city her circle of friends is limited only by that of her acquaintances.

Louis S. C. Schroeder.—For twenty-seven years Louis Schroeder was engaged in the drug business in Fort Wayne, and in that time came to be regarded as one of the successful and dependable business men of the city. He and his brother, Charles J. H., established themselves in their chosen field in 1871, locating at 1408 Calhoun street, and it was said of them that they were the two youngest druggists in the state of Indiana, Mr. Schroeder being only twenty years old at that time and his brother eighteen. They retired from the business, in 1904, and Mr. Schroeder lived quietly, with no business ties, until, in 1911, he was appointed superintendent of the State Free Employment Bureau, a position he held until January 1, 1917. Louis S. C. Schroeder is a native son of Fort Wayne, born on September 10, 1857, and his parents were Louis and Elise (Rippe) Schroeder both native born Germans, the father coming from Beneckstein and the mother from Bremen, Germany. An engineer and practical sawmill man, Mr. Schroeder settled in Allen county soon after his arrival in America and was connected with various sawmills during his life in Fort Wayne. He died there, in 1908, and the mother still survives. Their children were Louis S. C., of this review, and Charles J. H., who died in 1906. The brothers were reared and had their education in Fort Wayne, and when the elder was fifteen years old he entered one of the local drug stores to learn the business. He gained in that manner a practical experience that was worth vastly more to him in later years than the same time spent in book learning would have been. Both were licensed druggists and careful business men, and they built up a thriving business in the growing city with the passing years. When they retired in 1904, they were among the foremost drug men of the city, enjoying a prestige to which they were well entitled by reason of the nature of their methods and business procedure. They were prominent Democrats always, and the subject was secretary of the Democratic Central Committee in 1906, 1908 and 1910. His appointment to the post of superintendent of the State Free Employment Bureau was an especially appropriate one, and he had every qualification for the successful administration of the office. Mr. Schroeder is a thirty-second degree Mason, a member of Mizpah Temple, A. A. O. N. M. S., a member of the Knights of Pythias, of which he was trustee for nineteen years, the Benevolent and Protective Order of Elks, and is now serving as business manager of the Elks' Band. Mr. Schroeder has done excellent work in the interests of the city as president of the city council, in 1911-12-13, and was revenue collector at Fort Wayne during Grover Cleveland's first administration. On November 20, 1879, Mr. Schroeder married Miss Loretta Bradway, who was a Fort Wayne girl and the daughter of a well-known family of that city.

William C. Schwier has effectively shown his loyalty to his native city and county by effective service in various public offices of local order and is now the able and popular incumbent of the office of county commissioner, as representative of the metropolitan district of Fort Wayne. He was born in this city on August 3, 1868, a son of Charles and Catherine (Bernhardt) Schwier, both natives of Germany. Upon coming to the United States Charles Schwier first found employment in the city of Cincinnati, Ohio, where he worked at his trade, that of boilermaker, and within a few years he established his residence in Fort Wayne, where his marriage was solemnized, his wife having come with her parents to this county in 1853. Charles Schwier eventually became one of the successful merchants of Fort Wayne and was one of the city's venerable and highly honored citizens at the time of his death, in 1898, his widow still maintaining her home in Fort Wayne. Of the three children the subject of this review is the eldest; Catherine is a resident of Fort Wayne and gives the deepest filial care and solicitude to her venerable mother; and Sarah is the wife of Herbert B. Tobey, of Boston, Massachusetts. William S. Schwier acquired his youthful education in the schools of Fort Wayne and, in 1883, became associated with his father in the retail grocery business, under the title of Schwier & Son. The enterprise grew to be one of substantial order and eventually was greatly expanded in scope and importance, under the corporate title of the Montgomery Cash Grocery Company. With this representative mercantile enterprise Mr. Schwier continued his active association until 1913, when he disposed of his virtually controlling interest in the same, to give his time and attention to his duties as a public official. He is, however, still identified with the local business interests as a director of the Morris Plan Bank of Fort Wayne. Always a stalwart advocate and supporter of the principles of the Democratic party, Mr. Schwier has been influential in its affairs in his home city and county, and his strong hold upon popular confidence and esteem has been demonstrated by his being called upon to serve in various local offices of public trust. In 1905, while still active in the grocery business, he was elected councilman-at-large for the city of Fort Wayne, and served four years as president of the council. In 1912 he was elected a member of the board of county commissioners, his effective service needing no further voucher than the fact that he was re-elected, in 1914, his present term of office expiring in December, 1918, and his policies have been at all times progressive and yet marked by a constant desire wisely to conserve and foster the resources of the county and to bring about a consistently economical administration of fiscal affairs. In a fraternal way Mr. Schwier is affiliated with the Benevolent & Protective Order of Elks and the Loyal Order of Moose. Through his business and official associations he has become well known throughout his native county and it may consistently be said that his circle of friends is limited only by that of his acquaintances.

Samuel Scott has resided, since 1864, on his present fine homestead farm, in Section 16, Monroe township, and is one of the venerable, well-known and highly esteemed citizens of this attractive part of Allen county. He is a scion of the staunchest of English stock and finds a due measure of satisfaction in the fact that he can claim "fair Albion" as the place of his nativity. He is one of the three survivors in a family of nine children and was born in England on August 3, 1830, his parents, George and Jane (Cotam) Scott, having passed their entire lives in England. Samuel Scott gained his early education in the schools of his native land and upon attaining to his majority, in 1851, bade adieu to the "right little isle" of his birth and, with determined ambition and youthful courage, set forth for America, confident in his ability to wrest from the hands of Fate a due measure of independence and temporal prosperity. His initial experience in connection with American institutions and customs was gained during a residence of two years in Pennsylvania, and at the expiration of this period he made his way to Richland county, Ohio. About a year later he removed to Crawford county, that state, where he maintained his residence six years and there was solemnized his marriage to Miss Henrietta Salway, who likewise was born in England and has continued his loved and devoted companion and helpmeet during the long intervening years, the two having wrought side by side and having seen their earnest endeavors crowned with peace and prosperity, so that in the gracious evening of life they are compassed by those influences and benefices that are the merited reward for former effort and righteous living. Mr. and Mrs. Scott came to Allen county, in 1864, and established their home on the present farm, which comprises eighty acres and which is now one of the valuable and well-improved properties of Monroe township. When Mr. Scott purchased this tract of land most of the timber had been cut off, but there remained a plethora of stumps, so that he faced the most strenuous of labors in reclaiming the land and making it available for cultivation. The original family home was a log house of the true pioneer type, and this dwelling was made known for its unassuming hospitality and good cheer, especially as the family circle was augmented by sturdy sons and earnest and comely daughters who grew to adult age and assumed their share of the farm and domestic duties. This dwelling continued to be the family domicile until 1888, when Mr. Scott erected his present substantial and commodious frame house, the same being but one of the numerous permanent improvements he has made on the farm. Though in his venerable years Mr. Scott consistently has given over to others the arduous labors that were long his portion, he still takes an alert and helpful interest in the directing of the operations of the home farm and is fortunate in retaining splendid mental and physical vitality. He is aligned as a loyal supporter of the principles of the Democratic party and has at all times shown himself liberal and earnest in the furtherance of measures and enterprises tending to advance the communal welfare. He has had no ambition for public office, but in past years gave effective service as road superintendent, a position of which he continued the incumbent for several years. He was formerly in active affiliation with the Independent Order of Odd Fellows. To Mr. and Mrs. Scott were born twelve children, their names being here entered in respective order of birth: Lena, Winfield, George, Lillie, Harry, Ena, Cecelia, Jennie, Ida May, Marion, Pearl and Charles. Of the number Lena, George, Lillie, Marion and Pearl are deceased. Ene is the wife of A. Stevenson; Cecelia is the wife of William Zim; Jennie is the wife of Thomas Phillips; and Ida May is the wife of John Lighthoff.

Donald M. Sears is a man whose initiative energy and progressiveness have come into effective play in the furtherance of the commercial and industrial precedence of Fort Wayne. He is president of the D. M. Sears Company, which was organized in 1912 and is engaged in the manufacturing of food products, as a center of which line of industrial enterprise it has given a splendid impetus to Fort Wayne, for the business has grown to be one of broad scope and importance and now represents one of the noteworthy contributions to the vital commercial energy of the Allen county metropolis. In the organization of this company Mr. Sears was associated with Henry D. McLallen and John W. Caswell, and incorporation was based on a capital stock of $75,000. In 1914 the capital was increased to one hundred and twenty-five thousand and in the following year was raised to the present significant figure—one hundred and fifty thousand dollars. The personnel of the official corps of the company is as here noted: Donald M. Sears, president; Herbert B. Clugstone, vice-president; John W. Caswell, secretary; Henry D. McLallen, treasurer; and Donald M. Sears, general manager as well as president. The company erected for its purposes a substantial main building that is sixty-four by eighty-four feet in dimensions, two stories and basement; the annex boiler room is thirty-two by thirty-six feet, the pickle and salting house is one hundred and four by seventy-six feet, besides which are provided ample storage sheds and loading platforms. In the well-equipped plant employment is given to a force of about forty persons, and for the securing of its needed and large supplies, especially high-grade tomatoes, the company maintains fifteen stations for the purchasing, reception and shipping of the raw products. Such branches are maintained at Battle Creek, Reading, Union City and St. Joseph, Michigan; Columbia, Ohio; Grabill, Spencerville, Butler, Fremont, Angola, Berlin, Stroh, LaOtto, Columbia City and Newton, Indiana; and at Crocker, Humansville, Galloway, Republic, Monett and Springfield, Missouri, in which last mentioned city is also operated a branch factory. The company gives special attention to the manufacturing of tomato products of the finest grade, including pickles and bulk goods, and shipments are made in the special tank cars controlled by the concern. A vast acreage is retained as the reserve of the company for the growing of its products and under progressive and well-ordered management the business shows a constantly expanding tendency—the one mark of superiority in output and the popular estimate placed upon the same. Donald Merton Sears was born at Cortland, New York, on May 20, 1873, a son of Harvey A. and Jeanette (Willyard) Sears, the former of whom was born in Nova Scotia and the latter in Ohio. Harvey A. Sears was five years old at the time of the family removal to the United States and was reared and educated in the state of New York, where he learned the carpenter's trade. In 1854 he became one of the pioneers of Grand Rapids, Michigan, which was then a mere village, and there became a prominent contractor and builder. He served three years as a soldier of the Union in the Civil War—a member of the Nineteenth Michigan Infantry—and he was one of the venerable and honored citizens of Grand Rapids at the time of his death, his widow being still a resident of that city. He was a stalwart Republican, was a Presbyterian in his religious affiliation, as is also his widow, and was identified with the Grand Army of the Republic and the Masonic fraternity. Of the children Hal K. is now a resident of California; Clifford C. died at the age of eleven years; Donald M., of this sketch, was the third in order of birth; Benjamin G. is a resident of Sugar City, Colorado; and Hattie is the wife of **Forest** E. Manz, of Grand Rapids, Michigan. In the public schools of his native city Donald M. Sears acquired his early education and as a youth gained four years of strenuous experience in the great lumber woods of northern Michigan. Thereafter he was employed thirteen years by the famous H. J. Heinz Company, manufacturers of pickles, and in 1906 went to Chicago and entered the employ of Reid, Murdock & Company, one of the leading wholesale grocery concerns of the western metropolis. With this company he continued his association until 1912, when he came to Fort Wayne and effected the organization of the company which bears his name and of which he is president. He is not only progressive as a business man but also as a citizen and is one of the vigorous members of the Fort Wayne Commercial Club. His political allegiance is given to the Republican party, in the Masonic fraternity he is affiliated with the York, Scottish and Shrine bodies, and he and his wife are members of the Presbyterian church. April 29, 1902, recorded the marriage of Mr. Sears to Miss Maude E. Nelson, daughter of John B. and Sophia (Gibson) Nelson, of Allegan, Michigan, and the four children of this union are Harvey, Elizabeth, Margaret and Catharine.

Gideon W. Seavey.—Though the period of his residence in Fort Wayne covered little more than a decade, the late Gideon Webster Seavey became one of the dominating forces in the commercial and civic affairs of the city and was the founder of the extensive wholesale and retail hardware business that is still conducted under the title of the Seavey Hardware Company. Mr. Seavey was a man of fine intellectual powers and much business ability, his versatility having been shown in his having prepared himself for the legal profession, in which he achieved success, but his predilections led him more specifically into the domain of business enterprise, in which he proved his powers in no uncertain way. He continued at the head of the hardware business until the time of his death, which occurred on March 13, 1893, and his career was one of signal usefulness and honor, so that this publication may well give place to a tribute to his memory and accord recognition of the large place which he filled in the business and social life of the metropolis and judicial center of Allen county. Mr. Seavey was born on a farm near Prairieville, Lee county, Illinois, February 14, 1848, and was a scion of one of the sterling pioneer families of that section of the state. His alert mentality was coupled with an invincible ambition, and thus in his early educational work he made an exceptional record, as is shown by the fact that he was graduated in the literary department of the great University of Michigan when he was but twenty-two years of age. He was class poet and was popular and influential in student affairs at the university from which he received his degree of Bachelor of Arts. In the course of his career he not only gave evidence of his versatility of talent but also of his facility in expedients. Thus it is to be recorded that after his graduation he turned his attention to the newspaper business, by establishing a weekly paper, the Chronicle, at Hoopston, Illinois. In the domain of journalism he proved himself successful, as did he also in the practice of law, and he continued his residence in Illinois until 1879, when he came to Fort Wayne and became associated with his brother-in-law, the late Hon. Perry A. Randall, in the practice of law, Mr. Randall, who was one of the most honored and influential citizens of Fort Wayne at the time of his death, having been not only a fellow student but also the roommate of Mr. Seavey while they were attending the University of Michigan. Mr. Seavey demonstrated his ability as a resourceful trial lawyer and well-fortified counselor, but his assertive and vigorous individuality soon demanded expression in action aside from the routine of law practice. He became identified with the development of timber lands, and, in 1881, engaged in the hardware business, as the founder of the large and important business now conducted by the Seavey Hardware Company. At the time of the reorganization and incorporation of this company, in the spring of 1914, appreciative record was made in a local paper, and from the article it is but consistent that quotations be made in this context, as the data indicate the splendid development that has continued since the death of the honored founder of the business: "The Seavey Hardware Company was established in Fort Wayne, October 5, 1881, by the late G. W. Seavey, and has continued as a successful and growing business during the long intervening years. The company originally occupied the building at the northwest corner of Columbia and Clinton streets. In 1888 the business had grown so rapidly that new and larger quarters were necessary, so a new location was purchased in West Main street property, Mr. Seavey acquiring the building at 121 West Main street, where the business was continued twenty-five years. Owing to the continued increase in business this building also eventually proved inadequate properly to house the stock of merchandise and to execute the orders, so it was decided to change locations once more, and early in the fall of 1913 the company purchased the building at the northwest corner of Harrison and Pearl streets, formerly occupied by the Fort Wayne & Northern Indiana Traction Company, and the stock was moved to the new quarters in September, 1913." At the time of the reorganization, in the spring of 1914, the article from which the foregoing quotations have been made gave substantially the following record: "Endeavoring to enlarge its field of operation and extend its service to the public, the Seavey Hardware Company, one of the oldest and largest hardware establishments of northern Indiana, has just completed several changes in its organization, and articles of incorporation have been sent to the secretary of state. . . . The new company will take over the entire business and property of the Seavey Hardware Company on the 1st of February, 1914, and will continue the business of wholesaling, retailing and manufacturing, besides greatly increasing its sheet-metal products and roofing department. Walter R. Seavey, former manager of the company, who has spent sixteen years in assisting to build up the institution, is president and general manager of the new organization, and the other officials are: C. E. Greer, vice-president; W. S. Cutshall, secretary and treasurer; and A. S. Coverdale, chairman of the board of directors. Walter R. Seavey, president of the company, is the only son of the founder of the business. Mr. Coverdale has been closely associated with many of Fort Wayne's biggest and busiest institutions; Mr. Cutshall formerly served as city controller; Mr. Greer was actively connected with the business of the Seavey Hardware Company for twenty-two years prior to its reorganization. The other two members of the directorate are Henry J. Kaiser, one of the city's foremost contractors, and Charles Wermuth, a successful contractor who has aided in the building up of a greater city." Reverting to the honored subject of this memoir it may be said that he was one of the vital and loyal citizens and progressive business men of Fort Wayne, where he commanded inviolable place in popular esteem.

He was one of the organizers and vigorous supporters of the Fort Wayne Commercial Club, was a Republican in his political allegiance, and was always very active in the promotion of religious interests, as is also his widow, who still maintains her home in Fort Wayne. Mr. Seavey wedded Miss Catherine Amy Randall, the only daughter of Judge Edwin Randall, of Avilla, Indiana, and of their two children the elder is Walter R., president of the Seavey Hardware Company; and Irma Mary is the wife of C. Allen Merriam, of Portland, Oregon.

Adam Amos Serva.—Twenty-two years ago Adam Amos Serva became identified with Fort Wayne in his capacity as expert electrician in the employ of the General Electric Company, then known as the Fort Wayne Electric Corporation. His rise in the electrical field since then has been steady and consistent. In 1903 he was made assistant secretary of the company and in 1911 became sales manager of the Fort Wayne Electrical Works of the General Electric Company. He occupies that position today. Mr. Serva was born in Stark county, Ohio, January 15, 1869, son of Charles and Nancy (Sarver) Serva, natives of New York state and Ohio, respectively. The father was reared in Ohio, having been brought to that state by his parents when a small boy, and was long active in farming operations. His later years he spent in quiet retirement on his home place, and death claimed him in September, 1914. The mother still lives and has her home in Canton, Ohio. Of the nine children born to these people, two are living today—Adam A., of this review, and a daughter, now the wife of Doctor Flickinger, of Canton, Ohio. Adam A. Serva had his early schooling in the public schools of Canton, finishing a course in the local high school of his home city and then entering the Ohio State University, where he studied mechanical and electrical engineering. He was graduated, in 1893, with the degree M. E. During Mr. Serva's last year at the university he accepted a position with the Egypt-Chicago Exposition Company as chief of the electrical construction for the World's Columbian Exposition, and successfully carried on that work in conjunction with his university work, graduating with his class on schedule time. His work in connection with the exposition was considered very creditable, electrical displays at that time being in their comparative infancy, one might say, so that his accomplishment in that field were a good deal of an innovation. In the summer of 1893 he was appointed assistant engineer to the Board of Awards, under the United States government at the World's Columbian Exposition, where he continued to the close of the exposition. His next position was as foreman of an experimental telephone laboratory for S. D. McKelbey, Canton, Ohio, and, he says, "a little later on we organized the Independent Telephone Company at Canton." In November, 1894, he entered the employ of the Fort Wayne Electrical Company as electrical expert and salesman, and a little later on was appointed engineer of the Philadelphia (Pennsylvania) district for the Fort Wayne Electric Corporation, still later filling the same relative position in Boston, and in 1898 entering the employ of the General Electric Company as expert and salesman in their New York office. After a short stay there he was transferred to Fort Wayne to fill the position of assistant sales manager of the Fort Wayne Electrical Works, and, in 1903, the duties of assistant secretary were added to those of assistant sales manager. In 1911 came his appointment to the post of sales manager for the Fort Wayne Electric Works of the General Electric Company, and he has since continued in that position, as has already been stated. Mr. Serva has had about eight years of military service, though all of it has been of a peaceful nature. While in Canton high school he was a member of Company C, Canton Independent Battalion, and was a sergeant in his company. During his university days he was a member of Company A, a picked company, known at the time as one of the best-drilled military companies in the United States. It was challenged by a number of similar organizations from all over the country, and won out against all comers. Mr. Serva was a commissioned officer in the university regiment and was commissioned all the way up to the rank of first lieutenant. On September 15, 1896, Mr. Serva was married to Miss Antoinette M. Biechle, daughter of Leopold Biechle, a retired merchant of Canton, Ohio. They have one son—Albert Edward Serva, born January 9, 1902. Mr. Serva is a Republican in the matter of national politics, but in local issues always takes an independent stand. He is a member of St. Patrick's Roman Catholic church of Fort Wayne and of the Knights of Columbus. Other orders with which he is identified are the Elks, the Jovian Order, the latter being an electrical society, and the Phi Gamma Delta, his college fraternity. He is also a member of the American Institute of Electrical Engineers, the American Society for the Advancement of Science, the National Geographic Society, the Fort Wayne Country Club, and the University Club of Fort Wayne. He is now (1917) aide to the directors of the United States Naval Consulting Board.

Amasa Shaffer.—One of the prominent families of Madison township is represented by Amasa Shaffer, who was born in the community that is now his home on January 4, 1853. He is a son of John and Martha J. (Robinson) Shaffer, born in Ohio and there reared. They came to Allen county, Indiana, in 1841, and were here married. They settled on a farm, or on what promised one day to be a farm, though it was a good deal of a wilderness at that time, and they built a log cabin on the place, in which the family lived for some years. Later the cabin gave way to a more pretentious dwelling, but it is probable they were quite as happy in the log cabin as in the frame house. The father died, in 1903, and the mother passed away, September 26, 1916, at the advanced age of eighty-nine years. Of their ten children, two are now living. Amasa Shaffer was reared and educated in Allen county, and lived on the home place until he was twenty-two years old. He married Miss Samantha Jane Peckham then and set up an establishment of his own. Mrs. Shaffer was the daughter of William and Margaret (Heaton) Peckham, people of Ohio birth who came to Indiana soon after their marriage, and their daughter, Samantha Jane, was born in Allen county, Indiana. Eight children were born to the Peckhams, two of the number being deceased. Following his marriage Mr. Shaffer settled on a sixty-acre farm, situated in Section 35, in Madison township, and there resided until March, 1917, when he sold the place and the family established its home in Monroeville. The children of Mr. and Mrs. Shaffer are eight in number, and the family is distinguished by its possession of two pairs of twins. The children are here named in order of their birth: Oscar E., of Fort Wayne; Elmira P., the wife of R. Adams; Clyde W. and Claude J., twins; Edgar A., prominent in the Masonic order in Allen county; Nellie M.; Delma R. and Velma D., the second pair of twins. Mr. and Mrs. Shaffer are members of the Methodist Episcopal church and Mr. Shaffer is now serving as a member of its board of trustees. He is a

Democrat, it should be said in passing, and served the township as trustee for six years.

Jesse B. Shaffer.—To no one element of citizenship does Allen county owe more for her eminent precedence as a stage of advanced agricultural enterprise than to the large contingent of citizens of German birth or lineage who have been identified with the development of the county in the progressive stages of its history, many of the honored and influential pioneer families having been representatives of the sturdy German stock that has played so important a part in the civic and material achievement of our great republic. He whose name initiates this review may well take pride in being the scion of one of the fine German families that was founded in Pennsylvania in an early day and that in later generations was to wield much influence in connection with the normal development and progress of northern Indiana. Jesse B. Shaffer, who is now one of the substantial agriculturalists and stock-growers of Maumee township, with a fine farm of ninety-one acres, in Section 6, was born in Springfield township, this county, December 10, 1860, a son of Henry and Johanna (Gorrell) Shaffer, the former a native of Pennsylvania and the latter of Ohio, and both young at the time of the removal of the respective families to Allen county, Indiana, in the early pioneer days. After their marriage the parents of Mr. Shaffer settled on a farm in St. Joseph township, near Fort Wayne, and later removed to a farm in Springfield township, where the father continued his activities as an enterprising agriculturalist and stock-grower until he was well advanced in years. He then retired and established his home in the village of New Haven, but passed the closing period of his life in the city of Muncie, this state. His wife survived him and was a loved member of the family circle of her son, Jesse B., of this review, at the time that she too was called to the life eternal. Of the eight children the sixth and seventh, Henry and Charles, died in infancy, and the eighth, Earl, is also deceased. Those surviving are: Sophia, Gold, Mary, Laura and Jesse B., so that the subject of this sketch is the only surviving son. To the public schools of Springfield township Mr. Shaffer is indebted for his early educational discipline and as a youth he gave vigorous assistance in the work of the home farm. He eventually initiated independent activities as a farmer in Springfield township and later was a resident of the village of Harlan, that township, for two years. He then removed with his family to Antwerp, Paulding county, Ohio, where he engaged in the hoop mill business and there continued his residence six years, within which he served two years as a member of the city council. Upon leaving Antwerp he returned to his native farm, where he has since continued his progressive and successful activities as an agriculturalist and stock-grower. His is one of the valuable farms of Maumee township and on the same he has made the best of permanent improvements, including buildings, fences, tile drainage system, etc. He is a vigorous and public-spirited citizen and served two years as a member of the advisory board of Maumee township, his political allegiance being given to the Republican party. In the village of Harlan he maintains affiliation with Lodge No. 331, Independent Order of Odd Fellows. The year 1881 recorded the marriage of Mr. Shaffer to Miss Nellie Feighley, daughter of the late John W. and Matilda (Reichart) Feighley, the former of whom was born in Maryland and the latter in Ohio, where their marriage was solemnized and whence they came to Allen county and settled in Maumee township. Later they resided for a time in the village of Harlan, but finally returned to the farm in Maumee township, where they passed the residue of their lives, their children having been five in number—Theodore, Daniel (deceased), Viola, Nellie (Mrs. Shaffer), and Garry, who died when three days of age. Mr. and Mrs. Shaffer have two children: Jennie is the wife of Aaron Garrell, of Milan township, and they have three children—Roy, Myra and Dora. Herbert Shaffer, the younger of the two children, is engaged as a barber at Woodburn. He married Miss Bessie Burrier, and their two children are Ray and John.

William H. Shambaugh.—One of the most able and popular members of the bar of Allen county is William H. Shambaugh, whose long service in his native county has stamped him as a valuable citizen in many of the phases of active public life. Mr. Shambaugh was born in Allen county, December 24, 1858, son of Daniel and Sarah (Yeiser) Shambaugh, both of whom were natives of the state of Pennsylvania. The father was born in 1816 and the mother in 1830. From Pennsylvania they removed to Ohio and from the latter state came to Allen county, Indiana. William H. Shambaugh, the youngest in a family of five children, passed his boyhood days on the farm and obtained his early education in the rural schools. In 1877 he entered the normal school at Lebanon, Ohio, and in the same was graduated as a member of the class of 1879. In the autumn of this same year he took charge of the public schools of Fremont, Indiana, where he remained three years. He then, in the fall of 1882, established his residence in the city of Fort Wayne. His inclinations were toward the study of law, and he was afforded an opportunity to carry forward his plans in the office of Judge Samuel R. Alden. One year later he was admitted to practice in the courts of Allen county. Since 1885 he has been engaged in general practice in Fort Wayne, his talents summoning him to participation in some of the most famous cases heard before the local and state courts. Through the years of his active life since reaching his majority Mr. Shambaugh has labored diligently in the interests of the Democratic party. A public speaker of clear mind and impressive delivery, he has proved to be a powerful force in directing the destinies of his party in Indiana. In 1886 he was elected to membership in the general assembly of the state of Indiana, by a majority of nineteen hundred votes. In 1888 he was re-elected, by a majority of four thousand two hundred and thirty-three votes—a clear demonstration of his wide popularity and the value of his services as a public official. In the final session marking his service in the legislature he was awarded every recognition as a leader of the house of representatives. For twelve years Mr. Shambaugh served as city attorney of Fort Wayne, and during his incumbency of this office his keen vision and professional ability enabled him to contribute to the development of the many interests of the city. His service as a member of the board of trustees of the Fort Wayne schools is but another evidence of his true worth to his community. Mr. Shambaugh is an active member of the Masonic bodies—a Knight Templar and a member of the Scottish Rite class of 1889, and he is a Shriner and an Elk and a valued member of the Fort Wayne Commercial Club, the Rotary Club and other organizations which need the support and activity of a man of his strength of character and willingness to give of his talents to the general good. The maiden name of the wife of Mr. Shambaugh was Louise Robertson, and she was a daughter of Col. Robert A. Robertson, long an honored and influential citizen of Fort Wayne. Mrs. Shambaugh's death occurred in 1914 and she is survived by three sons—Willard, Howard and Robert. Mr. Shambaugh was the nominee on the Democratic ticket for mayor of Fort Wayne, in 1894, and he is the author of the present municipal charter of Fort Wayne, which was written in 1893 and became effective in May, 1894.

Thomas J. Sheehan is recognized as one of the vigorous and representative exponents of agricultural and live-stock industry in his native county and his well improved farm of seventy-five acres, in Sections 16 and 9, Monroe township, is a model of thrift and good management. In his farm industry Mr. Sheehan gives special attention to the raising of good breeds of live stock and has made this department of enterprise very successful, as he has studied means and methods and obtains the maximum returns, as does he also through his scientific agriculture. That he has secure place in the esteem of his home community needs no further voucher than the statement that he is serving as trustee of Monroe township. His success represents the direct results of his own energy and ability, and thus he has been in the true sense the architect of his own fortunes, besides which he is certain to make consecutive advancement in connection with productive industry. Mr. Sheehan was born in this county, where he was reared to the sturdy discipline of the farm and where he profited fully by the advantages afforded in the public schools. His parents, Daniel and Charlotta (Jones) Sheehan, were both born and reared in the state of Ohio, and the father became one of the sterling young pioneers of Allen county, Indiana, where he has maintained his home since 1844, and there he reclaimed and improved a productive farm, his cherished and devoted wife having passed to eternal rest in 1906, and of their six children all are living except one. Upon coming to this county Daniel Sheehan purchased a tract of land, the major part of which was still covered with the native timber. He erected a log house of the pioneer type and this continued to be the family domicile until circumstances justified its replacement by a more modern and commodious house, of frame construction. Daniel Sheehan still survives and is one of the sterling and honored pioneer citizens of the county. Thomas J. Sheehan, the immediate subject of this review, continued to assist his father in the work and management of the old homestead farm until he was twenty-seven years of age, when he wedded Miss Emma Smith, who likewise was born and reared in Allen county, a daughter of August and Sophia (Meyers) Smith, the former of whom is deceased and the latter still maintains her home in Allen county. After his marriage Mr. Sheehan began his independent career as a farmer and purchased his present farm. He has made many improvements on the place, has materially increased its productiveness in the domain of diversified agriculture, and, as before stated, has been specially prosperous as a grower and feeder of live stock. His political allegiance is given to the Democratic party and he is vitally interested in all things pertaining to the welfare of his native county, especially of Monroe township, of which he is now serving as trustee. At Monroeville he is actively affiliated with Lodge No. 293 of the Ancient Free & Accepted Masons. Mr. and Mrs. Sheehan have an interesting family of six children: Ruth A., who was graduated in the celebrated Valparaiso University, is now a successful and popular teacher in the public schools of her home county;

Nola M. is a student in Valparaiso University; and the four younger children are members of the ideal home circle.

Charles H. Sheldon, who was a resident of Fort Wayne for a quarter of a century, and who here developed a prosperous business enterprise, continued his active association with the civic and business interests of the Allen county metropolis until the time of his death, which occurred November 17, 1905. His active career was marked by earnest, worthy and successful endeavor and his high sense of personal stewardship was shown in all of the relations of life, so that he merited and received unqualified popular esteem. Mr. Sheldon was born at Northampton, Massachusetts, on November 10, 1854, and thus his death occurred exactly one week after the fifty-first anniversary of his birth. He was a scion of sterling old colonial stock in New England and his parents, Arnold and Melinda (Towne) Sheldon, passed their entire lives in Massachusetts, Charles H. having been the eldest of their five children; Herbert, the second son, likewise is deceased; Emma is the wife of Reuben Rich, of Providence, Rhode Island; Clara is the wife of William Marden, of Milford, Massachusetts; and Walter is now a resident of Columbus, Ohio. Charles H. Sheldon acquired his early education in the public schools of the old Bay state, and he was twenty-one years of age when he left Milford, Worcester county, Massachusetts, and established his residence at Columbus, the capital city of Ohio. There he established a shop for the re-blocking and repairing of hats for both men and women, and with this line of enterprise he there continued his association about three years, at the expiration of which, in August, 1878, he came to Fort Wayne, Indiana, and established himself in the same line of business. He developed a substantial and prosperous enterprise and became the owner of the building in which he conducted his flourishing business, his energy, reliability and progressiveness having conspired to develop the leading enterprise of this order in northern Indiana. After his death his widow sold the property and business, or, rather, exchanged the same for her present attractive home, at 1107 Hanna street. In politics Mr. Sheldon was a supporter of the Republican party, and in a fraternal way he was affiliated with the Ancient Order of United Workmen. On August 8, 1878, was solemnized the marriage of Mr. Sheldon to Miss Frederica Zuloman, of Columbus, Ohio, in which city she was born and reared, and their bridal tour was virtually their journey to the new home in Fort Wayne. Mrs. Sheldon is a daughter of Frederick and Henrietta (Sanbold) Zuloman, both of whom were born in Germany and both of whom were residents of Columbus, Ohio, at the time of their death. Of the seven children Mrs. Sheldon was the second, and her elder sister, Pauline, still resides at Columbus, as do also Elizabeth, Charles and Frederick; Amalie is the widow of Victor Orthofer and maintains her home in Columbus, as does also Minnie, the youngest of the children. Mr. Sheldon is survived by one son, Frederick, who remains with his widowed mother in Fort Wayne.

E. Clarence Shell, president and manager of The Pape Furniture Company, which conducts in Fort Wayne a most substantial business, is consistently to be designated as one of the representative business men of the metropolis of Allen county, and though he claims the old Empire state as the place of his nativity he is a scion of one of the sterling pioneer families of Allen county, within whose limits his paternal grandfather, Philip Shell, settled in 1833, having secured a tract of land near

Hall's Corners, where he developed a productive farm and there he and his wife passed the residue of their lives, as honored pioneers of this favored section of the Hoosier state. E. Clarence Shell was born in the city of Albany, New York, on February 4, 1859, his parents, Frank V. V. and Margaret Jane (Reid) Shell, both having been natives of that state, though the former had accompanied his parents to Indiana and was temporarily a resident of Albany at the time of the birth of the subject of this review. Frank V. V. Shell became one of the representative members of the bar of Allen county, where he was engaged in the practice of his profession, both at Monroeville and Fort Wayne, besides which he became identified with mercantile business in Fort Wayne, where he died in 1903, his widow, who celebrated her eightieth birthday anniversary in 1916, being still a resident of Fort Wayne and being revered by all who have come within the compass of her gracious influence. Of the three children E. Clarence is the eldest; Hattie is the wife of John C. Heller, of Fort Wayne; and Myron J. is a resident of Hicksville, Ohio. E. Clarence Shell acquired his youthful education in the public schools of Allen county and as a boy gained his initial business experience as a clerical assistant in the White fruit store, in which he remained two years. Thereafter he was employed about six years in a grocery establishment in Fort Wayne and then entered the employ of the old Fort Wayne Manufacturing Company, with which he continued his services about two years. In 1891 he became bookkeeper and manager for the Pape Furniture Company and continued the incumbent of this position until 1893, when he formed a partnership with A. C. Buetel and engaged in the furniture business. The firm built up a large and prosperous business and, in 1900, Mr. Shell purchased his partner's interest and assumed full control of the enterprise. To meet the increasing demands of his trade he effected the organization and incorporation of the present company, in which there are two other stockholders, and of which he has since continued president and manager. Mr. Shell is one of the substantial and progressive business men of Fort Wayne, is loyal and public-spirited in his civic attitude, is a Democrat in his political allegiance, and both he and his wife are communicants of the English Lutheran church. In the time-honored Masonic fraternity he has received the thirty-second degree of the Ancient Accepted Scottish Rite, besides which he is affiliated also with the Benevolent & Protective Order of Elks and the Royal League. On October 7, 1903, was solemnized the marriage of Mr. Shell to Miss Anna Thain, who was born and reared in Fort Wayne and who is the popular chatelaine of their attractive home.

Mary A. Shoup.—Among the estimable women who have helped to make Roanoke the pleasant village it is, Mary A. Shoup may be mentioned prominently. She has been identified creditably with community life since 1871 and her influence has ever been a worthy one. She is a native daughter of Wells county, Indiana, born on May 14, 1849, daughter of Evan and Eliza (Johnson) Belle. They were North Carolinians by birth, and came in youth to Indiana. Evan Belle early in life became a landowner in Wells county and was one of the responsible men of his community through his long and useful career as a farmer. To him and his wife were born four children. John, the eldest, died in 1868. Mary A. is the subject. Martha J. lives in Fort Wayne and William M. is in Zanesville. Mary A. Belle was married on October 19, 1882, to William H. Shoup, son of Jacob and Rachel (Cain) Shoup. They were Ohioans of German ancestry, and farmers all their lives. Their children numbered seven and are named in the order of their appearance as follows: Mary, Daniel, William, Sophia, Joseph, John and Jacob. The two first named are deceased. William is the husband of the subject. Mr. and Mrs. Shoup have three children, who are still to be found under the parental roof. They are Carrie, Chloe and Emma.

Bartlett W. Shryock is one of the successful and popular young representatives of the automobile business in his native city of Fort Wayne, where he has well-equipped salesrooms and is the enterprising agent for the well-known Buick and White automobiles. He established this business in the autumn of 1913, and his success has fully justified his choice of vocation, the while his record of sales indicates alike his ability and the popular favor in which are held the cars that are handled by him. He is one of the progressive young business men of Fort Wayne, is a loyal supporter of the activities of the Commercial Club, of which he is an active member, is independent in politics, and his religious faith is that of the Protestant Episcopal church, of which his parents likewise are earnest communicants, the family being one of prominence in the social life of the community. Bartlett Ward Shryock was born in Fort Wayne on March 17, 1889, a son of Dr. William Wilson Shryock and Louise (Ward) Shryock, both of whom were born and reared in this county, with whose history the respective family names have been long and worthily identified, the father being a leading representative of the profession of dentistry in his native county and having a large and successful practice. He whose name introduces this sketch is indebted to the public schools of Fort Wayne for his early educational discipline and after his graduation in the high school he completed a course in electrical engineering in the University of Pennsylvania. Since his return to Fort Wayne he has been engaged in the automobile business and is making of his independent enterprise in this line a distinctive success.

William W. Shryock, D. D. S.—Possibly the finest tribute which the dental profession can pay to a fellow-member is to give him prominence in its councils of deliberation. William Willson Shryock, of Fort Wayne, has been honored by the Indiana State Dental Society to election to every office in that body, with the exception of secretary. Such is the sort of recognition granted by the dentists of the state. At home, the honors have been still more marked, for Dr. Shryock has filled every office of the Isaac Knapp Dental Coterie, composed of leading members of the profession in Fort Wayne. He is an active member, also, of the National Dental Association. Dr. Shryock is a native of Hoosierdom, born in DeKalb county, May 27, 1857. He attended the public schools of Fort Wayne after the family removed to this city, and then entered the office of S. B. Brown, M. D., D. D. S., as a student. Here he remained three years. The natural fitness of Dr. Shryock for the practice of the profession which had attracted his early consideration was developed through a course in the dental department of the University of Michigan, followed by two years spent in the offices of leading practitioners, after which he entered the Indiana Dental College, from which institution he was graduated with the degree of Doctor of Dental Surgery. He is a member of the Delta Sigma Fraternity. Dr. Shryock, as an authority in his professional practice, is frequently called upon to give clinics dealing with unusual cases before local, state and national societies. He maintains a modern office suite at No. 129 West Berry street. December

3, 1885, Dr. Shryock was united in marriage with Miss Emily Louise Ward, of Fort Wayne, and to them have been born three children.

Mrs. Christina Siebold is the widow of John Siebold, a native-born German who came to America as a young man, in 1822. He came almost directly to Fort Wayne, where he engaged as a day laborer, but soon thereafter moved on into the farming center of the county and bought forty acres of timbered land in what came in later years to be known as Lafayette township. He farmed from then until the end of his life and was more or less successful, gaining title to land as the years went by, and becoming established as one of the substantial men of his community. He was a Democrat and a member of the German Lutheran church. He married Christina Krunna in 1865. To them were born eight children. John is a resident of Fort Wayne. Andrew died in Fort Wayne. Henry is located on a farm in Wayne township. Caroline is the wife of John Therne, of Fort Wayne. Maria lives with her widowed mother. Katherine became the wife of Simon Ambler, of Lafayette township and died in 1917. Dorothy married John Genth, who has assumed charge of the home farm, and Sarah became the wife of Elmer Hamilton, who died in 1916. Fourteen grandchildren have been added to the family in recent years. George is the son of John. Ella is the daughter of Audrey. Ralph, Glenn and Guy are the sons of Henry, who also has a daughter, Faith. Caroline has two children—George and Edith. Katherine has a daughter named Florence, and Dorothy has two sons—Jay and Gary. Sarah is the mother of Everett, Elsie and Howard.

Herman W. Sigrist is a young man who has shown individuality as well as initiative in the special domain of business enterprise to which he is devoting his attention and as a versatile and successful real estate auctioneer has gained a reputation that is far from being circumscribed or equivocal. His interposition has made him one of the most successful exponents of this particular policy of selling realty and his activities have extended in an important way through Indiana, Illinois, Ohio, Michigan, North and South Carolina, Georgia, Mississippi and Oklahoma, in which last mentioned commonwealth he had the distinction of making a record absolutely unprecedented and as yet unequaled, in the selling of the greatest number of town lots in the minimum time. This record was made on the 6th and 7th of December, 1910, when, within an actual selling period of nine hours and two minutes, he sold eight hundred and eight lots. This achievement is but one of many incidents in which he has shown his splendid resourcefulness as a salesman, and while his services have been enlisted in many different states of the Union, as above noted, he has maintained his home at Fort Wayne, where, since 1911, he has been engaged in the general real estate business, under the title of Sigrist & Company. Herman W. Sigrist was born in LaGrange county, Indiana, on March 31, 1882, and his parents, Adolph and Sarah (Long) Sigrist, now reside in the village of Brighton, that county, the father having been a successful farmer in the county for many years and being now retired. Of the other three children it may be noted that Lena is the wife of Lyoll E. Alspaugh, a farmer near Howe, LaGrange county; Weldon A. is a prosperous farmer near Brighton, Lagrange county; and Florence is a popular teacher in the public schools of the city of South Bend, Indiana. The parents are members of the Progressive Brethren church and are held in unqualified esteem in the county that has long represented their home. It is interesting to record that upon the death of Mrs. Sarah Long, maternal grandmother of the subject of this sketch, she was survived by more than fifty great-grandchildren, she having passed to eternal rest in July, 1915. After having availed himself of the advantages of the public schools Herman W. Sigrist entered the Tri-State Normal College, at Angola, Indiana, and in this institution was graduated as a member of the class of 1903. For two years thereafter he was a successful teacher in the public schools at Kane, Greene county, Illinois, and after his marriage, in 1905, he returned to the old home farm, near Brighton, Indiana. He had the control and management of the farm during the ensuing three years, and in the meanwhile was officially retained as one of the state lecturers or speakers at farmers' institutes in various counties of Indiana. He then went to the city of Chicago, where he completed a course in the Jones school of auctioneering and oratory, this requiring six weeks. Having thus fortified himself for direct auctioneering work, Mr. Sigrist then came to Fort Wayne, where he has since maintained his home and business headquarters. Within a period of about three months he received attractive overtures to go to South Carolina in the service of the Poag Real Estate Company, engaged in extensive real estate developments, and as official auctioneer for this company remained in the south one year. Though he then returned to Fort Wayne, he has since continued to spend from three to four months each winter in the south, where he has given each season effective service as an auctioneer, especially in connection with the development of new town sites and platted additions. His record has touched also the selling of farm properties, and within the course of eighteen months he sold at auction one hundred and eight farms, in different sections of the Union. In 1912 Mr. Sigrist published an interesting and valuable brochure on "the art of selling real estate at auction," and the booklet has had wide circulation, as it is an authoritative source of information on the subject treated. The previously mentioned and unparalleled record which he made in Oklahoma in the winter of 1910 was at Kenefick, on the line of the Missouri, Oklahoma & Gulf Railroad. In his local business at Fort Wayne Mr. Sigrist has been notably successful in the handling of both city and farm property, but much of his time is still demanded in his service as an expert auctioneer in the sale of real estate in divers states to which he is called. In 1913, he became one of the organizers of the Modern Way Furnace Company, a concern doing business in twenty-two states, and of which our subject is the manager. His political allegiance is given to the Democratic party and he and his wife hold membership in the Christian church. On June 15, 1905, was solemnized the marriage of Mr. Sigrist to Miss Sophia E. Showalter, daughter of Levi F. and Mary (Wigton) Showalter, of LaGrange, Indiana, and the names and respective birth dates of the three children of this union are as here noted: Pauline, June 28, 1906; Philip Franklin, May 2, 1910; and Allen Adolph, January 29, 1912.

Rev. William Sihler, Ph. D.—Among the strong and noble characters that have wielded great and enduring influence in the religious activities of Fort Wayne, none is held in more gracious reverence than the late Dr. Sihler, a pioneer in religious work in this community who held for forty years the pastorate of St. Paul's Evangelical Lutheran church—1845 to 1885. This publication emphasizes its consistency in paying tribute to this distinguished man. His lofty soul and great heart combined with the finest of intellectual forces to make him a power for good in the field in which he labored. Dr. William Sihler was born near the city of Breslau, capital of the province of Silesia, Germany, on November 12, 1801, and was a son of George and Elizabeth (Wiesner) Sihler, his father having been an officer in the Prussian army and a man of ability and influence. In a well ordered private school Dr. Sihler received his preliminary education, and his special mental precociousness enabled him to read the German language with readiness and exactitude when but five years old. He was ten years old when his mother died, and it was then he entered the gymnasium in his native city—an institution corresponding in large measure to the high school of America. His receptiveness and ambition as a student here became still more manifest, and by the time he was fifteen had attained a place in the highest class. In 1816, at the early age just noted, he entered the University of Breslau, and, in accordance with the laws of the country, he also entered military service, as a member of the Breslau battalion of infantry. In his military service he made an admirable record, as shown by the fact that in 1819 he was graduated with the rank of second lieutenant in the Twenty-second regiment of Infantry, and he was assigned to duty at Neisse. In 1823 Dr. Sihler entered the Prussian National Military University, in the city of Berlin, and there he was a classmate of Count Von Moltke, who, as Prussian field-marshal, became an historic figure. In this military institution Dr. Sihler remained until 1825, when he returned to Breslau and retired from military life. In 1826 he became a student in the University of Berlin, where he continued his higher academic studies and became so proficient in languages that he could read with precision works of the Spanish, French and English poets in those languages. In 1843 Dr. Sihler came to the United States. His purpose in coming was to engage actively in religious work, and on the 1st of January, 1844, he preached his initial sermon in the land of his adoption—at Pomeroy, Ohio. In 1845 he received a call from the congregation of St. Paul's Evangelical Lutheran church in Fort Wayne, and he forthwith assumed the pastorate of this pioneer church of the Allen county metropolis. Here he lived and labored with faithful zeal, abiding human sympathy and tolerance, for forty years, and it is to be remembered with appreciation that he continued in this pastorate until the time of his death. Under his pastoral charge was erected the first church building of St. Paul's parish, a frame structure that occupied the site of the present edifice. Under his regime the parish prospered in both a spiritual and material sense and he long held secure place as a leader in religious circles as well as in the directing of civic sentiment and action. He was one of the organizers of the Missouri synod of the Evangelical Lutheran church, under the jurisdiction of which the Fort Wayne church was originally placed, and he became known and revered as the "grand old man" of the Lutheran faith in Indiana and as one of the distinguished clergymen of Fort Wayne. It was primarily through his influence and earnest efforts that the Concordia College was removed from St. Louis, Missouri, to Fort Wayne, where it has continued as a stronghold in education work. In 1846 was solemnized the marriage of Dr. Sihler to Miss Susanna Kern, of Marysville, Ohio, a native of Germany, and who was loved by all who came within the compass of her influence. The names of the nine children of this union are: Christian, Marie, Gottlieb, Elizabeth, Frederick, Johanna, Lillie, William, and Carl E.

Carl E. Sihler, the youngest of the children of the late Dr. Sihler, to whom the preceding memoir is dedicated, was born in Fort Wayne, April 9, 1868, and here he received his early education in the parish school of St. Paul's church, of which his father was the pastor, this discipline being supplemented by higher academic study in Concordia College. In 1889 he was graduated in the Kansas City Dental College, but after receiving his degree of Doctor of Dental Surgery he decided that he would not give his attention to the work of the profession for which he had thus fitted himself. He remained several years in Kansas City, Missouri, where he held a clerical position in a wholesale dry goods house. In 1895 he returned to Fort Wayne and accepted the position of bookkeeper in the offices of the Fort Wayne Gas Company. He continued his services as one of the valued employes of this company until 1902, when he assumed the position of bookkeeper in the White National Bank. Seven years later this institution was consolidated with the First National Bank, with which Mr. Sihler has since continued his effective service. He takes deep interest in all things pertaining to the well being of his native city but has had no desire for public office or political activity. He and his wife are communicants of St. Paul's Evangelical Lutheran church. In 1895 was solemnized the marriage of Mr. Sihler to Miss Helen Jurgensen, of Fort Wayne, she having been born in Schleswig-Holstein, Germany, and having been a child at the time of the family immigration to America, her parents, Peter K. and Emma (Thomasen) Jurgensen, having established their home in Fort Wayne many years ago. Mr. and Mrs. Sihler have six children—Oscar, Olga, William (III), Emma, and Ruth and Esther, who are twins.

Ira B. Sleet.—Ira B. Sleet, cashier of the New Haven State Bank, and organizer of that financial institution, in 1909, has been identified with banks and banking all his active business life. He is a native Kentuckian, born in Warsaw, Kentucky, July 22, 1886, son of Marshall and Adelia (Rosell) Sleet. The father was also born in Warsaw, Kentucky, and is still living in his native state, where he has devoted himself mainly to farming activities. He is a Democrat and an active member of the Christian church in his home community. Ira B. Sleet was the fourth born in a family of five children, the others being Emma, living at home; May, now deceased; Allen, a practicing physician in the home town; and Lawrence, who is deceased. With his brothers and sister, Ira B. Sleet attended the local schools. He graduated from the Warsaw High School in his 'teens and then entered the Warsaw Deposit Bank, where he had his first training in that line of work. He was next associated with the Bank of Glencoe, at Glencoe, Kentucky, and in August, 1909, came to New Haven and organized the New Haven State Bank. He was elected to the office of cashier of the new bank, and also became one of its board of directors, and much of the success of the thriving concern is due to his excellent methods and praiseworthy administration of those matters he has in charge. In addition to his work as cashier of the bank, Mr. Sleet writes general insurance and has quite an extensive business along that line. He is a Democrat in politics, and is now serving his third term as city treasurer. He is a member of the Methodist Episcopal church and ably serves at present on its board of trustees, as well as being treasurer of the church. He is a member of the Masonic fraternity and affiliates with the Blue Lodge, Home No. 342, at Fort Wayne, the Consistory. He was married on August 19, 1912, to Miss Maratta

Kenney, daughter of W. C. Kenney, of Louisville, Kentucky, and they have one son—Marshall Clayborn, born May 22, 1913.

James Slusher.—On both the paternal and maternal sides Mr. Slusher is a representative of pioneer stock in Indiana and in the agnatic line is a scion of a family that was founded in America in the colonial days. Mr. Slusher has long been a resident of Allen county and owns and operates one of the well-improved farms of Maumee township, where he is known and valued as a substantial and upright citizen and as a resourceful and prosperous exponent of the agricultural and live-stock industry. He was born in Randolph county, this state, on October 9, 1859, a son of William and Katherine (Boddkin) Slusher, the former of whom was born in Virginia and the latter in Randolph county, Indiana, where her parents settled at a very early date. William Slusher was a young man when he established his residence in Randolph county, where he operated a sawmill and was engaged in farming for a number of years. He then removed with his family to Paulding county, Ohio, where he continued farming operations about twenty years. He then established his home in Pulaski county, Kentucky, where he and his wife passed the remainder of their lives. Of their two children the subject of this review is the elder, and the younger son is Charles. James Slusher acquired his early education in the public schools of Randolph county, Indiana, and Paulding county, Ohio, and in the meanwhile gained practical experience in connection with farm work. He assisted his father in the operations of the home farm in Paulding county, Ohio, until he had attained to the age of eighteen years, and his first independent operations as a farmer were prosecuted in that county. Later, he came to Allen county, Indiana, and here he owns a fine farm of one hundred acres, in Section 35, Maumee township. On the place he has made the best of improvements, including the erection of a modern house, good barns and other farm buildings, the well-kept fences, the tile drainage and other provisions likewise accentuating the general evidence of thrift and prosperity. Though he has had no desire for political activity or the honors of public office, Mr. Slusher takes loyal interest in all things pertaining to the communal welfare and gives his allegiance to the Democratic party, both he and his wife being active members of the Wesleyan Methodist church. On May 22, 1885, was solemnized the marriage of Mr. Slusher to Miss Louisa DeBoy, who was born in Indiana, a daughter of the late Abraham and Nancy Ann DeBoy. It is specially interesting to record that Mr. and Mrs. Slusher have become the parents of a fine family of sixteen children and that death has never invaded the gracious home circle. The respective names of the children are here given in order of nativity: Charles, Oscar, Frank, May, Forrest, Ray, Leo, Goldie, Chester, Stella, Louisa, Orville, Wyllie, Warren, Georgia and William.

Glenn A. Smiley is one of the able and ambitious young lawyers who has made for himself a secure prestige as a member of the Allen county bar and he has been engaged in the practice of his profession in the city of Fort Wayne since 1911, his attention being given primarily to corporation and damage law and his clientage being of representative order. His well-appointed offices are located in the Shoaff building, and in addition to his substantial law business he has further identified himself with local interests, as he is a stockholder and director of the Purity Products Company, representing one of the important industrial enterprises contributing to the commercial precedence of Fort Wayne.

Mr. Smiley was born in Fayette county, Indiana, on April 24, 1885, a son of Milton T. and Margaret A. (Hirchman) Smiley, the former of whom was born in Fayette county, in 1851, and the latter in Rush county, her death having occurred on June 18, 1912, and her surviving children being three in number. Milton T. Smiley has been a successful farmer and contractor in his native state and now resides in the city of Indianapolis. Glenn A. Smiley acquired his preliminary education in the public schools of Tipton and Monroe counties, during the period of his parents' residence therein, and finally was graduated in the high school at Bloomington, Greene county, in 1903. In that city he then entered the University of Indiana and in this institution was graduated as a member of the class of 1907, and with the degree of Bachelor of Arts. During the ensuing four years he applied himself with characteristic diligence as a student in the law department of the university, from which he received the degree of Bachelor of Laws in 1910, with admission to the bar of his native state, in 1908. Soon after his graduation Mr. Smiley established his home at Fort Wayne and engaged in the practice of his profession, his original office headquarters having been in the Shoaff building. He has worked earnestly in his chosen profession and his unequivocal success attests not only to this fact but also vouches for his effective application of his technical knowledge. He gives his political allegiance to the Democratic party, he and his wife are members of the First Christian church, of which he has served as secretary, and he is affiliated with the Knights of Pythias and the Loyal Order of Moose. On July 8, 1916, was solemnized the marriage of Mr. Smiley to Miss Marianne Morton, who was born at Newport, Vermilion county ,this state, and whose widowed mother, Mrs. Jane Morton, now resides in Newport. Mr. and Mrs. Smiley are popular factors in the social life of Fort Wayne and he is a popular member of the Wayne Coterie Club, with the organization of which he was actively concerned.

Burtis H. Smith, cashier of The People's State Bank since it opened its doors for business, in August, 1916, and a well-known man among the foremost citizens of New Haven, is a native son of Indiana, born in Roanoke, September 24, 1876. He is a son of Jacob J. and Elizabeth (Hoover) Smith, the father an Ohioan, born in the vicinity of Dayton, in 1841, and the mother born near Roanoke, Indiana, March 16, 1846. They were farming people all their lives. Mr. Smith came to Indiana, in 1852, with his parents and settled in Roanoke when he reached manhood, there engaged in farming on his own responsibility, reared his family and retired from active life in 1900. He is living there today in the quiet of his country home, but the wife and mother died there on May 5, 1911. Mr. Smith is a Republican and a member of the United Brethren church. Six children were born to him and his wife. They are Ephraim F., living in Roanoke. James C., who died in 1902. Ella M., the wife of William V. Hughes, of Roanoke, Indiana. Burtis H., whose name heads this review. Rilla C., the wife of James A. Mitchell, of Joliet, Illinois. Clyde W., living at Montpelier, Indiana. Burtis H. Smith had his education in the schools of Roanoke. He finished the high school and entered Valparaiso University, from which he was graduated in 1899, and completed a course of study in the University of Chicago in 1900. He became superintendent of the Zanesville (Indiana) schools, filled the position one year and accepted the post of superintendent of the Roanoke (Indiana) schools, which he held until 1910. He then went to Vienna, Illinois, as superintendent of schools for one year, when he came to New Haven in the same capacity and continued to fill that position with all credit until he was appointed to his present position as cashier of the People's State Bank of New Haven, August 3, 1916. He has brought to his duties in that position the same character of industry and intelligence that won success for him in his educational work, and his future in the banking business is well assured. Mr. Smith is Republican in politics, a member of the Protestant Methodist church, and in a fraternal way is identified with Masonic order. He was married on March 29, 1900, to Miss Nellie Welch, daughter of Leroy and Melissa (Wilkerson) Welch, of Roanoke, Indiana, and they have two sons and one daughter—Byron, Helen, and Ned. Mrs. Smith has found a host of staunch friends in New Haven since she and her husband came to the community five years ago, and both of them are filling useful places in the civic and social life of the place.

Charles J. Smith is one of the vigorous and progressive men of Allen county, is one of the extensive landholders of this section of the Hoosier state, and in his career of admirable achievement has manifested the genuine intellectual and practical verve of constructive enterprise. He is one of the leading citizens of Monroe township and his homestead farm is one of the finest in that opulent section of Allen county. Mr. Smith was born at Sandusky, Ohio, September 17, 1860, a son of Anthony and Mary A. (Courdad) Smith, the former a native of Germany and the latter of France. The parents immigrated to America in 1832 and established their home in Ohio, where they passed the residue of their lives, and there they reared their children to the benignant discipline of honor and usefulness. Of their twelve children only five are living, in 1917. Charles J. Smith is indebted to the public schools of the old Buckeye state for his early educational privileges and in that commonwealth continued to reside until 1891, when he came to Allen county, Indiana, and settled on a partially improved farm in Jackson township. Here he became associated with his brother, William, in establishing a well-equipped sawmill and hoop factory, to the successful operation of which they gave their attention for twenty years, the while they have been accredited with clearing from the stump status a greater area of Allen county than any other two men in the county. After supply resources had brought a termination to the effective operation of the mill and factory Charles J. Smith purchased his present valuable landed estate, which comprises four hundred and sixty-seven acres of the excellent land of Allen county and all of which is well improved, the homestead place of Mr. Smith, in Section 21, Monroe township, being one of the model farmsteads of the county. As a citizen and business man he has been ambitious, energetic and progressive and through his own efforts has achieved substantial and worthy success. His political support is given to the Democratic party, but he has had no desire for public office of any kind. He and his wife are communicants of the Catholic church. In 1892 was solemnized the marriage of Mr. Smith, his wife having been born and reared in Ohio, and to them have been born ten children, all of whom are living: Laura M., Cecelia, Pernetta, Esther, Ralph, Bernard, Erma, Harold, Armilda and Luella Mary, the family home being known for its hospitality and good cheer and Mr. and Mrs. Smith having secure place in the esteem of the community in which they live.

Enoch H. Smith has not faltered in his appreciative allegiance to his native township and county and has not only been a representative farmer and business man of Pleasant township, but has shown his loyalty by effective service in the office of township trustee, of which he is the able and popular incumbent at the time of this writing, in the spring of 1917. He maintains his residence in the alert little village of Sheldon, where he is manager of the Farmers' Elevator, which is now owned and operated by the Standard Milling Company, of Clarksville, West Virginia. C. F. Davis and John Starber were the builders of this well-equipped grain elevator, which was established in 1911, by the Farmers' Grain Company, of which Mr. Smith was one of the organizers, in June of that year, and of which he was made president, George Springer having been vice-president and Harley Somers secretary and treasurer. The company was incorporated with a capital stock of ten thousand dollars, and it continued the operation of the elevator until August 1, 1916, when the interested principals made an advantageous disposition of the business, which then passed into the control of the Standard Milling Company of Clarksville, West Virginia, and the title was changed to the present form, the Farmers' Elevator. Mrs. B. E. Madix is secretary in executive charge of the office of the elevator and Mr. Smith is retained as the efficient general manager of the business. The elevator has a capacity of ten thousand bushels, and in connection with the general grain operations the concern handles also hay, coal, binder twine, etc. Enoch H. Smith was born in Pleasant township, of which the village of Sheldon is the principal trade center, and the date of his nativity was April 11, 1869. He is a scion of one of the honored pioneer families of this part of Allen county, his grandfather, Jacob Smith, having come with his family from Ohio and settled in Pleasant township, in 1847, and having done well his part in furthering the social and industrial development of the township, within whose borders he and his wife passed the residue of their lives. He whose name introduces this article is a son of Finley and Elmira (Clark) Smith, both of whom were born in Ohio. Finley Smith was a lad of eight years at the time of his parents' removal to Allen county and was reared to manhood on the old homestead farm in Pleasant township. He made good use of the advantages of the local schools, as demonstrated by the fact that as a young man he devoted himself for a time to successful service as a teacher in the district schools. He became one of the prominent farmers and influential citizens of the township, was a Democrat in politics, and both he and his wife were zealous members of the Church of God. Mrs. Smith entered into eternal rest, in 1900, and the honored husband and father passed to his reward in 1909. Of the ten children the eldest is Orson C., who is a successful farmer in St. Joseph township; Emma is the wife of Daniel Prough, of Wells county; Jacob A. is one of the substantial farmers of Pleasant township; Enoch H., of this sketch, was the next in order of birth; Elizabeth is the wife of Isaac Johnson, of Pleasant township; Zaccheus still resides in Pleasant township; Martha A. and Wilmetta are deceased; Frank W. resides in Lake township; Nora is the wife of Floyd Prough, of Kalkaska, Michigan. Enoch H. Smith is indebted to the public schools of his native township for his youthful education and in the meanwhile gained a full quota of practical experience in connection with the work of the home farm. For some time he was employed at farm work for others and finally purchased a farm of one hundred and sixty acres, in Section 30, Pleasant township. There he continued his activities as an agriculturalist and stock-grower until 1915 and in the interim had become concerned with the establishing of the grain elevator at Sheldon, as has been duly noted at an earlier point in this context. He has maintained his residence at Sheldon since 1915 and gives his attention to the elevator business and to zealous and circumspect service in the office of township trustee of Pleasant township, which position he assumed in January, 1914. His political allegiance is given to the Democratic party, he is secretary of the lodge of the Independent Order of Odd Fellows at Zanesville, and at Ossian he is affiliated with the lodge of Ancient Free & Accepted Masons and the tent of the Modern Maccabees. Both he and his wife are active members of the Church of God. June 17, 1890, recorded the marriage of Mr. Smith to Miss Elizabeth Woods, daughter of James and Margaret (Herman) Woods, of Pleasant township, and of the fine family of ten children born to Mr. and Mrs. Smith all remain at the parental home except two. Howard C., the eldest of the children, now resides in the city of Oshkosh, Wisconsin; and Celia B., the third child, is in the city of Toledo, Ohio. The names of the children still remaining members of the home circle are as follows: Chauncey A., Gladys E., Gerald H., Emma Mae, Frona M., Raymond Carl, Freda and Amanda A. L.

Dr. Joseph L. Smith was born in Dayton, Ohio, February 7, 1852, a son of Joseph H. and Carolina (Frick) Smith, natives of New Jersey and Pennsylvania, respectively. They were farming people, and came to Ohio in 1835, locating on a farm and later moving to a farm in Mercer county, Indiana, where their remaining years were passed in the quiet of country life. Seven children came to them, four of the number now living. Joseph L. Smith had his early education in the common schools of Dayton, Ohio, and in 1872 turned his attention to the study of medicine. He was graduated from the Eclectic Medical Institute at Cincinnati, Ohio, in 1878, and soon after established himself in practice in Hoagland, Indiana, where he has been occupied with the exception of a four-year period when he was serving as auditor of Allen county. During that period he made his home in Fort Wayne and at the expiration of his term returned to Hoagland and resumed his practice. He is a Democrat, and has held other minor offices in his community from time to time. In addition to his home in Hoagland, Doctor Smith owns a fine farm of one hundred and sixty-eight acres in Allen county, and has some Fort Wayne property as well. He is a thirty-second degree Mason, and with his family has membership in the Lutheran church. Doctor Smith was married, in 1875, to Miss Allie Emenhiser, who was born in Ohio, and ten children have been born to them. Addie, the eldest, is the wife of Doctor Morris. Willard O. is a practicing physician in the county; Estelle is the wife of John Colter, of Memphis, Tennessee; Grover A. is a doctor, located at Bryant, Indiana; Pearl is married to Marion Shookman, of Urbana, Illinois, the cashier of a bank at that point; and five are deceased.

Mrs. Lena Smith is one of the estimable and prominent women of her community, in which she was born on January 10, 1854, daughter of John Harber, who came to Allen county from Germany in his young manhood and settled in Marion township on a farm of eighty acres, there spending the rest of his life. John Harber was a well-known man in Marion township and reared a family that has reflected credit on the name and added not a little to the development of the county. Gerhard Harber, the eldest son, is deceased. Catherine is a resident of Fort Wayne; Lena is the subject of this review; Frederick is a Pleasant township farmer; Gertrude, John and Anthony are the names of the other children. Lena Harber married Joseph Smith on January 21, 1872. He was a son of John Smith, who came from Germany and settled in Allen county. Joseph Smith was born in Hesse Cassel, in 1848, and was for years identified with his father in farming activities. He bought eighty acres of land from his father when he married Lena Harber and made his home on that land to the end of his days, death coming on September 26, 1890. To him and his wife were born nine children. Alice married Henry Gibson. Josephine is the wife of William Minich, of Marion township. Francis is at home with his widowed mother. Albert and Elia are located in Fort Wayne. Agnes married Andrew Rubb. Gertrude is deceased. Otto and Romer are at home. There are twenty-two grandchildren in the family at this time.

Marion Smith has diversified farming activities with educational exercises, so that his career has been probably a more interesting one to contemplate than might be that of a man who gave his whole attention to the cultivation of his land. Mr. Smith was born in Allen county, December 1, 1852, son of William Wilson and Christina Catherine (Glock) Smith, who came from Ohio, in 1845, and bought land in Allen county. They first owned a place of one hundred and twenty acres, but in later years came to own other tracts in the county and were prosperous for their time. The elder Smith taught the first public school in Marion township, being a man of more than average education, and was engaged in school work up to 1862, after which time he turned his entire attention to farming. He was a prominent man in his locality and was county commissioner of Allen county for two years. A lifelong member of the Methodist Episcopal church, he served its best interests faithfully, and was for years a trustee in the church of which he was a member. Mr. and Mrs. Smith were the parents of ten children. Louisa married Solomon Snyder and is deceased. Their second child was Marion, the immediate subject of this family review. Elizabeth married Simon Somers. Romanza is deceased. Eva is the wife of N. Snyder. William is no longer living. Henry is an attorney of Fort Wayne. Charles died in infancy. John is a resident of Wells county, Indiana. Mina married William Dalman. Marion Smith, with his brothers and sisters, had his early education in the public schools of his community. He later attended the Methodist College at Fort Wayne and the Academy at Ossian, so that his education was fairly well looked out for. He prepared himself for the teaching profession and for fifteen years gave his attention to teaching in the country schools during the winter months. He gave his summers to farm work, having bought a fine farm, in 1872, and while he began his farming operations with a forty-acre place, he later added to it until he had a farm of two hundred and fifty acres, well improved and in first-class condition. In 1888-9 Mr. Smith was engaged in teaching music in the schools of Allen county and is distinguished throughout the county for his work as the conductor of a singing school in various communities through many years. A Democrat, Mr. Smith has been active in local politics, but has never aspired to public office. He is a member of the Methodist Episcopal church, and is vice-president of the Hoagland State Bank, and a member of its board of directors. Mr. Smith was married on September 6, 1874, to Miss Mary Kansas Linden, daughter of Philip and Elizabeth (Snyder) Linden. Mr. Linden came from Virginia, in 1845, and it is a notable fact that he walked the entire distance from his native village to Allen county. He bought land and built himself a log cabin, there settling down to the arduous labors of making a home in the wilderness, and conducting what is popularly known in many circles as "bachelor's hall." When he felt himself sufficiently prosperous to warrant the taking on of family responsibilities, he walked back to Virginia, bought a team and built a wagon, and returned, bringing his two sisters. The trip was a long and difficult one, covering a space of three weeks, and they camped out nights along the wilderness roads, cooked their meals by camp-fires and experienced all the pleasures and privations peculiar to that mode of travel. Mr. Linden married, in 1852, and was to the end of his days one of the estimable and dependable men of his community, where he served his neighbors in various public offices during his lifetime. He and his good wife were the parents of a family of seven children. The first born died in infancy. Delilah married John W. Fanner and they live in Clare, Michigan. Their third child, Mary Kansas, became the wife of the subject of this sketch. Preston is living in Marion township. Emily is the wife of Horace E. Smithey, of Roanoke, Indiana. Minnie married J. J. Bollinger and they live in Arkansas. Charles B. is a resident of Fort Wayne. Mr. and Mrs. Smith have five sons and daughters. Stella May, who is deceased, married H. H. Roberts and was the mother of Glenn S. and Marion H. Roberts. Francis M. is living in Ossian, Indiana. Oscar Clement is still under the parental roof, as is also Roscoe Wayne. Oscar, however, married Maud Hiser, the daughter of David F. Hiser, of Marion township, the marriage taking place on April 19, 1909, and they have a son named Brice. The third child of Mr. and Mrs. Smith died in infancy.

Orson C. Smith.—Fifty-five years of continuous residence in one locality will give to any man the distinction of an old settler and when he has the added distinction of being a native son of that locality, he is properly entitled to the position that has long been accorded to Orson C. Smith, who has spent his life thus far as a farmer in Pleasant and St. Joseph townships, in the former of which he was born on March 22, 1861. Mr. Smith is a son of Finley and Almira (Clark) Smith, both of them native Ohioans, and they were wed in Wells county, Indiana, where she had settled with her parents. Mr. Smith came to live in Pleasant township with his family when he was a lad of ten years, so that the residence of the Smith family in this community has endured for upwards of a century and the connection of these worthy people with the township has been an influence tending to the development and growth of their immediate locality through the years. Orson Smith was one of eleven children born to his parents. Named in the order of their birth they were Jonas (deceased), Orson, Emma, Jacob, Elizabeth, Enoch, Martha, Zaccheus, Wilmetta, Frank W. and Nora B. The first, seventh and ninth born are deceased, but the others came to years of maturity and are today filling places of usefulness in their various communities. The parents of this goodly family are no longer living. The mother, who was born in 1839, passed away in 1899, and the father, also born in 1839, lived till 1907. Orson C. Smith had his education in the schools of Pleasant township. He grew up in the knowledge of farm life and gained an experience in his home that added much to his chances for material success in his independent life. He farmed on his own responsibility in Pleasant township until 1899, when he moved to St. Joseph township and has since carried on a successful farming enterprise on his well-developed farm of eighty acres in Section 18. He has devoted himself to general farming and dairying and has a fine herd of Jersey cattle of which he is justly proud. A family man, Mr. Smith was married on December 22, 1881, to Miss Martha Logan, daughter of James S. and Mary Logan, who were among the very early settlers of Allen county. Two children were born of this union—Arthur J. and Florence A. The wife and mother died in 1892 and Mr. Smith was married a second time, in 1894, when Miss Mary A. Robinson became his bride. She was a daughter of Horney and Amanda (Orn) Robinson, another of the old-established and highly esteemed families of Allen county. Of this second marriage there are six children—Albert N.; Clarence and Clara, twins; Edna G.; F. Rollin and Alma. The twnis are deceased. Mr. Smith has long taken an active part in the public life of his community, and is at present serving as trustee of St. Joseph township. He was township assessor for six years. He is a Democrat in politics, and with his family has membership in the Methodist Episcopal church of his community.

R. Parker Smith is one of the vigorous and and progressive representatives of the real estate business in his native county and in his independent operations is showing the discrimination, resourcefulness and energy that, coupled with fair and honorable transactions, have conspired to make him definitely successful and influential as an exponent of this important phase of business enterprise, his well-equipped offices in the city of Fort Wayne being in suite 422-425 Shoaff building. He is a reliable and enterprising young business man and is consistently accorded recognition in this history of his native county. Mr. Smith was born at Monroeville, Monroe township, Allen county, on January 4, 1889, a son of Willard P. and Lydia (Parker) Smith, who now maintain their home in Fort Wayne, where the father is successfully engaged in the lumber business. R. Parker Smith was two years of age at the time of the family removal to Fort Wayne and here acquired his early education in the public schools, including the high school. In connection with his father's operations he early gained practical experience in the lumber business, and when about eighteen years of age became a traveling lumber salesman for George W. Myers, of St. Louis, Missouri. Eight months later he severed this allegiance to accept a similar position in the employ of W. F. Furguson, of St. Louis, for whom he continued his effective services until September, 1909. From that time he was in the employ of John Vesey, of Fort Wayne, until June 21, 1910, when he established his present real estate business, in which his success has been unequivocal. He handles both city and farm property and has made numerous important transfers of realty in his home county, besides which he gives special attention to rentals and collections. He and his wife hold membership in the Wayne Street Methodist Episcopal church. On August 1, 1911, was solemnized the marriage of Mr. Smith to Miss Charlotte B. Chase, of Fort Wayne, and their one child is a daughter, Charlotte P., who was born June 7, 1912.

William Smith, one of the well-to-do men of Monroeville, where he has lived since he retired from active business pursuits, in 1902, was born in Erie county, Ohio, July 30, 1852, son of Anthony and Anna Maria (Cordat) Smith, concerning whom more extended mention will be found elsewhere in these pages. Mr. Smith was reared and educated in his native community and came to Allen county, Indiana, as a young man, ambitious for material success, and energetic enough to win it in the face of long odds. He settled on a tract of timbered land in Jackson township, and in company with a brother, established a saw and hoop mill. The business was a successful one from the first, and their own land and surrounding county furnished the raw material for the mill for many years. Prosperity rewarded their efforts and, in 1902, the brothers retired and settled down to quiet life. William Smith located in Monroeville and his modern and very comfortable residence is admirably situated on a plot of land equal in size to eleven lots. In addition to this property, he owns a fine farm of four hundred acres of improved land which yields to him a comfortable income as well as a good deal of pleasure in its operation. Mr. Smith is a lifelong Democrat and has rendered worthy service as a member of the county board. He was married, in 1882, to Miss Sophia C. Hagy, born August 3, 1857, a woman of German birth and parentage, who came to America with her mother as a child of seven years. Her father, Anthony Hagy, died when she was a small child, and the mother, some little time after her arrival in America, married again and with her husband located in Sandusky, Ohio. There they spent the remaining years of their lives. To Mr. and Mrs. Smith were born two children. Louisa, the eldest, is the wife of Dwight Castleman, a resident of Allen county, and Jay William is a resident of Jackson township, also in Allen county. He, too, is married, and the elder Smiths are the grandparents of eleven children. The family are Roman Catholic in their religious faith.

Zaccheus A. Smith.—Successful farming is a talent quite as much as is successful selling, or financing, or teaching, or any other of the many fields in which talent makes for success, and Zaccheus A. Smith has manifested the same talent for progressive agriculture that made his father one of the successful men of his community. Mr. Smith was born in Pleasant township on March 2, 1872, son of Findlay and Elmira (Clark) Smith, both of them Ohioans. They came to Indiana with their parents, also farming people, when Findlay Smith was a lad of nine years and the girl who came to be his wife in later years was about six years old. Findlay Smith grew up on a farm and when he started out to make his own way in the world naturally chose to follow the line for which he was best fitted by training and inclination. He was said during his lifetime to be one of the most capable and farsighted farmers in Allen county. In addition to his prowess in that line, he was a successful school teacher and gave some time to that work in his early life, when the schools were not so well organized as they came to be in later years. He was ever the friend of education and fostered the spirit of child-training in his community all his days. He spent his last years in practical retirement from farm life, though he never gave up his enthusiasm for the affairs of communal life, and was a good citizen to the end of his life. He passed away on December 8, 1907, when he was in the sixty-eighth year of his life, his wife having preceded him on January 28, 1900, when she was sixty-one years old. They were worthy people, highly esteemed in their community and wherever they were known, and a host of friends mourned their passing. They were members of the Church of God, and Mr. Smith was a Democrat in politics. Eleven children blessed their home. They favored the good, old-fashioned names and their children were named as follows: Jonah, who died in infancy; Orson, living in the vicinity of Fort Wayne; Emma, a resident of Wells county, Indiana; Jacob, of Pleasant township; Elizabeth and Enoch also live in Pleasant township; Martha died May 6, 1902; Zaccheus is the eighth born; Wilametta died in 1915; Frank lives in Wayne township; and Nora has her home in Kalkaska, Indiana. Zaccheus Smith had his education in the common schools of Allen county, in common with his brothers and sisters, and when he was twenty-one years old took possession of a farm of his own, consisting of forty acres in Pleasant township. He bought and sold farms on numerous occasions, and his last move was in 1903, when he settled on his present place of sixty acres, to which he has since added a forty, making his holdings one hundred acres in all. He has specialized in hog breeding and his spotted Poland hogs are his pride, and the source of a good deal of revenue as well. He usually has about two hundred "porkers" on his place at a time, and holds two sales a year. He finds a ready market for his thoroughbreds, and is widely known in and about Allen county for his success in this enterprise. Mr. Smith is a Democrat in politics and with his family has membership in the Church of God. He was married on November 23, 1893, to Miss Nellie Denney, daughter of Roland and Jane (Bell) Denney, Lafayette township people and well-known in the county. They were early comers to Allen county, the father a native Virginian and the mother born in Pennsylvania. To Mr. and Mrs. Smith nine children came. Flossie May, the eldest, is the wife of Floyd Green; Vila Marie lives at home; the third child died in infancy; Gale Rolands it at home; Clarence Findlay died in April, 1901, and the sixth child died in infancy; Leota Annie, Howard Clayton and Dorothy Irena are all at home with the parents.

Benjamin Snider has passed the psalmist's span of three score years and ten, has been a resident of Allen county from the time of his birth and is a scion of one of the sterling pioneer families that was here founded three-fourths of a century ago, the name having been closely and honorably linked with the civic and industrial development and upbuilding of the county and he himself having long been a substantial exponent of agricultural enterprise in the township in which he was born and reared and in which he still maintains his residence on his fine homestead farm of eighty acres. A man who has marked the passing years with constructive industry and whose life has been guided and governed by high principles, Mr. Snider is one of the venerable and honored citizens of Jefferson township and is specially entitled to recognition in this history of his native county. Benjamin Snider was born in Jefferson township on September 10, 1846, a son of George and Elizabeth (Platt) Snider, the former a native of Pennsylvania and the latter of Ohio, their marriage having been solemnized in Carroll county, Ohio. He to whom this review is dedicated was the fourth in a family of nine children and his sister Martha, youngest of the number, is the only other survivor. The names of the deceased children are here noted: John Anderson, Rebecca, Anna Elizabeth, Adolphus, Amanda Maria, James P. (died in infancy), and David B. The parents came to Allen county in the year 1842 and established their home in Jefferson township, where the father obtained a tract of wild land and instituted the arduous task of reclaiming a farm from the virtual wilderness. He cleared and improved his land, became one of the prosperous farmers of the county and lived a life of signal honor and usefulness, both he and his wife having continued to reside on their old homestead until their death and their names meriting place on the roll of the sterling pioneers of the county. Benjamin Snider was reared to the sturdy discipline of the pioneer farm and has been significantly one of the world's earnest and productive workers, his early educational advantages having been those offered in the pioneer schools. He has never severed his allegiance to the fundamental industry of agriculture and his is one of the well-improved farms of Jefferson township, the place being about five and a half miles distant from Monroeville, which is his postoffice address. Mr. Snider has been an enterprising and progressive farmer and the most of the permanent improvements on his homestead have been made by him. Though now venerable in years he is still alert and vigorous and gives a general supervision to the affairs of his farm, with secure status as one of the honored and well-known citizens of his native township. His political allegiance is given to the Republican party, his religious views are in harmony with the tenets of the Episcopal church, and he formerly maintained active affiliation with the Independent Order of Odd Fellows. The first marriage of Mr. Snider was celebrated, January 21, 1869, when Miss Elizabeth Seibert became his wife. She was a daughter of Barney and Elizabeth (Warheim) Seibert, both of whom were born in Virginia, of German ancestry, and they were early settlers in Allen county, where they continued to reside until their death. Mrs. Snider was summoned to the life eternal on March 26, 1890, and her memory is cherished by all who came within the circle of her kindly influence. Of the seven children the first was Maggie May, who died when about thirty years of age, and the names of the others are indicated in respective order of birth: George Ellsworth, Oliver B., Mabel Gray. Dora W., Grace and Edith, the last two having died in infancy. For his second wife Mr. Snider wedded Mrs. Ellen Erbine, and she presides most graciously over the attractive home.

Preston H. Snider.—As a farmer and a member of the directorate of the Hoagland State Bank Preston H. Snider has come to occupy a leading position in his community, in which he has spent his life. He was born in Marion township, November 28, 1859, a son of Philip and Elizabeth (Snider) Snider, natives of Virginia and Ohio, respectively. Philip Snider was born on August 18, 1818, and came to Allen county, in 1848, buying land and devoting himself to farm life. He was married in 1852 and lived quietly and prosperously in his chosen community until the outbreak of the Civil war, when he promptly enlisted for service and passed through the war. His children were Lulu Maud, May Kansas and Preston H., of whom brief mention has already been made. Mr. Snider married Tilla Felger and they have one son, Frank Boyd Snider.

Edmond J. Somers has been the author of his own success in the farming world and such accomplishments as have been his are the results of his own well-directed efforts and energies. He is a native of the Hoosier state, born in Wells county, April 8, 1873, son of William Henry and Maggie (Pierce) Somers. They were born of German parents in Adams county, Indiana, and spent their lives in devotion to the farming industry in Wells county. They were staunch members of the Methodist Episcopal church, good citizens and neighbors, and were the parents of a family of nine children, most of them coming to years maturity and taking their places in their respective communities where they are living useful lives. They are named here in the order of their birth: Lula died in 1901. Park is a resident of Ossian, Indiana. Edmond J. was the third born. Gurden is a resident of Wells county. Chauncey lives in Fort Wayne. Ora is the wife of William Sherer, of Allen county. Florence is married and lives in Fort Wayne. Minnie married Calvin Bea, and they also are residents of Fort Wayne. Ira is the youngest. Edmond J. Somers had the usual country school education and spent his early life in association with his father in the working of the home farm. When he married he settled on his present farm, a well-appointed place of one hundred and seventy acres, to which he later added fifty-three acres adjoining. He has farmed energetically and profitably and takes his place among the foremost agricultural men of his community today. He is a leader in his township and is identified with the Masonic order in a fraternal way. His politics are Republican and with his family he has membership in the Methodist Episcopal church. He was married on March 5, 1900, to Martha Felger, daughter of Christ Felger, who was an early settler in Allen county, and who bought land there when it might be had in any quantity for six dollars the acre. They were among the substantial people of their community as long as they lived. Mr. and Mrs. Somers have two children—Walter and Albert—bright boys who are growing up in the freedom of rural life, and attending the local schools, which are vastly improved in comparison with the district schools their father attended not so many years agone.

Harley H. Somers has become one of the representative business men of the younger generation in his native county and is secretary and treasurer of the Farmers' State Bank in the village of Sheldon, Pleasant township, where he is also associated with his brother-in-law, Charles E. Clark, in a successful contracting business. He is progressive both as a business man and as a loyal citizen, and was prominently concerned in the organization of the substantial banking institution of which he is now a valued executive. The Farmers' State Bank of Sheldon was organized July 22, 1910, and with Mr. Somers forty-one other substantial citizens were associated in the establishing of the new institution, which was incorporated with a capital stock of twenty-five thousand dollars and which initiated active business on October 22, 1910. The official or executive corps of this well ordered bank is as here noted: Charles F. True, president; George Fogwell, vice-president; and Harley A. Somers, secretary and treasurer. In addition to the president and vice-president, the directorate of the bank includes also the following representative citizens: George F. Buskirk, Peter Sorg, J. F. Springer, William Brindle, Simon W. Somers, Andrew Neireiter, and Nathan Snider. The brick building occupied is owned by the bank and was erected and equipped for the purpose, the attractive structure of one story being twenty by forty feet in dimensions and being up to approved modern standard in appointments and equipment, with a fire and burglar-proof vault and with time-lock safe of the most approved type, the building having been erected at a cost of five thousand dollars. The substantial and consecutive expansion of the business of the bank are indicated in the following record of its resources on the 1st of January of each successive year up to January 1, 1916: 1911, $38,251.37; 1912, $66,244.85; 1913, $90,745.61; 1914, $117,068.33; 1915, $121,685.71; 1916, $153,673.67. Within the six years of its operation the bank has paid nine thousand dollars in dividends to its stockholders, and its surplus and undivided profits at the close of the year 1916 are represented in the sum of $2,200. Harley H. Somers was born in Marion township, this county, on January 26, 1883, and is a son of Simon W. and Mary E. (Smith) Somers, who still reside on their fine farm in Marion township. Simon W. Somers is not only one of the substantial farmers and influential citizens of his home township but is also a stockholder and director of the Farmers' State Bank of Sheldon, as the foregoing list has indicated. He was born in Adams county, this state, but was reared and educated in Allen county, his wife having been born and reared in this county and having completed her education in the Methodist College at Fort Wayne. Both she and her husband are zealous members of the Methodist Episcopal church at Poe, and he has been a trustee of the same since 1901, his political support being given to the Republican party. Of the two children, Harley H., of this review, is the elder, and the younger, Lucius V., continued to be associated with his father in the work and management of the home farm. Harley H. Somers acquired his early education in the district schools of his native township and supplemented this discipline by a course in the high school at Middletown. Thereafter he taught in the district schools for nine years, during which he made a record of success as a representative of the pedagogic profession, but his predilection for business activities led him to assume the position of assistant cashier of the bank in the village of Hoagland, this county, where he remained eight months and gained valuable experience, so that he was well fortified for executive service when, at the expiration of the period noted, he effected the organization of the Farmers' State Bank of Sheldon, of which he has since served as the efficient and popular secretary and treasurer. In politics Mr. Somers maintains an independent attitude and gives his support to the men and measures meeting the approval of his judgment. He is affiliated with the Scottish Rite body of the Masonic order and both he and his wife are active members of the Methodist Episcopal church in Poe. On May 12, 1907, was solemnized the marriage of Mr. Somers to Miss Etna Trenary, daughter of John and Ellen (Snider) Trenary, of Poe, this county, and the two children of this union are: Byron T., who was born June 27, 1912; and Mary E., who was born July 21, 1914.

Simon W. Somers was born in Marion township, Allen county, Indiana, on January 17, 1857, son of Harrison and Elizabeth (Roe) Somers, who came as young married people from their native state, Virginia, to Allen county, in 1856. The father was a cooper by trade, and gave some attention to that work after locating in Marion township, later buying a farm and turning his energies to the cultivation of his land. He was a renter for many years, and only lived seven years after he came into possession of a place of his own. He was a good citizen and a man highly esteemed in his community all his days. He and his wife were members of the Church of the Disciples. Their children numbered seven. John lives in Aboite township; Oliver is located in Angola; Elmer calls Fort Wayne his home; Charles lives in Milwaukee, Wisconsin; Preston is living in Fort Wayne; Anna is in Williamsburg, Ohio, and Simon W. is the eldest of the family. Simon W. Somers had his early education in the public schools of his community and worked on the home farm for some years, later finding employment on neighboring farms for some few years. In 1883 he bought a place of his own. It was small, comprising forty acres, but it was ample to begin independence with, and he later added one hundred and four acres of excellent farm land, so that he has today as much land as he can comfortably work. He was married on February 23, 1882, to Miss Mary E. Smith, daughter of Wilson and Catherine (Glock) Smith, who came from Germany and settled on land in Allen county in pioneer days. Mr. and Mrs. Somers have two children—Harley and Lucius. Both are married and Harley has two children—Byron and Mary, while Lucius has one daughter, named Elizabeth. Mr. Somers is Republican in politics and with his wife has membership in the Methodist Episcopal church of their community.

Edward A. Sordelet.—The consistent and progressive policies maintained in connection with the government of Allen county have in recent years been exemplified in no more important and beneficent way than in the recent purchase of the Allen County Farm, a fine estate that is already well equipped in many departments but upon which the best of improvements are being made, so that it shall be made a model demesne for the varied uses to which it is applied. Special wisdom was shown in selecting Edward A. Sordelet as superintendent of the farm, and his administration of affairs is proving full justification of his preferment in this official line, the exactions and responsibilities of which are many. He is a scion of the third generation of the Sordelet family in Allen county and the name has been worthily linked with civic and industrial progress in the county since the middle-pioneer period of its history. Edward A. Sordelet was born in Jefferson township, this county, July 7, 1871, and is a son of Jacques and Armonce (Dupont) Sordelet, who were born in France and who were children at the time of the immigration of the respective families to America. Both families came to Allen county in an early day, and the Sordelets settled in Jefferson township, while the Duponts located in Perry township, both becoming successful exponents of farm enterprise. Jacques Sordelet engaged in farming and with the passing years he developed a fine estate, on which he continued until his death, which occurred November 15, 1910, his loved and devoted wife having passed to the life eternal on the 9th of the preceding June, both having been lifelong communicants of the Catholic church. He whose name initiates this review was reared under the sturdy discipline of the home farm, made good use of the advantages of the public schools of his native township, and in earlier years followed work as a carpenter as well as giving effective service in connection with farm enterprise. Prior to accepting his present office, that of superintendent of the county farm, he had been for thirteen years superintendent of a fine estate of six hundred acres in Eel River township, and the diversified service given, with incidental administrative experience, rendered him specially eligible for the important office of which he is now the incumbent. He is the owner of a well improved farm of eighty acres, near Wallen, Washington township, and on the same he is giving special attention to the raising and feeding of fine Aberdeen-Angus cattle and a large type of Poland-China swine. He has made many improvements on this farm, including a fine barn and modern silo. At the time of this writing, in the summer of 1917, Mr. Sordelet is giving special attention to dividing and systematizing the work of the various departments of the county farm, as well as to the construction of fences and drainage ditches and to the remodeling of buildings, his determination being to make the place self-supporting and relieve the county from taxation to maintain it. Since he assumed office he has constructed six miles of fence. Mr. Sordelet is affiliated with the Knights of Pythias and the Modern Woodmen of America, at Churubusco, and the Fort Wayne lodge of the Loyal Order of Moose. Reverting to the family history it may be noted that the father of Mr. Sordelet was twice married, and the one surviving child of the first union is Mrs. Mary Rorick, of Jefferson township. The children of the second marriage are: Frank; Jacob, deceased; Charles; Mrs. Louise Haines; Mrs. Ida Pio; Edward A., of this sketch; John; Mrs. Ailene Biskel. July 16, 1895, occurred the marriage of Mr. Sordelet to Florence, daughter of John W. and Jennie (Cartwright) Holmes, who were born and reared in Allen county and who now reside near Plymouth, Marshall county. Mrs. Sordelet was summoned to the life eternal, and is survived by three children: Isabelle Marie holds a position in the offices of the Fort Wayne Electric Light Company, her birth having occurred March 9, 1897; Florence May, who was born November 8, 1898, resides in the home of Mrs. William Clutter, of Fort Wayne; and Florence Lucile, born April 17, 1901, lives at the home of her father's sister, Mrs. Pio, at Hobart. On April 25, 1906, was solemnized the marriage of Mr. Sordelet to Jessie A., daughter of Horace and Clara (Geiger) McDuffie, who reside in Eel River township, Mrs. Sordelet having there been born March 15, 1881. Mr. McDuffie is of Scotch-Irish ancestry, has been a resident of Allen county all his life and is one of the extensive farmers and influential citizens of Eel River township. Mrs. Sordelet received excellent educational advantages and prior to her marriage had taught seven terms of school in her home township, an experience that has proved of much value to her in connection with her present effective service as matron of the Allen county farm. Mr. and Mrs. Sordelet have no children.

Mrs. Mary J. Sorg, the widow of the late John George Sorg and daughter of Lambert and Theresa (Bush) Raund, was born in Orange county, New York, August 7, 1856. She has been a resident of Allen county since she was an infant, the family having left New York state, in 1857, and located in this district. Lambert Raund, the father, was a stone-cutter by trade, but when he came to Allen county he bought forty acres of farm land and settled down to agricultural life, in which occupation he spent the rest of his days. He was a successful farmer and added considerably to his original holdings during his active years of farm life. He died in 1884, still a leader in his community, and left three children. George and Joseph are deceased, and Mary J. is the immediate subject of this brief family review. She had her education in the public schools of Allen county and was eighteen years old when, on November 4, 1874, she became the wife of John George Sorg, son of Michael and Theresa (Bower) Sorg, German people who came from their native land in early life and settled on a farm in Marion township, Allen county. They were industrious and steady people, who eventually came to own land in the township to the extent of several hundred acres, and were among the foremost citizens of their community. The father was twice married. By his first marriage there were seven children, named Joseph, John George, Theodore, John, Peter, Anthony and Julia. The second marriage took place in 1851, Barbara Laurer becoming his wife, and their five children were Katherine, of Fort Wayne; Charles, of Marion township; Minnie C., living in Wisconsin, and Michael and Henry, both residents of Milan township, Allen county. J. George Sorg, who became the husband of the subject, was educated in the public and parochial schools of Allen county and was for some time employed in the carpenter's trade. He eventually inherited a tract of one hundred acres from his father, and so withdrew from that work, thereafter devoting himself exclusively to farming, in which he enjoyed a very pleasing measure of success. He died on the home farm on December 17, 1904, leaving a widow and twelve children to mourn his passing. He was a devout Roman Catholic all his life and a Democrat in politics. His children briefly mentioned as follows: Theresa, the eldest, is the wife of Frank J. Steinacker; John M., Bernhard, Anthony, Lambert, Catherine M., Ferdinand S., Daniel, Francis M., Andrew G., Roman H. and Robert F. Ferdinand died at the early age of fourteen years. Andrew and Roman still live at home with the mother, but the others have found their places in the world and are engaged in their respective callings. Mrs. Sorg has twenty grandchildren. Her eldest child, Theresa, is the mother of George and Venita. John M. has eight children, named Alfred, Irene, Edna, Oscar, Stella, Agnes, May and Edith. Bernhard is the father of Sylvester G., Marion and Walter. Anthony's children are Antoinette, May, James, Harold and Gerald (twins), Alice and Arthur. Mrs. Sorg carries on farming operations successfully, aided by her two sons who still share the old home place with her, and hers is one of the fine places in the township, where she enjoys the confidence and undivided allegiance of a large circle of old friends.

Frederick B. Sorgen.—The Sorgen family is distinctly German in its origin, and the branch represented by the subject came to America as late as 1858. Jacob and Mary (Helbling) Sorgen came from their native land soon after their marriage and settled in Hardin county, Ohio, where they passed the remaining years of their lives. They gave their attention to farming and were successful in their work, as German farmer folk are reasonably certain to be, given a fair chance. They reared a fine family of twelve children, eight of whom are now living, and they died on their Hardin county farm when fairly advanced in years. Frederick B. Sorgen, their eldest son, was born on September 26, 1855, and was reared and educated in his native county. In early manhood he married Miss Ruth Fertig, of Ohio birth and daughter of Samson and Rebecca (Swain) Fertig, both natives of the Buckeye state, who in later life moved to Kansas, where the father died some years ago. Mrs. Fertig, however, still makes her home in Kansas. Mrs. Sorgen was one of eight children born to her parents, all living but two. After his marriage Mr. Sorgen took his bride to Indiana and they settled in Allen county, locating, in 1891, on their present home in Monroe township. It is a fine farm of eighty acres and the twenty-five years they have spent on it have brought many changes in its general appearance, due to the policy of continuous improvement that Mr. Sorgen rigidly adhered to during his lifetime, and which his widow carried out after his death. Six children were born to them, briefly mentioned as follows: Effie M., the wife of Warren Allison; Clarence G.; Ruth I., married to Charles Myers; Carl C.; Olga L., married John Hart, March 7, 1917, and is living in Ohio, and Elmer D. The husband and father died April 8, 1899, and is buried in Stevenson cemetery, Monroe township.

C. A. Spanley.—(See Paragon Cooperage Company.)

Alvin A. Sprunger.—The efficient and popular young postmaster of the village of Woodburn, Maumee township, has been a resident of Allen county since his booyhood, but reverts to the Sunflower State as the place of his nativity, his birth having occurred on a farm in Reno county, Kansas, October 29, 1888. He is a son of Christian J. and Mary Anne Sprunger, the former of whom was born in Switzerland and the latter in the fine Swiss colony in Adams county, Indiana, where their marriage was solemnized and where they continued their association with farm industry until their removal to Reno county, Kansas, where the father continued to be engaged in agricultural pursuits for seven years. He then returned with his family to the vicinity of Berne, Adams county, Indiana, but about a year later came to Allen county, in 1893, and purchased a farm in Maumee township. Here he continued his successful enterprise as a progressive farmer for the ensuing fifteen years and is now living virtually retired in the village of Woodburn—a sterling citizen who commands unqualified esteem, his devoted wife having passed to the life eternal in 1912, a zealous member of the Missionary church, to the faith of which the family closely adheres. Of the eleven children, all of whom are living, the subject of this sketch was the eighth in order of birth, and the names of the others are here recorded: Edwin, Josephine, Salome, Frederick, Huston, Franklin, Alberta, Elizabeth, Elam and Aldo. The present postmaster of Woodburn was a lad of about five years at the time of the family removal to Allen county and here continued his studies in the public schools until he had completed the work of the freshman year in the Fort Wayne High School. Thereafter he was for three terms a student in the Tri-State Normal College, at Angola, this state, and after leaving this institution devoted eight years to successful pedagogic service, as a teacher in the schools of Maumee township. In 1914, after a successful civil-service examination, he was appointed postmaster at Woodburn and is giving a most effective and satisfactory administration. The fact that he was appointed under the regime of President Wilson indicates that he is a staunch supporter of the cause of the Democratic party, in the ranks of which he has given effective service in his home county, both he and his wife being zealous members of the Missionary church at Woodburn, of which he is serving as secretary and treasurer at the time of this writing, in 1917. In 1914 was solemnized the marriage of Mr. Sprunger to Miss Sylvia Lochner, a daughter of Samuel and Leah (Neuenschwander) Lochner, of Allen county, the father having been born in this county, near the village of Leo, and the family having been founded in the county in the pioneer days. Mr. and Mrs. Sprunger have one child, Meredith, who was born April 16, 1915.

Thomas L. Staples has achieved a notable work in furtherance of the educational and general business interests of Fort Wayne, where he established and is the executive head of the International Businss College, an institution of the highest grade in its special domain of service and one that has gained a large and representative supporting patronage, its high reputation for efficiency in all departments constituting its most valuable advertising and best business asset. Mr. Staples has had broad and varied experience in his special field of educational work and in the development of his present fine school has shown marked progressiveness and executive ability, the college now having secure status with the best institutions of the kind in the middle west. Thomas

Leslie Staples was born in the city of Toronto, Canada, June 23, 1865, and is one of a family of seven children, of whom four are now living. He is a son of Thomas and Matilda (Brisbin) Staples, the former of whom was born in Ireland and the latter in the province of Ontario, Canada. He whose name initiates this review attended the public schools of his native province until he had completed a course of study in the high school at Harriston, and he supplemented this discipline by an effective course in the Canadian School of Commerce, at Chatham, Ontario. For three years thereafter he was a successful teacher in a business college at Chatham, Ontario, and then went to the city of Saginaw, Michigan, where he served one year as an instructor in the Bliss Business College. In 1890 he came to Fort Wayne and established the International Business College, of which he has since continued the head and which has been developed to its present high standard under his vigorous and able management. Mr. Staples is a man of civic loyalty and progressiveness, is a Republican in his political allegiance, has received the thirty-second degree in the Ancient Accepted Scottish Rite of the Masonic fraternity, besides being affiliated also with the adjunct organization, the Ancient Arabic Order of the Nobles of the Mystic Shrine, as is he also with Fort Wayne Lodge of the Benevolent & Protective Order of Elks. He holds membership in the local Commercial and Rotary Clubs, as well as the Country Club, and is a popular figure in both business and social circles in the city of his home. Both he and his wife hold membership in the Presbyterian church. The marriage of Mr. Staples to Miss Bertha Digge was solemnized, June 29, 1891, and they have two daughters—Louise and Jean.

William F. Stasell is the fortunate owner of one of the excellent farms of Jackson township, where he has maintained his residence since the spring of 1912, and in the intervening period he has made various improvements of permanent order, including the erection of minor farm buildings, the installation of tile drainage, the building of fences, etc. Energy and thrift are shown in the general appearance of the farm, which is given over to diversified agriculture and to the growing of a consistent amount of live stock. Mr. Stasell is a native of the old Keystone state and is of staunch German lineage, as are many other of the representative farmers of Allen county. He was born in Allegheny county, Pennsylvania, on March 14, 1869, a son of Gerhardt and Eva (Schubert) Stasell, both of whom were children at the time of the immigration of the respective families from Germany to America. The parents were reared in Pennsylvania and there their marriage was solemnized. They settled in Allegheny county, that state, and there the death of the devoted wife and mother occurred. Gerhardt Stasell later removed with his children to Missouri and finally established his residence in La Salle county, Illinois, where he passed the remainder of his life, his death having occurred in September, 1901, and his entire active life having been one of close association with agricultural pursuits. He was the father of a fine family of eighteen children, of whom the sixth, Clara, died in infancy. The names of the children who attained to adult age are here recorded in the respective order of birth: Dora, George, Elizabeth, Gerhardt, Frederick, Anna, William F., Henry, John, August, Louis, Emma, Philip, Katherine, Isabel, Charles and Walter. The early educational advantages of William F. Stasell were limited to a somewhat brief and irregular attendance in the public schools of Pennsylvania and Missouri, and he has matured his knowledge effectively in the great school of practical experience and through self-discipline. As a youth he found employment at farm work in Missouri, where he also was associated for some time in the work of a sawmill. After removal to Illinois he worked as a farm hand in that state for ten years, being employed by the month. In the spring of 1900 he took unto himself a wife, and she has proved his loyal coadjutor in the efforts that have brought to them independence and definite prosperity. After his marriage Mr. Stasell continued his operations as a farmer on rented land in La Salle county, Illinois, until his removal to his present homestead farm, on February 28, 1912. Here he purchased a tract of one hundred and sixty acres, in Sections 26 and 22, Jackson township, the farm being situated three miles distant from the village of Edgerton and seven miles from Monroeville, from which latter place the family have service on rural mail route No. 1. Mr. Stasell is known as one of the energetic and progressive exponents of farm enterprise in Jackson township, he and his family have gained a wide circle of loyal friends in the community, he is a Republican in his political proclivities, and was appointed a special deputy sheriff of the county in 1917, by Sheriff Gillie. February 14, 1900, recorded the marriage of Mr. Stasell to Miss Rosie Hagenbucher, who was born in Germany, a daughter of Tobias Hagenbucher, who came to America when Mrs. Stasell was a child. The family home was established in the city of Chicago, where he conducted a store and milk depot for a period of fourteen years. For two years thereafter he was on a farm near Crown Point, Indiana, after which he returned with his family to Chicago. Six years later he removed to his present farm of one hundred and sixty acres, near Crown Point, Indiana, his wife having passed to the life eternal a quarter of a century ago and the four surviving children being Caroline, Rosie, Louis and Louisa. Mr. and Mrs. Stasell have four children, whose names and respective dates of birth are here indicated: Harold F., January 12, 1901; Eva L., September, 1903; Leonard H., March, 1904; and Inez A., April 17, 1914.

Rev. John Steger, the able and honored pastor of the Catholic parish of St. Aloysius, near Sheldon, has given virtually all of his services in the priesthood within the borders of the state of Indiana, and his consecrated labors have been fruitful in the furtherance of the spiritual and temporal prosperity of the various parishes in which he has faithfully labored. Father Henry Hellbacher, who was pastor of St. Aloysius church, passed to the life eternal on August 11, 1909, and for one month thereafter Rev. Fessler was the pastoral incumbent. He was succeeded by Father John Biedermann, who here continued his earnest labors until his death, which occurred November 26, 1915, he having celebrated in July of that year the twenty-fifth anniversary of his ordination to the priesthood. Of this revered pastor Father John Steger became the successor, and he has found gracious satisfaction in continuing the faithful service that had been rendered by his predecessors. He has vitalized the work of the parish, which has a congregation of fifty-five families, the parochial school having an enrollment of sixty pupils and being in charge of three sisters and of two other teachers. Preparations are being made for the erection of a new church edifice within the near future, and in this laudable enterprise Father Steger is receiving the earnest co-operation of his congregation. Father Steger was born in the Kingdom of

Bavaria, Germany, on June 13, 1875, and is a son of Peter and Francesca (Heinz) Steger, both of whom passed their entire lives in Bavaria, where the father was a prosperous farmer and where he served also as a commissioner for the Bavarian government. Father John Steger continued his studies in the schools of his native land until he had profited by the advantages of the gymnasium, which compares to the American high school. In 1901 he came to the United States, and completed his philosophical and ecclesiastical studies in St. Mary's Academy, his ordination to the priesthood having taken place at Fort Wayne on the 19th of June, 1905. His first pastoral charge was at Decatur, this state, where he remained thirteen months. He was then assigned to a church in the city of Kokomo, where he continued his ministrations two years, the ensuing two years having found him the incumbent of a pastorate at Garrett, DeKalb county. He was then assigned to a charge at Covington, Fountain county, where he remained one year. During the following three months he was at Goodland, Newton county, from which place he was transferred to St. Mary's church in Fort Wayne, where he remained until the assumption of his present charge, in the autumn of 1915.

Louis C. Steger has been closely identified with business interests in his native city since his early youth and now holds the responsible office of purchasing agent for S. F. Bowser & Company, one of the important industrial and commercial concerns of Fort Wayne. He was born in this city on August 10, 1876, a son of Rudolph and Johanna (Baals) Steger, who still maintain their home in Fort Wayne, where the father is living virtually retired, after a long and successful business career. Rudolph Steger was born at Kiel, Germany, and was a young man when he came to Fort Wayne, where he found employment as a cabinetmaker in the shops of the Pennsylvania Railroad Company. Later he engaged in the hardware business and became one of the representative merchants of the city in which he is now living retired. He has been influential in community affairs, is a loyal and liberal citizen and served for some time as a member of the board of public safety of Fort Wayne. In this city was solemnized his marriage, his wife having been born at Reading, Pennsylvania, and having been a child of three years when her parents established their home in Fort Wayne, both she and her husband being zealous communicants of the Lutheran church. Of their children, Albert H. and Gustave C. reside in the city of Toledo, Ohio; Louis C., of this review, was the next in order of birth; Charles F. is employed in the extensive Fort Wayne plant of the Bass Foundry & Machine Company; Theodore C. is an employe in the Fort Wayne shops of the Wabash Railroad; and the other four children did not live to attain to adult age. After having profited by the advantages afforded in the parochial schools of the Lutheran church in Fort Wayne Louis C. Steger pursued a course of higher study in Concordia College, of this city. For two years thereafter he was associated with his father's hardware business in a clerical capacity and then assumed a clerkship in the offices of the Pennsylvania Railroad shops in his native city. Later he was for seven years employed at the Fort Wayne Electric Works and since that time has been connected with S. F. Bowser & Company, Inc., in the service of which he now holds the position of purchasing agent, as previously noted. Mr. Steger gives a staunch allegiance to the Republican party, he and his wife are active communicants of Trinity English Lutheran church, and in the Masonic fraternity he is a member of Summit City Lodge No. 170, and has also made advancement in the Ancient Accepted Scottish Rite, in which he is affiliated with the Summit City Lodge of Perfection, at Fort Wayne. January 16, 1901, recorded the marriage of Mr. Steger to Miss Lottie Whitney, who likewise was born and reared in Fort Wayne and is a daughter of Frank and Adelaide (Green) Whitney. Mr. and Mrs. Steger have a fine little son, Robert Whitney, who was born July 25, 1906.

Daniel Steiner, as manager of the Huntertown Grain Company, of which he is a stockholder, exercises important influence touching the commercial and industrial activities of his native county and is essentially one of the representative and popular young business men of his native state. Mr. Steiner was born at Berne, Adams county, Indiana, on September, 1885, and is a son of Peter D. and Barbara (Moser) Steiner, who are of staunch German lineage and who still reside on their fine homestead farm, near Berne, Adams county. The names of their children are here noted in respective order of birth: Amos, Sarah, Judith, Daniel, Levi, Noah, Katie, Emma, Albert, Samuel, Ezra and John. All of the children are living except Noah, who died about 1901, and the subject of this review is the only one of the number not residing in the home county of Adams. Daniel Steiner was reared to the sturdy discipline of the home farm and under the earnest guidance of his father he early learned the dignity and value of honest toil. He profited by the advantages of the public schools of his native county and thereafter continued to be associated in the work and management of the home farm until he had attained to his legal majority. For nine months thereafter he was employed as a farm worker on another of the farms of his native county, and he then became associated with the Berne Hay & Grain Company, with which he maintained his connection about four years. He then came to Huntertown, and here he has been manager of the Huntertown Grain Company since September 1, 1911—an aggressive, energetic and resourceful young man who has wielded potent influence in the upbuilding of the substantial and important commercial enterprise with which he is thus identified. The company was organized in January, 1910, and was incorporated with a capital stock of eight thousand dollars, the same having been increased to thirty thousand dollars in the spring of 1916. The officers of the corporation are as here noted, and they are its largest stockholders: Dr. Frank Greenwell, president; Charles Bleke, vice-president; C. E. Preston, secretary and treasurer; and Daniel Steiner, manager. The business has shown a substantial expansion, and in 1916 it rendered to its stockholders a dividend of ten per cent. The enterprise included not only the buying and shipping of grain but also the handling of lumber and coal, and its material and commercial facilities are of the best. The company has recently erected for the lumber department of its business a building fifty-eight by one hundred feet in dimensions. the grain elevator is of modern type, a new grain dryer has been erected, and the value of this physical property is about six thousand dollars. Continuous employment is given to three men, and the force is increased at such times as the activities of the business demand. Mr. Steiner gives his close supervision to all details of the business and also takes loyal interest in community affairs, his political allegiance being given to the Democratic party. Both he and his wife hold membership in the Methodist Episcopal church. October 31, 1913, recorded the marriage of Mr. Steiner to Huldah, daughter of Christian and Sophia (Bailey) Stauffer, the former of whom is deceased and the latter of whom still resides on the home farm, near Monroe, Adams county, this state. Mr. and Mrs. Steiner have a daughter, Frieda, who was born in 1915.

Charles J. Steiss has shown himself to be emphatically a man of thought and action and has been influential in connection with civic and business affairs in his native city of Fort Wayne. He is now the secretary of the park commission of Fort Wayne and as a progressive and popular citizen and efficient public official is properly given recognition in this history. Mr. Steiss was born in Fort Wayne on February 23, 1874, a son of John George and Maria Magdalena (Rapp) Steiss, both natives of the Kingdom of Wurtemberg, Germany, where the former was born in January, 1840, and the latter on January 4, 1845, both having been reared and educated in their native land, where their marriage was solemnized and whence they came to the United States, in 1869. Soon after their arrival in America the parents of the subject of this review established their home in Fort Wayne, where the father opened a well-equipped shop and engaged in the work of his trade, that of cooper. A skilled artisan, he developed a prosperous business and continued in the active management of his cooperage until the close of his life. He was a man of abundant energy, of sterling character and of marked civic loyalty—a citizen who commanded the respect of all who knew him. His political support was given to the Democratic party, and both he and his wife were lifelong communicants of the Lutheran church, in which they were members of the St. John's parish in Fort Wayne. Of the children the eldest, John G., Jr., died in 1907, at the age of thirty-six years; Charles J., of this sketch, was the second son; Frederick W. likewise remains in Fort Wayne; Gustave H. and W. Minnie occupy the old family homestead; and Mary is the wife of Michael Fritz, of Fort Wayne. The father passed to the life eternal on October 3, 1893, and the venerable and widowed mother was summoned to the "land of the leal" on February 4, 1916. Charles J. Steiss acquired his early education in the parochial schools of St. John's Lutheran church and as a boy began to assist in the work of his father's cooper shop, in which he served an apprenticeship of thorough order. Later he learned the barber's trade and to the same continued to devote his attention about twenty years. For eighteen months thereafter he was associated in the publication of the Fort Wayne Labor Herald, a weekly paper, and in 1906 was appointed to a responsible position in the finance department of the city government, with which branch of the municipal service he continued to be identified four years. For the ensuing two years he was cashier of the state bank of Nuttman & Company, and since that time has given specially efficient service in the office of secretary of the city park commission, in which connection he is able to make practical and productive his deep interest in all that concerns the welfare of his native city. Mr. Steiss is a stalwart in the ranks of the Democratic party, is actively identified with the Fort Wayne Commercial Club, and both he and his wife are communicants of St. John's Lutheran church. Mr. Steiss has been prominently and earnestly concerned with the affairs of organized labor and has done much to further the cause. For five years he was secretary of the Fort Wayne Trades & Labor Council and was an influential member of the executive board of the Indiana Federation of Labor, besides which he served as delegate to national and international labor conventions, in which he was assigned to membership on important committees. In 1912, while attending the annual convention of the League of American Municipalities as a representative of Fort Wayne, he was elected to the office of treasurer, which office he held for three years, being re-elected the following year, at Winnipeg, and again in 1914 at Milwaukee. Since he has been identified with the park commission he has also attended all the conventions of the National Conference on City Planning. On August 5, 1895, Mr. Steiss wedded Miss Jennie Blanche Flightner, daughter of Samuel Flightner, a well-known citizen of Williams county, Ohio. Of the six children of this union the first, Carl Luther, died in infancy; Helen M., Esther L., Irene A., Lucile M., and Ruth Mae are still members of the gracious family circle of the parental home.

Alfred Anthony Stentz was born in Ashland county, Ohio, January 24, 1885, son of Henry C. and Josephine (Petot) Stentz, both natives of the state of Ohio. Mr. Stentz is a traveling salesman, and the family home is in Fort Wayne. They have two children—Mrs. Fred Harber, who lives on Harrison Hill, Fort Wayne, and Alfred Anthony, of this review. He was born and reared in his native county and attended school in Loudonville, Ohio, there completing his high school course in due season. He entered the shoe store of his grandfather in Loudonville and there had his first instruction in the shoe business. His next location was in Cleveland, in the employ of the Walkover Boot Shop, where he spent three years, and then came to Fort Wayne to take charge of the Walkover establishment here. He was twenty-two years of age then, and though young to manage such an establishment, he made good from the start, and the business has grown steadily with the growth of the city. C. E. Petot, of Cleveland, his uncle, was the owner of the business, and Mr. Stentz has come to hold a half interest in the establishment since he became identified with it as manager. The shop is centrally located on the main business street of the city, and each season adds many new and satisfied customers to the firm's clientele. Mr. Stentz married Miss Rose Jamison, of Ashland county, Ohio, daughter of Mrs. Elizabeth Jamison. They are members of the Congregational church and Mr. Stentz is a Mason of the thirty-second degree, an Elk, a member of the Commercial Club and the Rotary Club, in all of which he is popular and prominent.

Leonard D. Stolte.—One of the well-known and capable farmers of Washington township is Leonard D. Stolte, now living on the old homestead of the family. Mr. Stolte was born in his present community on May 20, 1874, son of Adolph and Elizabeth (Peters) Stolte, both native-born Germans who came to America in their youth, first settling in Indianapolis and later moving to Allen county, where they settled on the farm that later represented the family home and is now the property of the subject. To Adolph and Elizabeth Stolte were born nine children. William is deceased. Charles, Frank, George and Fred were the next in order of birth. Henry, the next child, is deceased; Leonard D., the subject, was the seventh, and was followed by Elizabeth and John, the last named being deceased. The parents passed their last days on the old homestead farm, and Leonard D., who had long devoted himself to the development of the place, came into possession of it at their death. Leonard D. Stolte had a rather better education than the average farm youth, the Fort Wayne Business College affording him some excellent training after he had finished with the local schools, and he has been able to utilize the systematic training he had there to excellent advantage in the management of his farm. He has been successful in general farming and stock-raising, and is counted among the ablest farmers of the community today. In 1900 Mr. Stolte married Gertrude Ludwig, a daughter of Wilson and Clara (Holman) Ludwig, and six children have been born to them. They are Albert, Herbert, Henry, Donald, Eugene and Marie, all living at the present time. Mr. Stolte was elected to the office of township trustee, in 1913, for a term of four years, and has thus far given an excellent service in that office. He is a member of the Modern Woodmen of America at Fort Wayne, and with his family has membership in St. John's Reformed church at Fort Wayne. He is a Democrat in politics.

Thomas Wade Stone is known as a mechanical engineer of distinctive ability and as such is manager of the works of the Western Gas Construction Company, 919 Columbia avenue, Fort Wayne. He was born at New Corydon, Jay county, Indiana, on October 4, 1877, being of Irish ancestry on the paternal side and of English in the distaff line. He is a son of Dr. Michael and Mary M. (Elzy) Stone. Dr. Stone was a pioneer citizen of St. Mary's, Ohio, and, when the Civil war was precipitated he went forth from that place to do service in defense of the Union. He first enlisted in the ninety days' service, as a member of the Thirty-first Ohio Volunteer Infantry, in which he became captain of Company E. At the expiration of his original term he re-enlisted in the same regiment and he continued as an officer of this gallant command during the remainder of the war, at the close of which he received his honorable discharge. After the war he engaged in the practice of medicine at New Corydon, Indiana, and he was as earnest and resourceful in his labors as he was in his effective service as a soldier. Of his four children the subject of this review is the eldest and the only son; Maude E. is the wife of Hon. Theodore H. Tangemann, of Wapakoneta, Ohio; Bessie is the wife of Hon. O. J. Boesel, of the same place; and Margaret resides at New Bremen, Ohio, where the parents established their residence in the early '80s. John S. Elzy, maternal grandfather of the subject of this sketch, likewise was a Union soldier in the Civil war. He enlisted at Decatur, Indiana, and continued in active service until he was wounded and captured, it having been his fate to be in Libby Prison, liberation having come only after the victory of the Union arms. Thomas W. Stone gained his early education in the public schools of New Bremen, Ohio, and thereafter attended for one year the Armour Institute of Technology, in Chicago. He entered the University of Ohio in 1902, and was there graduated with the degree of Mechanical Engineer. In the work of his profession his entire active service has been with the Western Gas Construction Company, one of the important industrial concerns of Fort Wayne and one whose operations extend into the most diverse sections of the Union. In his professional and executive capacity Mr. Stone has the general supervision of all practical operations of the institution, except the sales and finance departments. He is a member of the American Society of Mechanical Engineers, the American Gas Institute, the Fort Wayne Commercial Club, besides being affiliated with the Sigma Chi college fraternity. In politics Mr. Stone is a Republican. In 1905 he was married to Miss Dorothy M. Greiwe, of New Bremen, Ohio, and they are popular in the social circles of their home city. They have no children. Mr. Stone is an enthusiast in outdoor sports, including baseball and general athletics, and in connection with his profession he is a close and appreciative student of scientific subjects, his private library containing many of the best standard scientific works.

Frank E. Stouder has proved specially circumspect and successful as a purveyor of amusement for the public and is president and general manager of the Palace Theater Company at Fort Wayne, the attractive and modern theater building of this company presenting the best class of vaudeville entertainments, through the medium of the celebrated Keith circuit, and its supporting patronage being of representative order. Mr. Stouder was born at Millersport, Fairfield county, Ohio, May 29, 1867, a son of Jacob H. and Catherine A. (Shoop) Stouder. The original American ancestors of the Stouder family came from Switzerland to this country in the early days of the republic, and the paternal grandfather of the subject of this review became one of the pioneer exponents of agricultural industry in Fairfield county, Ohio. There Jacob H. Stouder was reared and educated and in his young manhood served effectively as a pilot on steamboats plying the Ohio river. In later years he conducted a well-ordered hotel at Crestline, Ohio. In the maternal line Frank E. Stouder is of English and French descent, the original American progenitors of the Shoop family having settled in Maryland, and representatives of the name having later become pioneers in southern Ohio. The seventh in order of birth in a family of ten children, of whom seven are still living, Frank E. Stouder was about ten years of age when the family home was established in Fort Wayne, in 1877, and here his father was for a number of years proprietor of the old Tremont Hotel, his death having here occurred in 1900, and his wife having died, June 10, 1915. Frank E. Stouder continued to attend the public schools of Fort Wayne until he had profited duly by the advantages of the high school and, in 1885, he here became treasurer of the Temple theater. After serving in this capacity nine years he became the lessee of the house, of which he continued the successful proprietor and manager until March, 1915. His success in the field of popular entertainment led him to extend his operations, and, in 1910, he organized a stock company which purchased the Lyric theater. This likewise was successfully conducted under his vigorous and careful management until 1915, when the holding company sold the property. In 1913 Mr. Stouder organized what is now the Palace Theater Company and instituted the erection of this theater, which was formally opened to the public on January 25, 1915, and it has gained recognition as one of the most modern and attractive theaters in the middle west. It is conceded to be the finest house devoted to vaudeville entertainment in the entire state of Indiana, and the building was erected and equipped at a cost of two hundred and twenty-five thousand dollars. It is of thoroughly fireproof construction, has a seating capacity of two thousand, has the most approved appointments for lighting, heating and ventilating and the general equipment of the stage and general auditorium is of thoroughly metropolitan order, the house having been designed by C. W. and G. L. Rapp, the celebrated theater architects, of Chicago. In presenting the attractions of the unrivaled Keith vaudeville circuit this beautiful house has not been denied the full measure of popular approval and support, and it has added much to the metropolitan prestige of Fort Wayne. Mr. Stouder has fine musical taste and appreciation and in former years brought his individual musical talent into effective play through his active identification with various singing societies in Fort Wayne. He has been active in bringing to the city the highest grade of musical attractions, including grand opera, and in the '90s organized several choral bodies for the effective presentation of standard oratorios. It was under his progressive direction that, in 1916, the Boston National Opera Company, with the celebrated Russian ballet, was brought to Fort Wayne for the presentation of a number of operas. No citizen is better known or enjoys a more gracious measure of popularity in Fort Wayne than does Frank E. Stouder, whose loyalty to the city has been shown in manifold ways and who has done much to promote its finer art appreciation. He was chairman of the committee that had supervision of the fine historical pageant given in Fort Wayne in the spring of 1916, incidental to the centennial celebration of the admission of Indiana to the sisterhood of states. In the Masonic fraternity he has received the thirty-third and last degree of the Ancient Accepted Scottish Rite, and the Shrine, and he is one of the vigorous and progressive members of the Fort Wayne Commercial Club, and the Rotary Club, besides being a member of the Country Club and the local lodge of Elks. He attends and supports the First Presbyterian church, of which his wife is an active member. In 1893 was recorded the marriage of Mr. Stouder to Miss Julia Wilson, daughter of George H. Wilson, a pioneer hardware merchant and honored citizen of Fort Wayne, and they have one child, a daughter, Jane.

David C. Stout may consistently be designated as a man of remarkable vitality, both physical and mental, and he has brought to bear his full powers in connection with the various and effective activities that have marked his career since the days of his youth. He is one of the well-known and distinctively popular native sons of Allen county, is now serving with characteristic efficiency as clerk of the county court, and is a broad-minded and progressive citizen who is eminently entitled to representation in this history. Mr. Stout was born at Monroeville, Monroe township, this county, on May 15, 1869, a son of George W. and Isabel (Murchland) Stout, the former of whom was born in Ohio and the latter in Allen county, Indiana, where her parents settled in the pioneer days; she passed to the life eternal in 1875, and of her three children the subject of this review is the eldest; Margaret is the wife of George Edward Corville, of Hoagland, this county; and Nannie is the wife of William Biggs, of Decatur, Adams county. The father, George W. Stout, now venerable in years, is living virtually retired in Fort Wayne—a sterling citizen whose circle of friends is coincident with that of his acquaintances. Prior to 1892 he was variously employed, and in that year was appointed deputy sheriff of Allen county, and in 1900 there came further recognition of his good faith and ability, in that he was elected sheriff, of which responsible office he continued the valued incumbent four years. After his retirement from the shrievalty he was engaged in the agricultural implement business about three years, the ensuing three years having found him a representative of the real estate business in Fort Wayne. He then went to Indianapolis, where for five years he held the position of custodian in the great Soldiers' and Sailors' Monument that is one of the most imposing objects in the Union and is one of the most important objects of general interest in the capital city of Indiana. Upon his retirement from this position in the employ of the state, in 1915, Mr. Stout returned to Fort Wayne, where he has since lived retired. David C. Stout made good use of the advantages afforded in the excellent public schools of Allen county and remained at the paternal home until he was about eighteen years of age. Thereafter he devoted himself to successful service as a teacher in the public schools until he had attained to his legal majority, when he became a traveling salesman for dental supplies, as a representative of a leading wholesale concern in this line of trade at Chicago and Detroit. With this enterprise he continued his identification about thirteen years, and thereafter was established in a substantial real estate and insurance business in Fort Wayne until November, 1914, when he was elected clerk of the court of Allen county, the duties of which office he assumed, January 1, 1915, his service in this position having been careful, circumspect and altogether satisfactory, as voiced by the estimate placed upon him by members of the judiciary and the bar of the county in general. Mr. Stout shows rousing enthusiasm in his advocacy of the cause of the Democratic party and has been influential in its local ranks. His popularity in his native county is of the most unequivocal order and he is actively affiliated with the Loyal Order of Moose, the Knights of Pythias, the Benevolent & Protective Order of Elks, and the Fraternal Order of Eagles. He has served as secretary of the Fort Wayne lodge of the Loyal Order of Moose from the time of its organization and, since 1910, has been chairman of the finance and auditing committee of the world's supreme lodge of this fraternal order. December 30, 1896, recorded the marriage of Mr. Stout to Miss Emma F. Youse, who likewise was born and reared in Allen county, and they became the parents of five children—Frances, Howard D., John W., David C., Jr., and Mary Jane—all of whom are living except Frances, who died at the age of six years.

Charles T. Strawbridge, vice-president of the Bass Foundry & Machine Company, has literally grown up with this now extensive and important industrial concern of Fort Wayne and his energy and executive ability have come effectively into service in the upbuilding of the extensive and well-ordered business. He established his residence in Fort Wayne in January, 1877, and became the first stenographer and typewriter operator in the newly established plant of the Bass Foundry & Machine Company. He had previously been employed about three years as a telegraph operator, and in the meanwhile had learned short-hand and typewriting, so that he proved a valued employe of Mr. Bass. Besides applying himself diligently as stenographer he installed in the office of the plant a telegraph equipment that gave direct connection with established commercial lines and proved of distinct value as an adjunct of the office equipment. From this minor executive service he has advanced through various stages until he has become vice-president of the company, and his has been an influential part in the development of what is now one of the most important industries of Fort Wayne. Charles Thomas Strawbridge was born at Blooming Grove, Morrow county, Ohio, on January 7, 1857, a son of John and Mary Jane (John) Strawbridge, both natives of Richland county, Ohio, and representatives of sterling pioneer families of that section of the Buckeye State. John Strawbridge was reared to the sturdy discipline of the farm, but as a young man became a stationary engineer. In 1860 he removed with his family to Bucyrus, the judicial center of Crawford county, Ohio, and there continued to maintain his home until his death, which occurred in March, 1901, his widow having there remained until she too passed to the life eternal, in October, 1907, and both having been earnest members of the Methodist Episcopal church. Of their children, Elnora and George W., the first and third in order of birth, are deceased; Charles T., of this sketch, was the second; and the youngest, Phoebe S., of Bucyrus, Ohio, is the widow of Patrick J. Carroll. When the Civil War was precipitated on a divided nation John Strawbridge went forth as a valiant soldier of the Union. In 1862 he enlisted in the Forty-fifth Ohio Infantry and with this gallant command continued in service until the close of the war, when he was mustered out and duly received his honorable discharge. In later years he vitalized his interest in his old comrades by maintaining appreciative affiliation with the Grand Army of the Republic. He took part in many important engagements marking the progress of the war and served in the commands of General Thomas and General Rosecrans. He was long one of the honored and influential citizens of Bucyrus, Ohio, loyally interested in community affairs and unflagging in his allegiance to the Republican party. Charles T. Strawbridge was a child of about three years at the time of the family removal to Bucyrus, Ohio, where he was reared to adult age and duly availed himself of the advantages of the public schools. While serving as messenger boy at the Bucyrus station of the Pennsylvania Railroad he began learning telegraphy and after becoming an expert in the art was employed as a telegraph operator in the service of the Pennsylvania Railroad Company, from 1874 to 1879, in which latter year he entered the employ of the Bass Foundry & Machine Company, with which he has continued his close association during the long intervening period of thirty-eight years. He finally familiarized himself with the sales department of the business and through this and other means expanded his executive resourcefulness and influence. His experience has touched all departments of the business with which he has been long identified and, in 1900, he was elected secretary of the company, of which position he has continued the incumbent, his election to the office of vice-president having taken place shortly afterward and his administrative functions having consequently been materially amplified. Mr. Strawbridge is vice-president of the Carroll Foundry & Machine Company, of Bucyrus, Ohio, this being a substantial concern engaged in the manufacturing of locomotive cranes and other heaving machinery. As a broad-gauged and progressive citizen Mr. Strawbridge takes deep interest in all things concerning the welfare of his home city and in politics is aligned as a stalwart in the cohorts of the Republican party. In the Masonic fraternity he has received the thirty-second degree of the Scottish Rite and is affiliated also with the Mystic Shrine. He is an influential member of the Fort Wayne Commercial Club, and he and his wife are communicants of Trinity church, Protestant Episcopal. In November, 1879, Mr. Strawbridge wedded Miss Lillian Rogers, daughter of William Rogers, of Fort Wayne, and she passed to the life eternal in June, 1897. The two surviving children of this union are John and William H., the former being employed as salesman for the National Mill & Supply Company, of Fort Wayne, and the latter is, in 1917, a student in the University of New York. On the 14th of March, 1900, was solemnized the marriage of Mr. Strawbridge to Miss Anna Rauner, daughter of Joseph Rauner, of Fort Wayne, and she is the popular chatelaine of the attractive family home.

Herman Strodel has become one of the successful business men and influential citizens of his native city of Fort Wayne, where he was for a long period actively identified with the meat-market business and is now serving with marked efficiency as superintendent of streets, his loyalty and punctilious care being manifest in the excellent condition of the thoroughfares of the city. Mr. Strodel was born at Fort Wayne on March 31, 1874, a son of John G. and Christina Katherine (Werston) Strodel, the former of whom was born in Germany and the latter was born and reared in Fort Wayne, a member of a well-known family of this city, where she continued to reside until her death, which occurred, August 14, 1911. John G. Strodel was a butcher by trade and vocation and was long identified with the saloon business on East Main street in Fort Wayne, the same being the famous Nimrod Hall saloon, known to people in several states. His death occurred, December 27, 1914, both he and his wife having been earnest communicants of the Lutheran church. They became the parents of eight children: Emma died in childhood; Martha is the wife of Charles Jacobs, of Fort Wayne; Pauline is the wife of George Jacobs, of this city; Emma, second of the name, is deceased; Herman, of this sketch, was the fifth child; Otto F. and Frank B. still reside in Fort Wayne, as does also Emma, the third daughter to be given this name, she being now the wife of Henry Schell. Herman Strodel attended the Lutheran parochial schools in his boyhood and when but thirteen years of age began to learn the butcher's trade under the direction of his uncle. With this line of enterprise he continued to be actively identified for twenty-three years and in the meanwhile opened a meat market which he individually conducted three years. Thereafter he was for eight years in the employ of the Bash Packing Company and then associated himself with the firm of Coverdale, Archer & Company, of whose finely equipped Fort Wayne market he was made assistant manager. Of this position he continued the incumbent until February 1, 1914, when he was appointed superintendent of streets for his native city, his admirable administration having resulted in his uninterrupted tenure of this significantly important municipal office. Prior to his assumption of this position he had served three years as a member of the city council, in which body he effectively represented the Ninth ward. Mr. Strodel is a Democrat in his political adherency, and is affiliated with the National Union and with Fort Wayne Lodge of the Benevolent & Protective Order of Elks, of which he served four years as treasurer. On September 29, 1898, was solemnized the marriage of Mr. Strodel to Miss Clara T. Brossard, who likewise was born and reared in Fort Wayne, and of their two children the elder, Casilda C., is living, the younger, John George, having died in infancy.

Justin N. Study.—The reputation of the public schools of Fort Wayne constantly draws to the city representatives from other municipalities who seek to know the means whereby the institution has gained place in the highest rank among the free educational establishments of America. The people of Fort Wayne know that the advanced status of the schools of the city is due to splendid leadership and earnest co-operation. To no one person alone is to be accorded the gratitude and praise of the people, but to the late Justin N. Study, superintendent of the schools from 1896 until his death, which occurred on the evening of August 29, 1917, goes without question the honor of that high degree of leadership which produced the most fully developed and harmonious working of all forces for the most praiseworthy results. Justin N. Study was born in Wayne county, Indiana, son of Samuel and Sarah Study. Following the period of his studies in the public schools of Hagerstown, Indiana, he entered the Ohio Wesleyan University, at Delaware, and in this institution was graduated with the class of 1871. Immediately after leaving the university he entered upon his long period of teaching—in the acceptance of a position as superintendent of the schools at Anderson, Indiana. The success attendant upon his work at Anderson attracted the attention of the school authorities of Greencastle, Indiana, the seat of DePauw University, and he was chosen superintendent of the schools there. After a service of three years in Greencastle, he was elected to the superintendency of the schools of Richmond, Indiana, seat of Earlham College. Here he served with marked success until, in 1896, he was called to Fort Wayne, as the successor to Dr. John S. Irwin in the office of superintendent of schools. To attempt even to suggest the steps whereby the schools of Fort Wayne were developed through the leadership of Superintendent Study and his co-workers would be an impossible task. It is sufficient to say that the great result came through a conscientious application of principles known to be for the best interests of the community—principles recognized by the board of trustees and the instructors who served within the long period of the superintendent's incumbency. During this time, the schools, while keeping pace with all forward steps in educational methods, were free from hasty and unwarranted changes of system. All was accomplished through the quiet application of tried methods and rules. Evolution, not revolution, steady development, not spasmodic effort, marked the progress of the schools. Hundreds of students have been graduated in the high school—fully equipped to enter upon their collegiate courses without question of fitness. For the student who wills it to remain in school to the close of the course, the superintendent had the highest admiration, and to him was ever given the most helpful encouragement; but to the one who deemed it impossible or impracticable to continue to the end of the prescribed period, the superintendent gave of his deepest thought, for he looked upon the public schools as the means to fit the boy and girl for the battle of life, and he recognized nothing as more harmful to the individual and to society than the youth who enters upon life unprepared to meet the problems which must demand acceptance and solution by every individual. So, in order to meet the problems of the one who leaves school before the prescribed course is completed, Superintendent Study pointed the way to success through the medium of the vocational department of the school system, which is open to all legally qualified to enter. It is the design of the vocational schools to provide equipment for life's work to those who feel the handicap of a lack of educational preparedness. Within the period of his incumbency Superintendent Study saw the opening of the Lakeside and the South Wayne schools, in 1897; within his regime six old buildings—the Hanna, Washington, Jefferson, Rudisill, Bloomingdale and Harmar schools—gave way to splendid modern structures; the James H. Smart school was erected; a large number of the other buildings were remodeled or enlarged; the magnificent High and Manual Training school building was erected; and a site for a south side high school was purchased, at the corner of Darrow and South Calhoun streets. The board of trustees also purchased property in other parts of the city, in anticipation of the growth of the needs of the public schools. In every department the schools were provided with the most modern equipment. In the year 1897, through the re-establishment of the normal school, with an extended course of work, a new and higher standard of qualification for teachers was defined, and the same was thoroughly upheld. Reference has been made to the vocational departments. The original school was opened in the Washington building, but the widespread recognition of the value of the plan as applied to the needs of Fort Wayne soon made necessary the separation of the departments. Finally the former plant of the Kerr-Murray Manufacturing Company became available for school use, and this was fully equipped for giving the widest opportunities for education to those who need it in largest measure. In addition to his services in the schools, Superintendent Study took a deep personal interest in many of the movements for the betterment of general conditions. His enviable standing among the representative educators of America is suggested by his connection with the National Educational Association as its vice president; the Indiana State Educational Association as its president, and the Northern Indiana Educational Association as its president, in addition to his active efforts as a member of the Northern Indiana Superintendents' club. As the superintendent of the Fort Wayne schools, he was a member of the State Board of Education. Superintendent Study was for many years prominent in the Masonic activities of Indiana. He was a past master of Webb Lodge, F. & A. M., No. 24, of Richmond, Indiana; past eminent commander of Fort Wayne Commandery, No. 4, Knights Templars, and his influential status in the Ancient Accepted Scottish Rite of Masonry was indicated by his having received therein the thirty-third, and ultimate, degree. He was a Past Grand Regent of the Royal Arcanum of Indiana and a member of the Senate of the National Union Assurance Society, the governing body of that organization. In 1874 he was married to Miss Belle Wiggins, of Hagerstown, Indiana, and to this union five children were born, four daughters and one son, one daughter and the son having died in infancy. The eldest daughter, Mrs. Joseph D. Harper, lives at Dallas, Texas. The second, Mrs. Gibson E. Sisco, lives at Toledo, Ohio, and the youngest, Miss Margery, is at home. Mr. Study was a member of the Wayne Street Methodist Church of Fort Wayne. He also held membership in the Commercial Club of Fort Wayne, and in other civic societies and literary organizations, among them being the Delta Tau Delta College Fraternity.

Elmer W. Stump.—A native son of Allen county and a son of one of the pioneer settlers of this district is Elmer W. Stump, born in Lafayette township on October 16, 1869. His parents were Jonathan and Elizabeth (Bowman) Stump, who came from Ohio to Allen county in 1848, entered a government tract of 160 acres and settled down to grub a home out of the wilderness. Their experience was similar to that of practically every other pioneer of that time, and much credit is due them for the courage and tenacity of purpose that made possible their worthy accomplishments of later years. Mr. Stump added seventy acres to his original holdings and in time a prosperous stock farm took the place of the uncultivated tract he settled on. He was a Republican and served his township as assessor and supervisor for some years. He was an adherent of the Dunkard faith and reared his family in that religion, and no more honored or esteemed man was found in his community in his day than he. A brief period of two years was spent as a resident of

Fort Wayne, but the best years of his life were passed on his farm home, where he died in 1905, after several years of practical retirement from active work. He was twice married. His first wife was the mother of six children. Jennie lives in Lafayette township. Alfa is a resident of Nevada, Missouri. Amanda married Christian Ambler. Mary is the wife of Washington Bolinger, and Sarah and John are deceased. The second wife was Elizabeth Bowman, mother of the subject. Two children were born of this marriage—Elmer and Eli C., living in Fort Wayne. Elmer Stump had his education in the common schools of his community and in Mount Morris College, in Illinois. He prepared himself for the vocation of a teacher, but never applied himself to that work. He was a fireman in Gas City, Indiana, for two years and then entered the Hedge Tool Works of that city, where he was foreman for eleven years. Later he returned to his native community and rented a farm, still later buying a fifty-acre tract and engaging in stock-farming, in which he has been enjoying very favorable success. He has specialized in Durham cattle and his place is known for the cattle it produces. Mr. Stump has made many improvements on his farm since he became its owner and has justly earned the title of successful farmer in the years he has been occupied in his present work. He has various other interests in the township industries. Mr. Stump was married on April 7, 1889, to Miss Luly Morris, daughter of Thomas and Ellen Morris, who came from Ohio to Huntington county, Indiana, and were counted among the early settlers of that county. Mr. and Mrs. Stump have six children and five grandchildren. Gussie, the first born, is the wife of Arby Brandstrator, of Abbott, Indiana. Orval and Otis, twins, are dead. Goldie married Earl Hefner, of Roanoke. Bertha and Harvey live at home. Gussia Brandstrator is the mother of Gussie, Olive, Alice, Alta and Elmer, Alice and Alta being twins. Goldie Hefner has one son, Carl. The family is one of the well established ones of the township and Mr. Stump is recognized as the successor of his esteemed father in those elements of better citizenship that were dominant characteristics in the make-up of that sturdy old settler.

John Suelzer, Jr., was born in Fort Wayne March 30, 1884, son of John and Catherine (Suelzer) Suelzer, both natives of Germany. The father was born in the vicinity of Cologne and came to America, in 1880, the mother following one year later. Mr. Suelzer was a carpenter by trade and came directly to Fort Wayne on arriving in America, engaging in general contracting, which business he has since carried on. Of the ten children born to these parents, all are still living. John, Jr., was educated in St. Peter's Parochial School and completed a commercial course there that fitted him for a position in the offices of the National Biscuit Company when he left school. His next work was with his father in the general contracting business and it was largely due to the son that the father joined him in the organization of an enterprise known as the Fort Wayne Builders' Supply Company. The business was organized in 1904 and young Suelzer was installed as manager at its inception. In 1905 they found the business growing beyond their available capital, so they incorporated it, thus adding new capital to the enterprise. The Fort Wayne Builders' Supply Company began its business career with three city lots and a few small buildings. They have added to their holdings from year to year until they have at the present time almost two acres of ground space. Commencing with five employees, they now have thirty-five, and Mr. Suelzer feels justified in making the claim that their concern has made greater strides in advancement than any other similar establishment in the city. They handle a complete line of building materials, excepting only hardware, glass and paints. Lumber, lime and cement make up a large part of their stock. They operate a planing mill and are prepared to get out anything and everything in woodwork, with special attention to architects' details. The growth of the firm speaks more convincingly of the character of the service this concern stands for than any words might convey. Mr. Suelzer was married on June 22, 1916, to Miss Marie Berghoff, native of Fort Wayne and daughter of G. A. Berghoff, engaged in the soap manufacturing business here. They are members of the Roman Catholic church, and Mr. Suelzer is affiliated with the Knights of Columbus, the Benevolent and Protective Order of Elks and the Commercial Club of Fort Wayne.

Eliza Ann Suter.—Particularly worthy of mention in a work devoted to a record of the lives of the pioneers of the county is the name of Elizabeth Ann (Chaffner) Suter, who is a resident of Lafayette township. She came to this part of the state when it required a courage amounting almost to heroism to take upon one's self the burden of life in a wilderness region, and she bore her full share in the arduous work of carving a home out of the forest and establishing the family name in the county. She was born in Stark county, Ohio, November 15, 1833, a daughter of Martin and Susan (Leece) Chaffner, who were native born Germans, coming to America in the early days when the sailing vessel was yet in vogue, and it is a noteworthy fact that they were ninety days making the trip. They settled in Stark county, Ohio, reared their family and there spent the remainder of their lives in comparative ease. Their daughter, Elizabeth Ann, married Jacob Suter, in 1862, and together they came to Lafayette, Allen county, and applied themselves with all of courage and fortitude to their self-imposed task of making a home in a new country. They knew all the rigors of life in the wilderness, but many joys were theirs that later generations may not know. They gradually improved their land until it was one of the fine homes in the township and the land that was theirs for the taking then has come to have a market value they would not have guessed in the wildest flights of imagination. They were the parents of six children. Mary is the wife of William Feightner, of Lafayette township. Daniel is on the old home place. Emma is deceased. Elizabeth is the wife of Charles Smith, living in Lafayette township. Catherine married James Malon and Jennie is deceased. There are eleven grandchildren. Mary, the eldest daughter, is the mother of Anna, Charlie, Margaretta, Adda, Sadie and Russell, and Catherine, the youngest living child of the subject, is the mother of Clara, Ethel, Ralph, Clarence and Jennie, all living but the last named, who died in infancy. Three great-grandchildren should also be mentioned. They are Eveline, the daughter of Charles Feightner; Selda, the daughter of Margaretta, and Virgil, the son of Adda, all the grandchildren of Mary (Suter) Feightner. Mrs. Suter is living on the old home place at the advanced age of eighty-four years, and is one of the honored residents of the community she has so long called home. She is loved of all who know her and the record of her years of labor in the village she helped to make will go down in the hearts of many who knew her as well as on printed page.

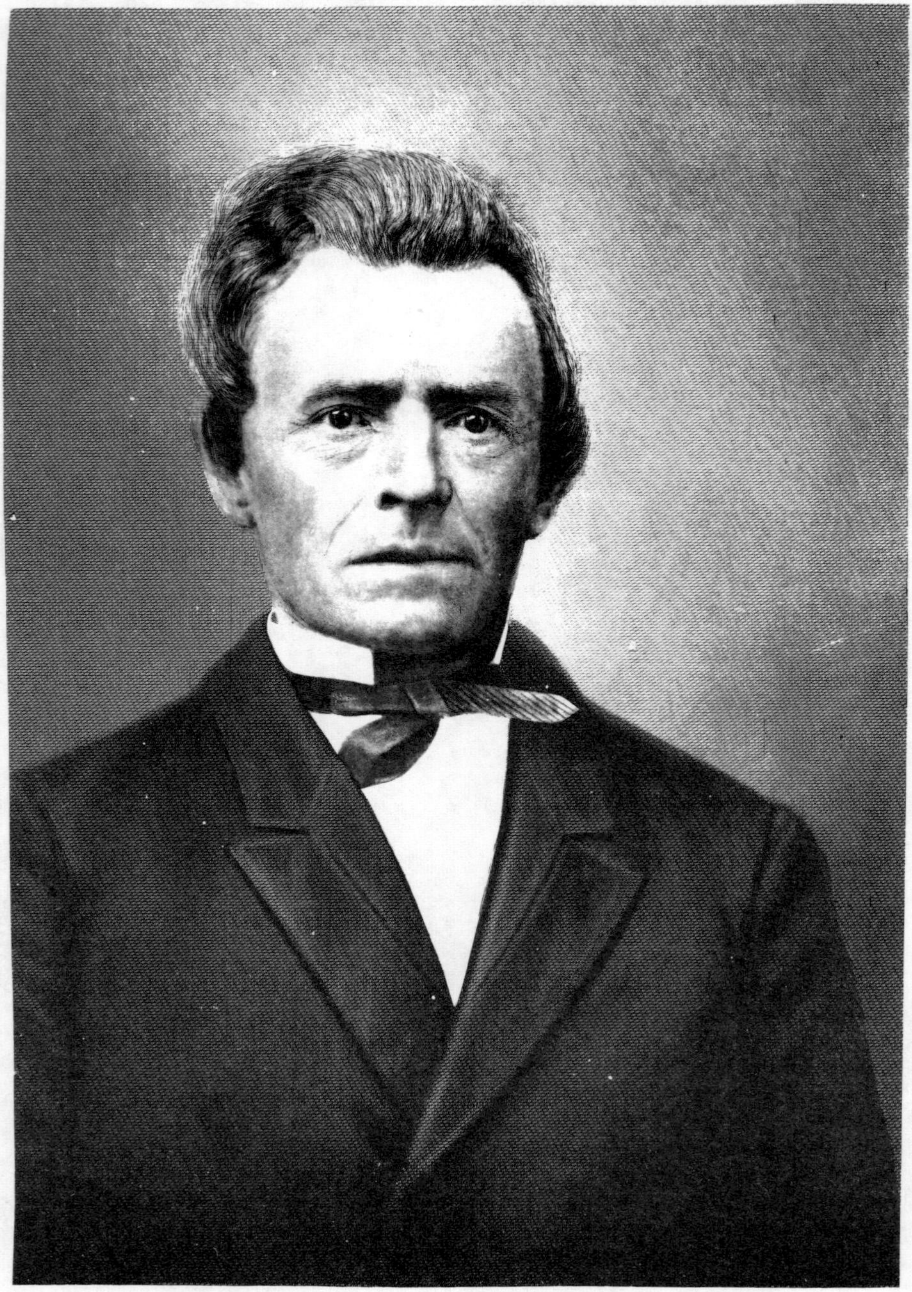

Thos W Swinney

Edward Swank, born in Pleasant township, Allen county, January 16, 1879, is a son of David and Anna (Stanton) Swank, who were native Ohioans. The father was of German descent but the mother came of Scotch and English parents. Mr. and Mrs. Swank came to Allen county in the late forties and settled on a farm of eighty acres, on which they have lived down to the present time, with exception of a period of about five years. Mr. Swank is a Democrat and was township assessor for twenty-five years, an office he filled with much satisfaction to his fellow townspeople. They were the parents of ten children. Irvin, the eldest, is a resident of Chicago. M. lives in Wallin, Indiana. Alonzo is a resident of Houston, Texas. Mason lives in Pleasant township. Thomas is a farmer in Sheldon. Stephen is in Fort Wayne, Indiana. Wesley lives in Sheldon, Indiana. Edward, the subject, is the eighth child. Flora is the wife of Stephen Kenert, of Fort Wayne. Grover is also a resident of Fort Wayne. Edward Swank had his education in the Pleasant township schools and never left the home farm. He has done his full share in building up the place and bringing it to its present state of productiveness and prosperity and has manifested the traits of a natural farmer. He is a Democrat and a man of influence in his community. He was married on November 26, 1902, to Miss Louisa Madden, the daughter of Dennis and Mary Madden, of Wallen, Allen county, both of whom are deceased. Mr. and Mrs. Swank have three children—Leslie, Howard and Helen, all at home.

Thomas W. Swinney.—The time shall not come when Allen county and the city of Fort Wayne can justly fail to pay a tribute of honor to the sterling pioneer to whom this brief memoir is dedicated and whose name is perpetuated, whose civic loyalty and generosity given enduring distinction in the beautiful Swinney Park, which was by him presented to Fort Wayne and which has been developed into one of the finest constituent portions of the park system of the Allen county metropolis and judicial center. This park passes into the full possession of the city upon the death of Misses Caroline and Frances E. Swinney, daughters of the honored pioneer to whom this tribute is dedicated, they having continued to reside in the attractive old homestead in Fort Wayne for the long period of seventy years, and the only other surviving child being Margaret, who likewise maintains her residence in Fort Wayne. Thomas W. Swinney was born at Piketon, Pike county, Ohio, on November 3, 1803, less than one year after the admission of Ohio as one of the sovereign states of the Union, and his parents were numbered among the earliest settlers of Pike county, where he himself was reared to manhood under the conditions and influences that marked pioneer life on the frontier. Mr. Swinney made good use of such educational advantages as time and place afforded and through self-discipline developed his strong mentality as well as the sturdy physical powers that admirably equipped him for the labors and responsibilities of a pioneer in Indiana, where he established his home within the first decade after the admission of the state to the Union. At some time between the years 1820 and 1824 Mr. Swinney came to Fort Wayne, which was then represented principally by the old frontier fort, around which had been developed a little settlement. He purchased a considerable body of wild land in Allen county and was one of the earliest and most successful exponents of agricultural industry in this section of the state. With the passing of the years and the rapid settlement and development of the county hereabouts, his land holdings greatly appreciated in value and he became one of the substantial men and influential citizens of Allen county, the closing years of his life having been passed in the old homestead now occupied by his two daughters, in Fort Wayne, and the place being one of the veritable landmarks of the city. Mr. Swinney passed from the stage of life's mortal endeavors on January 20, 1875, and his loved and devoted wife was summoned to eternal rest on May 20, 1860. He was a staunch advocate of the cause of the Republican party, with which he aligned himself at the time of its organization, and served for some time as justice of the peace, as did he also in the office of overseer of the poor. In December, 1827, was solemnized the marriage of Mr. Swinney to Miss Lucy Taber, daughter of Paul Taber, one of the prominent and honored pioneer citizens of Fort Wayne. Of the children of this union three are living, Margaret, Caroline and Frances E., the latter two, as previously stated, remaining in the old homestead which has been their place of abode for three score years and ten and which is endeared to them by the hallowed memories and associations of the past. They keep in touch with modern sentiment and progress, but find solace and compensation in holding themselves aside from the "madding crowd's ignoble strife." By the provisions made by their father in the connection they retain until death a vested interest in the beautiful Swinney Park, which thereafter is to pass into the absolute control of the city.

Robert S. Taylor.—Recognized and honored as the dean of the bar of Allen county, Judge Robert Stewart Taylor enjoys the respect of countless friends who, in his later years, exhibit in every way their appreciation of his value as a citizen and a lawyer. He was born near the city of Chillicothe, Ross county, Ohio, on May 22, 1838, son of Rev. Isaac N. and Margaretta (Stewart) Taylor. The father was a Presbyterian minister, a pioneer of his church in western Ohio and one who was located in turn at Celina and St. Mary's, Ohio, before removing, in 1844, with his family to Jay county, Indiana. The mother of Judge Taylor was born February 14, 1818, and died February 14, 1889. Rev. Isaac N. and Margaretta (Stewart) Taylor were the parents of eight children—Robert S., Esther C., William J., Sophia, Isaac N., Jr., Samuel R., John W. and Bertha. The father, after locating in Indiana, founded a school known as Liber College, near Portland, and in this well-conducted institution many young men of that section of the state received valuable instruction from the father of Judge Taylor. The latter here obtained the excellent preliminary training which naturally followed the instruction he received in the common schools. He was graduated in Liber College in the spring of 1858. Within a few minutes thereafter was solemnized his marriage to Miss Fanny W. Wright, of Randolph county, a young woman whose charming traits of character developed and ripened with the succeeding years; her death occurred in Fort Wayne, in 1913. Judge Taylor commenced the reading of law under the preceptorship of Judge Jacob M. Haynes, of Portland. In November, 1859, Judge and Mrs. Taylor removed to Fort Wayne, and here he continued his law studies, besides spending a portion of his time in teaching school. In November, 1860, he became a clerk in the office of Judge Lindley M. Ninde, a prominent member of the Allen county bar. Two years later the partnership of Ninde & Taylor was formed. In 1866 Colonel Robert S. Robertson became a member of the firm, and for

R. S. Taylor

six years it was one of the most prominent and influential in northern Indiana. In 1868, upon the establishment of the criminal court in Fort Wayne, Judge Taylor was appointed its first prosecuting attorney. In this same year the firm of Ninde, Taylor & Robertson was dissolved and Judge Taylor was appointed judge of the court of common pleas, which position he held until the following election, when he was chosen to represent Allen county in the Indiana general assembly. While a member of this body he introduced the bill that made possible the street car system of Fort Wayne. In 1874 he was the Republican candidate for Congress in the Twelfth congressional district, his opponent being Holman H. Hamilton. In 1880 he was again the candidate of his party for congressional honors, in opposition to Walpole G. Colerick. Both times he met defeat, but the normal Democratic majority was so greatly reduced as to indicate clearly his wide popularity. Judge Taylor has ever been recognized as a leader of his party in Indiana. A ready writer, clear in diction and forceful in logic, he speaks with influence upon any subject to which he gives his thoughtful attention. In March, 1881, Judge Taylor was appointed by President Garfield a member of the important Mississippi River Commission, to succeed Benjamin Harrison, and this position he held through successive presidential appointments for more than thirty years, his service having continued until March 10, 1913. Since 1883 Judge Taylor has devoted his attention to patent law. He is a Presbyterian, a member of the Commercial Club, and affiliated with organizations of various kinds which value highly his connection and his ever-ready assistance. The only child born to Judge and Mrs. Taylor is Frank B. Taylor, who was born, November 23, 1860. He is a geologist whose capabilities have been repeatedly recognized by the United States and Canadian governments. He is·an authority on the post-glacial geology of the Great Lakes region.

Rev. Charles Thiele, rector of St. Peter's church at Fort Wayne, was born June 22, 1863, at Leer, Oestfriesland, Hanover, Germany. At the age of three years he came with his parents to Baltimore, Maryland. A few years later they moved to Goshen, Indiana, where he spent his boyhood and received his early education. In 1879 he began a classical course at Notre Dame University, after which he was sent to St. Francis' Seminary at Milwaukee for his philosophical and theological courses. He was ordained priest by Bishop Dwenger in the Cathedral at Fort Wayne, June 29, 1888. In July he was appointed pastor at Monterey, remaining until August, 1898, when he was transferred to Sacred Heart church, at Whiting. June 7, 1905, he was named irremovable rector at St. Peter's church at Fort Wayne.

J. Gottlieb Thieme, vice-president and manager of the Thieme Brothers Company, was born in Fort Wayne on December 25, 1862, a son of Frederick J. Thieme, who was one of the old and honored citizens of Allen county at the time of his death. Mr. Thieme gained his early education in the parochial and public schools and supplemented this by a course in Concordia College. As a youth he learned the tailor's trade, to which he gave his attention about six years. He thereafter was associated with his brother, John A., in the conducting of a merchant tailor business, at 118 West Berry street, until 1907, when he assumed full control of the enterprise. In 1909 he sold the business and became one of the interested principals in the Thieme Brothers Company, manufacturers of silk hosiery, of which he is now vice-president and manager. His political allegiance is given to the Republican party and he is known as one of the liberal and progressive citizens and representative business men of his native city. He holds membership in the Fort Wayne Commercial and Country Clubs, is affiliated with the various York and Scottish Rite bodies of the Masonic fraternity, as well as the Mystic Shrine, and both he and his wife are communicants of Trinity Lutheran church. On June 14, 1898, Mr. Thieme wedded Miss Mary Adams, daughter of Morgan O. Adams, of Yellow Springs, Ohio, and the two children of this union are Morgan and Virginia.

Theodore F. Thieme.—In every progressive city of America a limited number of men are pointed out as the leaders of the public thought in their community. Theodore F. Thieme is one of these, and to his untiring efforts to make Fort Wayne a better and more representative city of America we owe much of the present position of Fort Wayne among the municipalities of the middle west. As the man who believed that Fort Wayne could become the seat of a great knitting factory and who, through his integrity, his energy and his courage, as well as through his initiative and executive ability, made the dream a glorious reality, he has the satisfaction of knowing that today the products of the Wayne Knitting Mills, of which he was the founder and is the president and general manager, are known throughout America. Mr. Thieme was born in Fort Wayne, on February 7, 1857, a son of Frederick J. and Clara Thieme, both of whom are deceased. The father was for many years a prominent clothing merchant and influential citizen. Theodore F. Thieme gained his early educational discipline in the public schools of Fort Wayne and in Concordia College of this city. Upon leaving school he determined upon a commercial career and decided to take up the study of pharmacy, with the result that he went to New York and entered upon a course of study in the New York College of Pharmacy, in which institution he was graduated as a member of the class of 1876. He engaged in business in New York city for a time and then came back to Fort Wayne, where he opened a drug store which became one of the leading retail establishments of the city. Even at this early period in his career Mr. Thieme was a deep student of large affairs and in 1889 sold his drug business in order to go to Europe to investigate several lines of manufacture that were influenced by the application of the McKinley tariff law. In Chemnitz, Germany, he became deeply interested in the knitting industry and here spent an entire winter investigating the business, with a view to the establishing of knitting mills in his home city. He was thoroughly convinced that the project could be carried to a successful conclusion, and so, upon his return, succeeded in interesting a sufficient number of citizens to organize the Wayne Knitting Mills, with a capital of thirty thousand dollars. Returning to Germany, Mr. Thieme purchased machinery with which to equip the mills and brought back a number of skilled knitters to operate the machines and to serve as instructors to others who would join them. The business was started in a small way, in rented quarters at the northeast corner of Clinton and Main streets. The chief difficulties to be overcome at the beginning were the opposition of foreign manufacturers and the ever-present stumbling block of local prejudice. However, dealers were finally convinced of the superiority of the Wayne Knit hosiery, and in 1892 the company built and equipped its first mill. From that time until today the plant has gradually been enlarged until its various departments now utilize 403,859 square feet of space. Fort Wayne has proved to be an excellent place of location for these mills and, fortunately, here has been found a class of workmen who appreciate the fact that the employer has their every interest at heart. This was early manifested when the company established a profit-sharing plan and every modern provision that bespeaks co-operation and fellowship. In 1910 the company established the Wayne Knit clubhouse, at a cost of fifty thousand dollars, in order to provide for its employes every social advantage as well as the means of athletic exercise. The building contains commodious dining-rooms, a lecture room with stage for dramatic and other entertainments, and various clubs and organizations composed of the employes of the mills use the clubhouse as a community center. Its influence has induced other Fort Wayne manufacturers to give deeper thought to the welfare of their employes. In 1909 Mr. Thieme took up, in a thoroughly businesslike way, the question of better city government. While on a trip to Europe he gave much time and thought to the methods followed by European cities in the attainment of objects which are not often found in American cities. Combining the result of his investigations with much that he had learned from the foremost students of this subject, Mr. Thieme has exerted a wide influence throughout the state of Indiana in bringing about improved conditions in the cities of Hoosierdom. He prepared the so-called "business system of city government" charter, modeled after the well-known plan in use in all progressive European countries. He was the organizer and is at present (1917) the chairman of the Citizens' League of Indiana, which was foremost in the fight for a new state constitution, home rule for cities, taxation reforms and other fundamental measures in the interest of modern economical government. Mr. Thieme is a director and officer in a number of leading industries, banks and trust companies, and while he has never held public office and is not engaged in partisan politics nevertheless takes an active interest in public affairs and especially in all political reforms. In 1894 Mr. Thieme wedded Miss Bessie Loring, of Boston, and they have one son, Wayne Thieme. The town house of the family is situated at West Berry and Rockhill streets, and the country home, southwest of the city, on the Covington road, is one of the handsomest rural estates of this community.

Theodore Thimlar.—One of the prosperous and prominent men of New Haven is Theodore Thimlar, director of the State Bank, retired farmer of Milan township, and prominently connected with a number of the leading lumber concerns in this part of the state. Mr. Thimlar was born in Milan township, Allen county, on September 6, 1856, and his parents were John and Annie Thimlar, both natives of Berlin, Germany. They came to America after their marriage and located in Salem, Ohio, where the father was identified with farming operations. In 1854 they came to Milan township, bought a farm and in connection with agricultural activities, Mr. Thimlar devoted some time to his trade as a stonemason. He prospered and was able to retire from active work some ten years before his death. He was a Democrat and a member of the German Lutheran church, and for a number of years was a member of the Board of Supervisers for his township. Nine children were born to these people. Theodore, whose name heads this brief family sketch, was the first born. Then came Charles, a resident of Milan township and a prominent man of his community. Adeline is the wife of Daniel Stauffer, of Milan township. Cora B. married L. B. Lindsay, of Lakeside, Indiana. Levi lives in Milan township. Franklin and John have homes in Springfield township. Byron is a resident of Adams township and Walter lives in Harlan, Indiana. Theodore Thimlar, as the eldest son, carried some of the responsibility of carrying on the farming operations conducted by his father. He had a common school education, and when he was twenty-one years old he left home for the first time. He went to New York state and there was employed for a year on a hop farm. Returning to his home, he next ventured into Michigan, where he made his first acquaintance with the lumber business. He spent a winter in the pine woods of that state, then famous for its lumber industries, and returning again to his native community, he bought a small tract of twenty-three acres of land in Milan township. This acreage formed the nucleus of his present fine place of about 460 acres, and for years he devoted himself almost exclusively to farming and its allied industries. He later identified himself with various lumber concerns, and at this time is a director in the New Haven Lumber Company & Green House and a part owner in the Monroeville Lumber Company. When the Peoples State Bank was organized he was one of the leading spirits in the enterprise and has from the beginning served as president of the institution and as a member of its directorate. Mr. Thimlar is a member of St. John's church (Roman Catholic) and is a Democrat in politics. He was married on May 29, 1882, to Henrietta, daughter of Bernard and Annie Barba, of Cedar Creek township, Allen county. Mr. and Mrs. Thimlar have the following named children: Wylie J., of Fort Wayne, Indiana; John, who is deceased; Almeda, of Fort Wayne; Hugh, living in Milan township; Cora, living at home; Cleatus, of Fort Wayne, Indiana, Barbara and Theodore living at home.

Barney Tibbet, whose death occurred August 23, 1912, about one month prior to the seventieth anniversary of his birth, had long been known and honored as one of the sterling citizens and representative farmers of Adams township and was a member of one of the pioneer families of Allen county, where he passed his entire life and where his character and achievement so marked him as worthy of the confidence of his fellow men that it is specially consistent that in this history be entered a tribute to his memory. Mr. Tibbet was born in Allen county on September 28, 1842, and was a son of Herman and Adeline (Holtal) Tibbet, both of whom were born in the Kingdom of Hanover, Germany, and both of whom passed the closing period of their lives on their old homestead farm in Allen county, their names meriting high place on the roll of the honored pioneers of the county. Of their five children the subject of this memoir was the eldest, and all of the others are now deceased—Katherine, Mrs. Mary Brames, Rosa and Theodore. Barney Tibbet acquired his early education in the parochial school of St. Mary's Catholic church in Fort Wayne, and he thereafter remained with his parents on the old homestead farm until they were summoned to the life eternal. He assisted his father in the reclaiming of the farm, near New Haven, and had his full quota of pioneer experience. Mr. Tibbet found profit and satisfaction in his continued allegiance to the fundamental industries of agriculture and stock-raising and his widow and children still reside on the fine old homestead farm of eighty acres, in Section 11, Adams township. Mr. Tibbet was a man of strong mentality, broad views and indefatigable industry. He accomplished much as one of the world's productive workers and in addition to his farm became the owner of a valuable business block in New Haven, this property having been sold since his death by his widow, who was made the executrix of the estate. Mr. Tibbet took a loyal interest in all things touching the communal welfare, was a Democrat in politics, and he served two terms as trustee of Adams township. At New Haven he was affiliated with the Catholic Knights of America and with St. John's Benevolent Society, and there also he was a zealous and honored communicant of St. John's Catholic church, in which his widow and children retain active membership. June 22, 1871, recorded the marriage of Mr. Tibbet to Miss Josephine Pripsing, whose death occurred February 19, 1888, the only child of this union having been Catherine, who died in infancy. On August 19, 1890, was solemnized the marriage of Mr. Tibbet to Miss Caroline Reville, who was born and reared in this county, the date of her nativity having been May 16, 1866. Mrs. Tibbet is a daughter of Adolph and Mary (Cramer) Reville, the former of whom was born in France and the latter in Germany, the father having come to America in 1852 and the mother, as a child, in 1839. Mrs. Tibbet was the second in a family of eight children, and the names of the others are here recorded: Fannie, John, Mary, Ernest, Eli, Alice, and Frank. John and Eli are now deceased. The children of Mr. and Mrs. Tibbet, and the respective dates of birth, are: John J., September 28, 1891; Helena F. was born April 12, 1893, and died on February 11 of the following year; Clarence J., December 31, 1894; Alice M., January 17, 1897; Anna J., March 17, 1899; Edwin F., June 6, 1901; and Eugene B. and Agnes C., twins, June 2, 1905. All of the surviving children remain with their mother on the old homestead and the family is one of prominence and popularity in the social life of the community.

Henry Till.—The fine farm home of Henry Till, long a resident of Washington township, is a splendid example of thrift and progressiveness and a credit alike to its owner and to the community. Mr. Till has demonstrated the practical value of every modern method known to successful farming in this section of the country, and has been ready at all times to accept the new idea and discard the old one, when he had proven to his satisfaction that the newer idea had more to recommend it than did its predecessor. These tactics have won for him an unqualified success in his chosen work, and his opinions are sought after by his fellow townsmen. Mr. Till was born on June 13, 1855, in Ohio, son of Nicholas and Catherine (Loss) Till, both of German birth and ancestry, who came to Ohio as young people, settling with their respective families in Hocking county. They married there and continued to live in Hocking county, Ohio, until 1885, when they came to Allen county, Indiana, settled on a farm in Washington township, and there spent the remainder of their lives in farming activities. Their six children were Nicholas, Henry, Fred, Michael, George and Joseph. Henry Till had his schooling in Hocking county, Ohio, and when the family moved into Allen county, in 1883, he accompanied them and turned his attention to farm work, in which he has ever since been actively engaged. Today Mr. Till is the owner of two hundred and twelve acres of valuable farm land in Washington township, and his place, as has already been stated, is a model of modern improvements, well tiled and fenced, and boasting fine and commodious barns and dwelling. Mr. Till was married on September 7, 1880, to Miss Mary Ellen Judy, daughter of Joseph and Catherine (Kinkler) Judy. The father was a native Pennsylvanian and the mother was born in Ohio and there reared. Joseph Judy came from Pennsylvania to Ohio, there met and married his wife, and there, in Hocking county, they spent their remaining years. They were the parents of eleven children, the first child being Mary Ellen, wife of the subject. The others were Frank, Louisa, John, Augustus, William, Charles, John, Victor, Thomas and Edward. It will be noted there are two named John. The first one died as a little child and another child was named for him in later years, who is also now deceased. William, Victor, Thomas and Edward are no longer living, and it is worthy of mention here that three of these died of smallpox in less than six weeks' time. To Mr. and Mrs. Till have been born ten children. They are Joseph, William, Michael, Nicholas, Leo, Thomas, Lawrence, John, Albert and Bertha. This is indeed a remarkable family, and it should be mentioned that five of the sons—Joseph, Michael, Leo, Thomas and Lawrence—are members of the Knights of Columbus, all having membership in Council No. 451 at Fort Wayne. One son, William, died in 1908. The family are communicants of St. Vincent's Roman Catholic church.

Albert Tomkinson.—When Albert Tomkinson came from England to America and applied himself to his trade as a plumber, he was a young man just twenty-one years old. He located at Youngstown, Ohio, first, and after five years came to Fort Wayne, spending ten years as a journeyman plumber, and in 1897 was able to open a shop on his own responsibility. He has since continued to enjoy a favorable patronage in the city, where his ten years of actual experience demonstrated incontrovertibly his native ability and his thorough understanding of his work. Mr. Tomkinson was born in England on December 10, 1861, a son of James and Mary (Leek) Tomkinson, both natives of England, where they passed their entire lives. The father was a prosperous contractor in brick and stone in his community. Their two sons came to America, in 1882, Leonard Tomkinson also being a resident of Fort Wayne, there engaged in business. Mr. Tomkinson has been established in Fort Wayne for the past twenty years, and conducts a thriving business in plumbing, heating and gas fitting, his establishment being one of the foremost of its kind in the city. On January 9, 1882, Mr. Tomkinson was married to Miss Pemila Ann Gater, who like himself was of English origin. Nine children have come to them—five sons and four daughters. Mary is the wife of Stillman Brokaw, who is mentioned elsewhere in this work. Joseph J. lives in Fort Wayne. Elizabeth is the wife of Thomas Hart, of Fort Wayne. Albert and John are both residents of Fort Wayne. Pemila is the wife of Wade Verweire, of Fort Wayne, and the three youngest children—Phoebe, William and Martha—are still at home. Mr. Tomkinson is a Republican and a member of the Episcopal church, his family also having membership in that body, and he is a thirty-second degree Mason, a Shriner and a member of the Sons of St. George, the latter identifying him unmistakably with his British origin.

John H. Trautman is another of the native sons of Allen county who is here doing his part in upholding the high standard of agricultural and live-stock industry, his well-improved farm, comprising fifty acres, being eligibly situated in Section 32, Aboite township. His homestead is about six miles distant from Roanoke, Huntington county, and from that village he receives service on rural mail route No. 4. Mr. Trautman was born in Fort Wayne, June 18, 1866, a son of Jacob and

Elizabeth (Swartz) Trautman. Jacob Trautman was born and reared in Marion township, this county, where his parents settled in the early pioneer days, and as a youth he learned the trade of blacksmith, under the direction of his father, who was a skilled workman. For twelve years Jacob Trautman was employed as a skilled mechanic in the Fort Wayne shops of the Pennsylvania Railroad, and for the ensuing seven years he farmed on rented land. Finally he purchased a farm of eighty acres, in Aboite township, where he is now living in retirement and in the enjoyment of the rewards of former years of earnest endeavor. His devoted wife is still with him in gracious companionship that has covered a period of more than sixty years. Of their children the subject of this review is the eldest; Frederick and David are successful farmers in Aboite township; Miss Catherine is a dressmaker by vocation and now resides in the city of Springfield, Illinois; Charles has established a home in the state of Oklahoma; Jay is employed as a brakeman on the Pennsylvania Railroad; William is a resident of Oklahoma; and Harry and Mary remain at the parental home. John H. Trautman profited by the advantages afforded in the public schools and after his school days continued to assist in the work of the home farm for several years. Thereafter he was employed by the month at farm work until he went to Fort Wayne and gave his attention to learning the plasterer's trade. He did not long continue in the work of his trade, for in the late '80s he resumed his association with agricultural industry. He farmed on rented land several years and, in 1897, purchased his present farm, on which he has made good improvements and which he has brought up to a high state of productiveness. Like his father, he accords a staunch allegiance to the Democratic party and is always ready to do his part in the furtherance of those measures that tend to advance the civic and material welfare of the community. On March 20, 1890, Mr. Trautman married Miss Lucy Jackson, who likewise was born and reared in this county and who is a daughter of the late John and Mary (Scherrick) Jackson, the former a native of North Carolina and the latter of Ohio. John Jackson, who was a valiant soldier in his country's service, passed the major part of his life in Allen county, and here both he and his wife died. Of their children the eldest is John, who is residing on his farm in Lafayette township; Jacob is deceased; Peter is a resident of Fort Wayne; Hannah is the wife of Alfred Heckman, of Huntington county; Lydia is the wife of Henry Adams, of Sheldon, Allen county; Thomas resides in Fort Wayne; and Lucy, wife of the subject of this review, is the youngest of the daughters. Mr. and Mrs. Trautman have but one child, a daughter, Fay, who is a member of the class of 1917 in the Roanoke high school.

John Trautman, who is now living retired in the city of Fort Wayne, is one of the well-known, venerable and honored citizens of the Allen county metropolis, which represented his home for many years and in which his activities in the past were of varied order, including effective and prolonged service as a member of the city police department. He was born in Stark county, Ohio, on October 23, 1835, and thus passed the age of four-score years, though his sturdy and vigorous life in the past has given him splendid vigor that is so pronounced that he has the appearance and vitality of a man many years his junior. Mr. Trautman is a son of George and Mary M. (Lameron) Trautman, both of whom passed the closing years of their lives on their old homestead farm in

Marion township, this county. George Trautman was born and reared in Baden, Germany, whence he immigrated to America in 1833. He established his residence in Stark county, Ohio, and there followed for a number of years the trade of blacksmith, which he had learned in his native land. After coming to Allen county, Indiana, he eventually became the owner of a farm of forty acres, in Marion township, and there passed the remainder of his long and useful life, his political support having been given to the Democratic party and both he and his wife having been members of the Lutheran church. Of their children the subject of this skecth is the first born, and the names of the others are here noted: Charles, Jacob, Peter, Henry, Casper, Frederick, Edward, Alice, Sarah, Margaret and George. John Trautman was about one year old at the time of the family removal to this county and acquired his early education in the pioneer schools of Marion township, in the meanwhile assisting in his father's blacksmith shop. As a skilled workman he was thereafter associated with his father in conducting the shop and business, and later was employed six years as a blacksmith in the Fort Wayne shops of the Pennsylvania Railroad. For several years he was engaged in teaming and next became a member of the Fort Wayne police force, with which he continued his effective service for the long period of eighteen years. In 1905 Mr. Trautman bought in Fort Wayne a well-equipped sporting goods store, to which he gave the name of The Emporium, and this he successfully conducted until 1914, since which time he has lived in well-earned retirement, his pleasant home, a property owned by him, being at 414 East Wayne street. As a city officer in the police department Mr. Trautman naturally took deep interest in municipal affairs and has always given unqualified allegiance to the Democratic party, in behalf of whose cause he has given effective service. October 8, 1864, recorded the marriage of Mr. Trautman to Miss Mary Gutermuth, daughter of the late George Gutermuth, who was a native of Germany and who became one of the sterling pioneers of Allen county, Indiana, where he established his home in 1836 and where he and his wife, Gertrude, passed the residue of their lives. To Mr. and Mrs. Trautman have been born ten children, namely: George, Emma, Henry, Louisa, Jacob, John, Jr., Sarah, Mary, Samuel and Rebecca. Mr. Trautman has lived a vigorous, upright and useful life and in the gracious evening of his days is enjoying the rewards for former endeavors, the while his circle of friends is limited only by that of his acquaintances.

Dayton S. Trease.—Dayton S. Trease was born in Cedar Creek township, Allen county, Indiana, November 3, 1859, son of George W. and Rosanna (Macafee) Trease, both native-born Pennsylvanians. George Trease came to Ohio with his parents as a boy, and later, in 1845, settled in Cedar Creek township, the parents both dying there well advanced in years. He married and reared a family of eight children—Mary, James, John, Elsie, Minnie, Margaret, Alice and Dayton S. Mary, John and Margaret are deceased. Dayton S. Trease had his education in the common schools of Cedar Creek township, and early identified himself with farm life, in which he is still actively engaged. He is owner of fifty-two and a half acres of land in St. Joseph township and has an interest in one hundred and thirteen acres of the undivided estate of his father, in Cedar Creek township. Mr. Trease has a well-improved farm, reflecting no little credit upon his energy and good management.

and his new and modern home is one of the finest in the township. He was married on February 14, 1883, to Harriet Tonkel, daughter of Henry and Frances (Cuttet) Tonkel, both born in France, and settlers in Stark county, Ohio, in early youth. They located in Cedar Creek township, in 1862, and there spent the closing years of their lives. They had ten children—Louis, Joseph, August, Hattie, Mary, Josephine, Henry, George, Frank and William, all living but Henry. Mr. and Mrs. Trease have no children.

Eugene G. Trenkley.—The late Eugene George Trenkley passed his entire life in Fort Wayne and from his youth until his death was here actively identified with the jewelry business, in which domain of enterprise he may consistently be said to have grown up, for his father had long been proprietor of the well-equipped jewelry establishment to which he himself eventually fell heir, his early and practical experience in the business having admirably fortified him for the conducting of the same when he assumed control, and his record having been that of a successful and prosperous jeweler and representative business man of his native city. Mr. Trenkley was born in Fort Wayne, at 336 West Washington street, on October 27, 1874, and died at his pleasant home at 1224 Fairfield avenue, in April, 1915. He was a son of Celestine and Emily (Greve) Trenkley, the former of whom was born in Siemonswold, in the historic Black Forest of Germany, and the latter was a native of Switzerland. Eugene George Trenkley was the third in a family of six children, the others being Edward, Theodore, Arthur, Clara and Edna. When the honored father passed from the stage of life's mortal endeavors none of the heirs seemed so well fitted to carry on the jewelry business as Eugene G., who had passed much time in the establishment and understood the business thoroughly. He admitted to partnership in the business Robert Koerber, and they successfully continued the business which had been established by Celestine Trenkley, the father, in the early '60s. When Eugene G. Trenkley died, in 1915, his widow came into possession of his share of the business, in which she has since continued her interest, as a principal in the incorporated firm of Trenkley & Koerber. Mr. Trenkley had a wide circle of friends in the business and social life of his native city and was actively affiliated with the Fort Wayne Lodge of Elks. On November 29, 1913, was solemnized his marriage to Miss Emma A. Bulger, who likewise was born and reared in Fort Wayne and who is a daughter of Patrick J. and Mary Jane (Ryan) Bulger, the former born in County Carlow, the city of Dublin, Ireland, and the latter in Fort Wayne. Mr. Bulger for many years conducted one of the largest trucking lines in Fort Wayne and in this connection handled the wares of many of the leading business houses in the city. He died, November 9, 1914, his wife having passed away, June 15, 1898. Of their six children Mrs. Trenkley is the only one now living. The names of the deceased children were Charles J., Ida, John, Nellie and George. Mr. and Mrs. Trenkley had no children.

George F. Trier may consistently be designated as a scion of one of the sterling pioneer families of Allen county and in the city of Fort Wayne has made for himself a place of prominence and influence both in business and social circles—in fact, his very vocation is one that touches most closely both the social and business affairs of the community, as he has been actively associated with his wife in the development and upbuilding of a thoroughly metropolitan dancing academy that receives a representative supporting patronage and figures largely in the social life of the city. George F. Trier was born at Fort Wayne on November 8, 1876, and has here continuously maintained his home save for a period of three years during which the family resided in Kansas, when he was a youth. In his native city his circle of friends is coincident with that of his acquaintances and he is specially entitled to recognition in this publication. George Frederick Trier is a son of Henry and Wilhelmina (Meier) Trier, the former of whom was born in Allen county, Indiana, November 27, 1838, and the latter in Hessen-Cassel, Germany, their marriage having been solemnized, November 25, 1864. Mrs. Trier was left an orphan in her childhood and was fourteen years old when she came with friends to America, her home finally being established at Fort Wayne, where her marriage later occurred. Of the eight children the eldest is Sophie, who is the wife of Fred Ludwig, of Denver, Colorado; William F. resides at Milwaukee, Wisconsin; Anna remains at the old home in Fort Wayne; Frank and Theodore are deceased; George F., of this review, was the next in order of birth; Oscar is deceased; and Lula Louise is the wife of Richard Elke, of Chicago. He whose name introduces this article received his rudimentary education in the German Lutheran parochial school of Fort Wayne, in which city his father became a successful contractor and substantial citizen, and when he was thirteen years of age the family removed to Newton, Kansas, where he continued his studies in the public schools until his graduation in the high school. On returning with his parents to Fort Wayne he here entered the International Business College, in which he completed an effective course. At the age of eighteen years he became stenographer in the law office of J. B. Harper, with whom he remained about one year. He then became stenographer and bookkeeper for the National Telegraph Company and about a year later was advanced to the position of superintendent of the local office of this company. A year later there came to him further and well-merited preferment, in his advancement to the position of secretary and general manager of the company, with headquarters at Fort Wayne. He retained this office about five years and until the time when the company consolidated with the Home Telephone Company. He then accepted a position with the Delaware & Madison Counties Telephone Company, for which corporation he was secretary and general manager about three years. In the meanwhile he had formed the acquaintance of Miss Estella Mulqueen, who had established a private dancing school in which he was one of her first pupils. That he developed marked facility in the terpsichorean art is shown by the fact that his instructor soon retained him as her coadjutor in demonstration work, but the more gracious sequel of this alliance was the marriage of the two young people two years later. Mr. Trier thereupon turned his attention fully to the teaching of dancing and has become one of the successful and representative exponents of the art in the middle west. The history of the growth of his classes has been in pace with the general advancement of Fort Wayne. When he initiated his activities in this field a class was considered numerically strong if it had thirty members, but within the intervening seventeen years the popularity of the Trier school has been such that it has three times been necessary to seek larger quarters for the accommodation of the ever-increasing patronage. In 1911, to meet the demands placed upon his metropolitan school, Mr. Trier planned and erected the Minuet building, which is conceded to be one of the best-equipped and thoroughly modern structures devoted to the teaching of dancing in the United States. At the Trier Academy of Dancing the average class organized at the present day involves an enrollment of from four hundred to six hundred pupils. The class organized in September, 1916, recorded an enrollment of five hundred and seventy-eight pupils the first day and one hundred and twenty-seven acquisitions the second day. It may be truthfully said that of the devotees of dancing in the city of Fort Wayne at the present time Mr. Trier has been the instructor of fully ninety per cent., and he reverts with pleasure to the fact that he has run as a teacher the gamut from childhood to venerable age, the year 1915, for instance, having given him one pupil who was but three and one-half years old and another who was "seventy-nine years young." In 1905 Mr. Trier was one of the first to advocate the expediency and consistency of establishing a privately owned and conducted dancing pavilion in a public park in the United States, and his conviction was one of action, as demonstrated by the fact that since that year he has conducted at Robison Park in Fort Wayne a pavilion of this order and one that is maintained on a high plane. It has ever been his aim in his profession to elevate the standard of the American ballroom and to provide for the people clean, healthful amusement and entertainment throughout the entire year. The popularity of the park pavilion was such, that, in 1914, he found it necessary to enlarge the attractive structure at a cost of about five thousand dollars, in order to meet the demand for admission to the well-ordered summer dances and classes. He is a thorough enthusiast in his profession and may well be satisfied to note the financial success which he has achieved and the high standard he has maintained at all times in his work as an instructor, with a constant determination to make dancing interpretation physically and morally effective and ideal. In national affairs he gives support to the cause of the Republican party, but in local matters is independent of partisan lines and supports men and measures meeting the approval of his judgment. He was reared in the faith of the German Lutheran church, of which he is a communicant, but customarily attends the Plymouth Congregational church, of which his wife is an active member. In the Masonic fraternity he has received the chivalric degrees of the York Rite, besides being affiliated also with the consistory of the Ancient Accepted Scottish Rite, as well as with the Benevolent & Protective Order of Elks and the Knights of Pythias. His civic loyalty is indicated by his membership in the Fort Wayne Commercial Club. On September 14, 1898, was solemnized the marriage of Mr. Trier to Miss Estella Mulqueen, daughter of John Mulqueen, a railroad man then residing at Bucyrus, Ohio. The attractive home of Mr. and Mrs. Trier is at 501 Washington boulevard and is known for its gracious hospitality and good cheer.

Joseph Lyle Tucker.—Joseph Lyle Tucker was born in Orono, Ontario, Canada, February 28, 1885, a son of Arthur A. and Viola (Staples) Tucker, both natives of Ontario. The father was a successful manufacturer of furniture in Canada, where he died on April 1, 1910, and the mother has since then made her home in Fort Wayne. Their children were Joseph Lyle, the subject; Leslie Staples, a dentist in Fort Wayne; Arthur Roy, also a dentist in that city, and Carl McPherson Tucker, of Fort Wayne. Joseph Tucker had his education in Ontario, and following his graduation from the Collegiate Institute in Orillia, Ontario, came to Fort Wayne, where the family was then established, and took a business course in the International Business College. He then entered the White Bank, later entering the employ of the First National bank, with which he was connected for eight years as bookkeeper. He left that institution to accept the post of treasurer of the International Business College, which position he now occupies and which he has handled most successfully and satisfactorily to all concerned. Mr. Tucker was married on September 6, 1911, to Miss Jeanette Morris, daughter of Samuel L. Morris, Sr., concerning which family more extended mention will be found on other pages of this biographical work. Mr. and Mrs. Tucker have one son, Joseph Lyle, Jr., born July 17, 1915. The family have membership in the Plymouth Congregational church, and Mr. Tucker is a Blue Lodge Mason. In politics he is a Republican, but is not a politician.

James Albert Turner.—When the Turner family made its way from Maryland to Indiana, in 1835, they settled at Fort Wayne, then a mere trading post. Many have been the changes that have been wrought in the face of the landscape thereabouts since that hardy pioneer, Enoch Turner, left the comforts of a settled country and dared the uncertainties of one that was not only unsettled, but unsafe. He, in company with nine other brave spirits, came by wagon train from Maryland, their native state. Their little families accompanied them, and while it is probable that the husbands and fathers were more venturesome and daring than their wives, they were not more courageous or self-sacrificing. A part of the little band left the company at Richmond, Indiana, but the others, including the Turners, Clarks, Jack Peacher and Daniel Welker, and one other family, pushed on deeper into the unknown country until the Indian village of Fort Wayne was reached. It was the wish of the majority of the group to settle in the village, but Enoch Turner was not of the same mind, and he chose to locate eleven miles west of Fort Wayne, where in the wilderness he settled upon a government tract of land comprising six hundred and forty acres, or one section. Today that piece of land is a beautifully improved farming tract, but at the time Mr. Turner located upon it, it was in the center of the Pottawattomie Indian Reservation, and their only neighbors on all sides were Indians. The first cabin home of the family was the approved log structure, which in later years was replaced with a substantial country dwelling, conforming to Colonial lines in architectural style, and being one of the fine places in the district. The family were old-time Methodists and Enoch Turner had the distinction of giving a building site for the first Methodist church to be built in that part of the country. They called it Friendship Church, and surely no apter name might have been chosen, for the people came to it from miles around to hear the circuit rider expound the scriptures on Sunday morning, and it was no uncommon sight on such occasions to see fifty to one hundred families gathered at the home of one of the neighbors near the church, a dinner being served the like of which no son or daughter of the present generation has been privileged to partake of. The church itself was builded of rough hewn logs with the puncheon floor common to that period, and it was the scene of many joys and sorrows that came into the lives of the simple folks who worshiped within its walls. Enoch Turner was a leader in his community all his days and died, well advanced in years. Levi Turner was born in Maryland on November 11, 1829, near Richmond, where the family had its home, and was about seven years of age when the family pioneered into Indiana. He was reared on the farm in the vicinity of Fort Wayne and on May 13, 1858, married Osa Jane Bayless, a daughter of Whitley county, Indiana. They were the parents of five children, of which number two are living at this time—James Albert, whose name heads this brief family review, and Delia, who lives at home with the mother. Levi Turner died, in 1907, when he was seventy-eight years of age. He had disposed of his country property a good many years previous, however, and for about thirty years was engaged in the grocery business in Fort Wayne, though he was living retired at the time of his death. James Albert Turner was born in Aboite township, Allen county, and had his early education in the public schools of Fort Wayne, following his training there with a course of study in the Fort Wayne Business College. He finished his studies there, in 1899, and his first position of a clerical order was that of bookkeeper for a wagon factory. He spent some months in that position and for several years thereafter was connected with a wholesale heavy hardware house, spending four years in Richmond, Indiana, as manager of the heavy hardware department of a prominent hardware house. He then went to Cleveland and was for a number of years a traveling salesman for the George Worthington Company, which was established in 1829 and is recognized as the oldest and largest house of its kind in the United States. Mr. Turner was transferred to Fort Wayne after some little time and for a number of years handled the Fort Wayne territory. In 1909 he withdrew from the concern and purchased an interest in the Protective Electrical Supply Company, becoming vice-president and sales-manager of the firm, which position he is now filling. On June 27, 1900, Mr. Turner was married to Miss Elsie M. Meiser, the daughter of John Meiser, a well-known farmer of Lake township, in Allen county. Mr. and Mrs. Turner have one son—James, Jr., born September 14, 1903. Mr. Turner is a Republican and a member of the Wayne Street Methodist Episcopal church, his wife also being affiliated with that church as a member. He is a member of the Commercial Club, the Odd Fellows and the American Insurance Union.

Henry C. Ulmer is the owner of a fine farm of one hundred and fifty-three acres in Jefferson township and is consistently to be designated as one of the progressive and representative exponents of agricultural and live-stock enterprise in his native county. He was born in Milan township, this county, on January 1, 1861, a son of Christopher and Catherine (Steele) Ulmer, whose marriage was solemnized in Allen county, where they passed the residue of their lives. Christopher Ulmer was born in Germany and was a young man when he established his home in Allen county and turned his attention vigorously to agricultural pursuits, in connection with which he achieved independence and prosperity, the while he was respected as a man of sterling character and of productive stewardship in the varied relations of life. All of his children are still living, namely: Frederick, Emma, Henry C., Rosa, Theodore, Gustave and Christopher. Henry C. Ulmer was afforded the advantages of the public schools of Fort Wayne and virtually his entire independent career has been one of close alliance with agricultural industry, of which he has become one of the successful and valued representatives in Jefferson township, the excellent improvements on his fine farm having been made by him and everything about the place giving clear indication of thrift and prosperity. The farm is about two miles distant from New Haven, from which village the family receives service on rural mail route No. 3. Mr. Ulmer is liberal and public-spirited as a citizen, always ready to aid in the support of measures and enterprises advanced for the best interests of the community, but he is non-partisan in politics and has had no desire for the honors or emoluments of public office. On November 10, 1890, Mr. Ulmer wedded Miss Margaret Monnot, daughter of Louis and Nancy (Snyder) Monnot, of Jefferson township, and the one child of this union is Christian H., who is associated in the work and management of the home farm.

Edmund M. Van Buskirk, M. D., has manifested the consistent solidarity of ambition and effort that are essential in preparing a man for the exacting work of the medical profession and it is by ability and earnest application that he has gained secure vantage-place as one of the representative physicians and surgeons of his native county. He is engaged in active general practice in the city of Fort Wayne, was for ten years a member of the health commission of the city, is an appreciative and valued member of the Allen County Medical Society and the Indiana State Medical Society, of which latter he served as first vice-president in 1910, besides which he maintains active affiliation with the American Medical Association. Doctor VanBuskirk was born at Monroeville, this county, on February 11, 1875, a son of Linford VanBuskirk, a well-known and honored citizen of the county. The Doctor is indebted to the public schools of his native village for his early educational discipline, which was supplemented by a course in the Jefferson school in the city of Chicago. In preparation for his chosen profession he entered the Fort Wayne Medical College, and in this institution was graduated as a member of the class of 1902, with the well-earned degree of Doctor of Medicine. Later he took an effective post-graduate course in the medical school of Harvard University, and has otherwise vigorously and circumspectly applied himself to study and research that have kept him in full touch with the advances made in both medical and surgical science. His initial professional work after his graduation was that involved in a year of effective service as resident physician of the Indiana School for the Feeble Minded, at Fort Wayne, and after his retirement from this position he engaged in the general practice of his profession in this city, his unequivocal success affording the best voucher for his ability and also for his secure place in popular confidence and esteem. His practice is now of representative character and he subordinates all else to the demands of his profession. His political allegiance is given to the Democratic party and he is affiliated with the Masonic fraternity. On January 10, 1906, was made record of the marriage of Doctor Van Buskirk to Miss Louise Schwarze, daughter of Henry Schwarze, of Fort Wayne, and the two children of this union are Edmund and Alice.

Otis W. Van Buskirk.—The state of Ohio contributed much to the settlement of Allen county, and many of the prosperous and prominent men of this section today claim Dutch parentage. Otis W. Van Buskirk is one of those whose parents migrated from Ohio and settled here more than half a century ago, and to these sturdy people and their contemporaries is due much credit for the development work they carried on so energetically and so successfully. The parents of the subject were

Linford and Mary E. (Knouse) Van Buskirk, born and bred in Ohio, and they came to Indiana in 1855, settling on a farm in Allen county, where they made their home permanently. The father died there in 1910 and the mother still lives on the old home place. Their four children are all living today. Otis W. was born on June 28, 1876, and had his schooling in the Allen county schools. He completed a course in a local high school, and made his home on the old place until he was twenty-four. He married then, Miss Nannie Clem becoming his wife, and bought a farm in Madison township, to which he took his young wife. He has had good success as a farmer, and is counted one of the solid young men of the community. He is a member of the Masonic order, thirty-second degree, and of the Red Men, and politically is a Democrat. He has been more or less active in party politics, having held a number of offices, and he is now serving his second year as township trustee. He was township assessor for six years.

William M. Van Horn.—The late William M. Van Horn, though a native of Ohio, was reared and educated in Allen county, whence he accompanied his parents as a small child, and was a contributor in no small measure to the development of this section of the country. His parents were Jonathan and Mary (McLachlan) Van Horn, the father of Dutch and the mother of Irish parentage, and they settled in Ohio in their early married life, later moving to Allen county, where they passed the remainder of their days in the quietness incidental to rural life. Eight children were born to them, all now deceased. William Van Horn was born in Ohio on December 1, 1843, and was reared and educated in Allen county as stated above. When the war broke out he enlisted for service as a member of Company F, 130th Regiment of Indiana Infantry. He was in active service during three years, and though he participated in that time in numerous important engagements, seemed to bear a charmed life and escaped the slightest injury. He was mustered out in North Carolina and, returning to his home in Allen county, settled down to farm life. In 1868 he married Miss Sarah Hess, daughter of Jacob and Harriett (Smith) Hess, who were people of Ohio birth, and who came to Indiana and Allen county in 1850. They were the parents of eight children, of which number four are now living. Following Mr. Van Horn's marriage to Sarah Hess he bought a farm and settled down to agricultural life in real earnest, continuing in that work until death claimed him in August, 1912. Success in a generous measure was his, and Mr. Van Horn was known in Monroe township for one of the stable citizens of the community. He had the esteem and friendship of all who knew him and his passing was conceded to have been a genuine loss to the town and county. Mr. Van Horn was a Republican all his life and was a staunch supporter of the party, though never an office seeker nor an aspirant to political favor. He was a Mason and a member of the Methodist church. Four children were born to him and his wife. The eldest, Amos, is deceased. The others are Charles, Jim and Mary, the latter the wife of Joseph Martin. The mother is still living on the family homestead of eighty acres in Section 10, Monroe township. She is a member of the Methodist Episcopal church of that community, and is a woman highly esteemed of all who have her acquaintance.

Homer L. Van Meter has shown much circumspection and energy in his business activities in the city of Fort Wayne, where he has developed a prosperous and representative enterprise in the handling of real estate, with special attention given to central and improved properties and general investments. As one of the progressive and influential exponents of this important line of business enterprise in Allen county Mr. Van Meter is properly given consideration in this work, and such recognition is the more consistent in view of his public-spirited attitude as a citizen. Mr. Van Meter was born on a farm near Antwerp, Paulding county, Ohio, August 28, 1872, a son of Perry H. and Anna M. (Hollis) Van Meter, the former of whom likewise was born in Ohio and the latter was a native of Wisconsin. The father was one of the prosperous men of Paulding county, Ohio. He died in Defiance county, Ohio, in 1887, and his widow survived him by more than a score of years, her death having occurred June 24, 1908. Of the children two died in infancy; Margaret is the wife of Albert C. Haviland, of Fort Wayne; Mary T. is the wife of Thomas Barber, of Antwerp, Ohio; Fannie J. is the wife of Wallace E. Doud, of Fort Wayne; Carry B. likewise resides in this city; Homer L., of this review, was the next in order of birth; and Alpha B. resides in Fort Wayne. Homer L. Van Meter acquired his early education in the public schools and was a lad of fifteen years at the time of his father's death. After leaving school he was employed about four years as a clerk in mercantile establishments, and in 1896 came to Fort Wayne, where he was associated with his brother-in-law, Wallace E. Doud, in the real estate business until 1909. He then engaged in the real estate and investment business in an independent way and his success has been of unequivocal order, his specialty being the handling of central business property in Fort Wayne, though his records at all times show other desirable investments, in both city and farm properties. He is a staunch advocate and supporter of the cause of the Republican party and is affiliated with the Fort Wayne Lodge of the Benevolent & Protective Order of Elks.

Garrette Van Sweringen, M. D.—The honored father of Doctor Van Sweringen established his residence in Allen county, in 1859, and for virtually a period of half a century here maintained high standing as one of the able and representative physicians and surgeons of this section of the Hoosier state. Under such conditions it may well be understood that it is a gracious family and professional heritage that has come to the subject of this review, who is well upholding the prestige of the family name both as a sterling citizen and as a well-fortified exponent of the profession that was signally dignified and distinguished by the services of his father. Doctor Van Sweringen was born in Fort Wayne on June 21, 1882, a son of Dr. Hiram Van Sweringen and Edna M. (Hanna) Van Sweringen. The father was born in Stark county, Ohio, and the lineage on the agnatic side traces back to staunch Holland Dutch origin. Dr. Hiram Van Sweringen brought to the work of his profession the full equipment of a strong and noble nature and the most careful technical training, his ambition and his fealty to his profession having never waned with the passing years and his study and research having at all times kept him abreast of the advances made in medical and surgical science. He came to Allen county, in 1859, as previously stated, and, with residence and professional headquarters in Fort Wayne, labored with all of zeal and kindliness in the work of his humane vocation for practically fifty years, earnest and self-abnegating in his ministrations to those in affliction and distress, so that his name and memory are revered in the city and county that so long represented his home and in which his death occurred in 1911. He served as health officer of Fort Wayne and for a long period was a member of the United States board of pension examining surgeons for Allen county. He was identified with leading professional organizations, including the American Medical Association and the Indiana State Medical Society, and was one of the most honored and influential members of the Allen County Medical Society. His political allegiance was given to the Republican party and he was long affiliated with the Masonic fraternity. Mrs. Edna M. (Hanna) Van Sweringen is still a resident of Fort Wayne. Of the children the eldest is Dr. Budd Van Sweringen, of Fort Wayne, who is individually mentioned on other pages of this publication; Frank is now a resident of Chicago, Illinois; Alice is the wife of Charles Fellowes, of Chicago; George likewise resides in the great western metropolis; Stella is the wife of William R. Hillary, of Toledo, Ohio; Dr. Garrette, of this review, was the next in order of birth; Howard resides in Chicago; and Newton and Harry died in infancy. Dr. Garrette Van Sweringen is indebted to the public schools of Fort Wayne for his preliminary educational discipline, which was supplemented by well-directed higher academic course in the University of Indiana. In preparation for his chosen profession he entered the historic old Jefferson Medical College, in the city of Philadelphia, and in this great institution was graduated as a member of the class of 1903. Immediately after thus receiving his degree of Doctor of Medicine he returned to his native city, where he has since been engaged in successful general practice, not depending upon paternal prestige but achieving success by virtue of his own ability and close application, the while his personal popularity has emphasized the representative character of his clientele. The Doctor is a Republican in politics, but has never appeared as a candidate for any public office save that of coroner, for which position he was nominated in 1906, his defeat being compassed by reason of the political exigencies involved in the superior strength of the Democratic party in the county. Doctor Van Sweringen is identified actively with the Allen County Medical Society and the Indiana State Medical Society, is affiliated with both the York and Scottish Rite organizations of the time-honored Masonic fraternity and is one of the popular and appreciative members of Fort Wayne Lodge of the Benevolent & Protective Order of Elks. In 1910 was solemnized his marriage to Miss Crete Zink, daughter of Gustave and Mary E. Zink, well-known citizens of Vincennes, Indiana. No children have been born of this union.

John L. Verweire has been identified with the profession of music all his life, and since coming to Fort Wayne has been connected with practically every well-known musical organization of the city. He is a Belgian, born in Ghent on November 3, 1869, son of John Bernard and Philomena (Peelman) Verweire, both of Belgian birth and parentage. The father was a merchant in his native land and came to America in 1885, settling in South Bend, where he died. The mother survives and has her home in that city today. Their children were Leopold, of Los Angeles, California; Charles Louis, of Fort Wayne; John L., of this review; Oscar, of Matanzas, Cuba, and three others who are dead. John Verweire had excellent educational advantages, as did also his brothers, having access to the best educational institutions provided by a land noted for her universities. He was graduated from the Royal Conservatory of Music at Ghent and came to South Bend as a member of the Lawrence Elbel Orchestra. A cornet player of unusual ability, he was in demand at all times, and from the Elbel organization went to the band of the First Regiment of Chicago. He was next with the Elgin Watch Company's band at Elgin, remaining there for about six years. He came to Fort Wayne, in 1896, to take charge of the city band, which later became known as the Packard Band, and still later as the Elks' Band. He was the director of the Fort Wayne Symphony Orchestra and is now director of the Mizpah Band, the Shriners' musical organization, and one of the finest musical bodies in the state. Mr. Verweire also has charge of the band of the General Electric Company, and the Concordia College Band, and has brought these organizations up to a splendid state of musical efficiency since they came under his direction. Mr. Verweire is a Republican and his fraternal affiliations are with the Masons and the Elks. He is a Scottish Rite Mason, is a Knight Templar and also a Shriner. He was married in LaPorte, Indiana, to Miss Minnie Wade, an Indiana girl, and their two sons are named Emel and Wade.

William J. Vesey.—In character, service and achievement it has been given Judge Vesey to maintain high vantage-place as a representative member of the bar of his native commonwealth and also to give characteristically effective administration during his incumbency of the office of judge of the superior court of Allen county. Save for the period of his service on the bench he has been continuously engaged in the active practice of his profession in the city of Fort Wayne for nearly forty years, and the impress which he has made as a lawyer, jurist and citizen has been dignified and benignant. The history of the bench and bar of Indiana shall enduringly record his name as that of one of the able and representative lawyers who have lent distinction to his profession, and this history of Fort Wayne and Allen county further enforces its consistency when it accords to him recognition as one of the leading contemporary members of the bar of northern Indiana. The genealogical history of Judge Vesey is specially interesting and its record virtually runs the entire gamut of American annals. It is gratifying that in this connection a large amount of ancestral data has been collected and that from the same a brief resume of the family history can be offered. As far as authentic records determine, it appears that the founder of the Vesey family in America was William, who was probably born in Lancaster, England, as was also his wife, whose maiden name was Elinor Tompson, their marriage having been solemnized in 1644. That William Vesey and wife had come to America prior to the mid-point in the seventeenth century is clearly indicated by the fact that their son William, next in order of descent, was born at Braintree, Massachusetts, October 6, 1647. William Vesey (II) and his wife, Mary, became the parents of Benjamin, who was born at Braintree, Massachusetts, and who there married Dorothy Spear, on December 19, 1720. Their son Benjamin was born at Braintree, April 11, 1740, and at that place solemnized his marriage to Abigail Brackett, who was there born April 17, 1740. The year of their marriage was 1764. William Vesey, son of Benjamin and Abigail (Brackett) Vesey, was born at Braintree in the year 1768, and in 1785 he married Polly Burridge. Of their children, William was born March 4, 1801, at Braintree, Vermont, showing that the parents had become early settlers in the old Green Mountain commonwealth. This son, William, married Adaline Copeland, who was born at Braintree, Vermont, January 29, 1823.

William J. Vesey

Their son Benjamin was born at Braintree, Vermont, February 8, 1829, and he wedded Sarah Penley Waterhouse, of Cumberland Center, Maine, where she was born February 26, 1837. Their marriage was solemnized February 8, 1853, and they became the founders of the family in LaGrange county, Indiana, where, on April 19, 1857, was born their son William Joseph, who is the immediate subject of this review. It will be noted in the abridged record just given that the name William, that of the founder of the American branch, has been retained in one generation after another, and Judge Vesey is of the eighth generation of the family in this country—a family that has given to the nation many men of distinction and sterling character. It is but consonant that a brief genealogical recapitulation be indulged at this juncture, in order to reveal further and interesting data: It is to be noted that William Vesey, the founder, came from England prior to 1640 and settled at Braintree, Massachusetts, where he was made a freeman on the 10th of May, 1843, this implying that he swore allegiance to the colonial government and was given a share in the common lands, together with special landed privileges. His wife, Elinor, was a daughter of Rev. William and Abigail Tompson, the former of whom probably came from Winwich, Lancaster, England. He was born in 1598 and died at Braintree, Massachusetts, August 10, 1666. He was the first minister in that part of Massachusetts and also the school teacher at Braintree for many years. He was associated with Richard Matler in the writing of some works for publication. The oldest headstone to be found in the ancient Hancock cemetery, at Quincy, Massachusetts, is that which marks the grave of Rev. William Tompson. Concerning the founder of the Vesey family in America further interesting data are available. He was one of the representatives of about twenty families who, in 1645, petitioned for the right to build a church, most of these petitioners having been members of the church at Braintree. October 20, 1647, the freeholders of Braintree mutually agreed to defend their ancient rights in regard to land in the town of Braintree, and among the signers to the agreement was Ensign William Vesey, this title indicating that he was a member of the militia. He served several years as selectman, held various other offices of public trust and was influential in church affairs. In 1677 he served in the colonial army. He built the old family homestead at Braintree and had farms on Hough's Neck. He died June 16, 1681, aged sixty-five years, and his remains were laid to rest in the old burial ground now known as Hancock cemetery, at Quincy, Massachusetts, where the inscription of his tombstone is still legible. His widow eventually became the wife of John French. In contracting this second marriage she and her second husband signed a peculiar contract, by the provisions of which all her property received from her first husband was to go to her children. Her remains were interred beside those of her first husband, she having been eighty-four years of age at the time of her death and having been mentioned in contemporary records as "an aged saint." Of the nine children of William and Elinor (Tompson) Vesey, their son, William (II), was born at Braintree, Massachusetts, October 6, 1647. He was very active and influential in town affairs, served for years as selectman and held other offices of trust. He was one of a commission of three appointed by the town of Braintree to represent the residents of that community against the demands of Boston relative to land and land rights, and these commissioners were given full power to act as they deemed best. It was the head of this family who, as Lieutenant Vesey, stands recorded in a list (in 1689) of "those sure, honest and well disposed persons that contributed their assistance for and toward erecting a Church of England." Thus it was that in 1704 Christ church, at Braintree, was fully organized, and several of the names found earliest in the town records, including that of Vesey, are found also recorded as those of wardens or vestrymen of the ancient church just mentioned. The name of William Vesey (II) is inscribed with two others on the bottom of a small silver cup belonging to the Congregational (Unitarian) church, to which it was given in 1649. This William Vesey and his wife, Mary, disposed of many pieces of land, as the records still extant indicate, among such records of deeds being noted the following: William Vesey deeded "to my beloved son, Benjamin," the homestead and other property. The family gradually spent more time at Hough's Neck. In 1696 Lieutenant William Vesey, church warden, was punished for deliberately plowing on Thanksgiving Day, as his protest against the appointment of days of fast and thanksgiving. August 26, 1725, William Vesey and his son Benjamin gave the land for the erection of a Church of England and for the cemetery or churchyard in connection therewith. William Vesey (II) was the father of Rev. William Vesey, who was the first rector of historic old Trinity church in New York city. Samuel Vesey, a brother of William (II), gave probably the first money that was bequeathed to the church of Braintree, Massachusetts. Benjamin Vesey, son of William (II), married Dorothy Spear on December 19, 1726, the ceremony being performed by John Quincy, justice of the peace. Benjamin Vesey was a soldier and was also prominent in town and church affairs. He was one of six men who provided funds and sent Rev. Ebenezer Miller to England to receive his degrees. He made his will October 19, 1762. Of his five children, Benjamin was born April 11, 1740. Benjamin Vesey (II) married, in 1764, Abigail Brackett, who was born April 13, 1740, a daughter of James and Abigail (Belcher) Brackett, whose marriage was solemnized August 2, 1733, by Rev. Samuel Chickley, pastor of the historic old South church, Boston. Benjamin Vesey was a selectman and otherwise prominent in town affairs in Braintree. He was one of the gallant minute men in the climacteric period leading up to the Revolution, and April 19, 1775, he took part in the battles of Lexington and Concord. He enlisted several times and served about two years during the war. He died in 1777. Of his three children, William (III) was born at Braintree in 1768. After the death of Benjamin Vesey his widow, Abigail, married David Bass, December 31, 1777. In the war of the Revolution there are entries of twenty Veseys from Braintree, Massachusetts. In 1785 William Vesey (III) and his brother Benjamin migrated to Braintree, Vermont. In the following year William married Polly, a daughter of John and Polly (Spear) Burridge, her father having served three years as a patriot soldier in the war of the Revolution. William and Polly (Burridge) Vesey became the parents of five children. Their son William (IV) was born March 4, 1801. In 1815 William Vesey (III) and his brother Benjamin removed with their families from Braintree, Vermont, to the west. The marriage of William Vesey (IV) and Adaline Copeland was solemnized January 29, 1823, and the latter was a daughter of Zion and Polly (Harwood) Copeland, who married in 1793. Zion Copeland was a very prominent figure in Braintree, Vermont, and it is a matter of record that four of his sons became clergymen of the Methodist Episcopal church. David Copeland, father of Zion, lived at Athol and later at Bethel, Massachusetts. He twice enlisted and served in the war of the Revolution. He was a descendant of Lawrence Copeland, one of the Pilgrim Fathers who landed at Plymouth Rock in 1620. One of the Copelands married a daughter of John and Priscilla (Mullins) Alden, whose names have been preserved in song and story, as well as in records of the early history of Massachusetts. William and Adaline (Copeland) Vesey became the parents of six children, and in 1834 they removed with their family from Braintree, Vermont, to Lake county, Ohio, and there the devoted wife and mother died in 1838. Later her remains were removed from that county and interred in a cemetery at Goshen, Indiana. In 1838 William Vesey (IV) removed from Ohio to Elkhart county, Indiana, and settled on a pioneer farm in Middlebury township. He was a gallant soldier of the Union in the Civil war, and served two terms as sheriff of Elkhart county, his death having occurred there in 1873. Of his six children, Benjamin was born at Braintree, Vermont, February 8, 1829, and he thus was about ten years old at the time when the family home was established in Elkhart county, Indiana, where he was reared to adult age. At the time of the discovery of gold in California, 1848-9, Benjamin Vesey was one of the adventurous young men who formed a company at Goshen, Indiana, and set forth to make the weary and perilous trip across the plains to the New Eldorado. There were one hundred teams with the party, for the transportation of supplies, and it was a recognized stipulation that none of the men should be permitted to ride unless he were ill. Thus it was that Mr. Vesey made virtually the entire journey on foot, and the trip was an exceptionally pleasant one as compared with those of many companies that followed, as the party set forth in 1848 and was early enough to avoid hostile Indians, as well as the subsequent ravages of cholera. After passing two years in California, Mr. Vesey returned by way of the Isthmus of Panama, and his experience in walking across the isthmus was unusual even for that time. Upon his return to Indiana he entered Asbury (now DePauw) University, at Greencastle, and there he pursued his studies two years. On the 8th of February, 1853, was solemnized his marriage to Miss Sarah Penley Waterhouse, who was born at Cumberland Center, Maine, February 26, 1837, a daughter of Joseph and Esther (Penley) Waterhouse, who married in October, 1823. Mrs. Waterhouse was a daughter of Joseph and Desire (Dingley) Penley, and, under three enlistments, her grandfather served about twenty months as a patriot soldier in the Revolutionary war. In 1843 Joseph Waterhouse came with his family from Cumberland Center, Maine, and established his home at Cloverdale, Putnam county, Indiana. After their marriage Benjamin and Sarah P. (Waterhouse) Vesey, the parents of Judge Vesey, removed to a farm in LaGrange county, Indiana, where they continued their residence several years. In 1885 they removed to Goshen, Elkhart county, and in 1890 they went to Cape Girardeau, Missouri, where they remained until 1896, when they returned to Indiana and established their home in Fort Wayne. Here the revered husband and father died May 3, 1908, and his remains rest in beautiful Lindenwood cemetery. He was a man of strong mentality and impregnable integrity and character, generous and kindly in all of the relations of life and loved by all who came within the sphere of his influence. His widow now resides with her sons in Fort Wayne, where her gentle manners have endeared her to a wide circle of friends. Of their five sons and one daughter, only two are now living—

William J. and Allen J. Judge William J. Vesey was born on a farm near Lima, LaGrange county, Indiana, April 19, 1857, and in the common schools of the locality and period he received his preliminary educational discipline, which was supplemented by a course in a well ordered private school or academy then maintained at Ontario, LaGrange county. At the age of seventeen years he taught a winter term of school, but his ambition and predilections lay elsewhere than along the line of the pedagogic profession and this ambition was one of determination and action, as indicated by the fact that he soon found opportunity to take up the study of law. For a time he pursued his reading under the preceptorship of Judge S. C. Coffinberry, at Constantine, St. Joseph county, Michigan, and later he continued his study in the office of James S. Drake, of LaGrange, who is now (1917) serving on the bench of the circuit court for LaGrange and Elkhart counties. It may well be said that, in all of his activities, thoroughness has been specially a denoting characteristic of Judge Vesey, and through consecutive study and ever broadening experience he has gained a comprehensive, accurate and readily available knowledge of the science of jurisprudence. He was admitted to the bar of his native state in 1878, and in October of that year he came to Fort Wayne, where he continued his law studies in the office of Ninde & Ellison. In 1881 he formed a professional alliance with the late Hon. Perry A. Randall, under the firm name of Randall & Vesey. This constituted one of the influential law firms of northern Indiana during the period of the partnership, which was dissolved in 1890. In that year Judge Vesey formed a partnership with Owen N. Heaton, and this alliance continued until Mr. Heaton was elected to the bench of the superior court of Allen county, in 1902. At this juncture Judge Vesey entered into a law partnership with his brother, Allen J., under the title of Vesey & Vesey, which is still retained. In 1910 Dick M. Vesey, eldest son of Judge Vesey, became a member of the firm, and in 1914 David S., a younger son, likewise was admitted to partnership. Dick M. was elected representative of Allen county in the state legislature in the autumn of 1916, and is an efficient member of the lower house. In October, 1899, Judge Vesey was appointed by Governor Durbin to serve on the bench of the superior court of Allen county, to fill the vacancy caused by the death of Judge C. M. Dawson, and he continued his service in this judicial office until the middle of November, 1900. In this connection it is worthy of record that he was, in October, 1900, the first judge to sit on the bench of the superior court in the fine new court house of Allen county. He has essentially the judicial cast of mind, and few of his rulings met with reversal by courts of higher jurisdiction. Judge Vesey would prove an ideal incumbent of higher judicial offices, and doubtless such preferment would long since have been his had he not been politically a representative of the minority party in this section of Indiana. The Judge is known as a resourceful advocate and has won many decisive victories as a trial lawyer. He is known also as an authority in commercial law, and has given the major part of his time and attention to this important department of professional work, with the result that his services both as an attorney and as a legal advisor have been retained by a large number of the leading corporations and other important business concerns and influential individuals in Fort Wayne. Thus it may be noted that he is at the present time attorney for the First and Hamilton National Bank of Fort Wayne, the Tri-State Loan & Trust Company, S. F. Bowser &

Company, the Fort Wayne Rolling Mill Corporation, the Dudlo Manufacturing Company, and Mossman, Yarnelle & Company. He is a member of the directorates of several banks and numerous business corporations. On the 25th of July, 1882, was solemnized the marriage of Judge Vesey to Maggie Studebaker, daughter of the late Judge David and Harriet (Evans) Studebaker, of Decatur, Adams county. As a young man Judge Studebaker served one year on the bench of the court of common pleas, and then resigned the office. Later he was for six years a member of the lower house of the Indiana legislature, and he was one of the prominent citizens of Adams county at the time of his death, in 1903, his wife having passed away in 1891. Mrs. Vesey was born January 17, 1863, and reared at Decatur. After her graduation in the local high school she entered the old Methodist College, Fort Wayne, in which institution she was graduated as a member of the class of 1882. She left upon the world the impress of the noble and gracious gentlewoman, was loved by all who knew her, and the entire community was shocked and manifested its sense of bereavement when came the news of her sudden death, April 8, 1910. Mrs. Vesey was prominent and influential in many civic enterprises and in the representative social life of her home city. In the entrance of the Fort Wayne Young Woman's Christian Association building has been placed a beautiful memorial tablet, in attestation of her aid in effecting the erection of the building and her loving and efficient administration as president of the association. Judge and Mrs. Vesey became the parents of six children, all of whom are living: Margaret Studebaker Vesey remains at the beautiful paternal home and is earnestly carrying forward many of the activities which had enlisted the attention of her loved mother; Sally Waterhouse Vesey is the wife of Cecil Alviere Max, of Muncie, Indiana, and they have one son, Benjamin Alviere; Dick Morrison Vesey married Miss Mary Glennis Life, and they have two children, Mary Margaret and William Joseph; William Joseph Vesey, Jr., married Bess Witte and is carrying on the floral and greenhouse activities with which the name of Vesey is so widely known. He is now serving in the U. S. Army. David Studebaker Vesey married Miss Lela Rich, and they have one child, Margaret Jane; Catherine, the youngest, remains at home. In politics Judge Vesey is a stalwart, effective advocate of the principles of the Republican party. He has received the thirty-second degree of the Ancient Accepted Scottish Rite of the Masonic fraternity, is affiliated with Fort Wayne Commandery of Knights Templars, as well as the Mystic Shrine and the Knights of Pythias. He has long been a member of the Wayne Street Methodist Episcopal church. July 6, 1917, Judge Vesey was united in marriage with Miss Grace Waters, born March 28, 1878, at Kansas City, Missouri. She is a daughter of Louis H. and Clara (Emerick) Waters, natives of Bridgeport, Connecticut, and Germantown, Ohio, respectively.

J. W. Vining.—The late J. W. Vining came of one of the old established families of the East and was himself born in Green county, New York, his natal day being July 13, 1827. He was a son of David and Hannah (Husted) Vining, native New Yorkers, and the father died in that state. His widow later came to Allen county, Indiana, but lived only a short time. They were the parents of a fine family numbering twelve children, briefly mentioned as follows: Robert, born March 21, 1806; Polly, born April 3, 1808; Jonathan, born April 8, 1810; Caroline, born July 26, 1812; David, born November 26, 1814; Elisha, born April

4, 1817; Sally, born June 10, 1819; Peter S., born September 25, 1820; Jane, born November 6, 1824; James W., the immediate subject of this brief review; Horace, born May 28, 1830; and Christine, born February 8, 1833. All are now deceased. James W. Vining was married to Catherine Antwerp. She was born, April 23, 1843, and died March 10, 1910, and was the daughter of Ludwig and Catherine Antwerp, both native-born Germans. The father was born on April 30, 1912, and the mother on January 23d of the same year. They were the parents of three children—Catherine, born April 23, 1843; Andrew Lewis, born February 26, 1845, and Frederick Wilhelm, born July 17, 1849. The first named became the wife of the subject, and to them were born three daughters—Carrie, Kitty and Myrtle. James W. Vining came to Allen county as a youth, accompanying his widowed mother and his brothers and sisters after the death of the father in New York state, and when he grew to manhood devoted himself to farming, in which occupation he spent the remainder of his active life, enjoying a success that was commensurate with his efforts and highly creditable to him in many ways. He was a leader in his community always, and was one of the five men who organized the first Methodist Episcopal church in St. Joseph township. He is also remembered as having assisted very materially in the building of the first gravel road in the township in the days when the toll highway was the rule instead of the exception. The second daughter, Kitty Vining, married Charles Parker, on August 10, 1895, and they now live on the old home place. They are childless and Mrs. Parker is the last living representative of this fine old family.

Christian G. Vonderau.—One of the newer and thriving concerns of New Haven is the Peoples State Bank, organized on May 23, 1916, and opened to the public on August 3d in the same year. Christian G. Vonderau was elected to the office of president of the bank, and he is ably filling that post. The bank opened its doors with a modest capital of $32,000 and total resources of $75,000, but the progress it has already made will warrant an increase in the capital within the next few years. At this time a fine new building is in course of construction, modern and sufficiently commodious for the needs of the establishment, and the cost of the building will be about $15,000. The board of directors is made up of the following New Haven men: Christian G. Vonderau, president; Dr. E. E. Morris, vice-president; B. H. Smith, cashier; Theodore Thimlar, John Zimmerman, Christ Goeglein, Fred Koellinger, Henry Heine, William H. Federspiel and Ernest Pruese. Christian G. Vonderau was born in Milan township, Allen county, Indiana, on May 16, 1866, and is the son of Jacob and Margaret (Kern) Vonderau. The father was born in Hesse-Dermstadt, Germany, and the mother is of Bavarian birth and parentage. Jacob Vonderau came to America in 1844, locating in Pennsylvania, where he engaged in his trade as a tailor. He remained there until 1857, when he came to Allen county and settled in Milan township, there buying a farm, and he continued in that industry the remainder of his life. He died in 1897 at the age of eighty-one years, and his faithful wife lived until 1908, passing on at the advanced age of eighty-two years. Mr. Vonderau was a Democrat in politics, a member of the German Lutheran church and an honorable and esteemed citizen to the end of his days. He and his wife reared a splendid family of eleven children. Susan, the first born, is deceased, as is also Casper. Peter lives in Fort Wayne, Indiana. Catherine is the wife of William

Grieble, and they live in Marion township, Allen county. Herman lives in St. Joseph township and is a prosperous farmer there. Frederick is deceased. Jacob is a resident of Maumee township. John is established in business in Toronto, Canada. Anna is the wife of Fred Wellman, of Indianapolis. Christian G., of this review, is the tenth child of his parents, and Martin J., a minister in the German Lutheran church, is in charge of a parish at Fort Dodge, Iowa. He is the eleventh and youngest of the family. Allen county common schools gave to Christian Vonderau such book-learning as he gained in youth. Up to the age of about twenty-two he remained at home on the farm, assisting in its management and learning the elements of successful agriculture under the guidance of his father. In 1888 he established himself on a farm of his own and he continued to devote himself to active farming until 1908, when he retired with twenty years of active farming to his credit and a splendid record for progressiveness and industry. He has always been a citizen who has manifested a wholesome interest in the affairs of his community, and for many years has been chosen to fill various offices of importance to his locality. He was township assessor for six years, member of the Board of Township Trustees for four years and a member of the Board of Review for three years. In all of these offices he has ably discharged the duties that came to his hand. He is a Democrat, a member of the German Lutheran church, and a member of the New Haven Commercial Club. He was married on October 6, 1889, to Miss Mary Griebel, the daughter of George and Fredericka (Wolf) Griebel, of Marion township, in Allen county. They were German people, and like Mr. Vonderau's own parents, came to Allen county and settled on a farm where they lived lives of industry and contributed much to the welfare of their community. Both are now deceased. Their daughter, Mrs. Vonderau, was born in Marion township on August 30, 1863, and she has been esteemed in the community all her life. Five children have come to their home: Freda, Anna, Herman, Jennie, and William. All share the parental home with the exception of Anna, who is a resident of Fort Wayne. The family is one of the foremost ones in New Haven, and they are leaders in the best social activities of their community, where they have a wide circle of friends.

Max J. Vonderau.—Max J. Vonderau, successful farmer of St. Joseph township, was born in Bartholomew county, Indiana, December 17, 1884. He is a son of John and Mary (Klopp) Vonderau and the grandson of Jacob and Margaret (Kern) Vonderau, the grandparents being natives of Germany, where they were reared and married. They came to America and settled in Marysville, Ohio, later locating in Allen county, Indiana, settling first in Milan township and later in St. Joseph township. Jacob and Margaret Vonderau had eleven children. They were Susan, Casper, Peter, Katherine, Herman, Frederick, Jacob, John, father of the subject; Annie, Christ and Martin. Susan, Casper and Frederick are deceased. John Vonderau has followed teaching and is now a resident of Ontario, Canada, where he is engaged in agricultual activities. Max J. Vonderau was educated in the public schools of the city of Cleveland, Ohio, Council Bluffs, Iowa, and the German Lutheran schools of Allen county, Indiana. He first took up farming in St. Joseph township and is now the owner of eighty acres of fertile and well-cultivated land, highly improved and showing evidences of intelligent industry in its operation. He has a fine brick dwelling house on the place, and the barns and fences reflect the general spirit of the place in their well-kept appearance. Mr. Vonderau was married, August 17, 1913, to Louise Behrman, daughter of John W. and Sophia (Harting) Behrman.

Edward A. Wagner.—All the business years of Edward Wagner's life have been devoted to electrical work and the past sixteen years have been spent in the employ of the General Electric Company in Fort Wayne as head of the transformer department of that well-known concern. Mr. Wagner has found both pleasure and profit in his chosen field of employment and is known as one of the best-posted men in his particular line to be found in his community today. Edward A. Wagner was born in New York city on August 8, 1873, son of Andrew and Adelaide (Schumm) Wagner, the father a native son of France and the mother of German birth and parentage. Andrew Wagner, after coming to America, engaged in the mercantile business in New York city and was engaged in that enterprise until he died, the mother still being a resident there. Of their five children Edward Wagner is the youngest but one. He had a substantial common school education, followed by a course of study in the College of New York City. He first gave his attention to a classical course, but after a year changed to a business course, to which he gave two years of diligent work. His first position after leaving college was with the Electrical World and it was there he had his introduction to the electrical field. He was so attracted by the possibilities offered that he left the World to enter a factory at Lynn, Massachusetts, in quest of practical experience in the work. He later moved to Schenectady, New York, where he added much to his already excellent knowledge of the work, and from there was sent to Mexico, where he spent two years in superintending the erection of a plant. That work completed, he returned to New York, where he decided to further his electrical knowledge by technical training in Cornell University. Entering as a special student he took the work assigned to students in the senior year, following it with post-graduate work, and made a record while there that marked him as one of the most brilliant men to be found in that field of study at the time. His post-graduate work finished, he returned to Schenectady to take charge of the transformer department of the General Electric Company at that point, where he continued until 1900, when he came to Fort Wayne in a similar capacity for the same company. He has manifested a wholesome interest in the development of electrical enterprises in the city and his work has been most praiseworthy along these lines. He was the organizer of the Electro-Technic Club of Fort Wayne and has been a moving spirit in that organization since that time. Mr. Wagner has taken his place among the up-to-the-minute men of the city since he first located in Fort Wayne and has shown himself to be the possessor of a commendable degree of civic pride and enthusiasm. A Republican in politics of national character, he has never permitted party lines to influence him in determining his line of action in local affairs, and has served the city creditably as a member of its council. He is a thirty-second degree Mason and a Shriner, and is a member of the Institute of American Electrical Engineers. On November 25, 1902, Mr. Wagner married DeEtta Davis, a daughter of Fort Wayne, and two children have blessed them—Ruth Davis and Frances Quait.

George Waldschmidt has been a resident of Fort Wayne since his boyhood, his early education having been received in his native province in Germany and he having been a lad of eleven years when his parents emigrated to America and established their home in Allen county, Indiana, where they passed the remainder of their worthy and useful lives, the subject of this review being the third eldest of their five children and the other four—Jacob, Louis, Elizabeth and Margaret—being likewise residents of Fort Wayne. George Waldschmidt has proved his energy and resourcefulness through connection with varied lines of business enterprise in Fort Wayne, and that he has developed an individual potential of assured order, besides entrenching himself securely in popular confidence and esteem, is indicated by his incumbency of the position of assistant cashier of the German-American National Bank of Fort Wayne, this being one of the strong and important financial institutions of northern Indiana. Mr. Waldschmidt was born at Krumbach, in the province of Hessen-Darmstadt, Germany, on September 3, 1869, and in the same section of the great German empire were born his parents, George and Katherine Waldschmidt, the father being employed by the Pennsylvania Railroad from the time he arrived in Fort Wayne until he was pensioned. Most of the time he was employed as mail carrier between the main office and the east office yards. Both he and his wife were most zealous communicants of the Lutheran church. After the family home had been established in Allen county the subject of this sketch attended the parochial school of St. Paul's Lutheran church up to the time of his confirmation as a communicant of the church, when he was about thirteen years old. For about a year thereafter he attended the public schools of the city and then completed a course in a local business college, so that he was well reinforced when he initiated his business career. After having held a few minor clerical positions he finally entered the employ of the Seavey Hardware Company, with which he remained about eight years. Thereafter he had charge of the office of the Fort Wayne Carriage Works about two years, and for the ensuing ten years was in charge of the general clerical work in the Nuttman Bank. With this institution he continued his effective service until May 20, 1905, when he resigned his position and assumed one of similar executive order in the newly organized German-American National Bank, of which he is now the efficient and popular assistant cashier. Mr. Waldschmidt has entered most fully into the best business and social life of Fort Wayne and his circle of friends is coincident with that of his acquaintances. He is a charter member of the local Rotary Club, of which he has served as treasurer from the time of its organization, is an active member of the Fort Wayne Commercial Club, and has been identified with the Fort Wayne Golf Club since the early stage of its existence, he having served nine years as its secretary. In the Masonic fraternity his ancient-craft affiliation is with Summit City Lodge, and in the Ancient Accepted Scottish Rite he has received the thirty-second degree, besides which he is affiliated also with the Mystic Shrine. He has been an active member of the Men's Club of the First Presbyterian church from the time of its organization: he was treasurer of this vigorous club for three years. Alert and progressive as a citizen and business man, Mr. Waldschmidt takes special interest in all things pertaining to the well being of his home city, and in politics he is found aligned as a stalwart supporter of the cause of the Republican party. On January 1, 1895, was solemnized the marriage of Mr. Waldschmidt to Miss Bessie P. Racine, who was born and reared in Fort Wayne, daughter of F. L. Racine, a well-known retired manufacturer of this city.

Noah A. Walker retired from business life about ten years ago, bought a small farm in Lafayette township, and has since lived there quietly, giving some attention to the business of cultivating the place, but taking life easily and enjoying the fruits of his labors of earlier years. He is a son of John W. and Rebecca (Dorry) Walker and was born in Lafayette township, Allen county, on October 24, 1857. The parents came from North Carolina to Allen county in an early day and were counted among the earliest settlers of this district. John W. Walker came with his parents as a boy, and his father was for some years a merchant in the community that in later years came to be known as Zanesville, in Huntington county. The boy, reared to manhood in Allen county, where his parents eventually settled, grew up with a working knowledge of farming in the wilds, and when he married Rebecca Dorsey bought a small farm and applied himself diligently to its development. He later added more land and in time found himself among the more prosperous men of his community. He was a Republican in politics in later life, and was township supervisor for several years. He was a member of the Christian church practically all his life, and was an example of many admirable qualities in his home and wherever he was found. Industry and honesty were salient traits in his makeup, and he was prominent in the financial affairs of the township for many years. He was twice married. His first wife, Rebecca Dorsey, was the mother of nine children, of whom brief mention may be made at this point. James is a resident of Lafayette township, and is a retired farmer. Mary E. was the next in order of birth. Noah A., the third born, is the immediate subject of this family review. Sarah married G. C. Miller, and they live in Fort Wayne. Ida became the wife of Martin Keplinger, now deceased. John M. and Rebecca Jane were twins, and the latter is married to William Jones of Huntington county. Ella died at the age of three years. William Clark is engaged in the grocery business in Zanesville, Indiana. The second wife of Mr. Walker was Louisa Warner, and three children were born of this union. Sanford lives in Zanesville. Laura is the wife of Jacob Erick, of Fort Wayne, and Paul is a resident of that city also. Noah A. Walker did not enjoy the best of educational advantages as a boy at home. The country school of his day ran about three months in the year and the advantages it afforded in that brief time were not to be compared with those of the remotest district school of today. The equipment was practically nil and the instruction most limited, so that if a child learned to read and write he did about all that was expected of him. Noah Walker's training was limited, but he is by no means illiterate, having made up in later years much of what was denied him in boyhood in the matter of schooling. He found much practical experience at work on his father's farm and after he left home worked by the day for five years, saving his money and gathering experience for the time when he should establish a place of his own. He rented a farm of 150 acres in Allen county which he operated successfully for twelve years, after which he engaged in the butcher business in Zanesville. He was engaged in that enterprise for a number of years, when he bought a small place near Sheldon and for the past eleven years has carried on farming activities on a small scale. He is a Republican and a member of the United Brethren church. Mr. Walker was married on October 28, 1877, to Miss Viola Florence Harvey, daughter of Harrison and Malinda (Connoway) Harvey, who came to Allen county about 1870.

Mr. Harvey is not living, but the mother survives and has her home in Lafayette township. They were farming people all their active days, and were old residents of Huntington county, Indiana. Mr. and Mrs. Harvey were the parents of five children. Viola is the wife of the subject. Isadore married Benjamin LeRoy Merchant, of Wells county, Indiana. Charles Monroe lives in Fort Wayne. John Randolph is deceased. Franklin Evert is an electrician with the Standard Oil Company and is located in Whiting, Indiana. Mr. and Mrs. Walker are parents of a son, Arvid D., of Detroit, Michigan, and he has four children—Leota Ferne, May Pauline, Asa Sodona and Ralph Harold.

William P. Walsh.—Marked by ambition and well directed activities has been the career of Mr. Walsh, who now controls a substantial insurance, real estate and loan business in the city of Fort Wayne and who, after identification with various lines of enterprise, has found in this sphere of business excellent opportunities for the achieving of success worthy of the name. He was born on a farm near Greenwick, Washington county, New York, and the date of his nativity was February 23, 1874. His parents, John and Mary (O'Keefe) Walsh, passed their entire lives in the old Empire state, where the father long held place as one of the successful farmers of Washington county, and both were zealous communicants of the Catholic church. Of their children the eldest, Thomas, died after having attained to man's estate; Michael died in infancy; Andrew is a resident of Plattsburg, Vermont; John resides at Port Richmond, New York; William P., of this review, was the next in order of birth; and Daniel still remains in his native county, where he maintains his home at Greenwich. In addition to receiving the advantages of the public schools and Washington Academy, William P. Walsh completed an effective course in the Albany Business College, an excellent school in the capital city of New York. As a youth he served an apprenticeship to the trade of mule spinner, but he did not long devote his attention to practical work at this vocation. Among his earlier business experiences in his native state were included one year of service as bookkeeper in the office of a woolen mill, clerk in a grocery store for a period of about equal duration, and resumption of work on the home farm for about three years. For four years thereafter he was engaged in the retail mercantile business at Fremont, Sullivan county, New York, and then came to the west and established his residence in the city of Chicago, where he held for one year the position of assistant superintendent of the shoe department in the great mail-order house of Montgomery Ward & Company. He then came to Fort Wayne as a representative of the Chicago Inter-Ocean, and his estimate of the advantages and attractions of the city has been best indicated by his continuous residence within its borders. After severing his association with the Chicago newspaper mentioned, he became a representative of the Columbian Relief Association, of Indianapolis, and this was the initiation of his connection with the insurance business. Through his resourceful energy and progressive and reliable methods he has developed in Fort Wayne a representative general insurance business, besides having become a successful exponent of the real estate and loan business. Though he is loyal and liberal in all things pertaining to civic fealty, he is independent of partisan lines in politics and votes for the men and measures meeting the approval of his judgment. Mr. Walsh and his wife are active communicants of St. Patrick's Catholic church, and he is affiliated with the

Knights of Columbus, the Benevolent & Protective Order of Elks, the Ancient Order of Hibernians, the Loyal Order of Moose, the Fraternal Order of Eagles, and the Buffaloes, besides which he is an appreciative and active member of the Fort Wayne Commercial Club. On October 16, 1901, was solemnized the marriage of Mr. Walsh to Miss Daisy Robertson, daughter of Clifford and Harriet (Larkin) Robertson, of East Greenwich, New York, and the two children of this union are Ruth and Doris.

Horatio Nelson Ward.—When Horatio Nelson Ward passed away, in 1909, he had to his credit sixty-one years of residence in Fort Wayne and was recognized as a pioneer in the crockery business in this section of the state. Mr. Ward was of English birth and parentage, born in Manchester on March 16, 1823, and was just twenty-four years of age when he left his native land to identify himself with life in America. He located first in New Orleans, Louisiana, but his stay there was a brief one and for a year he moved about a good deal in search of a suitable location. It was in 1848 that he came to Indiana, located first in New Albany and there establishing himself in the crockery business, to which he had been trained in Manchester. In 1859 he moved from New Albany to Fort Wayne, there engaging in the same enterprise, and was prominently identified with that business up to the time of his death, May 1, 1909. His first place of business was on Calhoun street, but the later years of his active business career found him located at what is now 108 West Columbia street, in a property owned by himself. In the years of his residence in Fort Wayne he prospered consistently and was able to accumulate considerable real estate in and about the city. He was a Democrat and took an active part in affairs of his party, and was a lifelong member of the Episcopal church, his parents having been members of the Church of England. He was a Mason of high degree and popular and prominent in Masonic circles locally. Mr. Ward was a man of splendid vitality and was able to give his attention to his business up to the last days of his life, though he had retired from commercial pursuits in 1899. In his passing Fort Wayne and Allen county lost an admirable citizen and a successful and enterprising business man. For many years he was the foremost dealer in crockery in Northern Indiana, the same being carried on both wholesale and retail. In 1855 Mr. Ward was married to Miss Christine Louise Shuler, a native of Germany. Two sons and five daughters were born to them, as follows: Albert H., deceased; William, deceased; Emily Louise, Lillie Caroline, deceased; Annie M., Pauline Rosaline, and Alice Christine.

S. Ren Warnock, Jr.—As one of the representative young business men and popular citizens of Allen county, the cashier of the Huntertown State Bank is specially entitled to recognition in this history. He is one of the progressive and public-spirited citizens of the thriving little city of Huntertown and was the prime factor in effecting the organization of the well ordered banking institution of which he is the efficient cashier. Mr. Warnock claims the old Buckeye state as the place of his nativity, as do also his parents, who still reside within its borders. He was born at Fort Recovery, an historic town in Mercer county, Ohio, and the date of his nativity was November 30, 1880. He is a son of S. Ren Warnock, Sr., and Clara (Kruse) Warnock, and his father has given the major part of his active career to agricultural enterprise, the subject of this review being the eldest of the three children, and the other two, Harry and Anna Louise, being still at the parental home in Mercer county, Ohio.

It may consistently be noted in this connection that the father of Mr. Warnock, while engaged in excavating for a public building at Fort Recovery, Ohio, disinterred what were supposed to be the mortal remains of General Butler, as the sword found with the remains bore the name of the general, the same being now on exhibition in the collection of relics maintained at the high school in Greenville, Ohio. S. Ren Warnock, Jr., is indebted to the public schools for his early educational discipline, which was supplemented by an effective course in a business college in the city of Cincinnati. For two years after leaving school he served as secretary to the superintendent of the telephone service of the Cincinnati, Hamilton & Dayton Railroad, and for eight years thereafter he was associated in the work and management of his father's farm. After his marriage he continued to be identified with farm enterprise in Ohio for two years, and the ensuing four years found him the incumbent of a position in the People's State Bank of Fort Recovery, Ohio. He then came to Huntertown, Indiana, and effected the organization of the Huntertown State Bank, which is incorporated with a capital stock of twenty-five thousand dollars and of which he has been cashier from the time of incorporation. The first president, Dr. Frank Grunwell, retired from this office and was succeeded by Charles H. Hartung, the present incumbent, Charles F. Bleke being vice-president of the institution. The bank was incorporated January 2, 1913, its business has been most ably managed, its success unqualified and its total assets being fully one hundred and fifty thousand dollars as indicated in the official report of January 2, 1917. Mr. Warnock has identified himself most loyally and fully with community interests and is treasurer of the Huntertown Live Stock & Agricultural Association. In Huntertown he is affiliated with Lodge No. 689, Ancient Free & Accepted Masons, his political support is given to the Democratic party, and he and his wife hold membership in the Methodist Episcopal church. On November 8, 1906, was solemnized the marriage of Mr. Warnock to Miss Clara Lee Straight, daughter of Charles and Harriet (Reprogle) Straight, who still maintain their home in Darke county, Ohio, where Mrs. Warnock was born and reared, the youngest of the three children. Her only sister, Gertrude, is the wife of Henry Hildbolt, of Fort Recovery, Ohio, and her brother, Ora, is, in 1917, a successful teacher in the public schools at Arcanum, Ohio. Mr. and Mrs. Warnock have two children—Raymond and Bettie Lee.

Dick F. Waterfield has had a somewhat varied and essentially vigorous career in connection with business affairs and is a recognized authority in the tobacco trade and commerce, of which he is now a leading representative in Fort Wayne, where he is secretary and treasurer of the Wayne Tobacco Company, the well equipped establishment which is located at 111-113 East Columbia street. A scion of staunch Pennsylvania German stock and of one of the sterling pioneer families of Clermont county, Ohio, Mr. Waterfield was born in the town of Felicity, that county, on the 30th of October, 1870, the fourth in order of birth of the six children of William W. and Mary Elizabeth (Frazier) Waterfield. His father was a prosperous general merchant and tobacco dealer in Clermont county for thirty years. After having duly profited by the advantages of the public schools of his native village, Dick F. Waterfield pursued an advanced course of study in Bethel Academy, at Nicholasville, Kentucky. At the age of eighteen years he went to Hutchinson, Kansas, where he completed a course in the Hutchinson Business College, and where also he made another and more important step in life, as he there married, when he was twenty years of age, Miss Florence May Folmer. Incidentally it may be noted at this point that of this union have been born seven children, all of whom are living and remain at the parental home, namely: Marydel, William, Sabina, Dallas, Richard, Helen and Camilla. For six years Mr. Waterfield continued his residence at Hutchinson, Kansas, and then established the family home at Covington, Kentucky, where he identified himself with the manufacturing of tobacco as superintendent of the large and well equipped plant of the Lowell & Buffington Tobacco Company. He continued his connection with this concern until 1904 and for the ensuing six years held an executive position in the Commercial National Bank of Covington. In March, 1913, he came to Fort Wayne as secretary and treasurer of the Wayne Tobacco Company, and in the development of the substantial wholesale business he has been the dominating force. Mr. Waterfield has been an active worker in behalf of the principles and policies of the Republican party, is one of the active and valued members of the Fort Wayne Commercial Club and the Rotary Club, in the latter of which he takes specially lively interest; he is affiliated with the Masonic fraternity, and both he and his wife are members of the Methodist Episcopal church. The family is one of marked popularity in the representative social life of the Allen county metropolis, with residence at 136 East DeWald street.

John S. Waters.—The Waters family has long been honorably identified with the agricultural history of Allen county, for it was as early as the year 1834, when Elias Waters, grandfather of the subject, migrated to Indiana from Pennsylvania, his native state, and engaged in farming. Elias Waters was a true pioneer, and he and his sons were leaders in the best development of their community in the early days. He acquired ownership of a thousand acres of land soon after his arrival and spent the remainder of his life in devotion to the task of developing and upbuilding that property. In his native state he had been employed as a teamster for years. He had saved his money carefully and when the time was ripe set out for newer fields, accompanied by his family. He first bought land in Wooster county, Ohio, which he later sold and bought a farm near St. Mary's, in Ohio, and in 1832 disposed of that place and came to Allen county, settling in Wabash township. It is said of him that he was about the only man in the neighborhood in those times who knew what money was, and it was a genuine treat for the men of the community to be employed by him, for he was able to pay their hire in cash and not in wheat or other produce, as was the custom. He was progressive and prosperous and was the first man in the township to build a frame barn. His grandson, the subject, tells many interesting stories of the experiences of that old pioneer, and it is worthy of record here that the journey of Elias Waters and his family from Ohio to Allen county was one fraught with many dangers—not the least of which was the attention bestowed upon the party by prowling wolves. At night they became so aggressive that it was necessary for them to protect the little party by building bright fires, and on the last night of the trip, when camping near what is now the junction of the Coldwater and Leo roads, they had felt themselves safe from attack, having seen no signs of wolves during the day, and so had retired to rest without taking the precaution of building up the fire. During the night Waters was awakened by a great commotion among the stock and hastily aroused his two eldest sons—mere lads, they were—to protect the stock from the wolves while he built up a fire. One of these lads was the father of the subject. Elias Waterfield died on his Allen county farm when he was sixty-five years of age. One of his sons was John, who married Sally Bowser. She was a daughter of S. F. Bowser, a native of Pennsylvania and a prominent man in Allen county for many years, concerning whom is to be found further mention elsewhere in this historical work. It is sufficient to say here that they came to Allen county as young people, and here met and married. They settled in Wabash township on a farm of forty acres and there spent the rest of their lives. John and Sally (Bowser) Waters spent their lives in devotion to the development of their forty-acre farm in Washington township, and John S., the subject, is the owner of that place today. They were the parents of five children—Lena, Elias, John S., Sarah and James Wesley. Lena and Elias are deceased. The parents died in advanced years, the father being seventy-six years old and the mother sixty-nine. They were worthy people, highly esteemed in their community, and were widely mourned in passing. John S. Waters had his education in the common schools of Washington township and all his active life has been spent in application to farming. He is today owner of four hundred acres of land in Washington township, on which he has made all modern improvements, with a fine farm home and appropriate barns and other buildings. The entire acreage is tiled and fenced and Mr. Waters himself cleared some of the land. In 1887 Mr. Waters was united in marriage with Miss Della Ramsey, daughter of Adam and Maria (Meyers) Ramsey, natives of Pennsylvania and Germany, respectively. They came to Allen county as young people, here married and settled down to a quiet life on a farm. Mr. and Mrs. Waters have four children. They are John Adams, Anna Elizabeth, Frank and Garnette. Mr. Waters is well advanced in Masonry and is affiliated with A. F. & A. M. No. 25 at Fort Wayne, and the A. A. O. N. M. S. at Fort Wayne.

The Wayne Knitting Mills.—No history of Allen county would be complete without a record of the Wayne Knitting Mills and also its subsidiary and likewise important adjunct, the Thieme Bros. Company. For the purposes of this history no better method of outlining the development of this representative industrial concern can be followed than by making liberal quotations from the attractive souvenir brochure issued by the Wayne Knitting Mills, in 1916, the twenty-fifth anniversary of the founding of the business. Owing to minor paraphrase and elimination in the reproduction it is not deemed necessary to use formal marks of quotation. About the year 1888-9 it began to dawn upon the American people that they were dependent upon Europe for certain manufactured products, as many leading industries were not then represented at all in our country. To find employment for our people and assure future prosperity demanded more factories. For the purpose of offering capital and labor the advantages of tariff protection the McKinley tariff bill was drafted and enacted into law. This was quickly taken advantage of by American business men, and the more adventurous proceeded to Europe to find and study those industries which offered opportunities for establishment over here. Among those who grasped the significance of the new tariff law was Theodore F. Thieme, of Fort Wayne, Indiana. He sold out his well established drug store, at the corner of Wayne and Calhoun streets, and started for Europe in the summer of 1889. Europe was full of attractions, but a selection was made in favor of the full-fashioned hosiery business, the home of which was in Chemnitz, Germany. Mr. Thieme returned home and effected the organization of the Wayne Knitting Mills, with a capital of thirty thousand dollars, and with original executive officers as here noted: President, Henry C. Paul; vice-president, Charles S. Bash; secretary and manager, Theodore F. Thieme; treasurer, William H. Dreier. This was in the spring of 1891. Another trip to Chemnitz followed, for the purpose of buying machinery and bringing over a colony of experienced hosiery-makers, both men and women. Men and machines arrived during the summer of 1891 and the mill started in a rented store building at the northeast corner of Main and Clinton streets, with twenty-five experienced knitters and finishers. Under the most trying conditions, with a gas engine furnishing power, wood stoves supplying heat, and a dye department in the basement, the first stockings were turned out for market in January, 1892. The first year's operation proved conclusively that the business had a future, but it also developed the fact that much more capital, as well as modern factory facilities, would be needed. Many discouraging features developed, and it seemed impossible to secure the additional capital. Mr. Thieme says that many evenings the key to the factory door was turned for good and all, but that new hope and encouragement seemed to come with the morning. Finally, in the fall of 1892, the company was enabled to increase its capital stock to one hundred thousand dollars, and plans were laid for a two-story brick building, with separate power plant and dye house. When completed, the new building, at the intersection of the Lake Erie and Nickel Plate railways, was equipped with additional machinery from Germany, and the old plant was removed to the new quarters in January, 1893. About this time the capacity of the mill was materially increased by the purchase and addition of the machinery and other equipment of a new mill that had been unsuccessfully operated at Dover, Delaware. In 1896 the capital stock was increased to $125,000, and in 1898, by the enlistment of eastern capital, the stock was raised to $250,000. A New York office and stock-room was opened, in charge of the firm of Spies & Nissen, who were given exclusive sale of Wayne Knit hosiery in the eastern market. This was the beginning of a New York office, which has been a most important factor in the growth of the business. Up to 1898 the Wayne Knitting Mills had confined itself to the manufacture of full-fashioned hosiery for men and women, but now began to feel the need of a line of children's hosiery, as well as a line of seamless goods. It was decided to make these in Fort Wayne, and under the direction of Fred J. Thieme the United Knitting Mills, an independent plant, began the manufacture of these goods, which were marketed by the Wayne Knitting Mills. The children's goods were put out under the now well known trade mark of "Pony Stockings," which is today the best advertised brand of children's hose in America. In 1902 the United Mill was taken over by the parent concern, the capital stock of which was then increased to $425,000. In this consolidation Samuel M. Foster became president of the corporation; Fred J. Thieme was appointed superintendent; Edward Helmcke became treasurer; and Theodore F. Thieme continued secretary and manager. In 1904 the board of directors adopted a profit-sharing plan, which included all officers and heads of departments and special employees, and the result is the present Textile Industrial Club, which has become a valuable aid in the development of the organization and the business.

In 1904 a fine exhibit of Wayne Knit hosiery was made at the Louisiana Purchase Exposition, in St. Louis, for which the jury of awards gave to the Wayne Knitting Mills the grand prize. In 1906 branch plants were established at Garrett and Roanoke, Indiana, and another on the east side of Fort Wayne. In this year also the capital stock of the corporation was increased to $700,000, and the Wayne Knitting Mills Benefit Society was organized. In 1908 the capital was again increased to $1,000,000. As the public demand for pure silk hose and combination stockings grew stronger, the management became impressed with the necessity of operating a special silk-hosiery mill. Since this work required separate handling and equipment, the Thieme Bros. Company was organized, in 1909, with a capital stock of $150,000, all of which was acquired by the stockholders of the Wayne Knitting Mills. A three-story brick building was put up, across the street from the main office, and the manufacturing of ingrain thread silk hosiery for men, women and children was instituted. This enterprise proved so successful that, two years later, the capital stock was increased to $200,000, and an additional building, with new machinery, was provided to double the original output. In 1909 John A. Thieme was made assistant manager, and both he and Mr. Helmcke became members of the board of directors of the Wayne Knitting Mills. At the annual meeting of the board of directors on May 10, 1910, Mr. Foster resigned the presidency in favor of Theodore F. Thieme, who still holds this office. The other officers of the company at the present time are as here noted: William E. Mossman, vice-president; Fred J. Thieme, secretary; and Edward Helmcke, treasurer. In connection with the profit-sharing plan that was instituted in 1904 a special fund was developed, and in six years this was sufficient to build and equip the present fine Club House for employees. This building, of two stories and basement, was completed in 1910, at a cost exceeding $50,000, and the Wayne Knit Social Center is without doubt the most important and far-reaching subsidiary activity of the Wayne Knitting Mills. In May, 1911, the capital stock of the concern was increased to its present figure, $1,200,000. The Old Fort Knitting Mills was acquired by purchase in 1912, and its full equipment under the new control made such provision as to warrant the closing down of the branches at Garrett and Roanoke. With the purchase of this mill the total floor space of the gigantic plant was increased to 403,859 square feet—about nine and one-fourth acres. The corporation now has an old-age pension fund, for which a definite distribution system is being brought into operation. The foregoing resume can not but show to even the casual reader the great importance of the Wayne Knitting Mills as touching the general commercial, civic and material welfare of Fort Wayne, and the history of the concern is one of which every citizen should be appreciative and definitely proud.

The Wayne Tobacco Company.—The advantages of Fort Wayne as a distributing center have gained due recognition and have enabled many ambitious and progressive citizens to develop substantial commercial enterprises of important order. Such a business is that conducted by the Wayne Tobacco Company, which controls a large trade in the wholesale handling of tobaccos, cigars, cigarets and general lines of smokers' supplies. The enterprise had its inception on February 13, 1908, and was originally conducted under the title of Albert H. Buuck & Company, with headquarters at 827 Madison street. In the following April, however, removal was made to 1022 Barr street, and in October, 1910, as a matter of commercial expediency and for the purpose of making proper provision for the constantly expanding trade, the concern was incorporated under the present title of the Wayne Tobacco Company, with operations based on a capital stock of twenty-five thousand dollars. At the time of incorporation Frank H. Bougher became president of the company and Albert H. Buuck the secretary and manager. About two years later the capital stock was increased to fifty thousand dollars, and at this time Mr. Buuck, the founder of the business, assumed the office of president, Henry F. Koeneman becoming secretary and treasurer and continuing the incumbent of this dual office until February, 1913, when he was succeeded by Dick F. Waterfield, who is still serving in the capacity noted. In the headquarters employment is given to fourteen persons, and eight traveling salesmen represent the house throughout its trade territory, the business having been expanded to an annual average of six hundred thousand dollars, so that it represents one of the flourishing and important commercial enterprises of the Summit City.

Jacob A. Weaver.—One of the pioneer families of Wells county, Indiana, was the family which Jacob A. Weaver is today representing in Allen county, where he settled in young manhood. The Weavers were of Ohio birth, David Z. Weaver, father of the subject, being born in Monroe county and there was reared to manhood. His first independent venture took him to Indiana, where he settled on land in Wells county. He was without means and was unable to buy improved land, but he compromised with fortune by homesteading a tract of government land, which he improved and patented in due time. His early life was not void of hardships, and with no near neighbors loneliness in those first years was a foregone conclusion. He was friendly with the Indians, who were numerous, and with whom he frequently traded, buying his first team of horses from them. He married Susanna Kohr and together they attained a pleasing measure of success in their work. In later years Mr. Weaver owned and operated a grist mill at Zanesville, and was for some time engaged in stock-buying. They were the parents of six children: John B., Catherine, Elizabeth, Emma, Jacob A., and Alice. Jacob A. Weaver was born in Wells county, Indiana, October 13, 1863. His young life was as uneventful as that of most farmer boys, and he divided his time until his later teens between the work of the home farm and his studies in the village schools. When he was twenty-three years old he left the family home and began farming on his own responsibility, beginning operations with an eighty-acre farm to which he later added one hundred and two acres, so that he now has a considerable acreage under cultivation. Stock-farming held his attention during most of the time, and he experienced a commendable success in that departure. In 1902 he withdrew from active farm life and settling in Fort Wayne identified himself with the Fort Wayne Lumber Company, with which establishment he was associated until March, 1917, when he returned to his farm, where he now resides and is again giving his attention to his agricultural interests. In 1886 Mr. Weaver was married to Kate V. Jacobs, daughter of Elijah Jacobs, an old Wells county pioneer, and they are the parents of five children: Merlie E., Goldie M., Ivan O., Lela F., and Floyd A.

Marion A. Webb.—Those familiar with the life record of the late Marion A. Webb, of Fort Wayne, are impressed with the fact that as a man, as a citizen and as a representative of important business interests, he measured fully up to the high standard of personal stewardship and honor which he set for himself and which gained and retained to him the confidence and high regard of those with whom he came in contact in the varied relations of a signally upright and useful life. During the greater part of his active career he was employed as a traveling commercial salesman in the dry goods line, and concerning him the following consistent statement has been written: "As a traveling salesman he continued his services for a term of years, covered his assigned territory with perfect regularity and made a record of salesmanship that placed him in the front rank of the men of his concern." From the age of fourteen years until his death Mr. Webb maintained his home in Fort Wayne, and here his circle of friends was limited only by that of his acquaintances. Mr. Webb was born at Germantown, Montgomery county, Ohio, March 28, 1846, a son of Jonathan P. and Helen Webb. He established his residence in Fort Wayne when he was a lad of fourteen years, as previously noted. Mr. Webb acquired his early education in the public schools of Ohio and Fort Wayne, and initiated his association with business affairs by obtaining employment in a Fort Wayne banking institution. Later he entered the service of the A. S. Evans dry goods house, of Fort Wayne, and, with characteristic circumspection and diligence so applied himself as to gain a thorough and comprehensive knowledge of material values and all other details pertaining to the dry goods trade, so that he was well fortified when he became a traveling salesman in the wholesale dry goods field. His course as a citizen and as a business man was marked by high ideals and his genial and kindly nature won to him hosts of friends. He was a member of a family of three children, of whom one, Marcus, died in infancy, and the one survivor is Helen, who is the wife of George Davis, of Fort Wayne. Mr. Webb was a life-long adherent of the Republican party, loyal and public-spirited but never a seeker of official preferment of political order. He was long and actively affiliated with the time-honored Masonic fraternity and was a zealous member of the Westminster Presbyterian church in Fort Wayne, in which his widow and daughters retain active membership. On May 9, 1871, was solemnized the marriage of Mr. Webb to Miss May Hamilton, of Fort Wayne. Mrs. Webb is a daughter of John and Agnes Hamilton, natives respectively of Albany, New York, and West Stockbridge, Mass. Mr. Hamilton was a saddler by trade and when he came to Fort Wayne, in 1842, established himself in the business to which he had been trained. He was one of the pioneers in the saddlery business at Fort Wayne but lived only a decade after here establishing his home, his death having occurred in 1852 and his widow having survived him by a number of years. Of their two children the son, Hugh, died in early youth, so that Mrs. Webb is the only living representative of this well known pioneer family of Fort Wayne. Mr. and Mrs. Webb became the parents of two daughters, Clara May and Marian Agnes, both of whom remain with their widowed mother in their native city. Mr. Webb passed to the life eternal on April 25, 1902, and to those nearest and dearest to him there remains a measure of compensation and reconciliation in the gracious memories of all that he was a devoted husband and father and as a man who stood "four square to every wind that blows." Though a measureable recapitulation, the following extract from an estimate that appeared in the Fort Wayne Morning Journal at the time of the death of Mr. Webb merits perpetuation in this memoir: "Mr. Webb was left an orphan at an early age, and somewhat later was taken into the home of D. S. Beaver. Mr. Webb first accepted employment at the old Bond bank, which occupied the site of the present First National Bank of Fort Wayne, and later entered the dry goods house of A. S. Evans & Company. He became a member of the firm, and when it was succeeded by the wholesale dry goods house of Evans, McDonald & Company Mr. Webb still retained an interest in the concern. When the firm failed, in 1882, he commenced work as a traveling salesman. In 1894 he accepted a position with the DeWald Dry Goods Company, and thereafter was accounted one of their best salesmen until his death.''

Fred Wehrenberg is secretary, treasurer and manager of the New Haven Lumber & Supply Company, which conducts a large and prosperous enterprise in the handling of lumber, building supplies, wire fencing, drain tile and various lines of farm supplies. The headquarters of the company are at New Haven, Adams township, and a lumber yard is also conducted at Monroeville, in Monroe township. The company was organized in 1906, by Henry C. Wehrenberg, Fred Albersmeyer, Charles Rodenbeck and Diederick Rodenbeck, and these men continued as the controlling principals until the spring of the following year, when the business was incorporated with a capital stock of twenty thousand dollars and with officers as here noted: Henry C. Wehrenberg, president; Charles Rodenbeck, vice-president; and Fred Albersmeyer, secretary, treasurer and manager. At this time Fred Wehrenberg, son of the president, began to assist in the practical management of the business, and his experience in the passing years covered all details of the enterprise. In January, 1915, a reorganization of the company took place and the ownership of the business passed to the control of Henry C. and Fred Wehrenberg, Theodore Thimlar and Diederick Rodenbeck. The present officers of the corporation are: Henry C. Wehrenberg, president; Theodore Thimlar, vice-president; and Fred Wehrenberg, secretary, treasurer and manager. In 1917 the capital stock was increased to $35,000. The business is founded on substantial basis of ample capital, effective service and fair and honorable dealings, so that the success of the enterprise has been normally and worthily achieved. Fred Wehrenberg was born in the city of Fort Wayne, December 29, 1890, and has gained place as one of the aggressive young business men of his native county. He is a son of Henry C. and Wilhelmina (Albersmeyer) Wehrenberg, both natives of Germany, the father having been born in the Kingdom of Hanover, February 22, 1859, and the mother October 24, 1862. Henry C. Wehrenberg was reared and educated in his native land and was a young man when he came to the United States, about the year 1880. He remained in New York city until 1881, when he came to Allen county, Indiana, and established his residence in Fort Wayne, where he worked two years at the trade of brick mason and then engaged in contracting business in the line of his trade, in which field of enterprise he still continues his successful operations, he and his wife still maintaining their home in Fort Wayne and both being communicants of the Lutheran church. Of their children the eldest is Fred, the immediate subject of this sketch, and the other four, Paul, Henry C., Jr., Wilma and Alfred, still remain at the parental home in Fort Wayne. Fred Wehrenberg attended in his boyhood the parochial school of St. Paul's Lutheran church in Fort Wayne, and supplemented this by continuing his studies in the Clay public school and the Fort Wayne Business College. After his course in the business college he was for six months in the employ of the Becker Paper Company, Fort Wayne, and thereafter was in the employ of the Western Gas & Construction Company. In 1917 he removed to New Haven, so he could better handle the affairs of the New Haven Lumber & Supply Company, of which he is now the active executive officer, besides being a stockholder in the New Haven State Bank. In politics he is not constrained by strict partisan lines but supports men and measures meeting the approval of his judgment. In his home village he is an influential member of the Commercial Club, and here he and his wife are active communicants of Emanuel Lutheran church. In Fort Wayne he holds membership in the Friars' Club, the One Hundred Per Cent. Club, and the Walther League of St. Paul's Lutheran parish. June 7, 1916, was solemnized the marriage of Mr. Wehrenberg to Miss Ruth Furste, daughter of George and Elizabeth (Waldron) Furste, of Huntington, Indiana, and they are popular factors in the representative social life of their home community.

Henry Wehrenberg, who has won through his own ability and well ordered efforts a secure vantage-place as one of the successful and representative contractors and builders in the city of Fort Wayne, was born in Hanover, Germany, on February 22, 1861, and is one of the two survivors of the seven children of Frederick and Mary (Schroeder) Wehrenberg, five of the number having died in childhood and the one other survivor being a daughter who resides in Bremen, Germany. The parents passed their entire lives in the German fatherland, and thus the subject of this review is the only representative of the immediate family in the United States. Henry Wehrenberg is indebted to the excellent schools of his native land for his early educational advantages, and there also he served his apprenticeship to the bricklayers' trade. In 1881, as a self-reliant and ambitious young man of twenty years, he severed the home ties and set forth to seek his fortunes in America. He landed in the port of New York city and remained in the national metropolis eighteen months, at the expiration of which he came to Indiana and established his permanent home in Fort Wayne. Here he was employed for several years as a journeyman at his trade, and since 1891 has here been engaged in contracting and building in an independent way. He has erected many private dwellings in this city, besides a large number of buildings of more pretentious order, including the Washington school and the school building on Holton avenue, the People's Trust Company's fine building and also that of the Lincoln National Life Insurance Company. Though he has not withdrawn from business as a progressive and successful contractor, Mr. Wehrenberg is at the time of this writing giving much of his time and attention to promotive service for the General Electric Company of Fort Wayne. He is a wide-awake and progressive citizen, is a Democrat in his political adherency, and both he and his wife are communicants of St. Paul's Lutheran church. On May 3, 1887, was solemnized the marriage of Mr. Wehrenberg to Miss Minnie Albersmeyer, who likewise was born in Germany, and they have five children—Frederick H., Paul, Henry, Wilma, and Alfred. The two older sons are active and popular young business men of their native county, Frederick H. being manager of the Lumber Supply Company at New Haven, and Paul is associated with his father in business, being a member of the municipal council of Fort Wayne.

Fred H. Wellman is a member of the firm of Wellman & Ulmer, which conducts one of the best appointed undertaking and funeral-directing establishments in the city of Fort Wayne, and from the same the most effective and considerate service is always assured, including that afforded through automobile funeral cars and carriages. Mr. Wellman was born in Fort Wayne on January 28, 1878, a son of Carl and Henrietta (Witte) Wellman, both natives of Germany. Carl Wellman was a skilled millwright by vocation and established his home in Fort Wayne in the year 1874, both he and his wife having here passed the remainder of their lives and the subject of this review being the older of their two surviving children. The younger child, Sophia, is the wife of William Koch, of Fort Wayne. He whose name introduces this sketch acquired his early education in the parochial school of Emanuel Lutheran church and later attended for a time the Fort Wayne Medical College, largely for the purpose of obtaining knowledge of anatomy, as an adjunct of the undertaking business. Later he completed a course in the Champion School of Embalming, at Springfield, Ohio, in 1896, and since that year has been actively associated with the undertaking business in Fort Wayne. In 1910 he purchased an interest in the well established business of his uncle, Henry Wellman, and after the latter's death, in 1915, obtained full control of the business, which he has since conducted in an individual way, until May 15, 1917, when he and C. J. Ulmer consolidated their undertaking businesses and the new firm name now is Wellman & Ulmer. Their well equipped establishment is at 211 West Berry street, and under the provisions of the Indiana laws Mr. Wellman is licensed both as an undertaker and an embalmer, having been one of the first in Fort Wayne to register under the laws thus provided. Both he and his wife are active communicants of the Lutheran church. On September 23, 1903, was solemnized the marriage of Mr. Wellman to Miss Edith Schwartz, daughter of Henry and Louise Schwartz, of Fort Wayne, and the one child of this union is a daughter, Valetta.

Joel Welty was a man whose sterling character expressed itself in earnest and consistent stewardship during the course of a long and useful life, and he achieved success and influence in connection with business affairs of important order. In 1895 he established a well equipped book bindery in Fort Wayne, and under his effective direction the Fort Wayne Binding Company became one of the important and prosperous business concerns of the Allen county metropolis. He amplified the enterprise eventually by engaging also in the manufacturing of paper boxes, under the title of the Fort Wayne Box Company, and of both of these substantial corporations he continued the executive head until his death, which occurred December 20, 1903, his widow still retaining his stock interest in the box company. Mr. Welty was a man of energy and mature judgment, of broad mental ken and of exalted integrity, so that his death was looked upon as a distinct loss to the community with which he had fully and loyally identified himself and in which his name is held in enduring honor. Joel Welty was born in Wayne county, Ohio, on April 15, 1857, a son of Christian and Magdalena (Lugenbuehl) Welty, the former of whom was born in the United States and the latter in the canton of Berne, Switzerland, the Welty family lineage likewise tracing back to staunch Swiss origin. Christian Welty continued his alliance with agricultural pursuits in the old Buckeye state until 1868, when he removed with his family to Moniteau county, Missouri, where he and his wife

J. Welty

passed the remainder of their lives and where he was a prosperous farmer and influential citizen, both he and his wife having been most devout members of the Mennonite church. Of their children the first born, Elizabeth, is deceased; Caroline is the wife of Andrew J. Moser and they reside in the state of Missouri; Daniel is a resident of California; Rosa is the wife of Michael Wenger, and they maintain their home in Idaho; John B. resides at Berne, Adams county, Indiana; Benjamin F. lives in Tacoma, Washington; Amelia is the wife of John Rhorer, of Winnie, Chambers county, Texas; and the subject of this memoir was the sixth in order of birth of the seven children. Joel Welty gained his rudimentary education in the Ohio schools and was about twelve years old at the time of the family removal to Missouri, where he was reared to manhood on the home farm and made good use of the advantages of the public schools of the period, this discipline having been supplemented by a course of study in the Mennonite college at Wadsworth, Ohio. As a youth he put his scholastic attainments to practical use by entering the pedagogic profession. He taught first in the schools of Wayne county, Ohio, and later was a successful teacher in the village schools of Berne, Indiana. There, on May 9, 1882, he opened a book and wall-paper store, and somewhat later established the first printing office in the village. From the latter was developed eventually a well equipped printing and binding plant that came into the control of the Mennonite Book Concern. Of this business Mr. Welty continued the manager until 1895, when he removed the machinery and general equipment of the bindery to Fort Wayne and here initiated business under the title of the Fort Wayne Binding Company. Of his excellent success in the upbuilding of this enterprise and also that of the Fort Wayne Box Company mention has already been made, but it may further be said that Mr. Welty gained secure and honorable place as one of the thoroughly representative businss men and valued citizens of Fort Wayne. He was a staunch Republican in politics, and while a resident of Berne, Indiana, served several years as postmaster. He was a man of the deepest Christian faith and service, and was a zealous and influential member of the Mennonite church. On April 3, 1887, was solemnized the marriage of Mr. Welty to Miss Dina Lehmann, daughter of Peter and Verena (Sprunger) Lehmann, of Berne, this state, and she survives him, as do also their six children. Of these Magdalena is the wife of Norman Tolson, of Chicago, and they have one child, Norman Welty Tolson; Harrison resides in the city of Detroit, Michigan; and Viola, Paul, Ivan and Carl remain with their widowed mother in the pleasant home in Fort Wayne. Peter Lehmann, father of Mrs. Welty, was born in Muensterburg, Switzerland, as was also his wife, and there their marriage was solemnized. In 1852 they came to the United States and established their home in Adams county, Indiana, where Mr. Lehmann engaged in farming and also gave effective service as a clergyman of the Mennonite church. For several years he was similarly engaged in Hickory county, Missouri, but later returned to Adams county, Indiana, where he and his wife passed the residue of their lives and he was living retired in the village of Berne at the time of his death. Of the children of Mr. and Mrs. Lehmann the following brief data are available: Anna is the wife of Christian P. Lugenbill, and they reside in the state of Kansas; Mary is deceased; Rachel is the wife of Peter Gilliom, of Berne, Indiana; Katherine is the wife of David C. Neuenschwander, of Berne, where also resides Japhet

F., the only son; Mrs. Welty was the sixth child and was born in Adams county, this state, on February 27, 1863, her education having been received principally in the schools of Missouri; Emma is the wife of James McCaslin, of Kansas; and Lydia is deceased.

Charles R. Wermuth.—One of the leaders in construction work in Fort Wayne is Charles R. Wermuth, who has carried on an independent business in that city for the past thirty years. He has to his credit the building of a good many of the finest specimens of the builder's art that the city possesses and has won a reputation for careful and honest workmanship that any man might envy. Mr. Wermuth is a native German, born in Saxony, Germany, August 18, 1853, son of Gottlieb and Johanna Wermuth, who passed their lives in their native land. Of twelve children born to them, three survive. Charles Wermuth left home at the age of twenty-three, going to Dresden, Germany, where he learned the trade of a carpenter and builder. He spent six years there and was wholly proficient in his trade when he came to America. He came to Fort Wayne, in 1881, and worked at his trade for about six years before he felt the time was ripe for the establishment of a business of his own. He was successful from the beginning, having already won a reputation in the community for reliable workmanship, and his progress has been steady and consistent with the character of his operations. Among the many well known buildings Mr. Wermuth has brought to completion are St. Paul's Cathedral, the Presbyterian church on Harrison street, the Sunset Building, the St. John's School, the Fort Wayne Knitting Mills, and the Deister Machine Shops. He has also built a large addition to the Wayne Oil Tank and built most of the Western Gas Company's plant. Mr. Wermuth was married, in 1876, to Miss Marie Pretchendorf, a native of Germany, whom he met in Dresden while located there learning his trade. They came to America soon after their marriage. Of nine children born to them, six survive. They are Helen, the wife of Harry C. Rehm, of Fort Wayne; Freda, Alfred, Martha, Selma and Thekla, all living at home with their parents. The two eldest, Clemence and Adolph, died in mature years, and the third child, also a boy, died in infancy. The family are members of the German Lutheran church.

John Wessel.—The late John Wessel II passed his entire life in Fort Wayne, as a scion of one of the honored pioneer families of the city and it was given him to achieve success in connection with business affairs, as well as to exemplify those sterling characteristics that invariably beget unqualified popular confidence and esteem. He was still a young man at the time of his death, which occurred March 1, 1889, and it is especially interesting to record that his parents, now venerable in years, still reside in Fort Wayne, where they have maintained their home for more than sixty years. He to whom this memoir is dedicated was born in Fort Wayne on November 6, 1856, and thus he was not yet thirty-three years of age when he passed from the stage of life's mortal endeavors. His parents, John and Elizabeth (Kientz) Wessel, were born and reared in Schleswig-Holstein, Germany, and their marriage was solemnized after they had established their home in America, the mother having become a resident of Fort Wayne, in 1854, and the father located in the city of Chicago, 1848, soon after his immigration to the United States. From the future metropolis of the west he came to Fort Wayne and here followed for many years the vocation of stationary engineer. In 1862 he enlisted for service as a soldier in the Civil war, but the exigencies of family affairs led him soon afterward to provide a substitute, and thus he did not see active service on the field of battle. The year 1917 finds him living in well earned retirement in Fort Wayne, at the age of eighty-five years, and his wife likewise is an octogenarian. Of their three children John II, subject of this memoir, was the eldest; Sophie, first of the name, died in infancy; and Sophie, second to be thus named, is the wife of Philip Graf, of Fort Wayne. John Wessel, Sr., and his wife have been lifelong and devoted communicants of the Catholic church, and his political allegiance is given to the Democratic party. John Wessel II, to whom this memoir is dedicated, acquired his youthful education in the parochial and public schools of Fort Wayne and for ten years prior to his death had been engaged in the retail grocery business in his native city. He was most vital and loyal in his civic attitude, was a staunch adherent of the Democratic party and served two terms as a member of the city council. He was a man of exalted integrity, and his genial personality gained and retained to him a host of friends, so that he was deeply mourned in his home community when he passed to the life eternal, in the very prime of his young manhood. He was an earnest communicant of St. Peter's Catholic church, as is also his widow, who still resides in Fort Wayne. On the 11th of February, 1880, was solemnized the marriage of Mr. Wessel to Miss Caroline Neidhofer, who likewise was born and reared in Fort Wayne, a daughter of the late William and Mary (Draker) Neidhofer, both natives of Germany and residents of Fort Wayne for many years prior to their death, the father having here been engaged in the grocery business for a long period. Of the four children Mrs. Wessel is the eldest; Anna is the wife of James Handley, of Fort Wayne; Joseph died in infancy, and Mary is the wife of Julian F. Franke, of Fort Wayne. Mr. and Mrs. Wessel became the parents of five children, of whom only one is living, John III.

William Westhoff abandoned his trade of brick mason to engage in contracting in Fort Wayne, in 1896. Since then he has been identified prominently with the erection of some of the finer buildings in and about the city, and has been gratifyingly successful in all his undertakings. Mr. Westhoff was born in Germany on January 18, 1859, son of Jule and Mary (Musman) Westhoff, who lived and died in their native land. Of their three children only the subject survives. He learned his trade in Germany and, in 1882, came to America, locating in Fort Wayne almost immediately. He followed his trade for some years, and was successful from the beginning. He gathered some capital together as a result of his labors, and, in 1896, embarked on a building career on his own responsibility. Among the more prominent pieces of work he has carried to completion might be mentioned the Jefferson school, the Elks' Building, the Broadway school house and Concordia church. Also, the remodeling of the Methodist church was a creditable example of his work, and the Presbyterian church on Harrison street should be mentioned in the list of his more notable work. Mr. Westhoff married Caroline Weigman, also of German birth, on October 15, 1886, and to them were born seven children as follows: Mary and Emma, deceased; Lena, Freda, Martha and twins who died at birth. Lena is living at home, as is also Martha, and Freda is the wife of Fred Everding, of Fort Wayne. The family are members of the German Lutheran church, and Mr. Westhoff is a Democrat in politics.

Henry A. Wetzel is a well known representative of a sterling German family that was founded in Allen county more than half a century ago, his father having become one of the substantial landholders and successful farmers of the county and having ever commanded inviolable place in the esteem of the community in which he continued his residence until his death. He whose name initiates this paragraph has well upheld in his native county the prestige of the family name, both as a loyal and public-spirited citizen and as an influential exponent of the basic industries of agriculture and stock-growing. He has served, since 1914, as a member of the board of county commissioners and has shown marked loyalty and progressiveness in administration of public affairs in the county. Mr. Wetzel was born in Springfield township, this county, on April 8, 1866, a son of William and Mary (Plummer) Wetzel, both of whom were born and reared in Germany. The parents established their home in Allen county, Indiana, more than fifty years ago and the father was one of the honored citizens and prosperous farmers of the county at the time of his death, in 1890, his widow having been venerable in years when she too was summoned to eternal rest, in 1907, and both having been lifelong and earnest communicants of the German Reformed church. Of their children the eldest is William, who maintains his residence in Fort Wayne; John W. is a resident of Tulsa, Oklahoma; Elizabeth is the wife of Frederick Fark, of St. Joseph township, Allen county; and the subject of this sketch is the youngest of the number. Henry A. Wetzel was reared to the sturdy discipline of the farm, was afforded the advantages of the public schools of Allen county, and here has been actively identified with farm industry from his early youth to the present time. He now has control of about two hundred acres of fertile and productive land, principally in St. Joseph township, and though he gives attention to diversified agriculture and stock-growing makes a specialty of the propagation of corn, of which he raises large crops each successive season. In his farm enterprise he brings to bear the most approved and scientific methods and is essentially one of the leading representatives of the agricultural interests of his native county, besides being an influential citizen whom his fellow citizens have called upon to serve in various offices of trust, the culminating preferment having come to him, in 1914, when he was elected to his present office as a member of the board of county commissioners. Mr. Wetzel is a stalwart and well fortified advocate of the principles of the Democratic party, he is affiliated with the Loyal Order of Moose, and he and his wife hold membership in the German Reformed church. His official duties demand his presence in Fort Wayne, the county seat, much of the time, but he still maintains his residence on his fine homestead farm in St. Joseph township. The marriage of Mr. Wetzel was to Miss Mary Smith, who was born in the state of Michigan. Of the three children of this union Elmer and Raymond are successful young farmers in St. Joseph township, and May remains at the parental home.

John Wilding is a native son of England, but has entered most fully into the progressive spirit of America and has here won advancement to a position of prominence and influence in connection with important business enterprise in the metropolis and judicial center of Allen county, where he is treasurer and manager of the Fort Wayne Printing Company, one of the largest and most successful concerns of the kind in Northern Indiana. Under the title of the Fort Wayne Paper & Blank Book Company this business was founded on July 20, 1903, with a capital stock of twenty-five thousand dollars and with the following named persons as the constituent members of the board of directors of the new corporation: H. C. Rockhill, I. G. Stafford, Joel Witte, Peter Boegli, A. H. Perfect, A. K. Mehl, and C. E. Hadsell. With headquarters at 214-16 East Main street, the company opened a well equipped establishment in which employment was given to a corps of thirty persons. In 1906 the business was incorporated under the present title, and in February of the following year the company purchased the plant and business of the job-printing department of the Fort Wayne Journal, the capital stock having been increased to fifty thousand dollars. The officers of the company at the present time are here noted: W. F. Graeter, president; A. H. Perfect, vice-president; John Wilding, treasurer and general manager; Harry Wilding, secretary; and Mrs. Rosa B. Ueber, A. C. Brase, A. J. Moynihan and Joseph Baum likewise being members of the directorate of the corporation, the capital stock of which was increased to one hundred and fifty thousand dollars in September, 1911. A thoroughly modern lithographing department was added to the large and well equipped plant in 1907, and in 1912 was established the special advertising department. The establishment now gives employment to fully two hundred persons and the annual business has attained to an average aggregate of four hundred thousand dollars—a status that marks the company as one of the most important printing concerns in the Hoosier state. In 1912 the company erected its present substantial and modern brick building, which is sixty by one hundred and fifty feet in lateral dimensions and four stories and basement in height. The company does a general job-printing business and manufactures and sells full lines of bank and office supplies, including blank books of the most approved modern type, and also various legal and general business blank documents. The mail-order business of the company, for 1916, reached the noteworthy aggregate of three hundred thousand dollars, and the importance of the concern as touching the general civic and business prosperity of Fort Wayne may be understood when it is stated that its weekly pay roll aggregates three thousand dollars. In connection with its general printing and binding business the company secured in 1916 an important contract for the state printing of Indiana—this being a notable recognition of the splendid facilities of the institution and of the effective and straightforward management of the business, which is an important adjunct to the industrial and commercial activities of Fort Wayne. John Wilding, the efficient and popular manager of this extensive enterprise, was born in Oldham, England, on August 9, 1873, a son of Robert Wilding, who came to the United States in 1890 and engaged in mercantile business in Indianapolis, where he continued his residence until 1905, since which time he has maintained his home in Fort Wayne, where he is now living virtually retired. John Wilding was afforded the advantages of the excellent schools of his native land and as a youth was there employed for some time in a cotton factory. He was seventeen years of age when he accompanied his parents on their removal to the United States and after the family home had been established in the capital city of Indiana he was there employed in a hotel for a few weeks. He then assumed the dignified position of "printer's devil" in the office of the Indianapolis Sentinel and there initiated his association with the "art preservative of all arts," in the intricacies and mysteries of which he has become an expert. After leaving the Sentinel Mr. Wilding was for six years employed in the printing office of the Baker-Randolph Company, in Indianapolis, and later passed six months in the office of William

B. Burford & Company, another of the important printing concerns of the capital city. In Indianapolis he next became foreman in the composing room of the printing establishment of Levy Brothers & Company. Two years later he was made general superintendent of this establishment and this incumbency retained five years, at the expiration of which he came to Fort Wayne and identified himself with the Fort Wayne Printing Company, of which he is now treasurer and general manager, with an experience and an executive ability that well fortify him for the manifold duties that devolve upon him in the handling of a business of broad scope and importance. He is actively identified with the Fort Wayne Commercial Club, the Rotary and Quest Clubs, is affiliated with the Masonic fraternity, including the Ancient Arabic Order, Nobles of the Mystic Shrine, and holds membership in the local ledge of the Benevolent & Protective Order of Elks, besides being a member of the Fort Wayne Country Club and the Knights of Pythias. In 1895 was solemnized the marriage of Mr. Wilding to Miss Clara Mellor, who was born and reared in England, a daughter of Joseph Mellor. The one child of this union is Lillian, who remains a member of the parental home circle.

The Wildwood Builders Company is an institution which by very virtue of its assigned functions and effective management has been destined to exercise large and important influence in connection with normal and progressive real estate development and improvement in the urban community of Fort Wayne, and it is proper that special mention of the same should be made in this history. The company was organized on April 1, 1910, and was duly incorporated under the laws of Indiana, with a capital stock of fifty thousand dollars. The interested principals in effecting the organization were Lee J. Ninde, Daniel B. Ninde, Frank K. Stafford, Samuel M. Foster, and Abe Ackerman, and all of these representative citizens of Allen county constituted the original directorate of the company. The personnel of the executive corps was as here noted: Lee J. Ninde, president; Daniel B. Ninde, vice-president; Frank K. Stafford, secretary and treasurer. The same officials still retain their respective offices, save that Mr. Safford is now serving as secretary only and Frederick B. Shoaff has been made treasurer. Besides these executives the board of directors includes also Clinton R. Willson, Joseph Slater and Victor V. Miller. The capital stock of the corporation has been increased to $625,000 and the company is giving its attention specifically to the development of the beautiful Wildwood Park addition and other leading suburban districts of Fort Wayne. In the spring of 1917, the company removed from its rooms in the Shoaff building to a commodious ground-floor suite in the Gauntt building, southwest corner of West Berry and Webster streets. The activities of the Wildwood companies mark a forward step in the methods of the extension of home building and the creation of outlying properties into beautiful and valuable residence districts. Lee J. Ninde, the guiding spirit of the organization, is a happy combination of the idealist and the business man. The same influence which he has exerted in elevating the plan of home making in Fort Wayne to a means of adding to the every-day happiness of the many, and taking out of it the sordid elements of mere house building, has extended to all portions of the state of Indiana, where Mr. Ninde, through his work as president of the Indiana Real Estate Exchange, has found ready acceptance of his modern ideas. It was he who inaugurated, in 1916, the plan of a state-wide automobile tour of the larger cities to spread the gospel of city planning. His interest in the publication of the Wildwood Magazine, his deep concern in boy welfare and his varied activities along many wholesome avenues of endeavor mark him as one of Fort Wayne's most valuable citizens.

Lewis S. Williams.—The late Lewis S. Williams, for many years a resident of Fort Wayne, was connected in his capacity as a timber buyer with some of the leading piano houses of the United States during the best years of his life. He was a man who knew the timber markets thoroughly, and was always a wise and careful buyer. His acquaintance with his field was wide and his knowledge of the subject in a large measure instinctive with him, for his father was in the lumber business all his life and operated in the virgin timber lands of Michigan for many years. He was Clark I. Williams, son of Dan Williams, who came to Ohio from Maryland. The family is descended directly from Roger Williams of early American fame and name. Clark Williams was born on January 31, 1823, and married Lucetta Helen Lane. Their children were eight in number and are here briefly mentioned as follows: Charles Reason was born on March 6, 1846, and died August 22, 1846. Milton Taylor was born April 26, 1847, and died in the service of his country on November 21, 1864, not yet turned eighteen. Thomas Rigdon was born February 18, 1850, and died January 14, 1911. Lewis S., the subject, was born March 20, 1852, and died March 2, 1903. Dan Norton was born August 24, 1854, and died January 3, 1910. Horatio Gates, born August 6, 1858, and died March 2, 1860. Ella Era, born February 6, 1861, died April 11, 1911. John William was born May 19, 1868, and is the only surviving member of the family. The father of this family died on August 1, 1878, and the mother survived her husband a number of years. Lewis S. Williams, after his marriage, went to Fort Wayne and there associated himself in business with the Mossman-Yarnelle Lumber Company, with which firm he was active for three years. He then settled on an Allen county farm and for six years devoted himself to the pursuits of agriculture, after which he took a position with the Packard Piano Company as a buyer of raw materials for the firm. He was next associated in a similar capacity with Mason & Hamlin, a rival piano house of Boston, his headquarters continuing to be Fort Wayne. He was connected with that firm for some time and left them to take a position with the McCracken Company of Louisville, Kentucky, and while there on a business trip met with an injury that compelled him to return to Fort Wayne and give up his work. After he had recovered sufficiently to resume activities, he became a deputy organizer for the Maccabee lodge and was employed in that work at the time of his death. Mr. Williams was married on December 9, 1875, to Miss Elizabeth Golden, daughter of Patrick and Mary Ann (Fitzgerald) Golden. Mrs. Golden is of the royal Fitzgerald family of Ireland and is a lineal descendant of early kings and queens of the Emerald Isle. The father, Patrick Golden, was born in Ireland and came to America in 1849 and located in Harrisburg, Pennsylvania, where he was employed as foreman in a coal mine, coming to Fort Wayne, in 1850, to take charge of the grading of the Pennsylvania road. He built the aqueduct at Logansport, Indiana, and has other construction work of similar order to his credit. In 1860 Mr. Golden bought a farm of one hundred and sixty acres near Monroeville and spent the remainder of his days in making a habitable and productive place out of it. He died on May 29, 1876, and his widow survived him until December

8, 1892. They had six children. The eldest, Elizabeth, was buried in the Atlantic ocean when the family were on their way to America. Mary Ann, who was born on Christmas Day, 1849, is the wife of J. Nesbitt, of Allen county. John is a resident of Fort Wayne. The fourth child is Mrs. Williams, widow of the subject. She was born on July 8, 1853. Catherine, who married James O'Leary, was born July 4, 1855, and died on December 23, 1892, and Mr. O'Leary died October 17, 1916. Julia Clara, the youngest of the six, is the wife of John Cleary, of Fort Wayne. Lewis and Elizabeth Williams were the parents of four children. John Clark was born August 30, 1876. Harry and Herbert were twins, born May 6, 1880; they died on August 3d and 5th, respectively, of the same year. Charles Bernard was born on December 10, 1883, and is a resident of Cleveland, Ohio, where he is employed as a foreman in steel construction work.

Clinton R. Willson.—A native son of Fort Wayne who has here become a representative factor in connection with civic and material affairs, Mr. Willson is a member of one of the well known families of Fort Wayne, where his father has resided for more than forty years. Mr. Willson has held positions of responsibility and trust in connection with several financial institutions of the city and in his more individual and independent activities his achievement has been noteworthy. Clinton Rusk Willson was born in Fort Wayne on May 27, 1877, a son of Martin S. and Emma J. (Robinson) Willson, the former of whom was born in Pennsylvania, and the latter in Fort Wayne, Indiana, where her father was a pioneer business man and an influential citizen. Martin S. Willson was for many years in the employ of the Fort Wayne Electric Company and since its consolidation with the General Electric Company has here continued to hold a responsible executive position with the latter corporation—his entire period of service with the local concern having covered more than thirty years. He and his wife have reason to be gratified in noting the success gained by their six sons, concerning whom the following brief data may consistently be given: Harry L. is the virtual owner and the executive head of the business of the Randall Printing Company, of St. Paul, Minnesota; Clinton R., of this review, was the next in order of birth; Frederick M. is engaged in the advertising business at St. Paul, Minnesota; James D. is a graduate of the United States Naval Academy, at Annapolis, ranking Lieutenant Commander, and is now in active service in the United States Navy; Ralph holds a position as purchasing agent with the C. O. Bartlett & Snow Company, of Cleveland, Ohio, a concern engaged in the handling of elevators and heavy conveyors; and August is employed in the engineering sales department of the S. F. Bowser Company, of Fort Wayne. Clinton R. Willson made good use of the advantages of the Fort Wayne public schools, including the high school, and at the age of seventeen years took a minor clerical position in the offices of the First National Bank of Fort Wayne. Through effective service he won consecutive advancement and remained with this institution seven years. He then resigned his post to accept that of assistant secretary of the newly organized Citizens' Trust Company, and six years later was called to the office of cashier of the Commercial Bank. He continued six years in this position and upon his resignation therefrom purchased the business of the Neireiter-Gumpper Insurance Agency, the second oldest institution of the kind in Fort Wayne. He assumed control of this business in July, 1914, and wisely preserved the old-established title of the agency, but added to the same his own name also. The large and representative general insurance business has since been continued, therefore, as the Neireiter-Gumpper-Willson Agency. Mr. Willson has not curbed his energy, and in connection with his insurance business is giving attention to the handling of high-grade securities. He is treasurer of the Morris Plan Company and the Lafayette Place Company, the latter of which has control of one of the most attractive residential subdivisions of Fort Wayne; he is treasurer of the Dreibelbiss Abstract Company; and is a director in the Fort Wayne Concrete Tile Company, the Wildwood Builders' Company, and the Home Supply Company. Aside from his business responsibilities Mr. Willson has found time to enjoy the best in the social life of the community and to make pleasing use of his musical talent. He has been a leader in the musical circles of Fort Wayne and for fully twenty years was a member of the choir of the Third Presbyterian church, besides which he has been identified with the musical affairs of the local Jewish synagogue for fourteen consecutive years. He is one of the valuable members of the Fort Wayne Commercial Club and the Rotary Club, holds membership in the Quest Club, is affiliated with the Masonic fraternity, his political allegiance is given to the Republican party, and he and his wife are members of the Third Presbyterian church. On June 13, 1901, was solemnized the marriage of Mr. Willson to Miss Lillie Wilding, daughter of James and Ella Wilding, of Fort Wayne, and the four children of this union are Helen, Kathryn, James and Robert.

Edward M. Wilson now has sole ownership and control of the long established and representative insurance business that is conducted under the title of Schrader & Wilson, although the senior member of the firm retired from the alliance on January 1, 1913. This is one of the oldest insurance agencies in the city of Fort Wayne and its functions include virtually all phases of indemnity underwriting except life insurance. Mr. Wilson is local representative for a number of the staunchest and best known companies that extend policies of indemnity for losses by fire, cyclone, accidents of various orders, plate-glass, steam-boiler, burglar, employers' liability, sprinkler leakage, automobile use and occupancy insurance, surety bonds and also the collection of rentals. In the well appointed offices, at the corner of East Main and Court streets, employment is given to four efficient clerical and executive assistants and the high reputation of the agency constitutes its best asset. This agency had its inception in 1875, when H. C. Schrader opened an office on the second floor of the Odd Fellows' building, on West Berry street. There he continued in an individual way until 1889, when Edward M. Wilson was admitted to partnership and the present firm name of Schrader & Wilson was adopted. This fortuitous alliance continued until January 1, 1913, when Mr. Schrader retired, Mr. Wilson purchasing his interest and having successfully continued the enterprise in the original firm name, which has long stood as a voucher for the best of service and for fair methods in all transactions. Edward M. Wilson was born at Wabash, September 6, 1867. He is a son of Solomon Wilson, who was one of the pioneer citizens of Wabash, where he lived until his death. In the public schools of his native city Edward M. Wilson completed the curriculum of the high school, and later he entered the University of Michigan, in the class of 1891, but he withdrew prior to graduation, as he became associated with his present business in 1889. He is a recognized local authority in all matters pertaining to insurance save life insurance, of which branch he has had no desire to become an exponent, as he has found ample field for successful activity in other forms of insurance. He is a broad-gauged and loyal citizen who takes deep interest in all things tending to advance the welfare and progress of his home city, and is serving as treasurer of the Indiana School for Feebleminded Children, at Fort Wayne. In the time-honored Masonic fraternity he has received the thirty-second degree of the Ancient Accepted Scottish Rite, besides being affiliated with the Ancient Arabic Order of the Nobles of the Mystic Shrine and the Benevolent & Protective Order of Elks. He is a member of the Commercial and Country clubs.

John C. Winte.—The late John C. Winte was one of the substantial self-made men who devoted his life to earnest manual toil but who, through the practice of industry and economy, earned much of the reward that is frequently denied to those more highly favored by fortune. Mr. Winte was born in Fort Wayne, April 24, 1861, a son of John D. and Wilhelmina (Homeyer) Winte, both natives of Germany. The parents were early settlers in Fort Wayne and here continued their residence until their death. They became the parents of four children: Sophia is the widow of William Hener, of Fort Wayne; John C., is the subject of this memoir; Minnie is the wife of Henry Bienz, of Fort Wayne; and Henry D. is a resident of Chesaning, Saginaw county, Michigan. John C. Winte became an expert in the work of the blacksmith trade, which he followed about two years while in the west. He returned to Indiana and located at Poe, Allen county, where he conducted a blacksmith shop about three years before returning to Fort Wayne. In his native city he established himself in business by opening a shop at 2206 Fairfield avenue, whence he later removed to No. 2139 on that thoroughfare. Mr. Winte was here engaged in the blacksmith business for a period of about twenty-four years and within this time accumulated property of considerable value. Mr. Winte was twice married. He first wedded Miss Minnie Meyer, of Poe, this county, and of this union were born four children—Herman F., who married Elizabeth Rank, of Detroit, and they reside in that city; Charles, who died in infancy; Alma, who is the wife of Arthur W. Young, cashier of the Aetna Life Insurance Company's general agency in Fort Wayne; and Oscar W., who married Evelyn Lordier, of Fort Wayne, and is associated with the Corrugated Paper Mills in the city of Chicago. For his second wife Mr. Winte married Miss Laura I. Hanker, who was born in Germany, a daughter of Charles F. and Wilhelmina (Walde) Hanker, who established their home in Fort Wayne nearly half a century ago, in 1871. Here Mr. Hanker engaged in the blacksmithing business and under his direction Mr. Winte, of this memoir, learned his trade. As sterling and honored citizens both Mr. Hanker and his wife passed the remainder of their lives in Fort Wayne, and besides Mrs. Winte four other children survive them—Hulda, who is a popular dancing instructor in the city of San Diego, California; William, deceased; Clara, who is the wife of Henry D. Winte, of Chesaning, Michigan; and Anna, who is the wife of Homer Hartman, of Fort Wayne. John C. Winte was a staunch supporter of the cause of the Republican party, was affiliated with the Knights of the Maccabees, and was an earnest communicant of the Lutheran church, as is also his widow, who still maintains her home in Fort Wayne. Mr. Winte was strong of mental and physical powers, loyal and true in all of the relations of life and worthy of the high esteem uniformly accorded to him. He served for a considerable time as treasurer of the local Horseshoers' Union in Fort Wayne. He was in the very prime of life at the time of his death, which occurred February 23, 1913.

Charles Winters.—One of the native sons of Allen county who has won a place for himself in his community and achieved material independence as a result of his labors is Charles Winters, born in Allen county on March 15, 1853, son of Christian and Louisa Winters. The father came from Germany in young manhood and settling in Allen county at a time when the Indian was not the least difficulty the early settlers had to contend with, established a home in the wilderness and gave the strength of his young manhood to the labors attendant upon such a task. Christian and Louisa Winters were people who possessed the true pioneer spirit, and no task was too great for their courage and hardihood. They reared a family of nine children, all of them living at this writing with the exception of Peter, the first born. The others are Charles, the immediate subject of this family sketch; Gustave, a resident of Allen county; Emma, living in Pleasant township; Elizabeth; Louisa; Jane, of Fort Wayne; Lucy, living in St. Louis, Missouri; and Frank, of Pleasant township. Charles Winters had his education in the public schools of Allen county and spent much of his time in boyhood and early manhood on the home farm. He has been a farmer all his life and today is the owner of one of the comfortable and productive farming properties of his township. He was married on August 24, 1904, to Miss Mary Burnell, and they have two children—Earl Wayne and Jennie Belle, both living at home. Mr. Winters is a Republican in politics, and a leader in his home community.

Joseph Witmer has been identified with farming and industrial activities of varied nature in Allen county practically all his life. He was born in Cedar Creek township, Allen county, January 31, 1848, and since he began to take an interest in the practical things of life has been a factor to be reckoned with in those circles with which he has been identified. The son of Peter and Anna (Sanders) Witmer was born on the farm on which the family located in the early forties. Peter Witmer was of French birth and parentage, and his wife was a native daughter of Wayne county, Ohio. Peter Witmer was a farmer all his life. He was born on February 16, 1815, and died on his farm in Cedar Creek township on August 5, 1851. The wife and mother was born November 2, 1824, and died February 22, 1904. They were the parents of a family of six children. John B. was born, December 18, 1843, and died on August 5, 1862. Jacob was born December 29, 1846, and is now living in California. Joseph, the third born, is the subject of this brief family review. Elizabeth was born, April 8, 1849, and is the wife of Henry Goldsmith, of Cedar Creek township. Annie was born, July 27, 1850, married Christian Klopfenstein and lives in Cedar Creek township. Barbara is the wife of Christian Sanders, of Cedar Creek township. Joseph Witmer had the usual training incident to life on a farm and has had a success that is rather better than average. For thirty-four seasons he did the community threshing, in conjunction with the operation of his own farm, and in later years has identified himself with the grain business. He operates a grain elevator and a grist mill and buys and sells grain, hay, flour, coal, cement, live stock and wool. In addition to this he still owns and operates a farm of one hundred acres in Springfield township, and is able to hold his own with those farming men who devote their entire time to that industry. Mr. Witmer was married on February 26, 1878, to Miss Susanna Goldsmith, of Adams county, and six children have been born to them. They are David, Henry, Rachel, Joseph S., Rosa, Caroline and Lilly. Rachel is the wife of Christian Shank, of Grabill, and Joseph is secretary-treasurer of the Witmer Grain Company, of which his father is the head. The two youngest children are still at home with the parents. A Republican in politics, Mr. Witmer has been more or less active in local matters of a political nature, though in no sense a politician. He is president of a local bank and of the Witmer Grain Company, which he organized and of which his son is also an official, as above stated. This grist mill has a capacity of fifty barrels per day and is equipped with Barnard and Lease rollers.

Herman Woebbeking.—Herman Woebbeking, born in Adams county, Indiana, November 15, 1875, is a son of Henry and Wilhelmina (Buuck) Woebbeking, one of the well known families of their section of the country, concerning whom mention is made in a sketch devoted to the life of another of their sons, William Woebbeking, a successful Maumee township farmer. Herman Woebbeking had his education in the common schools of Adams county and he might be said to have been meagerly educated in view of his five years of schooling. However, he was one who ever made the best of such opportunities as come his way and is today one of the well informed men of his community, despite his early disadvantages. He began farming in Maumee township when he was about ten years old and has been active in that township and occupation from then to the present time. Today Mr. Woebbeking is the owner of a farm of 160 acres in Maumee township, on which place he has made all modern improvements consistent with progressive and successful farming. Mr. Woebbeking was married on November 16, 1900, to Miss Minnie Lessenhop, daughter of William and Minnie Lessenhop, both native Germans. Mrs. Woebbeking came to Fort Wayne in 1893 with her mother, following the death of the husband and father. Seven children have been born to Mr. and Mrs. Woebbeking—Herman, Jr., Hilda, Arthur, Melinda, Laura, Herbert and Martin. Mr. Woebbeking has held no offices and is a member of no lodges. He is a Democrat in politics and with his family has membership in the German Lutheran church.

William E. Woebbeking has been a resident of Fort Wayne from the time of his birth, is a representative of one of the old and honored German families of this city, and from his youth has been closely identified with the business interests of Fort Wayne, with specially broad and effective experience in connection with the wholesale millinery business, of which he is now a prominent and successful exponent, as secretary of the C. T. Pidgeon Millinery Company, one of the large and important commercial concerns of his native city. Mr. Woébbeking was born in Fort Wayne, December 26, 1866, a member of a family of eleven children, all of whom are living except one brother and all have resided continuously in Fort Wayne with the exception of one sister, Mrs. Mary Kohlmeyer, who passed two years in the state of Montana and has since maintained her home in Fort Wayne. The parents, Conrad and Sophia (Piepenbrink) Woebbeking, were born in Germany and established their home in Fort Wayne more than half a century ago, their fiftieth wedding anniversary having been celebrated on Thanksgiving day prior to the death of the father, who was born in 1834 and was eighty years of age when he passed to the life eternal, his venerable widow being still a resident of Fort Wayne. Conrad Woebbeking was reared and educated in his native land and on his immigration to America made the voyage on an old-time sailing vessel which did not reach its destination until after the lapse of six weeks on the ocean. His loyalty to the land of his adoption was manifested in his service of three years as a valiant soldier of the Union in the Civil War, and in later years he was affiliated with that noble and patriotic organization, the Grand Army of the Republic. He was a skilled carpenter and for many years was one of the successful and representative contractors and builders in Fort Wayne,—a man of sterling character and one who ever commanded unqualified popular esteem. He was an eanest communicant of the German Lutheran church, as is also his widow, and was one of the honored pioneer citizens of Fort Wayne at the time of his death, in 1914. William E. Woebbeking acquired his early education in the parochial schools of the German Lutheran church in Fort Wayne and his initial business experience was gained through his service as errand boy for D. S. Low, who was engaged in the retail millinery business at 11 East Columbia street. After a period of about three years there was a change in the ownership of the business and Mr. Woebbeking remained with the new firm until it sold the business. He then entered the employ of Frank J. Noll and George B. Saylor, who at that time were local representatives of the wholesale millinery house of Adams, Steeley & Company, of Dayton, Ohio. Mr. Woebbeking had charge of the company's sample rooms in Fort Wayne while his employers were giving their attention to representing the house throughout their assigned trade territory. Finally the company opened a branch establishment in Fort Wayne, in a building that was on the site of the present Nuttman Bank, on Main street, and of this branch wholesale establishment Mr. Woebbeking had charge for two years. Mr. Adams, one of the principals in the Dayton company, then formed a partnership with his half-brother, Mr. Armstrong, and the latter assumed the supervision of the wholesale millinery house which they then established in Fort Wayne, on Calhoun street. The subject of this review was placed in charge of the silk department of the new concern and, in 1893, took the supervision of the buying department of the business. Later Mr. Adams sold his interest and a reorganization took pace, resuting in the former of the Armstrong-Turner Millinery Company. Still later this company was succeeded by the firm of Armstrong & Turner, and in 1904, the well established business was purchased by Charles T. Pidgeon and Mr. Woebbeking, who have since successfully conducted the substantial and prosperous enterprise under the title of the C. T. Pidgeon Millinery Company, this being one of the important concerns lending to the commercial prestige of Fort Wayne and its business extending throughout the large trade territory normally tributary to the city. Mr. Woebbeking is secretary of the company which bases its operation on ample capital, effective management and progressive policies, and he is essentially one of the alert and representative business men of his native city. He is president of the C. T. Pidgeon Realty Company and a director of the Fort Wayne Concrete Tile Company. Though never imbued with desire for public office, he takes loyal interest in all things touching the welfare and advancement of his native city and county, is a staunch Republican in politics, and holds membership in the Fort Wayne Commercial Club and the local Country Club. February 7, 1891, recorded the marriage of Mr. Woebbeking to Miss Cecelia H. Raidy, who was born and reared in Fort Wayne, where her parents, Mr. and Mrs. David Raidy, still reside, her father being now retired, after many years of service as a locomotive engineer on the Pennsylvania Railroad. Mr. and Mrs. Woebbeking have seven children, namely: Irene, Marie, Raymond William, Clarence Edward, Margaret, Georgiana Ethel, Robert William and Marian Agnes.

William Woebbeking.—Three generations of the family here named have contributed to the agricultural and industrial development of the state of Indiana in their respective localities, and a fourth generation is growing up to take its place in the world's work. William Woebbeking is the son of Henry and the grandson of the first American ancestor, the latter coming to America, in 1844, and bringing his family with him. They settled in Adams county and the German immigrant became one of the substantial and successful farming men in his community. After his death, his son, Henry, who had hitherto been engaged in the carpentering business, turned his attention to the operation of the home farm and continued actively in that work until his death, in 1913. Henry Woebbeking was born in Germany, in 1832, and was twelve years of age when he first saw America. He married Wilhelmina Buuck, who was born in Adams county of German parents, and who survives her husband at this writing. They were parents of eleven children, named Mary, Fred, (deceased), Carl, Ernest, Theodore, Henry, William, Herman, Paul, Martha, and Sophia, all living but the first, third and fourth. William Woebbeking was born in Adams county on September 21, 1873, and with his brothers and sisters had his education in the common schools of Adams county and the Lutheran school in Adams county. He began farming in Maumee township, Allen county, and it is there he is to be found active in his chosen enterprise at this time. He is the owner of a well developed farm of one hundred acres and his enterprise, industry and general good management have won him a place among the successful farming men of the township. The place is well equipped according to the best modern standards in agriculture and general farming is carried on, with special attention to the breeding of Shorthorned Durham cattle. On October 16, 1902, Mr. Woebbeking was married to Miss Minnie Rekeweg, a daughter of Deiderick and Louisa (Korte) Rekeweg, and they are the parents of two children—Luella and Welma, the latter deceased. Mr. and Mrs. Woebbeking are lifelong members of the German Lutheran church and Mr. Woebbeking is Republican in politics. He is not active in local politics, though fulfilling all the demands of good citizenship, and has no lodge memberships. He is content with his home life and finds occupation in the many duties afforded by the proper operation and management of his home and farm.

Paul E. Wolf came from Germany to America as an ambitious and industrious young man of twenty-one years, and within a short time after his arrival in the land of his adoption established his residence in Fort Wayne. A skilled workman at the trade of upholsterer, his energy and ability have enabled him here to develop a prosperous upholstering business of general order, and in connection therewith he has built up also an equally successful enterprise in the manufacturing of high-grade mattresses. He has been a resident of Fort Wayne for more than forty-five years, and each successive year has counted in worthy achievement on his part, the while he has been deeply appreciative of the advantages that have here been afforded him for the gaining of independence along normal lines of business enterprise and has shown himself unequivocally loyal and public-spirited as a citizen. He has been content to follow the quieter walks of life, has had no desire to bask in the glare of publicity, but his deep interest in community affairs has not been of merely sentimental and quiescent order, for he has given staunch and intelligent support to the cause of the Republican party and has served with marked efficiency as a member of the city council,—a preferment that indicates the high estimate placed upon him in the city that has long been his home and the stage of his fruitful activities. He is a substantial and popular business man and is well entitled to representation in this history. Mr. Wolf was born in the Kingdom of Saxony, Germany, on March 5, 1850, a son of Edward and Mathilda (Wehe) Wolf, who passed the closing years of their lives in Saxony, Germany, the father having been a tailor by trade and vocation and the family having held to the faith of the Lutheran church for generations. The subject of this sketch is one of the two surviving sons in a family of five children and was reared and educated in his native land, where also he served a thorough apprenticeship to the trade of upholsterer, of which he has continued an exponent during the long intervening years and through the medium of which he has built up his present thriving business, the headquarters of which are at 619-21 Clinton street. Both he and his wife, whose maiden name was Maria Knothe, are earnest members and communicants of the German Lutheran church.

Sol A. Wood is one of the representative members of the Allen county bar and is engaged in the successful general practice of law in the city of Fort Wayne. That he holds also the degree of Doctor of Medicine gives evidence of his versatility of talent and also of his broad mental attainments. He has been emphatically a man of ambition and resolute purpose, and in the various stages of his career has shown that high sense of personal stewardship that ever makes for effective service. Mr. Wood was born in Steuben county, Indiana, on April 11, 1857, a son of Dr. Warren A. and Louvina B. (Thompson) Wood, the former of whom was born at Bainbridge, Chenango county, New York, and the latter in Williams county, Ohio. The father prepared himself thoroughly for the exacting work of the medical profession and was for many years one of the leading physicians of Steuben county, Indiana, where his death occurred in 1868, the subject of this review being the only survivor of their four children. His widow continues to make her home in Angola. Sol A. Wood continued his studies in the public schools until he had profited duly by the advantages of the high school at Angola, the judicial center of his native county. In fortifying himself for the profession that had been dignified and honored by the character and services of his father, he finally entered the Fort Wayne Medical College, in which he was graduated as a member of the class of 1879, and from which he received the degree of Doctor of Medicine. For the ensuing two years he was engaged in successful general practice in Steuben county and was then elected county auditor, a position of which he continued the incumbent for eight years. Within this period he gave close attention to the study of law and after his retirement from office and his admission to the bar was for two years associated with Judge Frank Roby in the general practice of law at Angola. At the expiration of the period noted the partnership alliance was dissolved, and thereafter he continued in the independent practice of law at Angola, where he built up a substantial law business to which he gave his attention until 1901, when he found a broader field of professional endeavor by establishing his residence in the city of Fort Wayne. For two years he was here a member of the law firm of Gilbert, Berghoff & Wood, and since that time has controlled a representative general practice of representative order. He has served as referee in bankruptcy for North Eastern Indiana, embracing eleven counties, since 1905, but has otherwise given his undivided attention to the demands of his substantial law business, in connection with which he is known as a resourceful trial lawyer and able and reliable counselor. Dr. Wood gives unqualified allegiance to the Republican party and has been a loyal advocate of its principles and policies. He is an active member of the Indiana State Bar Association and the American Bar Association, is identified with the Fort Wayne Commercial Club, has received in the Masonic fraternity the thirty-second degree of the Ancient Accepted Scottish Rite, besides being affiliated with the Ancient Arabic Order, Nobles of the Mystic Shrine, and both he and his wife are communicants of the Protestant Episcopal church. On April 10, 1880, was solemnized the marriage of Mr. Wood to Miss May Huss, of Wheeling, West Virginia, she being a daughter of John and Emeline Huss, both of whom are deceased. Mr. and Mrs. Wood have two children—Carver C., who now resides in the city of Cincinnati, Ohio, and Harold L., who has established his residence in Louisville, Kentucky.

James Woods.—The Woods family came to Allen county from Wayne county, Ohio, in the year 1850, at a time when the subject, James Woods, was a lad of about fourteen years. He was born in East Union township, Wayne county, Ohio, July 15, 1836, son of George and Charlotte (Richie) Woods, the latter a native of Westmoreland county, Pennsylvania. When the family came to Allen county they bought a tract of 240 acres of land from one Josiah Hitchcock, a pioneer of East Union township, and paid for it the price of $2.50 per acre. That was considered a fair price in that day for wild land, and George Woods had no small task before him when he bought the land and settled down with the idea of making a home on it for his family. He proved himself equal to it, however, and neither the hard labor nor the danger from wild animals and Indians was sufficient to deter him in his purpose. He cleared the spot with his own hands where the first rude cabin home was erected, and lived to see his wilderness land grow into a productive and handsome possession. He was a Democrat in later life, active in the work of the party, and a member of the Church of the Brethren. He died in 1881 and his wife passed away in 1901. The children of George and Charlotte Woods were nine in number. Samuel, the first born, died in 1898. James was the second child. John, Alexander and Elizabeth are deceased. Milton lives in Fort Wayne; George is a resident of Pleasant township; Mary Jane became the wife of Allen Bushe and died in 1908 and Jacob is living on the old home farmstead. James Woods had his education in the subscription schools common to the period of his youth and was an important factor in the improvement of the farm his father settled on. Much of his youth and strength went into the development of the farm home, and he has spent all his life in Pleasant township. Mr. Woods is a Democrat, as was his father before him, and he is a member of the Church of God. He was married on March 10, 1858, to Margaret Hermine, daughter of George and Elizabeth (Kiester) Hermine, and they are the parents of five children. Augusta Ann, the first born, is deceased. Clement lives in Pleasant township. A third child died in infancy. Amanda is the wife of John Motz. Froney Elizabeth married Enoch Smith.

Charles H. Worden.—The elements which combine to prepare and equip a man for true service to his fellows are united in Charles Howard Worden. Although his energies are directed largely to the care and re-

Charles H. Worden

sponsibilities which group about his position as president and executive head of The First and Hamilton National Bank of Fort Wayne, his well ordered mind enables him to give attention not only to other business interests but to the needs of the people of his home city in many lines of endeavor. Mr. Worden was born September 14, 1859, in Fort Wayne. His parents were Judge James L and Anna (Grable) Worden. The mother was born on February 9, 1829. Judge Worden, the father, was one of Indiana's leading members of the bar. Born at Sandisfield, Berkshire county, Massachusetts, May 10, 1819, son of John and Jane Worden, of sturdy New England stock, James L. Worden remained in Massachusetts until he reached the age of eight when the widowed mother and an elder brother, John Babcock Worden, brought him to Portage county, Ohio, where he passed his youth on a farm. Later he studied law and was admitted to the Ohio supreme court. After a brief residence in Tiffin, Ohio, James L. orden removed to Columbia City, Indiana, and later took up his residence in Albion, of the same state. In 1849 he came to Fort Wayne and continued to make this his home until the time of his death. During the succeeding years he served as prosecuting attorney of the Twelfth judicial district, in a like capacity for the newly-formed Tenth District, as judge of the circuit court of Allen county, associate justice of the supreme court of Indiana, judge of the supreme court, mayor of Fort Wayne, judge of the Superior court of Allen county, and in other places of responsibility. Such were the type of the parentage of Charles H. Worden. Following his attendance at the public schools, Mr. Worden entered upon a course in the literary department of the University of Michigan, at Ann Arbor, and was a member of the class of 1883. In the previous year he had been admitted to the bar of Allen county, Indiana, of which his home was the county seat. He first read law in the office of Judge Robert S. Taylor, of Fort Wayne, and later was associated with John Morris, son of the late Judge John Morris, under the firm name of Worden & Morris, from 1887 until 1893, the fathers of these two young men having in earlier years been associated together in the practice of law under the same firm name. From 1894 until 1902 Mr. Worden was associated with Judge Allen Zollars, the firm being known as Zollars and Worden. During these years Mr. Worden, through his strong personality, his clear grasp of the true phases of intricate and involved questions at law, and his energy of thought and action, attained a high place in the legal circles of Indiana. However, in 1902, there came to him a call to another field of endeavor, and, withal, one which required the application of the same elements which marked his career in the law—that of the acceptance of the vice-presidency of the First National Bank, which included the responsibilities of chief executive officer of this important financial institution. For fourteen years Mr. Worden occupied the place of vice-president, or until January 9, 1917, when he was elected president and this office he continued to fill until April 7, 1917, when the Hamilton National Bank was merged with the First National and the title of the institution became the First and Hamilton National Bank, of which he was elected president. The bank opened for business under its new name on April 9, 1917, and the wisdom of the call and of his acceptance of it is shown in the remarkable progress of the institution toward higher and better things in the financial world during this period. Of him, another writer has recently said with truth and clearness. "Mr. Worden is a man who brings to bear knowledge, industry, public spirit and high character to a post with which he is qualified to deal, by long study, fine purpose and the possession not only of the facts of the case, but the confidence of all honored men interested in the duties and problems of the position. He knows what it is to struggle and what it is to achieve. He has worked up, until today he stands as a fine type of America's successful business man. He has the faculty of stating arguments, facts and conclusions in a clear, crisp and logical style—of saying without hesitation or embarrassment just what he means, and of using language precisely suited to the ideas set forth. He is a business man all the way through, and yet, with the air of a close student, fonder of books than of show and display. He has worthily earned the good will and respect of the most substantial and conservative members of the community and is looked upon as a man whose business ability, integrity and financial acumen have never been questioned. The thorough business training which he brings to bear is especially valuable to his important office, and there is every reason to predict for him an increased measure of success therein in time to come." Among the outside interests in which Mr. Worden is concerned in an official way are the Hartford Paper Company, of which he is the vice-president; the Fort Wayne Corrugated Paper Company, of which he is a director; and the Wayne Paper Goods Company, of which he is the vice-president and a director. He is an active member of the Masonic fraternity and holds the thirty-second degree in the Scottish Rite. He is a thoroughly loyal member of the First Presbyterian church, in which organization he has served as an elder from 1885 until the present time, and for many years also as the superintendent of the Sunday school. In politics, Mr. Worden has been a consistent supporter of the doctrine of the republican party. On January 10, 1884, Mr. Worden was united in marriage with Miss Elizabeth Marshall Hoffman, daughter of Jacob and Susan C. Hoffman of Fort Wayne, and a grand-daughter of Marshall S. Wines and Elizabeth Wines, two of the pioneer settlers of Fort Wayne. To them have been born three children—Mrs. Alice Worden Condit, wife of Gex Pullen Condit, of Gary, Indiana; Marshall Wines Worden and Charles James Worden.

James L. Worden.—Among the distinguished names of Fort Wayne's development is that of Judge James L. Worden, lawyer, jurist and statesman. Of strong mentality, invincible courage and a warmth of heart which made him a friend to all, Judge Worden was one of the best-loved men of his time. James Lorenzo Worden was born in Sandisfield, Berkshire county, Massachusetts, May 10, 1819, son of John and Jane Worden whose respective families were founded in America in the early colonial period. When Judge Worden was a lad of eight years, his father died, and the widowed mother removed to Portage county, Ohio, where she located on a farm. Here James L. Worden received the rudiments of his education in the rural schools and during which period the boy gave evidence of a strong liking for literary pursuits. At the age of nineteen he began the study of law, and in 1839 entered the office of Thomas T. Straight, a leading member of the bar in Cincinnati. In 1841 he was admitted to the bar of the supreme court of Ohio, at Lancaster, and for two or three years practiced at Tiffin, Ohio. In the spring of 1844 he came to Indiana and located at Columbia City, in Whitley county. In the autumn of 1845 Judge Worden removed to Albion, Noble county, Indiana, where he soon gained distinct recognition as a leader in his profession. At this time his reputation gained wider repute during the prosecution of a murder case which brought him to Fort Wayne on a

James L. Worden

change of venue from Noble county. His new friends induced him to locate in Fort Wayne, which he was pleased to do, in 1849, and here he spent his days until the time of his death. In 1850 Judge Worden was elected prosecuting attorney for the Twelfth judicial circuit, embracing the counties of Allen, Adams, Wells, Huntington, Whitley, Noble, Steuben, LaGrange and DeKalb. He held this office for three years. Two years after he was elected the state was re-districted for judicial purposes and Allen county became a part of the Tenth circuit, which also included the counties of Adams, Wells, Huntington, Wabash, Whitley, Noble, DeKalb, LaGrange, Steuben, Elkhart and Kosciusko. A year later the counties of Huntington and Wabash were taken from the circuit. Of this Tenth circuit James L. Worden was appointed by Governor Joseph A. Wright, in 1855, to fill a vacancy. At a general election, in the fall of that year, Judge Worden was elected to the bench of the circuit for a full term of six years, without opposition. Although he was disinclined to accept honors which would in any degree interfere with the further interests of his profession, his party associates made him the democratic candidate for congress, in 1857. The district was largely republican and he met defeat with the balance of the ticket. In 1858 Judge Worden resigned his position as judge of the Judicial circuit court, to which he had been appointed in 1855, to accept the appointment tendered him by Governor Willard as an associate justice of the supreme court of Indiana, to fill a vacancy caused by the resignation of Judge Stuart, of Logansport. In 1859 he was elected a judge of the supreme court for a full term of six years, ending in January, 1865. In 1864 he was renominated for another term, but the entire ticket suffered defeat. In January, 1865, upon his return to Fort Wayne, Judge Worden was induced to accept his party's nomination for mayor of the city and was elected in the following May. During his period of service in the mayor's chair, Judge Worden did splendid service, but, after serving about one year, resigned the place in order to give his undivided attention to his law practice which had grown to large proportions. From that time until January, 1871, he was associated in practive with Judge John Morris. In 1870 Judge Worden was again elected a judge of the supreme court, serving a full term of six years, at the expiration of which, in 1876, he was renominated by his party. He was re-elected by a large majority as the supreme judge of the court. Judge Worden entered upon his third term, in January, 1877. In 1882 his friends throughout the state insisted that he should become a candidate for re-election, but he felt that the exacting labors of the office during a period of nearly nineteen years entitled him to the right to decline further honors in this direction. However, upon his return to Allen county, he was nominated and elected to the office of judge of the superior court and remained in this office until the time of his death, June 2, 1884. Two days later, upon the occasion of a meeting of the Bar Association of Allen county, addresses expressive of the sorrow of the entire state were delivered by Judge Morris and Hon. J. K. Edgerton, and words of eulogy and sorrow came from representatives of the bar in all portions of Indiana. The late Judge Allen Zollars, writing of Judge Worden, gives this expression of the common estimate of the man: "Judge Worden made no pretense to florid oratory, but in his addresses to the court and jury he was logical, practical and convincing. In the trial of cases his thorough knowledge of the law and the rules of practice, his fine analytical powers and logical and methodical manner of thought, enabled him readily to discern and grasp the salient points and to handle them with consummate skill. As a nisi prius judge he had but few if any equals in the state. Of him it may truthfully be said that in no office to which he was called did he fail to come up to the full measure of its requirements. Judge Worden's work upon the supreme bench is what has most certainly secured him an honorable and enduring place in the history of the state. He went upon that bench when a young man, thirty-nine years of age. His mind was clear, logical and discriminating, and his sense of right and justice was broad and exact. He was not a man of circumlocution, either in thought or word. There is clearness, consciousness and directness of expression in his opinions, which may well serve for models for judges and lawyers. He was by nature a lawyer and judge, having the faculty, in an unusual degree, of brushing aside all that might tend to becloud and confuse, and, discerning the real question for decision, and determining what the decision should be to conform to the rules of the law and work substantial justice to the parties interested. His opinions not only show his ability and his learning in the law, but they give evidence also of careful and laborious preparation. He had no toleration for the weak and abused idea that the reputation of a judge on the bench of a court of final decision is to be established or the value of his labors measured by the amount that he may write, and he was governed by the one and only sensible idea that the reputation of the judge upon such a bench will finally rest upon the character and not the number of written opinions. He acted in conformity with the idea that care in the decision of causes and in the writing of opinions lessens the business in the supreme court by lessening the litigation below, while haste and the consequent looseness in expression, in an attempt to multiply opinions, necessarily results in misunderstanding on the part of the profession in the multiplication of suits below and the increase in the number of appeals. He knew, as every lawyer of observation and experience knows, that suits are very frequently instituted on no other foundation than a dictum which has been found in some previous case and which ought not to be there, standing only as the evidence of undue haste on the part of the judge who wrote the decision. Such cases invariably go to the supreme court, and thus haste in such a court increases rather than curtails business. Judge Worden wrote, perhaps, as few opinions in the length of time as any judge on the supreme bench of Indiana, but in the way of reputation he was in the front rank, if not the first man in the rank. By the lawyers of the state and by the courts, including the supreme court, his opinions are read and cited with a feeling of security. There is assurance that he was not only capable of deciding and stating the law correctly, but also that he had bestowed the labor and taken the time necessary to enable him to thus state correctly. It is for this reason that his opinions are the more frequently cited and relied upon, not only in Indiana but elsewhere. By his work on the supreme bench, as embodied in his written opinions extending over so many years, Judge Worden erected his own monument and wrote his own inscription. He needs naught else. While Judge Worden was a firm and conscientious advocate of the principles of the Democratic party, he was in no sense an aggressive or active partisan. The result was that he was singularly free from the assaults of party opponents, which, almost invariably, every public man has to meet. Indeed, Judge Worden always received a considerable support at the polls from those of the opposing political party who knew him well. On only one occasion was he assailed with anything like violence, and that assault was absolutely unfounded, while he never took the trouble to defend his position, deeming such action incompatible with the dignity of his position on the supreme bench. * * Judge Worden was a resident of Indiana a few months more than forty years. As prosecuting attorney, judge of the circuit court, mayor, judge of the supreme court and judge of the superior court of Allen county, he was in public service for more than twenty-seven years of that time. His life was thus, in a large measure, an open book, inviting the closest scrutiny and challenging it. When not in the public service he was in the practice of law at home and in a large number of surrounding counties, and he was thus still, in a sense, in public life. At no time did the people who knew him best have more confidence in his integrity and lofty character than in the later years of his life. The final manifestation of enlightened popular confidence shown in his election to the bench of the superior court of Allen county, after his long service on the supreme bench, is of itself more than sufficient to meet and overthrow the unreasonable and unjust imputation above mentioned. * * So long as Indiana shall be a commonwealth, so long as its people shall have laws and courts, his name will be known and honored. How much good he accomplished for the state may never be fully appreciated by the people in general, but it will be, in a measure at least, by the profession and by the more observing citizens in other walks of life." Judge Worden, in the spring of 1845, was united in marriage with Miss Anna Grable, daughter of Benjamin Grable, at that time county treasurer of Whitley county, Indiana. Three sons were born to this union: James Willis Worden, Charles H. Worden and Harry Lawrence Worden. Charles H. Worden, president of the First and Hamilton National Bank of Fort Wayne, is the subject of a sketch to be found in this work.

John B. Wyss.—One of the foremost men of his community, both in point of his farming accomplishments and his connection with the business and political life of Marion township, is John B. Wyss, who was born in the township on August 5, 1857. He is the son of Francis Joseph and Mary (Zuber) Wyss, who were Swiss people who came from their native land, in 1852, and settled in Fort Wayne. Francis Joseph Wyss was a tailor by trade but practically abandoned that work and turned his attention to farming. He first bought an eighty acre tract of what was known as school land, later adding an adjoining tract of one hundred and twenty acres. He was a successful farmer from the beginning and bought one parcel of land after another, as time went on, and was able to present each of his sons with a farm when he was ready to launch out to make an independent living. He was a splendid citizen and in his native land had served in the army. He was a Roman Catholic and reared his children in that faith, sending them part of the time to the parochial schools and partly to the public schools. Eight children were born to these people. Frank Joseph is living on a farm in Marion township; John B. was the second born; Nicholas J. also lives on a Marion township farm; Elizabeth is married to Geo. Hake and lives in Fort Wayne; Philip is a building inspector and is living in Fort Wayne, where he is in the employ of the city; Mary is the wife of Fred Herber, of Pleasant township; William P. is living on the old homestead; Gertrude is the wife of Frank P. Hoffman of Marion township. John B. Wyss had his schooling in the parochial and common schools of Marion township and remained at home on his father's farm until he was twenty-eight years old. At that time he was planning the establishment of a home of his own and his father in keeping with his practice along those lines, bought him a farm by way of starting him out in life and Mr. Wyss is living on the place today and it consists of 100 acres. Since he came into possession of it he has made many improvements in the buildings and in other ways, and it is one of the attractive places in the township today. Mr. Wyss carries on stock and grain farming and is remarkably successful in his work. A Democrat in politics, Mr. Wyss has served his township well, without respect to party lines. He was a member of the township advisory board, in 1900, and from 1901 to 1905 was a trustee of Marion township. In 1906 he was elected to the office of county commissioner, his re-election to the office following in 1908. His influence in local politics spread to county affairs and, in 1914, he was elected representative from Allen county and while a member of the state legislature was active in many worthy movements for the benefit of his county. He is financially interested in the German-American Trust Company and the Citizens Trust Company, and is a director in both concerns. Mr. Wyss was married on June 1, 1886, to Miss Margaret Beckman, daughter of Frederick and Catherine (Hake) Beckman, farmers of Marion township, and people of German ancestry. Mr. and Mrs. Wyss have thirteen children—Clara, George, Rose, Agnes, Bernard F., John F., Rosella G., Bertha E., Henry E., Albert M., Florence H., Marie G., Mabel M., and William W. Our subject and family are members of the Catholic church.

Philip Wyss, who holds the office of building inspector in the city of Fort Wayne, is admirably fortified for effective service in this important municipal position, for he had previously been one of the successful and representative contractors and builders of the metropolis of his native county. He was born in Marion township, Allen county, Indiana, on December 23, 1864, a son of Francis Joseph and Mary Anna (Zuber) Wyss, both of whom were born and reared in the noble little republic of Switzerland, where their marriage was solemnized and where they continued their residence until 1852, when they came to America, their home being established in Allen county, Indiana, in June of that year. The father, a man of energy, ambition and sterling integrity, became one of the substantial farmers of the county and here both he and his wife were honored pioneer citizens at the time of their death, both having passed away in the year 1911. On June 14, 1910, they celebrated their diamond wedding at their home in Marion township. Of their large family of children the first four died in infancy; Frank J., is a prosperous farmer in Marion township; John B. is a leading exponent of agricultural industry in Marion township and has served as a member of the board of county commissioners of Allen county and in the state legislature; Nicholas J. and William P. are representative farmers in Marion township; Elizabeth is the wife of George Hake, of Fort Wayne; Mary is the wife of Frederick Herber, of Pleasant township; Gertrude is the wife of Frank Huffman, of Marion township; Gerbard S. is deceased; and the youngest of the number is he whose name initiates this article. Philip Wyss passed the period of his childhood and youth on the old homestead farm, which was the place of his birth, and received his early education in the district schools of his native township. He continued to be associated in the work and management of the home farm until he was twenty-five years of age, when he removed to Fort Wayne and learned the carpenter's trade. After due preliminary experience of a most practical order he engaged in contracting and building in an independent way, and with this important line of business enterprise he continued his successful association until July, 1909, when he was appointed to his present municipal office of building inspector, in which he is giving a most efficient and acceptable administration. In addition to this preferment he served six years as a member of the city council of Fort Wayne, and he is specially loyal and progressive as a citizen. His political support is given to the cause of the Democratic party, he is a communicant of St. Peter's Catholic church, and is affiliated with the Knights of Columbus, the C. B. L. of I., and the Modern Woodmen of America. November 18, 1890, was solemnized the marriage of Mr. Wyss to Miss Mary Hoffman, and she passed to the life eternal January 8, 1910, a devoted communicant of the Catholic church. Of the seven children the eldest is Mary R., who is the wife of Andrew J. Muldoon, of Marion township, and the other children, all of whom still remain in Allen county are Frank A., Frances B., William S., Gertrude M., George J. and Philip H.

John R. Yaggy, the efficient and popular cashier of the Woodburn Banking Company, is a scion of sterling pioneer families of Allen county, where both his paternal and maternal grandparents settled in an early day, and in his native county he has found ample opportunity for the positive expression of his individuality through successful achievement and through appreciative loyalty as a citizen. He is one of the representative business men of the village of Woodburn and is properly given specific consideration in this history. Mr. Yaggy was born on the homestead farm of his father, in Cedar Creek township, this county, and the date of his nativity was October 17, 1872. He is a son of Andrew and Elizabeth (Sauder) Yaggy, both natives of Ohio and both reared and educated in Allen county, where the respective families settled in the pioneer days. Andrew Yaggy was long numbered among the aggressive and successful exponents of the agricultural and live-stock industry in Cedar Creek township, and after years of ceaseless toil and endeavor is now enjoying the just rewards thereof, he having retired from the active management of his farm and is residing in a pleasant home in the village of Grabill, not far distant from the old home farm. He is a consistent member of the Defenseless Mennonite church. The seven children are all living: Hannah, Henry, Andrew, Jr., Katie, Menno, John R. and Sarah. As a young woman Elizabeth Sauder, the mother, wedded Jacob Roth and he died after having become the father of five children—Anna, Levi, Elizabeth, Louisa and Lydia. Of these children all are living except Anna. John R. Yaggy attended in his boyhood and youth the public schools of his native county and in the meantime gave his quota of assistance in the work of the home farm. Later he attended Taylor University, at Fort Wayne, besides which he availed himself also of the advantages of the Tri-State Normal College, at Angola, Indiana, and the International Business College, at Fort Wayne. He proved a successful teacher in the schools of Allen county, continued his association with farm enterprise for a number of years, and finally found employment as a skilled bookkeeper, his effective services in this capacity leading to his active association with banking enterprise. He has been resourceful and energetic in the upbuilding of the staunch financial institution of which he is cashier and has held his present executive office since 1902. He has had no ambition for political preferment but gives unswerving allegiance to the Republican party, and both he and his wife are active members of the Methodist Episcopal church in their home village. In 1896 was solemnized the marriage of Mr. Yaggy to Miss Lydia Rupp, who was born in Fulton county, Ohio, a daughter of Christian and Elizabeth (Freiberger) Rupp, both natives of Germany. After coming to America Mr. Rupp removed to Fulton county, Ohio, where he became a prosperous farmer and passed the remainder of his life, his widow still remaining on the old homestead farm. Mr. and Mrs. Yaggy have four children—Prudence, Elizabeth, John and Eugenia.

Carl Yaple.—On the roster of those who have lent dignity and distinction to the bench of the superior court of Allen county, a place of special honor must consistently be accorded to the present able and popular incumbent, Judge Yaple, who as a lawyer and jurist is well upholding the prestige gained by his father, long a distinguished figure in professional and public life in the state of Michigan. Judge Carl Yaple was born at Coldwater, the beautiful metropolis and judicial center of Branch county, Michigan, on March 11, 1877, a scion of one of the sterling and influential pioneer families of the Wolverine commonwealth. He is a son of Hon. George L. and Mary H. (Hankinson) Yaple. Hon George L. Yaple was born at Leonidas, St. Joseph county, Michigan, and he and his wife now reside at Mendon, that county, where he is still actively engaged in the practice of law. Mrs. Yaple likewise was born in St. Joseph county, where her parents settled in the pioneer days. Hon. George L. Yaple received the degree of Master of Arts from Northwestern University, at Evanston, Illinois, and thereafter prepared himself for the legal profession, of which he has long been a distinguished representative in his native state. After having been for a number of years engaged in practice at Mendon he removed to Coldwater, Michigan, where he built up a representative law business and later was for a time engaged in practice at Beatrice, Nebraska. He finally returned to his native county and established his residence at Mendon, where he still gives active attention to the work of his profession, with standing as one of the leading legists and jurists of the state of Michigan. He served eighteen years on the bench of the circuit court for the district comprising St. Joseph and Branch counties and represented his district as representative in the United States congress, in which he made a characteristically admirable record and in which he was a contemporary with Hon. William J. Bryan, who was his associate member on various important committees of the house of representatives. He has been a leader in the furtherance of the cause of the Democratic party in Michigan, is affiliated with the Masonic fraternity and the Michigan Bar Association, and both he and his wife are members of the Methodist Episcopal church. Of the children the eldest is Edward, who is a resident of the city of Kalamazoo, Michigan; Frederick is deceased; Dr. Harry M., a doctor of dental surgery, is engaged in the practice of his profession in the city of Seattle, Washington; George L., Jr., is a resident of Fort Wayne and is a lawyer by occupation; Marie is deceased; Alice remains at the parental home; and Judge Yaple of this review was the third in order of birth of the children. Judge Yaple is indebted to the public schools of his native state for his early educational discipline, which was supplemented by high academic study in Kalamazoo College and Albion College, two of the excellent educational institutions of Michigan. Thereafter he was a student for a time in the great University of Michigan, and later attended the law department of the University of Indiana. He was admitted to the Indiana bar in 1900 and initiated the active practice of his profession in Fort Wayne, where he associated himself with the law firm of Vesey & Heaton. Later he formed a partnership alliance with Benjamin F. Heaton, under the firm name of Heaton & Yaple, and under these conditions continued in the active and successful general practice of his profession in Fort Wayne until his election to the bench of the superior court of Allen county, in 1910. In 1914 he was re-elected for a second term of four years, and as a jurist has shown the true judicial temperament as well as the broad and accurate knowledge of jurisprudence that insures a careful and equitable administration and conserves the ends of justice. Judge Yaple has been called upon to render decisions in many important cases and few of his rulings have been reversed by courts of higher jurisdiction. He is a stalwart advocate of the principles of the Democratic party, is a valued member of the Allen County Bar Association and the Indiana State Bar Association, is affiliated with the Masonic fraternity, the Loyal Order of Moose and the Benevolent and Protective Order of Elks, and both he and his wife are members of the First Presbyterian church of Fort Wayne. He takes lively interest in all things touching the communal welfare and is a loyal member of the Fort Wayne Commercial Club. On August 2, 1899, was solemnized the marriage of Judge Yaple to Miss Fannie Lois Russell, daughter of Benton and Sarah (Amidon) Russell, of Coldwater, Michigan, and the two children of this union are George R. and Kathryn Marie.

Christopher C. Young.—It is safe to assume that James Young, father of the subject, was of an adventurous turn of mind, or at least an admirer of the great adventurer, Christopher Columbus, for he named his first born son in his honor. Mr. Young is a native of the Hoosier state, born in Bush county on October 25, 1849. His parents were James and Elizabeth (Cross) Young, both natives of Ohio and representatives of well known families of Butler county, originally from New Jersey. The paternal great-grandfather of the subject was a soldier in the Revolutionary war, serving under General Washington. James Young came to Allen county, in 1853, and bought a farm of eighty acres from a Mr. Walker. It was wild land, and Mr. Young cleared a space on which to erect a house and another space for a barn. He planted potatoes in the bit of yard around the house and corn in the barn yard, utilizing every inch of space as rapidly as it was cleared of its timber growth. Mr. Young was a man of more education than the average man of his day and taught in the public schools of the county for many years, giving his winters to that work and his summers to his farm. He managed to keep busy, between the two callings, and it is presumable that he contributed as much to the progress and development of the county as did any one man of his time. He was township trustee for twelve years and a leader in his community always. He enlisted for service in the Mexican war, but was never called to actual service. He was a Democrat, a member of the Masonic order, and was long an active worker in the Christian church. To him and his wife were born four children. Christopher C. was born in October, 1849. F. Josephus is prominent in Allen county politics and is a resident of Fort Wayne. Mary Elizabeth is the wife of Gustave Williams, of Lafayette township. George F. is a resident of Chicago. Christopher Young was educated in the schools of his community, and though his advantages were few, managed to acquire the rudiments of an education and in later years built up a better than average education on that early foundation. He remained on the home farm until he was twenty-one years old, then turned his attention to carpentry for some years and still later was engaged in the tile business. In the early eighties he bought forty acres of land in Lafayette township, a little later adding twenty acres nearby, and engaged in stock farming. Today he has one of the well kept and productive places of the township. Mr. Young is a Democrat in politics, a member of the Christian church and in a fraternal way is identified with the Yeomen at Fort Wayne. He has served his township as a trustee, giving five and a half years to that office. He was married on October 1, 1874, to Miss Ella Bell, daughter of James and Catherine (Rodgers) Bell, who were North Carolinians, coming thence to Allen county. Mr. and Mrs. Young have two children and seven grandchildren. Homer, the son, is a prosperous farmer in Lafayette township and is also a school teacher. He has served in his township as a justice of the peace for six years and is one of the leading men of his community. He married Dessie Kiplinger on January 1, 1898, and they have five children—Mary K., Robert J., John H., Ralph W., and Samuel H., all at home. Bertha Young married Oscar Johnson, of Wells county, and has two daughters—Mabel and Hazel.

Julius Young is one of the foreign born citizens of St. Joseph township who has a long and honorable career to his credit. Not only is he one of the pioneer settlers of St. Joseph township, but he is a veteran of the Civil war, in which he served through three years under Sherman and Grant. In that time he saw much active service, participated in many of the hardest fought battles of the long war, and passed through the conflict without personal injury or illness. He was born in Hanover, Germany, December 25, 1828, son of Fred and Doretta Young, who never left their native land. Their son came to America, in 1842, coming direct to Allen county and settling in St. Joseph township, so that he has a record of seventy-five years of almost continuous residence in that community to his credit. It follows that he has been a witness to practically every stage of development that has taken place since St. Joseph township was settled by white men, and he has contributed no small share to the work that has gone to make up the sum of present day improvements. Today, at the fine old age of eighty-nine years, this pioneer is still active in the operation of his farm of one hundred and twenty acres, which he cleared and improved with his own hands. It was in 1862 that Mr. Young enlisted for service in the Eleventh Indiana Artillery, and he was mustered out of the service, in 1865, at Indianapolis, whereupon he returned home to the pursuits of peace and the enjoyment of the home and family he had left behind at the call of his adopted country. Mr. Young was married in 1859, to Miss Jane McBratney, daughter of James and Marguerite McBratney, and to them were born four children—William, Sarah, Julius and Fred. Mr. and Mrs. Young are members of the United Brethren church in their home town and he is a Republican in politics.

William F. Young.—Among the successful young farming men of St. Joseph township is William F. Young, born in the community he now lives in on October 11, 1871. He is a son of Henry and Louisa (Schaffer) Young, the father a native of Brown county, Ohio, who came to Allen county, Indiana, with his parents at the early age of three years. They lived in Cedar creek township for about ten years, then moved to St. Joseph township, where Henry Young spent the remainder of his life engaged in farming. He married Louisa Schaffer, in 1862, and ten children were born to them. The fourth born, William, is the subject of this brief family review. The others are Henry, Marie, Christine, Louise, Anna, Cyrus, Clara, Frederick and Louise. The fifth child, named Louise died young, and the youngest child was named for her. Frederick also is deceased. The father died on July 11, 1905, and the mother has her home in Fort Waynt at the present writing. William F. Young had his education in St. Joseph township, and in his teens entered the employ of the firm of Vebing & Company in Fort Wayne, with which he continued for a period of eight years. He then returned to the old home and turned his attention to farming. He has since added to the original acreage of the home place so that he now owns and operates 100 acres of the finest land in the township. His father, a progressive and prosperous farmer, made many improvements on the place, and the son is ably carrying on the work then begun. On August 22, 1895, Mr. Young married Miss Henrietta Kanmeyer, daughter of Frederick and Caroline (Bohde) Kanmeyer, both natives of Germany, who came to America at the respective ages of three and seven years, settling with their parents in Washington and St. Joseph townships in Allen county. Their parents were among the esteemed and honored citizens of the county for many years. Four children have been born to Mr. and Mrs. Young. They are named Werner, Lucile, Raymond and Iola. Mr. and Mrs. Young are members of the German Lutheran church and he is a Democrat in politics.

John S. Youse takes his place among the leading men of his community, not alone by reason of his material success, but because of his natural qualities of heart and mind, manifested in his every-day life. A successful farmer, he has stepped out of the usual trend of farm life and assisted in organizing the Hoagland State Bank, of which he is now serving as president. Mr. Youse was born in Allen county on December 18, 1855, son of Christian and Sarah (Adair) Youse. The father was born in Germany and came to America as a child three years old, settling with his parents on a farm in Allen county. Sarah Adair, mother of the subject, was born in Pennsylvania and came to Allen county as a young girl. Here she met and married Christian Youse. Her father came to Indiana in the hope of bettering his condition, and his first home in Allen county was one of the rude log cabins with clap-board roof and puncheon floor that the early pioneers were accustomed to building, and for several years his family made this shelter its home. Ten children were born to Christian and Sarah Youse, eight of them living at this writing. John Youse had a rather limited education in the schools of Allen county and was still very young when he turned his attention to farming on his own lookout. The first farm he bought was the one on which he now lives. It is located in Madison township and is a fine place of 310 acres, with every improvement and altogether a highly productive place. He married Sarah A. Gresley, in 1883, and they have lived happily on their farm home from then down to the present time. She is the daughter of John and Sarah (Bonenvito) Gresley, both natives of Pennsylvania, who came to Allen county in their early married life and, settling on a farm in Marion township, spent the remainder of their days there. Four children were born to John and Sarah Youse, briefly mentioned as follows: Amos D.; Lewis O., a teacher in Pontiac, Illinois; Dwight L., also a teacher, and Willard, living at home with his parents. Mr. and Mrs. Youse are members of the **Lutheran church.**

Walter G. Zahrt.—Among the men whose co-operative efforts down through the years have raised the manufacturing enterprise of S. F. Bowser & Company to a lofty place among the commercial industries of the middle west, is Walter G. Zahrt, treasurer and assistant general manager of this great concern. Mr. Zahrt was born, January 10, 1870, in LaPorte, Indiana, son of Henry and Katherine (Hering) Zahrt, both natives of Germany. The father conducted a hotel at LaPorte for many years. Following his attendance at the public schools at LaPorte, Walter G. Zahrt entered upon a business course of study in a commercial college, and there, by close application and a realization of the opportunities of the time, gained the foundation for his further successful career in the business world. In 1888 he went to Chicago and entered the employ of the Tiffany Refrigerator Car Company as a stenographer and secretary to the manager. After four years of service here he took a position as clerk of the Northern Indiana Hospital for the Insane at Logansport, Indiana, and, in 1892, succeeded Charles A. Dunkelberg as clerk and secretary to the superintendent. By successive steps he advanced to the position of steward, which is essentially that of business manager, involving the duties of secretary to the board of trustees and manager of the financial affairs of the institution. Incidentally, a clear view of the situation may be gained from the statement that the positions attained by Mr. Zahrt during his connection with the Northern Hospital were not gained through political appointment—indeed, the practice of selecting the right man for the right place in all departments of the institution has given the Logansport hospital the reputation of being one of the best institutions of its kind in America. Mr. Zahrt's worth to the institution is shown by the fact that for three years after his removal to Fort Wayne he was retained as a member of the board of trustees on the appointment of Governor Frank Hanly, but at the close of this period he was obliged to decline a re-appointment because of the pressure of new duties at home. Following twelve years of service at Logansport, Mr. Zahrt, in 1904, came to Fort Wayne to accept the position of sales manager with S. F. Bowser & Company, manufacturers of oil handling equipment, and one of the most widely known manufacturing concerns in America. Since then Mr. Zahrt has advanced through many positions of responsibility, all connected with the sales department of the enterprise. As office manager, general sales manager, and as assistant general manager and treasurer, which latter position he now holds, he has contributed constantly and intelligently to the success of the enterprise which has caused the name of Fort Wayne to be known in the farthest corners of the civilized world. In 1896 Mr. Zahrt was united in marriage with Rebecca Alice Shedron, of Camden, Indiana. To Mr. and Mrs. Zahrt have been born four children—Esther, Joseph, Walter and Robert. Mr. Zahrt is a member of the Wayne Street Methodist Episcopal church. In masonry, he is a Scottish Rite member of the thirty-second degree and a member of the Shrine. He is active in the work of the Commercial club and the Quest club.

Ernest Zelt is the owner of one of the well improved farms of Adams township, and is giving his attention principally to dairy farming, in connection with which he consigns his milk products to the village of New Haven, which is his postoffice address. Mr. Zelt was born at Arcadia, Hamilton county, Indiana, August 7, 1870, and is a son of Jacob and Sophia (Gallmeir) Zelt; the former was born in the state of New York, of German ancestry, and the latter in Germany. After their marriage the parents established their home in Hamilton county, and there they continued their residence until they came to Allen county and located on their present homestead farm of eighty acres, in Adams township, the father having so ordered his activities as to gain prestige as one of the substantial exponents of agricultural industry in this county. Of the eight children the subject of this sketch was the fourth in order of birth and all of the others are living except Herman, the seventh child, who died in November, 1916. The names of the other children are here noted: Theodore, John, Edward, William, Frederick, and Mary. Ernest Zelt received his early education in the Lutheran parochial school in Adams township, after which he attended the public schools two years. He continued to be associated with his father in the work of the home farm until his marriage, in 1897, when he located on his present farm, where he has shown much enterprise and progressiveness as an agriculturist and specially as a dairy farmer. In politics he is not constrained by strict partisan lines but gives his support to the candidates and measures meeting the approval of his judgment. He and his wife are active communicants of the Lutheran church, in Adams township. On April 29, 1897, Mr. Zelt wedded Miss Caroline Linker, who was born and reared in Adams township, where her parents, Henry and Caroline (Yergen) Linker, still reside, one of their ten children having died in infancy and the names of the others being here noted: Anna, Henry, Caroline, Louis, Dora, Elizabeth, Mary, Minnie and Frederick. Mr. and Mrs. Zelt have eight children, namely: Amandus, Paul, Walter, Carl, Ervin, Ernest, Jr., Lida and Alfred.

John Zelt is another of the native sons of Indiana who has become prominently and successfully identified with the business interests of the City of Fort Wayne, where he is now one of the interested principals of the A. C. Muntzinger Furniture Company, which conducts a substantial and prosperous business, as one of the leading concerns of this order in the city. Mr. Zelt was born in Hamilton county, Indiana, on August 4, 1865, and his parents are now venerable pioneer citizens of Allen county, where the father was for many years one of the active and substantial farmers of Adams township, he and his wife still continuing their residence in that township. He whose name introduces this article is a son of Jacob and Sophia (Gallmeyer) Zelt, the former of whom was born in the state of New York, January 22, 1837, of German parentage, and the latter was born in Rosenhagen, Germany, December 4, 1842. This sterling couple became the parents of seven sons and one daughter, concerning whom brief record is here entered: Theodore is a successful farmer in Adams township; John, of this review, was the next in order of birth; Edward resides in Fort Wayne; Ernest is a representative of agricultural enterprise in Adams township, as is also William; Herman is deceased and is survived by his wife and one daughter, Irene, who still reside in this county; Fred is identified with farming in Adams township; and Mary is the wife of George Dudenhoeffer, of Fort Wayne. John Zelt gained his early education in the Lutheran parochial schools in Adams township, where his parents established their home on a farm when he was a child, and later he attended the public schools for two years. Thereafter he continued to be associated with the work and management of the home farm until 1890, when he removed to Fort Wayne and here became a salesman for the Brudi Brothers flour mills at Bloomingdale. One year later he formed a partnership with his brother Edward and engaged in the retail grocery business. Two and one-half years later he purchased his brother's interest and for the ensuing thirteen years individually conducted a substantial and prosperous grocery store, after having erected for the purpose a substantial building at the corner of Gay street and Creighton avenue. He finally sold his grocery business and, in 1905, became a salesman for the D. N. Foster Furniture Company, with which he continued his connection in this capacity until July 1, 1916. In the meanwhile he had gained a thorough knowledge of furniture values and other details of the business, and on the tenth of the same month purchased an interest in the well established business of the A. C. Muntzinger Furniture Company, to the affairs of which he is now giving his characteristically effective attention. Mr. Zelt is aligned as a staunch supporter of the cause of the Republican party, and he was reared in the faith of the Lutheran church, of which both he and his wife are active communicants. In a fraternal way he is affiliated with the B. U. V. April 19, 1888, recorded the marriage of Mr. Zelt to Miss Minnie Rodenbeck, who was born in Adams township, this county, a daughter of Deitrick and Christina (Selter) Rodenbeck, both of whom were born in Germany and still reside in Adams township. It is pleasing to note that the parents of both Mr. and Mrs. Zelt have celebrated their golden wedding anniversaries and that all are old and honored citizens of Allen county. Mr. and Mrs. Zelt have three children—Winona, Elmer and Irma.

Fred E. Zollars had the very good fortune to receive his professional training at the hands of his father, who was one of the foremost lawyers of his time in Fort Wayne, and succeeded his father as counsel for the Pennsylvania lines in Indiana, the G. R. & I. and the Wabash and Vandalia railroad companies. Mr. Zollars, like his father, is known as a specialist in corporation law and stands high in the legal fraternity of the state. Born in Fort Wayne, February 7, 1869, Fred E. Zollars is one of three children born to his parents, Allen and Minnie (Ewing) Zollars. All three are living at this writing. Judge Allen Zollars was born in Licking county, Ohio, and died in Fort Wayne, in 1909, after having conducted a law practice in that city for forty-one years. The mother, also an Ohioan, was born in Lancaster, Fairfield county, and she died in Fort Wayne. Mr. Zollars had his early schooling in the public schools of Fort Wayne and Miami University furnished his college training. He entered his father's law office and there read law under the careful supervision of his parents, his admission to the bar following, in 1898. He joined his father in practice and they continued together until the death of the elder Zollars, when the son succeeded to the business of the firm as stated in a preceding paragraph. Mr. Zollars has identified himself with various enterprises in Fort Wayne and is connected prominently with the Federal Security Investment Company as a director of the concern. In politics he is a Democrat and fraternally is identified by his membership in the Masonic order, in which he has taken practically all degrees, the Elks and the Moose. He is also a member of the Country Club, the Rotary Club and the Press Club of Indianapolis. As a member of the Fort Wayne Commercial Club he has done good work in the best interests of the city and has helped to make that body one of the representative organizations of the community. On August 17, 1898, Mr. Zollars was married to Miss Gertrude Lindsay, who was born in Allen county, daughter of Charles and Angeline (Yahne) Lindsey.

Dennis C. Zook.—Fort Wayne has in Dennis C. Zook one of her substantial and dependable citizens, and the Pennsylvania system recognizes him as master carpenter of its bridge building forces between Pittsburg and Chicago. He has served the Pennsylvania from his youth on, and the road has no more faithful or dependable employee than he has proved himself to be. Mr. Zook was born on March 14, 1852, in Wyandotte county, Ohio, son of Daniel and Nancy (Steele) Zook, both natives of Pennsylvania. Daniel Zook was a farmer. He died, in 1852, when Dennis was two years old and the mother found herself with the burden of the support of their six children on her shoulders. Three of the six are living today, but the mother has gone to her reward. She kept the farm home and worked it as best she could, and the boy Dennis stayed there with her up to the age of eighteen years. He thought it time then to strike out into the world, and going to Nevada, Ohio, joined his brother who was there conducting a carpenter business. The young man applied himself to the task of learning the carpenter's trade, and after a time went to Upper Sandusky, there entering the employ of the Pennsylvania Lines, with which road he has been employed ever since. He advancd from one post to another until he finally was placed in charge of the carpenter work of the road between Chicago and Pittsburg, as has been stated above. Mr. Zook was married, in 1877, to Florence Turney, daughter of Dr. Joseph and Louisa (Welsh) Turney, both of them now dead. The children of Mr. and Mrs. Zook are five in number and are here briefly mentioned as follows: Edith May was a teacher in the Fort Wayne public schools for ten years, and is now the wife of Frank A. Taylor, of Cumberland, Maryland, master carpenter for the Baltimore & Ohio Railroad Company. Benjamin C. is located in Plymouth, Indiana, and is connected with the Pennsylvania road. Gertrude A. is a teacher employed in the Fort Wayne schools. Clarence L. is a civil engineer in the service of the McLain Fire Brick Company of Pittsburgh. Roscoe H. is an architect and is located in Chicago. All have had excellent educational advantages and are well established in life. Mr. Zook is a stockholder in one of the leading banks in the city and owns some real estate as well. He is a Republican and with his wife is a member of the Simpson Methodist Episcopal church. He is a Mason of high degree, and was at one time Master of the Chapter at Valparaiso, and was High Priest of the Royal Arch.

Joseph F. Zurbuch has proved himself strong, positive and efficient in connection with the directing of business enterprise of broad scope and importance and was the founder of the now extensive wholesale and retail coal business conducted in the city of Fort Wayne under the title of the Zurbuch-Baker Coal Company, with headquarters at 813 Taylor street, where he initiated business in 1905, with William A. Rinehart as his coadjutor. This alliance continued until July, 1910, and Mr. Zurbuch purchased his partner's interest, and thereafter he continued the enterprise in an individual way until August 1, 1914, when, to make better provision for the constantly expanding trade, he admitted Joseph J. Baker to partnership and the present title of Zurbuch-Baker Coal Company was adopted. The concern has ample storage facilities and the best of provisions for the handling of coal with expedition, as is demanded by the large volume of business transacted in both wholesale and retail departments. The company handles the various types and grades of coal that effectively meet the requirements of its trade and is one of the representative and substantial business concerns of Fort Wayne. Joseph F Zurbuch was born in Mercer county, Ohio, on the 11th of April, 1861, and was nine years of age at the time of the family removal to Lawrence county, Tennesee, where he was afforded the advantages of the public schools of Lawrenceburg, the county seat, and where he continued to assist in the work of his father's farm until he had attained to the age of seventeen years. He then served a thorough apprenticeship to the blacksmith's trade, at New Haven, Allen county, Indiana, of which county he became a resident when he was about seventeen years of age. In 1882 he engaged in the work of his trade in the city of Fort Wayne, and with this sturdy line of enterprise he continued his association until he engaged in the coal business, in 1905, as already noted in this context. Mr. Zurbuch is an ardent supporter of the cause of the Democratic party and has been influential in public affairs of a local order. In 1898 he was elected representative of the Fifth ward in the city council of Fort Wayne, and during his five years' incumbency of this office his course was marked by earnest and effective service in furthering the civic and material advancement and prosperity of the metropolis of Allen county. He is affiliated with the Knights of Columbus and the Fraternal Order of Eagles, and both he and his wife are communicants of St. Mary's Catholic church. On the 18th of November, 1884, was solemnized the marriage of Mr. Zurbuch to Miss Christina Rinehart, daughter of John Rinehart, a sterling citizen of Fort Wayne, and the one child of this union is Edward, who was born August 27, 1902.